Topsy-Turvy
1585

a translation and explication of
Luis Frois S.J.'s *TRATADO* (treatise)
listing 611 ways Europeans &
Japanese are contrary

by
robin d. gill

*"with a little help
from my friends"*

道可道
非常道

paraverse press

This is the third book published by paraverse press,
home of truly creative nonfiction, which is to say,
nonfiction that is neither journalism, nor history,
nor how-I-overcame-this-or-that, nor narrative.
Our books will not help you get rich, healthy
or up-to-date. Whatever their subject,
they offer one thing always the same
yet different; and that is ideas,
" food for thought,
all you can eat!"

but, please do not let that trouble you
for you may quote whatever you want, so long as
you cite this book and take care to check the **Errata** at
our web site:
http://www.paraverse.org/

We hope the Library of Congress will help us catalog
someday, for as you can see below, we need help! Meanwhile
our Publisher's Cataloging-in-Publication:

Topsy-Turvy 1585
– a translation and explication of
Luis Frois S.J.'s *TRATADO* listing 611 ways
Europeans & Japanese are contrary –
by robin d. gill
(with many other goodies)

ISBN# 0-9742618-1-5 (pbk)

1. Comparative Culture – Europe vs. Japan
2. Japan – Culture – 1500-1600 (Momoyama+Muromachi)
3. Europe – Culture – 1500-1600 (Renaissance+Reformation)
4. Identity – Collective – Europe/Japan(+China)
5. History – Jesuit – Accommodation Policy in Japan
6. Orientalism – Occidentalism (and contrary mores)
7. Nonfiction – Literature – Translation+Essay
8. Men, Women, Children, Religion, Food & Drink, Weapons, Horses,
Medicine, Writing, Architecture, Gardens, Boats, Entertainment . .
9. Luis Frois's *"Tratado em que se contem . . ."* (1585)
10. Luis Frois (Luís Fróis) S.J. (1532-1597)

1st edition (7/30/04), printed by Lightning Source
in the United States and United Kingdom. Distributed
by Ingram, at least. Amazon and other mail-order stores
should list it within two months of publication.
To learn more, please visit our website, or send a stamped envelope to:
Paraverse Press / pmb #399 / 260 Crandon blvd, suite 32 / Key Biscayne, FL 33149-1540

TOPSY-TURVY 1585 — *a full translation, explication and essay of Luis Frois S.J.'s famous treatise (**Tratado**) listing 611 ways Europeans and Japanese differ* — by robin d. gill [1]

"The Jesuits had aimed for Eldorado but landed in the antipodes" writes Professor George Elison in **Deus Destroyed.** *"There was no foothold to be had without an inversion of past attitudes. How difficult it was to perform to perform that headstand is apparent from a look at Padre Luis Frois's attempt at cultural analysis, a treatise he composed in 1585 on Contradictions and Differences of Custom between the Peoples of Europe and this Province of Japan."* (E:DD)

Frois's treatise (*tratado*) is bold and unique. Herodotus made *dozens* of black and white contrasts between Egypt and the Greco-Roman civilization he called "the rest of the world;" Alberuni (Il Bîrûnî) did the same, contrasting India to the West (mostly Arab world); but no one has made *hundreds* as did Frois, who was also the most prolific writer on Japan of the 16th century, and, probably, of all time. In this book, Frois's 611 (!) skeletal distiches — two lines we might call *heroic contrast!* — are translated into English, most for the first time. The author provides ample (and hopefully entertaining) commentary on the veracity and significance of the contrasts as well as their relationship to the Jesuits' attempt to accommodate themselves to life in Japan, something that preceded and paved the way for the more famous effort of Ricci in China described by Jonathon Spence (S:MPMR) and others.

The *topsy-turvy* is interesting in itself. Two slightly annotated Japanese translations of Frois's treatise have gone through countless popular pocket-book printings. Scholars value the work because most of Frois's contrasts are not judgmental but descriptive, resembling the more neutral stuff of cultural anthropology and history; and laymen enjoy it because the *Tratado* is also, to quote Elison again, "a booklet of amazing banality in which everything Japanese — from the man's head to the horse's tail" — is included. [2] Who but Frois would have noticed we pick our noses with different fingers and bothered to write it down!

Ideas raised by Frois's contrasts are explored when deemed significant or interesting. Additional *Faux Frois* contrasts are suggested, bringing the total distiches in the book to a thousand or so. Essays into the history of *topsy-turvy* and the way *China* (Japan's closest competition for being topsy-turvy to the Occident) fits into the general picture provide added perspective and, the author is not ashamed to hope, entertainment.

1. Robin D. Gill. A native Floridian (Key Biscayne). Worked 20 years as an acquisitions editor in Japan, where he is known for deconstructing the antithetical yet complementary cultural stereotypes of *Orientalism* & *Occidentalism* (the title of his most recent book). Descriptions of his seven non-fiction books written and published in Japan/ese (by publishers including Chikuma-bunko, Hakusuisha and Kousakusha) may be found at the Paraverse.org website. His first book in English, *Rise, Ye Sea Slugs!* (Paraverse Press: 2003), a translation and essay of 1,000 holothurian haiku, is highly acclaimed (Blurbs and Reviews in the appendix) but still unknown to most potential readers for lack of media coverage. Gill will publish the first volume of *In Praise of Olde Haiku*, an almanac of five seasons, in winter of 2004.
2. Elison's sentence continues, "[everything Japanese] is made to appear the precise opposite of its European counterpart." "Made to appear" implies exaggeration if not dishonesty. Where this happens, I point it out; but on the whole, there is remarkably little distortion in *Tratado* and it is mainly found in the selection of items that happen to be very different, something easy to do with cultures as different — mutually *exotic* — as Europe and Japan once were.

"I wonder
if I shall fall
right through the earth!
How funny it will seem
to come out among
the people that walk
with their heads
downwards!

The antipathies, I think –"

(Alice, as she tumbles down the rabbit hole)

..

日本人も http://www.paraverse.org の方へどうぞ！「わっパラ」もあるぞ。

TABLE OF
CONTENTS

桃山・室町時代に詳しい方のご協力を乞う。　本書に未解決の問題、まだある。

~~~~~~

貧乏は大変だから

~~~~~~

APOLOGY & APPEAL

All readers who are writers know that a book is never finished. But this book is in a class by itself, for circumstances (extreme poverty) have forced the author to publish long before he could chase down all the people and books needed to answer many remaining questions, and time better spent on that research, or on whittling down crude sentences into fine art, was instead wasted on details which could have been far more efficiently handled by others, had he the money to hire them. In other words, the book is too short because it lacks answers, and too long because it lacks editing.

~~~~~~

So, why publish if it is so far from complete? Because, the author is falling deeper into debt with every passing day and had to publish or perish (not in the ivory tower sense, but in the real world). Lacking a house, a car or other assets solid or liquid – his wealth is entirely invested in his books-to-be, of which a score are well along – he lacks the credit to borrow much more than he has already. But, if you have just bought this book, please do not despair at having bought an incomplete book. It is still a good read, boasts more research and thought than most "finished" books and is worth far more than what you paid for it and, with your help, shall be improved soon enough.

~~~~~~

Anyone with knowledge about 16th century Japan or Europe is cordially invited to help answer the remaining questions – the ones I specify, or any found – or, question any of my "answers." You will be credited by name, if you wish, or by initial. Quotes from previously published material are welcome especially coming from the author. Scholars and writers are free to peg on a line or two to plug their own book/s (in order to make helping me (and, hopefully, entertaining the reader) worthwhile for you, too.) So, as you read this book, please keep your pen in hand! But, before taking the time to write your gloss, please check the Gloss status at the Paraverse Press site to be certain no one else beat you to it.

..

~~~~~~

英語を読むのが苦手の場合、＜フロイス問答場＞　を訪ねてみて下さい。

~~~~~~

Scholars, please forgive the confusion respecting some Valignano citations. There were no less than 7 renditions of his summary of the contrary nature of Japan and most, if not all have the same words (*Principio* and *Sumario*) in them. They were not always abbreviated the same way by me or others. More info. on this is in the Annotated Bibliography. Where the date mattered most – where Valignano made a major change or reappraised his work – I was usually attentive to the order. I do not have the resources to fix this now (it is impossible for a poor man in the boondocks to get all the books together) and hope you will be understanding.

In Lieu of an
INDEX i hope a future edition can have a full index but, for now, this incomplete outline will have to do.

Introduction: The Appeal of Topsy-turvydom

Ch. 1 Men

Ch. 2 Women

Ch. 3 Children

Ch. 4 Monks & Bonzes

Ch. 5 Temples & Images

Ch. 6 Food & Drink

Ch. 7 War & Weapons

Midword: China *versus* Japan

Ch. 12   Ships

Ch. 13   Plays & Music

Ch. 14   Sundry

If any reader would like to make a contribution for the purpose of paying a student to thoroughly index future books, or like to volunteer their time, please contact me at Paraverse Press / PMB #399 / 260 Crandon Blvd. Suite #32 / Key Biscayne, FL. 33149-1540, or E-mail me at info@paraverse.org.   – rdg (publisher/publicist/editor/author&whatnot)

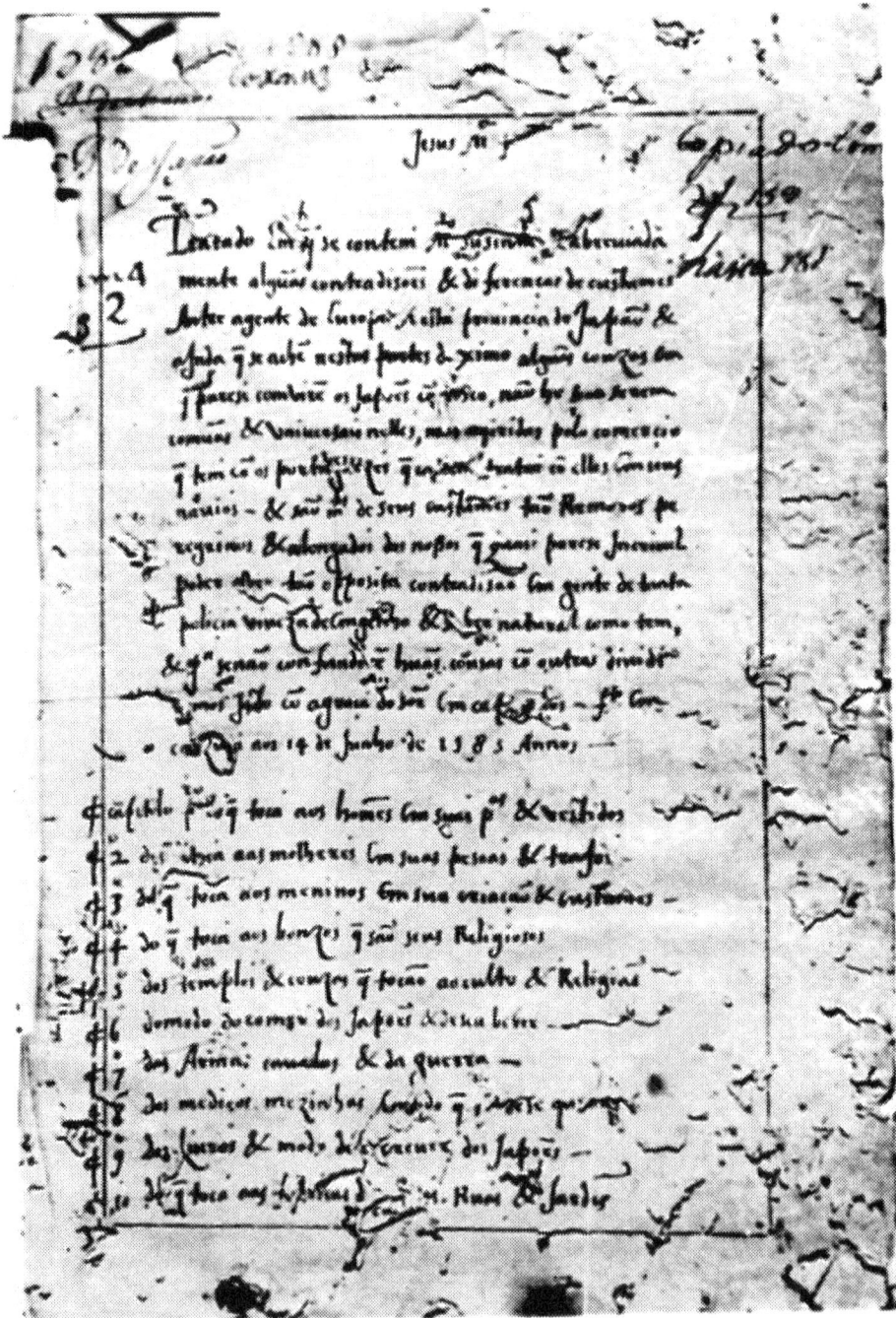

This is a copy of a copy of a photo of the first page of Frois's *Tratado* from mss Jes. 11-10-3/21 at the Biblioteca de la Académia de la História in Madrid borrowed (with apologies for not asking permission) from *Kulturgegensätze Europa-Japan* (1585) by Josef Franz Schütte, S.J. (Sophia University, Tokyo 1955 (F(S):T)). I hope to pay for a good copy from the Académia for the next edition, but am now out of time and money. I nevertheless include it, partly to prove it is real (for much will amaze the reader!) and partly to show its condition. The holes on the next page, reproduced in the pocketbook-sized translation by Matsuda & Jorissen (J/F(M&J):T), show much larger holes! It amazes me how few words Father Schütte failed to read or guess.

Preface

to the original untitled manuscript of Luis Frois S.J.

Jesus - Maria

This short treatise briefly outlines some contrasting customs and differences encountered among the people of Europe and the people of this province of Japan. Although there are a number of [cultural] items where Japanese appear similar to us in Shimo [today, West Kyushu], these were adopted to facilitate trade with the Portuguese who come here, and are not widespread. Many of their customs are so far removed, so alien from ours; it is hard to believe so radical a contrast can exist in a people blessed with such a high [level of] culture, lively ingenuity and natural endowment of intelligence as these [of Japan]. In order that the diverse matters concerning us and them are not further confused, with the help of our Lord God, I have divided them into chapters. – written in Canzusa [Katsusa] on the 14th of June, 1585.

a
Jesus-M

Tratado em que se contem muito [susinta e] abreviadamente algumas contradisões & diferenças de custumes Antre a gente de Europa & esta provincia de Japão & ainda que se achem nestas partes do ximo algumas couzas em que parese comverem os Japões connosco, não he por serem commuas & universais nelles, mas aqiridas polo comercio que tem com os portuguezes que ca vem tratar com elles em seus navios – & são muitos de seus custumes tão Remotos, peregrinos & alongados dos nossos que quasi parese Incrivel. Poder aver tão opposita contradisão em gente de tanta policia viveza de emgenho & saber natural como tem, & pera se não confundirem humas cousas com outras, dividimos isto com a graça do senhor em capitolos – feito em Canzusa Aos 14 de Junho de 1585 Annos –

This ↑ was borrowed from the transcription of Schütte S.J. with a few changes based on the photo of the original. The ampersands are restored and I tried to capitalize as Frois did (Schütte put it in all caps). I left the expansions of Frois's shorthand of "m" and "q" with lines over them for "muito" and "que," respectively, but restored "Maria" to her abbrev. state.) I think Frois meant to remove "susinta e" as redundant, and bracketed it. The photo is from Schütte:1955 work (F(S):T). A pg. from the body in F(M&J):T is far more worm-eaten. I couldn't have read it!

Now all this would not be surprising if they were like so many barbarians . . . To see how everything is the reverse of Europe, despite the fact that their ceremonies and customs are so discerning and reasonable for those who really understand them, is a thing of no little surprise.   Alessandro Valignano, S.J. (1583) [1]

When the Dutch laughed at their customs, they [the Japanese] laughed at the Dutch; but with submission to the learned commentator, that was rather an agreement than a difference.
Editor's note in Golownin (1824)

The discovery of the highly-developed Japanese culture and civilization, which had grown up quite independently of Europe came as a salutary shock.   Michael Cooper, S.J. (1965)

1. Valignano Restating the words of the Jesuit Visitador [i.e. plenipotentiary] to the East Indies brings out the otherwise indiscernible nuance of the penultimate line of Frois's preface: *We have come to expect strange things of savage, marginal peoples, but this is different: we have discovered equal but opposite people. That is cause for reflection, for who would have thought it possible!* (Cooper cites Wicki: I cannot tell if it is 1582, 1583 or both.)

As this is an important point, let me precede just once with a lot of translation detail. It will not happen often, for the notes in this book are meant to entertain. The first part of the Valignano translation comes from Cooper (C:TCJ), because his translation gets off to a fine start. I arbitrarily changed "cultured" (*politicas*) to "discerning" (both nuances are found in the original which was once Englished as "politicke" without any change in the meaning = behaving in a civil[ized] manner).

Less arbitrarily, I corrected his concluding phrase: "causes no little surprise to anyone who understands such things." The original suggests these words apply to the entire statement (*". . . sus ceremonias y costumbres, tan politicas y puestas en razon para quien bien las entiende, es cosa que puede causar no pequena admiracion."* where there is no comma after *razon*, but after *entiende* – another version has commas after both.): i.e., *the customs make sense to those who really understand them.* Valignano's phrase qualifying the things Europeans must learn from scratch in Japan (note 13, below) further reinforces my interpretation:

". . . and other thousands of new things[they do], which at first seem strange and unreasonable, seem fine once one grows accustomed to them" (. . *y hacer otras mil cosas nuevas, las cuales al principio parecen muy extranas y fuera de razon, mas despues que hombre se acostumbra a [ms L = "de'] ellas parecenle bien.* – SUMARIO (V(A):S&A)

Or, later, (V:1602), where Valignano expounds at greater length upon how one must actually experience and learn to understand such marvelous differences and contrariety (*differencia y contraridad*), and that means relearning

everything in a country as thoroughly regulated as Japan, where there is practically nothing without its particular rules (*casi ninguna cosa que no tenga sus leyes particulares*), he reiterates ". . . and all [Europe] find such difficulty in comprehending and accommodating themselves to them [different things]; still, after one has experienced and learned more, they seem fine and very reasonable, so much so that even to us they seem no less accommodating, courteous and rational than ours do." (*y todos hallamos tan grande dificultad en comprenderlas y acomodarnos a ellas, todavia, despues que se tiene mas experiencia y conociniento, parecen bien y puestas en mucha razon, tanto que a nosotros mismos no nos parecen menos acomodadas, corteses y racionales que las nuestras.* in Alvarez-Taladriz's notes (V(A):S&A)).

After this, Valignano gives the identical but opposite Japanese perspective, explaining that "many of our things come to be appreciated by them, because, for them too, experience (*uso*) makes them accustomed to our things." I believe it possible that Valignano's sentence reflects knowledge of Alberuni's India (c.1030), which, in the first paragraph of Chapter I includes this:

"For the reader must always bear in mind that the Hindus entirely differ from us in every respect, many a subject appearing intricate and obscure which would be perfectly clear if there were more connection between us." (Edward C. Sachau trans. A(S):AI p17)

Sachau, who first translated from Arabic into German admits, correctly, that his English is lacking, but I trust it is enough to make my point. We will explore more possible Al-Bîrûnî – Valignano connections later.

For me, the most trying question in translating the Valignano statement was whether to use the accurate but ungainly rendition "based on reason," or "reasonable," *a word so smooth to the ear that readers may fail to appreciate how literally it is being used here.* Valignano's concept of learned reason-ability is echoed by Knapp three hundred years later (intro. text ix)!

THE APPEAL OF TOPSY-TURVYDOM

foreword

i

six-hundred and eleven contrasts!

Herodotus, in (484 – 425? BC) contrasted the "rest of the world" with Egypt, where –

> women run the market and the shops, while the men, indoors, weave; and in this weaving, while the other people push the woof upward, the Egyptians push it down. The men carry burdens on their heads; the women carry theirs on their shoulders. The women make water standing, but the men do it squatting . . . [1]

Al-Bîrûnî, in 1030 (Islamic date: 420 or 421 [2]), contrasted "our country" to the Hindus where –

> they sip the stall of cows, but they do not eat their meat; in washing, they begin with the feet, and then wash the face; they wash themselves *before* cohabiting with their wives; on festive days they besmear their bodies with dung instead of perfumes; in all consultations and emergencies they take the advice of the women; they consider the *crepitus ventris* as a good omen, sneezing as a bad omen . . . [3]

There has always been a *Land of Topsy-Turvy*. The literature of cultural anthropology tells us of an *other* world, underground, inverted, a place where men walk upside-down and backwards, eat feces and spit up food. Knowing this, who can doubt the literal Antipodes, the crudely depicted foot-over-head folk we identify with the Medieval imagination, was born long before Pliny? But, listing numerous opposite features of another living and real culture – not the more easily invented monster – may well have begun with our entertaining "father of history."

---

1. *Herodotus's Egypt.* If the typical opposite culture is naturally explained by its antipodal location, Egypt – not *that* far from Greece – differed because of the radically different nature of the Nile, which, for a start, flows Northward rather than Southward? The quotation follows the translation by David Grene, except for the "make water," which I substituted for "urinate," a word too formal to match Pliny's style, or that of the translator himself! In this book, I use translations as they are whenever possible, because I tire of my own English; but, having worked as an editor checking translation for twenty years, I cannot resist an occasional improvement.

2. Islamic Time. Though the Islamic calendar's zero date is the *hagira* of Muhammad from Mecca to Medina in 622 A.D., one cannot merely subtract 622 from the Christian date to obtain the year as one might imagine because the fact that the calendar is *completely lunar* means the years are almost a week shorter than the solar one. If the two calendars are still in use after tens of thousands of years, the Islamic one will catch up to the Gregorian one. A practical problem: because the start and end varies year to year, a year cannot be exactly translated without knowing the exact month and day.

3. *Al-Bîrûnî's India.* The above quote is my arrangement of some of the dozens of contrasts from *Alberuni's India*. (trans. Edward C. Sachau). Unlike our Frois, Herodotus and Al-Bîrûnî mostly give but one side of the contrast, for it is assumed the reader knows well enough his own side. More of Al-Bîrûnî's contrasts will be introduced at appropriate places.

Scholar, missionary or merchant, world travelers have always hyped *difference* for it holds our interest – who doesn't enjoy hearing about strange things? The word "exotic" is proof. Literally, it means only *external*, or *foreign* – in linguistics, an "*exotic* tongue" is the opposite of a *cognate* one. But who can imagine the exotic without an element of *fascination*? Moreover, it is a useful tool of pedagogy. Nothing defines like radical *difference*.[1] Studying cultures depicted in black and white, i.e. high contrast, is a quick way to get a quick handle on a complex reality. What astounds us with the 16th century Portuguese Jesuit Luis Frois is the single-mindedness with which he pursues those differences. Things that impress strongly upon many visitors, such as –

> *We show much emotion when we lose our fortune or our house burns down;*
> *The Japanese bear everything with little expression.* (14-2)

> *We are terrified to kill a man, but think nothing of killing cows, chickens or dogs;*
> *The Japanese are afraid to kill animals, but kill men as a matter of course.* (14-6)

have been noted by many, albeit not so succinctly! But what about the next four contrasts, all taken from the last chapter (14), *On Sundry and Extraordinary Things*? They could only have been recorded by someone actively searching-out and collecting examples of difference.

> *With us, man, woman and child are afraid of the dark;*
> *In Japan, to the contrary, neither the old nor the young are ever afraid of it.* (14-14)

> *With us, killing flies with the hand is [considered] filthy;*
> *In Japan, lords and gentlemen do so, pulling off their wings and throwing them away.* (4-23)

> *We have no custom of giving presents of medicine;*
> *In Japan, it is a common thing to give medicine in clam shells.* (14-27)

> *When we warm our hands, the palm faces the fire;*
> *When the Japanese warm them, the back of the hand faces the fire.* (14-43)

1. *Black and White Comparison.* While contrast is found in many books, indeed whole theories of culture are built upon it – *shame* versus *sin*-culture (Ruth Benedict), *high-context* versus *low-context* culture (Edward Hall), *vertical* versus *horizontal* culture (Nakane Chie), etc.. – I know of only one book which contains a list of pure unabashed cultural contrasts. It was a paperback called *Nihonjin to Obeijin*, or "Japanese and Euro-Americans," (words, Tobioka Ken?) published in 1983 by PHP (an idealistic right-wing publisher affiliated with Matsushita electronics), supposedly "useful to international business and international exchange" by helping to create "true cosmopolitans" who "know how Japanese and foreigners differ and can explain it." There were a hundred or so differences explained in side-by-side English and Japanese, with witty illustrations.

In Japan, "Nature is the sacred province of the gods" reads the English, superimposed on a drawing of a smiling haiku-poet-like figure refraining from hitting a mosquito on his arm;

In the West, "Nature is the devil's province" says its contrary – a grim Westerner in modern clothing (horizontally striped tee-shirt) savagely brandishes a sword against the very elements.
In Japan, "A thief may receive a coin along with a reprimand." The drawing shows an

Tokugawa era (16 – 19th century) thief crying tears of joy before his benefactor.

In the West, "Forgiving a thief may result in your own demise." The drawing shows a man in modern dress grinning or perhaps chuckling with his smoking gun in hand after plugging three holes in the back of a fleeing thief.

Considering the grim twentieth century reality – 50% of Japan's coastline and 80% of Japanese river-banks straight-jacketed in cement, the "sacred province of the gods" is a sad laugh. As for the alleged mercy toward thieves, the very reason there is a story of such kind treatment is because no country was traditionally as hard on thieves as Japan (see 14-7)! This type of crude contrast – backed up with simplistic one-sided explanation – brings to mind something Jefferson once wrote about people who didn't read, and knowing nothing, were a good deal better informed than those who were misinformed by bad newspapers! But, by showing us that even bare contrasts can reveal prejudice, these examples help us appreciate the relatively high level of objectivity in Frois's TRATADO. (Since writing the above, I found Robert J. Collins: JAPAN-THINK AMERICA-THINK. Penguin 1992. This *"Irreverent Guide to Understanding the Cultural Differences Between Us"* ((C:JA) lacks the seriousness (?) of the Japanese work.)

611 contrasts! Surely, no one has ever managed to find and note even a tenth as many items as did this prolific Jesuit in 1585! [1] To my mind, Frois's discovery of common things is no less than the discovery of culture with a small *c*, and deserves to be far better known. [2]

ii
historical value of common things

Frois's observations are not merely interesting. Many have great historical value. Granted, the fact that "We use our index finger to pick our noses, while Japanese use their pinkie because they have small nostrils" (14-47) is only of entertainment value (I think Frois, God bless him, *meant* to be entertaining) to anyone but an anatomist; but just such an interest in trivia is what gives us observations about things so common they were taken for granted by others (especially, the Japanese themselves) and not recorded.

Taking three of thirty-nine observations on horses for example, who but Frois would tell us –

> *In Europe, teamsters load up their beasts and carry nothing themselves;*
> *Japanese teamsters, pitying the animal, divide the load and carry a third of it.* (8-36)?

> *Europeans roughly guess the weight of luggage before loading animals;*
> *In most parts of Japan they do not begin to load until it is weighed.* (8-37)?

> *Our horses stale upon the dirt inside the stable;*
> *Japanese horses' stale is taken by men using long ladles.* (8-24)?

1. *Frois's List as Unique*. The 11th century Muslim scholar Al-bîrûnî, who noted that "the Hindus entirely differ from us in every respect," came closest to matching Frois. Because his assumed contrasts often run-on, they are hard to count, but liberally dividing them we still find four dozen, at most. While Al-bîrûnî described the situation clearly – "in all manners and usages they differ from us to such a degree as to frighten their children with us" – he only gave up a few pages to pure contrast-mongering, for his main interest was in important matters, i.e., philosophy, science (especially mathematics and astronomy) and religion. These things may be what really counts for the scholar – and Al-bîrûnî's full presentation and analysis of Hindu knowledge and belief, involving ample comparison with the Greeks (making the Hindu less strange, for the Muslims were well-versed in the classics) and contrast with the best Islamic scholarship is so impressive a tour de force that we must view him as a critical modern scholar. True, he occasionally qualified his presentation of various Hindu belief in ways we might find reprehensible (i.e. *I only wrote this to show you how awful and ungodly they are*) but, we cannot help wondering if a man with so broad a perspective did so from the heart. Perhaps it is precisely because Frois was not enough of a scholar to be sidetracked by important matters, that he was free to observe and record so many trivial ones that please someone like me (also far from a scholar).

I only found Al-Bîrûnî because the brother of the man living next door to me got Alzheimer's and his books were put in the trash after he was institutionalized. I cannot help wondering if I might be missing others! If anyone knows of anyone I missed, please let me know!

2. *Common Things*. Frois's contribution here deserves special notice because scholars generally feel that Frois and other Jesuits made just two major contributions to the historiography of Japan. First, they recorded plentiful information about the personal life of Nobunaga, Hideyoshi, and Tokugawa Ieyasu, the three Shoguns who conquered, unified and solidified(?) Japan (and some other major figures), because they were uniquely close to these generally unapproachable rulers. It is hypothesized that the Shoguns could find respite from their high isolation through relatively free conversation with total outsiders. Nowadays, we think of foreigners being shut out from information in Japan; but in a period of history where trying to get inside would cost natives their lives, some Jesuits, including Frois, Valignano, Organtino and Rodrigues got to see more from within than any Japanese could. And, second, there was no native equivalent of the large dictionary (NIPO = Nihongo-Portuguese) made by Rodrigues et al, which I find cited everywhere in Japan's largest dictionary (Nihon Kokugo Daijiten – which I call OJD in this book), despite the large quantity of what we would now call reference books in Japan. I think Frois's attention to details meaningless to natives who take them for granted represents a third major contribution.

Joao Rodrigues S.J., writing only a decade or two after Frois, gives us an outstanding description of *The Way of Tea*. 50 solid pages. His comprehension of the finer part of Japanese culture, the "art of *suki*" or "good taste" that comes with the *chanoyu*, or tea ceremony, is, to my mind, nothing short of miraculous. Over a century before Chinese-style landscape would be the vogue in England, he wrote:

> "Everything artificial, refined and pretty must be avoided, for anything not made according to nature causes tedium and boredom in the long run. For if you plant two trees of the same size and shape, one in front of the other, and deliberately make them correspond to one another, they will end by causing tedium and boredom; the same applies to other things as well. But lack of artificiality and a note of naturalness (for example, in a complete tree made up of various disordered branches pointing this way and that, just as nature directed them) is never boring, because experience shows there is always something new to be found therein." (Cooper trans. THIS ISLAND OF JAPON = R(C):TIJ)

Compared to this, Frois's contrasts seem shallow indeed. But, Rodrigues gives us little if anything new to us today. A Japanese reader, or knowledgeable Western reader will not find much he did not know already, for other cultured souls *eventually* wrote about the same exceptionally worthy subjects. Frois, on the other hand, by being less discriminating, offers us much that is fresh.[1] History itself is topsy-turvy: *with the passage of time, it is the commonplace that becomes rare.*

iii
the nature of contrast

If, as the old English proverb claims, *comparison is odious*, then, *contrast* can be downright dangerous. Whether or not value-judgments are explicit, every cultural contrast has the potential to harm, because readers can not help but judge difference. We do *this* while they do *that* is what supports the largely uncomplimentary stereotyping called Orientalism and Occidentalism (Asian stereotypes about the West).[2] Take the following ostensibly harmless contrasts:

1. *Frois's Lack of Discrimination.* Frois wrote so many long letters that some would question his ability to have authored the sparely worded TRATADO. Matsuda & Jorissen joke away this discrepancy by pointing out that even if each distich is minimal and unlike Frois, *the fact there are as many as 611 of them* is *very* Frois! (J/F(M&J):T) Yet, we must be careful when charging someone with writing too much. Frois does not waste words. As D. F. Lach wrote in his magisterial ASIA IN THE MAKING OF EUROPE, "unlike many of the Jesuits, Frois was not given to sermonizing or verbosity." Frois's "avid concern for concrete data and detail" may fill up so much space that (as Cooper wrote in a note to TCJ) his letters are sometimes book-length; but it is all fresh reporting: content, not mere wordiness. Censors in Rome may have "felt from time to time that his letters were too "curious" and not "edifying" enough." (L:AME) but, that is because they did not fully appreciate that little things in a new world were of value in themselves as Frois, who deliberately studied many aspects and levels of Japanese society, did. This is why Frois (his letters and HISTORIA) may well be the single most valuable informant on 16th century Japan (and not only in European languages – the Japanese translators of his HISTORIA compare his reporting of certain events to that of Japanese and Korean reporters and find Frois the more observant). We are fortunate he was not discriminating enough to discriminate, that he did not whittle down his observations to concentrate on the things his employers would hold important. This – the pinkie in the nostril – is what makes the TRATADO so unmistakably Frois.

2. *Orientalism and Occidentalism.* Much more has been written about Orientalism, generally uncomplimentary stereotypes about the East than Occidentalism, generally uncomplimentary stereotypes about the West. The enormous difference in our tongues make both almost unavoidable for reasons I detail in ORIENTALISM AND OCCIDENTALISM: *Is mistranslating culture inevitable?* In an appendix, "Ways to Make a Difference," I give 16 reasons why apparent contrasts are often, if not usually misleading. Can publishing such a tool atone for the sin implicit to translating and annotating a book concentrating on differences, such as this one?

We count by quill [writing numbers down to calculate];
Japanese use jina [soroban: bead calculators] (14-25)

We express honor through our nouns [nomes];
The Japanese express it all through their verbs. (14-20)

We bury our dead;
The Japanese usually cremate theirs. (5-22)

Written calculation *vs.* mechanical calculation; nouns *vs.* verbs, earth *vs.* fire. We shall examine these distiches later (and the translation may change a bit), but I think it safe to say that Frois had *no intention to judge.* Yet we can imagine some Christians thinking the calculator black magic; nouns/names, being given by God, or His proxy Adam, worthier than verbs, and cremation a hellish way to treat the body . . . Or, *vice versa,* Japanese arguing the calculator was more advanced, the verb more fitting to reflect relationship because it links the actors and cremation more sanitary. Because of our tendency to value difference, we need to take care. Again, the Rodrigues-the-interpretor:

> They do not use gestures or movements of the body, as we do, in order to bring out a point, for this astonishes them greatly. *Instead,* they use special adverbs [1] which greatly abound in their language, for their noise and sound explain the matter without any movement of the hand or gestures . . ."(THIS ISLAND OF JAPAN *italics* mine)

A modern anthropologist or socio-linguist might note that Westerners – particularly those from Latin countries – actively gesticulate with their arms and hands, while Japanese tend not to, and simply put this down to *different body language.* The observation generally stops there, leaving us with an image of an active Latin and a passive Japanese. *Not that it matters. Everything is relative, you know.* [2] But is it not likely that active/passive images might lead people to think one side more *expressive/alive/ rude/repressed* than the other? More sophisticated, in the best sense of the word, Frois and some [3] of the other Jesuits in Japan knew it really *did* matter; so they went a little further and provided the important *instead.* It is my guess that Frois had intended for his distiches to be *explained,* so that he was not only playing up differences to exoticize the Japanese and show what the Christian mission was up against, but, as unlikely as this seems, to make them familiar as well! This cannot be proved – motive is hard to guess – but the only part of the missing first book (his Summary of Japan) of Frois's *History of the Church in Japan* (*Historia*) is so attentive to clearing up cultural misunderstanding due to insufficient information that I, at least, give him the benefit of the doubt. [4]

---

1. *Special adverbs.* Rodrigues apparently refers to what we call *onomatopoeia* and *psychological mimesis,* which are abundant in Japanese. In the foreword to the ARTE DA LINGOA DE IAPAM, the huge grammar published in 1604, Rodrigues writes that these adverbs "are plentiful, and extremely appropriate for expressing the circumstances of things and movement." The expressions – and his grammar lists hundreds with examples! – are usually repetitive (*jaja, pikupiku, tokotoko*) and pegged on to the front of the verb. Actually, these adverbs are but half of the story for emphasis in Japanese. The tip of the verb at the tail of the sentence, which I will discuss later, is also important. Be that as it may, the astonishment which Rodrigues mentioned with respect to our forceful body language on the part of the Japanese was still there when Japan was "opened" in the 19th century. Chamberlain wrote:

> "Old and young alike are remarkable for quietness of demeanor. The gesticulations of a Southern European fill them with amazement, not to say contempt . . . ." (THINGS JAPANESE: 1890)

2. *Everything is relative?* My cynicism is born of reading popular books of comparative culture in Japanese. I have seen too many writers talk up cultural relativity (deny the validity of value-judgment), while introducing material *which cannot help but cause readers to form good and bad opinions* about the people being compared, or, rather, *contrasted.* The assumption that difference does not matter gives the writer a *carte blanche* for writing down any alleged difference – totally irresponsible generalizations – without giving the matter serious thought. Far better that a writer honestly admits his or her preferences and tries to justify them so we may then be free to agree or disagree with the writer's judgment. See my *Orientalism & Occidentalism – is mistranslating culture inevitable?* (2004) for an elaboration of the problem.

3. *Some of the Jesuits.* There was no uniform Jesuit point of view. There were differing opinions at all times and change over time. Until the Bungo Consultation/ Consensus (see text and notes for iv below), some Jesuits were far from relative about cultural difference and not slow to admit it. In 1565, the same year Frois writes that "the Japanese are superior to the Spanish in more ways than I can say," his protégé in Japan, Gaspar Vilela wrote:

> Because the things that exist in this land are subject to the devil, they are so many and so diverse that to speak about all of them is never to finish . . . (CARTAS)

It is often said there is far more variety in ugliness than beauty. Vilela's statement implies that *things*, or should I say *Thing European* are correct, while all other things are not only wrong, but evil. This ethnocentric view might be summed up as: If there is but one God, then, by God there is only one way! To be fair to Vilela who was no dolt, in this context, he is not being mean but witty.

4. *Explaining Difference.* Many if not most of Frois's contrasts edify rather than exoticize, *if* they are explained. I think Frois may have done that himself. In the prologue for his lost *Historia* volume, his Summary of Japan, he wrote that one of the purposes of his book was to rid Europeans of mistaken ideas about Japanese they have come to hold from reading letters about the same written with the authority of "our brothers." And, he guesses the misunderstanding is largely the result of terms liable to being misunderstood when left as is without qualification. There are too many of these unexplained terms to list them all (least of all, in a prologue!), he laments, but it should be helpful to look at some found in letters from India (much information went to Europe via Goa, or was written by Jesuits in Goa who had been in Japan) or Japan, in order to see how matters dubious for their apparent qualitative or quantitative exaggeration may be but the result of terms insufficiently explained when used with respect to Japan. He gives ten examples: 1) units, 2) torches, 3) *botaos* (cautering irons?), 4) handkerchiefs, 5) gold-scabbards, 6) casks (of wine), 7) bars (of gold/silver), 8) grand architecture, 9) kings, 10) universities. Here, let us sample just two of Frois's explanations in their entirety.

> **1)** When someone, whoever he might be, sends notice that a lord or head of state in Japan leads three contos (units ?) into battle, they are using a Japanese expression that does not match our European system of counting because, in Japanese, "one *man* people" [*ichiman-nin*] means one unit (*conto*) and in their way of counting *ten-thousand* is one conto and a hundred-thousand is ten units (contos). So, if someone leads three units (*contos*) into battle, that is in the units of this country [Japan] and means only thirty-thousand men. [Hence,] it disagrees with the European way of counting." (J/F:HISTORIA)

If I have it right, a *conto* meant a million! (*Aurelio* defines it as "ten times a hundred thousand") So, the three *man* became "three million" in mis/translation! In English, we have no term simultaneously meaning a unit and a large

number, so this confusion could not have occurred in the first place. However, different notation probably caused confusion for people working with figures. When I first came to Japan in the early 1970's, old-fashioned people still wrote the place mark (comma or dot) after every fourth digit, rather than after every third one as we do. That is to say, the first mark makes a *man*, not a thousand. The next a *man man*, or 100 million, which is called one *oku*, was easy for me to remember, as it was the approximate number of people in Japan at that time. From the ubiquity of the term "ten-thousand" in the Bible, I would guess that Hebrew has an equivalent for *man*, and like *man*, it was probably also used rhetorically to mean *many*. The Chinese number system, which the Japanese adopted, has a term for "thousand" but not for a "million," which they must call either a hundred *man*, or *sen sen*, a thousand thousand.]

> **4)** Told that Japanese blow their nose but once per handkerchief, the European reader will find it odd if not ludicrous. It is like being told that the kings of Malabar eat just once from the same plate. They eat on banana leaves, so when the meal is over, they throw them away. Thus, when it is said that once a handkerchief has been spit in or blown upon, the Japanese throw it away without washing it, the following must be explained: that the Japanese, go about with many handkerchief-like thin, folded papers in their pocket[bosom], instead of handkerchiefs. As this paper is very cheap, for a very small outlay, they can use as much as they please. The gentry keep one white or blue linen cloth with the paper which is only used to wipe sweat. But merchants and ordinary folk, besides the paper, keep a cheap hemp rag tucked in their sashes for both wiping off sweat and for using when they wash their face or hands. (J/F:HISTORIA)

With no word for what Americans now call "kleenex" or even "tissue paper" – as such did not exist in the West – we can imagine it was easier to just write of a generic "handkerchief." The Japanese called this paper *chirigami,* literally "scatter-paper" (the gerund from the verb chiru which is what cherry blossoms do, rather than simply "fall") or *fukuro-gami*, "pocket-paper." The former is now the most common term for what we today call "toilet paper," while it is called instead *teishyu* (tissue), an abbreviation of "tissue paper." In 1998, I bought a box with a photo of a puppy on it and in large roman letters: TISSUE OF PUPPY. See 1-19+ on handkerchiefs, 1-50+,51+52+ for "pockets." We will encounter the same rag/washcloth/towel being used for the face *and* the feet in distich 14-46.

Seeing the thoroughness of Frois's explanations, can anyone doubt that whatever contrasts got into his Summary of Japan were not explained? In that sense, my lengthy notes to the TRATADO in this book do not betray its brevity, but fulfill its original intent to pose questions which could be, and perhaps were, for the most part, answered. More of the ten examples will be cited at appropriate places in the text.

For all my caveats, I really do think that contrasting generalization is a useful tool for intercultural studies for they bring out into the open much that more subtle essays, intentionally or not, sweep under the table. Differences are, I think, best dealt with by pointing them out. Sometimes Frois's distiches can broaden our perspective without explanation. When time stands a contrast on its head, contradicting contemporary stereotypes – the illusion of timelessness is one of the marks of all cultural stereotyping – we immediately realize that our ideas of "us" and "them" are too shallow. There are items in the *Tratado* which beautifully betray our expectations and emphasize the fact that not only is the past a foreign country but, at times, the very antipode of the present. How pleasant to read numerous items suggesting Japanese woman enjoyed far more personal freedom than European women. Contrasts 2-1, 2-20, 2-24, 2-30, 2-32, 2-34, 2-35, 2-38, 2-45, 2-54 show, respectively, that *they were not forced to be chaste, could walk barefoot, show their legs, own property (and lend it to their husbands), divorce their husbands, go where they please as girls, and as wives, have abortions, generally knew how to write, and could drink and even get drunk!*

Considering 20th century stereotypes about Japanese women as virtual slaves, such contrasts are refreshing. Yet, I must confess that even the confirmation of hoary differences can sometimes be useful. It is instructive to learn that even back then (before the Tokugawa Era with its long, in some ways, authoritarian rule) most Japanese clearly had more self-discipline than most Occidentals (14-2). That speaks well for Japanese, and suggests we had and still have something to reflect upon, or, better yet learn. Our criminal waste of resources (including clean water and air that is not too warm) better left for the future and shortsighted failure to stop the growth of human population ensures that we humans will need all the self-discipline we can muster to keep from turning the earth into hell. Frois was not much of a mechanic or farmer, so we miss out on all too many contrasts concerning tools and the agricultural life that occupied most Europeans and Japanese   He did, however, catch one farm-related item from the perspective of the urbanite.

> *We pay someone to haul away our human waste.*
> *In Japan, they buy it paying with rice or coin.* (11-21)

Now that is a fine example of a contrast where Japan, and not Europe, was clearly ahead of its time! Or was it? Is recycling our future? Do we *have* a future?

iv
frois, valignano and the origin of a contrary japan

The first *suggestion* of a contrast later to appear in the TRATADO is found a year after 16 year old Frois arrived in Goa. It is in a 1549 letter of [soon-to-be-sainted] Francis Xavier to the King of Portugal. Xavier, who went to preach in Japan that same year, explains that Japanese write vertically and includes an explanation by his young Japanese Christian companion, "Paul" (Yajiro), to the effect that, *as man's head is on top and feet at the bottom it is only natural to write from the former to the latter* (see 10-3 note). So, the first Jesuit in Japan discovers before he even gets there that culture can be different yet make sense on its own terms. There is, however, still no indication that Japanese are altogether *contrary*. Xavier was more impressed at finding a people so similar to Europeans (i.e., civilized and brave).

With respect to Japan, the earliest *list* of contrasts – not actually numbered, but sentences one after another – to bear a date is found in the original draft of the Japanese chapters of Alessandro Valignano's Indian Summary (1579) and revised for his later Japan Summary (drafted 1582, finished

1583). According to Schütte, the former was revised in August 1580, when a Japan-*China* contrast was deleted (S:VMP). We will discuss this in the *Midword*, where I try to grasp the dilemma of the "Middle-Country" China *and* Japan as *two* cultures topsy-turvy to the West! (Can that be!?).

As Visitador (an inspector with the Order's top authority) for the East Indies, Valignano had just come to Japan for the first time and from March of 1580 used Frois (who had become interested in Japan shortly after arriving in Goa as a teenage scribe, then Jesuit novice and moved there in 1563) as his interpreter. Since Valignano apparently had a predilection for contrast (*Chinese* vs Japanese, Japanese v.s. *Indian* and *Indian* v.s. European), it is possible that he suggested Frois draw up a list as Lach (L:AME) and others guess, but who knows whether Valignano's contrasts seeded Frois's more ambitious list, or were selected from a list already started by Frois. [1]   At any rate, the dozens of examples in Valignano's work are all found in the TRATADO, which was first written at least as early as the late 1583 (for a Table of Contents for the missing Summary of Japan is nearly identical) and neatly recopied, presumably with some additions in 1585. A score or so of Valignano's and Frois's later contrasts were already hinted at in the remarkably concise summaries of the Japanese found in Frois and Vilela's letters to the Company of 1565. [2]   But, as far as we know, the Herodotus-like distich, where both cultures are mentioned and the idea of their being generally at odds, was Valignano's invention.

1. *Valignano/Frois Priority*. I feel some scholars might not be giving Frois his due. Elison writes that Frois makes everything Japanese "appear the precise opposite of its European counterpart," and notes

> The author's nostalgia for Europe after an absence of thirty-seven years is understandable and his depiction of the Japanese topsy-turvydom is not without value. There is a lesson to be learned from this sort of view. It took the keen mind of Valignano to apply that lesson. (E:DD)

I share Elison's admiration for Valignano. But, Valignano's application predates "the Japanese topsy-turvydom" of *Tratado* by several years. So Frois had to know its uses. Or does Elison mean Frois began collecting items for contrast earlier but failed to use them? Even, if that were true, we could not be sure Frois did not help Valignano "apply that lesson," too. The prologue for the summary volume of Frois's *Historia* suggests he was not *that* naive. His discussion of incommensurate terms suggests to me that he may well have developed the subject further in the missing book. J. F. Moran, in his book on Valignano, quotes his last LIBRO (1601) in his chapter on "Full and complete information:"

> It has to be understood that the language and government of Japan are very different indeed from those which we have in Europe – there has never, after all, been any contact between them – and they also have different names for things. Now some of these names can in a sense be regarded as corresponding to our words, [literal trans.: some can, in some manner, accommodate ours] but they do not really match them very well, so that it cannot be properly said that they mean the same things. . . But since in Europe the Japanese titles are not understood . . . the Portuguese and Ours [Jesuits], so as to be understood, use our words for these things [Japanese titles] when they speak or write to

Europeans. In transferring titles in this way mistakes are frequently made . . . (M:JJ, brackets mine)

Did Moran not know that Frois discusses the "king" problem in that prologue and probably discussed other title translation problems in the missing book, which, for all we know, Valignano was looking at as he wrote, and had almost surely read? The Visitador=Valinano should have gotten it copied and shipped it off to Europe, as he did his own writing. In respect to this and Frois's slow promotion, Moran is, however, very sympathetic to Frois and critical of Valignano, whom he otherwise rates very highly, agreeing with Rodrigues, who called him "a solicitous and loving father, who deserves the title of Apostle of Japan and China." A chapter of his book detailing the Valignano-Frois relationship includes a half-page-long quotation of Valignano criticizing Frois's long style. Here, let me instead translate a sentence from a fictionalized Valignano-Frois letter in Inoue Hisashi's 1999 novel FUROISU (Frois).

> In Macao, while serving as a secretary for the Visitador [himself], . . . Frois is to rewrite his History of Japan, now longer than a Japanese *fundoshi* [a loin-cloth, so long the ends sometimes trailed on the ground] until it is as short as the Japanese stature.

2. *The 1565 Letters*. There was an explosion of letters cleverly orchestrated – or carried out (for the Superior Father Melchior might have suggested it) – by Vilela (_?_), Frois (4/20) and Almeida (_?_), all of which gave ample information about Japan. Frois and Almeida divided their writing duties on a trip, but the two long letters from Frois and Vilela which contain summaries of Japan's polity and culture, have obviously been *separately filled in from a common outline*. Perhaps they felt they would be more believable that way. Or, they wanted to be certain that at least one got through in mail, and rather than writing one letter and copying it, filled in one outline separately!

The Visitador's agenda was clear: convincing his superiors and colleagues that the Jesuit enterprise in Japan had to go native and gaining support for the tremendous effort this involved. He points out that Japanese, as highly cultured, literate, intelligent (rapid learners, capable of high-level logical argument) and dignified (he repeats Xavier's observation that money would not buy title, and poor gentry were still respected in Japan, unlike in Christian countries) "white" people, [1] deserve equal treatment and, besides, were so martial that any mistaken effort to use force (holy war) was bound to fail.[2] Since the Japanese are "so wedded to these customs and ceremonies that they will not veer even one point from their ordinary ways, though the world should drown," [3] the Jesuits had no choice but to "do in Rome as the Romans do." And this meant accepting that one was an ignoramus and relearning life as a child does in a world the reverse of that in Europe; [4] "for it is different and contrary in all, and conforms with us in hardly any respect."

1. "White" Japanese. St. Xavier found Japanese "the best race yet discovered" and his high opinion pretty much carried the day. When Frois in 1565, praised the Japanese as superior in many things – specifically, in their *policia, tratamiento* and *costumbres* (civility, manners and customs?) – he made certain to parenthetically include the words "as the padre maestro Francisco said." (CARTAS). But I cannot recall Xavier mentioning skin color. José Luis Alvarez-Taladriz's ample notes to Valignano's SUMARIO (1583) gives many citations going back to Fernandez in 1560 – "*esta gente es blanca.*" (See 1-8 for more). Valignano's constant use of the word when justifying the equal treatment of Japanese makes it clear that *blanca* has broader nuance than skin color. When he explains to his superior "The Importance of this Undertaking . . . in Japan" (1583:ch 6), his first of "many reasons" is because Japan is

"a big province with seventy six kingdoms all inhabited by whites (*habitada toda de gente blanca*) who are very discriminating, prudent, understanding and very subject to reason . . ."

Or, explaining elsewhere to the question as to whether Japanese should be received into the Order (found in note to the same by Alvarez-Taladriz): Valignano's second reason was

"because the population of Japan is as white, noble, ingenious, capable of virtue and the letters as the people of Europe . . ." (*es blanca, noble . . . tanto como son todas las mas gentes de Europa..*)

As Father Schütte writes in VALIGNANO'S MISSION PRINCIPLES (S:VMP), while still in India, Valignano regarded the Japanese (and Chinese) as "white people" far superior to Indian and African races," who were generally called "black." Even though some in India had great power and pomp (*fausto*) in some things and many possessions and gold, "still in other things they are as wretched and base that they seem like black people." (*todavia en otras son tan miserables y tan bajos que bien se parece ser gente negra.*) After visiting Japan, he further contrasted life in Japan and India as "living with cultivated and intelligent people in the former instance, and with base and bestial people in the latter." (in B:CCJ)

Unlike, the "honorary white" appellation granted to the Japanese by South African racists in the 1970's, economics was *not* the main factor involved, for Valignano and other Jesuits often noted that most Japanese, including many local rulers, were far from wealthy. While the Southern Europeans did not attach the devilish connotations to black that many (most?) other Europeans did – the Portuguese have traditionally prided themselves on not being racist – black was nevertheless synonymous with inferiority and often included as an adjective in descriptions of what we might *impoverishment, deprivation* or *ignorance*. In Japan's case, the widespread literacy and decorum would seem to be the deciding factors here, for the Chinese were likewise included as whites, although their alleged cowardice (see my *Midword*) cost them the respect of the West, and the Koreans, also highly literate, could be Jesuits from 1608. As Schütte points out, had Valignano known the more intellectual side of India (Goa was not the most civilized location), he might have felt differently about them, too.

I think we should credit the Jesuits for choosing as "whites" and our equals if not superiors in many aspects of civilized life the very people of the very cultures that did, in fact, end up our economic equals. Much can be said for India and its peoples, but, as Tagore admitted, only Japan was able to match the West in its own game. And now, we can see this being proven true for the entire Sinosphere. It is easy to sit back and chide Valignano for having a racist opinion of India. But, if "white" means close to Europeans and "black" means what we now call "Third World," or whatever the latest euphemism is, history has proven he was correct to exclude India and include the Far East. (Though I am rooting for India which has much I love!)

We might also note that Thunberg, a Swedish physician who was in Japan with the Dutch when the North American Colonies declared their independence from England, and is often cited as an early Japanophile, and seems like a progressive guy, independently came to the same opinion as Valignano. After spending time in South Africa and the East Indies, he wrote:

> It may with justice be alleged, that the inhabitants of the warmer climates have a dull torpid brain, and are less keen and sharp than the Europeans. . . And, without insulting the greater part of the dark-brown inhabitants of the East-Indies, one may truely say, that there is a greater difference between them and the Europeans, than between the monkies and them. (T:TEAAv2-p296)

This was mainly attributed to the climate (the same Aristotelian influence found in Valignano and pretty much every one), and Thunberg admitted that Europeans become likewise from the heat. Even "the most industrious man, against his inclination, frequently sinks into a state of inactivity and idleness." Like Valignano, he was hyped for Japan before he went. Leaving Batavia (Djakaruta) in 1775, he wrote of preparing for his visit by improving his wardrobe with clothing and decorative items of silk, cloth [cotton?], and lace, "in order that I might exhibit myself with propriety among the Japanese, who view the Europeans with greater attention than any natural philosopher can possibly examine the most rare and uncommon animal." (IbidV2 end) And, here is what he found:

> Of all the nations that inhabit the three largest parts of the globe, the Japanese deserve to rank the first, and to be compared to the Europeans; and although in many points they must yield the palm top the latter, yet in various other respects they may with great justice be preferred to them. (Ibid v3 preface)

At any rate, the color-line was drawn at China, Japan and Korea; i.e. the temperate Far East. The Southern reaches of the Sinosphere were not included. So we find Kaempfer, who, a hundred years after TRATADO, was the first to write in detail about isolated Japan, beginning his description of Thailand: "The Kingdom of Siam is the most powerful, and its court the most magnificent among all the black Nations of Asia." He even develops the blackness further:

> The Siamites represent the first Teacher of their Paganism in their Temples, in the figure of a Negro sitting, of a prodigious size, his hair curl'd, the skin black, but as it were out of respect gilt over . . (K(S)HOJ)

Even his apostles and disciples were likewise black. Kaempfer hypothesizes that the Teacher was not Buddha (or Shaka) but "some Egyptian Priest of note, probably of Memphis and a Moor." In Japan, shortly later, as the physician for the Dutch Embassy to the Emperor, Kaempfer made another interesting observation about skin color:

> As I was dancing, at the Emperor's command, I had an opportunity twice of seeing the Empress thro' the slits of the lattices, and took notice, that she was of a brown and beautiful complexion, with black

European eyes, full of fire, . . . (Ibid)

2. *Fighting Japanese.* Cooper writes "The remoteness of Japan precluded the use of European military might and the foreigners in Japan found that it was their turn to be despised and unflatteringly dubbed as barbarians. Here, then was to be the first confrontation between East and West on equal terms." (preface to C:TCJ) As Japan was hardly the only place remote from Europe, I think the military might of Japan as a deterrent might be stressed a bit more! (see note to 7-52)

3. *"Though the World Should Flood."* In the concluding chapter to Matsuda and Jorissen's critical presentation of TRATADO, they use Valignano's rhetoric to make a point.

> "As we have seen, the Visitador Valignano judged that the Japanese will never change their . . . customs even a smidgen. But, observing the customs of modern Japan it is all too clear how mistaken he was. . . . . if there is the assumption here that one nation or folk does not change their customs, it is held because that very tendency was so strong in the European ." (J/F(M&J):T).

Considering the tenor of Valignano's remarks, this comeback is not surprising, but let us see where Matsuda and Jorissen go next:

> With this in mind, perusing Frois's TRATADO, we cannot help but marvel at the enormity of the contrast with the case of Japan, when we compare the way most of the European customs have either not changed or remained with but minor improvements, while they have not adopted a single Japanese custom nor even been influenced by them. There are some items in TRATADO which haven't changed in Japan over these four centuries: in medicine, greeting with a slight grin, not being embarrassed to be drunk in public, and so forth. But, excluding those items that have improved or changed in the same [autonomous?] manner European customs have, almost all of the Japanese customs mentioned by Frois have fused with Western customs (*wayôsetchû*) or exist in symbiosis with them. (J/F(M&J):T)

There is not a little truth in this. But we should note that the Valignano was right in the sense that the Japanese adoption of some *namban* (southern barbarian) things such as cards, tobacco, *konpeito* (star-like pieces of sugar candy], *tempura* and sponge-cake represented little serious change and hardly touched the items in Frois's list. Almost all of Japan's real change was to await Perry's visit, when Japan's leaders, recognizing the overwhelming physical power of the West, decided they had to change or be changed. True, in the West, windmills, gunpowder and other major technological borrowings from abroad ended with the Renaissance – as Europe rediscovered the depth of ancient learning (thanks to Islam's scholarship), it may have belittled the cultures of contemporary others – but it was still in the process of adopting foreign things at the time TRATADO was written. In fact, part of the *De Missione* dialogues (largely written by Valignano) touching upon horseshoes (see 8-7) shows that in the late-16th century Europeans prided themselves in being more open to copying good things from others than the Japanese were. Most of this copying was between the very competitive Europeans themselves. But what about tobacco, potatoes, corn, tomatoes – the very idea of eating these raw vegetables – coffee, cocoa, porcelain and, not long after, Chinese-style gardens and, less obviously, Iroquois-style federal government in North America (see Weatherford: INDIAN GIVERS)? What Matsuda and Jorissen fail to mention is that Europe was in close contact with *so many places* that it could hardly be expected to find as much in Japan as Japan found in it. The relationship was not reciprocal and could not have been reciprocal.

Matsuda and Jorissen contrast an island culture eagerly taking in things from foreign cultures with

> "Europeans to whom not taking in things from heathen cultures, because their own Christian-based culture was held to be the best and highest in the world, became a tradition." (Ibid)

And they conclude that not only does reading the TRATADO teach us how different Europe and Japans customs were in the sixteenth century, but, in retrospect, makes all too clear the difference in the respective reception given by each culture to the other over the course of these four centuries. Again, they have a point. But, at the same time, for fairness's sake, they should point out that Japanese do not eagerly borrow from *one and all* – if so, they would drink *makali* as well as beer, eat sesame leaves, have heatable floors and use the most subtly beautiful spoons in the world (all fine things found in Korea, right next door) – *No!* They borrow from the most powerful or prestigious culture. And, conversely, as soon as Japan is seen to be pulling ahead, the West falls all over itself trying to copy from them. (*Remember the 'Learn from Japan' frenzy in the 1980's?*) True taste, rational discrimination, I fear, has much less to do with cultural exchange than we like to imagine. To my mind, the way mid-twentieth century white Usanians copied the "low" and marginal culture of the blacks – or sought a model for sexuality in the South Sea, even if it was a bit idealized! – is a far more revolutionary development than the cultural change that accompanied the modernization of Japan, because it was not accomplished under the gun or out of economic necessity.

Regardless, Valignano's "though the world should flood" statement was no naive misunderstanding. It was a hyperbole that accurately conveyed the strong cultural pride and self-confidence the Jesuits encountered in Japan. Xavier mentioned the Japanese being particularly convinced that no one could match them. In 1551, Cosme de Torres, explaining why great patience was required to work in Japan, wrote that the Japanese, being

> "very sharp and ingenious [*tan agudos de ingenerio*] make fun of all foreigners with their mouths and their hands [i.e. imitating them] in order to humiliate them, for, to them it seems that no one born exceeds them in knowledge and honor . . ." (CARTAS?)

In 1557, Vilela had more to say about the humiliation they had to put up with:

> Sometimes, going down the streets, they mocked us, calling us dogs, and, after that, boys threw stones at us. They treat us as the most abominable people in the world: and, thus, speak to us as to niggers, injuring us with numbing words [*palabras torpes*]" (CARTAS)

The reversal, with "us" as "niggers" (*nos hablan como a negros*) makes us smile. Lest, we exaggerate Japanese ethnocentrism, let me give Vilela's next sentence: "The riff-raff does this, the decent folk treat us with respect and reverence." But even decent folk could be proudly ethnocentric. Frois, in a long 1665 letter (which includes many observations found in the TRATADO), wrote:

> Despite holding their rites, religion and laws came from Sion and China, they prefer them to all and deprecate every other nation; for they are of the opinion that their society and understanding is the model and rule for all other nations [*por tener de si esta opinion, que son en policia y saber natural el methodo y regla de todas las otras naciones*] (CARTAS)

Perhaps the strong conceit was born of an inferiority complex versus continental culture, but that would not detract from its reality any more than feeling inferior about black physical prowess would nullify a white supremacist's conceit. That is why the terms "inferiority" and "superiority *complex*" are so apt. (Yes, it *is* always *complex*. That is why argument should be kind.) Perhaps the best testimony comes in a backhanded way from Balthasar Gago, a Jesuit who spent most of the 1550's in Japan – "When they wish to do us great honor, they say that we resemble them." (Sept 23, 1555 – CARTAS)

4. *Becoming a Child Again.* What Valignano means is that sociolinguistic fluency in Japanese means we must grow up all over again; it takes a decade of learning – not just living – in Japan for most Westerners. If the Jesuits wanted to compete with the erudite Buddhists, who were masters of calligraphy, poetry and the tea ceremony, etc.. they not only had to master an exotic tongue with more varieties of speech, reading and writing than found anywhere in the West, but a complex system of etiquette ("they have infinite books to teach them ceremonies and customs"), social and artistic skills attained by life-long study – or, true leisure if you may, on the part of the upper-class Japanese. Valignano was in favor of Jesuits trying just this, but he realized that, practically speaking it would be impossible on a large scale; and, hence, a Japanese church that could sustain the high level of Christian belief they valued most, would have to be run by Japanese.

Today, in Japan and the West, we grossly underestimate the amount of study needed to gain fluency in an exotic tongue. Graduate programs in exotic languages are a joke, for even with the extra credits given, they are generally based on cognate language programs and totally inadequate. We should take Valignano *very* seriously.

This was no academic matter. As Visitador[1] to Japan (and the whole Far East), with the support of Organtino, Frois and other sympathetic Brothers, Valignano was in the process of overturning the unabashedly discriminatory policies of Cabral,[2] the Superior in Japan in favor of a completely nondiscriminatory policy treating Japanese as full-fledged "whites," and doing this in such a way as to build consensus for making the greatest conscious effort at cultural acclimation the world had ever seen.

1. *Visitador.* As far as I can make out, the Visitador is in charge of appraising and overseeing the Jesuit Mission, which means doing *a lot* of traveling – I wonder what their average life-span was! – and had the power to make decisions, some delegated ahead of time, some in concert with others, and some after consultation with Rome. (Perhaps someone else can sum this up better! I hate technical detail.)

2. *To Discriminate or Not to Discriminate!* When Valignano arrived, Cabral was the head of the Jesuit mission in Japan. He had received correspondence from Organtino and Frois, among others, complaining of the Superior's attitude. Years later – after the battle ended – Valignano wrote that Cabral would:

1)   Treat Japanese harshly because they are prideful and speak disparagingly to them "calling them 'niggers.' "(*llamandoles negros*) to humiliate them, and habitually exclaim aloud "What do you expect from Japanese!" (*!al fin de cuentas, sois hasta japones!*) – how will this effect a people who despise impatience and don't even tolerate an impolite word from their own kings?

2)   Segregate Japanese brothers completely from Portuguese brothers in every way: dress, food and sleeping quarters to maintain their humility – how could our Company's unity and uniformity survive this?

3)   Make Japanese accommodate themselves to our ways and not the Portuguese ways to theirs, because in the final account they were niggers (*al fin de cuentas eran negros*) with barbaric customs – while he disgusted the Japanese serving beef on filthy table cloths.

4)   And, related to 3), find strange and speak badly of Japanese ways – the leader sets the example: with this attitude none of the Jesuits bothered to learn Japanese customs and vehemently expressed preference for ours over theirs.

5)   Forbid anyone to teach Japanese brothers Portuguese or Latin so they cannot hear our secrets when we speak to each other nor learn the sciences or become sacerdotes – otherwise, he thinks they will become uppity and ungovernable.

6)   Consent not to build seminaries for Japanese as they would live there in vice and impurity – argue against him as you will, he says they ought not study nor become priests.

7)   Maintain tenaciously his opinion that we could not learn Japanese well, could never preach it, nor

learn it from a gramatica (a book of grammar) – and so in his three years as the Superior in Japan, he learned only some crude phrases for necessities and saw no need to make a Japanese grammar. (My one-third length abbreviation – the original Spanish in V(A):S&A, and the full English translation in S:VMP are even more impressive, though the latter mistranslates the "*gramatica*" in 7).)

Cabral reminds us of a typical racist; it is Valignano's uncanny ability to portray him that astounds us. Has racist practice ever been described in such fine detail? The first point alone should have been enough to damn Cabral, for Valignano not only heard complaints first-hand from Japanese, but even had the backing of Xavier's 1549 testimony about the importance of treating others with respect in Japan; to wit:

"These [nobles and commoners alike] are people who will suffer no injury, nor a single word spoken with contempt. (CARTAS)"

No doubt Cabral rationalized that this was precisely why Japanese had to be broken. (*It is also ironic, for the Spanish have long been stereotyped in exactly that way by the English*). But Jesuits were not supposed to play the devil and use bad language to disrespect others into humility. Speaking well of others was, after all, their official Company policy. [What was that Latin phrase?] On the other hand, we have Organtino, who, to quote Schütte, "had become a Japanese with the Japanese; he championed a policy of transformation into the people to be evangelized." (S:VMP). From a 1577 letter to "a father probably stationed in Rome" –

I pray Your Reverence to get rid of the notion that this is an uncivilized people; for, apart from the faith we hold, no matter how wise we fancy ourselves to be, when compared with them it is we who are most uncivilized (*comparati a loro siamo barbarissimi*). I confess in all truth I am learning from them every day, and I believe that there is no nation in the world so singularly gifted and talented as the Japanese. (in S:VMP)

If Cabral found the Japanese *haughty, avaricious, unreliable, insincere, proud, grasping, ambitious* and *hypocritical* (all words taken from quotations in S:VMP), Organtino found them *patient, magnanimous, austere, polite* and *discerning* (ditto). His expressions of love for the Japanese Church written in 1589, *after* the persecution of Christians began resemble nothing so much as the raptures of female saints in the metaphysical arms of Jesus Christ.:

> I languish to death for love of this blessed spouse of God (*morior et digne consumor pro hac sponsa Dei benedicta*). Were I to limn her features for your Paternity, you would be amazed (*attonito*) at the result. .... Any Jesuit who comes to Japan and does not foster a love for this bride of wondrous beauty, not caring to learn her language immediately nor conforming to her ways, [deserves] to be packed back to Europe as an inept and unprofitable worker in God's vineyard. Perhaps, when I have time I shall sketch a picture of this bride; it would present to Your Paternity's gaze and that of our fathers and brothers in Rome such an entrancing image that, enamoured of her beauty, they could not take their eyes off her countenance but would petition God with great instancy to be sent to Japan as servants of this beloved spouse.

Valignano, like his translator and confident Frois, took a position midway between these two. His SUMARIO (1583?) gave almost as much play to bad characteristics as good ones. In the earlier version (1582?), he mixes them; e.g., pride that protects dignity and pride that leads to suicide he suggests are heads and tails of the same coin. In the revised version, Valignano takes more care to separate the good and bad elements in the national character. Schütte apparently feels this brought out the good more ("the bright features gain in clarity, though the somber qualities also are fully recognized" VMP). I felt it did the opposite, that is brought the bad into stronger relief! That Valignano did this partly for political reasons may be surmised from the way *he argued against himself* in his 1601 LIBRO (see my notes to 14-6). Regardless, Valignano still dwells upon the contradiction of combining the best of the best and the worst of the worst in a single people as something to marvel at (*cosa maravillosa*). This suggests the insight is thrown away as paradox. If Valignano had noted that the best and worst parts of a culture or a personality are often found together it might have been a revolutionary insight.

Yet, Valignano was far from neutral on how Japanese should be treated. Here, he takes after Saint Xavier who was disappointed in the bad name the Portuguese made for themselves in the countries they had already proselytized –

> "as it is, the heathen see that the converts are despised and looked down on by the Portuguese, and so, as is natural, they are unwilling to become converts themselves."

– and thought of Japan and China as a place where the Company could make a fresh start. While Cabral did some good things for the mission (he was a diligent Superior) Xavier's ghost would have been horrified with his attitude; and indeed it was, in the formidable person of the Visitador Valignano.

To my mind, the Bungo Consultation of 1580 [1], where the reasons for, and details of the new Japanization of the Jesuits in Japan was officially worked out is every bit as significant as the famous Chinese Rites controversy. [2] It is astonishing how few people know of it.

---

1. The Bungo Consensus. As Father Schütte points out, no trace of the opposing views of Cabral are found in the *acta* (whatever that means) of the Bungo Consultation.

> "All were agreed that the Japanese, owing to their knowledge of the native tongue and the written word, were marked out as the chief exponents of Christianity. By virtue of their fine intellectual qualities as a 'white' race, they stood on the same level as the Europeans, and, given a thorough training in the truths of the faith, and in the spiritual life, they bade fair to become good religious." [And that] "owing to the size of Japan, its remoteness, and its differing culture, it was essential that native elements should also cooperate in the building up of the Japanese Church." (S:VMP)

To bring the Europeans and the Japanese together in the spirit,

> four practical measures were decided upon at the consultation. They are found, in substance, in the *regimento* for the Japanese Superior: 1. uniform treatment of both elements, European and Japanese; 2. kindly treatment in the spirit of the Constitutions of the order; 3. exact observance of the rule which forbids Jesuits to think or speak unfavorably of other nations; 4. adaptation to Japanese ways of living. (Ibid)

To make this last rule a reality, they hammered out a complex program, details on dining and clothing alone taking pages, which shall not be elaborated upon here other than to point out that even Cabral went on the record for going completely native on the latter, partly because of the economic savings – he was reputed to be a penny pincher – whereas the Japanophile Organtino was in favor of maintaining the European cassock, or mantle. Schütte writes that in this Organtino seems "at first blush, to depart from the policy of adaptation." Since Schütte fails to explain why, at second blush, he does *not* really depart from it, I *will*. To Japanese, each human type, i.e. ethnicity/profession, has their authentic dress. As Buddhist and Shinto habits are quite different, the Jesuits would also do well to keep their identifying garb – perhaps with Japanese adaptations, such as vent-holes under the arms and sandals, for the hot summers – for *that*, not mere mimicry, is the Japanese *way of doing things*. Until the end of the 19th century, the Japanese stuck to their own dress *and expected others to do likewise*. That is why a Westerner in Japanese clothing is called a *hen-na gaijin*, or "weird foreigner." For a foreigner to assume the costume of the Japanese would not be accommodating but, rather, ignoring Japanese expectations! In other words, sometimes accommodation means following the spirit rather than the clothes.

To my mind, Organtino was not just in love with Japanese, but understood them like no one else. Even his lavishness with money, which Valignano feared could lead to financial ruin (and used as a reason to prevent his obtaining a higher post) shows me that *he knew how Japanese do business* – with large outlays at the onset – and I have no doubt that only he could have won the terrifying (many even say sadistic) tyrant Nobunaga's heart and, with it, not only protection but real estate for a mission in a prime location that no amount of money could have obtained, etc..

At the time of the Bungo Consultation (also called the Usuki Deliberation), Ricci, who was sent to China by Valignano, had already expressed his doubts on doing everything as it was done in Europe, and was soon to take up the robes of a Buddhist monk and even shave his head and beard. Since Buddhist monks were not as highly esteemed in China as they were in Japan (something already pointed out by a number of Jesuits) this was *not* a very good strategy. Still, "it took Ricci several years to learn he had developed the wrong external image . . . Supported in his conviction that he had to abandon Chinese priestly dress and appearance both by influential Chinese scholars and by his own superior Valignano, Ricci made the final break in the summer of 1595." (LR) For so brilliant a scholar, he was very slow to catch on, at least compared to the cross-cultural wizard Organtino!

2. *The Chinese Rites Controversy.* For readers unfamiliar with it, a brief outline. About a century after the Bungo Consultation consensus was reached, Paris and Rome saw a theological debate about the nature of Chinese "rites." Jesuits in Peking wrote up their understanding on what rites were and were not and presented it to Emperor K'ang Hsi to sign. The petition said that people don't *worship* Master K'ung (Confucius) but kowtow to show they *revere* his teaching; that the ceremony for the dead is to manifest a sincere affection and spirit of love and the setting up of tablets to the ancestors does not mean their souls are thought to be actually residing in the wood; and the sacrifice is only to help "concentrate their devotion as though the persons were present" to make them feel like they were "meeting them in the flesh," in other words to keep the memory of ones ancestors dear forever. (George Minamiki, S.J. THE CHINESE RITES CONTRAVERSY

FROM ITS BEGINNING TO MODERN TIMES / Loyola U. P.) It was a mature document that rose above the immature Western theology we can still find behind ridiculous terms like "ancestor worship" and "nature worship." The Emperor, naturally, liked what he read, signed it and wrote that *no part needed emendation*. Needless to say, this was a remarkable undertaking. Unfortunately, the idiots in Rome considered the opinion of the Emperor an affront, for he was a civil authority, not a religious one. They didn't come to their senses on this until the 1930's.

There is no doubt that the Rites Controversy was a historical happening of more importance than the Bungo Consensus *in Europe*. Moreover, the theo-philosophical effort on the part of Ricci required a higher level of scholarship – the man didn't only read but wrote books in Chinese! – than the work of Valignano. But, I do believe the significance of the Bungo Consultation (or Consensus?) *as a milestone in human history* exceeds that of the Rites Controversy. And, I think Valignano's role in bringing it about and developing a Japanese church that would be sainted if churches could be sainted, is every bit as praiseworthy. Moreover, the Chinese scholars who write about Ricci, willfully or not, fail to give Valignano and the Japanese church (Frois, Organtino, etc.) credit for their pioneering policies of accommodation.

Reading Spence (S:MPMR) and Mungello (M:CL), one might think Ricci invented accommodation and Valignano, his Superior, simply went along! Spence at least gives several pages to a biography of Valignano; but he wrongly leaves the reader with the impression that Valignano pretty much gave up on the Japanese in favor of the Chinese (See my Midword) and fails to mention what he accomplished in Bungo, except in respect to a main theme of his book, sodomy. That is to say, he treats Ricci, his protagonist fairly, but treats Valignano, a prop, cavalierly. Mungello is far worse, for he shows no knowledge of any Japan connection. He writes of "somewhat rigid and Eurocentric attitudes and approaches among missionaries" and how "distinguishing himself from them, Ricci stressed flexibility and sympathy in his approach to the Chinese people and culture and therefore *his* method is referred to as one of "accommodation." Indeed, he stresses this supposedly unique accommodation, but does not even mention Bungo, where a majority of missionaries, or rather, Consensus of Jesuits already supported accommodation in 1580 and by 1582, the year Ricci was sent to China, had even worked out specific rules (*viz* Valignano's *Advertimentos* of 1581). Ricci was following the policy of the Company. Mungello's only mention of Valignano, whose heroic efforts succeeded in making that accommodation (sensible accommodation, compromising in the right places) *the* policy, is mentioned only once, to tell us he *acceded to* Ricci's perception of a need to write books in Chinese of a high literary standard to persuade Chinese of the validity of Christianity.

While Japanese and Chinese were considered "white" by Xavier – whose biography was written by Valignano – two generations earlier, and the testimony of many visitors mentioned the equality or superiority of Japan and China to Europe in one respect or another, the Bungo Consensus may well be the first official act of cultural equality in the modern world. [1]

1. *First Official Act of Equality?* The fact that the Japanese gained equality *as whites* (that all colors were not included) should not completely invalidate the claim that the Bungo Consensus was a significant milestone in race relations for the West any more than the fact women were not given voting rights and slavery was tacitly permitted should make the American Bill of Rights a worthless development in the history of constitutional government. It was a big step in the right direction. It was not the only one. Almost a half century earlier, Las Casas excoriated the Spaniard's cruel behavior against the meek Indios. His seventh reason Lord Don Philip Prince of Spain should act quickly to stop the genocide is one horrendous metaphor after another:

> The Spaniardes doe sucke from the Indians the whole substaunce of their bodies, because they haue nothing else in their houses, They make them spitte blood . . . . To put the Indians into the Spaniardes handes, is, to giue the childes throate to a frantick and mad man when he hath the razor in his hande: or it is as much as to deliuer men into the power of the furious or capital enemies, who long time haue verye desirously wayted to put them to death. It is as a man shoulde commit a faire young virgin to the guiding of a young man snared, transported, and doting in her loue, whereby she shoulde be spoiled and deflowred, unlesse shee were miraculously preferued. To be briefe, it were as good to throwe them among the hornes of wild Bulles . . . (L(S) SC)

If Las Casas saw Indians as different but equal (or even *superior*), the equality was *purely moral* – they were obviously gentler than the Spanish devils (as he calls his countrymen). He does not validate their cultural practices in relative terms as Valignano does the Japanese, but, as Todorov (COA) puts it, rationalizes them as a developmentally primitive stage of one civilization, ours. (As primitives, he thinks they behave a bit better than we did at that stage.)

Needless to say, neither this Dominican's kindness, nor the Jesuits' relativity and tolerance won the West. Hundreds of years later in America, Japanese not only were no longer "white," they were no longer treated as humans. At the very time Edward Morse (in Boston) was extolling the Japanese – "a book might be written on the lower working classes of Japan; their honesty, frugality, politeness, cleanliness, and every virtue that in our country might be called Christian" (JDD) – people in California "threw stones and bricks" at Japanese brave enough to walk in the parks, threw "showers of pebbles" at Japanese on the street, and spat at them. White friends would pretend not to recognize Japanese in public. In A JAPANESE ARTIST IN LONDON, Markino has pages on the hell he went through in California. Besides the above examples of "our" barbarian behavior, bullies near the Cliff House destroyed all of the painting equipment he had worked three or four months to buy. In London, where he was much more kindly treated, even thirteen years after leaving California, he would wake up with nightmares. Even the lower classes were kinder in London. Here is the response of "a little shopkeeper" (someone running a newspaper stand) to his telling him how he was treated in the Land of the Free:

He said, *"Thut ain't fair, sir! Indeed, thut ain't fair!"* How sweet this world was to me! I carried this sweet "thut ain't fair" in my head, and slept with it all night so comfortably. (M:JAL:1910)

Though Valignano's SUMARIO was a secret epistle to the head of the Jesuit Order, the parts concerning only the Japanese culture (not the part on the Jesuit work in Japan) were released for use in Japan-related publications (in various languages) that accompanied the European tour of a handful of young Japanese Christians – an endeavor itself devised partly because Valignano realized that radical difference was a two-way street: if Westerners found a country as contrary as Japan hard to believe, the Japanese, for their part, could hardly grasp the reality of a nation they had never seen. They would have to see it with their own eyes, or failing that, the eyes of a fellow Japanese, to be convinced. [1]

1. *Showing Europe to the Japanese.* While the bits of technology and science – guns and astronomical knowledge – brought by the Portuguese gave some backing to their claims about the might of Europe, most Japanese were not convinced that the Europeans were more than just one more type of barbarian. This was a big problem for the Jesuits, because the treatment they received in Japan was largely dependent upon the way Japanese viewed their employers and employing countries. A tie-in with trade helped (if aid is tied with trade today, trade was tied with Christian "aid" for the souls, in so far that Japanese rulers feared losing it by angering the Jesuits.) But this trade pressure wasn't enough. For the Jesuits, and those they converted to be treated with respect – rather than as "Southern barbarians" – they had to prove they came from a lofty place. The exotic must be confirmed by a countryman to be believed. So an embassy of Japanese, by and for the Jesuits, was assembled at Valignano's behest. A fine retrospective summary by England's first Ambassador *to* Japan:

> Their reception at Rome was not only magnificent, but their whole progress through Spain and Italy was one continued ovation. 'A nation of thirty millions of civilized and intelligent people has been won from the heathen!' Great indeed was the joy and triumph; and this was the culminating point of the church's success. (Alcock A:COT)

I read somewhere that the worth of the Embassy was serious compromised by the youth of the ambassadors. But judging from their handwriting, these were precocious and extremely bright young nobles (three were princes (sons of daimyô) at the perfect age for rapid learning; and when they came back to Japan eight years later, they were in their prime. Frois writes (in his HISTORIA) that they were given a lot of what we would today call press. They were not ignored. If the impact on Japan as a nation – for it had pretty much turned into one nation over the eight year absence – was not large enough to make the trip worthwhile, it was not their fault or Valignano's that

> In the same hour, while the artillery of St. Angelo, answered by the guns of the Vatican, was thundering a welcome to the Japanese ambassadors, an edict had gone forth from the Kubo-sama, or sovereign lord of Japan, banishing all Catholic missionaries within six months, on pain of death; and ordering all crosses to be thrown down, and all churches to be razed to the ground." (A:COT)

When they returned, the church was hobbled. They were lucky not to be executed. Valignano was able to meet Hideyoshi (the "Kubo-sama" mentioned), who, Frois tells us, asked countless questions to the up-and-coming translator Joao Rodrigues and the senor ambassador "Don Mancio," whom he wanted to adopt. This would seem to indicate success, but I still wonder if the Embassy might not have ultimately hurt the Christian cause in Japan precisely because it succeeded all too well in proving Europe was indeed powerful and therefore dangerous to get involved with. The details of this or that plot – real or invented – that reached the Japanese ears were less important than the overall perception of threat, and may only served as pretexts for a crackdown. In this sense, Valignano's reasonable intentions to teach Japanese how powerful and advanced the West was may well have backfired.

The returning "Ambassadors" were to have received support in the form of a book printed in Macao. DE MISSIONE LEGATORVM IAPONEN [and more, abbreviated] (J/S:DM:1590) gave not only the itinerary of the visit but

> *"as complete an account, as it was then possible to give, of the state of Europe, its largeness and division, its government Monarchical, Aristocratical, or Democratical: Of the pomp and magnificence of the European Princes, the splendor of their Court, their riches and power: Of the manners, customs, and way of life of the nobles and inferior sort of people: Of the flourishing condition of trade and commerce: Of the way of carrying on war in Europe, both by Sea and Land . . ."* (from the translator's introduction to Kaempfer's K:HOJ).

According to de Sande, who evidently translated the manuscript for the book into Latin from Valignano's Spanish, the content for the dialogue between "Michael" (or, Miguel) the Christian name of one of the Japanese ambassadors and his relation Leo was constructed from reports sent back to Goa by the ambassadors during their long trip. As such, the report is as much Valignano's as the ambassadors' – I usually quote it as "Miguel=Valignano" or Leo=Valignano, etc. – and he uses the book to reiterate his reasons for the Embassy through Miguel's mouth:

> The first reason is that the Jesuit Visitador Pater Alexander Valignanus coming all the way from Europe to Japan, noticed right off that Japanese customs greatly differed from those of Europe and, furthermore, because the respective distance between the two was so great, news of the size and excellence of Europe's many republics and kingdoms, the kings' authority and power and many other wondrous things, arrived in Japan if they arrived at all, as faint wind-born rumor reaching only some of the islands; and even then, when the Company's padres speak about these things to us Japanese, the Japanese don't at all believe them; and, as they know from experience, this results in both countless inconveniences and psychological wounds [to the Jesuits], and less of the thing most desired, results in proselytizing. [Dang, I'd like to see the Latin for the "psychological wounds!" – I am translating from the modern Japanese translation of the Latin.] (J/S:DM)

As we have already seen, the Jesuits did not enjoy being treated as "niggers." The lifestyle changes agreed upon at Bungo and the increased credibility brought about by the Embassy's testimony were supposed to change this. But the latter was too late. Despite a tenuously maintained friendship with Hideyoshi and his successors, the Jesuits had to swallow their pride in Europe as the child of Christianity (and Portugal as its prodigy) and play humble pie in order to keep their toehold in Japan. Hideyoshi was intent upon proving his authority. He had, after all, massacred entire sects of Buddhists, not over a religious matter, but because they would not acknowledge his absolute authority. Introducing DE MISSIONE, with its Europe this and that, to Japanese at this time would be like throwing oil on a fire. As a result, the book was not translated (as far as we know, although Kaempfer's translator mentions a translation, he seems to have relied upon de Sande's (dedication) or "Leo's" (dial.34) statement of intention) into Japanese until the mid-twentieth century (1942), from Sande's Latin, which the Japanese translators claim is very poor, as does Sande, himself. In his delightfully honest "dedication and note to the reader," De Sande admits his head was full with his study of written Chinese at the time Valignano requested his participation and that as a result, he fears that he turned Valignano's original into something sounding as much Chinese as Latin! – and this poor Latin was damaged by the transcription of a poor speller. I don't much care for the Japanese either, for it tends toward a style I call *translationese*, but not a little of the dialogue touches upon contrasts made in the TRATADO, so I have dared to English substantial parts of it in this book.

Today, DE MISSIONE is perhaps most valuable for students of modernization. "Miguel," with some imput from "Mancio," gives many reasons for Europe's wealth and power. Peace, rich natural resources and trade are the main factors given, with the first condition, based on the bonds of Christian love, necessary to develop the other

two (dialogue 31 and elsewhere). The relative superiority of Europe and China , where de Sande had served, is also given ample attention, with Europe, of course, winning the laurels.

Post-script: Compare the Japanese sent to Rome with the talent brought back from the West Indies by Cortez.

> "Four Indians skilled in juggling with a stick with their feet, . . . skillful dancers who were accustomed to use some sort of contrivance, so that they seem to fly in the air while dancing; . . . three Indian hunchbacks who were monstrosities, for their bodies appeared broken, and they were very dwarfish" (Bernal Diaz in T:COA)!

At any rate, through Valignano's masterful summary, most well-educated Europeans already knew something about Japan's topsy-turvyness by the time the TRATADO manuscript was penned. This, and the facts that 1) the table of contents for Frois's unpublished HISTORIA DE IAPAM show that much of a "Summary of Japan" making up the main part of the first volume (unfortunately missing) written in 1584 was largely identical with the TRATADO; [1] 2) the TRATADO was neatly rewritten even though spaces and other things indicate it was not intended for publication as is; and 3) it was full of Japanese terms with no translations, suggest it was intended for showing to other Jesuits in Asia who, as Matsuda and Joressen point out, often included Japanese terms in their letters (for example, the *waza to* for "on purpose" Frois often uses, to emphasize the contrariness of an action) partly because they came from diverse language cultures. These knowledgeable men could then use it to explain what accommodation was about or, with some explanation, as a training tool for Jesuits coming to Japan, perhaps something we might call culture-shock therapy to make certain they left their racism behind. [2]

1. *Frois's "Summary of Japan."* Froi's HISTORIA is not only scattered through a half-dozen libraries, but most is copied rather than original manuscript and information about the missing first part found in letters and other documentation is contradictory. Page after page of explanation is given by the translators of the fullest version of the HISTORIA published to date (FUROISU NIHON-SHI, trans. and annot. Matsuda Kiichi and Kawasaki Momota Chuokoronsha 1977). Here, let us just note that the "Summary of Japan" is actually called a *tratado* by Frois (?) at the head of the Ajuda (?) library's Cod. 49-IV-54 manuscript. This *tratado* is intended for the head of the volume of history covering 1549-1578. But most references – including internal references in the Prologue – speak of a separate first vo-lume including this summary, or *tratado*, and an intro-duction to each of Japan's 66 provinces, and only disagree upon the order in which those two parts should appear.

At any rate, the text of this first volume is still missing and may never be found. All we have is a table of contents. And it was by no means final, for when a group under Josef Montanya (sp?) transcribed the HISTORIA in the 18th century, it copied that table of contents (found in some old un-named document!) and, unable to find the text, simply appended it to the HISTORIA. Here, let us only note the fact that some of the separate chapters of TRATADO are found together – architecture + food, war +

horses, boats + gardens – and, conversely, there are chapters for what are scattered contrasts in TRATADO (eg. the tea ceremony and judicial system) and religious matters get twenty-four (!), rather than two chapters.

Had Frois's Summary only survived, we would have a brief 16th century synopsis of not only many varieties of Japanese Buddhism but Shinto as well. With respect to Zen, the tea ceremony, Japanese writing and other things covered so well by Joao Rodrigues "the translator," this is no big loss. In fact, the similarity of many of the headings – and content (compare on handkerchief tissues!) – with the first part of Rodrigues's *Church History*, translated by Cooper as THIS ISLAND OF JAPON suggests that Rodrigues may well have read and used the missing Summary (the Japanese translators of Frois's HISTORIA list the *Church History* right after TRATADO as the two extant documents most closely related to it). But, for things *not* covered by Rodrigues, the loss is irreparable.

I would guess the un-named old document giving the table of contents of the Summary predates the TRATADO, because the amount and nature of the material we find in the TRATADO on what the Summary combines as "horses and war," "housing and food" etc. warrants their being given a separate chapter. That is to say, the bare-bones TRATADO probably has the greater number of contrasts. It is the explanations we are sadly missing.

2. Culture Shock Therapy. This term – where shock can link either way – is mine. I was reading the *"Relations of the Japanese to the Society"* (part of the *modus viviendi/operendi* worked out at Bungo), the part regarding the "close union" of the European and Japanese missionaries where the "greatest hindrance" was said to lie in the immense difference between their respective customs. "Many things which for us denote politeness and good breeding wound the feelings of the Japanese." Living in Japan, the Europeans had to "learn and observe Japanese etiquette." The following three sentences in particular made me think of "culture shock therapy":

> They should not speak disparagingly of the native customs, as newcomers from India usually do. As soon as they arrive in Japan, their attention must be drawn to the matter; the Superior is to see that from the start they impress on their memories Japanese usages in keeping with the "Rules for the ceremonial and customs which Ours are to observe in one another's company and with strangers." Someone well acquainted with Japanese etiquette should introduce them to these customs and drill them thoroughly in them for some days, so that they may not be taken for uncouth and unmannerly people. (S:VMP p340)

The Bungo Consultation made it clear that learning respect for an exotic culture *takes work*. The Jesuits did not stop at the need to learn proper behavior; they even thought to prevent the opposite, by unlearning it! Might not Frois's *Tratado* make a fine teacher's aid for this culture-shock training?

At the same time, as DR once speculated (corresp.), could the plentiful Japanese in the manuscript suggest the reverse, that the TRATADO might also have been intended for training Japanese, who were going to Macao, Goa or Europe? This does seem *possible* because, as exampled in the text, some of the words (eg. *waza-waza*) were rhetorical rather than necessary (such as *katabira*, a type of robe as we shall see later) and because awareness of difference would be important not only to Japanese traveling to Europe but for those who trained in Japan. To wit:

> Care has to be taken, too, that Japanese members of the order do not, through association with Europeans, grow remiss in observing their native forms of etiquette, as could easily happen. This would shock the feelings of externs. (S:VMP.)

However, so many of the distiches are "we" and "they" rather than "Europeans" and "Japanese" – not to mention the order, with "us" coming first – that the Tratado, as is, would not have been ideal for going in that direction!

My personal experience with what I term *the art of listing* is that it is addictive. Whether it be "good things," "bad things," "things that are unpleasant to see," "things without merit" – these last two from THE PILLOW BOOK OF SEI SHONAGON, which is full of lists, called *mono-wa-tsukushi*, or *"the exhausting of things"* in Japanese – once you get started, it is hard to stop. It is a form of intellectual collecting. Whoever or whatever sparked it, once Frois got started on his "contradictory things," he was hooked. And, the blank spaces show the typical wish of an amateur who wishes to involve others in one's hobby. Frois might have been going for an even thousand. This is not known, but with the additional contrasts – my *Faux Frois* – supplied in this book, we may come close.

V
topsy-turvy japan over the period of seclusion

Valignano's listing of dozens of contrasts, rather than Frois's hundreds, made their anonymous way into the drawing rooms of Europe. One finds them in almost every work on Japan published for centuries, often barely recognizable, for most popular books translated and rephrased the distiches found more or less as Valignano wrote them, in Maffei's popular *Historia*. Meanwhile, a Dutchman did an end-run on the Catholic press (remember they were fighting for freedom against the Spanish). THE VOYAGE OF JOHN HUYGHEN VAN LINSCHOTEN TO THE EAST INDIES (English translation, 1598) borrows – or rather steals, for no credit is given – several pages of contrasts from Valignano's earliest lists of Japanese contrasts.[1]

1. Van Linschoten and Valignano. The Hakluyt Society or later editors of the 1884 reprint of this 1598 English translation of THE VOYAGE give some of Maffei's distiches in the footnotes but fail to see that not only the contrasts but most of the condensed summary of Japanese mores were rather taken straight from Valignano! Linschoten's examples of "cleane contrary" Chinese and Japanese are not "us" (Europeans) *vs.* "they" (Japanese) re-edited to fit "this theory of Linschoten," as the editors assume, but taken from the first version (1579) of the PRINCIPIO. The editor does, however, tell us that V. Linschoten, a Dutchman, learned Spanish as a boy and gained employed in the suite of the Archbishop of Goa from 1583, when they went to the Indies on the same boat, until the Archbishop's death in 1588 (at which time he was house-sitting while the Archbishop traveled to Europe.) Needless to say, he was in the perfect place to read Valignano's draft! As Linschoten's VOYAGE was probably read by many Dutch before they went to Japan, the idea of Japanese being "cleane contrarie unto all other nations" may have received a bigger boost by this work than Carletti's slightly later VOYAGE.

Only one work evidently borrows directly from Frois's TRATADO. This is the oft-published work MY VOYAGE AROUND THE WORLD (*Ragionamenti . .*) of Carletti. Valignano is his favorite source. After describing a Japanese peasant who shook his feet "so much his shoes came off" and pardoned himself "instead of removing a hat – which they never wear," as he passed the Florentine merchant on a bridge, he writes:

> And as their customs are no less strange than varied, and as they are opposite to us in location of their land, I have made notes about them and contrasted them with ours in every way. But all that was lost with everything else of mine. But to report something that comes back to my memory, what greater strangeness could there be than their way of caring for the sick, whom they feed on fresh and salted fish . . . . and on various raw, sour, unripe fruits, and without ever letting blood, thus in everything doing the opposite of what we do? (transl. Herbert Weinstock)

The fine details of shaking off shoes and the humorous way he says they do not take off the hats "which they never wear" is pure Carletti – a fine observer and witty raconteur. But how strange that "their way of caring for the sick" should happen to be the thing to come back to him, for it just happens to be something stressed in Valignano's 1583(?) SUMARIO (*Mas cousa de espanto es ver la manera del curar . . .*) and is identical down to the details about the food! Yet, as Matsuda and Jorissen point out, part of the "notes" were almost certainly made from Frois's manuscript, which Carletti could have seen while staying in Nagasaki for ten months on the year of Frois's death, 1597; for a number of observations on contrasting maritime matters which are not in Valignano's work are not only treated by Carletti, *but in the same order in which they appear* in the TRATADO. Or might Carletti have "requisitioned" that missing first volume of Frois's HISTORIA, in which case it may be lost forever in a shipwreck on the bottom of the sea? [1]

1. *Carletti mystery.* Carletti lost everything he was bringing back to Europe in a shipwreck. The long explanations of subjects dear to his heart (on, say, *cocoa* and *metal balls implanted in penises* go on for pages) tell me the man either had a phenomenal memory or retained just enough of his notes to prove he was the best reporter that ever lived. Who can say? My guess is that he either hastily copied the TRATADO or parts of it, or had the missing prologue with him, but did not have time to really read it. If he spent time with Frois's contrasts, surely he would have had more of them in his book, rather than only having those mentioned in Valignano/Maffei! He probably only read – or kept notes (maybe sent them home in a letter to a friend?) for the part of TRATADO dealing with ships. It is also possible Carletti read a Valignano manuscript at Frois's in Nagasaki.

Forty years after Frois's death, Japan was sealed off to all but a tiny trade with the Dutch, which was conducted with as much care as we would with aliens, perhaps carrying germs that could infect and destroy us. So all news from Japan had to come from the Dutch and those who worked for them. A 1670 work ostensibly on the Dutch EMBASSY TO THE EMPEROR OF JAPAN, but actually a hodge-podge of history, second-hand reportage and imaginative explanation by Montanus and an early 18th century anonymous English translation of a late 17th century HISTORY OF THE CHURCH OF JAPAN, by "Monsieur L' Abbe de T." are full of contrasts borrowed from Valignano=Maffei.[1] Despite the sensationalism (monstrous depictions of idol-worship in the former and an entire volume on gruesome martyrdoms in the latter), Montanus admits the good characteristics of the Japanese as well as the bad, while Monseiur L' Abbe presents everything favorable Valignano wrote about the Japanese character and a few he did not, while touching upon only a couple of their shortcomings! [2]

1. *Montanus and Monsieur L' Abbe de T.'s contrasts*. I plan to cite both of these authors' second or third-hand contrasts deriving from Valignano's SUMARIO (i.e., Maffei) occasionally, for the late seventeenth and early eighteenth century English provides a bold and, I trust, entertaining counterpoint to my timid translation of Frois. In Montanus's case, the only thing new that is added comes from his bold glosses. Sometimes they are instructive, for they help us to find something wet between the lines of Frois's all too dry contrast; as often, they are wrong. *Such is the risk of explanation.* Here are two examples of the latter:

> "Yet in their Diet, they are no less curious or dainty than the Chineses, and like them use two Sticks, one in each hand, with which they take up their Hashed Service, needing neither Knives nor Forks . . .

> "We in heat of Summer affect cool and pure Spring Water, which they drink hot, liking what is muddy better than what is clear. (M:EEJ)

Montanus's explanation about the dishes (service=food) coming out already minced (*hashed*) happens to be correct, but *one in each hand!?* There is a tendency of Japanese to favor tea over cool water, but liking what is muddy? (Maybe he heard of *miso* soup?) L' Abbe is far more circumspect about his contrasts, makes no mistakes worth mentioning and adds something substantial. Here is a contrast that would have been one of the first for me to make yet, as far as I recall, missed by both Valignano and Frois (Does any one recall the source?):

> "As in France, we distinguish the Ladies of Quality by the length of their Trains, so in Japan they are known by the number of their Cloaths. There are some who have five, ten, and twenty at once . . . They are so delicately fine, and thin, that you may put several of them together in your Pocket. (A:HCJ)

2. *Monsieur L' Abbe de T.'s Praise of Japan and Montanus's Orientalism*. L' Abbe is only bold when improving upon the *good* things said about the Japanese character. Where Valignano and others wrote of the extraordinary lack of bad language and the way the very grammar dictates politeness, L' Abbe claims

> If anyone chances to come out in Company with an unhandsome word, the young Men rise immediately and retire in silence, with as much shame, as a modest Virgin wou'd do upon an Immodest Discourse. (A:HCJ) [This is silly because they don't use or make a big deal over bad words (White Usanians demonstrate the extreme with "our" hyper-sensitivity, as ludicrous today as it was in the Victorian Age. Such concern seems to peak when the Robber Barons rise, a sort of fake gentility justifying a cruelly unequal society.)]

Where others compared their mastery of their passions to the stoics, L' Abbe writes "that nothing of the very Stoics is like them." That is to say they make the Stoics look like cry-babies. Not only are they very strict about thievery, but "They are so just and free from Deceit, that if a Merchant gives them more than due, they immediately restore it of their own accord."(True. What Morse was to later applaud.) And, here is the best of all:

> The persons of the first Rank have a Custome amongst them, which we can never enough admire, they have for the most part one of their Domesticks of the best sense, ordering him to inspect their Actions, and admonish them of their Faults, believing all Men, but most of all the Great ones unjust; and that Flatterers who are about them rather serve to nourish their Vices, than to mind them of their Faults. (A:HCJ)

Until I read this I had never really thought much about the chamberlain scurrying about admonishing the judge (also a great swordsman because modern heroes must be supermen) on TV Easterns, called *jidai-geki* or "period drama" in Japan. My assumption was that the opinionated old gentleman was only a cute TV character who served to show the particular magnanimity of the great judge. Thanks to L' Abbe, I now know differently!

L' Abbe also reminds us of what I would call the spirit of Bungo when he tackles European conceit head-on:

> It is very usual for Civil and Polite Nations to look upon all others as Barbarians. The Grecians were once of this Opinion, and the Romans after them thought there was no wit or breeding out of Italy. In like manner, Europe being now the Seat of Learning and Science, where learned Academies are set up for the Discovery of hidden Secrets in Nature, we take all the Rest of Mankind for meer Barbarians: but those who have travelled into China and Japan, must confess those people far surpass us in the endowments, both of body and mind. (A:HCJ)

Montanus, on the other hand, sensationalizes all the bad qualities of the Japanese depicted by Valignano in his early writing, proving Valignano was right to qualify himself in his last, unpublished LIBRO, when, unfortunately, the cat was already out of the bag. With Montanus, in 1670, I feel, for the first time, that I am looking at the early modern stereotypically Orientalized East. A Byzantine Japan. Dozens of spectacular illustrations show absurdly realistic monumental idols – not sculptures, but depictions of what seem to be real people, animals and fantastic creatures (Did the artist believe that was how Orientals experienced them?), surrounded by people abjectly prostrating themselves. (Actually Japanese have always enjoyed themselves, frolicking about when visiting temple grounds.)

The German Kaempfer, who spent a few years in the tiny Dutch trading post, and enjoyed two annual visits to the Capital (then, Edo = Tokyo), observed much with the mind of a doctor and amateur botanist instead of a theologian. His thorough book, containing travelogue type observation and locally researched natural history, mythology, etc. with ample drawings, many copied from Japanese books, was the first to contribute substantial information not already found in the Jesuits' writing. It also includes justification for the Japanese policy of exclusion (and of capitol punishment for minor crimes) on the basis of the fruit: a crime-free and happy society. It reads as well today as Carletti's lighter fare and, unlike Montanus, Kaempfer does not Orientalize. While Kaempfer loved oddity as much as anyone in his baroque era – he introduces "the Shogun who loved dogs" twice and spends pages on blowfish – he stands out for *not* remarking upon any tendency toward *contrariness* on the part of the Japanese.

But the theme of *contrariety* was pretty much fixed in the literature. There are two footnotes regarding "some of the extraordinary differences between the Japanese customs and those of Europe" by the anonymous early 19th century English editor of the Russian Golownin's touching account of Japan and his captivity there (G:MCJ v3p81) While most of the differences given ultimately derive from Valignano/Maffei, the editor credits "Dutch writers" with the idea and Jesuits are not even mentioned! [1]

1. *Uncredited Jesuits.* It's bad enough that Valignano and/or Maffei are not credited (In Frois's case, with TRATADO unknown, that could not be helped). What hurts is that the Jesuits came to be wrongly identified with *criticism* of the Japanese alone. This could only be expected of the English who had long been at War with Iberia and Catholicism, but even the admirable Russian gentleman, Captain Golownin, who came to highly admire the Japanese over the course of his 27 month imprisonment there in the early 18th century, fumes:

> . . . the missionaries, expelled from Japan, represent the nation whom they could not succeed in deceiving, as cunning, faithless, ungrateful, revengeful, in short, in such odious colours, that it would hardly be possible to find a being who merited to be compared with a Japanese. These accounts, inspired by monastic rage, have been taken in Europe for genuine . . . This firm belief in the detestable character of the Japanese goes so far, that such expressions as Japanese malice! Japanese treachery! are [sic] become proverbial. (G:MCJ 1824)

The true tales of martyrdom (though most are about Japanese martyrs) were so horrendous (and interesting to read) that it wouldn't be surprising if the larger picture was lost, but Golownin was not fair to the Jesuits. Golownin's editor does mention Xavier's high opinion of Japanese and quotes our man "the learned jesuit" – i.e., "father Luigi Froes, in *'Lettere del Giappone'* published at Naples in 1580" – to the effect that Japanese have prodigious ability to acquire European knowledge and skills – or learn Chinese – speedily. But, the affection and respect the Jesuits expressed for the Japanese even after the martyrdom began does not come through. Valignano's splendid qualification of his own harshest criticism of the Japanese found in his LIBRO was composed in 1601, after some cruel persecutions – the Nagasaki Massacre – had already occurred. But his original tract was well balanced and hardly composed in "a monastic rage!"

After the unparalleled persecution of Japanese Christians in the first half of the 17th century, did the Jesuits (understandably) savage the Japanese and deserve to be maligned? I had not seen anything to support it and thought Montanus (*not* a Jesuit) may have started the Orientalizing, until reading about an article by Engelbert Jorissen in the *bulletin of Portuguese/Japanese Studies* ("Exotic and 'strange' images of Japan in European texts in the early 17th century") which credits (?) S. Gonçalves, S.J. with "creating a strange malevolent image of Japan" in his History (ca.1615), which was picked up by others with the result being the exotic became barbaric. So, the Jesuits may indeed deserve some blame for *bad Japan.*

To his credit, Golownin's editor also adds the first note of caution towards difference-mongering. With respect to a remark of the Swede Thunberg (like Kaempfer, a physician who served the Dutch to see Japan and equally a big Japanophile), claiming Japan was "totally different from Europe," he remonstrated:

> but, not withstanding this is generally true, it is not the less remarkable, that many of their institutions, and much of their manners . . . are absolutely fac-similes of our own feudal times, and demonstrate the existence of that system to a much greater extent than our ablest writers have hitherto imagined; at the same time, corroborating the similarity frequently noticed between Japan and Great Britian, and opening a wide field of speculation for the spirit of political prophecy . . . (G:MCJ)

I did not find that Thunberg (T:TEAA) stressed difference enough to earn such a riposte in a footnote to a third party's book, but Golownin's editor makes a good point: *differences reviewed from a developmental perspective can be understood as similarity.* Because this implies a ladder of progress, however, one might say that a neutral difference has been reinterpreted as one with a value: for, if Japan is indeed like us, then, by the yardstick of progress, it is inferior.

vi
modern topsy-turvydom: alcock

The later half of the 19th century saw an explosion of topsy-turvy consciousness in English Literature. The Age of Nonsense may well have been born in newly "opened" Japan, for the letters of the first English Ambassador to Japan, Sir Rutherford Alcock, were "printed and laid before Parliament" and published in leading journal/s during the decade before Lewis Carroll's *Alice* discovered the Antipathies. [1] They were published in book form in 1863. ALICE in 1865. In a page of Alcock's CAPITAL OF THE TYCOON captioned *"Paradoxes and Anomalies,"* a splendid reverie on the bathhouses of Yeddo (Edo/Tokyo), which includes mention of a young Caucasian who "emerged as red as a lobster, and much as that martyr to gastronomy may be supposed to feel before all feeling is boiled out of him" – ends with the dreamy sentence: "Here, if they have any cares, they seem to forget them all in the steamy atmosphere, and forming the very oddest assemblage that can well be conceived." And, as if that steam (rather than *looking glass*) created a mirage on the brain – in the very next sentence and paragraph Alcock is *there.*

> Japan is essentially a country of paradoxes and anomalies, where all, even familiar things, put on new faces, and are curiously reversed. Except that they do not walk on their heads instead of their feet, there are few things in which they do not by some occult law, to have been impelled in a perfectly opposite manner and a reversed order. They write from top to bottom, from right to left, in perpendicular instead of horizontal lines, and their books begin where ours end, thus furnishing good examples of the curious perfection this rule of contraries has obtained. Their locks, though imitated from Europe, are all made to lock by turning their key from left to right. The course of all sublunary things appears reversed. Their day is for the most part our night, and this principle of antagonism crops out in the most unexpected and bizarre way in all their moral being, customs and habits. I leave to philosophers the explanation – I only speak the facts. There, old men fly kites while children look on; [2] the carpenter uses his plane by drawing it to him, and their tailors stitch from them . . . and, finally, the utter confusion of the sexes in the public bath-houses, making that correct which we in the West deem so shocking and improper, I leave as I find it – a problem to solve. (A:COT)

---

1. *Alcock's Topsy-Turvy date.* I would be delighted if a library sleuth could tell me exactly when Alcock first announced/printed his topsy-turvy passage, because the Marquis de Moge has a similar, but less powerful passage on European and Chinese contrasts (see my Midword) in his book on *Baron Gros's Embassy to China and Japan* published in 1860 (M:BGE) and Cornwallis has a couple lines in 1859 (C:TJJ).

2. *Old Men Flying Kites* while children watch. In Japan, today, kite-flying is, basically, a children's game, as it is

here. The exception is festivals where large kites are flown competitively – these kites are so heavy they can kill people they fall on, for which reason, some participants wear crash-helmets and an ambulance waits by the side of the field! In Alcock's day, too, most kites were flown by children, even if old men also enjoyed it. An earlier, anonymously authored 1841 book summarizing the reports coming from "members of the Dutch Factory," edited, written (and translated?) by Mrs. Busk, with an aim toward presenting "a compendium of the curious and interesting facts which they contain" includes the kite:

. . . the prettiest [festival] is one in which lighted lanterns are launched at night upon the bay, to ascertain by their fate, the destiny of the souls of deceased relatives and friends; *the oddest, one in which men holding high official situations, and of advanced years, busy themselves in flying kites, the strings being thickly studded with broken glass to cut, if possible, the string of a rival's kite;* and the most absurd, one in which the foul fiend is simultaneously expelled from every house, by dint of pelting him with boiled peas according to Meylan, with stones according to Fischer. (MANNERS AND CUSTOMS OF THE JAPANESE. B:MCJ)

This book also contains the earliest use of the adjective *topsy-turvy* in a book about Japan; but it is applied in a literal manner rather than figurative: ". . . the first indication of mourning appears in turning all the screens and sliding doors in the house *topsy-turvy*, and all the

garments inside out. (*Meylan, in B:MCJ, my *italics*) But, returning to the kite, I hate to be a spoilsport, but Eliza Skidmore, describing "an unexampled aerial carnival" she saw from "Hideyoshi's bronze-railed Shijo bridge" on the Southern end of the Tokaido, has something to say about the proverbial kite-flying grampa:

> Thousands of giant kites float upward, and the air is filled with a humming, as they soar, sweep and circle over the city like huge birds. Kite combats take place in mid-air, and strings covered with pounded glass cut other strings, and let the half-animate paper birds and demons loose. Jinrickshaw coolies on bridges and streets must dodge the hanging strings, and boys run over and into each other while watching their ventures; but the traditional kite-flying grandfathers whom one reads about in Western prints are conspicuous by their absence." (1891 S:JDJ)

This sort of kite fight can be dangerous even to observe.

I skipped Alcock's comments on Japanese horses and lady's teeth, all of which will be noticed by all subsequent Victorian era visitors, as they are found in Frois. While Alcock found more than a few things to praise in Japan (he had a soft spot for simple but effective mechanical devices, the abundance of which mystified him in view of the low cost of labor), he was an opinionated Englishman, writing from the new perspective of progress-as-the-measure-of-man – which made him far less relative about culture (religion aside) than the Jesuits in Bungo. Yet, sometime over the course of the Victorian era, whether due to the spreading American ideology of equality, Alfred Russell Wallace's testimony of equality based on years of living with alleged primitives, romantic tolerance for the exotic – *the antipodes as cute* – or, whatever, *the modern relativistic outlook began to take root*, plumb in the middle of the heyday of Orientalism, long before the flourishing of the Boas school of anthropology with which it is usually identified. Kipling, a man all too often identified with Imperialism – who, by happy coincidence, was born the very year ALICE was published – penned a charming page-long children's verse called *"We and They,"* which is as relative as relative can be. The last stanza is especially charming and deserves to be better known:

> All good people agree,
>   And all good people say,
> All nice people, like Us, are We
>   And every one else is They:
> But if you cross over the sea,
>   Instead of over the way,
> You may end by (think of it!) looking on We
>   As only a sort of They!

We do : They do, or poems of ethno-relativity. Kipling was followed by Belloc, whose hilarious *On Food* starts –

"Alas! What various tastes in food, / Divide the human brotherhood! / Birds in their little nests agree / With Chinamen, but not with me"   and ends –

" . . . yet upon the other hand, / *De gustibus non disputand* – / – Um."

Both were followed by the American poet with the world's most irregular feet, Ogden Nash (who – to those who read and know Kipling and Belloc, ogdviously – playgarized them) did a more adult version: *"Goody for our side and your side too."* If the reader knows of any more such poems – was Kipling really the first? (England has many comic poets, there must be more!) – please let me know. Perhaps we may have enough for an anthology. (The title poem can be Piet Hein's Antipode Grook).

vii

modern topsy-turvydom: chamberlain

It would seem that Alcock's patent on the "principle of antagonism" was a short one, for by the end of the century, Professor Basil Hall Chamberlain, who, according to Charles E. Tuttle Co.'s book-jacket blurb, "taught Japanese and Japan to the Japanese," became widely identified with the term "topsy-turvydom." This is not surprising, for there is even a two page *"Topsy-turvydom"* heading in his classic THINGS JAPANESE (1890)[1] that includes dozens of examples. The heading begins –

> "It has often been remarked that the Japanese do many things in a way that runs directly counter to European ideas of what is natural and proper. To the Japanese themselves our ways appear equally unaccountable. It was only the other day that a Tokyo lady asked the present writer why foreigners did so many things topsy-turvy, instead of doing them naturally, after the manner of her country people."

1. THINGS JAPANESE. Bought used, my Tuttle Co. edition lacks a title page and date, but the name was tastelessly changed to JAPANESE THINGS during the boring conformism of the West in its era of the *Organization Man* in his *Grey Flannel Suit*. Luckily, Chamberlain's preface for the (very slightly) revised 1904 edition boasting about the success of the book – "years after its first appearance, newspapers and book-makers continue to quote wholesale from it without acknowledgment" – and the explanation of its original title remained.

> . . . and the title, which cost us much cogitation, and which we borrowed from the Spanish phrase *cosas de Espana*, has passed into general use, even coming to supply titles for similar works written about other lands in imitation of this one.

What a coincidence, as Jose Luis Alvarez-Taladriz points out in his SUMARIO notes, that the modern whose name is synonymous with Topsy-turvydom – both Japanese translations of TRATADO mention Chamberlain in that respect – chose the same name for his book as Valignano, whose chapter on *"las cosas de japon"* in the *Sumario of India* (1579? or a bit later) and whose book (1583?) titled *Sumario de las cosas de japon* were the first to publish the same type of topsy-turvy material! Since THINGS JAPANESE has a very thorough section for Books on Japan, we can be fairly certain Chamberlain was unfamiliar with Valignano (or Maffei)) – but, . . . see my next note!

Neither Valignano (Maffei) nor even Carletti are mentioned. Chamberlain may not have read them. He writes of an apparent fact, a strange but natural phenomenon born of our antipodal cultures. Or, perhaps, he wants us to believe it is only natural – what anyone with eyes can not fail to see is hardly patentable – to excuse his failure to properly credit Sir Rutherford Alcock, (whose book he read and reviewed) for developing the idea of topsy-turvydom.[1] But, then, Alcock, himself, failed to mention his predecessors in topsy-turvydom, and they, theirs and so forth. Time, the ultimate plagiarist, obscured the fathers of *contrary* Japan, Valignano and Frois.

1. *Alcock, Chamberlain, Things Japanese, and the Topsy-Turvy.* While Alcock's CAPITOL OF THE TYCOON (1863) is a good read even today, it is not so *practical* as Chamberlain's headings of *Things*, and did not survive the century in which it was written. Chamberlain read and liked it. In his *"Books on Japan"* heading, he gushed "Though published forty years ago, . . . this book is still delightful and profitable reading, "and in his "Japanese People" heading, he called Alcock "one of the most acute writers on Japan" and "one of the most difficult to quote" because "one would like to transcribe it all." Impressed by the page-long quote in Chamberlain, I ordered Alcock by Interlibrary loan. And what did I find? Every*thing*!

Stymied from getting a good view of Osaka by timid officials giving all sorts of strange excuses, Alcock uses that very phrase *Cosas d' Espana!* (I assumed he was using it as a cross between a cussword and what we now call a *Catch 22*. But, later I found it elsewhere. It means "there is no accounting for (ridiculous) customs." My guess is that *Cosas d' Espana* was a popular comedy with some entertaining clashes of culture. At any rate, Chamberlain would have heard it as a young man and subconsciously registered the phrase. Or might he have read and likewise buried in his subconscious the very title of his book? Alcock's note about how his book's Chapter IX, "Japanese Sayings and Doings," was suggested in part by an outrageous book on Japan, full of those marvelous

adventures one might write on a sofa, includes this: "My observations on *things Japanese*, passing daily under my eyes at the time, very different in kind . . ." (*my italics!*)

We are talking about two long volumes. Chamberlain may well have missed both of these seemingly relevant lines. We might be talking sheer coincidence. Still, considering Chamberlain complained about people quoting him without acknowledgement, this is ironic, and grows more so when we see that Alcock also beat him to the punch with the idea of a contrary Japan.

Or, perhaps, I nit-pick, I protest too much. As Swift wrote about his account of the Struldbruggs, as Gulliver headed for Japan:

> And if I am deceived [as to the uniqueness of my account], my Excuse must be, that it is necessary for Travellers, who describe the same Country, very often to agree on dwelling on the same Particulars, without deserving the Censure of having borrowed or transcribed from those who wrote before them." (S:GT, pt3 ch11)

That is to say, if one culture happens to be topsy-turvy with respect to another, that may be an obvious particular, in which case, perhaps Alcock and Chamberlain deserve the benefit of the doubt Gulliver requests.

Unlike Herodotus and Frois's contrasts, Chamberlain's instances of "contrariety" follow the style of Al-bîrûnî whose *India* was Englished but two years before *Things Japanese* (the German edition, having appeared a few years earlier). That is to say, he usually mentions only *their* side. After all, he wrote for an English-speaking audience who clearly knew *their,* I mean "our" own. Here are some items mentioned by Chamberlain that Frois missed, and which I have not introduced elsewhere in the notes to the TRATADO. I have trimmed the edges from some of them:

> Footnotes are printed at the top of the page.
> The reader inserts his marker at the bottom. [1]
> Sweets come before the pieces de resistance [main dishes]. [2]
> The Japanese do not say "north-east," "south-west," but "east-north," "west-south." [3]
> In addressing a letter they employ the following order of words: *"Japan, Tokyo, Akasaka district, such-and-such a street, 19 Number, Smith John Mr."* – thus putting the general first, and the particular afterwards, which is the exact reverse of our method. [4]
> Japanese women needle their thread rather than threading their needle.
> Instead of running the needle through the cloth, they hold it still and run the cloth upon it. [5]
> There are no actresses to speak of; it is the women who fall in love with fashionable actors.

---

1. *Book Marks.* Today, I find no difference in the use of book-marks – for books generally rest on their butts in Japan today, as they do with us, so marks must stick up – and the cloth type are all attached on top. Books in Japan were more plentiful than in the West and seldom had hard-covers. Naturally, they laid on their side. If you lay a book on its side in front of you, the bottom of the book is what you would see, hence that is where the markers should stick out. By the way, book-marks of all types far more plentiful in Japan than in the USA because 1) the word *shiori* is so beautiful (it comes from a poetic term for "branch-bending" to mark a trail in the woods) the

thing itself appeals more; and 2), because writing and art fit the vertically long format better than ours does and this results in many attractive *shiori*.

2. *Sweets Before Meals or After.* The comparison is not very good, for the Japanese are not much on desert, period. I would write

> *We eat deserts with our meals*
> *They eat them apart from their meals*

My contrast, however, would be flawed by an accident of vocabulary; namely, we would not then call it a "desert" but a snack.

3. East-north, West-south. This order comes from the Chinese convention, and is almost invariably used to designate places, but Japanese today often use the Western way for navigation purposes. I think a bolder contrast could have been made:

> *We think of North as up.*
> *They think of East as up.*

This was, no doubt already changing by Chamberlain's time, but Kyoto retains traces of this idea even today. The East of Kyoto is "uptown" for, as they say, it is the side where the sun rises, and the West is "downtown" for the opposite reason.   Pre-Renaissance European maps likewise often had the East on top. The Chinese convention may itself have come from the primary importance of the East-West axis for people who look up at the sky rather than down at a compass.

4. *Smith John Mr.* This is not half so fun an example as that of James Joyce's *Writer as a Young Artist*, who works down from the Universe to himself. If Frois missed this contrast, it must have been because addresses, as we know of them were not needed for mailing then. The contrast parallels our respective grammar, where English may modify/describe a subject with dependent phrases, which follow it, while Japanese piles them on in front – so that "the old lady" of the *Old Lady Who Swallows the Fly* ends up at the *end* of the sequence. In

the case of mail, at least, the difference is not relative: the Japanese system is clearly the more logical, for our Post Office is put in the position of reading our addresses from the bottom line up!   Direction and name order are apparently related.

But, unlike the Chinese and Koreans who generally retain the family-name-first in English, Japanese, like Hungarians, choose to use the English order. When I tried to use the original Japanese order when referring to Japanese – more for euphony than principle – in my letters, the Japanese-run *Japan Times* did not allow it! On the other hand, English names are often reversed in Japanese. (Sometimes it gets confusing. I recall finding half of my books under "Robin" and half under "Gill" in the Japanese equivalent of *Books in Print*.) It makes for an interesting cultural dilemma.   Had we best respect culture by following the *When in Rome* style of the Japanese? Or, had we best hold inviolate the phonetic order of the individual's name?

5. *Running Clothes On a Needle*. When one sews a thin broadly woven fabric using wide stitches proceeding in a simple porpoise-like manner – how I would describe most of the hemming work on traditional Japanese dress – that is the best way to sew. I have done it, without ever seeing anyone do it nor having read about it. You must, however, make subtle adjustments of the position of the needle's point, while you fold the clothing into it.

The *Topsy-turvy* heading was not the only place for the topsy-turvy in *Things Japanese*. After writing under "Time," that Japanese have six night-hours and six day-hours, twice as long as ours, beginning with 9 and ending with 4, with sunrise and sunset always at 6, Chamberlain gives us a prime example:

> Why, it will be asked, did they count the hours backwards? *A case of Japanese topsy-turvydom,* we suppose. But then why, as there were six hours, not count from six to one, instead of beginning at so arbitrary a number as nine? The reason is this: -- three preliminary strokes were always struck, in order to warn people that the hour was about to be sounded. Hence if the numbers one, two, three had been used . . . (C:TJ)

His explanation of why Japanese time was counted down to *four* rather than *one* is fine as it is. But how about the broader idea of *counting down*? If you think of time as something you use up – as, most of us do as we contemplate a deadline, or mark off days on a calendar – the idea of counting down seems far more logical than counting *up* (I am surprised Ben Franklin didn't advocate such a system to make us more frugal with it!). And, Chamberlain forgot to mention the most interesting aspect of Japanese time, the varying length of the hours. [1]

---

1. *Japanese Time.* Pivoting on sunrise and sunset, the length of the "night" and "day" hours naturally varied with the seasons. I personally find this far more attractive than our uniform hours. The fact some Japanese Edo era watch-smiths succeeded in making time-pieces that automatically adjusted the length of the day and night-time hours tells you why Japan was able to industrialize in no time flat! The three preliminary strokes to alert the listener fit very well with a Japanese observation of my own. I find Japanese often concentrate so hard – or,

screen out noise so successfully – that they start aloud when disturbed for something. Given this mental constitution, Japanese would need such an alert more than less-focused people. Before developing this further, we must find out what, if any, other society has used such an alert and whether Chamberlain's explanation is correct, for an 1841 book compiled mostly from Dutch sources gives a completely different explanation, namely:

Nine being esteemed the perfect number, noon and

midnight are both called "nine o'clock," the one of the day, the other of the night; while sunrise and sunset are respectively "six o'clock" of the day and "six o'clock" of the night [It's too bad Japanese didn't use Arabic numbers, where 6 and 9 are opposite in appearance!] . . . Nine . . . is considered the first hour. Twice 9 are 18; subtract the decimal figure and 8 remains, therefore [it] is the hour following noon or midnight . . . Three times 9 are 27; subtract the

decimal figure and 7 remains, and the third hour becomes 7 o'clock of day or night. . . . (Fischer paraphrased in B:MCJ 1845)

Since the hours are twice as long as ours, after 4 is reached by this method (based on multiplying up, rather than counting down as I imagined) the next hour brings us to noon/midnight when there is nothing left to do but go back to nine. (see, too 5-13)

On the whole, Chamberlain is fair, amusing and still may be the best and most thorough guide to the traditional Japan and its mind [1] – it is why he is still published today – but deep explanations are sometimes neglected for breathless "topsy-turvy" exclamations such as we saw above. Why such laziness in this prolific and generally conscientious writer? *Viz*, Chamberlain on "Logic" –

> Sometimes, after a recurrence of astounding instances [problematic business transactions], one is apt to exclaim that Japanese logic is the very antipodes of European logic, that it is like London and New Zealand, – when the sun shines on one, 'tis night-time in the other, and *vice-versa*. Were it really so, action would be easy enough: – one would simply have to go by the "rule of contraries." But no; the contradiction is only occasional, it only manifests itself sporadically and along certain, – or uncertain – lines . . . .

> *Race*,[2] yes, that is it. The word slipped accidentally from our pen; but racial difference is doubtless the explanation of the phenomenon under discussion, – an explanation which, it is true, explains nothing . . . . (C:TJ)

1. *Chamberlain and the Japanese Mind*. The heading *"Japanese People"* in THINGS JAPANESE has a sub-title: II. Mental Characteristics. This "phenomena of the mind" can't be gauged by the "tape-line, the weighing machine, the craniometer," etc. and no matter what your opinion, someone is bound to assail you for it. So, Chamberlain "decided to express none at all, but simply to quote the opinions of others." The first is one sentence from St. Francis Xavier: "This nation is the delight of my soul." After ten pages of fun reading, Chamberlain summed up the opinions of the writers who "lived some time in Japan" to the effect that, on the credit side, Japanese manifest "cleanliness, kindliness and refined artistic taste," and on the debit side, "vanity, unbusinesslike habits, and an incapacity for appreciating abstract ideas," while "imitativeness" went either way depending upon how it was interpreted.

As far as the "imitativeness" goes, I should point out that Japanese themselves are of two minds about it. In a brow-beating frame of mind, they decry their own supposed lack of creativity; in a celebratory frame of mind they boast of their imitation-as-learning, often comparing themselves favorably to the Chinese who have too much pride to learn from the West. But, actually, Japanese have *never* lacked pride (as they often claim). They have a different sort of pride. Chamberlain came as close as anyone to describing it when he contrasted Chinese "race pride" and Japanese "national vanity." The Chinese care nothing for their polity and would not die for such an ideal,

"but they are nevertheless inalienably wedded to every detail of their ancient civilization. The Japanese, though they have twice, at intervals of a millennium, thrown everything national overboard, are intense nationalists in the abstract. In fact, patriotism may be said to be their sole remaining ideal. No Chinaman but glories in the outer badges of his race; no Japanese but would be delighted to pass for a European in order to beat Europeans on their own ground. (C:TJ)

So as not to confuse, I would prefer a single term. The Chinese *take pride* in the trappings and the tradition of being Chinese regardless of whether they are in power or not (remember, the Mongols took over China, so the Han people couldn't base their identity on control), while the Japanese *take pride* in being in charge, even if it means superficially swallowing that pride (they who never were occupied until recently, and even then for less than a generation). If pure power is real, such nationalism is hardly abstract. But so much has changed in the world since Chamberlain's time, it is hard to say how far these generalizations still apply to either people.

3. *Race as an Explanation*. Chamberlain is only saying: the Japanese are like that because they are Japanese. That his "race" is not the same as our white, yellow and black concept is shown by statements like the following:

> People are fond of drawing comparisons between the Chinese and the Japanese. Almost all are agreed that

the Japanese are the pleasanter *race* to live with, clean, kindly, artistic. On the other hand, the Chinese are universally allowed to be far more trustworthy. (Ibid. *italics* mine)

This launches a page-long discussion arriving at a complaint dressed up in a splendid aphorism – "Japan the globe-trotters paradise is also the grave of the merchant's hopes." (Ibid)

---

viii

modern topsy-turvydom: lowell

The boyish belief that on the other side of the globe all things are of necessity upside down is startlingly brought back to the man when he sets foot in Yokohama. If his initial glance does not, to be sure, disclose the natives in the every-day feet of standing calmly on their heads, . . . it does at least reveal them looking at the world as if from the standpoint of that eccentric posture. For they seem to him to see everything topsy-turvy. (Percival Lowell: THE SOUL OF THE FAR EAST)

The earliest use of the word "topsy-turvy" to describe the Japanese – as opposed to the idea, which dates back to the 16th century Jesuits – to describe Japan that I have found so far belongs to "an intellect" Chamberlain calls "truly meteor-like in its brilliancy," Percival Lowell. The date, 1888. Chances are that Chamberlain, having been on the scene longer, had himself already used "topsy-turvy" in another less famous book or article.[1] Moreover, the nature of THINGS JAPANESE suggests it was a work long in the making, so I spot a few years to Chamberlain, and put Lowell after him in my chronology. [1] But, Lowell should have been mentioned – squeezed into – Chamberlain's *"Topsy-turvy"* heading because the essay appearing at the very start of his "dazzling display of metaphysical epigrams" attacking "the inner nature of the Japanese soul," as Chamberlain himself (C:TJ) describes Lowell's SOUL, is the longest and most entertaining ever written on the subject. It is with great difficulty that I refrain from quoting *all* of the first eight pages!

Whether it be that their antipodal situation has affected their brains, or whether it is in the mind of the observer himself that has hitherto been wrong in undertaking to rectify the inverted pictures presented by his retina, the result, at all events, is undeniable. The world stands reversed, and, taking for granted his own uprightness, the stranger unhesitantly imputes to them an obliquity of vision, a state of mind outwardly typified by the cat-like obliqueness of their eyes. (L:SOFE)

Lowell writes in a style somewhere between Thoreau and Barthes – the metaphysical retina for the former and the semiotic oblique eyes for the latter – although neither of them are so besotted with the insipid third-person.

. . . If personal experience has definitely convinced him that the inhabitants of that under side of our planet do not adhere to it head downwards like flies on a ceiling, – his early *a priori* deduction, – they still appear quite as antipodal, mentally considered. Intellectually, at least, their attitude sets gravity at defiance. . . . To speak backwards, write backwards, read backwards, is but the *a b c* of their contrariety. The inversion extends deeper than mere modes of expression, down into the very matter of thought. Ideas of ours which we deemed innate find in them no home, while methods which strike us as preposterously unnatural appear to be their birthright. From the standing of a wet umbrella on its handle instead of its head to dry, to the striking of a match away in place of toward one, there seems to be no action of our daily lives, however trivial, but finds with them its appropriate reaction – equal but opposite. Indeed, to one anxious of conforming to the manners and customs of this country, the only road lies in following unswervingly that course which his inherited instincts assure him to be wrong.

. . . Like us, indeed, and yet so unlike are they that we seem as we gaze at them, to be viewing our own humanity in some mirth-provoking mirror of the mind, – a mirror that shows us all our familiar thoughts, but all turned wrong side out. [2]

1. *Chronology of Topsy-turvy*. As a writer with books that have taken a decade or more to get published, my instincts tell me to go with Chamberlain rather than Lowell. Still, a guess is a guess. I welcome confirmable "sightings" from readers on the early use of the term "topsy-turvy" used with respect to Japan.

2. *The Mirror Metaphor*. Lowell's Mirror showing things "turned wrong-side out," rather than merely reversed is the first mirror metaphor for East-West cultural difference that I have noted. The most *recent* use of the mirror image I know of is in Inoue Hisashi's short novel about Frois (FUROISU). Not long after Inoue's Frois comes to Japan, he writes a colleague in Nagasaki wondering

"With everything reversed, how can the Truth ever root here as the Truth? I can't help doubting it."

The reply.

"Yes, Japan may well be, as you write, a country in a looking glass. There are indeed many ideas and customs opposite to those of Europe. But, Brother Frois, take out a mirror and look at it closely. For sure, everything in the mirror is reversed left and right, but are Heaven and earth upside-down? In a hundred countries, there are a hundred ways of doing things, but, in every one of them, the sun rises from the East. There is no reason the Truth should not take root in this country..."

The "looking glass" suggests the "wonderland" of the Japanese translation of Carroll's THROUGH THE LOOKING-GLASS and, as far as I know, was born in translation of the same and never used as a metaphor by the Jesuits.

If Lowell's philosophy/example ratio is a bit too high, it is because his book, like Barthes', describes not real Japanese, but idealizations fitting his meta-psychological theory: *"If with us the I seems to be of the very essence of the soul, then the soul of the Far East may be said to be Impersonality."* He does a fine job with a small number of contrasts which support his master contrast – the way Japanese share the New Years for a communal birthday whereas we have individual birthdays,[1] Japanese arranged marriage vs. Western love,[2] etc., but quickly poops out. That is to say, he does not notice (or write down) trivial differences unless they matter, in which case they are no longer trivial.

1. *Individual vs Communal Birthdays*. This is no mere contrast, but Percival Lowell's exemplar:

. . . the poor little Japanese baby is ushered into this world in a sadly impersonal manner, for he is not even accorded the distinction of a birthday. He is permitted instead only the much less special honor of a birth-year. . . . *New Year's day is a common birthday for the community, a sort of impersonal anniversary for his whole world.* . . . A communistic age is, however, but an unavoidable detail of the general scheme whose most suggestive feature consists in the subordination of the actual birthday of the individual to the fictitious birthday of the community. . . . *Then [New Year's day] everybody congratulates everybody else upon everything in general, and incidentally upon being alive.* Such substitution of an abstract for a concrete birthday, although exceedingly convenient for others, must at least conduce to self-forgetfulness on the part of its proper possessor, and tend inevitably to merge the identity of the individual in that of the community. (*my italics* L:SOFE)

This description of the New Year – the part I italicized – is *splendid*. Thoreau, with his broader metaphysics would have embraced the NY idea and celebrated it, rather than call it fictitious, abstract and dangerous for individual identity. Lowell himself seems to have been of two minds about it; he used it for proof of the backwardness of the Asian psyche on the one hand and in another chapter on "Nature" and "Art" praised it. As a matter of fact, the contrast is too sweeping. Pereira observed in the mid-sixteenth century that the Chinese not only observed birthdays but had birthday parties!

They are wont also to solemnize each one his birthday, where-unto their kindred and friends do resort of custom, with presents of jewels and money, receiving again for their reward good cheer. (B:SCSC)

Cruz would repeat this with added detail in the first book on China published in Europe (1569) and the editor of a Portuguese version I've read surmised that the great attention given to the birthday suggested that they did not much celebrate birthdays in Iberia at that time. So, on further consideration, Lowell's flippant East-West contrast can itself be flipped right over!

Here, my note was over until I read the following in Ball's CHINESE THINGS:

> As a general rule it may be said that the principle of topsy-turvydom comes into play in the differences in observing birthdays in China and England: here in China the 'grown-ups'' birthdays are kept and the child's almost entirely ignored, while with us, in our own lands, the contrary is more commonly the case.

This can also be said for Japan, and is only logical when you consider that a human grows, or should grow, more and more useful, more and more precious and worth celebrating with each passing year.

2. *Arranged Marriage vs. Love*. According to Lowell, marriage in Japan is "entirely a business transaction." We might counter that Japanese often had *some* choice – at least an informal veto – exercised after a preliminary meeting called an *omiai*, literally "look-meeting;" it would still be true that marriages usually did not *begin* with romance (as was true in parts of Europe, too) . But Lowell goes much further, claiming that *youth in Japan do not fall in love!*

> He does nothing of the kind. Sad to say, he is a stranger to the feeling. Love, as we understand it, is a thing unknown to the Far East. . . The community could never permit the practice, for it strikes at the very root of their whole social system. (L:SOFE)

Lowell makes a *big* mistake. If he had said Japanese "neither make love nor woo" as Caron (C:MKJS) wrote, it would have only been a small error (for peasants still had their night-creeping – something like our bundling, but was more likely to include consummation – and there was

other wooing as well (see note 2-16) ; but he makes a *major* error: he conflates a society's official attitude toward love and the hearts of men. Need I point out that not long before Lowell wrote, the Japanese government passed a new law about double suicides, so that a surviving lover "guilty of "Unlawful Sexual Intercourse"" (eg. with "a girl bound to a turn of service in a tea-house and a lover without sufficient means to redeem her") who tried to commit suicide but failed to die would only get a ten-year jail sentence, (Summary of The Japanese Penal Codes [of 1871] Englished in Transactions of the Asiatic Soc. of Japan v5 pt2 1877) rather than be executed as was formerly the case? If Japanese were only strangers to "the feeling" a lot of lives might have been saved. But, it is good that his illusions of difference inspired Lowell to write about love, for he does it so well!

> Seen by another besides ourselves, our castles in the air take on something of the substance of stereoscopic sights ... It would be more than mortal not to believe in ourselves when another believes so absolutely in us. (L:SOFE)

Those stereoscopic castles, make Lowell's entire book worthwhile, whether or not his contrasts are misleading. Lowell concludes,

> with a communal, not to say cosmic birthday, and a conventional wife, he [the Japanese/ Oriental] might well deem his separate existence the shadow of a shade and embrace Buddhism from mere force of circumstances. (Ibid)

This, when, unknown to Lowell, Japanese were and still are *more*, not less, self-conscious than Westerners (This is proven by their suffering from high rates of hyper-consciousness-related phobias and other such *Underground Man type* mental disorders) and, according to Keene, among the world's greatest diarists (K:CJL) .

> The light of truth has reached each hemisphere through the medium of its own mental crystallization, and this has polarized it in opposite ways, so that now the rays that are normal to the eyes of the one only produce darkness to the eyes of the other. (L:SOFE)

Lowell admitted the equality of the East and the West. And he even suggested that together they provide stereo-vision; but his overriding hypothesis holds that the Eastern personality, or rather lack thereof, to be in a form of arrested development.[1] That is to say, high level of culture or not, Japanese/Orientals are backwards, in the idiomatic sense of the word. No fancy metaphysics excuses this prejudice. The post-Bungo Jesuits, despite their belief that Japanese needed Christianity and their pride in their own wealthy global civilization and its power, did not exhibit such cultural conceit.

---

1. *Arrested Development* and the lack of a personality in the East. Here, a reader must be well versed in 19th century science to grasp the full significance of Lowell's rhetoric. The very fact that Japanese were, *on the whole*, more cultured and indulged in more intelligent pastimes was held against them.

An idea of how little one man's brain differs from his neighbor's may be gathered from the fact, that while a common coolie in Japan spends his spare time in playing a chess twice as complicated as ours, the most advanced philosopher is still on the blissfully ignorant side of the *pons asinorum*. (L:SOFE)

The reader may look up the "Bridge of Asses" himself. I will stop at pointing out that Lowell is only saying the same thing about Japanese that the sociobiologists of his day were saying about *women*: i.e., compared to men, they are more dependable and far less likely to be utter idiots or criminals; but the same lack of variety means they lack true genius, such as, say, *mine!* (See Cynthia Russett's *Sexual Science* to learn how women were *made*.)

The men whom Japan reveres are much less removed from the common herd than is the case in any Western land. And this has been so from the earliest times. Shakespeares and Newtons have never existed there. Japanese humanity is not the soil to grow them.

Utter bullshit! Japan is full of genius. Perhaps the most famous historical figure, the priest who brought over esoteric Buddhism from China and arranged the Japanese syllabary into a poem, Kobo Taishi, could write five separate things at once with brushes held in his feet and hands and mouth and was also credited with doing things that make Jesus Christ look very common, indeed. One Seki Takakazu, "born in the same year as Newton" developed a purely Japanese "method for solving cubic equations, or for dealing with negative and imaginary roots" totally separate from Newton and Leibnitz. Moreover, he introduced "the concept of the matrix in 1686, well ahead of Leibnitz's separate introduction of it in Europe." (See Perrin P:GUG) While aesthetic geniuses such as the painters Sesshu and Hokusai, the poets Basho, and Buson and tea-master Sen-no-Rikkyu are harder to judge, one might ask whether it is possible that the common herd in Japan might be closer to them rather than the vice-versa!

ix
modern topsy-turvydom: knapp

In his less well-known FEUDAL AND MODERN JAPAN published six years after Chamberlain's classic, Arthur Knapp developed his "Principle of Inversion." If Chamberlain and Lowell neglect to credit Alcock and Alcock neglects to credit Carletti or Maffei who neglects to mention Valignano who neglects to mention Frois or Al-bîrûnî who . . . . Knapp, too, faithfully follows the self-discovery tradition in topsy-turvy, for despite mentioning the opinions of "Professor Chamberlain" many times on other issues, he does not mention him (nor anyone else) in *this* respect. Why do I introduce yet another statement, when it merely echoes the others? Because, finding the Antipodes alive so far from Medieval times – so close to our times – is thrilling enough to bear repetition. Who says we have to go back a thousand years to find such enchanting naivité! We cannot fairly judge the Japanese=Oriental (Knapp conflates the two), he writes, "unless we can succeed in psychologically standing on our heads" because:

> Inversion is the confirmed habit of the far Oriental. It characterizes, not only the general mode as well as every detail of his outward life. but also his intellectual and moral being. It is not simply that his ways and thoughts differ from ours. They are the total reversal of ours. In our childhood we were accustomed to picture the inhabitants of the antipodes as standing upon their heads. We were so far right in our imaginings that that is really the only thing the Oriental does not do in the inversion of our ways. (K:FMJ)

These men are writing about the wonder of wonders: to the West, Japan (and the Japanese) was *the biggest wonder in the world*. After regretting he had not kept a memorandum of the "numberless and minute details of art, and thought and life" in Japan that illustrated his principle, his memory provided enough to show "something more than a mere bent of the Japanese mind; that bent is carried so far as to become a somersault." A number of the remembered "details" do not appear in Frois, Alcock, Lowell or Chamberlain:

> After-dinner speeches made before dinner, thus assuring brevity, and furnishing the topic for conversation.
> The absorbing desire of the young ladies to grow old that they may share the reverence given to age.
> Gimlets threaded the opposite way from ours. [1] (K:FMJ)

1. *Opposite Gimle*ts. To attach significance to something which may be the result of chance, we might investigate the ergonomics of un/screwing. No doubt, one direction allows more power for screwing in and one for screwing out. If I am not mistaken, ours favors the "in" and theirs the "out." This would certainly be true semiotically speaking, for the dexterous turn would appear to be favored. If we "push in" and "pull out," this different turn matches the push=West and pull=East equation below as well. Frois has a *different* gimlet contrast (11-26) which does not mention this. Does anyone know when Japanese gimlets were threaded, that is cut in a screw-like way?

Others were marginally different. Instead of Alcock's keys locking "left to right," Chamberlain's puzzling keys that "turn in instead of out," Knapp writes of "keyholes made upside down, [*so you find*] the keys turning backwards," [1] and teaches you that footnotes turning into headnotes makes more sense because "the larger margin of the page . . . [is] at the top instead of at the bottom." That is to say that despite Knapp's crude hyperbole of *inversion* as a "confirmed habit", he was not only "bright," but extraordinarily "sympathetic" (Chamberlain's appraisal) in his approach. He went a step further than the general relativism of Valignano, to whom familiarity made all difference (excluding religion, of course) equally reasonable, and found something missed by the humorous relativism of Alcock, the abstract relativism of Lowell, and the nihilistic relativism of Chamberlain, who thought he was writing the epitaph for a moribund culture. Here is what it was:

> Of course, our first conclusion is that theirs is the wrong way, because it is the opposite of that which we have been taught is the only right way. But an analysis of almost any one of their methods . . . . will show that it possesses manifest advantage over ours. . . . For example, by carefully experimenting with the use of the Japanese saw in comparison with the workings of our own, I am convinced that the former has superior merit in the ease and firmness with which it can be guided in the hand of the workman. So too . . .

Sometimes, *our* way also may have an advantage or two. But anyone who has used a saw that bites on the *pull* rather than the *push* can confirm the general *superiority* of the Oriental saw. Here, Knapp teaches us something very important: difference, even caricatured as "inversion" or "somersault" need not imply negative value-judgment. In fact, the opposite is equally possible. With the proper attitude – unbiased *judgment*, rather than dumb moratorium on judgment – and rational explanation, even radical contrast-mongering can prove that culture, *too*, makes all men kin.

1. *Keys and Key-holes.* If our key-holes were uniform then, they are not now! One of my keyholes takes the key teeth *up* and one teeth *down* and one of my mother's locks turns one way and one the other! Judging from key-holes, we might say that nowadays, our culture may be too sloppy to reveal patterns capable of generalization. That would make topsy-turvy observation difficult to say the least.

X
"topsy-turvy" in broader perspective

Take those opposite saws. Japanese cultural difference-mongers (*nihonjinron-ka*) tie it in to opposite *lifestyles*, which might be summed as *boxing* versus *judo*. They trace these back to different primal environments that gave rise to literally *pushy* Western (this West includes what "we" call the Middle-East) herders fighting off beasts in pastures undergoing harsh desertification *versus* pacific Eastern (the East beginning, perhaps, in Burma, according to some Japanese) farming folk peacefully *pulling* on their hoes in little plots tucked into a benevolent moist forest. [1] The only problem is that pull-saws were (and probably still are) common as far West as Turkey. Okay, then let's start the East *there* (and they share the Ural-Altaic language with Japan: does anyone know about Finnish saws?) – and the general push-pull contrast still holds, but the significance changes when we put this in a different perspective: *most of the civilized world* used pull-saws. It is not the Japanese who are the odd-guys out, but us! [2] This is no doubt true for many of Frois's items, too.

More interesting yet is the matter of *pulling* versus *pushing* as opposite. Vector-wise, you can not get more contrary than that. But is *direction* the all of it? As far as saws and planes go, it would appear that way. But consider another implement, the knife. They reverse the situation with the saw! As Frois points out in contrast 7-13, Japanese tend to whittle *away* where we whittle *towards* ourselves. But knives can generally be used in many ways and there is no settled Eastern or Western direction for cutting that I know of. At any rate, the pushing vs. pulling contrast is not so solid as *Nihonjinron-ka* have made it, and more important (if you, like me, like ideas – otherwise, all of this is not important), an Indian philosopher might laugh at *pull* vs. *push* culturology: *Away? Towards? What of it? In India, we generally do neither.* No, he is not talking about Indians doing nothing, even if some Indians are good at doing that, too! *We can cut with the knife in place.* People (Is it *women* only? Anyone?) slice vegetables and fruit by passing them through a knife imbedded blade-up in a stationary stone or wooden base. [3] Is not this lack of movement, as opposed to movement of the cutting device – and its being blade *up* rather than *down* – far more exotic than opposite vectors of action? Could this be called *deep topsy-turvy?*

1. Pushy-pully Stereotypes. I give no scholarly citations, for this is something I read countless times when living in Japan. As part of the *Nihonjinron* (Japaneseness defined largely in opposition to the West) worldview, it was just too common for a professor to claim for his or her theory.
2. Why Not Just "Pull-saws?" I have seen pull-cut saws sold in the US only over the last couple decades, but they are sold as "Japanese" – meaning, I assume, *high quality* saws. They now occupy ___% (statistics, anyone?) of the total manual saws sold in ____ (anyone?). Many years ago, it is at least possible that because most men pushed plows behind oxen or horses, they were much stronger at *pushing* than *pulling* and push-cut saws made sense. But this peculiar reason, hasn't held true for a almost a hundred years. And, as we can see by the Knapp quotation, the existence of, and superiority of pull-cut saws (they do not buckle when they stick and one can pull with the whole body) was an open secret. So why the

delay? Perhaps Matsuda and Jorissen had a point about our smug superiority complex.

3. Still Indian Knives. Practically speaking, there is an *advantage* to having heavy and solid cutting instruments when they are not very sharp. The stolidity partially offsets the dullness by reducing energy loss from vibration. Since such a knife tends to be heavier than the things to be cut, it makes sense to put the blade in a base and move the things. The mass of the base further reduces the energy loss by steadying the knife more than any hand could. While such a knife fits the metaphysically active=female / still=male image of Kali the Destroyer upon an inert male, I think we have to be careful here, for it also keeps knives out of womens' hands – and before the gun, the knife was a great domestic equalizer (See Zora Neale Hurston: *Of Mules and Men* , perhaps, for the way domestic violence was once stopped).

Here, the Far East and Far West are mirror-images of each other, while only India (the original Middle East, until the British military command of that name moved with said name to the Near East) may be called the true Antipode. If something as simple as using a knife offers three axes of contrast, we might ask, what about more complex, multifaceted things? What about the ultimate cultural artifact, without which we say culture itself is dead – what about *language?* Which is farther from English, Chinese or Japanese? [1] Is the all-character writing of Chinese, or the mixed Chinese character and phonetic syllabets of Japanese more alien to us? 100% *character* is the more perfect antithesis of 100% *alphabet.* Seen that way, *Chinese is more exotic*; but a *mixed* system is more perfect an antithesis to a *pure* one, and seen that way *Japanese is more exotic to both English and Chinese.* Or, what about the telegraphic nature of Chinese and the SOV (subject-object-verb) syntax of Japanese? Which is closer/further from us? Classical Chinese – at least, as written – is *unbelievably* spare (not Tarzan and Jane-like, but *utterly alien*), while the syntax is more-or-less the same SVO we use; while Japanese despite its alien SOV (mutually exotic word order) seems stylistically similar to English, i.e., equally redundant, or wasteful, and enjoying a similar degree of freedom with their syntax. Then there is poetry. Is the terse but rhyming Chinese, or the softer unrhymed Japanese closer to ours? The Chinese are part of "our" rhyming world, while the Japanese are not; but the perfectly matching lines of only a few (4-8 is common) characters comprising Chinese rhymes that come out looking like rectangles seem alien to us, where Japanese unrhyming poems seem of a more natural (*i.e., familiar*) design. With multi-cultural contrast, opposites quickly produce paradoxes.

There are dozens of ways which each language is more different from English than the other and more similar. The same can be said about so many things. That is why, every single one of Frois's contrasts (*contradicoes*) not only is a true contradiction in the sense Valignano made clear – i.e. they do not represent different levels on a developmental ladder of humanity, but describe equally developed cultures that contradict the very idea of a single ladder – but, in one way or another, can, indeed, be contradicted.

---

1. *Japanese and Chinese.* I contrast Japanese and Chinese from English, but the contrast between the two Eastern languages may be greater. David Pollack writes:

> [Japanese and Chinese] belong to two [language] groups that are not only entirely unrelated but appear almost entirely antithetical in their phonological, morphological, and syntactic systems . . . Chinese operates in a dominantly synchronic mode, relying almost entirely upon parallelism and rhyme, its logic governed by the association of like categories;

Japanese, to the contrary, is a diachronic language governed by hypotactic subordination, its logic predominantly that of the combination of dissimilar categories. (THE FRACTURE OF MEANING)

Please do not ask *me* what the Latinate words all mean. Think of it as a performance of which the finest aria – this is worth going to the library for – is a florid paragraph equating Chinese to a "black hole" and Japanese to a "supernova," surely one of the boldest metaphors of contrast in the history of philosophical linguistics!

---

xi
post-modern topsy-turvydom

The antipodes did not die with the 19th century, either. Ripley (*Believe It or Not*) , probably following Ball, vulgarized difference in 1932, contrasting the West, not to Japan, but to the *"Heathen Chinee"* (see *Midword*), and the German economist, Kurt Singer, anticipating the concise yet obscure style of the post-war French academics, glorified it in 1939, after an eight-year stay. Here is what he had to say about the culture shock facing "a stranger landing on the islands of Japan."

> . . . the sense of orientation and the scales of preference are subtly disturbed by a general "topsy-turvydom"[I cannot find it is a translation, but still wonder: is there a good German word for Topsy-turvy?] expressing itself in almost systematic exchanges of right and left, before and after, speech and silence. Every gesture, the shape of the vessels, the cadence of a sentence, the etiquette of a household or of a school-class, an arrangement of flowers in a vase – each bears an unmistakable mark peculiar to this country. (MIRROR, SWORD AND JEWEL — the Geometry of Japanese Life, first publ. 1973.)

So we see Chamberlain's favorite term, *topsy-turvydom* – as always with no credit – used in a book the good critic Donald Richie recently (reviewing the 1997 reprint in the Japan Times) called *the best ever written on the Japanese!* Personally, I much prefer the timeless work of Chamberlain's contemporary and close friend Lafcadio Hearn. I think he is the best and always will be. The misty fairyland quality of Hearn's writing on Japan comes in part from his affection for things quaint, old and mysterious, no matter what culture – his *Creole* (New Orleans) *Sketches* are a particular treat – and partly from the fact that *his* Japan is developed from a single controlling antithesis: *the*

Brobdingnagian West versus Lilliputian Japan. That idea is found only indirectly, if at all, in Frois. Europeans tend to be taller (1-1), Japanese value simple black and white artwork (11-29), give less presents to show love than Europeans (14-26, 14-55), etc.. A generation later, Rodrigues comes closer when he repeatedly comments on the more minimalistic Japanese taste, for the metaphors of *quantity/quality* and *luxury/austerity* are cognate with those of *big/small*. But, it would seem that the clear-cut "big vs. small" contrast is post-Perry, an invention (in the old sense of the word, including "discovery") that had to await an overgrown modern Europe and the *Aren't we a big baby!* America of Walt Whitman. Chamberlain certainly shared the still young idea with Hearn, for here is how he began his introduction of sumo:

> The wrestlers must be numbered among Japan's most characteristic sights, though they are neither small nor dainty, like the majority of things Japanese." (C:TJ)

Who does not love miniatures? Through Hearn, even the Japanese learned to love themselves in an age where the Western culture was – at least for a couple decades, it seems – worshipped. But we cannot swallow Hearn like a cormorant (I use a favorite Japanese expression). Like Lowell, we have cultural comparison/contrast *serving* a larger *a priori* topsy-turvy concept. As John Steadman pointed out in his groundbreaking deconstruction of Orientalism THE MYTH OF ASIA (1969) [1], Hearn thought nothing of matching Gothic cathedrals with Shinto shrines (rather than the much larger Buddhist temples) or sumptuous opera with geisha playing a *shamisens* (rather than the far fancier *kabuki*), i.e., he compared incommensurables to maximize contrast. But, that is one reason Hearn reads so well. What good writer does not exaggerate? I do not like Hearn any less for it. I only to wish to point out with respect to Singer and Hearn – and, let me add Barthes' *Empire of the Sign* (B(H):EOS) and Lee O'young's *Furoshiki Post-modern* (J/I:FPM) , both of which will be quoted at length in the text – that a heavy dose of the topsy-turvy can be found in our most sophisticated work, and our most beautiful. We may talk about the philosophical pitfalls of *dualism* and nitpick all we like, but *black and white*, *upside-down*, *inside-out* high-contrast still makes our day.

1. *THE MYTH OF ASIA.* John Steadman shows that Asia has presented many faces to the West, some good and some bad, but too multi-facetted to be summed up in a single Orientalism. There is no *Asia*, only *Asias*. Excluding the inane Cold War period preface by a political big-shot about how important our relations with the East are, the book is a better read and far more educational and balanced than E. Said's two-dimensional ORIENTALISM which was published about the same time. I have never known a good book to do so perfect a disappearing act as this one. It made a splash so small I have yet to find a single person who read it, or find it cited in books that should cite it. (I have taught some people about it over the past decade and hope to find it cited soon.) Does anyone know what happened to erase this book from history?

And, finally, I would add that the locus of creation of contrary culture, or what I call antithetical stereotypes of Occident and Orient (or, more vulgarly, the USA vs. Japan) is no longer in the West but in the East. I introduce *some* contemporary Japanese thought into my explanation of Frois's treatise but much more may be found in my *Orientalism & Occidentalism* (2004).

xii
the discovery of frois's treatise

In 1955, Josef Franz Schütte S.J. discovered Frois's forgotten manuscript in the Royal History Museum of Madrid, transcribed the badly worm-eaten 16th century Portuguese handwriting – which includes many Japanese terms only a bilingual scholar could decipher – and published it in Japan, together with a translation and notes in German. [1]   Since that time, two annotated Japanese translations were published by major publishers. Both became near best-sellers, pocket-books, going through dozens of printings.[2] Nonfiction does not sell well in Japan, too. So, how can we explain this success? I think it is partly because the modern Japanese identity is almost entirely based upon bi-polar contrast with the West – in short, "they" define themselves as what "we" are *not,* and the *vice versa.* [3]   Frois's style is very familiar to them, for it is *their* style, and yet the content is old enough to be fresh. *Nihonjin-ron,* books defining Japaneseness, sold exceptionally well in the 1970s and 80s and Frois, or rather his translators and publishers profited from it. But they (particularly Okada) also deserve credit for providing the supplementary information needed to flesh out Frois's skeletal distiches for the Japanese lay reader. I would think non-Japanese readers would require even more supplementary information, but the recent Portuguese and the French versions (all I have seen so far) offer surprisingly little such assistance.[4] So Frois is *out,* but not the presence he could have become if the needs of the Occidental reader were considered.

Frois is not totally unknown in the English language world. Michael Cooper's superb classic anthology of "European Reports on Japan, 1543-1640", *They Came to Japan* (1965) includes a couple dozen contrasts and Endymion Wilkinson's more journalistic *Japan versus Europe* (1980) about an equal number. Citations pop up here and there. I can understand why the list of 611 topsy-turvy items would not excite 'us' as much as 'them'.   Occidental intellectuals may point out that "without east there is no west, without natives there are no sahibs, without 'them' there is no 'us';" (Littlewood 1996?), but our identity, such as it is, is not dependent on one 'them' as is the case for Japanese. It is constructed against a host of antithetical boogaboos (Oriental, African, Puritan, Despotic, Primitive, Communist, Islamic, etc.). Thus, the psychological importance of the Far East in general and Japan in particular, is *to* us but a fraction of the importance *of* us to them. That, perhaps, is why 'we' tend to relegate Eastern things to a small number of publishers who specialize in it rather than any good general publisher, as the Japanese do for our books. Marginalized by definition, even a book with content of interest to the general reader may be overlooked or turned down. I assume that this, more than anything else, may explain why this is the TRATADO's first English translation.

1. Schutte's TRATADO. My German does not suffice to judge his translation in *Kultur-gegensätze Europa-Japan* (1585), but what I have checked suggests he has figured out as much as many of the later translations. So, the quality of subsequent translations owes much to his pioneering work. His quotation=translation-filled analysis of *Valignano's Mission Principles* (S:VMP) is magnificent, as explained in my annotated bibliography. I have great admiration for his scholarship. *We owe him.*

2. Japanese TRATADO.   See the Annotated biography about the Japanese translations. Both were a great help.

3. Japanese Identity as Contrary. Peter Dale sums up well: "As the anti-image of foreignness, Japanese identity can only be confirmed by stipulating a systematic, if

Borgesian taxonomy of the Other . . . What they attribute to themselves they must deny to "outsiders", and conversely what is ascribed to others is disclaimed within the indigenous patrimony." (THE JAPANESE MYTH OF UNIQUENESS). This brilliant but occasionally unfair (see my ORIENTALISM & OCCIDENTALISM) polemicist has pegged it here. I would only add that the tendency to make the West whatever another is *not* is not just Japanese. (See: PORTRAITS OF "THE WHITEMAN" (Keith Basso); the stereotypical "whiteman" varies considerably depending on the culture, but never fail to be contrary to the self-image of those who depict him.

4. Portuguese and French TRATADO. Beautiful books. See the acknowledgment and bibliography for more.

p.s. *note to Readers!*

Thanks to Frois, and the assistance of everyone mentioned in the *Acknowledgement*, all of us can now enjoy in these pages a world every bit as wonderful as that visited by Alice. That world, like Alice's is, you will see, not only *theirs*, but *ours*. I hope you will find me a satisfactory guide and heartily welcome your suggestions for addition and revision.   – r.d.g.

About the translation

Frois's original *Tratado* is in Portuguese. I first did a draft-translation from the Japanese translations in 1998. Then, I obtained the modern Portuguese edition and while checking my translation against it, another Port-Eng. translation by a native speaker (H) arrived. It was not bad for a quick job. But because the difficulty was less in the grammar or vocabulary (I will point out and explain exceptions, i.e. problems, in context) as in *knowing what Frois was driving at*, the native translation added little *for me* (The Japanese, who knew what was what and consulted with Portuguese did far better). Because of the extremely short sentences of the original, I felt a native speaker was needed only for *asking questions re. problematic phrases* that remained at the very end of the process, but DR (See *Acknowledgment*) judged – no doubt correctly – that academia required it. (Academia is far more foreign to me then, say, Japan!) DR rendered a translation for about half the chapters based on my translation (before I saw the Portuguese), the native speaker's translation and his good sense as a fine writer and incisive scholar. Finally, I rewrote my own based on a much closer reading of the Japanese translations (I made a few mistakes the first time) and the original Portuguese (with better dictionaries by my side), DR's rewrite (some words or phrases borrowed for the first 8 chapters), the French translation (particularly useful regarding Far East-derived Portuguese words but also for hints at better vocabulary and what one might get away with, for it is a very pleasant translation), the German translation (to the extent possible: see *Acknowledgment*) and my increased understanding based on further research and input from Japanese, Portuguese, French and German acquaintances. The biggest dilemma was not how to assure accuracy or beauty, but how closely to adhere to the original where it was awkward and the writer in me says "Pretty it up!" while *something* else says "No, just give them the closest thing to what Frois wrote!"   I fear my choice has not been uniform. I sometimes let the syntax slip a bit for a smoother translation, other times I go for an ugly direct translation to better make a point in the explication of the contrast.   I simply cannot pull it off in the smooth manner of the French (or, as I think DR might have). Part of it may be failings on the part of my English, but most of it is because of *my attitude toward translation*. I cannot help wanting to show people what does *not* get translated as well as what does. I want to be completely open and admit ambiguity where it exists. (This attitude gave birth to a new type of translation, multiple versions of single poems, in my recent book *Rise, Ye Sea Slugs!* (See Reviews at back of this book)) That is one reason why I thought it best to supply the entire original, at least in size 9 font, for reference. I give it, misspellings and all, as Schütte S.J. did (If he had typos, I may have copied a few of them, too, and hope that can be fixed in the future), for reality is like that. Ah, you may note that some of Frois's contrasts given in the *Foreword* are not translated identically later in my text. It doesn't bother *me*. Does it bother *you?*
..

Readers who want to know more about what translation involves will find additional information scattered throughout the book. Others who prefer not to see such details are always free to skip right over them. But, I warn you that details are sometimes very interesting.

I

OF MEN, *THEIR PERSONS AND DRESS*

do que toca aos homens em suas pessoas, e vestidos

~~~~~~

1-1   Europeans are for the most part tall and well built;
Pola maior parte os homens de Europa são altos de corpo e boa es[ta]tura;

Japanese are for the most part shorter and slighter of build than us.
Os Japões pola maior parte mais baxos de corpo e estatura que nós. [1]

While most of Frois's contrasts are in black and white, he deserves credit for qualifying the first with *pola maior parte*. The height difference that *generally* held true in 1585, still holds true, though the average height of a Japanese *today* [2] probably exceeds that of the average European in 1585. Frois's observation does not necessarily belittle the Japanese in his mind. As DR points out, the Jesuits, being from South Europe, where men tended to be shorter than in the North, may have had a different perspective: i.e. "large of body, small of wit." Still, tall and short do unconsciously embody the natural psychological difference reflected by the shared meaning of "looking up to" and "looking down on" in English, Japanese and many languages. Citing 19th century European literature on petite Japan, Littlewood comments "small may be beautiful but it's lower down the hierarchy than big and, even when the intention is to compliment, the language of size reflects this hierarchy. It is essentially patronizing. The moneyed middle classes in England invariably have at their disposal 'a little man' who can be called in to do the odd jobs for which they themselves are unfitted."(L:IOJ) As is the case with *black* and *white*, there may be some historical accidents at work here, too: the fact is that even *within* Japan, the short have tended to serve the tall. One of the Japanese translations of TRATADO (M&J) incorporates the inescapable belittling connotation of short/low/slight [*baxo*] by making the Japanese "inferior [*otoroeteiru*] in build and height."

Estatura (physique) is more complex than Frois's contrast allows, for both individuals and cultures disagree on what is a "good" and "bad" build. In 1547, captain Jorge Alvarez wrote "the natives are for the most part of middling height, *hardy, well made* and fair complexioned." (*italics* mine, an abridgment in Coleridge C:LLFX); Mrs. Busk's 1841 summary of the views of centuries of Dutch observers writes that "they are generally described as *well made*, strong active, and fresh-coloured." Most later (19th century) visitors agreed (B:MCJ). Some were impressed enough by what they spied in the public baths to be reminded of Eden (LFS) and they often noted the "well-turned leg" – *the* mark of male beauty in the West [3] prior to the ascendancy of what was women's clothing in much of the world: *trousers* – as Japanese, for their part, found "our" legs lacking. The notorious 18th century nationalist Hirata Atsune, pointed out that "the slenderness of their [the Dutch traders'] legs also makes them resemble animals." (K:JDE) [4]

Yet not all visitors were impressed. In 1880, superwoman Isabella Bird wrote "their physique is wretched, leanness without muscle being the general rule." That seems closer to Frois. But, Bird also claimed she "saw nothing like even passable good looks" among Japanese women, and this last contradicts almost *all* other writers (Japanese women have *always* had many foreign fans because petite women attract most males). At least we cannot accuse her of conflating inside and outside beauty: Japanese of both sexes "impress" her "as the ugliest and the most pleasing people I have ever seen, as well as the neatest and most ingenious." (B:UTJ)

Estatura is ambiguous for including elements of proportion and bearing. Frois probably means muscularity, for Rodrigues would soon write the mostly "medium build" Japanese "admire well-built men." (C:TCJ) Moreover, in a 1565 letter, Frois wrote Japanese were "very white and well proportioned" (*muy blanca y bien proporcionada*: CARTAS 1565/4/20).   At that time, Frois only knew the people of the Southern coast. He might have changed his mind about the proportions by 1585. The problem is there never was *a* Japanese build. In 1690, Kaempfer found "common people . . . of a very ugly appearance, short-siz'd, strong, thick-legged, tawny, with flattish noses," [5] nobles, "somewhat more majestick in their shape and countenance, being more like Europeans," and people in some provinces "short, slender, but well shap'd, of a good handsome appearance." (The same described in Frois's 1565 letter?) But stocky or slender, most Japanese were probably far from the Greco-Roman ideal. "Compared with people of European race, the average Japanese has a long body and short legs;"(C:TJ:1890). This still holds true today. The head-to-body-length ratio far exceeds the classical 1:8 proportion (a proportion many Japanese, but few Americans, are aware of). Moreover, the less recognized but more important shoulder-to-waist width ratio is noticeably different and relates to different ideals of beauty, or perhaps we should say *power*. Late twentieth century *Nihonjinron* (intro. note __) contrast the broad-shouldered heaven-oriented Occidental Atlas (a triangle standing on its tip) with the earth-bound stability of the sumo-wrestler with his low center of balance (a triangle on its base), and point out the more ecological(?) earth-bound nature of *their* side.

If height and build are considered *as a unit,* Frois's contrast strengthens, for robust tall Japanese are *very* rare.   And, when we include *posture*, the illusion of absolute difference grows yet stronger.[5] Permit a *Faux Frois* to close what I hope proves the most plodding explanation in the book!

Europeans go proudly about chin-up and chest-out, looking straight out at the world God made. Japanese are nekozei *[cat-backed=hunched-over] and think it immodest to appear so full of pride.*

1. *The Translation* is interesting for one adjective *baxos* (low/small/light) serves to modify both the height and the build in the Japanese half, where two, *altos* (tall/heavy) and *boa* (good), are used for the Europeans. The French translation uses *petit* for both height and build." English could use "compact" for both, but the connotation would be too good.

2. *Height Statistics.* I vaguely recall reading that most Japanese today are taller than most Europeans then but could not google to the information. *Statistics anyone?*

3. *Legs in the West.* I have a tremendous amount of proof about this going back to Bulwer who described a well developed male calf culture in the mid 17th century (suggesting it was already in existence in 1585) even involving debates on how to stroke them best to improve their form (B:A) Lest we think it a momentary fashion, let me add that the male leg fetish lasted for centuries. This obsession with the legs was still going strong in the in 1837 when Thomas Hood wrote a young lady:

Conceive him sitting languishingly – a Narcissus without his pond – seeing nothing, admiring nothing, but his own well-turned legs! Fancy him stretching them, crossing them, ogling them in all possible attitudes, taking back and front views of them, and along the outer or inner side. Imagine him coquetting with them, carelessly dropping a handkerchief over them, as if to veil their beauties: sliding his enamoured hand down them by turns, – and then, with great reluctance brought to dance on them, if dancing it might be called, so languidly, as if he feared to wear out the dear delicate limbs by the exertion . . . It is very well to marry a man with handsome legs, but one would not choose to have them always running in his head." (*Hood's Works* vol. III: 1870)

Anyone who reads the above, will not see old paintings of men the same way. Japan has nothing like it.

4. *Animal Legs.* Hirata has a point. Meaty calves *are* as human a phenomenon as wide nails. (Then, again, Hirata *also* had them lifting a leg to urinate like dogs! He knew better. Perhaps he had to lay on the insults to get away with his study and promotion of illegal Dutch science for the sake of his unappreciative country.) Though not so obsessed with human beauty as Occidentals, Japanese were calf-conscious, for thin shanks were *the* mark of being down-and-out, at least for men. Come to think of it, I am not sure Japanese men had any way to show off parts of their bodies in the European manner. (When did "we" first make that silly pose with arms held up crab-like at a 90+90 degrees? As soon as we hid our legs in trousers?)

4. *Honesty about Beauty.* While Kaempfer's honest appraisal of human beauty/ugliness *as he saw it* may offend some, I, who take offense, rather, with the muscle-

worshipping culture of the Romans and their clones in twentieth century America, find his evident respect for the short and slender male a refreshing change. Chamberlain, in the late nineteenth century, being more muscle-positive than Kaempfer came to the opposite conclusion about which class looked better!

> "The lower classes are mostly strong, with well-developed arms, legs, and chests. The upper classes are too often weakly." (C:TJ)

5. *This Postural Difference* is not *only* East-West, for the neighboring Koreans walk *ramrod-straight*, as do the Balinese partly, I would guess, because they have traditionally carried things on their head – whereas Japanese do not; or, conversely, that poor posture comes from the fact Japanese must nod vigorously and continually while conversing? (see 14-45) If, however, it turns out to be a post-Frois development, it might reflect the humble body-language required for fitness under Tokugawa Feudalism.

1-2   Europeans hold large eyes to be beautiful;
Os de Europa tem por fermozura os olhos grandes;

> Japanese think they are horrid, and find eyes beautiful that are pinched shut on the tear[duct]-side. *Os Japões os tem por horrendos, e os fermozos são fechados da parte dos lagrimais.*

The fact that the upper-class for a thousand years or so was a relatively tall *slit-eyed* Mongolian type, as opposed to the relatively *round-eyed* working-class "pudding-faced" (C:TJ 1890) type, obviously enhanced the appeal of the former. But, note, *shape* not *size* was the telling factor. It was *round* eyes that were considered ugly and beastly – "like dogs."(CP) Large eyes were admired in Japan too, so long as they were vertically narrow like the Chinese character "one" (一), in which case, the lachrymal part is hidden because eyes narrow most around the edges.   Still, the wide open eyes of the Europeans do show more of themselves than most Japanese eyes and would, indeed, look "large." A Japanese folk-history of the *Barbarian Temple* (*nambanji-kyôkaiki* c.1700) describes the eyes of Furukomu, a composite character, mostly Frois, as "round, as if they were eye-glasses"(J/E:NBJ). Thunberg, in 1775, observed how the Japanese, including children, would gather loudly calling out "*Oranda O-me!* (Dutch Big-eyes!)" whenever they saw Europeans (T:TEAA). Dr. Thunberg for his part, thought the "oblong, small," and deep-sunk "organs" of the Japanese and Chinese gave them "almost the appearance of being pink-eyed [conjunctivitis]."

I am surprised that Frois does *not* contrast eyelids, the *differénce* that so excited a certain 20th century French philosopher.[1]   The double-eyelid, or perhaps better put, eyelid with trimming, is almost universal in the West (most apparent exception being the pseudo single-eyelid not uncommon in North Europe where the overhanging skin obscures the fold), but found in only about half of Japanese. Having spent all his adulthood in Japan, was Frois no longer conscious of the difference? Or, were Europeans themselves less wide-eyed and more familiar with unfringed eyelids at Frois's time than in later centuries? We can see many Madonnas and Saints with eyes which might be considered "Mongolian" in 12-16th century European art.[2]

With the Westernization of the world in the 20th century, Japanese ideals have also changed. Operations to double eyelids, the better to frame eyes Western style and make them *look* larger – the double lid and large open eyes complement each other – have become all too common.[3] Since most Japanese now tend to see *their* single-fold, or rather, unfolded eyelid in terms of *lack,* I was delighted to read Okada's notes to this contrast not only explaining why Occidental show-everything eyes have an intrinsic aesthetic problem, but doing so in terms of a *lack:*

> Because European eyes *normally have little adipose tissue* on the upper lid, most lids are double, ... and the upper eyelid can look sunken and shadowed. When wide open, the red tear-duct can be seen on the inner canthus. (my *italics,* J/F(O):T)

The relationship or lack of relationship between double eyelids and insufficient padding is beyond my ken, but how could one disagree with the aesthetic complaint of the Japanese in Frois's day?   The inner quarter inch or so of the eye opening *is* ugly.   We see precisely the type of yucky red/pink membrane humans have managed to hide over the course of their evolution from the grosser apes. (The ape's ugliness is not only due to our similarity, but because of that unseemly exposure. Eyelids should conceal the inner canthus as lips conceal gum, the rump conceals the anus and both flesh and hair replace the disgusting genital welt of the non-human female primate.)   Membrane takes getting used to.   The 16th century Japanese were not used to it and, I believe, must have pointed it out to Frois. [4]   Today, they are, and no one would express different eyes in terms of its relative visibility as Frois did.

1. *Roland Barthes' Japanese Eyes.* A whole chapter of the *Empire of Signs* is dedicated to *"The Eyelid."*

> "The eye is flat (that is its miracle); neither exorbital nor shrunken, without padding, without pouch, and so to speak without skin, it is the smooth slit in a smooth surface. . . . it is quite mistakenly (by an obvious ethnocentrism) that we French call it *bridé* (bridled, constrained); nothing restrains the eye, for since it is inscribed at the very level of the skin and not sculpted in the bone structure, its space is that of the entire face." (trans. Richard Howard B(H):EOS)

I wish I could quote all of it. Many of Barthes' assertions are outrageous if for no other reason that they ignore the diverse reality of Japan/ese, but he admits he is playing with a semi-fictive "Japan." To me, his creative association of physiology and psychology as he develops "the possibility of difference" is delightful, and his relating the skin-level eye with the Japanese practice of snoozing on the train so funny I will feature it in the Sandman chapter of a Chinese Mother Goose book series I will finish up if/when I marry and have a child! *Imagine how hard it would be to pile sand on an eyelid without an edge! Imagine.*

2. *Renaissance Eyes* Please view the faces on my topsy-turvy1585 web-page at http://www.paraverse.org. See if you can tell the Japanese from the Occidental! Perhaps the most Japanese example – eyes more oriental than those of many Japanese! – is St. Elizabeth in Geertgen Tot Sint Jans's *The Holy Kinship* (c 1490) (Rijksmuseum Amsterdam). Perhaps eyes narrowed to a slit are more representative of a humble culture – as are the folds not visible (or stretched out?) when people look down – and large eyes representative of a proud culture where people look up? (My Mexican friend Maria Tonteria doesn't buy that. She says, indignantly, *No! The sad and the dead look down and the happy living look up . . .*).

3. *Blepharoplasty.* We who take our eyelids for granted do not realize that the fold comes in many varieties. But someone who is buying a fold must chose between parallel, tapered, lateral flare and semi-lunar designs. Counter-intuitively, fold-less eyelids are the more complex (and therefore problematic) of the two basic designs, for more people lacking folds experience difficulty due to down-pointing eyelashes. Because of this, I think it may not be racial discrimination to take the fold as "normal" and think of the lack of an eye-fold as the side-effect of an extreme adaptation for the cold. So an eyelid operation may be more natural (less harmful) than a circumcision.

4. *A Strange Practice.* But, for all this traditional delicacy with respect to mucous membranes, the Japanese in 1863 – I doubt this goes back to Frois's day – had an eye-related custom that could not be grosser. "The practice which prevails among the people" writes Alcock "of having their eyelids daily turned inside out – of which you may see an example as you pass that barber's shop – and then rubbed over, titillated, and polished by a smooth copper spatula, must, I should think, be eminently conducive to disease of one sort or another." (A:COT) Alcock, the British Consul, was a fine observer, so this observation is probably accurate. If so, why did Japanese do this? Gloss, anyone!

1-3   Among us, having white/bright/translucent eyes [1] is not strange or repulsive; [2]
Antre nós ter os olhos brancos não se estranha;

Japanese find them monstrous, and it is a rarity among them.
Os Japões o têm por mon[stru]oso, e hé couza rara antre elles.

It is hard to say what Frois means by *olhos brancos*. There is more than one possible interpretation of this distich, please bear with me.

First, let us take *brancos* literally, as "white." The German and one of the Japanese translations seem to do that. Because I have had operations for whitish fatty growths on my eyes called *pterigiums*, my first thought was that Frois meant disease that covers the iris and, eventually the pupil, causing blindness. In the days before sunglasses and eye surgery, such a disease (brought on by sun, salt-water and genetic proclivity) would have been common in South Europe but not in Japan, for it is rare among dark-eyed Orientals. Or, could blindness caused by syphilis, which causes the same "white-eye" appearance, have enjoyed a 50 year head-start in Europe?

Another literally "white" interpretation comes from Okada who takes it to mean the *sclera*, or white of the eye (Schütte's and the other Japanese translation simply make it "white eyes" and leave it at that.). Could Frois, having come to Japan early in life, forgotten the Japanese idea of *shirome* (exposing the white of the eye *shirome o dasu,* etc.) had no Portuguese equivalent? The white of the eye, taken alone, *is* indeed *monstruoso*, spooky. Even, if upturned eyes were not characteristic of the dead, an absent pupil in the days before sun-glasses would still scare and disgust those who saw it. This *white-as-scariness* is not so obvious when the iris or pupil are visible, but it is a fact that when eyes bulge with anger, draw a bead on someone, or open wide in "walleyed" fear, the sclera *does* stand out. Japanese were evidently not used to seeing eyes revealing so much whiteness – in the late-19th century, Edward Morse was told "You all have fierce, staring eyes" (M:JDD) – or the open displays of emotion (14-2) often accompanying that wild-eyed look. Moreover, exposing the sclera has another more far-fetched association in Japan: *cruel and unfeeling disdain.* This is reflected in the idiom: "to look [at someone] with white eyes" is to look at them with cold, merciless eyes, as a demon might. *Why?* Because, according to Okada,

> an eye with a large proportion of sclera showing *looks* cold and sharp. Wet, the white takes on the cold gleam of porcelain, which is one reason the eyes appear malevolent. (*italics mine;* Ibid.)

Melville might have liked this, but it is an open question to what degree the idiom reflects the Japanese perception of the eyes and whether color-psychology finds porcelain [3] cold. Be that as it may, I cannot help returning to the slits Frois did *not* mention and offering my own *faux Frois:*

> *Europeans find slit-eyes uncanny and associate narrowed eyes with anger;*
> *Japanese admire slit-eyes as discreet and associate narrowed eyes with contentment.*

To "narrow ones eyes" in Japanese means to be delighted. This narrowing implies a vertical rather than horizontal closure and holds true for cats as well as humans. Japanese draw happy specimens of either with closed eyes in the shape of gentle arch. Our lack of awareness of this is apparent in depictions of people smiling with unrealistically wide open eyes and captions accompanying cats with closed eyes in photographs claiming they are asleep when the rest of their body language says otherwise (see the "Smiling With Closed Eyes" chapter of *Hanchan's Dream: Essays in Felinity* when I publish it). People also do "narrow their eyes in anger" as per English idiom, but this is mostly narrowing *across* (scrunching together), rather than *up and down*. This difference suggests a culture's reading of narrowed/closed eyes can go either of two ways. My feeling is that the main difference is one of perception; but Morse suggests it lies in our respective expressions of displeasure.

> With us, we usually frown and compress the eyes, but the Japanese when "mad" open their eyes wide; and a boy who has done something wrong will get a scolding, or *Omedama chodai;* literally, "a gift of eyeballs." (M:JDD)

Close-eyed anger and open-eyed anger are associated with different sub-emotions of anger. I would expect a growl or bite more likely from the former and a yell or a pounce from the latter. But, it is generally accepted that wide-open eyes are the primary indicator of anger in our family of animals, so I suspect Occidental body-language may be less natural in this respect than the Japanese. [4] Perhaps our ocular ideology (the idea that sustained, unblinking eye contact is a mark of honesty and something good) has reduced the natural scare value of the open-eyed stare.

Once I introduced Okada's interpretation, one thing led to the next and I failed to introduce the more likely reading of *olhos brancos*.   The French translation makes it *yeux clairs,* or "bright/clear/translucent eyes."   Since it really is likely Frois would have known enough to write *branco do olho,* or "white of the eye" if that was what he meant – Portuguese are very eye-conscious, for they have a tremendous number of eye idioms and names (everything from "eye by eye and tooth by tooth" to "the eye of a mosquito") and this makes looseness on Frois's part less likely than otherwise – common sense suggests a slightly less common reading of *branco,* the 4th in *Aurelio, "claro, transparente, translúcido."*   That still does not quite solve it, for we cannot say for certain if he means *the eye overall,* in which case the big, bright, overly obvious eyes upset Japanese whose eyes do not jump out at you like that, or a pupil that is blue, grey or hazel and seems translucent, which might be spooky to people not used to iris's with what seems like layers (And I can recall that my father's grey-blue eyes had a spooky quality, but it might have been because of an association: he had a voice like thunder and, like the Occidental of 14-2, let his emotion out in a way terrifying to a child.). My French advisor says the spelling *clairs* favors the latter. Back to that description of Frois by *name* (but Valignano by *time*) in the folk history of the Southern Barbarian Temple, for it includes a relevant close-up of the Western eye:

> His eyes were round like eyeglasses and within them the eyes [pupils?] were gold colored, . . . he rode standing tall in the stirrups, smoking tobacco (a pipe?) lit from sparks that flew from his own nails, **. . .** spotting a crow in a tree he would ride closer while the bird would remain transfixed and break off the branch it sat on **. . .** (J/E:NBJ)

The story continues to credit Furukomu with being quite the magician, but the example of the frozen bird following on the *round gold eyes* suggests the bright *branco* to me. I suppose it is ridiculous to spend less space explicating the reading I think correct than I did explaining the one I think may be incorrect, but what more can be said? So long as we are on eyes, one more *Faux Frois:*

> *Europeans think strongly slanted eyes outlandish;*
> *Japanese find them either gallant or coquettish.*

Slit-consciousness is not *entirely* different East and West, for exceptionally straight slits are called "fox-eyes" in Japan, and considered hard, untrustworthy and merciless.[5]   Moreover, most Japanese do not have oblique eyes, so they are almost as conscious of them as Occidentals are. The difference is that they are common enough not to seem outlandish. I find it intriguing that almost all samurai and geisha are depicted with them and that Japanese prints often show people with eyes slanting up like those of cats.   On television *jidaigeki* (literally: "era-dramas" the Eastern equivalent of the American Western, which I shall just call *Easterns* from now on), every hero has eyes made up to look as oblique as possible, and even though "cat-burglars" are called "mouse-burglars" in Japanese, the pretty mouse-burglars, or *ninja,* always have big, yet extremely oblique pussy-cat eyes (suitably large for modern cartoon-derived taste). I find it remarkable that despite early-20th century Japanese propaganda art showing the Chinese very slant-eyed, and themselves like Europeans, we find this continuing *romance of the cat-eye* still going strong in this way! And these cat-eyed warriors are now taking over the world through the spread of Japanese animation! Does the beautiful example of the cat itself or the fact that eyebrows tend to stand up in anger make this emotionally true across cultures? [6]   But let us return to the days before animation to get a grip on reality. The humorist Douglas Sladen observed the following in 1905:

> ..
> The Japanese girl of the lower classes . . . is a most fascinating little creature. Her complexion is not yellow, but of a sunny brown, with rich blood showing through like the best Italian complexions. Her eyes are not obliquely placed or set in slits – she would only be too thankful if they were, for it is vulgar to have the eyes we admire. The paintings of Giotto would seem perfectly beautiful to a Japanese. The merry little maiden like Greuze's *Girl at the Fountain,* with

her bright healthy cheeks, and lips like cherries, and innocent round eyes, which Europeans admire so much in Japan, only strikes the Japanese themselves as plebeian: they prefer tragic queens, with lantern jaws and long hooked noses, and pasty white faces, and eyes like cats. (S:MQTJ)

Sladen refers to the women found in Edo era *ukiyoe*. I doubt Japanese taste is really so uniform.   As Arthur Marwick (BEAUTY IN HISTORY) argues, we cannot assume that stylized art reflects what men, or women, *really* find attractive.[7] Art-ificial *haute culture* ideals of beauty may misrepresent our real ideals of beauty, the beauty we would have if we could.

1. White Eye Search. Frois's expression is puzzling. Before I had Aurelio (a large dict.) on hand, neither scholar nor dictionary were of any help.   Googling the Portuguese did bring me some hits. *All were for blind drosophilia!*

2. The Portuguese Verb "se estranha" contains connotations of "strange" and, I would guess from the other half of the contrast, "repulsion." So, I used two words to translate it.

3. More Porcelain!   Barthes writes (on a photo of a contemplative Japanese boy) "under the porcelain eyelid, / a broad black drop: / the Night of the Inkwell, / of which Mallarmé speaks." (RB:EOS). Why *porcelain?*

4. Open Eye Experiment.   A psychologist might show people of various ages a picture of a wide-eyed Japanese macaque or almost any other primate (if any primates have different body language, I would like to know) – and ask them to select the proper emotion from a list. I expect we should find more Japanese, and, perhaps other Orientals, choosing "it's angry" and more Occidentals choosing "it's surprised."   It would be especially interesting to learn how early in life this different reading of emotion occurs.

5. Slit Hardness: Variations.   Most slits (I realize the term "slit" appalls, but has anyone come up with another? If not, we will just have to take a *slits-are-beautiful* approach.) actually curve slightly and the most beautiful *slit-eyes* are graced by a slight double-curve, or lazy "s" (The eyes of the Buddhist Goddess of Mercy, Kannon, are almost always such). To me this is more attractive than the almond-shaped eye which would seem to be the world's favorite.

6. Eye Angle. From the time I first saw a Korean tutelary deity carved in wood with eyes *completely vertical* (Perhaps to emphasize perfect upward and downward vision), I thought some day I would like to do a book on eye angle alone; but any work involving images requires one to be independently wealthy, so the would-be book was added to hundreds of others reserved for my good fortune, if it ever came. (Poor me, as poor as a church mouse!)

7. Marwick's Point: While much religious art and formal studies of beauty (i.e Venus or Eve) may vary enough from century to century to suggest a great relativity in our taste – extremely skinny or obese or pregnant bodies and various facial types – the nude mistresses painted for their masters and other boastful or salacious artwork shows women who are generally equally attractive to men now as then.

1-4   Our noses are high, some aquiline;
Os nossos narizes são altos e alguns aquilinos;

Theirs are low with small nostrils.
Os seus baxos e as ventas peqenas.

Frois's "ours" clearly does not hold for the round-headed peasants of parts of North Europe, but to South Europe where even the poor boasted beaks. And most of the 16th century Jesuits were of that ilk. An 18th century folk history 南蛮寺興廃記 description of Organtino includes this:

He was about 9 feet tall (kyu-shaku), with a head proportionately small for his body, a red face, round eyes, and a long, long (*takadaka to shite* high, high) nose so that when he looked sideways it would brush on his shoulder. His mouth was so large it reached to his ears . . . (E:NBJ)

In Japanese, big/long noses are called "high," with all the favorable metaphorical connotations that accompany (small noses, of course, are called "low" and bear the opposite connotation). As a glance at *ukiyoe* prints shows, the same association of high-bridged and finely shaped "aristocratic noses" with the nobility and administrative/warrior class and pug-noses with commoners found in parts of Europe was found developed to a higher degree in Japan, where farmers were often depicted utterly noseless. Naoko, a farm girl who worked as what is now called an *au pair*, whom I befriended on my first trip to Japan in 1971 (aboard the last voyage of the S.S. Wilson), told me how, as a girl, she had stroked her bridgeless button nose and sang a ditty to try to "heighten" it. To her, it was not *an* indicator but *the* indicator of personal beauty. She thought another Japanese woman no better looking than her – not good looking at all, I thought – a real beauty, solely for that reason!

Another Japanese friend says, *no*, it is not about class association or aesthetics. A "high" nose *means* someone is ambitious and going somewhere. She sent me a book, a best-seller year after year in Japan, which might best be described as an *almanac of fortune* for the year Heisei 12, or 2000 AD – the methods used are far more diverse than our astrology – and here is what it says about the nose:

> The nose (*hana*) is a flower (*hana*) that is the bloom of your life. The nose reveals the extent of your intellectual and financial fortune. No matter how capable you are, without a grand nose the *hana* of life will not bloom. Strange but true. There are hardly any people with small or somehow lacking noses who actually make it in society. (*Heisei-juninen unmei-hôkan*)

My friend's mother was a professional fortune-teller, so she admits to being more conscious of traditional physiognomy than her contemporaries, but whatever aspect is looked at, the size of the nose has more bearing on one's face-value in Japan than is the case in Europe. This may be because too many Europeans have bridged noses to make its presence or absence a matter for general concern, whereas in Japan and parts of China (where the physiognomy books derive) *variety is the rule*. [1]

The "high" Japanese nose also boasts a larger presence in literature than its West European counterpart. "We" do have our Cyrano, but in Japan it goes back to the book some call the world's oldest novel, THE TALE OF GENJI (c.1000), where the Shining Prince discovers the woman he courted (at night from behind a screen) has a long pointed nose with a red tip, who is punned upon by being called *Suetsumubana*, (end-pinch-flower, the source of lipstick), and Japan's oldest collection of poetry *Manyôshû* (TEN THOUSAND LEAVES), where a man is cruelly roasted for having a nose so red it could be mined for cinnabar! This nasal fixation may partly derive from the Japanese practice of pointing at, or touching the tip of their noses to identify themselves. This practice may still exist in parts of China, too, for the Chinese character meaning "personal" or "private" (used for writing one of the many "I's" used in Japan, today) comprises the *gathered-grain* radical and the *nose* radical, and folk philology says this was because people pointed at their noses to say "the grain is *mine!*" (This matter deserves more research, for the body-language of self-designation may be a fine cultural fingerprint). Marquis de Moge put it like this in 1860:

> When the Japanese wish to designate the I, that is to say their personality, they touch their nose; the tip of the organ being, according to them, the seat of individuality. There is nothing wonderful [shocking/surprising] in all this. When a Frenchman wishes to be very impressive, and to indicate his ego, does he not press his hand upon his stomach? [2] (M:BGE, *my bracket*)

Finally, the sexual nuances are more developed in Japan. Not only is nose size associated with genital endowment, as is true in many cultures, but nose-bleed is commonly associated with sexual excitement, a favorite gimmick in situation comedies and comic books today. If syphilis was mostly identified with pox-marks in Europe; in Japan, to catch the pox was *to lose your nose*, and this was a favorite theme for the black humor of *senryu*. (There might be a medical reason for the stress on different symptoms – even Herr Doctor Kaempfer in his short stay in Japan relates the case of "a Neighbour of my servant at Nangasaki" whose "nose was ready to drop off." "In order to get rid at once both his life and the distemper," the poor man ate poisonous blowfish, with soot from the thatched roof of his house to "make the poison still stronger." He fell "mortally sick" but then brought up "a large quantity of viscid, sharp, nasty matter" and, to make a long story short, miraculously recovered!) [3]

While Japanese today are still conscious of having noses smaller than those of Occidentals, the nostril is seldom given any thought. Large and small ones are discussed in the above-mentioned almanac, but nostrils are less value-laden than bridges. They do, however, share the class difference, for "small nostrils" or not, short noses tend to *show* their holes more than aristocratic ones. A typical drawing of a beastly peasant or a *busu* ("an ugly," as opposed to "a beauty") gives them swinish nostrils *instead of* a nose.

There was also a subtle difference between male and female ideals of nasal beauty. In Heian Japan (c.800-1200), there was a tendency to depict beautiful women with neither nose nor nostril. John Bulwer, in 1653, suggested that noselessness as an ideal had a Chinese origin:

> The *Chinoyse* doe hold them for the finest women who have small Noses, wherefore from their Child-hood, they use all the art they can possible, to prohibit the encrease of the Noses of their female Children. And indeed, their Noses are very little, and scarece standing forth. The People being in the composition of their Body short nosed, when they make the portraiture of a deformed Man, they paint him with a Long nose. (B:A)

Bulwer felt "the natural Sagacitie" of the Chinese would be somewhat hurt, for short noses do not smell as well as long ones; but beauty-wise, he admits their noses are "not unsuitable unto their broad Faces." A beak of a nose on a wide face would be literally "deformed" for even birds do not boast that combination. And, he adds something about Europe that suggests Frois's contrast may indirectly favor European men:

> With us, and with most of Europe, a long Nose is held more Beautiful, especially in Men; for the Midwives as soon as children are born, use with their fingers to extend the Nose, that it may be fairer and longer . . . (B:A)

These precious Occidental noses were extended yet further and turned into outlandish goblin beaks by Japanese *namban-e* (Southern Barbarian Paintings) and illustrations in anti-kirisutan literature (where said beak gives away the padre hiding in Japanese dress). [4]

1. *Variety of Nose and Race.* The highest bridges I have seen are on some Mongolians and Amerindians. So the idea that Europeans have them and Asiatics don't is wrong. Indeed, there is great variety in China. It would seem there is a link with the shape of the head and face but not with the eyes.

2. *Nose and Belly-touching First-Person*. Someone told me she saw it somewhere in China. This might provide a hint toward unraveling Japanese roots. Belly rather than chest-touching in Europe is also new to me. I would appreciate details on China and Europe!

3. **Pox, Sex and Noses.** The identification of syphilis and the sexual organ with the nose in Japan is only comparatively greater than in Europe.   John Donne's bold essay *"Why doth the Poxe Soe Much Affect to Undermine the Nose?"* says it all. After joking about whether said phenomenon was the merciful act of a disease not wishing one to "smell his own stinck," or a sneak attack of the low member upon the high, or an act of justice substituting for Revenge killing being recently made illegal, or a warning lest others shipwreck upon

that Coast, Donne concludes that the "Analogy, Proportion and Affection between the Nose and that part where the disease is first contracted, and therefore *Heliogabalus* chose not his Minions in the Bath but by the Nose . . . . is [the reason] nearest truth," or, in a word, "the Nose is most compassionate with this part," and, taking a dig at the big-nosed leadership, snickers "it is reasonable that this Disease in particular should affect the most eminent and perspicuous part, which in general doth effect to take hold of the most eminent and conspicuous men." (D/C:CPSP)

4. *Namban-e* I *know*. Everyone wants illustrations. But I enjoy the challenge of a picture-less book. For a future edition, I would like uniform black and white line-drawings (made from assorted photos, paintings and prints) of things in this book, perhaps one per page. But, first, I must find the right bilingual artist to do it, for I must keep writing. Meanwhile, I will try to put up some illustrations at on my website. If any readers wish to start gathering illustrations, I can make a link to your websites, too. So please visit the Topsy-turvy illustrations at http://www.paraverse.org.

1-5   European people for the most part have thick beards;
Pola maior parte a gente de Europa tem boa cópia de barba;

Japanese usually have sparse, poorly shaped beards.
Os Japões pola mayor parte pouca e naõ bem composta.

While Japanese often have so little beard Rodrigues once claimed one might say more appropriately they do not have them (V(A):S&A n99), he also noted that the owner of said [no]beard exercised more freedom over it than Europeans of that time. To wit:

> They also cultivate their beards in various fashions. Some wear only mustaches . . . and shave all the rest. Others follow the fashion which pleases them best and in this they are imitated out here in the East by the Portuguese, Spaniards and Moors, who have abandoned the traditional Portuguese style. (C:TCJ).

If thick beards were rare, one would have to allow a great variety of style, for otherwise they could not be kept trim. But the Jesuits arrived in an exceptionally wild era. Beards followed them out. The samurai in the Era of Seclusion ended up as clean-shaven as the 1950's corporation man of the United States. And in 1929, the *Encyclopedia Britannica* told us that along "with other traditions of their feudal age, the Japanese nation has broken its ancient custom of the razor, and their emperor has beard and moustache." Even allowing the hardly ancient razor to be a metaphor, from Frois and Rodrigues, above, we know such simple claims about "ancient" and "traditions" are utter nonsense. A people with a history – something all too often only accorded to the West – are too complex to be described in the bi-polar terms of "modern" and "traditional." Still, we could say that the Japanese have *tended to* shave or pluck their beards, which is not surprising, for they are relatively lacking in body hair and their culture had a long conflict with the Ainu, reportedly the most hirsute people in the world. Frois via Maffei via Willis (1577) described the latter as follows:

> North from Japan, three hundred leagues out of Miyako [the capitol: Kyoto], layeth a great country of savage men, clothed in beasts skins, rough bodied with huge beards, and monstrous moustaches, the which they hold up with little forks as they drink. (W:HOT)

The fact that many natives of North America were also hair-pluckers and some, like the Japanese, did not stop with the beard, suggests that even in the absence of a counter-example like the Ainu, the poorly bearded man may tend to go for an ideal of smooth skin. Bulwer, writing *cerca* 1650 on the way "the people of the whole world" treated their bodies observed that:

> The Chinese also have by their Beards, consisting not of above twenty or thirty haires, a thing wonderful to behold, and when they would describe a deformed man, they paint him with a thick beard. (B:A)

Since Bulwer cites Maffei, he is probably elaborating upon Valignano's description of the Japanese and playing the topsy-turvy game. Beards may have been secondary sexual attributes, but they numbered among the primary race indicators. About fifty years after Bulwer, Francois Bernier used "the lushness of the male beard" to categorize races. The "first species", the Europeans and north Africans had flowing beards, while the black Africans and peoples of east Asia had only "three or four hairs" and "three hairs of beard," respectively. The beard of his fourth species, the Lapps ("stunted little creatures") was not mentioned. (Londa Schiebinger: NATURE'S BODY, Beacon, 1993) And, "as late as 1848, Charles Hamilton Smith, friend and disciple of George Cuvier" made a chart geologically dividing the races where the West was occupied by "Caucasian or bearded type" and the East by "Mongolic or beardless type."(Ibid) Both the lack of beard and the practice of removal of the beard and other body hair may be connected to generations of living in cold climates, for animal fats were applied to the skin as protection against cold wind by the Amerindians.

1-6   The dignity and honor of a European is placed upon his beard.
A honrra e primor que a jente de Europa tem boa copia de barba;

The Japanese put it on a tuft of hair bound at the back of their heads.
Os Japões a poem no cabelinho que trazem atado detrás do toutiço.

The word "honor" was no exaggeration. European men even swore by their beards. "Among the Anglo-Saxons the penalty for damage to a beard was twenty shillings, while breaking a thigh bone was only twelve." (Phillip Camerarius writing in the seventeenth century, according to Schiebinger, Ibid. 1-5n)

Camerarius went on to recount that in many places in Europe serious criminals, such as fornicators, were punished by having their beards "chopped off publicly with a keen axe." (Ibid)

Sir Thomas More's first witticism as he was about to ascend to the block, was "I pray thee see me safely up, but as for my coming down again, let me shift for myself." (C. Hibbert: *Tower of London –* Newsweek 1971)   His third, less famous witticism, expressed after warning the headsman "You will never get any credit for beheading me, my neck is too short," tells us something about our subject:

Let me lay my beard over the block lest you cut it, for *it* has never committed treason."

The tuft of hair by which Japanese expressed their honor was not bound low at the back of the head like the Chinese queue, but near the top.   4 to 6 inches of the hair jutting up proudly 6 to 8 inches from the crown,   was bound into an erect trunk with chord spiraling up and down to create criss-cross intersections or diamonds (as found on sword handles).   The extra 1 to 3 inches bristled up and out freely like a brush. (O:KGB) I think of it as the most manly hairstyle in the world.   The thickness varied depending on how much, if any, of the head was shaven.   If the head was shaven it was usually relatively thin, waxed and bound.   Magistrates and samurai in Frois's time already kept it in this *chonmage,* or "bent" style (where the tuft curls forward like a pistol set on the head) that would be used by most classes in the Tokugawa era (1603-1867).   More precise descriptions:

. . . the front and top of the head being shaved, the long hair from the back and the sides being drawn up and tied, then waxed, tied again, and cut short off, the stiff queue being brought forward and laid, pointing forwards, along the back part of the top of the head. This top-knot is shaped much like a short clay pipe. (B:UTJ:1880)

. . . the Japanese beaux endeavor to improve it, by using a very fine pomatum; and take care that the hair lies very even and regular, so that it forms a solid mass; the hair tuft must perfectly resemble a four-cornered piece of japanned wood, which has at the top and two sides an opening. (G:MCJ: tr1824)

On TV Easterns – which remain more popular than our Westerns! -- the losing sword fighter's *chonmage* is often cut off by the victor as the camera pans the loser, whose remaining hair falls abjectly down. With this psychological baggage, it is amazing that less than a generation after Perry opened Japan, the Japanese cut off their own topknots as part of their effort to take on the West by becoming the West – what Lafcadio Hearn called "the most admirable system of intellectual self-defense ever heard of – by a marvelous national *jiujitsu* [judo]."(in N:MAR) The new national policy was accepted by most of the samurai class, perhaps because by that time, the *chonmage* was more common among the lower classes than the upper classes within which it started. (B:UTJ: 1880)

Koreans shared the practice of wearing topknots with the Japanese. Their knots, which were often bejeweled, stuck up "like a horn" and were bound around a shaved circular spot three inches in diameter on the crown of their head (B:KHN) In 1895, a Japanese effort to abolish the topknot in Korea, where it was as important a mark of manhood as wearing a sword was for the Japanese, set off nation-wide rioting that ended with a reduced Japanese influence in Korea and the heads of cabinet members who supported the measure rolling in the streets! (see Bird: KHN for details of this sorry affair.)

1-7   With us, men keep their hair trimmed, but consider it an affront to have it removed.[1] *Os homens antre nós andão trosquiados e tem por afronta pelarem;*

> Japanese make themselves bald, using a tweezers to be sure not a hair remains. Pain and tears accompany this. *Os Japões se pelão com tenazes pera não terem cabelos, e isto com dor e lagrimas.*

Apparently, "we" were hair moderates, if insisting on a medium-length can be so called. We did not allow long hair for men and shaved the heads of adults of both sexes for punishment. This lack of freedom was nothing to crow over, but keeping one's hair cropped was still easier than what the custom demanded of most (?) Japanese men. An earlier letter of Frois's, as Englished by Willis, is a good read:

> "bare-headed commonly they go, procuring baldness with sorrow and tears, rooting up with pincers all the hairs of their heads as it groweth, except it be a little behind, the which they knot and keep with all diligence." (The "tears" are in the original 1565 letter, but the connotation of what must be *dor* (i.e. *dolor*) in this case should be *pain* rather than "sorrow!").

Okada backs up Frois with a passage from the *Keichô Kenbunshû* written about 30 years after *Tratado* by the Japanese author (Miura 浄心) where the "old fool [self denigrating term]" in his youth observed hair on boy's foreheads removed "not with razors but with large wooden tweezers" in the Kanto (greater Tôkyô) area. He observed "a horrendous amount of black blood flowing down their foreheads." Valignano's short-lived China-Japan contrast of 1579 put it like this:

> The Chinese wear their hair long like women; here they not only cut theirs short but actually pull it out so they remain bald-headed. (in S:VMP or, was it V(W):HPP?)

When Frois wrote, the Japanese were in the process of changing from the excruciating process of plucking the hair out – this "fashionable but painful style" (Rodrigues:C:TCJ) being a perfect masculine rite for the Warring Period – to shaving the head "in a very handsome way." (ibid. It is hard to know if this "handsome" refers to Rodrigues's admiration of the hair-style or the skill of the shaving.) In the early 19th century, observing the toilet of ship-wrecked Japanese sailors seated on mats on the deck of the Dutch boat, someone, Seibold, perhaps, writes "above all, we admired their dexterity in shaving their own heads." (in B:MCJ:1841) The topknot, which stuck up from the crown and pointed forward on the shaven pate, was cut off "as a sacrifice to his patron divinity, in acknowledgement of his deliverance from imminent danger." Though I mention "Japanese" doing this or that, there really was more diversity of hair-style than one might imagine from the above. One particularly notable one (*otsugami* is what I would call an *anti-style* created by allowing the "moon forehead" clearing to grow into an ugly porcupine (shades of punk!), while the rest of the hair is unbound to hang down. This was worn by masterless samurai, some sick people, playboys wanting to look tough, etc.. In other words, it was cool or *bad,* which is to say, a kind of style that is scary to some. (J/O:KGB)

The origin of the partial head shaving is said to be the need to keep cool wearing helmets in the Warring Years. The part of the head that was shaved (i.e. the crown) was called the *tsukishiro* meaning "a place to lodge the moon), *tsukibitai,* or "moon forehead," i.e. the clearing looks like the moon, or *sakayaka,* a word of debatable etymology. It so happens that many of the most Japanese-looking natives of North Brazil and South Venezuela, the Yanamamo, Cayapo and Tchikrin shave the exact same portion of their heads and all of them consider the tonsure "a graphic representation of the moon's disc." (Robert Brain: *The Decorated Body* 1979) I cannot help but wonder if there is a connection somewhere!

1. *Pelarem* **Translation.**   To be "depilated" might be more accurate etymologically speaking, but the comparison with Japan suggests *shaved* or *cut close to the scalp* as well as *pulled out.* Unfortunately, English has no generic term for being *de-haired* such as for, say, guts, where "de-gutted" or "gutted," both mean "removed."

~~~~~~

1-8   We have many freckled men and women;
Antre nós há muitos homens e molheres sardas;

Japanese, though white, rarely have freckles.
Os Japões, com serem alvos, há muy pouqos que o sejão.

Japanese, as mentioned in the foreword, were considered "white." This was not only an honorable white status but how Japanese were literally perceived. Vilela, who proceeded Frois to Japan wrote that when it came to whiteness (*blanca*), the Portuguese had nothing over the Japanese; and in the same year (1565) Frois described "a Japanese youth much paler (*albo*) than the Spaniards" and another who "in his whiteness (*blancura*) of face resembles a German". (From notes to V(A):S&A) While lightly pigmented Japanese can sun splotch with age, they do indeed have *few* freckles. Frois's syntax [*with* being white] is not quite so clear as my "though," but his antithetical point must be that Japanese do not freckle *despite* being fair. I doubt this is *all* genes. Because Japanese are especially anxious about marks on the skin – rough and discolored skin is common to vengeful female ghosts and taboo for seeming impurity – Japanese may have taken more care than "us" to protect their skin. We had parasols and sun bonnets, too, but they – even today – do farm work with a towel draping down both sides of their faces under their hats. This greater care is reflected indirectly by an observation about the Embassy of Japanese youth sent to Europe in 1582 cited by Alvarez-Taladriz: "Although it is said that in Japan skin is white [*suele ser blanco*] and fits the great cold there, these gentlemen for the travail of the road have darkened to the point of appearing to be moors." In the late 17th or early 18th century, L' Abbe de T. wrote "the *Chinese* call them [the Japanese] whites [Perhaps L' Abbe refers to Japanese and Europeans being called the same name "Southern-Barbarian?"] , tho' they rather incline to an olive colour." As late as 1860, The Marquis de Moges, denied the "pretty legend" of Japanese originating in China as a select group of young pioneers seeking "the herb of immortality" who never returned, claiming:

> The Japanese, with skins as white as our own, cannot be descendents of the yellow sons of Han; and indeed they repudiate all idea of common descent with the Chinese . . . (M:BGE)

With Moges as pleased with the honorable Japanese ("cleanly to a miracle," "noble and proud") as he was disgusted with the cowardly Chinese ("dreadfully dirty" "sneaking, submissive and cunning"), it would appear that *white is as white does* influenced his perception which compares poorly to the observant Alcock who just 3 years later wrote of "the skin nature gave" Japanese women – as opposed to the Pict-like tatoos of some men – "in all its varying shades of olive, and sometimes hardly a shade at all." But, when did the ridiculous idea of "yellowness" found in Moges's above missive first appear? Was it born in the mid-19th century scientific studies of race? [1] Regardless, it soon spread from China to Japan and we find even a bright observer like Chamberlain writing "the Japanese are Mongols, that is, they are distinguished by a yellowish skin . . ." (C:TJ) The earliest *yellow Japanese* I have come across date back to the 1880 novel *Yellow Peril* and explorer Isabella Bird's book of the same year where she finds [Caucasian] Ainu features a welcome relief

> "after the yellow skins, the stiff horse hair, the feeble eyelids, the elongated eyes, the sloping eyebrows . . . and the general impression of degeneracy conveyed by the appearance of the Japanese." (UTJ)

While not a few Japanese good-naturedly lamented their lack of beauty as a race, they did not readily agree with their new *yellow* label. If they knew some English, they also knew the word had a bad connotation. Despite the auspicious connotations of yellow in the Sino-sphere, as far as I know there were no celebrations of yellowness. Any recognition of a yellow identity was a grudging one. On 4 January 1901, the sickly novelist who now adorns the 1000-yen bill, Natsume Soseki, notes that phlegm in London is black, imagines how dark the lungs of Londoners must be, and admits to shuddering every time he blows his nose. The next day he writes:

> It is hard to understand how people living in this smoke can be so beautiful. It can not be the climate or the weak sunlight. I saw a short, strangely dirty man coming toward me, and then I realized it was my reflection in a mirror. Coming here, for the first time, this matter of our being yellow made sense to me. (H:SN)

Yellowism on "our" side peaked during World War II, when Japanese were depicted as literally yellow, denigrated as LYB's (little yellow-bellies) and country stars sang the likes of *"We're gonna find a Fellow Who is Yellow and Beat Him Red White and Blue."* (D:WWM). It revived in a visual format during the Trade Wars of the 1970's, when the European press bannered bright yellow samurai and sumo-wrestlers. In this context, the yellowness was not cowardly, but outlandish and terrifying. (In America, Japanese, Korean and Chinese ethnicities would sue such racist press, so what yellow journalism there is, is minor by comparison!) As trade deficits with China grows at the dawn of the 21st century, we shall soon see whether this *yellowism* blooms yet again!

Living 20 years in Japan, I met only one person with yellow skin. Perhaps it was the combination of the chemicals he worked with (he was a lithographer), his consumption of tangerines (up to a half-box a day) and his chain-smoking. On the other hand, I knew a number of Japanese who thought they, as Mongoloids, didn't need to fear the sun (like whites) and got badly burned for it! Japanese never identify *themselves* as "yellow" except indirectly, when the press complains about a foreign politician allegedly crusading against "yellow peril," or reports on a Hawaiian metaphor, *banana,* the yellow equivalent of the black-inside white-outside *oreo.* On the other hand, Japan's yellow press does not hesitate to use the terms whites (*hakujin*) and black (*kokujin*). So, come to think of it, does ours. In the late 1960's, a Mexican cartoonist suggested his countrymen needed a color to *compete* in the brave new world of color "power" and color "beauty," so as not to be forced out of the running by their overbearing black and white neighbors: ergo, "beige power" and "beige beauty." Ruiz's idea (Could anyone find that issue of *Los Aguachados* for me?) apparently did not catch on. In matters of color, there would seem to be *a law of the excluded middle.* [2]

1. Genderizing Science   I believe Cynthia Russett's ***Sexual Science: the Victorian Construction of Woman-hood*** (Harvard: 1989) is by far the best summary of the way *male* and *female* were made out to be topsy-turvy by 19th century science. Her book should be better known.

2. *Beige Power?* Maybe I am wrong. In 2003, I heard a Mexican-American finally published a book arguing such an idea. I think he used "brown" rather than beige. Now, only *Yellow Beauty* remains silent. Since *yellow* is an Imperial and happy color in the Sinosphere and not all bad in the Eurosphere – think of the color of the smiling suns "our" children draw! (in Japan, they are red), it should be far easier to rehabilitate than "black" was.

1-9   With us, pockmarked men and women are rare.
Antre nós hé raro serem os homens ou m[olhe]res bixigozas;

In Japan, they are common and many lose their sight from the pox.
Antre os Japões hé couza muito commua e cegão muitos d[e] bexigas.

At the time Frois wrote, descriptions of missing persons suggest that about one in six Englishmen were pockmarked. (T:DMR←Lost the book name! Can anyone guess?) So Europeans on the whole were not exactly smooth-faced. Had the Iberians already gained enough immunity (or been sufficiently thinned out?) not to be hit so hard? Or, could the Japanese by the 1580's, already be suffering from strains the Europeans introduced which were new to them? [1] Whatever the reason, Japanese children, writes Okada, were especially hard hit by pock-mark-leaving diseases in this era. A proverb he introduced (common enough that I have read it many times) suggests a bigger difference, which reverses our common assumption on the respective deadliness of two diseases:

We fear measles, but we fear small pox most of all.
They say "smallpox takes your looks, measles takes your life." and fear measles more.

To be more precise, the proverb reads: "small pox will settle your looks but measles will settle your life." By Frois's time or soon thereafter Japanese evidently found *measles* the more lethal disease. Then again, it may have been because more lethal strains of measles got to Japan. The deadly measles was not something to joke about, but 18[th] century *senryu* (17-syllabet poems (or, black humor) about the foibles of city life) owes much to small pox. It is full of pitted brides, called simply "bring-dowries" (for the wealth that b[r]ought them husbands) and feared pimps, whose scars typically came from *the* pox – syphilis, brought East by the West shortly after the West itself caught it, presumably from Africa or the New World. The Japanese usually called it either *baidoku,* "plum-poison" (because the chancre resembles the tiny Japanese plum) or *togasa,* "Chinese chancre." It is unlikely this disease spread quickly enough in Japan to be a significant cause for the difference noted by Frois because the high number of pockmarked Japanese still observed when it was reopened in the mid-19th century dropped precipitously within a generation of Perry's arrival thanks to appropriate government measures encouraging vaccination for smallpox "which has always been epidemic" in Japan, according to Morse, who also noted in 1877 that "in this matter, as in many others, the Japanese are far ahead of occidental nations."(M:JDD) [2]

If the spread of small-pox and syphilis was a tragedy, the cholera epidemic that killed hundreds of thousands shortly after Perry's Opening of Japan was a crime and a permanent stain on the name of the United States of America, for the offending ship's captain took advantage of the unfair treaty to *refuse* to undergo the requested quarantine. As the first English Consul Alcock acknowledged, it went a long way to explain the frequent assassinations of Westerners in the following decades. Still, the Far East was not just the victim of disease from the West. With its intensive animal husbandry, the East was (and is) itself a major *source* of infectious disease.

1. ***Sorting Out Diseases.*** I cannot pretend to have sorted out what was what with small pox in Europe and Japan. "Until the sixteenth century, smallpox was considered an unpleasant, but not particularly dangerous, childhood disease. It is possible that it mutated to a more virulent form. An alternative explanation is that the more dangerous form already existed in Africa and was imported to Europe via the slave trade." (www.bignell. uk.com/plagues.htm) Like always, everything is changing right in the period I hope to explain! Queen Elizabeth caught it in 1562, the year before Frois finally managed to get to Japan. Because it kept coming and coming and anyone who caught it once never caught it again, it became pretty much a children's disease and, for that reason young servants who were pockmarked were favored over those that were not for it was known they were immune. (see David A. Koplow *Smallpox The Fight to Eradicate a Global Scourge* 2003 U. of California Press.)

2. ***Backwards Occident*** In respect to the slowness of the West to adopt vaccination, Morse lamented Christian fundamentalism that prevented the rational spread of scientific knowledge in the USA. It is depressing to consider how little progress has made in fundamentalist Usania even today at the start of the 21st century. We need the help of humor such as Adam Fitz-Adam's 5 June, 1755 article, published in his magazine *THE WORLD* wherein four objections were made to the practice. First, it was Turkish or Persian and "speaking as a man, I dread lest it should be a means of introducing, in these *opera days*, some more alarming practices of the seraglio." Second, it might work too well: i.e., "the world . . . is certainly much over-peopled" and the "inconvenience" born of this (which he elaborates) "had in a great measure been prevented by the proper number of people who were daily removed by the small-pox in the natural way" and without this help "unless we should speedily have a war

upon the continent, we shall be in danger of being eaten up with famine at home, through the multiplicity of our people . . . ." (Yes, yes, Malthus wasn't born yet. He was, however, 22 when the multi-volume 3rd ed. of the *WORLD* I quote was published: 1789. *I'll bet he read it.*). Third, it would mean a greater percentage of beauties, who "are naturally disposed to be a little insolent" and give rise to a shortage of "fit and ugly women," whose work kept the commonwealth prosperous, so that "this modern invention for the preservation of pretty faces ought, no doubt, to be abolished." And, fourth, without fear of disease the country gentry – especially their wives – will "evacuate their hospitable seats and roll away with

safety and tranquility to town to the great diminution of country neighborhood . . ." – I'd guess that Fitz-Adam actually favored "the unnatural and unconstitutional practice of INOCULATION;" but the fact that many people *seriously* divided the world into things natural and unnatural in the West kept the resistance alive until the twentieth century. No, the twenty-first. It should be noted that he was referring to the longstanding African and Asian practice of inoculating people with a bit of pus taken from the pock marks of a sufferer that Lady Mary Wortley Montagu was the first to succeed in getting established in Europe. It was said to have a mortality rate of about 2-3%, far better than odds the disease gave you.

1-10   We consider it filthy and uncouth to have long finger-nails.
Antre nós trazer as unhas compridas se tem por sujidade e pouqa criasão;

In Japan, men as well as well-bred women sport some talon-like nails.
Os Japões, asi homens como molheres fidalgas, trazem algumas como de gaviões.

Okada protests: "It is an exaggeration to write that our country has the custom of growing long nails. There were just days when nail-cutting was taboo; it was considered inauspicious to cut them at night or [for punning reasons] before departing on a journey." Indeed, most Japanese depicted in *ukiyoe* prints show nails cut so short the meat of the finger-tip bulges up. But, I beg to point out that while Okada and others translate Frois's second sentence as "*sometimes* have nails" or ". . . some *men and ladies* have nails . . . ," strictly speaking, the "some" (*algumas*) should refer to the *nails* (*unhas*), and may refer to the fact that priests, literatae, wealthy merchants and nobles in Japan often boasted long fingernails on at least *one* pinkie, i.e., *some* finger. [1] The practice is originally Mandarin-Chinese. [2] Since the Japanese adopted/adapted many Chinese practices, *viz* Rada and Cruz, respectively, on 16th century China:

> The men often let the fingernails of one of their hands grow very long, and are very proud thereof, as we saw by many of them whose fingernails were as long as their fingers. (trans. Boxer:B:SCSC)

> There are some Chinas who wear very long finger-nails, from half a span to a span long, which they keep very clean; and these finger-nails do serve them instead of the chop-sticks for to eat withal. (ibid)

The Portuguese editor for the Cruz reprint writes that the nails were coated with silver (*bainhas de prata*). He also notes that no other documentation on *eating* with nails has been found. No documentation, perhaps, but the idea got around. Here is Bulwer a century later:

> In *China* some of them weare Nailes of half a quarter and a quarter long, which they keep very cleane; and these Nailes do serve them instead of Forkes to eate withall; the use of silver Forkes which our Gallants so much used of late was no doubt an imitation of this. (B:A)

Bulwer writes tongue-in-cheeke, but chopsticks – called just "sticks" by the Portuguese and Spaniards – were often Englished as *forks*. Dyer Ball, mercifully drops the chopstick idea, and gives a late-19th century explanation:

> Long finger-nails are not considered a sign of dirtiness, but of respectability, and of being above manual labour, which, if necessary, would of course prevent them from attaining such length as an inch and a half, two inches, or even three, though it is seldom one sees them all of equal length on all the fingers. It is well that such is the case, as two or three on one or both hands give such a claw-like appearance to the fingers as to make them sufficiently repulsive; fortunately hand-

shaking is not in vogue in China, as it would be extremely unpleasant to feel the long talons gripping one's hand. (THINGS CHINESE)

Viewed in retrospect, there is no little irony in the contrast, for in Japan, where the same word was used for "fingernail," "claw" and "talon," having long nails had a strong beastly significance and, as it turns out, identified with Europeans! The retrospective folk-description of the kind and gentle Japanophile Organtino S.J., the nose of which we have already seen includes some animal metaphor:

> His teeth are like a horse's, whiter than snow. His finger-nails the claws of a bear. (J/E:NBJ)

Since the same word is used for *nails* and *claws* in Japanese, it might be overdoing it to say that Furukomu (Frois or Valignano) lit his tobacco by striking fire from his own *claws*" (As it is usually translated), but the practice of depicting the other side with spooky fingernails is undeniable. These "claws" disappeared with the opening of Japan, but were returned to the hands – or, rather, paws – of Churchill, Roosevelt and other Anglo-American enemy in WWII Japanese propaganda art! (D:WWM) This art reminds us that we should be careful about equating nails and elegant femininity. [3]

1. *One Long Nail*   Some elderly Japanese –very few today – still keep one long fingernail, and claim it is useful for removing ear wax, which it certainly *is* (I keep one long for that reason – and to remove cotton from my ear – and find the only problem with it is that the drug-on-the-brain people of my native Usania (*America* should refer to the continents) are constantly asking me if it is for coke!).

2. *China May Be India*   Just because I trace back Japanese practices to China doesn't necessarily mean China is the original origin. Here is Âl-bîrûnî on India/ns:

> They let the nails grow long, glorying in their idleness, since they do not use them for any business or work, but only, while living a *dolce far niente* life, they scratch their heads with them and examine the hair for lice." (A(S):AI)

The unwritten contrary are Muslims who keep them short. Is it possible that long nails traveled North with Religion?

3. *A Second Nail Tradition.*   In examining history, we must take care not to allow ourselves to conflate long nails with idleness and femininity. A Sung dynasty painting of Fu-hsi, legendary inventor of the eight trigrams of Taoism, by Ma Lin, is described by Anthony Christie as follows:

> In addition to their role in divination the *pa kua* were the basis of Chinese calligraphy, so scholars especially revered Fu-hsi who, *despite* his 'archaic'

dress, is seen with the long nails worn by scholars." (C:CM – oops, I forgot to put this in the bibliography!)

Though a total amateur in mythology and art history, I can *see* the "despite" here is *wrong*. The man's nails (finger and toe) do not look at all like those of scholars but seem a perfect match for his dress comprising two furs, probably bear and leopard. They look terrifying, a perfect match to the fur. Moreover, Fu-hsi has hair on his feet! To me, this suggests a second tradition of nails, a ferocious one, diametric to the effete one. Here, too, there may well be an Indian connection. In 1659, an unarmed Hindu leader (Sivaji) assassinated a Mogul General (Afzal Khan) using "steel 'tiger-claws,' which he had secretly attached to his fingers" which resulted in a decisive battle win and the liberation of Maratha. (C:TTM this, too lost in my room!) It is possible this creative guerilla fighter invented his nails from scratch, but I would guess we have a tradition. It is not irrelevant that in the Americas, real nails were used for tools by the Tehueco in Sinaloa (Mexico).

> If they do not have a knife to cut the meat [flesh of human's they kill] , they do so with their thumbnail, which they grow long. PDR:HTHF 2-16

I believe what Andrés Péres de Ribas S.J. reports in the seventeenth century because nails can be strengthened by use because of the effect of pressure on their growth and because I have peeled oranges with my thumbnail . . .

1-11   We think sword scars on the face are ugly;[1]
Antre nós se tem por d[is]formidade ter huma cutil[a]da no rosto;

Japanese are proud of their wounds and, not taking care with their treatment, make them so much the uglier. *Os Japões, se prezão delas e como são mal quradas são ainda mais disformes.*

If I recall correctly, Valignano sported quite a scar himself.[2] As a Jesuit who would not want to boast he didn't include anything on it in his *Sumario*, but we can imagine he was surprised at all the *praise* it brought him in Japan. Dueling scars were likewise valued in some parts and eras in Europe, but it would be hard to find a culture as utterly macho as 16th century Japan. Every visitor to Japan was favorably impressed with their bravery. This was on the tail-end of the long Warring States Period (Sengoku-jidai: 1338-1568). Continual wars turn people into either chickens or roosters. In Japan's case, it was the latter:

> They will not put up with a single insult or even a word spoken in anger. Thus you speak (and, indeed, must speak) courteously even to the most menial laborers and peasants because they will not have it otherwise, for either they will drop their work without giving a second thought to what they stand to lose, or else they will do something even worse. (Alessandro Valignano in C:TCJ.).

Jesuits, themselves *warriors for Jesus* and honor-conscious Latins (i.e. Arabized Europeans), found the Japanese recklessness praiseworthy as compared to the Chinese who, many noted, ran "like women." The Japanese served as mercenaries throughout Asia at this time, were proud of their bravery as a people, and did not hesitate to boast about it. This "we are the toughest dudes around" attitude continued throughout the Tokugawa isolation and is one of the main reasons Japan was not colonized by the West.

One still finds scars at work in the popular culture, but they serve a different role in a no longer brave society. Sitcoms and comic books frequently show a scarred *yakuza* (or, rather *chinpira*, a *yakuza* underling) intimidating people with his presence alone – for some reason, nine out of ten times he is in the subway. Beauty is not the only "face value," a scar's scare-effect can gain a man (who may be a coward at heart) a seat and the room to stretch out on it . . . . Perhaps, scars, then, functioned as a mark of identity. If sartorial and weapons-related restrictions did not permit many types of gallantry (I use the word in the Olde English sense of it), scars, at least, could hardly be outlawed! This also may be part of a broader phenomenon, for, in Japan, even blindness had its own sort of face-value. (13-24)

1. *Translation*: The original Portuguese used the terms (*disformidade*) "deformity" or "defigurations" (*disformes*) rather than "ugly" and "uglier." The original terms suggest to me the visual equivalent of "unnatural" being used in the sense of "wicked." The undesirable connotations of both *deformity* and *unnatural* are a result of the Christian tendency to equate what *is* (i.e., what God created) with what *ought to be*. (On the other hand, some Christians think said world is *not* what ought to be, so this is a gross simplification!) Still, the main connotation of these words is "ugly," so I will stick with it.

2. *Valignano's Scar.* I cannot for the life of me re-find my notes about Valignano's dueling (I think it was in S:VMP or V(W):HPP). A short gloss anyone?

Concerning male dress
quanto aos vestidos dos homens

(This is the first and last chapter with a double count. It shows Frois's treatise was unfinished.)

1-1+   Our dress is the same for almost all of the four seasons of the year;
Os nossos vestidos quasi em todos os 4 tempos do anno são, os mesmos;

Japanese change their dress three times a year: *i.e., natsu katabira, aki awase, fuyu kimono.*   *Os Japões os varião 3 vezes no ano: naccu catabira, aqui avaxe, fuyu qimão.*

Non-Japanese tend to use the word *kimono* to describe all robe-like clothing worn by Japanese. [1] Frois uses the Japanese terms *as is*. The *natsu katabira* is an unlined, sometimes gauze-thin, summer robe, after nature's the second best suit for the sultry Japanese summer. It was also raised above the head as a parasol of sorts. Today, we find something close, the *yukata*, worn at home, for some festivals, in hotels and even outside in hot-spring resorts (but no one holds it over their heads). Until Japanese adopted Western dress, it also served for underwear. The *aki awase* or fall style of dress is a more substantial two-layered robe which can properly be called a kimono. It was *officially* only worn for a short time, from the first day of the Ninth Month (now, mid-October) until the ninth day of the same, perhaps, partly to air it out before it was stuffed with cotton or flock-silk (for nobles) and turned into a *fuyu kimono*, or, winter kimono, and this was pulled out to turn it back into an *awase* on the first day of summer (the Fourth Month by the old calendar). This latter is called *hatsu-awase*, or "first awase" and the day is called "Clothes-Change" (*koromogae*) Day. (In case you wonder, Spring is missed because the Japanese calendar Spring began at the same time as the New Year, mid-February when Japan is freezing.)

Even if he did grow up in Portugal, Frois must have known that much of Europe is freezing cold in the winter, so what does he mean when he says "our dress" remains the same? First, Europeans could usually keep their tights and pompously plump pants [2] and skirts, etc. on year-round because Western Europe summers are relatively dry. Second, Europeans put a coat *over* their usual suit, where the Japanese replaced or stuffed the suit itself and were more formally attentive to seasonal colors.

While there were formal dates for changing suit, and Rodrigues noted "They are most punctilious in the observance of those ceremonies," (R(C):TIJ) (Ibid.) the Japanese were not absolute=irrational about it, for he also writes the *katabira* was worn in the summer "and when it is hot," and, more interesting yet, hints at the possibility of a compromise, the practice of, frequent, if not day-by-day stuffing and unstuffing: "this costume will be more or less padded in keeping with the natural temperature of the season." *That* is smart. I have long wondered why we don't use inflatable coats in the winter.

1. *Defining Kimono.* I googled across this correction of the misuse of the term for any and all Japanese clothing by foreigners:

"To begin, the word "ki-mono" is a modern term. It was invented in the Meiji era (1868-1912), a time of great openness in Japan after nearly three centuries of self-imposed seclusion. When pressed by foreigners to name their native style of dress, they used the word "kimono" which means simply "thing to wear."" (LR)

This, too, however is wrong. Kimono (including dozens of regional variations such as *kirimono* and *kimon*) was used to signify both certain types of robes *and* as a generic word for "clothing" as far back as Japan has written records. In that sense, it is similar to the word "dress." We use it to mean "all clothing" but we cannot point at a specific piece of clothing and call it "a dress," unless it is a certain type of garment. You would not call trousers or even a skirt "a dress."

2. *Plump Pants.* When Frois wrote, pompous plump pants were near their peak. To me, men in pants with *pumpkin-sized* thighs are far more ludicrous than women with their bustle that is, after all, a *bona fide* extension of a secondary sexual attribute. Nothing in the so-called exotic Far East is half so weird, except possibly the pant-leg extensions in Japan I will describe elsewhere.

1-2+   With us, colorful clothing is considered frivolous and ludicrous;
Antre nós trazer o vestido pintado se teria por liviandade e zombaria;

With Japanese, excepting bonzes and old men of shaven pate, wearing colorful clothing is universal. *Nos Japões hé universal trazerem-nos todos pintados, excepto bonzos e velhos rapados.*

Japanese *never* wore clothing as ludicrous as that of the Renaissance dandy, who boasted tights of different color on each leg! But Fashion is short-sighted. The West had tentatively begun the historical anomaly Pflugel [1] called the Great Sartorial Renunciation, i.e., the graying of male fashion, when Frois wrote. [2]   Until the mid-16th century when they warred ferociously with one another over who was the holiest and cut back on their proclivity to play the peacock, European men were second to none in their decoration. As Japanese pictures of Southern barbarians makes clear, European men still wore quite a bit of colored (as in, not white or black) clothing with fine adornment when Frois wrote. This makes me believe that his *pintado* probably does not so much mean colorful in the sense of bright colors, as covered with bold printed or painted *designs* – that might be better called *paintings*, though they were often printed. I am thinking of Japanese designs such as those Rodrigues described:

> The outer surface of the material of the robe, whether it be silk, hemp or linen, is generally printed handsomely with flowers in various colours, although some of the silk robes have a striped pattern, others are dyed with one colour, others with two. . . . they intermingle gold among the flowers painted in diverse ways, and they are especially clever in the use of crimsons and, even more, violets. (THIS ISLAND)

Japan, in the succeeding Tokugawa era, was to enact strict sartorial laws, but they were not nearly as restrictive as the black and white mindset of [some of] our puritan forefathers and the modern corporation man in his gray flannel suit! In the 1960's and 70's, conservative Japanese, appalled at the revival of color in menswear in the West, forgot about their own past and the America of a decade earlier and argued such freedom was the result of Occidental individualism, far from drab but productive and safe Japanese conformity. So, Japan came to hold the line on 1950's haircuts and fashions long after Usanians gave them up. Through all of this, only the young Japanese construction worker and truck driver remained true to their wild pre-Modern roots. They are the ones you'll find wearing purple and orange trousers and whatever hairstyle they please.

1. *The Great Renunciation.* I wrote "tentatively" because the 17th century ended up adopting colorful male fashion again.   Fashion tacks back and forth appearing not to go anywhere though it eventually does.

2. Pflugel?! On the whole, the internet is so convenient, so *kind* to those of us with poor memories! I can look up a name with two different spelling possibilities and choose the   most abundant (or, if close, the spelling chosen by the better sites.) But I was not prepared for not finding Pflugel's *Psychology of Clothing!* I thought I read it decades ago. His ideas were important for my book-to-be of 30-odd years, encouraging reflection about

and revolution against the cultural imperialism implicit in the bifurcated clothing forced upon men in robe, skirt and wrap-around cultures. (The main title will be *Redressing the World*) The book exists: *The psychology of clothing.* But Worldcat says it is by: Dearborn, George Van Ness, 1869-. (I would guess he is dead by now, but anyway). So, who is this Pflugel who has lived in my head all these decades? Worldcat has this, too: "The present discussion, a kind of scientific ghost of 'Sartor resartus,' developed as lectures in the Fruhauf school of salesmanship in New York in August, 1917." So then, should I conclude that Pflugel, like Carlyle's German professor, is a fiction invented by Dearborn ? Can any reader set me straight?

1-3+   We have new clothing and new designs almost every year.
        Antre nós quasi cad'ano se inventa hum novo traje e invensão de vestidos;

            In Japan, the fashions are the same and never change.
            Em Japão, sempre a feisão hé a mesma sem nunqa se variar.

Early modern fashion vs. traditional culture? It is hardly so simple. One way or another, men *will* seek novelty. Men *will* show off. Could restrictive color and graphic design rules in Europe have been offset by more structural changes in the costume from year to year and the vice versa with respect to Japan?   Almost a hundred years earlier, Sebastian Brant had snorted *"Shameless and fickle I do brand / Style-slaves who live in every land"* (JH:CER), but there is no question that Europeans – or, at least, the Jesuits who traveled to and from it – were very conscious of the rapid change of fashion in their part of the world.   Montaigne, writing at the same time as Frois, discovered what might be called "the fashion cycle," where the acceptable clothing circles back to the styles of earlier generations, and marveled about it using vocabulary that demands quoting in this book:

> The present fashion in dress makes them promptly condemn the old, with such great conviction and such universal agreement that you would think it was a kind of mania that thus turns their understanding upside down. ("Of Ancient Customs" DF:CEM)

At any rate, the "us" side of Frois's contrast about Europeans following fashion, was itself old hat. In the report of the contemporary Japanese Embassy to Europe, Miguel=Valignano first describes the sumptuous wall-hangings in Europe, then adds "you can imagine how much Europeans adorn their bodies." Indeed,

> . . . the first surprising thing is that since Europeans wouldn't think of wearing the same type of clothing all the time and dislike using one item over and over, every year, they think up new modes of dress. Whatever the dress is, the fabric tends to be very expensive thin wool weave, silk . . . and is adorned with gold brocade, so that an enormous sum of money must be spent to keep one's body properly attired. . . . The women, too, like the men, ordinarily invent things that are new and not yet worn by others . . . Moreover, this type of luxury is not confined to the masters, but found among domestic servants and squires as well. The higher the place [his master's social position] of the servant, the more elegant his clothing . . . In the end, the excessive competition with respect to beautiful clothing without regard for money sometimes makes it necessary to restrict this excess prolificacy by law, but whatever the punishment, whatever the threat, at least with respect to tailoring, has no effect on Europeans. (J/S:DM: 1590 ch 9)
>
> ..

I do not know what if anything Valignano or Frois really felt about European innovation. Perhaps they hated it, for the Jesuits usually criticized luxury *in the East* (eg. 4-8) as deriving from a culture with completely worldly interests. But, in *De Missione* – even granting the last line quoted above – Miguel=Valignano *uses* the prodigious expenditure of wealth on architecture and clothing and jewelry, where even servants are fitted out luxuriously, as proof of the overflowing – or rather, overwhelming – wealth of Europe, particularly with respect to their closest rival for global prestige, the Chinese. (J/S:DM, ch.33) Evidently, Christian modesty was overruled by the need to show what bounty the religion has brought to those who believed in it! Still, one wonders what Valignano would have thought of mid-seventeenth century (Philip IV) Iberia, when fashion extremes reached all-time peaks of absurdity – e.g., all the ladies in Spain wearing eyeglasses of different weird shapes (D:DLS)!

The Japanese had, in fact, not made *major* structural changes. Frois's observation was to be repeated by other Western visitors over the next several centuries. In 1776, Thunberg noticed that almost nothing had changed since Kaempfer visited a hundred years earlier. In a page-long sentence of particulars prefacing a short summary – "All this must appear as improbable, and, to many, as impossible, as it is strictly true, and deserving of the utmost attention." (T:TEAA) – he mentions the closure of the country with the support of the populace, laws that "have remained unaltered for thousands of years," no foreign wars for centuries, different religious sects living in harmony, and

> that the monarch and all his subjects should be clad alike in a particular national dress; that no fashions should be adopted from abroad, nor new ones invented at home (Ibid. Vol 3)

Paradoxically, Japan was in so great ferment during the time of Frois's stay, that fashions – which need a backdrop of normalcy – may have been invisible.[1] But, had Thunberg hung around a bit longer he would have realized that even if the basic structure of Japanese dress remained pretty constant, fashion was far from dead. Tokugawa intellectuals were self-conscious of their rapidly changing fashions *(ryuukou)*, and even "fashion" is too slow a word to describe Edo, where even a street vender could start a *fad (hayari)* by a clever advertising gimmick! By the late twentieth century, Japanese considered themselves, for better or worse, the *most* prone to fads or "booms" as they call them, of all the world's people. In the heyday of *Japan-as-Number-One*, the intellectuals of the Bubble went so far as to call the West (a traditionally-minded "stock culture" incapable of coping with the new) *a museum* for Japanese tourists, incapable of competing with the post-modern, ever-changing "flow culture" of Japan. In a word, modern Japanese managed to reverse the hoary stereotype of the sleepy, changeless East and active protean West.

Yet, for all these contradictions and qualifications, Frois has a point. Japanese traditional clothing (*wafuku*) and footwear even today (though confined to certain places and times) remains basically what it was a thousand years ago, or thrice that if the Chinese roots are included! If Japanese seldom wear it, at least they *do*, whereas Occidental ancient clothing only exists in books of costume. (And the exceptions, the Irish kilt, Greek skirt and Swiss shorts are not worn so often as traditional Japanese clothing.) In this sense, one could argue that the Europe has no *living* traditional clothing in the sense that Japan has. We lack alternative continuous threads of culture.

1. *Fashion in 1593*. It may well be that Japanese were not fashion-conscious in 1585, but it is doubtful when you consider that –

> when Hideyoshi set out from Nagoya on his way back to the capital, the members of his retinue were dressed in Portuguese style. Largely as a result of Valignano's embassy in 1591, every Japanese at court made efforts to obtain at least one article of European dress . . ." (C:RTI:pg104)

Does that sound like a fashion-dead culture!

1-4+   We are used to wearing a cape/coat over our doublet and shirts;
Antre nós sobre os jibões e palotes se usa de trazer capa;

> The Japanese wear a colored, very thin, open-fronted *sambenito*, over their *katabira* [see 1-1+] or *kimono*. *Os Japões sobre o qimão ou catabira trazem hum sambenito pintado muito ralo, aberto por diante.*

Frois lacked a generic term for a *smock* because "we" did not have one. The *sambenito* is a sleeveless smock not opening in the front, that was often covered with colorful symbolic designs worn by penitents during the Inquisition trials – to us, today, they appear to be something a fool might wear. I think Frois really refers to a *haori,* literally "wing-weave!" The translators of Frois split as to whether the *muito ralo* applies to the subtlety of the colors or the thinness of the cloth. My guess, with Okada, is that it is the latter, for the Iberian Cape was a substantial coat and the contrast is stronger this way, and because *haori* were not necessarily subdued at this time, as they came to be in the Tokugawa era when, as discussed in 1-11, below, sumptuary law forced them to be plain on the outside). But I may be wrong. The *jibao,* or *gibao* is a "doublet." But what *is* a "doublet?" Looking at several pictures, I'd say it was a fancy leather jacket with or without sleeves, and a belted waist. Clothing terms do not translate well across the ocean of space or time! Frois would seem to be contrasting an outside garment that is longer, heavier and closed in the West to one smaller, thinner and open in Japan. I wish Frois had used *more adjectives* and *less nouns!*

1-5+   Our sleeves are narrow and extend to the butt of the hand;
As nossas [man]gas são estreitas e chegão até o colo da mão;

> Those of Japan are wide; and male, female or bonze stop halfway down the arm.
As dos Japões largas, asi homens como molheres e bonzos, chegão-lhe até meo braço.

Wide sleeves were traditional with Japanese clothing; *short* ones were not. They were a century-long "tradition", perhaps a functional development of the long Warring Period. For most of Japanese history, the sleeves extended to, near or even past the wrist. Okada notes they were also rounded off at the ends at this time (in the centuries before and after the rectangular ends dangle down), but that they were still loose compared to the skin-clinging style of Europe, the land of tights where even loose sleeves and voluminous trousers had tight collars and cuffs – where people needed to unloop or unlace to remove their clothing. Van Loon attributes tights to European fashion's copying the "vertical stream-lines" of the Gothic era (V:AM). I.e., a *column mentality*.[1] In the looser, pre-warring times in Japan, the sleeves were often wider than they were long, and "long sleeves" actually meant *wide* ones, for in Japanese, as in English, the longest side is generally called "the length". At the time of Frois's visit, men probably did not wear their sleeves quite so "long=wide" as women did. As Isabella Bird wrote three hundred years later, "it is only women and children who have a prescriptive right to folly, who wear them so *long* as to nearly touch the ground." (my *italics* – UTJ:1880) If our early modern fashion was generally too tight to be functional, Japanese was too loose.

1. *European Exceptions* Because of Europe's diversity, there are probably exceptions to all generalizations we can make about clothing. I have seen a painting of a 16th century Venetian Senator in a red robe with white trimming (it looks a bit Santa-like) where the ends of a sleeve held out are so broad=long (in the same way as in Japan or China) as to reach to the floor. Unlike Japanese sleeves, however, it narrowed toward the armpit. In other words, it was an extreme bell-bottomed sleeve!

1-6+   Our breeches or drawers open in the front.
Os nossos calsões ou seroulas são abertas por diante;

Those of Japan open on both sides, and a loin-wrap [?] pommel of [. .?]
Os dos Japões tem duas aberturas nas ylhargas e hum tanga[nho] ou arsão de sela de [?]

Boy, did "ours" open in front! The Iberians tended to cover the top of their breeches with skirts (and were in the process of switching to very baggy pants), but even these tended to retain a trace of what might be called a bow-sprit. I am looking at a Giovanni Battista Moroni portrait (1565) of one Antonio Navagero, a serious looking, powerfully built middle-aged man with red breeches sporting a red codpiece curved upward as if he had a perpetual erection. And he is not alone in this. Frois chooses not to mention this Occidental vulgarity. His contemporary Montaigne mentions it as one of three examples (the other two were women's headgear) of "the most monstrous" perversions of the natural use of clothing, "which is the service and comfort of the body," – i.e., "that empty and useless model of a member that we cannot even decently mention by name, which however we show off and parade in public." The "empty" is telling. Unlike the Dani of New Guinea, who actually stick their penis into the long gourd tube, the European model at this time was a total fake. Time for another *faux Frois*:

We parade colorful abstract models of our manhood attached to our breeches every day. They parade huge realistic members about town on their shoulders once a year.[1]

Although Frois writes "or," all the other translations have "breeches *and* underwear." That may well be Frois's intention, but the "or" (*ou*) of the original does have a point. At this time, breeches had just been born in Europe of a mix between the body-stocking and legging as male dresses (skirts) turned into shirts. They were actually half-underwear, proto-pants, and their thin, i.e., tight nature is what gave rise to the modest covering that morphed into a baubled showcase for the male endowment. Exactly how one was *opened*, I do not know.

The Japanese side is harder because of lacuna in the manuscript. "Those" of the Japanese would seem to be *momohiki* (literally: thigh-pullers). Rodrigues describes them as "wide at the bottom and open on both sides from the top down to the knees" and notes that

> one part is in front without any opening but with ribbons attached by which it is tied, and another is behind also with ribbons . . ." (Ibid. = I forget what Ibid! Probably R(C):TIJ)

If I am not mistaken Frois's "loin-wrap" (according to Okada, *tanganho* = a diminutive of *tanga,* an African wrap-around) – if it is a loin-wrap [2] – alludes to the manner that not only the "ribbons," or ties but a large portion of the cloth itself wraps around to the other hip or further. Be that as it may, the truth be said, Japanese were never big on bifurcated male clothing. As Rodrigues notes, breeches "are not the ordinary attire of the nation" but purely formal wear, probably invented in "that part of China facing Japan . . . from which . . . Japan was populated."(Ibid) Nieuhoff, a half century later was to describe *Chinese* breeches as "not like ours, Gathered or Pleated, but . . . wide on the top" and made fast either by tying "a piece of String about them, or are like Aprons, with a Hem, through which running a String, they pull then together" (N(O):EC). Since, no trousers can be wide on top and stay up, we know he means that the cloth of the trousers *when they are not worn*. Okada thinks the puzzling "pommel" may refer to a frontal flap on some formal trousers called *hakama*. A type of these *hakama* worn by high-level administrators in Japan developed beyond, or rather, mutated from their Chinese prototype, until the legs extended down far beyond the man's feet! Rodrigues, on the uniform of magistrates:

> Those on duty . . . wear these trousers with their feet hidden within, the trouser legs trail along two or three spans after the feet, and they must exercise diligence lest they fall over. This is done, in addition to other things, out of pomp and because it is the custom of the kingdom. (Ibid.)

With us, trousers are generally associated with mobility, so trousers designed to trip one up must have seemed strange, indeed. How did Frois miss this next distich!

> *We wear pantaloons to separate our legs in order to ride easily and move about faster;*
> *They wear* hakama *which extend past their feet to slow themselves down and look dignified.*

Perhaps, he thought they were worn so rarely and by so few, that such a contrast would be misleading. Still, Alcock and Oliphant observed these *culottes* (the legs seem to join in the middle like skirts) still in use almost three hundred years later.

> . . . the most singular part of the whole costume, and that which, added to the headgear [earlier described as "a boat turned bottom up, with one half cut off and the edges folded in"], gave an irresistibly comic air to the whole presentment, was the immeasurable elongation of the silk trowsers. These, instead of stopping short at the heels, are unconscionably lengthened, and left to trail two or three feet behind them, so that their feet, as they advanced, seemed pushed into what should have been the knees of the garment. The consequence was, that they were compelled to shuffle along like so many people shorn by some general calamity of both legs, and walking upon their stumps, much as a man cut down to his knees might be expected to progress, an effect farther heightened by said prolongations trailing behind on the floor, collapsed and evidently empty. It certainly required some command of countenance to follow gravely these high officers . . . and how they managed to shuffle on, without tumbling at each step, was all but incomprehensible. I have seen none of the Japanese conjurors [Alcock elsewhere describes *monteblancs* at length] do any thing better. (A:COT)

> . . . the most singular portion of their apparel are the trousers which they wear at their audiences with the Tycoon; they seem to be cut upon *a principle precisely the opposite* to that which regulates our Court-dress. We consider that when we have brought our nether garments down to

the knee, we have not only satisfied decency, but have reached the highest pitch of refinement and elegance. The great object of the Japanese is to create an entire misconception in the mind of the spectator as to the situation of that important joint; he wishes it to be supposed that he shuffles into the royal presence on his knees; but finding that process attended with much practical inconvenience, he compromises the matter by having his trousers made about eighteen inches longer than his legs; by these means his feet are made to represent his knees, and he is enabled to walk upon them comfortably with his sham legs dragging after him.(O:LEM *italics,* mine)

Rudofsky, more recently, speculates:

Short legs look even shorter in overlong trousers, yet true costume emphasizes rather than hides body characteristics. The trailing pantaloons were intended to curtail the wearer's mobility, a wise precaution in an age of excessive sword play. (R:KM)

Rudolfsky's guess is tainted by his belief that Japanese suffer from – or, rather enjoy – "an entire web of pathological streaks" (he even claims the periodic disassembly and reconstruction of the Grand Ise Shrine every 20 years comes from "their propensity for destruction") but, let us leave these dragging trousers and go to the common man – or nobleman at rest – who was far more comfortable in his loincloth – "merely a sash, silk for nobles and linen for ordinary people" (Rodrigues, Ibid.) – which was indeed open on both sides, came in many colors, could be comically long and even sport a poem! Issa has dozens of loincloth haiku, my favorite of which concerns the custom of dropping them on the crossroads to get rid of, or, rather, pass on a jinx. In the summer, the loincloth was often the *only* thing worn, and even as late as early Meiji (1868-1912), the father of modern haiku, Shiki writes of:

loin-cloths
of every color
dusk cool

Isabella Bird, who traveled Japan during Shiki's lifetime, continually describes the summer costume of the Japanese as *nothing*. She claimed they were "naked." But a picture in her book shows the costume includes a hat, a fan and said loincloth, wedged up in back like a thong. Morse, who was in Japan at about the same time as Bird, wrote what *today* would be an oxymoron: "the men when naked always wear a loincloth." (M:JDD1) It is likely, then, that the following "strange sight" taken in by Bird (B:UTJ) includes a loincloth:

Could there be a stranger one [sight] than a decent-looking middle-aged man, lying on his chest in the verandah, raised on his elbows, and intently reading a book, clothed only in a pair of spectacles?

..

But the necessity of proving themselves a civilized people to a West that ignorantly – especially considering its own Classic tradition – equated clothing with culture resulted in a crackdown on the loincloth as an outdoor garment by Japanese authorities. Bird records one of what must have been countless incidents occasioned by the prurience of her compatriots. She writes of "traveling along a very narrow road" when

we met a man leading a prisoner by a rope, followed by a policeman. As soon as my runner saw the latter, he fell down on his face so suddenly in the shafts, as nearly to throw me out, at the same time trying to wriggle into a garment which he had carried on the crossbar, while the young men who were carrying the two *kurumas* behind, crouching behind my vehicle, tried to scuttle into their clothes. I never saw such a picture of abjectness as my man presented. He trembled from head to foot, and illustrated that queer phrase often heard in Scotch Presbyterian prayers, "lay our hands on our mouths and our mouths in the dust." . . . It was all because he had no clothes on. I interceded for him as the day was very hot, and the policeman said he would not arrest him, as he should otherwise have done, because of the inconvenience it would cause to a foreigner. He was quite an elderly man, and never recovered his spirits, but as soon as a turn of the road took us out of the policeman's sight, the two younger men threw their clothes into the air, and gamboled in the shafts, shrieking with laughter! (B:UTJ)

It *is* quite funny. A law made to satisfy foreigners not enforced in order not to inconvenience a foreigner! By the time Japan proved itself civilized by whopping Russia, the Japanese themselves probably didn't care to see loincloths in public. Today they are only worn in some local festivals and by a minute minority of men doing ablutions on Shinto religious retreats or on pilgrimages, in pristine rivers, under waterfalls or by sacred artesian wells. The loincloth looks much better wet than our underwear – it does not cling and blowing in the breeze has movement – and some day will no doubt make a return as swimwear.

> *We wrap long pieces of cloth around our necks to keep warm in the winter;*
> *They wrap long pieces of cloth around their privates for cool summer dress.*

> *We think of a loincloth as something primitive and made from crude material;*
> *They make them from silk so even a nobleman can wear one without shame.*

> *We would not think of wearing our underwear outside;*
> *They not only wear their loincloths outside but some even work wearing them.*

I do not know if Frois had a good word for a loincloth, but he could have burrowed the Japanese *fundoshi* had he thought of a way to make it a contrary. It would not be enough to say simply, they have them and we do not.

1. *Parading Members.*   The Japanese still have fertility festivals where huge priapae are shouldered through the streets to the amusement of all.   Dirty-minded Usanians do not even allow them in risqué festivals such as the Coconut Grove King Mango Festival which I was disappointed to find *purely breast fetish* (like the 1950's Playboy magazine!) – breasts so erect, however, that they seem to reflect what I would call the perverse machofication of feminized Puritanism. What in the heck is wrong with the lower half of the body? Here Miami is, down South, half-way to Brazil and half-Latin and breasts are given priority over butts!

2. *Loin-wrap?*   I think it possible that *nothing* was in the missing part of the manuscript (*tanga* by itself can mean a cloth) or something might have been there to suggest loincloths instead. The French translation brings in a "piece(?) of wood (<*brin* (?) *de bois*>) (笑) ! Not likely.

1-7+   Our skirt-pantaloons and imperial tights are made of silk with gold brocade.
As nossas calsas e muslos imperiais são de seda atroceladas d'ouro;

Even when the clothing of Japan is silken, the trousers are of cotton, or *nuno*.
Os vestidos dos Japões, ainda que sejão de seda, os calsões sempre hão de ser de canga [1] *ou nono.*

Nuno is simply a crudely woven cloth of cotton. Trousers would seem to have alternated between cotton and hemp. Even the gentry used these for trousers in Japan because they were cooler (Japan being very hot and humid in the summer).   Who can say whether Frois might have used this simply to illustrate the fact that "we" spend a lot even for the lower part of our body, whereas the Japanese (since *nuno* is relatively cheap, and used for sundry purposes including head-bands and house-cleaning) shortchange their extremities, or to explain the different climate of Japan that makes simple, cool trousers essential. But even finding additional signification for these contrasts, they are small stuff compared to Âl-bîrûnî's felicitous single-line contrast of the Muslim and Hindu:

> *They* [the Indians] *use turbans for trousers.* (A/S:AI)

Functionally, this is disingenuous for Indians do not really wrap their hats around their crotches; but there is a resemblance, as both look like swaddling. But even as I marveled at this creative topsy-turvy, I came across the following passage in Michael Cooper's *Rodrigues the Interpreter* describing what actually happened in Japan (as described by our Frois) when the Shôgun Hideyoshi presented white *katabira* robes to the retinue of black guards (the Portuguese always had their slaves with them) after watching their dance performance in 1593:

> Rodrigues indicated to the recipients that they should follow Japanese etiquette and raise the presents over their heads as a sign of reverence towards the donor. Obviously misunderstanding his directions, the men proceeded to wind the robes around their heads as if they were turbans, thus unwittingly causing further entertainment for the onlookers. (C:RTI)

1. *Canga* Translation. The French translation notes that *ganga* was a Chinese cotton fabric of blue or yellow hue known in India and this was corrupted as *canga*. The same, as *canque,* "a Chinese cotton fabric" or "cotton linen" (from Nanquin, says one quote) is in the OED, but I left the plain "cotton" so the reader could see the contrast with silk, which I feel is the point of Frois's contrast at a glance.

~~~~~~

1-8+   With us, male clothing can not be worn by women;
Os vestidos dos homens antre nós não hé couza que possa servir aas molheres;

The Japanese *kimono* and *katabira* are worn by both men and women.
Os quimões e catabiras de Japão ygualmente servem às molheres e homens.

Medieval illustrations show Europeans in what (to my untrained eye) looks like unisex dresses and robes. By the Reformation (16thc), such ambiguity is only found among children: little boys continued to wear pretty dresses for longer (until an older age and later in history) than most people, including some historians (who mistake little princes for princesses or wrongly assume they are being corrupted if not perverted) imagine! Japanese traditional male and female fashion is, on the whole, more similar than that of the Europe of 1585. As Okada points out, it is not tailored to the peculiarities of the human body, so gender differences would naturally be less pronounced even if the Japanese physique did not exhibit less sexual dimorphism than the European physique to begin with. As a result, Occidentals had great trouble telling the sexes apart. The visit of the first Japanese Embassy to America – and to the West (excluding the boys sent by Valignano in 1582) – in the mid-nineteenth century provided ample proof that Frois's contrast still held true. Witness these reports by two contemporary correspondents one of whom was laughing at the Japanese and one of whom was recording the barbarism of his countrymen.

> Don't I wish yeou'd a bin their, Uncle Jack; and if yeou had, yeou'd jave larfed fit tew split. Their wos we, awl in unerform, grate big men; and their wos they, little, peaked, slim chaps, dressed e'enermost like wimmen folks, but as bright and chippur as a school-marm on examanashun mornin.'

> Then at every halt each carriage was surrounded by a mob, who thrust their heads into the carriages, and passed all sorts of comments among themselves upon the appearance of the strangers. One burly fellow swore that all they wanted was to have a little more crinoline and be right out decent looking nigger wenches. (J-A:FJE)

Be that as it may, Japanese men and women do not *wear* clothing in quite the same way. Belts are tied in different places, left and right wrapping reversed, some colors taboo, etc.. Japanese had no trouble telling the difference.

1-9+   Our clothing fits the body and is tight and restrictive.[1]
Os nossos vestidos são justos, estreitos e apertados no corpo;

> Japanese clothing is so loose people can easily bare themselves above the waist and think nothing of it. *Os de Japão tão largos que com facilidade e sem pejo se desp[em logo] da sinta pera riba.*

In his outlandish KIMONO MIND, Rudofsky lets his designer eye portray "our" tight clothing that has, on the whole, held true for over 500 years:

> Western cloths are constructed with an eye to anatomy . . . . they represent a sort of hollow casting of their owner. Between airings they hang like human effigies from the gallows of our clothes closets. (R:KM)

If Frois had a contemporary European reader, he or she might have read loose morals into the loose clothing. But his wording suggests functional difference. Golownin, writing two hundred years after Frois, gives an amusing account of how such looseness was used to adjust the warmth of multi-layered *kimonos*:

> When a Japanese finds a room too warm, he pulls off the upper coat, and lets it hang upon a girdle [i.e. from the back of his *obi* belt]; if this is not enough, the second, third, &c. are pulled off, and he keeps on only one coat: when he feels too cold, one coat is by degrees put on again over the other. (MCJ3)

Frois describes the removal of that last layer – in the summer, the nobles wore these fine white cotton robes as underwear, but most people only wore one garment. Slipping out of the top part of it left their upper torso completely bare. And this was not only true for men. Bird later described women in the country working "with a blue cotton garment open to the waist tucked into the [waist] band," and "women unclothed to their waists . . . busy stripping mulberry branches." (B:UTJ) Mrs. Hugh Frazer, wife of the British Ambassador had to forbid her servants from keeping their grandparents with them because it was "impossible to impress these very elderly people with the necessity and propriety of wearing clothes in warm weather." When they were young – before the Opening – people dressed practically.

> Why be bothered with them [clothing] in August? And so it happened that, when Cook-San's grandmother was met in the kitchen one warm afternoon without a shred of rainment on her old brown body, then I found that there really wasn't room for more than three generations in our very inadequate servants' quarters . . .(F:DWJ:1899)

Most clothing, especially restrictive, hot Western clothing, was and still is totally unsuited for the muggy summer of Japan (and the Eastern seaboard of North America, if one would avoid, pace Mailer, *the air-conditioned nightmare* we now think a normal way of living). Loose clothing was *de rigueur* in Japan for ventilation, wiping off sweat and frequent washing (38+, below). But not all Japanese fashion is loose and comfortable. Far from it. When I appeared on Japanese late-night television to discuss men and non-bifurcated clothing, they cinched me up in a kimono as stiff as a straight-jacket torture (No wonder, thought I, that "binding" – rather than whipping or spanking – is the traditional form of sadomasochism in Japan). Luckily, I puffed out my belly like a sly horse when the fitter put his knee on my back, so I could breathe! Formality, East or West, can be excruciating. Rudofsky calls the enjoyment of such discomfort *sartoriasis,* and claims "the kimono fills that need to perfection." (R:KM)

1. *The original has three adjectives*. The *justos* means something like "just," as in just the same as the body, a perfect fit. I might have translated "tailored, tight and restricted," but chose instead to change the first adjective to a verb, "fits."

~~~~~~

1-10+   We, because of our buttons and lacing, cannot easily reach our bodies with our hands;
Nós por causa dos botões e atacas não podemos meter a mão no corpo fa[cilmente];

> Japanese men and women, not restricted by such devices, can thrust their hands into their bosom at any time, especially in the winter when the sleeves are left dangling. *Os Japões asi homens como molheres, como não tem nada disto, sempre, specialmente no Inverno, trazem as mangas por f[ora] caídas e as mãos dentro no corpo.*

With little heating (see the chapter on architecture) and no sweaters (Japanese sometimes wore rabbit fur, but lacking sheep, wool was not common), the ability to withdraw *into* one's clothing and fuse the body into one unit is vital to conserving heat. Call it *the mitten effect*. Arms may be pressed against the torso, or one arm thrust up the other arm's sleeve. This ability, it turns out, is also useful for hot weather:

> As the robes are very ample and have wide sleeves, people can insert their hands inside with the greatest of ease and wipe away body sweat [One place wiped was "under the arm-pits!" (Thunberg)] with a handkerchief. (Rodrigues: THIS ISLAND)

"But," Rodrigues observes, to put one's hands inside of one's sleeves "is a grave discourtesy and impertinence in the presence of the gentry, only a master will do it in front of his servants; but on no account whatsoever may a servant do it in the presence of his master." Nor, he continues, could anyone do so at a formal function. This is understandable, for, on television *Easterns*, the loosely hanging sleeves mark the "cool" gambler and other men-about-town. But impolite or not, there is something marvelously debonair about it.

Ancient Japanese clothing was, according to the Chinese, a light *poncho* or *muumuu*-like habit. So the "Japanese" robe, with a frontal opening good for sticking the hands in, that we call a *kimono,* comes from China, where it was somewhat less humid but, as a continental climate, far hotter in the dog days.   Dyer Ball:

> It is amusing to see the vigorous way in which a Chinese fans himself: not content with a languid stirring of air in front of his face and chest, he inserts the fan under his jacket, both front and back, and applies it vigorously till cooled, when his legs and arms will come in for an equal share of attention. (TC)

To Japanese or Chinese, "our" tubular clothing must have seemed like a straight-jacket. What heroism, what suffering (*what ringworm!*) must have accompanied their adoption of our unsuitable clothing!

~~~~~~

1-11+   We wear our best dress on top and the inferior underneath.
Antre nós se veste o milhor vestido em cima e o somenos debaxo;

> Japanese wear the best underneath and the inferior on top.
> *Os Japães o milhor debaxo e o somenos em riba.*

The metaphorical equations *top=outside* and *below=inside* are found in Japanese, Portuguese and English, alike. They speak from the perspective of the body. The Japanese seem to contradict the metaphorical equation, by putting the superior garment "below" the inferior one, and even go against nature, for animals wear *their* decorations on the outside. So, for this contrast, the Japanese side is clearly the one calling for an explanation. Did this reversal begin because of sartorial regulations (sumptuary law)? Because the best dress was preserved for ones intimates and not wasted on the rabble? To preserve good clothing from weathering? To avoid highwaymen or taxes? Or, to avoid envy? Who knows? I do know it is usually explained *today* in terms of subtle Japanese aesthetic preference. It is *shibui* (discriminating in a subdued way) to keep the best art under cover.

1-12+   With us, a garment must always be better than its lining.
       Antre nós sempre o vestido á-de ser milhor que o forro;

> With *dobuku* [vest] of the Japanese gentry, the lining must, as far as possible, be better than the [outside of the] garment. *Em Japão os dubuqus dos senhores hão-de ter o forro milhor que [o] vestido, se poderem.*

It would seem that in Portuguese, the outside of a garment/dress (*vestido*) is identical with the item itself, while the lining is not. That is why I had to add "outside of the" to make the meaning clear. I suppose that the same lining might be used for many different types of garments. The Japanese *dobuku* transliterates as "torso-wear;" it was usually sleeveless and, like Japanese trousers, originated in China Here, Frois probably refers to silk *dobuku.* I cannot say more about the *dobuku* of 1585, but the OJD says it evolved into the silk *haori,* literally "wing-weave," of the Tokugawa era (1603-1867), which usually had sleeves and always had a lining. The way the wealthy merchants and townsmen vied with one another over who could boast the most ornate lining for their plain black *haori* coats is common knowledge in Japan.

There is a pure and personal aesthetic pleasure in this inside-out-ism unrelated to fashion that must be experienced to be believed. I have a nineteenth or early twentieth century *haori* and am delighted with it. The plain black outside makes the inside (which really is not *that* fancy) seem magical, like the treasure trove in a dull shell called *oolite!*

..

1-13+   We wear our hide *dobuqus* with the fur on the inside;
       Nós trazemos os dobuqus de peliças com a pelle pera dentro;

> Japanese wear it on the outside.
> *Os Japões os trazem com as peliças pera fora.*

Since fur generally holds heat better when facing in, and Japanese, as Buddhists who should not kill animals, might be expected to hide the evidence, it is doubly surprising they wore the fur on the outside. But they *did* either for the beauty – for the love of natural texture, including fur – or because it was thought itchy inside (sheer guesswork), or simply – i.e., historical accident – because samurai first wore sleeveless *dobuku* over their armor with the fur out. Today, Japanese sometimes wear traditional down vests, but fur vests are rare – the only one I saw was rabbit on canvas: I bought it at a flea-market! Fur is now pretty much the prerogative of women in Japan, as in the West. One finds many kimonoed little old ladies out for their New Year's shrine visit, or young ladies celebrating their adulthood on the 15th of January of the year when they turn 20 (rather than 21) with weasel/ ermine/ferret/mink comforters, usually but not always white in color, and very memorable for having the heads – and sometimes even feet – attached. The eyeballs replaced with black beads glisten realistically out from the white fur.

Another possibility I have not seen broached is that hair on the inside, though warm, can be itchy and house lice. This would not bother Christian ascetics (not only monks, but sometimes laity) who wore a hair-shirt – painfully coarse hair (goat and camel were traditional favorites, but it was occasionally made of fine wire) against their skin! St Xavier, like some of the Buddhist ascetics, was happy to allow bugs to partake of him, though he did it because suffering was thought good penance, while they did it out of kindness to the bugs. Most Occidentals in 1585 were not ascetics, but they did not value cleanliness as much as the Japanese, either, so scuzzy fur would not have bothered them.

1-14+ We cut or shave the hair on our heads for relief from suffering;
Antre nós trosquia ou rapa hum homem a cabeça pera se aliviar de dores;

Japanese shave it off out of sadness, for sorrow, or falling out of grace with a master. *Os Japões a rapão por tristeza ou dó, ou por estarem fora da graça de seus senhores.*

The reasons Frois gives for Europeans shaving their pate are unclear. What relief is gained? He doesn't mean *head-lice*, does he? If he means an escape from secular suffering by joining a religious order or going on a pilgrimage, then isn't that the same as the Japanese? In Japan, one's head is shaved for Buddhist ordination – the "gain-road-ceremony" or *tokudôshiki*) – as well as to mark retirement from the world.

The only clear difference to me is the part about shaving *to take responsibility for something.* Japanese are good at that. *Taking responsibility.* And, it is better to shave off one's hair – literally "round one's head" (*atama-o marumeru*) – to show one is contrite and determined to make a fresh start than cut off a finger in the style of the courtesan or yakuza to express the same! But grief and falling out of grace are both but part of the bundle of significance of shaving ones head (as opposed to having one's topknot cut (1-6+)). More than anything else, it signified *do-or-die determination.* What Japanese call 必死 [1] Take the following episode recorded by Cocks on Oct. 10, 1616.

> Late towardes night was an uprower in the cittie of Edo, for that cavelero, called Deo Dono, gave it out that he would take the Emperours doughter as she went to morrow towardes her new husband, for that the ould Emperour in his life tyme had promised her to hym, in respect to his service donne in Osekay against Fidaia Samme. But the Emperour now would not concent theirunto, but sent hym word to cut his bellie, which he refuced to doe, in taking of his howse with 1000 men his followers, *whoe all shaved them selves,* with 50 women of his, lyke wais protesting to stand out till the death . . . (my *italics*, his misspelling!)

The "Emperor" (doubtless the Shogun), surrounded the 1000 with 10000 armed men of his own and told the servants that if they "would deliver up the master in quiet" the eldest son could inherit (meaning everyone would not be executed). Deo Dono learned of it and "kild the saide sonne with his owne hands; yet, after, his servantes killed their master and deliverd his head to the men without" to save themselves. Here, obviously, the head-shaving resolution was only scalp deep. Still, we are no closer to the clear-cut contrast Frois promises. Herodotus, the father of contrast as well as history, does much better:

> Among other people it is the custom in grief, for those to whom the grief comes close to shave their heads; but the Egyptians under the shadow of death let their hair and beards grow long, though at other times they shave. (H(G):HH)

Paradoxically, what Herodotus says about the Egyptians *growing hair* is *also* true for the Japanese, for when someone dies one purpose of shaving is to allow the mourning party to completely ignore grooming for months – as they also do not clean house. (Even today, men with the means to do so, let themselves go for a year after their father dies (I observed this twice but need more information). Perhaps the biggest difference in the shaving cultures is simply the fact that the Japanese one is so much more complex than Europe's. Yet, I think Frois must have had *some* contrast in mind, which we miss. If the Church he knew taught that reducing hair lightened one's sins and this "relief" was commonly provided for, say, the mortally ill, it might be associated in his mind with *liberation*, where the Japanese action would be associated with suffering and onerous duty. (I need the help of historians to properly *solve* this contrast.)

1. **Hisshi** (Today, these two characters so inadequately translated as "do-or-die" is often found on the headbands of students studying to pass high-school or university entrance exams in Japan and on martial arts related headbands in the USA. I think this tells you something about both cultures. My 2000+ page Kenkyûsha Japanese-English dictionary fails to come up with the *do-or-die* and gives us only "frantic" and "desperate" and "prepared for death." That is why machines cannot translate and people like me still come in handy.

‿‿‿

1-15+   We shave our beards when entering a religious order.
Antre nós rapa hum a barba quando se qer meter em alguma religião;

Japanese cut off the clump of hair on the back of their head as a sign of leaving the secular world. *Os Japões cortão o cabelinho do toutiço em sinal que deixão as couzas do mundo.*

European monks of some orders shaved part of their heads, too; but with full beards more universal than a full head of hair among Western men, sacrificing this precious symbol of manhood (1-6) to serve God made more sense than it would in the Far East, where many men had and still have little beard to lose (1-5), while baldness is relatively uncommon.

If beards are – or, *were* – more significant to Occidentals, hair in Japanese has a more powerful presence then in English or, as far as I know, any Indo-European language. The Yamato (native Japanese) word, *kami,* is homophonic with "god/s" and "upper," while the Chinese-derived pronunciation, *ke,* is homophonic with "filth/pollution." Hair on the head, now generally called *kami-no-ke,* was and is treasured by the native Shinto tradition, whereas hair below may have been thought dirty/impure. Ample body hair was first associated with the less civilized native people of Japan, the Ainu, and, later, the "barbarian" West – Furukomu (Valignano/Frois) is depicted by the Barbarian Temple tales as completely covered with grey hair, with the exception of a tonsure (E:NBJ) – and all hair was loosely associated with *desire,* whether from the pubic connection or the rhetoric of Buddhism (because it was myriad and grew and thus was identified with the world of generation?). This idea of hair-as-worldly combined with the significance of the *chonmage* (clump of hair) as a mark of manhood made it the prime candidate for cutting off.

I have seen the last remnant of the practice on TV, many times. I refer to the always tearful hair-cut ceremony of retiring sumo wrestlers! But, like head-shaving (1-14+), cutting off one's hair in Japan does not so much signify a change of status as having made up ones mind to do so. There is a determining quality, a *once-and-for-all* quality to it commonly expressed in Japanese by the double-verb *omoi-kitte,* or "think-cut." You might say it is the outer indication of a mental burning-of-the-bridges.

Here, again, the Father of History had the more perfect contrast, for if Frois finds different *parts* of the hair cut, Herodotus (H(G):HH) pegged the whole thing:

"In the rest of the world priests of the gods wear their hair long; but in Egypt they shave close."

Âl-bîrûnî captures an even broader hair contrast for it covers the entire man.   It is accompanied by an explanation of the contrary Hindhu custom:

They do not cut any of the hair of the body. Originally they went naked in consequence of the heat, and by not cutting the hair of the head, they intended to prevent sunstroke. (A(S):AI)

Here, we must fill in the "we" part. The Muslims (like the Greeks?) shaved off most of their body hair. The explanation is a bit confusing. There is one good unstated contrast there: "we" (the Muslims) used clothing to protect ourselves from the sun; but the leap from any hair of the body to head-hair is hard to follow. Perhaps, if the more hair the better the protection, then the rest of the body just follows the lead of the head if it were. The other possibility is that it should read something like: "Originally, naked because of the heat, they needed all their hair for protection from the sun, as head-hair protects us from sun-stroke." Either way, Âl-bîrûnî really ought to have brought humidity into the picture. Another Âl-bîrûnî hair contrast fills in a part of the picture Frois ignored:

As regards their not cutting the hair of the genitals, they try to make people believe that the cutting of it incites to lust and increases carnal desire. Therefore such of them as feel a strong desire for cohabitation never cut the hair of the genitals. (Ibid)

The Muslims removed all their pubic hair. The Japanese generally did not follow this Occidental practice, with the exception being public women, who shaved it (or ground it off between stones, (pumice?)) to avoid lice and hair-burn (I think this was true for Greek women, too – a gloss on Europe anyone?).

~~~~~~

1-16+ We wrap our clothing right over left.
Antre nós se dobrão os roupões da mão direita pera a esquerda;

Japanese do it left over right.
Os Japões dobrão os quimões da esquerda pera a dereita

..

The original does not clearly say "over," but doubling or "folding from right to left" and vice versa; but it is clear that the outer layer of clothing is what counts. In Japanese, wrapping the right hem of one's garment over the left is called something that might be Englished as "left flap" (*sajin*) and was used by the Chinese as a derogatory term for "barbarians," i.e., the Japanese, who evidently wore their clothes that way (when not just sticking their heads through a hole in a piece of cloth, Mayan style). In 719, the Japanese officially switched to the left-over-right style called "right-flap" (*ujin*),[1] and about eight hundred years later called Western visitors like Frois and Rodrigues "left-flaps!" (Note: my dictionary suggests "gusset" or "gore" rather than "flap." We are talking about the cloth additional to what is needed to surround the body.) As is the case with Western languages, the word "left" has sinister connotations in Japanese, mostly deriving from Chinese, where the "evil/unjust" connotation was even stronger. I would guess that were a right-over-left wrap called a "right-over," or anything else emphasizing the *right*ness, rather than identified with the side of the body where the visible edge of the flap ended, or cloth from the left side that was folded first (I am not sure of the etymology), the result would have been the opposite! I have not yet found any contemporary metaphysical reasons given for European clothing once wrapping right-over-left – and, might add that a search of 15th and 16th century artwork made it clear to me that such was not always the case, although it usually was for cloaks – but I did find a discussion of Jewish dress where the *right-over-left* wrap was considered to represent favoring justice and good over its opposite and men advised not to wear suits with the left side over the right which supports my guess that it is not the nature of the wrap but the way it is read! (Here, the side the cloth came from rather than the side where it tied, or the side folded first, and the fact it was on the outside which was deemed superior to the inside because it was "over" it.) [2]

Reading Morse's JAPAN DAY BY DAY, in a section on folk superstition, including *If one's head itches, it is a sign of being happy; if dandruff falls it's a sign of intelligence,* I discovered that "fold" – a term that gave me trouble here – may have been the proper and, apparently understood, term in English only a century ago:

> When a person is getting poor and unfortunate, the expression is used, "*Anoshito no uchi wa hidari mai [mae] ni naru*"; that is, "The man of the house folds his kimono to the left," which is considered unlucky. A corpse is dressed with the kimono folded to the left. (M:JDD2)

This *hidari-mae* is the colloquial term for "left flap" and literally translates as "left-before." Since it is the flap on the right-side of the kimono that is in front, the "before" either means the first side to be wrapped (the left=inside one) or the side where the edge of the wrapped fabric ends, which is on the left. Looking down on someone from directly above, we could call *hidari-mae* counter-clockwise, provided that we consider the outer edge as the leading edge of the spiral. One hardly wants to be dead or perverted, so it is not surprising that People in the Sinosphere of both sexes still wear their traditional clothing folded in the manner described by Frois which puts them on the opposite, *right* side.

Today, "we" wear our clothing in the Sino-Japanese manner. Why did men change? Was it the fact that Turks with whom we were warring in Frois's day wore right-over-left, and we wanted to contradict them? Or, was it the spread of buttons, which are easiest to undo with the right-hand alone (the left hand left for the reins) [3] if the left side with the holes is on the outside. The commonplace explanation for women's clothing in the West adopting right-over-left is that it was kinder to the servants who did the buttoning. *Perhaps*. But if Frois is correct, it was also going back to the traditional side. Since the 19th century when this happened was also *the* Age of radical genderizing (again, see Cynthia Russett's *Sexual Science* to understand how absurd it got), it might well have caught on simply because men and women were supposed to be contrary. One Korean website, forgetting that Europe, too, has a unisex past, boasts: "we created uni-sex." I would say, rather, you *preserved* unisex. But, when Chinese, Koreans or Japanese wear Western clothing, they follow the modern West with left-over for men and right-over for women.

1. *Ujin?* My OJD had *sajin,* but not *ujin.* Either it neglected to put it in or?

2. *Kosher Suits?* Here is what I googled, with some editing to fix up the plain-text and remove more citation than we need.

> "To quote from the fairly new English version of the Chabad-Lubavitch prayerbook, from Otzar Sifrei Lubavitch, p 413: "Customs relating to clothes" "It is customary for men not to button their jackets in the common fashion of left over right, but rather the right side over the left. This is because the "left side" in the physical world is an expression of the spiritual "left side" (evil, *sitra achra*). Putting the left side over the right could therefore give strength to its spiritual counterpart . . . ."

> "The following comes from "The [Lubavitcher] Rebbe's Advice" vol 2 *Single-Breasted Suit* "Many times the Rebbe emphasized the vital importance of wearing one's clothing in a manner that the right side of a suit is over the left, not vice versa. This is basically because right represents kindness and goodness, whereas left represents judgment and harshness. A Jew should practice the right (*chesed*) over the left (*gevura*), not the opposite."

> "A person was wearing a single-breasted suit, with the left side of the jacket buttoned over the right side. The Rebbe noticed it and told him to tell his mother to sew a button on the inside of the right side, enabling him to button the right side over the left side." (pp 3-4)

> "The Tzaddik of Rimanov, too, was very upset in his letters, 'about the new custom of the non-Jews, that they reverse matters and place the left lapel over the right side, buttoning-up as it is known, and by this

they cause the powers of the left to overcome those of the right.'" [In a letter printed by Guttman, MiGedolei haChassidus, IV, 55-]

I could not guess the dates, the years or the location of the debate. All the names and terms are to me what Japanese call "a Chinaman's sleep-talk." The reason I felt the above worth sharing is because it also included the following comments:

> One [reason for caring which way to button] is *halachic*: that the *Yidden* should *davka,* not emulate the ways of the *umos ha'olam* (YF: as above, only those of idolaters). Therefore, if they wear one color shoelace, we should *davka* wear a different color. So, too, with buttoning the jacket; since the *umos ha'olam* have the *minhag* to button menswear left on right, so the *Yidden* do just the opposite (YF: should we wear our hats upside down?).

Forget about the words I italicized, none of which I know!

It is rare to find a conscious attempt to preserve identity by being contrary (cultures are assumed to do this but it is not usually explicit), and the limits to such an approach are (wittily) stated.

4. *Ideas for Further Study*. The ergonomics involved with buttoning a tiny flap and the overlapping robe or cloak are so different that we really would need pages to sort this out properly. I think that the Chinese (and Tartars) had the left-over style because one can reach inside the clothing with the right hand while holding reins with the left. The Turks probably did the opposite because, as Muslims, they would prefer to reach into their bosom (or further) with their left hand in order to keep the right one pure. I also feel that the metaphysics of buttons can be developed further. When the right side is under the left, the buttons are on the right side and the holes are on the left. If we see buttons as male and, I wonder

. . . did Carlyle catch this?

1-17+ Our shirts have a mantle and are closed in the front;
As nossas camizas tem manteos e são serradas por diante;

The Japanese *catabiras* [thin-robes] open in front and have no mantles.
As catabiras dos Japões são abertas por diante e não tem manteos.

This is yet another *closed* vs. *open* contrast deriving from the different climate of Europe and Japan. We have mentioned the *katabira* before. A light robe with one side wrapped over the other and usually tied loosely with a thin and soft sash around the waist (rather than the thick and hot *obi* seen on the formal *kimono*) , it was indeed the nearest equivalent of a shirt. But is Frois's *camisa* a shirt in the modern sense of the word? "Dresses" might be more accurate, because our "shirts" were usually belted and stuck out at the bottom. (The English "shirt" and "skirt" are etymologically speaking and historically speaking one.) The *mantle* he mentions resembles a small built-in bib, decorative (lace about the edges, adorned with buttons, etc.) and not plain as those found on the Puritans. We see traces of it on our formal dress-shirts today. Frois forgot to mention what often went over the mantle:

> We use ornate collars to present our still living heads as if they were gifts to the world;
> They have no collars wrapping around the neck and only present heads that have been cut-off.

If the mantle resembles a pretty placemat, the collar resembles a dish, incredibly fancy China serving up the faces of the wealthy. Or should we think of the mantle instead as a huge sepal and the collars, which could be round or square (like Shakespeare's), the petals of a flower, although I hesitate to say what that makes the face! Or should we be talking, instead, about inner and outer picture-frames, clearly baroque before the Baroque Age?

Today, Western clothing – not quite that described by Frois! – is, of course, standard-wear in Japan. Shirts worn by white-collar workers are called *wai-shyatsu*, from "white shirt" though they need not be *white* any more than our "blankets" (literally, "white" + a diminutive suffix) do. The term sounds funny. But before we laugh we should remember that all Japanese at least know where their various types of clothing comes from. What percentage of Americans know where their pants originated? Or even their "pajamas?" (This last given in any dictionary)

~~~~~~

1-18+   We store our clothing by folding it up with the outside inside and the inside outside;
Antre nós se dobrão os vestidos pera se guardarem com o direito pera dentro e o aveso pera fora;

Japanese fold it up with the outside outside and the inside inside.
Os Japões os dobrão com o dereito pera fora e o aveso pera dentro.

This contrast Englishes horribly. One Portuguese-English dictionary suggests I try "face of the clothing" for *direito/dereito* (the second Frois's misspelling) and "wrong side" for *aveso*. It will not work.   The verb that became "store" alone in English, has the meaning of "guard" or "protect" in Portuguese, which seems to support the idea of folding the best part of the garment – if you recall from 1-11+ and 1-12+, "our" clothing had the best part *outside* – inside where it would be safer. And, by the same logic, the Japanese clothing with their precious linings would keep that side in. But there are more possibilities here. Were Japanese storage conditions cleaner so there was less risk of soiling the outside? Or were mantles of shirts and buttons on the coats of Frois's time so costly they just asked for being wrapped up in order not to tempt the servants?
..

While all the translations *seem to* take the above reading, the Japanese ones manage to leave the ambiguity of interpreting it in a different way, for *omote* can mean "outside" or "front-side" and the *ura*, "inside" or "back-side!" I feel jealous of that ambiguity which I cannot use in English, for I cannot shake off the feeling that maybe, just maybe, Frois is talking about *front* and *back* and nothing really gets turned *inside-out,* unless one considers the front of the garment as the rightful outside or face and does not count the back. But if that were the case, we would fold in the fronts and expose the backs while Japanese would fold in the backs and expose the fronts and this would contradict the following *Faux Frois:*

Europeans meeting up with a dangerous animal or person tend to stand and face the threat;
Japanese tend to fold up their bodies and present their back to the danger.

But I am not much one for folding – indeed, I do not even iron my clothes either with the result that my shirts tend to look best after I wear them for three days and the wrinkles are gone (so long as you do not look at the collar – and forget how it is done by "us" or "them" and think I it best to differ further discussion to people who know better.

~~~~~~

1-19+   Our handkerchiefs are of extremely thin fabric, embroidered and edged, etc.;
Antre nós os lenços são de pano muito fino, lavrados ou de desfiado, etc.,

The Japanese use ones of rags or paper.
Os dos Japões huns são como de liteiro groso e outros de papel.

The "rags" – *tenugui* (a cotton hand-towel) in one translation and "hempen refuse" in another – and paper" used for wiping brows, drying hands and such were probably as beautiful in their way as the ornate Western handkerchief mentioned.   I, at least, prefer naturally colored hand-made paper and the simple prints on Japanese *tenugui* (a handkerchief used either to wipe sweat, rolled up as a sweat-band or tied as a wrapped cap) today to the fancy but usually less tasteful Western handkerchief.   For blowing noses, Japanese used only disposable tissues, which is generally still the case. (Even today one can find plentiful boxes of tissues and even bare rolls of toilet paper on desks in offices)

Rodrigues noted they were also used for spitting into "when they are in matted rooms."

> This paper is used throughout the kingdom and is very necessary for the sake of cleanliness, and nobody, the gentry or the common folk, women or children, fails to carry this in their bosom. . . . Nobles and gentry observe great cleanliness by immediately throwing away the sheet of paper after they have blown their nose; for this reason there is a great abundance of this paper throughout the whole kingdom. (R(C):TIJ – compare this to Frois's earlier remarks: intro pt iii [1])

Don't get the wrong idea. The paper was not reused. It was collected and recycled. (Paper vats, according to Issa, were a very dangerous place for butterflies). Hygiene, ecology and literacy aligned! In old Japan, there was no telling who once blew his or her nose on the paper you wrote on. Before waxing poetic – imagining paper flying all about the Japanese landscape – however, let us observe that Rodrigues fails to say what people who were *not* "nobles and gentry" did after blowing *their* noses. Isabella Bird provides the answer:

> Certain charms and "pocket" idols are carried in the sleeve and food, and the paper squares used for pocket handkerchiefs, which when new are carried in the girdles, after being used once, are dropped into the sleeve, until an opportunity occurs for throwing them away out of doors. (UTJ)

I would guess that the lower classes had to take care not only when indoors but when outdoors to throw away their tissue in a manner that didn't anger the upper classes, and that meant they were carried, even if for only a short period of time. One hopes that the food and charms were carried in one sleeve and the used tissues in the other! If you believe the *ukiyoe* artist, however, the main use of tissue paper in Japan was not for blowing noses or spitting into. It was for love-making. You can estimate the amount of sex engaged in by counting the tissues, and the intensity of it by noticing how crumpled and far-flung they are. Popular brands of tissue paper were used as currency in the Yoshiwara Pleasure Quarters!

1. *Odd if Not Ludicrous Tissue* According to Frois's *Prologue* explanation, given in full in my Foreword, the Europeans find the idea of throw-away tissues ludicrous because they can not imagine cheap paper. Unfortunately, I have not found a contemporary Japanese view of the European practice, but I did find the next best thing in Montaigne. A French gentleman who made a practice of blowing his nose "in his hand" defended his infamous practice to the Essayist as follows:

> He asked me what privilege this dirty excrement had that we should prepare a fine delicate piece of linen to receive it, and then, what is more, wrap it up and carry it carefully on us; for that should be much more horrifying and nauseating than to see it dropped in any old place, as we do all other excrements."

When outside, I hold a finger over one nostril and blow the other clean the moment no one is looking, so I cannot help but wonder if the gentleman really blew his nose *in* his hand rather than *with* it, but Montaigne continues,

> I found that what he said was not entirely without reason; and habit had led me not to perceive the strangeness of this action, which nevertheless we find so [would find?] hideous when it is [if it were?]

told about another country. (M/F:CEM)

From here, Montaigne goes on to state what might be considered his central idea of relativity:

> Habitation puts to sleep the eye of our judgment. Barbarians are no more marvelous to us than we are to them, nor for better cause; as everyone would admit if everyone knew how, after perusing these new examples, to reflect on his own and compare them sanely."

I wish I knew if Valignano caught Montaigne's Essay (this one *Of Custom*: 1572-4). For he shares something of its spirit. In this essay, Montaigne goes on to give dozens of customs calculated to astound his readers including Herodotus's women who piss standing and men who piss squatting (strangely not attributed), women who show-off their loves by wearing tassels for each man they bed, people who drink the dissolved remains of the dead with wine or feed them to dogs, etc. and – this one takes the cheese – a people who, when "eating, wipe their fingers on their thighs, on the pouch of their genitals, and on the soles of their feet." Montaigne's world was too broad to stop with mere topsy-turvy! (all trans. by Donald M. Frame: M/F:CEM)

1-20+   We show our courtesy by removing our hats.
Nós fazemos a cortezia com tirar o barrete;

The Japanese show it by removing their footgear.
Os Japões a fazem com descalsar os sapatos.

As we, when we all *had* hats, once removed them to greet a superior on the street, Japanese removed their footgear. The pariah class, the *eta*, were not permitted to wear foot-wear in *anyone's* presence, ostensibly because it would be inappropriate for their animal (called four-footed, or simply indicated by four fingers) identity, but logically, because they were the inferiors of all others and had to remain physically lower. Note that both the removal of one's shoes and the removal of one's hat both make someone lower. There is a difference, however, the removal of shoes was something more than a mere *courtesy*, it was a sign of respect shown to one's *superior*, where *courtesy toward equals* was shown by a slight bow, in the manner that we might tip our hat for an equal, and removing the shoes when coming into a house would better be described as a custom and a *necessity* than as a courtesy. The eclectic (and occasionally wrong) English editor of Golowin's MEMOIRS has it right when he uses the hat *vs.* footgear contrast as one of four examples of why Japanese "have been called our moral Antipodes."

They salute the foot, instead of the head or the hands, &c (G:MCJv3):

This is not as ludicrous as it seems. The verb "salute" in mid-nineteenth century English meant *"to show respect using."* Today, no one in Japan removes footgear to show respect; neither do young idiots on both sides of the Pacific who wear baseball caps backwards because their poor posture makes their necks more likely to burn than their noses (I joke about this fashion that proves Montaigne's understanding of humans as an inane species well-founded) remove or even tip their caps – how could they, with the brim facing back? That (tipping), thanks to Frois, I now realize is another reason for a brim being in *front* of the hat.

1-21+   We use swords that cut on both sides of the blade..
Antre nós se uza d'espadas que cortão d'ambos os gumes;

The Japanese use a cutlass that cuts on only one edge of the blade.
Os Japões de traçados que não cortão mais que de hum gume somente.

The Occidental *espada* was first a stabbing and second a hacking instrument. Although it presumably cut better than its Gaelic prototype, it was crude stuff compared to the razor-sharp Japanese sword that was Japan's top export item to China (See 28 below on blade quality). Okada notes that in the West, too, if you go back to Rome, swords were originally single-edged. I find this intriguing because Hollywood *always* shows them with the double edged *spatha* they adopted (later than the event depicted) from the Gauls! Our topsy-turvy scheme is beautifully preserved in historical flip, when we consider one more fact: the ancient Japanese sword, the *tsurugi,* was double-edged and as long as our medieval "long-sword."

So we went from one edge to two, while they went from two to one!

1-22+   Our scabbards are leather or felt.
As nossas bainhas são de couro ou de veludo.

> Those of the Japanese are of lacquered wood, and the lords' covered with gold or silver. *As dos Japões de pao* vruxadas, *e as dos senhores cubertas d'ouro ou prata.*

The wood, which Frois describes as *vruxadas* (he has turned the Japanese *urushi*=lacquer into a Portuguese adjective!) was usually *magnolia hypoleuca.* If lacquer-ware to eat from was generally vermilion, scabbards were usually black. In Frois's list of ten sample misinterpretations of *things Japanese* in the prologue to his lost book, we find a reference to the lords' scabbards:

> When it is stated that Japanese scabbards are made of gold, this must be understood to mean that the scabbard is wooden and lightly gilded over. The thickness of the gilt depends upon the [financial] capacity of the person the scabbard is made for. (FH)

So much for Marco Polo and Columbus's *Zipangu* as El Dorado! The Japanese, like the Balinese observed more recently, were very big on gilt, not *fool's gold,* perhaps, but close to it from the Western viewpoint. When we consider the fact that we cannot see inside of objects, the more logical view would be that "we" are *fools* to use solid gold where it is not functional. Unlike leather and felt, lacquer-ware or gilt wood does not get damp and would have helped keep the blade from rusting. Still, one wonders what Sigmund Freud would have thought about that hard scabbard . . .

1-23+   Our swords have chapes, hilts and pommels.
As nossas espadas tem conteiras, cabos e maçãns;

> Those of Japan have none of these things.
> *As dos Japões nenhuma destas couzas tem.*

The chape is a protective metal fitting for the tip of the scabbard. I assume the fact the European scabbard was "leather or felt"(1-22+) requires it. The pommel is a big fancy butt for the handle. While the inlaid jewels and whatnot are functionally worthless, the extra weight below the hand improves both the balance (and, thus, control) and the cut (more momentum and reduction of vibration). This was not needed by Japanese swords because they had proportionately longer handles that were gripped with both hands (*viz* 7-2). Frois's assertion about the *cabo* is problematic for it generally referred to either the "hilt" or the "handle," and Japanese swords, obviously, had both (the hilt being the place the blade met the guard). The Japanese handle had a sword-guard, that in comparison with the huge cross-pieces that turned "our" swords into crosses (generally including a leading part slightly further up the blade and, sometimes, even fender-like knuckle-guards) must have seemed little more than a large washer. The handle grip also seems spare – almost a continuation of the blade – in comparison with the more heavily crafted horn handles found on Occidental swords. Frois may have meant the Japanese sword had nothing *we* would consider a proper handle.
..

1-24+   Our swords are tested on lumber or animals;
As nossas espadas se provão em paos ou em animaes;

> Japanese insist upon testing theirs on the bodies of dead men.
> *Os Japões fincão-se pera provar as suas em corpos de homens mortos.*

This is not Orientalism. Like Damascus steel, the best Japanese swords were indeed tempered and tested on flesh. Cooper has a wealth of information on this gory subject including: "a first-class blade sometimes cut through three corpses with one blow, although seven is on record." (see "Sword testing" in index of C:TCJ) Rodrigues marveled: "the delight and pleasure which they feel in cutting up human bodies is astonishing as is also the way that young boys sometimes indulge in this." (C/R:TIJ). No wonder there was a great demand for bodies. Executed criminals did not suffice even though the bodies were occasionally sewn together to be used a second time! And this testing continued long after the Warring Period ended. A century after TRATADO, Kaempfer mentions an execution place "where, 'tis said, young people try'd their strength, and the sharpness of their Scymiters, upon the dead bodies, by hacking them into small pieces, scarce an inch long and broad, which they afterwards permitted to be buried." A widely published illustration from this period shows the potential cuts on a headless torso in the same manner as "we" might show the "cuts" of beef or pork, marked on the body of the respective animals, with the difference only that the Japanese illustration names the cuts themselves, whereas the lines on the European illustration divide the meat into named sections.

Lest this makes the Japanese seem inhumane, let us carefully observe Kaempfer's above words. *"Burying the remains"* implies gratefulness toward the flesh/donor on the part of those using them, because executed people were usually not buried in Japan or the West, but either left to rot, be eaten by beasts or burned. In the West, people convicted of especially heinous crimes were *quartered* – pulled apart by horses – not so much for painful punishment (it was sometimes done after they were executed) but because it was popularly believed that those whose bodies were broken up would have a harder time getting it together in the After-life (Since they would seem destined for Hell anyway, I don't see the logic of this, but so be it). In that case, the only thing the victims served was Christian superstition and sadistic spectacle, whereas in the Japanese case of sword-testing, the corpses were not cut up in vain but served to improve a skill or an instrument that might well be used to save lives.

Our surgeons practiced the closest Western equivalent to sword-testing; but dissection was psychologically the more onerous practice because of the associations mentioned above. It is also why grave-robbing and *Burking* – murdering people to sell their bodies to surgeons – were considered especially horrific crimes. (*Death, Dissection and the Destitute* (1987) by Ruth Richardson is *the* book). But this is not to say the Japanese practice was harmless, for, in some times and places, criminal elements and bad people in authority (evidently including one Shogun!) took to testing swords on any poor-looking passerby. This was called *sujikire,* "crossroads-cutting" and is still a favorite theme of Japanese television Easterns, but it is hard to say how much actually took place (see note 14-6).

..

~~~~~~

1-25+   Our cutlasses and scimitar are worn with the convex side [1] downward;
      Antre nós os traçados ou alfanjes se trazem com o arcado pera baxo;

         The Japanese wear them with the concave side below and the bow on top.
         Os Japões os trazem com o concavo pera baxo e o arcado pera sima.

When children play with swords today they tend to wear them hanging straight down. But traditionally, East or West, the scabbard hung or swords were stuck into a belt so as to point diagonally or even horizontally. This is why we get the top and bottom side Frois mentions. The longer classic Japanese sword, the *tachi,* dangled horizontally from the belt with the convex side downward the same as the European weapons mentioned by Frois, but the *tachi* was out of fashion at the time *Tratado* was written [2] and the *uchigatana* ("striking-sword") was indeed thrust through the belt (see 7-3) diagonally with the curve, barely pronounced enough to notice in artwork, convex-side (that is cutting edge) up. As ER points out, I could also say the cutting edge points *back*. Note that these swords are *always* in the scabbard. The idea, however, was a draw that instantly go to work. This the Japanese got with their new arrangement, which puts the drawn sword out front, whereas ours comes out raised high (better for a cavalry officer showing off than for immediate defense).[3]

Although, the picture I paint in my head suggests Frois is correct with "our" side, I wanted to confirm his statement about "our" weapons, but all scabbards/blades depicted in the paintings I came across were straight, doubtless because paintings show mostly nobility and their straight rapiers.

1. Translation. I wanted to use "arc" or "bow" here, but in English, it does not necessarily mean the convex side. Readers are not only free to send glosses but criticize the translations, so I may improve them on the next edition.

2. Tachi Exceptions. There were occasional tachi still out there but they were generally worn in a back-scabbard with the handle peeking up over the shoulder (*seoidachi*). The most famous opponent of Musashi, Sasaki Kojiro carried one such sword. (W.S. Wilson: The Lone Samurai.).

3. Draw. I am not sure if I got that right.

~~~~~~

1-26+   In rainy weather, we wear felt caps, *beden* [Moroccan capes], rain capes and hats;
   Nós uzamos de feltros, bedens *e capas d'agoa e sonbreiros pola chuva;*

       Japanese, rich or poor, wear the same very long straw capes and hats.
       Os Japões altos e baxos de capas de palha muito compridas e sombreiros de palha.

The Japanese don't have or need a rain hat *per se*. Their traveling or working "hat" and "umbrella" are not only homophonic (*kasa*), *homomorphic,* which is to say that the Japanese hat is a good deal more effective for rain and, for that matter, UV protection than ours. Not clinging to the head, but supported by a harness, it is better ventilated and more suitable for a muggy climate, too.[1] A hundred years later Kaempfer describes one "made of split bambous, or straw, very neatly and artfully twisted, in the form of an extended Sombreiro or Umbrello . . . tied under the chin with broad silk bands lin'd with cotton . . . transparent and exceedingly light, and yet once wet, will let no rain come through." And, he adds, "not only the men wear such hats upon their journies, but also the women in cities and villages, at all times, and in all weather, and it gives them no disagreeable look." (K(S):HOJ)

In Frois's day, the Japanese had no simple raincoat, either. They only had capes of straw layered like a thatched roof; but, soon, this was to change. Kaempfer describes a "large cloak made of double varnish'd oil'd paper, and withal so very large and wide, that it covers and shelters at once man, horse and baggage." (KHJ) and adds what is still the accepted history: "it seems the Japanese have learnt the use of it, together with the name Kappa, from the Portuguese [*capa*]". At first, *kappa* meant any kind of cape, but in the Meiji era(1868-1912) *manto* (mantle) came to mean a cape or shawl and *kappa* came to mean only a rain-coat, and today, depending on the context, this word derived from Portuguese can even signify the straw cape, mentioned by Frois, that predates the word in Japanese (before, it was called something else). I am not sure if the "very long" refers to the straw or the garment. For both might be so modified. It is pleasant to imagine a man wearing one of these crosses between a thatched bungalo roof and a haystack getting out of the rain and shaking himself off like a wet dog. Had Frois only traveled to the North of his own country, he might have witnessed the same. *Vid* Ball on China:

> In rainy weather the lower classes of the South put on a cloak made of bamboo leaves sewn together, presenting a veritable Robinson Crusoe appearance; but in Swatow a similar one made of coir fibre is substituted, looking somewhat like the *capude palha,* or straw cloads, worn by the peasantry, in the northern provinces of Portugal. (B:TC)

It is *possible* that someone brought the idea back from Japan or China, but chances are this type of thing was common to peasants in many places and what made Japan unique, or rather contrary, was the sight of the rich wearing such crude-looking items.

1. *Decent Hats.* "Our" hats are still not even close to as good as the traditional hats of the East. Unfortunately, there are a couple details involving the harness that must be worked out to have a good commercial product. Contact me if you have money to invest in an ecological clothing venture and I'll explain.

~~~~~~

1-**27**+   We hold walking to be great fun, healthy and refreshing;
          Nós temos por grande recreasão, saude e alivio o pasear;

> Japanese have no use for them whatsoever, are puzzled by our doing so, and think we do it for some business or penance. *Os Japões totalmente ho não uzão, antes se espantão e o tem en nós por trabalho e penitencia.*

This contrast has held up for centuries. Wondering why Japan couldn't do with less executions and more jail sentences, America's first Ambassador to Japan, Townsend Harris, was told that prisons were not punishment for Japanese because they did not feel a need to walk about in the first place (14-11). The first Japanese Embassy to the West (excluding the 16ᵗʰ century mission) contrasted Occidentals who went *out* with Orientals who stay *in* (14-34). Alcock, the first British Ambassador, who arrived in Japan several years ahead of Harris, included *walking* among his "causes of mutual repulsion." Although his book CAPITOL OF THE TYCOON is about Japan, he makes it clear that this puzzlement belongs to the broader Sinosphere.

> The Chinese and the Japanese, like other people, are very apt to condemn what they dislike or do not rightly understand; and we may rest assured that the foreigner who finds the necessity for 'walking his thousand steps every day,' * or pulling like a bargeman for exercise, or shouting hurrahs with stentorian lungs after dinner for enjoyment, will be regarded as a 'barbarian' by the Chinese, and despised and disliked accordingly . . .
>
> *[Alcock's footnote] The way in which the daily exercise of the foreigners (when confined to the space within the Factory Gardens) used to be described by the Cantonese. It was supposed by the natives, in order to explain a proceeding otherwise so irrational and unintelligible to them, that this was the mode by which the foreign trader computed and made up his accounts! (A:COT)

Japanese and Chinese found the idea of "a constitutional" (or a "physique" as Pepys put it closer to Frois's day) ludicrous. To relax and think, they sat still. Considering the way habitual motion (shaving, washing in the shower and walking) strangely improves creative thought in a way meditation does not, I think the Far East missed out on something good. Who knows but this difference may explain the rise of the West!

That the Western practice of taking a walk did not catch on in Japan is reflected by the fact that the term for "a walk," i.e. *sanpô:* (scattered-steps) was only rarely used until the late-19ᵗʰ century. But it is a bit too much to say that Japanese only walked *to go somewhere.* There is, for example, *sozoro-aruki,* or "aimless walking," with pretty much the same connotations of my English translation which in Edo during the Tokugawa usually referred to a stroll through the so-called Pleasure Quarters, where the poor poet makes fun of people rather than actually making the women – but I don't know whether it dates back to Frois's time, for even the best Japanese dictionary is not so thorough as the

OED with first usages. Regardless, there were probably always some people who just liked walking:

> *time on his hands*
>
> *they're out! they're out!*
> i stroll about announcing
> the mosquitoes
>
> *himajin ya ka-ga deta deta to fure-aruki*

Issa wrote haiku of his "*nô-teppo*," literally, field-gun (discharging)," meaning *aimless walking* and, better yet, just walking about (*fure-aruki*) or, rather up and down his town (hickvilles like Issa's home town were usually one long street parallel to a highway), unemployed, informing the whole world about important matters. I might add that Issa and other haiku poets spent the better half of their lives on the road, which no doubt helps explain their creativity (Reader, please don't take me too seriously!)

There are two more qualifications for Frois's contrast of *we who walk* and *they who do not*. First, if we exclude nomadic migration, Japanese may well have led the civilized world in serious long-distance walking. People of all classes were constantly off on pilgrimages. They had good roads and used them to walk from shrine to shrine, from temple to temple for hundreds and even thousands of miles. Japanese may not have walked much, but when they did, they walked like it was nobody's business. Golowin's English editor cites Charlevoix to the effect that:

> whenever traveling was practicable, a stranger would suppose, that not a soul was left in the towns and villages, but that the whole nation was in motion; some traveling on business; others on pilgrimages; numerous beggars . . . (G:MCJ3)

I suspect, however, that the number of pilgrims on the road in Frois's time was not that high because of the dangers of War. (There would, I would guess, have been many refugees, instead.[1]) The second qualification is more spectacular and might best be introduced as a Faux Frois contrast:

> *Europeans marching in parades walk as fast or faster than they do normally.*
> *Japanese on parade move one leg at a time so slowly they resemble stickbugs.*

..
This refers to but one of the stylized walks of Japanese pageantry referred to as *neri-aruki,* or "polished walking." There were as many varieties of this walk as those invented by the Ministry of Silly Walks of the Monty Python Show, ranging from the rapid and tiny up and down toe-movements used by most Shinto float (*dashi*) carriers, which can be seen today, to slow-motion deliberate wobbling and rotating of each foot in turn by courtesans on parade wearing high *geta* clogs. Kaempfer describes a variety of *neri-aruki* I have not even seen in a movie, perhaps because it would take a circus troupe to re-enact it! The scene is the train of a great prince in 1692. Elegant rows of black silk marching in sublime silence, marred only by the "ridiculous" naked rears of the pike bearers and sedan carriers.

> What appears more odd and whimsical, is to see the Pages, Pikebearers, Umbrello and hat-bearers, Fassanbak or chestbearers, and all the footmen in their liveries, affect a strange mimic march or dance, when they pass through a Town, or Borough, or by the train of another Prince or Lord. Every step they make, they draw up one foot quite to their back, in the meantime stretching out the arm on the opposite side as far as they can, and putting themselves in such a posture, as if they had a mind to swim through the air. Mean while the pikes, hats, umbrello's, Fassanbacks, boxes, baskets, and what ever else they carry, are danced and toss'd about in a very singular manner, answering the motion of their bodies. (K(S):HOJ)

1. *History of Walking in Japan*. If there is such a book, I   and you have read it, please send a gloss so good I will
want to read it. If not, someone should write it. If there is,   not have to read it.

~~~~~~

1-28+   Our swords and valuable goods are highly adorned;
As nossos espadas e cousas de muito preço estão bem guarnecidas;

Their valuables have no artifice or adornment.
As suas preciosas nenhum aparato nem guarnisão tem.

"In our country there were golden and silver swords made for ritual purposes, but swords for use were not ornate like those of Europe" writes Okada. He overcompensates a bit, for Japanese working swords in Frois's time usually had hilts well adorned with fine metal work. But, even so, it was subtly done, not obvious from a distance. There were none of those globs of jewels that (to my opinion) vulgarize the possessions of the European nobility. The most treasured swords, which were not necessarily used anymore, might not even have a hilt. As Chamberlain put it – for there was no change in attitude over the centuries –

> to the Japanese connoisseur the great treasure is always the blade itself, which has been called "the living soul of the Samurai." (C:TJ)

The Japanese had something the Europeans lacked, extremely good sword blades valuable in themselves. As Rodrigues noted, "one of their ordinary swords" could "cut a man through the middle in two parts with the greatest of ease"(R(C):TIJ). There is ample literature attesting to the cutting ability of a good Japanese sword. Perrin quotes Dutchman Arnold Montanus to the effect that they could "cut our *European* blades asunder, like Flags or Rushes;" (P:GUG) and mentions a modern arms collector who "took part in a test in which a sixteenth century Japanese sword was used to cut a modern European sword in two." He also writes that "tolerably thick nails didn't even make an interesting challenge," and no wonder, for "there exists in Japan right now a film showing a machine-gun barrel being sliced in half by a sword from the forge of the great 15th century maker, Kanemoto II." Apparently *millions* of layers of steel of various degrees of hardness had to be hammered out to temper the blade of a sword like this. The Japanese were interested in the quality of a sword rather than its trappings. And, this practical value could be proven. [1]

Even disregarding the above mentioned "transcendent excellence," (B:MCJ) – a phrase used in 1845, for how else does one describe something as sharp as a razor that can cut nails without notching or bending?! – the elemental layered and etched beauty of the layers of steel on the blades of the best Japanese swords impress a person with a modicum of taste far more than glittery jewels. Western aesthetics was, and I fear, still largely is, the aesthetics of the child, or the magpie, rationalized by the value – i.e. high price – of trinkets. Valignano in 1583, does not go so far as to call jewels trinkets; but when he describes old sword blades – in particular, one that "had no adornment of any type, nor gold, but is only a blade of pure iron" for which the King of Bungo paid 4,500 ducats – together with tea utensils and *sumie* (black ink paintings), as the Japanese equivalent of our jewels, he pens a fine paragraph on the Japanese point of view:

> And when we ask why they spend so much money on things naturally of little value, they respond that they do it for the same reason we buy diamonds and rubies for so high a price, which they, no less, find shocking, saying that . . . . at least the things they buy and value so highly serve for something; and, for that reason, the imagination that leads them to pay so much for them is less faulty than that of Europeans who buy little stones that have no use. (in V(A):S&A)

Here, Valignano stresses a relativistic explanation of value, for his object was to convince readers of the reality of the Contrary Culture he and his Jesuit brethren had to cope with. But, almost a decade later, in dialogue 9 of DE MISSIONE report, Miguel=Valignano turns about and makes a spirited defense of jewels. After Miguel waxes enthusiastically over the unbelievable amount of gems and pearls adorning noble dress in Europe, gives examples of diamonds that even had names (as true for swords in Japan), and explains that Europe is so wealthy these expensive items (one worth 500,000 gold pieces) are even used as gifts, Leno=Valignano remonstrates about how foolish it is to pay so much for such tiny stones. Then, Miguel replies that

> if the value of large and small pearls were not recognized in most of Asia and Africa as well as in Europe, it would certainly seem absurd to pay so much for something so small; but, actually, the prices, as I have said, are standard almost wherever you go in the world and nobody doubts the value of these types of gem. Moreover, it seems even nature demands this price, for there is a wonderful shine and luster in these gems, some of which can be seen to shine even from afar, and many have the astonishing power to ward off disease or serve as medicine to save human life. So, now, considering our goods, the tea kettles and . . . . made of earth, clay or iron . . . , paying a sum as large as . . . for them, is, rather [more so than in the case of gems] strange. [Likewise for] only one piece of paper with a single tree, bird or something painted with black ink . . . considering the value of the materials, the artist's skill, there is nothing intrinsic or extrinsic to such a painting to make it so horribly expensive. (J/S:DM)

The sword blade is nowhere in sight. Valignano may have come to realize their undeniable value [2] and decided they would complicate his explanation of the value of gems within the framework of what we might today call the global vs. local culture debate. Miguel (I think it was Miguel, my notes are unclear)=Valignano continues –

> There is nothing wrong with letting these things be left to the judgment and opinion of each society, leaving each free to defend its own taste, feelings and customs. But if one should make a judgment based on natural law, not bound to the ideas of a people or nation, gems are first of all lustrous and shiny, second, they have the advantage of lasting a long time without loss and, third, have various special properties which are very useful to our lives. Accordingly, it is not unreasonable that almost all peoples throughout the world similarly value gems, and considering this agreement, we cannot think their judgment wrong, and we must hold it only natural for gems to be precious. On the other hand, those earthen and iron utensils valued in Japan are not valued in any other place you may go to. Generally speaking, an opinion held by only one people, is usually and fundamentally wrong about the matter in question, while one which most peoples agree about is correct. (Ibid)

Leo=Valignano replies, "That may be right, but if I am free to choose, I would still prefer Japanese things to the outside world's gems and pearls, whatever the reason, and though they be made of earth." To this honest confession, Miguel gives an sympathetic and charming reply, which confirms Valignano's globalism yet does not force it upon Japan's particularism.

> Of course what you say is fine, so long as you confine your trading and purchasing to Japan; but the Portuguese put such a high value on those tiny rock-like things that if many of them were found in Japan, we could sell them to them and buy a great quantity of our [tea] utensils! (Ibid)

I like this because to me, too, the aesthetic value of those utensils far exceeds the cool geometry of precious gems. I agree with the Japanese side, which in Montanus' words, looks upon our *pretious* stones "as Whitings-Eyes and Pebbles, admiring and giving Rates for old Iron and Earth Ware." (M:EEJ) But, Valignano=Miguel describes the real world, the vulgar place where we must, like it or not, live. The question of whether this or that part of their own culture (an item of food or clothing, a song, a book, a particular body language or way of speaking, etc.) is or is not internationally viable is *still* discussed in Japan. Such a multi-cultural perspective is part of daily life. In the Occident or, at least in the USA, where we tend to assume our culture is globally applicable, the question generally only comes up with respect to political matters: *i.e.* the suitability of democratic rule and individual rights for non-Western cultures.

1. *Practical Value of Japanese Sword*. These are pretty spectacular claims and despite finding them in decent books, I cannot help but wonder how they hold up to scientific study. The details on forging the swords make sense. A million layers sounds like a lot, but with the way things double it only takes 20 folds to get there, so it is not quite what the math-dumb might think. Apparently the best swords around the world (Damascus, Toledo and according to someone on the net, "Viking," too!) were better than mediocre Japanese swords, with a dozen or so folds and about as good as good Japanese swords with about 15 folds (32,000+layers). The superior Japanese sword is another story. It is created by varying the number of folds for different parts of the blade – sandwiching layers of different layer density – so the interior remains pliant while the exterior, especially the part closest to the edge of the blade is folded until it is brittle and razor-sharp. This sounds reasonable, too. But when we are told it becomes *incomparably hard* upon its final heating and rapid cooling (in water, not blood), how are we to take that? *Is it really possible that a razor-sharp blade can come through battle after battle without nicks? Have there been scientific tests on these things?* Is it true that only 19th century metallurgy could "make steel approaching 13th century Japanese steel in quality"(*Early Japan:* J.N. Leonard + eds. of Time-Life Books)? A good gloss on "the myth of the Japanese sword" would be welcome.

2. *Aesthetic Value of the Sword Blade*. When most of us imagine a centuries-old sword blade, we imagine a rusty thing valuable as a memento of some famous person or smith, but if I am not mistaken, these old blades were kept polished and people did not just take them out to feel how sharp they were. In the March 1967 *Horizon* magazine (if you do not have a trash-pile as prolific as the one next-door where I found it, and do not know of *Horizon*, be sure to hunt for it the next time you are in a big library), art critic Robert Hughes describes "the visual subtleties of the great Japanese *hamon* ('the band of frosted opaque steel crystals, between an eighth and a half-inch wide, that runs along the cutting edge . . . the "signature of the edge" – the physical sign of extreme metallic hardness')" as only a true connoisseur can:

> Light seems to bloom and settle like pollen along the matte, crystalline edge, and its delicately uneven flow is as replete with images of nature as a sumi-e painting. The *hamon* of the Kunimune [a photo of this Kunimune, "one of six greatest blades ever forged" is shown] suggests a distant landscape seen through mist: the running profile of the hills, flecked with innumerable deepenings of tone and floating clouds of darker steel. Other edge patterns conjure up rivers, the striations of high cirrus clouds, flurried snow, or the tempestuous march of foam-capped waves.

> Much of the visual complexity of the Japanese sword lies in the dialogue . . . between the edge pattern and the grain of the more polished surface of the blade. . . . . A battery of technical terms has been invented by Japanese sword scholars to classify the surface patterns: straight grain, wood grain, pear skin, burl grain, catfish skin, *ayasugi-hada* or concentrically curved grain, *matsukawa-hada* or grain like that of pine-tree bark." (The Art of the Japanese Sword: More than mere weaponry, the great blades of Japan are revered in shrines and prized among Western connoisseurs.)

Hughes noted there was a list of ten-thousand swordsmiths spanning 1200 years and matching up blade patterns with their makers was an art so demanding that, in the words of Dr Compton, "Two lifetimes of continuous dedication could not exhaust this field." When it comes to Japanese swords as art, debunking is impossible.

~~~~~~

1-29+   We think it a discourtesy for a servant not to remain standing when his master is sitting;
Nós temos por descortezia não estar o servo im pé quando o senhor estaa asentado;

> They think it poor breeding for a servant not to sit, too.
> *E elles por mao insino não se asentar tambem o criado.*

"Our" requirement is cruel for the tired servant, and, even today, we find employers (the new masters) forcing employees to stand out of respect to themselves or customers. But the second half of the contrast is not the result of Japanese being kind enough to allow their servants to rest. It is because Japan shared the extreme *up-down consciousness* of much of South East Asia and the Pacific island cultures where the superior had to be *literally* higher than others at all times. It might be more practical for a servant to remain on his feet, but one cannot have the servant above the master. K'tut Tantri writes of a Raja in 1930's Bali who would not go under an overpass for fear of losing his dignity should anyone chance to look down on him. They had to stop the car so he could get out and walk over it. (REVOLT IN PARADISE). [1] Heusken, translator for the first United States Ambassador to Japan, described an outing of "His Magnificent Majesty" of Siam: "All the bridges on the route of the Royal Gondola are removed because Royalty cannot bear to pass underneath a path where others place their feet." Also, for this reason one seldom sees two-story houses in Siam." Alcock described something similar in Japan:

> That they should be a ceremonious and punctilious people follows as a matter of course, for just in proportion as they are conscious of sensitiveness on these points, is their scrupulousness in avoiding any provocation or ground of offense to others. Indeed, to such a pitch do they carry this, that no equestrian statue is permitted – so at least they say themselves – because it would wound the dignity of anyone entitled to marks of respect to pass in the street, or to meet in a house, *a person riding, even in bronze, while the other was on foot!* (A:COT)

This *is* a matter of rules of etiquette for sure, but behind the individual rule lies a broader principle. As Rodrigues explained in his detailed pages on the etiquette of dismounting, a "man on horseback is in a higher and more exalted position than the man walking on foot, and to a certain extent looks down on him and is, as it were, his superior, while the man on foot is in a low and inferior position." (R(C):TIJ) Japanese could be ridiculously literal. To fold a wife's clothing on top of a husband's would disrespect him, to use a book as a pillow would disrespect the author. It is surprising that Japanese ever allowed the woman superior position in sex! Bowing, of course, was the most common site of up-down comparison. A Western compilation of Dutch observations in Japan published in 1841 claimed that

> Gentlemen wear a scarf over the shoulders, the length of which is regulated by the rank of the wearer; and this serves in turn to regulate the bow with which they greet each other, it being indispensable to bow to a superior until the ends of the scarf touch the ground. (B:MCJ)

Scarves were not that common in Japan. This would seem to be a gross generalization of an earlier observation (I have read it but can't find it) of a Buddhist sect for which it held true. But the general idea is right. Even today, old-fashioned Japanese can be seen bowing back and forth literally sizing each other up. Since people come in different sizes, the height has to be, at least in part, displaced by angle. Since men tend to gain higher status as they age, the angle of the upper part of the body becomes closer and closer to the vertical. This is, of course, the precise opposite of the case with the male's private part; and I have seen any number of cartoons demonstrating this as an inverse rule of thumb (the *open hand* is shown in front of the body with the thumb demonstrating a youth's erection and an elder's bow, the index finger as a young man's erection or late-middle-aged bow, the baby finger as a youth's bow and an old man's erection, and so forth.)

In Valignano's PRINCIPIO (1582?), we read "To pay honor, *others* stand up, the Japanese sit down." (my italics – S:VMP) Here, Valignano may be too quick to put Europe in the majority. I would guess that most people stay down or get lower yet (Anthropologists, I would appreciate input!). Yet Europeans certainly appreciated – at least, understood – the psychology of *up* and *down* in Frois's time. See this passage from the *Voyage of Van Linschoten*. When elephants and their keepers pay their respect to the authorities,

> the elephants come to the dore and bowe when any thing is given, they kneele on their knees *with great lowliness* [and thankefulnesse] for the good deedes so done unto their keepers (which they think bee done unto themselves)."(my *italics*).

A footnote says the English translator has written "lowliness" for the Dutch word meaning "reverence!"

1. *K'tut Tantri.* A red-haired painter born on the Isle of Manx, who accompanied her mother to Hollywood where she saw Chaplin's movie on Bali and moved there, intending to settle forever, but was forced by history to become a spy against the Japanese and, then, an agent for the independence of Indonesia from Imperialist European powers. If any of our movie producers read good non-fiction and understood what is most important in life, they would have turned her book *Revolt In Paradise* into a movie long ago. Together with Captain Golownin's *Captivity*, which should also be turned into a movie *yesterday* (it would be far better than the *Last Samurai*), this book depicts a foreign culture which is in many ways laudable and an author who is incredibly heroic yet believable and embodies the most important virtue of all, which is peacefully persevering in the face of adversity.

~~~~~~

1-30+   We use black for mourning;
Nós uzamos do preto por dó;

The Japanese white.
E os Japões do branco.

Today, *white* is far less prevalent than *black* at Japanese funerals. This is partly because of the Western influence and partly because the use of white in Japan was never as absolute as in neighboring Korea, where it is still *the* color of bereavement (and worn all the time by the elderly as if to say *"I'm ready to go!"*) or China, from where, Rodrigues wrote, the custom came. Even in Frois's time, Japanese men of the *bushi* (samurai) class, at least, only wore white to their *own* funeral, i.e., when committing *seppuku* (formal *harakiri*). Otherwise, they tended to wear dull-black hemp (Okada) and, as Frois himself noted in a letter Englished by Willis, the bonzes wore fine black upper garments to funerals. This makes sense, for the *dark=sad* metaphor is as much part of the Japanese language, as it is part of ours (One even finds a cherry tree blooming with ashen colored blossoms in the *Kokinshû* collection of poems (c.900). *White*, on the other hand, as befits a color made of the entire spectrum of light, boasts a more complex semiology. It is both the color of the *purity* at the heart of Shinto and the metaphorical "unknowing" (*shira* as in *shira-tsuyu*: "white-dew", or "dew, not knowing it will soon evaporate" – think of our going *blank*) of the Zen Buddhist poet. Together with *red*, white comprises the male half of the traditional pair of festive colors. Sometimes both the pure, festive aspect and the mourning aspect of white could and was fused, for the

> Japanese bride goes to be married in a pure white mourning robe, which is intended to signify that henceforth she is dead to her old home and her parents, and that she must henceforth look upon her husband's people as her own" (Lorimer in S:MQTJ)

This marriage-as-death idea was developed *much* farther in parts of China and South East Asia. Today, Japanese have little or no consciousness of it. The white veil or cap over the head, which once was "her destined shroud" (B:MCJ), is now known only as a "horn-hider," (*tsuno-kakushi*), a visible reminder that the bride is studying to be good despite her devilish female nature (whether from the Buddhist idea of women as bundles of desire or some part of Shinto, I do not yet know – anyone?), as in the West, it is the purity aspect of the color that is dominant and recognized. Given this complexity, it is ironic that black and white contrasts became so black and white. Montanus, in 1670, may have been the first to proceed one logical step forward and claim that –

> To be clad in Black or Scarlet, amongst them signifies Triumph or Joy, but their Mourning for loss of Friends and other Disastors, is White. (M:EEJ)

I have *never* found black so described by Japanese and they would have found it ludicrous. On the other hand, I have found white mourning in the West. *Plenty of it.*   First, Montaigne:

Argive and Roman ladies wore white mourning, as ours used to and should have continued to do, if they had taken my advice. But there are entire books written about this question. (M(F):CEM) [1]

And A. H. Oliveira Marques, writing about Frois's Portugal(!), suggests that one hardly need to go back to classical times:

> Because unbleached and undyed homespun and sackcloth were whitish or yellowish, just as is burlap, white became a badge of mourning during the Middle Ages . . . Only the king and queen could wear black as a sign of mourning. When Fernando dies (1383), the Count of Ourém, perhaps following a foreign custom, appeared dressed in black when all the other nobles were in homespun. That was criticized and reprimanded to such a point that the count had to resign himself to covering his black clothing with the customary white cloak. . . . Black had begun to vie with white as an indication of mourning toward the close off the Middle Ages. . . . But only in the reign of Manuel I (1495-1521) was it adopted as the official color of mourning in clothing. (M:DLP)

When Philip (Felipe) II (King of Spain, Portugal (and mucho more)) died five years after TRATADO, his lasting black legacy proved to be a problem, for after the civic officials purchased their black gowns and black draperies for the buildings at public expense, the fabric "began to fetch black market prices." In Seville, "poor people who could not afford the appropriate black mourning garb were thrown in prison. Apparently, the number of arrests was so high that Philip III had to modify the requirements, allowing the poor simply to wear unadorned hats."(E:MP) We tend to think of dark as natural and light as artificial, but the fact most fabrics are naturally closer to white than black probably ensures that the crude clothing favored by most cultures for mourning will be whitish. Indeed, Nieuhoff in 1672 cited just that argument by Semedo. Namely, silk and cotton were too fine for mourning, so hemp was *de rigor* in China; and, hempen white being "a naturally unpleasing colour," he argued, white came to be chosen as "the Colour of their Mourning." Nieuhoff also cites Martinus to the effect that the Chinese "themselves say" that it is because only

> White is Natural, when all other things are Dy'd, or Artificial, by which they say, is signifi'd that in Sorrow, neither Art nor Pride must be shewn, for where a true Sorrow is, Nature sufficiently expresses it. (N(O):EC)

The relationship of this natural raw white and brilliant white in the East is, however, a matter for debate. Lee O-Young has argued the Korean predilection for white clothing in terms of his countrymen's long-term poverty.[2] I contested in print, that, no, it takes a hell of a lot of labor to make and keep clothing as white as *that* – I did not know it at the time I wrote my article, but Bird had written a large paragraph on just that a hundred years before me!

> Washing is her manifest destiny so long as her lord wears white. She washes in this foul river, in the pond of the Mulberry Palace, in every wet ditch . . . . The women are slaves to the laundry, and the only sound which breaks the stillness of a Seoul night is the regular beat of their laundry sticks. (B:KHN)

True white (as opposed to undyed cloth), then, is no more a default color than black. Koreans may have originally adopted it because they had so much interest in the dead and the other world that life became a perpetual period of mourning, and as the white brightened, it became a necessary proof of spiritual purity, as black became identified with spiritual sobriety in the West.

---

1. Montaigne Citation. I lost the page and thus the name of the essay. You would not go wrong searching for it, for *Montaigne's Essays* are full of fun at every turn and even if you fail to find it you will find something!

2. Lee O-young. I think it was in *In This Wind and on this Earth*. But it might have been in another book he wrote about Korea published in Japanese. My article was in *Chuo-koron* May 1990.

1-31+   When we walk, we lift up our clothing in front so it is not soiled;
Nós quando caminhamos alevantamos os vestidos por diante pera os não sujar;

The Japanese lift it up so high from behind that the entire north[1] is bared.
Os Japões os alevantão tanto por detrás, que lhe fica todo o norte desquberto.

Today, with our high heels, it makes sense to lift up in front, but I am not sure why that would have been the case in Frois's time unless it was because keeping a clean front was the more important.

The Japanese side. When traveling in the hot half of the year, the hem of the robe was typically tucked into the obi belt high enough a man's rear-end, hopefully covered by a loin-cloth, could be seen. This makes eminent sense, for Japanese sandals would have flicked up mud, even if the amount would have been lessened by the shortness of the heels (1-59+) and, for a man, baring one's rear is, after all, less embarrassing than revealing one's front. For women, however, the rear-end is equally vulnerable, so the hems were usually tucked up – less radically, to be sure – in the front. It is possible, however, that men showed more than their asses, for loin-cloths were loosened for air in the humid summer and might be washed and, tied to a bamboo pole like a banner, dried while walking! Here is Kaempfer describing his First Journey to Edo:

> Ordinary servants, chiefly Norimonmen [*norimono* men = palanquin bearers] and pikebearers, wear no breeches at all, and for expeditions sake tack their gowns quite up to their belt, exposing their back and privy parts naked to every bodies view, which they say, they have no reason at all to be asham'd of. (KHJ)

Japanese themselves may not have been completely unconscious of the ugliness of this style, if it can be called so. Here is a haiku[1] written about the time Kaempfer was in Japan .

> *[kannazuki] secchin-no kami-no tabiji ya shiri-karage* – yusei (rakuyô-shû)
> ("god-not-month" – privy's god's travel-road: buttock [of robe] tucked up)

(subject: *the godless-month*)

the privy god is on the road, his robe tucked up high	our privy gods on the road, again, robes up out of the way

The Japanese term *shiri-karage* is standard idiom for this style and no one (aside from foreigners) usually notices the buttocks (*shiri*) in it. But, here, by making the god of the privy the butt of the haiku, Japanese, too, can see it. The gods of Japan all caucus in Izumo in the first month of the winter, which is called *god-less* because the Shinto gods are not around locally. Most travelers, let alone gods, would not hang ass in this cold part of the year, although Issa (see next item) found exceptions.

1. *The North as Down Under.* In the Chinese Buddhist tradition, the North was generally put down and the South up. Japanese privies were traditionally on the North side of the house. Frois's euphemistic *norte* does not, of course, come from that but, it would seem, from an Occidental equation of the North and Nether region (why some Medieval & Renaissance Hells end up in the Artic).

2. *Is This A Haiku?* Because the poem has that important seasonal element it can be considered a haiku, rather than a senryu; but the calculating manner in which it seems to play with the god's travel makes it seem more a senryu than a haiku. If the author wrote it alluding to a hard trip he had made or was making at that time, perhaps suffering from the runs, it would be a *bona fide* haiku. As it is, it is borderline, even granted the seasonal element.

1-32+ With us neither commoner nor noble dare reveal so much as a little toe when accompanying his master; *Antre nós os pajens e fidalgos acompanhando seus senhores não lhe á-de aparecer hum dedo do pee;;*

> Japanese on the road with their master may roll their breeches up clear to their groin. *Os Japões quando os acompanhão polas ruas arregasão os calsões [até às] verilhas.*

If Europeans found their inferiors' nudity insulting, and professed to be disgusted by it, Japanese rather enjoyed it. This attitude lasted well into the Edo era, when Issa wrote haiku of freezing cold winter moon-shine congealing on the rumps of butt-proud footmen. In Japan, a lord would be proud of, rather than embarrassed by the magnificent *gluteus-maximae(?)* on his charges, though he himself generally wore "very wide breeches with slits on both sides to put in the ends of their long gowns, which would otherwise be troublesome to them in walking and riding." (LR) Not that the lords were ashamed, either. The dignity of office forced them to wear too much for the summer and too little for the winter. Issa wrote several haiku which seem to show his enjoyment of the discomfort of the *daimyo* (feudal lords) in their regular parades back and forth from Edo (something they did not have to do in Frois's time) from the point of view of a poor man, who could lounge naked in the shade or sit at his *kotatsu* heater and watch the big-shots on parade suffer in the heat or sleet.

Today, the way many Muslims require women to wear veils seems oppressive to "us." But, we (especially in the USA) forget that we force women to cover their breasts and both sexes to cover their genitals and these laws are at heart based on religion, what we might call the *Adam and Eve just-so story for clothing*, and "we" have not only done this to ourselves but, less forgivably, to others:

> When our father, Adam, saw himself naked after he had sinned, he was so ashamed and humiliated that he immediately sought a way to remedy his nudity, even if it was only with leaves from the trees. . . Although the women in the nations we are discussing [Peoples of North Mexico] showed some concern for their nudity, the men paid no mind to it whatsoever. Today, in Christian fashion with modesty and propriety they all cover themselves with clothing. . . . In order for an indian to return to his lands with clothing for himself and his wife, he will spend half a year or more working in some mining camp or at one of the Spaniard's settlements, especially if the clothing is at all elegant, which they like. This is the degree to which nudity has been uprooted . . . (R(R&A&D):HOT7-7)

In this 17th century report by the Jesuit Andrés Péres de Ribas, walking "forty or fifty leagues" to work for months or even years at no small risk of death is considered a good bargain for clothing, which was considered the *sine qua non* for Christian=civilized living, called, not inappropriately, "reduction"! In the face of such sartorial imperialism, we who do not think the desert religions should dictate their rules of clothing to the rest of the world, are thankful to the Japanese for proving that bare skin and civil society are not intrinsically at odds.

1-33+ We spit at any time;
Nós em todo tempo deitamos o cuspinho fora;

> Japanese normally swallow their sputum.
> *Os Japões commumente emgolem pera dentro os escarros.*

"We" is not so simple. In England, Frois could even have pissed in the corner of a room, but if he dared the tiniest spit in a Dutch home he would have been brained by a frying pan (LR). There is some irony here, for in the twentieth century, it is Japanese men who have spit too freely for the taste of most Westerners, who forget that not long ago we were the big spitters (Especially Usanians – Dickens and Trollop entertain us for pages with outlandish depictions of tobacco-chewing Americans who never let up whether it was in a gale at sea or in the Senate). But the Japanese men only do it outdoors. Indoors, the existence of *tatami* (straw mat) pretty much rules out expectoration. It is curious that the Japanese of Frois's time also refrained *outside*. Okada wonders if it might have been considered impolite. Because most body noises have not bothered Japanese (see 6-60), that would be puzzling unless sputum was considered particularly impure or, like hair and nail clippings, something to be guarded from black magic). But there is another type of expectoration we do but Japanese don't that was probably true in Frois's day as it was when I lived in Japan:

> *We readily blow our noses and can not abide continued sniffling;*
> *Japanese find nose-blowing gross, while sniffling aloud all day long!*

Frois and others also miss the bodily function considered by some "a privilege of the male sex," that has aroused by far the most international controversy – judging from countless *letters to the editor* in English language papers in Japan – in the latter half of the twentieth century: namely, *tachi-shoben* or "standing-urination." Japanese men are infamous for doing it practically anywhere at any time. I know this habit goes back almost as far as the mid-Tokugawa (18th century) because of *senryu* about wise guys pissing on signs forbidding it. (See my ISSA BLUESMAN, if/when it is published, for a whole chapter on this subject!). Perhaps the contrast did not exist in Frois's day because European men *also* enjoyed the privilege of doing it virtually anywhere.

..

1-34+ The swords we wear are welded with one hand;
A espada que se singe antre nós se joga com huma mão;

Those of Japan are very heavy and all are welded with both hands.
As dos Japões, como são muito pezadas, todas se jogão com anbas.

European swords are thought to have lightened up to complement firearms.[1] (Because guns had the reach and power? Or, because of the additional weight of carrying both?). The rapier took this development to its spinal conclusion in the following century, while the Japanese sword did not change, thanks to firearms being banned (except for limited purposes, such as parades) and, I believe, a more reverent attitude toward tradition. By this, I do not so much mean love for the precise form of the traditional sword so much *as the manner in which it was held.* Polite drinking – a mark, not just of formality, but *sincerity* – was done with two hands. As a custom, this apparently comes from China, where –

> Both hands are used to pass anything, therefore a Chinese is not to be considered clumsy who hands any small articles, such as a cup of tea, in this manner: it would be thought the height of rudeness to do otherwise, for it would evince an unwillingness to take the little trouble necessary. (B:TC)

I feel there is more to this. For some reason, cupping an object with two hands seems to sanctify it and affect the cupper. *Something flows between person and thing.* I do not know what it is, but I have felt it. A one-handed grip does not satisfy the man who puts his whole heart into his swordsmanship, or the country that understands and admires that type of true dedication. There is no verb for *centering* and being *centered* in Japanese, but it is that English word that comes to mind here.

1. *Swords and Fire Arms.* The standard explanation is that, with fire-arms, heavy armor became useless and heavy swords for hacking were not worth their weight, especially when those new fire-arms (and their stands, etc. were very heavy! Can anyone come up with a more interesting explanation?

1-35+ We wear leather shoes and nobles felt ones;
Nós uzamos de sapatos de couro, e os fildalgos de veludo;

Japanese, high and low, wear sandals made of rice straw.
Os japões altos e baxos de al[pa]rcas feitas de palha d'arroz.

As mentioned earlier, the humidity for Europe is high in the winter and low in the summer, precisely opposite to Japan. In the summer, felt would have been too hot and leather would have given all Japanese ringworm (the bane of GI's in Vietnam, who lost more hours of active duty through this fungus – of the foot, calf and crotch – than to combat injuries!). It pains me to think of what suffering the spread of Western footwear has caused to people who happen to live in places with sultry summers. Yet, the Japanese have not always been so kind to themselves. Illustrations of Classic times (Heian Era (794-1185)) in my "Old Language Dictionary" (*kogojiten:* something all high-school students in Japan have) show four shoes worn by Japanese nobility: one looks like a lacquer-ware pram, one like a brocade canoe, one a leather rain-boot, that would also float and one, of thin cloth, with a boot-like extension and a thin sole for playing kick-ball (*keri*), which was perfectly rectangular.[2] The three remind me of boat-like Korean shoes (which are now often made of pure rubber!) I have worn. All would be excessively hot for much of the year and, I believe, reflect the strong continental (equestrian, dry summer) influence on Japan.[1] That Japanese, in the long run, did not go the way of shoes proves common sense can sometimes beat high fashion.

Frois's "high and low" in the Japanese side of the equation is right, but a bit misleading. Rice straw or not, the finely woven *zori* of the wealthy and the crudely macraméed (?) *waraji* of the poor were stylistically a world apart. The latter was also worn by begging bonzes (low level Buddhist priests), poets, tea-masters, people doing penance, and travelers. Eliza Skidmore:

> For long tramps the foreigner finds the *waraji* and the *tabi,* or digitated stocking, much better than his own clumsy boots, and he ties them on as overshoes when he has rocky paths to climb. (JDS:1891)

Today, this footwear is seldom worn except by old ladies and visiting foreigners. Japanese men have uniformly adopted the style of the West, the West of the Corporation Man and would rather fight athlete's foot than this new convention. Also, they tell me they dare not wear sandals on the subway *for fear of being trod on* – they evidently aren't as brave as women who do not hesitate to wear toeless shoes. And what sandals are found in Japan today are mostly hideous plastic slippers. To me, the footwear situation in Japan (i.e., more West than the West) proves that Japanese do not import things intelligently, as is so often claimed, but for the more common, all-too-human reasons of *prestige value,* i.e., going along with the world leaders.

Frois mentioned "the low" but I think one more contrast might be made concerning the lowest of the low. *Faux* Frois:

> *In Europe, poor people usually can not afford to wear shoes.*
> *In Japan, even the poor always have footwear.*

I do not *know* that European poor went barefoot. I suspect it because of Cruz's observation that *shoes were so cheap many of the poor could walk about shod in China.* Chances are he would not have written that if the poor in Europe had shoes.   While the dirt-poor in Japan, like China, generally were shod, there is one exception: the despised Eta (next to the Imperial family, the only blood lineage, or *caste,* once treated seriously in Japan) who were *not allowed* to wear anything on their feet.   This seems particularly ironic when we recall they slaughtered animals, cured hide and worked leather and might have made leather footwear open or closed (Perhaps this is why Japanese never had leather sandals.)

1. *Heian Summer Shoes.* Would anyone know if nobles had any sandals to wear at this time, or if they only wore those shoes?
2. *Rectangular Shoes for Football?* An active game such as "our" soccer would not work with soft shoes boasting soft corners sticking out.   It would seem to indicate that the flat of the foot (top, bottom or both) were used and the toes were not.   See 14-31 and 14-32.

1-36+   In Europe, a noble would have to be mad to go barefoot before a prince.
Antre nós em Europa seria doudice yr hum fidalgo descalso diante de hum príncipe;

In Japan, it is improper to wear shoes in the presence of any lord.
[Os Japões] tem por mao insino yr calsados diante de quaisquer senhores que sejão.

This is pretty much the same as 20+ above.   I changed "[a mark of] bad learning" (my attempt to approximate the original) to the simple "improper."   Content-wise, it bears noting that thanks to their cooler footwear, Japanese feet/socks would not have stunk as ours certainly would have. Still, considering the facts that feet get dirty when shoes are removed outdoors, I feel that the Occidental practice is the more practical one.   And, since taking off a hat is relatively easy, I cannot help wondering if it encouraged us to treat our equals like superiors.   Who knows but that hat-removing cultures might not have a greater tendency toward equality than shoe-removing cultures.

1-37+   We enter our houses wearing our shoes;
Nós emtramos nas cazas calçados;

In Japan, that is impolite and shoes must be left by the door.
Em Japão hé descortezia e hão-se de deixar os sapatos hà porta.

There seems to be a larger pattern here: the Pacific island cultures with the custom of removing footwear before one's superior also happen to have finely woven matting – usually made by women for their dowries – which required bare feet inside a dwelling.   For cleanliness's sake this had to be.   Japanese matting, *tatami,* may be resilient enough to serve as a judo mat, but the sharp edges on some soles and nail-heads would damage it, and dirt quickly works its way into the weave.

Removing shoes, the Jesuits were quick to discover, could be inconvenient.   As Valignano noted, it meant they could never go anywhere without *komono* (literally "little-people") child-servants "to keep count of the shoes, for to do otherwise was to risk walking home untrod on the street" (letter n.77 in A:VS).   This was not so much because shoes were stolen as they got lost amid hundreds of other shoes at some public places – even today, it can be like trying to find a car in a parking lot – or inadvertently worn away by the wrong party.   The shoe-carriers were still around when the West came back.   Here is Heusken, translator for the first American Ambassador in 1857.

I dismount, preferring to walk, my two samurai, the shoe-bearer [He probably carried straw horse-shoes, too!] and the umbrella-bearer still following me like my own shadow.   I am beginning to realize that grandeur has its disadvantages and that Sancho Panza was right when he divested himself of his governorship . . . The skies, fair so far, are getting overcast. Ah! It's all my fault! Why do I have that person with the umbrella always by my side?   (11/24 H: JJ)

In the Meiji era, I have often read (this could well be legend), many people took off their shoes to board the train and were disappointed not to find them waiting for them when they arrived at their destination. The train ride of modernity safely over, the custom of removing shoes remains. What *tatami* started now applies to carpet and clean wooden floors as well. A fine compromise has been reached between shoe and no shoe. Japanese today generally trade in their Western-style shoes for slippers at the office, and there is often a special rack or container with slipper for guests at homes as well. But all is not well, for unlike the open-heeled traditional *geta* or *zori*, the Western shoe, which modern Japanese seem stuck with, does not easily shake off, so salesmen, messengers and others who for whatever reason do a lot of coming and going are either wizards with the shoe-horn, which usually hangs by the door, or have permanently scrunched down heels! Moreover, the use of indoor slippers makes it harder to remember to slip in and out of the additional pair of slippers reserved for the WC! (There are just too many transfers for absent-minded people!) *Enough boring pragmatism*: Let us see Lowell's more metaphysical reading of this contrast probably repeated in every book ever written on Japan by an Occidental.

> If Japanese ways look odd at first sight, they look but more odd on closer acquaintance. In a land where, to allow one's understanding the freer play of indoor life, one begins, not by taking off his hat, but by removing his boots, he gets at the very threshold a hint that humanity is to be approached the wrong end to. When, after thus entering a house, he tries next to gain admittance to the mind of its occupant, the suspicion becomes a certainty. . . (SFE)

Morse has found the sole exception to the shoes-off-at-the-entrance rule. Like the clothes "folding" (1-16+), it is an instance of the topsy-turvy dead.[1]

> When the body is carried out of the house, the men performing this function do not remove their clogs as they enter or leave; hence, if one is seen trying on his first clogs on the mat, his friend will say, "Please do not do it; it is a bad sign." (JDD)

1. *Topsy-turvy Dead.* The idea of another world, below, where people are upside-down – a topsy-turvy, or inverse reality, or rather, supernatural, that proceeded the idea of a globe – is found in many cultures I am told. I would welcome a gloss (a whole page or two!) from anyone who has researched this.

~~~~~~

1-38+   We roll up only our sleeves to wash our hands and face;
Nós pera lavar as mãos e o rosto arregasamos os pulsos somente;

Japanese bare themselves down to the waist to do the same.
Os Japões pera o mesmo effeito se despem nus da cinta pera sima.

If it is easy to do, and 1-9+ shows it was indeed, stripping to the waist is much more hygienic, for it allows the neck to be included in the face-wash, preventing ring-around-the-collar and, for men, infection of hair follicles.   To restate and enlarge upon a weak contrast, ease of dressing and undressing encouraged cleanliness. Here is Kaempfer, one hundred years after Frois:

> Besides, as they can undress themselves in an instant, so they are ready at a minute's warning to go into the bagnio. For they need but untie their sash, and all their cloaths fall down at once, leaving them quite naked, excepting a small band [loincloth], which they wear close to the body about their waste. (HOJ)

1-39+   The obeisance we show by placing a knee on the ground;
As cortezias [1] *que nós fazemos com pôr hum jiolho no chão;*

> The Japanese show by prostrating themselves, legs, arms and head close to flat on the ground. *Essas fazem os Japões com se pôrem debruços com os pés e mãos e a cabeça quasi no chão.*

Europeans reserved the more extreme forms of two-legged prostration for God or, once in a lifetime, for their goddess: asking a woman's hand in marriage. In the West, it seems that only the Pope lies down on the ground – not quite in the style of the Japanese, who always folded their bodies up as they went down (and unlike Muslims, too, for they reach their arms *out*) – or, rather, asphalt, when he kisses it immediately after getting off the airplane.

As far as I know, the Japanese do not prostrate themselves before their gods. Shinto or Buddhist, they may hold their hands together and lightly nod their head or bow, but that is generally it. There is nothing like our kneeling on both legs. [2] Obeisance toward superiors, especially the most powerful is a different matter. Jesuits in Japan had to learn how to show obeisance in the Japanese manner to survive. See Rodrigues (R(C):TIJ) for more details on bowing. [3]   I shall only add one thing neither Frois and Rodrigues mentioned: the wordless, but auditory element of Japanese obeisance.

> *We bow or kneel silently or while saying appropriate courteous words;.*
> *They do so while making sounds like someone about to expectorate or hissing snakes.*

The first mention of these weird noises which seem to say *"I am tense and awed! I am tense and awed!"* may be by the English Captain Saris: ". . . and then clapping their left hand within their left, they put them downe towards their knees, and so wagging or mouing of their hands a little to and fro, they stooping, steppe with small steps sideling from the partie saluted, and crie *Augh, Augh.*" (LR) Alcock is the first to do the subject full justice:

> . . . suddenly, on some signal apparently, there is a general and long-prolonged silibated sound impossible to describe, something between a '*hiss*' and a long-drawn '*hish-t.*' It seems to circulate through the whole building far and near, and to be echoed through all the courts and corridors; and is supposed I fancy, to indicate some act or movement of the Tycoon bespeaking reverence and a hushed attention. It was immediately after one of these rustlings of the breeze of reverence vibrating through the lips of a thousand silibating courtiers, that I received the signal to advance to the entrance of the council chamber. I have never seen or heard anything like it, or, indeed, in the least resembling this strange but impressive way of bespeaking reverence. (COT, ch19)

Actually, he *had.* Earlier in the book (ch 9), Alcock described how the *Hai! Hei!* and *Ha!* (meaning, "yes, I follow you," "I'm listening") sounds emanated from his prostrate translator, "sometimes from the lips, but oftener from unfathomable recesses low in the throat and hovering between a deep-drawn sigh and an interjection," when listening to a superior. We are talking about *a welling up of awe.* Or, rather of *awe acoustically shared by allowing it to leak over.* Today, we hear something similar on the soundtrack for tensely building movie scenes; but if we heard it from a human, we would say *Relax! You're giving me the creeps!* Earlier yet, Alcock had described holiday greetings, when people "exchanging grave and courteous salutations" uttered

> *with a deep-drawn inspiration,* the depth from whence it was extracted appearing to be in strict relation to the degree of respect they wished to manifest, as though the joy and satisfaction of such a meeting were something too deep for utterance. (A:COT, ch3, *my italics*)

In the mid-nineteenth century, when Japanese still prostrated themselves, but Westerners, who no longer dropped to one knee in the manner described by Frois, experienced mixed feelings not felt in Frois's time, when inequality was taken for granted.   Some may have been delighted to find old-fashioned obeisance – as W.H. Hudson was thrilled to meet a country maid in England who could still do a proper courtesy – and Ian Littlewood cites such delight as a typical Western response to Japan.

> Sir Edwin Arnold showed a similar enthusiasm when praising his daughter's Japanese maid: "In bringing a message . . . or doing anything that is not absolutely instantaneous, she always goes down on her little knees, and often upon her little nose . . . (L:IOJ)

But, from the New World, I think it was more common to find criticism of what Usanians considered to be excessive servility and humiliation. Young Heusken,[4] shortly after arriving in Japan, traveled from the ridiculously far-off town where the Embassy was, to the capitol with the Consul (America's first Ambassador to Japan, Townsend Harris).

> I traveled from Shimoda to Shinagawa [outskirt of Edo/Tokyo], a journey of seven days, admist a kneeling population, while our heralds continually repeated the "*shita ni iro,*" kneel down[!], even in the remotest parts of the forests or on the tops of mountains where there was no one, as if the trees and plants should pay homage to the Embassy of the Republic Par Excellence. The sight of all these human beings, as good as I am or even better, on their knees began to disgust me. Here a white-haired old man bent his trembling knees and lowered his venerable brow; there a young girl turned her lovely face towards the ground and remained in a humiliating posture. It is certainly an excessive honor to see all the beauties of Japan on their knees before oneself; but this honor did not please me; if I had been allowed at least to kneel with her, this thing would have had a different complexion. (H(V&W):JJ)

Today, Japanese still occasionally suck air and make strange noises in the presence of superiors, and bow to each other; but they no longer prostrate themselves.

---

1. *Cortezias.* The French translation is "make our reverences." It is hard to settle on a word. "Obeisance" is a bit too strong, but "courtesies" would be too weak for some obedience is involved.

2. *Showing Reverence to Gods.* I would like to know more about the body-language of reverence used by Japanese in Shinto and in various Buddhist sects.

3. *Bowing by Jesuits*. This is so important a matter that I am embarrassed to admit at this stage, I am still not sure how much bowing the Jesuits did before the rulers of Japan. They were able to accept bowing as a courtesy and later in China even accepted bowing before name tablets of ancestors to show respect, so long as the tablets had nothing about spirits written on them . . . but I do not know how they felt about low-bowing (prostrating themselves) before rulers of Japan? Was it part of Accommodation? In England, the low obeisance of the Catholics was conflated with the Oriental practice as paryt of the general denigration of the "Papists."

4. *Heusken* This is not the first quote from Heusken and it will not be the last. Judging from the journal of this young translator who was cut down by a Japanese assassin long before he reached his potential, I feel that had he lived he probably would have become the first Occidental to understand and write haiku.

~~~~~~

1-40+   We wear hats of thick cloth that are square or round.
Nós uzamos de barretes de cantos ou redondos de pano;

> Japanese ones are silk, some pointed and others shaped like bags.
> *Os Japões de barretes de seda, huns agudos e outros feitos hà feisão de sacos.*

I do not see much of a contrast between the hats as Frois describes them, unless he means that ours with their corners and roundness are real geometric forms, while theirs are ugly points and bags.

Moreover, the great poet Bashô, who was born about the time Frois wrote, is usually shown wearing a hat the shape of a cake about two layers high. It is neither pointed, nor bag-like. Before and after Frois wrote there was a never-ending gallery of hats in Europe and Japan that defy easy contrast. To my mind, the ancient Japanese (but not in Frois's time) boasted more phallic hats than Europe ever knew and the Europeans of Frois's day sometimes sported broader flat hats than ever seen in Japan, where broad hats were always functional (umbrella-like). That is interesting for it contradicts/offsets the vertical bias of the West and the horizontal bias of Japan.

~~~~~~~~~~~~~~~~~~~~~~4~~~~~~

1-41+   With us, a patch is a lowly thing;
Antre nós hum remendo é couza mui baxa;

> In Japan, even princes put a high value on kimonos and *dobuku* [vests worn outside] made of nothing but patches. *Em Japão estima hum principe em muite hum quimão ou dobuqu todo feito de remendos.*

..

Sixteenth-century Japanese were hardly into grunge. The tea masters and poet-aesthetes were wild about patchwork, mostly of old brocade and other fine material (including not a little gold) and some nobles liked to be "in." This patchwork (*hagi*) was a far cry from that of the poor. The rage apparently became an aesthetic tradition of sorts; two hundred years later, Issa writes of a similar patchwork of paper kimonos – the poor man's winter dress – which was glued rather than sewn together from a collage of *hanko*, reusable paper scraps from old books, calendars, paintings, manuscript, etc..

kiritsuki no bi o tsukushitaru kamiko kana – issa (d.1823)

milking the beauty
of collage for all it's worth
this paper robe

~~~~~~

1-42+   In Europe, all our cloth is cut with scissors.
Em Europa todo vestido se corta com tizoura;

In Japan, all is cut by blades.
Em Japão todo se corta com faca.

I have had tiny *shears*, which is to say, cutting blades where the fulcrum is the end of the handle – or, tong-blades – introduced to me as "Japanese scissors." [1] They are beautiful for their simplicity but hard to keep in correct trim, so it is easy to see why knives were preferred. A specific knife (*monotachigatana* ("thing-cut-off-sword")) or, simply, *monotachi*) was indeed used for tailoring in Japan. So why didn't the Japanese use *real* scissors – i.e., two blades on a common fulcrum between the handles and blades, that opening make a cross? Logically speaking, if one blade is sharp enough – and Japanese were the best blade-makers in the world – two are not needed. Still, it is doubtful that most Japanese could have afforded a razor-sharp knife blade and it is puzzling that a culture where something as complex as guns were copied=learned=adopted in a jiffy did not adopt scissors from the Chinese. Or, did Chinese, too, not have them? Did the prior use of chopsticks strengthen the fingers and improve coordination enough to do away with the need for the small tongs with fulcrums that preceded the invention of such scissors elsewhere? [2]

Logic alone is not a good way to do history; I googled for true scissors in China and Japan. In chronological order. The *Hakata-gasami*, scissors made in Hakata (North Kyushu) was said to have come from Sung China about 700 years ago [3] (sounds more like early Yûan, to me), was sold as *Tôgasami*, or Chinese scissors (for, in Japan, Tô=Tang (Dynasty) was used to mean China/ese), improved in some details by sword-making technology in the Tokugawa era and came to be called its current name in the late nineteenth century. The *Tanega-basami,* bear the name of Tanegashima, the island where Portuguese introduced the gun to Japan in 1543. It is thought that Ming Chinese traders aboard the ships taught the islanders how to make scissors (hardly likely – if you ask me they just reproduced them), and these scissors are supposed to bear the unique ability to sharpen themselves with each use. [4] So, scissors probably did exist here and there in Frois's Japan, but had not yet caught on.

1. *Shears vs Scissors* We tend to think of shears as large scissors – scissors where more than one finger is wraps around or goes through the handle – but, the technologist defines them by the location of the fulcrum. Shears are tong-like scissors. The Japanese *hasami* written one way includes not only "shears" and "scissors," but [nail] "clippers" and hole "punches" – that is to say any blades that cut by squeezing together. Its homophone (actually the same word) written another way includes all pincer-like activity and its opposite, i.e. squeezing between something.

2. *Need for Tongs in Japan* Later, I found out that scissoring tongs were used for making swords and *sembei* (a type of thin, very hard cracker roasted in a waffle-iron type device), so the basic technology of the fulcrum between handle and object was extant.

3. *Age of Chinese Scissors.* While I would expect scissors to be in China for over a millennium, for they are found in the Classical world, the only date I could find other than that mentioned for Hakata scissors was 1651, when the recently defunct "Pock-marked King" (Wang Mazi) Scissors Factory opened for business in Beijing. (information on older Chinese scissors anyone?)

4. *Remarkable Scissors in Japan.* According to a Googled article (LR) by someone who had apparently not heard of the *Tanega-basami* and *Hakata-gasami,* the earliest true Japanese scissors were produced after the Opening of Japan in the mid-nineteenth century by a sword-maker who lost his job to modernization. Yajyûrô Yoshida (called Yakichi) a disciple of a sword-smith of Edo, Kinzou Kozukahara,) and his ten disciples and their disciples made such good scissors that all the scissors companies of Tokyo have inherited his technique, borrowed from sword-making. Questioned as to why it mattered whether one bought a Western scissors or a *wasei*, or Japanese-made scissors, the craftsman replied: "Japanese scissors are very sharp in the blades and the two blades are filed very lightly. So it's easier to cut clothing materials. (*What about the scissors from overseas?*) They are made in different ways with different materials and the blades are filed heavily. This is enough for the foreigners. (*Can Japanese people use them [Western scissors]?*) It's not impossible, but the hand will get tired. Tailors won't be able to use them. (*How do the foreigners use them?*) They have bigger hands and more power so they want to feel that their hands are actually cutting. On the other hand, Japanese people hold the scissors with four fingers and they want to cut lightly."

1-43+ In Europe, it would be considered effeminate for a man to carry and use a fan; *Em Europa se teria por cousa afiminada trazer hum homem abano e abanar-se com elle;*

In Japan, a man always has a fan in his belt and would be considered vulgar and wretched otherwise. *Em Japão hé baixeza e miseria não o trazer sempre na sinta e uzar delle.*

The original says a man would not "fan" (*abanar-se*) a fan (*abano*). Because "fan a fan" doesn't work in English, I changed the verb to "use." But using *fan* as a verb would bring out "our" attitude better, for *fanning* suggests "fluttering," a fine and, therefore, feminine movement. If you have ever faced a large barracuda fanning its fins, you can imagine a samurai with a fan would look tough enough, even if the fan itself was rarely if ever used as a lethal weapon (as shown on Japanese TV Easterns).

Lacking air-conditioning, only a masochist of either sex could summer in muggy Japan without a fan. The same thing could be said of most of South East Asia. That might seem the end of it. But fans, like so much "simple" technology, are no one-trick wonder like air conditioning; they were good for many things.

Among the men, the fan serves a great variety of purposes: visitors receive the dainties offered them upon it; and the beggar, imploring charity, holds out his fan for the alms his prayers may have obtained. The fan serves the dandy in lieu of a whalebone switch; the pedagogue instead of a ferule for the offending schoolboy's knuckles; . . . a fan presented upon a peculiar kind of salver to the high-born criminal, is said to be the form of announcing his death-doom, his head being struck off the moment he stretches it towards this emblem of his fate. (B:MCJ:1841)

The *gumbai uchiwa*, heavy war fans, often with iron or bronze outer-sticks, went with each suit of armor; and the oblong *uchiwa* [*uchiwa*: a fixed, rather than folding fan], descending from priests to *No* dancers and to umpires in games and contests . . . . Fans serve an infinite variety of purposes and speak a language in this land of their own, and no season or condition of life is without its ministrations. The farmer winnows his grain with a fan, the housewife blows up the charcoal fire with a fan, and gardeners, sitting for hours on patient heels, will softly fan half-open flowers until every petal unfolds. For specific gifts, specific designs and colors appear. One fan may be offered to a lady as a declaration of love. Another serves as her sign of dismissal, and the Japanese are often amused to see foreigners misapply the language and etiquette of fans. (S:JDJ:1891)

..
With all these functions, it is surprising Frois only made two contrasts (this one and 14-3) involving fans. A hundred years after TRATADO, Kaempfer described yet another function not mentioned by Frois or the above writers.

The Japanese of both sexes never go abroad without fans, as we Europeans seldom do without gloves. Upon their journeys they make use of the fan, which hath the roads printed upon it, and tells them how many miles they are to travel, what inns they are to go to, and what price victuals are at. (HOJ)

As Japan was officially *closed* at this time, the Dutch were not permitted "at least publickly, to buy any of these fans" or "road books" sold by "poor children begging along the road. Morse in 1877 could, and he further described a fan that was a complete Baeddecker. His page of observations includes the observation that fans are used to cool down hot soup – it *does* look more civilized than blowing on it! – and that "an oil-paper fan is dipped in water and thus, in fanning, the air is cooled." (M:JDD)

This last type of fan apparently didn't survive the electric age. But fans are still far more common in Japan than in the USA. They are distributed free in the dog-day *bon* dances – folk dances which survive in all parts of Japan (but are actually better in Honolulu's Palolo Valley than the Tokyo area, where only little children and elderly women do much dancing). The fans are used for some dances, but are mostly for cooling off or sitting on. The only two I clearly remember were graced with the face of an actor and florescent fireflies on one side, and an advertisement for a local store and a warning on safe driving, respectively on the other. (They made good coal shovels for dancing the *tanko-bushi.*)

If, for the sake of argument, fan usage were to be modified, the adjective "effeminate" would have to be dropped in favor of *elderly*. Constant fanning in Japan was *especially* identified with old age, for the elderly were more likely to have their hands free. Old man Issa haikus his young wife Kiku considerately "sticking a fan into his rear" (under his belt or in his loin-cloth) as he heads out. Other haiku tell us *why*: he couldn't buy them as fast as he lost them! I would guess, his fan was mostly used to jot down haiku, for Japanese spies and "spies upon the spies" in 1858 covered their fans with long notes of what they saw on a visiting Western ship (M:BGE), unlike the Chinese who, the Marquis de Moges wrote, came aboard only to sell things.

For all of this, only the *folding fan* [1] would seem to come from Japan. As with many things, much if not most of this complex fan-culture goes back to China.. This is reflected in the fact that

Ball's THINGS CHINESE waxes at far greater length on this subject than Chamberlain's THINGS JAPANESE.   The variety of fans is stupendous. It covers all the Japanese ones – even maps – but the War Fan (and that might just be an omission), and mentions not only round but "octagonal, sexagonal, or polygonal" shaped screen fans; the materials range from the usual bamboo and paper to silk actually spun on the frame by the silk-worm (!), the palm leaf, and goose-feathers arranged in bone or ivory handles in a lyre shape, to huge imitation wooden fans used to prevent officials from seeing one another and having to stop when meeting on the highway and, most incredible, fans of pure air, which is to say "open-work spaces are left in walls of the shape."

Still, the most fantastic *imagined use* of the fan is found in Japanese literature (if the risqué popular poetry of the Edo era may be so called). There was a fabled "Woman's Island" where women did without men and impregnated themselves, as Aristotle? Pliny? claimed some animals did, by the wind.   Some hilarious pornographic prints show these women exposing themselves to – i.e., in congress with – the sea-breeze. The horny *senryu* poets, most of whom lived in the 80% male city of Edo, combined the legend with one of their favorite themes (masturbation by either sex) to come up with: *Nyôgô no harikata kosaetaru Mieidô,* which transliterates as "Woman-Island's dildo/s constructs Mieido" meaning *the famous Kyoto fan shop Mieidô makes and exports fans for masturbatory use on Woman's Island when the love-wind is not blowing!* and might be versed:

> *doldrum's cure*
>
> the isle of women
> custom-made dildos
> from mieidô!

In 1858, great numbers of English got all the information on the fan found in Kaempfer and the 1841 compilation by Mrs. William Busk by reading William Dalton's well-researched children's book: THE ENGLISH BOY IN JAPAN, *or the perils and adventures of Mark Raffles among the princes, priests, and people of that singular empire.* The paragraph in question begins

> Mark had to go through a course of lessons in the fan exercise; -- no unimportant item, I can assure you, in a country where the people take to fans as ducks do to water, and where a man without a fan would be even a greater oddity than a man without a head; for in Japan the latter is not at all uncommon. All wear the fan – ladies, soldiers, and priests. (D:EBJ)

In Europe, the oddest piece of fan-lore found in the course of researching this book comes from an undated work by the Counselor to the King of France, Englished in 1635. It is of a quite different nature from what we have seen so far, and makes me suspect some men in France, at least, fanned.

> Q -- From whence comes it that where motion chaseth the Ayre, we refresh our Selves, nevertheless when we are hot, in beating the Ayre with our hats, hand-cerchiffs, or Fannes?

> A -- It is that in so moving and beating the Ayre, we chase behind us, that which was formerly chased, and that which succeedeth and followeth suddenly after the other, is more fresh; for there is nothing voide in nature. (D:R)

---

1. *Folding Fan and Other Fans*.   In Japanese, there is not one word for fan, but a multitude of words. A folding fan is a *sensu,* a solid one an *uchiwa* or an *ogi* (I forget the subtle difference between the two), and an electrical fan a *senpuki.* If you ask someone to, say, "turn on the *sensu,*" they would not know what you meant.

1-44+ With us, nobles and princes are preceded by torches of wax
Antre nós se uza de tochas de sera que vão diante dos fidalgos e principes;

In Japan, they are made from long bundles of old, dry cane[1] or bundles of straw.
Em Japão de molhos de canas velhas, seqas, compridas, ou molhos de palhas.

While Japanese commonly used portable lanterns by this time, the torch, as the ancient method, was probably considered more proper for nobility engaged in ceremony. The common Japanese term for torch is *taimatsu,* literally, "pine-light," because pine resin was generally the fuel, though it was not always rubbed on to pine. The straw might have been crudely bound by peasants, but a proper torch had it bound up within a bamboo framework.

This is one of the ten items Frois gives as an example of misinterpretation of terms in the Prologue to his missing summary of Japan. He writes that if it were reported that Nobunaga [the Shogun] met the Visitador [Valignano] on such and such a mountain in the light of "two thousand torches" a person would "have to know that they were not of wax, . . . because there is no beeswax in Japan and Japanese torches are made from straw;" and "likewise for India" when a "torch" is mentioned they are talking about a lamp of oil and not beeswax, "so from the European point of view, they are not torches." (J/F:Historia v.1) Linguistically, Frois has made an interesting point, but I may be missing something, for this still seems a piddling contrast to me unless the bee's wax has some lofty significance whereas cane and straw seem humble and even wretched materials to "us."

1. Cane? Bamboo? The other translations make the *canas* "bamboo," (the standard translation), but that would not explain the "bundles:" one piece of bamboo is enough! I think it is the finger-thick bamboo I call "cane" and Japanese call "arrow-bamboo" (see 7-23 re. *yadake*) in that it is segmented and has somewhat bamboo-like leaves and is hollow. It grows to about ten feet tall, dries in place and is easy to gather. But it might be made from the branches of *bona fide* bamboo, as are brooms. Anyone to carry the torch for me?

1-45+ In Europe, one would be strangely regarded for baring so much as one leg to warm himself before a fire. *Em Europa descobrir hum pé ao fogo pera se hum aqentar estranha-se;*

Japanese warming themselves, stand and openly bare their entire posteriors to the fire, without feeling any shame. *Em Japão quem estaa im pé ao fogo pera se aquentar descobre em claro sem pejo toda a trazeira.*

The eccentric Zen abbot Sengai, who lived in Issa's time, painted himself doing just that, with his testicles in plain view; and, punning on their euphemistic name, "golden gems," wrote an accompanying poem about breaking out the gold for all the world to share! (*kintama-o uchi-akete . . .*) (LR).[1]

Had Frois been writing in England fifty years earlier, the contrast might have been a bit more difficult. According to a Law passed by King Edward VI in 1548, "Any knight under the rank of a lord, or any other person [is forbidden to wear] any gowne, jaket or cloke unless it be of sufficient length on a man standing upright to cover his privy member and buttokkes." (from A. Parsons: FACTS AND PHALLUSES, 1990) But Europe turned prudish while lack of shame with respect to revealing ones private parts in a non-sexual connection survived Japan's feudal era to shock the nineteenth century West. It was one thing for fishermen to toss books with dirty pictures up to Perry's Black Ships to the joy of the sailors and the anger of the ship chaplain – ports are known for such behavior – and quite another to have a "respectable Japanese" gentleman at home open up his robe and, "taking his privities in his hand," ask "the names of the various parts in English" in plain sight of his mother, wife and daughter, as reported to the first American ambassador to Japan by his highly reputed Dutch-American translator-secretary Heusken! (THE COMPLETE JOURNAL OF TOWNSEND HARRIS: Jan. 21, 1857). (I should add that Japanese to whom I've related this story generally do not believe it, but I find Heusken and Harris very reliable reporters, so I provide it with the date!)

On the other hand, 19th century Japanese found the décolletage of Western women – not to mention emphasizing the figure by various devices – shameful in the extreme and, at first, even took umbrage at the showing of nudes in painting exhibitions, because they had no similar tradition of figure worship. (If the Japanese were as rude to *us* as we were to them, they would surely have called us a *figure-idolizing culture.*)

1. *Proper Use of a Fire.* But, by far the best writing on *how to properly warm oneself before a fire* is found in either Zora Neale Hurston's autobiography, *Dust Tracks on a Road,* or her masterpiece *Of Mules and Men.* I would introduce a passage here but poverty has stranded these books, with 90% of my library, in Japan. So, you will just have to take my word for it or go to the library, where you will find either book worth a read!).

1-46+ We consider it effeminate for a noble to look in the mirror;
Antre nós ver-se hum fidalgo a hum espelho se tem por obra afeminada;

Japanese nobles all have their mirrors to dress in front of.
Os fidalgos japões pera se vestirem tem commumente todos espelho diante de si.

Okada notes that even *Hagakure,* the classic manual for the samurai revival of the Edo era, recommends that warriors use a mirror to make certain they are properly dressed and groomed. He adds that looking at the mirror at least once before going out was thought to ward off potential disaster. I would add that the mirror was considered an instrument of self-knowledge, purity and cleansing. As part of the Shinto tradition, a gift from the gods; and identified with the redeeming light of the moon=buddha, its use by either sex was not thought to be narcissistic but, rather, *reflective* in the best meaning of the word. But, religion, philosophy and psychology apart, the use of a mirror was hardly surprising for men who spent so much time grooming:

They spend whole mornings combing and tying up their hair, smoothing it with great pains and anointing it with scented oils, to make it glisten. And if anyone unluckily happens to touch this hair-tuft... (Carletti in TCJ)

Basically, Japanese men resembled "our" ancient Celts, warriors who bleached their hair in lime-water and painted their eyelids black, the major difference being that the Celts paid more attention to muscular development and were reported to punish young men who exceeded "the standard measure of the girdle." (Peter Beresford Ellis: *Celtic Women* Constable 1995) By Frois's time, European men were evidently not supposed to care about their own appearance, though the paintings of the time suggest that not a few men did sneak looks into mirrors.

1-47+ With us, one would have to be joking or mad to clothe oneself in paper;[1]
Antre nós vestir-se hum de papel seria escarnio ou doudice;

In Japan, bonzes and many nobles wear paper [dress] with a silk front and sleeves.
Em Japão bonzos e muitos senhores se vestem de papel com a dianteira e mangas de seda.

On the one hand, paper was a high fashion material (1-41+). Robes made of fancy paper (glued together with devil's tongue paste) with a fine lacquered finish (persimmon sap), they were evidently a luxury item in Frois's time. On the other hand, paper robes called *kamiko* soon came to be associated with elderly poets and prostitutes. Believe it or not, the haiku association (i.e. seasonality) of the *kamiko* is with *winter*. (In the 1960's, I once went out with a girl wearing a paper dress. It was summertime. New Orleans. Sultry)   Recall that winter is the driest part of the year in Japan, so the paper would not dampen.   And, as the homeless know, many layers of paper make remarkably good insulation. There is another angle that Frois may have missed, which is given by Thunberg in 1776:

> A kind of a thick paper, which was of a brownish colour, with several single darkish streaks printed on it, was sold as a rarity. Several pieces, of more than a foot square, were pasted very neatly together, and were said to be used as night-gowns. These night-gowns . . . were worn by very old people only, and that in the cold season of the year, when they do not perspire, and over one or two other night-gowns. It was said, that young people were absolutely forbidden to wear them. As this dress was neither durable, or indeed necessary for want of clothing, it rather denoted the great age of those that were permitted to wear it. (T:TEAA)

~~~~~~

1-48+   What we would take for house-wear,
Ho que antre nós hé trazer roupão por caza, –

> This the Japanese use [to dress up?], wearing sleeveless *dobuqu* [vest/s] over *katabira* [robe/s].   *Disto uzão os Japões vestindo sobre as* catabiras dobuqus *sem mangas.*

I may well be wrong. [1] All other translations I have seen (Japanese, German and French) are as follows:

> When we would wear house-wear;
> The Japanese wear sleeveless *dobuku* [vests] over *katabira.*

The other translations seem a bit closest to the Portuguese but that makes the contrast a mere indoor repetition of 1-4+, i.e. Japanese wear vests over their robes while we do not. At the very least it needs to be supplemented: *The Japanese wear the same dobuku* [vests] over *katabira* they wear to go out. But as long as we are having to supplement information to make sense of it, is it not possible that by *vestindo* here Frois may not only mean dressing/dressed but *dressed up* as opposed to what one wears inside?   Either way, I think we *need* an *indoor* vs *outdoor* contrast. Montanus in 1670 wrote "they wear a Coat or Tunick of various Colours reaching to their Ankles, with which they go loose within doors; but going abroad, they tie like long Breeches about their legs." (M:EEJ) That is a bit off, but it *is* an *in* and *out* contrast. L' Abbe de T. in 1705 does even better:

> When we go abroad, we commonly put on Cloaks and Hats; they on the contrary wear Cloaks in the House, and lay them aside when they go to Town, and put on a large sort of Hose [*tabi?*], which they throw off presently at their return. (A:HCJ)

..

A note by Golownin's editor suggests something even more contrary: *"They [the Japanese] wear habits of ceremony or their Sunday clothes in the house: but lay them aside in going out."* (G:MCJ)   Could Frois have been driving at something like this –

> *Where we put on informal clothing at home and our best clothing to go out;*
> *They get dressed up to stay home but not to go out.*

– but got lost in particulars? This makes sense considering Japanese weather and because, as Frois notes elsewhere (14-34), "we" tend to do our entertaining in public while the Japanese do it at home.   Okada writes the *dobuku* was *de rigor* for what would be called professionals today: magistrates, doctors and tea-masters. The question here is whether they wore them inside – i.e. dressing up at home – while practicing their profession, outside, or both.

1. *I May Be Wrong.* Because the Japanese translators know more about Japan than I do, I suspect that for all of this my translation is wrong, but I want to encourage Japanese to think about it just in case.   日本人の専門家よろしく！胴服を帷子のうえにかけたとしたら、家の中のもの？外へ行くためのもの？など。。。

~~~~~~

1-49+   We wash our clothing scrubbing it with our hands;
Antre nós se lava a roupa esfregando-a com as mãos;

>   The Japanese wash, kicking the laundry with their feet.
>   *Em Japão a lavão pizando-a aos couces com os pees.*

I know by experience – years without a washing machine – that it is *remarkably* easy to stamp laundry clean in a bathtub. Not only are leg muscles bigger but the weight of the body can be put to work. Unfortunately, better clothing requires hand-eye coordination, so all cannot be washed that way. More recently, I discovered that the women in Edinburgh were known for washing by foot. Thomas Hood (H: WTH), the elder:

>   In walking one morning I came to the green,
>   Where the manner of washing in Scotland is seen;
>   And I thought it perhaps would amuse, should I write,
>   A description of what seemed a singular sight.
>   Here great bare-legged women were striding around,
>   And watering cloths that were laid on the ground.
>   While, on t'other hand, you the lasses might spy
>   In tubs, with their petticoats up to the thigh,
>   And, instead of their hands, washing thus with their feet,
>   Which they often will do in the midst of the street,
>   Which appears quite indelicate, – shocking, indeed,
>   To those ladies who come from the south of the Tweed! (dec. 1815 v10)

Okada says that most washing in Japan was done by hand (I would concur, for I have never known a Japanese to wash by foot, but come to think of it, I was in Edinburgh and saw no washer-women either) and that Frois is simply going for the contrast.   In Korea, a real contrast with Europe would have been easier to find, for most laundry was *pounded* clean or swung into smooth rocks in rivers.   In Japan, where bright white cloth was rarely seen, vigorous pounding was reserved for new silken-cloth. It was called *kinuta* ("clothes-board) and was the most common human sound found in haiku (No matter where a poet hears it, he thinks of *momma* or his hometown!) Be that as it may, the *hand* versus *foot* Topsy-Turvy Sweepstake goes elsewhere, i.e., to Herodotus:

>   *They [the Egyptians] knead dough with their feet, but mud with their hands, and they lift dung with their hands.*

I guess the Greeks kneaded the other way around. The dung would seem a gratuitous dig unless Greeks lifted it with their feet!

1-50+   We carry our handkerchiefs and tissue in our pockets or sleeves;
Nós trazemos lencos e papeis na aljibeira ou manga;

The Japanese stuff it into their bosom; the more there, the more gallant.[1]
Os Japões tudo trazem metido no seio, e quanto mais alevantado é mais primor.

"Our" *pockets* (*aljibeira=algibeira*) are a problem.   If the same *aljibeira* did not appear in 51+, "purse" would be the more likely translation.   The reason is that the transition from an external purse to an internal pocket was not finished and the word applied to both.   But even that is not quite right, for the first pockets were often purses worn within one's clothing and reached through an unmarked slit.   Unfortunately, even the vocabulary escapes me.   Take this googled sentence elaborating 16th century garments "with pockets" ("with" meaning built-in) found in Arnold's *Patterns of Fashion*:

> "Most of them are hidden in the side-seams, but the paned slops worn by Don Garcia, a pair of Venetians, and all of the *pluderhosen* have pockets, done in several different styles." (from Stefan's Florilegium pants-msg - 11/10/98)

If that is not enough, the most common pocket of the time may well have been (in the words of Chaucer's Wife of Bath) "his nether purs," which is to say the codpiece! As might be expected, Shakespeare played with these baubles:

> Enter AUTOLYCUS.

> 'twas nothing to geld a codpiece of a purse; . . .   and had not the old man come in with a whoo-bub against his daughter and the king's son, and scared my choughs from the chaff, I had not left a purse alive in the whole army. *Winter's Tale* 4-3

Sleeves are also a problem.   While I knew how Japanese carry things in *their* capacious sleeves (which Frois left out so as not to spoil the contrast!), I thought *our* practice was confined to magicians, so I had to google for that, too.   My first find was Rabelais, who, as might be expected, was also big on codpieces (Gargantua's "purse" was made from the cod of an elephant, and others he drew were so large as to require wheels, etc.), and my second, *Webster's*.   Respectively:

> After dinner Panurge went to see her, carrying in his sleeve a great purse full of palace-crowns, called counters, and began to say unto her, "Which of us two loveth other best, you me, or I you?"

> *To have in one's sleeve* is to offer a person's name for a vacant situation. Dean Swift, when he waited on Harley, had always some name in his sleeve. The phrase arose from the custom of placing pockets in sleeves. These sleeve-pockets were chiefly used for memoranda, and other small articles. (www.websters-dictionary-online.org/ definition/english/sl/sleeve.html)

Seeing neither illustration nor further description of these sleeve-pockets, I can not say, for example, whether people first rose their hands when they were held up so as to dump the contents. But, I think this is enough on the European side of the contrast: in Japan, the sash about the lower belly turns the entire garment above the waist into an enormous pocket.   Rodrigues describes it as "the bosom formed by the two sides of the robe." (R(C):TIJ) The contents were by no means limited to tissue. Okada cites two Tokugawa era sources – one Japanese and one Russian (Goncharov?) – marveling over the way men turned their kimono into "warehouses" or "entire stores full of goods!" Even "cakes from receptions" were mixed in with a list of items putting the twentieth century woman's purse to shame!   Isabella Bird, in the 19th century, makes it clear that some of the goods were heavy:

> Men sometimes carry their children in the fronts of their dresses, and I have seen as many as seven books and a map taken out of the same capacious reservoir. (B:UTJ)

One wonders if the Japanese were not the model for Jonathon Swift's philosophical linguists at the Grand Academy of Lagado who carried everything on their person. Bird also noted how sleeves were used "for stowing away all sorts of things" – "I call them bags, for the sides are sewn up from the lower end to a short distance below the arms." She means sewn up perpendicular to the arm if the arms are held out. She also notes a gruesome use for sleeves. Women were ashamed to hang themselves like men, so when a woman wished to kill herself out of "a sense of shame, lovers' quarrels . . . the loss of personal charms through age or illness" etc. those sleeve bags came in handy:

> In these cases they usually go out at night, and after filling their capacious hanging sleeves with stones, jump into a river or well. I have passed two wells which are at present disused in consequence of recent suicides. (B:UTJ)

There may have been a closer equivalent to this Japanese bosom-stuffing in the West than the sleeves and/or pockets/purses mentioned by Frois. In 1653, Bulwer wrote of the capacious breeches comprising the best part of "the garbe of old English Gallantry," about whom a "Chronologer" wrote "that they bestowed more cost of their Arses than they did on the rest of their whole body. These breeches were aped – to use the English critics favorite term – from the continent, where the thighs of male breeches got so fat on the inner as well as outer thigh that men had to walk bow-legged. Evidently the idea of stuffing that originated in the common practice of bolstering one's manhood expanded to encompass the entire garment. A man who fell astray of sartorial law against "wearing Bayes [*baize* = a fine cloth introduced by Dutch and French fugitives in the 16th century and subject to sumptuary restrictions, for even the types of cloth people wove was regulated!] stuffed in their Breeches" stands in court before a judge and –

> began to excuse himselfe of the offense, and endeavouring by little and little to discharge himselfe of that which he did weare within them, he drew out of his breeches a paire of Sheets, two Table Cloaths, ten Napkings, foure Shirts, a Brush, a Glasse, and a Combe, Night-caps, and other things of use, saying, (all the Hall being strewed with this furniture) your Highnesse may understand, that because I have no safer store-house, these pockets do serve me for a roome to lay up my goods in, and though it be a straight prison, yet it is a store-house big enough for them, for I have many things more of value yet within it. And so his discharge was accepted and well laughed at . . . (B:A) [2]

1. Gallant and Primor: Frois constantly uses the term *primor*. Here, he wrote the more junk stuffed in the bosom, the more *primor*. The only perfect equivalent I can think of is the slangy "cool." I first used "dandier," but after reading too many old English texts, settled on *gallant* instead, because it seemed to me more befitting the martial age. DR, on the other hand, favored *dandier* as "more consistent with Frois's thoroughly male-gendered perspective on reality." There are other good reasons to favor either word.

2. Capacious Breeches. In Bulwer's anecdote, the man proves he is neither smuggler, nor show-off but either homeless or a hermit crab. We will return to these breeches later, for within decades of TRATADO, they were put to use smuggling things into Japan. I am careful to include our outlandish side lest telling of the Japanese side makes them seem *particularly* strange.

1-51+   We use pockets;
Antre nós se uza de aljibeiras;

The Japanese, small purses suspended from the belt.
Os Japões de bolsinhas pinduradas da sinta.

Because of this contrast, we may guess the *algibeiras* in 1-50+ are probably *bona fide* pockets in or under the clothes. The strings by which the Japanese pouches dangled were the purse strings, so they kept closed naturally. These strings wrapped around the *obi* sash or simply passed under it. To prevent the purses from slipping off, a counter-weight large enough not to slip or be easily tugged through the space between belt and belly (it would catch on the edge of the belt) was tied to the other end of the string. This is the *netsuke,* collected throughout the world today for the fine miniature carving. The pouches were made of leather, cotton or wood (with the last, the two strings pass through the lid).   The advantage of a pouch as opposed to a pocket is that they rarely spill things when you sit or lie down. Perhaps for this reason Japanese did not adopt the pocket from the Portuguese or, later, the Dutch. When the West returned 250 years after Frois, pockets were still eye-opening. Morse:

> You try to effect indifference, and yet you are guilty of performing acts specially to excite their attention, such as turning your pockets inside out in search of something, for a pocket in Japanese clothing is as unknown to them as it is to a woman nowadays; you raise a laugh by some gesture of annoyance; sometimes you find you are making a fool of yourself, when all the time the effort is to appear calm and natural. (M:JDD)

1-52+   A purse in Europe is used to carry money;
As bolsas servem em Europa de trazer dinheiro;

In Japan, that of a noble or soldier serve for scent, medicine and flint.
Em Japão as dos fildalgos e soldados servem de cheiros, mezinhas e pederneira.

Japanese men, especially nobles, were *very* big on scent. If the TALE OF GENJI is any indication, they used to roam about all night making love to their women, leaving a personal scent trails that could be identified by others a whole day later. Unlike tom cats, the scent was pleasant to most, though rivals no doubt thought it stank to high heaven! A generation after Frois wrote, I am afraid tobacco was the main scent left by all men, gentry or peasant. Bird noted – after her translator tripped and cut his head on the brazier while trying to get a light! – that Japanese men even woke up for a puff at night!   Medicine might be carried in a wooden or enameled purses, if such is the right word for them. Frois might also have mentioned "purses" for writing equipment (to which pipes would soon be added). We shall return to *flint* later. Not everyone was allowed to carry it. With all this hanging paraphernalia, we may guess that if Japanese had pick-pockets, they were evidently not so common as in Europe!

1-53+   We bathe at home to completely avoid the eyes of others;
Antre nós a jente lava o corpo em suas cazas muito escondido;

In Japan, man, woman or bonze, they bathe in a public bath or, by night, in front of their homes. *Em Japão homens, molheres e bonzos em banhos publicos ou à noite aas suas portas.*

In a discussion of transparent *katabira* and skimpy loincloths, Rodrigues wrote "in this respect, the Japanese are not very bashful by nature" and that neither nobles or common folk felt shame in stripping to their loin-cloths or birthday suits for wrestling or "other activities which require the body to be naked or nude." (R(C):TIJ) Some modesty may be natural to our species, but I think it safe to say, "we" are in the cultural minority, i.e. the weird ones here. The Christian mythology of shame and sin made Europe, once a land of naked Pics and barely robed Greeks, pathologically averse to nudity, even as we continued to worship the ideal human body! Still, we were not always the filthy hydrophobic barbarians shown in the movie *Shogun*, either.   Europe once enjoyed public baths. Unlike the Japanese bath, which was primarily a place for bathing, European baths (or baths in parts of Europe, anyway) were once entertainment centers.   Renaissance paintings show people of both sexes sitting in tubs eating and drinking off boards, with musical accompaniment!   14th century England seems quite Japanese:

> Men and women could go naked, or nearly naked, through the street to the baths in a way which today would be impossible, except perhaps at a bathing resort, or for undergraduates living out of college at one of the major British universities. (LR: know date because of this: "The daughters of the nobility thought it an honour to parade naked in front of Charles V.")

Unfortunately, these baths were put out of business by the Plague and the Reformation, and syphilis (brought back from Africa or America), probably, drove the final nail in the coffin.   But even in the heyday of the European public bath, "we" probably never bathed as often as the Japanese. Had Frois been in Japan a hundred years later, he might have also written this:

> *Our gentry bathes occasionally and many of us almost never bathe.*
> *Japanese rich or poor bathe every day.*

The Jesuits, like the English depicted in SHOGUN had to learn to bathe more often as part of their efforts to accommodate the Japanese. But they did not have to bathe every day, for that practice developed later after public baths became popular, then taken-for-granted in the Tokugawa Era (1603-1868).   This occurred in Edo (the water-city, now called Tokyo which was nothing in Frois's day), where the first commercial bath-house (*sentô*, literally: penny-hotwater) was opened – jumping the gun a bit – in 1591. Frois would, however, have seen pay bathhouses in Kyoto, where some (called simply *furuya* =bath-rooms) date back to the Muromachi Era (1338-1573). They were not so open and bright inside as we now imagine, for the people had to duck under a low door for the room to maintain its heat. The Japanese bath began as a sauna + cold-water, then (at Frois's time) added a shallow hot water tub. It was not enough to soak the entire body in and the dark and steamy room would not have offered quite the eyeful of mixed genitalia modern readers might imagine! Moreover, it is debatable how much full nudity existed in mixed baths at this time, for there are reports of wrap-around skirts on women and small loincloths on men.

Most of Japan's public baths were probably still run by Buddhist Temples in Frois's time. If Christianity tended to discourage bathing, Buddhism introduced it as a religious good. According to some sources the practice started to clean Buddhist sculptures (I hate the connotations attached to *idol* and *icon*) and the laity who got wet caught the habit.   Other sources put it in terms of *purification*. I identify this more with Shinto.   Prior to Buddhism coming to Japan in the 7th century, Japanese used the sweat-house (or grotto) + cold river combination similar to that found in native American culture. Presumably, that would have served equally well for purification purposes.   Be that as it may, bathing eventually brought Buddhist brownie points and the faithful were encouraged to bath on certain days where the benefit was thought the greatest.   And, in Edo, where the bath-houses came to offer full emersion and a second-floor where people could play *go* (see 14-39 notes) and engage in other light recreation, the daily bath was born. Alcock, who came to Japan on the tail of the Edo Era, called the bathhouse in Japan "what the baths were to the Romans, and what the cafe is to the Frenchman – the grand lounge."

> . . . passing along the streets of Yeddo [Edo=Tokyo] on a summer's evening, at every hundred steps a bath-house is visible. You know the vicinity by the steam escaping through the open doors and windows, and the hum of many voices, bass and tenor, in full chorus. And here all the gossip of the neighborhood and town is no doubt ventilated.

Neither Frois nor Rodrigues directly contrast the single-sex bathing in Europe (unless female bath employees are included) *versus* mixed bathing in Japan. After the bath-inspired topsy-turvy revelations quoted in the *Foreword* (vi), Alcock devises a splendid *just-so story* to explain and "make correct" the "shocking" fact of "the utter confusion of sexes in the public bath-houses in Japan."

> But if this great institution of the bath be the source of the public opinion – said by the ministers to exist, and so often invoked – it rises in dignity as the people's *parliamente* or house of assembly (the only one, certainly, they are permitted), and we may overlook some of its deficiencies of costume and other eccentricities in the contemplation of its political and national uses . . . It certainly has a recommendation wanting in all other parliaments, of acknowledging to the fullest extent the rights of both sexes, and their equality. Not only is woman not excluded as in more pretentious parliaments, but their voice is unquestionably heard! The gentler tenor often prevails over the deep bass of the men; and the frequent laugh and shrill hilarity of tone, heard from afar, ought to be sufficient guarantee to the government that no deep schemes of treason or sanguinary revolutions are being discussed, at the same time that it offers a pleasant contrast in other respects to many debates in more solemn places. The sex is the State's protection; for, though one woman may plot a deed of vengeance, the history of the world does not record an instance of a *conspiracy of women*, or of any mixed assembly of men and women, for the enactment of scenes of violence and political convulsions. Long experience, or a deep insight into human nature, may have given the jealous rulers of Japan full assurance of the fact, and thus have supplied to the *vox populi* a free vent as a sort of safety-valve, without any of its attendant dangers. Assuredly, they would allow no such gatherings of men alone. If so, they have made a discovery by which Western States may hereafter profit, with such modifications of drapery and costume as our more refined habits would dictate," (A:COT)

Nothing changed during the first quarter-century after the Opening, for Isabella Bird wrote "As I rode through on my temporary biped [she preferred quadruped transportation], the people rushed out from the baths to see me, men and women alike without a particle of clothing."(B:UTJ) – No wonder they bathed in front of their homes: the better to watch the passerby! Bird, after acknowledging Alcock's argument without giving his name, shows us that change is underway:

> . . . but the Government is doing its best to prevent promiscuous bathing; and though the reform may travel slowly into these remote regions, it will doubtless arrive sooner or later." (B:UTJ)

Bird was right about mixed bathing. [1] It was quickly chased out of the cities and only remained in a number of medicinal spas that mostly cater to the elderly. But Japanese public baths – with men on one side, women on the other – only began to close down in the last half of the twentieth century as more and more people came to have convenient facilities at home. I have fond memories of public baths in Tokyo, a pleasant pandemonium, with little boys pulling around choo-choo trains of linked stools and wash-tubs (gallon-sized pails used for washing prior to getting into the baths), the owner's daughter coming in to clean up with me still washing, etc.. Soon, I fear, few Japanese will have such memories. Another *Faux* Frois:

> *Europeans wash themselves with soap inside of the bath;*
> *The Japanese wash themselves first to keep the bath water clean.*

Japanese are warned not to do this in Western hotels where the bathroom floor lacks a drain.

But to return to the matter of Frois's contrast, *a different standard of modesty*: every culture divides the private (shameful) and public (show-able) in its own way. In Bali, not long ago, women gave birth in public view – with younger children shouting "come on, mommy, I see its head!" – yet people ate individually facing the corner behind closed doors, and there was even a fine for disturbing families while they were eating. Birth, including a ringside view of the vulva, was public, while dining was very private. (LR) Japanese may not have minded nudity, but they enjoyed eating together and childbirth was taboo for men (and they would not dream of exposing a child to it). In this sense, they were like us, opposite to the Balinese.

Since it is unlikely that one culture should be more immodest than another in every way, it behooves us to think of how Japanese may have been more modest than Europeans in 1585. Frois, elsewhere mentions *feelings*. Japanese hid *them*. We will examine *kissing, embracing* and *eye contact,* all avoided by Japanese (at least in public), later.

1. *Mixed Bathing in Japan.* A short essay cannot do justice to a complex subject. While Japanese macaque have joined humans bathing in hot springs in Japan without embarrassment, Japanese, as humans, are conscious of their bodies and the authorities did occasionally regulate exposure. In the Kansei period (1789-1801), the authorities separated men and women in Edo baths, and a half-century later, in the more conservative (Confucian?) Tempo (1830-1844) Reform, the older baths of Kansai (Nara, Kyoto, Osaka, Nagoya). Or, who knows? Maybe morals had nothing to do with it. Perhaps the popularity of back-scrubbing women (*yûna*) who used the baths to solicit night-time trysts antagonized the owners of the Pleasure Quarters. At any rate, mixed baths were always *somewhere* in Japan. I do not know if Alcock's "utter confusion of the sexes" was accurate, for one door on the outside may have masked a split between baths inside. Apparently, the male and female sides are reversed in Tokyo and Kyoto. This probably derives from a different approach toward left and right as reflected in their respective placement of Prince and Princess dolls (Pages could be written on this alone!). But I like the explanation a journalist got from a bath-owner in Kyoto:

> in Kyoto, men used to go to the bath with their wife or girlfriend and when they left at the same time, he would see the better side of her face, the right-side, so the woman's side is on the right side of the entrance. (粟津 征二郎 DISCOVER KYOTO -No.13- 女湯は右か左か、都の銭湯)

1-54+ We wear boots or regular footwear when it rains;
Antre nós pola chuva se trazem botas ou o calsado comum;

Japanese go barefoot or elevated on wooden chapin with staff in hand.
Em Japão ou vão descalsos ou levão chapis de pao e bordões nas mãos.

The two Japanese translations differ on the Japanese footwear and walking aid. Okada writes "wooden shoes with pole in hand;" whereas Matsuda and Jorissen write "raised-sole-shoes (*geta*) (with an additional gloss for the chapin!) with an iron cane." I was tempted to turn the *chapin* into a *clog,* but considering the fact that clogs have solid soles of cork or another light wood, whereas the chapin [1] actually had the same stilt-like extensions as found on the Japanese wooden footwear, I decided to use the obsolete word and explain it instead. Basically we are talking about two boards attached at vertical angles to the solid sole – the best resemblance is Π (Thank God for the Japanese in my computer, by which I could easily call up the pi symbol!), with a bit more overhang fore and aft. Most Japanese chapin, or *geta,* are not very high, but the type called *ashida* raised about six inches high on stilts. In Frois's time, they were pretty much used for wading mud puddles. They were later worn by prostitutes in parades and some men in the water-trades (entertainment industry). Though a mountain magician on a single stilt chapin (*tengu-geta*) might use a metal staff, wood was normal. I guess the Portuguese term also meant *pike.* But why wear gear unstable enough to require a staff? I think it is because, in the summertime, when it rains the most, boots would be too hot in humid Japan.

1. *Chapin, Chopine, Choppines*: Okada writes this shoe came from the high-heeled cork shoes worn by women in the Ancient/Classical world. According to my Shogakukan-Random-House dictionary, the *chopine* came into Europe from Turkey in the 18th century; but Bulwer, in the mid 17th century, writes "what a prodigious affection is that of Choppines, wherein our ladies imitate the Venetian and Persian Ladies" and he also shows "the English Gallant" standing upon something at least as high as the above-described *ashida,* with two stilts per shoe and all, the only difference being the way they are fastened to his feet. My guess is that this fashion was copied from Japanese footwear brought back to England (perhaps by Saris), or depicted by artists. Young gallants also wore what are now called high-heels (*gig-like heeles*) "which puts them into so tottering a condition, that when they have spun a while in the streets, usually come hobling down, and in this fashion are emblematically presented to be unstable in all their waies." (B:A) These male fashions do not seem to have proper names; I introduce them to show that the West in no ways lagged behind the East when it came to wearing unlikely footwear. Moreover, we did it not to navigate mud-puddles but just to show off!

1-55+   We make our footwear from stiff, thick leather;
Entre nôs fazem o calsado de couro forte e grosso;

The Japanese make *tabi* [*foot-bags*] of glove leather.
Em Japão os tabis *são de couro como luvas.*

The "leather as with gloves" probably was meant to have double significance. First, the *tabi* was made from glove leather (according to Carletti, "goatskin" – regardless, within a century, most were made of cotton.) and second, the *tabi* were a sort of glove for the feet. As they were generally worn with sandals or *geta* providing the soles and, if clean, could be worn indoors, they are not really commensurable with shoes and might better be called socks. Frois could have written:

We wear delicate stockings of knitted silk;
They wear short thick ones made of woven cloth.

Or, seeing them as slippers that double as socks for sandals:

We change from our slippers to our shoes when we go out.
They wear their slippers upon their shoes when they go out.

Our socks usually cover the entire foot and do not divide the toes;
To Japanese that looks like horse hooves, for theirs separate the large toe from the others.

And I cannot help but wonder why he did not catch at least the second of the above unless Europeans of his day either wore split socks or no socks. I read (perhaps in Gwen Terasaki's heart-warming book *Bridge To the Rising Sun*) of an American maid, who, seeing *tabi,* jumped to the conclusion that Japanese had only two toes, which amused her Japanese husband who told her that Japanese, for their part, thought Occidentals lacked heels because their shoes were only raised high in the back, rather than having two stilts (or none) like Japanese shoes.

Our shoes have heels to prevent them from slipping through the stirrup and to raise us higher.
Their shoes, raised on stilts or flat on the ground, are all level with no heels.

In 18th century Edo, the term "heel-less ones" become slang for Westerners. A *senryu* quips "in Maruyama / once in a while they bear / heel-less ones" (OJD) (In this Period of Isolation, the authorities tried to discourage sex with foreigners, and, failing that, the birth of mixed-blood babies. But, occasionally there still were accidents.) Frois did not overlook the *heeled/heel-less* contrast: Occidental male shoes generally did not have heels to speak of in the 16th century. But he could have written this:

Our shoes are like boats and usually cover the entire foot;
Their shoes are only raft-like soles held to the foot by a strap between the first and second toes.

Today most Japanese only wear *tabi* when they wear Japanese traditional clothing. For informal traditional clothing or simply for wearing any sandal/zori with a toe thong, Japanese (mostly elderly ladies) wear socks with a single divide. They can be pulled on like any sock whereas the *tabi* must be painstakingly fastened up the side.[1] Carpenters prove the exception to the rule. Young or old, they wear special *tabi* with rough corrugated rubber soles, thin enough to let one get a feel for whatever lies beneath. (Everyone I have shown my pair ro thinks they are *ninja* shoes!) They are the opposite approach to safety of our heavy steel-plated boots. Japanese want to be able to climb and walk across beams with little danger of falling; we are afraid of things falling on us (or stepping on nails)! Such "heavy *tabi*" were worn by some coolies in the late-19th century (S:JDJ), but I do not know about Frois's time. I also wear cheap cotton Japanese socks with not just 2 but 5 toes each; they keep the toe-crotches cool and healthy in the summer and, under wool, in the winter. Called *gunsoku,* or military-socks, they are identified with the older generation and athlete's foot ("water-worm" as Japanese call it) – for which doctors occasionally prescribe them – and are entirely blue-collar. I never knew a white collar or young Japanese to wear them. My co-workers at a publisher thought them outlandish and agreed that only a foreigner like yours truly would wear them!

1. *Tabi Closing Problem.* With practice tucking tiny metal tabs into loops becomes relatively easy, but it really is too much to ask of us lazy moderns to tuck in 20 or 30 tabs! Sometimes there are several rows of loops which enable a perfect fit. If *tabi* and the carpenter/ninja shoes would only try velcro, they might make a *big* comeback.

~~~~~~

1-56+   Our gloves fold back at the wrist;
As nossas luvas dobrão-se no colo da mão;

Japanese ones sometimes extend to the elbow.
As dos Japões chegão-lhe às vezes até os cotovelos.

Old paintings show the European of Frois's time with a few inches of the glove turned back like a cuff (the "cuff" itself, originally meaning glove or mitten). While such a cuff might, once in a while, serve to prevent blood or some other liquid from flowing up the wearer's arm, I suspect it is 99% a matter of fashion. The long Japanese "gloves" were open palmed, and would appear to derive from archery arm-guards if it were not for the back of the arm being covered as well as the front. The fingers were usually not covered, so we might better call them arm-sleeves![1] Japanese also had – and Buddhist priests in traditional outfits still wear – a bamboo mesh tube on the fore-arm that keeps the sweaty skin from rubbing on the inside of the sleeve. But the main difference between gloves in Europe and Japan has nothing to do with the above details. To *Faux Frois* it:

> In Europe, gloves are thought elegant, symbolize power, signal duels and serve romantic ends;
> In Japan, they are purely practical tools and nothing else whatsoever.

Kings gave out gloves as tokens of this or that favor granted to a subject, gauntlets, as gloves were called, were thrown down in front of opponents as a challenge, or dropped on purpose to pick up a man by having him pick up said glove, etc.. As the fan was far more than a fan in the Sinosphere, the glove was, to Europeans, far more than gloves. I do not have Japanese writing about this exotic glove culture in Europe – by which we can match the European writing about Japanese and Chinese fans but, luckily, one contemporary Occidental who has reproduced examples of "The King's Glove," an ornate right-hand glove the Kings in England gave as tokens of land-grants which the recipient Baron (or Baroness) could then show to the illiterate ("It gave the holder domain over the lands and the people who worked it. It was a bond between the holder and the King that would not be disputed.") also gives a fine summary of the culture in question on her website.

From title, favor, approval, love, payment and challenge the glove is a personal representation of the person who gave it. They were used as vessels to convey bribes and payoffs tucked inside the hands, and even as possible weapons [poisoned gloves were used for assassination]. They have reflected wealth, power, status and nobility. From protecting hands from the cold to a promise of protection by a King, no greater sphere of diversity can be found in an accessory throughout history. (Mirianna Wrenne (Valerie Oswald) http://www.glove.org/gallery/mirianna.htm)[1]

Scottish legends speak of chieftains cutting off their own right hands and throwing them down on the land they claimed. "Not so smart," she adds, if the King needs to do battle again. The glove as proxy for the hand makes more sense. And, in an age where reality was more magical than today: "the touch of the King's hand was thought to remain within the glove and was held in esteem and respected as his hand would have been." White gloves were sometimes submitted to grantors as a sort of tribute. And the city of Konigsberg signified its submission to the Duke of Prussia by presenting a left-hand glove. In Aethelred II's reign, 979-1016, gloves were used as import duties by some German merchants. Perhaps the idea began further East: the Central Europeans, she writes, "used gloves to signify a transfer of property." Gloves as symbols of power have survived modernity – "In 1953, the ritual of the presentation of a right-handed glove to the Sovereign was re-instated in England. A Peer that had inherited the duty originally presented it to the Crown, . . . the Company of Worshipful Glovers by the order of the Earl Marshal . . . did the presentation." But, to me, the most exotic glove tale of all is the following isolated usage of the glove serving as proxy for a metaphorical hand:

In the 20th [?] century, a Dutch woman had to be married before she could travel alone to the East Indies. Often, the fiancé could not return for the ceremony so a MAT (marrying apart together) was developed; the bride stood beside her groom's portrait and held his glove. This was called *Het handschoentje* and was in all ways legal. Often the couple would re-marry when they were reunited but it was not required. (Ibid)

Today, gloves in Japan and in the West are considered to be a female accessory – males only wearing them for work – but in Frois's time gloves were still a predominantly male fashion and were just beginning to catch on with women (thanks largely to the example of Catherine de Médicis, queen consort of Henry II of France, and one person rumored to have used gloves as a weapon for assassination).

1. *Japanese Gloves.* What about when protection for the palms was needed? I would not mind more information about Japanese gloves.
2. *Glove Research*. Mirianna Wrenne (Valerie Oswald) writes she researched gloves as part of "a special project for Estrella war" [the movie Star Wars!?]. But she also writes that "in preparing the King's Gloves, I hope to enhance pageantry of our Courts with the use of some of the symbolism that was such an important part of medieval life." There is a bibliography on her site.

1-57+ With us, it would be madness to wear unfinished clothing;
Antre nós seria doudice trazer o vestido por agorentar;

Pelt *dobuku* [vests] worn by the Japanese seem just as they were torn off the buck.
Os dobuqus de peles dos Japões asi os trazem como se tirarão dos veados.

Japanese tend to preserve natural textures and shapes in their architecture, utensils, food and clothing. The natural grain of the wood was preferred to paint (11-7), unglazed pottery was used for formal occasions (6-30), and clothing was worn as it was woven, in the best form (rectangular) to show off the fabric, rather than the human body beneath. Animal pelts, unlike woven cloth, come in different shapes. We have already seen that the fur side is on the outside (1-13+). By leaving the pelt in its apparently natural shape as well, the material is revealed rather than hidden. If you would wear animal fur, then give the animal its due! (14-37) Another way of putting this is that Japanese value the material (fur or fabric), where Europeans value the tailor. Of course, someone must prepare the clothing in Japan, but the main thing is not *how* clothing is cut, but *what* is cut, if it is cut at all.

1-58+　Our shoes, boots and slippers have leather soles or removable foot-pads;
　　　Antre nós os sapatos, botas e calsas tem solas ou palmilhas postiças;

　　　　　Japanese *tabi* have no separate sole, [and are] just one continuous piece of leather.
　　　　　Os tabis de Japão não tem solas sobre si mas todo o couro hé contínuo.

Note 55+ explains part of why *tabi* had no soles: they were not worn on hard surfaces, but as socks. A better contrast would be to forget about the *tabi* and say that Japanese shoes were *all* sole, for the *zori* (good woven sandal) and *geta* have almost nothing *over* the foot. Still, it cannot be denied that the lack of any cushion between the foot, the wooden *geta* and the ground is literally jarring. Though Japanese roads tended to use less stone or brick than European roads, there were probably some hard stretches even in Frois's time. The greater health of Japanese feet (thanks to using open footwear) and joints (thanks to squatting) may have been one factor allowing this. It is also one reason why everyone wore cheap *waraji* (sandals made of thick twisted straw) for travel: they provided some shock absorption.

1-59+　In Europe, wearing shoes with the foot but halfway in would be ridiculous.
　　　Em Europa seria couza rediqulosa trazer o calsado até meio pé somente;

　　　　　In Japan, it is stylish.[1] Only bonzes, women and the elderly fit fully into their
　　　　　shoes. *Em Japão hé primor, e o inteiro hé de bonzos, molheres e velhos.*

Because a Japanese shoe is open and can accept feet of various widths (which can hang over the side if necessary, too), an entire population can use a single medium size. Cooper introduces the opposite truth to Frois's observation, Avila's "homely remark that 'it does not matter if the shoe be an inch or two longer than the foot, because even a child of four summers can wear the shoes of his father or mother.'"(C:TCJ Avila was a merchant contemporary of Frois.) Since grown-ups, not kids once decided what's stylish, an overhang, rather than under-hang became stylish. (笑)

　Not all Japanese footwear can be standardized. If Japanese shoes are one-size, the *tabi* must fit just right, for they do not stretch as much as "our" socks do. Amazing to say, the idea that it is cool to hang a heel remains until the present day. With my feet large by Japanese standards to begin with, I find Japanese demitasse *geta* and *zori* uncomfortable to say the least, but have been taught by Japanese friends that I did not even need the (too small) largest size, for a smaller one allowing more hang-over was more manly. Since I walk and once ran long-distance on the balls of my feet, I could accept *that*, but I could *never* accept the plastic indoor and bathroom slippers all too common today. They are just too hot – I can remember fearing I'd develop athlete's foot while wearing a close-toed plastic slipper at a dermatologist's office (Or was that the idea?). Lacking a toe-grip or thong, these plastic atrocities also slip off little feet.

---

1. *Primor* Translation. The same *primor* Englished as "dignity" (dignified) in 1-6 and "gallant" in 1-50+, here, with women and elderly mentioned as well, "stylish" seemed more fitting.

1-60+   We walk with all of our foot touching the ground;
Antre nós se anda com todo o pé asentado no chão;

The Japanese, only on the ball of the foot on shoes covering but half of their feet.
Em Japão somente com as pontinhas sobre o calsado de meyo pee.

Because of the reason given in the last contrast, people had to exercise their arches or soil their heels. No wonder, they didn't walk for relaxation! (1-27+)

1-61+   We do not wear clothing thin enough to reveal the body either in the winter or the summer.
Antre nós nem por Verão nem por Inverno se usa de vestidos ralos polos quais se veja o corpo;

In Japan, summer clothing is awfully thin, so thin almost everything is visible.
Em Japão são polo Verão tão ralos que quasi tudo se enxerga.

Japanese used to wear clothing that showed more than a wet tee-shirt (1-53+). About 600 years before Frois, the great complainer – or witty connoisseur of life, if you prefer – Sei Shonagon, had something to say about thin clothing in her listing of *"Things that are unpleasant to see:"*

> A dark-skinned person looks very ugly in an unlined robe of stiff silk. If the robe is scarlet, however, it looks better, even though it is just as transparent. I suppose that one of the reasons I do not like ugly women to wear unlined robes is that one can see their navels. (THE PILLOW BOOK OF SEI SHONAGON, trans. Ivan Morris)

When Frois wrote, cheap summer linen was so thin and weak that *haikai* (proto-*haiku*) joke about poor women unable to ford waist-high rivers. Be that as it may, the West (here, I include the makers of Western fashion in Japan who are blind to traditional wisdom) still has *a lot* to learn from Japan when it comes to fabric for hot weather. Traditional Japanese sheets soak up and evaporate sweat extremely quickly; sleep between them and you will *hate* our sheets (Unfortunately, the makers of these traditional sheets make them the size of traditional Japanese *futon*, i.e., tiny. You simply can not keep them tucked in.) and *jinbei* (a bermuda-length shorts-suit) boast cotton and hemp fabric far far cooler than our seersucker. Unfortunately, most of "us" prefer air-conditioning to a natural cool and the clothing industry is run by idiots. [1]

---

1. Why I Detest the Clothing Industry. I realize opinions on lifestyle may seem out of place in this book, but living in an ecologically responsible manner is my religion. The clothing industry is making it hard for me to practice it. In Miami, I use no air conditioning. Women are able to buy cool clothing, but male fashion demands we wear excruciatingly hot trousers (despite it being particularly bad for males). Hemp would be OK but it is priced higher than silk though it should be cheaper than cotton! So as I type, I wear women's trousers (bought at a garage sale) with the waist cut apart a bit to fit my belly. Anyone with real money to invest, contact me and I will spell out what is needed to make and market truly *cool* clothing and bedding that could let us raise thermostats on AC's (or turn them off) and save both our money (unimportant) and energy (that matters).

1-62+   The hems of our skirts and long robes do not reveal the foot at all;
As bordas dos nossos sayos ou roupões compridas não são desfalcados em nada;

In Japan, the front hem of the *katabira* and *kimono* of men and women wants a span. *Em Japão as catabiras y quimões de homens e molheres falta-lhe hum palmo nas bordas dianteiras.*

Frois's contemporary Rodrigues suggests that the difference was not so clear-cut for at least one sex:

> Both men's and women's robes are of the same style and fashion, although those of women are *very long and reach right down*, and they wear underneath a white petticoat from the waist downwards." (R/C:TIJ *italics* mine)

Either there was a change in the fashion in the two decades spanning Frois's and Rodrigues's writing, or they are describing different classes of woman or robes. That wonderful metaphysical (or was it cavalier?) poem about a woman's feet as mice hidden below the hems but occasionally peaking out at the world show Frois was not exaggerating about the length of "our" clothing, and it does *look* better to take a hem all the way down to the ground without a break, as Europeans did, but it must have been hell to keep this clothing clean and I only wonder what percent of the population could afford to wear it! No one who had to wash their own clothing I would bet!

~~~~~~

1-63+   We never stitch black clothing with white thread.[1]
Antre nós ho vestido preto não se coze com linhas nem r[etrós=mod Portuguese trans.] branqo;

> Japanese are not troubled when black (clothing) is sewn with white (thread).
> *Os Japões não têm por inconviniente com branqo cozer o preto.*

"This is presumably about the thread used for fitting kimonos. Sometimes part of this is left as 'decorative fitting,'" writes Okada. The neat stitches can be seen as mere adornment, but the fact they are not extraneous makes them a revelation as well. There is a beauty in *not* concealing human work, somewhat akin to the attraction of the grain of the wood or the fur mentioned in 1-57+. If I may wax poetic for a moment, in these stitches we can see the prototype of the pipes on that art museum in Paris, of a functional modern aesthetics. Unlike the pipes, however, we can appreciate the skill of the sewer, who is seen rather than forgotten.   Isn't this idea reflected in the open movement of props on stage and the presence of the puppeteer, albeit wearing the invisibility of black, moving about on stage with the puppet in Japanese traditional drama? That, too, is part of the show.

1. *Com linhas nem retros.* Translation. If the modern about two types of stitching and/or thread. That is beyond Portuguese editors' guess is correct, we may be talking me. Like the other translators, I kept it simple.

(Several blank pages, probably intended for additional contrasts, follow. The same is true for other chapters.)

M*en*

~~~~~~

The clothes may be the *man*, but so many items in the chapter rightly pertain to *both* sexes, that Frois ought to have made a chapter for *Costume* alone. One wonders if he did not do so because he had far more contrasts specifically about *Women* in the next chapter – and sought to equalize the length. The second, women's chapter is also more interesting, for many contrasts do not only treat appearances but concern lifestyle and, quite incidentally, some overturn current stereotypes. Reading this chapter, I couldn't help wondering if men had lives! The very title of the chapter specifies *"vestidos,"* as if males are but clothes-horses, whereas the next chapter gives Women *"custumes,"* or *customs* as well as *costumes* (only 1 of 4 other translations chose the latter meaning). I also couldn't help noticing all those *swords*. Arms are thoroughly contrasted in a later chapter on *Weapons and War*. That there could, nonetheless, be that many (seven!) entries about *swords* in this first chapter indicates just how much a part of the male *pessoa*, or person, they were considered.

<p style="text-align:center">男　　　　　　　男　　　　　　　男</p>

The most important part of the European's *persona*, skin color, was not touched upon because there was no contrast. Most of the Jesuits thought of the Japanese as whites. Although skin color has already been treated at length in my Foreword notes, it was and still is so salient an issue, that I will give a brief summary of the dozen or so pages treating it in DE MISSIONE (J/S:DM ch 2, 5,14,15), the dialogue-style report of the young Japanese embassy to Europe, based partly upon the youths' letters, but largely reflecting the views of the *Visitador* Valignano.

After Miguel=Valignano mentions dark-skinned men spear-fishing from little canoes in the Singapore Strait, Leo asks, But aren't there dark men like that in Portugal, too? Having seen the black slaves with the Portuguese, he wonders if the low folk in Portugal are "born with a black color as if to mark them out for becoming slaves, while the nobler people are white." Miguel replies that if Leo visited Portugal he would realize his mistake:

> Whether speaking of Portuguese or other Europeans, they do not have black and ill-proportioned features; they have noble features and well-proportioned bodies and are of a beautiful color . . .

Black or dusky slaves, on the other hand, come from the East; and "the various somatic differences, originally, have no relationship to differences in wealth and poverty." Climate explains why "there are no people in Europe that do not boast the noble color of white, while all the people of Africa and most of Asia are dark."(ch2) The later dialogue (ch5) is far more thorough, with Miguel spending pages on the relative influence of climate and heredity and coming to the perfectly modern understanding that *both* are involved as a result of considering the movement of peoples in time. As long as the Ethiopians [blacks, as opposed to relatively light bushmen?] have lived in the South [below and away from the equator] after moving there, their color should [by the climate hypothesis alone] have completely faded out, but they are black and keep bearing children as black as they themselves." Indeed, Miguel even discusses the way "the blemish branded by the first mother" will, over generations slowly disappear from the descendents of a white man and a black woman living in all-white Portugal, while a white couple will still have white children after moving to Ethiopia. "So"

Miguel concludes, "we can conclude that skin-color comes not from heat but from some reproductive cause."

..

Before long, the conversation drifts to Ham who disrespected his father Noah and was, together with his potential progeny, turned black. Leo correctly points out that the story is not in the Bible. Miguel agrees, but wonders if there might not be *some* truth in it, that not only the heat but "some invisible heavenly power" might also be involved, for not only was the skin blackened, but "most of their facial features are sadly deformed and their characters so very crude and they tend toward cruel and inhuman things." Here, Miguel wanders. If Ethiopians are set off from other races by different features as well as color, "we Japanese and Chinese, too, have features that differ from those of Europe, such as small and deep-sunk eyes and flat, low noses and so forth." [The "deep-sunk" is curious, for Caucasians are the one's with the deepset eyes. Perhaps the chain of translation broke somewhere.] In the final event, Miguel admits three causes for *blackness – whiteness* being taken for granted (!) – climate, an invisible cause, and the parents' seed.

This whiteness also appears in other contexts. Toward the end of the book (ch 34), Miguel and Leo discuss the significance of *size* and *position* in geography. When Miguel points out that the quality of the land and the work people put into it count more than sheer size – Europe being considered the smallest of the five continents – Leo readily agrees, but adds an interesting thought of his own:

> Now, if we were to judge the merit of the continents, of course, we ought to give first place to our Japan and China; but, gazing at a world map, seeing Africa in the middle of the others, I think it would be right to give Africa first place because, as we say, morality lies in the happy mean.

Miguel mercilessly pounces on this Leo's fancy, saying the "mean" has nothing to do with physical placement, then, gratuitously, that "Africa is probably the most inferior continent." Finally, Miguel (Here is where we especially feel Valignano putting words into the mouth of the young men) sums up objectively (?) – "temporarily setting aside my identity as a Japanese, and thinking of myself as a *world-man* – as Socrates was proud to be "Europe's philosopher" – as a citizen of the entire world, not being biased by feelings good or bad toward any country," – concluding that Europe was superior to all other places by virtue of 1) its being in the temperate zone, 2) its race and 3) the grace of Christianity. Again, white is identified with beauty and intelligence, while black/dark/dusky is identified with a crude and unrefined character.

All this pumping up of Europeans included the risk of antagonizing the Japanese. Despite the occasional references – or, rather, *because* of the occasional references – to the Japanese being not quite the equal of Europeans in appearance, the reader is periodically reassured that Japanese are "somewhat similar to Europeans in their intelligence, elegance and nobility." (ch 34) Indeed, "our being by far the most similar to Europeans of all other races in terms of high-mindedness, culture and deportment is incredible if not wondrous" explains Miguel, "considering the fact our countrymen had no help from either of these [*Christianity* and *stability*? – I cannot say for sure because I do not have the next page (252) and it is too difficult to obtain the book again]." But, to my mind, all this praise would probably not have sufficed to heal the wounded pride of Japanese asked to accept second place in the race of races.

..

Jesuit thought is often identified with sophistry. "Jesuit" as an adjective in the dictionary tells us that much (and not only in anti-Catholic England, but in Portuguese as well!). I do not know how much validity is in the charge. But, one thing is certain. The academic question of the worth of the *noble primitive* position (expounded in imaginary debates between Indian ascetics and Alexander the Great, etc.) which engaged Medieval scholars is child's play compared to the task of understanding then explaining a different but equal people to an intellectual tradition that had already placed itself on the top of the pyramid. And this, precisely, was one of the first tasks that the newly formed Company had to do. The Jesuit tradition teethed in a suddenly complex world, where simple black and white explanation was impossible. Skin color provides a good example of this.

男   男   男

Today, skin-color no longer matters for Japanese-Western relations, except in so far that the relative uniformity – few blacks or whites – in Japan makes it difficult for Japanese to comprehend the problems inherent to more obviously poli-ethnic and poli-racial societies (I write *"more obviously"* because Japan *does* have some variety and problems I will not go into in this book). But physical differences *other than skin color* still matter and these differences, I believe, create a gender difference. In a word, Far Eastern women fare better in the world than Far Eastern men. This is because *size* matters: petite finely featured girls are loved by men and women alike in much of the world. In her 1890 work, JAPANESE GIRLS AND WOMEN, Alice Mabel Bacon gives us the first clear exposition of what we might call *the beauty advantage* of small Japanese women and self-hate on the part of large Western women. This important testimony is found at the end of a long footnote (taking up most of two pages and part of another), occasioned by this line: "A young man, who finds himself in a position to marry, speaks to a married friend, and asks him to be on the lookout for a beautiful* and accomplished maiden, who would be willing to become his wife." So, Bacon asked, *what* then *is* "the Japanese standard of beauty?"

> . . . the eye-socket should not be outlined at all, either by the brow, the cheek, or by the nose. It is this flatness of face about the eyes that gives the mildness of expression to all young people of Mongolian type that is so noticeable a trait always in their physiognomy. [i.e. a gentle neotony] . . . the complexion should be light, – a clear ivory-white, with little color in the cheeks. The blooming country girl syle of beauty is not admired, and everything, even to the color in the cheeks, must be sacrificed to gain the delicacy that is the *sine qua non* of the Japanese beauty. [and, we think Victorian tastes were tubercular!] The figure should be slender, the waist long, but not especially small, and the hips narrow, to secure the best effect with Japanese dress . . . . In walking, the step should be short and quick, with the toes turned in, and the foot lifted so slightly that either the clog or sandal will scuff with every step. . . [Here, we can imagine a *faux Froix.*]

> Contrast with this type, the fair, curling hair, the round blue eyes, the rosy cheeks, the erect, slim-waisted, large-hipped figures of many foreign beauties, – the rapid, long, clean-stepping walk, and the air of almost masculine strength and independence, which belongs especially to English and American women, – and one can see how the Japanese find little that they recognize as beauty among them. Blue eyes set into deep sockets, and with the bridge of the nose rising as a barrier between them, impart a fierce grotesqueness to the face, that the untraveled Japanese seldom admire. The very babies will scream with horror at first sight of a blue-eyed, light-haired foreigner, and it is only after considerable familiarity with such a person that they can be induced to show anything but the wildest fright in their presence. *Foreigners who have lived a great deal among the Japanese find their standards unconsciously changing, and see, to their own surprise, that their countrywomen look ungainly, fierce, aggressive, and awkward among the small, mild, shrinking, and graceful Japanese ladies.* (B:JGW, my *italics*,)

There is one contradiction in the overall difference. Broad hips and large busts (which are, strangely, neglected), are neither masculine nor threatening. They were considered attractive, and commonly cited by Occidental social scientists as proof that the Caucasian race was more highly evolved than Asian races, for sexual bimorphism meant *specialization* and a high degree of specialization brought about Higher Civilization (by the thinking of the time). That a Western superiority complex complete with scientific backing could not only disappear but flip over while one lived in Japan – and I would guess that the first of her "countrywomen" who felt less than happy with herself was Bacon herself! – is remarkable! Some of the early Jesuits went over to the Japanese side with respect to *character* (Organtino being the clearest case), but they never admit to feeling *ugly* or seeing their countrymen or women with such Japanese eyes. As men of religion, from a culture where men were not supposed to look in the mirror (1-46+) we wouldn't expect them to, either. But the fact that European males were on the large/tall/powerfully-featured=attractive side of the equation, makes it unlikely that even the merchants from a mirror-viewing part of the West would have found grounds to feel inadequate. Living in Japan for most of the last quarter of the twentieth century, I never came across sobbing white or black men, but I often ran across remarks similar to Bacon's on the part of Caucasian *women* visiting or living in Japan who worried about their own low self-esteem and seemed disappointed or even *angry* that Caucasian males in Japan usually favored Japanese women. Such jealousy is understandable. So much has been written by Western men on the wondrously wonderful Japanese women that one could make a whole library of their adulation. I must have read the geisha's wit praised at least a dozen times, with each writer pointing out that she is not just a "giggling girl," but, in Menpe's words "a little genius." (M:JRC) Hearn, who was married to a very kind and intelligent Japanese woman, has every right to *his* adulation; but I would guess most Occidental males simply liked the fuss Japanese women made of them and were happy to jump on the bandwagon for sanctifying Japanese women in masse. This made a certain Mr. Crosland, writing in 1904, very cross:

> In brief, if we are to believe the books, there is not a shrew in all Japan, and consequently not an uncomfortable husband. On the face of it this is ridiculous. Where you have women you are bound to have shrews; where you have marriage, you are bound to have a considerable number of husbands who are sorry for themselves. (C:TAJ)

He also put in a most effective counterpunch against "geisha worship" by writing what a Japanese male tourist might have to say about British women.

> Ah, the dear big British barmaid – who could take Bass without her! . . . She is a glorious bird among the bottles and the mirrors. Sure her hair is of gold. She has a large, sad, sweet face as of the moon. She wear flower if you buy it to her . . . England could not be so merry if it were not for the bun-shop girl. She bring your tea with laughs like angels . . . (C:TAJ)

But, let's be serious – how many laments like Bacon's can be found coming from a Caucasian *male*? Kipling is the only writer who even comes close. In a fine passage from his *First Letter from Japan* (1889), when he admitted to feeling uncomfortably large in the "doll houses" of Japan." he writes "I tried to console myself with the thought that I could kick the place to pieces; but this only made me feel large and coarse and dirty." (C&W:KJ) But, this is a *bull-in-the-china* situation-induced lament, the "we-as-barbarian" amusement of a humorist that doesn't go nearly so deep as true apprehension over one's appearance. As far as I know, Japanese – and other oriental males – are *never* envied for their *looks*. As Golownin's editor put it in 1824, "all the early writers [mostly 17th century Dutch] describe the women as extremely handsome; and yet they represent the men as very ill made." The only exception I know of was Morse, who found Japanese men to be "better-looking than the women," among peasants, who were "on the whole rather plain-looking." Still, he doesn't go so far as to call them handsome. And this was not only true for Japan but for Mongolians in general. Take Cruz on China in 1569. Here is how he began his chapter "Of the apparel and customs of the *men*."

> Although the Chinas commonly are ill-favoured, having small eyes, and their faces and noses flat, and are beardless, with some few hairs on the point of the chin, notwithstanding there are some who have very good faces, and well proportioned, with great eyes, their beards well set, and their noses well shapen. But these are very few and it may well be that they are descended from other nations . . . (in B:SCSC translation)

..

The original is even harsher, for it uses no euphemism like "ill-favoured" but says simply *feios,* "ugly"! (C:TCC) Compare that to the beginning of the chapter "Of the apparel and customs of the *women,* and whether there are slaves in China."

> The women commonly, excepting those of the sea coast and the mountains, are very white and gentlewomen, some having their noses and eyes well proportioned. From their childhood they squeeze their feet in cloths, so that they may remain small, and they do it because the Chinas do hold them for finer gentlewomen that have small noses and feet. (B:SCSC)

Today, in an Americanized world where maleness is identified with powerful chins, broad shoulders and, ridiculously large muscles – not to mention porn-star penises – which Westerners and blacks, with their larger and less neotonous physiques more frequently embody, the Far Eastern male is at an greater disadvantage than ever. Until, *unless* they break free of Western fashion and create an entirely different ideal, they are pretty much doomed to inferiority. Here is Isabella Bird on a troupe of Japanese actors (*who would have looked fine in their own dress*) doing a stage call in European evening dress:

> Where was Ichikawa Danjiro, the idol of the playgoers, with whose stately figure in brocaded robes I had become familiar with from countless photographs, and where the host of grand, two-sworded luminaries in the rich draperies of the old *regime*? Fanny Parkes [daughter of the outspoken English Ambassador], age six, said, "Papa, how *very* funny all those ugly men look!" and if she had been aged sixty she could not have made a more apt remark. The yellow, featureless faces, all alike, the bullet-shaped craniums, the coarse cropped hair bristling up from the head, the flat chests, round shoulders, and lean, ill-shaped legs, were exhibited in all their ugliness in western dress, for the first time, and I hope the last time. The clothes looked as if they had all been made for one man, and that man not one of the forty who were present. . . . They stood in one deplorable attitude, with lean arms hanging limp by their sides, hands badly cramped into badly-fitting white kid gloves, and looking like miscreants awaiting castigation." (B:UBT:1880)

The "all alike" comment is nonsense; Japanese look better than *that,* and, today, Western clothing for both sexes by Japanese fashion designers does well in Paris. But it does so with far more Japanese female models than male models, almost all of whom are foreign. Sure, there are some very handsome and powerful Japanese men. There are always exceptions. But the difference – although none would dare put it like Bird did today – is still there. What the little girl said, still holds true today, albeit to a less obvious degree. Moreover, little can be done about the mean difference in the dimensions of the part nobody mentions (though, the less endowed can rest assured that they have far less danger of prostate cancer and, possibly, a longer active sex life) – which, to men counts for a good portion of their self image – but I believe that the right fashions could pretty well offset the rest of the gap. Not Chinese characters, but Western clothing and hair-styles are what the Japanese (and other largely Mongolian people) should get rid of, the sooner the better, if they would be happier and more confident in the greater global society, that all of us, thanks to mass media, live in today. Unless the idea is to stay ugly as an incentive to work harder and gain the attractiveness of the rich, I think the Far East should ditch the narrow-waist broad-shoulder dress of the Occident in favor of a robe and show off the thick and shiny hair by tying it up on top of the head.

男   男   男

I have a vague childhood memory of seeing a town of tiny houses our family drove through in Florida. It belonged to dwarves. I remember feeling very attracted to the houses because they were seemed so make-able (like the tree-houses I had made) and magical, compared to normal houses, which have always seemed forbidding and, even inhuman to me. This, I thought, was the type of house I wanted to grow up in. But, then, I sadly thought, I'd soon be too tall for such a house anyway. For the only time in my life I truly felt envious of dwarves, for they could *always* live in such houses. Physically, the Japanese are not small enough for dwarf-size dwellings. Although Japanese harp on the small size of their land and lack of natural resources, the global wealth of the Japanese does not demand downsizing for economy, either. Yet, the run-away bigness in the world today needs to be challenged with another model, one which *shows* that small is beautiful.

The original fairy world, or toy world of Japan described by Lafcadio Hearn and others came about naturally, i.e. by default. Hearn's horror at the destruction of Japan's miniature world is often treated as Western condescension, Orientalism or even racism. But if Hearn worried about the Occidental *overliving* in the Far East, he also worried about Orientals *underliving* in the Far West. I think it is more fair to give Hearn the benefit of the doubt and recognize his deep-felt aesthetic appreciation for cultural diversity and his genuine fear that we would inadvertently destroy it and end up with a uniformly shallow world.

Today, a century later, some of us still pray for the world he so loved. Not that it rest in peace, mind you, but that it comes back. We see nothing belittling about "diminutive scale and picture-book appearance." (L:IOJ) Like the legendary bicycles of Beijin – now largely replaced by the car – we think of it as the future rather than the past. Look around! Why must the current reality of ugly urban sprawl, ugly clothing, and criminally wasteful modes of transportation be taken for granted? Not only the Japanese, but all of us are dwarves in need of our own dwarf-town, though we may not even know it.

..

# #
MS-Word wasted half of my day and shortened my life ten times that by *refusing* to do the page numbers right. I cannot express my fury at BG and crew for their lack of consideration. (Finally, I have had to down a bottle of wine so as not to overheat and perhaps get a stroke) OK, maybe I made a booboo by doing three different captions before setting the page numbers, but, damn it, if I can try and fail for *3 hours* to fix the page numbers, something is wrong with your software. I had to set each page number *by hand* for this chapter (which meant fake double columns to change the section (another idiocy, we should be able to just check a box and say we want that) – another 3 hours wasted! – and even then, when i got to the note part, for opaque reasons, i could not get my page number to get to the margin! For God's sake, you guys, try working with *writers* instead of computer nerds! Do the folk at MS have any idea how much creativity goes to waste thanks to this bad design? (At least, make it so one can specify that the *entire file* is properly paginated regardless of whatever may have been previously, accidentally asked!) [later, I found that even worse, making sections in the course of editing makes numbering go haywire. I ended up doing the rest of the book completely with headers, not using the page-number function.] Then again, if you have been selling Word, now, for what 10 years? and still offer such a lousy half-assed spell-check, . . . *I just do not get it.* Are you doing this on purpose? Or are you just incompetent?

II

OF WOMEN, *THEIR PERSONS AND MORES*

do que toca as molheres, e de suas pesoas e custumes

~~~~~~

2-1   In Europe, the supreme honor and treasure of young women is their chastity and the preservation of their purity; *Em Europa a suprema honrra e riqueza das molheres moças hée a pudicicia e o claustro inviolado de sua pureza;*

> In Japan, women never worry about their virginity. Without it, they lose neither their honor nor the opportunity to wed. *As molheres de Japão nenhum cazo fazem da linpeza virginal nem perdem, pola não ter, honrra nem casamento.*

Christianity made premarital sex taboo and turned chastity into a fetish. The "preservation of their purity" in more direct translation would be "the inviolate cloister of their purity," (*claustro inviolado de sua pureza*) and the simple "virginity" the Japanese failed to value would be "virginal cleanliness=purity" (*limpeza virginal*). The outlandishness of such vocabulary owes something to the fact that English is not Portuguese, but it is also due to our unfamiliarity with a culture where virginity was so highly esteemed. One need not go back to Frois's time to find out. Here is a snippet from *Nihil Obstat,* an article published in *The Catholic Encyclopedia* less than a century ago that conveys something of the right feeling:

> Elisabeth Gnauck-Kühne says truly: "The esteem of virginity is the true emancipation of woman in the literal sense." This elevation of woman centres in Mary the Mother of Jesus, the purest virginity and motherhood, both tender and strong, united in wonderful sublimity. The history of the Catholic Church bears constant testimony of this position of Mary in the history of civilization. The respect for woman rises and falls with the veneration of the Virgin Mother of God. (*The Catholic Encyclopedia*, Volume XV Copyright © 1912 by Robert Appleton Company Online Edition Copyright © 2003 by K. Knight *Nihil Obstat,* October 1, 1912. Remy Lafort, S.T.D., Censor Imprimatur. +John Cardinal Farley, Archbishop of New York.)

Prior to the Reformation, North and South Europe were equally enthralled by Virgin Mary (the North had more Churches under her name) but, by the time Frois wrote, the sanctity of marriage was valued higher than that of virginity in the Protestant countries where the attention given to Mary at the cost of Jesus had come to be considered misguided. Nevertheless, premarital sex and adultery were thought to damage the sanctity of marriage and the general level of anxiety with respect to sex itself was higher in the Calvinist parts, so Frois's generalization probably held true for most of Europe.

In Japan, on the other hand, the ancient courtship practice called "night-crawling" (*yobai*) sex preliminary to marriage – if the girl got pregnant or the guy slept-in, the knot was tied – was doubtless alive and well in Frois's time, for it survived right up to the mid-twentieth century in rural areas. The fertility-worship element of culture survived occasional repression by Buddhist and Confucian authorities and men and women exchanged bawdy songs as they planted rice and laughed with their children on their shoulders when gigantic phalluses (phallae?) paraded through town. In other words, "they" were still as "we" were, once upon a time, when natural generation rather than the fiat of Creation was venerated . . . . [1]

While Christian missionaries like Frois struggled to implant their chaste ideals in their Japan congregations (*cultural rape for virginity?*), other Portuguese, according to the Florentine merchant Carletti, found "this Land of Cockaigne [2] much to their liking." One of the sexual opportunities worldly visitors might have enjoyed was leasing girls for live-in maid+mistresses. The young women (probably in their teens) prostituted themselves for the sake of their poor families. Carletti explained the benefit in it for the girls themselves, observing that not only do they not "lose the occasion of marrying" for "having thus been used," but "many of them never would be able to marry if they did not acquire a dowry in this way." (C(W):MVAW)

In 1585, the Japanese would no longer have considered virginity a spiritual liability as some claim was true in ancient times [3], but Frois and Carletti did not exaggerate its insignificance, either. Since the poor "used" girls had not acted from desire – what Buddhism found sinful about sex – but to help others, they actually furthered their salvation. And they behaved admirably by obeying and assisting their parents, cardinal virtues in the Confucian ethics common to the Sinosphere. For the same reason, an upper-class girl slated for an arranged marriage who engaged in premarital sex would be in serious trouble, not for losing her virginity [3] but for losing her heart and disobeying the wishes of her parents.

KT remonstrates, *"But didn't Shintô demand virgin priestesses [miko]?"* Many Japanese folklorists and students of religion wonder about that, too. Today, mostly high school girls who work at shrines, dancing, handing out predictions, anti-misfortune arrows, etc., but originally they were probably of any age. The theory I find most convincing is that Buddhist ideas of "purity" considering women the less enlightened, or, to be blunt, the dirtier sex (Buddhist priests are never female and there are temples out of bounds to women (see 2-58)) supplanted Shinto ideas of im/purity which originally may have required abstinence because a *miko* was supposed to be occupied by the *kami* (spirit/god), [4] but would not have required virginity because sex was not thought of as permanent pollution. It only contaminated the body *temporarily* – there were rules for men, too, in this respect – but did not permanently corrupt it (This is the impression gained from the earliest Japanese literature, the myths about the gods, the poetry of the men and women and some Buddhists). My feeling is that the Buddhist-inspired misogyny may have given men an excuse to run the women off the mountain and set apart Japanese religion from the largely woman-run shamanism of Korea and Okinawa (where it survives until today). Most professional *mikô* (i.e. shamanness or medium who wear white and identify with Shinto) today are not virgin and do not live within shrine precincts.

1. Once Upon A Time "We" I may exaggerate the contrast a bit when I mourn the disappearance of pre-Christian joy, for there were still reports of May-poles and hanky-panky in the woods in England the very year Frois is thought to have written the first Draft of TRATADO, 1583:

> Against Maie, Whitsondaie, or other time, every parishe, towne and village assemble themselves together, both men women and children, olde and yonge . . . they run gadding to the woods and groues, hils and mountaines, where they spende all the night in pleasaunt pastymes, and in the morning they return, bringing home birch bowes and braunches of trees.... Their cheapest jewell they bring home from thence is their Maiepoole, which they bring home with greate veneration. They haue twentie, or fortie, yoke of Oxen, every Oxe hauyng a sweete Nosegaie of flowers tyed on the tippe of his hornes, and these Oxen drawe home this Mai pool [this stinckyng Idoll rather] which is covered all over with Flowers and Hearbes . . . and some time painted with variable colours, with twoo or three hundred Men and women, and children followyng it, vith great deuotion. And thus being reared up, with handkercheifs and flagges; streamyng on the toppe, they . . . sett up Sommer Haules, Bowers and Arbours hard by it. Then fall they to banquet and feaste, to leape and daunce about it, as ye Heathen people did at the dedication of their Idolles, whereof this is a perfect pattern, or rather the thyng it self. . . . I have heard it credibly reported, and that *viva voce* by menne of great gravitie and reputation, that of fourtie, three score, or a hundred maides goyng to the woode over night, there have scarcely the third part returned home again undefiled. (Stubbes, *Anatomie of Ahuses*, fol. 94, 8vo. London)

But the fact that such an event was *reported* itself proves it was already "survivals," whereas the Japanese tradition was as vigorous as ever. And, there was "a parading of phallic ornament" in the Venetian Carnival (H:CER). It continued a while longer, but the point of carnival is to do what ordinarily is taboo, so it may be counted either way, as affirming or contradicting Frois..

2. Cockaigne   From MF meaning an idler's paradise, orig. from MD meaning *cookie-land.* The popular (androcentric) version included plentiful drink and easy women.

3. Virginity as Bad   I once read a book that was largely conjecture about the ancient matrilineal society in Japan (by Aoki Yayoi?) and recall that a woman who had the misfortune to die still a virgin was buried by or under a crossroads so her spirit could be metaphysically consoled by the traffic   Here are two parallels from the New World: "One of Peru's most famous colonial era churchmen, Jesuit José de Acosta, wrote in 1590 that "virginity, which is viewed with esteem and honor by all men, is deprecated by those barbarians as something vile," according to *Family Values in Seventeenth-Century Peru*, an article by Duke University anthropologist Irene Silverblatt. ("Once taboo, erotic ceramics a link to ancient Peru" in the *Miami Herald* 2004 Feb.29) And, "Father Joseph Och (Treutlein 1965:133), noted in the mid 1700s . . . that "Opata [in NW Mexico] buried deceased children in the middle of a road, so the child's spirit could accompany or enter the body of a passerby and presumably experience the life it prematurely was denied." (R:DPC)

4. *Virginity Per Se*   To me, the fixation on material virginity on the part of the Christian culture was crude and misplaced. But I should qualify my description of a more mature Japanese morality with this: If *senryu* (seventeen syllabet – my term for phonological equivalent of the letters of a syllabary – poems on the foibles of life) are to be trusted, intercourse with a virgin was supposed to gain an old man 75 days of additional life. This sort of superstition was, I think, not believed by many and rarely if ever acted upon, and I only mention it as a rare instance of virginity *itself* mattering in Japan.

5. *Room for Gods/Spirits*   Since a medium must pretty much give him or herself over to the spirits/gods, the heart really should be open. Some folklorists (Origuchi being the most noted example) go further and believe that the mikô originally were not only not virgin but supposed to sleep with the stranger-as-god, and were the original model for the prostitute, etc.. While there are historical documents about this throughout the world, I do not think there is much evidence for such a practice in Japan.

~~~~~~

2-2   European women[1] prize golden hair and do many things to obtain it;
As d'Europa se prezão e fazem muito por ter os cabelos louros;

Japanese loathe it, and do all within their power to make it black.
As japoas os aborrecem e trabalhão quanto podem polos fazerem pretos.

Apparently, blond was big in Iberia in the 16th century.   In "The Perfect Wife" (*La Casada Perfecta*), Frois's contemporary, Fray Luis de León wrote:

It often happens that a man of letters does not spend as much on his books as a lady on having her hair dyed blond. May God save us from such ruination! (L(J&L):LPC)

DR hypothesizes that this urge to lighten up might have something to do with Spain's long struggle against the darker haired Islamic and Moorish people to the South. De Leon was less understanding.   Those "who alter the color of their hair," he wrote, "are offended by their own nationality; they regret not having been born German or English, and so they try to denaturalize themselves at least in their hair." Up in England, anti-fashion criticism directed equally at men and women likewise played up the shame of aping foreigners, but with Spain self-consciously the world's leading power at this time, it was not just the ignominy of copying at issue but of copying ones inferiors. Moreover, because *rubio* denotes blond *and* red in Spanish, de León could even claim that *with this fiery hair,* women "become omens of their own evil" (burning desire and sooty dirtiness)! If that wasn't enough, he claimed it harmed their health because too much hair-washing dampens the head and this hurts the brain and, worst of all, the practice was doubly sacrilegious.

For the Christian woman to place safron on her head is the same as putting it in front of an idol on the altar; for what is offered to evil spirits . . . may be seen to be offered in sacrifice to idols.

But the Lord says: "Which one of you can change a single hair from black to white or from white to black?" Who? These women who deny God. "See," they say, "instead of changing it from black to white, we change it to blonde, which is an easier change."

In Japan, the ideal mentioned by Frois and morality were fortunate enough to be on the same side. Ancient poetry overflows with *nubatama,* or "raven-black" hair. (The Chinese characters most commonly used for the word are "crow-wing" or "crow-gem," though the actual metaphor is "leopard-flower seeds (berries?)"). In the late nineteenth century, Alice Mabel Bacon added *texture* to the contrasting color ideals:

> The hair should be straight and glossy black, and absolutely smooth. Japanese ladies who have the misfortune to have any wave or ripple in their hair, as many of them do, are at as much pains to straighten it in the dressing as American ladies are to simulate a natural curl, when Nature has denied them that charm. (Japanese Girls and Women: 1890 (B:JGW))

For much of the twentieth century, any hair not jet-black and smooth was considered *ipso facto* proof of juvenile delinquency – both because of the suspicion of dyeing/permanents and the association of immorality and Western women [2] – and girls with natural reddish hair sometimes had to dye their hair in order not to be criticized or even sent home from school! The hair of some Japanese lightens noticeably with exposure to the sun, and, even in Frois's time, this was evidently the mark of a *marginal* lifestyle, for Valignano writes not only that hair and teeth were dyed black, but "white teeth and blond/red hair are left to the meaner class and the fallen." (*dejando para la gente baja y abatida los dientes blancos y cabellos rubios* = SUMARIO:A:VS). Shortly later, Rodrigues wrote: "Their hair *must be* black; *on no account* may it be fair, and for this purpose they dye it after their manner." (*my italics* TIJ) Reading Valignano and Rodrigues together, we can guess that it is possible *some* Japanese women felt forced. But who knows.

We take for granted observations such as those by Frois, Valignano, Rodrigues and Bacon above. One must read the clearly jaundiced description on the part of late nineteenth and early twentieth century writers to appreciate their objectivity. Take the "hair" of *Ideal Mongolic* and *Caucasic Types* compared in Dyer Ball's THINGS CHINESE (1890).

> Dull-black, long, coarse, stiff, and lank, cylindrical in section.
> Long, wavy, and normally light brown, but very variable – glossy, jet-black, flaxen, red, etc., elliptical in section. (B:TC)

Ball cannot even find the shine in *their* hair! But, that is nothing, *their* "expression" is "heavy, inanimate, monotonously uniform" while *ours* is "bright, intelligent, infinitely varied;" and *their* "temperament," is "dull, taciturn, morose, lethargic, but fitfully vehement," while *we* are "energetic, restless, fiery and poetic." (B:TC) *This* is prejudice. *This* is looksism (unless anyone can come up with a better word for this). Nothing like it is found in our Jesuits. Neither, I think, is it representative of the way hair was generally viewed: in spiritual and aesthetic terms. Lafcadio Hearn wrote what I feel the best summary of the classic Occidental view of hair color in response to "a pretty translation (by 'Q') of some Spanish fancies in regard to the character of the fair woman as compared with the dark woman," who "ventures at last to express his preference for the darker style of beauty, and his decision is commendably loyal, and well supported by the opinions of poets and artists."

> ..
> Yet how much remains to be said in favor of the fair woman! The Greeks, who were surely master-judges of beauty, made fair the limbs and the locks of their marble entities. . . . Was not Venus called 'the Golden'? The artists of antiquity gilded her hair. . . . Most of the glorious old gods were represented with golden hair; and the dainty flesh tints given to their statues are supposed to have been of exceeding fairness. For the fair beauty surely comes nearest to our ideal of divinity – a loveliness typical of light and life and immortality – a comeliness as of golden summer and golden suns. . . . We might picture Lilith as a brunette; but Eve we dare not think of save as the loveliest of blondes . . . Perhaps we feel more reverence for blond beauty, not only

because it seems a reflection of celestrial loveliness, but because it bears with it the suggestion of force and will and strength and royalty . . . White beauty inspires awe, like the calm beauty of the gods. Dark beauty – save in the purest Oriental types – inspires only love. . . . All the most famous canticles of love have been devoted to the darker types of beauty . . . for the dark eye is the eye of love itself . . . (*Fair Women and Dark Women* in (New Orleans) *Item*, August 25, 1878 in EDITORIALS)

The way that this hair color pops up in Frois's contrasts right after the item on chastity suggests a spiritual connection, ironic, for blond icons of pure women doubtless influenced women to behave in an impure manner by dying their hair. Given this attitude – and it includes a page on the effect of dark versus light eyes as well – how remarkable that "we" managed to progress (?) so quickly to the opposite image of the blonde bimbo!   Yet all this cultural ephemera may conceal another perspective, neither classical nor Hollywood: Is it not possible that the two extremes of golden/light blond and jet-black ultimately represent the same ideals of luster and youth? The brilliance of blond hair goes without saying, but smooth blackness is equally bright. The Mende of West Africa connect a natural phenomenon – black water reflects most clearly – with their ideal of skin color. What we might call "dark," they would call *shiny*. (This concept is developed in the only truly *reflective* look at black beauty I know of: Sylvia Arden Boone: *Radiance From the Waters* Yale 1986) There is only one difference with the case of Japan.   There, black hair was a foil for white skin, much as black waiting women "set off the splendour" of fairer beauties in the Middle East (B:A). Dark skin was far from ebony in Japan, and generally *not* admired. (see note 2-15, below.) The youthfulness common to light blond and jet-black may be explained, respectively, by fine, fair hair being more common in infants, while thick black hair is farthest from the thin white crown of age.

1. *Translation*:   European women in this chapter are almost *always* called "as d'Europa" or "as de Europa," i.e "those of Europe" or "European ones," where Japanese women are "as japoas" or "the Japanese (of feminine gender)". To refer to the *first* side of the contrast as "those" was too awkward even for this occasionally lenient translator to permit. Note also that the *japoas* are never capitalized while the *Japões,* i.e., the men in the last were! The modern Portuguese translation (1993) quietly fixes this so the women are equally capitalized. I do not know what the story is here.

2. *Promiscuous Foreign Women*   In the twentieth century, Japanese came to see Occidental women as loose. First this was due to seeing them in paintings (for nude bodies were not "art" in Japan) and seeing them kissing in public. After World War II, Japanese so thoroughly adapted the white panties and virgin-until-married ideals of the Usanians that the freedom of the 60's shocked them. Sexual license (including homo-sexuality) was, then, seen as a mark of the individualistic West. In the last quarter of the 20th century, Japanese began to come to terms with their own history and became increasingly aware of "our" (Usanian) conservatism as manifested by the hysteria about Pres. Clinton's peccadilloes. On the whole, Japanese are more relaxed than Usanians (I hesitate to speak for various European peoples!) about sex and the body, but I think tourists overestimate the amount of casual sex in Japan because they frequent parts of cities where people seeking sex tend to go (in pursuit of foreigners in some cases).

2-3   European women make their part on their forehead;
As de Europa fazem sus espertaduras na t[esta];

   Japanese women shave their foreheads and conceal their part.
   As japoas rapão as testas e emcobrem a espertadura.

European women also had a brief fling with shaving to reclaim some scalp as forehead in the fifteenth century. This was to keep their hairline from sticking out under their tall hats (hennin) and emphasize the size of their brows.   But most paintings from all ages show European women with parts, which were particularly common and well-defined in Frois's time With Japanese, on the other hand, one finds almost no examples of parts at that time and I do not think Japanese ever used the parts "we" think natural on the right and left of the head. Center parts were almost universal in the Heian Era when hair was tied on both sides or low in back and naturally slipped a bit right and left, but shortly before Frois, even the nobles abandoned this hairstyle. For the remainder of pre-modern Japanese history, hair was tied in the middle of the head, high enough that parts had no call to form.

The part-less Japanese engineered their hairlines. Unlike Europeans, they did not think large brows were particularly noble or beautiful, but they did have preferred shapes for the boundary of skin and hair. Young woman in Frois's time probably [1] tended to round their brows, while middle-aged women went for "the ideal of the beloved Fuji," or Widow's peak, [2] which Bacon mentions. I feel there was a bit more variety, but historians tend to pay more attention to the hairdo itself than the boundary, so it is hard to be specific. It would seem to say that all women cleaned up around the edges of the hairline to banish irregularity – this unnatural perfection is one reason why the women look like they are wearing wigs in old prints (and must wear wigs on the TV Easterns to mimick that).

The Japanese side of the contrast is puzzling. Could it mean "shave their foreheads *to* conceal their part?" But, doing away with something altogether is not usually considered concealment. And did Japanese really *conceal* parts? Okada, who shows a picture of a woman (Oinu, who died at age 32 in 1582) whose hair has a clear part, must have had his doubts, for he translated *testas,* generally thought of as forehead, as head and wonders if the *espertadura,* or "part," might not include a clearing (?) shaved into the scalp called a *nakazori,* or "middle-shave," where a *komakura* (pillowette) was set as the base for a chignon. Presumably, this was useful for stability and the sake of the scalp, but the practice is more closely associated with male hairdo, so I will stick to the majority reading, though I feel the case is not closed.

Even today, there is a lot more *brow-shaping* on the part of Japanese than Europeans. It is probably done by men more than women. I think one reason for it is that many people have relatively low brows – or hair that grows low enough to give that appearance – while the ideals of Europeans/whites who tend to have larger hair-free brows are now accepted.

1. "Probably" History I took the information from a Warring Era Museum exhibition site (http://www.sengoku -expo.net/text/tf/J/) which covers a period ending decades before Frois wrote his TRATADO. It is probably valid. There is little detailed information available on the turbulent period the Jesuits worked in Japan.
2. Fujibitai v.s. Widow's Peak These terms do not really describe the same thing. *Widow's Peak* refers to an upside-down pyramid whereas *Fujibitai* ([Mt.]Fuji-brow) is right-side-up. The slight upside-down pyramid is the mouth of the volcanic mountain whose slope goes clear down to the temples. Needless to say, the slopes define a hairline far narrower than the "noble brow" demanded by Western women.

2-4   European women perfume their hair with aromatic essences;
          As de Europa perfumão os cabelos com cheiros odoríferos;

          Japanese women go about reeking of the oil with which it is anointed.
          As japoas andão sempre fedendo ao azeite com que os untão.

There is no small irony in this contrast. European women who rarely bathed smelled good thanks to perfume, while Japanese who bathed regularly stunk of oil. I doubt, however, that noblewomen reeked. I do not know if cloves – worth their weight in gold – were still added to their hair oil, i.e., *mizu-abura,* (literally "water-oil") were still used in the sixteenth century, as they were hundreds of years earlier, but Okada cites a work of literature where a woman is advised to trade in her sesame oil for the less smelly walnut oil if she would get into the good graces of her master, and this suggests to me that not *all* women smelled. I suspect also that this was a period when more and more common folk began to copy upper-class hair-styles that required oil. As few could afford the best oils, they had to settle for the somewhat cloying camellia (*tsubaki*), itself not cheap, or the pungent sesame (these oils, like olive smell wonderful fresh but turn smelly almost immediately in contact with the body). But it is a fact that smells are a very subjective matter. Most Japanese were probably used to the "reeking." On the other hand, as KT points out, most Japanese today "don't use perfume and don't like people who do." (I can attest to great antagonism when I dared to splash myself with bay rum before going to work.)

I do not think European perfuming needs any explanation.[1] But, I cannot resist introducing a certain method of toiletry used by some Spanish women a generation after Frois.

> if the lady had no scent-spray, her maid sucked in the water and projected it in little drops through her teeth all over the face and body of her mistress. (D:DLS)

This is, "if one can believe Madame d' Aulnoy," who reported it (Ibid).   Though the description – or, translation? – is poor, I believe it, for this is the same method used by Jonathon Edwards, the New England preacher of Fire and Brimstone fame, to research the nature of the rainbow; and I believe him because I have often made such a fine mist by blowing in the manner that one toots a fairly high note on a trumpet. while pretending to be a whale, but that is another tale.

1. Perfuming.   I hate to contradict myself too often, but there is one historical detail that begs for explanation. In both Europe and Japan, perfume began with smoke, i.e. incense. In the West, I can trace it back as far as Egypt, for in a book about the sexual life of Egyptians I saw a prostitute squatting over a large jar with a small top (the author, an art historian and amateur Egyptologist (and a woman) astounded me by explaining that it was the oldest picture of a woman masturbating(!)) *per-fuming* her vagina, a practice recorded in recent centuries in Africa. In and after Frois's time, there was still a much broader use of literal per-fuming, in medicine, at least. But it is hard to say just when the smoke was exchanged for the liquid variety which became the norm for perfuming the body. My guess is that it already was in Frois's time. (Anyone?)

~~~~~~

2-5   European women rarely add any other hair to their own;
As de Europa raramente uzão de cabelos estranhos ajuntados aos seus;

Japanese women buy a large quantity of wigs imported from China.
As japoas comprão muitas cabeleiras que vem de viniaga[1] da China.

In Roman times, the "fashionable ladies of Rome" were said to favor golden hair imported from Germany; but, in the sixteenth century, it would seem that men were the big-wigs with "us." The practice was mainly English, upper-class and professional, but, by the next century, most men with any pretensions to being fashionable had to wear their powdered wigs that were so important marks of manhood that even the statues in the Louvre were crowned and re-crowned with the newest fashions (all of this from the 1929 Encyclopedia Britannica). This wig-wearing habit was apparently not known to the first Japanese Embassy to the USA. According to the diary of the vice-Ambassador Muragaki-Awaji-no-Kami – for here is what they *thought* they saw in the Smithsonian!

> On the wall were also hung specimens of the hair of the successive Presidents. What a disgusting custom to exhibit the hair of dead men in a public place! (A-J:FJE)

The Embassy also took umbrage with the mummies: "Poor once-proud human beings! Here they lie side by side with birds and animals, publicly exhibited as objects of curiosity in the name of science!"

To return to the contrast, Frois's contemporary Rodrigues suggests one reason why Japanese women needed so many wigs: "The longer the hair is, the more dignified it is, and so some find it necessary to insert wigs into their hair."(Ibid.) Some noble women did wear several lengths of hair in serial, but they, doubtless had their special sources (I imagine the hair of young widows who go to nunneries or something like that).   Okada notes that most women desiring hair-pieces (for bald spots or some supplementing of their natural hair, I guess) would have used Japanese hair, for there was a profession of *ochyanai* who went around buying the hair that normally comes out when brushing for recycling as inexpensive wigs, and that the hair imported from China that Frois mentions was almost certainly yak hair, red, black or white, that was not used for wigs proper, but to stuff *mage* (buns that could be very large: call them the original beehives!) This is backed up by Ôhara Reiko, who notes, as Okada does, that Frois is wrong to call them *kazura* ("wigs" = *cabeleiras*) when they are properly speaking *kamoji*. ("tresses/rats.").

1. *Viniaga=Veniaga.* To oversimplify the explanation in   meaning to engage in commerce, especially with China.
the French translation: this is from a Malaysian verb

~~~~~~

2-6   European women use many coiffures to adorn their heads;
        As de Europa uzão de muitos toucados pera ornamento da cabeça;

> The Japanese go about with uncovered and unadorned hair, and the noblewomen with their hair loose. *As japoas andão sempre em cabelo, e as fidalgas com elle solto.*

I do not know much about the specifics on our side, but paintings show coronet, tiara and other headwear, or rather hair-wear in Europe, combined with fancy hairdos I lack the vocabulary to describe.   The prize contrast is that between the noblewomen because, in Europe, only the poor would let it hang down loose.

Be that as it may, "our" and "their" hair ornamentation, or lack thereof, is a fleeting contrast. Within a hundred years, Japanese women – at least the harlots, or if you prefer, courtesans – depicted in *ukiyoe* – boasted a great variety of sculptured hairdo and sported enough large hairpins to scare a porcupine, and the hairpin man with his straw-wrapped pole stuck full of his diverse chopstick-sized ware would become an accepted part of Edo fashion! Shortly after Japan reopened, Alcock wrote:

> Trinkets for women, especially metal pins for their hair, and combs, almost the only ornaments they appear to indulge in; and perhaps, to make up for any restricted use elsewhere, they sometimes carry a forest of these on their heads; pins with hollow glass beads, filled with bright-colored liquids, also seemed to enjoy great favor. (A:COT)

And, fifty years later at the turn of the century, Douglas Sladen likewise noted that not only do these pins take the place of other head ornament but of all jewelry, for Japanese generally wore none (no rings, no bracelets, no necklaces).

> Hairpins are the hatpins of Japan. To rival the fine diamonds and pearls with which girls in the suburbs pin on their home-made hats, she uses hairpins which have nothing to do with keeping her hair up. According to her wealth and refinement, her hairpin-heads vary from little bits of choice lacquer to gaudy imitation flowers and butterflies. In the Whitechapel Exhibition there were even hairpin-heads of Japanese soldiers dragging Chinese soldiers by their pigtails. But these were not good style . . . (S:MQTJ)

Edward Morse, in his book from earlier notes but printed later than Sladen's wrote that these "ornamental hairpins" called *kanzashi,* were made of "cloth, gold paper, delicate spiral springs, straw, spangles, red coral, etc." – he means the decorative part, not the generally two-pronged or comb-like pin part.

Quite half the designs represent flowers. I do not remember ever seeing a natural flower worn in the hair of a person. Many of them represent a story or act of some kind; a child painting a kakemono, a bird-cage, a bird in bamboo. Elaborate as some of them are, the cost is trifling – a cent or two. Hardly a visit is made without a present of some kind being offered, and these *kanzashi* are favorite objects for that purpose. (M:JDD – the numbered illustration of the bird-cage shows a tiny *cricket* in it, instead!)

When Frois wrote, at the tail end of centuries of war, men had most of the decoration. This would change in the peaceful centuries to follow, when women came to enjoy the lion's share of the decoration. For poor women, that apparently meant hairpins.

~~~~~~

2-7   European women tie it [their hair] with ribbons at the end of their braids;
As de Europa os atão com nastros até baxo emtrançados.

> Japanese women tie it with a scrap of paper in just one place in back or with paper string in the middle of their head. *As japoas os atão com hum pequeno de papel em hum só lugar detrás, ou os emrolão com hum fio de papel no meyo da cabeça.*

Japanese women, or rather, *ladies,* for Frois has the nobility in mind, who let their hair hang down unbound in his last contrast, now *tie* it. This apparent contradiction resolves when you know that for all practical purposes the hair *was* loose. The tie – obvious half bow-ties with the loop on the left being standard – were so low-down (at mid-back or lower) that viewed above the tie, the hair appears to be unbound. For practical purposes, nothing could be worse than this style, because such hair would catch on things very easily, whereas things would pull through loose hair without such a tie. The second Japanese style mentioned will make far better sense to the reader in a figurative translation: *pony-tail.* This was the style a noblewoman would use if she went riding and it was not restricted to noble women. The paper cord wrapped around the base sometimes continued upward – or *outward,* for the position of the ponytail varied – for several inches, creating a very perky effect.

So, Frois's contrast is between hair kept tightly bound from scalp to tip, on the one hand, and hair that is bound in only one place, i.e., *free* for the rest of its considerable length.   Presumably, the latter – I can't help thinking of the old C & W hit *Behind Closed Doors* (*"but when she lets her hair fall down . . ."*) –would have been found "loose" in both senses of the word in Europe at this date.

~~~~~~

2-8   European women wear fine bonnets or silk scarves on their heads;
As de Europa poem beatilhas ou volantes na cabeça;

> Japanese women *wataboshi* of silk refuse or a length of white cloth under a mantle. *As japoas hum* vataboxi *de borra ou hum pedaço de pano branqo debaxo do manto.*

The Portuguese for this common European headwear, *beatilhas* and *volantes,* interest me. The former has a beatific, or blessed ring to it, reminding one of our "Sunday best." The latter, literally means "flying" and was, no doubt, a means of increasing a woman's attractiveness even as it veiled her. Both items are fine, while the Japanese items, on the other hand, are crude. The *wataboshi* is cloth beaten out of substandard silkworm cocoons, the remnants, dredges or, in slang *merda* (which I shall not translate) of the silk. [1] The white cloth is also plain, the antithesis to the gossamer silk covering European hair. *Wataboshi* is soft and warm, while the plain cloth was absorbent and cool, so the

Japanese headwear, if not much to look at, was practical. In fact, only generations before Frois wrote, the *wataboshi* was worn by men, too.

In Philip Stubbes ANATOMIE OF ABUSES, published in 1583, we learn that the above-mentioned hats are but a beginning, for among the "hats that defy virtue" we find that

> sometimes they use them sharp on the crowne, peaking up like a sphere, or shafte of a steeple, standing a quarter of a yard above the crowne of their heades; some more, some lesse, as please the phantasies of their mindes. Othersome be flat and broad on the crowne, like the battlements of a house. An other sort have round crownes, sometime with one kinde of bande, sometime with an other,; nowe blacke, now white, now russet, . . . never contente with one colour or fashion two dayes to an ende. . . Ande as the fashions bee rare and straunge, so are the thinges whereof their Hattes be nade, diverse also; for some are of silke, some of velvet, some of taffetie, some of carcanet, some of wooll: & which is more curious, some of a certaine kind of fine haire, far fetched and deare bought, . . . [others must have] a great bunche of feathers of diverse and sundrie colours , peaking on toppe of their heades . . . and these fluttering sayles are fethered flags of defiance to vertue . . . (in AOV[I lost the book behind this acronym!])

Today, the head-wear of both sides mentioned by Frois share something. Both have developed into wedding dress. I will skip describing "our" side. In the century after Frois, the *watabôshi* lifted up off the head so it seems to float like a huge upside-down soup bowl and now it is easy to find on the internet because it hides the "horns" of the bride in the Shinto part of the ceremony.

1. Silk and Cotton   The word *wataboshi* reads "cotton-hat/cap." This is because *wata,* or "cotton" has the connotation of *crudity* (and it is homophonic with "guts"). With *tofu,* for example, the soft, smooth blocks are called *kinu* (silk) and the harder, rough blocks are called *momen* (cotton-cloth).   Since the connotation of the former suggests greater value, most young Japanese who have been too busy with school and office work to do their own shopping wrongly assume it is the more expensive, when the opposite is true (at least for tofu sold by traditional shops that make it themselves) because the hard and rough tofu requires more squeezes (?) of the beans.

~~~~~~

2-9   European women wash their hair and head in their houses;
As de Europa lavão em suas cazas os cabelos e cabeça;

> Japanese women do it in public baths where there are special lavatories for the hair. *As japoas em banhos publicos onde ha partiqulares lavatórios pera os cabelos.*

Here, Frois is probably *not* referring to Japanese noblewomen, who, I think, would not be caught dead in a public bath (see 1-53). But it is hard to find any solid information about these things. Okada found proof that there were special parts of baths to wash hair 25 years after *Tratado.*   I cannot say more. I can only wonder why Frois wrote "hair and head" – why not just "hair"? – and why Japanese women should have relied upon public baths as completely as they evidently did, while Korean women showed a preference for rivers right up to recently – I saw it done many times while thrice visiting Korea in the 1970's – Is it possible that the group bathing and heat is more appreciated by the Japanese because they eat less spicy food?

But all this is old. In the 1990's, *asa-shan* or, shampooing every morning at home (thanks to powerful showers), was *the* thing for young Japanese women. Older people, this foreigner included, found it a waste of time and the world's limited energy resources. I enjoyed the fragrance of the freshly washed hair on the subway, but I suspect older Japanese put it in the same negative category as perfume (11-47) and resent having it pushed in their faces.

2-10   The noblewomen of Europe wear long trains;
As nobres de Europa trazem grandes rabos nas fraldas;

> Japanese women in the house of the *Kubo* [shôgun] wear four or five wigs attached one to another that drag three *couvades* [about 6 feet] behind them when they walk.   *Os japoas em casa do* Qubo *trazem 4 ou sinco cabeleiras apegadas humas nas outras, que lhe andão arrojando tres covados por detras polo chão.*

Ambrose Bierce – who was convinced that all of us unconsciously crave the tail our ancestors actually had – would have been delighted to know that "our" *trains* were called "tails" (*rabos*) by the Portuguese, and that there were women who dragged their hair (not to mention the male equivalent in trousers = *hakama*) mentioned earlier (1-6+notes)).

The *Kubo*, literally, "public-direction=person=way" was used (by the missionaries, at least) to refer to anything from the Emperor to high-level administrators. Frois usually used it to refer to the *Shogun* Hideyoshi, whom he had met and who ruled Japan at the time he wrote TRATADO. Hideyoshi's women – we know he had at least thirteen, far more than his predecessor Nobunaga, who only had one wife and two mistresses. [1] – would have worn what *looked like* a train of wigs on formal occasions. Actually, *they were not "wigs"* (*katsura*) serially linked, but a single long "tress" (*kamoji*)[2] linked to the real hair a bit below the shoulders with a cord (generally tubular cloth decorated with auspicious natural motif tied in a way to leave both ends sticking out cleanly a few inches each way) and red and white *mizuhiki* paper decoratively tied with half-bows at intervals. I can understand Frois's confusion, for it is hard to see how any unbroken hair (be it from a 4 or a 2-legged animal) can be so long.

All of this presumed extremely clean surroundings, for hair was not washed daily. The hair generally rested on the long train of the kimono which in turn rested on spotlessly clean tatami mat or floorboards. The women only wore their hair like this on formal occasions, but my impression is that there were many such. (And, long before, in the Heian era, real hair was worn to dragging length all the time, if illustrations are to be believed) In Europe, where even castles of kings had dirty floors, I would assume there was far less dragging of any type.

1. *Rulers and Their Women* Japanese rulers had many wives and/or mistresses but they were not many at all in contrast to the harems of the stereotypical East (some of which were true).

2. *Wigs and Wigs* Ohara Reiko (J/O: KKB), points out Frois's error in detail. Okada uses the *kanji* for *katsura* in his translation, because that is how Frois had it, but explains it is really a *kamoji.* Like Frois (?) no such distinction is in my working vocabulary, but I note that *kamoji* in my Japanese-English dictionary (KNJE) does not include "wig." It has: "a tress of false hair; a switch; a rat (USA)," whereas *katsura* is defined as: "a wig; a periwig; a false head of hair; a toupee; [and with adjectives] a scratch-wig; a bagwig."

2-11   European women value beautifully fashioned, symmetrical eyebrows;
As de Europa prezão-se das sobrancelhas bem feitas e concertadas;

> Japanese women pluck them all out with a tweezers, leaving not one hair.
> *As japoas as tirão todas com tenas[1] sem lhe fiqar hum só cabelo.*

Citing Castiglione's *Il Libro del Cortegiano* (*Venezia, 1528*), Matsuda and Jorissen note that in parts of Europe, too, women plucked out all their eyebrows, "as seen in some fifteenth century paintings." Yes, I have seen *Mona Lisa*, among others. "In this case," they conclude, Frois's contrast "loses its significance." *I disagree.* In Europe, this was only a fashion.[2] In Japan, it was age-old custom; it was *the* style for their civilization. The oldest poetry writes of eyebrows like the new-moon or the crescent moon, etc. in the Chinese style, but the eyebrows began to disappear as early as the Heian Era (c.800-1200). Although we find some skepticism in the 12th century voiced by *"The young woman who loved caterpillars"* ["hair-bug" in Japanese!] (she argued it was illogical for people to hate them, considering what they turn into) who refused to shave her bushy eyebrows (frightened off potential suitors in the bargain). (DK:AJL), the practice outlived Frois.

The Japanese may have loved nature, but they were not so constrained by a philosophy or rather, theology of the natural, that confused *what is* with what *ought to be.* Europeans justified or condemned everything as "natural" or "unnatural." If Portuguese – and most men in Europe – had natural beards, their women had natural eyebrows. When Rodrigues despite his long years in Japan fumed "This [eyebrow plucking] is considered very fashionable, but in reality, it is an abuse and is against the decoration which nature herself places on the human face,"(R(C):TIJ) he was a typical man of his age. In a sense, though, he may be *wrong.* This eyebrow-plucking (or, soon, as in the case with the male pate, *shaving*) may well be a cultural extension of an unconscious strategy for maximizing natural beauty in a relatively hairless race. The best book ever written against artificial beauty, John Bulwer's ANTHROPOMETAMORPHOSIS: MAN TRANSFORMED OR THE ARTIFICIAL CHANGLING (1654), or, rather the chapter, or "Scene," as he calls it, titled: *Eye-brow Rites, or the Eye-brows abus'd contrary to Nature* has the evidence:

In the *Indies,* the *Cumanans* pluck off all the Haire of their Eye-brows, taking great pride, and using much superstition in that unnatural depliation.
In *Nombre de Dios,* the Women with a certaine Hearb, make the Haire of their Eye-brows fall off.
In *Peru* they use offerings in pulling off the Haire of their Eye-brows, to offer unto the Sun.
The *Brazilians* (also) eradicate the Haire of their Eyebrows.

These are all, basically, Mongoloid peoples with relatively little facial hair to begin with. And, if I am not mistaken, the women in the 15th century European paintings Matsuda and Jorissen mention are mostly blonds, who tend to share this neotoneous trait with Mongoloids. (Moreover, these thin-haired women were generally put in a *damned if you do and ugly if you don't* situation in Europe, because eye-liner was considered not only artificial but, as painted enticement, *sinful* as well!).

Natural or not, there may be something more to this. Today, some Japanese feminists believe this eyebrowlessness, combined with make-up minimizing the size of the mouth, helped make women *less expressive,* for it left them bereft of the physical signs of an outgoing personality.[3] Bulwer made the association with expressiveness in the first paragraph of the Scene, which is memorable because it also reveals that one can both *have* yet *not have* eyebrows in that sense.

The *Russian* Ladies tie up their Foreheads so strict with fillets, which they are used to from their Infancy, that they cannot move their Eye-brows, or use any motion; the meaner sort also affect it . . . . *what a plot have these Women upon Nature, thus to bind their Eye-brows to the observation of so strict and unnatural a silence, to hinder her in one of her most significant operations, and to exclude that part of her mind which useth to be exhibited by the Eye-brows.* (B:A)

KT asks: *But weren't they drawn back in?* For most of Japan's long eyebrow-plucking history, the eyebrows were indeed redrawn, but it was not upon their original location; it was far higher, near the hairline, or, considering the fact that the hairline was usually shaved (i.e. *shaped*), more or less *upon* the hairline. Such is the case for Oinu, used as an illustration by Okada. Her thick painted eyebrows are so high up that they bear some resemblance to sunglasses resting on the top of the head. In that respect, the fashion should not be conflated with the Chinese practice of drawing a thin line to replace the eyebrows in more or less the correct place.[4] These Japanese eyebrows, if they can be called eyebrows, were short and thick, and in the most radical version, completely round![4] More important, sitting way up there, they served a purely decorative function, for the upper brow is virtually stationary.   However, the fake eyebrows were not drawn all the time – women relaxing are often shown without them – and I have seen enough pictures of women dressed up yet without them that I would guess that sometimes it was accepted if not fashionable not to draw in the eyebrow at all. (誰か確認を!)

Originally, shaving the eyebrows was done by upper-rank noblewomen (*kuge*) after they gave birth. I would guess there is a post-partum purification element here, if nothing else because the verb for removing the eyebrows was once *harau* and this is the same verb used for exorcism. It came to be the mark of a married woman and was copied by commoners.   Noble children of both sexes also had their eyebrows shaved and redrawn. Cooper notes that "As late as 1868, the youthful Emperor Meiji had high artificial eyebrows painted on his forehead when he received European diplomats." (LR maybe note to C:TCJ) I wonder whether some ancient folk belief in a second pair of eyes might have anything to do with this. (What about the Chinese?) Lest "we" find all this very strange, let me throw in one more piece of "our" trivia: seventeenth century European women made false eyebrows out of mouse hide! *Honest to God.*

1. ***"Tweezers" and "Tenaciousness"*** are the same *tenas=tenaz* in Portuguese. The fact that tweezers called *ke-nuki*, or "hair-removers," were a popular item for street-vendors helped me to decide which possibility to go with.

2. ***Shaving Eyebrows in the West.*** Since Queen Elizabeth in 1595 seems to lack eyebrows, and this is several generations since the hennin, I wondered if the fashion that is identified by Renaissance Florence might not be more widespread and long-lasting than I thought, or traveled slowly from country to country getting to England last (Queen Elizabeth might have just covered her eyebrows with white powder in a base of puppy fat) – but found googling got me nowhere. Everywhere it was the same *Did you know that Mona Lisa . . .?*   And whatever was not Mona Lisa was *dead cats*: when one died in an Egyptian house, the (human) family shaved their eyebrows to mourn for it.

3. ***The Psychological Significance of Shaved Eyebrows Revisited***.   Ishida Kaori, in her *Keshô sezu ni wa ikirarenai ningen no rekishi* (The history of humans who cannot live without being made up) gives a completely different perspective. After giving the standard take on this fashion as anti-expression, she asks "Why do people with shaved eyebrows seem spooky?" and answers "It is because you do not know what a person who has shaved eyebrows might be thinking." Put that way, I suppose you could call the fashion empowering! I suppose the last word is context. The following article is a good example of how a fashion can be turned on its head. ***Japan Bans Judo Kids with Thin Eyebrows*** Sat Jul 13, 4:06 AM ET TOKYO (Reuters) - *Six Japanese high school students were ejected from a judo tournament to teach them a lesson after they shaved their eyebrows to a fashionable but intimidating thin line. Kyodo news agency, quoting organizers Saturday, said the six had been disqualified from a judo tournament in Utsunomiya, north of Tokyo, on the grounds that the current Japanese teenage fad gave them an unfair advantage. "We have banned thin eyebrows because they are intimidating to opponents and cause displeasure," . . .* This would seem to contradict the basic natural psychology of eyebrows where large bushy ones are threatening. The reason they spook here is because shaving eyebrows and painting in or tattooing a thin line is something the yakuza and other violent gang members do. And the reason they were disqualified is because the students knew they were not allowed to do it, yet did. Someone who did *that* might lift you in a T-bone, drop you on a shoulder and break your collar-bone or something.

4. ***Chinese Eyebrows.*** It is possible the Chinese painted their eyebrows outlandishly high at about the same time Japanese imported so many other Chinese things. If so, they did not stick with it for long, because one does not find it in later Chinese art. One reason I would like to think Chinese began it is that the Chinese had a mythological four-eyed deity – the legendary inventor of so-called "ideograms." Then we could imagine the high eyebrows to serve an imaginary higher set of invisible eyes . . . Anyone?   中国では四つ目のが、かの漢字の神 だけ？ まゆげの神話学はない？

5. ***Eyebrow Shapes***   According to books of makeup history, most women knew to make thin eyebrows if they had small faces and thick ones if they had large, especially long faces, which is just what cosmology teaches today, but noblewomen could not do this because they had to make theirs in whatever was the proper shape for their position and the occasion. This hints at a new "right," the Right to Make Yourself Attractive! 水尾順一 「化粧品のブランド史」中公新書 or 日本化学会「お化粧 と科学」大日本図書

2-12   European women put cosmetics on their brows to make them white;
As de Europa p õem posturas na testa pèra a fazer alva;

Japanese noblewomen put some pictures on their foreheads with black paint on festive occasions.   *As japoas nobres lhe poem per festa humas pinturas de tinta preta.*

Both Japanese translations have Japanese noblewomen painting their brows with *some black paint* on *formal* occasions. Indeed, *festa* includes a stronger ceremonial connotation than the English "festive." But Frois really *does* write "pictures" (*pinturas*)! As noted above, Japanese women painted the edges of their hairline and painted in stubby false eyebrows on the upper part of the forehead. Since these varied in thickness and shape depending on the shape of the woman's face, her preferences and, perhaps, the occasion, were they hyperbolized into "pictures"? The Japanese translators retain the possibility these eyebrows, or a false hairline is what Frois refers to. But, if we take Frois at his word on those *pinturas,* as the French edition does, *it would seem there was a brief-lived fashion of decorating brows with pictures,* [1.] or he was impressed by New Year's games where black circles and other designs are painted on the face when the shuttlecock is dropped, etc.. The contrast seems *black* and *white,* but the meaning is not.

1. *Pictures on the Face* The only pictures I recall (in Bulwer:1643) have been on European women's faces. Googling says decorative patches were used in Frois's century, made of Spanish leather or felt, cut into crescent moons, stars and other shapes, and glued to the face to cover smallpox scars. In the eighteenth century it grew into a fad for both men and women. 万が一フロイスのいう如く絵を額に画いた日本人の記録がご存知ならば...

2-13   European women all too soon find their hair turns white;
As de Europa, em breves annos, se lhe fazem os cabelos branqos;

Japanese women's hair does not turn white though they turn sixty, because they oil it. *As japoas são* [2] *de sesenta e não tem cabelo branco polos untarem com azeite.*

If European men were more fortunate in their full beards, Japanese women were blessed with lasting beauty in their hair, even if their fountain of youth made them smelly (2-4)! Walnut oil, in particular, was reputed to keep hair black, according to a period publication *Onna-kagami,* or "Woman's Mirror (with the punning meaning, "Paragon of womanhood")" cited by Okada. I suspect genetics and diet have more to do with it; but wonder if the oil might not protect from sun damage and include something beneficial to the hair that may be absorbed by the scalp.

2-14   European women open holes in their ears and fill them with earrings;
As de Europa furão as orelhas e emchen-nas de arrecadas;

Japanese women neither open holes in their ears nor wear earrings.
As japoas nem furão orelhas nem trazem arrecadas.

It is surprising the Japanese did not do this when the Chinese, whose habits they usually adopted, did.   In China, according to Ball, every woman and girl wears them; and so accustomed does one get to see them in a woman's ears, that it looks almost as queer to see a Chinese woman without these indispensables, as it would to see an English lady going barefoot; and a Chinese woman would feel ashamed to appear in the one condition, as an English lady would in the other. (B:TC)

So the West would seem to lie somewhere between Japan and China on this matter! Thunberg, at the end of the 18th century, explained the lack of this adornment in Japan in moral terms: "Vanity has not yet taken root among them to that degree, as to induce them to wear rings or other ornaments in their ears." (T:TEAA) But, at this time, they did go in for fancy combs and pins in their hair. I think there must be another explanation. A museum exhibit text states matter-of-factly that decorative clothing absorbed all of the decorativeness leaving no need for any *akusesari* (Japanese call jewelry *accessories*) (http://www.sengoku-expo.net/text/tf/J/kaisetsu_keppatsu.html). But I think that is too simple. I can't help noting that not a few Japanese women *even today* think of ear-piercing as *unnatural* – as most of us view any other body-piercing (or viewed it until recently) – and damaging the body their parents gave them at birth. They refrain from getting pierced even though they must wear clumsy clamp-style earrings and have accepted without protest tight Western-style shoes which deform their toes, as they do "ours." With large earlobes (*fukumimi*) synonymous with good fortune, is it not also possible Japanese once felt puncturing the site of one's fortune was not a good idea? Could Chinese, who also had the fortune-ear idea, have concluded the opposite: that puncturing it and hanging valuable metal from it would stretch it and serve as a sort of pump-primer? Maybe the two people have a different assessment of *holes* . . .

Or could this be a case of *historical trauma* dating back to a time when Japanese were not yet Japanese. According to the historical reconstruction of Tanikawa Kenichi, Japanese did wear ear ornaments from the Jomon period (10,000-300 BC) to the Kofun period (300-c.600). These ancestral Japanese hailing from the sea-people tribes of the Hainan (South China) area were called the *mimi*, or "ear" people and ancient Japanese gods/spirits with names including *mimi* are theirs. Over the millennia, these adornments included large rings, strings of heavy *magatama* (comma-shaped beads [1]) strung on string and, most notably, ear-lobe plugs, or rather discs up to about 4 inches in circumference. In the Yayoi (300BC-300AD) period, Ear ornaments stopped being worn by live people but continued being used as funerary dress. Meanwhile the Ear people and the Eye people intermarried and created Japan. Why the ear-plugs and ear-rings had to go, though, I do not know. [2]

Be that as it may, most Japanese women today are perfectly happy to supplement their natural complement of 10 holes. [3] I can recall a young woman at the local butcher's shop (Ikuta, Japan, 1998) who boasted a half-dozen small rings in each ear.

1. *Magatama* The literal translation is "bent-gem." They are usually jade or what seems to me to be plain ole stone or even clay. My dictionary calls them "comma-shaped beads." They might also be called dull saber-tooth tiger teeth. But they are a bit too short for such fangs and far thicker than even the boldest comma. The OJD claims they derive from boar tusks. Perhaps. But the only accurate description would be that they look like tiny embryos. Considering the fact that similar "bent-gems" are not found elsewhere (unless we include shell) and that they are deeply associated with rebirth, for they (usually on necklaces) are *the* most common "gem" found in grave offerings, I guess that even if they were originally fake boar tusks, they were consciously identified with embryos. After these hunting and gathering people – who would know what an embryo looked like – were replaced (or faded out in favor of) by rice-cultivating people, this

consciousness disappeared and with it, eventually the *magatama*.

2. *Ear-lobe Holes* in Japan FK taught me what she knew and warned me it might be wrong and not to believe it, which needless to say goes without saying. I doubt that ear-plugs would disappear so easily and suspect that the ear-people were repressed and the slightest hole in the ear avoided by the Eye people who turned into Japanese. You may take that with an even larger grain of salt . . .

3. *Perfect Tens* I've always though the invention of the zero will eventually be traced back to the decimality of women, but I had better leave further discussion of that to another book!).

ところで、朝鮮・韓国人の場合、耳はどうなるでしょうか。日本人みたいに穴明けはしない？　明ける？、

2-15   European women think heavy make-up and embellishment of the face unattractive [a
vice];   *Nas de Europa hé defeito parecerem-lhe muyto as posturas e afeites do rosto;*

Japanese women think the more layers of [white] powder applied the more
elegant [gentile].   *As japoas, quanto mais alvayade poem, tanto o tem por maior gentileza.*

In 1583, Fray de Leon warned that "with the excessive use of these corrosives" women
"wither their own flower and thus turn yellow and render themselves easy prey to illnesses through
having their skin wasted by the make up they put on it" (L(L&P):LCP). The powder was the same
"white lead" about which Swift later wrote

> *When Mercury her Tresses mows*
> *To think of Black-head Combs is vain,*
> *No Painting can restore a Nose,*
> *Nor will her Teeth return again.*

But health was not the real reason the Occident was, generally, down on cosmetics. To be
heavily "painted" was to be a harlot and any obvious make-up was the mark of someone behaving in a
fresh manner toward the catechism of humility. This sometimes gave rise to great enmity, such as
that expressed by the following words spit by an English Puritan a few decades after Frois: "a painted
woman's face is a liver smeared with carrion." (LR) De Leon, more diplomatically, did not insult the
body nor "want to talk about the sin which some people find and link to make-up." He acknowledged
that most women did use *some* make-up, yet were not by any stretch of the imagination harlots. So,
he tried to expose Make-up *himself* as a problem, "a deceitful trickster, who gives them [the women]
the opposite of what he promises them, and that as in the game children play, so he saying that he
paints them, blackens them . . ." De Leon's logic is often as silly as it is impeccable: since women
wash off their make-up before they sleep, they *know* it is dirty, *ergo* "how can they persuade
themselves that it beautifies them?" (Ibid) But a hundred pages of scintillating logic always come
back to one thing: Make-up is unnatural=false=deceitful=wrong.

I have not come across anything in Japanese literature suggesting that make-up is a moral
issue, unless it is about the social sin of not getting properly made up to fit whatever role one might
have in society.   This does not need any explanation. With most cultures different or excessive
decorations might be thought odd or unattractive but immoral? *We* are the ones needing explanation.
Of course, the freedom to plaster oneself can be overdone. The prolific playwright and novelist
Saikaku (1641-93) has a protagonist whose face is already white, rubbing in 200 layers of *hachya*
(mercury-based white make-up) with freezing cold water [2] in *Honchô Machinin-Kagami* – those were
bountiful times, indeed, for Saikaku, on his part, polished off 10,000 haiku in a night and that is no
hyperbole! This "two hundred," however, was. It was probably a Chinese convention, for "The
Bride" in I.T. Headland's CHINESE MOTHER GOOSE happens to use "two hundred rouge-sticks," and,
unlike 800, 1000 or 10,000, this 200 is not a common idiom for plentitude.

When faced with Japanese make-up, all European visitors I have read become instant Puritans.
"We" *insist* upon the natural look. Mrs. Busk's 1841 summary of Dutch observations on Japan
sneers: "The face is painted red and white, to the utter spoiling of the complexion; the lips are stained
purple, with a golden tint."(B:MCJ)   Decades later, Alcock wrote he saw "many as fair as my
countrywomen, and with healthy blood mantling in their cheeks . . . when freshly washed," and
detested the way they "powdered all the face and neck with rice powder until they look like painted
Twelfth-night Queens done in pastry and white lead." (A:COT) This is not just men, who, after all,

were the biggest complainers in Europe. Women had the same opinion. "I decline to admire" wrote Isabella Bird, "complexions which owe much to powder and paint. The habit of painting the lips with a reddish-yellow pigment, and of heavily powdering the face and the neck with pearl powder is a repulsive one." (B:UTJ)

Thank goodness, I say, for the likes of Baudelaire, Huysmans and Wilde, who challenged this unnaturally narrow naturalism with their unabashed defense of the artificial, or rather, the natural artificiality of life. None of these famous characters visited Japan. The painter Menpe, who did, gives us the type of argument only a more enlightened thinker and true aesthete is capable of:

> There is nothing of the British scheme – no powder puff hidden in a pocket-handkerchief, no little ivory box with a looking glass in the lid, no rouge-tablet concealed in a muff to be supplied surreptitiously at some propitious moment. The Japanese woman has the courage to look upon her face purely as so much surface for decoration, a canvas upon which to paint a picture; and she decorates it as one might decorate a bit of bare wall . . . the white makes no effort to blend with the natural tone of her neck: it announces itself in a clear-cut, knife edge pattern above the folds of the kimono. (M:JRC)

In other words, pure materialism – i.e. *allowing the make-up materials to speak for themselves* – of the Japanese approach is the more honest one. It beats our naturalism, which is fake by nature. Moreover, the Japanese approach is *kinder*. Heavy white make-up is the equalizer par excellence. It lets everyone have an equally attractive second skin. In the dark, every cat is grey. In the light, every Japanese woman was white. *Bright white.* And, this equality of second nature was not only kind to the dark-skinned woman, but to the light-skinned as well. I owe this idea to Edward Morse. When, for the sake of balance, he mentioned a few absurd Japanese customs after a long talk extolling Japanese good manners as an example of higher civilization Vassar girls might well emulate, he brought up that white powder. "Young ladies going to a party" he wrote, "paint or powder their faces conspicuously white, and presenting a rather objectionable sight to those who associate this habit with the class who usually heavily paint at home." Here is the momentous discovery:

> Yet on inquiry about this practice I found it was extreme modesty that prompted it. Did a girl not paint on these occasions, it would assume she possessed so fair a complexion . . . (1894)

History tells us that Japanese have liked white skin – especially on women – from time immemorial. For all their *theorizing* about skin color, the young Ambassadors to Europe – who were probably the first Japanese to meet white *women* – had nothing specific, nothing personal to say about it (or Valignano did not record it for us, anyway). The first time a Japanese *woman* met a met white-skinned women that has been recorded,[1] was *far* more revealing. *The situation* was as follows. In 1812, Captain P. Rikord of the Imperial Russian Navy captured a Japanese merchant vessel and took hostage the incredibly bright and courageous merchant king Tachatay-Kachi as a means to free his beloved ex-Captain Golownin, who was held in captivity by the Japanese on shore. Since Captain Rikord was an admirable man, he and the merchant were soon fast friends, cooperating to gain Golownin's release (Will Adams is OK, but these guys impress me *far more*. They deserve a movie, a better one than *Shogun*, too!) Before heading back with the merchant and five of his sailors to winter in Russia (because the Japanese government was slow to make decisions), Rikord invited "a Japanese lady" on the captured vessel, "who had been the inseparable companion of Tachatay-Kachi" aboard to see his "ship, and the strange people and polite enemies, as she called us."

> On entering the cabin she placed both her hands on her head, with the palms outwards, and saluted us by bending her body very low. . . Fortunately for this unexpected visitor, there was on board our vessel a young and handsome woman, the wife of our surgeon's mate. . . . Our countrywoman endeavored to entertain the foreigner with what the women of all countries delight in: she showed

her trinkets. Our visitor examined the ornaments with great curiosity, and expressed her admiration by an agreeable smile. But the fair complexion of our countrywoman seemed most of all to attract her attention. She passed her hands over her face, as though she expected it had been painted, and with a smile exclaimed, *"yoee! yoee!"* which signifies *good.* I observed that our new visitor was somewhat vain of her new ornaments, and I held a looking-glass before her, that she might see how they became her. The Russian lady placed herself immediately behind her, in order to shew her the difference of their complexions. She immediately pushed the glass aside, and good humouredly said, *"varee! varee!"* (not good). She her self might have been called handsome . . . her countenance was expressive and interesting, and she was altogether calculated to make a good impression. She could not be older than eighteen. (Account by Rikord in G:MCJ bk2) [2]

Here, we can see from real life rather than literature how much Japanese adored white skin, and indirectly, why powder was so important as a beauty aid, or equalizer, in Japan. Still, it would be wrong to identify Japanese women in masse with heavy make-up. The Spanish merchant, Avila Giron, writing a couple decades after Frois, came to a contrary conclusion about who relied the most on beauty aids:

The women use neither perfume nor oil on their faces, neither do they use those filthy things which the women of our country are want to employ . . . yet, for all that do not have a better complexion than the Japanese woman who merely washes her face with water from any pond. But it is true that, as a mark of honour, married women are accustomed to putting on a little powder dissolved in water (although it is not really necessary) and a touch of colour on their lips to hide the dye which comes off on their lips when they stain their teeth. These days, worldly women and those married to Chinese whiten their faces exceedingly. (Relacion, in C:TCJ)

If "these" days are *more* heavily made up, those days when Frois wrote should not be as heavily made up as he writes.   Indeed, it is generally believed that the long Warring Era favored outdoor activity and *buke* (samurai class) women wore relatively light make-up. Perhaps, Frois observes the styles of make-up used by high-class women on formal occasions, whereas Giron describes the every day life of most women. Giron also makes what may be the first observation of the finer skin *quality* – as opposed to *color* – of the Japanese.   I do not know what "filthy things" Giron refers to, but he is a bit unfair to "our" women, for the Japanese, on their part, used bird-shit (especially *uguisu,* the harbinger of spring with a beautiful voice) for facials.   And, finally, to be fair to Frois, "our" side changed very quickly at the start of the 17th century.   The King of Frois's generation, Phillip II was austere of lifestyle and costume and expected others to follow suit. After he died, Iberia was ready for a bit of color.

1. *Translation of posturas and afeites.*   The former means both *posture* as in English and beautifying agents such as cosmetics.   The latter means artificial devices, imitations, similitudes, things lacking naturalness (From the NDA, I think it a derivative of *afetar* something like the modern *afetação*). Perhaps the English "make-up," a splendid word with ample connotations when you think about it, by itself would be enough.

2. *Movie Material*   It was hard not to quote the entire passage, twice that long, with more detailed description of the irrepressible young woman, whose way with words survives multiple translations. Since the 3-volume set of books of Captain Golownin's Captivity and Rescue are expensive, readers who are not specialists will have to await the movie for more!   *Send me an honest-to-goodness advance and I'll script it, anytime!*

2-16   European women do all they can, use all means to whiten their teeth;
       As de Europa trabalhão com arteficio e confeisões por fazer os dentes alvos;

       Japanese use iron and vinegar to make their mouth and teeth as black as [. . .]
       As japoas com ferro e vinagre trabalhão por fazerem a boca e os dentes pretos como [. . .]

The original is missing a word, but "black as *pitch*" is Rodrigues's term in Cooper's translation. Chances are Frois used the same idiom. I like the idea of "as a crow" (*carvão*) suggested in brackets by the modern Portuguese translation.

Rodrigues wrote that noble women and boys did it, but that "the practice has now been given up completely by men and largely by women who now leave their teeth in their natural condition." As it turned out, the custom – black teeth being the mark of a betrothed or married woman – was soon to revive and continue to the second Opening of Japan and then some. Cooper notes that the (boy) Emperor Meiji still had his teeth dyed in 1868! (C:TCJ)

Iron and vinegar were probably not the only ingredients.[1] Good dye was hard to make and often included secret ones. *Senryu* (haiku-length poems about human foibles, often of a risqué nature) mention men dangling their genitalia over tubs of dye to magically increase its blackening power for women who couldn't afford to buy the good stuff! "A noseless maid's tooth-black is always badly made" goes one from YANAGITARU (*hanakuta-na gejo ohyakuro-ga denu toiu* – Y 1-3), with the implication being her pox was so bad that she couldn't find a man to cooperate. Thunberg suggests the source of this superstition, for he describes the *ohaguro* as "prepared from urine, filings of iron and sakki [*sake*]." He also writes it was "so corrosive, that the gums and lips must be well covered while it is laid on, or it will turn them quite blue." (T:TEAA) Apparently, women began their day with this vile substance. Everyday was said to assure top quality black teeth. Every other day, decent black teeth. And, every third day, not so good black teeth.

This habit was perhaps the most widely reported example of Japanese contrariness that was not also Chinese. And it was nowhere made to appear so odd as in the English edition of Van Linschoten's Dutch translation[2] of what had to come from Valignano, judging from the proximity of the hair and teeth with the *black* vs. *white* mourning colors:

> . . . and as among other nations it is a good sight to see men with white and yealow hayre and white teeth, with them it is esteemed the filthiest thing in the world, and seeke by all meanes they may to make their hayre and teeth blacke, for that the white causeth their grief, and the blacke maketh them glad. (1598)

Ridiculous or not, it is a game attempt to make sense of a topsy-turvy custom. Alcock introduces another theory (and quashes it):

> When they have renewed the black varnish to the teeth, plucked out the last hair from their eyebrows, the Japanese matrons may certainly claim unrivaled pre-eminence in artificial ugliness over all of their sex. The mouths thus disfigured are like open sepulchres, and, whether given to 'flatter with their tongues' I cannot undertake in this my novitiate to say, but they must have sirens' tongues or a fifty-horse power of flattery to make those red-varnished lips utter any thing which could compensate man or child for so much artificial ugliness. . . . If this be a sacrifice offered on the shrine of conjugal fidelity, the motive is no doubt very laudable, but it leads to the inference, not altogether complimentary, that either the men are more dangerous or the women more frail than elsewhere, since such extreme measures have been found necessary to achieve the same results. Surely something less than the whole womanhood of Japan deliberately making itself hideous might have sufficed to prove the absence of all wish to captivate admirers! For my part, I cannot help thinking the husbands pay rather dear for any protection or security it is supposed to bring, since, if no other man can find anything pleasing in a face so marred and disfigured, the husband must be just as badly off, if he has any sense of beauty in him. Perhaps, custom and that 'deformed thief,' fashion, may have brought him to *like* it; but if so, where is the protection? If he can like it, so may others. . . . (A:COT:1853)

When Japan's greatest polymath, Minakata Kumagusu, visited America to study on the way to England at the end of the 19th century, he removed his artificial front teeth, so the women wouldn't interfere with his studies (he was so strong, handsome and bright that he supposedly attracted women everywhere), or so he claims in his autobiography. But I have never seen anything indicating that

Japanese thought blackened teeth ugly. So, we might have to consider other explanations. Could the black stand for the *Yin*, or female part of the Yin-yang universe? I find slightly inward pointing teeth make a woman look more cultured, refined, gentle, whereas buck-teeth make her look tomboyish and less unattractive. Are the black teeth, perhaps, are an extension of this psychology, making women less bone-hard looking and thereby more feminine? Or, going even further for the sake of argument, could the black teeth under the red lips rather advertise a woman's sexual readiness by increasing the affinity of the mouth above to that below? It was, after all, originally part of Coming of Age and only later became the mark of a married woman.

1. *Vinegar and Iron*. Romans imported many of their cosmetics from Egypt but they did have recipes of their own, like this one for hair dye: "Take a pint of leeches and two quarts of pure vinegar; pound them into a pot and ferment for sixty days. At the end of this time rub into the scalp in the sunlight and the hair will become beautifully black" (56.) I presume the leeches were full of blood and the blood full of iron, so we have almost the same recipe here as that Japanese used on their teeth!

2. *Linschoten's Dutch*   I would be curious to learn whether L. combined the funeral black and white contrast with the hair and tooth contrasts in this manner himself or if it was a creation of his English translator.

2-17   European women wear bracelets of gold and silver on their arms;
As de Europa trazem manilhas d'ouro e prata nos braços;

The noblewomen of Ximo [Shimo] wear thin strings wrapped around [their wrists] five or six times. *As japoas nobres de Ximo humas linhas delgadas em cinco ou seis voltas.*

Precious metals versus paltry threads. No wonder Miguel=Valignano went on and on about the ornaments worn by Europeans. (see 1-28n) While the extent to which "we" delighted in these materials was abnormal, the relative lack of interest in jewelry on the part of the Japanese was even more unusual, possibly even unique in South-East and Far-East Asia. Japan does seem to have been naturally shortchanged – there is a paucity of some interesting minerals, but there were sufficient jewels and precious metals to go around; and, unlike earrings, bracelets require no special operations. All they need is to be put on. Perhaps I paid too much attention to the hole issue with earrings. Is it possible they just did not like the *feel* of these things? I, who don't even wear a wristwatch could appreciate that, but I realize that is no explanation. *Or, does it need an explanation?* What if an examination of anthropological evidence showed over half the cultures in the world did not go in for metal bracelets? In that case, "we" would beg for explanation, rather than "them."

In respect to those strings, Okada wonders if Frois might be referring to a charm worn when the arm or fingers were sore, but he does not guess why they would be sore. Young noblewomen wove clothing for their boyfriends. Could it have come from long hours on the loom? Or could it be from too much *koto*, a zither that sounds feminine and was, indeed, generally played by women, but is actually one of the most muscularly taxing instruments in the world? (the thick strings are pressed on the outside of the bridge to bend notes, with the amount of bending dependent on muscle power) Be that as it may, my first guess is that the strings were indeed charms, but for romance. I have no evidence whatsoever.

2-18   European women wear jewels and golden chains around their necks;
As de Europa trazem joyas e cadeas d'ouro ao pescoso;

Gentile women in Japan wear nothing, and Christians relics or rosary beads.
As jentias de Japão nada, e as christãs relicairos ou rozairos de contas.

In ancient times, Japanese women *did* wear necklaces and these were not only adornment, but – at least in poetry – they and their lover's very souls.   These were called *tama-no-o,* or "tama-string." The word *tama* is a good example of how homophonic punning went to the very heart of Japanese culture.   A *tama* is a round and/or shiny object that may be translated according to context as *gem, jewel, ball, bead* or (rain or dew) *drop.* And, as beads were strung up, by extension, any small object with a whole in it, though it looked like *macaroni*, might even be so called. Japanese were so *tama*-oriented that they even took to using it as an adjective for something pretty and precious, such as the boat and oars the Herdsman uses to meet the Weaver when they make their annual rendezvous across the Milky Way.[1] A *tama* also means "soul." A different Chinese character is used, but the pronunciation is identical. Accordingly, these precious necklaces abound in ancient poetry. A widow in the MANYOSHU (Japan's oldest poetry anthology) is propositioned by a man wanting to restring her soul. *You wish! she* replies, *I've already found a better guy to restring me!* The under-belt as well as the neckless became a soul-string. And, the soul in Japanese could stand for what becomes the heart in the West, too. So we may think of the English word "heart-string."   Later, as longer poems were polished down to the more impersonal haiku, even a dewy spider's web might become a *tama-no-o* for the now Buddhist world. *Poof! Poof! Poof!* little souls return to the *Atman.* Come to think about it, "head" in Japanese is *atama.* Before Chinese characters turned the two *tama* into heteroscript the ancient *tama* was not a pair of homophones, but a singularity.

Yet, the Japanese abandoned their necklaces! *Why?* As noted already, the Japanese never really got into jewels – and, consequently, jewelry and it is not for a lack of resources. A fellow editor at the Japanese publisher where I worked for almost twenty years, published a book in Japanese but titled (in Arabic letters) MINERALIUM INDEX, in which he gave a wild theory (*muchi-o shochi-de*) as to why there is not only small interest but even a small vocabulary to discuss gems in Japanese. Yonezawa Kei hypothesizes it may have something to do with the birth of language. Finding so wondrous an object as a gem – an obviously symmetrical crystal, completely unlike all the far less obviously geometric things all around us – shocked us into thought=speech. You might call this the *Wow!* theory of language. This is supported by, or rather explains the Japanese word/concept of *kotodama*, or word-soul/gem. Since we know it is hard for soul to talk about soul, for language to lift itself up with by its own bootstraps, (the self-reference problem), Japanese lacks a vocabulary for the gems that gave birth to their tongue.   But, he adds, unfortunately (for one who is in love with minerals), "the axis of interest of all East Asia [including Japan] lies in rocks, not crystals." (1996)

Be that as it may, I cannot help but think that Frois, as a man of religion, valued Japanese more highly for not adorning themselves. If we were to score the contrasts, this one would go to the Japanese.

1. *Tama* as an Adjective. This usage has survived up to the present day. Once, a highly literate magazine editor was kind enough to call an essay I sent him *a gem of an* essay (*tama no zuihitsu*). While it does not work as an adjective in English, it does work, and that is amazing , too, amazing!

~~~~~~

2-19   European women have sleeves reaching to the wrist;
As de Europa chegão-lhe as mangas [até] o colo da mão;

> Japanese women have them reaching to mid-arm, and do not think it wanton to disclose their arms and breast. *As japoas, chegão-lhe até meio braço e não têm por dezonestidade descobrir os braços e peytos.*

The Portuguese I translated as "wanton" is *desonestidade,* or "dishonest." Old English used the word in the same way. Talk about contradiction! The Europeans claimed the use of make-up to *cover* the skin on the face was *dishonest* on the one hand, yet uncovering the skin on the arms, legs or breast *dishonest* on the other.   I do not feel Frois's *descobrir* is quite right, for it implies a willful revealing or showing of the body.   That was not the case, at least for the body parts in question, for they were not considered particularly sexy.   With the wide sleeves and loose collars, the breasts might be spied through the sleeve-hole or underarm hole –

> *We sometimes double the cloth under our arms to stop the sweat from running;*
> *The Japanese leave a space open under the arm to let heat out and cool air in.*

– of a raised arm, or from in front of a bowing body.   But the Japanese man would presumably peek elsewhere, at, say, the nape of the neck, if he were being dirty-minded . . .

Though Japanese clothing was relatively open, Japan was far from a nudist colony. The acceptable degree of revelation depended on the class of the woman and the situation.   There is a splendid *example* of a Japanese who failed to recognize this in Frois's description of the astonishingly rapid construction of Nijô castle for and by the first unifying Shogun of Japan, Nobunaga:

> Everybody, both men and women, who wanted to go and view the work passed in front of him;
> while on the site one day, he happened to see a soldier lifting up a woman's cloak slightly in order
> to get a glimpse of her face, and there and then the king struck off his head with his own hand.
> (Historia: in trans. C:TCJ)

Neither was the relatively more revealing nation completely free of fetish, men wanting to see more than custom allowed.   There are *senryu* about men using the still rare telescope to spy on women and even men sneaking a peek at women micturating, this last was considered a perk of being a guide for blind women! But it is possible that sort of thing did not begin until the heyday of Edo about a hundred years after Frois.

~~~~~~

2-20   Among us, a woman who walked about barefoot would be thought mad or shameless;
        Antre nós, andar huma molher descalsa ter-se 'ia por douda ou dezavergonhada;

   Japanese women, rich or poor, walk about barefoot for most of the year.
        As japoas altas e baxas a mayor parte do ano andão sempre descalsas.

One might say the culture of Europe was literally out of touch with the earth.   Everyone who could wore shoes, inside and out.   But I did Japanese really walk about *barefoot*?   Inside, yes. On the beach, sometimes.   Otherwise, they had to take care to keep their feet clean as not to soil their immaculate *tatami*.   For this reason, even small children were generally not allowed to walk barefoot outside.   Hence, this contrast provides a perfect example of the kind of misleading term Frois mentioned in the Prologue to his missing Summary. "We" assume "barefoot" – *descalcas,* or "unsocked" in Portuguese – is tantamount to being *shoeless*, because *we* always wear socks with shoes. But Japanese rarely wear *tabi* (the closest thing they had to socks: see 1-55+) during the hot half of the year. They walk about with bare-feet, for sure, but those feet are not bare on the bottom as we might suppose because they are *in their sandals* or *on their clogs*.   Considering the high humidity, this is only natural. But why did Frois put this contrast into the woman's chapter?   The answer is probably that he was not so much thinking of what we think of when discussing bare feet, i.e., the soles, as of the *upper part of the foot*, i.e., the scandalous revelation of skin on the lower half of a woman's body.

As a literal antipode for Japan, China would have been far better than Europe.   For Chinese women not only kept their feet hidden when they were dressed, but when they were not.   In China, feet were a woman's surrogate private part. If Japanese women were loose with their feet, Chinese women were tight, and Europeans somewhere in-between. This is not only true for the degree of exposure, but for the degree to which the feet were tortured. The Japanese were kind to them, the Europeans, with their pointed and symmetrical toes, hard on them, and the Chinese with their foot-binding, very, very cruel to them. Considering this, it is *ridiculous* to find Occidentals conflating Japanese and Chinese foot traditions, as S. Cockburn did in his privately printed *"Japanese Ideas of London . . ."* (1873). After he has his Japanese "scout" denigrate the pannier ("a large vulgar cushion/ invented, I think by a Russian") and bustle (and what's that below them so odd – do you ask it?/ Behold on their backs is a great *baker's basket!)* worn by "our" women, he has an Englishman retort:

> The vulgar barbarian, tho' colleague of mine
> Who made him a judge on a subject so fine?
> He forgets that his women are beauties too small;
> They totter about as if ready to fall,
> And can't even walk for *they've no feet at all!*

Some illustrations of *Chinese* women really do seem to depict a footless race! Presumably Cockburn saw one of these and jumped to the wrong conclusion. This was one Chinese custom the foot-free Japanese wanted no part of!

~~~~~~

2-21   European women wear their belts very tight.
As de Europa trazem seu sinjidouro muito apertado;

> Japanese noble women [wear them] so loose, they are always dropping down.
> *As japoas nobres tão largo que lhe anda sempre caindo.*

Okada writes matter-of-factly that the reason *obi* sashes – bands of cloth "as wide as a horse's girth strap" (de Avila Giron in C:TCJ) and just as stiff – were tied loosely was because of their greater width and the fact they are wrapped around the body several times (In TV Easterns, bad guys strip women by grapping hold of the end of the *obi* and spinning them like tops!). But, from what Rodrigues writes decades after Frois, *fashion* was probably at the heart of the matter, and Frois was catching the tail end of it:

> In olden days and up to the time when we went to Japan, and even long afterwards . . . It was thought fitting to wear them very loose and they always placed both their hands inside the sashes as they walked about the house in order to stop them slipping down to their feet. Nowadays, all the women tie their sashes in the same way as the men do . . . (R(C):TIJ)
..
Today, the *obi* is usually thought of as *very* restrictive. The rude French traveler Paul Theroux described it as "an armor compressing and flattening the breasts." The Austrian-born American Rudofsky more lyrically(?) depicts "breasts flattened out like flowers in a herbarium." KT adds more concretely, "you stick towels and padding under the obi to take away the bosom and hips' shape." This is definitely a strange development from the socio-biological perspective. If the Japanese were rubbing shoulders with a large-bosomed, wide-hipped people, one might argue this was an unconscious ploy to create an identity by *alternity*, as some call it. This not being the case, we might hypothesize that the relatively small difference between the male and female body was compensated for by raising and thickening the belt for women to further contrast it to the far lower male belt (which is explained by the claim that traditionally a long-belly was considered handsome in a male), but such a strategy would have been easier to develop by having men wear the thickest belts (like sumo

wrestlers) and women thinner waist-making belts.   So, I think it best to go with the common explanation: it is a strategy to best show off the kimono design – fabric, not form – the woman as clotheshorse.

The Japanese did not compress the breast for anti-erotic or misogynic reasons. And, I do not doubt that women who have grown used to the firm support find it reassuring, but, rationalizations aside, I still cannot help feeling the *obi* is a form of national masochism. *How good to learn from Frois that it was not always tight!* On the other hand – though two wrongs do not make a right – the West, too, has not always been supportive of the female breast. Desmond Morris writes that early English Puritans flattened "the breasts completely with a tight bodice" and, in seventeenth century Spain (geographically and chronologically close to our Frois), young ladies had "lead plates [!] pressed in to their swelling bosoms in an attempt to prevent their development." (INTIMATE BEHAVIOR)

~~~~~~

2-22   European women wear rings with gems and other jewelry;
           As de Europa trazem aneis com pedraria e outras joyas;

           Japanese women wear no jewelry made of gold or silver.
           As japoas nenhuma peça nem joya feita de ouro nem prata uzão.

When one considers the old association of trinkets with trade, where "we" the West laugh at the willingness of "they" the non-West to accept useless pretty objects in exchange for things of real worth, like, say, Manhattan, the existence of a people less interested in trinkets than Westerners is a wonderful object lesson. Okada notes that Japanese called rings *yubigane,* "finger-metal," rather than the contemporary term, *yubiwa,* or "finger-ring," and that some were imported from the Dutch in the 17th century, but may have been used for other things, such as fastening the strings of a pouch (one area where a certain amount of ornamentation was traditional). Finger rings seem such a natural to us that it is hard to imagine a people who would have nothing to do with them.

Since most cultures possessing precious metal has always worn it, the Japanese side is the one most in need of explanation. We have already addressed this, but it is worth more attention. Here is Thunberg, writing in the late eighteenth century:

> That idle vanity, so common amongst other Asiatic as well as many African nations, who adorn themselves with shells, beads, and glittering pieces of metal, is never observed here; nor are these unnecessary European trappings of gold and silver lace, jewels and the like, which serve merely to catch the eye, here prized at all; but they endeavour to furnish themselves from their manufactures with decent clothing, palatable food, and excellent weapons. (T:TEAA)

Thanks to Japan, European culture is seen for what it is, a culture of primitive magpie-like taste focusing on things that shine. Thanks to a cache of art books found in the trash pile next door, I have recently seen scores of jewel-filled European jewelry, including sword handles and the crowns of kings that are now kept in Museums. *As art, they are almost all atrocious. If they did not happen to have millions of dollars worth of precious gems in them, anyone with any sense would say they are junk of zero value.*   This is even true for those by famous artisans.   In a word "we" as a culture were (and still are, I think) *nouveau riche* in the worse way. Our art would have been far better if it had to *create* what was precious rather than merely taking it. If a king had outlawed the use of anything precious for art, we might have had art.

Today, aside from the matter of earrings (2-14), Japanese women have largely caught up (become equally magpie?) with their *akusesari* (accessories), as they call jewelry, and almost everyone uses engagement rings, mostly platinum with diamonds.[1]

1. *Wedding Rings in Japan.*   The wedding ring – an unbroken and therefore forever circle around the medicine=spirit-finger on the left hand that was thought to link directly with the heart – goes back to Greece or Rome, but in Europe was also associated with the Christian vow – eternal vow – of marriage. The Germans prefer the right hand on the strength of their right=straight/correct vs. left=wrong philosophy. Japanese generally use the left hand, but some follow the German style.

~~~~~~

2-23   European women wear purses or keys on their girdles[1] and belts;
As de Europa trazem bolsas ou chaves em seus cordões e singidouros;

> The Japanese gird themselves [above the broader *obi* bands] with some thin strips of silk decorated with gold leaf, but hang nothing from them. *As japoas sinjem humas tiras de seda delgada pintadas com folhas d'ouro, mas não lhe pindurão nada.*

With the loose sleeve corners and bosoms serving as large pockets, Japanese had no need for purses. And if 2-21 was right, and the belts were always dropping down . . . But this is, more strictly, a contrast of the use of chord or chain-like devices to hang things from. The Japanese men did not wear baldrics (thin rope-like belts, usually over one shoulder) for swords, either. The thin European belt may have been functional, but the thin strings or colored bands (not all were gilt) wrapped around the *obi* pure decoration and something possible only because of the extreme width of the *obi*. But I feel Frois missed a better contrast here involving those keys. Can the reader guess?

> *We present the house-keys to a bride to use and wear with pride.*
> *They are presented with a wooden spoon, for they have no locks.*

The image of a housewife with keys dangling from her waist is a very Western one. Japanese houses could only be locked from the inside, and there were no locked rooms or cabinets, so the women would have had no use for keys from the start. "In Japan, the key to privacy is in the human heart, not in hardware, like in the West" as some *Nihonjinron-ka* (a Japanese writer on Japaneseness versus Westerness) once put it. Actually, this could be inconvenient, for in a house with something worth stealing it meant that someone always had to stay home. In fact, there is even a word for precisely that, a *rusuban,* or "remain-guard/duty" and corollary expressions such as *hana-no rusu,* or "blossom's remain/duty," which is to say someone who guards the house while everyone else is out enjoying a cherry blossom viewing. He also missed another cord contrast:

> *We wear our clothes loose or tight and clothing cannot be both.*
> *They wear their clothes loose but tighten it for work by crisscrossing cords.*

That is, Japanese crisscross their torso once with a thin but tough band of cloth or chord called a *tasuke*, which trusses up the loose robe (and, if the sleeves and hems are pulled up a bit, holds them in too) in order to keep it from getting dirty by touching the pail one is carrying, the pot one is throwing or whatever. Personally, I think it looks cool and should be imitated by the fashion world.
..

~~~~~~

2-24   European women's dress is closed in the front so the feet are concealed all the way down to the ground; *Os vestidos das de Europa são serrados por diante e cobren-lhe os pés até o chão;*

> Japanese women's are completely open in the front so that the feet are visible all the way up the instep. *Os das japoas são todos por diante abertos e chegão até o peito do pee.*

"We," if only Europe is included, often think about the concealment of the face by many Muslims, but we do not often consider how strictly we guarded all female skin from view for centuries.

"Open" with respect to the Japanese dress does not mean cut-away or slit *in order to show the leg*, but only that the overlap of the flaps in front is but a foot or two, so that a large step (since Japanese women walked with small steps, a medium step by our standards) shows the foot up to the lower calf. It was possible, however, to show more if one were determined to do so. Tokugawa era courtesans made yearly parades through town on high-teethed chappin called *takageta,* wearing a half dozen or more layers of clothing, yet still managed to flash their goods by virtue of all the layers opening in the front.[1] Good women, however, usually had some inner layers that wrapped around to the side, which kept most of their legs well covered, and walked in short, mincing steps – "as tho' her legs were tied together at the knees"[2] – with toes pigeoned inward as if consciously hiding their insteps, which, together with the nape of the neck, were the official focus of men's oogling.

Until the Takashimaya department store fire of 1928, when women who jumped to their deaths were caught on film showing what should not be shown, most Japanese women wore no confining underwear with kimonos, because, I've been told, the lines would show through the silk. I suspect, however, that in the days before air conditioning, the ventilation was important.

1. Showing Ones Goods   I cannot recall where I read this and it may be wrong. I do know that despite the relatively easy-going attitude toward innocent nudity, Japanese men could still be titillated. Or, at least that senryu a hundred years after Frois speak of see-through crepe cloth and what would amount to stripteases. There were even women who specialized in the introduction of snakes. But, remember, Edo was a city 80% men, so we should pardon their horniness. Here is a *Faux Frois* that would have horrified him:

In Europe, our pornography delights in the beauty of the entire male and female human body;

In Japan, the pornography shows nothing but the genitals, which are grossly exaggerated.

2. Leg-tied   *Some Unpublished Letters of Townsend Harris* ed. by Shin Sakanishi 1941 in R:TKM

~~~~~~

2-25   European women wear valuable scented gloves;
As de Europa trazem luvas preciosas e odoriferas;

Japanese women wear mittons of silk reaching to mid-arm, with all the fingers showing. *As japoas huns manguitos de seda até meyo braço com todos os dedos fora.*

We pretty much covered gloves in the last chapter (1-56). If European men wore gloves first as armor, then as signs of authority, women apparently wore them to hide their hands, supply something good-smelling for people to kiss, or to accidentally drop in order to attract a man's attention. The Japanese equivalent of this last use, was a broken clog strap, though it would see a hard trick to cause such an accident. Evidently, the first sex of gloves (gauntlets), were themselves tempted to use perfume, for I googled across a sixteenth century Portuguese document, ORDENAÇÃO DA DEFESA DOS VELUDOS E SEDAS ([royal] order [by Dom João III] for defense of velour and silk) which includes a clause that forbids men of whatever status, quality or condition (*qualquer estado, qualidade e condição*) to wear or carry perfumed gloves of any scent whatsoever (*não possa trazer , nem traga luvas perfumadas, nem adubadas de nenhuns óleos e perfumes*) – very specific legalese! – while permitting women to wear them as they wish (*como quiserem*). (Biblioteca Nacional de Lisboa, reservados, códice 3395.)

The "sleeves" (*manguitos* [1]) on the Japanese side confuse. Is there no better word for a cloth tube that does not connect with the real sleeve of the clothing or close at the end like gloves or mittens in English? (In French, *manchon* is perfect for just such apparel.). If it were on the leg, we could say "legging," but, unfortunately, we have no "arming," and "arm-guard" would not seem right for a silken fashion worn to protect the forearm from the sun or cold and keep the inside of the sleeve clean. In Japanese translation, the word *teôi* or "hand-covering" is used. It, too, is a bit odd, for we would think that "arm-covering would be better, but at least it is a separate word from the totally encompassing "glove" which is called a *tebukuro,* or "hand-bag."

1. *Manguito*   While a small dictionary defines it as a mitten, a large one defines it as a small *manga*. (A *manga* is a *sleeve; mango; waterspout, cloudburst, lamp-chimney* and *cattle-chute*) which, among other things, is used as adornment and protection of the wrist (*dos pulsos*). The French *Manchon,* or "little sleeve" shares this last meaning.

2-26   European [noble[1]]women generally wear very long black mantles.
      As de Europa trazem mantos muito compridos e pretos

      Japanese noblewomen wear short ones of white silk.
      As nobres japoas curtos e de seda branca.

An Iberian mantle might be described as a cross between a hat, a veil and a cloak. Okada adds that the Japanese mantles were usually made of figured satin or silk crape. Long and black vs. short and white seems about as different as different can be, but considering the fact that both women kept their hair shielded and that both colors are manifestly pure and somber, even funereal – though they could be worn on festive occasions – they are at some deeper level, similar. While most Japanese headgear was not colorful, it is my impression that many European women wore colorful mantles, which is why the first part of the distich probably deserves the same "noble" qualification as the Japanese one. (Any one?)

2-27   European mantles have neither sleeves nor colorful designs;[1]
      Os mantos de Europa não tem mangas nem pintura alguma;

      In Japan, the same figured *katabira* [light robe/s] they wear also serve for
      mantles. *Em Japão as mesmas* catabiras *pintadas que vestem servem tambem de mantos.*

I mean The image of a light robe serving as a mantle, or veil – imagine someone warding off a rain shower with a coat – would seem so absurd to the reader that Frois has redundantly put "the same" (*as mesmas*) before the *katabira*, where "also" (*tambem*) was grammatically sufficient. Indeed – confession! – before researching to write this book, I mistakenly assumed that the *katabira* I had encountered in haiku was a summer hat! I had no idea it was a robe! (It turns out that most Japanese today, conversely, know it was a robe, but do not know it served as a mantle.)

Okada adds that the color (aside from white) was usually "pale-scallion" or "water-pale-scallion" – light greens and blues – and other light shades. Japanese still feel such colors are *cooling* and even today utilize them, not for mantles but for window and door-screens (which I find very ugly).

1. *Colorful Designs.*   My first translation was "nor any figures," but I feared that would be ambiguous and changed to "nor colorful designs." Another possibility would have been "nor any pictures." I had considered using the word "painted" or "painting," but since most are actually *printed . . .*

2-28   European soldiers wear uniforms on festive occasions;
Os soldados em Europa por festa se vestem de libré;[1]

Japanese women ordinarily wear *kimono* uniforms in full decor.
As japoas vestem ordinariamente qimões de libré e quarteados.

The translation of *quarteados* is a problem. The Japanese translations take it to mean a four-color scheme,[2] but I think we can extrapolate the idiomatic meaning of being well-proportioned, broad across the shoulders, etc. found in the dictionary (NDA) to mean what we now call dressed to the T, which in military idiom suggests "full décor." This gives the clothing a correct but still formidable air (lost to the French translation's apparent waffle, *richement colorés*) and fortifies Frois's intended contrast of the informal, far-from-uniform women's wear in Europe (indirectly alluded to by the soldiers) with their formal well-starched counterparts in Japan. This reading is backed up by Rodrigues who was soon to write, Japanese garments "are all cut in only one plain style, and this is true of the dress of men and women, laymen and religious"(TIJ) and Thunberg two hundred years later:

> the Japanese always have their coat of arms put on their clokes . . . with a view to prevent their being stolen, which in a country where people's clothes are so much alike in point of materials, form, and size, might easily happen. (T:TEEA)
>
> ..

This sounds like folk-ethnology, as if Thunberg asked a Japanese, who came up with an answer to please him. (I would say "lost" rather than "stolen" for clothing folded into little boxes at public baths and would be easily confused.)   The reverse side of this is the fact that kimono designs, perhaps *because* they had a fixed shape – and a fine rectangular shape for a canvas at that! – reached artistic heights of graphic design that Western costume has never reached. These "coat of arms" found not on all clothing but on all formal outside wear also suggest martial dress, though I doubt it was so common in the less regulated sixteenth century. A *Faux Frois*:

> *European women go to dances hoping each to boast her special dress unlike any other;*
> *Japanese women at bon dances come in regiments, outfitted with identical uniforms.*

Since the Jesuits in Japan were so down on festivities that they even criticized Japanese for their efforts to create Christian fun, we have no reports of bon dances, which probably would have been considered proof of the popularity of the devil. But, I have been impressed by groups of identically dressed women (including neighborhood groups and the employees of medium-sized companies) participating in bon dances. I recall feeling they resembled athletic teams and comparing them to colorfully dressed groups of women participating in an African (I wish I could recall the country) festival I had seen in National Geographic. These uniforms are far from drab and are a joy to behold. If, despite all this circumstantial evidence, I am mistaken and *quarteados* does indeed refer to a four-color scheme that happened to be big in Frois's time (if so, only for a short time or else Okada would have added an annotation), we would still need to explain whether it meant colors found on a single item, or four different robes worn one over another. With respect to the latter, another *Faux Frois*:

> *European women wear and show only one or at most two layers of clothing;*
> *Japanese ones wear up to twelve layers of clothing and often show them all.*

I regard this as perhaps the most spectacular difference of all with respect to clothing and am puzzled Frois never made it. What fascinates me is that with Japanese clothing generally fastened in only one place – thin sashes might tie each layer but still they only did so at the waist – the rest of the vertical hem, from the collar to the waist (and, sometimes from the waist to the feet) was loose enough that each layer of color would show like the layers of tissue opened up by a large surgical incision. To return to the young woman described by Captain Rikord:

> Her dress consisted of six wadded silk garments, similar to our night-gowns, each fastened round the lower part of the waist by a separate band, and drawn close together from the girdle downwards. They were all of different colours, and the upper one was black. (in G:MCJ)

1. *Vestem de Libre*. Frois's word for "uniform," libre, is fascinating. It does not derive from the fact that Japanese with a stronger tendency to uniform themselves than Westerners are liberated from wasting time and money on choice which as often as not leads only to clothing uglier than the uniform.. It comes from the same roots as "livery" in the sense of delivery=distribution, where masters/employers retainers bestowed set of distinctive clothing to their retainers or servants or soldiers so they could be recognized. I find this ironic.

2. *Color Schemes*. Japanese color conventions are too complex to develop in this book if nothing else because of the difficulty of coming up with suitable names for the colors that are note necessarily matched in English. Suffice it to say that Kogo-jiten (old-language dictionaries used mostly by high-school students studying old Japanese) provide color charts for the help of Japanese and that there are many formal color schemes devised for the various seasons and these could be further broken down to pairs of colors.

~~~~~~

2-29 In Europe, the men walk in front and the women behind;
Em Europa vão os homens diante e as molheres detrás;

In Japan, the men behind and the women in front.
Em Japão os homens detrás e as molheres diante.

Both Japanese translations turn the subjects into *husband* and *wife* (*otto, tsuma*) rather than "men" and "women." This contrast, *though mistaken* – especially before I *knew* it was mistaken – astounded and delighted me, for Europeans visiting Japan after the Tokugawa period of seclusion observed Japanese men walking in front of their wives, who were supposed to lag back a bit to avoid stepping on their husband's shadow, or for another reason that reminds me of our reason for men walking on the curbside of a woman.

> When they go out, she walks a dog's pace behind him – a relic of the good old days when it was the fashion for your enemies to stab you in the back. (S:MQTJ)

The Japanese, for their part, were shocked to see our convention of *"ladies first!"* Chamberlain, describing "Woman (Status of)" in THINGS JAPANESE, makes some interesting associations in this respect:

> Two grotesquely different influences are now at work to undermine this state of slavery [i.e. "the three obediences" to father, husband and son] – one, European theories concerning the relation of the sexes, the other, European clothes! The same fellow who struts into a room before his wife when she is dressed *a la japonaise,* will let her go in first when she is dressed *a l'europeenne.*

It is hard to believe something so value-laden as walking order should reverse; and I couldn't help wondering if Frois might have made a slip of the pen, but Okada made no comment as he usually did to indicate doubt about a contrast, and Matsuda and Jorissen are reputable scholars, so I introduced the inverse husband and wife in one of my books published in 1984 (*Nihonjinron Tanken,* an anti-stereotype book written in Japanese.) What a disappointment to find out the contrast was not half so interesting as I thought, that Frois was only contrasting an accompaniment of servants! This cannot be ascertained from the Portuguese original alone. Frois's *homens* (men) and *molheres* (women) are terms with broad connotations (He often used them to mean *husbands* or *wives*). Without further information, "husband/s" and "wife/wives" (Japanese has no number) is a figurative translation, rather than a mis-translation.[1]   That the translators figured wrong only becomes apparent when we see what Valignano wrote, in my translation, or in Van Linschoten's or in Montanus's:

> The women ride horses like the men, and when they bring with them maids (*senoras mocas*), maidens and other women, all of them go in front of them, and the men-servants (*criados*) behind, the opposite of the women in Europe. (V(A):V&S)

> The like [contrarie] custome is among the women, for as they goe abroad they have their daughters and maydes before them, and their men servants come behind, which in Spaigne is cleane contrarie, . . . (L:VJHVL) [2]

> . . . and so [contrarily] amongst their Women, who when they walk abroad, order their maids and Daughters to go before them, whereas ours follow their Mistresses. (M:EEJ)

And, finally, according to the editor of Golownin (1824), the "Ambassades Memorables" of the 17th century Dutch include the fact that "In Japan, husbands walk before their wives" in their potpourri of differences.   Had Frois visited in the twentieth century, he might have observed, as I did, the following:

> *In Usania (I cannot speak for Europe), husbands and wives often go out together.*
> *In Japan, husbands and wives rarely if ever go out together, unless it is to a foreign country.*

1. Mistranslation.   By writing "husband" and "wife," (*otto, tsuma*) the Japanese translators show they did not guess what Frois meant.   The French and German translations are literal (*men* and *women*) and both they and the Portuguese version do not supply any explanation, as they undoubtedly would if they knew what it meant. Since, in the lack of explanation, readers assume Frois means the relative positions of men and women walking together, though literally correct, these are as mistaken as the Japanese.   Unless, someone can prove that European men walked in front of their wives and men behind them in Frois's time, we must follow Valignano.

2. Linschoten's Sources: I recall reading he relied on Maffei, but if I am not mistaken, Maffei wrote only: *Foeminas in publico viri et cognati praecedunt, famuli subsequuntur.*   This suggests Van Linschoten borrowed from Valignano.

2-30   In Europe, property is shared between spouses;
           Em Europa a fazenda hé commua antre os cazados;

> In Japan, each owns his or her own.   A woman sometimes lends hers to her husband.   *Em Japão cada hum tem a sua separada e às vezes a molher onzena com o marido.*

As DR points out, "common property would seem to accompany the Western concept of 'becoming one'."   That is doubtless the main contrast and parallels that of 4-5,   where Frois contrasts the individual economy of Japanese Buddhist monks with the common property of the Christian Brothers.   But the European concept of commonality was belied by the fact that, practically speaking, the fortune generally belonged to the man.   Matsuda and Jorissen cite a mid-17th century text which advises that while not all responsibilities should be divided between spouses, the purse should be in the firm control of the husband and "a lady should fear the touch of money as one would fear fire." This was because money was thought to become a "despicable weapon" in the hands of a woman.   In Portugal, at least, the marriage contract usually specified an allowance to be paid by a husband to his wife.   (J/F(M&J):)   That is to say Frois's idealistic contrast might be restated in terms of who held the purse strings.

Okada notes the rules for *buke* (samurai class) about a hundred years before Frois came to Japan.   The brides were expected to bring a trousseau, supposedly for make-up and clothing, but really to ensure her proper support and this was to be returned after an unspecified period or upon her death. And women generally could bring their own farming plots and money with them into a marriage and lend them to their husbands at their pleasure. Perhaps I should add that his Japanese translation specifies "at high interest." This reflects the fact that the *onzena* was an onerous tax of 11% that suggested loan-shark-like behavior or engaging in *usury*. The respectively high position of Japanese women vis-à-vis European women continued up to Modern Times, though the picture is hardly simple. A half-century after Frois, Caron wrote:

> Daughters have no portions at all, nor nothing given them at marriage; sometimes it happens that rich Parents send a good sum of money with their Daughters, upon their marriage day . . . which present is returned by the Bridegroom and his Parents with much thanks, being unwilling that the bride should have any colourable excuse to raise her into an opinion of having obliged her Husband: The poorer sort do but seldom return these offers as needing them, and glad of any augmentation of their Friends. (C:DOJ)

This lets us know that the poor had no choice but to enjoy equality, but not all Japanese men (or their families) wanted to be indebted to their wives. This next from Sladen in 1905 includes a new element:

> The maddest thing of all about a Japanese marriage was the trousseau. A girl whose parents were only moderately well off, who was marrying a man no better off than herself, might have a trousseau worth five hundred pounds, in which she was provided with everything she could want during the first few years of married life, except the food which perishes. The theory was, that it might make her husband dissatisfied with her if she had to go on asking for things . . . (S:MQTJ)

Sladen's theory suggests women were so lowly valued parents had to pay men to marry their daughters and this was conversely the reason they had money to lend. Be what may, a wife could and generally did *own things* in Japan. They even got them back when she divorced (see 32, below). She could not, however, keep "her" children (unless hers by a previous marriage), for they belonged to, and stayed with, her husband's family.   This is not because children belonged to men so much as because they belonged to the house in which they were born and bred.   When a man married into a woman's family, she and her family kept the children if he left.   But, whether or not the wife enjoyed an independent fortune or living in her family house or not, women generally were in charge of money.[1]   Men, unless merchant class, were supposed to be above pecuniary matters and were perfectly content to let their wives control the family's purse strings. A housewife in all her glory – as opposed to a young bride who was typically hen-pecked by her mother-in-law – was called the *daikoku-bashira* , literally "big-black-post," which is to say the central pillar of the house. She was the family accountant – female fingers are most deft on the *soroban* calculator (see 14-25) – made sure debts were paid on time, knew where the family cash (*hesokuri* = navel-juggling) was hidden and doled out her husband's allowance. In the mid-nineteenth century, Alcock, apparently not knowing about this, expressed surprise that

> the men . . . all over Japan, seem to be wretched accountants . . . [while] the women, strange to say, are much better than their lords at figures; and when it came to a matter of addition or multiplication, we always had recourse to the more ready wit of the wife. (COT)

Despite men being more likely to major in mathematics in Japan as in the West, today, women still tend to be the family accountant (perhaps this helps explain the high savings rate?) and not only the matron of the house but young wives do so; for even if the husband's mother is in the house, the newlyweds nowadays generally do their own thing. *Faux Frois:*

> *In Europe, men handle the family finances;*
> *In Japan, all accounting is left to wives.*

Generations of Japanese men have joked about being cormorants made to regurgitate their pay for their wives. I have been told that the wedding ring (a Western import) symbolizes the neck-choke worn by this fishing bird to make certain he can't swallow any of his catch.[2] It is reported that Japanese companies often cooperate (or did in the last half of the 20th century) with their cormorant "salarymen" by giving them two paychecks, one of which is kept secret from the wife.[2] This might also have something to do with the size of the infamous corporative entertainment accounts.

1. *Significance of Control.* A letter to *The Japan Times* from Christina Tsuchida notes that Prohibition was "a result of the new enfranchisement of women" and the fact that, "U.S. women, unlike Japanese wives, lacked control of the purse strings" so that "Husbands were drinking away their paychecks before they could be used to pay family bills."("Money and patience needed" =LR=1980's or 90's). It would seem the whole ecology of a society is affected by which sex controls the purse-strings!

2. *Companies and Paychecks.* If men once fought to keep a bit of spare change, now (2004), with a divorced wife entitled to 30 to 50 percent of her husband's salary (house and other possessions, aside) as alimony according to Japanese Law, and divorce initiated by middle-aged and elderly women rising rapidly a new scam has begun. "The weekly magazine *Shukan Hoseki* recently explored the "divorce savings plans" and found that $285 to $425 a month is common, and men go to extraordinary lengths to conceal the plans, such as forging pay statements." (Googled article: LR) I have no idea if 1 in 10,000 Japanese men do this or 1/10.

2-31   In Europe, repudiating a woman is a serious sin and the greatest dishonor;
Em Europa, alem do pecado, hé suma infâmia repudiar a molher;

In Japan, one may repudiate as many as one pleases. The women do not lose their honor for this, nor their marriageability. [*Em Japão dá hum repudio a quantas quer, e ellas não perdem por isso honra nem casamento.*]

In reality, separation and divorce may have been more acceptable if not common in parts of Europe, including Iberia, than Frois would admit or we would assume. Take this passage from Sara T. Nalle's *God in La Mancha: Religious Reform and the People of Cuenca*, 1500-1650:

Fiancés cohabited, people married within prohibited degrees of consanguinity, couples separated and lived freely with other partners. Many believed that one could separate legally from his or her spouse simply by going to the town notary and obtaining a so-called letter of separation. Others, who sought to annul their marriages, found witnesses willing to lie for them.(97) (found on IBERIAN RESOURCES ONLINE)

Still, if we are thinking about the professed attitude of responsible parties, the European side of the contrast is beyond dispute. Even Kings were not free to "repudiate" their wives. One English King who wanted to do so found it simpler to behead them, until he divorced his nation from the Catholic church. Even so, Henry VIII's new Anglican church did not permit others to divorce. It is interesting that Frois frames his contrast in terms of moral approbation or acceptance and not on what was legal or illegal. If people were that afraid of sin, why were laws needed? Be that as it may, the Japanese side of the contrast was first noted as early as 1565, twenty years before TRATADO by Frois:

They commonly have no more than one woman [wife], but for very slight reasons, they may divorce her, even though she may have born many sons, and take others [for a wife], and they also leave their husbands, although it is less common, still divorce is so frequent among them, from kings to laborers, that they are not at all upset or astounded about it [*que de ninguna manera se extrana*] (20-11?2?-65 /V(A): S&A?))

I would guess the Jesuits in Japan had nixed feelings about this attitude toward divorce. On the one hand it was proof of sinfulness, but when they forced nobles who wished to become Christian to ditch all but one wife, the fact that the others would not be ruined by the divorce was doubtless a relief. [1] The final part of Frois's above note was picked up by Valignano, and skillfully expanded:

And it is surprising how peacefully they do this, because no ill-feeling remains among the relatives, indeed, they visit, speak and treat one another as they did before. (A:VS)

The reality was complex.   With samurai, where marriage tended to be political, divorce required the permission of the lord of the domain. The "no more than one woman" suggests Frois is contrasting the commoners who made up about 94% of the country. Most of their divorces were probably early in the marriage. In many cases, the man may not yet have brought his bride home but was himself commuting to her house until his mother saw fit to turn over the house to her. If either spouse was thought to be a poor worker, they might be deemed unsuitable and the marriage, that might well be called a trial marriage, annulled by their families. It is commonly noted that in the Tokugawa era (there is almost no information on Frois's time [2]) women could not remarry without an official letter of divorce which only the husband was free to *grant* or *not to grant*. This gives us the impression that the freedom of repudiation was of greater service to men than to women. As Alvarez-Taladriz wrote in his notes to Valignano's *Summaria*, the husband-wife relationship was one of master and vassal in a feudal relationship. Indeed, the threat of simple divorce seems to have been a way to keep women in line. About a hundred years after Frois wrote, moralist Kaibara Eiken in his classic *Onna Daigaku,* [3] "Woman-Great-Study" or, to use a free rendition suggested by Chamberlain "The Whole Duty of Woman," gave seven reasons for divorce allegedly based on Confucius. They were: disobedience to the father or mother-in-law, barrenness (but an otherwise good wife might be kept if they adopted children), lewdness, jealousy, leprosy or any like foul disease, disturbing the household harmony by talking too much and too disrespectfully, or being a kleptomaniac. I have seen longer lists. The Tokugawa government (authorities in some fiefdoms, at any rate) decreed *Reasons for Divorce* in order to promote frugality, and included things like "too much sightseeing" or "too much tea-drinking!"

The reality was *more* complex. At the time Kaibara wrote the above list, the husband *also* needed proper proof of divorce (which meant he needed his wife to write a receipt (*kaeri-issatsu*) for his writ of divorce.) If she could be shaved bald and returned to her parent's home for remarrying without being clearly divorced, he could be banished (*tokoro-barai* – exactly where to I do not know [3]). Women whose husbands philandered away their fortune might lend them money against such a signed permission of divorce(!).   And, Japanese families, being careful, sometimes included pre-signed divorce writs (*sakiwatashi-rienjô*) among their prenuptial agreements. The property of the wife was also detailed so that most men could not divorce their wives even if they wanted to because they did not have the wherewithal to properly return them, as was required.[4] The wording of the writ of divorce includes the phrase "*katte*," which implies fiat, but it also has the connotation (still common today) of selfish individual behavior and came at a price, namely, the responsibility to compensate the other party.

The West was still surprised at Japan's high divorce rate when Japan reopened to the world in the mid-19th century. Alice Mabel Bacon wrote there were men and women who had divorced two or three times over and were none the worse for it (B:JGW).   The Meiji Civil Code of 1898-9 attempted to improve Japan's international reputation, and in a single year the official rate (which vastly understated the reality) dropped from approximately 3 divorces for every 1000 people/year to 1.5, and this rate dropped year to year. By the mid-twentieth century, Japan boasted its Confucian family values explained its extraordinarily low rates vs. the high and rising rates in the USA (the rest of Europe, which included many nations with lower rates yet were conveniently overlooked). The main reason given by Japanese – especially the men in power – for fighting hand and tooth against liberalizing divorce law in the last quarter of the century was concern lest easy divorce would permit men to throw away their wives for someone younger.

Finally, in the late-20th century, the law did change. As it turned out, it was not so much women as men who had something to worry about, for a 19/1/04 AP article cites a Nagoya marriage counselor to the effect that "in well over 80% of cases he sees, the wife is demanding the divorce and it has usually come as a shock to the husband," and (slightly lagging?) family court statistics from the Justice Ministry show "the number of divorces sought by women is 2.5 times more than those sought by men." A large and rapidly growing portion of these are elderly women freeing themselves of dead-weight husbands disparagingly called *sôdai-gomi,* or large crude trash (things too big to fit in the garbage, put out on a special day for collection)!

1. *Ditching (and Taking) Wives for Christianity*   After my rather glib evaluation of the double-edged sword of easy divorce for Church policy, I found out that in 1592 Valignano had delivered questions about Japanese matters including divorce to Father Procurator Gil de la Mata who was to submit them to famous casuists at the universities. He had 11(!) questions with respect to marriage. The fourth of these is:

> "A Christian has repudiated in good faith his first wife. He had married her before the publication of the works of the Council [of Trent, which dealt with marriage as a sacrament]. Now he has asked to marry another woman before the Church. He has not concealed in his confession that he has repudiated his first wife. He is admonished to return to his first wife. He does not do so and will not do so. Question: Should one in confession tell the truth to a Christian of this sort, and above all, should one administer to him before the Church the sacrament of marriage?"

The reply by the Casuist (Gabriel Vázquez, a scholastic theologian by specialty) was, in my opinion overly long – as if he were paid by the word – but to sum up, the traditional Japanese marriage was evidently contracted with the sole intention of testing the wife's behavior and as such was not an authentic marriage which presupposes perpetuity. (From Jacques Proust: *Europe Through the Prism of Japan* (P(B):ETPJ))

In other words, *the first marriage not being a proper marriage, the divorce is not a divorce, and you are free to have a real marriage with a Christian.*

Had the Jesuits in Japan only known this 20 years earlier, it might have made the conversion of Japanese in cases where one spouse objected a lot easier!

2. *Frois's Time and Marital Matters.* See Note 3 for a pre-Frois example. When Frois wrote, the rules were not yet nationalized. The Tokugawa laws officially allowing only men to seek divorce were not yet in place and the situation probably varied from place to place as well as from class to class. Takagi Tadashi notes that the extent of the difference can be exampled with the rules for what

to do with the older brother's widow. In some parts, a commoner was legally obliged to marry his older brother's widow, whereas in all parts samurai were forbidden to do the same, for the widow shared the older brother's superior status and status was rigidly preserved. (*Marriage and Divorce in the Edo Period* in *Japan Echo* Vol. 30, No. 5, October 2003) One could write a book on the Topsy-turvy *within* Japan by contrasting these two classes!

3. *Onna Daigaku*   I fear the existence of this ludicrous list of divorceable shortcomings has encouraged overly facile generalizing on the behalf of smug Christians. A Catholic explanation of why only Christianity elevates women fails to notice any of the relative freedom of Japanese women as observed by Frois and simply pegs Japanese women on to Chinese women as follows:

> "The binding of the feet is in reality only a means to keep the women at home. The absolute dependence of the wife upon the husband was also maintained as an unyielding custom in old Japan until the late reorganization, as is proved by the *"Onna Daigaku"* of Kaibara Ekken (1630)." (The Catholic Encyclopedia, Volume XV Copyright © 1912 by Robert Appleton Company Online Edition Copyright © 2003 by K. Knight *Nihil Obstat*, October 1, 1912. Remy Lafort, S.T.D., Censor Imprimatur. +John Cardinal Farley, Archbishop of New York)

4. *A Wife's Property*   A description of the types of property a wife owned – which had to be returned and which did not and other proof of how seriously this rule was taken in Tokugawa Japan may be found in a lengthy article about *Divorce in Law and in Practice* by Takagi Tadashi (Ibid). He cites a document showing a husband having to get his wife's possessions out of pawn before divorcing her and a senryu (satiric poem) of complaint for having to return more money than the man got for a dowry, because the portion of the match-maker (10%) is included. Takagi also gives cases where poor women who wanted divorces worked to gain the money needed to convince their husbands. It is not clear, however, what would happen if the husband could not be convinced.

2-32 In accord with [our? their?] fallen nature, men are the ones who repudiate women [in Europe]; *Segundo a natureza corrupta, os homens são os que repudião as molheres;*

In Japan, the women are often the ones to repudiate the men.
Em Japão, muitas vezes, as molheres são as que repudião os homens.

If Frois meant "their," and "their" meant the men (as most of the translations suggest [1]), it would be a bit odd, for in England, at least, it was women who were generally accused of having an especially sinful nature at this time. As crooked as the rib they came from, they were accused of having given in to the snake and corrupted Adam.   Late sixteenth and seventeenth century feminists countered that God made woman of man's flesh that" she might bee purer then he" that is to say, she was not second-hand but double-refined! (Jane Anger 1589 in Travisky ed. THE PARADISE OF WOMEN, but A. Goreau THE WHOLE DUTY OF WOMEN is the best book on the subject).   Assuming Frois did mean that men in Europe followed "their natural depravity"(what one translation seems to say) and this represents a Virgin/Mother Mary-loving Catholic understanding of what modern day sociobiology claims (the male had the stronger tendency to live dissolutely and seek other sex partners), should we then cheer for the men of Europe being rightfully put down? Why not? But we should also note that Frois's contrast was not necessarily a compliment to Japanese women, for the inference is that *they* are more "corrupt" than their European counterparts.

While women in Japan did not did gain a formal right to sue for divorce until 1873, there were circumstances when they could do what amounted to the same in the Edo period. As Okada notes, a husband who spent a wife's savings and sold her property could be divorced by her family and she could gain a divorce by his failing to send her an official Summons to Return (after she went home because he abandoned or maltreated her. In 31, above we have already seen other details of how a woman could divorce a man in the Edo era, but it is hard to be precise about what Frois saw. One hint comes from the Japanese Middle Ages. In Tale 10 of book of Buddhist tales called *Shasekishû* (vol.5) written in 1283 describes a husband who goes to the constable (*jitô*) for his assistance in capturing his wife who left him, but the constable found she was a kind person, so she got to stay in the house and he was banished from the (shall we call it) county. In the Middle Ages of Japan, it seems, a man could divorce his wife and both could remain in the same county, while a man who was divorced by his wife had to leave. This was good, obviously, for protecting the woman from revenge. (M:KZJ ch3)

The above concerns commoners. The samurai class would be a different story. The men did not need to divorce to enjoy new love (they could take another wife or a formal mistress), whereas the women would certainly have a better reason to *want* a divorce than a man would. But in their case, politics and economics made it hard.

When it comes to divorce, poor women probably had the advantage. Nineteenth century Europeans observed that, among lower class wage earners, the women were likely to divorce their husbands, mostly for being hopelessly dissolute drinkers or gamblers (if she waits too long he might even sell her for his debts) but sometimes for lesser reasons. Bacon mentions a woman who got married on the promise that the bossy Mother in Law would remain with her older son, and when this turned out not to be the case, "sued for divorce and obtained it, and was back in her old place, all in a month's time from the date of her marriage." (B:JGW) In *Queer Things About Japan,* Douglas Sladen *lauded* the high divorce rate in Japan, noting that it was far more reasonable to allow a working woman to divorce her no-good husband than to chain them to utterly irresponsible and violent men by unfair laws of property, as English Law did at the time. And, in his next book wrote:

Until quite recently one marriage out of every three ended in a divorce, which was perhaps, as the American woman said, one way of making enough husbands go around." (S:MQTJ)

One final qualification. It is possible that some or even most of the divorces of men by women that Frois learned of were not really by the women but by their parents. In Edo, 20% of marriages adopted a groom into the bride's family (*yôshi engumi*) either because the family had no sons (or young ones). In this case, Takagi writes,

> the adoption took legal precedence over the marriage, and the right to dissolve the relationship rested with the bride's father. If he decided he did not care for his son-in-law, he could cut the adoptive tie, and this would automatically end the marriage, even if the couple were happy with each other. This arrangement, under which property is inherited on a matrilineal basis, is an unusual one; other than in Japan, it is found only in the Pyrenees region of France, parts of Scandinavia, and parts of India. (*Japan Echo* Oct. 2003)

We can imagine more cases where the couple was unhappy and the daughter said "Papa, ditch him!" It is also possible that the 20% of Edo was the most common situation in parts of Frois's Japan, though it might not have always been called adoption. Many Japanese folklorists emphasize matrilineal survivals in rural areas. It is not hard to imagine that women living at their own homes would have been able to kick out their husbands in one way or another.

1.   *Corrupt Nature.* I am unsure of Frois's phrase *Segundo a natureza corrupta.* If he wanted to specify "their," Frois could have written *seus.* That is why I feel I suppose he means it in a broader sense, and, with English (a language that needs pronouns), I feel an "our" might be good, even if Frois did not specify that either. The French, by the way, is *leur naturel corrompu.* Comments are welcome!

2-33   In Europe, the abduction of a female relation threatens the survival of all her family;
Em Europa polo rapto de huma parenta se põe toda a gerasão[1] a perigo de morte;

In Japan, her father, mother and brothers conceal it and just let it pass over.
Em Japão os pais e as mãis e irmãos desimulão e pasão levemente por isso.

"*Rapto*" is hell to translate. I have no idea if Frois means only forced intercourse (*rape* in our sense of the word), merely the elopement of a young female without the permission of her family, both or something in-between the two. The Japanese translations use a term generally meaning *kidnapping* a term close to the central meaning of the term "abduction." (We can see it used that way for old paintings such as *The Rape of Europa* by Zeus in the persona(?) of a bull.) Apparently, European, or, at least Iberian males were under cultural if not legal obligation to risk death trying to wrest back (or *kill*, as we see in some Islamic countries even today [1]) a stolen or, perhaps, wayward woman and those responsible for taking her in order to defend the family honor even if it resulted in the destruction of said family in the course of the vendetta. I cannot tell if Frois refers to families giving up their daughters and/or wives to lecherous leaders (the Shogun Hideyoshi was one such robber of women) and choosing to survive, families who choose not to pursue their daughter's elopement, an epidemic of kidnappings or actual rape, which I feel was probably rare because women in Japan were not push-overs (See 2-35, below).

The moderation on the part of the Japanese that Frois describes here does not cover the whole picture. Adultery is another matter altogether. The Florentine merchant Carletti describes a horrific punishment he or someone apparently witnessed in Japan. After the adulterers are bound and carted to the husband's house:

> ... in his presence they cut off the man's penis and take enough skin from his body to make a sort of cap, this is put on the head of the adulterous woman. And from her shameful part they cut a strip of flesh from around the vagina, making a garland of it to place on the head of the adulterous man. And thus ornamented and adorned with those members, they go naked through the city, making a miserable and shameful show of their bodies to all the people during the time when the flowing out of their blood from the wounded parts ends their lives. (C(W):MVAW)

This is doubtless an anomaly, a show put on by a furious big-shot. Dutchman Caron reported at length an even more grotesque story, where the wronged husband has his dazed wife unwittingly open a box with her lover's privities in it in front of all her friends before he cuts her head off! (C:DOJ) Unlike Caron, Carletti put the cruelty in perspective, writing that the Portuguese were even stricter than the Japanese in this regard! *Not only adultery, but mere suspicion justified homicide.* Portuguese law (in Goa [2nd account E. Indies p214]) permitted husbands to kill their wives at whim, so that women "frequently die unjustly." He sadly mentions hearing of a "young wife of only a few months, killed by her husband because of a jealousy that he felt of a man who had fallen in love with her when she had been a girl, but who continued to pass through the street in which she lived with her husband." (I might add that the legacy of this Portuguese law is still found in Brazil, where news of and, thank goodness, controversy, over perfunctory killings of wives by jealous husbands continues today.)

If Frois writes nothing whatsoever about *adultery,* it is doubtless because there was no contrast. Europe and Japan *both* punished it with death. [2] We might add that the men East and West always make it sound like *they,* not women, are the victims. This lament by a character of Ben Jonson's, written shortly after Frois wrote his *Tratado,* helps explain why men believed they had to restrict their wive's freedom:

> Alas, sir, do you ever think to find a chaste wife in these times? now? when there are so many masques, plays, Puritan preachings, mad folks, and other strange sights to be seen daily, private and public? If you had lived in King Etheldred's time, sir, or Edward the Confessor, you might, perhaps, have found one in some cold country hamlet, then, a dull frosty [frigid] wench, who would have been contented with one man: now, they will as soon be pleased with one leg, or one eye. I'll tell you, sir, the monstruous hazards you shall run with a wife. (*The Silent Women*)

The Commandments treat neither virginity before marriage nor adultery afterwards, except for the one about men coveting other men's livestock and women. In LA CASADA PERFECTA, de León wrote that the reason for this was that God assumes women are "like a canvas on which other virtues are painted" – that is to say pure *tabula rasa* and that merely bringing up the question of chastity or purity would be a mistake, for

> it should not even enter their heads that it could be otherwise, they must not imagine that the contrary is possible, anymore than fire can be cold or snow hot. They must realize that a woman breaking this fidelity to her husband is the same as the stars losing their light and the heavens tumbling down, and nature breaking its laws and everything reverting to that ancient and primeval chaos. (L(L&P):LPC)

1. *Killing Women.* Every time I read of the murder of a woman by men, usually her own brothers and/or father it infuriates and saddens me, but until reading Frois, above, I did not reflect enough on the pressure put on the family. If they did not kill the woman who eloped, one can imagine that the family of the other man to whom she had been promised would come after her family for the loss of honor. The brothers may sound disgustingly righteous, but they may be doing what they have to do to prevent the start of a vendetta that would end in many more deaths. In other words, the root of the problem is not in *misogyny* so much as in the absoluteness of *honor* and how conflict is settled.

2. *Adultery Execution in Europe.* After introducing Japanese cruelty, it behooves us to see "our" side, too. Here is a typical Iberian execution, not so horrible as ones that begin by parading mutilated adulterers but cruel enough! "In 1565, the Plaza was filled with people who wanted to see the execution of an innkeeper's wife and her lover.   By ancient law, the wronged husband was permitted to execute his wife and her lover. Despite the pleas of monks to pardon the guilty couple, the husband remained adamant. He walked up to where they stood bound and repeatedly stabbed them with a knife. Finishing them off with his sword, he threw down his hat and said, "So much for the horns." (*Crime and Society in Early Modern Seville* by Mary Elizabeth Perry found at THE LIBRARY OF IBERIAN RESOURCES ONLINE)

2-34   In Europe, the seclusion of daughters and maidens is important and rigorous;
Em Europa, o emcerramento das filhas e donzelas hé muito grande e riguroso;

In Japan, daughters go out for the whole day, or many, wherever they want to, without telling their parents. *Em Japão as filhas vão sós por onde qerem por hum dia e muitos, sem ter conta com os pais.*

Ah, to breathe the free air of Japan! The freedom of Japanese women was noted by the captain of the very first European ship to visit Japan, Alvarez (in Boxer's words below) and to Frois's superior Valignano, who contrasted them to Chinese women:

That Alvarez [see 2-35n] was no uncommon observer, is seen from his remark that, despite the nominally inferior position of women, the gray mare was frequently the better horse. He alludes wonderingly to the relative freedom of movement enjoyed by women who could go out unaccompanied by their menfolk or chaperones – something very daring to an Iberian, for as a result of centuries of Mohammedan rule, Moslem ideas on the seclusion of women were much stronger in the Peninsula than elsewhere in Europe. (B:CCJ)

The Chinese women are very retiring and modest and are seen in public rarely or never; the Japanese enjoy more freedom and are looser in their conduct than women anywhere else. – Valignano (PRINCIPIO, first redaction (1580?), in S:VMP).

I am not sure what Frois thought of girls and women having license to roam, but it was convenient for the Jesuit mission because it meant that they could proselytize women as well as men.

Since women were not so secluded in Japan as they were in most Asiatic countries (or in sixteenth century Spain or Portugal for that matter), the Jesuits were permitted to receive female visitors, although in a *zashiki,* or a room with sliding doors ajar so that the occupants were visible to those elsewhere in the building. (B:CCJ)

It is hard to say which culture is the odd man out here, Japan or Europe (Iberia, at least). The lack of freedom for Iberian woman may be inferred by the following comments about the natives of Sinaloa (North Mexico) by Ándres Peréz de Ribas in the seventeenth century. Despite constant warfare, drunkenness and adultery,
..

Another sign of temperance among these people which I confess amazed me, was how safely the women and girls walk around alone through the fields and along the roads without being assaulted by anyone [nadie las ofendiense]. I do not know whether they could have done this as safely in some Christian countries. (R(R&A&D):HOT)

The Japanese situation was not common to the Sinosphere. Marquis de Moge describes the rare chance encounter in mid-nineteenth century China. His small party observed three elegant ("daubed with rouge") young ladies limping toward them on bound feet.

When they saw us they screamed aloud and rushed against the wall, hiding their faces in their hands, and turning their backs toward us in the most contemptuous manner possible. The attitude was so ridiculous to us "foreign devils" that we could not help bursting into a hearty laugh. (M:BGE)

Whereas, in Japan, "the women do not run off as they do in China." It is not, strictly speaking, right to judge gender relations of a foreign culture by the manner in which men or women respond to foreigners, but they do give us an indication of what's what. Women generally kept out of sight of men in China. Li Yu's novels show the telescope being used to bridge the distance between the sexes. But, despite the generally accurate reporting from China and Japan, writers back home continued to confuse the two cultures. In 1873, Cockburn's literary creation, the "Japanese Scout," is amazed that in London *"you'll see the most lovely young 'lassies' / Taking a walk without any young 'laddies'"* to protect their perfectly figured classical bodies ("Oh Darwin, thine ape / could never have ever conceived such a race / Despite thy wild notions of time and space!") from harm. This tells us that London, at least, was finally modern, but an amazed *Japanese* scout? As if young lassies *ever* needed escorts in Tokyo!

~~~~~~

2-35 In Europe, a wife cannot go out without her husband's permission;
As molheres em Europa não vão fora de caza sem licença de seus maridos;

Japanese wives are free to go where they please without informing their husbands.
As japoas tem liberdade de yrem por onde qizerem, sem os maridos o saberem.

This difference may owe something to the lower level of public order in Europe, but for the most part it probably reflects a moral philosophy of total control over women on "our" side. The normality of this oppressive state is reflected by an observer of the Carnival preceding Lent in late sixteenth-century Barcelona:

The women, too, take their part . . . throughout the year they are so severely restricted that they are not allowed to talk to strangers. But at carnival there are no such shackles and hindrance. They put on masks and run through the streets in complete freedom . . . So, for more than one husband, the cuckoo sings before the Spring [summer?] comes." (Felix Platter in H:CER)

The Japanese, not being shackled in their daily life, did not *need* such carnivals to go to town (I exaggerate a bit, for there was something called zakone, sundry-fish-sleep, where great crowds of people slept together on the solstice in Shinto temples. But it was just a sleep-with-anybody thing and not a city-wide abandon of the classic Occidental topsy-turvy carnival.). An abridged Englishing of the testimony of Alvarez,[1] the ship captain and merchant who visited Japan and was the very first Westerner to write about it, at the request of St. Francis Xavier in 1543, contains this line:

Good wives are held in much esteem by their husbands; indeed they altogether rule them, and go hither and thither as they list, without ever thinking of asking leave of their lords." (in C:LLFX)
..

Bernandino de Avila Giron, a Spanish merchant contemporary with Frois, also thought highly of Japanese married women who "may be trusted completely for they are the most upright and faithful women in the whole world." "And," continuing with tongue in cheek, "she who errs in this matter pays for it with her head." (C:TCJ) Fifty years later, Francois Caron of the Dutch East Indian Company gave a more astute, if not sophisticated explanation of the goodness and freedom of wives in Japan. Since men who were not happy with their wives could freely divert themselves with concubines and prostitutes, "this liberty that the Men have, obliges the Women to observe their Husbands and endeavor to endear them to them, by an humble compliance and submission to their humors, being sure else to lose them, and see their Rivals preferred before them."(Ibid.) In a word, these men argue Japanese women are free because they are not free.

Be that as it may, Japanese women in the warrior class and among town-folk emulating them, were not only more likely to read and write than their European counterparts (2-45, below), but to have studied enough martial arts to make them no push-over. You don't hear of *them* fainting away like the European lady. Moreover, if overpowered, they were liable to kill themselves – on Television Easterns, at least, they stab themselves, or lacking a knife, bite off their tongues and bleed to death as soon as the bad guy touches them, which brings on the revenge of the hero, not to mention her vengeful ghost.[2] Television exaggerates; but the threat of suicide must have been a major deterrent of violence against women, unless the man was so utterly cruel as to want his victims dead. (The authorities thought of this possibility, for "terrifying a person into the commission of suicide" was a capitol crime). Here is a story of this practice of *suicide-as-last-defense*, chronologically, but not psychologically far removed from the 16th century – exactly as it was written by a Japanese man for English readers.

> Some years ago there was a most innocent and sacred little girl, like an angel, in Japan. By some misfortune she was captured by some American blackmails. The poor girl found out she was going to be sold as a prostitute in America. There was no way for this helpless creature to escape her future doom. She committed suicide, leaving a poetry which is even now repeated incessantly by every Japanese mouth. It ran this: *Tsuyu-wo dani itoo Yamato-no Ominaeshi / Furu America-ni Sode-wa nurasaji.*
>
> Even a drop of dew is dreaded by the little meadow flower of Japan.
> How could she bear to let her sleeves be soaked by Ame[=rain]rica?
>
> Indeed she was too pure to be ruined by those barbarous Americans. The Japanese judge had sense enough not to pass sentence of "unsounded mind" on her. But we all worship her as the sacred mirror[=paragon] of highest ethics.
>
> There is always something higher and nobler than our life. That is human dignity. . . . Not only for her own dignity, but for the dignity of her country, the daughter of Japan killed herself. But she is immortalized forever!
>
> We, each individual, have each our own bodies, but our conscience is only one conscience, common to all of us. Therefore it is most selfish to kill the sacred conscience, which is common to others, for the sake to save our own life. (M:JAL:1911 – I left the awkward English as is except for the poem which read "how could she bear to *make her sleeves wet*." Luckily, the Japanese lyrics were provided so I could catch the puns!)

..

Still, lest *all* Japanese women appear braver, or rather, more heroic than they probably were, I must qualify. While the women mentioned by Frois may have been going out *without their husband's permission,* if they were anything more than a servant, they probably did not go out *all* alone. A 1565 letter of Gaspar Vilela put it like this: "They [noblewomen] are not used to being accompanied by men when they go out, but with many other women, their servants. (con otras muchas mugeres criadas suyas)" These words suggest that the women did not have male guards as they had in Iberia, but it does not suggest the image a modern reader might get reading Frois: a woman walking all by herself. [3] About three hundred years later, Chamberlain wrote that while Japanese women neither wore veils nor were beaten, they were nevertheless poorly treated:

> . . . women are all their lives treated more or less like babies, neither trusted with the independence which our modern manners allow; nor commanding the romantic homage that was a woman's dower in medieval Europe." (C:TJ)

This is a very different contrast, indeed. But, if I am not mistaken, the status of Japanese women changed little between Frois and Chamberlain. That of Europeans did, and with it their perspective reversed.

1. *Alvarez's Testimony*.   I have not found the full account yet. Anyone with access to it is welcome to suggest glosses. Remember to send the original words of any quotes with the gloss, where possible.

2. *Suicide and Honor*.   This willingness to die rather than be assaulted does not contradict the lack of concern for chastity. It is a matter of the honor-over-all-ism discussed elsewhere in this book, but I doubt that there were as many assaults or suicides as the television dramas suggest!

3. *Women Who Walk Alone*   There has been some debate among Japanese scholars on the freedom of women to walk about in the Era that ended about the time Frois came to Japan. Some say that *tsujidori* (crossroad-snatching) and *medori* (woman-snatching) was winked at by the authorities. (My OED defines the latter as rape and the former as "a way to get a wife if a good-looking poor woman is found walking alone." (It was a serious crime to commit adultery but this was what we might call a misdemeanor.)   Others point out that society was generally safe enough to guarantee women to walk about safely. Hosokawa Ryôichi leaves that question open, but shows that the only women who were depicted as traveling (as opposed to moving about one's own county) alone were the emotionally distraught, i.e. the crazy women, so popular in Noh. Nuns, professional dancers and even prostitutes never traveled alone, but always in groups of two or more. (M:KZJ ch7)

2-36   In Europe, the love between relations of both sexes for one another is very great;
Ho amor dos parentes e parentas entre si hé em Europa muito grande;

In Japan, it is very little; they act like they hardly know one another.
Em Japão muito pouco, e se hão huns pera com os outros como estranhos.

My English "relations" is vague, but "family" to many readers would not include extended relations, or "relatives," while "relatives" would not include "family."   The Portuguese *parentes* and *parentas* include both family members and relatives.   Thinking about it, I recalled reading international politics at Georgetown School of Foreign Service, in particular how personalism and nepotism made democracy difficult in cultures colonialized by Iberians with close extended families. And, I recalled a translation job at the Nihon Honyaku Center, where I Englished a Japanese spouse's application for divorce from a Philippine spouse whose extended family was sucking up his (or her, I cannot recall) entire fortune – as the spouse thought it only natural to share it all. This difference of thinking was cited as the prime instance of "incompatibility." And, finally, I sadly recall but only half-regret not trying as hard as I might have to win the heart of a certain someone because I feared I could not handle her relation-centered life (there was always someone flying in from South America who had to be attended to).   So, while all pre-modern Europe may have had families far more extended than what we now call family, I suspect the Iberians were especially close to their kin (and, maybe Northern Europeans with their clans and Russians, if their complex vocabulary for relations is taken at face value).

The Japanese, on the other hand, did not constantly dwell on or cherish such relationships. While the reserve Japanese of the upper classes maintained even between family members (see 3-16) exaggerated their distance somewhat, as the proverb confirms, Japanese have traditionally favored *"the stranger close by, over the relative far off."* (*tôi shinseki yori chikaku no tanin*). [1] Japanese families were more liable to adopt children (or husbands) to carry on the family line, despite their pride in lineage, than Europeans. Perhaps, the idea of lineage and rights of heredity had less to do with blood and more to do with pragmatic relationships, the ability to learn skills and trustworthiness to keep secrets transmitted down the generations in Japan. After all, in a culture where skill was highly valued, it would do no good to keep the name and lose the art. As far as why Japanese were not so cozy with their relatives (see 3-20), I would guess that they chose to invest their time with their more limited nuclear family and with their business or employer.

Many Japanese might find it surprising to be put on the nuclear or individualistic side of the contrast. East Asians in the nineteenth century and twentieth century have continually talked up the family-like nature of their corporations and politic. But corporations functioning *like* families [2] is not the same as a society where everything depends upon blood relations. I think Frois called it right and that this attitude of the Japanese was conducive to modernization in general and the building of a powerful skill-based economy that vaulted Japan over the Iberian cultures to become an economic super-power.

1. *New Proverb* One Japanese friend, who will remain nameless, quips that in the internet age, she would rephrase it "the stranger far off rather than the relative nearby."

2. *Corporations Functioning Just Like Families*. This metaphor is one of the worse ever invented. The reason is that there are many *types* of families. In Japan, there are two major family models, both traditional: one is extremely hierarchical and the other egalitarian. As discussed I forget where, the extent to which either is the dominant model is debatable. Nevertheless, attempts have been made to define prototypical Japanese families, or houses (*ie*) and contrast them to Western ones. The first element of Murakami Yasusuke's description of Japan's "family civilization" is "kin-tract-ship, which indicates that membership can be based on kinship or social contract." That element is probably common to both major family models. (For the other three elements and a critical discussion of Japanese familism, see Steven Heine's chapter "*Ie*-ism and the Discourse of Postmodernism" in S/F:JTPP)

2-37   In India, barefoot boys hold up parasols/umbrellas to keep the rain and sun off the women;   *Na Índia levão os moços sonbreiros [1] de pé aas molheres pola chuva ou sol;*

        In Japan, the women hold up parasols/umbrellas for each other.
        Em Japão as molheres os levam umas às outras.

This is the only time Frois refers to India instead of Europe! Is it because Europeans didn't yet use umbrellas at all? [2] Presumably, most Jesuit recruits in Japan or bound for Japan or leaving Japan for Europe would spend some time in Goa and become familiar with Indian life, so India is a good proxy for "our" side. The French translators turn the boys into what they were, "young blacks" (*jeunes Noirs* – why the capital letter?). Matsuda and Jorissen make them "barefoot," not quite the original "on foot" but I like it and borrowed it.

Frois is not talking about women in general, but the women in Japan who have a similar social position to those served by others in India or in Europe (though not yet for umbrellas). It is true that Japanese women could do things for themselves. While upper-class ladies did have help in Japan for almost every aspect of their lives, including the classic "fart-cut-nuns" (*hehiri-bikuni*) who took the blame for their social indiscretions – i.e., the responsibility for their literal and figurative farts! – even such pampered courtesans (women living in court) would usually *fan themselves*, something not true in much of the world. In Japan, only the Emperor's dog had someone to fan his flies away and put bits of ice in his mouth, according to A DIPLOMATIST'S WIFE IN JAPAN, Mrs. Frazer, who sighed "I wish some kind fairy would fan me all day and put bits of ice into my mouth!"

    Reading of women who held up parasols/umbrellas for one another, we conjure up a vision of women walking side-by-side each extending their parasol out and over the other. That would be exotic, very artsy and a poignant illustration of how equality and dependence can go together if it could be done which in reality it cannot, unless a line of women each held umbrellas over the one in front of them. So my first guess at what Frois really meant was that women often *shared* their parasols/umbrellas. Sharing them was so common there are even terms for it in the dictionary (*aiaigasa, aiyaigasa, aigasa*) and in the Edo era it came to signify a romantic relationship. Imagine, if you will, a Japanese Don Juan, umbrella in hand, waiting for rain and the right woman. Even today, where "we" would draw a *heart* within which to insert the names of lovers, Japanese will draw a simple *umbrella* and put the names under it, one on each side of the handle.

But, the most common depiction of women with umbrellas has them each carrying their own. Frois must be referring to noblewoman whose heads were indeed shielded by parasols/umbrellas held by *other* women, who are not lowly servants but (judging from pictures) lower level ladies of the court. *Relatively well-off women doing the menial work of holding up umbrellas* would be contrast enough with women using lowly servants.

1. *Moços sombrieros de pé*   I believe we might have something called "umbrella-boys," but lacking corroboration and facing a confusing grammar (German is not the only language that likes to split things in weird ways, Portuguese sometimes does it, too) that requires the umbrella separate from the boys, too.

2. *Umbrellas/Parasols in Europe.* Umbrellas eventually made their way to Europe (more information, please!) and centuries later the metal-spoke modern improvement returned to Japan where it came to be called kômorigasa, or " bat-umbrellas," presumably because of the black color and small size.

2-38   In Europe, granted there are abortions, but they are very infrequent;
Em Europa, posto que o aja, não hé frequente o aborsio das crianças;

In Japan, it is so common there are women who have aborted twenty times.
Em Japão hé tão comum, que há molher que aborta vinte vezes.

Frois's colleague Vilela writes that not only were "one or two sons considered enough to conserve a family [line]" but that "the devil has persuaded them that a woman who gives birth to a girl will go to hell where she can't be saved, and because of this fear women drink a certain thing that the creature dies before birth." (cited in note to V(A):S&A)   Since Japanese, as far as I know, had no way to sex a fetus, I would guess that Vilela conflated abortion and infanticide. In respect to the former, Andrés Pérez de Ribas wrote that native women (in what is now North México) already nursing aborted on purpose and, on being "reproached for this abuse and cruelty" replied " 'Can't you see that i am looking out for the life of this child that i'm holding in my arms?' thus making it clear that she was killing one child to raise another."(PR/DR:HTHF 4-3) [1] In Japan, where nursing was long, chances are that the abortions were carried out for reasons that made more sense than some strange, presumably Buddhist superstition such as mentioned by Vilela.[2] Be that as it may, if Frois is right about those numbers, Japanese medical care for women was far in advance of that in Europe, where I wouldn't give a million–to-one chance to anyone surviving so many abortions! Montanus (perhaps from a letter of Frois's?) wrote:

> They employ a cruel Dame, who laying them in a fit posture on their best and softest Bed, crushes and kneads the infant in the Womb, til it becomes like a lump of Dough, which departs from them with [no?] more extreme torture than if it were naturally delivered. (M:EED:p51)

Montanus in English translation also claims that until they are thirty-seven, Japanese mothers kill all children. This last is almost surely a mistranslation (perhaps mistaken in a report from Japan?) for information about aborting if one had a child younger than 3 or two younger than 7 (three and 7 being important marks in a child's age) and that, only in some provinces in hard times. But, exaggeration or not, abortion was common enough a century or two later that one there are many *senryu* (risqué poems) roasting lady-doctors who specialized in abortion – called colloquially "droppings" (*oroshi*) – salaciously(!?) imagining their work "below the hair-line," and how bold their sons must be with their maids, etc.. That is to say, Japanese were familiar enough with the practice to joke about it. Obviously, abortion was no laughing matter for the women who drank poisons, had pressure put on their bellies and worse. Still, it was far less dangerous than the major killer of women (but not men) throughout human history, childbirth.

After the Opening of Japan, militarists eager to push up the population and compete with the West in colonizing the world came down hard on abortion, but once Japan was forced out of the war game and back to peace in the last half of the twentieth century, women were once again free to choose.   This does not mean all was well, for it was far too common because doctors who profited greatly from it, blocked the pill as too dangerous a medicine for birth-control. The medical lobby is despicable, but Japanese women who abort their fetus rather than raise it under unfavorable conditions show a far greater love for children than women who would give birth regardless of their capability to provide a good childhood. On the whole, I think these women are intelligent enough to realize that a fetus is *not* human, but only a *potential* human. Nevertheless, the guilt felt by some women is sometimes taken advantage of by Buddhist temples that take high fees to pray for the so called "water-baby's" soul (the idea being to help the soul have a better chance next time). At these temples, one can see thousands of small stone statues, many with bibs and candy or toys placed before them.

1. *People Who Control Their Population.* I have the impression that people/cultures that permit abortion and infanticide were generally gentle and did so in preference to making war on others or allowing starvation to do the dirty work, whereas people/cultures that force women to have children generally kill others in order to expand, or exist in a state of mutual war with others of their ilk.   I hope an anthropologist will test this correlation (that suggests an unrestricted "right to life" may actually be a "license to kill.") on a large number of cultures. The aborting indians mentioned by Pérez de Ribas, the Mayo, are described as *"not as fierce as these other nations . . . rather, they are tractable and gentle . . ."* (R(R&A&D): HOT 4-1) In other words, they fit the bill and I think it no accident.

2. *Buddhist Superstition* Vilela may be partly right. There *were* some bad beliefs out there.   A woman who died while pregnant (or giving birth when the child was not released) was doomed to suffer six years of torture in Hell within a *chi-no-ike* or Pool of Blood (that of birth and menstruation)!   One way to lessen this punishment was for a woman to be cut open after death to remove the fetus that wanted out (Based on the belief the fetus wished to be born based on tales of babies being born in graves, probably true, because of the build up of gas in the abdomen).   A still-birth could also put a women in the pool, how long I do not know. According to Hank Glassman, the idea of such a place in hell originated in China with the Ketsubonkyô (blood-bowl sutra) –

"It claims that the blood spilt by women from menstruation and childbirth had defiled the god of the earth (*chijin*), and that by washing their soiled clothes in streams and rivers, they not only polluted the water but also the tea served to various sages. For that sin, women had to suffer the retribution of falling into a "Blood-bowl Pond" after death." (G:RCM (?) Also found at Toshie Kurihara: *a history of women in japanese buddhism nichiren's*

perspectives on the enlightenment of women: Institute of Oriental Philosophy).

It came to Japan in the late twelfth century where its use at funerals was documented in the fifteenth century. Japan was ready for it because the long Warring Era had resulted in a denigration of women to the degree that the fetus came to belong to the father and the "belly is borrowed goods" (*hara-wa karimono*) – not owned, but only borrowed by the woman whose body it is in – idea, the same as the Western one of woman as a field planted with male seed. The Bloody Pool found its way into very popular tales (*otogizôshi*) of the fifteenth and sixteenth centuries and was further spread "by a network of traveling nuns who brought this cult into the homes of women across japan." (G:RCM)

These are the original roving *bikuni* mentioned in 4-23, below. With metaphysical burdens added to the very real fear of pain and dying in childbirth, it is not surprising that women would be willing to pay these nuns a lot for amulets for safe childbirth on the one hand and medicine for abortion (if they dealt in herbs, too, and that I do not know) on the other. It is dubious that all women bought this. In the Ujishûmonogatari (date?), a widower who dies finds himself before the Judge of Hell and finds it is because of the still-death of his child and that his wife, who died earlier had argued successfully that it was unfair that only she was made to suffer. The story was introduced in the context of women retaining some autonomy despite centuries of patriarchal rule. (M:KZJ: ch2) As a final note (sorry to be long but it is an interesting subject and salient so long as we have women who are fully human valued no more than fetuses that are mere potential) the course of my research, I was most surprised to discover that Nichiren, whom I had disliked for his nationalist proclivities and the rabid evangelism (if I can use such a word for Buddhists) of his sect, was absolutely *magnificent* in his defense of women! Toshie Kurihara's *A History of Women in Japanese Buddhism – Nichiren's perspectives on the enlightenment of women* (Again, the

Institute of Oriental Philosophy) opened my eyes. Nichiren (1222-1282) critically noted a whole range of misogynic Buddhism including the Shingon=Pure Word sect's rites to turn female fetuses into male ones and observing that the blame was partly with Buddhist writings (he lists and describes the problematic passages), including the Flower Garland Sutra ("Women are messengers of hell who can destroy the seeds of Buddhahood. They may look like bodhisattvas, but at heart they are like yaksha demons.") and Nirvana Sutra, said to be Buddha's last teaching, ("If all the desires and delusions of all the men throughout the major world system were lumped together, they would be no greater than the karmic impediment of one single woman.") (Ibid) and recommended the only sutra he found satisfactory, the Lotus Sutra. He accepted the idea that woman had a very different nature than man, admitting they were less stable, more likely to change their mind, but he did not hold it against them.

Indeed his poetic metaphor reminds me of D.H. Lawrence.

"A man is like a pillar, a woman like the crossbeam. A man is like the legs of a person, a woman like the trunk. A man is like the wings of a bird, a woman like the body. If the wings and the body become separate . . . ." He held we owe a debt of gratitude toward our mothers for the great pain we cause them and his description of pregnancy and birth is unexcelled:

"At that time her belly is swelled as tight as a drum and her neck as unstable as a needle. She can only exhale but not inhale, and her complexion is the color of withered grass . . . When the time for her delivery draws near, the pain is so great that her hips seem to be torn apart and her eyes stare as though they would fly out of her head into the heaven . . . Once she has succeeded in giving birth to this enemy who has caused her such pain, one might suppose that she would fling it to the ground, tear open its belly and toss it aside. But such, of course, is not the case. On the contrary, she forbears to think of her own pain, but hastens to take the child in her arms, wipes away the blood, washes off the unclean matter, and clasps it to her breast, and for a period of three years assiduously nourishes it." (Ibid)

More to the point, he responded at length to questions by women who were very troubled with their alleged impurity. In response to a woman who wondered whether she could read sutras during menstruation without defiling them, Nichiren's answer included:

"In my own study of the sacred teachings, though I find clear prohibitions on certain days of the month against the impurity of things like meat or wine, the five spicy foods, or sexual acts, for instance, I have never come across any passage in the sutras or treatises that speaks of avoidances connected with menstruation. // While the Buddha was in the world, many women in their prime became nuns and devoted themselves to the Buddha's teachings, but they were never shunned on account of their menstrual period. Judging from this, I would say that menstruation does not represent any kind of impurity coming from an external source. It is simply a characteristic of the female sex, a phenomenon related to the perpetuation of the seed of chronically recurring illness. In the case of feces and urine, though these are substances produced by the body, so long as one observes cleanly habits, there are no special prohibitions to be observed concerning them." (Ibid)

But, even more impressively, he wrote that "if you feel so inclined, dispense with the reading of the sutra and simply recite Nam-myoho-renge-kyo. " and that "when making your devotions, you need not bow facing the sutra." That is to say, if despite knowing intellectually that you are not impure, if you *feel* unclean and want to do these things, it is not sinful." (Toshie Kurihara, Ibid). Interestingly, Pure Land's Shinran, who married a woman, did not debate the idea of female inferiority and, sadly, Dogen, the Zen priest whose suggestion that we had "better not try to become Gods but rather strive to become human" is so beloved by all of us, who came out strongly against the prohibition of women from ritual grounds ("space is space . . .") as a young man, chickened out and caved in after he got a juicy post. (Ibid) Finally, let me add two things. First, like the Christians, the Nichiren sect, because of its strong evangelism, was prohibited in Tokugawa Japan. Second, today Nichiren's teachings are promulgated by Sôka Gakkai, (lit. "Value-Creation-Society/Group"). Its ten million followers are a powerful political force in Japan (Because of proportionate representation they have a viable political party). A lively woman in the Japanese neighborhood I lived in ran a choir at their temple/church. They remind me of fundamentalist Christians for they even have people giving testimonials!

4-39   In Europe, it is very rare if ever that an infant is killed after birth.
Em Europa, depois da criança nacer, raras vezes ou quasi nunca se mata;

Japanese women put their foot on the baby's throat and kill all that they don't think they can raise. *As japoas lhe põem o pé no pescoço e matão todos os que lhe parese que não podem sostentar.*

Okada cites a late Ming (1368-1644) Chinese report [1] that there are more women than men in Japan because young and poor women tend to have more boys and the fief administrators cruelly encourage them to be strangled because they only desire a supply of women to serve as common-law wives and mistresses! [2] Frois, however, writes in a letter (April 4, 1565) that it is the *girls* who are liable to be killed (*especialmente a las hijas*). I suspect it depends upon location and date. We might also guess that the Chinese author, coming from a country where girls were the more frequent victims, was especially attentive to instances of the opposite.

As a farming people, Japanese called infanticide *mabiki,* or "thinning," a term neither metaphor nor euphemism. You do not "thin" out of cruelty, you do it to get healthier survivors. When crops failed or didn't keep up with taxes, parents had to make hard choices on how to maximize the chances of survival for their offspring. Or, to put this in human terms, they wanted to do everything possible to keep their children fat and happy. (I bet you could prove that these "killers" kept more children alive and happy than their "right-to-life" Europeans) Since a bad year could not be predicted, abortion was not always an option. In 1557, Vilela wrote with obvious sympathy, "We fear the lean cows of Pharaoh and pray the Lord will not let them come here, because it is heart-breaking to see how many children are killed in such times." (in C:TCJ) He also wrote:

> It [Japan] has many people; and if they don't kill the children they bear, they will eat up one another, because the number of children killed at birth is infinite. There are women with 15 or 20 dead [children], and with this, they still have infinite people. (note 49 to V(A):S&A)

Vilela seems to have had a far greater understanding of the population problem than the Popes of the 20th century. Reading between the lines, I cannot help wondering if he realized that killing the youngest child was actually the *kindest* way to cope with famine, and a more benign way to regulate the population than allowing starvation, war and disease to kill older children and adults, whose lives were and still are much more valuable, in so far that they already have the humanity an infant only promises. (See Nancy Schieper-Hughes: DEATH WITHOUT WEEPING, on infanticide by neglect in Brazil, today, for an honest witness of reality.) In this respect, it is interesting to note that the most outspoken critics of infanticide in Japan – as was the case with abortion – were *those who wanted Japan to "move on and spread all over the world,"* as exemplified by Satô Nobuhiro, who devised programs for the reconstruction and expansion of Japan in the early nineteenth century (T:SJT).

Infanticide is harder on the parents than abortion, but far from homicide. St. Xavier writes matter-of-factly "Poor women who have many children kill the youngest that they may not grow up to suffer poverty, and this is not punished." (Coleridge trans.) *Should it be?* Carletti writes of the situation elsewhere in the East Indies, where parents "driven by poverty" sell their children, or "apparently feeling greater pity, drown their children as soon as they are born, particularly if they are females, not wanting to be forced to see them living in dishonour." [1] The modern American ideology holds "life" at any cost to be the ultimate value. Unless overcome by a wave of patriotism, when we willingly sacrifice our lives for the sake of the American Way, we forget that culture in most of the world means and has always meant that *ideals were more important than life* and all life is not equally precious. Still, infanticide had little support from philosophy. One finds no official recognition for it as a moral act even in China, where infanticide was an open fact of life in some provinces. Ball, nevertheless, found one tale – one of twenty-four encouraging filial duty – where a man and his wife resolve to sacrifice their infant in order that its grandparent would have enough to eat, and

> "taking the child for the purpose of burying it alive, the misguided and wicked parent . . . was rewarded for this murderous act of filial piety by discovering a pot of gold in a hole he had dug for his own offspring. And this is held up as an example . . ." (Ball:TC)

Are they misguided? To me, this is not half so bad as "our" Abraham offering to kill his son because voices told him to, merely to obey an abstraction called God!

Frois does not mention the related practice of *abandonment*. While a parent could rationalize that the baby might find good parents, most babies did not and suffered far more than those strangled at birth. The poet Buson haikus a winter-dead field, without even a thicket big enough to abandon a baby in (*ko-o sutsuru yabu sae nakute kareno kana*). Such a thicket by a roadside, a *jizo-san* statue at an intersection, or a temple are usually mentioned in connection with abandonment in Japan. The arrangements in China could be more formal. Near Swatow, Ball wrote, a basket hung from a wall just outside the city of Ch'ao Chou, where a baby could be left. If no one chose to adopt the baby, it "ultimately met the fate of so many of the inhabitants of babydom in China." [3] In Europe, the Catholic Church had institutions to accept abandoned infants, but I wonder if as many of them survived childhood as those abandoned in Japan.

1. *Pronunciation, Anyone?* In Japanese, the author's name 鄭舜功 is Tei Shunkô. The book is 日本一鑑 (Japan One Model). Despite the numerous on-line dictionaries, there is no help that I know of for the pronunciation of Chinese names and book titles.

2. *Boy Killing.* There might have been another reason for the boy-killing. In the case when there was a marriage between a peasant class freeman (jiyûjin) and a serf/servant (*genin*), the girls would become serf/servants like their mother whereas boys inherited their father's class. Generally, there was always more room at the bottom and competition for the top in a feudal society. An abundance of free men may have been perceived as a threat. Be that as it may, claims have been made that

"whenever infanticide is practiced, girls are first eliminated, followed by deformed and sickly children, offspring unwanted for reasons of magic (such as multiple births, twins or triplets) . . ."

But the observation of boy-killing in Japan is not alone. Most of the 100 or so infant corpses found crammed in the sewer of the fourth-to-sixth-century Baths uncovered in Ashqelon in 1986 were predominantly male. The Greek inscription "Enter and Enjoy" by the entrance suggests it was a brothel so that baby girls could have been brought up to work with or take over from their mothers. (found at http://www.ucd.ie/~classics/ClassicsIreland.html CLASSICS IRELAND 1996 Volume 3 University College Dublin, Ireland) This association of infanticide with prostitution in the Occident may help explain why it was held in such bad repute.

3. *Abandonment in China*. Elsewhere, Ball notes that out of 1,000 infants born in Hong-Kong "only 72 survived for a period of twelve months in 1900." He also mentions "a large hole in a city wall into which the infant was cast" in a large prefectural city in Amoy, and most spectacular of all:

In the North of China, baby towers are provided, perhaps amongst other reasons, for the same purpose, though they are principally used for receiving the dead bodies of infants. Occasionally a separate hole is provided on different sides of the tower to keep the sexes distinct, and thus prevent any incentives to immorality amongst the ghosts of the little babies! No wonder the Chinese consider themselves so far superior to us in this all-important virtue of morality! (B:TC)

North China once had little infanticide. We can largely credit the West for introducing the potato, banishing most famine and thereby making it necessary. How ironic that Christian fundamentalists, who could care less about overpopulation (*Oh, goodie! Armageddon!*) presume to judge the Chinese, who are doing their best under the circumstances to keep their population down (without infanticide), and sabotage global family planning in the name of human rights.

2-40 Pregnant women in Europe loosen their belts in order not to hurt the baby; *As molheres prenhes em Europa largão os singidouros por não fazer mal à criansa;*

The Japanese tie on a belt so tightly before giving birth that even a hand cannot be squeezed between the belt and their flesh. *As japoas até que pairão se apertão com huma precinta tão rijamente que antre a precinta e a carne lhe não possa caber a mão.*

Valignano introduced the Japanese side of this contrast here, together with that of contrast 2-21, above. Here it is in my translation of his dramatic description (1583), the English translation of the same by Van Linschoten (1598), Montanus (1670) and L' Abbe (1705):

Nor is it less surprising to see what women do when they are with child and give birth; because, when they conceive, all the wives and maidens who, before conceiving, went about wearing a belt of silk so loose and wide that it was always liable to fall off, and took pride in walking about so disheveled, bind themselves up so tightly with a *faxa*[?] that it seems they would burst, in such a manner that they seem to have thinner bellies on the point of giving birth than they had before conceiving. And I don't understand how, in doing this, they do not kill themselves with their babies – with all this, they say they know from experience that if they do not go about so restricted, the parturition is bad. (historica indica 1.teil,18 from V(W):HPP?)

. .

. . . and when they are great with childe, they tye their girdles so hard about them, that men would thinke they shuld burst, and when they are not with Childe, they weare their girdles so slack, that [you would thinke] they would fall from their bodies, saying that by experience they do finde, if they shoulde not do so, they should have evill lucke with their fruict. (VVL)

. . . and as other Women when with child, expatiate their bodies by unlacing to give more liberty to their growing issue, they on the other side, contract, imprisoning the Infant in a narrower Circle, by pinching and girding closer their swelling Waste, supposing else they would Miscarry. (M:EEJ)

Married women wear their Girdle so large, that they seem always to be at Down-lying: On the contrary, being big with Child, they tie them Selves about very strait, and believe this much helps to a happy time. (A:HCJ)

Valignano's principle point was that not only are their customs contrary, but they are so because, they attest, *experience* has taught them it is best. He is amazed that experience could teach people such contrary things. Perhaps there are advantages and disadvantages to *both* ways. In a later SUMARIO, Valignano further specifies that the tight *obi* (which was put on ceremoniously in the fifth month of conception) was thought to prevent miscarriage *and premature birth*. My guess is that looseness would improve circulation while support would prevent strain. Inactive European women would benefit most from the former and more active Japanese would require the second. *Opinions, Doctors?*

~~~~~~

2-41   European women remain lying down and rest after giving birth;
As molheres em Europa acabando de parir deitão-se e descansão;

Japanese women must remain seated day and night for twenty days after birth.
As japoas hão-de estar depois de parir asentadas 20 dias de dia e de noite.

Childbirth in Japan was done sitting (as it is in most cultures) rather than on flat beds. The wealthy sat on special legless chairs covered with cushions – if we can call something legless a chair, we can call it a sofa and say "they" invented the sofa or soft arm-chair – and poor farmers improvised the same with straw. A document quoted by Okada mentions no less than twelve bundles of straw covered with a futon. Between day 17 and 21 some of the straw is removed each night until the woman is flat on her back again on the 21st day.   Since said document dates to the early nineteenth century, we know the custom Frois introduces was no medical fad but a real tradition.   But considering what was written about the poverty of much of the country, I cannot help doubting that commoners stayed seated all day.

The idea of this contrast would seem to be that "we" think new mothers should take it easy, but "they" think not. Valignano has them not only being forced to remain seated (because lying down would allow the blood to rise to their head, but bathed with cold water (mother and baby) and only given "things of little substance" to eat. "And, with all of this," he rhetorically marvels, it "takes place among people who live with as much discernment and dignity [*regalo y nobleza*] as we do in Europe." There might be some truth to this easy vs. hard idea, but, in my opinion, sitting would not be as bad as most readers might imagine. For one, Japanese, lacking chairs in their daily living generally had no back support, so this would be more of a vacation for them than for us. And, second, a slightly curved body is better for the circulation of the belly – something that must mend after the tumor called a baby comes out – than a straight one (if you have intestinal gas problems, you will find it helps to raise your knees and shoulders a bit).[1]   Third, since Japanese never had the practice of walking about for exercise to begin with, it would not be felt as confining and the woman would, after all, get sufficient exercise every time she got up to go to the outhouse (for the benefits of squatting, 11-20n). We will discuss the cold water below, but as far as the diet goes, they were given some food the Europeans may not have thought nutritious such as the celebratory red beans on white rice (azuki-han) – red and white being an auspicious and joyous combination – and shell-fish. Regardless, the immobility of the mother would reduce the need for much food.

At least two possible *origins* for a custom of not indulging a woman's appetite come to mind. For the commoners, who desired to space-out births, weight gain meant a quick return to unwanted fertility, and for nobles, who turned over nursing to their maids, there was advantage in keeping a slim figure, which noble men thought appealing.

1. *Sitting Back Around the Clock*.   I wrote my first published book lying on a *futon* upon a beach-chair with a partially raised back, sleeping only several hours a night for about three weeks and can attest to the benefit of such a position when you are not well, yet must work around the clock – like a mother, nursing her newly born.

2-42   In Europe, we are strongly on guard [against] air and wind after birth;
    Em Europa se guardão muito do ar e do vento depois do parto;

> The Japanese, as soon as they give birth, wash themselves and leave the doors and windows open. *As Japoas em acabando de parir se lavão e estão com portas e janelas abertas.*

Europeans were afraid of the mother and child catching something from outside. Fear of such "wind" is not restricted to the past or to childbirth either. Most of us know, or have known someone deathly afraid of *drafts*.[1] My grandmother, who lived to be 106 avoided them like the plague. I who slept with an open window and fan on in Florida recall my surprise at her solemn warnings. It is hard to draw a line between *drafts* and *air*. If *influenza* (in-flow) can be associated with drafts, *malaria* (bad-air) can be associated with air. But it has also long been thought good to go out and *"get some air,"* so, as in many things, it would seem a matter of balance or degree.

The Japanese, presumably, wanted to vent the pollution of birth, which is, after all, a bloody experience. In fact, for most of Japanese history, birth took place in a special separate birth hut, so the main house would not be polluted.[1] However, the Japanese were also wary of the wind, for the very word for "cold" (the disease) in Japanese *is* "wind." The 1604 Japanese-Portuguese Dictionary includes *ubukaze,* or "birth-wind," meaning a cold caught by a newly born, and a disease of the newly born called "wind-eye" (*fûgan*) which it defines as "an eye sickness, the cause of which is wind or airs." Actually, it is from gonorrhea, and may lead to blindness, but, the wind, if not the air, is in the original word, so it is clear that Japanese, too, were concerned about exposure to the elements,[2] though L' Abbe, after Valignano, claimed Japanese washed the newly born "in Cold Water to harden and fortify it against the injuries of the Weather," i.e. *because* they are concerned for the same. Montanus, as usual, gives the most outlandish elaboration:

They much exercise their patience in all manners of sufferings and are so inur'd by Custom, that Hunger, Cold, Heat, & Thirst, Watching [?] & Travel are their Play-Fellows; for as soon as they are born, though the weather happen to be extream cold & pinching, they carry out the Infants, & wash them in the Running Streams, where whilst they are cleaning, they let them paddle in the Water to save themselves from sinking. (M:EED p63)

But I doubt this (even without the swimming!) was done by most Japanese. It sounds like a samurai idea, and not the most common practice in Japan, for in most dialects of Japanese, the bath after birth is called *ubuyu,* "birth-warmwater [3]," and is only rarely called *ubumizu,* "birth-coldwater," as it was in Shikajima prefecture, which happens to be the area where the Jesuits began their work. But, even then, it was generally only a little cold water used *after* the warm water and may have depended on the location, season and other things. From my limited reading of diary literature (haiku poet Issa's journals), I know that a couple hundred years after Frois, even couples could have disagreements over what was best. The grief-stricken Issa excoriated his wife Kiku for "killing" their son Ishitaro by not waiting 100 days before taking him into the (hot) bath with her (she only jumped the gun by a couple weeks), as he suggested. If only she'd waited until the "rock" (the boy's name translates as "rocky") solidified, he lamented, he wouldn't have caught a cold and died.

1. Birth-house   It puzzles me that Frois did not write: *Women in Europe give birth in the same bed they always sleep in; Women in Japan give birth in a special hut.* But, I have not been able to find as much information on the web as I thought I could, so perhaps the practice was far from universal. What I did find (in Ôhara, near Kyoto) shows a tiny A-frame – a house 100% roof! The straw is a foot or two thick, so it would hold up to a blizzard. There is a sickle dangling from the entrance supposedly to keep bad-luck out and we are told that the women were supposed to remain seven days. Seven days is the same as the period a woman having her menses could not enter Shinto grounds. As a matter of fact, these huts generally called *ubugoya* (birth-small-hut), were also used for women having their periods While we tend to think of this segregation as a sort of imprisonment, women probably found it a place for pleasant sorority and respite from work. One hypothesis is that the hut originally was meant to hide the newly born from evil spirits to improve the chance of survival and that the pollution idea came later. I am not sure how such a hypothesis fits with its use by women having periods, but it is worth pointing out that the Japanese were, as far as I know never religious enough or too pragmatic to overdo the idea of pollution as was done in some parts of Christendom:

> "In Russian and some Eastern orthodox church areas, the wet-nurse was a necessity, since no-one, including the child, could eat in the presence of a postpartum woman until she had completed the 40 days purification and been 'churched'. How this was arranged is unclear but prominent women used wet-nurses." (Jennifer A. Heise: *Women and Medicine in the Middle Ages and Renaissance* © 2003. As a result, medicine to encourage or discourage lactation was developed. [LR: found at Lalecheleague site?]

By Frois's time, I believe these huts had already begun to be replaced by use of the *tsuchima,* or *doma,* a dirt[floored]-room within the house which almost always had a stove (good because flames were thought to be purifying and useful for heating water). Or, perhaps, many women already had come fully inside to give birth and convalesce in the *nando,* a sort of pantry, then the innermost bedroom. Today almost all Japanese births are in medical facilities, as in the West. (The source cited by the Japanese website Babycom is Kaneda Hisako: *Nihonjin no ko-umi, ko-sodate, Ima Mukashi*: 1990 == unfortunately, the web selection is unclear on the exact timeline).

2. *Japanese and Drafts.* In Okada's note for 3-3, an undated (but presumably old) Japanese instruction book for infants includes the advice that a *byôbu* (folding screen: see 11-5) partially encircle the bed to keep drafts off the infant sleeping next to his wet-nurse. This is not immediately after birth, but it does prove what the vocabulary suggests.

3. *Birth-Warm-water.* The enormous vocabulary of Japanese includes short words for cold and warm water, unlike English, which must use adjectives. Here, by the way, is a summation of the first-bath practice (same source as first note): "In the old days when people gave birth at home, the first thing someone would say when they heard the baby was about to come was "we better get the water boiling!" This would have been the thought of as only normal by any Japanese, but in Europe they never had a practice of bathing a newly born in warm water. . . The mid-wife would wash the baby and the bath was generally not just warm water. The most wide-spread practice was to salt the water as it was thought to prevent colds, but in some provinces we find rice-mill syrup, egg-white, boiled fig-leaf juice, *sake,* vinegar, a silver coin and other things. We even find examples of including mouse shit and a piece of lacquerware! This shows that the purpose of the bath was not only to clean but to give the infant life-power . . . . (Babycom. Ibid)

2-43   In Europe, the cloister and seclusion of nuns is strict and rigorous;
Em Europa a clauzura e emserramento das freiras hé estreito e riguroso;

In Japan, convents for the *bikuni* (nuns) are as good as pleasure quarters.
Em Japão os moesteiros das biqunis *quasi que serve de rua de meretrices.*

This is a *bad* contrast. Frois, Christian partisan, is not being fair to the real thing. Much of the most charming female letters in Japan are the work of real Buddhist nuns who do not deserve the libel. But Bikuni whores were indeed a very visible part of Japan for hundreds of years. They were a staple of Edo senryu and ukiyoe prints. There even were "boat-*nuns*" (*funa-bikuni*), who plied the canals. And this was not *just* a nun fetish where girls having absolutely nothing to do with religion put on habits to titillate men who liked innocent looking things (today Japanese men are big on stewardesses and high-school girls – especially their sailor uniforms!). There was *some* connection. Englebert Kaempfer, who wrote his HISTORY OF JAPAN a hundred years after Frois's *Tratado*, explains why "a certain remarkable religious order of Young Girls" call'd Bikuni" were more than a mere habit:

> "They live under the protection of the Nunneries at Kamakura and Miaco [Miyako: Kyoto, the capitol], to whom they pay a certain sum a year, of what they get by begging, as an acknowledgement of their authority. Some pay besides a sort of tribute, or contribution, to the Khumano Temples at Isje . . . . They are, in my opinion, by much the handsomest girls we saw in Japan. The daughters of poor parents, if they be handsome and agreeable, apply for and easily obtain this privilege of begging in the habit of Nuns, knowing that beauty is one of the most persuasive inducements to travelers to let them feel the effects of their generosity. The Jammabos, or begging Mountain Priests . . . frequently incorporate their daughters into this religious order, and take their wives from among the Bikuni's."
>
> ..

So, the religious authorities (some, at least) could indeed be charged with complicity in creating these roadside angels sometimes identified with Kannon, Buddhist Goddess of Mercy! [2] Frois is only wrong for what he neglects to write – not a word on *real* Buddhist convents (even in his chapter on religion) and nothing to indicate that whores in habit were but one kind of whore in Japan. It was almost as if he wanted the Buddhists to get the whole blame. Kaempfer devoted a good dozen pages to prostitution of one type of another, not to criticize, nor to boast – at that time, foreigners were not allowed such contact – but simply because it was interesting. The *bikuni* just mentioned "particularly watch [for] people of fashion" to whom they

> "draw near and address themselves tho' not all together, but singly, every one accosting a gentleman by herself, singing a rural song: if he proves very liberal and charitable, she will keep him company and divert him for hours. . . Their voices, gestures, and apparent behavior, are neither too bold and daring nor too much dejected and affected, but free, comely, and seemingly modest. However not to extol their modesty beyond what it deserves, it must be observ'd that they make nothing of laying their bosoms quite bare to the view of charitable travelers all the while they keep him company, under the pretence of its being customary in the country . . ." (K(S):HOJ 1692)

So, before radio, here was how Japanese men, at least, kept diverted on the road! Kaempfer also describes how they generally made out in town.

> As to the other necessaries travelers may have occasion for, they are generally serv'd by the house-maids, if they be natives of Japan. These wenches also lay the cloth, and wait at table, taking this opportunity to engage their guests to farther favours. But 'tis quite otherwise with us. (Ibid.)

These women, commonly called *han-mori,* or "rice-pilers" in Japanese, were usually hard-working farm-girls (In her novel *"Hinekureta (warped) Issa,"* top female novelist Tanabe Seiko claims haiku's most country character much preferred their meaty bodies to the anemic women of the pleasure quarter he couldn't afford, anyway) with one-year contracts with the inns. Besides standing in front of the inns to draw travelers, they washed and massaged the traveler's feet, sewed his clothes, lit the fire . . . And, finally, as part of the package, kept his bed warm. Kaempfer guessed that "very seldom any Japanese pass thro' these villages but they pick up some of these whores and have to do with them." That is very understandable. They were getting a full-service pit-stop for almost nothing. Kaempfer had only one *complaint* to make about them. In the daytime, when there were a number of inns in a row, he found "their chattering and rattling no inconsiderable noise, and prove not a little troublesome." My biggest problem is trying to make out how much of this went on a hundred years earlier, *when Frois wrote.* Cocks, the Englishman whose diary provides a window on a time closer to Frois, the second decade of the 17th century, makes it clear that the dancers we will meet again in chapter 13 also slept with men:

> *September 8. a* – We dyned, or rather supped, at a merchantes howse called Neyem Dono, where he provided *caboques,* or woman plears, who danced and songe; and when we retorned home, he sent eavery one one of them. (1616)
>
> ..

About twenty years after Cock's, however, Caron wrote a laudatory paragraph on Japanese women minimizing the amount of prostitution. Kaempfer jumped on it, and in doing so provides us with an interesting reference for the late-20th century "comfort woman" – or, "war-slave" – controversy. [1]

> I cannot forbear mentioning . . . a small mistake of Mr. Caron, in his account of Japan, where he shews so tender a regard for the honour of the Japanese sex (perhaps out of respect to his lady, who was a Japanese woman [with whom he had 6 children!]) as to assert, that besides the publick and priviledg'd bawdy-houses, this trade is not carried on in any other city or village in the Empire. It is unquestionably true that there is hardly a publick Inn upon the great Island Nipon, but what may be call'd a bawdy-house; and if there be too many customers resort to one place, the neighboring Inn-keepers will friendly and willingly lend their wenches . . . . Nor, is it a new custom come up but lately in this country, or since Mr. Caron's time. On the contrary, it is of very old date, and took its rise many hundred years ago, in the times of that brave first Secular Monarch Joritoma, who apprehensive, lest his soldiers weary of his long and tedious expeditions . . . thought it much more adviseable to indulge them in this particular and indulge their carnal appetites, by allowing publick and private bawdy-houses.

The only problem is that Hideyoshi (Joritomo was one of his many appellations) unified the country about the time TRATADO was written, and his long-lasting invasion of Korea began in 1592 – hardly many hundred years ago! Since the brothels in question were begun at about that time (in Shimonoseki, a seaport facing Korea), Kaempfer's claim is clearly overwrought, but circumstantial evidence does suggest that many forms of prostitution were found in Frois's Japan. If Frois does not contrast prostitution *per se,* but sticks to the allegedly Buddhist *bikuni,* it is probably because he knew that, in the words of historian Defourneaux's composite visitor to Phillip II's Spain,

> the public *puteria* [whorehouse] is so common in Spain that on entering a town, many people go there before going to church. (D(B):DLS)

Frois might well have contrasted the respective cultures' *attitude* toward the world's oldest profession, but he certainly could not have done so with the *practice,* for it was similar. And, considering the power the Church had over Spain, it *had* to be involved, [3] even if the women in the *puteria* were not allowed to assume the habits of nuns. But, if we are allowed a longer and broader perspective, even such differences between our civilizations disappear:

Eleventh-century Byzantine emperor Michael IV built in Constantinople "an edifice of enormous size and very great beauty" (according to chronicler Michael Psellus). The emperor issued a proclamation that prostitutes might there adopt nuns' habits "and all fear of poverty would be banished from their lives forever ... Thereupon a great swarm of prostitutes descended upon this refuge ... and changed both their garments and their manner of life." Michael's example was imitated in the West, from the twelfth century on. In 1227, Pope Gregory IX gave his blessing to the Order of Saint Mary Magdalene, which established convents in several cities. The nuns wore white and were known as the "White ladies." Louis IX, after a vain effort to abolish prostitution, endowed similar establishments. ("Prostitution in the Middle Ages" From: Gies, Frances and Joseph. *Women in the Middle Ages* New York: Harper & Row, 1978, 56-58.)

It seems a kind policy turning prostitutes into nuns. The question is how many really changed their way of life. At any rate, the Occident did come to believe that hiding prostitution was proper while publicly acknowledged prostitution was still acceptable in Japan when the Seclusion ended in the 19th century. This scandalized "us." "We" – particularly American (Puritan) Victorians – even pretended to be repulsed by man-to-man *discussion* of sex. Here is the American Ambassador about a year after he arrived in Japan, having tea with the "Prince" of Shinano (the earthy part of Japan Issa came from):

The conversation now took the usual Japanese turn. The lubricity of these people surpasses belief. The moment business is over, the one and only subject on which they dare converse comes up. I was asked a hundred different questions about American females, as whether single women dressed differently from married ones, etc., etc.; but I will not soil my paper with the greater part of them, but I clearly perceived that there were particulars that enter into the Japanese marriage contracts that are disgusting beyond belief. Bingo-no-Kami informed me that one of the Vice-Governors was specially charged with the duty of supplying me with female society, and if I fancied any woman the Vice-Governor would procure her for me, etc., etc., etc.

I was asked if their people could receive some instructions in beating the drum when the next man-of-war came ... They asked me about the various signals given by beat of drum, which I answered as well as I could. Then – oh, shame! They asked me if *we* had a beat of the drum as a signal to our soldiers to go to the houses of *ill fame,* and I emphatically replied *no.* They evidently did not believe me; for, said they, "We know the Dutch do so at Nagasaki, and all your armies are much the same." I gladly took my leave at three P.M. and reached home quite jaded out. (2/22?/1857)

Poor Mr. Harris! He just couldn't take the Japanese honesty with respect to sex. It is too bad he did not see fit to share his "etc.'s" with us! And how ironic an episode, when we consider the problems caused by horny GI's stationed around the world, including Japan, over the last decades!

1. *Comfort Women* The contemporary "problem" is that Japanese did not only use volunteers from Japan but enlisted Koreans and others and were very slow to admit that some were kidnapped or hired under false pretenses. But the idea of a troup of "comfort-women" accompanying soldiers goes back as far as we care to check, for it was necessary for any long campaign if conflict with local people is to be avoided. The German armies had such *Hurenweibel* prior to the Protestant crackdown (which may have encouraged raping) and in the Low Countries Wars that were taking place about the time Frois wrote, "official whores in the Catholic Spanish forces was cut to a maximum of eight per two hundred men." (H:CER.)

2. *Buddhist Wandering Nuns* The prostitute "nuns" not only wore habits and shaved their heads, but sang Buddhist invocations/chants/prayers, and sold amulets from Mt. Kumano, as Kaempfer noted. It was a cover that fooled no one, but gave the authorities an excuse to wink at what was going on. At the time Frois wrote, there were real singing-nuns (*utabikuni*) based in Kumano who traveled the country explaining Buddhist stories often employing pictures to gain donations and win converts. Also called "picture-solving-nuns" (etoki bikuni) or "soliciting-nuns" (kanjin bikuni), the Japanese Architecture and Art Net explains: "they gradually added elements of romance to spice up their narratives. Over time, love as related to salvation changed to love (and sex) for money, the real basis of their profession." While such an explanation is as charming as Kaempfer's, I believe we are talking about a different generation and different type of woman. The real ones, on fund-raising missions (*hongansho*) for their temples mostly preached *to women* – not men! – and told them stories and showed them pictures mostly related to female problems as we will see in chapter 4.   The first such mission was at Zenkôji (an esoteric Tendaishû and Jôdôshû (Pure Land) temple in Nagano) founded in 1264 by the mother of the great monk Hottô Kokushi Kakushin and was run and staffed by women (and still exists today as the Pure Land sect convent Daihongan. (see Hank Glassman: http://www.haverford.edu/east/glassman/PDFs/ (possibly from: a dissertation in the Religious Studies program at Stanford on "The Religious Construction of Motherhood in Medieval Japan").

3. *Prostitution and the Church.* By pushing more people to get married (including clergy) and direct oppression, Protestants pretty much killed prostitution in North Europe by the time Frois wrote the TRATADO, but it was still alive in Catholic parts.   I do not have anything specific on Spain, but Hale writes that "in Catholic Perpignan (France) the Dominicans were still contributing in 1608 to the upkeep of the municipal brothel. (H:CER). My impression is that Catholic countries kept prostitution up to modern times, for it was considered good for maintaining morals (discouraging premarital sex by women, adultery, homosexuality, etc). Rome and Venice, with their particularly large numbers of "influential unmarried men" (H:CER) were, like Edo in Japan, red zones.

~~~~~~

2-44   Our nuns ordinarily do not go outside of the convent;
             As freiras antre nós ordinariamente não andão fora de seus moesteiros;

> The *bikuni* of Japan are always going out, sometimes visiting military camps.
> *As* biqunis *de Japão andão sempre em folguedos e às vezes vão de* jindachi.

"Our nuns" include women in over a dozen orders. As I write in English, let me add that none were in England, for the English crown had dissolved both monasteries and nunneries in the 1530's (*compelling* monks to marry nuns, to boot!), ostensibly for the sake of Reformation and for the punishment of abuse, but actually to gain the resources they had built up over the centuries.   And, as Frois belonged to the Society of Jesus, we might note that of all the Catholic orders, the Jesuits alone had no parallel order for women. This does not mean they were particularly down on women. If anything, they were progressive. They had "a special ministry for prostitutes and their children."(LR) They supported the education of women and thought they could be as valiant as men. But they were very strong believers in chain of command and were very clear about women being under man's command.   Be that as it may, "our" convents were a mixed blessing. They provided a refuge for widows and other women without a place to go, but they *also* served as prisons for the innocent. "One scholar believes that convents were designed primarily to be a means of controlling the surplus female population of the wealthy or noble classes," writes Mary Springfels (Newberry Consort Repertoire Behind Cloiser Walls: Nun's Music (Googled:LR). That helps explain why we have so many stories of nuns with lovers.[1]   She provides an "eloquent and angry condemnation" of forced claustration by Archangela Tarabotti, herself a victim of this practice.

..

> It is well known that the majority of nuns cannot attain perfection because they are forced to the religious life by the force exerted by their fathers and kin . . . these unhappy girls, born under an unfortunate star . . . singing pretty love-songs and with their tender limbs forming graceful movements, please the ear and delight the soul of the base fathers who, deceitful, weaving nets of deception, think of nothing but to remove them from sight as soon as possible and so bury them alive [2] in cloisters for the whole of their lives, bound with indissoluble knots. *Paternal Tyranny, or Simplicity Betrayed*, 1654.

There must have been many fine cloisters full of genuine religious volunteers and my only apology for dwelling on the bad is that when it comes to Japanese "nuns," so did Frois. Besides, the *bad*, especially when it is beautiful, is more interesting. About a hundred years after Tarabotti's

Paternal Tyranny, the paternalistic seducer Giacomo Casanova describes one "sort of convent" which amounted to a life sentence, for of hundreds of girls who were there, only 4 succeeded in marrying out in 20 years, mostly because men were not allowed to see them.

> "And who are those who ask permission to put a poor girl in this prison?"
> "A poor relative, a devout mother or father, who fears that the girl will succumb to sin. For this reason girls are not accepted here unless they are already very pretty."
> "Who pronounces on their prettiness?"
> "Relatives, some ecclesiastic, a monk, the priest of the girl's parish, and in the last instance the Cardinal, who, if he does not think the child pretty, sends her away, for an ugly girl is believed to run no risk by remaining in the world. So you can be sure that, unhappy as we are here, we curse all those who declared us pretty." (Vol 12 ch 1 of *History of My Life,* transl. Trask)

On the Japanese side, Okada does not bother to point out the mistake of equating such *bikuni* with nuns – too obvious for the Japanese reader – and wryly observes with respect to the camp visits mentioned by Frois, "it appears that *bikuni* sell-color [prostitution] was really flourishing." I might add that Valignano blames Buddhist bonzes wishing to cover up accidental issue with "their nuns, whom they call *bikuni"* for inventing abortificents and claimed they dispensed them to those who request them! (*muchos de ellos dan ahora hierbas y medicinas, a los que las piden, para hacer mover –* SUMARIO=1583. V(A):S&A p31) If Frois conflates real nuns with prostitutes in the garb of nuns, Valignano neglects to point out that the Chinese herbalist tradition was introduced and largely carried on by bonzes headquartered in temples. (See note at end of ch. 9)

1. *Nuns with Lovers.* The old stories about horny nuns are usually pornography (or, misogyny if you think of it that way), but there are now fine books letting the lonely nuns who were not nuns tell their own stories. Look at these publisher comments about Mary Laven's *Virgins of Venice: Enclosed Lives and Broken Vows in the Renaissance Convent.*

> "Far from being precincts of piety and silence, the convents of Venice were hotbeds of political scheming, colorful pageantry, gorgeous decoration, and illicit love affairs. One nun was so determined to sleep with her lover that she painstakingly chipped a hole in a stone wall so he could climb through under cover of night. Another expressed her individuality through obsessive gift giving while keeping records of the dangerous flirtations going on around her."

In Venice there were "fifty convents housing three thousand nuns, many of them refined, upper-class women who had been immured against their will."

2. Buried Alive? How bad could it be? Frois does not exaggerate about the strict sequestration. He wrote at a time when nuns were being treated with great severity. In *A Convent Tale: A Century of Sisterhood in Spanish Milan* (New York: Routledge. 2002), P. Renée Baernstein writes of the convent of San Paolo Converso. It began as a progressive institution but times changed and

> "when Borromeo was appointed archbishop of Milan in 1564, the nuns were already primed to fall in with his plans for convents to be utterly segregated from the outside world in every respect. The deranged nature of this impulse is illustrated at many levels by the Catholic Church's general ruling that "nuns could take in washing only if both the wearer and the washer were anonymous" ; the Angelics were therefore not only not allowed to see or be seen by the Barnabites [their monk counterparts], but they were not allowed to wash the Barnabites' liturgical vestments."

2-45   Among us, it is not very common for women to know how to write;
Antre nós não hé muito corrente saberem as molheres escrever;

> The honorable[1] women of Japan think not knowing how to do so lowers their worth. *Nas honrradas de Japão se tem por abatimento as que o não sabem fazer.*

At the time Frois wrote, literacy was on the rise and education was bullish throughout Europe. But, not for women. Even when some made it into a lower school, they were not permitted to go beyond the basics. According to the Banbury Grammar School statutes (1594), "none were permitted to attend 'above the age of nine or longer than they may learn to read English'" (G:WDW). "Thus," an anonymous feminist wrote a generation later, "if we are weak by nature; they strive to make us more weak by our nurture. And if in degree of place low, they strive by their policy to keep us more under." (G:WDW) The logic of man's oppression of woman in Europe is puzzling. If women were inferior, as claimed, why would their literacy be a threat? But, that is how all true discrimination operates: it seeks to create by artificial means the difference it claims is natural. Perhaps the repression is best understood as men jealously guarding their *property* rights, their two-legged treasures. As Lady Carey put it only a decade or so after TRATADO, for a woman to be published is wrong, for her wedding vow made her husband the sole proprietor of her body *and mind*.

> Then she usurps upon another's right,
> That seeks to be by public language graced;
> And tho' her thoughts reflect with purist light
> Her mind, if not peculiar, is not chaste.
> For in a wife it is no worse to find
> A common body, than a common mind.

That is to say, writing involves *sharing* and women in Europe – or, much of Europe, much of the time, for there were pockets of literacy [1] and times/places when troubadours, paramours and such were not only accepted but *de rigor* – were monopolized. Yet, by the last quarter of the nineteenth century, when Alice Mabel Bacon taught noblewomen (the relations of the imperial family, perhaps I should say *peerage*) in Japan, the situation for women in the West had improved enough that she worried on behalf of her students in particular and Japanese womanhood in general, lest "the higher courses of study only serve to make her kick against the pricks, and render herself miserable." (B:JGW) Was she, perhaps, speaking from experience? Here is D.H. Lawrence on Western woman a generation later:

> *The great mass of humanity should never learn to read and write – never* . . . . At all cost, try to prevent a girl's mind from dwelling on herself. . . . Anything to keep her busy, to prevent her reading and becoming self-conscious . . . ("Fantasia of the Unconscious")

I went on at length about *us* because "our" side has changed the most with respect to this contrast. We, not Japan, are the foreign country. This does not mean Japan was a modern country with close to 100% literacy. It means that the men and women were more or less equally literate. As Frois wrote in his 1565 Meaco (Miyako=Kyoto) letter, "in the more cultured parts of the land, and wherever there are nobility, both men and women know how to read and write." [2] And, I would add that the accomplishment was more phenomenal than his words suggest, for it was not enough to write. One had to write beautifully (content and calligraphy-wise) and correctly. To do so required a tremendous investment and it was made for both sexes. And this went back over a half-millennium. In Murasaki Shikibu's *Tale of Genji* (debatedly the first full-length novel ever written: c. 1100-1110) letters rather than looks were the key to a lover's heart as poems written out of sight were passed back and forth in the night. Women were not, however, expected to master and use as many Chinese characters as men and, mostly wrote with the phonetic syllabary. In fact, that is the usual reason given for why they, not men, developed the essay and the novel. And there were other male-female differences, but Frois, as we shall see in Chapter X, missed a lot of contrasts he could have made about language. *Faux Frois*:

> *In Europe, the women always speak a language men can understand;*
> *In Japan, the women say things men cannot make sense of.*

But perhaps, Frois skipped this because he had already written somewhere and heard it caused confusion. I write this because Rodrigues claimed something gave rise to the mistaken idea among some Europeans that women wrote in a code the men couldn't understand and felt he had to clarify: "They should have said that women, especially the noble and high-born, use among themselves, in addition to the ordinary language of the kingdom, many words, nouns and verbs which the men do not ordinarily understand, and this actually happens." [3] Even today, we find a greater gender difference in Japanese than in English (and I would guess all European tongues). This makes Japanese novels, or, at least the flow from dialogue to dialogue, better than ours, because it is so obvious who speaks that novelists can skip the "he said" and "she said" stuff altogether.

Lest we get the mistaken impression that all Japanese men were gentlemen about female literacy, let me add that an item included with *"Hateful Things"* (things so enviable they are hated) in the "exhaustive listing" (*mono-wa-tsukushi*) titled INU-MAKURA (the dog-pillow: just about Frois's time) [4] includes "a woman's writing well" (Edward Putzar trans.), and a senryû from the MUTAMAGAWA (17th century) reads "a man boasting / an illiterate wife / lives in paradise" (*muppitsu no nyôbo motte, gokuraku*). No doubt the idea is: She cannot receive love letters, nor read his.

1. Honourable? Samurai class is included, so "noble" will not do. "Upper-class" would seem artificial. "Respectable" would imply moral judgment. So?

2. Pockets of Literacy. There was an abortive "golden age" of female letters in Tudor England (which concentrated so much on classics that one does not get the fine literature produced by Japanese women in their native tongue), but the "women who actually benefited from this . . . was limited to royalty and a handful of daughters of very eminent and privileged noblemen,"(G:WDW). It lasted little more than a generation (1520-60). There are doubtless more such pockets of literacy and abundant examples of extraordinary women who overcame their disadvantage. Those who were known, however, were usually vilified or treated as oddities, so many did not publish=publicize their learning. DR notes "nuns in Spain and the New World such as Sor Juana de La Cruz, who we only recently learned penned fabulous poetry, plays, commentaries and auto-biographical pieces." I fear I do not know enough about the European traditions or Japanese (outside of older classic work and women in haiku (my specialty)).

3. Respective Male and Female Literacy   Europeans learned about Japanese equality of education. The Editor of Golownin's *Captivity* (1824) noted "the Jesuits assure us that . . . no difference whatever is made between the sexes" while "cultivating the mind of youth." (G G:MCIJ).

4. Woman Words. Much of the difference is similar to that found in the West, certain adjectives or adverbs used more frequently by one sex than the other. Where "our" women (at least up to my grandmother's generation) would speak greater tonal range then men, Japanese women would put different emotive tails on the verbs that generally end the Japanese sentence. But, I think, there was and still is a larger difference in vocabulary between the two sexes in Japan. In both cultures we find women using more baby words and more euphemism for body parts and enjoying a larger vocabulary in certain fields (food, clothing), but the Japanese women had them for many more things and, thanks to honorific suffixes such as *o* or *mi* or *sa* could sweeten words that were otherwise identical. Rodrigues, in his *Treatise on Epistolary Style* (part of his second, brief GRAMMAR), includes examples of a type of woman-speak that I have never heard of and seems to belie his assertion that women did not speak in code, for it resembles pig-latin! Eg.: *fumonji* for *fumi* = letter; *somonji* for *sonata* = you; *pamonji* for padre=father. (R(L):TES)

5. Just about Frois's Time. The version of Dog Pillow Putzar translated in the *Harvard Journal of Asiatic Studies (1968 issue # lost, sorry!)* was "printed in movable wooden type" in 1607 but the original was made a couple decades earlier by Hata Soen (1550-1607). The listing is not so elegant as that of Sei Shônagon.

~~~~~~

2-46   The letters we write to women are signed by the men who write them;
  Nas cartas que se escrevem antre nós a molheres, se asina o homem que a escreve;

> In Japan, letters written to women need not bear a signature; nor do women sign their letters nor record the month or year. *Em Japão as que se escrevem a molheres não hão-de levar sinal, nem ellas em suas cartas se asinão, nem poem mes nem era.*

I thought Frois might have been conflating *informality* with gender difference here, for letters between friends need not be signed when each recognizes the other's hand-writing. But reading the short section "On the Letters of Women" in Rodriguez's *Treatise on Epistolary Style*, we find that –

"Letters from women to men have no courtesies [formal phrases to end the letter] at the end of the letter, are not signed and do not give the day of the month." (R(L):TOES)

As far as letters from men to women go, Rodrigues writes they are signed and bear the day of the month (but not the month or year). This does not necessarily contradict Frois, for Frois does not say they *never* are signed, but we can see how he improved the contrast. It is possible that formality vs. informality is not the whole story. Sei Shonagon in her *Pillowbook* (c.1000) writes about a man extremely aggravated by her cryptic messages (she sent him a piece of seaweed [1]) and it might be that women who prided themselves on their fine discrimination found signatures boring whereas men did not want to guess and that this difference became recognized if not formalized by Frois's time.

1. Sei Shônagon's Seaweed. If it were *wakame* kelp, she might have meant he'd be better with a younger woman, for *waka* is homophonic with "young" and *me* with "woman". But, I believe it was the laver, *nori* In that case, the verb *noru* means to be aboard or, in the case of a plan, to agree with it or join it. But if she had such intentions, his temper quickly abused her of it. 清少納言の「糊」に関心ある。欄外注、誰か？ Even though I reduce the Japanese to font size 8, MS-Word makes it virtually impossible to line up things when 2 columns are used. I PROTEST!

2-47   With us, women receive the name of a saint;
Antre nós os nomes das molheres são tomados das Sanctas;

Japanese women's names are as follows, namely: kettle, crane, turtle, sandal, tea, bamboo. *Os nomes das japoas são: tacho, grou, cagado, alparqa, chá, cana.*

A sampling of female names in Lisbon in 1565 did show one saint (Maria 74, Isabel 71, Caterina 56, etc.) after another. With few exceptions, even the less common names (9 Branca [white/bright/clear] 13, Graçia 6, Luzia 6, Crara 2, Cosma 1, Esperança [hope] 1) were spiritually uplifting. [1] If I am not mistaken, men, too, often received the name of Saints in Catholic countries. During a home-stay in Mexico (1968), I was asked where I got my name since there was no St. Robin in the calendar (I replied, *he stole from the rich and . . .* wasn't that saintly?). The kindly matron of the house had searched the calendar to confirm my birthday, only to find it missing altogether!

Of the Japanese names given – in Japanese, *Nabe, Tsuru, Kame, ___?, Ocha,* and *Take* – only the "slipper" would be unfamiliar to Japanese today. Okada, looking up the Portuguese word in the NIPO Dictionary found *gege,* a horribly cacophonic woman's word for straw sandals and guesses it *might* be what Frois intended. According to the OJD, it is a homophone for the lowest of the low and was used for low-level male servants, so it may have been used for women, too. Aurelio suggests a leather shoe, too, so I wonder if Tabi (those sock/slippers) might not be the name intended. Regardless, as Michael Cooper notes,

Frois has certainly chosen some unflattering examples to emphasize the differences between Japanese and European usages; he might have also included more pleasing names such as Spring, Plum, Bounty and Purity. (C:TCJ)

Indeed. Isabella Bird gave the following examples "among the children's names" in a large family she visited: "*Haru,* Spring; *Yuki,* Snow; *Hana,* Blossom; *Kiku,* Chrysanthemum; *Gin,* Silver;" (B:UTJ) and Lafcadio Hearn left us 48 charming pages, with *hundreds* of fine examples of "Japanese Female Names" broken down by type (SHADOWINGS: 1900). The variety is tremendous. *Faux Frois:*

Europeans have a large number of family names and a small number of given names;
Japanese have a small number of family names and a large number of given names.

I do not know about Frois's time, but today there are over a million different personal names in use in Japan, though many of these are homophonic, so the number of different sounding names would be an order or two of magnitude less.   People combine Chinese characters like copywriters creating a new name for a product. "We", on the other hand, have a large number of *family* names primarily because of the diversity of our roots. Were this the other way around, the *Nihonjinron* (pop-culturology of the Japanese character) mill – not to mention Mr. Lowell back in 1888 – would have used it as "proof" of how individualistic Westerners are.   But even with millions of choices, popular names in Japan, like those in the US show large variation from decade to decade. Women's names in particular, show systematic changes in Japan of a greater magnitude than anything the Anglo-American world has seen. Early in the twentieth century, their names had varied endings, but in mid-century, *most* were given names ending in the syllabet *ko,* written with the Chinese character for "child" (eg., Ono Yoko) that was previously used by the nobility (eg., Empress Michiko), then, in the last quarter of the century, the *ko*'s quickly thinned out and were replaced by *mi*'s, *ri*'s, *ka*'s, *na*'s etc..

1. *Names in Lisbon and Elsewhere*.   The exceptions include one Eva, one Galinda, one Neta (Grand-daughter?). Were the 11 Violantes still-death girls who "flew" to heaven? The list was @ *Portuguese Feminine Names from Lisbon, 1565* by Aryanhwy merch Catmael (Sara L. Friedemann). // Could anyone give me a comparative study of the spread of *family* names in Europe and Japan that would fit in one or two paragraphs?

2-48   In Europe, women wear *chapin* [1] [raised/fancy shoes] made of leather or Valencia gilt;
Em Europa trazem as molheres chapins de couro ou dourados de Valença;

The Japanese wear ones made of *vruxado* [1] [lacquered] wood, with the big toe separated from the others.   *As japoas os trazem de pao* vruxado *com o dedo polegar dividido dos outros.*

The *chapin* can mean either sandal or clog-like shoes that are open to one degree or another or, simply, fancy shoes. [2] Since some of these European chapin had stilts somewhat like those of the typical Japanese *geta,* or because Japanese were not yet as uniformly up on stilts as they soon would be, [3] Frois concentrates on the material and tops rather than the stilts, which *today* mark the *geta* as unique. Today, we are familiar enough with wooden shoes not to gasp, but to Iberians of his time, they might have been considered odd, and certainly would not have been identified with fine footwear. The beautifully laquered female footwear in Japan usually had a triangular front stilt tapering out to the tip and is called *bokuri* rather than *geta*. Shiny black was probably most common.   All varieties of Japanese footwear came to have the toe separation.   The thongs – never mentioned by Frois – are generally the most decorative part of the shoe for they are what is seen above the tabi-wearing foot. But the contrast would have to be with shoe-laces. Did "we" have them yet?

1. **Frois's** *vruxado* turns the noun *urushi*, or "lacquer" into another part of speech. *Urushi* was also verbed by English, but in a stranger way yet: as *japaned* and *japaning*. Had Frois written in the 17th century, I would have written "japaned wood."

2. *Chapin* **problem.** The Japanese translators also had trouble with this. Okada uses the Japanese generic term for "shoes" and Matsuda+Yorissen use a modern *gairaigo* (imported term) *haihiru,* or "high-heels!" The French team uses *patins,* a version of the word chapin. According to the OED, the *patten* is "a name applied at different periods to various kinds of foot-gear." Still, from the examples given, almost all tend to share one characteristic. In one way and to one degree or another they are raised.

3. *Raised Shoes.* If I am not mistaken and the geta we know were not yet that common, then it would seem that shoes rose in Japan and Europe at about the same time. Rudovsky points out, it was the trade city of Venice where Italian engravings of the 17th century show "courtesans walking upon chopines twenty inches high." As noted already, Bulwer points out the same in England. Rudovsky guesses, "the vulgar form of Venetian walking contraptions, whittled down to a few inches are today's high-heeled shoes" (R:KM).   But before we credit the East (Venetia as the most Oriental city in the West) or Japan for "our" high heels, we really need to tease out two different threads. It is one thing to walk on raised shoes and quite another to walk on raised heels. *A gloss regarding the spread of high shoes is wanted!*

2-49   European women ride side-saddle or on a seat [sedan-chair];
As de Europa andão en silhões ou andilhas;

Japanese women ride in the same manner as men.
As de Japão cavalgão da mesma maneira que os homens.

It would probably be easier for the reader to find a side-saddle in an encyclopedia than for me to explain exactly how they were made and, if I am not mistaken, the traveling-seat, or *andilhas,* was somewhat like the platform we see people riding on elephants or camels. I was tempted to translate it as "perch." Frois's "Japanese" are family of nobles and high-ranking samurai. Others had no horses to ride.

Japanese nobles or *buke* (samurai class) women generally had riding experience since childhood, and rode in the same style as their brothers. Why did Japanese women ride "like men?" One explanation is that with Japan coming off several hundred years of warfare, people of both sexes had to move fast or die. But I doubt if that is the main reason or even a good one. Rather, we might turn this around and ask why European women did *not* ride in a natural way like men. "Our" weird idea that it was obscene for a woman's legs to split (or dangerous for a virgin) [1] is what needs explaining! Other people who were transported on horseback, such as the middle-class townsmen, wealthy farmers, and most especially the brides, often depicted in prints taking the only ride they would have in their life, generally "rode" in the manner ascribed to European women. I say "rode" because these women did not really ride (take command of a horse), but were simply transported.

1. *Women on Horses.* Though Japanese did not joke about samurai women riding horses, they did not entirely divorce horse-riding from sexuality either. Senryu claimed that *exercise before sex* was good for women (but bad for men) – a claim recently confirmed by modern research! – and debated as to which was the ideal exercise for warming them up (senryu were written from the point of view of men), *riding* or *walking,* though both were considered better than being carried in a sedan.

2-50   For our women, some pads are placed on the back of the mule under the seat;
Pera as molheres se põe em cima das mulas nas andilhas humas almofadas;

In Japan, a white sheet is draped over the saddle of the horse of noblewomen.
Em Japão pera as molheres honrradas se põe em riba da sela do cavalo hum lençol branqo.

The Portuguese in the first half of the distich is sloppy and ambiguous. All the translations of the European and Japanese side I have seen put cushions on top of the seat rather than pads under it, on the mule. But a draft translation by H, the opinion of the librarian at the National Library of Portugal (BNP) and the long saddle-cloths mentioned in 8-26 affirm the above reading which improves the contrast in an over-under way. A 1560 Japanese text cited by Okada calls the sheet something that translates as "oil-cloth" and describes it as a *aka-tori,* or "dust-remover" and cites another source to the effect that these hung way down like skirts. I do not know if the sheet *over* the saddle would have seemed odd for the people of Frois's time. Paintings of the caparisons of knights I have seen show them *under* the saddle, but the OED has them *over* it. Either way, a sheet on a horse was considered knightly (a male thing), and that may have been the prime *aren't "they" odd!* element of the contrast.

But, I/we could be wrong, and the European *almofada* are *pillows* on the seat, not *pads* below it, in which case the contrast would be one of pampered European behinds vs. knightly Japanese women, also not bad. In this case, however, it would need to be pointed out that Japanese had cushion, called *futon* (like the bedding that has recently entered the English language), because their saddles were wooden and they needed them!

~~~~~~

2-51   In Europe, women generally prepare meals.
            Em Europa ordinariamente as molheres fazem de comer;

In Japan, men prepare them, and noblemen are proud to go into the kitchen to do so.
Em Japão o fazem os homens, e os fidalgos tem por primor y-llo fazer hà cozinha.

Matsuda and Jorissen claim Frois exaggerates the contrast, citing Ruperto de Nola (*Libro de Guisados* (1529)) as an example of a male cook in court, but this hardly destroys Frois's contention that there were *more* men in the kitchen in Japan (Frois's "*ordinariamente*" is not absolute). And it is also of little account that cooking became the fashion for noblemen in 17th and 18th century Europe, for Frois never claimed his contrasts were timeless. One thing is certain. The Jesuits were impressed. Rodrigues gives a detailed description of the "public kitchens in the palaces of the lords and other noble people." Said kitchen was one of the best parts of the dwelling. Perhaps, the fact cooking was deemed "a dignified and honorable occupation," and the preparation area was so spacious, beautiful and clean, may help explain the comparatively greater role of men. And, perhaps more important than anything else, carving was a major activity in the kitchens of nobility, where there was plentiful game (including fish). It was one of the ten principal "liberal arts," and "a very common and noble office among them" (R(C):TIJ). In the West, too, men have always dressed game outside and carved meat on the table. In Japan, where, because of chopsticks, everything is carried to the table bite-size, there was a high demand for knife-work and this presumably drew men into the kitchen.

In fact, there were even a number of competing schools of professional carvers boasting the "shi" (master) suffix on their title and, judging from illustrations, fine dress, both of which indicate theirs was, indeed, one of the most honorable professions. Such knife-masters (*hôchôshi*) could even be found working, or rather putting on a show, in front of eaters, something I had assumed was invented by a certain Japanese restaurant in America. Yet the art was, evidently, not restricted to professionals. Here is a description of some of the visual delights accompanying a dinner given to Baron Gros's Embassy by the governor of Shimoda in 1858.

> First, there were dwarf trees, cut into the shape of flowers and animals; then there was a large fish in a dish of water, imitating a pool of salt water with seaweed floating on it; and lastly there came superb flowers, constructed out of lobster-flesh and sliced turnips. The governor told us with evident satisfaction, that these flowers were the work of his officers; which certainly gave us a high idea of the neat handiness of these gentlemen, although it somewhat lowered our opinion of the character of their occupations. That the principal functionaries of state are free to spend their time in making artificial flowers out of carrots and turnips and lobster-flesh, proves the social machine is well ordered and works smoothly without watchful supervision. (M:BGE)

I cannot sort through the edible and non-edible part of the Marquis's description. The topiary art, if that is what it is, was, no doubt done with the aim of pleasing the foreigners, whose [bad] taste was well known by the Japanese hosts. But what would ole Nietzsche have thought about all those Japanese men in the kitchen? *Viz.* Item 234 of BEYOND GOOD AND EVIL, a vintage piece of misogynist blather :

> Stupidity in the kitchen; woman as cook; the terrible thoughtlessness with which the feeding of the family and the master of the house is managed! Woman does not understand what food *means*,

and she insists on being cook! If woman had been a thinking creature, she would certainly, as cook for thousands of years, have discovered the most important physiological facts, and should likewise have got possession of the healing art! Through bad female cooks – through the entire lack of reason in the kitchen – the development of mankind has been longest retarded and most interfered with: even to-day matters are very little better . – *A Word to High School Girls.*

And this from a man who waxed hysterical about the "de-feminizing" of women and the feminization of European "manliness!" Compare Nietzsche's ideal and Frois's reality to that found in a late-20th century Japanese food product advertisement where a young woman says "I'm the one who makes it" and the young man says "I'm the one who eats it!" [1] The mass media generally slights feminist complaint in Japan, but a few voices raised against this ad developed into a national controversy, or rather, reflection, because it called attention to the sad but true fact: that few Japanese men did *any* cooking. Indeed, things got so bad that, judging from Japanese television, at least, when wives visit their families for a few days, they usually prepare a number of meals ahead of time for their husbands who wouldn't know where anything was in the kitchen even if they could cook. To be fair to men, the 70-80 hour work weeks of the post-war economic miracle did not leave any time for diddling in the kitchen. By the time the work week dropped to 50-60 hours, or they retired, most of these corporate warriors (or, company slaves) were totally at sea in a kitchen. But, young men didn't have that excuse, and the ad featured a young couple.

1. *Famous Ad Copy.*   One reason this advertisement could not be overlooked by the feminists is that the Japanese grammar used, which does not English well, but is fine colloquial Japanese (seems to equate the behavior with the very identity of the person. *watashi wa tsukuru hito!* (lit., "I'm a making-person") *Boku wa taberu hito!* (lit., "I'm an eating person").   The product was either curry or instant ramen and I guess the idea was that if you must cook for someone make it easy on yourself and buy our cheap ready-made food for your easy-to-please but lazy boyfriend who will love you for it. The company caved in to the criticism.

~~~~~~

2-52   In Europe, men are tailors;
          Em Europa [os]homens são alfayates;

          And in Japan, the women.
          E em Japão as molheres.

Tinker, Tailor, Soldier, Sailor . . . – as the nursery rhyme goes.   OED dates the word tailor back to 1297.   That was about the time when the loose robes of the Medieval period were being supplanted with clothing cut to fit the body. Whether that followed the new classical reverence for the human form or helped create the new reverence for the human form I do not know, but with the Renaissance the primary importance of the cloth gave way to that of the cut and the draper (cloth merchant) to the tailor, who was in some cases actually two people, a cutter, or pattern expert, and a sewer, or assembler. The title of a book printed in Madrid, then (1589) the fashion capital of Europe, "*Libro de Geometria, Pratica y Traca*" (Book of the Geometry[measurement], Practice [construction] and Tracing) by the master tailor Juan de Alcega, [1] reveals something of the nature of the trade: highly skilled and male (What little I saw reminded me of ballistics and other male sciences). There are a dozen different trades involved in the making of clothing, many of which (eg. *broger, capper, carder, lister*) most of us would not even recognize. While few women were engaged in any of these as recognized professionals (guild members), they often worked on commission and sometimes managed to succeed a deceased husband. As the tailor reached the top of the pinnacle and, by the sixteenth century ranked with the merchant class, women were pretty much shut out, though in North Europe, at least, they are reported to have done work for master tailors on commission. [2] *Officially speaking,* then, Frois is right.

On the Japanese side, the dyers (the merchant-manufacturer, not the listers who got their hands wet,) and drapers were still on the top and the cutters and assemblers, or, *tailors* were considered menial labor. In that sense, women in Japan did not really enjoy the prestige of being tailors in the Western sense of the word. They were not an independent calling but *seamstresses* working for drapers. In that sense, Japanese men *always* had a hand in the sewing business in Japan. They ran it. From a customer point of view, leaving out gender difference, it might be *Faux Frois'ed* like this:

> *When we buy cloth, we hire someone to sew it or do so ourselves.*
> *The Japanese buy the cloth only, and the tailoring comes for free.*

Japanese did not buy their kimonos; they bought rolls of cloth so expensive that the creation of the actual product by the in-house labor was free. [3]   Upper-class clothing in the West resembles this to a degree, but the proportion of expense and labor that go into the cloth production and tailoring are very different, if not the reverse (I simplify, for the tailors in London eventually played a role in the production of cloth that would form well.)

When Japan reopened in the 19th century, Japanese-style clothing (*wafuku*) continued to be assembled by women, while most cutter-sewers of Western style clothing (*yofuku*) were men who were called *shitateya* (lit. outfitter) now translated as "tailor" or "dress-maker." The *ya* on the tail of the word makes it clear that this is someone with his own shop. While more women may have possessed the requisite skills, men created or took over the business of making Western clothing because in the 19th century it was prestigious (as the newest fashion, a nationally endorsed effort), risky (both because it was new and because at first, a tailor largely dealt with foreigners) and predominantly *for* men, because more males visited Japan and Japanese women, following an abortive early attempt to introduce Western dress, largely reverted to their native wear and only Westernized in mass after World War II. [3] Considering the wholesale import of European social institutions at the time, men-as-tailors was also tried simply because it was a male job in the West. Logically speaking, this makes perfect sense, but one still wonders if Japanese men might not have better left the entire business of making clothing to their women, for Westerners in Japan throughout the 19th century unanimously put down their product. Considering the praise they had for Japanese craftsmanship even then this is extraordinary. To get a decent suit, they all recommended Chinese tailors. But, this may be unfair to Japanese men. The Chinese, besides their robes, had a tradition of tubular clothing, where the Japanese only knew rectangles. It is possible even Japanese women would have failed.

1. *Source of Information* Mostly: http://www.lone-star.net/mall/literature/tailor4.htm   *The History of Tailoring: An Overview* by G. Bruce Boyer.

1. *Juan de Alcega's Book*. There is an English facsimile and translation: *Patterns of Fashion: The Cut and Construction of Clothes for Men and Women* c 1560-1620 by Janet Arnold. Unfortunately I did not see it.

2. *Summary of Guilds*   My information came from *Women in Medieval Guilds,* a 1999 article by Robert G. Ferrell in www.virtualworldlets.net/Papers/Hosted/ Women Med.php. His main source (3 books cited) was the records of the city of York from 1273 to the early sixteenth century. He notes that because wives who took over from husbands were not officially recorded (but there are records of husbands leaving items such as looms to wives), the female role in all aspects of the trades is surely much larger than records indicate.

3. *In-house Seamstressing.*   Buying cloth to buy a kimono is still true today! As a result, it is almost impossible to find anyone to adjust a kimono or make one from cloth bought elsewhere. I once bought an old used kimono and ended up letting it out myself.

GENERAL NOTE: *Gender and Cultural Diversity.* It is my theory that the survival of clearly differing gender roles in and out of the workplace has helped Japan preserve separately, rather than fuse and lose, items of Eastern and Western culture, such as Japanese and Western clothing. When a monoculture follows suit it loses its entire past, whereas one which has some firewalls – whether between genders, classes or localities – built in can keep a number of threads alive simultaneously.

2-53   In Europe, men eat at high tables and women at a low ones.
          Em Europa os homens comem em mezas altas e as molheres em baxas;

          In Japan, women eat at high tables and men at a low ones.
          Em Japão as molheres em mezas altas e os homens em baxas.

Women and men tended to eat separately in Europe and Japan and the logic of psychology would suggest a *higher* place for men in *both* cultures.   Indeed, the Japanese observation seems contrary to practices suggesting that Japanese had a clear cut sense of up=high=exalted and down=low=base. *So what is happening here?* First, I think it bears noting that the tables in the two lines of the distich are not really the same thing. Our tables are large raised surfaces where people eat together; theirs, a tiny portable writing-desk-like devices with tiny folding legs. Okada shows a picture with a nobleman eating with his table directly in front of him resting on the *tatami* (legs folded up) while the woman diagonally across the room has a table by her side about eight inches high. Since both sit on the floor (see 6-5) no one is looking down on anyone. I can imagine the early visitors (male) to Japan wishing they had the higher tables so they would have a sporting chance of getting the food to their mouth!

2-54   In Europe, it is thought offensive for women to drink wine;
          Em Europa se tem por afronta beberem as molheres vinho;

          In Japan, it is very common, and on festive occasions, they sometimes get drunk;
          Em Japão é muito freqente, e em festas bebem às vezes até acavesarem [or, avinhaçarem ? [1]];

Granted that Iberian ideology held that it was worse for a woman to drink than for a youth to drink (both improper according to the 1529 *Libro de Guisados* (N:LDG)), write Jorissen and Matsuda, but does it hold true for the rest of Europe? They cite a number of European travel writings recording women in a Tyrolian castle downing several large servings of wine at a sitting without being criticized for it, and Bernado Bizoni recording that the wife of Henry IV took a sip of wine now and then at a banquette, etc.. Indeed, we have all seen the Flanders-school paintings of riotous peasant festivities without a sober adult of either sex to be found. I thought the Islamic influence might have made Frois's claim correct for Iberia, at least, but this was not necessarily the case. Reff writing about the Missions in the New World:

..
> . . . the Jesuits wrote disparagingly of native feasts and celebrations that degenerated into bacchanals, implying that such behavior was at odds with Christian practice. And yet the profanation of sacred places (dancing, feasting, "lewd and enormous sins") was apparently commonplace in sixteenth-century Spain, so much so that communities found it necessary to include in their constitutions requests that people keep their clothes on when they slept at shrines (Christian:1981:164)" (in R:DPC)

Japanese women, especially those in the business of entertainment and older women who were retired from active duty if it were, did indeed imbibe as freely as the men whose *sake* they heated. Still, there was a gender gap. While women did enjoy a wee cup or two now and then, they did not get drunk as much as men. They were, after all, meant to stand by their men, not lie plastered with them.[2]   The Spanish merchant de Avila Giron summed it all up very well: "the women drink very little, although their menfolk are like Frenchmen."

1. *Acavesarem? Avinhaçarem?* The meaning of "until ~" is so clear that the apparent messiness or corruption of the manuscript that led Father Schütte to read the first and the modern Portuguese translators to read the second, does not matter. The first word seems to suggest getting high/giddy (but is not too clear in my dictionaries) whereas the second is clear.

2. *Stand By Your Man* The best line in this country classic that is widely thought to reflect the opposite mentality of feminism advises women to forgive and help their mate who is too drunk to stand up, for he is "only a man." That phrase "only a man" suggests the gap between feminism and country may not be so large as imagined. Condescension is condescension.

2-55   European women, for the most part, eat meat and fish;
As molheres de Europa pola mayor parte comem carne e pexe;

Japanese noblewomen generally don't eat meat, and many don't eat fish, too.
As japoas fidalgas ordinariamente não comem carne, e muitas nem comem pexe.

Europe is on the rare side of the contrast here, for in most cultures, meat is a male thing. I believe this is less because males hunted or herded (though it may have begun that way) than because men tend to have less efficient intestines – they tend to absorb less – than women. [1] This is why famine kills men at a much higher rate than it kills women, even in cultures such as Japan, Korea and China, where no rules of chivalry said to help "women first." Where many women thrive on flour, water, and a bit of greens (I exaggerate a little, here), men usually end up emaciated from such a diet. They need meat, something easily digested in the stomach, more than women do. I think that is why women in Japan could earn Buddhist brownie points on their karma by forsaking meat and most animal protein, whereas most men, although they may have wanted to, could not do so and remain healthy. Men in this Buddhist culture called their four-legged animal meat "medicine," (see 6-24) and that, was not merely a euphemism. They *needed it.*

Notice the "noblewomen" (*hidalgas*) on the Japanese side. Frois specified them because if any woman should be able to afford meat it would be them and, thus, abstaining is doubly contrary for it means they eat like poor women in Europe. But more is involved. Noblewomen were freer to worry about their spiritual betterment than commoners who had other things to worry about and they had a diet diverse enough (plenty of tofu, sea-weeds and whatnot) not to *need* animal protein. Commoners needed to eat fish or *anything* nutritious *when they could,* which probably was not often, because (his) parents, husband and children came first. Even in the first half of the 20th century, we hear tales of young women having to fight to get a single *egg* now and then from the monopolizing mother-in-law![2] Since one would think that the nutrition of young women would be evolutionarily speaking more important than the mother-in-law's appetite, it is possible this worked as birth-control (I am not sure how true this stereotype of starving young wives is – gloss anyone?).

Today, while one does find big eaters among Japanese women, they tend not to compete with men as women do in the USA, for they take it for granted that genitalia are not the only difference between the sexes.

Note also that Frois's exceptionally nuanced contrast includes 3 qualifications: *most, generally* and *many.*

1. *Carnivorous Women* Millennia of history can effect human genes. I cannot help feeling that women who chose to eat very meaty diets for years (as is the case for many in the USA) are playing with fire in the long-run.

2. *Suffering Young Wives* A tear-jerking soap opera about just such a perpetually hungry young wife was a big hit in Japan in the early 1980's. Oshin was given little

attention in the USA (as "our" worthless Dallas," failed to gain an audience in Japan) but became a big hit throughout Asia, indeed all the way South to Indonesia and West to the Middle East (supposedly big episodes caused major traffic jams in Iran), for the women in these countries were still living it or had escaped it even more recently than Japanese women did. I wrote in the past tense, but a quick Google reveals that Oshin has been revived!

> "The drama, 'Oshin,' will be supplied to Iraq's IMN television station through the Japan Foundation, the Foreign Ministry, which has jurisdiction over the foundation, said.
>
> 'We hope that people seeing the life of a Japanese woman who overcame various difficulties to survive a tumultuous period will offer encouragement during the period of rehabilitation after the war,' a ministry official said.
>
> The move is being promoted as a 'soft contribution' that differs from the approach of dispatching Japan's self-defense forces to Iraq. The shows will run in English, and an Egyptian television station will supply subtitles in Arabic. (Mainichi Shinbun, Japan, Oct. 23, 2003)

I hope the US GI's watch, too. In difficult times, we cannot have too much self-control and perseverance.

2-56   European women wearing mantles cover their faces all the more when speaking with someone. *As molheres de Europa, se estão com manto, cobrem-se ainda mais pera falarem com jente;*

> Japanese women must remove their head from their mantle, for it would be discourteous to speak with it in place. *As japoas hão-de tirar o manto da cabeça, porque falar com elle hé descortezia.*

   Though the Muslims had been driven from Iberia almost a hundred years before, European clothing still reflected the influence of what had been, and outside of Europe, perhaps still was, the most powerful civilization in the world.[1]   Remembering the fervor with which I have heard Muslim women defend their veils, I am unsure as to whether we should speak of women suffering "centuries of Islamic as well as Christian enclosure of the body." (DR) But, when I consider how hot veils would be in the summer, I feel "enclosure" too mild a word for the torture. (It is a lot easier to be pro-veil today, with air-conditioning.) There is also an ironic twist in the assertion that hiding the face serves modesty.   In Frois's time, some argued that veils – especially the *tapado de medio ojo* or half veil, had become "an instrument of the seductive art" for by only giving "a hint of the face beneath" it could "add piquancy" to pretty features or "lend imaginative charms to those women who were lacking real ones and knew how to use it to excite the attention of men who without this disguise would not give a second glance." (D:DLS) So, we find the veil in essence equated with heavy makeup! If that wasn't bad enough, as the Council of Castille complained to Philip II, family members can't recognize each other, men mistakenly accost others wives or innocent girls, prostitutes pass off for good women. The King forbade its use in 1590. Despite big fines and confiscation, the veil was not suppressed, for, as Defourneaux quips, "his successors periodically tried to renew the prohibition."

   Okada points out that Japanese dramas of the time show women carrying on a discussion, mantle in place. But, the dramas were *Kyogen*, meaning "crazy-talk," so Frois's contrast has hardly been compromised. I think this contrast may show that while Japanese women tended to cover their faces, the reasons for it probably were not quite the same as they were in the West. In the case of noblewomen, it might stem more from the principle of social importance being indicated by degree of separation (the Emperor the most hidden as reflected in Japanese architecture; and in the case of samurai and merchant class it might have been mainly about protection from the sun and dust or simply being coy.   As far as I know (and I am not at all confident about this), it does not seem to have been thought *sinful* to show a face nor was it ever a punishable offense (as, I would guess it was in certain times and places in the West) in Japan. Or, if it was, it was not by Frois's time. Over the course of the Tokugawa era, commoners, especially townswomen (nobles held out to the late-19th century) began showing off their faces more and more. While Western feminist scholars might identify attention to the personal beauty of women with female oppression, some Japanese feminist writers see the cult of public beauties in the Tokugawa era, represented by the *bijin-e* (lit. *"beautiful-women-paintings,"* mostly of *yûjo* (lit.: *play-woman:* usually translated as harlot or courtesan or geisha)), as a mark of a new freedom of women to exist as *persona*, rather than the faceless belongings of men. When this or that *yûjo* or street-vendor caught the imagination of Edo and, recognized for one or another characteristic (often, a creative way of dressing or advertising), even spawned fads, women began to come into their own, to gain individual identities. But, for all this progress (?), I have to add one *Faux Frois* about something that may go back a long way:

> *European women laugh with their hands wherever they might be.*
> *Japanese women cover their mouths with their hands when they laugh.*

Even without the veil of the West or the *byôbu* screen of the noblewoman described in the next contrast, there was a tendency for *all* Japanese women to hide their faces, which we can still see today, though less and less young women now cover their faces when they laugh. When "we" think of modesty, we imagine Adam and Eve clutching their crotches (or crotch and breast). I think if Adam and Eve were Japanese "they" might, rather, cover their faces.[2]

1. *Muslim Influence Paradox* On the one hand, we might find the veiling of women due to the Islamic influence. On the other hand, considering the strong tendency to sequester women partly due to their identification with the Virgin Mary, it is possible that only the existence of the Muslim other *prevented* the Catholics from covering up their women completely. When measures were proposed to unveil the Moriscos (Islamic Iberian residents who converted to Christianity to survive) in 1565, Francisco Nuñez Muley objected, "The dress of our women *is not Moorish but merely provincial, just as in Castile and other regions* . . . To require our women to unveil their faces is only to provide opportunity for men to sin after beholding the beauty of those they are attracted to, while the ugly will find no one to marry them." (in H:CER, *italics mine*)

2. *Places To Cover.* I recently came across an old report of what may have been Cost Rican natives in which the women when asked why they only covered their breast when meeting men while bathing in a river replied that the bottom part was what we were born with so there was no shame in revealing that, whereas the breast grew differently on each of them and was embarrassing to reveal.

~~~~~~

2-57   European noblewomen speak openly with people who call on them;
As fidalgas d'Europa falão descubertamente com quem vem falar com ellas;

> Japanese noblewomen speak to someone they don't know from behind *byôbu* [paper partitions] or bamboo blind.[1]   *As senhoras de Japão, se as pessoas não são conhecidas, falão-lhe por detrás de biobus ou esteyras.*

So European noblewoman were not as free as Japanese outside, but freer to reveal themselves inside of their architectural enclosures even when facing people who might be strangers (Frois implies this from what he wrote about Japanese). I am not sure what exactly this implies. Is it deemed useless to pretend to modesty when the wolf is already inside? Is revelation outside thought as advertising whereas this was not so within the house? Or were there always enough guards that the women felt particularly secure?

This does not contradict what Frois wrote about the freedom of Japanese women (2-34, 2-35) or the previous item, 2-56, because here we are only speaking of noblewomen, who were a special case. The Wizard of Oz-like custom of talking from behind screens goes back at least a half millennium and is why the beautiful "shining" prince Hikaru Genji got stuck with a bony, incredibly ugly mistress with a long pointed red-tipped nose, Suetsumuhana, who, as it turned out was not too smart to boot: he was fooled, or rather misled himself, by not realizing the letters they exchanged at night were actually produced by her retainers! (at least, she was kind, and so was Genji to keep her!).[2]

1. Bamboo Blinds. We are talking about very thin strips of bamboo that let through more air and allow for better visibility (for the person closest to it, but not from a distance) than our curtains, yet block the sunlight perfectly. They are called *sudare* and hang from most doors and some windows. You might call them hanging, temporary walls.

2. Suetsumuhana   The OJD writes that Suetsumuhana had compensatory qualities: she was shy in an old-fashioned way (funny how shyness has remained old-fashioned for thousands of years, isn't it!) and kind-hearted. Her name means "dyer's saffron" (according to my Jp-En dict.) or rouge-producing plant, as it is known and is written "end[tip]-pinch-blossom."   (Since "blossom" is homophonic with "nose," her name evokes her, as Genji's given name Hikaru means "to shine.")

2-58   In Europe, women may enter any church they want to;
        Em Europa podem entrar as molheres em qualquer igreja que qerem;

> The gentile [1] women in Japan cannot enter some temples that are prohibited to them. *As jentias em Japão não podem emtrar em alguns templos que lhe são prohibidos.*

On the balance, Japan offered much more freedom of worship – or, more important by far, the freedom *not* to worship – than Europe; but women were and occasionally still are taboo (*nyonin-kinsei, nyonin-kekkai*) in some (Buddhist) temples. Some mountains – usually, it was an entire mountain rather than one temple – opened up to women only one day a year (In Japan the mountains and the seashore have official "openings," i.e. times of the year when certain activities are acceptable).[2] Issa fondly haikus old women, who visit such a temple, noting that they *". . first of all, look at the sea."* If they were hard-working farm-wives, chances are it was their only look at the sea for the entire year, so one can forgive them for paying attention to nature before the gods!

Buddhism was not sexist at the outset. According to Toshie Kurihara, roughly a century after Shakyamuni's death, a doctrine arose that denied women the opportunity for Buddhahood unless they transform themselves into males, either literally, before a public gathering . . . , or symbolically, by becoming a nun. This idea later came to Japan as *henjo-nanshi* in Japanese – the idea, if I read right, was for nuns to pray to overcome their sex at the moment of death to have a shot at paradise: for there were no women in the Pure Land (M:KZJ ch 7).   But, note, Buddhism in Japan, too, was not sexist at the outset. "It is generally acknowledged that the first three individuals in Japan to renounce the world and devote their lives to Buddhist practice were women" and "throughout the Nara period (710–794), nuns were accorded the same status as monks." Presumably this mean they were not kept out of temples.   In the Heian Period (794–1185), however, monks took the lion's share of the public functions reducing the need for nuns while the harsh ascetic regimes of ascetic Buddhism – marked by male comradery and misogyny – literally gained ground that became off-bounds to women, and "by the Kamakura period (1185–1333), formally ordained nuns were a rarity, while their lay counterparts grew in numbers. For the most part, women were treated merely as religious subjects needing to be saved." I would add that, reading Kenkô's *Tsurezuregusa* (1330-31),   I get the impression that *fear* of women as forces attracting men to stay in this world – rather than denigration or hatred of them, as our term misogyny implies – may have been the salient problem. If you think of the temple as a sort of monastery, it does not seem so outlandish to have female visitors forbidden to the men who want them.

In Europe, too, women may have occasionally been denied church entrance. In England, writes Keith Thomas, there was a purification aspect of religious service, so that some vicars refused communion to women who were menstruating or had sex the night before. As with the Shinto gate guards in Japan, one wonders how these men *knew!*

1. Gentile? Since no woman was allowed where women were not allowed – that is to say, Christian Japanese   women would be denied entry, too – it seems redundant to use the term "gentile" (heathen). Perhaps Frois used it to indirectly identify the temples as neither Christian nor Jewish.

2. *Buddhist Temple Sexism*. I am a bit confused about just how many Buddhist Temples were off to women and whether it was true for any Shinto Shrines (other than those sharing a mountain with the Buddhists (Gloss, anyone?).

There is also the alive vs. dead problem. A chapter in a Japanese history book (M:KZJ ch 6:) tells us that: "In the Chûsei (Middle Ages (1185-1568), women were prohibited from temples but, *after death,* women could be buried even on Kôyasan (the main mountain for the Shingon (True Word) Buddhist sect). I think that by the end of this period there were many temples women could visit, but I could be wrong. At any rate, compared to cultures where women and men are even buried separately, Europe and Japan are both egalitarian.

~~~~~~

2-59   With us, it would be very strange for women to carry things by *pingah* [shoulder-poles];
Antre nós seria muito estranho levarem as molheres couza à pinga;

In Japan, it is normal for maid-servants to carry water in buckets.
Em Japão hé ordinário acarretarem as servas agoa em baldes.

The apparent reading of the first half of the distich, *based on Portuguese alone,* has women not carrying what seems to be "dripping things." That *astounded* me and I was disappointed not to find any annotation in the Japanese translations and the modern Portuguese version. I searched for an explanation, any explanation, in vain.[1] The French *Traité* saves us on this one, pointing out that the word *pinga* here is not "dripping" but a Malay word *pingah* used in Macao (a Portuguese colony on the edge of China that served as a sort of Jesuit headquarters in the Far East) for poles of bamboo or wood shouldered to carry things suspended from the ends. There is no good Portuguese term, as there is no English term for this. There is a Japanese one: *tenbinbô,* literally, "scale-pole." If artwork is accurate, the poles tend to be more slender and bend more than those in other countries I have seen pictured. It is hard to find maids in painting and print, but there are many illustrations of "brine-maidens" (*shiokumi*), who used such *tenbinbô's* to carry brine to the vats (run by men) at salt-works. That is because said maidens were associated with romantic poems and drama, whereas Frois's servants were not. Japanese men also used poles, but Frois chose to confine his contrast to women, for the greater psychological contrariety.

I never fail to be amazed at how poor the West is at carrying things on foot and wonder whether it is the result of "our" using more pack animals and better wheels or the cause of it![2]   I recall reading scientific studies proving skinny women put marines to shame in their carrying ability, thanks to the weight being centered on the top of their heads. Head-carrying is more common in Korea than Japan, but is difficult to adapt to, and would probably not be good for the neck in the long run; but the use of carrying sticks is just as efficient[3] and easy to adapt to. I find myself wondering further whether the problem with the West might not be in our mindset, which makes the assumption that carrying things is supposed to be uncomfortable and a good way to show off what we so highly value: *muscles.* Or, forgive the excess of theories, could it be that masters and mistresses in the West were less attentive to the needs of their servants and too stingy to provide a pole?

1. *My Original Befuddlement* with 2-59, translated as "with us, it is very extraordinary for women to carry *dripping things*; In Japan, it is normal for maid-servants to carry pails full of water." My last draft prior to finding the answer in the French translation. In retrospect it is pretty funny:

This is beyond doubt the *strangest* of Frois's contrasts. The European side of the contrast doesn't make sense. In most parts of the world, women have always done the drudge-work because, as noted in 55, above, they are the more efficient machine. So why weren't "our" women carrying water? (to DR: *Was this true for all Europe???*) Was there a superstition based on the metaphor of woman-as-vessel which kept Iberian women from carrying anything that dripped (*cousa a pinga*)?! Was there more to Jack and Jill than even the Freudians – and Egyptologists – know? Or was it because the Iberians carried things on their heads but lacked both the gourds of the Africans and the slosh-stop devices of the Far East – Morse (M:JDD) mentions floating circular pieces of wood in the buckets, not that the Japanese had much of a need for them, carrying buckets on poles, so they wouldn't get wet anyway. Who, then, carried water in Iberia? (I didn't know Latin men did *any* labor!) Is that why Rome built its aqueducts? In the Old Testament, one of the early links in the chain of begetting picked up his wife (Sarah? Ruth?) by the well-side – was the well-side considered a dangerous place? Japanese women evidently found the well a very pleasant place, for a group of women chatting is called an *idabata-kaigi,* or a "well-side conference!" In the publisher I worked for, that's what they called a periodic "girls only" meeting (which, by the way, included the chief editor)!

I had better qualify my comment re. Latin men. Farmers, herders and others obviously worked. It would be nice, though, to know what percent of the actual labor was done by men vs. women in various parts of Europe. I was not talking about Latin men today but from 1550-1600.

2. *Horses and Poles.* The relationship to four-legged carriers and the pole is suggested by the following seventeenth century description of "the unusual way they carry burdens" in North Mexico:

The weight is borne on the bare shoulder, across which there is laid a pole of smooth, strong wood that has a long net at both ends, like a scale. These nets are large enough to hold a fanaga of maize and with it, if need be, two small children, just as if they were in a cage. At times they carry such a heavy load it makes even a strong pole bend. The indian will, nevertheless walk with it for three, four or more leagues. . . . Today, this way of carrying loads is used less frequently because the indians have many horses which they buy from the Spaniards. (R(R&A&D):HOT 1-4)

3. *Efficiency of Poles* Carrying by pole does not allow one to center the weight quite so well as carrying something on top of the head, but it offers one very valuable benefit: the flexibility of the pole serves as a shock-absorber, and reduces the strain on the shoulders by allowing the burden to bob up and down (taking off much of the weight in part of the cycle) in rhythm with the walking. Bamboo allows this and is cheap. Perhaps we should add the lack of bamboo in the West to the reasons for poles not being in common use.

2-60   In Europe, women stand up to greet guests;
Em Europa recebem as molheres os ospedes alevantando-se em pee;

Those of Japan remain seated as they greet them.
As de Japão os recebem deixando-se ficar asentadas.

Frois has already mentioned this in 1-29+ and did not need to make it a woman-thing, when both sexes behave the same in both cultures. I forgot to mention then that this did only apply to *greetings.* Since *accommodation* had been adopted a few years earlier, Japanese celebrating the Eucharist were allowed to remain seated for the Gospel rather than rising, as it was how *they* showed *their* respect. (This was spelled out in Valignano's *Advertimentos* as the official new policy).

On a superficial level the behaviors are opposite: *getting up* vs. *staying down.*[1] On a deeper level they are similar. Both represent the most formal – should we say *stiff?* – postures of the respective cultures. We are all familiar with standing up and, in the case of men, snapping to attention, as the more formal posture in Europe (as opposed to and combined with the actual gestures of greeting: bows, hat-tips, curtsies, kisses, handshakes, etc.). We find it harder to understand how remaining seated could be formal, much less *stiff?* While Western women in finishing schools (What a word! *Finishing schools!*) may learn how to keep their knees together and angle their legs slightly to the side, this is not a posture proper for attentively facing a guest. The Japanese posture of proper seating puts the entire body into a tight rectangle and has a formal name, *seiza,* or "correct-seating." It is tiring to maintain for long periods because the weight of the body rests entirely on the folded legs (see 63, below).

Frois's contrast is not quite perfect: it should be "sit down *or remain seated,*" for the Japanese sat down if they were standing, or – this, too, should be noted – changed from a less formal way of sitting to the proper way to show respect for their guests. In short, the Japanese, to use a horrid expression, hopefully obsolete in the lifetime of this book, were as *pro-active* as Westerners when greeting their guests.

1. *Different vs. Arbitrary.* There is a tendency to see   apparent radical difference as proof of the arbitrary nature of signs, but I am not *so sure*. Wittgenstein or the linguist I just punned (my memory is excellent, but only in a fuzzy way) once noted two suggestions for honoring the manuscripts of a famous composer: 1) his students sending them off by burning them or, 2) dividing them up to keep as *mementos*. This was supposed to show how even something important like honoring a dead teacher proved the arbitrary nature of the signs/symbols humans use to do so. To my mind, *neither* possibility is arbitrary. Both come from a limited number of possibilities rooted in a single psyche. The idea of *determination* vs. *chance* or, *logical* vs. *arbitrary* (no matter how complexly described) does not do justice to the complex nature of reality.

2-61   European women wear *rebuco* [a high collar] in order to walk about unrecognized;
As molheres de Europa, pera caminhar desconhecidas, levão rebuço;

> Those of Japan fasten a towel on their head that hangs from both sides of the face when they walk about. *As de Japão quando caminhão atão huma toalha na cabeça, que lhe cay ambas as pontas diante do rosto.*

Since we have already seen contrasts involving mantles, it is evident that women East and West once had many ways of going *incognito*. The *rebuço* sounds very interesting. The dictionary says it was a high collar or lapel of a cloak or coat which turns up to conceal or protect the face. English had their "French collars" which did the same.   (Were these collars were combined with hats/hoods and frontal veils?)

Japanese women generally hung their whole light robes (*katabira*) from their heads, but some dangled *zukin,* literally head-clothes from their head. Today, these light, usually colorful, two-foot-long pieces of cloth are used for headbands for work, neckerchiefs+sweat-wiper at bon-dances, washcloths/towels and cleaning.   Regular white hand-towels (the same weave called towel in the West) are hung about the head for sun protection and wiping sweat while working in fields or the garden. I would not be surprised if such a practical use rather than the desire or need to be concealed was behind the behavior described in the Japanese side of the contrast.   Be that as it may, Frois opposes an up-raised collar to a dangling cloth.

2-62   European women keep their hair [long] until they die.
As molheres em Europa conservão seus cab[elos] até morte;

> In Japan, old women and widows cut their hair in place of mourning and sadness.
> *Em Japão as velhas e as que viuvão em lugar de dó e tristeza se rapão.*

To fully understand what hair once meant to European woman, consider Pope's *Rape of the Locke*. Mock Epic or not, the symbol depended on the view of a woman's hair as an inviolable treasure.

Frois's "in place of" (*em lugar de*) in the second half of the distich is not quite right, for it suggests that by renouncing this floating world and all its attachments together with the hair, the Japanese magically get over the loss of loved ones and their own beauty (or whatever else they would escape). This, of course, would be impossible. It reminds me of the *nihonjinronka* (writer of pop=Japanology) who wrote that by saying "thank you" a Western person had no lingering feelings, like Japanese who still feel much obliged. (Doi: *Anatomy of Dependence*). [1]   I suspect that Frois may really mean only that Japanese women cut their hair off and retire to a convents – as men do with their temples (Why don't we use the term "monastery" for bonzes?) – to age and die gracefully, rather than hanging on to their hair and suffering the grim end at home. In the West, too, widows sometimes withdrew from the world and became nuns, but apparently they did not cut their hair to do so.

Entering a convent in Japan could mean a total break with the family, as if the person died. This was generally the case for women who divorced or committed a crime or simply wanted to die alone in peace. On the other hand, it could be to *maintain* family relationships. Widows often went to pray for the soul of their husbands. In the case of the former motive, all the hair was cut off, for it symbolized cutting off all ties to house/family as well as the world. In the case of the latter, sometimes the hair was only cut half way off (a bit longer than shoulder length) and the woman, after a few years might return to the world and even remarry.

1. *Nihonjinronka*. The reverse side of Japanese Japanology is "us." If the readers wonders *how modern Japanese view the West*, I recommend my recent book *Orientalism and Occidentalism – is the mistranslation of culture inevitable?* The remark in question is found in Doi: *Amae no Kozo (The Anatomy of Dependence* = I do not know how it reads in the generally fine English translation by John Bester.).

2-63   In Europe, women sit on divans, chairs and stools;
As molheres de Europa se asentão em estrados, cadeiras ou tanhos;[1]

In Japan, women always kneel down, with their feet turned up together behind, with one hand resting on the *tatami*. *As Japoas sempre em baxo com os pés juntos virados pera trás estribando com uma mão sobre o* tatami.

No need to describe what Europeans do. Readers who do not know exactly how Japanese sit should note that the legs of the women are neatly tucked back under, shins flush to the *tatami*. Male or female, the legs are folded *straight back under* when sitting formally, with the hands resting symmetrically on their respective thighs, or in front, if the person also bows. Here, Frois describes a slightly informal posture (one arm down) which men never use, because they sit informally with crossed legs (the greater formality of the female way of sitting is probably why Frois made this a female item for contrast). The arm is needed to support the body, because the legs are allowed to stray in parallel a bit to one side. More informally yet, some women let their legs, still bent back, slip out to *both* sides so that their seat comes in direct contact with the *tatami* – this, a Taoist posture for meditation, is even harder for most Westerners than sitting on their heels. *How do they do it?* Here is Bacon:

The flexibility of the knees, which is required for comfort in the Japanese method of sitting, is gained in very early youth by the habit of setting a baby down with its knees bent under it, instead of with its legs straight out before it, as seems to us the natural way. To the Japanese, the normal way for a baby to sit is with its knees bent under it, and so, at a very early age, the muscles and tendons of the knees are accustomed to what seems to us a most unnatural and uncomfortable posture. (B:JGW)

There is also a footnote showing that this was one thing this Japan-lover did not go for

– "That the position of the Japanese in sitting is really unnatural and unhygienic, is shown by recent measurements taken by the surgeons of the Japanese army."

I don't know exactly what measurements proved her point (probably the relatively short legs), but Chamberlain pooh-poohs the idea that sitting on one's legs was bad for them, yet despite his prestige such criticism kept going and going and probably *still* is maintained by Westernizing types in Japan today. To my mind, it is Occidentals who might learn something from the Japanese in this regard, for "we," and not the Japanese suffer from bad knees.[2]

1. *Tanho* Translation.   Because the Japanese trans-lations indicated a stool, I went with it though I could find nothing in the Portuguese dictionaries. It was a relief to find the French translation, *tabouret,* which is included in the OED as "a low seat or stool, without back or arms, for one person: so called originally for its shape [i.e., like its first meaning, a *tabor* or a "drum."]. As written in the biblio, the OED is not only for English!

2. *Learn from Japan.* The Western doctor mistakenly assumes that tightening the knee-cap is the first step to aligning it, whereas it is often more important to *open* the space between the knee-cap and the underlying bone, especially if the damage is by a high impact blow (such as I have suffered) or the natural drying out of cartilage with age. Sitting back on ones feet is the best way to do this.

2-64   With us, women hold a cup of water in the right hand, and drink from the same;
Antre nós as molheres tomão o pucaro d'agoa com a mão direita e com a mesma o bebem;

Japanese women take up a *sakazuki* [sake cup] with their left hand and drink it with the right. *As japoas tomão o* sacanzzuqi *do vinho com a mão esqerda e bebem-no com a dereita.*

"Our" side does seem the normal human default here and the Japanese one a special custom learned in a particular culture. I have not been able to find any verification of it. Okada cited a contemporary Chinese (?) source *Karanishiki* to the effect that "according to someone, the women take up *sake* bottles and drink with their *sake* cups using not both but only one hand," whereas, it went without stating, Japanese men usually held the tiny sake cups with both hands in what was considered the proper and, indeed, only sincere manner, when someone filled it for them, and formally drank that way, too. (6-28)   There was no direct confirmation on that left hand, but I can think of two logical explanations. First if Japanese women were not expected to be as sincere as men in their fashion of drinking and, unlike men, were permitted or even expected to pour their own drinks, the bottle would be in the right hand and the cup in the left. Second, when Japanese hold cups with both hands, the left one is always under the butt of the cup. This would make it the main hand for *taking* the same and if, when it was passed to the mouth, the right hand lifted it up off the left one, this could be described as taking the cup in the left hand and drinking it with the right. (I just erased further guesswork, but would welcome a gloss from anyone in the know.)

2-65   European women braid their hair with silk ribbons;
As molheres em Europa transão os cabelos com fitas de seda;

The Japanese tie them behind in just one place, sometimes with a very dirty rag.
As japoas os atão por detrás em hum só lugar, às vezes com hum lenço muito sujo.

..

The contrast is clear enough – and almost identical with 2-10 – but one wishes Frois was more specific about the class of woman he contrasts. After all, in 2-28 we have the women as uniformly neat as soldiers in full décor. Why should they use dirty rags in their hair? I can only think of two possibilities: 1) Even poor women in Europe were careful to tie their hair with pretty things such as ribbons or colored yarn, whereas women who worked (women and men both worked in Japan, it is strange Frois did not find any contrasts there) in Japan simply tied there hair back with whatever was at hand. The most common item would be a *tenugui,* the piece of cloth already mentioned. Some were probably worn, faded and stained. While not *literally* dirty, i.e., unwashed, they might have *seemed* dirty, i.e., ugly.   2), a far less likely possibility is that samurai women whose husbands were off on campaigns had *lucky hair-ties* which couldn't be washed until a loved one returned safely or *faithful hair-ties* waiting for the loved one to untie them or something. [1]

1. *Unlikely Explanation*. In classical times, women were not only allowed but expected to let things go to seed when their husband was away for a long time, so I hypothesize their hair adornment suffered for it. My Japanese correspondents overwhelmingly favor the first explanation and not this one.

~~~~~~

2-66   In Europe, one box of make-up powder would satisfy the demand of an entire country;
        Em Europa bastará hum caxão d'alvayade pera todo hum reino;

In Japan, many Chinese junks full of it come and still this does not suffice.
Em Japão vêm muitas somas[1] *de chinas carregadas delle e ainda não basta.*

A poetic corollary to contrast 2-15! We can imagine how impressed/shocked Frois must have been with what Japanese women did to their faces. Yet, with noblewomen on horses and sometimes even going to war by the end of the Warring Period (Frois caught the tail of it) the make-up (in Portuguese, *alvaide* = whitening) was lighter than any time before or after (until modern times), but, the demand for the powder, of which there were two types, the very expensive mercury (this expense makes the 200 layers of it applied by Saikaku's character a case of conspicuous consumption) and lead, swiftly grew over the time Frois was in Japan, because the commoners – starting with the wealthy merchant class – began to use it. In a word, it was *popular*. Japan at this time (and later, when it began to industrialize) still had sufficient reserves of most minerals – the idea of Japan as a nation exceptionally poor in natural resources that "has to be diligent" is a modern invention, a useful tool of government – but, *nevertheless* imported mercury and lead from China.[1] What was probably the most popular powder was called, literally *"Chinese dirt."*

The application of these poisons seems dumb – not that we who have given ourselves skin cancer by roasting ourselves in the sun are much brighter – for the danger, as we have seen, was known.   (Though it was not known that the high death-rate among the infants of women who were heavy users – 2 of 3 samurai class children died in infancy (LR)) – People wanted *that much* to be white. *Viz,* Frois's contemporary Montaigne:

> I have seen some swallow gravell, ashes, coales, dust, tallow, candles and for the-nonce, labour and toyle themselves to spoile their stomacke, only to get a pale-bleake colour. ("The Taste of Goods or Evils" old transl. in VICE: AN ANTHOLOGY)

When palour as an ideal most recently peaked in the late-19th century heyday of romantic consumption – slightly different than Montaigne's plaintive melancholy – the Occidental ideal and Japan's briefly met, as can be seen in the paintings of women in both cultures.   In 1585, I would guess make-up in Europe and Japan similarly made women look frail and sickly. This took both cultures away from China, for the Chinese traditionally applied "a coarse big daub" of rouge "on each side of her face," something Ball (B:TC) attributes to a Northern race descending to the South while attempting to maintain their natural appearance. Geo-historical considerations aside, the Chinese usage would create an image of health, quite different from the Euro-Japanese approach.

1. *Soma and Junk*. According to the French translators, citing Du Halde:1735 *, *soma* (*somme* in French) is "a Malay word for ancient Chinese ships used for war or commerce resembling junks called *somas* or *sommes* by the Portuguese." I wonder if the word goes back to the huge ships that dwarfed those of the West until the advent of the super-freighter. * P. Jean-Baptiste Du Halde: *Description géographique, historiique, . . . de l'Empire de la Tartarie chinoise*. Paris. 1735)

2. *Chinese and Japanese Make-up.* We do not know exactly what the relative quantities of home-made and Chinese whitening powder was, but we know that the best "white-powder" = make-up was from Ise and made of mercury, while the cheaper lead-based white powder = make-up was from Kyoto (or at least the two types bore such geographical names. (main source: http://www. sengoku-expo.net/text/tf/J/kaisetsu_ohaguro.html)

2-67   European women do their stitching with copper thimbles on their finger-tips;
As molheres em Europa cozem suas custuras com didais de cobre na ponta do dedo;

> Those of Japan do it with a strip of leather in the palm of their hand or some paper wrapped around mid-finger. *As de Japão com uma tira de couro na palma da mão ou com hum pouco de papel emrolado no meo do dedo.*

As Okada explains, Europeans put it on the tip their middle finger of the right hand and push the needle through with each stroke, while "in our country" (Japan) a long needle is held steady with its butt upon the leather or paper for a type of sewing called "grab-needling" (*tsukami-bari*), where the fingertips help fold and push the cloth into the needle, before pulling the needle through from the tip. In the Edo era, a small round metal dish was devised for this, where the needle rested against the *concavity* – another contrary!

Today, Japanese push the needle through individually as much as they telescope fabric on it – with big jobs done by sewing machine, darning buttons or repairing tears is the most of it – but they still use thimbles that are actually broad-banded rings rather than tiny fingertip-covering cups like ours. Perhaps the name has something to do with it. In Japanese, thimbles could hardly be closed on one end when they are called *yubi-nuki,* or "finger-pass-throughs!"

2-68   With us, a knife is used to cut the stitches when a garment is taken apart at the seams;
Antre nós, quando se [quer] descozer hum vestido, cortão-se as custuras com faca;

> Japanese women unlace the thread complete.
> *As molheres de Japão tirão-lhe as linhas inteiras.*

This has nothing to do with fine-tipped fingers and the legendary dexterity of Asian women. It probably has nothing to do with reuse of thread, though that is possible, either. I have taken apart an old kimono, and can testify that this contrast is born of different types of stitching – with the loose (but perfectly straight) Japanese-style stitching, it is simply far easier and faster to pull out the thread than to cut it. (Note that the Portuguese *custuras (costuras)* means both the "seams" and the "stitches".)

endnote **II**

Women

The reversal of our expectations with respect to the relative freedom of "our" and "their" women makes this chapter an especially attractive part of TRATADO even if the value of the contrast is diminished to the extent that Frois describes Iberian women, who were especially confined. The reversal occurs because "we" changed sometime between Frois and the End of the Seclusion (1853). The Russian Captain Golownin left us a very finely nuanced description of Japan at the beginning of the nineteenth century:

> Only the princes and the nobility, and the rich who imitate them, keep their wives almost constantly in rooms, to which no person of the other sex, except the nearest relatives, is admitted. This measure, is adopted by the husbands, not so much of jealousy as pride. As for the women of other classes, they may visit their relatives and friends, and appear in the streets and public places with their faces unveiled, but they must not converse with any persons of the other sex, in the absence of their husbands. On the whole, the jealousy of the Japanese cannot be compared to that of other Asiatic nations; I even think that, if female frailty is considered, the Japanese should not be called jealous, but only prudent, or more jealous than the Europeans. (MCJ:1824?)

Japan had changed, but only a little. The West, however, was no longer the Europe of Frois's contrast. Sometime after 1585, the segregation of the sexes broke down. Many Europeans began to think of life as a partnership, even if the fair sex was still considered the inferior partner. Where Japanese women had been placed in opposition to the more secluded Europeans and Chinese, now, they were placed somewhere between Asian and Europe. In a book edited by Mrs. William Busk published in 1841 (London), all mention of classes of women disappears and we find only a general fiction, "Japanese women." It was still the case that "the sex . . . approaches more nearly their European condition" than holds true in "other parts of the East" and "are subjected to no jealous seclusion, hold a fair station in society, and share in all the innocent recreations of their fathers and husbands." The fact "their minds . . . are cultivated with as much care as those of the men" is also mentioned. Yet, we *also* find a completely new element of criticism, which we might call *the modern view of Japanese women:*

> At home, the wife is mistress of the family: but in other respects she is treated rather as a toy for her husband's amusement, than as the rational, confidential partner of his life. She is expected to please him by her accomplishments, and to cheer him with her lively conversation, but never suffered to share his more serious thoughts, or to relieve by participation his anxieties and cares.
>
> ..

While this popular book (reprinted by the Harper Bro's in New York 1845) was about Japan, the editor writes of "the difference between Asiatic and European civilization" of which "so much . . appears to be intimately connected with, if not actually to result from, the different treatment and condition of woman in the two continents." For the reader who might be surprised to find such a feminist worldview in 1845, here is another example, though the contrast is not Japan. It was written by a male New Yorker two decades earlier.

> Under the mild influence of Christianity and the easy sustenance to be procured in our republican states, the condition of women is undoubtedly preferable to that of their sex in any part of the

globe. They ought to know that Fredonia [the USA] is women's terrestrial paradise. Here they are the rational companions of men, not their playthings or slaves. (from footnote to Samuel Mitchell's long poem "*Address to the Fredes*" 18__ – will try to get date by 2nd ed.)

Once we start going in this direction, the Japanese can't help looking backward; but, as Harriet Martineau pointed out in 1837, the American reality did not exactly live up to this first round of "you've come a long way, baby!" cockle-doodling (see her *Society in America*). With the reopening of Japan in the mid-nineteenth century, the extent of freedom enjoyed by Japanese women became a subject for first-hand observation and debate. Alcock, who evidently read much written by the Dutch and German writers and, thereby, indirectly, the Jesuits, and therefore expected more outgoing women, was strongly disappointed in the paucity of conversation with cultured women.

> Of the *ladies* of Japan no chance passenger can speak; they are never visible to a stranger . . . . I cannot help thinking some rather erroneous notions have been disseminated by the writers on Japan in respect to the position and relations of the wife here. That she may be more of a companion to her husband, and on a greater footing of equality than in other Eastern countries is possible; but she is strictly forbidden by the laws and customs of the country from entering into society, or being seen by any bit those of her own family, as any inmate of a harem. When traveling, or passing from house to house, it is always in a *norimon* [sedan] hermetically closed and surrounded by her husband's attendants. I speak of the upper classes; the lower and working orders, here as elsewhere, by the necessity of labor, can not be shut up. (A:COT 1863)

女　　　　　　女　　　　　　女

I should add that the treatment of women – or, more precisely, the assessment of the treatment of women – in the West, as opposed to the East was no academic matter. *The condition of women became a litmus test for civilization.* America's first Ambassador to Japan, Townsend Harris, wrote something while still en route to Japan that echoes the opinion of Mrs Busk:

> The following lines, translated from a Cingalese poet, show that females do not occupy a high position in their estimation:
>
> I've seen the *udumber* tree in *flower;*
> *White* plumage on the *crow*;
> And *fishes' footsteps* o'er the *deep,*
> I've seen through ebb and flow;
> If man it is who this asserts,
> *His* word you may believe;
> But all that woman says, distrust,
> *She* speaks but to deceive.

> The *adumber,* almost alone of the Cingalese trees, *never blooms.* In my wanderings in almost every part of the world I have applied one test, which I find to be unvarying, and that is, that the social position of the women in any nation will indicate the amount of its civilization. Therefore, given her social status and you can at once find the mental state of the men. (H:CJTH:1/11?/1856)

Not surprisingly, women, like slaves, were a powerful excuse for colonialist rule. Today, it is easy to laugh at Kipling's phrase "the white man's burden," but try, if you will, to read through his emotional poems on the murder and maltreatment of women in India (not just suttee, but other horrible things) – many of the poems can only be called *feminist*! – and tell yourself that the British should *not* have interfered! (I do not mean to excuse Imperialism, which was 90% selfish, but . .) . But Japan had no worry in that department. Foreigners might quibble on the finer points, but no one denied that women were much freer there than in most of the Far East. Isabella Bird's description of the social position of women in neighboring Korea is chilling.

> Daughters have been put to death by their fathers, wives by their husbands, and women have even committed suicide, according to Dallet, when strange men, whether by accident or design have even touched their hands, and quite lately a serving woman gave as reason for her remissness in attempting to save her mistress, who perished in a fire, that in the confusion a man had touched the lady, making her not worth saving! . . .

> A man wishing to repair his roof must notify his neighbors, lest by any chance he should see any of their women. After the age of seven, boys and girls part company, and the girls a re rigidly secluded . . . Girl children, even among the poor, are so successfully hidden away, that in somewhat extensive Korean journeys I never saw one girl who looked above the age of six, except hanging listlessly about in the woman's rooms . . .

> There are no native schools for girls, and though women of the upper classes learn to read the native script [something that takes about ten hours to do], the number of Korean women who can read is estimated at two in a thousand . . .

> In the capital a very curious arrangement prevailed. About eight o'clock the great bell tolled a signal for men to retire into their houses, and for women to come out and amuse themselves . . . From its operation were excluded blind men, officials, foreigners' servants, and persons carrying prescriptions to the druggists'. These were often forged for the purpose of escape from durance vile, and a few people got long staffs and personated blind men. At twelve the bell again boomed, women retired, and men were at liberty to go abroad. A lady of high position told me that she had never seen the streets of Seoul by daylight. . . .

> The name bestowed on her by her parents soon after her birth is dropped, and she is known thereafter only as "the wife of so and so," or "the mother of so and so." . . . Silence is regarded as a wife's first duty. During the whole of the marriage day the bride must be mute as a statue. . . . The custom of silence is observed with the greatest rigidity in the higher classes. It may be a week or several months before a husband knows the sound of his wife's voice. . . . With the father-in-law the law of silence is even more rigid. The daughter-in-law often passes years without raising her eyes to his, or addressing a word to him. (B:KAN – a long quote on a subject only indirectly related to this book, but unlike Bird's *Unbeaten Tracks in Japan*, it is a rare book so I thought I would treat you to it.)

Bird, however, was the first to admit that the Korean women, not knowing any other life, do not "fret or groan under this system, or crave for the freedom which European women enjoy."

> One intelligent woman, when I pressed her hard to say what they thought of our customs in the matter, replied, "We think that your husbands don't care for you very much"! (B:KAN)

Japan was already in Korea at the time Bird was there, manipulating the government and doing its best to help shoulder the white man's burden. Her observations show us that Alcock was wrong to cavalierly write that lower-class women were visible in any country (some servants Bird called *virtual slaves* were the only women visible in Korea, while the vast majority of women were visible in Japan). There were tremendous overall differences, even if the nobility tended to resemble each other. I strongly suspect there were Japanese who cited the condition of women in Korea as one reason for colonizing their neighbor (researchers?). If they did, it would be ironic because the Europeans, even admitting degrees of difference between Japan and other non-Western nations, generally held that Japanese women were "their husband's slaves" (S:MQTJ) and that only Christianity could ever truly free them. Even Ms. Bacon, whose JAPANESE GIRLS AND WOMEN is, in many ways the best single work of cultural anthropology I have read could not help writing:

> Buddhism and Confucianism were elevating and civilizing, but failed to place the women of Japan upon even as high a plane as they occupied in the old barbaric times. To Christianity they must

look for the security and happiness which it has never failed to give the wives and mothers of all Christian nations.

This is hogwash, or, rather whitewash! Christianity has justified horrid treatment of women in different times and places. Even today, there are places it is called upon to support genital mutilation. Frois's TRATADO unwittingly tells us that much and it bears mention that the greatest equality of the sexes – confident and absolutely ebullient girls and women – found by the globe-trotting Bird, were not in the Christian West but in Eastern Tibet: i.e., The Man-tze people, where *"men and women are always seen together,"* where *"a woman can be anything, from a muleteer to a Tu-tze."*(B:YVB)   To be fair to Bacon, she wrote the above because she was upset that the noblewomen she taught and had deep affection for would be unable to do much if anything with their higher learning. Her usual objectivity lapsed because she was so afraid that her teaching would only hurt them and they would all end up frustrated.

女   女   女

Elsewhere, Bacon provided the best analysis of the place of woman in Japan ever written. After describing, *yoshii,* the practice of adopting a man into a *samurai* family (as the husband of the daughter) to carry on the family name, where the wife usually wears the britches so to speak, she writes:

> From the custom of *yoshii,* and its effect upon the wife's position, we see that, in certain cases, Japanese women are treated as equal with men. *It is not because of their sex that they are looked down upon and held in subjugation, but it is because of their almost universal dependence of position. . . .* Wherever the table are turned, and the men are dependents of the women, and even where the women are independent of the men, – there we find the relations of the men to women vastly changed. (B:JGW? my *italics*)

This is an extremely significant point (so, I repeat what has been covered in 2-30). In not a few Eastern cultures – including Japan's closest neighbor – women were viewed as *intrinsically* inferior, and not permitted to take advantage of their family's economic situation or their own labor. (Such a difference doesn't disappear overnight. In Korea (1972 and 1980), I was horrified to find some well-educated men who still thought of women as inferior beings and treated them so. I *never* met a Japanese man who did this.)   But, in Japan, the position of women was not a *given,* it was *ex*trinsic to their nature. After this, Bacon argues for equal inheritance rights and other measures to improve the independence of Japanese women and then goes into depth on a matter Frois neglected and others only broached:

> The wife of a peasant or merchant is much nearer to her husband's level than is the wife of the Emperor. Apparently, each step up the social ladder is a little higher for the man than it is for the woman, and lifts him a little further above his wife. The peasant and his wife work side by side in the field, put their shoulders to the same wheel, eat together in the same room, at the same time, and whichever of them happens to be the stronger in character governs the house, without regard to sex. (B:JGW)

To this claim, she added personal testimony and more general information on the equality of women in the silk and tea districts where they are the main wage earners and "the equal of the stronger sex." (I would say, rather, that at certain tasks requiring endurance and finesse, women *are* the stronger sex, but her observation stands) and, finally, concludes:

The Japanese peasant woman, when she marries, works side by side with her husband, finds life full of interest out of the simple household work, and, as the years go by, her face shows more individuality, more pleasure in life, less suffering and disappointment, than that of her wealthier and less hard-working sister. (B:JGW)

There is a Froisean *contrast* with the West in this, too. It is a big one, but, to tell the truth, I might have passed right by it had it not been for the humorist Douglas Sladen. His words contain little not in Bacon:

> ..
> One of the queerest things about this queer land is the fact that the humbler the wife is socially, the more is she on a footing of equality with her husband. It is the well-born woman who is content to be treated as her husband's inferior in almost everything. She is not allowed to work outside her own garden as her humbler sister may; she may not mix with her husband's friends and enter into conversation with them when he invites them to his house . . . (S:MQTJ)

Because Sladen crudely calls what he is about to describe *queer*, or rather "queerest," he tells us clearly that *in the West, we expect the opposite thing.* Indeed, the poor wife who was the bottom of the pecking order in England at this time was, by all accounts, treated dismally. "Our" poor were not *gentle*-men. Chivalry was upper-class. Misogynic behavior is *traditional* in the lower classes of the "Christian" West (and those from Africa who incorporated them in America).   The same contrast can be observed with Xenophobia. In Japan, the lower classes have always seemed the more open-minded, whereas in the West, right to the present day, they have traditionally been the stronghold of bigotry.

女   女   女

The reader may have noted one perspective missing from this chapter: **the Japanese point of view.**

The first Japanese to officially travel to the West on Japanese business (The *Missione* of the 16th century went on Christian, or rather Jesuit business not Japanese business) had an experience in the United States relevant to the subject in 1860. Just before the Japanese were about to depart from a treaty ceremony held at the house of General Cass, the general's grand-daughter, who all reports claim to be a stunning beauty, led a "charge" of the fair sex:

> ..
> And now the ladies crowded in from an adjoining room with great rapidity, making the room quite warm, when General Cass remarked to the Japanese that he did not know how they regulated their ladies, but in this country the ladies regulated the gentlemen, and went just where they pleased. This was an apology for the presence of the ladies, and [but] the Ambassadors replied, in a very grave manner, that they observed that there was a very marked difference in the discipline of the two countries. The General could scarcely control his countenance with this sally from the Japanese, who evidently thought they possessed an advantage over this country in this respect. ("Times Herald" reporter in A-J:FJE)

Here, the Western reporter (a male) portrays a contest of male pride, with the Japanese winning because the American women got away with being uppity. I have not, however yet seen what the Japanese themselves wrote (Glosses welcome if you have!).   The report of the *next* Embassy, the Iwakura mission, which spent much of the 1870's in the West, made it clear that Occidental culture was as exotic to Japanese as theirs was to us, and that the relationship of the sexes stood out more than anything else.   The Japanese were shocked to find women were not forbidden to enter military headquarters in the United States and to find them not only sightseeing on the grounds of army and navy schools, but visiting them for dances and enjoying themselves there. Such an observation is immediately followed with this Topsy-turvy philosophical statement:

These are the mores [*fuzoku*] of republican government. Think of the East and the West as lands separated by a mutually insurmountable gap from the start, where each and every more and even our temperaments are opposite. . . When our entourage boarded the American boat in Yokohama, it became a completely unique land, [a place] where our behavior raised their eyebrows and their behavior made astounded us in turn. . . . I did my best with [mastering] the many fine points [of their etiquette], but of all them, the one which seemed the weirdest of all, was the intercourse of men and women, of husband and wife. The way a bride acts toward her mother-in-law or children act toward their patients in Japan is the way a husband here acts toward his wife . . . he brings her trays of food, brushes off her dress . . . helps her up, offers her a seat on the sofa, . . . if the wife is angry, he must curry her affection [*ai-o okoshi*], or to regain her respect [*kei-o okoshi*], prostrate himself and apologize and if she still won't listen, stay and even eat outside . . . and with men and women riding together on boats and trains, the able-bodied man rises and gives up his seat to the woman [three lines about this follow!]. This [men serving women rather than vice versa] is generally true throughout the West, but it is particularly well developed in England where it has grown stronger because it is a country with a queen and America because, with its republican government, arguments in favor of male and female equality have taken root. . . . The teaching of the East is that women have control over the inside and do not work outside and the roles of men and women are naturally separate . . . (I:TZK pt13)

Basically, this is the mirror-opposite of the Western perception, and the only difference was in the observers' respective evaluations of which way is ideal. If Frois's contrast was a bit exaggerated because of Iberian conservatism, this Japanese report is extreme because it contrasts the East with the relatively liberal United States and England.

III

OF THE CHILDREN AND THEIR CUSTOMS
do que toca aos mininos [1] e a seus custumes

~~~~~~

3-1   Boys in Europe keep their hair trim;
Os meninos em Europa andão trosquiados;

> Those of Japan always let it grow freely up to the age of fifteen.
> *Os de Japão até os qinze anos sempre se lhe deixa crecer o cabelo.*

In Portuguese, the generic term for "children," *meninos,* is the same as the one used for "boys" and even can describe children young enough that English might insist on "babies." To translate, one must guess which is appropriate for the context, which depends on knowledge, rather than grammar. In the case of the title, the fact the chapter includes material pertinent to both sexes requires the broadest possible term, "children." In the case of this contrast, it must be "boys" because, in English, "children" means both sexes and Frois clearly describes but one of them. But, how short was short in Europe? In North Europe, paintings suggest a boys hair was little different than a man's and that was what we now might think of as medium length, at longest down to the shoulder. Bowl cuts were not uncommon. But paintings of Iberian youth, or the Japanese boys shorn by the Jesuits show hair that would not have looked out of place in the USA of McCarthy, or the Germany of Hitler, or Stalin's Soviet Union (Face it: uniformly short hair is a mark of ideological fanaticism and intolerance). [2]

In Japan, a baby boy's hair was shaven four to five times a month [3] until he was three (to my mind, the relatively large size of their heads gives them the appearance of bright bonzes) at which time there is a ceremony called "hair-placing" (*kami-oki*), after which it is allowed to grow until he is five at which time it is trimmed neatly around the edges in the manner of a bowl-cut. Then it was allowed to grow freely, i.e., without being cut, until the boys coming of age [4] (between ages 11-16), but it was not *free* in the sense of being wild. Japanese have traditionally considered a shock of loose hair the mark of a vengeful ghost or an outlaw. The Japanese boy's was generally bound in a ponytail in the manner of Japanese women (or Chinese men) or bundled higher up at the crown in the case of nobility (*kuge*). In some parts, a *kappa* cut, or page-cut was, like in Europe, not uncommon. After becoming an adult, the front of the pate was shaven and the remaining hair bound and set as described in 1-6. Since tiny children were traditionally allowed to do as they wished, it is paradoxical to find their heads shaved, while older children, who generally followed a harsh regime of studies, were allowed to wear theirs in a relatively free style!

Frois's observation is gender-neutral. "Like women" was the more common description. Valignano wrote: "The boys until age 14 wear their hair long and tied on top of their head like women." (1583). Since boys were regarded as beautiful, it is not surprising that Ribadeneira could write, further, that they valued their hair "as much as the most coquettish [*galanas*] women of Europe prize their red/blond hair [*rojos cabellos*]." (n.100 in V(A):S&A) This was not an academic concern for the Jesuits. According to Organtino, the reluctance of young Japanese to give up their hair was said to be a major hindrance to their joining the Jesuit seminary in Kyoto! (Ibid.)

Westernization in the Meiji era again meant cutting this hair, submitting to a sort of voluntary cultural castration in order to be considered men by the West. For, as Chamberlain noted, cultured people may lament the change and even implore Japanese to keep their own fashions, but

> The Japanese would be blind indeed, did they not see that their best security . . . lies in the determination to be strong, and in the endeavor not to be too different from the rest of mankind; for the mob of Western nations will tolerate eccentricity of appearance no more than will a mob of toughs. (C:TJ)

1. *Chapter Name.* *"Mininos"* is usually *"meninos,"* today. Frois, like the English of his day spelled words in many ways. I happen to like the *mini* feeling.

2. *Hair Length* The closest I could come to the question of short versus long-hair in the Iberia of Frois's day was information about Seville, Spain: In 1639 the city published a

> "Proclamation that His Majesty orders, because the abuse of long hair and hair pieces with which some men walk about, and the curls with which they set their hair, has come to be scandalous in these kingdoms, no man can wear long hair nor hair pieces." (LR)

The opposite sort of restriction was found in parts of North Europe where "round-heads" and some other fundamentalist Christian sects kept their hair so short that short-hair came to be outlawed by the authorities. (I do not have any literature confirming regulations either way involving Japanese. (お願い、誰か！)

3. *Shaving Babies* This, according to Okada and the OJD, might have been true a generation or two later in the Tokugawa Era, but I wonder if commoners could afford razors. (お願い、誰か！) Regardless, the fact that a two or three year-old could be shaven by his parents is in itself amazing. In the West, could a baby keep still enough? Would parents be deft enough?

4. *Coming of Age* The OJD gives 12 or 13 years. Valignano gives 14 and Frois 15. The OJD may be biased a bit toward the Tokugawa period. Early sixteenth century rebellion statistics give the age of participants as from 15 or 16 to 60, and this suggests that the age may have been a bit higher in the Warring Age when growing up could have more serious consequences. Criminal code held children responsible as adults from age 15.

3-2   European babies spend a long time in swaddling clothes with their hands kept inside of them; *Os d'Europa andão muito tempo em queiros e com as mãos prezas dentro nelles;*

> Japanese wear *kimonos* from the time they are born and their hands are always free. *Os de Japão logo em nacendo lhe vestem* qimões *e sempre andão com as mãos soltas.*

Frois wrote only *Os d'Europa* and *Os de Japão* (Those of ~) for his subject. By the rules of logic, that would mean using the same subject as that in the previous distich, which in Portuguese where *meninos* could be "boys" or "babies," is the same, while it is not in English. So common sense dictates that we fill in "babies" here. There is one slight exaggeration on the Japanese side. While Japanese babies were not so sadly(?) restricted as "ours," they didn't immediately don adult-style clothing, as the *qimões*, suggests. Rodrigues elaborates:

> Up to a certain age, children wear a robe which is fastened from behind by two ribbons sewn on either side; but when . . . their childhood comes to an end, they throw away these ribbons and gird themselves with an ordinary sash as a sign that they are now men and can carry a sword." (R(C):TIJ)

The leap from ribbons-to-sword may not have been that abrupt. The ribbons were exchanged for a more or less adult-style belt and outfit when the baby became a child capable of dressing himself (perhaps with help tying the belt). Isabella Bird:

They have no special dress. This is so queer that I cannot repeat it too often. At three they put on the *kimono* and girdle, which are as inconvenient to them as to their parents, and childish play in this garb is grotesque. I have, however, never seen what we call child's play . . . (B:UTJ)

But, let us not jump so far ahead. With respect to Japanese baby-wear there is more worth pointing out, things that evidently required a female observer to be noticed. Alice Mabel Bacon:

The Japanese baby's dress, though not as pretty as that of our babies, is in many ways much more sensible. It consists of as many wide-sleeved, straight . . . garments as the season of the year may require, – all cut after exactly the same pattern, and that pattern the same in shape as the grown-up *kimono*. These garments are fitted, one inside of the other, before they are put on; then they are laid down on the floor and the baby is laid into them; a soft belt is tied around the waist, and the baby is dressed without a shriek or a wail, as simply and easily as possible. The baby's dresses, like those of our babies, are made long enough to cover the little bare feet; and the sleeves cover the hands as well, so preventing the unmerciful scratching that most babies give to their faces, as well as keeping the hands warm and dry [keeping them out of the mouth]. (B:JGW – brackets from another passage in the book)

Bacon felt so strongly about the sensibility of Japanese baby's dress that she introduced it twice in her otherwise not particularly redundant book. I think this was because she thought it was one reason babies were less irritable in Japan. To *Faux Frois* her findings.

In Europe, we put clothing on a baby.
In Japan, the baby is put on the clothing.

In Europe, babies are dressed one piece of clothing after another.
In Japan, babies are dressed with many layers of clothing, all at one time

In Europe, we stop our babies from moving their limbs by tightly wrapping them up..
In Japan, they allow them to move, slowed down with loose long sleeves.

Kipling soon would *un*dress the Japanese baby. After attributing the cheerful nature of the Japanese to the large number of children (the Japanese population was sky-rocketing) – "You see they have such thousands of children in their streets that the elders must perforce be young lest the babes should grieve" – and describing how a four-foot child accompanies a three-foot child holding the hand of a two-foot child with a one-foot child on her back, he tells us that these "dolls" who "wriggle and laugh"

are tied up in a blue bed-gown which is tied by a sash, which again ties up the bed-gown of the carrier. Thus if you untie that sash, baby and but little bigger brother are at once perfectly naked. I saw a mother do this, and it was for all the world like the peeling of hard-boiled eggs. (1889: K:KJ)

I am sure Ms. Bacon must have mentioned the biggest remaining question *somewhere*; but I find no *diapers* in my notes. Because the Japanese *tatami* is the ultimate horror to clean, there is probably no contrast to be found, anyway. Japanese surely had them. If there is a contrast, one that holds true throughout most of the twentieth century, it would be with Koreans who had none. They dressed (and maybe some still do) their wee ones in robes so short, the slightest bend of the body leaves their privates uncovered. They can go, whenever they please, without dirtying their clothing. That is possible because Koreans have hard, seamless floors, Moreover, unlike our (European and Japanese) floors, there is no chill from below, for the flooring is warm in the winter (heated from beneath) so infants can remain open for doing their business year-round.

3-3   In Europe, cradles are used to help children sleep, and carts to teach them to walk;
          Em Europa se usa de berços pera os mininos dormirem e carretinhas pera se insinarem a andar;

          Those of Japan have none of that and only use the help given them by nature.
          Os de Japão não tem nada disto e somente uzão das ajudas que lhe dá a natureza.

"Nature" (*natureza*) implies a hands-off policy for the Japanese, but Okada introduces an undated book advising that a wet-nurse cradles the sleeping baby in her bosom for the first 15 days and later stays right by its side. There is also a mandatory night-lamp, hardly "natural." While neither the rocking cradle nor the prison-like crib was found in Japan, wicker baskets holding babies and love-sick cats – not together, mind you – appear in haiku. Farming women and widowers who could not afford wet-nurses probably made much use of those baskets (in the summer, a basket under a shade tree would beat being on a sweaty back), one type of which depicted by Morse shows a baby surrounded by loose swaddling up to the neck, so that the head rests like a head of cabbage in the middle of a pot or a butterfly peeking from its cocoon but these served more to keep a baby than to help it sleep.   In that sense, it seems a cross between swaddling and a crib.   There is no native Japanese name for "crib," but today, with baby baskets extinct, they are used during the day-time and called *beibi-sahkuru* or, "baby circles."   But Japanese infants still rarely if ever sleep alone at night. Japanese parents do not feel obliged to teach them to sleep alone, nor do they fear being arrested for child-neglect in the unlikely case of accidentally crushing a baby in its sleep (something perfectly natural – young cat-mothers do it more than old ones) or being accused of child molestation, as seems to be the case at the end of the 20th century in America, should they sleep with their children. [1]   While families slept together more in Frois's Europe, the infant was apparently the odd-one out, in which case the cradle part of the contrast might be Faux Frois'ed as follows:

> *In Europe, we think babies should sleep alone and have cradles to help us.*
> *In Japan, the babies never sleep alone and do not even have their own beds.*

I have not yet found the cart (or wagon [2]) mentioned by Frois which is charmingly Frenched as *petit chariots*, and will not try to guess what it looked like.   The only thing I have ever read about training a child to walk is the following observed by Thunberg in Amsterdam, 1770:

> In my landlord's house I observed a very ingenious method of teaching children to walk. – A ribband was fastened under the child's arms, which passed through a ring that slid on a long iron rod fixed horizontally in the roof, so that the child could walk backwards and forwards along the room, without falling or taking up the time of an attendant. (TEAA)

On the one hand, it seems remarkable to me that a device used to encourage children to walk would be forgotten.   On the other hand, considering the advantage of a child's *not* walking at a tender age, the loss is probably not missed.

1. *Sleeping With Children.* My observation is that most children continued to sleep with their parents up to grade-school in the last decades of the twentieth century. When there is more than one child, it was common for one to sleep with *papa* on his futon and one with *mama* on hers. I have had the experience of small tyke crawling in with me when I spent the night at a friend's house. He mistook me for his father in the dark and I grunted to cover up my identity so he would not awaken everyone (he was asleep when I arrived that evening). The next morning, I woke up to his crying, which was not helped by his older brother telling him that his dad had magically turned into a *gaijin* (foreigner)! In Frois's time families slept in big beds in much of Europe, but it is possible that the babies were left in cribs in some countries. Information anyone?

2. *Carts or Wagons or?* OED says carts have 2 wheels and wagons 4. Should we instead waffle with *walkers*?

3-4   With us, ordinarily, grown women carry babies on their bosom;
Antré nós ordinariamente molheres grandes trazem as crianças ao collo;

In Japan, very little girls go about with the babies almost always on their backs.
Em Japão mininas muito pequenas andão quasi sempre com as crianas aas costas.

In the twentieth century, every Japanese visitor to the United States returned to Japan excited by their close encounters with . . . squirrels!   The equivalent topic for nineteenth century Europeans would seem to be little Japanese *musume* of five or six jumping rope – or, weeding if a bit older – with infants on their backs.   An abundance of squirrels may be unique to the United States, but little children looking after littler children was hardly a Japanese monopoly. Even with the higher infant mortality rates in Europe, there were many children, and we can imagine *some* little girls took care of babies.[1]   Was the extraordinarily high level of employment among Japanese women (who could keep what they earned unlike most European women) one reason for baby-care being so completely left to little girls as to astound Europeans? And was this the cause for the method of carrying used? Or, was it *vice versa*, with little girls enabled as helpers as the natural outcome of back-style carrying? Illustrating his claim that *"Japan is the Antipodes as much as Australia,"* Douglas Sladen does a good job of relating the two elements of Frois's contrast:

> There is generally, it must be confessed, method in Japanese madness, but it does look very mad to the unreasoning globe-trotter. Take for instance, the matter of the woman carrying her baby behind instead of in front: that is because girls begin carrying babies so very young in Japan that it becomes second nature not to remember the baby at all, but to go on doing whatever one is doing without regarding it. . . . the first duty of a Japanese woman in home life is, when she is about four years old, to carry the next baby in a *haori* (shawl) on her back. The baby is fastened so securely that its little mothering sister can play ball or shuttlecock in spite of the pick-a-back . The baby does not cry or laugh – Japanese babies are solemn – but nods its head and runs at the nose. . .
> (QUEER THINGS ABOUT JAPAN: 1903 S:QTJ)
..

In his later *MORE   QUEER THINGS . . .* , Sladen writes "the babies are fastened on their backs with shawls, in much the same way as they are shawl-bound to the woman's sides in the streets of South Wales." *There go the Antipodes!* But Sladen found a new way to play up the contrast, which may be *Froised* as follows:

> *Among us, little girls have dolls to carry, hug and kiss.*
> *Japanese little girls have babies on their backs but don't know how to play with dolls*

 The method of carrying the babies, then, was less surprising to the European than the young age of the girls. Even granted technology made it possible, a four or 5 or 6 year-old capable enough to be entrusted with so heavy a responsibility seems miraculous to us. So how did an intellectual from Boston explain it in 1888?

> The diminutiveness of the nurse-perambulators is the most surprising part of the performance. The tiniest of tots may be seen thus toddling around with burdens half their own size. Like the dot upon the little i, the baby's head seems a natural part of their childish ego. . . . That it should be practicable thus to entrust one infant to another proves the precociousness of children . . . that which has less to grow up to, naturally grows up to its limit sooner. (L:SOE)

Can the reader guess where Percival Lowell is heading? Well, he has just found the reason for "the abnormally early development of the Chinese race, and its subsequent career of inactivity."

Ontogeny doesn't just recapitulate phylogeny, it causes it! To paraphrase one of his numerous metaphors, *a short race is a fast race, and soon the race is done.*

> Meanwhile the youthful nurse, in blissful ignorance of the evidence which her present precocity affords against her future possibilities, pursues her sports with intermittent attention to her charge, whose poor little head lolls about, now on one side and now on the other, in a most distressful manner, an uninterested spectator of the proceedings. (L:SOE)

We shall return to the important matter of precocity in 3-6, below. Here, let me only add that the description of that *poor little head* can easily be seconded. "It rolls from side to side, swaying to and fro, as if a dislocation of the neck must inevitably be the result."(Alcock) *Thirded.* "Wobbling about as though they must drop off, their eyes as nurses say, 'looking over their heads.'" (Bird) And *fourthed.* "A Japanese baby can hang on like a fly, and seems to enjoy trying to shake its head off." (Sladen) Even today, although tiny tots no longer carry babies in Japan, we occasionally find a baby on its mother's or, more commonly, grandmother's back, with its little head hanging to one side or another, or even straight back lolling so loosely that more than once I have shivered, remembering the head on a bird with a broken neck! But Japanese apparently don't even notice it. That, to them, is just *how babies are.* It is as normal to them as a bouquet of flowers carried upside-down (How did Frois miss *that* one!). Their only complaint – and I have only heard it from a few people – against the piggy-backing custom of their own country is that being carried about, tightly tied on, for too long, gave them bowlegs or a squashed nose (this last attributed to large-breasted nurses by our *Tristam Shandy*!).

A more interesting theory (heard from a man at a copy machine in a Florida library, who read it *somewhere* – I have not traced down the originator yet) gives our respective manners of carrying babies credit for our respective styles of eye contact which was already mentioned but not *Faux Frois'd* in chapter I:

> *Europeans think it is natural and good to look directly into each other's eyes.*
> *Japanese think it is rude to do so and tend to avert their eyes or close them.*

In the West, where babies are cradled at the breast, there is a lot of eye-contact for the first years of life, whereas in Japan and China, where infants do not spend much time face to face with their mother and other caretakers, there is very little. The difference is certainly hard for adults to overcome. We find it hard to believe that looking down or closing the eyes as we listen is more polite than looking attentively at the speaker, where they find it almost impossible to look into our eyes. Indeed, I have seen books instructing Japanese to *stare at a spot between the eyes if it is too hard to look into the other person's eyes as expected by Occidentals!*). Now that less babies are carried piggyback in Japan, we will have to see if there is an effect on eye-contact!

1. *Girls Caring for Babies in the West* Country singer Dolly Parton once ascribed her penchant for writing "dead baby songs" to her never getting over the death of baby number I-forget of her large Appalachian family, for each girl, beginning with the elder, got to "have" a baby to care for, and it had just worked down to her turn.

2. *Nobles and Babies.* Here Frois's contrast is clearly *not* about noble Japanese, whose babies were carried by nurse-maids, not siblings. According to Bacon, there was even a particular village of large and extremely fit, red-cheeked women who performed this service as a hereditary calling for the Emperors' children!

3-5   With us, babies [their clothing] has one plain sash tied in front;
Antre nós as crianças trazem hum só ourelo singido e atado diante;

Those of Japan have a mass of ribbons, all tied behind the *kimonos.*
As de Japão trazem nos qimões *hum monte de fitas e todas atadas detrás.*

It is easy to explain why baby's clothing in Japan was tied in back. With babies carried piggyback, the belts would have to be tied in back if the knot/s were not to come between its belly and its mother's – or older sister's – back. (I would imagine the native American papoose, who faced backward – too bad, this direction would have been perfect for Frois and Sladen's Japan – had his or her clothing tied in front.) Bows in back are also easier to untie when a small child squats to go to the toilet. And, without chairs, Japanese had no practice of leaning back, so there was no reason for knots *not* to be in back. A *Faux Frois*:

> *We fasten our belts or tie our sashes in front or slightly to one side;*
> *The Japanese, when properly dressed, always have the knot in back*

I qualify "when properly dressed" because most so called *kimono* may be kimonos in the generic and literal sense of the word, i.e. a "wear-thing," but are not what Japanese generally mean when *they* call something a kimono, but rather a *yukata*, i.e., "bath-robe" (also used for resort town wear and house-wear), or *negi*, i.e. "night-wear." These are often tied in front (to one side or another I always forget which). Frois's *quimõe* is confusing because it cannot help but conflate the two levels of meaning. It is like the confusing English word "dress." Japanese would not allow that a baby was "dressed in *a* kimono" any more than we would say that a boy in men's *dress* was *"wearing a dress."*

I do not know why there was such a mass (*monte,* literally "mountain") of ribbons. Period illustrations show women and children sometimes wore multiple thin sashes. I think it was mainly decorative, but would guess a baby's would have included a red one for warding off bad spirits.

~~~~~~

3-6   With us, a child of 4-years still does not know how to eat with his own hands;
Antre nós hum menino de 4 annos ainda não sabe comer com sua mão;

Those of Japan eat by themselves from age three, using *hashi* [chopsticks].
Os de Japão de três anos comem por si mesmos com faxis.

The European side of the contrast is puzzling, for if 6-1, the first item in the food chapter is correct, Europeans ate *with* their (bare) hands, so one would think even a baby would do fine! The Portuguese hand (*mão*) is, however, singular in case. Was there some one-handed, bare-handed etiquette (such as Indians have to eat rice) to follow that we have not heard of?

The Japanese side is one of what we might call the "genius Japanese" contrasts. And, speaking of genius, in the economic "bubble" days when E. Vogel's JAPAN AS NUMBER ONE was still selling like hotcakes, Morita Akio, the head of Sony, hypothesized that chopsticks (I know "chop" means food, but I *hate* that word! Do we eat with "stabsticks" and "scoopsticks?"), being more difficult to use than modern Western utensils, were good for the brain and helped to explain the success of the Far East. If doing delicate work with the hands did indeed develop neurons in the brain as neurologists say, then this additional stimulation at meal time would be good for the child's IQ. It's not *what* you eat but *how* you eat that gives you the smarts. And Frois has Japanese children doing it the hard way, *and* at a younger age! You might think the *hashi* were easier to manipulate than the child's own fingers! In his presentation of "Etiquette at the Table" which begins with the memorable line: "I will not praise Japanese food for it is not good, albeit it is pleasing to the eye, but instead I will describe the clean and peculiar way in which it is served," the Spanish merchant Bernardino de Avila Giron made it clear that the Japanese children weren't just going through the motions either!

Two clean sticks, or *hashi,* as thick as a quill and about a span and a half in length, are placed on the table. They take these up with four fingers and eat with them, and a child of four summers can remove the bones of a sardine with them. (C:TCJ)

What have these children got that "ours" do not? A November, 1978 *National Geographic* article describes a four year-old Inuit boy who, equally impressively picks up an honest-to-god adult's *knife* and walks down to the seashore to fillet a fish! Careless negligence on the part of his parents? *No.* The mother was quietly watching all of it with pride. Basically, this and the fine chopstick work and the baby-sitting described in 3-4, above, are describing the same thing, the *precocity* described by Lowell – or, viewed from the Japanese perspective, our children's unruliness. Lowell's explanation is clearly racist. It was also deceptive, for missing the ways in which Japanese and most other Asians are *less* quick to grow up than we are. Lowell might have been surprised to learn that in Japanese, too, a proverb states that *the slow-developing vessel ends up the largest.* (As a premature baby who developed late, I was told the same by my father in the USA!) He would have flipped out to see that same expression used by Japanese (in the bubbly exuberance of the 1970-80's) to explain why they were going to leave the flash-in-the-pan West behind!

But there *is* a difference. I have found little Japanese children and the one Chinese girl I knew [not much of a sample, I will admit!] to be years ahead of their American counterparts. They *are* as bright as they look. And it is dishonest and cowardly to *ignore* this difference, as the West has, by and large, (there are *some* studies by educational psychologists – mostly comparing American and Chinese children – but not nearly enough considering the importance of the subject) in the latter quarter of the twentieth century. As far as I know, the first person to give a possible reason – actually two causes – for the superiority of Japanese children was Alice Mabel Bacon. The first, we have already broached upon in 2, above: thanks to the sensible system of dress, "the poor little weak thing does not have to go through the complicated process of dressing which causes our babies such trials and shrieks every day." This saves "the daily physical fatigue and nervous strain of our manner of dressing" the infant and might improve its relations to others. The second cause:

> Here nobody ever makes a noise at a baby, or jiggles or shakes it, to stop its crying. If it cries and cannot be stopped by quiet and gentle means, it is not yelled at or trotted, but just goes on until it stops of its own accord, which it pretty soon does. . . . When they grow a little older, they are fully as bright and active and wide-awake as our children, so I do not think the quiet in which they are kept at first has any effect except to make them less nervous and irritable than American babies. (B:AJI)

Bacon wrote in a day when run-down *nerves* were believed *the* mark and the bane of civilization (there are parallels with our fixation on stress and differences because the skinny and the fat suffer differently). She was, then, suggesting that letting babies be would improve our health as adults. More recent surveys, which have largely confirmed the difference (LR), were done for reasons directly touching upon Frois's contrasts: i.e., because tiny-tots in the Far East were observed to be better mannered and more willing to study than in the Far West (America), and people were naturally curious as to *why.* Since *nature* (I.Q.) depends on the content of tests (though the math seems equivalent and therefore a safe measure) that measure it, and *nurture* includes pre- and post-natal diet, parental expectations, and other environmental factors, any short presentation is misleading. Let us just say that Lowell's idea was doubly wrong, for, on the whole, Mongoloids are a *slow*, rather than fast-maturing race (the big heads = neotenous [1]). Unless, one is to hypothesize that their minds are as fast as their bodies are slow – that is to say a body/mind split in the rate of development (an interesting theory, I'll admit), we must find other explanations for "precociousness."

---

1. *Neotenous Microsoft* Come on, Bill Gates, get a vocabulary! This basic word (including its root version *neoteny*) is not found in the MS-WORD dictionary. Try adding *literacy* to your next Service Pack!

3-7   With us, it is ordinary to whip and castigate children;
Antre nós hé ordinário açoutar e castiga[r os] filhos;

In Japan it is very rare and they are only rarely reprimanded.
Em Jãpao hé cousa mui rara e somente de [r?]aro os reprendem.

Three of the four published translations I have seen chose the gendered "son" rather than the generic "children" here, but I follow Schütte and DR+H with "children," for I would bet that both sexes were whipped and punished in Europe. Elsewhere, Frois clearly wrote that *children* in Japan are not physically punished and that "even children of six or seven were disciplined with words, spoken as seriously as one might speak to a seventy year-old." (correspondence dated 1565/2/20 noted by Okada). And Valignano wrote in 1580:

> They are a people universally accustomed to living as they wish, for *both men and women* are brought up from childhood that they are allowed to behave as they please, without their fathers checking them in the smallest degree, for they neither whip nor scold them. (B:CCJ Boxer tr. *Italics mine*)

Caron, writing a generation later, shows this was as true in school as at home:

> At school they begin by degrees, by sweetness and not by force, the Masters imprinting a desire in each of them to outdo his fellow . . . The children are so accustomed to this way, that they learn sooner and more then by any correction or whipping; for generous spirits, and an obstinate Nation, such as this is, are not to be forced, but rather won with gentleness and emulation. (C:DOJ)

It is interesting that Valignano thought gentle parenting created willful children and free-minded adults, whereas Caron thought willfulness required gentle teaching. Neither recommends harsh treatment. As the Jesuit policy in teaching was *not to use harsh words,*[1] so Valignano and Frois would not have been neutral about this contrast. They would have understood it as one item proving "them" superior to "us." This meaningful difference was long-lasting. About two centuries later, Thunberg "very seldom heard them rebuked or scolded; and hardly ever saw them flogged or beaten, either in private families or on board of the vessels. While," he adds with no little irony, "in more civilized and enlightened nations, these compliments abound." (T:TEAA) You can bet that the Dutch cabin boys were not so lucky! Or, was the rod only spared because the Japanese child was not spoiled to begin with? Valignano mentions willfulness, but he knew it did not go too far, for he also expressed surprise that –

> not even the boys use bad language, nor do they fight with slapping and fists like ours, but speak with great courtesy, never losing respect for one another, with such deliberation and gravity that they don't seem children, but serious men. This is true to such a degree that it is unbelievable. (A:VSA)

Reading Isabella Bird it is obvious that nothing changed over 300 years of isolation. She even worried about the docility of the Japanese child. "They are gentle creatures" she wrote, "but too formal and precocious." Indeed. "I have never seen what we call child's play, that general abandonment to miscellaneous impulses, which consists in struggling, slapping, rolling, jumping, kicking, shouting, laughing and quarrelling!" (B:UTJ) So, what *did* Bird see?

> Two fine boys are very clever in harnessing paper carts to the backs of beetles with gummed traces, so that eight of them draw a load of rice up an inclined plane. You can imagine what the fate of such a load and team would be at home among a number of snatching hands. Here, a number of infants watch the performance with motionless interest, and never need the adjuration, "Don't touch." (B:UTJ)

I have observed the same, and, to tell the truth, would trust the average Japanese 3 or 4 year-old with something breakable before I would trust an average American 6 year-old. How can this be? Mrs. Busk in 1845, give us this seemingly knowledgeable explanation, based on the testimony of the Dutch Meylan:

> Children are trained to habits of implicit obedience; which, independent on its beneficial effects on their future character, prevents, in a great measure, the necessity of punishment. (B:MCJ)

Yes, but *how* were – and how are – the Japanese children so trained, while ours were – are – not? Valignano thought it the natural result of the "concord and quiet" of Japanese domestic life, itself made possible by the total avoidance of confrontation (see 3-16, below). That was a good theory. The favored 19th century theory was *heredity*. Might not a difference in our racial nature, perhaps make it more likely that children would end up severely punished in the West yet not in Japan? Bacon, again:

> A Japanese child seems to be the product of a more perfect civilization than our own, for it comes into the world with little of the savagery and barbarian bad manners and behavior that distinguish children in this country, and the first ten or fifteen years of its life do not seem to be passed in one long struggle to acquire a coating of good manners that will help to render it less obnoxious in polite society. How much of the politeness of the Japanese is the result of training, and how much is inherited from generations of civilized ancestors is difficult to tell; but my impression is, that babies are born into the world with a head-start . . . and that the uniformly gentle and courteous treatment they receive from those about them, . . . produce with very little difficulty the universally attractive manners of the people. (B:JGW?)

This nature (head-start) theory gives me an idea. It is often said that baby *boys* cry a lot more than *girls*. Is it not possible that this would make a parent more likely to hit them? Would this not make boys more likely to be mean even before the testosterone kicked in? And, what if Japanese babies were, for the most part, quiet as girls, or even more so? And, then, what if this advantage were helped by the practice Bacon described of not reacting whenever a baby cried, something relatively infrequent because the baby was less likely to be in a cradle. Or, to put it conversely, might we be training babies who already have a genetic tendency to cry, to cry even more? And might this not drive enough parents to violence to start a vicious cycle of beating that continued for generations? At any rate, there is ample testimony of the wonderful, and to us incredible, silence of "good" Japanese babies. Bird wrote: "I have never yet heard a baby cry." I have; but, to tell the truth, it was almost always because the baby was frightened . . . of *me*! Morse never tired of the subject:

> A rare thing is to hear a baby cry, and thus far I have never seen the slightest sign of impatience on the part of the mother. I believe that Japan is the only nation in the world that yields so much to babies, or in which babies are so good. I saw one mother shaving a baby's head with a sharp razor; the baby was crying, but, nevertheless, standing perfectly still. I contrasted all this behavior over and over again with that found in certain tenement regions back at home. (M:JDD?)

> I have never yet seen a cradle, nor have I seen a baby left alone to squall its eyes out; indeed it is the rarest sound in Japan – a baby's cry. [note: when Morse wrote Japan was experiencing a population explosion, so the silence was not for lack of babies!]

Morse also had something to say about what the quiet babies became:

> There is one subject, . . . that foreign writers are unanimously agreed upon, and that is that Japan is the paradise for children. Not only are they kindly treated, but they have more liberty, take less liberty with their liberties, and have a greater variety of delightful experiences than the children of any other people. As infants forever riding on their mother's back or somebody's else back; no punishment, no chiding, no nagging; such favors and privileges they are allowed that one would certainly think they would be spoiled, and yet no nation possesses children that can approach the Japanese children in love of parents or respect for the aged. . . .

From the appearance of their smiling faces they must be happy from morning to night. They work [helping their parents] contentedly and happily, and I have never seen a sulky child or any personal chastisement. . . . The Japanese have certainly solved the children problem, and no better behaved, kinder children exist, and no more patient, affectionate, and devoted mothers are found. However, this is all trite, as every book on Japan has said the same thing again and again.

But it bore repetition and still does, because it is so hard for our conceited culture to realize that it is not necessarily God's gift to earth. However, I am not certain if Morse (or Alcock who coined the phrase) are right to call Japan "a paradise for children" without also calling it a paradise *for parents!* Let me add that all the above is still true today. Twentieth-century child psychologists have noted how Japanese mothers squat down and *explain things* at length to recalcitrant children – from what I have overheard, the most common appeal is to the child's conscience by putting it in the place of the other (injured/troubled) party and asking pointed questions, but there are also appeals to a child's pride and its reverse, a sense of shame – where Usanians would more likely *demand* obedience.[2] Sad to say, the contrast Frois points out probably has been true for hundreds, possibly thousands of years! One wonders when the West began to go wrong.

I hate doing so but cannot help but qualify this abundant testimony for the no-spank way by giving a counter example of Chinese children generally as well behaved – "a veritable chip off the old block, he takes his pleasures gravely" (B:TC) – as Japanese children, despite considerable corporal punishment. Ball:

..

> Severity is held up as a proper treatment for children; natural affection, however, often carries the day, so that there is, as the outcome, a constant conflict between the two principles, such as the Persians represent as existent between the principles of good and evil; neither in the case under question, being, however, an unmitigated good or an unqualified evil. If the child cries, as a rule everything it wants is given to it. At other times, the parents give way to violent fits of temper in their efforts to bring the child to obedience, when it is beaten with great cruelty, on the head or anywhere, with sticks of firewood, or anything that comes handy, and, like a typhoon, these violent outbursts upset everything. (B:TC)

This may only be relevant to *parts* of China in *certain times* (for Fernao Mendez Pinto testified that Chinese as well as Japanese had enough self-control to shame the emotionally childish European). Seaport residents were famous for violent outbursts, bad language. They behave/d more like what we expect of poor people in the West. Even tiny tots could deliver strings of invectives and gangs of what we would now call juvenile delinquents roamed the neighborhoods, etc. (I read a great autobiography of growing up in Shanghai but forget the name of the author and book). Nevertheless, Nieuhaus, in the 17th century writes that the Chinese "are amazed when they hear that the children of Europe are whipp'd on their Buttocks, looking upon it as a severe and cruel punishment." This speaks very convincingly of their overall gentle treatment of children because the Chinese were the world's leading culture for caning bare buttocks of *adults!* This they did to punish men *right in court* and to "Women of Quality" in public (but not to women who were known to have lost all their shame, who were "beaten upon their Drawers.")! To Frois Nieuhoff about the Chinese: *We* whip the bare asses of bad children; *They* cane the bare asses of bad adults. In Singapore, as one eighteen year-old American spray-painter found out in 1994, they still do.

---

1. *"No Harsh Words"*. This good trait of the Jesuits is generally known. Here is an example from a hagiography of St. Peter Canisius, a Jesuit contemporary of Frois (died in the same year, 1597) who met the Protestant Reformation with some fine reforming of his own in Germany:

"As intent as Peter was on keeping people true to the Catholic faith, he followed *the Jesuit policy that harsh words should not be used,* that those listening would see an example of charity in the way Catholics acted and preached." (*italics mine*: from http://www. catholic.org/saints/saint.php?saint_id=93)

2. *Obedience, Conscience, Sin, Shame*. The standard contrast of inner-directed Western morality with outer-directed Japanese morality with the former being *individual sin-based* and the latter *social shame-based* is, partially correct, but horribly misleading for it neglects the far more important contrast of morality based on *reward and punishment* versus natural morality based on having *a conscience.* If the only reason you do not do bad things is because your parents demand you don't do them and you know you will be overpowered or hurt if you disobey, or because the *Bible* says they are "sinful" and you fear the ultimate punishment, your morality is other-based. If, on the other hand, you do not, say, hit another kid in the face because it hurts you to even think of doing so, then you are following your conscience. It is amusing to read, a wee malefactor rationalizing his malfeasance on grounds that the Bible doesn't say anything about not throwing cupcakes at another child's face in KIDS SAY THE DARNDEST THINGS, but that is a perfect description of *the artificial nature of sin-based morality!* (There is nothing in the Ten Commandments about parents not whipping their children, either!) Because little children in Japan were treated very gently, and accordingly had consciences, they did not need an artificial construct to compensate, or whips to terrify them into submission if they could not be convinced of the reality of Hell. I think that if a culture must rely on the fear of sin – i.e., believe in Heaven and Hell, which is to say a sort of *"Santa Claus is Coming to Town"* threat for adults to behave – it

is a good indication that something has gone wrong with early childhood. Shame, on the other hand, is like the conscience, a natural emotion and, correctly comprehended, is not opposed to but strengthened by having a conscience. (If you do not have a *conscience* you can be embarassed but not really feel *shame*.)

3. *Un-noted Note*. Reading of the gentle treatment of children by their mothers, we might wonder how women could have been treated as badly by Buddhism as we noted in 2-58 and elsewhere. As a matter of fact, there were ways *the good mother* made herself felt in Japanese Buddhism. According to Hank Glassman's dissertation "The Religious Construction of Motherhood in Medieval Japan" (Stanford), *Japanese* Buddhist hagiographies always bring in *the mother of the Buddhist saint* unlike the case in China, where his patrilineal roots are stressed. She does good things and has extraordinary dreams when pregnant and the saint usually makes some special effort to save her soul. In fact, he may have become a bonze specifically to save his beloved mother. Because of this, we even have men sneaking relics down from the all male mountain to their mothers for an effective ceremony and a sort of para-temple for women in the form of shrines to the mothers of eminent monks sprouted outside the gates to the sacred space at the foot of the mountain and they became "particularly famous for their efficacy in granting their female petitioners safety in childbirth and an ample supply of mother's milk." (Ibid)

3-8   With us, reading and writing are learned from secular teachers;
Antre nós se aprende a ler e escrever com mestres sequlares;

In Japan, all children study in the *varelas* [1] [temples] of the bonzes.
Em Japão todos os meninos aprendem nas varelas dos bonzos.

Pangur the white cat,[2] his master and many other diligent monks did help bring books through the Dark Ages but they were not, on the whole eager to educate people. Faith was important, learning secondary and one factor sparking the Reformation in North Europe may have been the fact that the clergy lagged the laity in learning and thereby lost their respect. The Society of Jesus was to change this in a big way [3] – a bit too late to recover North Europe but soon enough to save the South for Catholicism – but Frois did not experience that change, for he received his training as a scribe from secular teachers and left Lisbon for the East the year he joined the Society of Jesus at age 16, which, as it happens was the very same year the Jesuits opened their first school, 1548. It was a secondary school in Messina, Italy and by 1585 the Society had opened thirty more primary and secondary schools. I am not sure what percent were primary schools and whether they were open early enough for news to have reached Frois. Regardless, it would have been true that the majority of the schools (and tutors) in Europe were secular. Most of the Jesuits primary schools were probably for orphans some of whom later joined the orders (see C:RTI), but there was not yet anything as broad-based as the temple-based elementary school system in Japan.

Okada seconds Frois to the effect that the nobility, samurai and commoners alike attended. But Rodrigues only decades after Frois wrote that the sons of lords are tutored at home while the rest of the gentry studied in the temple schools (R(C):TIJ) Since whole mountains of monks were obliterated in the last decades of the 16th century, and the new Shôgunate, wary of Buddhism (as they were wary of Christianity) as a competitive power, was deliberately Confucian, which is to say secular, my guess is that part of the education was removed from Buddhist hands. Unfortunately, Frois wrote in such a mercurial age that we can not say with certainty just how far down the social ladder schooling extended (and, sorry, I do not know how many girls were included) but literacy was, beyond doubt, higher than in the West.   Children who boarded, generally became pupils at age six or seven and "came down the mountain" as apprentice monks four or five years later.   These bonzes-to-be were often good-looking peasant boys, who appear in haiku as poppy flowers (*keshi-no-hana*) because poppy is a homophone for obliteration (no secular life, no progeny, and a high death rate) because its petals quickly fall leaving what resembles a shaved pate.   Most small temples were not up the mountains. The majority of the pupils attended these day-schools and did not join the orders.

Buddhism was a major source of letters in Japan.   An esoteric Buddhist abbot was credited with devising one of the phonetic syllabaries and the Buddhist scriptures were written in solid Chinese characters, even if the original came from India. Some of Japan's top literary work was written by Buddhist priests and the bonzes enjoyed a degree of public respect for their literacy and generally good calligraphy.   Despite this Buddhist literacy having been transmitted from China to Japan centuries earlier, this was apparently the opposite of the situation in China, where, from what Ricci and others wrote, the Buddhist priests ended up largely illiterate and all the learning and respect was monopolized by the government scholar-bureaucrats.   Considering the role of the clergy in preserving literacy through our "dark age" – that is in many ways not so dark, but, like the Tokugawa isolation of Japan, "enlightened" in its own way – it is surprising to me that more of *our* primary education was not in the hands of our religious orders.

1. *Varela.* Frois foreign terms are usually Japanese, but *varela*, like *pinga* (2-59) is one of the exceptions.   R. Catz defines it as: "A term that the old Portuguese writers applied to the Buddhist pagodas and monasteries of Indochina and China.   It is probably derived from the Malay *barhala,* or the Javanese "*brahala* meaning "idol." An idol temple is *rumah-barhala* or *barahla,* "a house of idols" . . ." (P(C):TMP). The spiteful term "idol" was, of course, meaningless to a tolerant religious culture. If it had such meaning in Malay, it was because of the presence of monotheistic prejudice introduced by Islamic culture from the West.

2. *Pangur Ban.* If you are not familiar with the pleasant medieval poem comparing a monk hunting knowledge in books and a cat mice in nooks, or even if you are, please visit the *paraversing* section of my paraverse.org site, where, with any luck I will upload a page with a few paraverses (versions of translations, for the original is old Irish) before long.

3. *Jesuits and Education.* The good the Jesuits did for education cannot be overstated.   When the Society of Jesus was formed in 1541, the Church did not even have a system for training its own clergy.   The Jesuits created one in decades and by the end of the century, had what we might call a non-profit corporation with a smoothly operating system of pedagogy (largely based on the Parisian method of progressive classes which we now take for granted) and funding – Jesuits were masters of commerce and gave all of the proceeds to the schools which were free to all and admitted equally all classes (as the Buddhists did in Japan) – which mass-produced high quality schools including, eventually *most* of the best higher education in Europe!   By 1773, the year the Society of Jesus was suppressed by papal edict, they ran 800 educational institutions around the globe.   Far from holding back the birth of modern science, they helped to both educate and fund many of the best scientists of the day.   Indeed, some were themselves top scientists the top mathematician of the 16th century, *were* Jesuits – Diligent at their correspondence (Frois was not alone there!) and believing in collaboration, i.e., the open sharing of knowledge, they sent back information from around the world to scientists in Europe, many of whom were not even Catholic (Even Kepler, who was Protestant received financial assistance and a free telescope from a Jesuit scientist) .   Arguments can be made that they were the first Scientific Society in the World.   (Most of this information comes from two fine articles, each with many excellent leads: *.How the First Jesuits Became Involved in Education* by John W. O'Malley, S.J. Published in *The Jesuit Ratio Studiorum: 400th Anniversary Perspectives.* Vincent J. Duminuco, S.J., Ed. (New York: Fordham University Press, 2000, pp.56-74.) ©Fordham University Press. found on the Boston College site: www.bc.edu/ offices/mission/exploring/jesuniv/omalley_education/; and *Partners and Rivals During the Scientific Revolution* [could not find a name but Wow! What a page! The illustrations are wonderful and there is a full bibliography] at http://www.faculty.fairfield.edu/jmac/sj/ cj/cj5science. html.

3-9   Our children first learn to read and later learn to write;
            Os nossos mininos aprendem primeiro a ler e depois a escrever;

            Those of Japan commence with writing and then learn to read.
            Os de Japão começão primeiro a escrever e depois aprendem a ler.

Japanese children did indeed write Chinese characters before they could read them. Since most characters have multiple readings in Japanese (eg. 頭 head," is pronounced *atama* for a plain ole head, *zu* as part of a headache=*zutsû* and *tô* when used for counting heads), it does indeed take much more time to master *reading* them than *writing* them, with the exception of the more complex characters, which most people never learn *to write*). Writing also plays a more important role in learning than it does in the West. Japanese, today, are still big on *memorizing-by-writing*. The thick, brushed line impresses the visual memory deeper than a penned one, and it is important for mastering the order of the strokes. Moreover, such writing is an aesthetically satisfying incentive for the child (We will come back to this in the writing chapter). I don't know how many times I have seen the calligraphy of elementary school children – usually just one or two large brushed characters – on exhibit at the railway/subway station (which is pretty much the center of any town in Japan). Many are just magnificent, for there is a beauty and a power that only repetition can create in art. Framed and exhibited in an art gallery, they would put to shame the largely worthless modern art found in Japan or here. Imagine if you can, samples of our children's writing – or, for that matter any one's writing – on exhibit in art galleries and hanging in homes as art. Impossible, isn't it. *Our calligraphy is an art, but the product is not art.* It is only decoration.

If Frois was not seeking contrast, he might have noted that young pupils in Japan also learn a phonetic syllabary; but with these syllabets (see 10-1) they can read *immediately* – or learn to read as they write – because they are far less ambiguous than spelling with "our" alphabet – here, I refer to English, not Spanish or Portuguese, which is more similar to Japanese in having only one possible pronunciation! Whereas we spell-out words so as to make them incomprehensible to children, Japanese do so to make them clear; for, in Japanese, spelling out *is simply saying a word slowly.* (I once laughed so hard I cried to hear a Japanese expert on American pop and country music in America tell his NHK (Japan's national public radio or BBC) audience that Tammy Wynette "spelled out all the 'hurting words'" in *D.I.V.O.R.C.E.* in order that her child could understand them better!) The Japanese practice of *spelling-as-speaking* is not even possible for a Latin language because consonants and vowels are spoken separately and a small child or an illiterate adult could not put them together.

3-10   Our tutors teach catechism, [the lives of] the saints, and virtuous customs to children;
            Os nossos mestres insinão a doutrina, santos e vertuosos custumes aos meninos;

            The bonzes teach them to play [musical instruments], sing, gamble [1] and fence, and practice their abominations on them. *Os bonzos os insinão a tanjer, cantar, jugar, esgrimir e com eles fazem suas abominasões.*
            ..

Frois grew up during a time when the Inquisition, having discovered gaps in the knowledge of the Christian doctrine on the part of a surprisingly large number of adults, [2] encouraged reformers to educate children. The Jesuits were among the first to do so. By the third article of the founding document (1539) of the Society of Jesus, members of the new order were bound to "hold esteemed the instruction of children and the uneducated in the Christine doctrine of the Ten Commandments and other similar rudiments." Here is a description of their modus operandi in the mid-1550's by Sara T. Nalle and testimony as to the efficacy of catechism (vs preaching) by one Diego Xuárez:

> During the afternoons, one Jesuit would walk through streets, ringing a bell, and the children followed him to the place of instruction. There they were first be encouraged to accuse one another of having sworn or lost their temper. Then they were taught how to sing their prayers, and at the end of the course the best catechumens won a prize. (Nalle: *God in La Mancha*)

> It melted my hard heart to see the eagerness with which the children came to doctrine, and they went singing it in the streets and fields, so that almost nothing else was heard. Some women were crying with devotion, and when we asked them why they didn't know the Ten Commandments, they said, "Because they didn't teach it to us like now in the streets." (from N:GIL)

The Jesuits also taught in elementary schools and presumably helped guide secular teachers, so I do not know just what "our" tutors/teachers/masters (*mestres*) includes, but it could be said that the Jesuits in Iberia helped to spark the Catholic Reformation child-first.

The Buddhist temple-schools, on the other hand, obviously had a broader agenda. They were a creative space with what we now might consider a progressive curriculum!   All those Chinese characters were hard work, but little Japanese, at least, did not have to endure too much catechism. Many probably did have the "abominations" problem. Rodrigues put it like this:

> After studying in these monastery schools they become children of the devil on account of the many bad customs and vices the bonzes teach the children there under their care. They not only do not feel these vices to be wrong, but they teach them in such a way that it is considered a virtue to consent to them and a despicable vice to resist and oppose them . . . For this reason, the Society, in keeping with its Institute, runs schools for the young sons of Christians in the regions where it has a house . . . (R(C):TIJ)

We are talking about *pederasty*. Judging from the literature going back a thousand years, there was quite some competition for the cutest boys. In Japan, as in Mexico [3] or ancient Greece, grown men unabashedly had young boyfriends with whom they enjoyed sex. Neither were necessarily homosexual in our sense of the word. Usually both were not. An Edo era erotic print by Koigawa Shôsan showing a samurai apparently sodomizing a youth, includes conversation with these words from the older to the younger: *"Let me suck your mouth [tongue-kiss]! For that, I'll buy you a whore tonight, too!"* Risqué poems (*senryu*) – like *Martial's Epigrams* – tell wives not to even try competing with hairless young asses, and, better yet, chuckle that even a *wakashû* (literally "young-crowd") – the closest phenomenon to what we call "gay," but invariably transvestite as well – are frightening, *when they eat chili peppers!*

But, as the term for a professional catamite, *kagema* or "shade-place" suggests, "male-color" (homosexuality) was nothing to boast about.   For bonzes, however, practicing sex with boys was considered far less reprehensible than intercourse with women.   They were supposed to avoid "the wide way" (vaginal intercourse) because of the supposedly greater pollution of women, the greater danger of falling into lasting love with the illusory beauty of this world as embodied by women and for fear of issue, i.e., the social repercussions of fatherhood and adultery – and stick to "the narrow way" (anal intercourse). Like prostitution licensed in order "to prevent the debauching of young Maids and married Women" (Caron) and masturbation, encouraged to preserve female chastity and save men from wasting money and sexually transmitted disease, pederasty was generally considered a relatively harmless vice. Of course, not doing it at all was as much the ideal for Buddhist clergy, as it was for Christian men of the cloth.

The amount of pederasty in Japan was not exaggerated by the Jesuits. They were only wrong to identify it so completely with Buddhism (4-2). The relationship of the samurai and his page-boy was socially more acceptable, even thought highly of. [4]   The short book of "exhaustive listings" *INU-MAKURA* (dog-pillow) – published with moveable wooden type in 1607 but "unequivocally a product of the Muromachi period" (Frois's era) and attributed to a bibliophile physician employed after 1599 by Tokugawa Ieyasu – contains a score of references to "boy favorites." Indeed, these boys are far more present than the female "sweetheart," "lover" or "beloved!" Except for one item in the "Dangerous Things" list: *leaving one's boy favorite to a priest's charge*, these boys have nothing to do with Buddhism. Between "broken promises" and "being awakened during a nap" in "Things That make One Angry:" *one's boy favorite pretending romantic attraction to someone else.* Between "teeth the color of loquats" and "a food-server with skin-diseased arms" in "Unclean Things:" *nail dirt and nose hair of a boy favorite.* Between "a guest with whom one talks too long" and "a willful horse" in "Things One Would Like To Stop:" *what follows evening stories with a boy favorite.* Between "one's only daughter giving birth to a son" and "one's illness being cured by a quack doctor" in "Joyful Things When One Has Been Apprehensive:" *the groundless jealousy of a boy favorite.* Between "biting into sand while eating food" and "to tear one's skin when scratching an itch" in "Bad Things In Good:" *imprudence in a fine boy favorite.* Between "that all is well in one's native village" and "that one has guessed the name of a famous perfume" in "Things Joyful To Hear:" *of a boy favorite speaking well of one behind one's back."* (trans. Edward Putzar: in *Harvard Journal of Asiatic Studies* _? 1968)

While Buddhism was not kicked out of Japan like Christianity, its power was drastically weakened by the Shoguns who united the country, yet the practice of "bogering boyes" (to borrow Cocks' term), if anything, became more popular after Japan kicked out the Jesuits. Kaempfer in 1691 reports:

> I cannot forbear taking notice . . . that on the chief street of this town, thro' which we pass'd, were built nine or ten neat houses, or booths, before each of which sate one, two, or three young boys, of ten to twelve years of age, well dress'd, with their faces painted, and feminine gestures, kept by their lew'd and cruel masters for the secret pleasure and entertainment of rich travelers, the Japanese being very much addicted to this vice. However, to save outward appearances, and lest the virtuous should be scandaliz'd, or the ignorant and poor presume to engage with them, they sit there, as it were, to sell the abovesaid plaister to travellers.

Indeed, the practice became so much the rage in the *kabuki* days of the seventeenth and eighteenth century that all the major pleasure quarters had *wakashû*, "young-crowd" houses and not a few female street-walkers impersonated these male female impersonators. The better looking women apparently did not go for this, but it was a great boost to the plain Janes, called *hashi-jorô*, or "marginal-prostitutes," for they stood a better chance of appealing to a man as a man, as *wakashû-jôro,,* or "young-crowd-prostitutes"! (Sasama Yoshihiko: KOSHOKU-ENGO_JITEN)   Golownin, in the early-19th century, confirmed that "the abominable vice, common to all Asiatics" was still practiced in Japan and the government did not suppress it. Moreover, he added that "the province of Kioto, in which the spiritual emperor lives, is celebrated for the beauty of its male in habitants, and furnishes the greater part of the youths for this infamous traffic." Since Confucius and company were not pederasts, while Plato and platoon [5] were, we might *Faux Frois:*

> *Our ancient philosophers were lovers of boys, and all of them would be burned alive today.*
> *Their ancient philosophers were not like that, but loving boys is now thought to be admirable.*

Homosexual relations, like public nudity and male long-hair, was persecuted for the sake of international relations (pleasing the West) and a tradition over 500 years old was driven underground so successfully that the coming out of homosexuality in the West in the late twentieth century, shocked Japanese who, for the most part, knew nothing about their own bisexual past.

Just to set things straight, while the Catholic Reformation did indeed crack down on sex (not just between men, but against clergy who seduced women who confessed their sins), there were some exceptions that suggest the West was by no means innocent of what was charged against Japan. In his eccentric *Sex in History*, Gordon Rattray Taylor writes that

> on the Continent, where the matrist movement had started earlier, and had now proceeded to the extreme of general licence, to the point where Alfonso d'Este could be called "the virtuous" because he confined himself to buying girls from their mothers for seduction instead of just seducing them, homosexuality was being erected into a virtue, as we may judge from the appearance of a work entitled *"De laudibus, sodomiae seu pederastiae"*, written by the Archbishop della Casa [1503-1556].

Giovanni Della Casa's erotic poem, usually Englished as *In Praise of Sodomy*, was well known. Yet he was a Jesuit, sent Protestant reformers to the death as an Inquisition judge and was responsible for at least one *Index of Prohibited Books!*. What gives? Was the practice winked at until the alleged pederast Pope Julius III (1550-55) died[6] and the Church got serious? But, if they did, how could Lithgow, a straight-speaking Scott , report the following in Padua in his book published in 1632?

> The Schollers here in the night commit many murthers against their privat adversaries, and too often executed upon the stranger and innocent, and all with gun-shot or else stillettoes: for beastly Sodomy, it is rife here as in Rome. Naples, Florence, Bullogna, Venice, Ferrara, Genoa. Parma not being exempted, nor yet the smallest Village of, Italy: A monstrous filthinesse, and yet to them a pleasant pastime, making songs and singing Sonets of the beauty and; pleasure of their Bardassi, or buggerd boyes. (in T:SIH)

I only bring up these things to complicate matters and do not think I have disproved Frois's contrast which may, *as a generalization* hold true.

1. *Gambling!?* The "gamble" was a hard decision for an ambiguous verb *jogar*. I believe Frois refers mainly to gambling but the word would also encompass the various board games such as *shogi* and *go* (see 14-39), which are, like our chess, games of skill and not intrinsically gambling, but often associated with it. As such, by using the word "gamble" I am a bit too narrow. I tried the verb "game" on some readers and they could not follow it, though it is perfectly good English and would have been perfect.

2. Inquisition as Inquiry. The Inquisition surveyed the accused it brought to court. So we have a record of what percent of the defendants knew this or that aspect of the Doctrine. In 1544-67 in one town, only one third knew by heart the basic four or five prayers, whereas, by 1568-1579 that number had doubled and by the time the TRATADO was written it was pushing 80%. So, we know that the catechism campaign worked. (more details in Sara T. Nalle: *God in La Mancha: Religious Reform and the People of Cuenca*, 1500-1650   THE LIBRARY OF IBERIAN RESOUCES ONLINE)

3. *Mexican Pederasty* I first became aware of this when there was a party at my house in Hawaii in 1977 and a Mexican friend, whom I had only known to be obsessed with seducing women (his lines praising their eyes as the most beautiful he ever saw etc. made me laugh) failed to pick up a woman and in his drunken condition tried instead to convince my male house-mates to sleep with him. My friends informed me he was "gay" and I asked E what he was up to and he explained that in Mexico if a man could not find a woman he would . . . . The idea was that so long as you were the one doing the poking, screwing men made you even *more* macho, for macho meant getting into anything with a hole. I had some doubt about his claim, but years later read about a practice in parts of Mexico of heterosexual men having boyfriends, but they were usually younger boys than my house-mates, so I suspect E was behaving more like a goat (I don't really know if goats behave like this, but I think you know what I mean) than the Mexican he was.

4. *Socially Acceptable Pederasty* Today, with thousands of lawsuits against the Catholic priests for pederasty (how ironic, or is it poetic justice for hubris with the respect to bonzes?), we need to remind ourselves that the damage to the young men is only damage because they are taught it is sinful and our culture is hysterical when it comes to young sex. One can find just as many cultures throughout history that considered such relationships to be part of growing up – even necessary for growing up! – and something to be sought. Here is Frois's contemporary Montaigne:

> And Socrates, when older than I am, speaking of an object of his love, said: "When I had leaned my shoulder against his and brought my head closer to his, as we were looking into a book together, I suddenly felt, without prevarication, a stinging in my

shoulder like some animal's bite, and I was more than five days with its prickling, and a continual itching flowed into my heart." A touch, and an accidental one, and one by a shoulder, to inflame and alter a soul cooled and enervated by age, and the first of all human souls in reformation! Indeed, why not? Socrates was a man, and wanted neither to be nor to seem anything else." (*On Some Verses of Virgil* in M(F):EOM)

Japan, like Greece, was a boy-loving culture and the relationship of a samurai with his boy – was considered beneficial to both. Ideally it lasted about 5 years – until the boy grew hairy. Montaigne writes that the Greek sophist Dion "called the downy hairs of adolescence Aristogeitons and Harmodiuses" because, explains Frame, "these hairs deliver lovers of the boys who grow them from the tyranny of love, as H & A delivered Athens from tyranny."

5. Pardon the Puns (Platon+Platoon)! But, get the following! When I mentioned a movie on the Vietnam War called *Platoon* to a Japanese friend, she expressed surprise to hear what it was about. The pronunciation for the title, left as is by the Japanese, was *puraton,* from which she thought it meant "platonic love" which to Japanese suggests homosexuality more than sexless relationships. I haven't seen the movie "Lost in Translation," but I doubt it could be better than that (For more extraordinary examples yet, see G:O&O)!

6. How "Bad" Were "We"? An internet list of "Papal Impropriety" claims Pope Julius III (1550-55) sodomized young boys, of which one was his own, illegitimate, son. He appointed several handsome teenage boys as cardinals. Cardinal della Casa's famous poem *In Praise of Sodomy* was dedicated to said Pope Julius III. (www.geocities. com /missus_gumby/papal.htm). A "leatherarchives" site puts it like this

"Reign of Pope Julius III who, upon election as Pope, made his 17 year old lover a member of the College of Cardinals, and also appointed him Secretary of State. His orgies with teenage Cardinals were common knowledge. Most were horrified but the Archbishop of Benevento wrote a book, *In Praise of Sodomy,* dedicated to the pope."

I have always taken such accusations or even worse accusations about earlier popes (courtesans crawling about between candles picking up chestnuts with their __, etcetera . . .) with a grain of salt. But there would seem to be something here. An in-depth, fully footnoted article by Oliver K. Olson, describes della Casa's persecution of the admirable *Baldo Lupetino, Venetian Martyr* and includes this telling passage: "Aren't you ashamed, you wretched Archbishop?" wrote the legate, Peter Paul Vergerio, about Della Casa's 1549 Index of Prohibited Books, published at the command of Paul III. "You dare come forth and damn holy books – you who have written poems in which you have extolled the most excreable

evils of Sodom as a divine work?" Vergerio had in mind the *Capitolo del Forno,* for which the homosexual cleric had earned a reputation as a pornographer. Here is a sample in English translation of one of his verses:

By day I used to search the woodlands through / For cave or rill, where griefs might sing and preen / Themselves in rhyme, and I on nights serene / Would lie awake with Love and Phoebus too; / Nor did I fear, Bernard, to climb with you / That secret mount where few men now have been. (from Olson: from part of Rime XXV, translated by Rudolf B.Gottfreid: *Fifteen Fourteens from Giovanni Della Casa*)

Erotic, perhaps, but pornographic? (Does anyone have the real thing? Or is that all! If so it is nothing compared to Ikkyû's poems). But, let me leave you with one image (or two, one pleasant and one not) about another pope before Frois's time, the very gentleman who excommunicated Luther: I found it while searching unsuccessfully for Della Casa's poems. Pope Leo X:

"he served dinners with sixty-five courses at which little boys jumped out of puddings . . . . cardinals wanted to assassinate him by injecting poison into his "formidable hemorrhoids." ("derived fully or partly from Wikipedia" but found at http:// encyclo-pedia.thefreedictionary.com /Pope%20Leo%20X).

Because the English-speaking world was at war with the Catholic one for centuries, I cannot help but wonder how much if anything of all this stuff was true. After all, look at all the lies about Jesuit Powder and the false idea that the Jesuits had it in for Japan, etc.. Yet, when I see one of those old oil paintings of a certain Pope, I must admit, the man looks evil. And it certainly wasn't painted by a Protestant. If anyone has a graciously written, finely nuanced, well-researched neutral opinion on this nasty matter, I would like to add it.

7. An Extra Note on Sunday Schools in case anyone wondered about the place synonymous with catechism. Robert Raikes (1735-1811) was the first person to set up an actual Sunday school in 1780 in Gloucester and even has a statue in London commemorating it. But a Methodist, Hannah Moore began a school in her own home in 1769 and there is a window in the Town Hall in High Wycombe to commemorate her. Here is what is interesting:

Raikes' idea behind Sunday school was the fact that the young children (most of who worked in the factories) could be stopped from turning into criminals if they were given a basic and religious education. Seeing as Sunday was the only day they did not work then that became the day that they went to school. (Googled: LR)

That reason for doing it on Sunday: "the only day they did not work." Those poor kids!

3-11   Ours as young men do not know how to give a message;
Os de Europa são mancebos e não sabem dar hum recado;

> Japanese children ten years old do so with the judgment and prudence of a 50 year-old. *Os meninos japões de dez annos paresem de 50 no sizo e prudencia com que o dão.*

Japan wins. This contrast, as with 3-6, 3-13 and 3-14, prove that Frois is not just following an agenda to idealize Europe, but calling it as he sees it. Not long ago, in both in the West and Japan, being entrusted with messages was an accepted way for youths to gain status and make connections. While carrying written messages – and, as DR reminds me, filling in the details as necessary – were part of the boy's duty, I believe that the ability to recall an invisible, and therefore safe, oral message may be what Frois means here. Our verb "to page" suggests that was the case in the West, too. Okada, who translates *recado* (message) as *kôjô* (mouth-above=oral message) quotes at length instruction for training children from the age of eight to relay messages properly, and notes that "becoming a messenger was considered *the* goal of learning the proprieties." Because the instructions suggested repeating simple greetings a hundred times over so they would become second nature (*shizen to narete*), we can see that *practice* may have had a lot to do with the "judgment and prudence" found in Japan.

3-12   With us, even a man of 20 rarely carries a sword;
Antre nós hé um homem de 20 annos e quasi que ainda não tras espada;

..

> The children of Japan, go about with a *katana* [Japanese sword] and *wakizashi* [dagger] from age 12 or 13. *Os meninos de Japão de 12, 13 anos andão com* catana e vaqizaxi.

In 1547, Alvarez "noted that males customarily carried swords from the tender age of eight years."(B:CCJ) Gago (1555) claimed they wore swords from the age ten.(CARTAS). Frois (1565) wrote "From a very young age, the boys wear swords and daggers, and when they sleep place them by their pillow." (CARTAS). Valignano dittoed that, and L Abbe d' T improved it, saying they do so "to shew themselves Souldiers in their very sleep." This could not have been true for *most* boys in Japan, even in this most warlike age; but it apparently was true for the 5-10% that belonged to the *buke*, or samurai stock and not a few commoners, though they would only wear one sword (two being a samurai privilege). From artwork I have seen, I think it safe to say that before the modernization of Japan in the late-19th century, even wee samurai far younger than "12 or 13" wore the standard set of "big and little" [sword] set. It is a good thing the swords were sheathed, for looking at the mid-19th century photos, one wonders how often they tripped over them!

Matsuda and Jorissen write that Frois's contrast is exaggerated, for the young ambassadors from Japan to Europe record (1584) a visit to a certain Count in Portugal, whose three sons, aged sixteen, fourteen and ten, all wore swords. *Touché*? Not quite. A formal occasion is not the same as wearing them *all the time*, as was the case for little samurai. As Noel Perrin has pointed out, in Japan, the sword was "the only embodiment of honor" that formed part of one's costume. With no signet ring, no jewels, no military decorations, the sword was *the* mark of somebody. "Occasionally a commoner would rise in the world and be granted a sort of life peerage. This was called *myoji-taito,* the privilege of surname and sword."(P:GUG) The swords were, as we have seen in chapter I, part of their clothing.

This contrast reflects not only the utterly martial orientation of the Japanese gentry but the precocious self-control already noted. Young Japanese who could handle chopsticks at 4 and deliver an oral message at ten could also be entrusted with a lethal weapon. Why? Because Japanese children did not fight each other. This was and is largely true right up to the present day. Morse wrote that kite fighting was "the only way I ever saw boys fight among themselves." He also noted that he saw only one street fight in his three years in Japan and he was the only one who watched (and it was only a bit of hair-pulling at that). There was none of that *"fight! fight!"* enthusiasm where all gather round to watch "admiring the punches and regretfully departing when the battle is finished or the police interfere" common to Morse's America and mine (several times per week behind the water-tower near Key Biscayne Elementary in the 1960's).

There was one downside to armed precocity. Valignano, writing about *harakiri*, notes: "To cut the belly in this way is so common in Japan that it sometimes happens that very small children do it in front of their parents when they are angry at them." *Ouch!* On a more amusing note, a couple hundred years later, a *senryu* mentions wee samurai children "kindly" (the word "kind=*shinsetsu*" written with two characters, one of which is "cut," probably a pun in this context) instructing commoner friends on how to cut their stomachs.

~~~~~~

3-13   Our children show little judgment or grace with respect to our manners;
Os nossos mininos tem pouqo asento e primor nos custumes;

> Those of Japan, in this regard, are so wonderfully perfect in every respect they are admirable. *Os de Japão são nisto estranhamente inteiros, em tanto que poem admirasao.*

This distich drove me crazy. "Customs" wasn't quite right. I thought *comportment* would be better for it includes the etiquette+behavior aspect of the original. But, then it would have to be "their." "Our" would not work. So, finally, I came to "manners." But no matter how it is translated, the idea gets across.

Should we ask why "our" children were – and are – so rambunctious? Perhaps, exceptionally rambunctious. (How do cultures neither Far Eastern nor Western, stand in this?) Did "Europe" in Frois's day already have a *youth culture* sufficiently different from tradition to estrange children from their parents and give them an excuse to misbehave? Keith Thomas writes of English children pretty much ignored by adults and running wild, *pissing in the aisles of churches to make ice to skate on*, and so forth. (T:RAD) How typical was this for European children? Was it the result of ebullience? Or was it a reaction to domestic violence? Or, was the importation of sugar, perhaps, already creating hyperactivity? Or should we, rather, ask why the Japanese children were so culture-positive, so ready to try finer things? Ruth Benedict once hypothesized that the *excessive* (her idea, not mine!) artistic activity and ritual observance in Bali derived from the way Balinese mothers continually frightened their children with imaginary ghosts, after which they gleefully cuddled and reassured them so they grew up insecure in the world at large and needed art to feel reassured in a well-ordered little world of their own. I suppose a similar explanation, turning punctilious behavior into abnormality born of neurosis could be made for the children of Frois's Japan. (We have already seen some of this, although Bird and Bacon never go so far as Benedict.) But I think the most likely reason for the goodness of Japanese children is that there is much in the culture that is good for, i.e., satisfies them. [1] (see my notes to 3-15)

I also wonder here if Frois is really thinking only of children. It would seem to me that he carved this contrast off a larger one he could have, but did not state. After all, Valignano, right after expressing his amazement with the docility of Japanese children, pointed out that Japanese in their dress, dining and so forth were remarkably "clean, trim and properly dressed" (*limpio, ataviados y concertados*) indeed:

> all of the Japanese have the same order and manner of proceeding, so much so it seems they were all taught in the same school. (V(A):S&A)

On November 13, 1857, Heusken, the young interpreter for the first American Consul to Japan, noted the same:

> It seems that the Japanese do everything they must do at the same time, prescribed by law. They take their breakfast, lunch, and dinner exactly at the same hour. They change clothes four times a year on the same day. One day, everybody is busy drying fish; another day is to dry fabrics woven by the women. Apparently they go even further, for today everybody without exception has a cold certainly by order of the government. (JJ)

An entire nation literally composed. The children could hardly fall astray, for there was no other way. Morse, after visiting the closest thing to slums in Japan, ventured that a random sample of even those children would prove "more polite and graceful in manner, less selfish, more considerate for the feelings of others" than their counterparts from upper Fifth Avenue, New York! (M:JDD) Today, this East-West politeness gap has closed considerably, particularly among males. Much of the remaining politeness is a female thing (for some reason, honorifics in Japanese are particularly pleasant to say, so this is no burden on women in my opinion) or the natural outgrowth of timidity or goodness, for good people tend to be gentle. Bacon made it clear how this happened. It was not a rebellion. The initial move away from etiquette was a *choice* on the part of the Japanese leadership.

> The Japanese are rapidly finding out that this busy nineteenth century gives little time for learning how to shut and open doors in the politest manner, and indeed such things under the newly established school system are now relegated entirely to the girls' schools, the boys having no lessons in etiquette. (B:JGW)

Basically, early modern civilization required men to be jerks in order to get ahead in the world and leave their culture in the care of women.

1. Child-friendly Cultures. I recall reading that white Americans kidnapped by natives were generally far happier than the vice-versa and that this is backed up by statistics on what might be called cultural recidivism. A good gloss would be welcome!

~~~~~~

3-14   Our children are, for the most part, embarrassed to act in public performances;
Os nossos mininos, são pola mayor parte pejados em autos públicos e reprezentações;

> Those of Japan are at ease, lively, adorable, and bold in their roles.
> *Os de Japão despejados, libres, e graciosos e muy ayrozos [1] no que representão..*

Why is this? Isn't stage-fright normal? If Frois restricted his observation to the children of nobility it might be explained as experience, for judging from Fernao Mendez Pinto's detailed account, they were fond of putting on skits for guests (see 6-1). But there might be more to it. Hundreds of years after Frois, Bacon wrote that "the Japanese girl seems never at a loss, even under unusual circumstances, but bears herself with self-possession in places where young girls in America would be embarrassed and awkward," perhaps because of "regular teaching in the ways of polite society." (B:JGW) That is to say, contrary to our assumption that manners (including polite phrasesof speech) are restrictive, they can free those who incorporate them, much as the mastery of a certain type of music (to the exclusion of other possibilities) allows one to improvise freely. Someone – perhaps Eliza Skidmore? – called Japanese "a nation of poseurs." If there is anything to that, acting would be nothing out of the ordinary to them. Posing would in no way make the poseur lose his or her composure. The ease with which Japanese *of all ages* perform in front of audiences is still apparent today, is by no means restricted to drama, and suggests the following *Faux Frois:*

> *Europeans freeze up in formal situations and are at ease giving informal opinions.*
> *Japanese have difficulty giving personal opinions but are at ease when performing in public.*

In *informal* situations, or when asked for their *opinions*, Japanese above the age of eight tend to be *more* rather than less uptight than Usanians and, possibly, all Western peoples. Indeed, they see themselves as extremely bashful and even lacking in self-expression compared to "outgoing and brave" foreigners. The Jesuits alternated between praising such bashfulness as discretion and humility and damning it as being secretive. In the early eighteenth century, the extraordinarily objective Golownin gives a fine and long example (which really should be picked up by socio-linguists!) of the reticent style of Japanese argument where "they bring forward their opinions politely, and with many apologies, seeming to doubt the correctness of their own judgment." (G:MCJ) In the face of obnoxiously confident turn-of-the-century Americans "with an attitude" – all too many tougher-than-thou wise-ass sound-alikes who *think* they are original – such gentleness and humility seems too good to be true!   But, excessive reticence was and still is a problem, for, as even the supreme Japanophile Morse lamented, the Japanese are not only afraid to contradict one another "as it is with us," but "consider it rude to have a different opinion," with the result that all statements are given "submissive agreement" and the result, "to the uninformed, endless confusion." (M:IGM) There is truth in this lament. Without the unstated agreement to disagree found in the West, lively discussion in much of Japan (Kansai is more like the West and Korea in this respect) is all but impossible while sober.

But in *formal* situations, it is the Western man or woman who is far more likely to be at a loss and claim the cat got their tongue, or blush red as a beat, when asked for a speech at a wedding or to sing a song in front of colleagues, where many if not most Japanese do so with the aplomb of an old pro. In formal or public performance, most Japanese are still as awesome as the children mentioned by Frois. They seem to find what is essentially role-playing – acting out a public *persona* – less stressful than the informal argument most Westerners find relaxing rather than stressful. If this broader difference, or paradox was not mentioned by Frois, it may be that the Iberian culture was also quite performance-oriented (and shared some of the Japanese view on argument (I think of the oft-quoted Spanish proverb "Better to lose an argument than to lose a friend" which is used as proof of the more human virtues of the Latin American – as opposed to the logically relentless Anglo – by authors who fail to realize that argument need not be taken personally.)

Or, am I am barking up the wrong tree. Should I have stopped at children doing skits? Are Japanese children more at ease simply because Japanese were spared the rod (3-7)? One thing is certain, the Jesuits were unabashed humanists who, following the Greeks, were so big on plays that they deserve some credit for the seventeenth century being the century of drama (see chapter 13) in Europe.   As DR points out, they doubtless used plays as learning aids in Japan, so Frois's observation probably comes from hands-on experience. Perhaps because there is a separate chapter on drama, indicating that Frois did not necessarily stay home, Okada feels this may instead refer to the dancing and Noh plays that samurai children participate in which impressed Frois.

1. *Ayrozos=Airosos.* This wonderful-sounding word I translated as "bold" includes the following nuances: *jaunty, decorous, graceful, elegant, refined.* Perhaps we should, then, just say the Japanese children were really "cool" actors and leave it at that!

3-15   Children of Europe are raised with many dainty gifts, sweet words, caresses, good food and dress; *Os de Europa são criados com muitos mimos, branduras, bons comeres e vestidos;*

Those of Japan grow up half-naked, with hardly any gifts, affection or treats.
Os de Japão meos nus e quasi que de todos os mimos e dilícias carecem.

If Japanese were not whipped (3-7), they were not hugged either! Okada quotes a period child-rearing book to the effect that small children should to be "starved by a third and frozen by a tenth." This was thought good for their long-term health. Such advice was probably for the upper classes and wealthy merchant/townsman. The majority of children in Japan, and I would bet, Europe, and were automatically treated to the same! [1]   Something of the attitude survives, for even today, primary school children must wear shorts in the winter (*yes, it snows in Tokyo*), and every year a few foreign mothers with children attending Japanese schools write letters to the Japan Times to complain about this "cruelty" and suggest the teachers and administrators follow suit, etc.. Moreover, Japanese still aren't big on hugging each other and don't tell their children that they love them. Then again adults don't do these things to each other, either.

But let us consider one item at a time. The "half-naked" encompasses at least four different phenomena. First, health, as explained above. Second, the generally different attitude on nudity we have already discussed already. The Japanese were fine with it. Third, superstition. Mrs. Busk's 1841 summary of Dutch observations:

> The Japanese children are very meanly clad; and, when accompanying their mothers through the streets, their shabby appearance contrasts most strikingly with the parent's splendid attire. This, it is said, is to preserve them from the blighting effects of the admiration which, if well-dressed, their beauty might excite; and it is not a little curious that we should thus find the same strange superstition of the *evil* eye in the most remote and dissimilar countries, where intercommunication would seem to have been impossible. (B:MCJ)

And, fourth, assuming "half-naked" (*meos nus*) in Portuguese includes the figurative nuance it does in English, we should note that the Japanese by and large *did* let their little children run wild – except, as we have already seen, they were wild in moderation, encouraged to make their own little worlds, not modeled, thank goodness, on "our" *Lord of the Flies* model. Bird was impressed:

> I admire the way in which children are taught to be independent in their amusements. Part of the home education is the learning of the rules of the different games, which are absolute, and when there is a doubt, instead of a quarrelsome suspension of the game, the fiat of the senior child decides the matter. They play by themselves, and don't bother adults at every turn. (B:__?)

Even W.C. Fields might have appreciated such children! Moreover, they were allowed to play for a long time. Caron wrote that "None go to school under seven or eight years of age, as being until then incapable of its rules, and more inclined to play than to learn, unless it be waggishness and wantonness." In Europe, I suspect that children of the nobility, even if they were treated ever so sweetly as Frois describes, were generally tutored from a much earlier age.

> John Evelyn, writing on the death of his five-year-old son, said: 'So insatiable were his Desires of Knowledge, that upon a Time hearing one discourse of Terence and Plautus, and being told (upon his inquiry concerning these Authors) that the Books were too difficult for him, he wept for very Grief, and would hardly be pacified.'(Oliver Dick, intro. to AUBREY'S BRIEF LIVES)

Japan, on the other hand, was the original Montessori. In the mid-19th century Alcock wrote "I should say the children of Japan have a merit the tendency of modern education is to deprive ours of at home, namely, they are natural children . . ." (A:COT). At the end of the century, Mrs. Frazer wrote "Here, children are always welcome; they come and go as they like, are spoilt, if love means spoiling, by mother and father, relations and servants; but they grow imperceptibly in the right shape . . ." Today, when Japanese are liable to be identified with *artificial,* this type of observation is good to read. The late twentieth century obsession in Japan with starting schooling early so children can pass an exam for an elite nursery school so they can pass an exam for an elite kindergarten and so forth, all the way up to the university guaranteed to make them part of the power elite – all this is very new; only the patience and determination which the "education-mothers" (*kyoiku-mama*) bring to the task might be considered traditional. (I have pointed out the fact these mothers bear no small resemblance to Jewish-American mothers. Both can successfully push their children in their studies precisely because they *also* treat them with respect, and appear to – but actually do not – spoil them. (J/G:NRT))

So what exactly was it that Frois thought European children had and Japanese did not? The single Portuguese word *mimos* translates as "dainty, delicacy, gift, caress, petting" (DEIPPI) "dainty gifts," (SPED),. The *branduras* translates as "softness, gentleness" (DEIPPI) "endearments, loving words" (*carinhosas*) and "tender words" (*palavras meigas*) (my trans. from NDA). I added nouns and adjectives but still doubt the translation covers it. [not all dict. acronyms are in biblio – i promise they're real]

I believe one thing Frois had in mind was the type of thing I have overheard in Miami: Latin American mothers pouring loving words over their children as one might pour free syrup over pancakes. I do not know if I have ever heard it reproduced and I have a very poor aural memory. Suffice it to say that Anglos only talk that way to their lap-dogs or pampered cats. In the last two decades of the twentieth century, Usanian parents have started to feel like they must constantly tell their children "I love you," so they majority of Anglo- and African-Americans can now get an idea of where Frois's "our" comes from, but I believe they are still midway between the Japanese who do not feel a need to say the obvious and the Latins who take it for granted that words are for endearment. This is not just about children. A Faux Frois:

> We like to tell others we love them and think it a proper thing.
> Japanese think love needs no words and if it does it is not love.

As far as physical caresses go, Japanese will walk a child by the hand, *for it serves a practical use,* but they are just not into touching for touching's sake: hugging, stroking and patting. (see 14-30) Is it possible that Japanese stored up a life-time worth of contact in the first several years when they spend all their time riding on someone and enjoyed enough contact in later childhood by continuing to sleep with siblings and parents, not to mention touching in the baths, when different generations soaped one another (though this might be a post-Frois development) that they did not need such reassuring contact? Or, is it, rather, that our violence – the need to make up for whipping, emotional outbursts and other not so obvious selfish behavior that create resentment, etc. – is what necessitates so much making-up? [2]

As far as the gifts and treats go, there was no tradition of birthdays and, obviously, Christmas presents (assuming we gave such presents both back then) in Japan,. Officially speaking, there were only gifts of money and new clothing every New Year. Moreover, the lack of close ties with relatives (2-36, 3-20) drastically reduced the potential number of present-givers. Don't get me wrong. Gifts were plentiful in Japan, but they were of the type cultural anthropologists so like to study, they were between adults and confirmed the nature of their social relationships.

But it is misleading to put Japanese children entirely on the side of the have-nots, as in this contrast, without explaining where little Japanese children enjoyed blessings their counterparts in Europe did not. *Faux Frois:*

Among us, festivals and places of entertainment outside the house always serve adults.
In Japan, there are festivals just for children and many fun places just for serving them.

By festivals, I first mean what Lowell called "the great impersonal anniversaries of the third day of the third moon and the fifth day of the fifth moon" or, as they are usually called today: Girl's Day" and "Boy's Day." In Frois's time, they would have been called Doll-festival (*Hinamatsuri*) and Carp-banner (*Koinobori*), respectively. On 3/3 and 5/5, respectively:

> The great fire-proof storehouse gives forth its treasures of dolls; – in an old family, many of them hundreds of years old; – and for three days, with all their belongings of tiny furnishings in silver, lacquer and porcelain, they reign supreme, arranged on red-covered shelves in the finest room of the house. (L:SOE)

> Tokio is suddenly transformed into eighty square miles of aquarium." (L:SOE)

But, we must grant that neither of these aesthetically pleasing festivals provide much entertainment for children. Such fun is found in the Shrine visit on these days and both shrine and temple visits on many other holidays when collections of booths selling things or offering fun challenges for children set up on the street near the shrine or temple, or even within their grounds. (Even today this is so common, you cannot go two weeks without seeing a miniature children's fair somewhere in the neighborhood, and that despite competition from Toys-R-us and television.) Moreover, there were, at least in Edo – perhaps not yet in Frois's time – innumerable individual venders of services and toys catering to children. Everything from soap bubbles – the soap *shabon,* coming from the Portuguese *jabon* – to tiny kinetic toys, such as those Japan would become famous for in the Twentieth century, were available, and cheap. The most common booth today – or at least the most memorable *to me* – is the booth where children use paper-strung spatulas to catch (and take home) goldfish. It is pretty tricky business catching a fish before the wet paper breaks, but the seller always gives the smaller children a hand when necessary, so that everyone gets something. Morse, in 1877, describes *his* favorite, a booth where an old man had a stove and batter that he would

> sell by the cupful and provide a little tin spoon and they were allowed to spread it out a little at a time on the stove, cook it, and then, scrapping it off, eat it, or give it to their little friends, or feed the baby perched up behind. One who recalls the delight of getting into the kitchen and scrapping dough out of some vessel in which gingerbread had been made . . . The old man's booth was portable; he could fold up his huge umbrella and pack the other things compactly and move to another place. This might be introduced into our cities in regions where children swarm, and with this hint some poor man or woman may do it. [P] There was another booth where children could peep through openings and see pictures of some kind, which were being described by an old man. Again I must repeat that Japan is paradise for children. (M:JDD)

Nineteenth century visitors were impressed at the existence of this adorable children's world, which, more than anything else, inspired Lafcadio Hearn to describe Japan as a sort of *fairyland*. The question, again, is whether, the long isolation created it or whether it was already there, but for some strange reason, failed to impress the Jesuits. Bird makes it clear that it is not just things, either, but the way people acted:

> I never saw people take so much delight in their offspring, carrying them about, or holding their hands in walking, watching and entering into their games, supplying them constantly with new toys, taking them to picnics and festivals, never being content without them, and treating other people's children also with a suitable measure of affection and attention. (B:UTJ)

Still, this does not necessarily contradict Frois's contrast, for when children became old enough to know what's what, the discipline – what we might consider *deprivation* – mentioned by Okada and Spartan training described by Nitobe in BUSHIDO gradually came to replace the license of the younger child. There was a fall from Paradise. There is no contradiction here, either. The inner strength needed for children to study hard and do without, bearing their burden for the sake of a future dream was gained in those exceptionally pleasant years. The one makes the other possible. What is hard to say is how many Japanese fell how hard from their children's paradise; i.e., what portion of Japan's children were raised by Spartan *buke* (samurai class) standards at any particular era of Japanese history? Many Japanese hold that Japanese, being almost completely a farming people were, with the exception of a tiny percentage of samurai families, raised in a soft, loving egalitarian manner, until forced to copy the West to defend themselves. If so, it happened quite rapidly, for the diaries of the children of Hawaiian immigrants (peasant stock, indentured to work the pineapple and sugar fields) who left Japan before WWII complain that their parents withheld obvious affection, so much so, in fact, that they felt jealous of the more loving Hawaiian and *haole* (white) families [3] and a Canadian survey by La Violette (1945) concludes the same for a larger sample of "Americans of Japanese ancestry," citing a *nisei* [second generation immigrant] informant to the effect that the "age of constraint" (when a child is forced to behave) as beginning at age 8, with considerable variation according to the family at which point, the Japanese way of treating children turns topsy-turvy and –

> It is generally agreed that there is little possibility of discussion in parent-child relations . . . In the Japanese family, there is apparently very little "reasoning" with a child, even after he is fifteen or sixteen years of age. The technique of parental control is essentially that of ordering and forbidding. . . . A traditional mode of punishment is the *moxa* treatment . . . . The *nisei* [object to this painful mode of punishment . . . (L:AJN)

This was only the obvious part of the discipline. Withholding of praise and constant appeals made to a child's sense of responsibility toward the family name and the Japanese reputation were an even heavier cross to bear. Perhaps I am wrong, but I doubt that Japan's opening was traumatic enough to have caused drastic change in parent-child relations in one or even two generations. My guess is that many Japanese commoners (both merchants and farmers) had already adopted the Spartan values of the more prestigious class, to a degree higher than generally recognized, in the Tokugawa era. [4] The extent to which the denial of affection may be called artificial will be discussed later.

1. Treated to Moderation. What a coincidence! The day I proofed this page with my quip about the automatic benefits of poverty (which, I myself am now being treated to), I read the following exchange (?) in the 16th c Iberian novel, *The Life of Lazarillo de Tormes* (see biblio =T(M):LLT). After the cheap Squire who was not sharing food with Lazarillo pontificates "You'll live longer and keep your health better," . . ."Because, as we were saying, there's nothing in all the world like eating little to make you live long." this:

> "If that's the way of it," I said to myself, "I'll live forever, because I've kept that rule religiously, and for that matter I expect I'll have the bad luck to keep it all my life."

2. On Touching Yes, I have read the book of this title by A.M. but the proven importance of touch to infants does not translate into unqualified support for more touching as natural=good for adulthood. One can no more argue that lots of skin contact is good than one can that lots of eye contact is good.

3. *Hawaiian Studies.* I read all the diaries I could when I was at the University of Hawaii in 1977. The character of the Japanese described was not at all like what a Japanese teacher of mine claimed it was.

4. *Spartan Values.* Because of continual controversy about the nature of Japanese culture, in particular, the extent to which it was militaristic, one finds most that is written on this subject utterly worthless.

3-16   European parents deal directly with their sons/children;
Ois pais em Europa tratão os negocios inmediatamente com seus filhos;

In Japan, everything is done through messages and intermediaries.
Em Japão tudo hé por recados e por terceira pessoa.

"Our" side here seems too natural to require explanation. Valignano wrote at length about the Japanese side. After a paragraph on how prudent and discreet they are in their dealings with others, and how they never mention their troubles, he writes

> For this reason (and also in order not to become heated in their dealings with others), they observe a general custom in Japan of not transacting any important or difficult business face to face with another person, but instead they do it all through messages or a third person. This method is so much in vogue that it is used between fathers and their children, masters and servants, and even between husbands and wives, for they maintain it is only prudent to conduct through a third person such matters which may give rise to anger, objection or quarrels. As a result, they live in such peace and quietness . . . (1583? in C:TCJ)

The quote picks up, in my translation (note 3-7), where Valignano credits this domestic calm with producing nonviolent boys. Okada writes: "With *bushi,* it was normal for even parents and children to kept a strict distance as if they were strangers." Again, I am not certain it was only a samurai thing. There are regional variations but, to a degree, may have been true for all Japanese. The *bushi* only intensified and formalized the tendency. Japanese have probably never leveled with each other except when they exploded with anger, which, thank goodness, was and is seldom. Even face-to-face talk was – and still is – generally not eye-to-eye, but down, off to the side, or past one another. Swords or no swords, they dislike confrontation. (My personal feeling is that a syntax which weights pronouns in the manner of Japanese will either have speakers who argue ferociously, like Koreans (who share that syntax) – or no argument. No matter how many first and second-person pronouns are devised to soften things up, argument in these languages cannot help coming across *ad hominine* because those pronouns are intrinsically all-or-nothing affairs.[2]

Reading Valignano, we can see how this contrast lends itself to two contradictory interpretations. On the one hand, it might seem to serve as an example of how the consensus-loving close-knit Japanese avoid the pitfalls of the "confrontation culture" of the West. But, on the other hand, it might show that the Japanese are the more atomistic culture, as family members grow up so estranged from one another that they must rely on a third party. One modern playwright, Betsuyaku Minoru, apparently saw the humor of this. The very first *dogu* (tool/device/dojigger)In DOGU-ZUKUSHI (*a compleate book of doojiggers* 1984) was the *oitokesama,* a wooden manikin that could be set down by a party of two in order to help them in the absence of an actual third party, found in the isolated Tohoku (Northeast) region.

> Now, it no longer exists, but the way it was once used is that the *oitokesama* was set down in front, and the two sat side by side facing it, and told it everything that they wanted to tell to each other. In this way, everything said to the *oitokesama* was communicated to the other party and it was possible to have a conversation or dialogue, with no "meeting of eyes or shyness" coming between.

Betsuyaku's *dogu* is one of those things about which the Italians say *se non e vero e ben trovato.* Be that as it may – and I write no more (he has four pages on it) for I may try to translate that book some day, and don't wish to give too much away – the *oitokesama* is a fine sort of metaphysical proof of the accuracy of Valignano and Frois's contrast. There is, however, one thing still missing in my explanation, the matter of *inequality* and how it is treated. All of the examples given by Valignano involve unequal parties. The deeply Confucian samurai class expected the *inferior* to take great care in what they said to their *superior.* A son could no more remonstrate with a father than a servant could a master. As Rodrigues explains in his *Treatise on Epistolary Style*, a son could not even address his father directly *in a letter.* He was supposed to do what all vassals did, write him through the auspices of a third party using a level of honorifics suitable for the third party, rather than the father, and the clear (unambiguous) style proper to a "heraldic letter (hirôjô) (R(L):TES). While the father could theoretically skip the intermediary, he usually replied through the same so as not to impose himself on his children.

1. *Filhos Translation:* The French who had "sons" (*garçons*) for 3-7 have "children" (*enfants*) here, whereas Father Schütte, who had "children" (*kinder*) for 3-7 has "sons" (Söhnen) here! Here, it is hard to say whether to translate *filhos,* "sons" or "children." Both Japanese translators make both "son" (*musuko*), but Cooper's translation of Valignano on the same subject turns the Spanish equivalent *hijos* into "children." DR+H favor "children," too. So it is a tie.

2. *All-or-Nothing Pronouns.* I fear that only a thorough explanation of the pronoun dilemma in Japanese stands a chance of being comprehensible. Readers with interest in socio-, psycho, or philosophical linguistics might see Chapter 2 of my *Orientalism & Occidentalism.*

3-17   We take godparents with baptism or confirmation;[1]
Antre nós no baptismo ou crisma se tomão padrinhos;

> In Japan, one is chosen when a youth gets to wear a sword anew and takes a new name. *Em Japão quando o moço singe de novo espada e muda o nome então o toma.*

Baptism is in some ways analogous to purification rites, [2] but includes elements of renunciation, manumission, initiation and adoption. The 1911 Encyclopedia believes the heart of baptism as a concept came from the procedure of *Emancipatio,* a Roman law for freeing slaves from masters and sons from fathers, or *patria potestas*, who had the legal right of death or life over them.

> Like the legal ceremony, baptism freed the believer from one (Satan) who, by the mere fact of the believer's birth, had power of death over him. And as the legal manumission dissolved a son's previous agnatic relationships, so, too, the person baptized gave up father and mother, &c., and became one of a society of brethren the bond between whom was not physical but spiritual. The idea of adoption in baptism as a son and heir of God was almost certainly taken by Paul from Roman law. (found online at "LoveToKnow" Corp)

Iberian children were generally baptized at birth and the godfather and godmother were supposed to be "firm believers, able and ready to help the newly baptized – child or adult – on the road of Christian life" (as catechism #1255). Confirmation was a later ceremony, which generally took place at "the age of discretion" which was seven or eight in Iberia but at the age of fifteen or sixteen in England where a mature adult decision was desired. At this time, the god-parents could be reconfirmed as sponsors or another party could.

The Japanese side of the contrast describes a secular coming-of-age ceremony, *genbuku,* which is delightfully Englished by Kenkyûsha's Japanese-English dictionary as "assuming the *toga virilis.*" In this ceremony, held when a (samurai class) boy was 12-16, he acquired a valuable sword, adopted an adult style hair-do, over which a "crow-hat-parent," put a "crow-hat" (a tall black phallic-looking thing), and dropped his milk-name for a new one, which usually included a character taken from a posthumous family name (a Buddhist name acquired by any ancestor at death), the name of the crow-hat-parent or a nobleman (presumably related in some way). Rodrigues's description of the ceremony provides an interesting detail:

..

> The sponsor asks his godson the name he wishes to take, and if he leaves the choice to the sponsor, he writes down three names on paper, and the godson then chooses from them the one he most likes and the sponsor gives his approval. Or else the godson produces a name which he wants or which is common in his family, and the sponsor confirms it as if he had given it to him, and he calls him by this name. (R(C):TIJ)

Perhaps the reader has noted how our basic vocabulary forces the use of Christian terms where they do not really belong. Frois avoids calling a Japanese crow-hat-parent a "godparent" or "godfather" but must imply it with his pronoun, and Rodrigues uses "godson" in Cooper's doubtless accurate translation. Rodrigues suggests another *Faux Frois*:

Among Europeans, others always choose our names;
Japanese are perfectly free to name themselves.

Have young Europeans ever been offered a choice? Allowed to help chose their own name? If it were the other way around, would it become yet more proof of supposedly special Occidental individualism?

Today, there is nothing like the *genbuku* in Japan. Then, again, *genbuku* for most Japanese never was like it was described above. The masses knew nothing of those fancy *crow-hats*. They were more likely to simply shave off the hair in front in the adult style or in earthier parts, to celebrate the wearing of a *loincloth* (*fundoshi-iwai* and *heko-iwai*). In fact, we even had *loincloth-parents* (*heko-oya)* and *loincloth* sons (*hekomusuko*)! Sometimes, the loincloth celebration occurred early on (at 7 in Nagano) and sometimes late (15 in Kagoshima). I like to imagine both parents for both parts of dress and both a high name and a low name, but enough fantasy. Nowadays, Japanese do not have such ceremonies. Their names, like ours are generally fixed at birth. Young men and women who turn twenty within the year enjoying a common coming of adulthood celebration on the 15th Day of the New Year when the young men more often than not wear Western suits while the women almost without exception wear kimonos, which are often rented at astronomical prices. It is fun watching them flock to the proper venue for auspicious ceremony, Shinto Shrines, stadiums, etc.. using public transportation rather than isolated in cars as in Usania. I do not know exactly what they do, but they do not get new names.

1. *Confirmation=Chrism?*   The original has *crism.* Chrism, as it is written in English, is an unguent of Biblical pedigree. What baptism is to water, it is to oil, olive oil, of course, and we may readily guess what kind and it must also contain some balsam (an aromatic resin) of a kind sanctioned by the usage of the church and be blessed by a bishop, or at least by a priest delegated by the Holy See – its sanctification requires an incredibly complex ceremony involving many people and taking place on a Thursday – and that blessing must be a special kind for chrism only. Why olive-oil and balsam? Because olive oil, "being of its own nature rich, diffusive, and abiding, is fitted to represent the copious outpouring of sacramental grace, while balsam, which gives forth most agreeable and fragrant odours, typifies the innate sweetness of Christian virtue. Oil also gives strength and suppleness to the limbs, while balsam preserves from corruption." (PATRICK MORRISROE Transcribed by Dorothy Moloney The Catholic Encyclopedia, Volume III Copyright © 1908 by Robert Appleton Company Online Edition Copyright © 2003 by K. Knight) . This chrism is used to administer baptism, confirmation, and holy orders as well as the consecration of churches, chalices, patens, altars, and altar-stones, and in the solemn blessing of bells and baptismal water. One meaning of the word *crism* in Portuguese is the rite of Confirmation and the context suggests it is correct for Frois's contrast.

2. *Purification Rites* English lacks sufficient terms such rites. Purification for entering some sacred site or participating in a ritual is not the same as purification in the sense of ridding oneself of bad luck or sickness, but exorcism is too strong.

3. *Baptism.* Most readers may, like me, know as little about Christian ritual as Buddhist ritual. So a word more about baptism. Here is Tertullian on the meaning of baptism in the second century.

1. The flesh is washed, that the soul may be freed from stain.
2. The flesh is anointed, that the soul may be consecrated. 3. The flesh is sealed (i.e. signed with the cross), that the soul also may be protected.
4. The flesh is overshadowed with imposition of hands, that the soul also may be illuminated by the Spirit.
5. The flesh feeds on the body and blood of Christ, that the soul also may be filled and sated with God.

(© 2002-2003 by LoveToKnow, Corp. 1911 encyclopedia) It also bears noting that

"adult baptism was a capital offense in sixteenth-century Europe because it threatened the marriage of civil and religious authority that had developed over the centuries. Infant baptism conferred membership into both Catholic and Protestant churches. It also granted automatic citizenship, which gave civil authorities the power to tax and conscript ..." (Ibid)

Christianity was heavy stuff back then, as Islam, in some parts, still is today.

3-18   With us, children accompany their mothers when they go out;
Antre nós os filhos vão acompanhando as mães quando vão fora;

In Japan, children rarely or never (when they are full grown) accompany them.
Em Japão raramente ou nunqa (como são grandes)as acompanhão.

We have a translation problem to address first. Father Schütte has *sons* accompany the mother *when she goes out*, the French translators have *children* doing the same, while Okada conversely has the *mother accompanying when sons goes out* and Matsuda+Jorissen, escalates that interpretation so we have s*ons, when they go out, having their mother accompany them*. I would have waffled if I could have but, I fear my English was not up to it, and I ended up going along with the Europeans, i.e. reading the contrast as an extension of the idea broached in some other contrasts in this chapter, namely, in Japan, children and their relations are not very close, rather than it being an issue of freedom.

Whichever it may be, there is something misleading about stressing the independence of Japanese children and their mothers. Valignano, who had mentioned the Spartan upbringing of boys, how they were inured to the elements "going about without hats in the winter as well as summer, wearing clothing open to the cold" – two decades later, rectified, or rather *balanced* the picture, writing, "in contradiction to Maffei" (who translated him!), that boys were not separated from their mothers and nurses at a tender age, but "raised at home with much *nobleza* and *servicio,"* that "they suffer in their time great incommodation" to be turned into soldiers. (LIBRO PRIMERO) Alvarez-Taladriz introduces many items showing Japanese children were, "in reality, *muy enmadrados,"* (note 92 to V(A):S&A) that is to say *mother's boys*. "We see them in church, taking the hand, at the breast, or on the back of their mothers, " he writes, citing Frois's HISTORIA among others. The weaning was then, like now – or, until very recently – far later than in Europe. Almeida in 1561 wrote of children who could talk still nursing while being taught catechism. Bacon provides a simple explanation for this long nursing that is interesting for the light it sheds on the relationship between our diet and our lifestyle:

> Born into a country where cow's milk is never used, the Japanese baby is wholly dependent upon its mother for milk, and is not weaned entirely until it reaches the age of three or four years, [1] and is able to live on the ordinary food of the class to which it belongs. (B:JGW)

Seen this way, a cow is a mixed blessing, for it comes between a baby and its mother. One might find a cultural pattern, a difference in psychology, dividing those that hasten weaning by using another animal's milk (the goat and mare are also possibilities) and those that stick to human milk. And, if mother's milk, has a more natural opiates than cow milk, then, this difference, too, might help explain why Far Eastern babies are, by and large, more docile. On the other hand, cow milk was probably not broadly drunken before Pasteurization. If there was a diet gap, it was more subtle.
..

> In the sixteenth century supplemental foods were generally introduced between seven and nine months. Though medical writers recommended breastfeeding for two years, most German and Italian mothers had stopped by the thirteenth month and most English mothers by the eighteenth month. (Weaning as a Natural Process by Brylin Highton Dunedin, New Zealand From: LEAVEN, Vol. 36 No. 6, December 2000-January 2001, p.112-114 (found at www.lalecheleague.org/llleaderweb/ LV/LVDec00Jan01p112))

With an abundance of pudding-like foods and love for slim women, the Iberian nursing period was probably even shorter than the German and Italian one. Maybe it is ridiculous to correlate the length of the nursing period and the degree to which mothers and children stick together, but why not throw out one more wild guess? Could the longer nursing period create gentler, more trustworthy children and satisfy mothers so that separation could more naturally occur?

1. *Three-year Nursing.* Indirect and interesting proof that three years was the standard length for nursing comes from Kumano no Honji (the Deities of Kumono) a "staggeringly popular late medieval [pre-Frois] and kinsei [post-Frois] tale" about an ancient Indian king with 1000 wives of whom one favored by the king was executed at the behest of the other 999. Swords break on Gosuiden's neck and she, seven months pregnant, insists she must give birth first. She called on Buddha etc and succeeded after which her head was cut off. Her limbs slowly discomposed but "her breasts remain warm and golden to feed the baby for three years until he is found by a local holy man who raises him." (G:CMM)

There it is, *three years.* I also like to contrast this to the bodies of "our" female saints that remain fresh in their graves, but to no purpose other than to prove they were saints (Perhaps, I am being unfair, for the relics were used for healing).

3-19   With us, our names don't change after confirmation;
Antre nós não se muda o nome depois da crisma;

In Japan, the name changes five or six times in a lifetime.
Em Japão pollo discurso da ydade se muda sinco ou seis vezes.

François Caron wrote that all men had "three names, the children a childish, when they are men a more manly, and becoming old get others suitable to the decays of nature and old age." He might better have put it "at least" three names, or three basic names, for there were any number of possibilities. One is reminded of the "heathen chinee" in Ripley's (*"Believe It or Not"*) who "does not receive a permanent name until he is dead."[1] Some names changed serially, with better names reflecting higher status replacing previous ones, whereas others were more in the line of pen names or paint names (for artists did it, too), which could be used concurrently to one's other name. One can imagine that a peasant who stays on the farm would have three names at most, while a samurai or a merchant enjoying many changes of status in a lifetime would have more. The encyclopedic Joao Rodrigues found ten categories of names, some given, and some taken. It is a bit of an exaggeration to say with Arthur Hatch (like Caron, quoted in C:TCJ) that "everyone as hee pleaseth may make choyse of his owne name." If "they are commonly named either by the King, or else by some Noble or Greatman with whom they are chiefley in favour," (Hatch) which is to say, the name served as a sort of title, people could not have been completely free to claim names they had no title too. We may also wonder just when official names ended and nicknames began. Here, from the diary of the head of the English Factory in Japan:

February 14. – Sinze, our barkman, brought me a present of a *barso* wyne and 2 fyshes, desyring me to chang his name, according to order of Japon, which is held a greate honer amongst them. So the China Capt. sayid it was good to call hym Sinemon Dono. (1617) [For Cinnamon!?]

Frois's "five or six" might be a good guestimate of the average number of names per lifetime, but such details do not matter. It is far more significant that Frois failed to list a contrast so obvious he must have *imagined* he already wrote it down when, in fact, he did not! To wit:

We speak or write our Christian names before our family names;
They always put their family names before their given ones.

Caron, did not miss this and even included an explanation as to why "they" do it that way.

"The surnames are first pronounced, for being their parents were before them, they think it but reasonable that their names should likewise precede. (C:MKJS)

Actually, this is the only logical way to make a name, for the same reason the Sino-Japanese system of address (country-state-city-street-number-name) and dating (era-year-month-day) is superior to our system. Ours is the one in need of an explanation.

1. *Posthumous Names* Even today, the last name is a Buddhist one, good for the repose of the soul, suitable for the worth of the deceased and, not uncommonly, influenced by the amount of money donated to the temple! Presumably a good posthumous name would be of use for the prayers of salvation and theoretically, the names had great value, for deathdays were generally recalled rather than birthdays, but in reality these names usually end up pure trivia, which is to say they are not remembered.

3-20   With us, children often visit their relatives' houses and are close to them;
Antre nós os meninos vão muitas vezes a caza dos parentes e lhes são familiares;

In Japan, they rarely go to their houses, and treat them like strangers.
Em Japão hé raro yrem a suas cazas e os tratão como estranhos.

As explained in 2-36, the Japanese have stood at the opposite end of the spectrum from Latin culture with its extended families. The lack of a close relationship between relatives must have made Japanese seem like cold fish to visiting Iberians. I can also imagine that the difficulties finding Godparents (something for which relatives were favored) for Japanese Christians made Jesuits *practically* all-too-aware of this difference.

3-21   In Europe, children inherit on the death of their parents;
Em Europa os filhos herdão por morte dos pais;

In Japan, parents retire from life very early to surrender their fortune to their children. *Em Japão os pais se dezerdão muito cedo em vida pera emtregar a eransa aos filhos.*

This can be interpreted in two contrary ways. One is that wealthy parents in Japan, unlike in the West, do not selfishly (and, often, with disastrous consequences when they begin to lose their judgment) hold on to the family fortune and power as long as they can, but share it early enough to improve the lives of their loved ones, and probably improve the family business. That is to say, the parent gives *more* by giving it *earlier*. Even Feudal Lords and Shoguns tended to give up their official position as ruler to their sons [1] where an Occidental ruler would hold out until the end (*"The King/Queen is dead! Long live the King/Queen!"*). However, it is *also* possible to say that by handing over the business and retiring, the Japanese parents are selfishly getting out of work and onto the dole while they still are well enough to really enjoy themselves. Either way, the Japanese side of the contrast comes off best. So why haven't we done the same? Bacon, who seems to take the latter interpretation, gives a plausible reason.

The feeling, so strong in America, that dependence is of itself irksome and a thing to be dreaded, is altogether strange to the Japanese mind. The married son does not care to take his wife to a new and independent home of his own, and to support her and her children by his own labor or on his own income, but he takes her to his father's house, and thinks it no shame that his family live upon his parents. But in return, when the parents wish to retire from active life, the son takes upon himself ungrudgingly the burden of their support, and the bread of dependence is never bitter to the parents' lip, for it is given freely. To the time-honored European belief that a young man must be independent and enterprising in early life in order to lay by for old age, the Japanese will answer that children in Japan are taught to love their parents rather than ease and luxury, and that care for the future is not the necessity that it is in Europe and America . . . A Japanese considers his provision for the future made when he has brought up and educated for usefulness a large family of children. He invests his capital in their support and education, secure of bountiful returns in their gratitude and care for his old age. (B:JGW)

In other words, Americans (and most Western ethnic groups) push their children into being independent all too successfully. Excluding the stereotypical Jewish-American, we are all *A Boy Named Sue*, [2] forced not by our names but by our ideology of standing alone to forego a more efficient and loving lifestyle.

I am not sure how this contrast holds up today. I would guess that Japanese give more to their children and vice versa. But, turning over the family fortune and retiring are, in most cases, no longer related. Japanese are notoriously *poor* at retiring. They don't enjoy it at all. Like many Western men, and increasingly women, work is their everything. This probably was not true in pre-modern times when retirement was a quasi-religious experience, a retreat from the driven world of work into a free world of leisure. I believe the great joy of writing provided by the bottomless well of Chinese characters and the physical pleasure of the brushed letter played a major role in this. Big strokes of jet-black ink on white. Though your eyes dim so you can barely read, *by God you can still write!* (You can still write though you cannot read: *the circle closes*) And pilgrimages from temple to temple in a narrow land made for easy foot-travel.   And the game of *go* (see 14-39), far more enjoyable than chess. Anyone with half a brain never tires of it.   And raising – or, rather, training – Chrysanthemum and *bonsai.* Participating in the local festival committees. In my opinion, Japanese had far more fulfilling, truly stimulating leisure activities than we in the West. I say *had* because the mid-20th century was such a trying time that most Japanese had no time to learn *go.*

1. *Giving Up Power* In his *Historia* Frois writes about Hideyoshi handing over his official position to a son who is, however, too young to really exercise it. Here is a ruler who was hungrier for power and world domination than any in Japanese history.   Though sacred, Emperors, too, often retired. Compare this too our Popes!

2. *A Boy Named Sue.* A country music song, which also climbed to number one on the pop-charts where a boy named "Sue" grows up vowing to take vengeance on the no good SOB who named him, but meeting his father and beating him up pauses before the *coup de grâce* to hear his side of the story, which was that the father knowing he was a bum who would soon leave, wanted his son to grow up tough so he could fend fore himself and thought naming him Sue would do the trick, so Sue and his Dad hug and make up. Sung by Johnny Cash, but judging from the style, maybe Shel Silverstein lyrics?

3-22   For the health of our children, we scarify them and let their blood;
Pera a saude das nossas crianças os sarrafão e lhe tirão sangue;

In Japan, blood is not drawn, rather, they are treated with clumps of fire.
Em Japão [se] lhe não tira, a[ntes] os qurão com botõis de fogo.

Frois does not use the same term for blood-letting as he does in 9-2 when contrasting types of medical treatment. This *sarrafão (sarrafam)* "scarify," sounds scary! We are reminded of painful rituals to decorate the skin. But, actually, it is a "mild" method of bleeding (unless scarification also was used for immunization for smallpox (I haven't heard of it at this early date, but . . .)) by making many small puncture wounds – in the seventeenth and eighteenth century spring-loaded devices came to be used – which, with the aid of cupping glasses and syringes took the place of, or supplemented, the more radical venesection. [1] Bleeding, as elaborated in chapter 9, served both to balance over-all body humours (a practice compatible with Chinese medicine) and to treat local disorders. Since "we" were used to blood, such treatment would not have seemed as horrible as "their" burning.

The Sinosphere preferred burning to blood-letting. It was not because it hurt less. Moxibustion, or treatment by burning a pinch of *moxa* (made from mugwort leaf: see 9-2) set upon the skin is not pleasant. It was just that they did not care for blood. In some ways the two practices were quite similar. *Moxa,* too, was used to treat specific illnesses (hence Frois's "treated/cured"), as well as to build immunity. According to Okada, in Japan, a pellet of moxa was ritually burnt on top of the three-day-old infant's head and, in some parts of Japan, on the navel with a the aim of preventing future sickness (Perhaps this explains why Japanese children came to be so afraid of the thunder gods stealing their exposed navels, presumably by zapping them with lightning!) There was also an annual moxa-treatment ritual, that functioned as booster shots on top of this basic "vaccination." Children in Japan didn't like it anymore than we like shots. Although it took place in the coldest part of the year – early spring – Issa's haiku records a naked child fleeing from his "medicine." In contradiction of 3-7 above, it bears noting that even if children were not whipped, they sometimes were threatened with corporal punishment and, as mentioned in n3-15, the mode was . . . you guessed it, none other than moxa-treatment!

1. *Scarification.* Now, I know exactly what my mother's cat (a big Russian Grey who was abandoned or fled shortly after he had been spaded and grew very sharp nails to better defend himself next time) does to me every time I play with it. I am being *scarified* by my feline phlebotomist.

~~~~~~

3-23　　With us, only women use paint [1] and powder;
Antre nós as molheres somente uzão de arrebiqe e alvayade;

> With honorable Japanese, boys up to ten also wear some cosmetics when they go out.
> *Antre os Japões honrados,* [2] *quando os meninos até dez anos vão fora, tambem levão alguns posturas.*

The pre-Christian West boasts the Picts whose name says it all. But, the powder European men were supposed to wear in Frois's day was for their wigs – making them artificial elders? – and such were only worn by men engaged in legal or other administrative functions in some countries.

Male make-up in Japan was pretty much restricted to boys from the samurai class and above. Okada cites a contemporary Chinese report about "barbarian [i.e., Japanese] boys made up with thick powder like women." Most Japanese fashion has Chinese roots and would not have been worth reporting back to China, so the very fact it is mentioned tells us it surprised more than the Europeans.

In the last decade of the 20th century Japanese boys began to use make-up again. One sees many male *tarento* (minor TV personalities that usually last only a few years until the bloom is off their adolescent cheeks) that can only be described as "cute" and "adorable," rather than handsome and manly like "our" muscular "heart-throbs." These cutie-pies (what else can you call them?) take good care of their hairline, partially pluck and darken their eyebrows and, less obviously, use lipstick. In Tokyo, I even saw such eyeliner advertised on television! The object is not to become feminine but to look really good because young women are picky and want perfectly featured young men (most women deny this, but studies have shown they fall for fine features and symmetrical faces.)

1. *Paint Translation:* The "paint" was *arrebiqe* =*arrebique* in the original. It generally meant "makeup," but the second term *alvayade=alvaiade,* which I made "powder" clearly refers to white-lead, so here *arrebiqe* suggests rouge, eye-shadow, etc. (for Frois almost never uses synonyms). To include all the possibilities and include the fact that *Arrebique* in its various forms also means "fripperies," "garishness," "gaudy," "tawdry," "ravishing," and "enchanting," I made it "paint."

2. *Honrados.* The word *honrado* as ambiguous and we must guess the proper translation from what we know about the contrast. Here, samurai families are clearly included, so "noble" will not do.

3-24   With us, youths have sleeves that are narrow and tight about the shoulders;
Antre nós os meninos tem as mangas estreitas e fachadas polos onbros.

Those of Japan are loose and slit across under the arms.
Os de Japão as trazem muito largas, escaladas ao traves por debaxo dos bracos.

Matsuda and Jorissen remonstrate that the young Japanese ambassadors from Japan were "delighted" to find the youth in Ebola (Portugal) wearing clothing with "sleeves so broad as not to differ from those of Japan." Their delight suggests to me, rather, that such sleeves were rare in Europe and that Frois's observation was, on the whole, valid!

Those slits are still found in some traditional Japanese garments. They are generally not seen, and thus, not remarked upon because even in Japan men do not walk around with their arms held up (笑). If Frois could look up men's nostrils (14-47), he could do the same to their underarms. As far as I know, slits were not in anyway associated with *children's* dress; but they are common to informal dress, so it is possible adults in the upper classes, who were always formally dressed, did not wear them, whereas their children did. Perhaps that explains why Frois puts it with children. At least one fashion – informal resort wear called *jinbei* which do not date back to Frois – takes the slit all the way around the arm, using a mesh or little strings to keep the sleeves from falling off. Underarm slits are very cooling in sultry weather and should join sandals as ecological – who-needs-air-conditioning! – "world clothing."

Actually, "we," adult males at any rate, *did* air-condition our European clothing, too. I do not recall seeing slits under arms, but opening slits in clothing was considered to be gallant from early on in the Renaissance to well into the seventeenth century. Alvaro Semedo, who met a 1630 expedition to China (where Joao Rodrigues and company went to help the Emperor defend the capital and gain brownie points for Macao, but that story is beyond our scope) in the provincial city of Nan-ch'ang, observed that –

> the local Chinese nobles were greatly intrigued by the Portuguese costumes, and they "commended and admired all, except the Slashing and pinking of their cloathes, not being able to conceive, why, when a piece of stuffe is whole and new, men should cut it in severall places for ornament." (C:RTI)

I, too, had only thought of this practice as ridiculous, but upon consideration of the function of those underarm slits, it suddenly occurred to me that the European practice was probably long-lived because the foot-soldiers realized it kept them cool. While these men may not have been as uniformly muscular as our anatomy-besotted artists rendered them, they were doubtless more muscular than average and muscles tend to generate heat, especially when used. *Think of it!* A functional necessity justified as a "cool" fashion!

Children

There was one important *possible* child, or rather, *child-rearing* related contrast found in Alcock and Bird, but not in Frois.

> The mothers are not the sole guardians of the infant progeny. It is a very common sight in the streets and shops of Yeddo, to see a little nude Cupid in the arms of a stalwart-looking father, nearly as naked, who walks about with his small burden, evidently handling it with all the gentleness and dexterity of an experienced hand. It does not seem there is any need for a fondling hospital . . . (A:COT)

> Both fathers and mothers take pride in their children. It is most amusing about six every morning to see twelve or fourteen men sitting on a low wall, each with a child under two in his arms, fondling and playing with it, and showing off its intelligence. To judge from appearances, the children form the chief topic at this morning gathering. (B:UTJ)

I would guess from the way he is described, that *the paternal nurse* (as an illustration in Alcock is captioned) struck the 19th century visitor as something *odd*. (Morse shows a large boy with infant on back fishing! (M:JDD)) Alcock's words suggest that widowers in Europe would not be able to care for *their* babies and Bird's "amusing" makes it clear that this sort of thing would not be seen in her England. *Faux Frois.*

> *Among us, it would be laughable to see a grown man caring for a baby;*
> *The Japanese are used to seeing fathers carrying their babies and think little of it.*

While I have yet to see any comments on men and child-care in 16th century Jesuit writing – were Iberian men *also* paternal nurses, in which case it wouldn't be worth noting? – a note to Frois's *HISTORIA* provided by his Japanese translators includes a marvelous example, provided by none other than Shogun Hideyoshi, a commoner by birth and upbringing, who had just unified the country. It was recorded by someone in a Korean Embassy that had visited Hideyoshi months before Valignano was more graciously received. The Korean ambassador complains that instead of proper banquette-style dishes, they had to exchange drinks of *sake* that was murky (Hideyoshi may have preferred this raw, white-colored *sake,* but it was considered inferior to clear *sake*) from earthenware cups, and that they had no time to exchange the proper verbal greetings, much less discuss anything, because

> . . . Hideyoshi suddenly got up and disappeared into the interior [of the castle]. But none of his retainers moved at all. Shortly, a man in plain clothing carrying a baby [Tsurumatsu] came out from the interior and began walking about the great hall. Looking closely we could see it was Hideyoshi . . . Eventually, he called out our country's musicians and had them put on a big show, during which time the infant he held peed on his kimono. . . . Then and there he changed to another kimono. He acted as if no one else was around. It was brazen and shameless behavior. With that banquette, our ambassadors saw their last of Hideyoshi. Hideyoshi gave the Ambassador and Vice-Ambassador 400 silver pieces each and gifts proportionate to their qualifications to the secretaries, translators, and so forth. (J/F:HISTORIA)

Hideyoshi was famous in Japan for being the clown to beat all clowns. He hardly qualifies as a standard example of Japanese male behavior. But, still, as a man of commoner upbringing, I would guess he grew up around men acting like those described by Alcock and Bird hundreds of years later. And, as an eccentric who would behave as he damn well pleased, he brought his peasant behavior right into a banquet.

子   子   子

In the late twentieth century it would seem that things turned upside-down. Many Occidental men – at least, those in countries where women have either been forced to work outside the house, or chosen to spend less time with their children – have become part-time house-husbands, while Japanese men became absentee-fathers who spend only a few minutes per day conversing with their children – which could hardly be otherwise, given their incredibly long work hours. As the customs of decades quickly become traditions, it behooves us to show that things were not always so and need not always remain so. That, I think is why records of child-friendly Japanese fathers mean a lot.

子   子   子

I am sure that there are other child-related contrasts that could be added and welcome (for a later edition) contributions from cultural anthropologists. I know, for example, that Japanese children throw their upper baby teeth under their porches and throw the under baby teeth up over the roof, so the new teeth will grow rapidly in the appropriate direction. Wouldn't it be fun to learn that Europeans threw said teeth in the opposite manner?

IV

OF THE BONZES AND THEIR CUSTOMS

da que toca aos bonzos e a seus custumes

4-1 Our men join religious orders to make penitence and save themselves.
Os homens se metem antre nós em religião pera fazer penitencia e se salvarem;

> The bonzes[1] enter religious orders to live in idleness and luxury and escape work.
> *Os bonzos entrão na religião pera viver em dilícias e descanso e fojir aos trabalhos.*

I am not so sure that Frois's description of "our" side is as complimentary as he may have thought it was. Doing something to save one's own tail, *especially one's eternal tail*, is hardly something to boast about, though the good works performed by Jesuits and others seeking salvation are not to be scoffed at, either. Though many of "our" men joined because they wanted to help others in *this* world and save them in *that* world (though these two altruistic designs occasionally clashed), others, including, heaven forbid, some Jesuits, may have been attracted to the religious life by "the promise of leisure and pleasure, derived from communion with fellow religious [clergy] and, if possible, God himself." (R(R&A&D:HOT)) So, more precisely, what was the idea here? In Dialogue 7 of *De Missione* (1589), Leo=Valignano, a Christian cousin of Miguel, confesses that hearing about pious rich people in Europe was very interesting, because "looking at things from the Japanese standard," he had assumed religion was a refuge for people with no fortune or in a bind, but now he realized that "the situation is completely different in the East and West." The young Ambassador Miguel=Valignano is kind enough to give a reason for the gold-digging in Japan.

> If we investigate the difference between the two [Japan and Europe], first, this is because we Japanese suffer from poverty and material want, so that when people seek religion they . . . try to find a monastery with the most wealth . . . if there were another way [for them] to win a large income, honor, a prestigious position, . . . they would never sit tight within the four walls of a monastery. (J/S:DM)

On the other hand, he added, "the [Jesuit] *padres* were not originally people who had nothing, but men who could enjoy a far easier and comfortable life in Europe than in Japan." In a parenthesis, someone (Japanese often do not use brackets so it is hard to tell if it was in the original or added by the translator) wrote that a large fortune is often given up when entering the Company, but that the Jesuit lifestyle in Europe is not a poor one. Frois and Valignano knew well that what they wrote did not apply to *all* Buddhist sects, least of all to Zen, which shared with the Jesuits the distinction of a largely aristocratic membership.[2] But, it is questionable whether they felt Zen was a *bona fide* religion, seeing that many Zen-Buddhists professed belief in *nothing* (see 4-23, below).

This chapter and the next, also about Buddhism, are the least objective part of the TRATADO. Today, even the most benighted bible-thumper dares not write such harsh things about other religions as Frois and the other Jesuits did. I am not sure if that is to the fundamentalist's credit, either. If you really believe that lack of baptism dooms a soul to Hell, how can you justify *not* engaging in Holy

War against the infidels? I do not for a minute feel people today are kinder or more tolerant than they were in Frois's day. If you accept religious diversity, it is either because you, like me, do not believe in the absolute truth (Truth) of "our" religion – you are not Christian in the way most of "us" once were – or, because you are a coward. Yet, there is a kernel of truth in the Jesuits' criticism of the Buddhists, for corruption in Japanese Buddhism was indeed rampant. The problem is rather that the Jesuits conveniently overlook the equally bad corruption of Christianity in Europe that led to the Reformation and, for that matter, the creation of the Society of Jesus to fight it by example!

1. Bonze. A *bona fide* word in most European languages for Buddhist monks, which is convenient because by using bonze we need not specify monks are "Buddhist." It derives from Japanese.

2. Largely Aristocratic Jesuits. The Jesuit Order was founded by half-dozen young aristocrats who met at the University of Paris. The greatest correspondent, Frois and the greatest interpreter Rodrigues, were conscious of not being one of the well-educated elite. But if you assume that aristocratic means spoiled, read a biography of St Ignatius Loyola, founder of the Order of Jesus.

~~~~~~

4-2   We vow to be clean of soul and chaste of body on joining an order;
          Antre nós se profesa logo[1] limpeza da alma e castidade no corpo;

> Their bonzes [pledge themselves] totally to polluting their interior and all the nefarious sins of the flesh. *Os bonzos toda a sujidade interior e todos os pecados nefandos da carne.*

It is remarkable that Frois does not contrast how "we" *are* and "they" *are* but, rather what the respective parties profess to. This difference, then might partly be one of style, where padres vow to what they would pretend to be, whereas the bonzes tell it straight. Europeans reading reprints of the stories of Boccaccio – my favorite is the tailing – and new ones by Marguerite de Navarre (1559) encounter very different monks (and nuns). While stories prove little, they do suggest that, as DR puts it, "it is one thing to make a vow and another to live up to it." In his masterful *The Civilization of Europe in the Renaissance*, John Hale gives documented instances of what we would call rape and child-molestation by clergy. The former was sentenced to be married and the latter executed. Considering the enormous scandal involving Catholic clergy in the United States at the start of the second Millennium – doubtless, fueled by hysteria but not without basis – has given the following words by John Hale new life:

> There is a remorseless familiarity about what the sources reveal. (H:CER) [2]

But, there is no denial that there was a different attitude toward the body on the part of the Jesuits and the Buddhists. While any number of It is safe to say that no Occidental who wrote about Japan from Marco Polo to the reopening of Japan in the mid-nineteenth century failed to mention the sin that couldn't be mentioned! Even St. Francis Xavier, who thought the world of the Japanese, found this habit of "their priests, whom they call bonzes." (the word derived from the Japanese *bonzo*, low level clergy, the equivalent of monks) beyond redemption:

> These men are so given up to the most abominable kind of lust as to make open profession of it. This plague is indeed so common to all here, men and women alike, that the mere custom of it has taken away all their hatred and horror of the crime . . . . . we find the others listen to us with favor and are well disposed, but the bonzes themselves, when we admonish them to abstain from such filthy lusts, try to turn the edge of what we object to in them by laughter and jokes." (c.1550, H. J. Coleridge trans. C:LLFX)

I wish Xavier had recorded some of the jokes! The "common secular people" were, he wrote "less impure and more obedient to reason" than the bonzes – I assume he means with respect to which hole is natural for sex and which is unnatural. Seriously. When Xavier, with the help of a translator, first preached in the streets of Japan, sodomy was one of the three grave sins he targeted, the other two being, the abandonment of God to worship the Devil through his various idols, i.e., *idolatry*, and the practice of abortion and infanticide, i.e., *killing* (1550 *J/F:Historia* ch3). The Jesuits seemed genuinely puzzled to find so much sodomy in Japan and China both because a people thought particularly quick of reason, as were the Chinese and Japanese, ought to have hated sodomy which was, to use Valignano's words, a "vice so abominable and prejudicial *as reason shows.*" (*... como muestra la razón.*), and because it surprised them that God should *allow* such sinners to prosper so. Fernao Mendes Pinto – himself a Jesuit for a while – wrote "it utterly amazes me to see our Lord's generosity in sharing out the goods of the world among these people [the Chinese]" despite their ungrateful sins "that continually insult Our Lord, whether in their bestial, diabolical idolatry or in the depravity of the sin against nature." (P(L):TMP) Indeed, Frois, in his *History* of the Church in Japan, time and time again gave instances of God stepping in to punish sinners in *this* world.[3] In Goa, where the Iberians ruled, they burnt sodomites, but with no one killing sinners for God in China and Japan, He was expected to do it himself. Even Gaspar da Cruz, a Franciscan clearly against slavery, believed that *Deus* did not let the sinning Chinese entirely off the hook, for in the last chapter of his mid-sixteenth century book on China, he interpreted a disastrous series of earthquakes as "a grievous punishment" that "God was willing to send them" because of the commonness of this "accursed sin of unnatural vice." (C:TCC in B:SCSC) And Valignano explained that this was the reason Japan, despite being highly civilized, was not so affluent as befitted such high promise:

> They say that in ancient times they didn't have this sin in Japan, and so they all lived in much peace under only one king, until a perverse bonze whom they took for a saint and a prophet introduced it among them in the manner that we have seen, after which followed the uprisings, destruction and wars there are in Japan today, which shows that the sword of the Justice of God (Dios) is upon them, castigating this sin, so that the greater part of the men die by the blade and cities and families are leveled and destroyed and all live with continual misery and work. (1583?)

This just-so-story was included in Valignano's description of sodomy as "the first bad quality" of Japanese. As he doesn't mention China as the place the "perverse bonze" (Kôbô-daishi=Kûkai, founder of the esoteric Buddhist sect Shingon (Pure Word) and author of the syllabary-as-poem (10-1 or 10-2) was said to have picked up the habit – older paintings suggests the Japanese hardly needed to import it, but that has no bearing with this story! – it would seem that blaming the Buddhists rather than history was his agenda. Japanese folk history does indeed *credit* Kôbô with introducing the practice – his name actually became a synonym for it! – but the idea that it harmed Japan is Christian invention. Still, this was not merely an academic problem. The Jesuits could not afford to be philosophical about this for they ran training houses in Japan where young men slept. Spence cites a 1580 letter of Valignano's which suggests that one reason for the students were "falling into course and sinful ways" was to "seek consolation" or "force [the Jesuits] to open their eyes ..." was none other than the harsh treatment (see intro part iv, on Cabral) which made them live "such unhappy lives." In other words, he thought they sought each other out of despair. But he had to try to stop it. Seminary rules Valignano helped draw up that same year "stipulated with meticulous care that the students should sleep on tatami mats, separated by little wooden benches, and that a light was to be kept burning all night." (in S:MPMR) I would only add that these students probably slept with their brothers at home and that it was more likely there was some touching and masturbation than honest-to-goodness sodomy, which was, in Japan, generally pederasty, i.e. an unequal relationship (see 3-10).

In West Europe, the Catholics were on the receiving side of the charges. Luther in a 1542 letter to a friend complained about the hellishness of a world where "Sodomites torment our souls and eyes day and night" and, by Sodomites, writes Spence, "Luther made clear ... he meant "Turks, Jews, papists, and cardinals." (S:MPMR) And about a hundred years later, the generally tolerant Englishman Bulwer wrote that "the ancient Sin of Sodomy" was "in *Italy* nothing more common, and not only tolerated, but held convenient, especially for the Clergy, who are the chief Commanders of these *Ganimedes;* concerning the use of whom, a great Cardinall could prophanely say, it was *suave & divinum opus.*" (B:A) Europe was obviously *obsessed* with homosexuality and it would seem that the charge was loosely thrown about.

We covered the Japanese side enough in 3-10; suffice it to say that it was no big deal there!

1. *Se Professa Logo*. The Portuguese *logo* generally means "immediately/promptly."   I wonder if a minor meaning, "exatamente, justamente" (NDA) might not be possible here.   Since *se professa* can also mean "to join a religious order," I am guessing Frois meant that joining a religious order was *tantamount to* or coincided with an avowal of chastity.   If so, however, his grammar leaves something to be desired.

2. *Remorseless Familiarity*   One more item that might have been mentioned with regard to the religion wars in twenty first century America.   The homosexual marriage idea is not new: "While in Rome in 1580, Montaigne was told about the wedding services held for homosexual couples in the church of San Giovanni a Porta Latina, a practice continued until 'eight or nine Portuguese of this fine sect were burnt.'" (H:CER)

3. *Punishment for Sin in This World*. The most *dramatic* example Frois gives in his *Historia* was of how two of three young men who stole the crosses from Christian graves at the instigation of the bonzes got into a fight which ended up through a remarkable chain of circumstance getting all of them killed, showing, to Frois's all-too-evident delight, that the Christian God was one powerful dude. The most *important* example was of how the ruler Hideyoshi, whom Frois had known and liked and held great hope for, was punished by God for his destruction of the church of Nagasaki "in an extremely unjust manner." After quoting *Deus* to the effect that "he who smites you, smites my own eye," (?) and predicting that this was just the leading-edge of the eternal torment Hideyoshi had coming to him, Frois lists four recent punishments: 1) the death of the tyrant's mother which happened too fast for him to get to her bedside and on the same day he gave the orders to destroy the church; 2) the bad portent of having his ship wreck on a reef , leaving him "naked on a rock," and causing his captain to commit suicide; 3) the anguish and blow to his pride of receiving bad news from the Korean campaign, including that of the destruction of the largest Japanese fleet;   4) the inexplicable and ominous failure of the great bell of one of Japan's greatest temples [Miidera] to ring when struck, which portended great change. (ch102 = pt3-32) The last chapter (37) of his missing summary volume is entirely devoted to describing how god punishes those who persecute Christianity in Japan! (This type of thing is standard in Christian histories.)

4-3   We make a vow of poverty before God and flee from worldly riches;
Antre nós se promete a Deus voto de pobreza e se foge das riqezas do mundo;

The bonzes rip off their *dana* [patron/s] and seek to enrich themselves in a thousand ways. *Os bonzos esfolão os dannas* [1] *e buscão mil modos pera enriquicer.*

Frois is unfair to contrast ideal Christians with worldly Buddhists. His contemporary, the Florentine merchant Francesco Carletti gives us the ideal Buddhist. Between a rare description of what can only be local shamanism and another of "those who adore the lord of the heavens and the earth (Shinto), he describes "the one of Pythagoras," i.e. an austere vegetarian Buddhist sect:

They all lead a sterile life, in imitation of the founder, who introduced it [to Japan?] They say of him that he never ate anything but cooked rice, and sometimes raw rice, and that to do greater penitence he always wore an iron chain tight against his flesh, where it had made such a sore that it became putrid, generating and nourishing a quantity of worms. And if one of these worms happened to fall to the ground, he would pick it up lovingly and with charity and put it back in the sore, saying: "Why are you fleeing? Are you perhaps lacking something to eat?" (C(W):MVAW)

Moderns, who, like Carletti, tend to view asceticism as Eastern should not scoff at the Western tradition. Pinto describes, as no one else could, how the Jesuits, in collusion with their countrymen, *used* voluntary poverty to sell their religion. Fr. Xavier *insisted* on walking everywhere, and carrying his own things even though he was very sick. When Pinto and his party went to help him, "He wouldn't accept a ride on anybody's horse, so we had to dismount and walk along with him although he wouldn't hear of that either." When they finally reached their destination, an awaiting carrack, "every gun on the ship fired four rounds from bases, falconets and camels, never mind all the rest," so the King of Bungo, who was nearby, "supposed we had been attacked by a pirate fleet." The Portuguese explained to the messenger sent by the king that they were celebrating the safe arrival of "a priest we considered a saintly man, a man for whom the King of Portugal himself had the greatest respect." This astounded the messenger who confessed –

> Our bonzes have told him that this man isn't a saint at all . . . They say they have seen him at different times talking to demons with whom he has dealings and that he uses sorcery to trick the ignorant and gullible. They also say he is not just poor, but so poor that even the lice crawling all over his body are so sickened that they will not taste his flesh. (P(L):TMP) ch 209)

Fleeing lice!   For once, the West wins the *I-am-more-austere-than-thou* contest. The messenger tells the King that Fr. Francis was far from the beggar they had imagined because "the ship's captain and all the Portuguese traders assured me that if Fr. Francis asked them to give him the ship and all its cargo, they would gladly hand it over to him there and then, with no questions asked." All of this made the high-minded noblemen and king *adore* Francis to the chagrin of the bonzes, who "lost all credibility" with the king, and were fit to "hang themselves."

1. *Danas*   Frois pluralized *danna*, a Japanese Buddhist term which derives from the Sanskrit *dana* meaning alms or charity and meant these things as well as the parish, or local temple which supports the bonze and the head of that temple, or the landlord. Donald Keene uses *donor,* but I think *patron* is the best catch-all translation. During the Edo period the term came to become a common address used when sucking up to a superior (servant to master, wife to husband), a synonym for a wealthy man, an honorific title for another woman's husband used by a woman and probably many other things. (OJD)

~~~~~~

4-4   We vow obedience to our Superior when we join an order;
Antre nós se profesa e faz voto de obedientia ao Superior;

> The bonzes, do what each wants to, obeying their prelate only when their wishes happen to coincide. *Os bonzos cada um faz o que quer e, per accidens, no que lhe vem hà vontade, obedecem ao prelado.*

Again we have a vow, which is to say "our" *ideal,* versus "their" *reality* or, rather, a caricature of reality.   If *Tratado* were intended as a learning aid, Frois's hypothetical students would have chuckled at the phrase about wishes agreeing *by accident.*

While the Japanese predilection for disobedience, for following their own wishes, was legend in that era – and one reason given by Cabral for his authoritarian rule before the Bungo Consultation decided on a different course (intro n. pat iv) – most Buddhism was not quite *that* anarchistic! I can only imagine some radical Zen sect encouraging *that* much freedom or pretending to that much freedom. As Blyth puts it, "Zen has much in common with Panglossism, but this is balanced by *the abuse of Buddha and the Patriarchs.* In Western culture we find this freedom only in the history of the Rationalists, where it has almost always been accompanied by a complete lack of poetry, not to speak of religious feeling." (B:MM, *my italics*) In the Zen, Blyth shows us, students are taught to be contrary. It is part of the catechism. In his postscript to Zen and the Zen Classics (vol. 4, *Mumonkan*), Blyth writes:

> The best thing about Mumon is his speaking ill of everything and everyone. (ibid)

This does not mean the Zen *practice* was really that wild. But it does mean that if Zen bonzes were asked whether they always did what they themselves wanted to do, they would feel obliged to say *"Yes!"* or *"I try to!!"*   This *flaunting of disobedience* and *independence* would have horrified the Jesuits with their Order built upon absolute vows of obedience. But, for the bonzes, doing things out of obedience rather than nature would have been thought demeaning if not sacrilegious. So we may assume that Zen bonzes exaggerated their *badness* as much as the monks of the West exaggerated their *goodness*. Though the contrast in behavior – the real difference – was doubtless far less, I find the contrast between Western religion with its strict (militaristic?) order and more individualistic Eastern religion a welcome contrast to the Orientalist image of obedient Orientals.

Perhaps, I am being too cautious at stopping with Zen. Japanese in general were not so obsessed with vows as "we" were and the superior-inferior relationship was not thought of in terms of giving and obeying orders, but *asking* and *responding*, *leading* and *following,* or *teaching* and *studying*. While superiors in Japan, like their European counterparts, could be abrupt and did not feel obliged to explain themselves, they knew that they could not behave in a way their inferiors thought was unfair if they hoped to retain their loyalty.

4-5   The temporal possessions of a religious order, among us, is held in common;
     Os bens temporais da religião antre nós são comuns;

          The bonzes all have their own property and work for their own gain.
          Os bonzos todos têm suas propriedades e ganhão pera aqirir.

A new member of the Society of Jesus gave up (or gave to the Order) all his possessions upon joining. A Jesuit officially owned *nothing.* Anything they earned went straight to the corporation (or was supposed to). Like not a few nonprofit CEO's today, some Jesuits in Europe were said to live as if they were wealthy, but that is another story . . .   One reason they did not need to keep any possessions was because once they became a Jesuit they were expected to remain one for life.   One would no more think about leaving the Society than one would think of leaving the Family (as in Mafia).

Like other Japanese, monks had their own bowls, chopsticks, tea cups, brushes, ink-stones, clothing, bedding, artwork, books . . . and, we assume, money.   Yes, they were free to leave at any time.

..

4-6   With us, parishioners belong to the entire parish, not to particular clergy;
     Antre nòs os freguezes todos são de huma parroch[i]a e não de clerigos partiqulares;

          The bonzes have them divvied up, and each is fed by those in his own charge.
          Os bonzos os têm repartidos antre si, pera cada hum comer dos que tiver a carrego.

Evidently, the source of support for "our" and "their" clergy/bonzes followed the same pattern as that for possessions in 4-5.

If Frois's "us" means the Jesuits, the first part of the contrast is doubtless true. Policy is policy. But looking at Europe as a whole, and considering the widespread corruption that made the Society of Jesus stand out like a gem in the dirt, a more cynical appraisal might be "With us, the wealth of a parish belongs to the canon of the cathedral; [1] With them, the wealth of the parish is divided among the monks of the temple." In that case, "they" would come out smelling rosy for at least sharing it!

I do not know exactly how large temple finances worked in Japan. Some of the income, such as that for the upkeep of the temple, was surely collective. People who visit the temples did not leave any money with individual bonzes but threw money into collection boxes called *waniguchi* (crocodile/alligator-mouths). Issa's poetry mentions temples bringing in cherry trees to draw people and make more money in the Spring. But, Frois has a point. Bonzes did wander out from the temples to make their living. The territoriality of the bonzes – at least, young bonzes and begging bonzes who went door to door gathering alms (and sniffing out potential funerals? 4-36) – is recorded as late as the Meiji period when a haiku by Shiki jokes of an alms-gathering monk walking dead-end into another alms-gathering monk! (See the explanation for haiku #136&137 in *Rise, Ye Sea Slugs!*)

This matter of how bonzes made a living was not academic to Jesuits. Frois's *Historia* describes cases where a Christian takeover of a certain district (they convinced some leaders who became Christian to force it on their vassals) angered bonzes who were left without income, where protracted conflict was avoided by paying the bonzes enough to allow them to make the transition to another line of work..

4-7   Our clergy condemn people's sins without regard to civilities or circumstance;[1]
Antre nós os religiosos reprendem os pecados do povo sem uzar de respeitos humanos;

> The bonzes court their patrons and praise their sins in order not to lose the income. *Os bonzos grangeão os* dannas *e lhes louvão os pecados, pera que lhe não tirem a renda.*

English can use "religious" as a noun meaning, as it does in Portuguese (*religiosos*), "a monk or friar," but the usage, while not officially obsolete or even archaic, would be unfamiliar to all but specialists and the literati. Difficult words ought not be used more than once. So, "ours" are *clergy*.

Frois contrasts the ideal situation in Europe with sordid reality in Japan, hardly fair when you consider the exchange of sin for money called *indulgences* practiced by all too many Catholic religiosos in Europe. But the Jesuits were not *that* corrupt! It would be fairer to point out that the Jesuits were already on good terms with the nobility of Europe and "as we all know, power corrupts . . . it is ludicrous to think that many Jesuit confessors didn't refrain from condemning the sins of the innumerable kings, dukes, counts and lords whom they served as spiritual advisors." (DR) To go a bit beyond fairness and give Frois his due for his prejudice in this chapter, let me translate a few lines from the apostate Fukan Fabian's *Ha-deiusu* (destruction of "deus/deusites: 1620):

> "One person asks me: "Are all the Deus [clergy] free from avarice and only interested in mercy?" My answer is as follows: It is beyond the matter of having or not having avarice. They invented the game of ringing out the gold and silver they are so crazy about from their patrons. "That patron (*danna*) really obeys the commandments well, he is a good man" they say, praising when if he were a poor man they would make fun of him . . . even an unbeliever who breaks the commandments, if he is wealthy . . . ." (J/E:NBJ)

..

But I think I know where Frois is coming from. Could not his constant carping on the bonzes' Mammonism reflect his jealousy and his anxiety about "our" lack of income in Japan? [2] Valignano had to *repeatedly* explain the poverty of his beloved church of Japan to the head of the Society. The title of the 28th chapter of his SUMARIO (1583) is "of the cause and reason why the Christian lords cannot sustain the padres and their churches in Japan." To summarize: *First*, the lords in Japan are themselves poor. They receive little rent, own little personal land and cannot escape from continual warfare so they have neither income nor wealth, and this is especially true in the provinces where Christianity has made the most headway such as Shimo, which is "mountainous and sterile." *Second*, they have not converted any wealthy lords from the capitol region, but only a number of fine gentlemen. And, *third*, Christianity in Japan is very new and the Japanese cannot be expected to give a lot to "foreigners such as us."

On the other hand, "in respect to what is said about the bonzes" (i.e., *Then, how can the Japanese support so many?*) "there is much difference in their situation and ours," writes Valignano defensively as he begins another enumeration: "*First*, they began their sects at a time when Japan was flowering, prosperous and under one king" [2] who gave them great support, which "is impossible now that the reign is so divided in warfare;" and "*second*, because they were natives, sons and brothers of the major lords of Japan" and received good rent and land from their fathers and brothers, which religious motives aside, meant their temples remained, if it were, in the family, while we are . . . [in a word, outsiders]; and, "*third*, because the bonzes preach a different law from ours, for theirs leaves their charges to their appetites yet promises salvation, while we put an end to all sensuality and even with this cannot promise them salvation;" and "*fourth*, because, as natives, they know well the language and the customs and teach all their children," pragmatically accommodating themselves to the society irrespective of religious right or wrong, "and we, knowing nothing of this, with our laws and natives/customs [naturales] so contrary, destroy all this . . . for which, I say, it is a very great blessing from the Lord, and ought to be taken for something supernatural, that we are suffered to remain on their land." (V(A):S&A)

To my mind, the third point is especially relevant to Frois's contrast. Most noblemen had more than one wife, or a wife and several recognized concubines. This was probably the largest obstacle to gaining the nobles support and converting Japan. The repudiated wives often came from politically powerful families and, as might be imagined, sometimes turned their families into enemies of the Jesuits. Of course, holding the line against sin had already cost the Catholics England, so it was not *only* a Japan problem . . .

In retrospect, sucking up to patrons on the part of bonzes reflected a not-so-bad situation, where the customer (layman) was king. This was to change. About fifty years after TRATADO, the Tokugawa government made Buddhist temples responsible for making certain that no one belonged to a proscribed religion (Christian or Nichiren Buddhist). Everyone had to belong to a specific sect and be registered at their temple – defined as the one with their family plot – which checked that everything added up once every year and reported to the government.[3] This gave the bonzes great power to demand support. As Aramata Hiroshi put it, "finally the Buddhists got control over the living, too." (*Haka-wa Otera . . .* in J/A:NGK) And he writes there are records of some saying things like "if you don't pay up, you might end up under suspicion for being Christian." This not unnaturally gave rise to exorbitant prices for funeral-related services and eventually backfired when the last rulers of the Tokugawa decided to knock Buddhism out of the funeral game and give the right to Shinto and Confucian institutions, not to mention doing away with thousands of temples and melting down Buddhist images to create cannons such as the great cannon of Mito which became a symbol of National=Imperial=Shinto power. After World War II, Buddhism bounced back and retook the lion's share of the dead.

1. ***Translation.*** I had great difficulty with *sem uzar de respeitos humanos.* The temptation was to use simply "personal circumstances," but there seems to be a hint of civilities, which is to say etiquette proper to social position, also in the term. Someone expert in old Portuguese and fluent in English is welcome to correct me if needed.

2. ***Buddhist Riches*** I do not know if Valignano means over 500 years earlier when those 1 million stupas were distributed by the Empress or just two centuries earlier when Zen sects grew quickly with over 200 monks from China there at a time and "ships were assigned by Japanese authorities to trade with the Chinese, with the profits to be used to construct large Zen temples." (S(R):WTUD)

3. ***Fixed Family Plot*** This *danka seido* system is the prototype of the modern koseki, or "family register," something not found in the USA. (One thing still puzzles me: since most Japanese (the poor) had no plot, one wonders how they were kept track of. My guess is they simply could not move beyond their neighborhoods.)

4-8   Our clergy, out of contempt for this world, do not wear silk clothing;
Os religiosos antre nós, por desprezo do mundo, não usão de vestidos de seda;

All the bonzes who can, wear silk to parade their worldly pride and vanity.
Os bonzos todos os que podem andão vestidos de seda pera maior soberba e ostentasão no mundo.

If Orientalism means sumptuous Byzantine splendor, then Frois reinforces our "bias;"   but if it, rather, suggests the asceticism of yogi and Zen, he contradicts it.

While bonzes did strive to limit their worldly pleasures – as in Europe, sometimes by themselves and sometimes with reinforcement from sumptuary law – they did not want to disgust others with dirty clothing. Japanese Buddhists were one of the most evangelical – if you will allow a Christian term – Buddhists in Asia.   They wanted to wear *what worked*.   Perhaps, they found that most people prefer the prayers of a bonze whose very clothing shows that fortune smiles upon him over those of a down-and-out beggar   And, let's be honest, Buddhist or Christian, attractive clothing and, for that matter, good looks never hurt a preacher-man. Sei Shônagon (born c. 965) put it like this:

> A preacher ought to be good looking. For, if we are properly to understand his worthy sentiments, we must keep our eyes on him while he speaks; should we look away, we may forget to listen. Accordingly an ugly preacher may well be the source of sin . . . (S(M)PBSS)

Even Frois, in one of his fine 1565 letters, indirectly supported Shônagon's impertinent observation:

> He was clothed in flowing silk vestments, the under-robe being white and the outer one coloured, and he carried a gold fan in his hand. He was about 45 years of age and the paleness of his face made him look like a German; certainly he was one of the most handsome and engaging men I have ever seen . . . His soft and mellow voice and the gestures which he made during the sermon were all worthy of note. His method of preaching was to read a passage from the book in front of him and then to explain it with such elegance that father Vilela (who could understand the sermon) and all the others present marveled at his great skill and technique. We gained no little profit from this outing, as we learned a great deal about how to preach to the [Japanese] Christians in accordance with their liking and language . . . (in C:TCJ)

Still, the contrast between the Buddhist religiosos professed denial of the world and the ostentation of Buddhist high priests was noticed in Japan, too, and became a minor literary theme. The poets Buson and Issa (second and third to Bashô as the top three haiku poets) depict *Their Excellencies* shitting al fresco (called *noguso,* or "field-shit"), dressed in their bright silk and shielded by a servant's umbrella.

4-9   Among us, good clergy abhor and greatly fear to gain titles and honors;
Antre nós os bons religiosos repugnão e temem muito subir [1] a dignidades e honras.

The bonzes in Japan are all dying to gain them and spend great sums to that end.
Os bonzos em Japão, custão-lhe muito dinheiro e todos morrem por subirem a elas.

Frois, to his credit, did qualify the European side by only making the claim for "good" religiosos, but his declamation of the bonze side is like usual, irresponsibly catholic (*todos*). And, qualifications aside, all nine contrasts in this chapter so far depict "them" as worldly and arrogant and "us" as truly humble. The Jesuits took great stock in their humility. As DR points out, the Society of Jesus policy was "not to accept religious appointments (e,g, benefices)," though they sometimes had to accept positions conferred by "Kings and other powerful leaders."   On a more humble level, I note our "Luys Froes" signed his letters: *Sieruo inutil de todos* ("I serve uselessly in all"), *Sieruo inutil de todos, y su indigno hermano* ("*ditto,* and your unworthy brother"), etc.; and, as already noted, Valignano, though Visitador of the entire East did not publish his work on Japan with his name on it. Not all Japanese were, however, convinced. Fukan Fabian, the Japanese ex-Jesuit quoted in 4-7 complained:

> They (the *padres)* are always telling people to be humble because pride is the root of all evil and humility the foundation of all good; but, even the King of devils cannot match their own pride, be it their national propensity, or whatever. Because of this pride, secular folk better steer clear when they struggle for power and quarrel with other *bateren* (padres) [2] . . . and because they are such arrogant men, they don't even think Japanese human." (from Fabian's Ha=deusu trans. by F(MJ) [?not in biblio!] (but I found it in J/E:NBJ) and trans. is accurate.)

Japanese of all classes probably did indeed hanker for the honors of high rank and what Kaempfer, the German doctor who visited Japan a hundred years later, had to say about the *Ranks and Titles of the Jammabos* (ascetic mountain priests) does support Frois's assertion:

> If they return home from this hazardous Pilgrimage [climbing a dangerous mountain peak once a year], they repair forthwith, each to the general of his order, who resides in Miaco, make him a small present in money, which if poor, they must get by begging, and receive from him a more honourable title and higher dignity, which occasions some alteration in their dress, and encreases the respect which must be shown them by their brethen of the same order. So far is ambition from being banish'd out of these religious Societies. (K:HOJ)

Needless to say, the behavior of one rather weird sect does not speak for all sects, but I think there is something to it as a pattern of behavior. I think it also needs to be pointed out that given the Japanese sense of honor, where money meant little, but asking for the help of strangers (incurring obligations) meant a lot, begging was a very humiliating act, more so, I think, than it would have been for the religious in the West. So it could be argued that at the very least, these Japanese priests had to swallow their pride and learn to eat humble pie in order to make the world their oyster.

1. *Subir a*   The original speaks of "our" fear or "their" desire to *rise to (subir a)* the titles and honors. The idea of wishing to remain literally debased comes across well that way. If "titles" were changed to "ranks" it might work in English but another verb would then be needed for the "honors."

2. *Bateren*   The word derived from the Japanese pronunciation of padres→patere→bateren. Since they were in South Japan first and Koreans next door have a common phoneme between a "b" and a "p" (studying Korean, I wrote it with the tail going both ways!) this makes sense to me. It is sometimes written in the stiff *katakana* syllabary used for foreign words, but more often with Chinese characters which for friendly writers was generally 伴天連, or "accompany-heaven-clique," and unfriendly writers,   破天連, or "bust-heaven-clique."

~~~~~~

4-10   Our clergy always desire peace and simply cannot stand wars;
Os nossos religiosos sempre desejão a pax e lhe peza sumamente das guerras;

> The *Negoro* make war their profession and are hired by lords to fight their battles.
> *Os* nengoros *professão guerra e são alugados dos senhores pera yrem pelejar nas batalhas.*

While the Jesuits did not do much physical combat, they were not averse to *participating* in "just' wars. [1]   In the early 1580's, Valignano contributed gunpowder and other logistical help to

Christian rulers in Japan, but soon changed tack, discouraging a plan to convince the governor of the Philippines to send ships and arms to Nagasaki, then under the government of the Jesuits, because Japanese Christians felt safer *not* possessing such might, given the turbulent political situation in his country. The Shogun Hideyoshi, as Alcock surmised, had no doubt heard about the way the Pope tried "to dethrown the Queen of England in favor of another pretender to the crown, to raise up conspirators among her subjects, and release them from all oaths or ties of allegiance" (A:COT) – in 1580, as Accommodation was beginning to be worked out in Japan, Felipe (Philip) II even sent troops to Ireland – and, in 1587, he suddenly changed policy and cut the Christians in Nagasaki down to size. Valignano realized defiance was a losing game, and in his *"Obediencias"* of 1592 "laid down that on no account were the Jesuits to encourage or foment any fighting among the Japanese even if it was in support of a Christian daimyo against a heathen, or Christian vassals oppressed by a heathen overlord . . . but were to confine themselves to praying to God for the success of Christian arms."(B:CCJ) So, in the end, the Jesuits in Japan *became* as peaceful as Frois prematurely claims.

Martial arts in Buddhism came from China early as the 8th century. When Nobunaga utterly destroyed a Sangakuji temple in 1570, he wiped out a tradition that had lasted for 760 years. Founded in 807, it was one of a number of Tendai sect temples whose fighting bonzes (*sôhei*) opposed the excesses of the warrior-clan politics of the time by sending fighters to help the gentler side. I guess they opposed one warrior too many. The bonzes of the True Word (*Shingon*) sect, headquartered on Mount Negoro also had a tradition of martial arts that predated the Warring Era and at their peak had a coalition of 2000 temples.[2] Valignano mentions them in his SUMARIO in the context of explaining the natural love for arms on the part of the Japanese (i.e., *even* the clergy . . .). Quick to adopt and make firearms, they played an important role in the some major battles of the Warring era, but they were almost exterminated by Hideyoshi, the great warlord who unified Japan. Exasperated by their support of various rebel causes and unwillingness to submit to his authority, Hideyoshi burnt everything on their main mountain the very year Frois wrote TRATADO. Since they comprised one of the hundred-man rifle units, called *negoro-gumi,* for the man who wrested power from Hideyoshi's clan, Tokugawa Ieyasu, some Negoro obviously not only survived but revenged their nemesis. As Alvarez-Taladriz notes, Vilela and Maffei compared these bonzes to the Knights of Rhodes, and Frois described their character and massacre in his *Historia*. As he did so, little did Frois guess the Christian's turn was next.

It is hardly surprising to find fighting bonzes. We had "our" own tradition of "fighting monks" of which the Knights of Rhodes are but the most well known. [3] Religion and fighting are soul-mates, for true believers (provided their families share their faith or they are single) have no reason whatsoever to fear death. Who better to play the soldier, to serve as mercenaries for people who value life in this world more than life in the next? Be that as it may, with respect to the fighting bonzes of Japan, history is poetic if not just. When Japan began to modernize in the mid-nineteenth century and the state dropped its financial support of Buddhism, "the priests, having no income, were advised by the government to enter the army as soldiers!" ("The Daily Evening Bulletin" of San Francisco quoted as an accurate source in L:JIA).

1. *Just Wars* Reff provides a finely nuanced introduction to de Ribas's *The History of the Triumphs of Our Holy Faith . . .* (R(R&A&D):HOT) touching upon the relationship of Society of Jesus and war in the account of the "reduction" of the bellicose natives of North Mexico by the Jesuits working hand in hand with the Spanish military in the early 17th century. My own less nuanced impression is that while the Jesuits never engaged in combat, they provoked military action primarily by martyring themselves. A website with the aggressively anti-Christian name of www.christianism.com is harsher:

"IF DISEASES WERE THE SHOCK TROOPS OF THE INVASION OF AMERICA, CHRISTIAN MISSION-ARIES WERE ITS COMMANDOES, DISGUISED IN FEMININE BLACK ROBES AS MEMBERS OF A PEACE CORPS. Although they came bearing a message from a "Prince of Peace," they uncon-sciously bore a whole civilization that would not tolerate the America they had found." [That is to say, Christianity made war on the world. And, among all the missionaries ~] "PERHAPS THE BEST AGENTS OF ALL WERE THE JESUITS. By history and design, the Society of Jesus was destined to change the

American world. It was a fraternity designed for war, the greatest human engine of social change. Its founder [Saint Ignatius of Loyola 1491 - 1556] was a stubborn Spanish-Basque courtier-soldier, much taken with the "exercise of arms" in young manhood. The Society he founded was sanctioned by the pope in 1540 in a bull entitled *Regimini militantis Ecclesiae,* which accurately reflected its pugnacious stance toward the Protestant Reformation and international "paganism." The Spiritual Exercises that Loyola devised for his recruits sought to dissolve their individual wills in Christ's, which, they were reminded, was to "conquer the whole world," particularly "all the lands of the infidel."

University of Oklahoma, for I see he has presented a paper called *"The Fighting Servants of Buddha"* which (in its summary, for I have not seen it)* makes some good points: that there is an unfairly bad image of these bonzes due to badmouthing by later sects, a misunderstanding of their duties (mainly protective in an era of privatization [*we could have used some to protect the little old ladies from Enron's capitalist sharks*]) and their estrangement from society with the total dominance of the warrior class from the 14th century. I would only add that the losing side almost always gets shafted in history and this is no exception. * (*My only lead: Session 177: Fighting Monks and Praying Samurai: Redrawing the Social Landscape of Medieval Japan = www.aasianst.org/absts/1998abst/japan/j177.htm*)

While this is all true (except for the ridiculous modern Occidental prejudice about the gender of robes) *to read the Jesuits and to meet the Jesuits is to like the Jesuits.* If only the environmental movement had leaders of the quality of Loyola, Xavier and Valignano, we would be saved where it counts, here on earth.

2. *Fighting Bonzes*. I get very confused following their history because the "same" sect can evolve into a number of sects which themselves can splinter and only a taxonomical tree could possibly make this history clear at a glance. There is what seems (from the internet outline) a very thorough book by 日置英剛Hioki Eigô, a high school teacher whose main work is finishing a year by year chart of Japanese history begun by his father. I hope to find and read his book 僧兵の歴史法と鎧をまとった荒法師たち(a title I will not even try to translate for reasons my readers who read Japanese will immediately understand) by the next edition, or better yet, someone else will, and will give me such a good gloss, I will not have to. Perhaps, it could be Mikael Adolphson of the

3. *Fighting Monks*. On "our" side, I must confess that I have not yet read Desmond Seward: *The Monks of War: The Military Religious Orders* (1972). Amazon top 500 Reviewer Roger Albin notes that these orders "were founded initially to help and safeguard pilgrims to the Holy Land," were a "Medieval hybrid, combining Cistercian monasticism and Chivalric knightly values. . . . gaining influence in the Crusader Kingdoms and considerable wealth . . . , the military orders were significant actors in the complicated politics of the Eastern Mediterranean. Similar orders developed on other important frontiers between Christian Europe and non-Christian polities, notably in Spain and the eastern Baltic littoral. In Spain, the military orders were the shock-troops of the Reconquista. In the Baltic, the Teutonic Knights led the conquest and Christianization of Prussia and what is now a good part of the Baltic states." I would not be surprised if the book also mentions the founder of the Jesuits, for St. Loyola was a military man and his first intent was to head straight for the Holy Lands, something he was luckily dissuaded from doing by the Pope.

4-11   We struggle with all our might to keep our promises to God;
        Antre nós o que se promete a Deus se trabalha de guardar inteiramente

> The bonzes publicly profess not to eat meat or fish, but secretly almost all of them do it, only refraining for fear of being seen, or because they cannot.[1]
> *Os bonzos no de fora profesão não comer carne nem pexe, mas ocultamente quasi todos o comem, senão por temor de serem vistos ou por não poderem.*

About fifty years earlier, Xavier wrote that "formerly the bonzes or bonzesses who had broken one of their five precepts [sex/theft or lying/ homicide/killing any creature/eating the same or drinking wine] were punished with death by the princes and nobles of the place where they lived. . . . But at present, this discipline is entirely relaxed and corrupted; the greater number drink wine, eat meat secretly . . . ." (C:LLFX) So, even when the bonzes were good, the Jesuits attributed it to physical punishment rather than piety. There may be some truth to that charge, too. As we will see in chapter 6, Buddhist food restrictions are somewhat arbitrary and ambiguous. Thus , it is not surprising that only sumptuary laws could assure their compliance. But, Frois is only using food for proof that Buddhist priests are weak and untruthful even to their own faith. This is part of the larger issue of an absence of vows and hence loyalty in Japan that was lamented by Valignano and others. In Dialogue

13 of DE MISSIONE, the Ambassador Mancio=Valignano explains the concept of a European vow to Leo. He explains that when men are given honor (titles/positions) by their King in Europe, they pledge their fealty to said King, and that this pledge or vow is bound = *religio,* so that any disloyalty would be extremely dishonorable, whereas in "our country," Japan, this type of vow does not exist, with the result that, according to the circumstances, one can betray one's lord without dishonor. The Japanese translators of De Sande's Latin were right (for once! [2]) to leave in the word *religio* (a word with the double meaning here of *religion* and *ties*). No Christianity, no dependable relationship. *That* was the message.

Today, even in America with its supposed separation of Church and State, people vow with their hand on the Bible, as if this *religio* were the *sine qua non* for speaking the Truth. In Japan, people simply give their word. All told, "we" Occidentals – here, I include the Islamic World, for Muslims share as high a percent of our memes as chimpanzees share our genes – might be called *a swearing people*, for "we" have long sworn things upon This or That (some, very odd things indeed, if we think of the etymology of "testify!"), while Japanese, and one would presume most people, have no such cultural compulsion (see 10-11 re. notary publics).

1. *They cannot.* I.e., because no meat or fish is available to eat or they lack the money to buy it or the ability to digest it, etc.. This seems to me to share some of the same dry humor (a Mark Twain type of humor) as in 4-4 when the bonzes only obey when they agree by accident.
2. Latin, *"For Once!"* Considering the fact that at least a Japanese translation exists (not true for English) and the ample notes provided by the translators, it is churlish to complain, but I would have appreciated more Latin. Any reader who has access to the Latin *De Missione* and reads Latin is welcome to supply the proper word for anything I quote in this book.

~~~~~~

4-12 Our clergy, under no circumstances, act as envoys for princes and lords;
Os religiosos antre nós por nenhum cazo andão em recados de principes nem senhores;

The *tonos* [feudal lords] in Japan use bonzes for envoys and war strategists. [1]
Os Tonos *em Japão se servem dos bonzos pera recados e* buriaqos *da guerra.*

According to DR, "a wonderfully detailed study" by Dauril Aulden (The Making of an Enterprise . . .) shows that the Jesuits "undertook many diplomatic missions on behalf of the Crown of Portugal." Was Frois, perhaps, too low level an operative to have known what was going on? But what about Valignano forbidding Jesuits in Japan "to act as military intelligence agents, or to pass on news of the progress of a campaign, even if it was in the interests of a Christian daimyo against a heathen" (B:CCJ)? Frois had to know that, for he recorded it in his *Historia.* Perhaps Frois *meant* that the bonzes are *hired* in hat capacity, whereas the Jesuits might *dabble* in the information business, but only as agents of their Society on the behalf of spreading their religion.

Okada points out that each Shogun had his famous bonze envoy or diplomat and that there were actually terms such *shizô* (messenger-bonze) and *jinzô* (encampment or army-bonze). Is it possible that in the Warring era, other envoys might have been tortured for information or summarily executed? Or was it the greater literacy and, often, medical skills of the bonzes (4-29) that was in high demand? Originally, it would seem that Ippen and the bonzes of his sect, whose name *jishû* stood for the last moments of life 臨命終時, made a vow to remain by dying warriors (when they were not dancing! (see 4-22) to help them invoke the divine mercy of *Amida* and assure they, thus, made it into the Pure Land Paradise. This was similar to the role of Christian priests in "our" armies. Soon, they came to live "near their lords and aid them in both combat and death." (S(R):WTUD)

1. *Strategist or Tactician?* According to the Japanese-Portuguese (NIPO) dictionary, the term *buryaku* was understood to mean both tactics and strategy. I do not know if *tactician* or *strategist* is the better translation.

4-13   With us, a clergy who gets married becomes an apostate;
           Antre nós cazar-se hum religioso hé ficar apostata;

> The bonzes, when they get tired of the religious life, can marry or become soldiers. *Os bonzos, como se enfadão da religião, ou se cazão ou se fazem soldados.*

"Us" here means Catholic *religioso*. Ex-Catholic priest Luther married a former nun about a decade before Frois went to Japan.   Luther felt that the enforced celibacy of the clerics was one reason for their hidden concubines and tolerance of prostitution (H:CER).   By this time, Frois probably had heard about this.   A few Buddhist sects, like Lutherans, went even farther and permitted marriage.   Senryu joke about how these married priests both *bore* and *buried* people, or how happy they were to hear their wives crying out *"[I'm] dying! I'm dying!"* (*shinu shinu*) when they made love, because such words (a common Japanese love-call) were propitious for their *business* (Buddhism was associated with *burial* in Japan, as Christianity was hundreds of years later in Africa, when the priests were riddled as vultures, both for their habit of rushing to the dead and dying and their white-collared black dress).

But this contrast is not primarily about marriage *per se* (if it were, the "or soldiers" would not make sense); it is yet another instance of the *vow* vs. *no-vow* contrast. For the Jesuit, a decision to join the Order was, as we have already explained, *irrevocable*. To quit was to go back on your word, to betray the Church and God and your Superiors to whom it was pledged. The same type of stigma was attached to it as one might to a divorce.   *Apostate* was and still is a dirty word. For Japanese, however, the religious life was not so much a life-long commitment as a day-to-day choice. Japanese remained in their temples out of their own free will (disregarding cases involving political refugees).

This may be out of order – wrong country, wrong age – but, when I spent some time in Korea in 1972, I recall visiting a mountain temple where a friend of my friend was living as a monk. My friend said that many, if not most of his friends had spent some time (usually a few months but up to a year) living as a monk. It was part of their life experience. In the West, the assumption would seem to be that one is either on the *outside* (visits churches to worship) or the *inside* (one either ministers or becomes a monk/nun). The closest "we" come to enjoying an impermanent half-in/half-out religious experience is the relatively short practice we call *a retreat*.

4-14   Within our orders, the succession is made on the basis of election and virtue, not inheritance. *Nas nossas religiões não há socesão por heransa mas por eleisão e vertude;*

> Among the bonzes, the successor is a disciple raised and taught for that purpose since childhood. *Antre os bonzos herda o discípulo que o superior cria de pequeno pera lhe soceder.*

As DR points out, "during the century following the founding of the Jesuit Order, the ranks of the Professed [1] were dominated by Spaniards and Italians from aristocratic families who discriminated against Jesuits born elsewhere (R(R&A&D):HOT)" One can't help wondering if Frois, a boy from a humble family who did not rise in the ranks as fast as he should have considering his obvious skills was entirely satisfied with his position, considering the fact that his superior, Valignano, who, coming from a family with the right Papal connections, despite jail time (or house arrest? I cannot recall precisely) for seriously injuring a man in a fight, shot up like a rocket to the upper ranks of the Jesuit order, becoming a Visitador in charge of all the East Indies (churches from India Eastward) at age 37 (S:MPMR). Humble soul that he was, perhaps it never bothered him. But, that is unlikely.

The Japanese side sounds like Tibetan Buddhism, where a boy enters the monastery as the Lama-to-be; but in Japan, as Okada notes, a disciple might be chosen from a large number of young bonzes (or bonzes-to-be) on the basis of his apparent intelligence and ability. He was indeed groomed for succession, but it was hardly so arbitrary a process as the contrast implied. Yet, some Zen monasteries took in younger brothers of samurai families, who would give up their inheritance (cut of power) and expected promising opportunities in exchange, so Frois is not all wrong.

1. *Professed?* Since the Jesuits were modeled on a military order, they are full of ranks. The professed, I believe is a ful-fledged Jesuit.   I believe Frois did not achieve that rank until very late in his life, despite all he did. But I am bad with details like that. If someone would like to gloss the next edition . . .

4-15   We enter the orders out of devotion and an inner calling to virtue;
Antre nós entrão na relegião por devosão e movimento interior de virtude; [1]

Bonzes do it to inherit each others wealth and gain worldly glory.
Os bonzos entrão por erdarem huns aos outros o fato e terem a gloria neste mundo.

This is **4-1** all over again. We can be sure people became *religiosos* for many reasons in Europe, not all of which were virtuous, and likewise for Japanese.

1. *Movimento interior de virtude* I am indebted to DR for the excellent phrase: "an inner calling to virtue." My draft translation, "virtuous interior motives," was *very* lame.

4-16   Our clergy strive most of all for interior purity and cleanliness;
Os nossos religiosos fazem a principal força na pureza e limpeza interior;

The bonzes are extremely clean when it comes to their dwellings, gardens and temples, and filthy of soul. *Os bonzos são limpissimos nas cazas,* nivas *e templos, e abominaveis nas almas.*

"Our" side is getting a little boring. I almost feel like saying *"yeah, yeah, yeah!"* The "they" side in the contrast is more interesting for it seems to imply that interior and exterior cleanliness correlate inversely. This had been previously suggested in a 1571 letter by Vilela in which "He could not repress his whole-hearted admiration of the cleanliness and neatness of their persons and surroundings, which he noted as forming a glaring contrast to "the filthiness of their consciences." (B:CCJ)
Japanese cleanliness was constantly noted by the missionaries and it was always suspect. In 1565, Almeida, after writing that a Buddhist monastery's kitchen was spotless, added that it was so because it was "a thing very common with the Japanese, being very clean in all their exterior works." He let the dirty *interior* lie quietly between the lines of his letter. Frois in his parallel letter described the same temples as both clean and boasting wood so brilliant that it leaves "our" tapestry of gold, silk and brocade in the shade. (*se nos representaba ser como una sombra en comparacion desto*). He cleverly prefaced his praise with a disclaimer to his "dearest brothers," to the effect that they (the Buddhists) have all this loveliness, "solely for their happiness and glory in this world." (i.e. at the expense of neglecting *that* World.) In his HISTORIA, Frois later explains the same thing in reverse, i.e., that lacking hope of salvation and eternal life, the Buddhists concentrate on this world. *Worldly Buddhists and otherworldly Christians.* This, too, turns on its head the contrasts we have become familiar with since the nineteenth-century.

Christians have long had a problem with external cleanliness and beauty. On the one hand, they profess to despise the world of appearance, but on the other, as members of the Establishment in the West, they had to keep clean to differentiate themselves from radical or marginal elements. Moreover, with stench associated with the Devil and lack of odor or a good scent (even after death), the mark of a saint, even Christians in hair-shirts probably felt obliged to practice *some* personal hygiene. Yet, they obviously did not practice too hard, for "in Catholic Europe" at least, "lice were regarded as the inseparable companions of monks and soldiers." (B:CCJ) Cleaning might have been included in "good works," but was not in itself considered to be soul work.

In Japan, on the other hand, "cleanliness emphatically came next to godliness." (B:CCJ) The mirror is one of Shinto's (the native "purity religion") main symbols; and keeping it clean was identified with keeping a pure soul. "During impurity, access to any temple, and most acts of religion, are forbidden, and the head must be covered, that the sun's beams may not be defiled by falling upon it." (B:MCJ). As Kaempfer pointed out, "scrupulous adorers" not only must keep physically unpolluted, but "carry things still further, and think it unbecoming to appear in the presence of the Gods, even when the thoughts, or memories of their misfortunes, possess their mind." This is actually a deeper idea of internal cleanliness than the Christian one which stopped at not thinking of sinful things.

This Shinto concept of purity was not foreign to Buddhism, either. The Buddhists cherished the moon, which was identified with the Wheel of the Law, and that moon in Japan was likened to a mirror which had to be *kept free of dust* (or, in a unique interpretation in Issa's haiku, a purifier of all the sins that might come to its light). Buddhism probably *had to* emphasize cleanliness to root in the land of Shinto. Frois did not understand – or, could not accept – that *cleaning* and *reflection* were one, and that Japanese Buddhism and Shinto both aimed for "inward purity of heart" (the first of Shinto's five "chief points," according to Kaempfer). In this respect, the Moslems are closer to Japanese Buddhists and Shintoists than Christians; for they even pluck the hair from their armpits and pubic region (sticky paper for this purpose is apparently sold in the supermarkets today). As the Messenger of Allah said "He who performed ablution well, his sins would come out from his body, even coming from under his nails (Sahib[?] Muslim Book 2 #0476 – found on the internet) This sounds almost Shinto, with pollution exchanged for "sins." [1-]

The Jesuits' accommodation to the Japanese lifestyle ordered by Valignano included not only the introduction of clean kitchen and dining habits, but more subtle things such as always sending a messenger ahead of time to be certain and give the other party time to clean up as needed and put on clean clothing, and always wearing something clean when visiting. (1583? 1592? p231 ch23 in V(A):S&A) If the beautiful and the good were equated in ancient Greece, in Japan, in Japanese today, *kirei* means "clean," "pretty," and "right" – as in "doing it right" (*kirei-ni-shite*). But for all Valignano's apparent awareness of this, "in his "Obediencias" of 1592, he laid down that none but the very sick or aged were to be allowed the frequent use of a *furo* [Japanese bath], and all other personnel, European and Japanese alike, could only take a proper bath once in eight days." Boxer *sighs* "To such ridiculous lengths had the mediaeval Christian reaction against Roman cleanliness and personal hygiene carried the men of the Renaissance." (B:CCJ) I think Valignano's rule had less to do with hygiene *per se,* and more to do with *avoiding sensual pleasure*, for the physical comfort of a good hot bath is not to be reckoned lightly. (To put it the other way around, I suspect Valignano, himself, was a bath-lover.) Presumably, Valignano did allow other less pleasurable means of keeping the body clean enough for Japan.

Perhaps a word more on the "filthy of soul" is needed. It was not just *sodomy* that bothered the Jesuits. It was a general laxity with regard to sex and the genitals. The Buddhists only thought badly of sex in so far as it provoked strong desires and bound one to the sensual world of appearance. Sex *itself* was not sinful and certainly nothing to get excited about. This casual attitude did not only surprise the Jesuits but prudish mid-nineteenth century American visitors, such as John Preble, an officer who came with Commodore Perry's squadron in 1854.

Resting at a temple near Hakodate, he notices a pretty unmarried girl among the crowd. A man comes up to her, whispers, then takes her behind a screen five feet away: Her companions were not slow, to show us, by the most indecent signs in which the old priest joined, what they had gone for. The women laughing heartily as though it were a first-rate joke and no uncommon occurrence to so pervert their Temples. (L:IOJ)

A Buddhist priest – unless of one of the sects that would be the equivalent of our fundamentalist sects – would be above it all. Were he to get huffy-puffy about such things, Japanese might wonder about his spiritual maturity, for a clean soul is calm and laughs off little things like a liaison behind a screen, whereas, an upright Christian *religioso* would have been expected to act outraged, and a bonze who observed such outrage would, then, have been shocked at the priest's passions (a devilish thing) and lack of insight into what matters and what does not.

But to return to the *cleanliness*, the contrast need not be restricted to temples. It was true for most Japanese buildings (like the Chinese, but cleaner, as many have observed) and for the country *as a whole*. Thunberg's complaint of a *lack of weeds for botanizing* (we will find this in ch 11) was later confirmed by Kipling:

But all I can write will give you no notion of the wantonness of neatness visible in the fields . . . The young rice was transplanted very much as draughts are laid on the board; the tea might have been cropped garden box . . . while the beans ran up to the mustard and stopped as though cut by a rule. K(C&?):KJ)

1. *Ablution Correlation.* It is interesting that the Muslims, also into pederasty. Is there a correlation here?
Japanese and Romans, all deeply into cleanliness, were

~~~~~~

4-17   We are keen to avoid deceit, hypocrisy and adulation;
Antre os nossos se foje muito ao fenjimento e ipocrezia e adulasão;

> The bonzes of Japan live off these, and find them a super[1] way to make a livelihood. *Os bonzes de Japão disto vivem, e o tem por potíssimo meo pera poderem viver.*

Thanks to enmity between Protestants and Catholics (and quarrels between 17th century Catholics as well), in the English speaking world, it is "we" – if *we* means the Jesuits [2] – who now have this unjust reputation. The very word "Jesuit" became synonymous with "a dissembling person, a prevaricator" and "black intrigues," and "Jesuitical" with "deceitful, dissembling, practicing equivocation, prevarication, or mental reservation of truth." (OED) To my mind, the reality is complex and the simple ferocity of Calvinism and the Papacy that eventually turned on the Jesuits is what deserves criticism. An attack on equivocation is along the same line as attack on science for being less than certain. Unfortunately, the Jesuits did not equivocate when it came to describing Buddhism. Even gentle St. Xavier showed no Christian mercy for bonzes:

. . . our greatest enemies are the bonzes, because we expose their falsehoods. . . . they used to make the people believe that it is impossible for persons in general to keep those five commandments . . . and that, therefore, they would observe them for the people, on the condition of the people giving them maintenance and honour. They give their word that if anyone goes down into hell he will be delivered by their intervention and labour. We, on the contrary, proved to the people that in hell there is no redemption, and that no one can be rescued from it by bonzes and bonzesses. At last, by the help of God, the bonzes themselves were forced to confess the truth that they could not save anyone from the punishment of hell by their prayers, but that unless they gave out that they had this power, they would infallibly be reduced to die of hunger. [3] And, indeed, soon after this, the bonzes, as the assistance they received from their disciples gradually failed, experienced great difficulties as to their maintenance, and had to live in a state of degradation. (C:LLFX)

In one sense, I would agree with Frois and Xavier. Most Japanese – even bonzes – were probably not true believers, that is to say not the supremely confident fanatic, absolutely sure of his faith, as confident in the existence of God and Heaven as a three year old child is of Santa Claus, which is to say a *bona fide* Christian. Unlike Occidentals – unlike all too many Americans who *today* would teach Creationism in science class – the bonzes were emotionally and intellectually mature and humble enough to know they did not know everything. While the Jesuits who went to Japan were sophisticated Christians in the best sense of the word, their sophistication was on behalf of Christianity, which was and is, for better or worse, a very simplistic religion.

1. Super!? *Potíssimo.* The original word is hard to find. I think it is a augmentation of *potici* which according to Aurelio's means *superabundance* or a *copia* and derives from potosi, which, of course comes from "the great font of riches" Potosi, Bolivia. It is a clever word to emphasize the bonze's wealth and suggest it is obtained by exploitation.

2. "Jesuits" The name "Jesuit" itself is not a happy one. The idea of calling themselves the Society of Jesus rather than giving their Society a name per se, was to avoid names. But, in a vacuum, a name will appear. Today,

"Jesuit" has become acceptable even to the Jesuits.

2. *Promise and Power.* DR points out that if we replace "*hell* with *purgatory,* in the above quote, Xavier's argument against the bonzes could readily be said to apply to the Jesuits and other Christians." Moreover, that "like the bonzes, priests and nuns are quick to point out that they have no power to rescue a soul from purgatory or hell, still they accept money for masses, rosaries and prayers that are offered to God in the hope of winning his mercy."

4-18   Our clergy wear no beard and have tonsures;
Os nossos religiosos trazem a barba rapada e a coroa feita;

The bonzes shave their heads and beard every four days.
Os bonzos rapão a cabeça e barba cada 4 dias.

You might say "our" monk only shaved the part of his head that looked at heaven, while the bonze turned his whole head into a round object, which, in Japan is a similitude for the soul itself (*tama* means "soul" and "gem" or any round smooth object, and *atama* means "head"). The frequency of shaving varies. The frequency of shaving depended on the sect.. The first Occidental observer of Japan, Captain Alvarez wrote:

The bonzes are all shaven with razors; they have rooms built at a short distance from their monasteries, where they go twice a day to perform their ablutions. They heat the necessary water at stoves erected for the purpose, the wood for the fires being given them for the love of God. (C:LLFX)

This must be one of Frois's most unsatisfactory contrasts because there is more similarity than difference. As DR points out, the Jesuits are not included in "ours" here, for they did not shave *their* heads. It is too bad that the Jesuits did not also wear beards, for that would have allowed for a real contrast!

4-19   Among us, clergy wear hats or berets; *Antre nós trazem os religiosos capelos ou barretes;*

> Bonzes generally go about with nothing on their head, but when it's cold they wear baggy barrettes, or *wataboshi*, and others wear caps like the neck and head of a horse, with ears. *Os bonzos o mais do tempo andão sen nada na cabeça e polo frio uzão de barretes como bolsa, ou de* vataxboxis *e outros hum capelo como pescoso e cabeça de cavalo com orelhas.*

I think Frois may exaggerate the bare-headedness. When bonzes did field work or traveled, I believe they usualy wore umbrella-like hats that do not fit the above description, for shade (could I be wrong?). I wonder if the fact that these large umbrella-like hats did not actually rest right on their scalps but were trussed around a ring meant that they did not count as something on the head?   But these are never worn indoors. See 2-8 for a description of the *wataboshi* (cotton-hat), which sounds like it might actually *be* the baggy barrettes. The bonzes' caps tended to have neck-pieces attached, which kept the chill off the nape of the neck. That may explain the horsy simile. Orfanel writes of a "two-pointed hat." (C:TCJ). Perhaps the "ears" appear when the middle part of the rectangular hat settles down leaving the corners protruding a bit! Frois seems to be trying too hard for a contrast that is barely there.

4-20   Our clergy greatly value decency and setting a good example.
Os nossos religiosos estimão em muito a honestidade e bom exemplo;

> The bonzes always go about with their legs bare and wear robes so thin they show almost everything in the summer, and no one thinks it bad or embarrassing. *Os bonzos andão sempre em pernas e polo verão com catabiras tão ralas que lhe parese quanto tem, sem disso terem nenhum pejo nem vergonha.*

My "decency" is *honestidade* in the original. One meaning of "honest" in old English was "chaste" (e.g. *She was poor but honest*). How ironic to find it *dishonest* to show the body! How sad that Western *religiosos* were so hung up on this world that the entire body had to be covered up. That the fig-leaf had grown to such utterly insane proportions! "Men of the cloth," indeed. There is no small irony here when you consider the fact that this ridiculous disgust for the body came from the same civilization that so worshipped the figure of man that it even gave God a muscle-bound body. [1] In Japan and China, where bodies were not idolized in fresco or in oil, no one was the least bothered by thin clothing (the same see-through *katabira* robe mentioned in 1-61) in hot muggy weather, unless it was Sei Shônagon with her snide complaint at how bad thin, dark and hairy bodies looked through them. While nudity and sex are not equivalent, the terms Frois uses do make the Buddhists seem *dirty* by way of contrast with the *decent* Christians.

Valignano was the first Jesuit I know to cut the Buddhists some slack on the moral side. In his LIBRO (1601-03), he qualified his earlier views and admitted that Buddhism had a clean origin, for the Buddha did not practice the dishonesties of Jupiter, Venus and Cupid, so adored by the Romans, and the Buddhists did not have fiestas for Venus, the Priapus and Bacchus, but only ones that are "modest and honest on the exterior." (in n.6 ch3 V(A):S&A) [2] As he wrote this, however, he came down hard on Shinto for having "very impossible, dirty and burlesque histories as was always the case for the histories of the gentile gods." Someone must have told him about the first god with the part left over and the first goddess with a part missing,[3] and the shuttle-in-the-vagina homicide and clever red arrow flying up from the privy into the same, and the birth of grains from the dying goddess's vagina and so forth!   Yes, not only does Shinto have earthy "histories" (at least our patronizing modern(?) term "mythology"[4] was not used!) as most religions with a small "r" do, but was and still is one with the folk tradition of parading large straw or wooden phalluses about in local festivals in Japan. (Christians should not mind *that* as it is about generation, begatting.)

Aside from the numerous allusions to Buddhist sodomy in TRATADO, Frois completely neglects the relation of religion and genitalia. We shall make amends for it with the following long quote from Cock's diary (26 Feb 1616[17]):

> Mr. Nealson going a walking, p'r chance fowned an alter of the antient god Priapus (or the lecheros god) w'th a greate towle [tool], wherevnto women goe on pilgremadge carying wooden prick's with them made lyke vnto a mans member, the w'ch they first put into their nature (or membr) and after offer it vp to the god, as well women that are w'th child, to haue speedy deliverance, as also them w'ch are barren, to be frutefull. One of w'ch prickes he brought away w'th hym, & shewed it to me, & learn'd by them w'ch dwelled by to what vse they were ordayned, w'ch was as aboue said. I remembr when I was in France, & passing thorow the landes betwixt the citties of Bourdeaulx and Bayon, I had knowledg of an image & alter, whereon stood a pickture w'th a greate toole (w'ch as I remember), they called St. Puchin, to w'ch all baron women went on pilgremage, to the extent to proue frutefull, & to that extent shaved (or scraped affe) a littell of the prick, & put it into wyne and drunck it, p'r w'ch meanes they verely beleeved they should be frutefull, but of late yeares there were som women taken, going thether on pilgramadg (not of the meanest sort), & carid ruffians w'th them to curry them over, to the extent to get vp their bellies before they retorned. This a m'rchnt of Bourdeaulx tould me in whose company I traveled, &c. (C:DORC2)

Note how Mr. Cocks makes this Japanese practice perfectly familiar to his Western reader by introducing the European equivalent (as Valignano did writing about Shinto, with the difference being that Valignano pretended it was only *ancient* history in the West). And, let me add that the perfectly secular English Hakklyut Society's version of Cock's diary (C:DORC1) cut out all the detail – reducing the quote by a half – something I only realized upon finding the real thing in an edition of Cock's diary published in Japan![5]

It would be wrong, however, to give the impression of Japan as utterly lacking moral qualms about nudity and sex. In 1840, that is over a decade *before* Perry reopened Japan, the Confucian element in Japanese society prevailed upon the government to crack down on open promiscuity and religion-related sexuality. The pleasure quarters were left as is, but age-old stone phalluses, sculptures of, shall we say, Yin-Yang in action, and the life-size models on their "god-shelves" of courtesans were forced into hiding or destroyed. A large number of the last, according to the journalism of the time, was tossed into a river where they made quite a sight bobbing up and down in the current (most were weighted on the bottom so they wouldn't capsize, so the glans penis, particularly large according to the Japanese aesthetic tradition, poked up from the water!).

1. Schizophrenic West   At the time Frois wrote the anti-nudity campaign was reaching a zenith in Catholic Europe. In the Catholic Netherlands a censor even objected to the Christ child being shown naked and in Spain even tortured martyrs had to keep their clothes on.   Yet, the body could not be completely done away with (as it was in Protestant countries where old statues were destroyed) and Hale writes about Frois's King Phillip II that, "though having a scarf arranged round the loins of Cellini's naked marble Christ when it arrived for installation in the church of the Escorial [his private hermitage-palace] continued to enjoy Titian's glowingly physical mythological scenes in his other palaces." (H:CER) It seems to me that "our" infatuation for the body and "our" disgust for it come from the same place. If one does not live in a society where the body is dwelt upon, one does not get fed up with it, either.

2. Historical Buddhism and Sex   While there was Tantricism in Japan, it was far too small a practice to be worth noting. Valignano was wise to stop associating Buddhism with sex by contrasting the sexlessness of its *historia* with that of Shinto.

3. One part Too Many and Too Few If this book is ever done offset, I will add a half-page note here, for the history of the translation of the meeting of Izanagi and Izanami into bowdlerized English is very funny.

4. *"Historia" and Myth.* "Myth" is not intrinsically a bad word. It comes from a Greek word meaning "story." But "mythology" in its modern meaning is denigrating for it means that "their" beliefs are fiction while "ours" are true. The *"historia"* used by Valignano is better.

5. *Censorship of "Our" History.*   Censorship infuriates me for it presents us with a lie. The worst instance of it I know occurred in the USA, where "our" perverse fear of obscenity *ruined* our standard source of folk and cowboy song (Lomax). To see how witty obscenity was turned into trite Roy-Rogery, read the fine commentary and dirty (i.e. *real*) songs in Guy Logsdon: THE WHORE-HOUSE BELLS WERE RINGING! (U. of Illinois P. 1995)

~~~~~~

4-21   Our clergy show great sobriety and temperance with respect to drink, especially wine;
Os nossos religiosos tem muita sobriedade e temperansa no beber, maxime *vinho;*

The bonzes, though it is prohibited, are often [encountered?] drunk on the road.
Aos bonzos, com lhes ser prohibido, muitas vezes [se achão?] por esses caminhos bebados.

With wine (*vinho*) *especially* noted, it would seem there were problems with *other* drinks as well. Would they be tea drinking, cocoa (a favorite of Jesuits, that was considered addictive) and coffee, [1] or, were there other alcoholic drinks such as beer to take care with? [2]

Since there were many fake bonzes around; if nothing else because being a bonze was a good way to get around (professional poets, who had to travel a lot often did so in order to get through the fief checkpoints (*seki*) more easily), we cannot know how many of the drunk bonzes were the real thing. Not that it matters.   The prohibition in Japanese Buddhism had more to do with sumptuary law than morality. Like meat-eating, drinking is relatively wasteful. Fermentation may help otherwise lost food keep, but taking rice out of its limited circulation to make *sake* from it was, on the whole, an inefficient way to feed a large population. So there had to be some limits imposed and who better to bear them then bonzes? But Japanese saw and still see nothing wrong with being drunk *per se*. Since there are almost no mean and violent drunks in Japan (6-38 notes), the association of drink with the Devil was simply not there. And is it not true that *walking around drunk is a religious act in itself*, giving up the hubris of being "captain" of your soul, and letting fate, do as it likes with you?

I once stayed at a temple that enjoys a quiet renown for its 500 *rakkan*, stone statues of *arhat* (one of which is said to resemble anyone who searches) placed here and there throughout the grounds, rather than in stiff rows as is common. With a hip-joint ruined by pole-vaulting – or rather by an inattentive doctor – I had not so much come for the usual cross-legged meditation, but because I admired the natural placement of those *rakkan*. And I realized the very old and tiny hunch-backed grounds-keepers – so tiny, indeed, that I thought and still think them a different race (the legendary mountain *sanka,* perhaps?) – could not clean the rubbish (cans and cigarette cartons left by Japanese tourists, for no foreign tourist would be so sacrilegious) off the steep slopes, so I volunteered to do that rather than meditate (though I did meditate once to have the pleasure of being whacked by a bamboo stick and noticing that the incense was mosquito repellent of the type we used when I grew up (those green coils)). That night, the abbot, whom I guessed to be about 85, invited me out for dinner. We walked miles up down and around mountains. It was a chilly fall night, yet he wore *geta* and a light two-layer robe with an open collar and coughed now and then. After finally arriving to a mountain inn, we had wild boar (or, rather "mountain-whale" for Japanese Buddhists favor "fish" over meat – now, for the environmentalist's sake, perhaps they should speak of "sea-boar" for the whale!) *nabe* (stew cooked on ones table), and drank *sake* together, while singing the *Kurodabushi,* a macho samurai *sake*-drinking song and, unless I am mistaken, the *kazoe-uta* (a dirty counting-song) to the mama-san's amusement. We must have drunken quite a lot for I can't remember the return trip!

1. *Coffee and Jesuits.* I identify cocoa with Jesuits   because I smelled it whenever I cut through a certain hall at Georgetown, where I went to school. It was invented by nuns in Mexico (the Aztex's hot chocolate was bitter and fermented), but obviously, found its way to the monks. I read wonderful warnings about cocoa addiction somewhere and lost it. The original home of coffee is said to be Ethiopia and the Jesuits got there shortly after they got to Japan and had the King and his court converted within a half-century, but a revolution (1632) ended all that, and with it, I suspect, the possibility of a Jesuit coffee business. But, before that happened, coffee, despite being under-suspicion as an Islamic drink, did get all the way to the Pope (Clement IV) who, according to internet sources, baptized it and said either "coffee is so delicious it would be a pity to let the infidels have exclusive use of it" or "We will not let coffee remain the property of Satan. As Christians, our power is greater than Satan's; we shall make coffee our own." I do not know if the Jesuits had anything to do with this.

2. Beer etc. Distilled drinks were just beginning to move from the laboratories of alchemy to the bars about the time Frois wrote, so he would not have known about them, but beer is another matter. Unfortunately, I know nothing about it. Anyone?

4-22 Our clergy are not accustomed to singing and playing accompaniment at skits and profane comedies; *Os nossos religiosos não costumão cantar, nem tanjer em autos e farças profanas;*

The bonzes are old hats at it and accustomed to divert themselves that way.
Os bonzos tem isto por suas mangas e nellas se costumão recrear.

Not only were "our" fathers in Japan not big on performing, but worse, they could be wet-blankets when others wished to. In a letter written by Almeida in 1565, we find a church of Japanese Christians visited by dancing gentiles. In return, they created a dance lauding the Virgin Mary and took it to the gentiles' neighborhood. (This letter of Almeida's was the first time I ever read of dance exchanges! What a delightful custom!) On the return trip, they dropped by the church to show off the dance to Father Cosme de Torres, who not only locked the door and refused to see them, but the next day said mass early behind closed doors! He then made them understand how great a disgrace to God, not to mention their *padre,* their behavior had been. A Japanese nobleman took full responsibility for the dance on himself alone, and made *"notable penitencia"* disciplining himself so strongly "that he was left bathed in blood." This sense of personal responsibility greatly impressed Almeida about the quality of the Japanese Christians. He says nothing about whether he felt Cosme de Torres was right to be so strict. [1]

All bonzes were no more performers than they were warriors, but some were. A part of the Pureland (*Sôdo*) sect called the *jishû* was particularly noted for its rousing sutra performances, which irreligious literature reports could attract hundreds of good-looking wives into the temples. Basically, we are talking about a popular proclivity for what might be called Buddhist gospel music. It was centered on vocals, percussion and dancing and was considered enlightening. [2] The trader Caron, in Japan with the Dutch a generation after Frois, gives supporting evidence of a more neutral nature than that given by the Jesuits:

> The best of these [twelve Buddhist] Sects make Taverns of their Temples, which are most commonly built in the pleasantest and best places, sumptuous and well planted with trees and orchards: When the Inhabitants have a minde to rejoyce, they assemble here, and in the presence of their Gods, and company of their Priests, (who are likewise good fellows), they debauch and do those extravagances, which are the concomitants of excess and folly; common whores are permitted to enter and dance, the Priests themselves allowing of this jolity, and a further use, so it be in secret of these immodest females. (C:DOJ)

That this was not meant in criticism is clear from the next sentence: "I never heard that those people trouble themselves to dispute or argue in their religion; neither do they break their heads in converting others to their opinions; but leave every one to the freedom of his own, as indifferent and reasonable, as being infused into him by their Gods." The 1661 edition adds that "anyone who has need for money will readily change his sect for a hundred crowns" but, still, I read this as *approval* rather than criticism.   Having witnessed the disgusting carnage, the massacres and cruelty of the religious wars in Europe, Caron was evidently relieved at Japanese sanity and pragmatism with respect to faith.   He also showed up in Japan at the right time, for the Buddhist sects that *had* competed vociferously in Frois's time were quashed, so Japan was a peaceful spiritual free-market.   If men did not badger their neighbors as persistently as some Christians did (and still do), temples, sects and bonzes did continue to actively compete for clients.   They were not great orators for nothing.   Indeed, religious performers of all types may have been more active in Japan than in Europe. I can recall reading in Issa's diary (late-18th-19th century) of a sect that paraded a woman about naked (the excuse being that she was going from temple to temple to pray) for a publicity stunt (the object being to draw a crowd into the temple) on several occasions before – no doubt at the behest of a competing temple – the authorities cracked down!

Indeed, a strange, diverse street drama flowered throughout the Edo era, which began about the time Caron visited and continued until the Opening of Japan. Aside from the major sects, there was a host of begging bonzes, real and pseudo, with a variety of dramatic gimmicks to sell themselves. In Mitani Kazuma's masterful sketches of the street venders of Edo (EDO-SHOBAI-ZUE), we find a score of "voluntary bonzes and beggars" (some Shinto in motif) including:

1) *konpira-mairi* – pilgrims who individually carry about a huge mask (half the size of their body) of a *tengu* (long-red nosed goblin) on their back;

2) *nanatsu-bozu* – groups of young bonzes who suddenly appear at *nanatsu* (four in the afternoon), hitting wooden rhythm sticks together and fast-stepping dance a sutra;

3) *waiwai-teno* – who wear a tengu mask and go door to door;

4) *komosô* – who play flutes from under hats that look like garbage cans over their heads;

5) *gorishô* – who make the head of a fox spring out of a hole under a mock-up of a Shinto shrine entrance (*torii*) and dance about on a long springy neck (the movement and name suggests the male's member!);

6) *ongyô* – who dance while ringing a bell and scattering about tiny drawings of monsters for children;

7) *yamabushi* – mountain priests who dressed uniquely and walked about blowing on a welch shell;

8) *sutasuta-bozu* – bonzes named mimetically for the rustling sound their straw skirts made when they danced about;

9) *sange!zange!* – bonzes who walked about shaking his partial shakujô (a pole with iron rings on it) and singing out "repent! repent!" and bringing luck;

10) *chobokure-bozu* – who rattled coins strung between the ends of a bamboo pincers while shouting out tongue-twisters;

11) *oshaka* – who walked about with an adorned pail containing a statue of Buddha in it on Buddha's birthday (8th day of the 4th month) calling out *"oshaka! oshaka!"* (Shakamuni);

12) *konôgyo-nin* – who walked back and forth on foot-high sandals with a pail of water containing some sprigs of star anise (*Illicium religiousum*), while bonging a gong with a hammer yet not spilling a drop of water;

13) *Handa-ina-ni* – who carried a big load of red things including a big banner and rag-doll measles monkey while dancing about and singing "measles are light (nothing much) small-pox is light, if you are devout . . ." and handed out clay dolls to children;

14) *otenki-o kitô* – four or five men would dance about under big umbrellas ringing bells and loudly yelling for the rain to let up;

15) *kangaemono* – a bonze-like man would distribute riddles to houses, then go about explaining and collecting money for them . . .

..

If some of the Jesuits in Japan were not much on singing and instrumental performance, their Society was, nonetheless, on the forefront of drama-as-a-teaching-device in Europe and it is no accident Frois devoted a chapter of the TRATADO to it.

1. *Discouraging Play?* DR notes that in New Spain, "crosses with feathers on them and dances to the Virgin Mary were tolerated if not encouraged" and wonders if the difference might not derive from the Jesuits being less tolerant of the Japanese precisely because they thought of them as their equals. I think that a good guess, but my first assumption would be that it depended on the date: whether the dance was a native embellishment of a Christian tradition or Christians flying their colors if it were in a native context. It was also before Valignano and his policy of "accommodation," which not only took effect in Japan and China, but North India where the Jesuits "mounted lavish festivals, fireworks, parades, and choral services, even going so far as to hire tightrope walkers and jugglers and to decorate the Christmas crib with mechanical apes and birds." (For more, see Gauvin Alexander Bailey: *Unto the Indies* www.companysj.com/v132/ untoin.html)

2. *Dancing for Buddha Tradition*. The Buddhists in Japan had a long history of dancing. For some reason, *it goes together with the sects that claim faith is everything,* just as it does with Usanian Christianity. Is that because there is something parallel between losing one's self in faith and in dance? Pure Land Buddhism held that having faith as represented by simply repeating *Namu-amida-butsu* was enough, but some of that faith danced. In 1279, the traveling Pure Land priest Ippen "revalued and systematicized the Amidist dances. It was an extraordinary success: commoners danced with him and recited *Namu Amida butsu.* Ippen gave to Amidist dances the rhythms of the peasant dances . . . As the dancers approached a state of ecstasy, their movement took on magical aspects . . ." (S(R):WTUD) They were, in short, purified and fortified against disease. They went around the country fomenting(?) dance and "whether or not they believed did not matter." He wasn't allowed into Kamakura "for fear that his enraptured dancers would cause disruptions."

〜〜〜〜〜〜〜〜〜〜〜〜〜〜〜〜〜〜〜〜〜〜〜〜〜〜〜〜〜〜〜〜〜〜〜〜

4-23   We have faith in the glory and punishment of the future and the immortality of the soul;
Nós temos por fé a glória e pena futura e immortalidade da alma;

The Zenshû [zen sect] bonzes deny all of this and [claim] there is nothing more than being born and dying. *Os* bonzos Jenxus *negão tudo isto e que não há mais que nacer e morrer.*

Today "we" would be more likely to associate "joy" with Heaven than "glory." The *pena* of the future, suggesting Hell, encompasses both *imprisonment* and *sorrow*, so I chose a word containing both: *punishment*. The "we" means the clergy. I do not know if Frois could have imagined a European like Montaigne (and, doubtless, many who read him), who was unsure about immortality.

Had Frois been writing a book on *similarities* rather than differences, he might have skipped Zen's missing spiritual geography altogether, and observed instead that of all Asian people, only the Japanese had a decent Hell [1] – or rather a pandemonium of hells – capable of competing with the Christian one! (This was true for Heaven, too, but to a far more limited extent). Japanese depictions of Hell are fantastic, more terrifying, and better art than ours. Did the artists have more fun with it because they believed in it less?). Evidently noticing the great variety of demons, Valignano perceptively guessed that the divinities of conquered peoples were incorporated as such. (S:VMPpg82) Yet, if the Japanese Buddhist Hell was equally full of fire and poking and cutting, etc., how you got there and how long you stayed was another matter. *Faux Frois:*

> With us, anyone who is not saved by Jesus ends up in Hell forever.
> With them, only people who commit major sins go to Hell and for a limited time.

Is not the Japanese Hell *better* than "ours" from the moral standpoint as well as the aesthetic? Much of the Christian Hell, in my opinion, is a damnable idea. Can anyone not *feel for* the poor Japanese and kind St. Xavier, who wrote the following about the effect of "our" unforgiving theology?

> One of the things that most of all pains and torments these Japanese is, that we teach them that the prison of hell is irrevocably shut, so that there is no egress therefrom. For they grieve over the fate of their departed children, of their parents and relatives, and they often show their grief by their tears. So they ask us if their is any hope, any way to free them by prayer from that eternal misery, and I am obliged to answer that there is absolutely none. Their grief at this affects and torments them wonderfully; they almost pine away with sorrow. . . . They often ask if God cannot take their fathers out of hell, and why their punishment must never have an end. We gave them a

satisfactory answer, but they did not cease to grieve over the misfortune of their relatives; and I can hardly restrain my tears sometimes at seeing men so dear to my heart suffer such intense pain about a thing that is already done with and can never be undone. (C:LLFX)

Is *that* not Hell on Earth! What a *horrible* belief! If you ask me both the Japanese Christians and St. Xavier were too good for Christianity! For Christ's sake, was "our" God too small to make exceptions!? Mandatory fixed-punishment is sometimes necessary when time and money does not permit case-by-case judgment, but wasn't *Deus* supposed to be omnipotent? To the Catholic's credit, I should add that since the Second Vatican Council, things have not been so simple.[1]

Frois is right on about Zen's belief, or rather absence thereof, though it may be put in a more poetic way: *getting born is dying.* Or to put it in the words of a nineteenth century resident of Concord, *one world at a time.* The Zen-shû, or Zen faith (there is more than one sect of Zen) is one of three main faiths of Buddhism in Japan, the other two being the Pure Land sect, which emphasized egalitarianism and mercy and the Nichiren sect which combined Buddhism with nationalism. Skeptical down to the bone and marked by the practice of meditation with the goal being direct experience of reality rather than paradise, Zen had more appeal to the intellectual upper class than common folk. Because the Jesuits tended to take the high road – try to convert the rulers who could convince their subjects to follow them – in Japan, they quickly discovered they were in competition with Zen. In his HISTORIA , Frois describes a debate between Fr. Lourenço and Shôzaemon, who came walking into their Miaco (Kyoto) church looking for someone who would preach to him. Since Lourenco didn't know how much Shozaemon knew, he began by describing the "great differences" between the Japanese *kami* (Gods) and *hotoke* (Buddhas) and *Deus.* Shozaemon smiled and said it was a waste of time to bother with details about the existence and powers of gods "for all that is a laughable illusion" which "wise and knowledgeable men value not a whit." He then explained that in his faith, Zen, besides the four elements, there was a fifth essence (*quinta essencia*) and that was called *mu,* or "nothing," although that, too, did not define the essence which was called many things. To better grasp this *mu,* people practiced meditation and struggled to solve *koans* (paradoxical puzzles). Yet even the most learned people could not really pin it down. So what do you think about this *nothing* that is the core and focus of Zen? Lourenco's reply to all this was

> I am delighted you ask that. For, with you (unlike others) it means I can skip explaining . . why the reason cannot be satisfied with *kami* and *hotoke.* You tell me that there is great debate over the nature of the fifth essence in Zen . . . Well, you should know *that* is the main reason and motivation why the *batenren* (Jesuits) came here from afar. . [solving this question] is their [our] mission and goal. . . . First, you should know that the ancient philosophers of Europe held that, besides the four elements, there was a fifth essence, which they called "heaven." (ch8p102,3)

This Lourenco was quite the preacher. He was more famous for out-debating, or rather goading an old Nichiren priest into attempting to cut off his head (to see if a soul came out) in front of Nobunaga, who apparently favored the (slightly) cooler Christians. (HISTORIA and C:TCJ) Nobunaga was probably *agnostic*, as were most upper-class Japanese. Huxley's term fits because Japanese were usually not so black and white about it as our atheists, whose intensity often echoes that of their opposition. This did not just come from Zen Buddhism. Confucianism, which tended toward a sort of deistic animism, was even more influential in Japan. Indeed, Kaempfer, in 1692, described *Siuto* (*judo,* meaning "Confucian-way,") as "the Philosophical Sect" in Japan. Not believing in the transmigration of souls, they "admit of none but temporal rewards, or punishments." They "believe in an *Animam mundi*, an universal Soul, Spirit or power, diffused throughout the whole world which animates all things" but, "admitting no Gods, they have no temples, no forms of worship." This was similar to the belief system of the literati in China described as *Epicurean* by Ricci in 1584. (S:MPMR) In the early-19th century, with nary a mention of Zen or Confucianism, Golownin introduced a new, more contemporary vocabulary, writing about "free-thinkers" in Japan, who "deny the existence of a Supreme Being, ascribe the creation and government of the world all to chance, and doubt of every thing." The Japanese translator whom Golownin called "our friend Teske" did a fine job of explaining his philosophy, and I would bet a bottle of Vodka that the end of his argument was read by Dostoevsky, for the *Inquisitor* chapter of the BROTHERS KARAMATSOV echoes his every line!

> But as it is not to be expected, that a whole nation should become philosophers, and comprehend this truth, and as the majority would probably make use of this doctrine only to the injury of others, it is absolutely necessary to deceive the common people, and convince them that there is a superior power which sees our most secret actions, and to which we must some day give a strict account of all the evil done to our fellow-creatures, and severely atone for it. In a word, he considered every religion as a fraud, necessary for the good of the people.. (G:MCJ)

Golownin's editor notes in a footnote that "all the early writers assert that, notwithstanding the infinity and variety of the Gods introduced into Japan, all the grandees are decided Atheists, and actually disbelieve the immortality of the soul, although they preserve public appearance by professing an adherence to some particular sect." I suspect the same could have been said for the classically-inclined upper-class in Europe. Golownin, at any rate, included a strange qualification which suggests he didn't want to be stamped an atheist: "We made our objections to such principles, but as he understood very little Russian, and we as little Japanese, our arguments entirely failed of producing any effect." (Strange, because they had no trouble understanding *his* argument.) Teske elsewhere defended the usefulness of preserving ethnocentric belief, no matter how "ridiculous and incredible," as useful to the state!

If Confucianism was similar to Epicurean thought, Zen, which we might call Tao-Buddhism to better reflect its similarly Chinese roots, [2] bears resemblance to Christian mysticism in both the rigorous discipline with its aim of unity with the ALL and NOTHING, and in the free behavior of the enlightened. But such an understanding was apparently beyond Frois. He saw Zen temples as places for aristocrats who had no concern whatsoever for their souls and concentrate on one thing: worldly pleasure (J/F:HISTORIA ch19). To a degree, he may have been right. Many of the aristocrats may well have been dilettantes practicing Zen because it was cool (especially with the tea ceremony link). Yet, Joao Rodrigues, writing two decades later, was clearly impressed:

> Their vocation is not to philosophize with the help of books and sermons written by illustrious masters and philosophers . . . . Instead, they give themselves up to contemplating the things of nature . . . Thus, from what they see in things themselves, they attain by their own efforts to a knowledge of the first cause, and putting aside what is evil and imperfect in the mind and reasoning, they reach the natural perfection and being of the first cause. . . . the monks of this sect are of a resolute and determined character, without any indolence, laxity or effeminacy. . . .they do without a great number of things which they consider superfluous and unnecessary. They maintain that a hermitage should first of all be frugal and moderate, with much quietness, peace of soul and exterior modesty. (in C:TCJ)

Rodrigues qualifies his remarks by going on to claim it was so much "hypocrisy;" but the context – a description of the tea ceremony (tea-masters were generally of the Zen sect) Rodrigues and the other Jesuits clearly admired – made me wonder if he only wrote that to keep from getting in trouble with Rome. [3]

> *We believe that a man or woman has only one life on this earth which settles our fate forever;*
> *They believe that people are born over and over into higher or lower states depending on their conduct.*

Reincarnation is not so perfect a contrast with the Christian belief as the lack of reward and punishment of the Zen faith, but it is better than many contrasts Frois did not forget to make and it was far more representative of the religious belief of most Japanese than Zen. And that may be true for Chinese, too. According to Ricci "the pervasiveness of ideas of reincarnation, accounted for the great amount of infanticide in China, since the very poor would kill infants in the hope that they would be reborn soon into a richer family" (S:MPMR). So, *that* sin, too, could be laid at the door of Buddhism, although Ricci took care to blam "our" Pythagoras for inventing the mistaken idea of reincarnation he hoped the Chinese would abandon for the correct religion.

1. *Non-Christians and Hell*   According to www.scarboromissions.ca/Interfaith_dialogue/global_dia-logue.php: "In past centuries, Christian missionaries tended to view other cultures and religions as corrupt and godless. The modern missionary is more likely to see God as already present and active in other religious cultures. Christian mission, therefore, does not consist of a movement toward theological and cultural imperialism. It can, however, involve the experience of inculturation." This is a wonderful development that seems to go one step beyond the Bungo Concensus and even recognize the relativity of religion. It began with Pope Paul VI and the Second Vatican Council of 1967 and was developed further by John Paul II, who even apologized for historical "mistakes." I do not know what this does about the Hell problem, but Rev. Arimasa Kubo writes that it is not true that non-Christians go to Hell. That idea is a corrupt understanding that arose in the Middle Ages, he writes, citing the Bible to prove his point. They go to Hades [Sheol], which is temporary, "where they await His court of judgment, when "God will determine their final destiny: either the kingdom of God [new Heaven and new Earth] or ("the lake of fire" [Hell] www2.biglobe.ne.jp/~remnant/ hades.htm). So there is at least a chance God might exercise judicial restraint in the final event.

2. *Chinese Roots of Areligiousity*. The lack of interest in the other world is not just Zen or Cha'an, to use the Chinese word for the same. It may be the natural outcome of millennium of civilization. Enroute to Japan from China in 1555, Padre Maestro Melchior (later, as Secretary for the Jesuits very supportive of Frois's writing) observed that Chinese were –

> "very ingenious with works of the hands and very able in matters of buying and selling and all that touches upon sustaining the corporal life; but never have I seen a people blinder about things of the soul . . . . they don't know of a sole God creator of all things, nor expect reward or punishment in the other life, and from this little interest in the business of the soul (*negocios del alma*) is born." (CARTAS)

3. *Rodriguez and Zen* Reading Cooper's *Rodrigues The Interpreter* disabused me of the notion that Rodrigues really did not feel antagonistic to Zen. It also made me wonder if it were not possible that he was helped in his efforts by that missing first book of Frois's.

~~~~~~

4-24   We profess just one God, one faith, one baptism and one Catholic Church.
Nós profesamos hum só Deus, huma fee, hum baptismo e huma Igreja Catolica;

> In Japan, there are thirteen sects and almost all disagree on their faith and devotions. *Em Japão há 13 ceytas e quasi todas discrepão no culto e adorasão.*

Frois *wishes* "our" side were so united. With the Reformation well underway, most of Europe was in a constant state of religious war. "We" contended over infant vs. childhood baptism, predestination vs. salvation by good works, celibacy vs. marriage for clergy, sacred images vs. iconoclasm and, most important, regional vs. Papal control. We are not only talking about armies fighting armies, but numerous gruesome civilian massacres (St. Bartholomew's Day is just one) of the type we now associate with machete or AK-14 wielding ethnic groups in Africa or Central Europe and the torture and execution of the clergy on both sides. English-reading readers have read plenty about the atrocities of the Spanish Inquisition. How about one from "our" side of the channel?

> He left with three other priests for England on April 24. He was asked if the Pope could err. His response was "No." This response was taken as a plea of guilty and he was sentenced to death. He was drawn at Tyburn, where he desired all Catholics to pray for him. He was cut down and disemboweled while still alive. (from WELCOME TO KEEPING CATHOLICS CATHOLIC PAGE XXV THE TIMELINE OF THE CATHOLIC CHURCH THE SIXTEENTH CENTURY CONTINUED)

If there was "one church" it was only "catholic" in the sense that everyone thought their side was the one rightful faith and the others invalid if not criminal. Frois wrote shortly after Phillip II re-conquered the Netherlands. They would almost immediately rebel again. Things were already horrible and would only get worse.   Soon, Lutherans from Holland and England would be warning the Japanese against "Papist plots," and, with some help from the Franciscans (who insisted on confronting the Japanese), poison the atmosphere too heavily to permit Christianity to survive in Japan. If we think Frois is slow to catch on, even four years *after* TRATADO, when knowledge of the failed Armada should have reached Macao and the *padres* church in Nagasaki had been demolished, largely because of fears spread by other Westerners, we find Miguel=Valignano blithely going on and on about the *single aim, single spirit, and singularly perfect unanimity of belief* in the West. (dialog 7 DE MISSIONE)   Did they 1) wish to keep religious discord in the West a secret? 2) think that writing something down might help make it come true? 3) fail to recognize reality because it spoiled their dream?   Is this political, or is it wish-fulfillment?

But let us proceed to the second half of the distich. About Japanese Buddhism, Xavier wrote:

There are nine kinds of sects, all of them different from each other, and both men and women may freely chose whichever one they please, and there is no compulsion to join one sect rather than another. The matter is left for the individual to decide and it is not considered at all strange to find a family in which the husband belongs to one sect, the wife to another and the children to a third. (in C:TCJ)

Did five new sects appeared in the half century between Xavier and Frois?[1] Does it matter? No. The important observation is that, as Frois wrote, there was open disagreement and as Xavier noted, probably without approval, there was individual religious freedom in Japan that was unheard of in Europe.[2]   Indeed, members of families of Japanese could simultaneously belong not only to different sects, as he observes, but individually to more than one religion – i.e., Shinto and Buddhism – at once.   This did not stop the sects from fighting one another.   Xavier also writes that "little love is lost between" the bonzes who wear gray habits and those that wear black "because black bonzes loathe the gray ones, declaring that they are ignorant and lead bad lives . . ." (Ibid.) But they did not drag everyone into it and murder each other in the European fashion. This charming sentence from Cock's diary, coincidentally written just one day before an edict banning Catholic religion was issued in Edo on 9/8/1616, transmits the atmosphere of that murderous era better than anything on the other side I could translate from Spanish or Portuguese:

But that it were good he [the Kynge of Firandos [Hirado's] brother] advized the Emperour to take heed of them [the padres], lest they did not goe about to serve hym as they had donne the Kinges of England, in going about to kill & poizen them or to blow them vp w'th gunpoulder, & sturing vp the subiectes to rebell against their naturall prince, for w'ch they were all banished out of England, &c. (C:DORC1)

Be that as it may, Frois's contrast emphasizes "our" unity – there is but one way to go to heaven – and their disunity – there are many ways to go to hell.   In 1585, he clearly knew a lot more about Buddhism than he did in a letter of 1565, when he belittled its theological riches by claiming "the diversity of the sects of Japan, China and Sion (Thailand) is very little; their *Pagodes* [temples=sects?] have different names while being the same." In his HISTORIA chapter dealing with 1565 written simultaneously and after TRATADO, Frois not only noted that St. Xavier wanted them to be able to explain how *each different* Buddhist sect's beliefs differed from the Christian Belief but, following a passage on how he and Vilela had a hard time converting Zen-Buddhists, who wanted concrete rather than logical proof, added, *but it's worth the trouble*, for they (Zen-Buddhists) have particularly good-quality minds and later can grasp the truth so much the better, and

For us, it is a great advantage that Japan has different sects and diverse and opposing beliefs. It made it easier for us to introduce our Lord *Deus* [into this country]. If all [the Japanese] solidified around the same religious principles, it would probably have been very difficult to get them to accept our teachings. (J/F:Historia ch18)

What I like about the Jesuits is the way they find *something good in everything*. Whether it is because they want to justify all that happens for the sake of God's reputation or because they are apprehensive lest complaining should hurt their own reputations, or were trained in what we now call "positive-thinking" I really can't say! Of course, this wasn't just a Jesuit trait. It was shared to a degree by all good Christians. After Mary Rolandson slaughtered her indian captors and returned to New England civilization, she felt very grateful for the *opportunity* God gave her to suffer and gain brownie points for Heaven. (See her 1682 work, *A True History of the Captivity and Restoration of Mrs. Mary Rolandson, a Minister's Wife in New England*).   While Valignano and his able crew in Japan overcame the setbacks of the late 1580's and succeeded in keeping the church membership growing for over two more decades, the heart-wrenching epic of torture and martyrdom that was to put an end to the whole effort was just around the corner. Even though I am very happy that Japanese did not become Christian, it makes me sad to think about it.

1. *Number of Sects*   There were traditionally 13 Buddhist sects in China and 8 in Japan. (The number 8, however, is hard to take literally for it also means "many" in Japanese.) That explains the difference.

2. *Religious Freedom*   The early modern West was spiritually totalitarian. In the mid-sixteenth century (following the 1559 Elizabethan Act of Uniformity), English were legally bound to go to church on certain days and *put in jail for non-attendance.* A mayor of York "was hauled before the Northern Ecclesiastical Commission to answer for his wife's absence from church."(LR)   In Calvinist Geneva,

> the Registers reveal that bridesmaids were arrested for decorating a bride too gaily. People were punished for dancing, spending time in taverns, eating fish on Good Friday, having their fortunes told, objecting when the priest christened their child by a different name from the one they had chosen, arranging a marriage between persons of disparate ages, singing songs against Calvin, and much besides. Pierre Ami, one of those responsible for bringing Calvin to Geneva, was imprisoned for dancing with his wife at a betrothal; his wife later had to flee the country. . . . Attendance at church on Sundays and on Wednesdays was compulsory, and the police went through streets, shops and homes to see if anyone was evading his duty. On the other hand, it was a punishable offence to go to church except at the hour of service. Grant observes: '. . . the dress of citizens, male and female, the mode of dressing the hair, the dishes served on ordinary days and on festivals, the jokes in the streets, the character of private entertainments − all were enquired into, and what seemed wrong was censured and punished. . . . In Geneva, seventeen sermons were given every week, two on each weekday and five on Sunday, and attendance at all was compulsory.' (T:SIH)

By the mid-seventeenth century, Puritan England followed suit:

> "there was a flurry of acts . . . . prohibiting maypoles, abolishing Christmas, Whitsun and Easter as pagan festivals, ordering the Book of Sports to be burnt, and even banning "idle sitting at doors and walking in churchyards". . . . . . The only behavior which was permissible when not actually at church was the singing of psalms or the repeating of sermons. Richard Baxter records with satisfaction how he walked through Kidderminster in 1660 and heard nothing on all sides but the sound of families singing psalms and saying sermons, which had not been the case (he noted) when he first went there in 1641. Baxter's walk must have been privileged, for the law was that Communion was to be denied to anyone who Played football, travelled, or walked on Sunday." (T:SIH)

In Iberia, confession and communion were mandatory. In Rome, even two hundred years after Frois, the names of people who failed to take the Sacrament at Easter were posted on the door of the church and people encouraged to hound such heretics (Casanova, missing his "Easter duty" had to confess to a Franciscan monk and beg a certificate explaining he was confined to bed that morning to get his name cleared (C(T):HML v11-2).

There were exceptional periods and places of toleration, but totalitarianism was the rule.   In most of the world, including Japan, no one could even *imagine* forcing people to attend religious services! This does not necessarily mean the Japanese were *always completely* free. As Gulick wrote in 1903, "though perfect liberty is the rule, one topic is even got under official embargo. No one may express public dissent from the authorized version of Japanese history."   Gulick writes of a professor who was fired for making an attempt to interpret ancient myths, as his work was thought to undermine the claims of divine descent of the Imperial line. And, a century after Gulick wrote, messing in such territory carried some risk of reprisal from the fanatic right. This type of thing was probably not true, or far less true, in Frois's time.

Note that the sources for most of this note on intolerance in the Christian West are sex-related. Taylor's *Sex in History* and Casanova's *History of My Life.*   That says something, though I am not sure exactly what.

4-25   We hate and abominate the devil above all else;
Nós sobre todas as couzas avorrecemos e abominamos ao demonio;

> The bonzes venerate and worship him, build him temples and make him great offerings. *Os bonzos o venerão e adorão e lhe fazem templos e grandes sacreficios.*

..

The Devil.   What a concept! Most cultures have no such thing, unless it is a trickster hero/villain of the type of Creation legends we would call *just-so stories.* That is because the idea of a singular Devil is the flip-side of the coin of the idea of a singular God.   If there is just one God and he is accountable for all, one must either admit that he has a heartless side or invent the Devil. The most influential Kabbalistic text, *The Zobar,* written by the Spanish mystic Moses de Leon in about 1275 found the original "root of evil in God himself" and suggested it became "evil and destructive" only when it broke away from working in harmony with divine Mercy. (A:HOG). With the 1484 Papal Bull *Summa Desiderantes,* the Devil broke away with a vengeance. He took concrete form to the extent that even his freezing cold forked penis was seriously described. If God was contrasted to the Devil, the Holy Virgin (who, over the Medieval period took over a large portion of religious interest) was now contrasted to the diabolic Witch. With Germany and the other North countries taking the lead, all of Europe, except for Italy, indulged their psychotic fear (a devil that through his followers, i.e. women, spread impotence as well as sexual license) fantasies in the trial, torture and execution of thousands if not millions of people that ended in Spain only with Salazar's report of 1611 that found not one *bona fide* – or, should I say, *mala fide?* – witch among 11,300 accused he examined in Spain.[1] Even as the Church battled the heresy of the Manichees, it, itself, turned as radically dualistic as a religion could possibly be. Indeed, Taylor hypothesizes that "the persecution of Manichaeism became inevitable, because it made the whole Christian position ludicrous." (T:SIH[2])

According to "our" thinking even the gentle Buddha was ultimately a tool of the Devil. In 1569, Vilela wrote "They have a dozen sects and all different one from the other; but, in the end, all give signs of their [common] inventor, who is the devil.[3]" Frois, in a 1565 letter, Englished by Willis, also wrote of "how artificially [craftily]. how cunningly, under the pretext of religion that crafty adversary of mankind, leadeth and draweth into perdition the Japanese minds, blinded with many superstitions and ceremonies, [so that the reader] may the more pity this nation." But I believe Frois, on the whole less vituperative than Vilela, probably refers in this distich to the fact that in Buddhist temples from India to Japan, one *does* often find the closest thing the Buddhists have to the Devil. Kaempfer introduces him in 1690:

> Jemma, or with a more majestuous Character Jemma O [king], (by which same name he is known to the Brahmines, Siamites, and Chinese,) is the severe Judge and sovereign commander of this place of horror and heinousness, by means of a large looking-glass, placed before him and called, Ssofarino Kagami or the looking-glass of knowledge. (K:HOJ)

Enma, or *Yama*, if you would go back to the Sanskrit roots, kept score of one's sins (in writing: so, Enma's ledger is slang for a report card) and commanded an army of demons to carry out the punishments. Kaempfer goes on to explain that the "poor unhappy Souls" in Hell may receive "great relief" (lighter punishment, early release, etc) by the "*virtuous life and good actions of their family friends and relatives*" and by "the prayers and offerings of the Priests to the great and good Amida" (a Buddha of mercy). I would only add that it was also possible to appeal for mercy directly to the Judge, and that doing so had none of the nefarious connotations as our "deals with the Devil." Frois, himself describes a "temple, dedicated to the god and judge of hell" where people did just that in his long letter about the temples of Kyoto of 1565:

On the walls are painted the many kinds of torments in hell, with many figures of men and women suffering these pains, and of the demons inflicting them. Many people visit this temple to pray and give alms, and they usually repair there to beg the king of hell to deliver them from these torments. (in C:TCJ)

The reason Japanese could pray to Enma is simple: *he is not evil*. He did not lure people or pursue them. He did not delight in bad behavior nor seek to increase it. If anything, his existence discouraged it. He only judged them for their sins, and made sure they got what was coming to them. I first became acquainted with this Jemma, called Yama or Emma(o) in Japan today, editing a book of CHINESE MOTHER GOOSE rhymes. A lullaby suggests that your baby's brains will get squeezed with a hoop to provide oil to fry *tofu* and the fearsome King Yama, wearing his own iron crown, will come for that *tofu* and make your little body shake like you have malarial fever *unless you go to sleep, like a good kid!* Reverend I.T. Headland's translation drops the deadly shakes and turns this Pluto into a simple "king." It was a good decision, for "our" Devil could not be so lightly joked with. That relates to a problem with Frois's contrast: the Occidental reader cannot help but construct the Japanese Devil in the image of their own demonized Satan. It is one of the worse *apples and oranges* comparison ever made (There are more demons that are not devils in 5-8.). Had Frois been neutral on religion his contrast might have gone like this:

> *Our Devil is cruel and wants to seduce us away from God by causing us to do evil things;*
> *Their Devil is kind, for he wants to frighten people so as to not do any evil and stay good.*

There was a shrine/hall for Enma that was part of the Inshôji Temple in Kyoto that was so popular the temple came to be known as Enma-dô and boasted one of the top three annual big-praying events (*dainenbutsu* = public-marathons-of-prayer) in the city. There were also two days a year for visiting Enma shrines/halls (part of larger Buddhist temples) throughout Japan. On these days (January 16 and July 16 – on the first day of the waning moon of Spring and Fall in the old calendar), the lids were said to be taken off the cauldrons in Hades, as the demons employed for the torture were allowed to take their vacations. It was thought a good time to communicate to relatives who might be undergoing punishment. Issa (d.1823), whose compassion even extended to what we would call "objects" wrote this haiku about that day:

sanichi-wa fumaruru usu mo yasumi kana

on enma day
even treaded mortars
get a day off

Finally, there is the matter of Frois's *"grandes sacreficios,"* which I translated as "great offerings." Japanese did not kill animals such as might be imagined by such language. The offertory boxes, called, as noted earlier, "alligator-mouths," are what made a killing on such days.

1. *Salazar.* We need to make a list of the real heroes in history, not your conquerors, but people who stood up to oppression and cruelty. *Las Casas, Salazar, . . .*

2. *Sex and Intolerance* Summing up the Inquisition's rational for the witch-hunt, Taylor writes: " In short, we find the Church alleging similarities between a somewhat diverse group of sects, a diversity which is rather marked in the case of the Cathars and the witches, since the former abstained from all intercourse while the latter made it the centre of their religion. . . . Thus heresy became a sexual rather than a doctrinal concept; to say a man was a heretic was to say he was a homosexual, and vice versa. . . . the Church sought to bring together all its enemies into a common pattern, and to tar them with the same brush." (T:SIH) This provides one more reason why the Jesuits, despite their not being particularly interested in pursuing witchcraft, still harped on sodomy.

3. *Devil and Capitalization.* My impression of old writing in Europe was that capitalization was more common than today. This was not as common in Latin languages as in North European ones. Still I expected the Devil would be capitalized. In Vilela, as in Frois's contrast, it is *"el demonio."* I do not know if such a usage suggests a policy of not o granting Satan's appellation the honor of being a proper noun or Latin language. *Experts?*

4-26   With us, the temples and offices of the monastery belong to the whole Order;
Antre nós o templo e as oficinas do moesteiro hé da Religião universal;

> In Japan, if a bonze becomes disenchanted, he sells off the temple and its offices.
> *Em Japão se hum bonzo ali se eemfada, vende o templo e as oficinas e [tudo?]*

Yet another contrast of collectivist=humble us vs. individualist=selfish them. By "offices," Frois means the rights and duties conferred by the authorities to do what the temple does. Perhaps "dispensations" would also do for a translation. Okada believes Frois alludes to the fact that when a Buddhist temple lost its backing, or the prelate retired (without a successor?), it was declared a *haidera,* or "derelict temple" and might even be bought for use by a different sect (or, even different religion, such as the Christianity?).

Today, one finds many privately owned Buddhist temples (お寺の私有率は？) throughout Japan. That a private property could be "declared a derelict temple" implies a sort of communal ownership that lets the Buddhists (of whatever sect?) use it or what we would now call zoning but I do not know the details (さて、この点も困っています！)

4-27   Our priests wear a stole to administer the sacraments;
Os nossos sacerdotes uzão da estola pera ministrar sacramentos;

> The bonzes wear them for appearance sake when making their visitations.
> *Os bonzos uzão dela por honra quando vão fora a suas visitasões.*

What exactly *is* a stole? Here are parts of a description from one of the "articles written by our parishioners" (in this case, Dean Rose) of the Anglican Church of Saint Peter:

> The stole is a long scarf-like cloth that hangs around the neck, over the shoulders and down the front of bishops and priests [generally, two-four inches across]. Deacons wear the stole around the neck and across the chest. The stole was the insignia of Roman magistrates and governors .It was originally a symbolic towel *indicating that the magistrate was sweating or working hard on behalf of society.* It was worn at the Imperial court and for public ceremonies. In the Roman era it meant that power also required becoming a servant. . . . [my added *italics*]

> The stole was made of white sheep's wool symbolizing that like Christ the good shepherd a bishop must care for the sheep of his flock. [I do not know about Frois's time; now it is generally silk] . . .

> Before the sixth century the priest's stole was called an *orarion* (from the Latin word *orare* - to pray) and indicated the role of priests in leading the prayers in public worship. Stole is a Greco-Latin word meaning "garment" or simply "cloth" and may be the origin of the phrase "man of the cloth". . .

> Wearing the stole symbolizes the taking on of the yoke of Christ's service (*Matthew* 11:29,30). The stole has a small cross in its middle at the nape of the neck. The bishop or priest may kiss this cross before putting on the stole as a symbol that they take on Christ's yoke and carry his cross in the spirit of willingness and love. (http://www.geocities.com/saintpeter_oshawa/articles-Vestments.html)

The Buddhist equivalent to the stole was the *kesa,* a scarf-like cloth generally worn diagonally over their robe like a baldric (belt for a weapon in the West) when going out on official religious duties such as conferencing with other bonzes. It would seem what Frois is really saying is *we adorn ourselves to pray to God ;they do so to go out and meet people.* But, it is unfair, for getting around *is* the business of bonzes. Frois's *honra* makes it seem that the bonzes dress just to show-off (why I translated "for appearance sake") and not to any religious purpose.

~~~~~~

4-28　Our priests wear it draped about their necks;
Os nossos sacerdotes a trazem deitada ao pescoso;

> The bonzes wear it as a baldric [diagonally], and it is larger and a different shape.
> *Os bonzos como tiracolo, mais larga e feita doutra feisão.*

The *stole* again. This would seem to be for the clergy what the sword was for the Men in chapter I. Funny that the cross is not mentioned. If it were, it might have to go like this:

Our clergy and many faithful wear a cross around our necks.
They wear nothing, but, then again, Japanese never wear anything around their necks.

..

The fact the priests and bonzes wore something similar enough to be the same "it" is far more remarkable than any difference in detail. According to Hendrik Van Loon in his ambitious volume THE ARTS OF MANKIND, when Rome fell under the cultural influence of "her Oriental possessions "the more austere and more truly Roman toga" was replaced by "ceremonial robes of Asia . . . gorgeous robes of silk, stiff with gold thread" and that we can still "see them being worn by the priests officiating in Roman Catholic churches and reading mass in the former law-courts of a Roman basilica." (V:AM). Could we surmise that Frois's interest in pursuing details of difference here derives in part from the all too obvious similarities between the dress of our respective *religiosos*?

~~~~~~

4-29　Our clergy, if they know how to cure [illness], cure for free out of love for God;
Os nossos religiosos, se sabem qurar, qurão gratis polo amor de Deus;

> Most Japanese *medicos* are bonzes who live on their fees.
> *Os mais dos medicos de Japão são bonzos que vivem de seu estipendio.*

Not a few Jesuits did indeed know something about medical care for "Jesuit novices were required to spend time each week working in hospitals"(DR). One of the earliest Jesuits in Japan, surgeon Luis Almeida founded a hospital in South Kyushu and Frois, who, as far as I know, had no hospital experience, himself became what we might call a faith-healer when it was necessary and was remarkably successful, as will be detailed in the chapter on Medicine. Needless to say, curing was useful propaganda for God. Religious men like Frois often worked wonders, for the "Doctor" himself believed in his spiritual placebo (and the efficacy of placebos depends on the faith of the Doctor as well as the patient!). Be that as it may, it is a shame there were not more medically trained priests in Europe, for it would have mooted the awful question of *which to fetch first*, the doctor for the soul or the doctor of the body for a badly wounded person!

Okada writes that while there were bonzes who attended to medical matters in the large temples in Kyoto and Nara, most doctors in Japan shaved their heads and otherwise looked like bonzes – useful for free travel as well as cleanliness – so Frois probably assumed (wrongly) they were. I think the involvement of bonzes in, and the relationship of bonzes to medicine was greater than that implies (Frois may not have been mistaken). It begins in the literature with the fifth chapter of the

Hokkekyô (*kyô=sutra*) on herbs and their effects and the twenty third chapter on the Herb-King Boddhisattva (yakuôbosatsu) which includes the following:

> The *Hokke Sutra* is good medicine given to all people with disease who, if they believe in it, will recover from their sickness and become both ageless and immortal (not-old/age, not-die). (東京都薬剤師会北多摩支部薬と歴史シリーズ　第二　http://www.tpa-kitatama.jp/museum/museum_05.html)

While the *Kojiki* (Record of Ancient Matters) in 715 and the *Nihonshoki* (The Chronicles of Japan) in 720 mention *a native God of healing* (who treated an injured white rabbit by putting it in a pot) by several names, in 602 a Buddhist priest well-versed in medicine and astronomy came to Japan from Kudara (a Kingdom on the West side of Korea.).   In 615, a statue of a healing buddha (*yakushi-nyôrai*) [1] was finished at Hôrinji temple.   And, in the Nara Era (710-94), one Chinese bonze with medical knowledge and a photographic nose (I mean a nose with a perfect memory) made it to Japan on his seventh try (after six turn-backs or shipwrecks), and soon after we find large temples with rhinoceros bone, dragon bone, ginseng, etc..(ibid)   Not surprisingly, a few hundred years before Frois, most physicians were herb-doctors (*kuzushi*) and they were generally bonzes, as the practice of this medicine from China, required familiarity with a large body of written knowledge and the ability to grow or import the materials (*ninja* spies were also good at gathering herbs, but that is another story).   But over the Warring Period (1338-1568), a different type of military doctor – a quick-fix artist rather than a herb-doctor, who was often not a bonze – began to gain in prestige, so things were more complex when the Jesuits came to Japan.   Bonze, or not, incantation was part of the treatment, and the words (whatever they mean) accompanied by dramatic gesture (something like making the sign of the cross in the air) were usually:

臨・兵・闘・者・皆・陣・烈・在・前

rin-byô-tô-sha-kai-jin-retsu-zai-zen

This did not change the fact that the common folk still relied on herb-doctors and the most popular medicines still had Buddhist names.[2]   And, at the same time, to complicate matters, for all the Buddhist inroads, "the Gods of the herb-doctor" remained native (i.e. Shinto), Ônamuchinokami and Sukunahikonanokami.   Not having read any statistics on the number of doctors who were bonzes, I hesitate to contradict Okada outright, but we do know that the bonze-doctor continued to practice into the Edo era – despite the Buddhism being bypassed by the new Confucian-based medicine [3] –for bonze-doctors were treated with (black) humor in *senryu:*

yuube-ni-wa isha ashita-ni-wa zoo to nari
(in evening, a doctor, in the morrow=morning priest becomes)

1 x 3

playing both sides	***the doctor-priest***
at night a doctor	as a bonze
at dawn, *knock! knock!*	he comes at dawn to bury
he returns a bonze	his mistake

two fees, if you please!

the patient dies
but ole doc is okay
he returns as the priest
the very next day

The humor in the poem comes, of course, from the main role of the bonzes in Japan: *carrying out funerals.* We will soon get to that.

1. *Name problems.* Yakushi: *Bhêchadjaguru*; the physician of souls. Nyorai: *tathagata;* a person who has attained Buddhahood.

2. *Medicine Names.* Daranisuke, the "Dara Nun's Helper," a very bitter medicine to help bonzes keep awake when doing marathon sutra readings is one example. Another popular cure-all, Hyakusô, or one hundred herbs, was connected to the esoteric Buddhism of the mountain bonzes and thought to cure a hundred diseases.

3. *Buddhism and Confucianism and Medicine.* The Tokugawa government in the seventeenth and eighteenth century strongly favored the secular Confucian school of morals and learning and as a result many people who were not bonzes became very literate in Chinese and that, together with tight governmental control on trade and great interest in Chinese herbal medicine on the part of the leadership, helped ensure a shift of herbal medicine (called *kanpoyaku,* or "chinese medicine/drugs") away from the temples. But, this was doubtless more true for the upper-class than the lower-class which had to rely on a more local pharmacopoeia and bonze doctors. (This is my impression. Specialist glosses are welcome).

~~~~~~

4-30   Our clergy, if they were to go about with gilded fans in their hands, would be thought **crazy;** *Os nossos religiosos se andassem com abanos dourados na mão tê-los hião por doudos;*

> The bonzes, when they preach or go out, have to carry a gilded fan to be dignified.
> *Os bonzos, por honra, quando pregão e vão fora, hão-de levar hum abano dourado na mão.*

These fans belong to a class of fans called either *suebiro,* i.e., "end/tip-open/wide," or *chûkei,* i.e. "middle-open," where the "open" is written not with the most common character but with one meaning "light/bright" which includes connotations of *enlightenment.* But even without this symbolism, these partially open fans reminding one of the opening of a fish-tail palm leaf are, in my humble opinion, a far more elegant symbol of authority than, say, a cross. Frois is not quite right to give the bonzes *en masse* the right to carry such a fan. Only the higher ranking Buddhist clergy were allowed that honor. The fans were used to emphasize points in conversation, as fans still are used with devastating effect by traditional stand-up (or sit-down?) comics called *rakugoshi,* who pop them open or crack them shut and whack them smartly against their thighs, etc., but, judging from the next distich, this was apparently beneath the dignity of bonzes.

~~~~~~

4-31   We stand when we preach and make our gestures by moving our hands; *Nós pregamos em pee e fazemos as acsões com o movimento das mãos;*

> The bonzes preach seated, without stirring their hands, and gesture with their heads.
> *Os bonzos pregão assentados, e as acsões, sem bulirem co[m] as mãos, as fazem com a cabeça..*

That "we" should stand while Japanese should sit to preach might seem strange considering the fact that our culture is more dependent on chairs; but it is natural when we consider another of Frois's contrasts (2-60) points out that "we" stand for formality, while "they" sit.

Europeans *still* express far more with their hands than Japanese. The contrast is greatest with the Southern Europeans who, when they get going, might be said to *talk off their hands.* This might have something to do with "our" more outgoing personalities, but it was not only a natural complement of culture: the use of gesture was taught as part of classical rhetoric or, as we might call it, speech-making.[1] I assumed such activity might have looked aggressive to Japanese, but from what an Edo era anti-Christian folk-historian wrote of Organtino's preaching, it may have simply seemed ludicrous:

His voice was like a dove/pigeon's cooing and no one could make out the words and his mannerism was like a bat stretching out its wings, a painful sight. (*Nambanji* in E:NBJ)

Japanese moved and *still* move their heads so much when they converse that they may be differentiated not only from Europeans but from Koreans or Chinese from a hundred yards away (see14-45).   Reading Frois's contrast, I wonder if there may have been less noticed aspects of gesture in Japanese, such as the cocking of the head to indicate doubt, but, as far as I know, we are talking about one thing: *nodding, lots of nodding.* Frois was obviously more interested in evangelizing than religious practice itself or he might have caught the following:

> *We meditate while lying down, sitting comfortably on a chair, or kneeling as one does to pray;* [1]
> *They always meditate seated, legs crossed, with the knees low and the soles of the feet pointing up.*

A hundred years after Frois, Kaempfer gave a fine description of the latter as, "a posture very singular in itself, but reckon'd very proper for this sublime way of thinking."

to wit, sitting cross-legg'd, with his hands in the bossom placed so, that the two extremities of the thumbs touch'd one another: A posture , which is thought to engage one's mind into so profound a meditation, and to wrap it up so entirely within itself, that the body lies for a while as it were senseless, unattentive, and unmoved by any external objects whatsoever. This profound Enthusiasm is by them call'd Sasen [*zazen*], and the divine truths revealed to such persons Satori. (K:HOJ)

1. *Gesture as Rhetoric* I have read Bulwer's mid-seventeenth century work on gesture and assume that it was, as was true for many things, about 50-100 years behind the Continent. Which is to say, the Jesuits probably taught classical body-language rhetoric in their schools at the time Frois wrote. *Gloss, anyone?*

2. *Meditation in Europe* The kneeling is obvious, but I believe that though we required kneeling for prayer, it was not necessarily so for meditation. I recall reading of Druids lying in caves with a big rock on their chests or something like that. Did Christians have any recommended positions? *Gloss, anyone?*

~~~~~~

4-32   We preach in Europe wearing a white surplice without a stole;
Nós pregamos com sobrepelix[1] branca em Europa sem estola;

   The bonzes preach with a black *koromo* [a religious habit], a stole and a gilded fan.
   Os bonzos com coromo *preto e estola e abano dourado na mão.*

More clothes! Are you, too, tired of it? A googled definition of "surplice" is "a loose, full-sleeved white vestment, worn over the cassock [a long, close-fitting tunic, usually black, buttoning up to the neck and reaching the feet] as part of the customary dress of a priest. This is the most basic vestment which belongs to all grades of ordination;" but color-wise, Frois's "we" is a bit too pat.   The Benedictines wore *black*; Cistercians eschewed dyed material and dressed in undyed *off-white* wool which became *white* when they lost their ascetic edge; Carthusians, a contemplative order, wore *white*; Franciscans were called the Grey Friars because of their *grey* habits, exchanged for *brown* ones in the 15th century, whereas Carmelites were the White Friars; Dominicans wore a *black* robe over a white gown; and Augustinians were styled *Black* Canons against the Premonstratensians, or *White* Canons. (abbrev. from Googled, LR). Doubtless the balance-of-color in the 16th century was in favor of the white, or Frois would not have so generalized.

The stole, mentioned in 4-27, was evidently only used for certain services by "us," while the bonze equivalent (also mentioned in 4-27) was more or less standard wear. Orfanel, a Dominican who came to Japan a generation after Frois, described the *koromo* as "a black robe of fine hemp with sleeves so wide and long that they almost reach the ground" (C:TCJ) which is worn over a "very clean white robe" (Ibid.). The word *koromo* is also the traditional generic term for clothing in Japanese. Or *was* until recently. Now, the term *fukusô* or, even *yofuku* ("Western/ocean-dress(!)") is usually used instead.   I have even heard *Japanese items,* properly *wafuku* (Japanese/peaceful-dress), casually referred to as *yofuku.*

The religious use of white in Japan was pretty much reserved by Shinto, the traditional Way of the Gods and the mountain wizards, a cross between esoteric Buddhism and Shamanism (with Shinto elements). People on pilgrimages also still stick to white. It is part of their orientation toward purity and, today, provides a powerful visual contrast not so much versus Buddhist gloom, as against the corporative society and its dark suits.

All I know about the *sobrepelix* is that in the Middle Ages, monks in cold countries were allowed to have fur garments, and the linen gown worn over these was the *superpellicium* or surplice. In the century after Frois, they were ornamented with lace.

~~~~~~

4-33   We preach at pulpits; *Nós pregamos em pulpetos;*

And the bonzes on chairs like our lecturers. *E os bonzos en cadeiras como dos nossos lentes.*

No need to describe the pulpit, though I cannot help noting that were I a Spanish cartoonist, I would picture a padre standing on a small octopus, for if a pulpo is an octopus it stands to reason that a *pulpeto* (*púlpito*) is a small octopus.

The chair is another matter. I had imagined the Japanese legless chair, where the seat (with a cushion on it) is flush against the tatami mat. These are offered to old people and foreigners today. *I was wrong.* I found a picture of the Buddhist preaching chair, called a *kyokuroku,*[1] in my OJD and it turns out they are rather tall chairs with 1) "X" legs when viewed from the side (which probably means it could be folded up), 2) runners(?) extending between the feet of the front legs and the back legs (one has the support of two parallel lines rather than four points: useful if such a chair sits on mud or snow, I guess), 3) a foot-rest built upon the front runner, 4) a curved back that seems to allow a partial armrest (next edition may have a picture, sorry!) and, 5) a flat seat, which I imagine a cushion was placed on. And the explanation says they were generally vermilion or black lacquer. In short, it seems a remarkably complex chair for a generally chair-less culture!

1. Kyokuroku Chair Before going to my OJD, I tried googling and was surprised to find almost no information in Japanese. I did find something in Chinese with said chair's name as the title. Since I do not read Chinese, I tried the machine translation offered on line. Because the vocabulary that comes with most software is unnecessarily limited (it lags the development of search-engines by decades) the chair's name is not part of the translation software's vocabulary (as it is not part of my Microsoft Word) so the parts of the name split into one character that by itself means nothing to speak of and turns into boxes (I turned them to blanks) or equal-sign etc. and the one which means *bent/twisted* (because of the way the back twists around to become a Gaudiesque(?) armrest?) follows another of its meanings: *melody/song/tune music.*

Here is Babelfish:

Qu? is the chair one kind, Chang?yu in the _ancestor involved legal matter. Original _is Hu I is vulgar _. Also __chair, position in a hierarchy, __chair. Its shape __tune, some four _, __overlapping, has the chairback; Because of _its shape _flexure, therefore a _tune 彔, is refers to its quarter wooden flexure _. Latter _"the tune 彔" one _also uses in to refer _the bed, like "Cloud _Wen Yan?? __" in volume center _: "_Fang Lao? the slave, 曲木 _the bed seat of honor place, 求名求利, _Buddha answers Buddha, _ the ancestor answers the ancestor, the excrement delivers the urine." "Ming Dynasty Eminent monk _" volume in six also _: "20 years _sit Qu?ch'uang." In "Pu ___Hut ___Chapter" center _: "The tiger earthen mound death anniversary, burns incense at a temple to say that, 'Always __, hits __the Italian wisdom senior buddhist priest, makes _the skill _, _ anchors must. _ this unloads _ the arms, _ a minute clothes is eating _. 20 years _, sit Qu?mu, _ the sheep _, _ 狗肉, knows him to have really _ according to? _however, _ the fragrant date, the eternity will make one hate once a year _ to be deep.'"

And, here is Excite:

Music = is in the desk of the Zen sect of 於 which is one sort of a chair and often exists. A basis is the common name of the chair of 胡. Moreover, it is called the chair and chair to realize and participates in a chair. ; which the form winds and has 4 pairs of shoes, and 2 pairs of shoes crosses and has a remote chair -- since the form bent -- music = -- saying – it – wooden music – pointing out mincing signs that it is -- だ And the thing of "music =" for which 1 Language was also used and the bed is measured is pointed out. It has said to the inside which analects>> of the Zen priest of 文偃 of the door of <<clouds rolls – if it becomes, they will be :" many directions – bed 座って of the zen by which the slave to whom さん wears out, and music are stunned, and grade go to stool by asking for asking for profits, hearing replying to a Buddha at a Buddha, and hearing replying to 祖 at 祖, and send to urine "<< -->> from which a large and bright priest of high virtue is transmitted sits on the over [: "20 year] music = bed which was rolled and has been said also in 6 "<< – the

anniversary of person's death of : " 虎丘 said in うじて which a universal light follows to the chapter of the Zen priest of the flower of a hermitage, and>> to record, and: burned incense and said collide with, it must not write and give old Kazuhisa of the wisdom which it is not intentionally [this], must not render くち, and must not gather and anchor without prospering throughout life And it has a meal by taking down war, making it suitable and writing clothes. Did you sell the meat of a dog, had sat on the music = tree since 20 years, and having applied the head of the sheep, and does he know that there is proof very much? It rotates forever and – is made to blame the day which will burn incense once in 1, and a deep thing.'"

Judging from this, human translators will not be lacking for work for quite some time to come!

4-34   We give to others blessed rosaries and the relics of saints, gratis;
Nós damos aos proximos contas bentas e reliqias de santos de graça;

The bonzes sell a great number and variety of charms written on paper for much money. *Os bonzos grande numero e diversidade de nominas escritas em papel por muito bom dinheiro.*

Perhaps, the Jesuits did not sell the religious paraphernalia Frois mentions, but when I think of the sale of *relics* and pushing of *indulgences* and God knows what else in Catholic Europe (a major cause of the Lutheran Reformation) it is hard not to laugh at Frois. Still, he may have a point. The Church received ample funding in Europe, possibly even as high as the proverbial ten percent – when you consider that we chafe at donating even one percent of our vastly greater income to foreign aid, one can realize how cheap morality has become – through offerings accepted at the mandatory church services and a variety of direct or indirect rents or taxes, whereas, in Japan, the amount of money tossed into the fixed collection boxes at temples or the bowls of traveling bonzes was miniscule by comparison. The clergy were part of a church with money to spare, while the bonzes had to sell things to eke out a living. I suspect that many of the charms were Shinto/shamanistic, for such abound even today. Some bonzes (or sects?) may also have gone beyond proper Buddhist behavior with their guaranteed "tickets to paradise" that believers might keep on their body at all times, as Europeans kept their crucifixes, and even worse, as Frois reported to Maffei:

> They borrow likewise money to be repaid with great usury in another world, giving by obligation unto the lender an assurance thereof, the which departing out of this life he may carry with him to hell. (?W:HOT?)

Ha, ha, ha! Frois must have chuckled as he wrote that letter! Of course, he never mentions any of the ways in which the Church profits on the afterlife in Europe. In Spain, and I would guess Portugal, at the time Frois wrote, one had to write a will to be properly buried, and *the law required all wills to request masses.* Needless to say, these masses were not free. The "Eager for Heaven" chapter of Carlos Eire's FROM MADRID TO PURGATORY was a real eye-opener for me. During Frois's lifetime, the number of such masses, believed to help speed up one's passage through purgatory, which might otherwise take thousands of years, with time discounted by suffering in this world ("a day of suffering in this life could count for a year or more in purgatory"), inflated from an average of a little more than 100 masses per testator in Madrid in the decade when Frois was born to about 800 masses when he died! Felipe II, who died a year after Frois, wanted all the priests of the Escorial (the royal cathedral *cum* mausoleum) to say masses for his soul for nine days (non-stop, I presume), that 30,000 such masses be said in the shortest time possible by the Franciscan monastery that "could do so with the greatest devotion (to be chosen by his executors)", a high mass, read from the altar directly above the royal mausoleum, "every day until Christ's second coming" (*Anyone, are they still doing it?*) not to mention a prayer to be said for him daily added to the canonical hours of the monks of the Escorial, nor the two perpetual anniversary masses for his birth and death date! As a warrior King, Felipe knew he had committed enormous sin and would need a hell of a lot of help to get out of purgatory.(E:MP) Not a few men left their entire estate for saying masses. Eire quotes the will of a Father who was canon of a cathedral and administrator of a hospital for poor students to the effect that

> I declare that I wish to make my soul the heir of all that remains of my possessions . . . because I have worked for fifty-three years, toiling and struggling along diverse roads and towns, and I have done all I could for my brothers and my sisters, out of my own sweat and the income I earned through it . . . . Therefore, it is fitting that my soul . . . should now enjoy the fruits of this labor, and that my earnings all be spent in masses and sacrifices [sic: offerings?], so that through these devotions and through His mercy, God, my redeemer may desist from damning me, and save me. (E:MP)

..

"Father Juan," writes Eire, "was making an investment in his future . . . as if he fully expected a return on his investment, very much like present-day wage earners who divert part of their salaries into retirement plans." If a man in the Father's line of work needed that much help to make it through purgatory, pity the poor layman! – no, seriously, despite my own disbelief, I find myself feeling sorry for God when I read things like that. Can you imagine him sitting up there counting masses? [1]

I cannot help but note that this is the only contrast where Frois mentions relics. A Japanese Frois would probably have found *our* practice worth a distich or two of its own:

> *In Japan, the remains of a holy man is treated with respect, left whole, or cremated.*
> *In Europe, a saint is cut up into bits as one would cut up a criminal.*

> *With us, the very idea of fondling parts of the dead is disgusting.*
> *With them, parts of Saints are kissed and placed over wounds.*

When Felipe II lay mortally ill, he asked for and received "the entire knee of the glorious martyr Saint Sebastian, with all its bone and skin," which he kissed and held against his bad knee. He also got "a rib of St. Alban," in some way useful for releasing his soul from purgatory, and "the arm of Saint Vincent Ferrer" possibly because of his connections to "the angel of judgment." (E:MP) The way Saints' bodies were cut up and distributed in this century – Saint Teresa (not yet canonized, but nevertheless known to be sainted) died in 1582 and was dug up in 1585, the very same year the TRATADO was penned – is, to the modern Western sensibility, too, incredibly ghoulish. Two convents had dibs on Teresa, so even before the gradual dismemberment began, we have a Father cutting off her left arm at the order of his superior, in order to compensate the sisters of the convent from which he was removing the body. He hated to do it, but

> It was marvelous. Using no more force than would be needed to cut a melon, or some soft cheese, so to speak, he instantly severed the arm at the shoulder joint. Though he had not spent a long time trying to do it, the arm was cleanly separated from the body. (Ribera in E:MP)

> According to Yepes, "Her bones were white, and her flesh was soft, white and red. The shoulder remained dense and solid, as if she had died a few moments before." (E:MP432~)

This practice had already died out in Protestant Europe, so the *us* must be divided in any contrast with *them*. But, this was not the result of a change with respect to the *efficacy* of dead bodies for curing, just a change with respect to what mattered in religion. I say this because what might be called *mummy medicine* would continue to be as popular in North Europe as South (see 9-17).

1. *Counting Masses.* We cannot say if God counted the masses, but the authorities sure did. In a town (Cuenca) in La Mancha, the peak lagged Madrid by a bit so that the biggest jump occurred in the decade following TRATADO: an average of 150 masses per person in 1585 to almost 500 in 1595 when one Vicar M Juan de Viana, an inquisition notary, paid for 11,038 masses. The most masses for a woman in the town was the widow F Mari Gómez de Caravallo with 3,005 in 1555 (N:GIL). So, how did this come to pass? For one it would seem to be a carry-over of the pagan idea of offering sustenance to dead souls; but it may also be the indirect result of the

excessively idealistic Doctrine that held that priests were supposed to perform spiritual functions for free and burial, as a spiritual function was not supposed to demand a fee. Apparently, the gifts that could be given to the clergy after the funeral were insufficient, so . . . The Protestants did away with these masses by doing away with the idea of Purgatory that accompanied it. Because the Last Judgment was somewhere around the corner, even Protestants could not completely kill purgatory, but they could change it from a lively place where things could happen to, as someone put it, a holding cell which was not at all accessible.

4-35 The friars of St. Francis give some deceased the habit of their Order for free;
Os frades de S. Francisco dão gratis o abito da sua Ordem a alguns defuntos;

> The bonzes make living men and women buy paper *katabira* [robes] with *hokekyô* [short title of the Lotus Sutra] written on them to wear when they die, and gain a lot from it. *Os bonzos fazem tomar em vida aos homens e molheres humas* catabiras *de papel com o* foqeqio *escrito nelas, pera levarem vestidos quando morrerem e os bonzos ganharem com isso pr[emio].*

From what I could google, within a century of St. Francis's death, wealthy knights and ladies who made donations to Franciscans were able to be buried in their habits and before long, sympathizers, such as Columbus, who shared their millennialism, were also buried in the robes of their secular order (I do not know exactly how such robes would defer from that of the brothers) and that, today, there are still lay Catholics who ascribe to the Franciscans' simple life who still get buried in those robes though they probably no longer believe with the medieval noblemen that their doing so might cause St Peter to mistake them for friars and give them a fast track through the traffic jam at the Pearly Gates. I could not ascertain why Franciscan robes were thought especially suitable and can only guess that their ascetic lifestyle made them most obviously deserving of reward in heaven and the hoods were the better for concealment!

Frois's description of Nobunaga's cold-blooded execution of everyone related to a political rival (Araki) in his *Historia*, contains an aside on these undergarments worn under the formal dress of 120 women who were crucified. He writes of *secret teachings and histories*, but I would guess it was these sutras which were written in Chinese characters on robes which brought great offerings and incomes to the bonzes who "took advantage of this fraudulent practice." Frois claimed that only wealthy people could afford such robes (J/F:HISTORIA)

"The Sutra on the Lotus of the Wonderful Law" is the full title (*Myôhôrengekyô* or Saddharma Pundarika Sutra). According to Wicci, Organtino and Frois devoted almost a year to studying this sacred book of the Hokke[1] sect, under the tutelage of an erudite and highly-cultured former bonze. The call of the *uguisu* (translated either "yellow bush-warbler" or "nightingale" depending upon whether the bird's denotation or connotation is the more important to the context) happens to be the short version of the Sutra's title. Since it was enough to skip the sutra itself and just say or write its *name* to invoke its content, when the haiku poet Issa joined the bird with his flute he was able to make gospel music with nature! But written language in the Sino-cultural sphere did not need to be evoked to be invoked. The writing could be cast upon the wind, each flutter of a sutra-lettered flag comprising a read; burnt or exploded to float up into heaven or be absorbed into the air; vibrated into heaven by being written around the bonze's hand-drum or upon a temple bell that is struck; "read" to the universe by rotation [2] using human, hydraulic or wind-power; dissolved and drunk, or simply worn, like the robes here mentioned by Frois.

1. *Hokekyô (the sutra) & Hokkeshû?(the sect).* If 日本 can be *nihon, nipon* or *nippon,* 法華 can be *hoke* or *hokke.* One of the little things proof reading teaches us.

2. *Rotating Prayers to Heaven* The prayer-wheel is to my mind the most fascinating religious gimmick in the world. I think of it as "fast-prayer." Later, reading Golownin, I found I was not the first one to think of it as a sort of economy:

> On their high roads, every mountain, every hill, every cliff, is consecrated to some divinity; at all these places, therefore, travelers have to repeat prayers, and frequently, several times over. But as the fulfillment of this duty would keep pious travelers too long on the road, the Japanese have invented the following means to prevent this inconvenience. Upon these spots, consecrated to divinities, they set up posts, in case there are none already there, to mark distances. In these posts a long vertical cut is made, about an arsheen and a half, above the ground; on which a flat round iron plate turns like a sheave in a block. Upon this plate the prayer is engraved, which is dedicated to the divinity of the place; to turn it around is equivalent to repeating the prayer, and the prayer is supposed to be repeated as many times as it turns around. In this manner the traveler is able, without stopping, and merely by turning the plate with his fingers, to send up even more prayers to the divinity than he is obliged to do. (MCJ)

The one-prayer wheel is, I think, rare. So long as you are turning something, you might as well turn thousands or millions of prayers at a time. That is to say, why just a *sutra,* when you can put a whole *stupa* to work! Morse:

> In a smaller temple we saw a curious object of devotion, an immense wooden affair richly carved and painted, ten or fifteen feet high, which rested on a shaft in the ground. With some strength this could be rotated by certain beams sticking out of the side against which one pushed. The casket contains the Chinese library of a famous Buddhist priest, and devotees come in to turn it. If it turns easily their prayers have been answered, and if with difficulty it is doubtful. Here is a prayer gauge that all of Tyndall's arguments could not avail against! I have tried it , as shown in figure 208 [illus!] (M:JDD)

Needless to say, this is not a Japanese invention as Golownin thought. It is most closely identified with Tibetan Buddhism. Here is Isabella Bird's description of a "lama-serai house of worship" she came across somewhere beyond the Yangtze Valley.

> At its entrance are two large prayer-wheels. Close beside it the road passes under an arch, on each side of which are six prayer-cylinders, which revolve upon being brushed by the hand; and mear it is a much decorated "prayer-wheel," in a house of its own, bestriding a stream, worked by water power, the lama in attendance receiving so much for each revolution. This cylinder is twelve feet high, with a diameter of four feet, and is said to contain 100,000 repetitions of the well-known Buddhist mantra "*Om mani padme hun.*" (YV&B)

Considering the cost of the countless funeral masses said in Iberia – In Eirie's words, "the dead made off with much of the nation's wealth" (E:MP) – right at the time Frois put down the Buddhists' fees, it is a shame the Catholics couldn't come up with such labor-saving devices!

~~~~~~

4-36   Our priests hold funeral services for the deceased in churches;
Os nossos sacerdotes fazem os saimentos [1] aos defuntos nas igrejas;

> The bonzes hold it in the house of the deceased many times over, in order to eat and drink there. *Os bonzos em casa dos defuntos grande numero de vezes, pera comerem e beberem ali.*

Starting with "our" side, let me be rude enough to say that it just so happens priests did not always stay in church. First from fiction, the 16th century Spanish picaresque classic, *The Life of Lazarillo de Tormes.* In chapter 2, the perpetually hungry Lazarillo is working for a priest who has just claimed he is, as is proper for a man of the cloth, temperate in his eating and drinking –

..

> But he was lying, the miserable creature, because when we went to pray at meetings and wakes, where somebody else was paying, he ate like a wolf and drank more than a quack doctor. And, speaking of wakes, God forgive me, I was never a foe to humanity except on those occasions. Because then we ate well and I stuffed myself. I yearned, I actually prayed to God to kill off one of His Servants every day.   And when we went to give the sacrament to the sick, especially when it was Extreme Unction, when the priest asks everybody present to pray, I wasn't the last to start. I prayed to the Lord with all my heart and with a right good will, but I didn't ask Him to dispose of the person according to His will, as they usually do. I begged that the object of our prayers might be removed from this world. (A(M):LLT)

That is fiction and also a one-time-per-person wake. Frois has "them" doing it "many times over." A highly documented study of the people of Cuenca (a town in La Mancha) by Sara T. Nalle reveals that, after an intense nine-day period of grieving, masses, and grave offerings,

> every day or on Sundays a female member of the deceased's household placed on the grave a gift of bread, wine, and wax which would collected by the priest. Despite the pagan connotations of the practice, the *añal* [annual] was considered a form of suffrage and was not openly condemned in the diocese's constitutions. The añal's function was very different from the ritual funeral banquets that existed at the time in most countries and until recently in some villages of Spain. The wake served to bind the living together in one cathartic dinner; the añal, on the other hand, in a sense prolonged the deceased's life, because for an entire year the dead person continued to be a mouth to feed and a drain on the family budget. (N:GILM)

This was true for the entire 16th century. Unlike the cases with most pagan offerings which were eaten by animals (or the poor), here, the priests got it! The only difference is that the bonzes ate at the house of the deceased, whereas the priests apparently gathered theirs wholesale from the graveyards!

> The añal gifts in the first half of the century were modest compared to what they were to become. Typically, the testator asked for one maravedi's worth of bread, a blanca's worth of wine, and a wax tablet for weekdays, and double that amount on Sundays and feastdays. . . . No more did the testator ask for the simple chunk of bread and cup of wine. In 1575 Esteban de Palomares, a bonnet maker and familiar in the Inquisition, required on Sundays six pounds of bread, including a loaf of blessed bread, two maravedis' worth of wine, and two wax tapers; On Easter and the feasts of Our Lady, two pounds of stew and the same quantity of wine and wax; and finally, on weekdays, a pound of bread, one maravedi's worth of wine, and a wax tablet. . . . As a group, noble women gave most generously (an average of forty-two ducats per testator!), followed by the priests (thirty-two ducats) and bourgeois men (fifteen ducats). Artisans gave the least, about eight and one-half ducats a year. (ibid) [2]

Still, *as far as Japan went,* it was a fact that Christian funerals were a good deal compared to Buddhist ones. In his HISTORIA, Frois pointed out that these services were such a burden on Japanese families that the much cheaper yet attractive Christian alternative was a major draw. Moreover, because missionaries were not averse to burying people for free, poor people without relatives (for only relatives were allowed to bury or cremate someone) who would otherwise end up dragged to dunghills or the woods at night and left for the dogs to eat – or, worse, still alive and liable to be kicked out from their tenement as they lay mortally ill (so it would not be polluted by their death) – were strongly tempted to convert before dying. So, the contrast was not academic for Frois.

Despite whatever excesses may have occurred, funerals are still Buddhist in Japan today, though the service – in many ways more a long wake or vigil – is generally held at home, rather than a temple or funeral home. (People important enough to draw hundreds or thousands of mourners hold memorial services at Buddhist temples or other institutions, too.) Relatives gather to help with the cooking, cleaning, reception of guests, recording of gifts received, etc.. People sit around, reminisce and occasionally look at the deceased. Everyone lights a joss stick. Bonzes come and go and intone sutras. They surely played a much larger role in these affairs in Frois's time and, not unnaturally, enjoyed the repast. Some, supposedly enjoyed the widows, too. In Frois's missing HISTORIA summary volume, a whole chapter is devoted to "Japanese funerals and the bonzes' gain from them." Japanese themselves kidded about the fact death profited the bonzes in their country – there are countless senryû about that – but it does not justify Frois's biased contrast. Most bonzes probably believed they were doing their work for the repose, or rather *bon voyage* of the soul. Here is a fine story in Eliza Skidmore's JINRICKSHA DAYS IN JAPAN which provides balance to the picture of selfish Buddhists:

> When the American man-o-war *Oneida* was run down and sank with her officers and crew by the P. and O. steamer *Bombay,* near the mouth of Yeddo Bay, January 23, 1870, our Government

made no effort to raise the wreck or search for it, and finally sold it to a Japanese wrecking company for fifteen hundred dollars. The wreckers found many bones of the lost men among the ship's timbers, and when the work was entirely completed, with their voluntary contributions they erected a tablet in the Ikegami [temple] grounds to the memory of the dead, and celebrated there the impressive Buddhist *segaki* (feast of hungry souls), in May, 1889. The great temple was in ceremonial array; seventy-five priests in their richest robes assisted at the mass . . . The scriptures were read, a service was chanted, the Sutra repeated, incense burned, the symbolic lotus-leaves cast before the altar . . . . No other country, no other religion, offers a parallel to this experience . .

Here, pace Shakespeare, we see it is not birth but *death* that makes all men kin. They are quick to say mass for anyone. "No other country" is overdoing it, but Skidmore's point is that the Buddhists are *kind.* I would add that when Toby, Alcock's favorite Scotch terrier was buried, sure enough, a "priest of the temple brought water and incense sticks to burn." (A:COT) *Good.*

1. **Saimentos** The Portuguese *saimentos* means "farewells" or, a *send-off,* and . . . *funerals.*

2. **Spanish Practices.** I did not find the type of material found on Iberia on-line respecting Portugal. This is one of many cases where I wonder whether the Portuguese situation known by young Frois would have justified his claims so easily contradicted by "Iberia."

~~~~~~

4-37   For our clergy, yellow is a garish and indecent color;
Pera os nossos relegiosos a cor amarela hé garrida e indecente;

The bonzes think yellow or green decent and delight in wearing them.
Os bonzos a tem por honesta e folgão de se vestir d'amarelo ou de verde.

It is interesting that the West should put down *these* colors in particular: *yellow*, which is close to gold and the color of our sun (pictured red in Japan) and *green*, the color of vegetable life! Is it, perhaps, that these colors are not so closely associated with the body? [1]   Then, again, Frois does not say Europeans, but the clergy, so maybe I should ask another question. Is it proof of "our" failure to find the sacred in Nature?

Different sects wore different colors according to the seasons. The yellow and green traditional Buddhist robes I have seen are, respectively, closer to *manilla* and *moss*, i.e. far from the primary colors one might imagine. Only esoteric Buddhist high-priests (like "our" high priests), *hari-krishna* evangelists (now found, together with Jehovah's witnesses, in Japan) and marginal cults go in for truly bright colors.

1. **Why Not Yellow?** I can understand the problem with *green*. It makes natural green look faded. (Red is better, for it brings out natural green.). But yellow is tough. We could divide up cultures by those that love yellow clothing and those that detest it. The yellow=cowardly idea is only found in English, so it will not do for an explanation. A Mexican friend thinks that it is a bad color because only a very beautiful person (who looks good in it) or someone who is conceited (and does not look good in it) dares to wear it. Gloss, anyone?

~~~~~~

4-38   Among us, the clergy of one order do not hate those of another;
Antre nós não se tem odio humas religiões aas outras;

The bonzes do, as it adds to their own *isei* [authority] and profit to abhor other sects.   *Os bonzos antre si, pera seu yxei e proveito, aborresem as outras ceytas.*

All that needs to be said about "our" loving brothers has been said in my notes to 4-24. I would only add that the respective sides of the distich are not really commensurable because the orders to which Frois alludes are all fellow Catholics in broad agreement on the doctrine as interpreted by the Pope – Dominicans, Franciscans and Jesuits all belong to a single, albeit large, sect of Christianity – whereas the bonzes belong to sects as different as (to use contemporary examples) Mormons, Baptists and Catholics. As far as I can see, "we" not only hated but did not permit two sects in a single country, and if it were in "our" power would not have allowed two in the entire world.

As Okada points out, the precepts of the Pure Land sect include Renyo's admonition against bad-mouthing other sects (written about 200 years before the TRATADO), but in the sixteenth century this sect (known by its detractors as Ikkô-shû, or One-way-cult) was spreading by aggressive proselytizing and friction was inevitable. Frois begins the chapter 51 (chapter 29 of part 2) of his HISTORY as follows:

> Because all of Japan's religious rites were invented by the creator of evil himself, the devil, the bonzes live in a state of perpetual argument with one another and this is not only from enthusiasm about matters of doctrine for even people belonging to the same sect debate each other out of pride or to show-off.

Frois went on to explain that the most common arguments are between the Hokke sect which calls their Buddha "Shaka" and the above-mentioned Pure Land sect that calls their Buddha "Amida."[1] Then he recounted how a bonze from one sect challenged the other to a debate that ended up being refereed by Nobunaga, a Shôgun who did not think much of religion. The losing side literally forfeited their heads and, if I read correctly, had their head-temple demolished! The questions began with things like whether or not the Hokekyô sutra actually had the *nenbutsu* (the prayer they chant) in it or not, whether the Buddhas of the two sects was one and the same or not and other such (Frois does not give all of them). The Hokke side was stumped by the question of what the character 妙 (myô),[2] which Shaka preached for 44 years, meant and the victors did some fan dance and onlookers laughed and tore the robes of the Hokke bonzes and Hokke books that had been brought were shredded on the spot and, to make a long story short, Nobunaga forbade the Hokke sect to engage in argument from then on, not only with the Pure Land sect but with *all* sects!

Considering the mean things Nichiren's Hokke side said about other sects, and the fact that the Hokke sect pioneered the use of force as a means of spreading religion, one feels like applauding, but the truth was that Nobunaga was ready to take advantage of any opportunity he could to cut-down to size both of these sects. Because many Japanese who were not part of Hokke found them obnoxious, I think Nobunaga chose to attack them first in a way calculated to gain public support.; but, actually, the "winners" in the debate were his real enemy, for they had managed to unify with large independent peasant communes, that paid a tithe to the main temple of the Honganji (main temple of the Pure Land / Ikkô sect) and little or no more rent to the lords. They "liberated, "i.e., gained control over a large swath of central Japan and played the king-maker (or, more usually, breaker) role in the fight to gain control of Japan on the part of the war-lords. Left alone they had a tendency to spread like wildfire and to the rulers (and, now, historians) the very name Ikkô is associated with *uprisings*. Nobunaga fought a bloody running battle with the rural leagues of the Ikkô sect from 1570-80, and as Souyri (who has almost ten pages on peasant organizing [2]) puts it, "they were crushed one by one." (S(R):WTUD)

---

1. *Myô?* I think the best definition of 妙 *myô* might be "sublime." How would *you* define that on the spot?

2. *Peasant Communes.* As I read Souyri, I could not help thinking that an in-depth comparative study of similar(?) movements in England might be interesting. Anyone?

4-39   The sorcerers among us are punished and severely disciplined;
Os feiticeiros antre nós são punidos e castigados;

The *Ikkôshû* and *Yamabushi* are delighted with sorcerers, for being sorcerers.
Os bonzos Ycoxos e Yamabuxis *folgão com eles por serem feticeiros.*

The Yamabushi, literally "mountain warriors," dressed in robes (white or colored) and leggings, with strange necklaces, adorned conch trumpets and, sometimes, even weird one-stilt shoes, actually *look* wizard-like to us. They combine elements of esoteric Buddhism and shamanism. After undergoing terrifying ordeals and inhuman austerities in their mountain headquarters (see Frois's *"The Place of Confession"* in C:TCJ), they wander around the country, to put it crudely, exchanging magic for money. Frois writes that this company "with curled and straying hair . . . . make a profession to find out again things either lost or stolen. . . ."

> They set before them a child, whom the devil invadeth, called up thither by charms: of that child then do they all ask that which they are desirous to know. ("Yamabushi" in C:TCJ)

Frois also writes that they sold curses as well as blessings!

The large Ikkô sect is another matter all together. Their "sorcery" is more like evangelical Christianity practiced under a charismatic leader, where the spiritually charged atmosphere – or mass hysteria, if you prefer – gives rise to faith-healing and other such "miracles." The head of the sect was venerated as a reincarnation of Amida (Amithaba – a manifestation of the Buddha). Faith in Amida alone was supposed to be sufficient to save one – again, we are reminded of the evangelical "Jesus saves!" This excerpt from Frois's fellow Japan-hand Vilela's description of "the Ikkô sect" says it all.

> They give this bonze so much money in alms that he controls a large part of the country's wealth [and like so many of our TV preachers, but more brazenly "he publicly maintains many women"] Every year a great festival is held in his [Amidabutsu? The sect leader?] honour, and so many people wait at the gate of the temple to enter that many die in the stampede which results when they open the gates. Such people, however, are considered very lucky to have died in that way and some at their own request are dropped into the crowd around the gates and are thus killed. At night he preaches them a sermon during which they shed many tears . . . (in C:TCJ)

Frois's contrast of "our" disenchanted religion and "their" sorcery-corrupted religion is ironic in that the first popular Christian inroad made in Japan, as described at length by St. Xavier, concerns Portuguese merchants who were unwittingly lodged in "some buildings left without inhabitants, because experience had proved that they were much infested by ghosts." Knowing nothing of this, "For some nights they were continually surprised to find that when they lay down to rest the clothes and the coverings of their beds were pulled off, without their being able to see anyone." To cut a long story short, they also saw "a terrible spectre" and discovered from a servant that "figures of the cross" repelled it. They made such a commotion, their Japanese neighbors heard, and after they told them what happened, "the Japanese confessed that the building had for a long time been infested by a certain evil spirit." The Portuguese told them about the efficacy of the cross and soon

> crosses made either of paper, or wood, or any such substance, were to be seen at the doors of nearly all the houses in the town; the natives, who were often wont to suffer great molestation from the visits of hellish ghosts, making use with great eagerness of the defense against such assaults which had been made known to them. (C:LLFX)

And so the Japanese were primed for Christianity! This seems to me a description of a *kitsune-tsuki* or fox-possession epidemic which sometimes jinxed entire neighborhoods. Remarkably, something similar happened fifty years later to Ricci in China. Ricci accepted an uninhabited palace known by "the whole town" as "a favorite resort of demons," a place with "perpetually strange noises and plaintive moanings, and in the night terrific apparitions." Not only would none dare live in it, but the whole neighborhood was "overwhelmed with terror and consternation." Ricci, who had found it almost impossible to find good real estate bought it "and the missionaries with great joy, installed themselves in their palace, though not without having previously sprinkled it well with holy water." They encountered no spectors whatsoever

> and from that time all Nankin was talking, not only of the knowledge of these foreign doctors, but of their power over evil spirits; and it was inferred also that their religion must be a holy one, since their presence was thus sufficient to silence and put to flight a whole army of demons. This event did not fail to make a great impression on the Chinese, and disposed them strongly in favour of the European ecclesiastics. (H:CCTT)

That such a success would impress the Chinese is certain but it would *not* have proven the Jesuits were *holy*. It is more likely the Chinese thought: *These water-sprinkling cross-waving fellows are powerful sorcerers!* Could we not say that sorcery and Christianity (or Islam) go hand in hand.? Does not religion thrive in a climate of fear, where supernaturalism (by whatever label it choses to give itself) will most readily be given a chance to prove itself? Is it purely coincidental that the country where Christians (albeit Protestants) were to make the biggest comeback in the 19th and 20th century, Korea, boasted a phenomenal amount of daemons requiring a phenomenal amount of sorcery? Isabella Bird was horrified by how much shamans charged: "At the lowest computation, Daemonism costs Korea two million five hundred thousand dollars annually. . . . In sickness, the very poor half starve themselves and pawn their clothing to pay for her [the shaman, or *mudang* is usually a woman] exorcisms." So why has "her power" been, to use Bird's strange expression, "riveted upon the country"?

> In Korean belief, earth, air, and sea, are peopled by daemons. They haunt every umbrageous tree, shady ravine, crystal spring, and mountain crest . . . . north, south, east, and west they abound, making malignant sport of human destinies. They are on every roof, ceiling, fireplace, *kang* [?] and beam. They fill the chimney, the shed . . . they are on every shelf and jar. In thousands they waylay the traveller as he leaves his home, beside him, behind him, dancing in front of him, whirring over his head, crying out upon him from earth, air and water. They are numbered in the thousands of billions, and it has been said [by Rev. G.H. Jones] that their ubiquity is an unholy travesty of the Divine Omnipresence. This belief, and it seems to be the only one he has, keeps the Korean in a perpetual state of nervous apprehension, it surrounds him with indefinite terrors, and it may truly be said of him that he "passes the time of his sojourning here in fear." Every Korean home is subject to daemons, here, there, and everywhere. They touch the Korean at every point in life, making his well-being depend on a continual series of acts of propitition, and they avenge every omission with merciless severity, keeping him under this yoke of bondage from birth to death. (B:KAHN)

Bird makes it clear that this is not "daemon-worship" as some Occidentals call it, and about 80% of the daemons are "malignant" while the rest are "partly kindly" but "even these are easily offended and act with extraordinary capriciousness." Bird supplies a detailed classification of the daemons by a Dr. Landis. Here, I only want to point out that, her above description is a perfect ringer for two other cultures I have read a lot about: the Malays and the Irish (just substitute "fairy" or "good folk" for "demons' for the latter). Many of the former are Moslems and the latter famously Catholic.

Today, Japanese intellectuals *talk* a lot about myriad spirits (*yaoyorazu-kami*) inhabiting everything from computer chips to industrial robots (I have read serious articles explaining that is why we animistic Japanese get along better with these robots than Christian Occidentals!). Such talk is a welcome counter to "our" tendency to allow God to monopolize spirit, leaving a disenchanted world. Vilela wrote:

They worship everything. They worship the sun, the moon and the stars. They worship sticks, stones, snakes, foxes, and many other things." (1565).

But I would guess that even at the time Vilela wrote many Japanese and most of the upper class may not have believed whole-heartedly in such spirits, but only humored them, which is, after all, the safe thing to do. Japan was simply not as spirit-ridden as Korea, Ireland and Indonesia. I take the controversial ancient statement that Japan was the country where words were not evoked (*kotoage-senu kuni*) to mean the Japanese were conscious of this difference and proud of not constantly appealing to the gods=daemons like their neighbors. To my mind, the West in Frois and Vilela's time was probably closer to the Korea described by Bird than to Japan. The strict punishment for witchery found in the West was, after all, proof of the depth of "our" belief in what we call superstition when we find it in other cultures. Take, for example,

> the case of Margaret Harkett, a sixty year old widow of Hammore, Middlesex, who was executed at Tyburn in 1585. She had picked a basketful of peas in a neighbor's field without permission. Asked to return them, she flung them down in anger; since then, no peas would grow in the field." (T:RDM)

This English *conte* that would be amusing had it not ended as it did, occurred the very year Frois penned his TRATADO. At this time, it was usual for mediums in England (I do not know the case in Iberia) to try to locate stolen goods for which they would receive 25% – far more than the Jammabo in Japan! "In France, a decree of Henry III., in 1579, forbade all makers of almanacs to prophesy, directly or indirectly, concerning affairs either of the state or of individuals." (C:CBD) This was not because it was thought to be nonsense but because it was thought to be *diabolic*. As Frois wrote, "we" took sorcery seriously. That is because "we" believed that strongly in it (If the almanac was allowed to continue with the same in England, it was because the belief was weaker). In England and Germany, the first rational challenges to torture and murder in the name of fighting witchcraft were being published about the time Frois wrote. Fine refutations of the concept of witchcraft by several brave Jesuits and one extraordinary Inquisitor (Salazar, mentioned earlier) would soon follow and put an end to the persecution of witches in Spain.[1] And, shortly after that, folk-history in Japan turned the Jesuits into sorcerers themselves. I think even Frois would have been amused to see himself (possibly Frois, for the following comes from a context suggesting his involvement) depicted doing this:

> Making handkerchiefs [*tenugui*] look like horses, throwing dust into the air where it turns into birds, making dead trees blossom, turning pebbles into jewels, sitting in the air, hiding in the earth, or instantly creating black clouds to rain or snow . . . (J/E:NBJ)

1. *Over in Spain But Salem?* Yes, Usanian readers, "our" Salem came later. It is a touching story and Cotton Mather, who is usually misrepresented as a cruel gung ho witch-burner, made a tremendous effort to keep the hysteria from getting worse (His bad reputation came from his effort to prevent further recrimination against the judges *after* the hysteria had ceased in the interest of getting the community back on its feet). I highly recommend Chadwick Hansen's *Witchcraft in Salem.*

4-40 The *tabi* [socks] of [Japanese] laymen are black or olive brown;
Os tabis *dos sequlares ou são pretos ou almecegados;*

Those of bonzes and noblewomen are white and made of cotton.
Os dos bonzos e das fidalgas nobres são branqos feitos de canga.

Both sides of the above distich are the Japanese side.   Assuming a contrast with Europe is intended, I would guess it means our clergy and noblewomen wore dark socks/stockings and laymen wore white ones.   What more can be said?

~~~~~~

4-41   In Europe when a master dies, his servants, crying accompany him as far as the grave;
Em Europa por morte dos senhores os criados chorando os acompanhão ató à cova;

> In Japan, some cut their stomachs, and many cut off the tips of their fingers and toss them into the burning pyre. *Em Japão alguns cortão a barriga e muitos as cabeças dos dedos e os deitão no fogo onde os queimão.*

There were many types of funerals in Japan.   Frois describes at great length (for pages) a sumptuous funeral in the capital city of Miyako (Kyoto) with no split bellies nor chopped fingers (C:TCJ).   In this contrast, he deliberately gives the most outlandish example.   Some more details may be surmised by the English factory director Richard Cox's description of the send-off for a member of the royalty in Hiradox (Nagasaki area) in 1621.

> And there was one *bozu*, or prist, hanged hym selfe in a tree hard by the place of funerall, to accompany hym in an other world, for *bozu* may not cutt their bellies, but hang themselves they may.   And 3 other of the dead mans servantes would have cutt their bellies, to have accompanid hym to serve hym in an other world as they stidfastly beleeve they might have donne; but the king would not suffer them to doe it.   Many others, his friends, cut affe the 2 foremost joyntes of their littell fingers and threw them into the fire to be burned with the corps, thinking it a greate honor to them selves and the least service they could doe to hym . . . (C:TCJ)

The belly-cutting is, as far as I know, uniquely Japanese. The finger joint cutting – today, a monopoly of apologetic *yakuza* – is found in many Pacific island peoples and suggests Japanese are a partly Southern race.   Gruesome fare, for sure, but no more bloody and less outlandish than a good old-fashioned Norse funeral of a type not extant in Frois's time to be sure, described by the diplomat Ibn Fadhlan in 921-2.[1]   This dead chieftain was joined by a favorite slave girl who supposedly volunteered and was treated kindly, feasting and going from tent to tent enjoying sex with many men (or, according to some recent internet interpretations, being *raped* by many men) before taking drugs and drinking, seeing her Master in the Other World, and in the grand finale having sex with (*ditto:* being raped by) six men and being strangled in a ritualistic way under the supervision of an old woman called the Angel of Death after which the ship was burnt to ashes in an hour thanks to strong wind and the interpreter enthusiastically told the envoy that such was a far better send-off to heaven than being buried and slowly eaten by worms in the Arab way.

1. *Ibn Fadhlan.* What incredibly detailed reporting! The story and more is quoted in The Lure of the Vikings by Lionel Casson: Horizon (Spring: 1975). If Ibn Faldan wrote more, I want to read it!

~~~~~~

4-42   In Europe, Christians beat their breasts when begging for the mercy of God;
Em Europa os cristãos batendo nos peitos pedimos a Deus misericordia;

> In Japan, the gentiles rub very vigorously on their beads.
> *Em Japão os jentios esfregão as contas muito rijo nas palmas das mãos.*

In Latin the words, *Mea culpa, mea culpa, mea maximo culpa!* or, in Spanish, *Por mi culpa, por mi culpa, por me gran culpa!* or in English, *Through my fault, through my fault, through my most grievous fault!* [1] are vocalized while beating the breast with the right hand while reciting El Credo right before saying that Christ was crucified. Apparently, this practice was once not confined to the Creed.

One of Issa's most famous haiku features a fly rubbing his hands and feet for mercy. (*yare utsuna hae ga te o suru ashi o suru*) Harold Stewart indirectly suggests that the idea comes from an old Zen *koan,* asking whether it was OK to swat such a fly. Most Japanese commentators neglect to consider this and only point out naively that Issa looked closely at little living things (shades of Robert Burn's "timorous beastie"). No one – not even the most heavily annotated anthologies in Japan – mention the *senryu* from which (I think) Issa borrowed the structure of his poem: *yare tatsuna tatsuna de musashi jûzu o suru* (see my *Fly-ku!* for the whole story). In that *senryu*, the famous warrior Benkei (nicknamed Musashi, but not the same as Miyamoto Musashi) rubs his "rosaries" to try to keep down waves in a tempest. (The poem is a *senryu* because someone not knowing about the event, popularized in the drama *Funa-Benkei* is supposed to misinterpret it wrong and imagine the chaste young fighting bonze praying to keep down his hard-on! The verb *tatsu* or "stand up" suggests large waves or an erection in Japanese.). In the absence of an icon like the crucifix, it would seem that prayer beads played a bigger role in Japanese Buddhism than they did in Christianity. Frois wrote *gentiles* rather than *bonzes* because Japanese Buddhist laymen also had beads.

I have walked by a houseful of praying believers of one popular Buddhists sect and the grating of the beads by ten or twenty of them together made a deafening roar which set off the oil-cicada (*abura-semi*) coming from the trees above very well. Perhaps, I thought for a moment, that is what made the cicada here so loud, *Nichiren* rosaries! Or does "Rosaries" sound wrong for anything but the Catholics with whom they are identified? I hesitate to write "sutra prayer beads" because it is not a term but a description and in Japanese, a single word *juzu* does the trick as well as "rosaries: does. While Frois brought up the beads as a matter of contrast, I am amazed this item (more in 5-18) could play so similar a role in two religions as distant to one another as Buddhism and Christianity.

---

1. Translation of *Mea Culpa* into English. The middle phrase in the English was "through my *own* fault" until recently when the Catholic Church (Vatican II) removed the "own" to "restore" it to an earlier translation. Note the "grievous" not found in the original. That is because *culpa* includes connotations of sin that makes it heavier than a mere "fault" would be. DR Englishes that meaning with verve: *"It's my fault, I'm the guilty one, Oh, how I have sinned."*

"If approved by the U.S. bishops at their November 2004 meeting, and if Rome subsequently approves it, the text could be ready for use in American parishes by early 2005."

<u>endnote</u> **IV**

Bonzes

~~~~~~

> From the sociological point of view, the whole missionary system, irrespective of sect and creed, represents the skirmishing force of Western civilization in its general attack upon all civilizations of the ancient type .   – Lafcadio Hearn (H:JAI)

In CURIOUS LAND: JESUIT ACCOMMODATION AND THE ORIGINS OF SINOLOGY, D.E. Mungello found Ricci "morally, more complex than many historians have described him." He did well by most of the Mosaic commandments but disobeyed his parents in becoming a Jesuit [then, again, didn't Christ welcome such disobedience if it were to follow *Him*?] and "showed some highly human equivocation in that most fundamental of Christian commandments – love." Why?

> His intolerance and dislike of the Buddhist monks in China was surprising in its intensity. The tendency has been to treat this dislike as part of a quite orthodox Christian opposition to idolatry and it was true that Ricci's dislike for Buddhists as idolaters pales to only moderate dimensions when compared to the standards of his times. Nevertheless, his dislike of Buddhists sharply contrasted with a normally sympathetic attitude toward the Chinese. (1985/89)

Mungello is surprised for the same reason he gave Ricci all the credit for inventing a policy of *accommodation* (see n. in pt iv of the Foreword), he failed to give sufficient attention to the Japanese side of the church (Perhaps forgivable when you consider the book's focus was closer to its 1985 title: STUDIA LEIBNITIANA, SUPPLEMENTA 25!). By the time Ricci went to China, the Jesuits had been at war with the Buddhists in Japan for almost four decades. Any number of reports from Japan (dating back to St. Xavier) respect the people and *dis* the bonzes. Genius or not, Ricci was part of that *tradition*.

When, from day one, the Buddhists were attacked for allowing sodomy and infanticide, not to mention worshipping the Devil, they were more than ready to respond. Some sects were well-stocked with preachers, whom they dispatched from afar to take on the Jesuits. Both sides apparently *relished* the fight. A 1551 letter of Iuan Fernandez, whom Xavier had left in Japan, and probably knew more Japanese than any other Westerner at that time tells of Bonzes who refused to receive them "saying we were devils, and on our account much bad had come to the land [there was a war going on]" and of their "saying many bad things about us because we reprehend them for their sins . . . and said we were his [the Devil's] disciples, and many saw a ray of light (?) [un rayo??] fall on the house of the King, which was cast there by the Devil on account of us. Others tried to libel us, saying we ate human meat." (CARTAS p53)

As we have discussed already, Some Buddhist sects were every bit as aggressive as fundamentalists(?) in 20th-century North America who were not beneath shooting gynecologists (or rationalizing it, which is just as bad). They were not about to take things sitting down. They didn't only argue with each other and the Jesuits but sometimes tried to get them killed. If the de-facto ruler of Japan, Nobunaga, had not quickly become fond of Frois, our author would probably have been assassinated long before TRATADO was written, for in 1569, one enemy bonze managed to get the Emperor to sign a death warrant for any Jesuits found in the capitol. Nobunaga gave Frois a safe-pass and "told him, on the eve of his departure, in front of a vast concourse of Kyoto nobility, "Do not worry about either the Emperor or the shogun, because I am in complete control of everything. Only do what I tell you, and you can go where you like."(B:CCIJ)

僧   僧   僧

The obvious guts and personal charm of the intrepid Jesuits, their scientific knowledge (especially cosmology that served to prove they knew about things and gained brownie points with Japanese intellectuals) and their becoming inseperable from the Portuguese trade, not to mention Nobunaga's hatred for Buddhists who opposed his authority, gave them an advantage over their adversaries. They used it. And they misused it. Frois's HISTORIA *gloats* over the horrendous destruction of idols on the part of himself and Fr. Coelho in 1582 (ch44=pt2-36). Sometimes, considering the cultural terrorism "we" did, I regret "we" had that advantage and almost wish Nobunaga let Frois reap the rewards of rudeness by getting killed! Then, again, when Nobunaga, still ostensibly serving the Ashikaga Shogunate, built Nijo castle in 1569, he did the same himself, for more a more practical purpose, the construction of Japan's first genuine stone castle. Frois observed with no reprehension:

> As there was no stone available for the work, he ordered many stone idols to be pulled down, and the men tied ropes around the necks of these and dragged them to the site. All this struck terror and amazement in the hearts of the Miyako citizens for they deeply venerated their idols. . . . and as all were eager to please Nobunaga, . . . they smashed the stone altars, toppled over and broke up the *hotoke* (buddhist statues), and carried away the pieces in carts. ("Portrait of a Ruler" chapter in C:TCJ)

While the Christians could not do such things in the Miyako, the boondocks of Kyushu were another matter. There was a natural cavern that could only be entered by climbing a dangerous rock mountain on an island. "The Devil," Frois writes, "long ago occupied this terrifying place in order that it could be used for his worship." The bonzes borrowed "the wiles of the Devil" in devising ways up the sheer rock clifts using iron spikes and chain-link hand-holds. As Frois admitted, the extreme difficulty of visiting the site made it a popular place of pilgrimage when Arima belonged to the Pagans. They found the cave to "be close to overflowing with Buddhist idols, all of which were strange figures, very intricate, exquisitely made, so that it would be impossible to think of any better ones than these." Yet, our Christian vandals removed them – burning the ones too large to take out without breaking up – and with the help of their Japanese followers, paraded them back to their quarters where they used them as firewood, basking in the heat of their exploit the whole winter long!

Two things make this *especially* reprehensible. First, many of these statues were there because of earlier Christian persecution. It is bad enough to persecute others, but to *pursue* them in that way is cruel. Eight years earlier, "because the Japanese are born with such a quick intellect," the local people after hearing only one sermon, turned into a Christian mob and went out burning down temples and destroying idols (and worst of all, some non-Christian retainers were forced to use their own "idols" for firewood). All of this Frois records matter of factly in his HISTORIA. And only two years earlier, at Valignano's bidding, the lord of Arima dismantled or destroyed all the Shinto and Buddhist temples – more than forty in all, and some renowned throughout Japan – in his realm and forced the bonzes to convert or emigrate. (S:VMP) Since Shinto was included in that religious cleansing campaign, we can see the action was not just a case of competitive exclusion, for Shinto, unlike Buddhism, is not at all like Christianity. Coelho had correctly surmised that some idols were saved from this destruction and hidden in that cave! And second, that very year, Valignano wrote that "we must show great love for Buddhist bonzes. We should especially refrain from rejoicing at their misfortunes, despising them and others and saying bad things about them. This attitude is particularly disliked by the Japanese; not only does it not raise our prestige, but gives us a bad reputation." (found in japanese notes to HISTORIA citing Schütte (maybe S:VMP?))

The Japanese translators of HISTORIA also note that the local tradition of the cave is completely different from Frois's story. What is remembered by Japanese is how some Christians hid out there after the Shimabara insurrection (the war of 1538, where thousands of Christians and oppressed peasants held out in a castle for so long that the Bakufu – Tokugawa government – gave up its plan to try to liberate Luson! ("Liberate" because some Tagalogs had, according to Boxer, requested it.) and would have escaped had not the departing officials noticed some white smoke coming out of the cave as they departed. They landed again and climbed for the Christians. When the Christians had nothing left to throw at their pursuers they cut off and threw the heads of the statues at them and when these ran out they were captured. As the blues refrain goes: *You reap what you sow!*

While cultural destruction is a crime and a tragedy, sometimes the little triumphs of "our" benighted crusaders found in Frois' HISTORIA are so funny one can't help but laugh aloud. A Buddhist monk shoots into a house in revenge after idols are destroyed and, missing the priests, tells them he will convert if only they don't tell his master and get him in trouble. Of course, they let him and gain a good Christian. A typhoon tosses the head of a popular Kaizodera (a temple for seamen) image into "the really dirty [cesspool beneath the] toilet of one of its biggest believers" and "the next day it was discovered there in the place most fitting for an idol." I am grateful for the amusement, but cannot help saying "Come on, Frois, *grow up!*" But, then, Frois's intellectual formative years (age 16-31) were spent in Goa, a city built on religious spoil. From a letter written by a Florentine in 1515:

> In this land of Goa and the whole of India there are innumerable ancient edifices of the gentiles and in a little neighboring island called Divari, the Portuguese have destroyed an ancient Pagode in order to build the land (town) of Goa." (G:PPI)

Does Frois have any other excuse for his behavior? As many Jesuits, including Frois himself, observed, *Meaco* (Kyoto), where he spent so many years, was "the sanctuary of the infidelity and idolatry of Japan, where the enemy continually worked to prevent the law of God from being introduced, and after it was introduced to throw it out." (Vilela:CARTAS:2/4/1570) Frois was constantly under-fire in what was essentially enemy territory (Kyoto was and is ringed with hundreds of Buddhist temples!). As Frois wrote to a friend in Portugal,

> Think of a man from Morocco come to Lisbon, where Christianity prospers, to build a mosque. That is how I stand in the Japanese capital, . . . (M:RPJ)

Given this beleaguered atmosphere, it is not surprising to find Frois going out with Coehlo on that search-and-destroy mission while enjoying the (to him) free atmosphere of a part of Japan that was ruled by a Christian. But, I cannot help wonder whether Frois, who had by this time surely known some morally impeccable Buddhists, had any qualms about it; or whether the more Japanized Organtino, who was also in *Meaco* for a long time, would have gone along with such mean-hearted behavior. I also wish I could see into Valignano's heart to see whether he pulled the above-mentioned about-face only for the pragmatic reason he gave – the Jesuit image in Japan – or because, after getting to know the heathens better, he had begun to feel ashamed for his and his Society's behavior!

僧   僧   僧

In the end, it was the Christians' turn to cry. The destruction of shrines and temples, and the persecution of Buddhist priests, not to mention compelling people under Christian lords to adopt their faith were two of the main reasons given by Nobunaga's successor Hideyoshi for outlawing Christianity, after which martyrdom followed upon martyrdom until Tokugawa Iemitsu's regime took the art of torture to new heights. Boxer writes "the new shogun chastised Christianity with scorpions where his father had used whips." Horrific details are provided by the far from popish Caron in his 44 page-long description of *the persecution of the Romish Christians.* Since the Christians seemed to welcome such easy executions as crucifixion, beheading and even getting burned at the stake, we find women dragged naked through the street, "ravished and lain with by Ruffians and Villains," or worse (attempts to force bestiality or incest were recorded), then thrown "into deep tubs full of Snakes and Adders, which crept by several passages into their bodies;" executioners putting out parents eyes "and placing their little Children by them, pinched and plagued them whole daies long, enforcing them with tears of blood to cry to their helpless Fathers and Mothers for an end to their sufferings." Every major martyrdom was treated as a touchdown on the way to winning God's game and fested in the Macau with "horse-races, fencing matches, fireworks, masquerades, comedies and plays" (B:CCJ?).

Since the object was not so much killing Christians as making them recant, eventually, a master torturer arose who managed to break Christians without killing them. Caron claims this Governor *Onemendonne* rooted all Christians out of Hirado/Nagasaki in 45 or 46 days with only one casualty. His method was to take all the Christians to Arima, where there was a sulfurous "Hell-spring" and continually ladle corrosive hot water over them by day and keep them awake in cramped huts built over the boiling water on the seashore at night, while treating them as needed by skilled physicians to keep their torture as constant as possible without killing them. During this period, "he would not suffer the Justices of *Nangansacque* [Nagasaki] nor of *Arima* to come near him, so that he might have the sole honour and glory of this work." (C:DOJ) Boxer, speaking of Iemitsu's reign (1623-51) summed it up as follows:

> Neither the infamous brutality of the methods which he used to exterminate the Christians, nor the heroic constancy of the sufferers have ever been surpassed in the long and painful history of the martyrdom of man." (B:CCJ)

僧　　　　　　僧　　　　　　僧

Lest the chapter leave a bad impression of Japan – for destroying things is not as cruel as killing people – I would like to peg on another observation of Boxer's:

> . . . at the martydom of de Angelis and his forty-nine companions at Yedo in December, 1623, no attempt was made to prevent the Jesuit's preaching to the crowd, and to such effect that two of the bystanders rushed forward and vainly begged the presiding judges to let them join the martyrs . . . It is perhaps worth reminding the reader that in contemporary Europe no such evidence of sympathy for the victims would have been permitted among the onlookers [sometimes the crowd even sang *hymns* with them!] at the hanging of the Roman Catholic priests in London, nor at the *autos da fé* for the Jews in Lisbon." (Ibid)

The Catholic and Protestant powers were at war and religion was probably less important than politics – we see the Irish and English completely flip over, so the English side, which had been pro-Pope became anti- and the Irish, who had rebelled against the Pope's rule became the Catholics they remain to this day. Unlike the case in Japan, the above-mentioned killings did not reflect any real danger but derived from a sickening combination of greed, religious righteousness and cruelty. While the Portuguese *only* slaughtered Jews now and then, the Spanish, thanks to their seven or eight-hundred year-old struggle with Islam, had a burning agenda to rid Europe of all infidels for good. After Felipe II united most of Europe, including Portugal, under his favorite state, Spain, in 1580, the earlier tolerance (?) whereby Jews were allowed to be baptized and pretend to be Christians and so forth, that had weakened with the coming of the Inquisition to Portugal in 1536, disappeared completely, and all Jews were fair game. Even Neo-Christian *dead* Jews! One such was Jerónimo Dias, a leading physician in Goa whose remains were "exhumed and solemnly burnt . . . in accordance with the posthumous punishment inflicted on crypto jews who escaped the stake in their lifetime" (G:PPI) – this in 1580, *while Valignano was pushing through his policy of accommodation in Japan!* And, in 1585, our very year:

> "a bizarre edict was issued commanding that only Indo-Portuguese with Brahminical (Hindu priestly) blood would be accepted in the colony's [Goa's] seminaries to train for the priesthood of the Roman Catholic Church." (William Dalrymple: *White Mughals.* Viking 2002)

It is hard to tell if this should be pointed to as an example of the paradox of accommodation – *it is not always progressive* – or a marriage of convenience between Hindu and European blood-prejudice.

V

OF TEMPLES, *IMAGES AND THINGS THAT TOUCH ON THE WORSHIP OF THEIR RELIGION*

dos templos. imajens e cousas que tocão ao culto de sua religião

5-1   Our churches are long and narrow; *As nossas igrejas são compridas e estreitas;*

The temples of Japan are broad and short. *Os templos de Japão largos e curtos.*

Frois's perspective is from the front of the building. To enter a Christian church of the type with which Frois would have been familiar would be to enter a long hall called a nave from the end, or vestibule, which traditionally was to the West. Since this corresponded to the foot of the cross,[1] a wedding procession that goes down the aisle actually goes *up* it. But what matters is that it is an aisle, something long and deep.

Buddhist temples, on the other hand, are usually *faced*, as one might face a stage, rather than entered. Like most Japanese traditional buildings, they are open and if there is any aisle it is the veranda that encircles it. One can generally walk *around* that and peer in. Often, that is far enough. Or, one can ring the bell outside from the ground and talk to the priest seated within and go no further, for all can be seen from without. This could be *Faux Froised* as follows:

> *Our churches have a door that is larger than a house's but smaller than a barn's;*
> *Their temples have doors wider than a barn's for they are as wide as the building itself.*

Valignano warns of the importance of guarding this difference while constructing Catholic churches in Japan, lest the church resemble a "devil's temple." (Okada)

As was the case with the last chapter which the title claimed was on *bonzes,* whereas from out perspective, it was on bonzes *and* the clergy of Europe, the title here only mentions the Buddhist "temples." While the Portuguese word *igrejas* has a different root than "church," they translate cleanly because both words are only used for Christian places of worship, whereas "temples" as a generic term can be used for other faiths. Japanese are even more discriminating in their vocabulary, for, as with many things, they use completely different terms for native and foreign religions. A small Shinto shrine – a simple wooden building with roof-beams crossing in the fashion of a two-dimensional tepee – is a *yashiro* and a larger one a *jinja*, a Buddhist temple, a *tera* or *otera,* and a church a *kyôkai*. The *kyôkai*, literally "teach-meet" means a society of people sharing a common teaching and, as a building, came to refer specifically to a (Christian) church..

1. ***Church as Cross*** The church was never just a building but the heavenly city of Jerusalem, the Virgin, or most commonly the cruciform body of Christ. The North and South Transepts three quarters of the way up the Nave are the arms of the cross. The r-side of the body (the l-side for people facing East) was the Gospel or Mary side and the left-side the Epistle or Joseph side, the center the chancel (choir and sanctuary) or heart, and the altar the head.

5-2   Ours have choir-lofts, and pews or chairs on which to sit;
As nossas tem coros altos e banqos ou cadeiras em que se asentão;

> The bonzes pray before their altar seated on *tatami* [mats].
> *Os bonzos rezão diante do seu altar asentados nos* tatamis.

The pews and chairs were a relatively recent addition to the church. Eastern and Orthodox Christians remain standing throughout the service. The choirs were in the heart of the church and the religious (clergy and novices?) generally sat there and sang (while the attending masses stood?). Even if Japanese Buddhists had a choir, which they did not, I could not imagine it being *above the altar and the abbot.* Could the angel metaphor have made it possible in the West: i.e., while the social position of the singers may be below that of the priest behind the altar – and many in the congregation – are they free to occupy an exalted position because they serve as proxy for a form of existence between man and God?

When you think about it, a broad room (5-1) in which people face forward is not ideal for aiming at an altar. I am not sure if Japanese always prayed *before an "altar"* in the temples, any way.[1] In fact, in the case of the Zen temples, is it even right to say they "pray?"

Yet, despite widespread agnosticism in Japan, almost every Japanese family has an altar, whereas it is uncommon for even religious Christians in the USA to have the same. Perhaps that owes something to the fact most Japanese Buddhists did not go to temples regularly the way we *attended* church. This is because of one intolerant reason – when the Christians were being kicked out of Japan, the Tokugawa authorities made membership in local Buddhist temples and the owning of Buddhist altar mandatory in order to keep track of people [2] – and one tolerant reason – because, in actuality, the Shinto (reflection-and-cleansing), Confucian (ancestor revering?) and Buddhist (ancestor soul-helping?) aspects are all generally combined – although there are separate Shinto and Buddhist altars [3] for sale – in said altar.

1. *Altars in Temples.* I would appreciate a short gloss on what an altar is in Buddhist temples of various sects!

2.   *Keeping Track.*   Today, generations of family registries established at this time are still kept by authorities (a marriage is not really considered official until entered in these registries), but the authorities are the municipal government rather than the neighborhood temples.

3. *Various Altars.* The eclecticism is expressed by the items going on the shelves, but the overall design is not mixed and is either Buddhist, in which case it is called a *butsudan,* or Shinto, in which case it is called a *kamidan.*

5-3   We have books put on a common stand for all there to sing together;
Nós temos os libros postos em estante pera todos ali cantarem juntos;

> Each bonze has his altar in front of him, and each his book.
> *Os bonzos tem cada hum diante de si hum banquinho e cada hum seu livro.*

Another case of Japanese individualism – or, should we just say, private usage? This may reflect, as DR opines, the more individual meditation or devotion of the Buddhist as opposed to the emphasis on communion on the part of the Christians sharing in the "body of Christ." It may also have physical causes: 1) the Japanese (partly because of the highly humid and hot summers?) are not a very touching people; 2) the Japanese had better (i.e. cheaper) printing available; 3) sitting cross-legged does not permit people to get close. But DR has a point, for the singing/chanting by the Japanese is also far less orchestrated.

5-4　　Our books are folded and bound with clasps;
Os nossos livros são dobrados e fechados com brochas;

> Those of the bonzes' are rolled up and tied with a ribbon.
> *Os dos bonzos emrolados e atados com huma fita.*

After spending oodles of time googling but finding only "red clasps," "ivory clasps," "missing clasps" (made of brass stock),"metal clasps,""rawhide clasps," and one paltry picture of something that resembled a large fat needle with a long slit for an eye, which I took to be a button-like device, I was close to giving up on "our" side. Then I found:

> A metal fitting attached to the boards at the fore edge of a binding in order to hold the book shut and to preserve the parchment (unless kept at an appropriate temperature and humidity level, parchment tends to cockle and return to the original shape of the animal skin). Clasps became popular during the fourteenth century initially as a combination of metal fittings and leather straps and then entirely of metal. (www.ceu.hu/medstud/ manual/MMM/glossary.html).

Finally, E-bay let me *see* one. It was a hinged catch that squeezed together the covers of the book on the open-side. The next week, I found (at a garage sale) a large 1871 Bible with two clasps for the open side. Too bad the other side, the cover, had split in two!

The Japanese translations of Frois just say they are tied up with strings (*himo*). The reason Frois writes "ribbon" is probably because the finely woven cords are tape-like (indeed, the same type can be used as a book-mark.). But, I am not so sure about the validity of the contrast, itself, because scrolls were not yet extinct in Europe and bound books not *that* rare in Japan.[1] *Their* peculiarity (or difference, compared to "ours"):

> *Our books are printed on many folded sheets of paper thick enough for writing on both sides;*
> *Theirs are printed on one side of one strip of thin paper folded up so the writing is on one side.*

Because Japanese had a tradition of long, long picture scrolls, the paper could be so long that the entire book could be made from a single leaf, or vice versa.[2] This leads to a second difference:

> *We must carefully cut open the leaves of our new books in order to read them.*
> *They leave their leaves uncut, for there is nothing but air between the closed pages.*

All that can be read is on the outside part. This contrast, described in a way far harder to understand by Frois brings up the tail of chapter 10 (10-29). But why was this *book contrast* made part of a religion-related chapter rather than put into chapter 10, on Writing? Is it because the switch from scroll to book was slower inside temples than on the outside, so the contrast was greater? The flat rectangular books in Japan were made of paper much better than "ours" which, like the books we now own, could stay as shut as a sleeping mimosa without a clasp to help![2]

1. How Long Japanese Paper? Has anyone studied this?

2. Clasp Use. But I think there are other advantages to the clasp. If tight enough, they can prevent silverfish from squeezing in between the pages to steal the food of thought. Some may also have served as locks.

5-5　　Our images are, for the main part, painted retabulo;
As nossas imajens pola maior parte são de retabolos pintados;

> The images of the *varelas* [temples: see 3-8] of the Bonzes are all sculpted.
> *Nas varelas nos bonzos todas as imajens são de vulto.*

The *retabulo* is a stand placed behind or above the altar, generally made of ornate wood or marble and containing one or more panels with paintings or low relief (NDA) generally of Christ's passion and/or saints. The Buddhist images – and, to Frois's credit, he does not use the prejudicial term of "idol" here – were generally cast or carved in wood.

In order to justify this contrast, we must focus on the central images, near the altar. If we open up the entire church and temple for comparison the contrast falls flat. First, we can find abundant Catholic sculptures which, I think, need no description – though I cannot help adding that the next generation of churches, the Rococo style (also called *Jesuit style* for their love of classical elements) abound in statuettes in the classical style, particularly dozens of little cupids, known as Putti, which float throughout the church! And, second, we have no shortage of Buddhist paintings, ranging from the black and white Zen *dharuma* and portraits (usually not hanging in the show-off part of the temples) to the luridly colored paintings of Hell – usually sequences which could be explained for visitors – some so imaginative as to make Bosch look banal. Frois himself once noted them. As far as I know, none of the Jesuits mention the most important type of painted image in esoteric Buddhism, the *mandala*. Let me try:

> We learn our faith by concentrating upon our doctrine of words;[1]
> The mikkyô [esoteric Buddhism] bonzes reflect on complex paintings.

Mandalas, extraordinarily elaborate symbol-filled pictures painted or made of colored sand, are *not* my *forte*. I can take complexity only in small doses and unmixed with meaning: i.e., I prefer the kaleidoscope. The reader who wishes to know more about the types and uses of the mandala can do his or her own research![2]

1. *Words vs. Image*   DR provides an excellent gloss: "Thomas Aquinas argued that natural reason and contemplation of nature (the emphasis in Zen Buddhism) revealed the existence of God but not his nature; the latter was knowable from scripture and, ultimately, an infusion of God's grace."

2. *Mandhala Connection to the West*   I believe the closest thing to mandalas in the West are the elaborate carpet designs created by Islamic artists (Remember, Islam is every bit as Occidental as Christianity from a Buddhist point of view.). I also once tried to convince my employer in Japan to publish a book of the best of Sufi stories as Western Zen *koans,* for the intelligent absurdity is identical in style and sometimes even in details.

~~~~~~

5-6   We use diverse colors for our images;
Nós uzamos nas imagens de diversas pinturas;

They gild all of theirs from top to bottom.
Elles dourão as suas todas d'alt'abaxo.

Our images, in retabulo or sculpted, were generally painted in color, as were those of the Classic world.[1]   In the Japanese case, here Frois would seem to mean images for adoration,[2] the same ones referred to in 5-5. The figures inside the main temple, generally the manifestation of Buddha best reflecting the philosophy of the sect (and/or the founder, himself such a manifestation) are usually gilt but, as Frois knew, the rest usually were not. Some are red (guardian demons), plain stone (*jizo* = a guardian deity of children), or, more rarely, as life-like (Frois saw and described the terribly realistic – wooden, with implanted hair – Basura, a skinny saint) as the fake people "installed" by some any modern artists.

I wonder if Frois means to indirectly suggest that *ours* are not sinful *gilt images*. Think about it. The Old Testament decried not "images," but "*gilt* images" (or silver ones). And, loh and behold, the Japanese ones were just that! The Christians have a problem with gold, as they do with cleanliness (see 4-16 note): on the one hand, it is the perfect symbol of truth, for it is incorruptible and, together with the sun, was identified with Christ; on the other hand, its impermanence is of the material world, and contradicts faith in the truly eternal immaterial world. Alchemy in the West might be seen as an attempt to resolve this contradiction, or should we say cultural schizophrenia. In China and Japan, alchemy was so completely absorbed in the matter of longevity, not wealth, that gold played a far smaller role. Be that as it may, secular Western visitors found the gilt much to their liking. The Englishman Richard Cocks, writing in 1616 about one temple's gilt statues: "The truth is, all of it is to be admired." And another temple's 3333 idols: "made after an excellente forme neare to the life, and clothed with a gowne (or loose garment) over them, and all gilded over with pure gould, very fresh and glorious to behould." (C:DORC)

The whole idea of images created by "our" Old Testament is one big mistake. I am delighted to find a best-seller such as Karen Armstrong's *A History of God* get that straight. After quoting a particularly detestable passage of Hosea on sacrificing and blowing kisses to silver calves, she comments:

> This was, of course, a most unfair and reductive description of Canaanite religion. The people of Canaan and Babylon had never believed that their effigies of the gods were themselves divine; they had never bowed down to worship a statue *tout court*. The effigy had been a symbol of divinity. Like their myths about the unimaginable primordial events, it had been devised to direct the attention of the worshipper beyond itself. (A:HOG)

I doubt Frois understood this. And, I wonder how many Usanian Christians do.

---

1. *Classical Color.*   Lafcadio Hearn wrote an essay – editorial ("Tinted Art") on how our mistaken belief that Classical sculpture was plain white colored our image of Greek and Roman culture. Since most good nonfiction is not reprinted, I will share a big chunk of it with you.

> The White Art, as the French critic termed sculpture, is a modern art . . . . To the Greek mind an endless succession of purely white architectural masses would have seemed spectral, weird – perhaps even shocking. The temples and public buildings of the Hellenes were not only painted, but painted with diverse warm colors – so that the uniformity of stone effects might be agreeably relieved or broken by the polychromatic decorations. Their statues were never left in the condition which modern sculptors consider complete; they were painted or varnished in illusive imitation of flesh . . . they were overlaid with an encaustic varnish, partly formed of wax and oil, which produced a startling imitation of pale transparent flesh . The marble having been carefully chosen with a view to tint and grain, and the surface worked minutely in imitation of human skin, the effects of this varnish may be imagined . . . Pygmalion. . . . It was reserved for another age and another people to find beauty in perfect whiteness; and it is not too much to aver that the spirit of Christianity had much to do with this . . . The joyous, materialistic, sensual Greeks had occasionally heard of those who felt "world-sickness," who found little delight in natural enjoyment, and longed for things beyond their reach; but such men were deemed to be victims of a strange malady – were looked upon as men enamored of phantoms . . . For more than a thousand years that simple word *White* has been connected with our spiritual ideas and holy traditions; it has become sacred as a tomb, awful as a ghost. (Lafcadio Hearn: *Editorials* H. Mifflin 1926)

Yet, if I am not mistaken, most of us do not discover that classical whiteness is a myth until we grow up, which is to say, after our ascetic taste has developed. This is a subject worth an entire book. Is there one?

2. *Images for Adoration*   I do not know if "adoration" is quite right. But it is better than "worship," for Buddhists, at least, "do not worship the Buddha. But they often have an altar with statues or images. And they often make offerings at the altar. The statues and images are used as a reminder of the need to follow the Buddhist path and the offerings are symbolic of the wish to give up wealth and selfish actions for the sake of others." (Googled from *The Buddhist altar: Introducing Buddhism course*, tutor: Mike Horne).

5-7   All of ours [the images] are proportioned to the human stature;
As nossas são proporcionadas todas hà estatura dos homens;

Some of theirs are so big that they resemble giants.
Algumas das suas tão grandes que paresem jigantes.

In medieval European paintings, as in paintings throughout the world, important personages were often depicted larger than others around them. Why, then, no huge statues of Jesus or Mary? Did the counter-example of ancient "pagan" sculpture make anything large a "graven idol?" Or was largeness, thought rightfully a monopoly of God alone? Regardless, Cocks, who was not a religious, was enthralled by "The Hudge Collosso or Bras Imadg (or rather idoll)" – the *Dibotes*, or great-buddha (*daibutsu*) statue in Kyoto – "of a wonderful bignes, the head of it reaching to the top of the temple, allthough he sat croselegged" and other idolls, all of which he called "the most admerablest thing that ever I saw, and may well be reconed before any of the noted 7 wonders of the world." [1] (11/2/1616) Ten years later, the Dutchman Conrad Cramer described the same sweet-looking colossal Buddha as "incredibly big," "the mother of all devils." (in C:TCJ/notes)   "Wondering how I could describe it when I returned home," the Mexican-born Rodrigo de Vivero y Velasco (who served as interim Governor of the Philippines and was shipwrecked off the coast of Japan in 1609) had a servant climb up the statue – where he "tried to encircle the thumb with both his arms" but was "two spans" short. Velasco finished up his account of this temple with its colossal and 33,000 other gilt images as follows:

> Only the devil could have devised this waste in order to make the Emperor use up his wealth and riches. (in C:TCJ)

Kipling fell into a revelry over the *daibutsu* in Kamakura: "Little blue and grey slated figures pass under its shadow, buy two or three joss-sticks, disappear into the shrine, that is the body of the god, come out smiling, and drift away through the shrubberies. A fat carp in a pond sucks at a fallen leaf with just the sound of a wicked worldly little kiss. Then the earth steams and steams in silence, and a gorgeous butterfly, full six inches from wing to wing, cuts through the steam in a zigzag of colour and flickers up to the forehead of the god." Then, after describing some images to put the yet-to-come imagist school to shame, this wonderful question:

> To overcome desire and covetousness of mere gold, which is often very vilely designed, that is conceivable; but why must a man give up the delight of the eye, colour that rejoices, light that cheers, and line that satisfies the innermost deeps of the heart? Ah, if the Bodhisat had only seen his own image. (in C+W:KJ)

While Frois's contrast is couched in neutral terms, his idol-destroying past tells us that he probably felt the Japanese side was *bad*. I cannot help wondering what he would have thought about the fundamentalism in Northwest Europe, which came close to destroying all churches – as Moslems did to all images of the human body – for even churches were considered idolatrous by the purist of the Puritans! "The plain and functional Quaker's meeting house was," as Keith Thomas writes, "the ultimate achievement of this line of thought." (T:RDM) We came damn close to losing our entire architectural heritage: it could have followed the great ancient libraries and the holy clumps of trees and been razed to the ground.

1. *Wonders of the World.* The eight wonders of the Ancient World included two huge statues, that of Rhodes astride a harbor entrance (one worries what a tall mast could do to his crotch) and that of Zeus in Olibina (?). The standing Chinese Buddhas and those of Bamiyan, Afganistan (175 ft tall) recently razed by Islamic bigots are the tallest ancient sculptures on earth, though they are not so tall as our Lady of Freedom. The Christians got into the game recently, with a 100-foot tall Christ overlooking Rio de Janeiro from atop the 2,300-ft peak of Corcovado mountain since 1931 and a slightly smaller one in a suburb of Lisbon since 1959.

~~~~~~

5-8　　Ours are beautiful and inspire devotion;
　　　As nossas são fermozas e que provocão á deva[>o]são;

　　　Theirs are horrid and frightening with figures of flaming demons.
　　　As suas horrendas e temerozas com figuras de diabos abrazados em fogos.

Since "theirs" cannot be both gilt (as in 6 above) *and* burning red, Frois should have said "*some* of theirs." More important, the contrast, though true, could as easily have been the other way around:

> *Our chief religious image, Jesus, is usually depicted expressing horrible agony upon the cross;*
> *Their chief religious image, Buddha, is usually shown sitting relaxed with a serene smile.*

The Buddha with his eyes often shut and looking content more than offsets the dreadful bulgy-eyed muscle-bound demons that served to ward-off evil spirits or guard this or that Buddhist treasure. Actually, Frois knew by first-hand experience that some of "theirs" were like "ours," i.e. beautiful.[1] In a letter (Englished by Willis) he wrote:

> In the midst of their temples is erected an altar, whereon standeth a wooden idol of Amida, naked from the girdle upward, with holes in his ears after the manner of Italian Gentlewomen, sitting on a wooden rose, goodly to behold.

In another letter, he describes a thousand sculptures of "Kannon, the son of Amida" (actually, Kannon is Amida (Buddha) as the *Goddess* of Mercy and the thousand are her progeny, if I am correct, but that doesn't matter, here.) as follows:

> There is a shining halo behind each statue. All these statues are gilded from head to foot with pure gold, and when you look down the length of the temple, the sight is enough to blind you with its brilliance. The beautiful faces are so well carved that, but for the fact that it is a temple of Amida, this scene would make a good composition of place for a meditation on the ranks and hierarchies of the angels. (in C:TCJ)

Many, if not most of the "horrid and frightening" demons have a conversion story and were originally incorporated from local deity. The cynocephalic St. Christopher, whose beastly powers were enlisted on behalf of his new religion, was perhaps the closest Christian equivalent (See David Gordon White: DOGMAN). Such demons are peripheral presences for most Buddhist sects but one, the Konpira sect "worshipped" (for lack of a better word) the powerful tengu goblin. Like St. Christopher, he was the patron "saint" of travelers and, most of all seafarers. Fishing villages generally prayed at Konpira temples. Tengu were related to the man-of-the-mountain type local guardian demons=gods of shamanistic Buddhism, rain and storm-influencing dragon-gods (which farmers put big stock in) and thunder-demons, the last of which are a folk favorite and the source of many amusing folk-tales.[2] The tengu's connection with the wind is suggested by this haiku by Shiki (c1900) :

> *raising a kite*
> *the children implore*
> *mister tengu*

Fearsome red statues are not always *tengu* or minor guardian demons. One reason for the "flaming" aspect noted in the contrast may be surmised from the following description of a Japanese traditional blacksmith's ceremony and his patron deity, the "Metal Mountain God" by the contemporary Japanese designer Sugiura Kohei:

> This god's more well known manifestation is the fear-inspiring Fûdômyô-ô, literally "the unmoving-light/bright-king" (identified with the Hindi Acala) who was thought to sit fast upon a metal-filled mountain, his countenance glaring like molten ore, with an upraised sword (to severe the deep-seated appetites of the flesh) in hand. (robin d. gill trans.: MOJI-NO SHUKUSAI or "a celebration of letters," 1995 Shaken)

In Buddhism, different gods tend to have different personalities, whereas the Judeo-Christian God traditionally is *both* pacifistic, though never so gentle as Buddha, *and* more terrifying than this fiery Acala, whose sword, you may note is put to a less bloody and far more edifying use than the indiscriminate slaughters "our" God carried out according to the Old Testament. Moreover, it should be noted that the prevalence of red is not just to express the molten power described by Sugiura above but because it was the color identified with charms against evil. But I *still* oversimplify. A marvelous passage by Meylan found in the MANNERS AND CUSTOMS OF THE JAPANESE (1841) suggests even more delightful complexity:

> I know not whether it be to do the devil honour or to jeer at him that the Japanese, in their eigth month, take pleasure in contemplating a grotesque dance, performed in the streets by persons attired as demons, and duly horned and vizarded. These mummers have, besides, a drum hung about them . . . but what deserves mention is that their dresses are of various colours, to wit, black, white, red, and green. It is well known that white men represent the devil as black, while the negroes make theirs white; but red and green devils are, I believe, wholly and solely Japanese. I long sought their reasons for these colours, and at length received the following explanation. Among the theological disputes of Japan, one arose concerning the colour of the devil; one party affirming it to be black, a second white, a third red, and, finally, a fourth declared that the fiendish hue was green. This difference of opinion seemed likely to produce a civil war, when the judicious idea was started of submitting the question to the spiritual emperor, the *mikado*. The *Son of Heaven,* after a short deliberation, prevented the threatened evil by declaring all parties to be in the right . . . Since that time the Japanese devils have adopted the four colours; and, thus tinted, dance up and down the streets, to the delight of the curious spectators, who, while they look on, no longer dream of menacing disputes. (B:MCJ)

I suspect that "the devil" is, rather, *demons* and that each color [3] stands for a season of the year and point of the compass.

It is about time to qualify Frois's "ours." Half of "us," meaning Europe, is no longer with him. Did Frois *know* about the wholesale destruction of Christian images by Protestants (Lutherans, Calvinists, Puritans, etc) in Switzerland in the 1530's, England in the 1540's, the Netherlands from the mid-1560's and elsewhere that makes his decimation of the Buddhist art of South Japan seem small peanuts? In East England, for example, "all but one of the two hundred and sixty-two statues decorating the Alcock chantry in Ely cathedral were smashed or mutilated." (H:CER) Here is the tolerant Reformist Erasmus describing an early 1529 outburst in Basel and :

> Not a statue had been left in the churches, in porches, on facades, or in the monasteries. Everything frescoed is lost under coats of whitewash. Whatever would burn has been thrown into the pyre, everything else has been hacked into small pieces. Neither value nor artistry prevailed to save anything. On the first of April, the city magistrates approved the outburst . . . (H:CER)

Fearing that the mass destruction would end up destroying all authority, in most of North Europe the attack on Catholic "idolatry" was managed less dramatically by dismantling, storing and selling. Regardless, it is a sad story.

---

1. *Beautiful Images.* While Buddhas and Buddhist saints (bodhisattva) are never muscular, they need not be fat either. There are slim and elegant sculptures dating back to the 7th century in Japan.

2. Thunder-Demon Folk Tales. In my favorite, a fallen thunder-demon baby is raised on the milk made from the lint collected from the navels of an entire town (for adult thunder-demons were said to eat navels) and given a sweet send-off. Compare that adorable folk tradition to "our" clergies' practice of getting electrocuted while desperately ringing the church bells to ward off what they thought were The Devil's doings! (See Cohen's BENJAMIN FRANKLIN for a fine summary) These thunder-demons have horns on their head like our devil and usually also have large canine teeth on the bottom (like the boar, upon which Emma sometimes rode in Japan), though I have seen in sushi shop posters (demons are connected with a type of toasted tofu-wrapped rice called *inarizushi*) demons with extended upper canines; but that may be from the modern influence of werewolves and vampires, and is very rare. Regardless, these creatures are so jolly-looking that they remind me of our cherubim (who, if you recall, chased the sinning couple out of Eden).

2. Demon Colors. I apologize for pure guesswork, if guessing can be called work. There must be a doctorate out there, somewhere, on the colors of Gods and Demons! A gloss, anyone?

5-9   We have our bells on very high towers;
Nós temos os sinos em torres muito altas;

They, low, so close to the ground they may be touched.
Elles em baixo muito perto do chão, que lhe chegão com a mão.

Japan, as we shall see in the architecture chapter, did not have tall structures. Low architecture did not prevent bells from being heard in Japan for temples with large bells were usually on mountain-sides, and had the advantage of being on solid ground yet still high up so that the sound would permeate the town below. I need not point out the height of our bells, only remind the reader that it was because they stood out (as it was the policy to maintain the commanding view in a town) as they did that they attracted that diabolic lightning, which was far less of a problem with the Japanese temples which were generally lower than the surrounding trees. [1]

Perhaps it bears pointing out that the Chinese were *not* topsy-turvy to us here, for they had bells on the top floor of high pagodas. A 13-story Dragon Pagoda is depicted in Headland's Chinese Mother Goose Rhymes. I suspect that competition with Muslim minarets in West China would have fueled a race for the sky which the Japanese, luckily (considering the earthquakes), never had to engage in. Alternatively, it may reflect the more heavenly orientation of the Chinese (Pardon the guesswork: glosses anyone?)

1. Temple Grounding. Can anyone tell me if those chains hanging from the corners of the roofs which look like they would ground them actually do so, and if they predate Franklin or not?

5-10   Our bells are tolled and have the clappers attached within;
Os nossos sinos se dobrão e tem o badalo da banda de dentro;

Those of Japan do not move and are struck from without by a pole like a battering ram. *Os de Japão estão sem se moverem, e tanjen-nos de fora com huma tranca como vayvem.*

When you think about it, our method of tolling bells is matrist, or feminist, if you prefer. The ding or the dong called a clapper hangs there and the concavity does the moving, swinging back and forth until contact is initiated! Actually that is also how a small hand-bell works, as opposed to the gong where only the striker is moved. Hanging and swinging the huge bells that became common in church towers during medieval times was no easy business and required wheel-like devices the function of which I will not even try to explain. By the early-16th century, Europe's great cathedrals boasted 10-ton bells.[1] Meanwhile bell-ringing has became increasingly elaborate as the reader can ascertain by visiting the website of , say, the CCCBR or Central Council of Church Bell Ringers.[2]

While we tend to identify large bells with the West, the world's largest *working* bells are actually found in Burma, Korea, and Japan (the Russians made the largest bells but their largest are out of commission) and all are close to the ground and struck in the manner Frois describes for Japan despite being concave bells rather than gongs. The 70 ton bell of Chioninji Temple in Kyoto made in 1636, is the largest in Japan today.

The striking pole is correspondingly huge. It can be 10-20 feet-long and weigh 3-500 pounds. It is swung back and forth horizontally, building up momentum like a pendulum using a pair or more of ropes attached to each side until, with one final swing, it is launched into the bell like a battering ram, at which time a monk letting go sometimes does a backwards flip around the rope. Unfortunately, my English is not up to a really good description of this process which I have seen. *Kipling is*. He writes of being awoken by what he thought was an earthquake in Kyoto and discovering it was a great bell ("twenty feet of green bronze") hanging with its lower lip only five feet from the ground "under a cut in the hillside." A knuckle rapped lightly on the lip

> made the monster breathe heavily, and the blow of a stick started a hundred shrill-voiced echoes round the darkness of its dome. At one side, guyed by half a dozen small hawsers, hung a battering ram, a twelve-foot spar bound with iron, its nose pointing full-butt at a chrysanthemum in high relief on the belly of the bell. Then by special favour of Providence, which always looks after a loafer, they began to sound sixty strokes. Half a dozen men swang the ram back and forth with shoutings and outcries, till it had gathered sufficient way, and the loosened ropes let it hurl against the chrysanthemum. The boom of the smitten bronze was swallowed up by the earth below and the hillside behind, so that its volume was not proportionate to the size of the bell . . . An English hanger would have made thrice as much of it. But then he would have lost the crawling jar that ran through the rock-stone and pine for twenty yards round, that beat through the body of the listener and died away under his feet like the shock of distant blasting. . . . (1889 – K:KJ)

Reading Kipling I thought *Eureka!* So that is why the anus in Japan (especially in the context of sodomy) is usually drawn as a Chrysanthemum! I had thought it was either because the *kiku* was the flower that brought up the end of the year or because, being the Imperial flower, it was ideal for symbolic blasphemy. More likely, the chrysanthemum-pounding bonzes and their proclivities fused into the symbol! Sometimes, the bell is as high as ten feet or so above the ground, or on the edge of a slope in which case a platform is provided for the bell-pounders. The most powerful sex scene in modern cinema (Itami Junzo's *Sôshiki,* or "The Funeral") shows such a bell being pounded while the protagonist rams his belly against the ample white rump of his old flame in the woods. But not all bell clanging in Japan is so powerful an affair:

> Their priests, with gong and incense, pursue a stately service, quite undisturbed by the fact that the worshippers are ringing bells, just as we ring up the Central Office on the telephone, to inform their gods that there are prayers for them to listen to . . . (S:MQTJ)

This would seem to describe a large temple with things going on here and there in the clamorous manner that always astound Occidentals who expect something more dignified and singularly focused. Shinto Shrines and temples with Shinto connections have yet another type of bell, a gong which visitors (usually after making an offering and a wish but often just for fun) sound very gently by swinging a rope with a knot higher up – they are usually about ten feet up, just under the eaves of the temple. Because one has to put a wave into the rope to get anything more than a muffled sound from the gong, it is ideal for little children to play with: they cannot make enough noise to disturb anyone – speaking of which, Thomas Paine once wrote with respect to the proposal of Camille Jordan to restore the Catholic privilege of Bell-ringing which was taken away by the French Revolution:

As to bells, they are a public nuisance. If one profession is to have bells, and another has the right to use the instruments of the same kind, or any other noisy instrument, some may choose to meet at the sound of cannon, another at the beat of drum, another at the sound of trumpets, and so on, until the whole becomes a scene of general confusion. But if we permit ourselves to think of the state of the sick, and the many sleepless nights and days they undergo, we shall feel the impropriety of increasing their distress by the noise of bells, or any other noisy instruments. (1797? http://www.infidels.org/library/historical/thomas_paine/worship_and_church.html)

While the fact that going to church was mandatory, bells were expensive (people were poor), and (some argue) the vesper bell was first used by conquerors to enforce a curfew, give credence to Paine's apprehension, his aesthetic sense is not mine.   Most people in the West and Japan would, I think, agree that one need not be religious to appreciate bells ringing at dawn, mid-day and dusk. They add a patina of pathos to the natural world and quicken us in ways hard to describe. (This is not true for "any noisy instrument." I would prefer to hear a cannon on much rarer occasions such as, say, the first appearance of the new moon or the rising of the full-moon.)   Russians go even further than Japanese or most Western Catholics by ascribing scientific healing properties to bells.[3] My feelings are mixed only in so far that bells no longer tell real time (when the sun rises or sets) but only indicate our artificial hours.   I can hear church bells from where I write, but only the colony of parrots in the Kapok tree a hundred yards away tells me when the sun appears if I have slept in.

1. *Large Bells?* A large elephant weighs 6 tons. A Rouen bell (1501) weighs 16, the Maria Gloriosa of Erfurt Cathedral (1497) 13, the post-Frois Cologne Cathedral bell, made from captured French cannon, nearly 27 (info from *Catholic Encyclopedia*). So we have 2-5 elephants swinging up there!   Obviously, that is a hell of a feat! Tsar Bell III (Tsar-Kolokol) in Moscow.

If you include bells that did not work well, we have the broken Tsar Kolokol III which was cast thrice, more metal added each time. The present incarnation (1733-35) weighs about 180 tons (400,000 pounds). The Shi-tenno-ji (temple) in Osaka, Japan (1902), at 310,000 lbs. the largest photographed bell cast in Asia was melted down in 1942 for its metal. A Burmese Dhammazedi bell (1484) that may have been *much* larger yet was lost by a Portuguese adventurer, Filipe de Brito y Nicote in 1608 when he removed the bell from the Shwedagon Pagoda, rolled it down hill to a raft in the Pazundaung Creek, hauled it by elephants to the river where bell and raft were lashed to his flagship for the journey across the river to Thanlyn (Syrian) to be melted down and made into ships cannons before which (off a place now known as Monkey Point) the raft broke up and the bell went to the bottom, taking the ship with it, after which, the surviving Portuguese garrison was killed in an attack by angry Burmese and the Portuguese leader died a slow death on bamboo stakes.

The largest working bell is the Mingun Bell, which rings near the city of Sagaing, at the Mingun pagoda, some 11 km (7 miles) upriver from Mandalay, in the center of Burma. It was cast in 1808 and weighs about 200 US tons kg. (Info from http://www.russianbells.com/)

2. *The Central Council of Church Bell Ringers* is the representative body for all who ring bells by rope and wheel in the English tradition, the majority of whom

practice the art of change ringing. Change ringing is an English tradition which consists of ringing bells so that the order in which they sound is systematically changed. The bells are tuned to a normal (diatonic) scale and it is usual to start with ringing down the scale, a sequence which ringers call "rounds". Much of this evolved in the 17th century so it is nothing for this book but Google them out if you wish. (www.cccbr.org.uk/)

3. *Bells and Health*   A splendid article by Tatiana Kharlamova starts like this:

Above me, the dark bronze tent of the bell. Above it, only gold domes and the sky. My hands hardly fit the thick kapron ropes. A team of ringers take their places at the four bell towers of the Cathedral of Christ the Savior. They allow me as newcomer to make the first stroke of the blagovest. I swing the tongue and . . . BOOM!— an enormous sound overwhelms me with its compunctionate triumph. Slipping out of the arch of the belltower, the sound floats away as a silver cloud above the streets and alleys of Moscow. People below crane their necks and the alarms of the cars parked near the church go off. . . . And miracles begin." (http://www.rus-sianbells.com/ interest/zdorovie/zdorovie.html)

She continues. According to engineer-physicist Yuri Kornilov,

"bell construction is very harmonious with the human body, whose internal organs respond to every vibration of the outer world. Bells are made in such a way that their vibrations harmonize with the state of our physical vessel. . . . alarm bells are cast in such a way as to awaken in the hearer a feeling of disturbance. It seems that blagovestnik bells, on the other hand, fill you with peace and attune you to joy."

A psycho-neurological clinic in St Petersburg finds bells particularly effective against depression.   The special festal, triumphal, and joyful peal known as "raspberry" (*malinovy*) turns out to be the best for this. Because "bell ringing protects from illnesses and other troubles" bell-ringers tend to live long and healthy lives.   Bell-ringer Sergei Vaganovich. suggests it effects "the functions of breathing, digestion, and endocrine glands," Kharlanova writes she checked her own senses the day of the interview and "though sick with a fever, runny nose, and cough." and out "in the rain and wind at a great height, there was nothing left of my cold when I came down."

"Bell Ringing Heals Illness and Depression" Tatiana Kharlamova   (I find all the articles at http://www.russian-bells.com/ just marvelous).

~~~~~~

5-11   Our bells toll for festivals, and do it many times.
       Os nossos sinos se repição polas festas e isto muitas vezes;

           Theirs never toll for they do not have clappers.
           Os seus nunca se ripição porque não tem badalos.

       The Portuguese *dobrão (dobram)* in 5-10 and the *repição (repicam)* above both become "toll" in English.   In the case of the first it is literally a *doubling* motion and the second *repeating*. "toll" works, but barely. I say *barely*, because Japanese did sometimes repeat the bell sound even if they did not cling-clang. Since the Japanese used bells to mark the time, there *was* repetition, it just wasn't the frantic cling-clanging the clapper makes possible. In particular, I recall hearing the bells struck over and over and over on New Year's Eve. I did not count, but the *joya-no-kane*, literally, casting-off-[the last]night-bell which now rings from before-to-after midnight (I am not sure when it used to ring, maybe at sunset ——誰か？) is/are supposed to sound 108 times. If you live in a hilly area with many echoes, believe me, it sounds like solid bells! It was supposed to purify (or perhaps exorcise?) the 108 sins of mankind and that idea came from China some time before Frois.

       But, what did we ring *and* toll "our" bells for? Romans expressed gratitude to the gods for success in battle by ringing bells mounted on chariots in victory parades. In the first half of the first millennium, church-bells came to summon the faithful to religious services and sound an alarm when danger threatened.   The pope sanctioned their use in 604 and a ceremony for blessing them soon followed.   By the eleventh century, church-towers began to boast the large bells we take for granted today. These bells often had poems inscribed in them in Latin:

       Laudo Deum verum plebem voco congrego clerum
       (I praise the true God, I call the people, I assemble the clergy;)
       Defunctos ploro, nimbum fugo, festa decoro.
       (I bewail the dead, I dispense storm clouds, I do honour to feasts.)

       Funera plango fulmina frango sabbata pango
       (At obsequies I mourn, the thunderbolts I scatter, I ring in the sabbaths;)
       Excito lentos dissipo ventos paco cruentos
       (I hustle the sluggards, I drive away storms, I proclaim peace [after bloodshed].)

Note the peal of the rhyme in the Latin! Or, in English with a wee couplet in each line:

       Men's death I tell by doleful knell;
       Lightning and thunder I break asunder;
       On Sabbath all to church I call;
       The sleepy head I rouse from bed;
       The tempest's rage I do assuage;
       When cometh harm, I sound alarm.

I do not know the date for the last poem, but following England's break with the Catholic church, Latin inscriptions such as the above poems or simply *"Ave Maria,"* or *"Sancte, ora pro nobis,"* were replaced by very English doggerel, such as the following credit, complaint, warning and boast respectively, from *Chamber's Book of Days* (C:CBD).

> This bell was broake and cast againe, as plainly doth appeare,
> John Draper made me in 1618, wich tyme chvrchwardens were
> Edward Dixson for the one, whoe stode close to his tacklin,
> And he that was his partner there was Alexander Jacklin.'

> Of all the bells in Benet I am the best,
> And yet for my casting the parish paid lest.

> Repent, I say, be not too late, Thyself al times redy make.

> My sound is good, which that you hear,
> Young Bilbie made me sound so clear.

Those English! I think you can see why Catholics liked to stick to Latin! But better is yet to come: Catholic countries had something called a "passing bell," which

> was rung slowly when a death was imminent in the parish. When the sick person was near his end the solemn tones of the bell reminded the faithful of their Christian duty of praying for his happy death and for his eternal repose; and after his spirit had departed, the bell tolled out his age – one short stroke for each year . . ." (LR)

And, something called "the ringing of the Angelus." The Catholic site from which I borrowed the bell verses trumpets:

> There was nothing resembling it in Jewish and pagan rites. All religions, it is true, have had certain times for prayer; but they have had nothing at all like our Angelus, which consists essentially in the reciting of certain prayers at the sound of a bell at fixed hours." (LR)[1]

More precisely, it is "the triple repetition of the *Hail Mary* with certain versicles[?], responses and a prayer" at morning, noon and evening. But most interesting of all is the existence of a period when bells were *not* played.

> No bells, large or small, are rung between the end of the Gloria of the Mass on Holy Thursday and the beginning of the Gloria on Holy Saturday, when the Church begins to anticipate joyfully the Resurrection of our Lord. Then both the sanctuary gongs and the tower-bells peal forth triumphantly, to announce that Christ has risen from the dead, to die no more.

I can recall an eskimo (Inuit) in the early-20th century explaining what most impressed him about Christianity. It was the idea of not working on the Sabbath. "We have a taboo about many things, but to think that a day could be taboo! We never thought about that!" (maybe in one of Steffansson's books?) Japanese did have days where various things could not be done, but there were no bell-less days. I wonder what Catholics do to with their cuckoo clocks?

5-12   At our monasteries, there are iron clocks;
Em os nossos moesteiros há relogios de ferro;

The clocks of Japan are only of water.
Os relogios de Japão são somente de agoa.

In the Middle Ages most clocks in the West were not mechanical in the sense we now think of. Water-powered clocks did have gears but those gears were used for moving the fancy automata that put on a show and told the time: *clock*, itself comes from OHG *glocka,* OIr *clocc*, etc. meaning "bell." Gears to move hands and dials which could be *read* did not appear until about the 14th century. In a word, clocks were not for *keeping* time, but for *sounding* it. By the mid-15th century, most towns had mechanical clocks. They pretty much had to both in order to show they were not lagging other towns (European towns in the Renaissance exhibited a *keeping up with the Jones* quality) and because both the ecclesiastical and secular authorities demanded it.

> Clocks were seen as conducive to good order. A familiar if rather obscure saying of Holy Roman Emperor Charles V [1364-80: also called C. the Wise] makes the point: *"Portae, pulsus, pueri*: gates, bell strokes, children." Solid walls, proper schools, and the orderly measurement of time were for the emperor the characteristics of a well-governed city. (Andrew Pettegree *Time and Space: Living in Sixteenth-century Europe* Blackwell 2002)

The only problem was that with time being told loudly, a problem similar to our radio band problem arose. In cities with both Protestants and Catholics who, as might be guessed, might have different ideas on how to tell time, there was a struggle for the legal right to control the bell-tower and when neither side gave in, ugly "bell wars." Unfortunately, I do not know how deeply monasteries figured in this. I do know that by 1585, European clocks gained a second-hand and not only monks but hired workers were already following the clock in their chores. While time-consciousness is often tied in with the development of capitalism in Europe, I do not, however, think it meant a heck of a lot, for the industry of Japanese and Chinese who lacked the European-style mechanical clocks was immediately obvious to the European visitors. Both the punctilious work habits of the Chinese bureaucrat and the temple connection with time-telling (the Chinese character for "time" is comprised of the sun/day radical and the character for "temple") went back thousands of years, does it not?

The water clock mentioned by Frois is a "leak-hour," (*rokoku*) in Chinese characters, but the pronunciation was reversed at times and given a native Japanese pronunciation (*tokimori)*: the calendar and time department of the Imperial government includes "hour(time)-leak-doctors" (*tokimori-no-hakase* (Okada), though *sand* clocks were quickly gaining ground. These, together with sundials, did the trick for hours and another element, *fire*, also contributed to marking smaller units of time. Rodrigues mentions bonzes using a "very ingenious fire-clock" burning a dry scented powder in "a continuous line of furrows of a determined length, breadth and depth in the form of a square." (in C:TCJ) and, within a century, in the pleasure-quarters, a customer's time would be measured by slow-burning sticks of incense. Since incense in Japan was more commonly burnt for the repose of a dead soul – the hippie-inspired incense boom in the West did not catch on in the East for this reason! – senryû about courtesans burning them for dead Johns are particularly poignant.[1]

The Jesuits had the latest in European technology with them, and this included the portable clocks invented in the first part of the sixteenth century such as the "Nuremberg Eggs" of Peter Heinlein. They served the Jesuits not so much for keeping time as for proving Western technological superiority (naturally, attributed to Christianity) and keeping in the good grace of the rulers they presented them too.

---

1. *Time References.* Most indebted to the Time chapter of William G. Roy's *The Historical Construction of Reality* which includes citations of Dohrn-Van Rossum 1996. Googled.

2. *Courtesan Incense* I cannot locate one of these poems offhand, but I do recall Kipling's line "And tell the Yoshiwara girls to burn a stick for him" from the *Rhyme of the Three Sealers* because my father remembered it shortly before he died. I believe he thought it was a request from the dying owner of *The Mary Gloster* (on the whole, a better poem and addressed from a father to a son). I do not know if my father knew that incense was also used by the Yoshiwara girls as it was used.

5-13   We have twenty four hours between night and day;
Nós temos antre noyte e dia[1] *vinte e quatro oras;*

The Japanese have but six hours of night and six of day.
Os japões seis oras de noyte e seis de dia somente.

Until the spread of the geared clock in Europe, "we" had twenty-four uniform hours only twice a year, at equinox, for the twelve hours of day and twelve hours of night divided the actual night or day length, which varied according to the season, into equal units.[2] Japanese still used different lengths of night and day hours in 1585 and that is why Frois wrote "six hours of night and six of day" rather than twelve hours between the night and day. I must admit, however, to being confused as to what the church did with its *matins* and *media-dia* and *vesper*, for, to my mind at least, they would not match a system of twenty-four uniform hours.[3]

Actually, the Japanese had the modern system before we did. In the Nara and Heian eras (8-12c), the Court had a system of uniform length hours (*teijihô*), but changed, in the opposite direction as Europe, back *to* the varying length system (*futeijihô*) which better accommodated the common folk who could not afford a good water-clock and had to depend on the sun, i.e. follow the seasonal variance. But, this method was paradoxically, hard on the classes that did have good clocks, for convenient though it may be for marking *dawn* and *dusk*, cutting up hours of a different length every day with good clocks (water or mechanical) was *more* difficult as it requires constant adjustment. Rodrigues described how, with the above-mentioned (5-12) *fire*-clocks, "the furrow is made proportionately longer or shorter according to the length or shortness of the day and night." (Ibid.) When Japanese automata masters copied the new mechanical timepieces, some managed to accomplish the difficult task of making them adjust (in a semi-automatic manner) to the seasonal change.[4]

Were Japanese hours uniform, they could arguably be said to have had the same number of hours as we did, for the *six* hours really subdivide into *twelve* units because each numerical hour marked the *midpoint* of a time-unit called by a Chinese zodiac animal's name,[5] rather than the end of one unit and the start of another as is the case for our hours. This meant that half of the zodiac animal's time was over when the (two-of-our-hours-long) hour struck, and half remained, and if we think of the *before* and *after* portion as separate hours, eg. the *pre-rat* and the *post-rat* hours, the usable units come to a dozen for the day and a dozen for the night. In the older uniform system of the Court, the 12 big hours called *shinkoku* were subdivided into four quarters so one could speak of Rat 1 or Cow 3 and thereby be specific to within 30 minutes! So if Japanese in Frois's time might be said to have had *half* as many hours as we did, they once had *twice* as many! But, as confusing as this may seem, I am oversimplifying. Rodrigues has the hours of a square fire-clock divided into "*eight* quarters," mentions a system with "ten divisions, that is, two short ones and eight long ones [!]" (C:TCJ) and even another similar, he claims, to that of the Hebrews, Chaldeans and Church (note in C:TCJ). My Old Language Dictionary[6] further shows a system called *Kô* which divides the night (into *five* parts (because the hour is the time around a center – this is *even, i.e.* two hours on each side of a central midnight one!) with the daytime hours plus the dawn and dusk hours) left completely blank! And if this were not complex enough, a *hundred* hour-per-day system was used for astronomical and calendrical purposes!

1. *Night and Day?* Is Frois's word order, contrary to English's "day and night," simply idiomatic? Or, does it reflect the Christian idea of dark first, then light? How late did Italians, like the Jews start the day at nightfall? Gloss, anyone?

2. Seasonal Hours in Europe I oversimplify the relationship between the geared clock and end of seasonal hours in Europe. There was a messy in-between period when clocks were adjusted every few weeks or a different number of hours put into the night and day to preserve a constant length of hours . . . The same sort of problems incurred in the switch from a lunar to a solar calendar, but on a diurnal scale.

3. *Adjusting Church and Secular Time*   Religious observances that ought to be done as the sun rises or sets or at mid-day would be disturbed by uniform hours. In some areas, different sounding bells might indicate the religious hours without confusing secular hours, but I doubt such a luxury was an option in most places and I would welcome a gloss telling us how this was worked out!

4. *Japanese Seasonal Watches*   欄外注お願いします！

5. *Animal Names and Number of Hours*   Because there are twelve animals in the Chinese zodiac, the diurnal cycle did have 12 names and this fit the 12 hours perfectly. This was true with both the uniform and the varying systems.

6. *Old Language Dictionary*   Japanese in high school all buy these dictionaries, kogojiten, in Japanese. They generally combine a dictionary of archaic and obsolete usage with some encyclopedia-like presentations of costume, era schemes, time, old-fashioned carts, Buddhist statue symbolism, etc..

5-14   We count hours, one, two, three up to twelve;
Nós contamos as horas de huma, duas, tres, até doze;

The Japanese count them in this manner: six, five, 4, 9, 8, 7, 6, etc.
Os Japõis as contão desta maneira: seis, sinqo, 4, 9, 8, 7, 6, etc.

Here, "our" side is as natural as can be, while the Japanese side is *apparently* unnatural, for it is incomprehensible without an explanation, such as Chamberlain's in the introduction (part v.), though Chamberlain began at *nine* rather than at *six* like Frois. If you recall, there was no 1, 2 or 3, *because the first three strokes of the bell that told time were for the purpose of catching one's attention.* So 1 o'clock is 4, and 6 is 9. [1]   To me, this distich is clear proof that Frois intended TRATADO to be used as a teaching tool and did not expect it to be read without explanation.

Frois probably began with 6 because most people in Japan in Frois's time thought of the dawn as the start of the day. .Judging from the fact that midnight is the rat-hour (or "mouse-hour" if you prefer, for the Chinese term includes both), and said animal leads off the Chinese zodiac, I imagine that once upon a time, midnight was the start of the day, as it has been since I-forget-when in the West. (*Glosses welcome!*)

5-15   We adorn our churches with boughs and strew it with rush and narcissus;
Nós hornamos as igrejas com ramos e as juncamos com junqo ou espadana;

The Japanese mock this, saying we turn our churches into thickets or gardens.
Os Japões zonbão disso, dizendo que fazemos das igrejas matos ou ortas.

There is no little irony here, considering the fact Buddhist temples and Shinto shrines long occupied and thereby protected Japan's best old-growth forests,[1] while the Christians went about making cutting down the same because it was revered by the native religions of Europe. The church adorned in green: *an oasis in a desert partly of its own making!* Today, we associate this with Palm Sunday (the palm fronds thrown before Jesus on his last entry into Jerusalem). Chambers described the ceremony when England was still Catholic:

The flowers and branches designed to be used by the clergy were laid upon the high altar; those to be used by the laity upon the south step of the altar. The priest, arrayed in a red cope, proceeded to consecrate them by a prayer, beginning, "I conjure thee, thou creature of flowers and branches, in the name of God the Father," &c. This was to displace the devil or his influences, if he or they should chance to be lurking in or about the branches. He then prayed – "We humbly beseech thee that thy truth may [here a sign of the cross] sanctify this creature of flowers and branches, and slips of palms, or boughs of trees, which we offer," &c. The flowers and branches [local trees such as box, yew or willow were substituted] [2] were then fumed with frankincense from censers, after which there were prayers and sprinklings with holy water. The flowers and branches being then distributed, the procession commenced . . . When the procession had moved through the town, it returned to church, where mass was performed, the communion taken by the priests, and the branches and flowers offered at the altar. (C:CBD)

There were also funeral garlands for women who died unmarried=virgin that were hung in church (at least in England), and evergreens of Christmas decking churches as well as homes – not until the New Year as we think, but until February! – which periodically were attacked as being of pagan origin as they indeed were.[3] But, I think there is a very good chance that Frois is not just talking about Palm Sunday and Christmas, but the way the churches were decorated every Sunday. If you recall, "we" did not have clean floors. How did the church cope with this? In England,

> In the Herball to the Bible, 1587, mention is made of "sedge and rushes, the whiche manie in the countrie doe use in sommer-time to strewe their parlors or churches, as well for coolness as for pleasant smell." The species preferred was the *Calamus aromaticus*, which, when bruised, gives forth an odour resembling that of the myrtle; in the absence of this, inferior kinds were used. Provision was made for strewing the earthen or paved floors of churches with straw or rushes, according to the season of the year. [4] (C:CBD)
>
> ..

The strewing of rush not only in church but everywhere in England was noted by travelers from the continent [5] I failed to find anything on nature and the (Luso-Iberian Catholic church of Frois's time, but the following snippets from an essay called *God's Flowers* by John S. Stokes, Jr. suggests that there may have been less rush but more flowers:

> St. Paul taught that from the visible things of creation we can know the invisible things of God . . . Thus, Christians saw flowers as special signs of heaven and the unfolding of spiritual life, and adopted them as symbols of everything pure and holy in Christ and his Virgin Mother.
>
> Flowers were gathered joyously for the house of God, and in time were placed on the very altar itself. On the principal feasts, when the liturgy was performed with splendor, churches were regularly decked and strewn with flowers and greens, and priests wore them as garlands and crowns.

According to Stokes, special sacristan's gardens, generally built around a circular pool (the symbolism of which requires two paragraphs to explain) were established as sources for church flowers by the ninth century.

> Venerable Bede wrote in the ninth century of the white lily, later named the Madonna Lily, as the emblem of the Blessed Virgin: the white petals symbolizing the purity of her body and the golden anthers the beauty of her soul. Other flowers were associated with her from their use each year to deck churches for the "Lady-Days," the feasts of Our Lady, for which they were in bloom, including snowdrops (Purification Flower), Lily of the Valley, Marygold and aster (Our Lady's Birthday Flower).

Stokes goes on to claim that "documented research has listed over 1,000 flower names and symbolisms referring to Our Lady in popular religious tradition, evidencing the widespread use of flowers as intuitive symbols of her purity and sweetness, the beauty of her holiness and the splendor of her heavenly glory as the worthy Mother of God." But he also writes that at the end of the Gothic period, with the urbanization of culture, live nature came to be largely replaced with painted images of the same. [6] That time of transition was when Frois wrote. (Glosses on the amount of nature remaining in sixteenth-century churches welcome!)

To my mind, it is at least possible to hypothesize that the Christian practice of bringing *fola* into the church, while ostensibly based on religious symbolism, may reflect the exigencies of the architecture. Western buildings (excluding the open Roman public buildings) tend to have tiny windows. In the event they are large, as DR aptly notes, they "function not to reveal nature, but employ nature (sunlight) to relate a narrative in stained glass." In Japan, the windows are as tall as doors and as wide as the walls are wide. They go from corner post to corner post. The Japanese temple (or house, for that matter) is wide open to nature and/or the artificial nature of the garden. So there is little call to bring it *in*. Even today, Japanese are still not as liable to fill their homes with greenery as we are. The *bonsai* generally sit on the verandas which fringe the house and which become entirely visible when the windows which are bigger than our doors are open. All this holds true for temples as well.

Nevertheless, Japanese were not completely averse to using greenery for adornment. They stand two cut branches of pine in artistically cut green bamboo vases in front of their houses on New Years Eve (One red pine, one black pine, Yin and Yang, respectively). And, according to Cocks, there was another occasion which was even greener, Buddha's Birthday:

> This day is a feast in Japon, of their great profit or god, Shaka, whoe, as they beleeve, died a month past & rose againe this day, being the 8th of their moneth of *Singuach* [*shigatsu*=fourth-month]. Wherevpon they deck all the eaves of their howses w'th greene bowes, in remembrance of his rising from death to life ... (1617)

Buddha's *death*day was on the equinox – in Japan identified with the falling cherry blossoms – but, as far as I know, his birthday, which took place quite a while *before* his death, was not thought of in the Easter-like manner Cock's interprets it. [7] Aside from these holidays, the only place in Japan that was identified with greenery was outdoor water-closets. Here is Kaempfer on the fine road from Nagasaki to Edo in 1692:

> People of great quality, in their Journey's, cause the road to be swept with brooms, just before they pass it; and there lie heaps of sand in readiness at due distances (which are brought thither some days before) to be spread over the road in order to dry it in case it should rain upon their arrival. The Lords of the several Provinces, and the Princes of the Imperial blood in their Journies, find every two or three leagues distance, huts of green leav'd branches erected for them, with a private apartment, where they may step in for their pleasures or necessities.

I assume the branches au naturál proved the freshness of the facility and entertained the dignitary with a classic touch, for the WC in Japan was traditionally surrounded by greenery and over running water. Perhaps, this also explains why the Japanese were so shocked with the green church!

1. *Temples and Forest Protection* The Shinto practice of feting large old trees was not denied but incorporated into Japanese Buddhism (after all Buddha sat under the Bodhi tree to obtain enlightenment) and we find prohibitions against cutting all but some very carefully designated trees. The objective rationale is that between heavy monsoon rains, typhoons ands earthquakes, slopes that were not forested in Japan were liable to slide down upon the villages or cities below. When the modernizing government in the late-nineteenth and early twentieth century wanted lots of good timber fast, they simultaneously closed many of these Buddhist temples and cut their trees.

2. *Palm and its Uses.* In England, the willow branches which served for palm to strew in the street in front of Passion processions were gathered up and kept as "infallible protection against storms and lightning during the ensuing year," while the limited amount of palm that was available was made into tiny crosses and blessed by the priests, and sold to the people as safeguards against disease. In Cornwall, the peasantry carried these crosses to 'our lady of Nantswell,' where, after a gift to the priest, they were allowed to throw the crosses into the well, when, if they floated, it was argued that the thrower would outlive the year: if they sunk, that he would not. It was a saying that he who had not a palm in his hand on Palm Sunday, would have his hand cut off. Even the Reformation failed to kill the palm. Chambers writes "It has continued down to a recent period, if not to the present day, to be customary in many parts of England to go a-palming on the Saturday before Palm Sunday: that is, young persons go to the woods for slips of willow, which seems to be the tree chiefly employed in England as a substitute for the palm, on which account it often receives the latter name. They return with slips in their hats or button-holes, or a sprig in their mouths, bearing the branches in their hands." (C:CBD)

3. Pagan Christmas Decoration. Until the Reformation hardened, only Mistletoe was taboo'ed by the Church in England. Chambers cites a "quaint old writer" who "spiritualists the practice of Christmas decorations" claiming the "bayes and rosemary, holly and ivy, and other plants which are always green, winter and summer, signify and put us in mind of His Deity, that the child that now was born was God and man, who should spring up like a tender plant, should always be green and flourishing, and live for evermore" and gives samples of the carols he introduced:

Holly

Here comes holly that is so gent,
To please all men is his intent.
                    Allelujah!

Whosoever against holly do cry,
In a rope shall be hung full high.
                    Allelujah!

Whosoever against holly do sing,
He may weep and his hands wring,
                    Allelujah!

Ivy

Ivy is soft and meek of speech,
Against all bale she is bliss,
Well is he that may her reach.

Ivy is green, with colours bright,
Of all trees best she is,
And that I prove will now be right.

Ivy beareth berries black,
God grant us all his bliss,
For there shall be nothing lack.

4. *Extent of Rush.* We find entries in parish accounts about rectors who "Paid for 2 Borden Rysshes for the strewing the newe pewes, 3d." or "For 3 Burdens of rushes for ye new pews, 3d." which suggest rushes for special occasions rather than every Sunday, but we also find "charges for strewing the church floor with straw or rushes, according to the season of the year" (C:CBD).

5. *Rush in England.* *Chamber's Book of Days* includes this gem:

When Henry III, King of France, demanded of

Monsieur Dandelot what especial things he had noted in England during the time of his negotiation there, 'he answered that he had seen but three things remarkable; which were, that the people did drinke in bootee, eate rawe fish, and strewed all their best roomes with hay; meaning blacke jacks, oysters, and rushes.'" (*Wits, Fits, and Fancies*, 4to. 1614.) If, however, we may trust to an epistle, wherein Erasmus gives an account of this practice to his friend Dr. Francis, physician to Cardinal Wolsey, it would appear that, the rushes being seldom thoroughly changed, and the habits of those days not very cleanly, the smell soon became anything but pleasant. He speaks of the lowest layer of rushes (the top only being renewed) as remaining unchanged sometimes for twenty years; a receptacle for beer, grease, fragments of victuals, and other organic matters. To this filthiness he ascribes the frequent pestilences with which the people were afflicted, and Erasmus recommends the entire banishment of rushes, and a better ventilation . . . (C:CBD).

6. *Church-Nature Split.* Stokes claims that a change in the architecture so where new Churches were no longer "'oriented' (turned to the East) in nature" was concurrent with "those who furnished their [church] interiors" becoming "less and less able to 'find time' for the cultivation or gathering of flowers, now considered of little religious importance." (I would *bet* the Orthodox churches which have continued until the present with the practice of offering flowers to icons of Saints, etc. still insist upon properly *orienting* their churches.) Stokes laments that

this decline of the religious use of the things of nature in churches was accompanied by a corresponding decline in the religious sense of nature on the part of churchmen. Nature came to be considered optional as an approach to God, to be used or not, depending upon convenience and personal preference. (John S. Stokes, Jr. *God's Flowers*)

7. *Buddha's Birthday.* It is very rare for a birthday to be so celebrated in Japan. I think it reflects the continental influence and may be one reason why his birthday is still celebrated in a big way in Korea where it is celebrated at the proper time on the combined Lunar-Solar calendar, but barely noted in Japan where it keeps the 4/8 date (on the Gregorian Calendar). Buddha's enlightenment is feted on his deathday.

5-16   Our candles are thick at the base and thin above;
As nossas candeas são grosas no pee e delgadas em riba;

Those of Japan are thick above and thin at the base.
As dos Japões grosas em riba e delgadas no pee.

The West usually made candles from tallow (animal fat) – bee's wax candles were a luxury item – and the dip-drip method of candle-making was common, whereas the Japanese relied on sebiferous trees (mostly the "wax tree" sumac) for vegetable tallow, which was best shaped by hand (Okada). The Western method of production explains their shape, but the Japanese does not. There are three factors. First, Japanese wax drips less, so it needs not run down the candle to the base. Second, it runs just enough to look good hanging down from the upper edge, while not covering the surface of the candle, which was often decorated with an auspicious and artistic motif. Third, the Japanese are one of a minority of cultures that almost always puts very wide heads on phallic-looking things (the male member is often depicted as a veritable mushroom) so that the candle just seems natural designed wider on the top.

The Japanese candle is not only broader on top but slightly convex when viewed from the side. This gives it a crisp elegant silhouette compared to which ours, for all their fancy candelabras (another missed contrast), lack.

~~~~~~

5-17   Ours have wicks of string; *As nossas tem pavios de fiado;*

Theirs of wood and rush stem. *As suas de pao e miolo de junco.*

We find it hard to *feel* how important candles once were.

The 1579 procession inaugurating the Royal Chapel of the Cathedral, for example, consumed 25,000 pounds of wax candles. Candlemakers thrived when the Inquisition held an auto in Seville . . . (Mary Elizabeth Perry *Crime and Society in Early Modern Seville* THE LIBRARY OF IBERIAN RESOURCES ONLINE.)

Here and in the last item, Frois contrasts *expensive candles used in churches and temples.* The candles of the common folk in both countries was cruder. In England, at least, (I do not know about South Europe), lard-saturated rush candles provided light for the poor man. Rev. Gilbert White in his *Natural History of Selborne* explains the process of preparing such candles from start to finish. (also in C:CBD)

I am not confident about the exact nature of the Japanese candle referred to. The following observation by Morse suggests it is the central *tube* of the rush which is used:

The wick consists of a hollow tube of paper; the candlestick has a barb of iron instead of a socket, and the opening in the wick allows the barb to fit into it securely. Such a candlestick, long extinct, was known in England as a "pricket" candlestick. . . . The economy of this shape is seen when the piece of candle burning low is taken off the pricket and adjusted to the top of the new candle, so that not a particle of candle is wasted. (M:JDD)

The reader may find three contrasts with our candles in Morse's short but dense description! But, reading it, still does not explain the wood.   (I do not get Okada's Chinese quote. Did a thin stick of wood serving as a wick pass through the tube of the rush? 欄外注をお願いします。)

~~~~~~

5-18   We pray advancing our beads to the front; *Nós rezamos deitando as contas pera diante;*

They pray drawing theirs always to the back. *Elles rezão deitando-as sempre pera detras.*

The correct name for a string of Catholic beads is a *chaplet*, but it is usually referred to as a rosary, from *rosarium*, or "rose garden," considered a good place to pray with thorns and red blossoms to evoke the passion and red ones to evoke the holy virgin. A *rosary*, strictly speaking, is not the *charm,* a non-Catholic might takeit for, but a device by which a set number of prayers are recited with the beads helping to keep tally. One Catholic website says that monks as early as the third century in Eastern Christianity used beads, while another bead-centered website finds the first documented use of a Rosary among European Christians in the tomb of a seventh century holy abbess (Gertrude of Nivelles). Meanwhile the more common 33-bead (age of Christ at death) "worry beads" favored in Greece, Turkey, and Armenia were, Marcia Jo Myco writes, likely inspired from Islamic 99-bead prayer strands of which they were a common divisor (a larger 100th leader bead marked the coming full cycle and stood for the 100th name of Allah which only a Camel knows.)[1] Islamic traders brought the practice of prayer beads from the East, where

> Buddhist states the origin of rosaries as follows: "Sakyamuni, the founder of Buddhism . . . paid a visit to King Vaidunya. Sakya directed him to thread 108 seeds of the Bodhi tree on a string, and while passing (them) between his fingers to repeat . . . 'Hail to the Buddha, the law, and the congregation' . . . (2,000) times a day". (Dubin: The History of Beads, Lois Sherr Dubin, © 1987, by Harry N. Abrams, Inc., New York, NY found in a lecture *History of Prayer Beads* © IBRAG. by Marcia Jo Mycko first presented to the Tampa Bay Bead Society, in January 1997.)

"Hail" doesn't sound right to me, but sutras *never* sound right in translation, which is why the Japanese, who got their prayer beads called "*juzu*" (gem-count?) in the 7th century usually chant in the original (or as close as their phonetic system via Chinese characters allows) and are content to have no idea what most of it means other than it implores the Buddha's aid. The early use of beads by the Christians was generally not what it is (or is supposed to be) now. Serving as talismans against disease, with coral thought particularly efficacious, and adornment when other adornment was forbidden, they were not a little pagan and only were officially *sanctified* while Frois was in Japan, when Pope Pious V decreed St. Dominic (1170-1231) the official inventor of the Rosary.[2]

Of course, the Japanese *juzu* are used in different ways. Quite aside from the different vector of movement – which a Catholic friend assures me does not hold true for Greeks (Orthodox?) who use one hand and pull the beads as the Japanese do rather than using two hands and pushing them forward – the Buddhists tend to zip along at a syllabet a bead,[3] whereas the Catholics recite a *Hail Mary* prayer for each bead, they sure *look* alike! Percival Lowell irresponsibly simplifies:

> The resemblance so struck the early Catholic missionaries that they felt obliged to explain the remarkable similarity between the two. With them, ingenuous surprise instantly begot ingenious sophistry. Externally, the likeness was so exact that at first they could not bring themselves to believe that the Buddhist ceremonials had not been filched bodily from the practices of the true faith. Finding, however, no human agency had acted in the matter, they bethought them of introducing, to account for things, a *deus ex machina* in the shape of the devil. They were so pleased with this solution of the difficulty that they imparted it at once with much pride to the natives. You have indeed got, they graciously, if somewhat gratuitously informed them, the outward semblance of the true faith, but you are in fact the victims of an impious fraud. Satan has stolen the insignia of divinity, and is now masquerading in front of you as the deity; your god is really our devil, – a recognition of antipodal inversion truly worthy of the Jesuitical mind! (L:SOFE)

Lowell knew nothing of the Jesuits' achievements in Japan, for he continued "perhaps it is not matter for great surprise that they converted but few of their hearers." Actually, they did *far* better than the Christian missionaries in Lowell's era, or *ours*, for that matter. Moreover, I am not certain that Jesuits were really *that* upset about the similarities. True, Xavier, before he even got to Japan, learned of "monasteries" and "habits, with long sleeves almost like our friars", people "praying on their knees as we do at home," while their men of religion "also recite prayers at sunrise, at midday and in the evening," and this "in a language not understood by the common people, just as our priests in Latin," and, finally, that they teach there is "one Supreme God" and a "Purgatory, Paradise and Hell," (LR) etc.; but he seemed to regard it as some distant if benighted, offshoot of Christianity. If the Catholics had any reason to react as Lowell claimed they did, it would have been, perhaps, in reaction to the English, Dutch and German visitors who took every opportunity to exaggerate these similarities to make Catholics look bad. One of many such remarks by Cocks:

> And from thence they led us into the bushops chappell or oratory, all sett out with idolls and lamps, neither more nor lesse then in the papist churches, before which idolls the Japons did likewais fall downe and worship. (10/24/1618)

The Jesuits, for their part, found something *Lutheran* about the more popular Japanese sects of Buddhism. Here is Valignano in his 1583 SUMARIO, ch 3 *"On the religion and sects of the Japanese,"* complaining about what we might call unfair competition in the salvation market!

> And to better gain the good graces of the Japanese and facilitate the acceptance of their sects, they [these sects] make salvation so easy, coming to say that though they [men] commit as many sins as they desire, because of the great sympathy and love Amida and Shaka hold for them, by invoking their names with firm belief in them and their deeds, they will remain purged and cleaned of all their sins, without the necessity of making any other penance or good works, for with these they would only harm the penance they [Amida and Shaka] are performing to save men. *In this manner, they say what is properly the doctrine of Luther.* (V(A):S&A(p66-7) *my italics*)

In his notes, Alvarez-Taladriz cites Cabral, Maffei and others who made the same observation and, best of all, a 1596 *Lettera annua* from our "Luigi Frois" to Rome:

> "If your powerful God could create the world with just a single word, then why cannot men be saved with another single word?" asked the *bonzos* to the *cristianos,* who gave an adequate response. (IBID n48)

So, if the Devil cleverly modeled Buddhism on Christianity, he did not stop with the Catholics but even had room to include Protestants, although it is true that they do not use prayer beads.

1. Islamic Beads. I really must stop wandering, but must add that the Muslims thought it good to do 100 reps morning and night to achieve forgiveness. 100x100 is 10,000, a quantity which has a singular name in Japanese and Chinese but not in English. *Does it in Arabic?*

2. Conflicting Accounts of the Rosary. Another claim has them invented by one Peter the Hermit d 1090 AD.

3. Japanese Speed Beads A small group of Japanese of a Buddhist sect I can't recall that used to meet in a house near me made a phenomenal racket with their prayer beads. The noise was in-between the gear-crunching sound made by slow old library computers and the overwhelming din of the *aburazemi,* or "oil cicada." It bears close resemblance to the noise made by an abacus and, as it turns out, the combination of large and small beads and main and smaller strings of beads in one Tibetan system, according to the *History of Prayer Beads* cited in the main text "act as an abacus, capable of counting up to 10,800 prayers."

5-19   Our deceased go with their hair as it is when they die;
Os nossos defuntos vão com seus cabelos asi como morrem;

Those of Japan, men and women, must go shaved.
Os de Japão asi homens como molheres hão-de yr rapados.

Europeans find nothing particularly off-putting about hair. Jesus had long hair and a beard and so do many saints and angels are all pictured with hairy heads. Blonde hair in particular even took on the positive aspect of purity and light. When the tonsure was invented, it was more for the purpose of distinguishing the humble world-renouncing monks from the proud world-loving aristocrats who happened to cultivate long hair. Some orders of knight also required full or partial head shaving for the Vigil of Arms that preceded the knighting ceremony because "sacrificing one's hair was seen as a sign of devotion to God," according to one web explanation. (LR) Later some symbolic meanings were found for the monks: a ring-like tonsure stood for Christ's crown of thorns or, the corona, according to Isidore of Seville, a crown of authority such as the tiara worn by Hebrew priests, etc.. She also came up with an explanation that sounds Buddhist:

> By this sign, the vices in religion are cut off, and we strip off the crimes of the body like hairs. This renewal fittingly takes place in the mind, but it is shown on the head where the mind is known to reside. [1]

The significance on the Japanese side needed no explanation. All Buddhists knew that hair stood for decoration and the worldly desire=sin that went with it. Hair was not something one would want to take to the other world. More precisely, because death was departure from this world, it was parallel to joining an order, and one who wanted to get particularly good treatment on the other side really should join an order *first*. Thus, the shaving was a sort of cross between an *ordination* (as you may recall, the deceased got a Buddhist name) and a *last-rite*. In 1585, the traditional idea that a person was supposed to have his or her head shaved just *before* dying (and, becoming an apprentice bonze-at-home, get a good earful of sutras on one's deathbed) was in the process of changing to the easier Edo era practice of shaving the dead (who, as a *fictive neophyte* heard the sutras while being borne off to be cremated). Eventually, the shaving itself was often economized to just part of the head or even making a motion as if it were being shaved while intoning the proper words.

Frois's "*go* with their hair" and "*go* shaved" is *ambiguous,* but, as we shall see in 5-22, many Japanese were cremated rather than buried, so he could not be more specific.

1. *Hair as Crimes/Sins* Citation: This quote and half of the info. in the preceding paragraph was from SCISSORS OR SWORDS? (social aspects of medieval hairstyles) *History Today*, May, 1999, by Simon Coates (www.findarticles.com/cf_0/m1373/5_49/54700 553/ p5/article. jhtml?term=Mero). Another older indication that Judeo-Christian literature did have some similarity to Buddhism:

"St. Jerome recalls the precept of Deuteronomy: 'If you desire to marry a captive, you must first shave her head and eyebrows, shave the hair on her body and cut her nails, so must it be done with profane literature, *after having removed all that was earthly and idolatrous*, unite with her and make her fruitful for the Lord' (Epist. 83)." (LR)

5-20   Our caskets are long and narrow;   *Ha nossa tunba hé comprida;*

Theirs are round, i.e., half a cask.   *E a sua redonda, id est, huma mea pipa.*

The first half of the distich applies to all classes in most parts of Europe. The second half refers to the coffins of the commoners in some, possibly most parts of Japan. Cornwallis, in 1858, describes the Japanese casket as "a sort of tub about three feet high by two and a half in diameter at the top and two feet at the bottom." (C:TJJ) That seems about right, for a Japanese source has one meter twenty centimeters.

Sitting coffins (*zakan*) are the most common type for people who bury their dead in clay pots. In Japan, they go back to the Jômon age (10,000 ~300 BC). In the Kôfun, or mound-building age

(300-600 AD), more variety is found with stone and wooden boards creating house-like, ship-like, square, rectangular coffins as well. Eventually, most wealthy people ended up with sleep-type (*nekan*) coffins, often with two layers (i.e. a casket inside a coffin). I say "most" because I once read about a luxurious sitting coffin which gave the deceased space to be properly seated (the cross-legged meditation position called *agura* or legs under in the formal *seiza* (see 1-39). Considering the shaven hair mentioned above, this would let one go out like a saint.

The "half a cask" coffins mentioned by Frois were no longer pottery but wood, which was lighter to transport. All the websites claim they became *the* way for commoners to be taken off for burial or cremation in the Edo era, when they were honestly named "quick-tubs" (*haya-oke*), for they were constructed on-the-spot if it were by specialists in barrel-making (there were no undertakers per se). All viewers of television Easterns are familiar with them and I would guess that many Japanese do not recall how long they survived. As late as 1946, 72% of people cremated in Kyoto were in sitting coffins. This dropped to 55% in 1952. (web LR) With the Westernization of culture, the idea of *death as sleeping* caught on and with cars for transportation, lightness is no longer a problem, so sitting went out. Doubtless it remains in small communities with crematories not made to fit lying coffins. (Statistics anyone?)

5-21   Our dead go lying down, with their faces up;
       Os nossos defuntos vão deitados com o rosto pera riba;

Theirs go seated, bound up with the face placed between the knees.
Os seus vão asentados e amarrados com o rosto metido antre os jiolhos.

"Our" posture is ideal for viewing someone and, perhaps more importantly, as DR notes, "in keeping with the Book of Revelation, Christians have long anticipated that the resurrection of the dead would begin with trumpet calls and other great signs in heaven. Thus, the logic of being buried face up." Of course, "we" did not look *straight* up but *toward the East*, and this was assured by placing the head of the coffin to the West. The wealthy minority who were buried or cremated on their backs in Japan ask for a *Faux Frois:*

Our dead lie with their heads to the West so they can better look East for the Awakening.
Their dead who lie, do so with their heads North and faces turned to the West, their Paradise.

The North was associated with death and the West, which is, after all, where the Sun sets, was the Pure Land Paradise. Here, I think, an argument could be made for the Buddhists being linear (East → West) and the Christians cyclic (East → East)!

The curled-up position Frois describes is that of the true economy-class coffin, for it reduces the volume of the casket making it lighter and easier to carry (two men typically sufficed) and less space-hungry in the graveyard. The only difficulty involved the *stiffs*. People do not usually curl up when they die. Cornwallis:

. . . for when the Japanese do not reduce the body of the defunct one to ashes, they bend it so it may accommodate itself to the described coffin, the joints being rendered flexible by means of a certain *dosia* powder[1] which is universally applied to that end after death. (C:TJJ:1849)

As far as the details go, on February 20, 1565, Frois wrote "the hands are pressed together like someone praying, and the head bends toward the ground looking at the place the unfortunate soul will be buried" (back-transl. from Okada's Japanese). Actually, the hands may not always have been in this position, for Oliphant wrote that "according to old Arnoldus Montanus, the old women are placed in these [caskets/graves] in a sitting posture, *with their hands separated, and their faces turned as though looking over their shoulder*" (*italics mine*: O:EMC) while the men, "seated in a devotional attitude with their hands clasped" are as Frois describes. Either way, it seems to me that the position is basically fetal. With the hair shaved off, we get an image of a baby getting reborn into the womb of the earth. In this connection, I might point out the obviously mons veneris+vulvic tombs found in the parts of Japan that were not completely Buddhified, such as Okinawa. Maybe Buddhism picked up on that and found the posture suitable for they too spoke of rebirth.

1. Dosia Powder. Thanks to Cornwallis, I finally understood where the sand came from that Edo era *senryu* have widows throw at the standing part of their dead husbands – embarrassing because such was how men with *jinkyo* (a wasting disease where the bed-ridden men are marked by priapism that poets blamed on good-looking wives) were reputed to die! It must have been that *dosia* powder! (Whatever *that* is!)

~~~~~~

5-22   We inter our dead; *Nós emterramos nossos defuntos;*

The Japanese, for the most part, burn them. *Os Japões pola mayor parte os qeimão.*

It puzzles me how Christians, whom one would assume could keep the dead body and soul apart better than, say, animists who find soul everywhere, could come to feel that the corpse needed to be kept entire (or the parts in close proximity) the easier to be reassembled for the Judgment Day. Apparently, the idea that only burial was sanctioned by the Bible was further justified by taking the *dust to dust* idea literally. The part that goes up in smoke would be cheating the earth of its own. Still, martyrs and people with communicable diseases, etc. were occasionally burnt, and in 1972, the Catholic Church finally came to accept cremation, with the qualification that the ashes be buried and not taken home (as is done in Japan and much of the East) or scattered in the air or sea (wrong elements). Before Christianity, cremation was common in many parts of Europe, but by Frois's time burning was thought of as a punishment and was done to punish the bodies and hence the souls of the executed.

The Japanese changed in the opposite direction. In ancient times, the dead were buried or, especially in the case of the nobility, entombed in mountain caves – one of my favorite *MANYOSHU* (c760) poems (#3806) has a brave girl taunt her cowardly lover that if worse comes to worst they can always hide from her father by holing up forever in one of those "stone-forts" – and their spirits were identified with the clouds wafting off such mountains. Buddhism introduced cremation. It allowed descendants to keep clean shards for *memento mori*, and provided a speedy visible demonstration of the immateriality of existence. The smoke of cremation conflated with the animistic clouds born in the mountain caves to remain a favorite topic for the noble poet. A thousand years later, a far from noble haiku poet Issa, celebrates surviving yet another serious illness:

still alive

new tobacco!
not becoming smoke, myself
i take a toke

keburi to mo nara-de kotoshi-no tabako kana
(smoke not becoming, this year's tobacco tis)

Unless Issa uses poetic license, this proves he had enough money to be considered middle class, despite his peasant upbringing, for in his time, most Japanese were buried, not cremated, for the fuel to burn a man cost more than burying (or abandoning) him. In Frois's time, only the upper 10% or so of the population, if that, would have been cremated, so we can observe how for *this* contrast he chose the burial method of the elite, whereas in the previous contrast he chose that of the commoners in order to create his contraries.

Today, cremation is the first choice, for Japanese have more money than room and feel more comfortable with a clean burn than the idea of slowly rotting. Most families have small "grave" sites, where a portion of the cremated shards may be interred but a portion is often kept at home. [1]

> *We visit the deceased at the cemetery and only keep the relics of Saints at hand;*
> *They keep shards of their loved ones at home and do not have relics.*

The finely crafted wooden shrine, usually about the size of a large bathroom mirror-box, which is to say the Buddha-shelf/altar or Kami-shelf/altar, gives a proper place to such remains which rest within a small urn. In this way, the living, and if you believe in them, the dead, may be consoled without going all the way to the cemetery. Now that most of "us" (I hope!) no longer confuse this tender and good custom with "worshipping one's ancestors," we might do well to adopt and adapt such a device for cherishing *our* dead.

1. *Shards in Japan* Since Japanese cremation is not as *hot* as Western cremation, the bones are not completely pulverized. One website points out that when bodies in the sitting position were cremated the bones got all jumbled up, but now they are cremated while lying down, the bones are very clearly laid out and this gave rise to the custom of picking out a few choice bones to keep (the so called throat-buddha (larynyx?) or *nodo-botoke*, in particular).   Lest this sound strange, let me add that no-thing in Japan comes close to matching the two Capuchin churches in Rome which arrange bones into fanciful flower shapes, chandeliers, and many other whimsical designs! (For a finely nuanced blog discussion of the Capuchin churches and the Catholic perspective on the new possibility of *turning one's loved ones into diamonds* (no joke!) by Fr Jim Tucker (priest of the Diocese of Arlington, in Northern Virginia) *Dappled Things* donjim. blogspot.com/2002_12_01_donjim_archive.html).

~~~~~~

5-23   We keep our images and prayers inside of our rooms;
Nos temos nossas imajens e nominas dentro nas camaras;

The Japanese nail them up outside their doors to face the street.
Os Japões as tem pregadas(!) foro das portas pera a banda a rua.

Nominas does not English well. The Japanese translation (*gofu*) back-translates to "amulet" or "talisman" or "charm," the best the French translation could do was *"les livres de prières"* (can you imagine a "prayer book" nailed to a door!?). Only the German does fine: *"Andachtszettel"* or, "devotion-slips[of paper]". We do know what it is, for a Portuguese dictionary defines it *nomina* as "a sack/purse for relics" *or* "a written prayer/sentence[*orácio*] kept inside of a sack/purse to free us from evil." (LR)

A charm – though Catholics might not like the word, what other English is there for this? – in a room, even if it is inside of a pouch, would fill the room like perfume and protect it by our residing in a blessed atmosphere. But the Japanese, like most people, concentrated their efforts on *keeping out* the bad and *bringing in* the good. This meant concentrating one's charms *on the portals*. The gate, door or door-frame were the most common places to stick or nail them. Kaempfer described a number of these protective devices "printed upon one half sheet of paper."

> The most common is the black-horn'd Giwon . . . the Ox-headed Prince of Heaven, whom they
> believe to have the power of keeping the family from distempers, and other unlucky accidents,

particularly from the Sekbio, or Smallpox, which proves fatal to great numbers of their children. Others fancy they thrive extreamly well, and live happily, under the protection of a countryman of Jeso, whose monstrous frightful picture they paste upon their doors, being hairy all over his body, and carrying a large sword with both hands, which they believe he makes use of to keep off, and as it were to parry all sorts of distempers and misfortunes, endeavoring to get into the house. On the fronts of the new and pretty houses, I have sometimes seen Dragons , or Devil's heads painted with a wide open mouth, large teeth and fiery eyes. (K(S):HOJ)

The Chinese make an even more perfect contrast with "us" in the way they use charms, for they not only post them on the door but sometimes put them on walls *a distance from the house* so strangers could read them and thereby heighten their efficacy! (Something like the 20th century Usanian practice of people praying for others in church.)   Here is a rhyme about such a charm found in I.T. Headland's CHINESE MOTHER GOOSE in *my* translation, for his (though a nice rhyme [1]) makes no sense:

sleep spell

Lord of the Land!
Lord of the Sky!
Our house is a home
to a little Sir Cry!
Pray stop, Upright Man,
and three times recite
that we may, at last,
have sleep tonight!

As DR points out, Frois (and my) inside=us, outside=them equation is a bit too pat, for "Europeans also placed gargoyles, crosses, and other Christian and pagan symbols on the outside of homes, churches and castles to ward off evil spirits."

1. *Headland's Translation.* "The heaven is bright, / The earth is bright, / I have a baby who cries all night; / Let those who pass read what I write, / And they'll sleep all night, / Till broad daylight." One can understand that a Christian minister such as Headland would not care for Chinese Gods/Lords, and we suspect that the idea of the charm (also unChristian) was deliberately lost in translation. But, the self-deprecatory idea of putting others to sleep with one's writing has a certain charm of its own; yes, Headland is alright by me!

~~~~~~

5-24   With us, after the funeral, relatives of the deceased go into seclusion;
Antre nós emserrão-se os parentes depois das exequias do defunto;

In Japan, after the funeral, they give a banquette for the bonzes and others attending.
O Japões depois do e ter emterrado dão hum banqete aos bonzos e aos que o acompanharão.

The Catholic wake was typically held for a couple days *before* the funeral. A man in Buffalo told me he saw his father stumble in with a dead uncle he took barhopping. Polish Catholic, if I am not mistaken. I do not know how rowdy it was in Frois's time, but presumably the partying took place when the deceased was laid out and not *after* he was buried.   Still, the web tells me about Eastern Europe funerals where banquets are held upon the grave, so chances are that in Frois's time there was post-burial eating, drinking and reminiscing of the same sort found in Japan in some parts of Europe.

Actually, the Japanese *did* practice seclusion. They just did not do it *immediately* after the funeral. Even today, people who can afford to do so take a long time off work and, if male, don't bother to shave – I have known a couple respectable men (one in his 50's another in his 60's) who looked like homeless alcoholics for an entire year after the death of their fathers! It is also virtually universal for the bereaved not to exchange the usual beautiful greeting cards or visits on the following New Year; instead, they send out a special card ahead of time asking others not to send them greetings. While I do not yet have the facts about 1585, I find it hard to believe that this type of thing was invented in modern times. (欄外注、誰か？)

5-25   Among us, someone who changes faith [1] is considered a traitor and apostate;
Emtre nós se tem por elche e arrenegado o que muda e lei;

In Japan, one may change sect as often as one likes without infamy.
Em Japão se troca a ceita cada vez que hum qer sem nenhuma infamia.

A direct translation of *lei* is "law," but the 7th meaning in the *Novo Dicionário Aurélio* is "religion" or "faith." The Japanese translations have *oshie,* or "teachings," Schütte's German and the French translation "his belief/faith" (*seinen Glauben / su croyance*). But it is hard to tell if Frois means the faith=law of a particular order, such as the Society of Jesus or those of the entire Catholic religion as represented by the words of the Pope, who, I might add is called the *Law-king* (*hôô*) in Japanese!

The Japanese side confirms the greater religious *tolerance* (a good thing!) or *laxity* (a bad thing!) of the Japanese, compared to the, spiritually-speaking, authoritarian West, as already contrasted in 4-13 and 4-24.

5-26   Our baptism is done with many ceremonies and solemnities;
Ho nosso baptismo hé com muitas sirimonias e solenidades;

In Japan, it suffices to put a book on the head to join any sect.
Em Japão basta pôr hum livro na cabeça pera ficar daqela ceita.

I cannot imagine Japanese actually placing a book on their head. Frois describes how they lift it up, over and slightly in front of the head, as they would offer something to a superior or receive something from a superior (even out of his presence) in order to show their reverence for the teachings or sutras of that sect. This would be *the public part* of someone's first step to becoming a bonze. There is certainly more *in private* – training and tests, head-shaving ceremonies, etc.

5-27   We ask one omnipotent God for favors in this life and the other;
Nòs pedimos a hum só Deus todo poderoso os bens desta vida e da outra;

The Japanese ask *kami* [Shinto *god/s*] for temporal good, and *hotoke* [Buddha/s] only for salvation. *Os Japões pedem aos* Camis *os bens temporaes e aos* Fotoqes *a salvasão somamente.*

The chapter *"On paying visits"* in Rodrigues's book on Japan gives us a fine window upon the significance of this division. On the New Years everyone visits the Shinto Shrines, but the bonzes, who regularly make house calls –

do not normally convey New Year's greetings to layfolk, nor do they visit their homes on these appointed days [when every one else calls on each other] . . . For people regard it as an ill omen for the bonzes to enter their homes at the time of the festive New Year which they wish to begin well so they may live long years. But it is the bonzes' office to teach the way to the next world and the people have no desire to go there too quickly; nor do they wish to speak with the bonzes for their talk is about the things of death. Many people are so superstitious that during these days they will not use certain words which either signify death or have a similar pronunciation . . . (R(C):TIJ)

In Japan, unlike Europe, both native and imported religion managed to survive by retaining separate niches. Native gods for *this* life and foreign gods for *that*. When Buddhism first came to Japan, there was friction, with rulers pushing their favorite, epidemics and other natural disasters taken advantage of to argue that the behavior of one side or the other was being punished, and so forth. But in the end, live-and-let-live won: there was some amalgamation and a division of interests – call it, specialization – and competitive exclusion was avoided! This happened to a degree in Europe (see Flint: THE RISE OF MAGIC) but not so successfully in the long run (see Thomas: THE DECLINE OF MAGIC).

Today, it is still common to hear of *Shinto for birth* and *Buddhism for death, or Shinto for happy occasions* and *Buddhism for sad ones*. But, this millennium-old division was threatened when the modernizing Japanese leadership took away that Buddhist privilege at the end of the nineteenth century and gave it to Shinto.   Death was restored to the Buddhists after World War II, but the anomaly is brought to our attention every year when political debate arises about the propriety of politicians attending the Yasukuni-jinja (a head Shinto shrine) observance for those who fought and *died* for their country (right or wrong). [1]

This is the only contrast in these two faith-related chapters that even mentions *Shinto!* I am not certain why the Jesuits paid so little attention to Shinto, other than the fact that it was and is one of the most low-profile religions in the world. A few obvious *Faux Froises* to close the gap:

Our priests and educated worshippers generally have read and know the Bible.
Even their priests, if so they can be called, often know nothing of their own faith.

That is what is so delightful about Shinto. Its hodgepodge of folk custom is *something,* but it is wonderfully beyond intellectual grasp. They have their "sacred and sublime mysteries" (as do our shriners), as Kaempfer writes, but, as Kaempfer also writes, the temples "are not attended by priests and ecclesial persons, but by laymen, who are generally speaking entirely ignorant of the grounds and reasons of the Religion they profess, and wholly unacquainted with the History of the Gods, whom they worship." (HOJ) Moreover, Japanese themselves often made fun of their own Shinto mythology *in print* – I have read an Edo era *senryu* that discovers a model of the island of Japan congealing from the primordial sea in a clump of fecal matter floating in a septic tank! [2]

Our churches are not in the business of predicting fortunes on any basis.
Their shrines sell omikuji, *pieces of paper with good and bad fortunes written on them.*

Obviously, no one will deliberately buy a bad fortune – or a bad answer to a question/wish asked from the heart. The fortunes are written on pieces of paper folded up tightly and you draw for them. If you get a great one you may make another contribution if you wish; and if you get a bad one, you tie it up on a tree-branch or a fence or something at the shrine and leave it there to get purified so it hopefully won't come true and draw another, hopefully better fortune! Trees covered with these look very pretty, but it is probably uncomfortable for them, and I think they would run away if they were only animals. (A Japanese friend of mine educated in a private Christian school thought the *good omokuji* were tied up! No, *you bring the good ones home with you.*)

Our God is always in.
Their gods are out for a month every year.

They are bound to caucus in Izumo and wait on the Emperor "'tho in an invisible manner, during the tenth month." (K:HOJ). The subject is a favorite for Edo era haiku poets who found many ways to metaphysically relate the absence of the Gods to the falling leaves, fine fall days and other natural phenomena of the season. Poor Issa has a poem easier for this equally poor writer to relate to:

the gods are off!

Poverty my pal
it's high time even you
hit the road!

yoi tsure zo binbôgami mo tachi tamae
(good companion [+emphatic] poverty-god, too be off[+honorific])

I added the title. To tell the truth, most Japanese today would *need* such a title or explanation, too. I learned recently that the gods came together for the Emperor's sake, I had thought they just wanted time off from people so they could party by themselves in which case, they must have been thrilled when the Buddhists brought their deities(?) to baby-sit for them. I knew that the Emperor was supposed to be directly descended from the top Shinto gods, but know little about how he (or she – once Empresses could be on top) relates to them, other than performing some rites such as the well-publicized rice-planting and attending a special sumo match related to the prognosis for that year's agricultural production, etc..   But these are modern ceremonies. In Frois's time, we might have said

> *Our Pope is a man who, with God's guidance, runs the only true Religion;*
> *Their Emperor is himself (supposedly) a god who, like their idols just sits and does nothing.*

I wrote the above on the basis of an amusing explanation of the role of the Emperor found in Mrs. Busk's 1841 medley of Dutch and Dutch-related reports on Japan in the 18th century.

..
> He determines the days on which certain religious festivals [of Shinto] are to be celebrated, the colours appropriate to evil spirits, and the like. One other sovereign act, if act it may be called, he daily performs, which would seem to show that, in virtue of his identification with the goddess of the sun, he is considered quite as much the patron divinity as the temporal lord of Japan. He every day passes a certain number of hours seated upon his thrown, perfectly immovable, lest by turning his head he should bring ruin upon that portion of the empire towards which or from which he might happen to direct looks, thus by his complete immobility maintaining the whole realm in a state of undisturbed happiness and tranquility. After he has been seated the requisite number of hours, he resigns his place to his crown, which continues on the throne, as his substitute, during the remainder of the day and the following night. (B:MACJ)

While the information is absolutely ridiculous hearsay, it was just too interesting to leave out! It does, however, help us understand why Frois, with his down-to-earth contrasts based mostly on observation, *avoided all mention of the Emperor!* But there are other things he might have caught:

> *Our churches have a door, a portal that opens directly into the building;*
> *Their shrines, a pair of pillars with two bars on top at a great distance from the building.*

These *torii* mark the boundary between sacred and profane ground. The ends of the cross-bars slightly over-reach the pillars and the upper one is especially large and slightly upturned.. A simple sketch of this *torii* on a map designates a shrine, as a reverse swastika serves for a Buddhist temple.

Usually they are either natural wood or bright red!

> *Our churches have a vertical-horizontal cross on top of the steeple;*
> *Their shrines have no steeple, but the roof-beams cross diagonally like the letter X.*

Symbolism aside, the basic design of these buildings harks back to the teepee-like structures of ancient times.

> *Our most celebrated churches took decades if not centuries to build;*
> *Their most famous shrine is torn down and rebuilt every twenty years.*

The great shrine of Ise. *Always new, it is the oldest extant shrine (as opposed to ruins) in the world.* A conceited Austrian-American pundit put it like this: "Their propensity for destruction is sometimes worked off in rituals: unwilling to wait for lightning to strike or some such sign from the gods, they tear down the Great Ise Shrines every twenty years to rebuild them in their identical image." (R:TKM) *Nonsense!* I see it as a monument to *the power of mortality*, an expression in architecture of the choice made by the ancestor of a people in Africa (or was it South America?) who was asked to chose the way of stone or the way of wood. An individual stone outlasts a tree, but eventually wears down to nothing, while a tree can survive forever in its offspring. The ancestor chose right and gained the life we still enjoy in our turn.

> *We have no mirrors in our churches;*
> *Their shrines always have mirrors.*

Golownin's editor describes the use of the mirror thusly: "On the door of this central building [of the Ise Shrine] hangs a gong, on which every worshipper strikes at his first arrival, to inform the God that he is come to worship him: after which, the votary looks through a window where hangs a mirror, as a symbol that as he sees his own countenance, so does God see his heart and thoughts – and this seems to end the ceremony." (G:MCJ) Oliphant later wrote they "commence by washing themselves in the font; they then pray opposite the looking-glass, asking for their necessities as we do; then chink a few coppers into the wire-covered box, strike the bell thrice as a sign that it is all over, and retire. Some with a metaphysical turn of mind suppose that God sees into their heart as plainly as they do into the looking glass, and therefore do not pray at all. (O:EMC) A more rational explanation of the use of the sacred mirror at Ise is given by Mori Arinori, the charismatic intellectual who oversaw the hundreds of Japanese students in the USA in the 1870s and returned to become the Minister of Education:

> They look in this mirror and examine their own eye, the eye being the index of the soul, the gazer can the more easily determine the honesty of his intentions. (L:JIA)

Personally, I see the mirror as something like the ones found at our better zoos. *You, too, are an animal, and the world's most dangerous one!* say ours, while the Shinto mirrors say, *You, too are a god!* or rather, *this* is where you had better look for godliness, within yourself!

1. *Yasukuni-jinja*. Every year the visit of the politicians and the criticism from the left repeats. I feel that what is needed is a simultaneous acknowledgement of the *bad* (not excused as unfortunate things that happen in wartime) Japan did on the one hand, and the heroism of not a few individuals who tried to do *good* under difficult circumstances on the other hand.

2. *Poking Fun at Mythology* The senryû are out of my reach at the moment, but having just read young Jesuit Fukan Fabian's put-down of Shinto mythology (1605), I cannot resist sharing his hyper-rational humor. First, he quipped that the proof that the gods began their creation with Japan, not China or India, must be that "all things start small." Then he noted that the August Halberd of the god dropped down right on a letters Big Sun (大日) that floated on the waters said halberd stirred to create the Great Sun Source Land (大日本地), anyone could see the 大 was a person lying with her legs apart (with the writing vertical, the sun 日 lies between them). Basically, the entire Shinto creation story is an extrapolation of what husband and wife do: *make children by sex.* If said god could create land out of the water just like that and knew there was nothing down there, why did he insist on stirring his thing around (*kakisaguru*)? Because, Fabian replies to himself, the idea was something vulgar (*geshin*) that he dared not put into words . . . After this, he explains that Japanese as an island people originally migrated from the continent and that the Shinto dating (well over 20,000 years: far more years than in the Judeo-Christian scheme) was false, because there was no writing that far back to record anything. . . Then, returning to the Creation, he wondered how big Izanami's belly would have had to have been to bear all she bore, including not only Japan but the Sun and the Moon, the former of which

was far bigger than the entire world and pointed out that sexual intercourse created things of the same nature as the parents and this made it ridiculous for human Gods that could be the ancestors of Japanese to bear such things to begin with . . . (妙貞問答 in E:NBJ – As Ebisusawa's annotation explains, in 1587, when Hideyoshi turned against the Jesuits and thought to conquer East Asia, he decreed Japan "Gods' Country (*nihon wa shinnkoku taru tokoro*). In 1605, Hideyoshi was out of the picture, but Shinto, to the extent it was identified with the new national polity was still a threat(?) to the Christians. So, Fabian's polemic was neither academic nor written just for the hell of it.) – This is the same Fabian who will turn apostate and "Destroy Deus" decades later . . .

5-28   Our images are painted on wood; *As nossas imajens se pintão em pao;*

Those of theirs on paper scrolls. *E elles as suas em papel emrolado.*

The *canvas+oil=painting* we take for granted began to be used in the first half of the fifteenth century in the Low Countries and soon after in Venice where it was particularly welcome because the high humidity and salt air on that low-riding island was hard on the tempura (on wood) and fresco (on plaster) paintings. It was not uncommon in South Europe when Frois wrote, but, apparently, was not the usual medium for painting Christian images. Here, the contrast intended may be one of *permanence* versus *fragility* and *impermanence.* If so, it is not quite right. Although painting on paper does not *seem* very permanent – almost like writing on water – because the pictures were commonly rolled up when not viewed, in reality they usually remained fresh as long, if not longer than wooden and canvas-board pictures which suffer more exposure to the light from constant display. The pictures usually have cloth backing and margins, as well as thin wooden ends on the top and bottom of the scroll – so they can still be rolled up – which not only help the hanging but improve the image, as a frame does.

5-29   Among us, a good retabulo done in oil-color is sometimes worth a lot;
Antre nós val às vezes muito hum bom retabolo d'olios;

In Japan, oil-color is not used and [yet] sometimes a black-ink portrait is worth many thousand cruzados. *Em Japão não se uza d'olios, e val às vezes muitos mil cruzados hum[a] figura em tinta preta.*

While one can find black and white sketches in European art that seem finished (see Rembrandt's simple "portrait of Saskia" or, much later, Turner's incredibly dynamic sketches) today – *after* we have been influenced by Japanese art? – in 1585 such a thing would not have been considered finished works of art, but *studies* preparatory to the real thing, the colored painting. Hence Frois's unstated wonder in the fact that quickly done paintings in black and white could be worth so much.

Painting was a subject close to the hearts of the Jesuit missionaries. This contrast couched in terms of "worth" seems secular if not commercial, but "our" main *use* art was religious. Seven years after the TRATADO was penned, Frois records in his HISTORIA that students at a Western Kyushu theological school up in the mountains where they could sing masses, practice Gregorian chants and play the organ as loud as they wanted (without fear of being found out – for Christianity was periodically repressed by this time – as they would be in town) were doing very well at Latin and *some were producing fine engravings, water-color and oil-color.* The last could reproduce pictures brought back from Rome by the four envoys so perfectly that it was impossible to tell which came from Rome and which did not. Some visitors "insisted the paintings by the Japanese had to have come from Rome" and even Portuguese who were shown the pictures thought they came from Rome and were impressed. "So, with God's help," Frois concludes, "Japan won't lack men who can keep all her churches full of fine images and satisfy the [aesthetic needs of] gentry(*tonotachi*)."

Japanese with any social pretensions (samurai class up) were heavily into present-giving and receiving. They delighted in paintings and from the time of Xavier's visit, the Jesuits could not keep up with requests for paintings of Mary and the Christ child. At the same time, paintings both in church and the living quarters had particular significance for the humanist-schooled Jesuits:

> From the very beginning, the Jesuits were fully aware of the potentiality of art as an evangelistic media. Artists of the Jesuits were adept in using painting and architecture to create drawings and space resembling the setting of stage, rendering visual stimuli to the believers of God during religious ceremonies and worshipping activities, and providing visible illusive images and memorable places for retreat and medication. To achieve the aim, the application of theory and technique of perspective, a visual science established by the precise manipulation of mathematical relationships, in painting was enhanced. (from a beautiful exhibit presentation by the Museum of Art of Macao at www.artmuseum.gov.mo/exile/english/preface1_e.htm)

Though the black and white paintings may have been valuable (more on this elsewhere), they failed to grab the viewer in the *emotional way* a realistic color painting could. At the time Frois wrote there were several seminaries such as the one he described in Japan teaching, among other things, painting. With perhaps 200,000 Christians and over a hundred churches, this skill was in great demand and the Japanese novices rose to meet it.

~~~~~~

5-30   Our prelates go about on mules;   *Os nossos prelados amdão em mulas;*

Their prelates go about in sedans.   *Os prelados de Japão em andas.*

The Japanese sedan is a box-like car hanging from a carrying pole which is shouldered by two men.[1] It seems appropriate enough for someone of status, for Japanese did not use horse-drawn coaches. True, they were not as fast as "our" horse-drawn carriages, but they had springs intelligent enough to read the road and were probably faster than a mule, for the men took great pride in their speed.

But, why *mules* for "ours"? The Japanese translation *roba* means "donkey" or "ass," as in Abbysinian ass, the humble animal with the mark of the cross Jesus was said to have ridden. My first guess was that this was an imitation of Jesus or perhaps to show humility by riding close to the ground, but, Defourneaux, in his book on daily life in Spain in the Golden Age, writes that "persons of quality, who wish to travel comfortably, hire a litter which is carried *by two mules*" (D:DLS – I wish there was a picture: I imagine each mule like the hull of a catamaran and the man in the center, but maybe he is dragged behind . . .) while ordinary travel was, indeed, on muleback, and, as was the case in Japan with horses, it involved the services of a helper, a *moco de mulas,* or muleteer. The Jesuits chose the later form of travel, as the more humble. Horses on the highway were generally fine runners reserved for the Royal Mail alone.

In Japan, the Jesuits usually walked – something associated more with the Franciscans and their vows of poverty in Europe – in order to differentiate themselves from the high-living Buddhist high priests as their first member in Japan, Saint Xavier had done.

1. *Sedans?* We will have more in the *Horse* chapter. Suffice it to say that at Frois's time the two-pole four-man sedan that catered to the nobility in ancient Japan had probably been replaced by the two man one-pole variety. The sedan only really caught on in Europe in the seventeenth century and, even then, was primarily for short distance only, because the carrying poles were below and *grasped* rather than *shouldered* as in Japan.

endnote V

T*emples*

I have two good stories, both of which I would title *A Matter of Good Faith* which I would share with all who are interested in pursuing religion across cultural borders.

The first comes from the kind and wise Bostonian Edward S. Morse, who found thousands of things to learn from the Japanese, not in their economic heyday, or even after the proved themselves by beating Imperial Russia, but before most of "us" thought they were considered worth copying. He even found the manner in which seeds are sold to feed the pigeons that fly down from the roof of the temple worth noting – a footnote added later suggests he succeeded with this cultural transmission:

> Within twenty years we have vastly improved in this respect, and now one may see flocks of pigeons fed on the Boston Common by men and boys, some of these birds actually alighting on the head, shoulders, or hands of the feeder. (M:JDD)

I love pigeon stories and have collected quite a few, but let's return to the temple and what Morse had to say about it, for the following testimony reveals more about the relationship between Christian missionaries and Buddhism than most entire books do.

> The curious objects one sees in the temple often excite surprise and even contempt. an American missionary journal, reflecting on this subject, held up to derision an object which was seen on the walls of this religious edifice, namely, a framed lithograph of the Pacific mail steamer, City of China. I could not believe it, and so, on this first visit to the temple, I specially searched for it, and found it among the souvenirs and emblems adorning the wall. It was, as described, a cheap, colored lithograph of the steamer, and from its rather soiled appearance I judged it had been there some years. On the glass on one side was an inscription in a few vertical lines. A few days afterwards I got a student to go to the temple with me and translate the inscription, and this is a free rendering: "This vessel rescued five shipwrecked Japanese sailors and brought them back to their native land. To commemorate this kind act on the part of the foreigner the priests of this temple have secured this picture and placed it among its relics." This was done at the time of bitter feeling against the foreigner and revealed a true Christian spirit on the part of the priests, and this picture is venerated by the Japanese. (M:JDD)

Morse continues, remarking how alike many features at the temple are to "the Catholic cult," as noted by Kaempfer. *Monks and nuns, holy water, incense, rosaries, celibate priests, masses, chants.* "He [Kaempfer] was forced to say *"Diablo simulanti Christum."* But all that is old hat. The above story of the American Christians is new. The missionaries, not being "Christian" enough to give the temple the benefit of the doubt, as Morse did, put down what they did not understand. They treated the Buddhists in *bad faith.* Morse's terms "relics" and "venerated" seem Orientalist, but in this context I think they suggest *mementos* and *treasured.* Morse checked out what *really* was what because he treated the Japanese as equals. He did not patronize them or their religion. Inter-religious understanding requires one thing: *good faith.*

寺　　　　　　　　寺　　　　　　　　寺

The second story comes from Yoshio Markino, who was, as the title of his book puts it, A JAPANESE ARTIST IN LONDON. Not long after moving to England from America, where he had been terribly bullied, he was "a frequent visitor to [the house of a] Mrs. Dryhurst, who introduced me many interesting peoples." (I leave his Japanglish as it was published):

One day those friends of hers surrounded me and asked me how was about the religions in Japan. That was a very difficult question to me. It is fact that I was at an American Missionary College in Japan and studied the Bible lessons for four years. But among us, the young schoolboys, the Christians were looked down as "not highly educated." I think the main reason was that those terribly ignorant and uneducated American missionaries in Japan were talking and doing too much nonsences. While I was in America when anybody asked me if I were a Christian I always answered negatively to prove that I was not one of those "Uneducated." But to my astonishment I was entirely knocked down. They called me "Pagan," "Heathen," and "Barbarian," and they treated me as if I were not a human. Fancy! that one whose duty is supposed to be "to seek the lost sheep" should act himself not at all humanely!

Now, facing to all my dearly respected friends in Hampstead, I was rather too timid to express my opinion so freely. Besides, it was not my intention to injure the Christian faith in this country. So I shamefully acted myself as a fox. I said: "Japan is a free country for religions. You may find quite numbers of Christians there."

"How pity! How Pity!" were the expressions from every one's mouth.

Some one shouted, "How about your beautiful philosophies, then?"

Mrs. Dryhurst asked me, "Have you ever forgotten Laotze, Confucius, and Mencius?"

I exclaimed, "Ahé, ahé. Wait, wait, wait, wait, wait a second, please."

I could not speak immediately. When those ancient Chinese philiosophers' names were mentioned my heart was so stricken with joy, as if one was told the name of a woman to whom he devoted his love . . .

My first words to my friends was, "I am not a Christian."

"You are right," was echoed and re-echoed in their mouth.

Then I confessed how timid I was before them, and they all heartily laughed.

If we find the eclectic mix of religion in Japan a mystery – they find us no less hard to understand. On the one hand, most of "our" intellectuals do not think Christianity is *the* Religion, but only *a* religion. Still, in the United States, at least, an intellectual Christian is not yet an oxymoron and even the agnostic usually puts up a Christian front with talk of God, especially if he or she happens to be in politics. As far as I know, Jesse Ventura, the wrestler-turned-governor is the first Usanian politician in history to come right out and admit he was not Christian and even opined, if so refined a word can be used for his off-cuff remarks, that religion was *a crutch for people too weak to face reality*. (Victorianism was nothing compared to the intellectual cowardice of the now-ended American Century and we should be grateful for Jesse's guts, even if we don't like his style!) Please do not misunderstand me. I love the *Orthodoxy* of a Chesterton and admire people who can keep the faith today, even in America. So long as they keep it on a high enough level – do not make the mistake of forcing their faith into science education – I am in no rush to dampen their spirits with my relatively dry brand of reason, and, to tell the truth, I don't mind quaffing a bit of those subtle spirits now and then. Watching the sun rise on Easter morning, I, too, am almost a believer.

寺   寺   寺

VI

OF THE JAPANESE MODE OF EATING *AND* DRINKING

do modo do comer e beber dos Japões

6-1 We eat everything with our fingers;
Nós comemos todas as couzas com a mão;

The Japanese, men and women, from childhood, eat with two sticks.
Os Japões, homens e molheres, desde crianças, comem com dous paos.[1]

    In the 1589 report of the European Embassy, DE MISSIONE, Miguel=Valignano enthusiastically describes the enormous amounts of gold paid by the wealthy in Europe to attend banquettes with equally plentiful silverware. His cousin Leo, who remained in Japan, remonstrated: "But, still, aren't they uncleanly? Don't they eat with their fingers and allow completely uncouth black people to serve them?" Miguel replied that most European visitors to Japan are sailors and merchants, poorly educated and lacking whatever personal belongings they might have at home. "Cultured people in Europe ordinarily use silver forks and spoons to take up food from their plates," he reassured Leo; and black slaves were an anomaly, a special feature of life in the Indies. In Europe, the servants were "free people, elegant and well educated"(J/S:DM) True, the hands are *sometimes* used, but they are, then wiped clean on the table-cloth and washed after the meal. (Here, I can't help introducing Marques' observation that "the utility of forks actually led, in the last analysis, to reduced hygiene" (M:DLP) because some people stopped washing their hands!) With Miguel=Valignano selling Europe, we can not be certain just how much, or rather how little these utensils were used; but since Valignano himself earlier wrote "there are no . . . knives, forks or spoons" on the table *in Japan,* (1579?1583?) some Europeans must not have used their fingers exclusively.

    Was this because Frois grew up in humble circumstances and had not seen enough service on the table in Europe to mention. (Unlike his superior and the young Japanese ambassadors, Frois was never wined and dined by the like of the Medici.) Or was it because the fork was mainly used to hold what was cut, while fingers were still the main utensil(?) for moving food into the mouth, and Frois chose to define "eat" *(comemos)* in terms of the latter action alone. Regardless, his failure to mention European utensils here enhances the contrast of *bare* v.s. *instrument, crudeness* vs. *culture*" and *clean vs. dirty.* In a much earlier letter, Frois observes that "to be delicate and fine they put their meat into their mouths with little forks, accounting it great rudeness to touch it with their fingers" (W:HOT – The translator, Willis, probably imagined the two sticks were joined together like prongs, or "forks"). The cleanliness aspect may echo Valignano, for he wrote the Japanese manipulate their "two small sticks with such cleanliness and skill that they do not touch any part of the food with their hands, nor let even a crumb fall from their plate on to the table." (in C:TCJ). Since Europeans, with their new-fangled telescopes and guns, even at this early date, considered themselves to be the masters of material culture as well as spiritual culture, this reversal of fortune at the table must have been a jarring experience. It gave birth to the best passage in Mendez Pinto's PEREGRINATION – and perhaps the best cultural contact story *ever* written.   Were it not four pages long, I would quote *every word* of it. I tried to pare it down to a page but ended up with two.

The background: The King (*daimyo*, in retrospect) of Bungo, having met Xavier earlier, was considering baptism. Xavier died, proving his Sainthood with his uncorrupt corpse and Belchior, the Jesuit's top priest East of India has come back to Japan in his place. He is invited to dinner, along with four other Portuguese, including Pinto, who had been there before with Xavier and enjoyed the King's hospitality.

> When we arrived the daimyo begged us, for the love we bore him, to eat in front of him using our hands, just as we did at home in our own country, because his wife would greatly enjoy seeing this. He ordered a meal to be prepared and platters of clean well-cooked delicacies were brought in by beautiful girls. We eagerly got stuck into everything they set before us but the comments and the teasing and the mockery they made of us when they saw us eating with our hands was far more enjoyable to the daimyo and his wife than any comedy that could have been performed for him. (Lowery tr. P(L):TMP ch 223)

Here, Lowery's translation continues with the Japanese regarding it "the depth of piggery to eat with the hands as we do;" Catz's earlier translation simply calls it "a very dirty thing;" and Cooper's (from a 1663 English translation) "a great incivilitie, to touch the meat with ones hand, as we use to do." With respect to the *daimyô,* since no European yet had used that term for a major feudal lord (Catz, in her translation uses the word Pinto must have, i.e. "king" – Lowery jumps ahead in time, while the translator in the olde version used by Cooper goes back and clarifies matters, slipping the words *"as we use to do"* (with respect to eating by hand) right into the text!

But, to return to the story. One of the king's daughters "a marvelous fair Princesse" of fourteen or fifteen asked for and received her father's permission to put on a play about their guests. As she and six or seven other girls prepared in another room, the ladies-in-waiting "drove away time at our cost, by jeering and gibing at us, who were much ashamed" (the 1663 transl.)/"enjoyed themselves immensely at our expense with all sorts of jokes and witticisms which shamed us all."(Lowery trans.) Unless Pinto was wrong (I have not seen the original), Lowery's translation must be right. It fits the Japanese character better.

> We were sitting there feeling humiliated – although suffering it as best we could because we saw how much the daimyo and his wife were enjoying it – when the beautiful princess came back into the room dressed up to look the part of the Japanese merchant, with a sword embellished with gold stuck in her waistband. [Note that the academic's technically correct "daimyo" backfires on Lowery because the daughter remains a "princess!"]

The "merchant" then knelt in front of her father and, after apologizing, "Oh most powerful Daimyo and Lord" for his boldness, explained he was old and poor with great numbers of children from four wives to support, and helping him would be "a great example of charity." (the detailed dialogue was obviously improved by Pinto, for even if they had a modern simultaneous interpreter it would have required a tape-recorder to get that much right!)

> You could also do a great favour to the Tenjiku-jius who have come in their great ship, because this merchandise of mine is something which would be more useful to them than to anyone else; it would help them with a great handicap under which they continually labour.

The Daimyo was laughing so hard to see his daughter "done up as an old merchant, with so many white hairs, so many children and so much need" that it took him a while to reply that he would see the merchandise and recommend it to the Portuguese – *tenjiku* was an old word for India, with heavenly connotations which was also used to refer to "us," while *jius,* was *deus,* for said "god" was always on the lips of the visitors – if he agreed they could make use of it. The merchant

> gave a deep bow and then withdrew to the other room again. We were all so embarrassed by what we had seen so far and we didn't know what would be coming next!

> As soon as the sixty odd women in the room – the Daimyo and Portuguese being the only men – quieted down, six of the merchant's children, all, in reality, "daughters of leading courtiers" came out with wrapped parcels and sang a song with a witty verse "in sweet voices that were a delight to listen to" – *this is, as far as I know, the first time any European admitted to liking any Japanese singing!* Then the girls all knelt down and the old merchant gave another "pleasant speech" thanking the Daimyo for allowing them to sell him their goods.

> Then the six girls unwrapped their parcels – and a great pile of wooden hands fell out onto the floor, just like the ones that are offered up to St Amaro in Portugal!

> The merchant remarked gracefully with well chosen words:

> "Since nature subjects the Portuguese, for their sins, to such filthy wretchedness that their hands must forever be stinking of fish or meat or whatever else they eat with them, this consignment of wooden hands would be of great use to them because while their own hands are being washed, they will be able to eat with these wooden hands."

> Of course, the daimyo apologized to the Portuguese and explained his daughter only dared to put on a play like that "because you are like brothers to her." The ebullient daughter, then pipes up:

> "If your God wishes to take me as a serving girl, I will put on better and more enjoyable plays than this one; but I'm sure that He won't forget about me anyway."

> After which these Portuguese, who recognized true nobility when they saw it, fell to their "knees and kissed the hem of her kimono and told her,"

> "We place our hopes in God that one day you will become a Christian and then we may yet see you as the Queen of Portugal!"

> And that set the girl and her mother off laughing uncontrollably again. (M. Lowery trans. P(L):TMP)

I can imagine the young princesses asking a servant or one of her brothers to rush off to a temple to borrow those hands as they composed their little song for that skit! And I can imagine some of the untranslatable puns on hands that must have drawn laughs. I do not know if the upper-class Chinese ever joked about "our" table manners in that way. Ordinary Chinese evidently did, for Pinto had previously recorded an old Chinese man's daughters "exchanging many amused remarks with their brother when they saw we ate with our fingers." But, being more cosmopolitan, noble Chinese, no doubt, *expected* the Southern Barbarians to eat that way. Needless to say, much of the Japanese side of Frois's contrasts about dining were shared with the people who invented the chopstick. Cruz's 1570 treatise on *Chinese* things (which Pinto apparently borrowed from) includes phrases echoed by Valignano and Frois.

> . . . there were two small sticks [*pauzinhos*] very fine and gilt, for to eat with, holding them between the fingers; they use them like a pair of pincers, so that that they touch nothing of that which is on the board with their hand. Yea, though they eat a dish of rice, they do it with these sticks, without any grain of the rice falling. And because they eat so cleanly, not touching with the hand their meat, they have no need of cloth or napkins. [see 4, below] All comes carved and well ordered to the table. (TCC in B:SCSC)

In 3-6 we saw why those "sticks" are supposed to make you smart.   But there may well be more *significance* in this difference – with the anomalous *fork* and *knife* substituted for Frois's *fingers* – than you ever dreamed. The great Korean essayist I O'ryon (Englished Lee O-Young), expanding Roland Barthes' contrast of "our knife (and of its predatory substitute the fork)" with the chopsticks, "an alimentary instrument which refuses to cut, to pierce, to mutilate" by which food is "no longer a prey to which one does violence" (EMPIRE OF SIGNS), writes that Orientals eating with chopsticks remind one of sparrows picking for grain, whereas Occidentals "tear apart" their food, "like a cat eating a mouse." (Barthes mentioned "pecking" and birdfood, but Lee is better with metaphor). Why stop with sadism? How about *masochism*? Isabella Bird describes people in inner China who thought the fork must "prick the mouth and make it bleed." (YVB:1899)

But this is not where Lee's main interest lies. Everyone (in the Far East, at least) already *knows* Occidentals are on the savage side of life (One wonders how Barthe and Lee would handle Frois's *bare-hands* – the Portuguese says *mão,* or "hand," but I translated it as "fingers" for the sake of comprehension – would they have us practicing *karate* on our food?). No, Lee is going straight for his Oriental reader's heart-strings:

> Western food – steak, of course, but bread, too – can not be picked up with chopsticks. That is to say that if Asians ate with chopsticks, it means the food was prepared to eat bite-size. The amount of food chopsticks pinch is just the ideal amount for a mouthful. One might even say chopsticks are a scale or measure for food. That food could be eaten without inconvenience, with no need for a fork and knife, is because the person who prepared the food always did so from the eater's point of view. . . . Here is a warm and sympathetic frame of mind only found in the chopstick cultural sphere. (FUROSHIKI BUNKA-NO POSUTO-MODAN 1989)

'Tis the *chop*, not the *stick* that matters. The Westerner's implements show a do-it-alone Robinson Crusoe mentality. "With fork and knife in hand, a man gains the freedom to render the world, and solitude," while the Eastern choice reflects people who love people, people chopping for people, who stick together to make a meal. In fact, Lee goes on, *hashi* (chopsticks) in Japanese are a homophone with *bridge*, and not only do they link people horizontally, but *vertically* as well. Unlike the spoon and fork, which infants can master by themselves, the old generation must *teach* the new generation how to eat with chopsticks. A bridge across the generations. *How sweet!* (Reading Lee, we can't help wonder *how it ever got started!* Were two sticks used to remove turtle-shell oracles from the fire, in which case Chinese characters and the chopsticks have a common origin?) But while playing at this psychological contrariety we may call Oriental/Occidentalism, let us not forget the contribution *Japanese* – not Chinese or Koreans – made to the chopstick culture. (*Try to guess!* I save the answer for the chapter endnotes!)

If the Japanese of Pinto's and Frois's day were curious about *our* eating manners [2], we were curious about theirs, too. Usanians were disappointed to find the first Japanese Embassy of 1860 already skilled in the use of "our" utensils, which they may have practiced using (not that it takes much practice!) while crossing the ocean; but the Japanese were, nevertheless, kind enough to demonstrate their use during a visit to the National Mint:

> A luncheon was served to them in the mint when the display of chop-stick skill – picking up one pea at a time at high speed with two sticks, for instance – was recreated to observant America. (A:FJE)

1. Chopstick *Translation*   In Portuguese, Frois calls chopsticks *paus,* a *very* broad term including sticks, twigs, poles, pieces of wood, wood, and even lumber! I do not know the expression used for chopsticks in his earlier letter, but would guess it included the same. From Spanish, they usually English as "slender reeds." While chopsticks are never hollow, as *reeds* are, they are often very lithe, so reed does have the right feeling. The French translation has two *baguettes,* "'baguette' the name for anything long and skinny, including drum sticks, strips of wood, etc.," and Schütte's German *Holzstäbchen* or, wooden-rod (the second by itself now suffices for chopsticks. Also, when you know that "chop" does not refer to *food* but to "quick/nimble" (according to the OED), the word "chopstick" seems better than it sounds.

2. *Manners, Literally.*   Manners, "from *manuarius* of, or pertaining to the hand." (Shogakukan-Random-house)

6-2   We ordinarily eat bread of wheat.   *Ho nosso comer ordinario hé pão de trigo;*

The Japanese, rice cooked without salt.   *Os Japões arroz cozido sem sal.*

The "we" for Europe is more inclusive than "the Japanese," for commoners in Japan ate as much millet and barley and buckwheat (always as noodles, not bread) as rice, which was, in their case, unpolished. To the poor, good white rice was a luxury item reserved for special occasions or sickness. In that sense, rice was less important though more highly respected than our "staff of life," which (eaten alone) came to be considered the food of our poor, until the easily grown potato replaced it in some areas (as the yam did in China and Japan). But if rice was not universally available, it functioned as something common yet valuable in a way that bread (or grain) did not in Europe:

..

> *In Europe, we measure a country's wealth in terms of acreage, gold or soldiers;*
> *In Japan, the weight of annual rice production is the measure of its wealth and status.*

Eventually, most Japanese could eat rice every day. Rice came to be called the *shushoku*, or "main-food," i.e. *the* staple of the diet. Japanese in the 20th century would speak of rice as the *shushoku* of Japanese and bread as the *shushoku* of Occidentals. Among themselves today they speak of people belonging to the "rice-party" (*gohan-ha*) or the bread-party (*pan-ha*)." But this idea of allegiance(?) to a single staple is foreign to "us." We take our bread and potatoes, rice and riceroni for granted and insist upon calling meat the "main-dish." (The only exception is pasta. You don't order a "main dish" of meat-balls with pasta on the side. But note, pasta came from the East!) The Japanese have picked up on this with a vengeance. The title of a popular *nihonjinron* book by Tsukuba Hisaharu says it all: "Rice-eating Civilization, Meat-eating Civilization" (*Beishoku, Nikushoku-no Bunmei* – NHK 1969). Lacking the word "rice-ivore" I could not write "carnivore" here, but the general idea is to juxtapose *gentle vegetarians* with *ferocious carnivores*. A 1960's best-seller, and far more original book by Sabata Toyoyuki titled "Carnivore Thoughts " (*Nikushoku no Shisô*: 1966) also set pastoral meat culture against paddy-rice culture, but, more importantly did the same for *bread* and rice. Milling grain into powder and baking bread was a far more complex process than cooking rice ("which they boil simply in water" (Carletti)).) The inhabitants of a medieval community in the West had to pay a miller to turn their grain to flour and, in many cases, a baker to cook it. (As Alcock put it in the mid-19th century, "boiled rice takes the place of *baker's bread*" my *italics*: A:COT) The taxes and inconvenience occasioned by this collectivism were much more onerous than that of a rice culture, where everything could be done at home, and *it was the reaction against this oppression that paradoxically gave birth to individualism.* (Sabata provides a fine come-uppance for the simplistic *Great Irrigation* explanations of "Asian authoritarianism" (and I suppose the same case could be made for religious totalitarianism.) often encountered in the West!

There is a reason Frois did not make a big deal of our *meat*-eating. Most Westerners ate very little meat at the time. Sure, there were big "beef-eaters" among the rich and professional athletes like the Royal Guard in England, who went by that very name. And the growing English middle-class was exceptionally fond of meat. In Pepys' diary (1659/1/26), we find:

> Home from my office to my Lord's lodgings where my wife had got ready a very fine dinner – viz. a dish of marrow bones; a leg of mutton; a loin of veal; a dish of fowl, three pullets, and two dozen of larks all in a dish; a great tart, a neat's tongue, a dish of anchovies; a dish of prawns and cheese. My company was my father, **...**

While the average family in Europe only saw meat once a week, and that usually in the form of a little mince-meat pie (LR?[1]), Pepys has a zoo on the table – and, note, not a word about non-meat dishes! Pepys aside, when Perry opened Japan, bread, potatoes and pasta were still the main dish and meat a condiment, as fish was in Japan (and Holland), for most of "us.". Moreover, the main condiments were generally butter and cheese, not meat. The English of all classes may have been the exception, for the Iwakura Mission to the West reported (1872 ch 91) that they were exceptionally heavy meat-eaters, while most working-class Europeans, like the French, made do with potato.   The olfactory adjective that the Japanese were to peg on Occidentals was not "bloody," but "butter-stinking *(bata-kusai)*." Only over the last decades of the twentieth century, has the per-capita meat-consumption in Europe doubled, making the West clearly carnivorous. This is also true, however, for Japan. When its economy took off in the 1970's, its consumption of animal protein caught up to South Europe (I have read statistics but do not have them. Anyone?). But, in one way, Japanese held the line on tradition:

> *Our dogs and cats eat meat or meat products.*
> *Their dogs and cats eat rice like they do, or used to do.*

Since Japanese rarely reheat rice, there is always a lot left-over. Some elderly Japanese, remembering the old days when every grain was a blessing because the rice often ran out, scold about this waste. But it isn't wasted. I was astonished to see rice as the main food for many Japanese dogs and cats. Some paper-thin and irresistibly aromatic smoked bonito flakes *(katsuo-bushi)* and perhaps the miniscule leftovers of a fish tail or scraps of fish-cake or whatnot convinces them to eat bowls of the stuff! This rice-is-good-for-all-animals mentality, like so many things, would seem to come from China. In the mid-sixteenth century, Gaspar da Cruz, describes how his "nightingales" were fed:

> I kept two males and a female, and they sang in December as if it were April. They fed them with cooked rice wrapped in the yolk of an egg, somewhat on the dry side, which deceives them into thinking they are eating little insects. (TCC in B:SCSC)

1. *LR?*   I thought I learned about what was what with meat-eating, or rather its paucity in a book called *Holland In Rembrandt's Time* by Paul Zunthor because I wrote that 20 years ago, but I cannot find any confirmation that such a book exists! So it is a Lost Reference.

~~~~~~

6-3   Our tables are there before meals are brought out.
          As nossas mezas estão antes que venha o comer postas;

          Theirs come together with the meal from the kitchen.
          As suas vem juntamente com o comer da cozinha.

The tables were small and brought out from the kitchen by the woman of the house, as easily as waitresses carry trays of food. This was a more labor-intensive process than our collective table setting and serving. Isabella Bird in 1880, applauds an inn serving guests "from the high Government official down to the ... baggage coolies."

> It might not be difficult to provide a dinner for forty, but then it must be forty dinners, *i.e.* each person must have his separate lacquered table and from four to twelve dishes or bowls containing edibles. I abhor the viands, but I have never seen a coolie taking his midday meal without fresh admiration of the neat and cleanly mode of serving, and the adaptability and elegance of the *solitaire* dinner service. (B:UTJ)

In Japan, today, this is only true for some traditional style restaurants. In Korea, however, food is still often served this way at home. Frois might also have written:

We eat around large collective tables.
They eat at small individual tables.

"We" were more collectivist than Japanese. In medieval Portugal, tables were not the only thing shared. "It must be emphasized" writes Marques, "that each bowl or plate was always used by two guests, seated side by side." He adds that this explains the Portuguese idiom *"comer com aguem no prato,* literally "to eat with someone on the plate" [i.e. from the same plate] "signifying to be very close to someone" (M:DLP). In 1670, Montanus sets the social Occidental against the lone-wolf Japanese:

> Their manner of Diet is also opposite to ours; whereas we delight in Friends and Strangers at our private Tables, or at least admit Relations and Concerns to sit with us, never willing to eat alone; they on the contrary have each their peculiar Boards, where they dine and sup by themselves in a churlish manner, and serv'd but meanly, are satisfi'd with a slender pittance. (M:EEJ)

As usual, Montanus takes a dry kernel of fact and makes heavily buttered popcorn of it. Perhaps (judging from the present day) the Japanese were not as liable to join strangers in food or conversation as people in some Occidental nations (or in Korea, where people not only engage in talk with strangers but dip into the same soup bowl with their spoons, or did in Pusan 30 years ago), but individual tables were placed in close proximity and had nothing to do with churlish separatism at meal-time. There are cultures, such as traditional Bali, where eating was so intensely private that members of a family faced their separate corners of the room and strangers were fined for intruding at meal time! Japan was not such a culture. Meals were generally convivial.

~~~~~~

6-4   Our tables are high and have tablecloths and napkins.
As nossas mezas são e tem suas toalhas e guardanapos;

> Those of Japan are *urushi'ed* [lacquered] trays, rectangular and low-down, without tablecloths and napkins. *As dos Japões taboleiros vruxados, quadreados, razos, sem guardanapo nem toalha.*

Most of the little tables – which might be lined up when many people ate – had legs long enough to lift them four to eight inches off the *tatami,* "tea-trays, with legs like dachshunds" to use Sladen's description. (S:MQT). This contrast was no academic matter for Frois. Five years before our TRATADO, at the Bungo Consultation, the Jesuits officially decided to eat in the Japanese style. Schütte S.J. sums up the situation with respect to tables:

..

> Hitherto, in the fathers and *irmaos* [novices] refractory, the community sat at high tables and made use of tablecloths and napkins. Naturally, these could not be changed and washed after each meal. In the eyes of the Japanese, accustomed to extreme cleanliness, such unchanged table linen was always soiled; in other respects, too, there was a general lack of neatness. All this could be avoided by conforming to the Japanese mode . . . (S:VMP)

In the *"Resoluciones del Padre Visitador,"* Valignano was concerned that the dirtiness of their kitchens and diners was giving the Jesuits a bad reputation among Japanese, "especially all the bonzes . . . who take us for a filthy and unworthy people *(gente sucia y de poca estima)"* (in V(A):S&A) Decades later, Rodrigues reiterated: "they are much amazed at our eating with the hands and wiping them on napkins, which then remain covered with food stains, and this causes them both nausea and disgust." (R:TIJ) These tablecloths and napkins were not only used for hands, but for *knives.* As each person generally brought their own knife to eat with, they had to wipe them clean before they departed. The proper etiquette was to first wipe the knife on the manchets (round bread used for a plate that would be given to the dogs or the poor) and, then, the table-cloth, but such rules were not always followed. (M:DLP) How ironic that the very items the Occidental diner used to stay clean gave "us" the opposite reputation! (Put this way, one wonders if the linen reminded Japanese of paper used in a similar fashion after defecation or sex!) What is most remarkable of all is the fact that the more thorough-going Japanese cleanliness, which was observed in the nineteenth century with the equal surprise and delight – but more in contrast with China, than with the European observers themselves – as it was by the Jesuits in the 16th century, was not a monopoly of the fastidious bourgeoisie, but shared by everyone! *Get this:*

> However dirty the clothing and even the houses of the poorer classes are, I have never seen anything but extreme cleanliness in the cooking and serving of meals, and I have often preferred to spend an hour by the kitchen fire to a dignified solitude in my own room. (B:UTJ)

Ms Bishop was no Japanophile – she never hesitated to call a spade a spade, or more – so we can bet the Japanese were *extremely* clean cooks! I write "were" because at present the difference is no longer that clear.

~~~~~~

6-5   We sit on chairs to we eat with our legs extended.
Nós asentamo-nos em cadeiras pera comer com as pernas estendidas;

> They [sit] on the *tatami* or the ground with their legs crossed.
> *Elles sobre os* tatamis *ou no chão com as pernas emcruzadas.*

This, too, *mattered* to Frois. When the Jesuits asked themselves whether or not to observe Japanese table manners, the question

> reduced itself to whether one was to squat at a low table on ones haunches after the Japanese manner (a radical proposal, this) or sit at a high table as in Europe? If Europeans, for reasons of principle dictated by their task in Japan, decided in future to take their meals squatting on the ground (and every European who has tried to accustom himself to the Japanese method knows what it means), it was only to be expected that such efforts at adaptation would not stop there. (S:VMP)

Father Schütte's pair of parentheses reflect great sympathy for the excruciating personal sacrifices the Jesuits would have to make after Bungo. A 20th century *conte* by George Mikes:

..

> You can carry this passion of going Japanese too far. Once, with a number of English residents in Tokyo, we went to a very Japanese Japanese restaurant . . . . We were led to one of those small special rooms . . . and on the way up one of my companions discovered one of his friends – another Englishman – having dinner, squatting on the floor with apparent ease.
>
> 'I envy you,' he said. 'The one thing I cannot learn is this squatting.[sic]'
>
> 'Quite easy, really," the other replied, a shade patronizingly, I thought.
>
> We proceeded to the neighboring room, ate our dinner and would have forgotten about him but for his unexpected reappearance. He had wanted to straighten his tired legs – squatting [sic] was easy but not that easy – had lost his balance, rolled over, fallen against the thin paper-wall, burst through it and ended up – with proper British apologies – in my soup." (M:LRY – my *sics*)

One should not quote and criticize; but neither sitting cross-legged in the informal style mentioned in Frois's contrast nor sitting on ones shins in the formal style as suggested in Mikes' story and described by Thunberg as making "a chair of their heels," (T:TEAA) ought to be called *squatting* (because of our lack of a word for this, the author or editor chose the yuckiest verb for sit they could find and it was *squat*),. A squat is a natural way of lowering one's buttock, without a chair to meet it halfway. All people not addicted to chairs do it naturally. It is the natural posture for defecation. Japanese may sometimes gobble down a box lunch *without a table* while squatting, but no Japanese has *ever* squatted *at a table!* These Japanese ways of sitting are proper (i.e. learned), while squatting is far from it. If anything, they are similar to the postures and movements of Bali – where babies were not allowed to crawl! -- which may be expressed in a single word: *rectitude*. Still, there seems to be no way for us to avoid the wrong word here, for even the very knowledgeable Cooper uses it when he quotes Valignano, who, as a giant, must have suffered more than anyone:

> Their way of sitting causes no less suffering because they kneel on the floor and sit back on their heels, or, as we would say, squat. This is a very restful position for them, but for others it is very wearisome and painful until they gradually become accustomed to it in the course of time. (1583? PRINCIPIO in C:TCJ)

Men may begin formal meals in this *seiza,* or "proper-seat" position (see 2-63), but they rarely ate entire meals in it. As Thunberg noted in 1775, "being used to this posture, they [the Japanese men] could endure it for a while, but it was easily seen that it proved tiresome to them at length, by their rising up, and sitting for some time like the Europeans." They usually switch to the informal cross-legged style before the meal is over. Women, however, almost never sat cross-legged. As social inferiors, they sat more or less formally all the time and, I would guess, rarely enjoyed leisurely meals.

Valignano, who suggested sitting was one of the things someone had to relearn as if they were a child in this contrary culture of Japan (1583) realized it went both ways. In DE MISSIONE, the ambassador Miguel=Valignano and Leo, who remained in Japan, had a splendid dialogue.

Leo – Say what you will about how they [European visitors] are elegant in their own way. We still think our Japanese way of sitting best. Sitting in their chairs, their legs can't help dangling down – how can a body relax [1] on a chair?

Miguel – Good point! It really is so Japanese a thing to say. The European thought on this is just the opposite. They think sitting with the legs folded-up almost unbearable. But considering things from a natural viewpoint, the European way of sitting is much more appropriate. Using a chair preserves a type of dignity. With the feet resting on the floor or a foot-rest, while the rest of the body maintains a fitting, stable posture, the body is at ease. Sitting directly on the floor, however, does not only look ignoble [prostrate/dejected], but is hard because most of the body is supported by the legs [knees/shin] alone. Even the padres [tough and adapted to Japanese ways] find this way of sitting so hard that they cannot easily bear it.

Leo – If you like their way of sitting that much, it would seem you have lost your birthright as a Japanese and turned into a person of European birth! But, those other peoples you saw, how in the world did they sit? If we could only know that it would be easier to judge the relative merits and demerits.

Miguel – If we pay attention to the customs of other people, our way of sitting comes off even worse. Excluding the Europeans, the only people polished and elegant enough to bear comparison are the Chinese, who sit on chairs like Europeans. The rest are primitive [2]. We have seen that primitive people sit directly on the ground. Still, the Japanese have the most elegant floors and way of sitting, but, then again, every people has found out their own way of sitting which fits their own country and adapted their bodies to it over the course of many years, so such debate is not very meaningful. That is to say, the Japanese way of sitting fits the Japanese wealth and housing, while the European way suits their income and wealth, and it costs a good deal more. So, we might say that when customs differ, each people have their respective reasons for it, so all customs make perfect sense. (J/S:DM dialogue 9).

Imagine Leo on something even more disconnected from the ground than a chair: *a rotating bar stool!* Might he not feel something akin to the experience of *paling,* a nauseous terror that assaulted a Balinese person who didn't know his exact orientation? If the Balinese needed to get out from a car and find their bearings with respect to the mountain and/or sea, would the Japanese have to bail out from the bar stool and sit down upon the firm back of mother earth, or rather *tatami*?

1. *Translation Note: Relax* The Japanese word I translated as "relax" was a negative form (the Japanese is a double negative rhetorical question) of *ochitsuku.* The word means to feel right at home, or utterly at ease, and literally translates as "fall-stuck," – like our "settled down," but used more often for more things. Should I have translated as "can not *settle* on a chair"? I feel it reflects a Japanese psychological cosmogony which seeks stability in being grounded and is terrified of suspension. To be left hanging in Japanese has stronger connotations of anxiety than it does in English – one thinks of the haiku image of a turtle or an octopus suspended from the awnings of a shop. This may be part of a cultural complex including the tendency of Japanese dancers to seldom leave the ground – or, conversely, is the opposite of the tendency of chair-cultures to leap a lot (See 13-27).

2. *Translation Note*: Primitive The Japanese translation *mikai* is a *modern term,* i.e., "undeveloped." Not seeing the original Latin of *De Missione,* I do not know whether such a word existed, but guessing it did not, I used "primitive."

6-6   Theirs, either all together – or on three tables. *As suas ou todas juntas – ou em tres mezas;*

Our dishes come out a little at a time. *As nossas yguarias vem pouqas e poquas.*

More proof that TRATADO was not finished: the order of the contrast is *backward.*

Details of formal three, five and seven-table banquets are provided by Rodrigues. For example,

> in the banquettes of three tables, . . . there are twenty dishes and they include four *shiru* [soups, see 7 below] . . . with five tables they serve twenty-six dishes, among which are included six *shiru* [soup] . . . six tables or trays, there are thirty-two dishes, among which are included eight *shiru,* that is five of fish, one of shell fish and two of meat; one of these is crane . . . (R(C):TIJ)

Myriad choice rather than item after item, as in our "production line style of eating," accompanied by "social talk," admits Lee O-Young (I O'ryon) in his best=worst Occidentalist vein, "but it is just an exchange of [self-serving?] words." This is not surprising, for, "when it comes to eating, [with Occidentals] it is every man for himself, the food piled up on his individual plate." As Lee is happy to boast, in this respect, Korea is the most Eastern of all, for Korean tables today have the most food items, both because the dishes are tiny and because (my impression, not his) Korean women have the upper-torso power needed to carry out such full tables. When tables are set side-by-side, the dishes are usually for collective use. With each person's rice bowl remaining the home-base to return to, the chopsticks "dance about over the table like a butterfly" picking up this and that.

> To beautifully pull off this space-performance, with no conductor and no signal lights requires a harmonious spirit with heaven, earth and man as one. (J/I:FPM)

Since I have always liked to eat more than one dish at a time – mix my food – I enjoy the Far Eastern freedom to choose, freedom to really choreograph ones own meal more than our sequential method. Here, the musical contrast we will see later is reversed. *They* enjoy polyphony of the palate; *we* plod on not knowing true harmony. Still, living with butterfly eaters is not always easy. The ex-wife of a Japanese acquaintance was a *go-for-the-good-stuff-while-the-getting-is-good* Edoite type, while he was a *save-the-best-stuff-for-last* Tohoku type.[1] Until they divorced, his wife and three daughters – when it comes to food most children are natural Edoites – left him without goodies. Every meal was a miniature Tragedy of the Commons with Inoue Hisashi the victim (to be fair to

Yoshiko, he writes comedies and is prone to hyperbole).   Worse yet, the "space performance" became a popular television quiz game, not one show, mind you, but a *genre* found on channel after channel, day and night in the 1980's in Japan.   A personality would be shown eating and game-show participants would be asked either to guess the *next* dish he or she – usually a very pretty she – would reach for, or, harder yet, the *order* of the first five or so items.   So far, tolerable if boring. But the close-ups of the personalities chewing – often talking at the same time – were just too much to stomach.   In Frois's time, this quiz would have necessarily skipped the first couple items in the meal, for people eating formally always began with a few "morsels of rice" followed by a sip of soup repeated thrice over according to Avila Giron ("Etiquette at the Table" in Cooper – I find it a fascinating observation because it mimics the 3X3 *sake* drinking exchange at weddings and would seem to turn the banquette into a binding occasion).   It is at least *possible* that Roland Barthes, who, as an avant-garde intellectual was feted in Japan – unlike, yours truly, who was largely ignored – was responsible for the idea of such shows. To wit,

> . . . a chopstick – as its shape sufficiently indicates – has a deitic function: it points to the food, designates the fragment, brings into existence by the very gesture of choice, which is the index; but thereby, instead of ingestion following a kind of mechanical sequence, in which one would be limited to swallowing little by little the parts of one and the same dish, the chopstick, designating what it selects (and thus selecting there and then *this* and *that*), introduces into the use of food not an order but a caprice, a certain indolence: in any case, an intelligent and no longer mechanical operation. (B(H):EOS)

The practice of introducing small amounts of many different things at once and preparing the food ahead of time which is common to chopstick cultures may also explain the Chinese cultural sphere's fancy, multi-compartment lunch-boxes – I translated an article about a Qing Dynasty Imperial snack box with *18 compartments*, partially hollowed out to make the entire box into the Chinese character for "ten-thousand."   While that many compartments is unusual, the lunch-box tradition in Japan today is still going strong and makes our paper-bagging and tin lunch boxes seem very, very primitive. Not only carry-out lunches, but cafeteria-style lunches and dinners, and *gourmet banquette food* is often served in these boxes, which are generally lacquer-ware, or, today, imitation lacquer-ware, i.e. plastic. Or, perhaps, it would be better to contrast collective banquette smorgasbords in the West, with pre-divided individualized smorgasbords in the Far East.

> *We put only simple meals into boxes and only use them for picnics.*
> *They put elaborate full-course dinners into boxes and even eat them indoors.*

Even lunch-boxes for children are so complex by the simple standards of the West that Occidental mothers sending their children to Japanese schools find their preparation a major trauma! Their letters to the editors of English language newspapers appear every year, or did when I was there.

~~~~~~

6-7   We can eat well enough without soup; *Nós podemos muito bem comer dem caldo;*

The Japanese can not eat without *shiru* [soup]. *Os Japões não podem comer sem* xiru.

Rodrigues suggests soup was *indispensable* because of the method of serving. With the old style three, five or seven plate banquette, "the food was insipid as it was cut up in portions and brought in on tables, and the only thing hot was the *shiru*, or broth, which one was able to enjoy." That banquette style was already changing when Frois wrote TRATADO and was largely superseded by the time Rodrigues wrote, when more food was brought out hot but I think the fact Japanese rarely drank anything substantial with their meal (*sake* was too strong to drink like beer or watered-down wine and tea was only drunken after the meal) was also important: there had to be *something* to wash the food down with.

While fancy restaurants still serve fish and fowl in *shiru*, as described by Rodrigues, today the soup is usually either *miso-shiru*, a cloudy fermented bean-curd soup, or one of a number of clear *suimono* – literally "sucking-thing" soups. The ingredients of both are almost entirely vegetable, but tiny shellfish (*asari* or *chijimi*) in the shell are often added to improve the flavor of the former, which is now well known among health-food devotees in the West. When my father worked in Japan, he avoided *miso-shiru* at first, because he was suspicious of what the *murk* hid. He thought it the potage equivalent of that mix of god-knows-what called a hotdog. Once he learned that it was wholesomeness itself, he became a *miso-ite*. In Japan, *miso* receives as much good press as wine in France. Hardly a week goes by without the publication of a new study showing this or that new medical benefit (never the opposite, see 6-57) – usually anti-carcinogenic – deriving from it.

Miso in Japan is sacred. Usanians associate apple-pie, mother and country. But the relationship is weak. If Usanians away from home were asked what they miss most of their mother's cooking, perhaps one in fifty would say "her apple pie." Almost all Japanese, however, would probably say her *miso-shiru*. Abroad, they generally *long* for that soup in a way we who don't have such an emotionally-invested food cannot know. The difference is that we don't eat apple pie with almost every meal, and when we do eat it, chances are it's bought. Most Japanese may not ferment their bean curd from scratch nowadays, but they still select and mix it and add other ingredients to make their soup. Because there is a much greater difference between each mother's *miso-shiru* and the only other thing almost sure to appear at every meal, the rice, the flavor of that *miso* becomes the most important part of the taste-identity of every Japanese. So long as a Japanese can return to sip his mother's miso-shiru, one senses an invisible umbilical cord still passing fluid. I suppose it is something like the flavor of the water of your home town in the USA.

As I once pointed out in public debate in Japan (Aera (lost the date)), today, *miso-shiru* has one disagreeable quality: the Japanese establishment *pushes* it on young Japanese for the *principle* rather than the flavor! It comes with *everything* at university cafeterias. Imagine ordering already too salty *kareraisu* (curry on rice) and being given *miso-shiru* to drink – Japanese slurp it from the tiny bowl (another *reason* it serves as a drink) – with it! Not only is the flavor *wrong* for curry, but considering the high salinity of *miso,* the combination of two salty foods is unhealthy. Moreover, institutional *miso-shiru* is generally horrible. If, by the time university students graduate today, not a few are alienated from the national soup, it is the tasteless Establishment, not the long-surviving boogey-man called "Western influence" that is to blame! But, then again, Japanese *miso,* itself, is green and tasteless compared to the more mature *miso* found in Korea. Sorry, mothers of Japan, but to me, the difference is as great as that between American cheese and French, or American beer and German.

There is one interesting contradiction about Japanese and "their" *miso.* The people of the city that was the capitol of Japan, Meaco as Frois called it, did not drink – soup requires the verb *nomu,* or "drink" – *miso-shiru.* Kyotoites only have a very light colored "white" *miso* stew on the first couple days of the year. In his book on the spirit of Kyoto, Umesao Tadao, director of Japan's National Museum of Ethnology writes

> I hate *miso-shiru.* I can't eat *takuwan* [*radish* pickles], much less *umeboshi* [dried plum]. *Sukiyaki*[1] disgusts me. This kind of Japanese abounds in Kyoto. (U:KNS)

---

1. *Sukiyaki* Selections from Barthes' description of this party dish: "a stew whose every element can be known and recognized, since it is made in front of you;" "garbed in an aesthetic nakedness;" "stew before your eyes;" "an entire minor odyssey of food you are experiencing through your eyes: you are attending the Twilight of the Raw." (B:EOS) By the way, the Japanese pop hit *Sukiyaki* has nothing to do with *sukiyaki*.

~~~~~~

6-8   Our service is silver or pewter.
        A nossa baxela hé de prata ou estanho;

        ## That of Japan is vermillion or black *urushi'ed* [lacquered] wood.
        A dos Japões feita de pao vruxado, vermelha ou preta.

Perhaps "tin" would be the more precise translation of *estanho* but *tin* today connotes *cheapness*, whereas that was not Frois's intent and pewter is, after all, generally about 95% tin.[1] (The German translation *Zinn* means either one, and a German acquaintance tells me she read it as "pewter.")

Frois may well have explained the benefits of this lacquered wood in his missing Summary. Unlike ceramics it is light; unlike metals it does not conduct much heat, unlike paint it is permanent and unlike unpainted wood it is waterproof and can be completely cleaned. The only reason I never came to like it very much is because it reminds me of plastic. Indeed, *today*, most ostensibly lacquered bowls – rarely plates – and spoons in Japan *are* plastic. In a world of slick thin things, we need thick earthenware to retain our material sanity. (It is just like realistic painting which I don't care for today, but would probably have loved before the photograph was invented). That my lack of interest in lacquer was not shared in Europe is proven by the fact that only decades after the TRATADO was written, it became a household word in English. Moreover, it became identified with the name of its country of origin, *japan* and was made through a process called *jappaning* by the *jappaners* who *japanned* it! Here is Kaempfer, a century later:

> The *Urusi* or Varnish-Tree, is another of the noblest and most useful Trees of this Country. It affords a milky Juice, which the Japanese make use of to varnish, and as we call it, to japan all their Household goods, dishes and plates of Wood, and this from the Emperor down to the meanest Peasant. For even at Court, and at the Imperial Table, services of lacker'd ware are preferr'd to those of gold and silver. (K(S):HOJ)

For a people whose very dreams revolved upon precious metals,[2] this *japan-ware* was a tremendous shock, or . . . revelation. To love it was to love Japanese art, to accept another aesthetic tradition. Here is a sentence from "a do-it-yourself of great value to furniture-makers" by John Stalker and George Parker published in 1688 and titled *A Treatise of Jappaning or Varnishing*:

> Let not the Europeans any longer flatter themselves with the empty notions of having surpassed all the world beside in stately Palaces, costly Temples, and sumptuous Fabricks; Ancient and modern Rome must now give place: the Glory of one Country, Japan alone, has exceeded in beauty and magnificence all the pride of the Vatican at this time, and the Pantheon heretofore. (in John M. MacKenzie: *ORIENTALISM: History, Theory and the Arts*)

The complex art of *urushi* (see Chamberlain for details!) originated in China, but Japanese artists were and are credited with taking it up to a higher plane. And, unlike China's china, it was never matched by Europe.

---

1. ***Tin and Pewter.*** For readers who, like me know *tin* only as stuff used for cheap cans and *pewter* as an ugly cross between silver and lead that only looks good on a shiny young dolphin, a note. *Tin* is an honest-too-goodness element, #50 to be precise. Re. *pewter*: "The Worshipful Company of Pewterers, starting in the sixteenth century, authorized three grades of pewter: Fine, for eating ware, with 96 percent tin, and 4 percent copper; Trifle, also for eating and drinking utensils but duller in appearance, with essentially 92 percent tin, 4 percent copper, and up to 4 percent lead; and Lay or Ley metal, not for eating or drinking utensils, which could contain up to 15 percent lead." (From Charles Hull, in *Pewter* (United Kingdom: Shire Publications Ltd., 1992) quoted in "Lead in Britannia Metal Fittings," by Gene Larson publ. in the issue of the *Nautical Research Journal* (12/1997))

2. *Gold Fever*   Read Columbus's journals and you will come to the conclusion that Columbus's constant harping on precious metals, especially *gold, gold, gold!* was not merely politic (for his backers), but from the heart. "Our" avarice was pathological. Oviedo wondered whether the explorers' strange disease (*malaria*) "evolved from the 'lust for gold' by which they were possessed" (P:EAE). Indeed, *gold=yellow fever!*

~~~~~~

6-9   We use earthenware pots and porringers [1] to prepare our food;
Nós uzamos de panelas e tijelas de barro pera se fazer o comer;

The Japanese, cast iron kettles and pans.
Os Japões de tachos e vazos de ferro coado.

This contrast seems a bit too pat. *Japan* is the first place I have ever seen stews being slowly boiled in earthen rather than metal-ware! Japan has fine traditional cooking utensils of *both* materials. Perhaps, in Frois's time, the gentry in Japan used metal-ware for cooking, while Europeans preferred earthenware in a curious reversal of their, I mean, "our" usual love for metal. "Kettles and pans" is not quite right. The original seems to say "pans and vessels." The problem is the a pan is a type of vessel. Something is wrong, so I just put what I think was.

1. *Porringer.* A pot/bowl with a handle. Most words for cooking utensils used in the past or abroad do not translate. When an exact name can be found it is usually only known to the gourmet or historian, i.e., "porringer." More commonly we get an overly broad selection.

2. *Tachos* According to the DEI dictionary, *tacho* is "shallow, wide pan, pail." In English, pails cannot be shallow by definition. I suspect Frois might mean something like a wok, but without an illustration, who knows!

~~~~~~

6-10   We place tripods with the legs down. *Nos pomos a trempe com os pees pera baxo;*

The Japanese, with the legs up. *Os Japões com os pees pera cima.*

Valignano begins a section of his elaboration of Japanese contrariness with this example, adding that, with the leg-up Japanese tripod, the "ring" was on the bottom (1583?). The classic Greeks, who gave tripods, together with pretty slaves, to winning athletes, might have found much of interest in this contrast. But for most modern readers, like me, it is a good thing the contrast stops where it does, for we now have only a vague idea of how these devices also called "trivets," "spiders" and "kettle-holders" were used in the West. Moreover, the tripod is but one cooking device in Japan. The fascinating *irori* contraption – by which pots are hung over fires – used in common Japanese homes is too complex to even *try* a simple contrast. All one can do is picture it (which I will do when/if the next edition is offset).

~~~~~~

6-11   Men in Europe ordinarily eat with their women.
Os homens em Europa comem ordinariamente com suas molheres;

In Japan, it is something very rare, for the tables are also separate.
Em Japão hé cousa mui rara, porque tambem as mezas são divizas.

Even if Japanese women were freer than European women in some respects, the two sexes were not considered equal, and women were only allowed at the table of men in a serving capacity. This was true at least for the gentry, but among the peasantry in much of Japan, husband and wife often ate together, and it was not uncommon for men of most classes to eat with their mistresses, at least in private. As the 20th century began, this matter of men and women eating together became part of Japan's *national agenda* in its valiant drive to Westernize in order to gain the respect of the world powers. The Imperial family led the way!

> The [Crown] Princess [Sada] enters the carriage ahead of him [the Crown Prince] when they drive together, and they habitually take their meals together – an astounding revolution in Japan. (S: MQTJ: 1905)

Today, husband and wife *still* eat and party together far less than they do in the West. The reason, however, has little to do with the traditional segregation of male and female. Japanese working and commuting hours are usually so long that people eat and party with their colleagues alone. I am, rather, surprised that as many eat as home as do. Married men often eat nothing at the normal dinner hour, persevering until they get home to eat with their wives who wait for them at 10, 11 or 12 at night! (At least this held true for the small companies I knew, where the hours were far longer than reflected in the official statistics).

Frois's "separate" tables may mean divided into male and female types, as described in 2-53. But one might also point out that with the men sitting with their knees sticking out to the right and left, people could not sit as close together as they did in Europe.

~~~~~~

6-12   Europeans like fish brazed or stewed. *A jente de Europa se deleita com pexe asado e cozido;*

> The Japanese delight even more in eating it raw. *Os Japões folgão muyto mais de o comer cru.*

After Valignano mentions how remarkable it is that things in Japan could be so contrary to those in Europe – yet perfectly reasonable for those who really came to know them – even though Japan was a very civilized place (my introduction quote), here is how he continues:

> What is much more astonishing is that they are so different and even contrary to us, as regards the senses and natural things; this is something I would not dare to affirm if I had not had so much experience among them. Thus, their taste is so different from ours that they generally despise and dislike the things we find most pleasing; on the other hand, we cannot stand the things which they like. (1583? Cooper tr. C:TCJ)

The last phrase in the original Spanish reads *nosotros no lo podemos meter en la boca,* "we cannot even put in our mouth." And the prime example of this was generally raw fish. Let me lift an entire note (note 85) from Alvarez-Taladriz:

> The Japanese custom of eating raw fish caused no little suffering to the missionaries at the banquettes where it was offered. If they found it a "continual torment," and "extreme mortification, seeing them eat was edifying for the natives "because they say people who suffer that much to accommodate themselves to them can not but be saintly and come from heaven." (Mejia 1584) Just how repugnant eating raw fish was to them is revealed by their belief that eating it was the reason there were so many lepers in the country. (Ribadeneira) (Both in V(A)S&A)

Raw, perhaps, but, as a rule, not *as raw* as that eaten today. Carletti on fish: "They usually eat this in a practically raw state, after having dipped it in boiling vinegar." (C(W):MVAW) The diverse and extremely appealing *sushi* we know was not yet fully developed. That required the creativity of food preparation in the heyday of Edo culture. Eventually, the advent of refrigeration expanded its possibilities yet further and made *sushi* a world-class food, even if television sitcom writers in America Inc. cannot resist baiting it. But one cannot blame the sitcom writers, for *sushi* took off less for its flavor than for the same reason Western food has reached around the globe, because of the high prestige of a wealthy Japan in the 1970's and 80's. Before Japan got rich, the prejudice of the West against raw fish, or *sashimi, – sushi,* being thin slices of the fish on rice – not only prevented us from trying it, but prevented Japanese visitors to the West from eating it. When the 1862 *Bakufu* mission stayed in France

> . . . they actually resorted to cutting up raw fish in *sashimi* style and eating it with the soy sauce [500 bottles!] they had brought with them. Their sense of pride, however, forced them to abandon the habit, such was their indigence when a British newspaper compared their partiality for raw fish with the diet of natives [sic: the word must have been *"savages"* or "barbarians," not "natives"!] in South America. (JDVB? = LR)

The classic vinegared fish still survives in the sushi-shop repertoire and does not impress me as all that different from the herrings the Dutch were beginning to pickle in earnest (they made it a huge industry) about the time Frois wrote. The tendency of Japanese in the past century to avoid spicy food, however, has resulted in the total demise of the far more interesting *karashi* (mustard) marinated *sushi* of Edo on the mainland. One must go to the Ogasawara (Bonin) islands a thousand miles due South of Tokyo where it barely hangs on (an island survival); and, as far as I know, no one eats raw bonito as gamey as it was in Frois's day. This expensive delicacy (?), which became a veritable cult in Edo soon after the country was closed, was reputed to make those who ate it as high as if they were drunk. (But I have had far worse from Norway!). Few in Japan, today, realize that vinegared or fermented, i.e. *semi*-raw fish, was once what sushi was all about.

> "(for us, rawness is a strong state of food, as is metonymically shown by the intensive seasoning we impose on our *steak tartare*)." (B:EOS)

Frois writes *comer cru* for "eating [it] raw." In Spanish, judging from Alvarez-Taladriz, they also spoke of *pescado crudo.* The Portugues *cru* includes connotations such as "cruel" (savage) and "hard-hearted." "strong" and "savage." When Barthes call rawness "the tutelary divinity of Japanese food," he mentions the French equivalent(?) *crudité* ("an inner essence of the foodstuff . . . the sanguinary plethora by which we assimilate vital energy by transmigration" unlike the Japanese rawness, which is "essentially visual . . . not deep." B:EOS). I suppose the English "raw," while not so *cruel* as the Portuguese nor so *crude* as the French, has the same rough quality belying the complex preparation of *sashimi* or *sushi* which is, in most cases, more difficult than cooking a fish. I was delighted to find that where Valignano touches upon raw fish, he writes *pescado salada y fresco,* i.e. "uncooked [[salted?]] and fresh." I would bet that Valignano learned to like it.

6-13   Among us, all fruits are eaten ripe, and only cucumbers green.
Antre nós se comem todas as frutas maduras, e somente os pipinos verdes;

The Japanese [eat] all fruits green, and only cucumbers very yellow and ripe.
Os Japões todas as frutas verdes, e os pipinos somente muito amarelos e maduros.

The Japanese pickled most "fruit," with the apparent exception of the cucumber.[1] The Portuguese must not have exercised one iota of influence on Japanese taste in fruit, for the first British ambassador after the Opening, Sir Rutherford Alcock writes:

> Every tea-garden in the vicinity of Yeddo [Edo] tries to rival its neighbor in the beauty and size of the peach blossoms, but it is very difficult to get good peaches to eat. They are all habitually plucked unripe. It does not seem to me that the Japanese have any idea what ripe fruit means. They certainly never treat themselves to it, and after two years' practice, my market coolie could

never be made to understand what constituted ripeness. When pressed by threat of dismissal if he did not buy ripe peaches, and his attention was drawn to the colour and softness as signs, we found he used to pinch them 'black and blue' as the readiest means of meeting one of the conditions at least of softness; and no doubt, in his own mind, thought he had unreasonable people to deal with, when, instead of praise for his ingenuity, he fell into deeper disgrace.

About a quarter century later, Morse likewise described the Japanese and their green peaches. They made a great impression on his ears for he has two passages on the *noise* they make:

> . . . the peaches small, unripe, hard, and green. One can hear a boy bite a peach from across the street, yet in this hard, green state the Japanese seem to prefer them.

> They offered me a drink of sake` and one of the clerks brought to me on a dish two peaches nicely peeled, but they were very green and hard as brickbats. After the first bite I complained of being sick and rubbed my stomach pantomime fashion, which they promptly interpreted. While I am writing this I can see two domestics across the way leaning over a piazza rail eating peaches. The fruit is so green that I can actually hear them as they tear off the bites. They clutch the peaches firmly in their hands as if they were eating the hardest of apples. (M:JDD)

Today, one finds ripe peaches just like ours and nectarines, but no green peaches whatsoever. Unless it is – *it must be!* the large green "plums"(*ume*) that go into *ume-shu,* or "plum-liquor" or the smaller but apparently similar plums (?) that are pickled in vinegar and sold dyed bright red under the name *su-momo* or "vinegar-peach."   I find the vinegar hard to take, but the plums that have soaked in *sake* for a long time are as tasty as they are intoxicating. I always drank a glass-full (it is sold in glasses with lids!) of *ume-shu* with two of these plums in it – all for the equivalent of only two dollars, the best deal in Japan! – that I ate last, while I made copies of rare-books or manuscripts at the local fast food (and rice) store.

Of all the Japanese fruit, Alcock found only watermelon, persimmon and grapes passable. He and Frois failed to note that the persimmon – most of which are large and not astringent even though hard – are not only eaten ripe, but often left on the tree until they shrivel up like enormous raisins and turn white with the exuded sugar after which (or, it might be *before*, I do not know the details) they are strung up on straw-cords and sold. One cannot get riper than *that.* In the USA, I greatly miss the wonderful taste and great variety found in Japanese persimmon – not to mention the decent price – and wonder why we don't either import them or raise them ourselves! Isabella Bishop, who in 1880, agrees with me that the persimmon is "the finest fruit of Japan," wrote that her favorite was "the hard kind, which after being peeled, is dried in the sun, and then tastes like a fig." (As far as I know, the skin does not peel. We shall leave this a mystery.)

Another strange shortcoming in the Japanese "fruit" diet is their lack of interest in berries. In the early-19th century Golownin wrote:

> In the course of our journey, we often met with raspberries and strawberries, which, at first, they would not allow us to pluck, as they conceived them to be unfavorable to the health. [The Japanese feared their prisoners would commit suicide!] We asserted, however, that quite the contrary opinion prevailed in Russia, and were at last permitted to refresh ourselves with the fruit. (G:MCJ)

I noticed the same thing in the late twentieth century and wondered if it were just the urbanization of the population; but apparently it goes way back and is part of a general ignorance and fear of the woods of a purely farming immigrant people who probably came from parts of Asia where there were few berries. Indeed, there is no generic "berry" in the Japanese vocabulary, and I believe, Chinese. The closest word, *kinomi,* is so unspecific that it stands for nuts as well as berries and other fruit. Since Iberia had few berries – berries want wetter summers – Frois had nothing to say about this. In China – at least South China – however, Europeans had only praise for all the fruit, from the first.

Gaspar Da Cruz praised the taste of many Chinese fruit including some not found in the West. This one about an un-named fruit is too good not to quote:

> There is a fruit whereof there are many orchards, and it groweth on great and large-boughed trees; it is a fruit as big as a plum round, and a little bigger; it casts the husk and is a very singular and rare fruit. None can have his fill of it, for always it leaveth a desire for more, though they eat never so much, yet it does no hurt. (in B:SCSC)

The difference between fruit in Japan and in the West cannot be described in these matter-of-fact contrasts about availability or taste. Most fruit in Japan, until the last two decades of the twentieth century, was more of *a gift item* than a grocery item *per se.* One bought fruit at the vegetable shop, or occasionally, at a fruit-shop, and carried it to wherever you visited, where they would serve part of it and you would get some, too. That is one reason why the huge ten-dollar apples and other incredibly expensive fruits sell so well in Japan. People are not buying them for themselves but as gifts. Fruit is also seen in abundance at *funeral receptions*. The local green-grocer still often makes much of his or her income making baskets of fruit for funeral decoration! They assemble them as kits, with baskets, unfolding adornment. If they are good calligraphers, they also write in the name of the deceased and whatnot on the placards. I think that this fruit is eventually served to the guests during the funeral services which extend in one way or another for days if not weeks. But, I don't really know. Maybe it is sent back to the store and sold!

1. *Cucumber As Fruit?* Evidently, the highly liquid cucumber was thought of as a fruit in Frois's day. A Mexican friend tells me they mix cucumber and pineapple and avocado into a vitamin drink that is identified with *fruit* juice rather than with vegetable juice in Brazil, today. So, there would seem to be a bias for *fruit*-ing things.

~~~~~~

6-14   We cut melons length-wise. *Nós cortamos o melão ao comprido;*

The Japanese cut them cross-wise. *Os Japões o cortão ao traves.*

Okada writes that although Japanese generally cut *melons* length-wise, too, the *makuwa-uri* (*Cucumis melo var. Makuwa* = a Japanese melon the Japanese do not call a *meron*) was cut cross-wise in thin rings when offered to guests., the implication being that is what caught Frois's eye. Logically speaking, it would make sense to cut across if melons that had not been turned (in the garden) taste different on each side – or, just for looks, if one wants uniform slices, while a length-wise cut would be best for melons whose flavored varied from stem to butt, to ensure each person gets an equal deal. But there are other matters that come into play than logic or even taste. Morse:

> In serving *daikon,* a kind of radish, two pieces are always put upon the plate, one piece is called *hitokiri* **. . .** it also means "man cut"; three pieces is called *mikiri,* and also means "body cut." Eggplants and other vegetables, except *daikon*, must be cut longitudinally and not transversely, because cutting transversely seems cruel. (JDD (2-p311))

Cutting transversely, i.e. in a cross-cut would also be a *yokogiri,* or a "betrayal" – think of our "*crossing* someone" – and Japanese with their mania for significant punning would have tried to avoid it, but a *yokogiri* all the way through a melon with a hollow (where seeds are removed) within makes a *wagiri,* or ring-cut, and "ring (*wa*)" is homophonous with "peace/harmony (*wa*)." That, evidently, was fine. It would not, however have been permissible with a watermelon, for a watermelon is solid and no ring would be made.

In the last half of the 20th century in Japan, concern over the direction of the slice was of less concern than the price, which was sky-high. Despite that, they were almost never sold piecemeal at the grocers, so single people with low incomes (like *yours truly*) rarely ate any. As already noted, fruit was mainly sold for gifts – one melon or a few apples when visiting a house, a watermelon beautifully bound for carrying up a mountain (!) to a Buddhist temple or platters including pineapple and citrus as well as melon for funeral display and wakes – and only affluent families regularly ate fruit. (The exception being tangerines in season and, toward the end of my stay, bananas). I tried to convince a number of grocers to try selling *slices* but was always refused. The idea of selling pieces was most *unJapanese* they told me. It was an idea that would only fly in American, a society infected with selfish individualism (they do not put it quite so plainly, but that was the gist of it, as I recall) could come up with. Later, I discovered that in that most Japanese of times, the Secluded Edo era, melons were commonly sold *by the slice* to individuals at a price they could afford. (Since Edo had many times more men than women and most of those men were single, it could hardly have been otherwise!) So much for the stereotypes of modern *Nihonjin-ron!*

6-15   We sniff a melon from the top. *Nós cheiramos o melão pola cabeça;*

      They from the bottom. *Elles polo pé.*

If the anonymous English saying *"a woman, like a melon, is hard to choose"* came from Frois's Iberia, there might be a whiff of humor lying between these lines: it would turn the Japanese into cats, but I was at a total lost for a logical explanation of this difference until, the day before I wrote this [the first draft], when it just so happened that an 85 year-old farmer brought two cantaloupes and a watermelon into my sister's house [in Newberry, Florida]. He carried the huge watermelon resting, to all appearances very lightly, upon one forearm. Another time I saw him carry two big watermelons that way. But this book is not about the phenomenal Mr. Hadsock . . . . Well, I sniffed and found the cantaloupes smelled *much* stronger from the top, or "head" as Frois puts it, than from the bottom, or "feet" (to transliterate the Portuguese, a detail which would much improve Robert William Wood's rhyme *"The Antalope and the Cantalope!"*) But, I also noticed that there was a navel-like depression on top and thought, hmmm, *in Japan, this would not be the case.* That is not because Japanese melons are born of immaculate conception (I can't help mentioning an old Japanese folk-tale where a woman bears the child of a traveler who poked a melon she later ate!) and lack navels, but *because Japanese leave a portion of the stem on the melon for display.* It includes a bit of the main vine as well, so it stands up from the round surface like the letter "T." The "T" on the "O" not only looks good but is profoundly satisfying for literate people because that "T" is found upside-down in the Chinese character for "melon" (瓜) Later, I tested a melon with a piece of the umbilicus still attached and found, sure enough, that without the bare navel, the melon does not smell more from the top as is the case for us. If anything, the bottom is a bit more revealing!

      I should probably stop here and leave well enough alone; but, to tell the truth, I have seen a number of Japanese mothers *sniffing* rather than feeling their baby's diapers, and cannot help but wonder if this bottom-sniffing – in Japan, the bottom of a melon is called its "butt" (*shiri*) – habit might not have been carried over into the grocery store!

6-16   We eat it and afterward throw out the rind.
      Nós o comemos, e depois lhe deitamos a casca fora;

      They pare it and throw out the rind before eating.
      Elles o aparão e lhe tirão primeiro a casca fora que o comão.

This is related to what was discussed in 1) above with respect to chopsticks; the Japanese tend to completely prepare their food before serving it. The watermelon was an exception; slices were eaten with husk in hand, as we usually eat it. Big pieces of watermelon, smaller melons, persimmon and pears are first peeled, and then cut into bite-size pieces which are either picked up with chopsticks or with a large bamboo toothpick. The inner-skin of the tangerine is an exception for it is usually chewed and spit out. But even then, the outer skin or peel is first removed and set aside, usually in a single piece that looks somewhat like a large plum blossom, which serves as a neat receptacle for the spit-out inner skins. It takes quite a bit of practice for most foreigners to learn how to properly peel a tangerine that way! As long as we are discussing things done to produce, let me add another *Faux Frois:*

> *We sometimes turn produce into faces;*
> *They turn it into make-believe horses.*

On our side, I mean shaped apples with clove eyes and Jack-o-lanterns. (but I have no idea whether we did any of this in Frois' time!). A thousand years ago, the first of Sei Shônagon's *Adorable Things* is a "the face of a child drawn on a melon" and, according to the translator Ivan Morris, "drawing faces on melons was a common pastime, especially for women and children," but that is something I never saw, and I don't know how common it was in Frois's time. On the other hand, I have seen *countless* horses made of cucumbers and egg-plants, and more rarely, potatoes and daikon (radish). Morse did too.

..

> On the lower shelf [of the Buddhist household shrine], in the right-hand corner, are seen a sweet potato and a radish propped up on four legs, looking like a toy deer or beasts of some kind. Whether this indicated the work of children or represented the horses upon which the gods could take a ride, was not ascertained. (M:JH&S)

Not ascertained, my fundament! Morse was so delighted to be able to teach his biology without Christian mythology interfering, so satisfied to be in what seemed to him a largely agnostic country where men (but not most women) had "outgrown these superstitions," that he didn't even bother to ask! The horses (or cows) are for transporting the souls of family members and ancestors back home from the Milky Way for the Bon holidays. At the end of the Bon (I can never remember how many days-long), the horses and cows are taken from the god-shelf and set adrift in a river (nowadays, I fear they are often just left out by the side of the road in the rain). I do not know how seriously adults take this, but children find something akin to the magic of Santa Claus and his sled in it. And what better way to keep in psychological touch with one's family past and loved ones who have departed? I would bet (and hope) even Christian families in Japan do this if they have children.

6-17   We pick green grapes to season our food. *Nós colhemos o agraço pera temperar o comer;*

They pick them for pickling. *Elles o colhem pera o salgar.*

We once used the juice from green apples and grapes for a condiment called *verjuice,* evidently very sour, for a sour-puss was called *verjuiced.* The philogy is obvious *verte* or "green" juice. I don't know why Usanians stopped using fruit in that way except for cranberries on Thanksgiving and mango chutney. When I worked my way back from Japan on a Swedish freighter, I found that at least part of the Occident still puts sour fruit on its meat – the lingonberries sold at outrageous prices as gourmet food in America are as basic as salt and pepper to the Swedes. (I was delighted to gain a lot of weight while I worked, so I would guess the berries may be very good for the digestion, too.)

But, I found them as *sweet* as they were sour. I would guess this was true for Frois's grapes and that we should realize the word used for season (*temperar*) also means "soften." This may increase the contrast, for Japanese pickling tends to be heavy on salt – why the Portuguese original says "salted" (vinegar is only used for a few items, and chili, sugar and other spices were and still are not used as much as they are in most of South-east Asia). Since tiny portions of these things are eaten together with, or between bites of, rice, I think of them as the equivalent for the salts, pepper and sauces we put on food. Because rice, unlike bread, has no unseen salt content (with bread, most people only realize how salty it is when they taste low-salt content bread) it requires salty condiments more then bread does.

It is hard to tell exactly what grapes are being compared. Probably the Japanese side refers to the tiny (i.e., wild) grapes called *yamabudô* and *ebikazura* whereas "ours" are unripe cultivated grapes, but maybe I am wrong.

~~~~~~

6-18   All of our food, except for bread, is carried out covered.
Todas as nossas yguarias vão cubertas, somente o pão;

> With that of the Japanese, on the contrary, only the rice is covered.
> *As dos Japões pollo comtrairo, e somente o arroz quberto.*

Why was everything of "ours" carried out covered? I think it was because we ate almost nothing raw or pickled/salted. Most of our dishes were cooked and served hot. The "raw" salads we eat today were yet to be. Evidently, bread was an exception. Generally, it was bought at the bakers, as noted previously, so it was not served freshly-made, i.e. hot, like, say, tortillas, which come from the kitchen wrapped in cloth.

The comparison works well because, as we have written, bread and rice are equivalents, the backbone of the meal. Even today, rice is usually set in a covered pot near to the table, so it can be dished out piping hot. Soup, too, is often carried out covered in a traditional Japanese restaurant – the bowl has its own little cover which must be twisted as it is opened, for there is inevitably a vacuum inside – but that was either a post-Frois development or, as I rather suspect, he overlooked it for the sake of a simple, more perfect contrast.

~~~~~~

6-19   As much as Europeans are friends of the sweet;
Quanto em Europa são os homens amigos de doce;

> The Japanese are of the salty.
> *Tanto os Japões o são de salgado.*

Okada explains the difference as a result of the fact that salt has long been produced in abundance in Japan, while sugar was an expensive import. *Perhaps*. But the paucity of interest in most ripe fruit that caught Frois's eye makes one wonder whether some other factor may be involved. I experience more craving for sweets when I eat a few meals based on bread or noodles than I do with a largely rice one, probably because Japanese rice (unlike the *indica* variety popular in the West, it is short and fat and glutinous) *itself* has a relatively high sugar content. Moreover, Japanese *sake* is very sweet, so adult males, if they drank, certainly got *their* sugar. Isabella Byrd's translator Ito

> invested in sweetmeats everywhere. They seemed as essential to him as tobacco, and he said that all who abstain from *sake* crave for sugar. (B:UBJ?)

The Japanese love for saltiness, in addition to the bread/rice issue already mentioned, may reflect their low use of other spices. Salt, in the guise of soy sauce and *miso* and pickles must do the trick by itself. But it was also natural for a hard-working people who ate little meat. (Even with their chili peppers, the Koreans likewise overdo salt, while the Eskimos, who ate *only* meat, used *no* salt, for it was in the meat/blood.) Today, people in office jobs sweat far less but keep eating the salty flavor they have grown up with. That is why *miso* soup is not always the godsend most Japanese believe it is. In some particularly salt-loving provinces in the North of Japan, middle-aged men are suffering strokes at rates so high one is reminded of the Swiss province where ridiculously high egg consumption caused a dreadfully high rate of heart-attacks.

There is still much that does not fall into place here. Though Japanese, in accord with Frois, claim to be astounded by the sweetness of *our* pastry, *their* traditional cakes – if that is what they can be called – that go with tea astound *us* equally, for they are solid sugar! (Granted, they are tiny) And, their bean-jam, *an* (which is found in the *Nipo* (Japanese-Portuguese) dictionary proves it was eaten in Frois's day), tastes *horribly sweet*, although this may be largely because *we are not used to beans-as-jam*. Moreover, all fruit in Japan is advertised as "sweet," (*amai*) – a curious thing for people who supposedly don't care for sweet things. I love tartness but found it hard to get a merchant to tell me the truth, for merely requesting "sour" (for "tart" and "sour" are a single word which never fails to draw a grimace in Japan) is to suggest he might have inferior fruit in stock! That the use of "sweet" as synonymous with "good" and "tasty" in Japan – contrary to Frois's assertion – is no modern development is proven by haiku of Issa portraying tiny peasants innocently learning a lie for their very first word, as their siblings selling bad persimmon repeatedly cry out *"sweet! sweet!"* to those who pass by their tree. Even fish (!) are not uncommonly advertised as sweet, although good fish is usually called "fat-ridden." (*abura ga notteiru*).[1]

Yet there is one factor, that supports Frois's general claim. Japanese do not call things or even people "sweet" (*amai*) in the complimentary sense we do in English (or, Chinese, for that matter!) – it is only used to mean "slut" (*ama'kko*) or, as a predicate adjective, "soft" "shallow" or "a sucker."   Owing to our common human nature most metaphors work in most languages, but there are no "sweet" babies or lovers in Japanese! The corollary of this is that there are no *sweetiepies, honeys* or *sugarbuns,* either.   Perhaps, this lack of a sweet vocabulary in Japanese proves Frois's point. Then, again, it might only be a linguistic quirk.

1. *Sweet Tooth New?* Still, to be fair to Frois, it is possible that the trade with Europe and China that took place during the time of his stay introduced enough sweets to change the Japanese taste by Issa's time (about two hundred years later). Anyone?

6-20   Among us, the servants clean up our tables.
Antre nós os pajens alevantão as mezas;

In Japan, nobles often clean up after themselves.
Em Japão os mesmos fidalgos que comem aleva[ntã]o muitas [ve]zes as suas.

This may be misleading, for, if Okada is correct, it applies only to etiquette *in a tea-hut,* a place where the host does the serving. He cites a contemporary document instructing that the participants arrange everything on their trays and take them to the entrance/window(?) to the kitchen (*katteguchi*) after the ceremony ends. I suspect that not only Way of the Tea equality, but the fact the *dogu,* or tea-ware, was often the host's most valuable possessions – the equivalent of large diamonds in the West, *but breakable* – may have had something to do with this! (But I hope there is more! *Anyone?*)

6-21   We wash our hands before and after a meal.
     Nos lavamos as mãos no principio e fim da meza;

> The Japanese, since they don't touch their food, have no need to wash them.
> *Os Japões, como não põem a mão no comer, não tem necessidade de as lavar.*

This is one of the relatively rare contrasts that included the explanation. The exception is for the tea ceremony, where the priceless vessels, needless to say, are taken in hand and respect dictated that hands were washed, much as they are washed entering some Shinto shrines. Today, Japanese restaurants do, however, offer a hot wet washcloth-sized rolled towel to wipe ones hands and face before eating. This is an idea adopted from China and is more for refreshing ones senses than cleanliness.

6-22   We eat our vermicelli hot and cut up.
     Nós comemos a aletria quente e cortada;

> [*They*] place it in cold water and eat it very long.
> *[Elles a] metem em agoa fria e a comem muito comprida.*

The cold water referred to is not a condiment but part of the preparation of the noodles. The hot noodles are quickly cooled down to preserve the "hips," that is to say the bite. Long before *instanto ramen,* Japanese noodles were quicker cooking than most pasta. With the thinner noodles such as the hair-thin *somen,* Okada guesses Frois is referring to here – the Portuguese *comprida* has a *stretched long and thin* feeling, not found in any English word – the line between *al dente* and sogginess is very fine. All Japanese noodles may be eaten cold. I think Frois may be thinking of *soba,* or buckwheat noodles, and possibly even the wheat *udon,* which is generally slightly thicker and square-edged and eaten hot. Today, *somen* is almost always eaten cold, *soba* about half the time, and *udon* rarely. The Koreans have far more varieties of delicious cold noodles – perhaps because they are heated sufficiently by chili peppers – and sometimes put ice cubes in with them!

It is much easier to eat any type of noodles in the East Asian style, using chopsticks and slurping from a raised bowl, than in our slower and, when you think about it, *amusing* method of spooling it on a fork twirling in a spoon! After having experienced the *ease* of eating it the Japanese way, I sometimes feel we should either eat our spaghetti "their" way, or cut it up, as the Portuguese of Frois's day did and have done with it!

6-23   We eat [vermicelli/pasta] with sugar, egg and cinnamon.
     Nós a comemos com asuqre e ovos e canela;

They eat it with mustard and chili pepper.
Elles a comem com mostarda e pimenta.

The pasta we are familiar with was not yet popular. I knew Latinos, with their rice pudding and bread pudding, had teeth so sweet that all grains often turned into desert, but *noodles?* This "we" was a new one to me. Matsuda and Jorissen back it up with a sentence from De Nola's famous *Book of the Glutton* (*Libro de Guisanos*: 1529):

> the pasta, after being rinsed in water is boiled (simmered?) in chicken or meat (beef? pork? lamb?) and seasoned with sugar and goat or lamb milk. After it is finished, it is served with sugar and cinnamon are sprinkled on. [1] (*the (?)'s are mine*)

The Japanese often include some sweet sake in their sauce for *somen* (thin noodles) and, rarely, mandarin orange slices, too – there is a sweet style of eating them – so the contrast was probably not *that* black and white (or, did they learn it from the Portuguese?). While Japanese do use mustard with some Chinese dishes (egg-rolls, like us), I have never encountered it with noodles in Japan. I wonder if Frois's "mustard" is not *wasabi,* or, horse radish (see note to 40, below), which is found in some sauces [2] (especially with cold buckwheat noodles).

1. *Translating via Japanese*. I wonder about whether the pasta (whatever type it was) was really washed *before* boiling, etc. but not having the original here to check .

2. *Sauces*. The liquid substance which noodles are eaten out of (and often not all is drunken afterward) or *dipped into* seems too thin and clear to be a "sauce". Sometimes it is flavored with bonito flakes in addition to soy-sauce and sweet sake. In that case, I almost feel like calling it "broth." I wonder what Julia C. would have called it.

6-24   Europeans love chicken, quail, pie and blancmange;
           Os de Europa folgão com galinhas, perdizes, pasteis, e manjar branco;

> The Japanese, wild-dog,[1] crane, monkey, cat and raw seaweed.
> *Os Japãos com adibes, grous, bojios, gatos e limos e limos da praya cruz.*

Matsuda and Jorissen, who translate *blancmange* as "creamy white jelly" note that De Nola called it "the king of dishes." *Manjar blanca* [2] was created by boiling a fat and succulent [*gorda y tallosa*] chicken, rice flour, rose-water, sugar, goat's milk, or white almond and saffron, until the chicken looks like melted white cheese, then sprinkling pretty fine sugar upon it (J/F(M&J):T). They also note that a 1485 German cookbook does not mention beef. It was not as popular as pork and poultry. I would guess that in Frois's own Lisbon, fish was more common than pork, too. But, let's see the strange potpourri of Japanese items one at a time:

Dog. I assumed it was eaten in the dog-days when a dish today called "*sutamina*" (food for increasing one's stamina) – usually liver and leek, or fatty eel on rice – thought necessary for men doing fighting, heavy labor outdoors or in bed and people of either sex suffering from *natsuyase,* or "summer-thinning," [3] because that is what dog is deemed good for in Korea, where, I confess to once eating it by accident. But, Okada quotes contemporary writing about dog having been considered a good *shimojimo-no* gift (one given to one's inferiors) for samurai or town-folk in the *Winter*.[4] This suggests *kusurigui* (mostly men gathering outside to eat for warmth and health in early winter: see 6-41) instead.

Crane was a banquette food for nobility. Since the bird was a symbol of longevity, it was an auspicious food. Since Frois was lucky enough to know and eat with the rulers of Japan, he was familiar with this extraordinary food. He never had such an opportunity in Europe, or he might have known that the nobility *there* ate not only cranes, but *flamingo* and *peacocks*. When the daughter of Ferdinand and Isabella of Spain married, all the tables got a bevy of "roasted peacocks with their entire tails and the heads and necks with all the feathers intact, which looked beautiful because there were so many of them." [5] There was a pair of roasted whole steers, with gilded horns and hooves, pulling a golden cart . . . .(chronicle of Joao II in M:DLP).

Monkey.[6] Japan had and still has a few monkey temples – havens for these macaques, something like what is done on a larger scale in India and the Japanese have never done the cruel things done to monkeys in parts of South East Asia (where, the brains are eaten out of live ones!). But, judging from what I saw on the TV news, a large population can sure cause trouble: not only do they raid crops, but make love to bitches and kidnap puppies! Japanese farmers doubtless welcomed their hunting. Okada quotes a document about the items available at a Hunters' Market one station beyond Yotsuya (the edge of Edo) which includes monkey. Today, the very idea of eating monkey would horrify Japanese.

Cat is probably a mistake. Okada believes Frois mistook *tanuki* (racoon dog), weasel or something else for cat. However, considering the fact that cat skin was used for making *shamisen,* and it is unlikely the rest of the cat went to waste, I would bet that *some* cats were eaten by *someone.* [7] The irony here is that, if cat was eaten *anywhere,* it was in Europe! According to Matsuda and Jorissen, De Nola's famous book included a recipe for *roasted cat.* "After removing the hair (singed?), the cat (Pyrenees wild cats are best) is wrapped in hempen cloth and buried in the ground overnight, then (?) garlic and oil is rubbed in, and the cat roasted, after which it is carried (whole?) to the table like rabbit or veal." The author also advised that "the brain not be eaten, lest the diner become crazy in the head." (J/F(M&J):T) This is no obscure joke. The cookbook by the chef of Rey Hernando de Napoles was *the* best-selling book of 16th century Spain!)

Raw seaweed is still eaten today. Unlike the other items, this (finally!) is an everyday food. But one rarely hears about something called "sea-weed" (*kaiso* actually sea-*grass*) in Japan. Japanese no more eat "sea-weed" than we eat "land-weed." They eat *nori, ishinori, konbu, wakame, mozu, hijiki,* etc.. Most of these are processed or cooked, but many varieties of raw "seaweed" whose names are only known by gourmets are served on a *sashimi* platter. Frois's *limos da praya,* or "scum/slime/ ooze of the beach" suggests two of the six varieties above-mentioned, for they really are slimy. Today, *seaweed* in Portuguese is "alga" and *sea-grass* "sargaço."

This is not one of Frois's better contrasts. The selection of food is too arbitrary. Three of four Japanese foods were rarely eaten (or never eaten by most Japanese), while three of four of the European examples were everyday and nothing was included that might surprise or disgust Japanese (chicken and quail were eaten but they were mainly raised for eggs in Japan). Montanus, hyping Valignano, wrote:

> And that we account delicate, dainty or a well-seasoned Dish, that they spit out, and their Stomacks rise at: In like manner, what they highly commend, and seems to have a most delicious gust, that we as much abhor. (M:EEJ)

With Frois's examples, such a claim would fall flat. Meat ground-up and *stuffed into intestine* (sausage), stuff *squirted from cow, sheep or goat tits* (milk), left to age and harden (cheese) – now that type of thing would have disgusted the Japanese! Here, I can't help thinking of a different contrast altogether. Europe and Japan *versus* China. *We in Europe and Japan eat some things but not others; In China, they eat everything!* All visitors to China were *amazed* at the omnivorous taste of the Chinese. Pinto, who, if you recall, visited Japan, too, describes it several times:

> These people eat every kind of meat there is: lamb, mutton, goat, pork, horse, buffalo, deer, tiger, lion, dog, mule, donkey, zebra, tapir, otter, badger – indeed the flesh of every animal that you could name.

> . . . they slaughter, salt, smoke and cure as many kinds of game and meat as are to be found on earth: mountains of pork, sucking-pig, bacon, goose, duck, crane, wild turkey, emu, venison, beef, buffalo, tapir, badger, horse, tiger, dog, fox --- indeed the flesh of every animal that breeds on earth. (PB:SCSC – Refer. has prob. Maybe someone else in Boxer B:SCSC or he quoted Pinto in a note?)

Even when it comes to fish, Japan's forte, the Chinese eat a far greater variety. In THINGS CHINESE, Ball writes that "it is said that in Macao one may have a different kind of fish for breakfast every morning of the year." I am surprised Pinto neglects rats. Ball does not:

> It is a mistake to suppose that Chinese live on rats, etc. They are eaten occasionally by the very poor . . . These people, if they come across a large, fat one may cook it. Dried rats are to be seen hung up for sale in dried meat shops. The wealthy do not eat them as a rule, though there is a notion that rat's flesh will produce the growth of hair: so some, though feeling squeamish about such meat, will force themselves to eat a little in order that their hair may grow again. (B:TC)

These rats were euphoniously called urban venison – usually named for the respective city, eg. *Peking-deer.*

1. Wild-dog?   *Adibe* is probably Frois's translation of *nora* a word used for cats or dogs without owners that wandered about wild. Maybe he was reassured (rightly or wrongly) by the Japanese that only *nora* were eaten. Schütte made it *wilde hunde,* and added, in parenthesis, *Schakale*, which is what the French wrote: *chacals*. I suppose a thin Japanese dog would look a bit like a jackal.

2. Blancmange: I was very lucky *manjar branco* can be Englished in French (though it reads like a dog disease to me). Food terms can be as troublesome as clothing terms. Today, for example, the Japanese use the word *pudein* (pudding) for *flan,* which they learned to make from the Portuguese, but have no generic term for what we call "pudding," while they call Jello "zeri" (jelly) – this is how Okada described *manjar branco* to his readers, as "white jelly" and *clear* fruit-preserves, *jyammu* (jam!) and . . . Natural foods can be translated well enough, but processed food opens up a whole new bag of vocabulary.

3. Natsuyase or Summer-thinning.   The Chinese character for "thin" includes the "sickness" radical, for wasting away is, as only the *involuntarily thin* know, a real disease. In Japan, not only men, who suffer from thinness as they do in much of the world, but women, too, had to be careful of losing weight. In JAPANESE GIRLS AND WOMEN, Alice Mabel Bacon wrote

> "at thirty-five her fresh color is usually entirely gone, her eyes have begun to sink a little in their sockets, her youthful roundness and symmetry of figure have given place to an absolute leanness . . ."

4. Dog Meat Here and There The writing Okada cites includes the advice to cut/beat (*uchikorosu*) them to death on sight at the appropriate season (If I interpret right). That sounds cruel, but it has no suggestion of slow beating as I have read was even recently done in Korea to soften the meat (?!) and does not compare to what Las Casas described in Mexico: Spaniards feeding their dogs with butchered Indians!

5. Peacock Do not think the peacock was only popular in Iberia. Chambers, in the 19th century described how it once was in England:

> "Next in importance to the boar's-head as a Christmas-dish came the peacock. To prepare Argus for the table was a task entailing no little trouble. The skin was first carefully stripped off, with the plumage adhering; the bird was then roasted; when done and partially cooled, it was sewed up again in its feathers, its beak gilt, and so sent to table. Sometimes the whole body was covered with leaf-gold, and a piece of cotton, saturated with spirits, placed in its beak, and lighted before the carver commenced operations. This 'food for lovers and meat for lords' was stuffed with spices and sweet herbs, basted with yolk of egg, and served with plenty of gravy . . . . . The noble bird was not served by common hands; that privilege was reserved for the lady-guests most distinguished by birth or beauty. One of them carried it into the dining-hall to the sound of music, the rest of the ladies following in due order. The bearer of the dish set it down before the master of the house or his most honoured guest. (C:CBD)

6. Monkey And Macaque. The Japanese use one generic term *saru* for all primates. The Japanese "monkey" is a macaque. It has no tail and a slightly baboonish red face which looks most appropriate in a hot spring surrounded by snow.

7. Eating Cat. It is possible Frois assumed a missing cat was stolen for food when it was really taken for the skin. But, again, I can not imagine cat meat going to waste. 三味線に皮を差し上げた猫の肉は、どうなったでしょうか？捨てるともったいないから、塩漬け猫などなかったでしょうか？ For a horrific story of kidnapped cats in the good ole US of A, read the introduction to Steinbeck: *Log of the Sea of Cortez* (a book I got translated into Japanese).

6-25   We eat trout lightly broiled or stewed/baked/boiled; [1]
Nós comemos as trutas asadas brandamente ou cozidas;

They spit them on wood and roast them until they are burnt.
Elles as espetão em paos e poem a asar até ficarem torradas.

In the old country hotel where I spent my first few months in Japan, the smoke always gave away breakfast and I can remember my father explaining "they never *cook* fish, they always *burn* it! As most of the blackened part was on the skin-side of the slices, and the heavily salted skin might be discarded anyway, this was not so crazy as it might seem. A sympathetic view would be that Japanese have learned how to barbecue on a plain gas range (Honest to goodness, they do it on the stove!). From reading Frois, we can see they had centuries of practice at it, and had only to adapt themselves to gas. (I have never used or seen an electric range in Japan, and I hope I never will.) With the traditional fire, the end of the spit for the trout was stuck diagonally into the sand around the fire/coals so the fish, head up, leaned over the heat. This was more commonly done for the smaller *ayu,* or sweetfish, than trout, but Frois probably did not want to introduce a new fish to his imagined audience.

This contrast is weak, for broiling and roasting are hardly contrary even if one is done lightly and the other – at least on the outside – well-done. Here is a better contrast

> *We drop lobsters alive into boiling water but don't eat them until they are good and dead;*
> *They cut up fish alive and eat them while they still quiver with life.*

It is pretty shocking to see a fish with its meat diced up and sitting on it – like the yellow of a devilled egg returned to the white – with its tail still flickering with life. Apparently (I have not seen it), the slices were sometimes left tenuously in place and a drop of vinegar applied to the fish's eyes to induce a convulsion and pull the slices apart. It is puzzling to find such a "cruel and disgusting spectacle" (de Hubner, cited in L:IOJ) in Buddhist Japan, where the traditional poets went on and on about the sinful occupation of the cormorant-fisherman! (In defense of the Japanese, let me say that fish are not very sensitive animals. Once, I caught a large mackerel, hammered it on the head, cut off fillets on both sides flush to the backbone and tossed the skeletal remnant into the water, where it immediately revived and swam off!) But I do not know if Japanese ate sashimi like this in 1585.

1. *Stewed/Baked/Boiled.* The Portuguese word can mean any of these. Only someone familiar with both English cooking terms and how trout was cooked at this date could choose the right word.

6-26   With us, wine is chilled.
Antre nós se esfria o vinho;

In Japan, it is heated for drinking practically all year round.
Em Japão, pera se beber, quasi todo ano se aqenta.

Imagine coming home for *a hot one* rather than a cool one! In the absence of ice, it is easier to heat something than to cool it. But ice was as available in Japan as in Europe. Issa even mentions an ice-seller shivering at the first sign of fall – when the demand for his product would drop. *Sake* lovers explain how the heat brings out this or that quality of the *sake,* but I believe the wariness Japanese had, and still have for all cold drinks was probably the main incentive here. To me, nothing tastes more refreshing than good cold *sake* (the one with a resinous scent called masuzake) in a pine or cedar cup with a pinch of salt on the corner. *Corner?* Another *Faux Frois:*

> *Our cups always have circular rims;*
> *Some of theirs are completely square.*

As far as I know, drinking from square cups is a far rarer phenomenon than warm drinks. I am not certain whether these cups evolved from high-sided square trays for *sake* cups sometimes used at banquettes in Frois's day, or from square *measures* adopted for cups; but suspect that one reason they are used on celebratory occasions today is because their name, *masu,* happens to be a homophone for "increase!"   But, to return to the subject of Frois's contrast, twenty years after the TRATADO, Rodrigues shows us how difficult it is to generalize on temperature. The "true and ancient custom," he writes, was for warm wine to be

> drunk from the ninth day of the ninth moon until the third day of the third moon, except for the first wine which is brought out on New Year visits, . . . For the rest of the year cold wine should be drunk, although nowadays this is neither usual nor definite because everybody now drinks warm wine all the year round." (R(C):TIJ)

He also did not neglect to mention that the Chinese also drank "warm wine throughout the year." He did not, however, mention that in mid-16th century France, the physician to King Francis I recommended warm wine for the health or that the custom of drinking wine warmed by the fireplace or diluted with warm water was popular among all classes in all seasons. Stranger yet, wine was warmed by dropping hot pieces of toast, white hot pieces of iron, gold or, in the case of the poor, burning coals into it! (Matsuda and Jorissen (J/F(M&J):T), citing Margolin and Sauzet: *Pratiques et Discours alimentaires a la Renaissance*) But the medical theories changed with the century, and shortly later, another doctor was advising young people to drink *chilled* wine while sitting in fountains. (Ibid) Be that as it may, Frois had the big picture right.

6-27   Our wine is of grapes. *Ho nosso vinho hé de uvas;*

Theirs is all of rice. *O seu hé todo de arroz.*

The rice wine is occasionally, however, flavored with fruit, and turned into *umeshu,* the plum wine (dictionaries often translate it as a "brandy") mentioned in 13, above, or persimmon wine, which is made by some Zen temples, etc.. I would add another contrast:

Our wine, even the red, is clear;
Theirs comes in two types, clear and cloudy.

The latter is called *nigorishu* or "murky *sake.*" It is usually translated as "raw sake," but it does not taste as raw or sour as Korean *makali* or Mexican *pulque,* both of which I love. Once, I suspect, it was the most common type of *sake,* but it is rarely drunken today. Japanese, like most people, tend to go for clear alcohol if given a choice. The last time I went to Korea, beer was beating the pants off *makali* and my Korean friends thought me terribly old-fashioned to prefer *makali.* I suspect the same thing would happen in Mexico.

6-28   We drink with one hand. *Nós bebemos com huma mão;*

They always drink with two. *Elles sempre bebem com duas.*

Men, that is (see 2-64). Although Japanese *sake* cups were bigger than Chinese ones, they were still usually smaller than ours. There was no physical reason for using two hands. To receive something with both hands shows it is not taken lightly and to continue to cup it while drinking, I think, was an unconscious token of sincerity (see 1-34).   But, I cannot imagine Japanese "always" drank with two hands. I wonder if men used two hands to drink in the presence of women or inferiors alone (I could be wrong, here), or when by himself, unless it were in front of a deceased soul, showing respect to the full moon, or before committing ritual suicide. Frois may be describing the etiquette of men with their equals and superiors or a tea ceremony where all were equal before the tea.

Today, two-handed drinking is as polite as it is rare. The most obvious type of two-handed drinking today – or at least, alive in literature read today – is the drinking of water from cool mountain springs, by scooping it up with two hands, which is called *tamusubi,* or "hand-joining." This word appears in countless haiku for it makes what might be the common act of a hot traveler seem like something reverential. In those two hands full of pure water, we feel the enchantment of the mountain and its spiritual fountain of youth, before the days of the cable-car and asphalt tops.

Frois contrast also concerns only the receiving end. He probably could have complemented it with a contrast on *pouring* wine:

> ..
> *We pour wine with our arm in a natural manner;*
> *They pour theirs with both arms held straight out and rigid.*

This idea of propriety through stiffness – straight arms rather than bent ones – is still understood in Japan, but adhered to less dramatically than in Korea, where the straight right arm was often braced by a straight left arm with the hand clasping the wrist of the right arm as recent as the 1980 (when I was there).

6-29   We drink seated on chairs. *Nós quando bebemos, estamos asentados em cadeiras;*

They, setting on their knees. *Elles postos de jiolhos.*

Again, this is *formal* drinking where men sit "back on their feet with their knees pointing forward." (Rodrigues) Men did not always drink like that – they also sat cross-legged – and today seldom do. The Jesuits tried very hard to master Japanese customs, and, with friends in high places, this included their etiquette. Luckily, Frois only touches upon a few points, for the intricate details described by Rodrigues at length could only hold the interest of someone with a far more Victorian mind than mine.

6-30   We drink from cups of silver, glass or porcelain.
Antre nós se bebe por copos de prata ou vidro ou porcelina;

The Japanese from *sakazuki* of wood or clay *kawarake* [unglazed earthenware].
Os Japões por sacanzuqi de pao, ou cavaraque de barro.

A *sakazuki* is a *sake* cup. It is the shape of a martini glass – but, sometimes wider than deep, i.e., veritable bird-baths – with a tiny foot rather than a long stem – unstable, but good for viewing the reflection of the moon – but generally much smaller, though sumo tournament champions down their sake from cups as large as a garbage can lid. Rodrigues mentions cups made of "gold, silver, unicorn, or rhinoceros horn, red sandalwood," "the very large red and beautiful beaks of certain birds found in China, very fine red scented wood with delicate work on the outside, while the inside where the wine is poured is overlaid with silver . . . . and finally there are others of porcelain and they are the meanest of them all." (R(C):TIJ) In his paragraph-long descriptions of "five kinds of cups which they use when they entertain guests with wine [sake]," one is a "lacquered cup, gilded or plain," two "simple earthenware," one "completely gilded or silvered, or half-gilded or silvered, both inside and out" and one "gilded and silvered earthenware." And even more remarkable, the last types of cup mentioned were placed on a three-legged cedar "salver" or tray shaped in "imitation of a jagged seashore with its entrances and exits like the bays and capes of a shore, . . . painted entirely blue, or the colour of the sea, and decorated with various patterns of flowers or small trees, especially the pine which grows along the coast . . ." (Ibid). Up to five cups might be placed here and there on the colorful landscape! Considering this, we might think Frois's contrast of "our" luxurious items with apparently crude materials on the Japanese side disingenuous. *But, actually, it is a very good contrast once we know what Frois is driving at or should be driving at.* To understand that, we need to know the occasions when the type of cups Frois mentions were used and how they were used. The wooden and unglazed cups were *always new*[1] and *only used once* and that made them appropriate for the New Years and, perhaps because of their primal appearance, other "ancient ceremonies." Some reports say that the Emperor used such cups because everything he used was used only once, then destroyed so no one else can use them. There is much wondrous lore concerning the Emperor but, unfortunately, nothing in Frois' contrasts gives me an excuse to really go after the fantastic hearsay about the *mikado*. I can and should, however, confirm the value of *the unpainted* and the *unglazed*. To wit, the December 8, 1857 testimony of the first American Ambassador to Japan, Townsend Harris.

> I omitted to state yesterday that the dinner sent to me was placed on some forty to fifty trays made of unpainted wood. These trays were eleven inches high for me and about five inches for Mr. Heusken [his Dutch-American translator]. . . . I was told that the trays and other utensils, after having been used by me, could never be used by another person, and therefore they were made of unvarnished wood, this being the custom of Japan when presenting food to persons of exhalted rank, etc., etc. (H:JJ)

The poor man, who had long suffered from the same cruel complaint as that which has afflicted your writer for most of his life – namely, a strong appetite, but weak digestion – was particularly sick that day, and, torture of tortures, "unable to eat a morsel" from those forty or fifty trays! Perhaps I should add for the consolation of Mr. Harris's soul that those who are most commonly served in unglazed pottery don't really eat it either. I refer to offerings to the ancestors and gods left on the "god-shelves" of the household shrine.

Since "we" use our most valuable utensils (a value that usually is monetary as well as sentimental, deriving from the history of the item) on important occasions or to show appreciation for our guests, even Rodrigues, for all his evident appreciation of the naturalism of the tea ceremony and its apparently simple, but incredibly expensive *dogu,* was not impressed with these throw-away items. First, he complained, the unglazed pottery was literally worthless: "there is a great number of them on sale . . . and they are so cheap that they are hardly worth anything at all." And, second, "this sort of new earthenware cup is dry and therefore sticks a good deal to the lips, people who are not careful sometimes find themselves in trouble because they cannot easily unstick them; before they drink, they first of all must moisten their lips . . ." (A good Japanese drinker barely touches a cup to his lips. He moves his whole head back lightly as the cup meets his lips rather than turning the cup edge in his mouth as we do. Someone who drank with the proper alacrity might not need to wet his lips. Evidently, for all his smarts, Rodrigues was not a good drinker in the Japanese style.). Here is his last word on the glazeless *kawarake*:

> Whence can be seen the power of ancient customs and notions of countries that could well use precious and convenient things which do not have such drawbacks, but instead leave them aside in favour of those of little worth, whose use offers such difficulties." (R(C):TIJ)

Japanese simply did not let globs of metal and oodles of jewels monopolize value as was the case in the West (extending to India at least). They rarely adorned themselves with objects made of metal, for they did not think of shiny things as the ultimate of fashion. They *did* use a lot of gold-leaf (though not a lot by Balinese standards!). Not long after he met Valignano and told Frois all about his retirement plans, Hideyoshi returned from a hunting expedition with "two thousand five hundred large birds, each one dangling from its own gilt bamboo pole" (J/F:HISTORIA) and the 1845 Englished testimony of the Dutch claimed that "at a Japanese banquette the dishes are tricked out with gold leaf, and upon very grand occasions the bills, legs, and claws of the birds served up are gilt."(H:MCJ) They may also have served *sake* with flecks of gold-leaf in it, for I have had a bottle of such *sake* and the label claimed it was something traditional.

An unglazed earthenware cup of chilled *sake,* with some flecks of gold-leaf floating on it – to me, such an aesthetic experience beats drinking, say brandy from a jeweled cup made of precious metal!

1. *Newness and Unglazed Pottery* The Japanese word for unglazed pottery, *kawarake,* is fresh even in metaphor as it was a common idiom for a young woman's still hairless *mons veneris.* As far as I know, our "terracotta" never picked up such nuances.

~~~~~~

6-31   With us, no one drinks more than he himself wants to, without being persuaded by others. *Antre nós não bebe cada hum mais que aquilo que qer, sem persuasão dos outros;*

> Japanese are so demanding they make some throw up and others drunk.
> *Em Japão se importunão tanto, que a huns fazem arrevesar e a outros embebedar-se.*

Forced drinking in Japan was the child of pushiness on one side and pride on the other. Rodrigues devotes a whole page to it. Basically, men took pride in their drinking and would not refuse when challenged to a drinking match, "because they regard it just as if they were fighting a battle or duel." Moreover, there were professional instigators. Rodrigues writes of "woman dancers and singers and other types of depraved people, who, when they drink, challenge whomsoever they wish to partake as well; they take the cup from which they have drunk and give it to a person, and pride prevents his refusing to accept it and drink from it." Sometimes this escalates until some "challenge others to drink wine from hand-basins and other large vessels." Finally, Rodrigues blamed the "thousands of kinds" of tasty appetizers concocted "as incentives" for drink. He found it

> astonishing to note the various devices and means, which the devil has taught them to encourage much wine drinking, and those who drink next to nothing are often obliged to partake. There are cases in which such people cannot avoid doing so, nor will any excuse be accepted, so they are obliged to drink even when it is injurious to their health. (R(C):TIJ)

So Frois was right about Japan. But Europe may have been a bit less angelic than he paints it. Matsuda and Jorissen quote a February 12, 1528 letter of Erasmus of Rotterdam criticizing a banquette where he was forced to drink and Thomas Coryat (*Coryat's Crudities*, vol.I,II:1611) on how a wine-glass full of wine would be given to a man in Germany, who would be, then considered impolite unless he drank it down to the others health and handed it back (Even without reading such evidence, can anyone imagine Occidental drunks not being pushy?). Yet, I think it is true that despite the generally mild nature of the Japanese, even today there is a stronger tendency for drinking men to *push drinks* on others in Japan than in the USA at least. This is doubly bad for Japanese because almost half the population (versus less than 10% of Caucasians) has some degree of alcohol intolerance, caused by lack of a certain enzyme. A late-19th century traveler, who evidently did not know that, mistook it for a peculiar property of *sake,* declaring its "first effect is to loosen the tongue and limber the joints; its second to turn the whole body flaming red" (S:JDJ) Even that is not quite accurate, for many if not most Japanese turn beet red *after only a sip*, and, of these, many experience heat, headaches, sleepiness and other uncomfortable symptoms. Not surprisingly, the Japanese themselves have long been aware that pushing drinks on people is bad. Here is the Buddhist priest Kenko about 250 years before TRATADO:

> There are many things in the world I cannot understand. I cannot imagine why people find it so enjoyable to push liquor on you the first thing, on every occasion, and force you to drink it . . . the victim's head aches even the following day, and he lies abed groaning, unable to eat, unable to recall what happened the night before, as if everything had taken place in a previous incarnation. He neglects important duties, both public and private, and the result is disaster. It is cruel and a breach of courtesy to oblige a man to undergo such experiences . . . If it were reported that such a custom, unknown among ourselves, existed in some foreign country, we should certainly find it peculiar and even incredible . . . Buddha taught that a man who takes liquor and forces another to drink will be reborn a thousand times without hands. . . (K(K):EI)

Reading of the many social uses of drinking in Japan – the various types of exchanges of multiple cups, sequential drinking from single cups (something the Chinese never do, according to Rodrigues), etc. – we can see that half of the forced drinking problem was systematic rather than individual.

First, there was a tradition of drinking as manly. This can be seen in the Easterns on television where the majority of the swordsman heroes are never without their *sake,* but still manage to cut cleanly through their stupor as soon as the bad guys attack. It can also be seen in the early-20th century drinking song (based on a much older traditional song), *Kurodabushi,* about a samurai who bet everything on his being able to gulp down an enormous basin of *sake.* This popular song that every man and many woman could sing up to the last two decades of the twentieth century – the solemn yet complex vocals are beyond the ken of a young generation raised on pop music [1] – makes *sake* drinking *the* mark of a real Japanese warrior. So, one man can turn to another who wishes not to drink and chide him: "And you call yourself a Japanese!" (*soredemo nipponjin kai*)

And, second, there were the customary *ways of drinking,* similar to that Coryat described for Germany. I can imagine how it *was* in Frois and Rodrigues's Japan because I taught for a while in Korea and saw such a system in action. A dozen or so students of mine (middle-level government employees from top universities) each brought me their glasses of beer and we exchanged drinks one at a time. That is to say, I drank a dozen times more than they did. That is why, explained one, a certain member of the Korean faculty (whom I thought would make a better dean for the graduate school) preferred to allow another, less qualified man to have the post. He simply could not drink enough to fulfill his duties as an administrator! Some years after this, I read a filler article to the effect that the Korean government was trying to make it easier on administrators (and politicians who are in the same situation) by decreeing that glasses be only half-filled for toasts. Japan reformed itself about a hundred years earlier. Morse wrote that according to a Japanese friend who was "informed by the Chief of the Sanitary Bureau," saké was once offered to guests who then *had to* drink it, but now (1878-9) might refuse it without giving offense. Tea served as a substitute. Also,

> at that time one cup was used in a convivial company and the cup had to be emptied when passing. Now each has his own saké cup and can regulate his desires without constraint. (M:JDD)

While the open drunkenness and lavish banquettes, i.e. parties, found in Japan was attributed by the Jesuits to the pagan propensity to favor flesh over soul, Occidental observers from Xavier agreed the Japanese were, *generally*, moderate eaters and drinkers. Valignano's last word on the subject is that even the wealthy and the grandees of Japan are more parsimonious eaters than Europeans. The Japanese are "content with few things, which is something that puts to shame the Christians of Europe, who, parting from the teachings of *Jesucristo,* go looking for so many inventions=discoveries of food to satisfy the palate (that more seem to live to eat than to eat to live), and justly, in punishment for over-eating, suffer from many and grave illnesses, and also shorten their lives."(LIBRO (1601) in V(A):S&A (n.101))

1. *Singing the Kuroda Bushi.* While not all Japanese can still sing this old song, some Usanians can. If Henry Clay W. ever reads this, he should ask his mother E. to sing it, for she sings it like a samurai.

~~~~~~

6-32   To us, it would be nauseating to drink from a bowl that held chicken, fish or meat.
Antre nós beber pola tijela de caldo, de pexe ou carne se teria por nojo;

> In Japan, it is common to empty one's *shiru-goki* [soup-bowl] and drink from it.
> *Em Japão hé muito uzado despejar o xiru goqi e beber por elle.*

I have known Japanese to drink their tea this way, but not *sake*. Okada writes it must have been common in Frois's day and documents it with two episodes from a journal whose name Englishes as "drunk-sleep-smile/laugh," one of which tells of drinking 4 servings of desert (?) sake, each from a larger bowl, the last being the rice bowl! (And *sake,* I should point out is always poured to the brim. Another way to put this would be:

> *We flavor our food with a little wine;*
> *They flavor their wine with a little food.*

For some reason, *sake* tastes alright like this, while wine does not. I have even drunk *sake* in the shell of a crab after eating out the inside. The after-taste of crab eggs is said to enhance the *sake!* There is another way sake was supposedly drunken by some men, but it will be left to a footnote.[1]

1. *Adult Sake.* I have not yet tried *wakame*-[a seaweed: *undaria pinnatifida*]*zake,* where a woman is the cup. Theoretically, the *sake* is supposed to fill and be warmed by the vagina, but as this is easier said than done, the usual method – supposedly done by cabaret-girls for extra pocket-money – is to cross and raise the legs slightly while leaning back so the *sake* is cupped in a sort of pubic nest. The under-hairs (to use a Japanglishism) covered by its *sake* are said to resemble the sea grass swaying slowly in its natural habitat (女陰万考 pg 211). *Wakame* is a homophone for "young woman." A traditional *kyôgen* comedy features a young man who goes out to buy *wakame* as an appetizer and is tricked into buying a young woman instead, but I had better cut that story short! Let us just say that where "we" would use whipped-cream or champagne; they use *sake.*

~~~~~~

6-33   Our everyday drinking water has to be cold and clear.
Antre nós a agoa que se bebe antre-dia á-de ser fria e clara;

> For the Japanese, it has to be hot and have tea powder frothed up with a bamboo whisk [in it]. *A dos Japões à de serqente e à-de levar pós de chá batidos com huma escova de cana.*

While cocoa, an invention of nuns in Mexico, would become very popular in another decade or two, Iberia was and would remain the cold drink capitol of Europe. According to Defourneaux, there was a great demand for orange juice, strawberry water and orgeat (almond and orange), things generally tastiest cool. "Great quantities of snow were taken during the winter from the Sierra, which is some 40 kilometers from Madrid, and deposited in 'snow-pits' . . . [and] sold in turn for cold drinks and sherbets." (D:DLS) Presumably, this predilection for cold extended to water and, the religious who wanted to keep simple would drink a lot of it rather than the more expensive juices. In Japan, tea was *de rigor* at temples.

Here, Frois describes only one way of making tea – to quote Bishop, with "the appearance and consistency of pea-soup" – with the expensive bright green powder now identified with the tea ceremony, which was once drunken with meals by the well-to-do. Usually, tea was made from leaves lightly steeped. Frois might better have written a more generally valid contrast about water, such as "it has to be hot and served either as tea, medicine, flavored by barley or left over from cooking noodles." (my experience) Perhaps some of these flavors were too weak to be tasted at times. Valignano claims to have experienced water, as he called it, "so hot it can not pass [the throat] but in gulps" that was "drunken after eaten." (V(A):S&A).   Perhaps he was, in fact, thinking primarily of the tea-ceremony (cha-no-yu), for the same items appear together in Rodrigues's explanation, which may well have been influenced by Frois's missing *Summary*.

> In all the kingdom water is plentiful and there are excellent springs; although they do not usually drink it cold, the Japanese appreciate this good water for use in their *cha-no-yu* [tea-ceremony]. . . Neither in the summer nor in the winter do the Japanese, especially in the regions west of Gokinai, usually drink cold water; but in the regions of Kanto and eastwards they drink cold water even in the winter, although they also make use of hot water. (R(C):TIJ)

Frois did not know the Kanto (Tokyo area). But even in Edo where cold water was sold in the streets in the summer, cold water was viewed with trepidation by many. For all the nakedness of the young and healthy workers, Japanese have always thought it important to keep the belly warm. Most Japanese of middle age and up have, until recent years worn belly-wraps around the clock. Many still do. If ordinary cool water was believed bad for the digestion – and still is: I was often advised to avoid drinking it by people concerned for my excessive thinness – colder spring water, such as the ice-water-drinking Usanians think nothing of, was considered quite capable of bringing on a stroke! I have even found it tied to the poetic phrase *inochi ni naru,* meaning that indulging in something will cost your life! Perhaps more plebian concerns of dysentery might also have played a role in this, for even if Japan had good water, the populated area was very crowded. Whatever the reason may be, even something as hard to digest as watermelon was sold – if we are to credit *senryu* with realism – with the following advertisement:

a cold slice

"water, sir,
is poison!" says the vender
of watermelons

mizu-wa doku de gozarimasu to suika-uri
(from Mitani Kazuma: SAISHIKI EDO MONOURI ZUE)

"Watermelon" in Japanese is written "west-melon," but the pronunciation of the "West" is *sui,* or "water." I assume the author of the *senryu* imagined the melon vender competing against an ice-water vender because that enhances the humor. The fact that this *senryu* describes Edo shows that even in a city where water was drunken, that water was not beyond suspicion. In the "Tokio" chapter of her book Eliza Skidmore finds some new water paradoxes in her 1891 book:

> The Japanese seldom drink water, although they splash, dabble, or soak in it half the time; yet men who are working in moats or lotus ponds, grubbing out the old roots or stalks, and dripping wet to their waists and shoulders will quit work on rainy days. (S:JDJ)

..

Even today, water fountains are relatively scarce in Japan and not used much, partly because they are all too often lacking water pressure or tepid and taste awful. In Korea, however, I found even *less* drinking of fresh water than in Japan. So much so, in fact, that water in which roasted barley has been steeped is often simply called "water" (*m/bul*: the Koreans have a consonant pronounced midway between "m" and "b.") with the "tea" (ja) left off! In Korea, 1897, this hydrophobia even extended to ponies!

They are never allowed to lie down, and very rarely to drink water, and then only when freely salted. Their nostrils are all slit in an attempt to improve upon nature and give them better wind. They are fed three times a day on brown slush as hot as they can drink it, composed of beans, chopped millet stalks, rice husks, and bran, with the water in which they have been boiled. (Isabella Bird: KOREA AND HER NEIGHBORS)

West Japan, where cold water was not drunken, is closer to Korea. But, until the other day, when I happened to read *Drink: A Social History Of America*, I had no idea how close 17th and 18th century English and Americans were to the Japanese and Koreans in this respect. If the past is a foreign country, these snippets from Andrew Barr's book are the proof:

Water is not wholesome solely by itself for an Englishman . . . If any man do use to drink water with wine, let it be purely strained, and then boil it . . . let him put it in his wine – 16th century English dietitian.

Would you believe it, though water is to be had in abundance in London, and of fairly good quality, absolutely none is drunk? In this country . . . beer . . . is what everybody drinks when thirsty. – 18th century Swiss visitor.

In those days God did cause his people . . . to be contented with mean things. It was not accounted a strange thing in those days to drink water. – 17th century New England emigrant.

The host, next to whom I sat, whispered in my ear, asking with a smile if I could not drink something else, because the unexpected request for water had upset the entire household and they did not know what they were about. – 18th century Italian visitor to Virginia (Invited by Jefferson to try his hand at growing vines.)

My companion at the press drank every day a pint before breakfast, a pint at breakfast, . . . in all six pints a day of strong beer. – The eccentric man called a "water American", Ben Franklin.

There is unquestionably too much spirituous liquors drank in the newly settled parts of America, but a very good reason can be assigned for it. The labor of clearing the land is rugged and severe, and the summer heats are sometimes so great that it would be dangerous to drink cold water. – early-19th century English visitor.

During hot weather thirst is so widespread . . . in all American cities that several persons die each year from drinking cold pump water when hot. Printed handbills are distributed each summer to warn people of these dangers. Strangers especially are warned either to drink grog or to add a little wine or some other spirituous liquor to their water. – a Frenchman in Philadelphia, late 18th century. (all from B:D)

Barr explains that it was probably not really shock from the difference in temperature – although some people must have gotten the cramps from gulping down cold water to have made coldness the culprit – but pathogenic bacteria. Moreover, unless the water was at least 50% spirits, it would not have been decontaminated, with one exception: *wine*. The skins of grapes are rich in bacteria-killing compounds. Unlike the Persian and Roman armies who used this knowledge to their advantage, America had little wine. Their reliance on hard liquor (beer, which did not keep well was not an option for most localities) inevitably led to a reaction. "At the end of the 1820's, the first temperance societies were established, and the number of people who died from drinking cold water in hot weather increased." (B: DSH) Yet, in a remarkable reversal, The United States of America soon became the ice-water mecca of the world!

Since Japan has the same muggy summers as the East coast of America, it is not surprising the population shared a particularly strong aversion to cold water. (I assume other reasons – unhygienic waste treatment – was the main problem in England where the average per capita beer consumption was over a quart and a half in the 17th century! – in 1684, anyway, (T:RDM).) When it came to mountain springs, however, most Japanese were more than willing to risk shock, and a naive haiku in one of the earliest anthologies, the *chirizuka haikaishû,* or "trash-mound haikai" (17th century) reads: "what i want is mountain spring-water with broken ice. (*hoshii-wa kohri-o kudaku shimizu kana).* It was in the middle of a series of poems bewailing the summer heat.

I hate to qualify what Barr wrote about liquor. But a Cambridge professor of anthropology (whose name I failed to catch when I saw a television program I also failed to record), credits the anti-bacterial properties of tea (together with boiling the water I would think) for the same.   Without tea breaks, he claims, the industrial revolution would have collapsed because the factory cities were so crowded that water pollution would have sickened and killed the workers that did not flee back to the country. It is also why Japan could have such populous cities he explained, strangely forgetting to give at least a bow in the direction of China.

6-34   Among us, the burnt rice at the bottom of the pot is thrown out or given to the dogs.
Antre nós o arros qeimado do fundo do tacho se deita for a ou se dá aos cães;

> In Japan it becomes the after-dinner fruit or is thrown into the hot water drunk at the end. *Em Japão hé fruta de sobremeza ou se deita na agoa q[ente] que se bebe no cabo.*

Okada explains that the Japanese practice is due to the respect paid by Japanese to every last grain of rice. In this era, where each lord's holdings were described in terms of potential rice harvest (not what actually belongs to said lord, but the total for his fiefdom) rather than acreage, rice had indeed become more than a food. Still, it wasn't yet turned into a sacred=imperial=japanese object, for the neo-nationalism a hundred or two-hundred years ahead (the fundamentalists selected myths to show that the only rice worthy of the name was the *nipponica* deriving from the body of their Sun Goddess Amateresa-omikami).   Nor did even those myths manage to control the meal – people use myths as they like, rather than the vice-versa. I also question the assumption (that comes from what Okada wrote, not Frois) that all the rice was always eaten. Many Japanese may well have felt it better to leave rice for servants or pets or fertilizer or other reasons such as this one noted by Isabella L Bird in 1880:

> For children to eat the charred rice which sometimes remains at the bottom of the rice-pot is to ensure their marriage to persons scarred with small-pox. (B:UTJ)

It was also a matter of taste and mouthfeel. I know many Japanese who *like* the crispy "burnt" part (which is to rice what toast is to bread and "burnt" or not can be an attractive gold color, rather than black). It sometimes comes out cracker-like, tasty even for this Westerner. Perhaps, too, Japanese who were not from the part (North) with the superstition recorded by Bird, were allowed to scrap off and eat it as children, as we lick mixing bowls, and this psychologically endears it to them as adults. So, as ridiculous as it sounds to Occidentals who assume meals must end on a sweet note, it would make a good "after-dinner fruit," which doubtless means *dessert.*

Since roasted barley tea is drunk in Japan (although not as much as in Korea) and so are many teas mixing roasted rice kernels with tea leaves – something like Rice Krispees (a cereal from the USA) without so loud a *snap, crackle and pop* – the *koge* (burnt-rice) "thrown into the hot water" would have the flavor of a tea, yet, lacking the caffeine, be a more appropriate drink for the evening meal. At lunch, on the other hand, it was probably a good way to get a few more calories. I must confess, however that I have never seen the rice at the bottom of the pot thrown into hot water. Rather, by putting the water into the pot when it is still hot one gets a head-start on the cleaning. *And*, so as not to waste it, and because it tastes good, you drink it. Arthur Hatch in a 1623 letter quoted by Cooper:

Their ordinary drink is Water, and that is made most times hot, in the same pot where they seethe their Rice, that so it may receive some thickness and substance from the Rice. (C:TCJ)

While Japanese can still get excited about their rice – and I, too, defend rice-nationalism because paddies mean *frogs and ducks* – most of the rice at the bottom of the cooker or, worse, the bowl, no longer religiously consumed or superstitiously avoided, goes to *wan-chan* and *nyan-chan,* the dogs and cats of the house. Despite the dear price of rice in Japan, one is amazed to see more old rice than pet-food in their feeding bowls!

~~~~~~

6-35   With us, the drinking commences as soon as [the meal] starts;
Antre nós logo depois do principio se começa a beber;

> In Japan, they start bringing out the wine toward the end of the meal.
> *Os Japões, quasi no cabo da meza emtão começa a vir o vinho.*

Japanese also drank *before* eating – "a man who is fond of his cups drinks heavily before dinner, and not afterwards, as he does in England" (S:MQT:1905 – I think that custom was the same in 1585) – but Frois is only contrasting drinking *as part of a formal meal*. Avila Giron wrote "About halfway through the meal, along comes a page with hot wine in a flask, but does not pour it unless the diner holds out his cup, which, in Japan, may be *no other than the bowl which covered the rice*." (my italics – C:TCJ) This sentence has an important point we will return to. But even formal culinary events offered more than one way to drink. Here is how Kaempfer enjoyed *sake* with a "Japanese Treat" given to his party by the Imperial Commissioners toward the end of the 17th century:

> At the first commissioners the treat consisted of the following things. 1. Tea. 2. Tobacco, with the whole set of instruments for smoking. 3. Philosophical, or white syrup. 4. A piece of Steenbrassen, a very scarce fish, boil'd, in a brown sauce. 5. Another dish of fish dress'd with bean-flower and spices. 6. Cakes of Eggs roll'd together. 7. Fried fish, which were presented to us on green skewers of Bambous. 8. Lemon peels with sugar. *After every one of these dishes, they made us drink a dish of Sacki, as good as ever I tasted.*" (my italics, K(S):HOJ)

I think "dish" is as fine a way as any to describe the shape of some *sake* cups, but, here, Kaempfer (or his English translator) is humorously making the 8 *dishes* turn into 16, not bad for a "treat." It is possible the Japanese heard that foreigners drank through-out a meal and adjusted their treat accordingly, but I would not be surprised if the Japanese did this themselves, and even in Frois's 16th century. After all, the Japanese did follow the Chinese in many things, and *they* did not wait long for their rice-wine. Cruz, again:

> They also had a very tiny gilt porcelain [cup] that carried one mouthful [*bocado*] of wine, and had a waiter for it by the table. They drank so little because for each mouthful of food they had to take a mouthful of drink, and for that the cup is so tiny. (*Translation:* The Portuguese *bocado* is more like a "bite" than a "mouthful," – for the mouth is not filled with wine – but "a bite of food and a bite of wine" does not work. (C:TCC)

Frois was so busy contrasting the crude materials of the Japanese sake cup, and worse yet, the yucky manner of drinking from dirty dishes with the more elegant West, that he forgot to contrast the thimble-sized *sake* cup with the huge (by Japanese standards) glasses we use to drink from! Thanks to Cruz, we can even guess the origin of those Lilliputian cups: *an aid to moderation*. Or, I wrong Frois. For *if* Giron is correct about the tops to the rice bowls being the *only* sake cup permitted, then Japanese did not yet use the tiny cups we know. (I'm sorry to leave this hanging. Anyone?)

6-36   Among us, we do not drink out of the porcelain in which we eat our soup or rice without washing it. *Antre nós na porselana em que se comeo caldo ou arroz não se bebe por ella sem se lavar;*

>The Japanese dump out the *shiru* [soup] from the rice *goki* [bowl] and then drink hot water from it. *Os Japões, deitando xiru no goqi do arroz, bebem depois a agoa qente por elle.*

According to OED the word *porcelain*, which came from the Portuguese (and was taken from the shiny cowry shell) got to England in the 16th century, whereas China didn't until the 17th and so I use the former though it does not read very well. But to get to the subject itself, Bishop (Bird) called *hot water*, which was also drunken by the "Ainos" (Ainu) "the ancient national beverage" of Japan (B:UTJ or B:KAHN?). This contrast is the water equivalent of 6-32, where *sake* was drunk from the same. One contrast naming both liquids would have been sufficient! If 6-32 was about the etiquette of formal dinners, this one is about everyday meals, when, I might add, *sake* was rarely drunken. Unlike the French with their wine, Japanese, like most Usanians today, generally *drank to drink* – and still *drink to drink* – rather than simply drinking with their meals. I believe this was inevitable in Japan, because of the high percentage of people allergic to alcohol. In the United States, it is probably because of a lingering prejudice against alcohol and fear of addiction in a society that does not have, and so, does not (or cannot) believe in self-control.

6-37   Our quills[1] for the teeth are very short.
As nossas penas pera os dentes são muyto curtas;

>The sticks for the teeth of the Japanese at times surpass a palm [8-9"] in length. *Os paos pera os dentes dos Japões passão às vezes dum palmo.*

To us, today, this contrast might be too trivial to mention, but in the 16th century toothpicks were considered *fashionable accessories* by some of "us." A bit of googling found me a treasure of information which I will compress into a single quote-like section:
..

>*One sixteenth century antique, a tooth-pick that looked something like a fancy screwdriver used for eye-glasses except that it was silver and had a big jewel embedded in its butt-end and a finely engraved silver cover.* And it taught me: *That Sixteenth century teeth from Europe occasionally show a notable loss of enamel accompanied by scratch marks as a result of metal toothpick usage-which was popular at that time.* And, that this made "us" similar to our ancestors, for *"Grooves on the approximal [proximal?] surfaces of molars in Paleolithic persons are attributed to the sustained use of bone needle tooth picks used to remove food from between teeth. The bone needles have been found in the same cave strata as the skeletal specimens."* (C. Johnson at the Orthodontic Department at the UIC College of Dentistry) And, less importantly, that the nine-day queen of Henry VIII *Lady Jane Grey collected "a motley assortment of fish-shaped toothpicks"* and *Shakespeare's character Clown (The Winter's Tale) recognized "a great man . . . by the picking on's teeth"* or perhaps by the fact (?) the toothpick in its jeweld case might be dispalyed in the hatband (!?). The only thing I could find on the Spanish or Portuguese toothpick in particular was *a line in Cervantes (ch.44) "Poor gentleman of good family! always cockering up his honour, dining miserably and in secret, and making a hypocrite of the toothpick with which he sallies out into the street after eating nothing to oblige him to use it!"* (trans. Ormsby). Since *George Gascoigne's foolish traveller – an "Italianated character" (or fop) – "came home in 1572 with a toothpick hanging out of his mouth,,"* we can assume the habit came from the South side of Europe.[2]

Okada writes that Japanese toothpicks were generally between three and fourteen inches in length. The short ones, called "fingernail toothpicks" (*tsuma-yoji*), used today for tooth-picks in Japan, caught on in the Edo era that was soon to come. More importantly from the usage point of view, Japanese toothpicks are cut rectangular rather than round and are almost always made of bamboo. Anyone who has used both prefers theirs. But the Japanese can keep the sucking noise that so often accompanies the use of said toothpick (Young Japanese readers may resent this sentence, for this habit is largely obsolete today).

1. *Quill.* The use of a *quill* for a *pen* is evident in the Portuguese original. An indication of the "pointed" nuance of the quill (which we no longer feel) may be gained by reading the following how-to for vaccination:

The first thing to be done is to obtain some of this fluid from the vesicles of the udder, then puncture the skin slightly on the arm with a crowquill, sharpened fine like the nib of a pen or toothpick; dip it in the fluid, and insert it under the skin where you have previously made the puncture . . ." (*Dr. Coffin's Treatise on Midwifery and the Diseases of Women and Children, with Remedies.* London 1878)

2. *Googling "Tooth-pick."* Did you know that *"the first thing he [Mohammad] did when he came home was use a toothpick."*? That *"a toothpick is the object most often choked on by Americans"* ? (I would guess it is pills and that the trivia site means *items for which a doctor is called*). That there may have been *"True Cross Toothpicks"*? That the Seventeenth Chapter of the Zoroastrian sacred book(?) *Sad Dar*, that "had the reputation of being a very old work in the early part of the sixteenth century," teaches that *"when they cut a toothpick ('hilal), or a splinter which they wish to apply to the root of the teeth, it is necessary that they retain no bark. 2. For if a small quantity of bark be on it when they apply it to the teeth, and they cast it away, if a pregnant woman puts her foot upon it, the danger of that may be that the child comes to harm"*? (Trans. by E. W. West).

〜〜〜

6-38   Among us, to be drunk is offensive and to a man's discredit;
Antre nós hé grande injuria e descredito embebedar-se hum homem;

In Japan, they are proud of it and asked: "How is your Tono [master]?" reply "He's drunk." *Em Japão se prezão disso, e perguntando: "Que faz o Tono?" dizem: "Está bebado."*

There was "us" and then there was *us*. True, the Iberians may not have drunken much. Even in the more decadent mid-17th century, the Countess d' Aulnoy noted their dryness and that: "One could not enrage them [the Spaniards] more then to accuse them of being drunk" (D:DLS). But the rest of Europe cannot be so neatly described. As Matsuda and Jorissen point out, the writing of the time often singled out the French, and even more so, the Germans for being big drinkers. Still, they admit, even liberals like Erasmus and Montague, who might be expected to support their countrymen, found drunkenness ignominious if not immoral, though the latter's attitude is more complex than that might indicate. Montaigne thought drunkenness "a particularly gross and brutish vice" because men lose their rational facilities; but admits not all men forget themselves when they drink. He also describes styles of drinking:

The Germans drink almost all wines with equal pleasure. Their aim is to swallow rather than to taste. They have much the better part of the bargain. Their pleasure is much more plentiful and right at hand. ("Of drunkenness" M(F):MEM)

To drink French style, at two meals and moderately, for fear of your health, is to restrain the god's favor too much. You need more time and persistence. The ancients spent whole nights at this exercise and often added the days . . .

And shortly after Montaigne wrote, that is to say about the time Frois wrote this, the hitherto sober "English in their long wars in the Netherlands first learnt to drown themselves with immoderate drinking and by drinking other people's healths impair their own." (Camden's *History of Queen*

Elizabeth quoted in *Curiousities of Literature* v5, London 1823). The "spirited writer" Tom Nash, in *Pierce Pennilesse* (1595), wrote that this *Sin* of "superfluity in drink" that came from the *Low-Countries* was previously "held in that highest degree of hatred that might be" and

> Then if we had seen a man go wallowing in the streets, or lain sleeping under the board, we should have spet at him, and warned all our friends out of his company. (in *Curiousities*)

His "previously" describes Frois's "us." While laws were passed to try to stem the rising flood of spirit, they failed. Pepys & co. a couple centuries later drank until they spewed or dropped. In this, they might be called classic, for, as Montaigne pointed out, antiquity had a high opinion of this alleged vice, "and even among the Stoics there are some who recommend that we sometimes allow ourselves to drink our fill, and get drunk in order to relax the soul." Indeed, hemlock was only Socrates' last drink. In his later essay *"Of experience,"* Montaigne clarified his opinion: he was only concerned lest too much drink numbed and therefore reduced a man's potential sensual pleasure. Still, no one (unless it be Rabelais, indirectly) came out clearly and asked: *"Why not? Why, the hell, not!"* The Christian West insisted drunkenness was *bad.* In that sense, the spirit of Frois's contrast holds true for all of Europe.

In Japan, on the other hand, Rodrigues writes,

> all the banquets, revelries and recreations are aimed at persuading them by various means to drink too much wine until they end up drunk and many of them completely lose their senses. The Chinese and the Japanese do not consider drunkenness in banquets and revelries as something wrong.(TIJ)

And Japanese are not alone. Let me add the Koreans to this happy company.

> I should say that drunkenness is an outstanding feature in Korea. And it is not disreputable. If a man drinks rice wine til he loses his reason, no one regards him as a beast. A great dignitary even may roll on the floor drunk at the end of a meal, at which he has eaten to repletion, without losing caste, and on becoming sober receives the congratulations of inferiors on being rich enough to afford such a luxury. (Isabella Bird Bishop: KOREA AND HER NEIGHBORS, 1897)

Despite the Confucian stress on propriety (or, is drunkenness needed as an escape *because of* it?), they – the Koreans, the Japanese and in a more qualified manner, the Chinese – *still* don't think it *wrong*. And why should they? Why should it be wrong? (see 4-21, too) If it is wrong to lose our senses, then we sin every day, *by sleeping*. If the Ancients in the West were not ashamed to get drunk, why are we? Is it just a silly Christian taboo not found in the Ten Commandments? Or, is the problem a deeper one? Is alcohol bad because *we* are? Here is Eliza Skidmore on heavy drinking in Japan:

> Mukojima's carnival rivals the saturnalia of the ancients. . . . one half expects to find a flower-crowned statue of Bacchus . . . Men dance like satyrs, cup and gourd in hand, or, extending a hand, make orations to the crowd . . . But with all this intoxication, only glee and affection manifest themselves. No fighting, no rowdyism, no rough words accompany the spring saturnalia; and the laughter is so infectious, the antics and figures so comical, that even sober people seem to have tasted of the insane cup . . . the most confirmed drinker is only a little redder, a little happier, a little more loquacious than the rest. (JINRICKSHAW DAYS IN JAPAN, 1891)

Most testimony from the 16th and 17th centuries likewise find Japanese harmless drunks:

> I never saw anybody there completely drunk, because when they overindulge they lie down and sleep it off. (Alvarez 1546 in Cooper's trans. C:TCJ)

> Drunkenness is apparently unknown, for as soon as one feels himself getting out of his own control, he ceases his potations, and betakes himself to sleep (Ditto in a 19th cent trans. in C:LLFX)

They are much given to feasting and do not regard intoxication as anything disgraceful, for usually at such times they abstain from evil conduct, merely dancing or singing or playing instrumental music . . . (Organtino: 1577 in S:VMP)

They never quarrel in their debauches, but he who is first drunk retires and sleeps, until the fumes of the wine be evaporated. (Caron c 1630 10)

Being allergic to alcohol, many Japanese cannot help getting drowsy. But the sleepy and kind drunk is contradicted by others. R. de Vivero wrote that "the Japanese are mean when they drink (*viciosos en beber*), and this results in other [sic] worse harm, for they are not content with the women they have, which sometimes is more than a hundred." (*Relaciones de la Camboya y del Japon*). However, he was not in Japan for more than a few months and apparently had the misfortune to drink with some very lecherous lord (?) – a hundred consorts exceeds anything I know of, and is hardly representative of Japanese on the whole – at his worst.   Arthur Hatch, an English preacher who visited the English trading outpost of Hirado in 1620, likewise claimed that when they "drink largely" and are "moved to anger or wrath in the heate of theire Drinke, you may assoone perswade Tygres to patience and quietnesse as them, so obstinate and wilfull are they in the furie of their impatience." (in C:TCJ) I think this concerns relatively unruly bachelor soldiers in the vicinity of the trading post, but even here, we do not find talk of serious fights, whereas Cocks' diary, as we have seen, mentions any number of injuries and even murder committed by drunk Europeans. Or, it might depend on the *part* of Japan reported. Edoites also have long been known in Japan for "selling quarrels" when drunk. I think that, and the exceptional political situation – masterless samurai running rampant – shortly after the Opening of Japan, made Alcock in 1863 stress over and over how Japanese intoxication was, *contrary to what he had read*, "noisy, dangerous, and pugnacious." But Morse, only 15 years later, wrote:

> . . . where in our blessed country (America) would a foreigner of another race pass crowds of men more or less affected by liquor and fresh from an animating exhibition of wrestling without receiving some slurring word or gesture? (M:JDD)

There is an interesting paradox in Frois's contrast. Rodrigues also mentions men who "in order to show more gratitude towards the host and to excuse themselves from drinking many times in the middle of the feast, or because of the strength of the wine, say, "I am completely tipsy and cannot manage any more (as if they were owing themselves beaten), nor am I capable of returning home." (R(C):TIJ) The paradox here would be that a European, who could not himself – or by way of a servant – admit he was drunk for the shame of it, would have to drink more! Still, whether or not people get drunk or not is not, *by itself*, a moral issue. Since Japanese enjoyed, and, to a degree, still enjoy, the virtue of moderation, they had and have every right to get drunk in public when they want to. Golownin in the early-19th century gives the fairest summary of all observers:

> Strong liquors are in use among the Japanese. The common people are very fond of them, and frequently drink to excess on holidays; but this vice is not common in Japan, as in many European countries. To be drunk in the daytime is looked upon as very disgraceful, even among the common people; the lovers of drinking, therefore, do not indulge their propensity until evening, after the termination of all labor and business. Besides, it is only on few occasions, and in a social circle, that they drink, and not as common men do among us. (G:MCJ3).

6-39   We esteem things of milk, cheese, butter and marrow.
Nos estimamos couzas de leite, queijo e manteiga e tutanos

The Japanese abhor all this and it smells very bad to them.
Os Japões abominão tudo isto e cheira-lhe muito mal.

Eating raw fish is no big thing. Many mammals do it. But squeezing a substance from the living body of another species and eating it? We are the only mammals to act like ants with their aphids! Van Linschoten gives a reason for the Japanese distaste for dairy products:

> they doe likewise refuse to eate Milke, as wee doe bloud, saying that Milke although it is white, yet it is verie bloude (VVL)

Philosophy lost. Today, most Japanese like milk and flan. But, at the end of the 20th century, Japanese still ate very little sour cream or plain yoghurt – sourness, rather than milkiness has proven an unsurpassable barrier. Why? Many Americans *learn* to like a sour flavors as a part of growing up. But Japanese tend to make it an ethnic thing. Forgetting about their own mouth-puckering plums, vinegar-drenched *tokoroten* noodles and other things of their own culture that they must grow used to, they pronounce "*We Japanese* don't like sour foods," which prevents them from making the effort and ensuring they never will like the foods in question. I should add that coming to Japan in the early 1970's, nothing Japanese ate shocked me half so much as how men in bars *ate butter*. Thick slices of butter, with two or three raisins embedded in each, were eaten with tooth-picks as appetizers. *We* may be called "butter-stinky" (*bata-kusai*), but only Japanese actually *eat* the stuff!

While I, like any Occidental who is not vegetarian, suck the marrow from bones, it puzzled me that Frois put an item so minor as marrow together with dairy products until searching out enough 16th century recipes to see that this marrow was thought of as a "dainty" and served as a thickener and flavor enhancer for pottage, broth, stuffing, tarts, pies, cakes, puddings and other pastries. [1] Obviously, the sweets and the meats had more in common in those days than today.

1. *Marrow in Recipes* A first course in an Elizabethan feast: "Miniature pastries filled with cod liver or beef marrow." A c1420 "curd" cheesecake (Harleian MS. 279) "contains bone marrow for added richness." (the English is too difficult to follow) A pear tart and quince pie in a 1553 cookbook: "Take pears and peel them and cut them into thin strips, take beef marrow, cinnamon, sugar and raisins and let it bake." "Peel the quinces and cut the core cleanly out with a knife, fry them in fat. After that stuff the quinces with currants, sugar, cinnamon and cloves. Afterwards take beef marrow or finely chopped kidney suet or skimmed fat from some other meat and put good Malavosia or Reinfal on it, sugar, cinnamon and cloves, however it seems good to you." (LR)

Readers who like novels may enjoy Kathy Lynn Emerson: *Face Down in the Marrow-Bone Pie*, described as "a delightfully cozy Elizabethan mystery."

6-40   We season our food with diverse spices;
Nós temperamos o comer com diversos adubos;

> The Japanese with *miso* [bean-paste], which has rice and rotten grain blended with salt. *Os Japões com* miso, *que hé arroz e graos podres misturados com sal.*

Yes we did, and many of those spices came from "the East Indies" – they helped get the Jesuits *to* Japan – but they were not *in* Japan.

Japanese *miso*, or at least most modern Japanese *miso* is, as already mentioned, boring, but Frois's "rotten" rather than *fermented* grain suggests that the *miso* at that time might have been nastier=better than it is now! That Frois does not mention the main ingredient of *miso*, namely *soy beans* (mentioned in the Nipo dict.) suggests, again, that the contrasts are meant to be explained, or for the enjoyment of those in the know.

Frois is right. Miso and the condensed liquid *miso* called soy sauce aside, traditional Japanese *cooking* lacks spice (Unless you allow the bonito shavings and sugar simmered into the sauce, which is used for some types of noodles). Some Chinese and/or Portuguese-influenced biscuits (sweet confectionary) bake in some cinnamon, and stews in some parts of Japan may have come to include sugar (usually as sweet cooking *sake*) and chili pepper, which as we know from 6-23 was already used in 1585, but that was about it.

After the dishes are cooked, however, spices could be added. Three common ones used today with Japanese food are 7-flavor red pepper (*shichimi togarashi*) clearly post-dating Frois and supposedly invented to keep people doing waterfall prayers (you let the cold water fall on your head as you pray) warm, a finely ground feather-light brown-green Chinese pepper, *sansho,* which numbs the tip of the tongue – something found in none of our spices (unless anyone uses cocaine for a spice) – and is most commonly used with eel, a sweet miso which is put on cooked egg-plant, hot sesame oil and vinegar for some Chinese dishes, and my favorite, *wasabi.* I would think that the effect of this *wasabi* or horse-radish would be too spectacular not to report in detail but, strangely, have found nothing so far (other than Frois's mention of "mustard"). Most people feel it in the nose, between the eyes, or inside the forehead, but I am one of a minority who feel a sharp pang an inch or so inside the crown of the head! (Perhaps it shoots back to the inner end of my perpetually blocked sinus and activates a sympathetic nerve that seems like it is inside my brain!). Then, there is *sohsu,* or "sauce" (a Worchester-like sauce) put on dishes of a Chinese or Western origin that probably post-date Frois.

I am afraid I over-reached myself with the above survey. If any cooking historians feel my it is off, they are free to take it from scratch.

~~~~~~

6-41   We avoid [eating] dog, and eat cows.
Nós fujimos de cãis e comemos vaqa;

They avoid cows, and eat dogs decorously, as medicine.
Elles fojem da vaqa e comem lindamente os cãis por mezinha.

Dogs again (see 6-24)! Frois knows what will amaze us. The clear mention of *mezina,* or "medicine" indicates he also knew dog was not *usually* eaten but only indulged in by some men in their "medicine-eating" (*kusurigui*) when Buddhist guilt at taking life was overridden by health, and, I think, appetite. This early winter barbecue was a common theme for haiku, where the meat, more commonly "mountain whale" (wild boar) or venison was euphemistically called *momiji,* or colored leaves. Is this, perhaps, why Frois writes *lindamente* (decorously)? Japanese had eating taboos with respect to domestic animals – one reason they would not come out and say "dog" as Frois does this time (*cãis*) unlike before – which was one reason they did not eat beef, but Japanese taboos are rarely absolute, so even horses were, and still are, occasionally eaten.[1] But, I believe most Japanese had mixed feelings on eating dogs and there may have been periods when they abstained completely. When Kaempfer visited a hundred years after Frois, thanks to the "reigning Emperor," Japan was a veritable Dog Paradise!

> They have their Masters indeed, but lie about the Streets, and are very troublesome to passengers and travelers. Every street must, by special command of the Emperor, keep a certain number of these Animals, and provide them with victuals. There are Huts built in every street, where they are taken care of when they fall sick. Those that die, must be carried up to the tops of mountains and hills, as the usual burying places, and very decently interr'd. Nobody may, under severe penalties, insult or abuse them, and to kill them is a capital Crime, whatever mischief they do. In this case, notice of their misdemeanors must be given to their keepers, who are alone empower'd to chastise

and to punish them.[2] This extraordinary care for the preservation of Dog-kind is the effect of a superstitious fancy of the now reigning Emperor, who was born in the Sign of the Dog[3] . . . and hath for this reason so great an esteem for this Animal, as the great Roman Emperor Augustus Caesar is reported in Histories to have had for Rams. The natives tell a pleasant tale on this head. A Japanese, as he was carrying up the dead carcass of a Dog to the top of a mountain, in order to its burial, grew impatient, grumbled and cursed the Emperor's birthday and whimsical commands. His companion, tho' sensible of the justice of his complaints, bid him hold his tongue and be quiet, and instead of swearing and cursing, return thanks to the Gods, that the Emperor was not born in the Sign of the Horse, because in that case the load wou'd have been much heavier. (K:THJ)

Though beef, as already noted, was not eaten on a modern scale by European peasants, it was much more part of the diet of the wealthy classes than was dog in Japan.   Moreover, Europeans were not completely innocent of eating man's best friend. Keith Thomas notes that in hard times in early 17th century England "dog's flesh was thought 'a dainty dish' in many houses, and cat's meat was turned into 'good pottage.," (T:MNW)

20 years in Japan and I *never* encountered any dog meat or even heard of anyone eating it. But Korean men still do – or did until the Seoul Olympics turned it into an international hullabaloo – and use ample sesame leaves to mask the strong doggy(?) flavor (They told me it was *lamb*, until I wondered aloud part way through the meal). In the late-19th century, Bishop wrote that "dog meat is in great request at certain seasons, and dogs extensively bred for the table." But, Korean men with the means to do so had a *way* of eating meat that was in itself more surprising than the *type* consumed.   Bishop writes: "I have seen Koreans eat more than three pounds of solid meat at one meal." She also saw "twenty to twenty-five peaches or small melons disappear at a single sitting" and attributed this gluttony – unknown in Japan – to "the enormous consumption of red pepper, which is supplied even to infants." (KOREA AND HER NEIGHBORS) But even red pepper does not explain how or why Koreans, unlike the Japanese (and any other people I know), easily eat all but the very largest fish bones!

Most Japanese ate less mammal meat than Europeans or their Korean neighbors.[4]   Why? Kaempfer, after noting the scarcity of "*desart* [wild] places" for wild four-footed Beasts to "increase and multiply," gave the official line, i.e. Buddhism:

> Pythagoras's doctrine of the transmigration of the Soul being receiv'd almost universally, the natives eat no Flesh-meat, and living, as they do, chiefly on Vegetables, they know how to improve the ground to much better advantage, than by turning it into meadows and pastures for the breeding of Cattle. (Ibid)

Kaempfer doubtless found the Japanese abstention from eating cow further proof of their exceptionally close relationship with the Middle East (support of his Japanese-as-Babylonia theory) – but the use of the term Pythagorean with respect to the Sinosphere was, I think, started by Ricci – for he observed cow worship thinned out on to the East of the Ganges, so that "in Siam and the more Eastern Kingdoms, even the Priests themselves make no scruple of eating Cow's Flesh, provided they have not given occasion, nor consented to their killing." This sort of rationalizing is also found in Ruth Benedict's 1943 war-time study of the Thai culture.

> The theory is that fish are not "killed," they are taken out of the water and if subsequently they die a natural death, no man is responsible . . . no man could without guilt send to the market or give orders to his servant for some particular animal or type of meat which he would then be responsible for having had killed, but if he sent for an animal or fowl which was dead already he had no guilt."

Reasons aside, the example of Frois and company did convince Japanese to try beef. Etchu Tetsuya writes "the Japanese taboo on beef-eating gradually disappeared after the Europeans established themselves in Japan." Avila Giron, who came to Japan about the time Frois died, "related how the price of beef had skyrocketed over the years. He claimed that the reason for the high cost was that all the citizens of Nagasaki had begun to eat beef." Japanese accounts concur on the popularity of beef. Matsunaga Teitoku (1571-1653), a linked-verse poet sometimes called the first haiku poet, wrote in *Nagusamegusa* that "around the time when Christianity was introduced to Japan, even people in the Kyoto region referred to beef as *waka* and ate it as a highly prized delicacy." (Etchu Tetsuya EUROPEAN INFLUENCE ON THE "CULTURE OF FOOD" IN NAGASAKI trans. Fumiko F. Earns www.uwosh.edu/home_pages/ faculty_staff/earns/etchu.html). But, *because of the association with Christianity*, the eating of beef had been outlawed before Kaempfer visited.

While Japanese today are not big meat-eaters, they are rarely vegetarian either (in food, like religion, they are not extremists). Today, the greatest populations of vegetarians are probably found in the West, with England and its mad cows leading the herd.

1. They Do *Eat Horses*.   Horse is sold in packages of paper-thin slices as *sashimi* called *sakura-niku*, or "cherry meat!" I have bought it at the local supermarket. Like petals, it is velvet to the teeth and very sweet – much better than the goat *sashimi* (which stinks like a petting zoo in August) – I had on one of Japan's Southernmost islands. The flesh melts in the mouth like butter (though there are ligament-like threads better removed). Note: I fail to see why the sin is greater than our feeding it to dogs or using it for glue!

2. Dog Lovers   The laws of the "Dog Shôgun" Tsunayoshi surprise us. I cannot find anything quite like it in Europe, but if we look at the 31st subject of the Zoroaster treatise *Sad Dar* (Written in Persian Translated by E. W. West, from Sacred Books of the East, volume 24, Clarendon Press, 1885.) from the *near* West (from the Japanese perspective), we can find something almost as crazy and far too pleasant not to introduce, namely,

"1. Every time they [believers] eat bread, it is necessary to withhold three morsels from their own bodies, and to give them to a dog. 2. And it is not desirable to beat a dog. 3. For, of the poor no one whatever is poorer than a dog, and it is necessary to give a tethered animal bread, because the good work is great. 4. And in revelation it is declared in this manner, that, if a dog is asleep upon the road, it is not proper that they put a foot violently on the ground, so that he becomes awake. 5. And, in former times, an allowance (*raitib*) of bread would have been made every day for the sake of the dogs, three times in summer and twice in winter, on this account, that one wishes them to come to the assistance of his soul at the Chinwad bridge. 6. In the worldly existence they are the guard of men and cattle. 7. If there had not been a dog they would not have been able to keep a single sheep. 8. Every time that he barks, just as his bark goes forth, the demons and fiends run away from the place."

Unfortunately, ch 43 of the same book say it is

"great good work to try to kill noxious things such as the frog in the water, the snake and scorpion, the ant (marchish) that flies, the common ant (morchah), and the mouse. . . . every time that they bring a frog up, out of the water, and make it dry, and, after (ba'hd) that, kill it, it is a good work of a thousand and two hundred dirhams in weight. . . . every time that they kill a snake, and recite the Avesta that is appointed for that occasion, it is just as though they have slain an apostate (ashmogh) . . . . every one who kills a flying ant (marchish) it is as much good work as for any one who is reciting inward prayer for ten days. 6. Among the creatures of Ahriman nothing whatever is more harmful than this; for, if it dies in the air (hava) it becomes a gnat, if it dies in the dust it becomes a worm, if it dies in the water it becomes a leech, if it dies among the excavators of flesh it becomes a venomous snake (mar-i af'hai), and if it dies in dung it becomes creeping things . . . For every one who kills a corn-dragging ant it is as much good work as for any one who recites the Ohrmazd Yasht. . . .. For every one who kills a mouse it is as much good work as if four lions are killed. . . . Therefore, it is incumbent on every one to make an effort to kill a noxious creature."

The Bible, I am afraid, shares not a little of this deadly un-ecological attitude.)

3. Sign of the Dog   Did any Chinese rulers likewise take their birth animal seriously, i.e., in the manner of a tribal totem.

4. *Koreans and Meat*.   Japan and Korea are equally Buddhist. Why the difference? One reason may be Koreans are closer to the Tibetan Buddhist school of thought that prefers the meat of large animals, to, say, insects. I think the long cold winters may also have a lot to do with it. I think, also, that nineteenth century travelers found Koreans much more handsome than Japanese partly because their high protein diet raised the bridges of their noses (Biologists, am I wrong on this?).

6-42   To us, putrid fish gut is something abominable.
    Antre nós as tripas podres do pexe se tem por abominasão;

The Japanese use it for *sakana* [*appetizers*] and like it a lot.
    Os Japões uzão dellas por sacana *e folgão muito com ellas.*

Once, Japanese salted and aged many varieties of fish tripe and roe. Today, *shiokara,* or salt-tripe almost invariably means the fermented guts of the squid, though (if I recall correctly) strips of squid are often mixed in. There is, however, another far more expensive fermented tripe, *konowata,* or sea cucumber guts.   This *konowata* was one of the tribute items delivered annually to the Imperial Court for hundreds, possibly thousands of years and is considered as one of the three top gourmet foods in Japan, though some who have not learned to like them compare the taste to s__t. [1]   Here is one of the score of *konowata* haiku I translated in *Rise, Ye Sea Slugs!*

like dad
i use scissors on
slug guts

chichi no seshi gotoku hasami de konowata o   Fukushima Masato

Because it is as slimy as silk, and so salty only a tiny bit is eaten at a time, or rather, at a sip of *sake,* some *konowata* fans have found a modern way to eat it (Maybe we should try it with spaghetti!)

1. *The Taste of Konowata*   One person to whom I offered retsina (Greek wine with a pine, rather than oak bouquet – pine barrels for wine predate oak ones) claimed it tasted like cat piss. One wonders how people know what these things taste like! Be that as it may, I wanted to taste *konowata* myself, but failed to obtain any in Miami, Florida.   Because it is fermented, shipping requires a direct plane flight or a cooperative distributor. Perhaps a professional wine-taster living in or close to Japan could try and describe it in my stead.

~~~~~~

6-43   Among us, making loud noises while we eat or gulping down wine is considered gross.
Antre nós mascar[1] muito alto o comer e escorropichar o vinho hé tido por sujidade.

The Japanese think they are both just dandy.
Os Japõis antre si huma e outra couza o tem por primor.

The noise Japanese make while eating has long upset Western visitors. Men in particular often chew with their mouths open amplifying each bite of the daikon pickle (the loudest culprit), making smacking sounds with open mouths – the "tongue-drum" noise a sign that the food is being relished as "lip-smacking" is, at least in the idiom, for "us" – and drink down whatever is not hot enough to prevent it in audible gulps.   In the case of the "wine," I am not certain if Frois only refers to the way a tiny sake cup is downed in a single movement (the toast, *kanpai!* means "drain/dry-cup") – rather than sipped – or the atrocious practice of chugalugging *sake* from large cups or bottles (When was this first recorded?). Loud slurping is common to both sexes. This is because it is proper to drink soup or noodles hot and said behavior both sucks the food in and cools it down enough to prevent one from being scalded at the same time.

Today, there is disagreement about the appropriateness of making excessive noise chewing, but slurping is still proper and gulping is, shall we say, popular. It serves as *the* main subliminal (but very obvious to a foreigner) part of beer, sports-drink or soft-drink advertisements in Japan. The *gokugokugoku* (to use Japanese mimesis for "glug, glug, glug") sound is so loud one feels that a microphone is embedded in the actor's Adam's Apple – usually a large and active one shown bobbing up and down in synch with the noise. This is soon followed by an even louder *ahh!* of thirst-quenched ecstasy, which mercifully gives way to triumphant music or some clever catch-phrase. Frois may have only been referring to the way a cup of *sake* is downed in a single gulp, in itself indecorous to a wine-sipping European, but I can't help wondering if he heard the all too common sound of chugalugging.

1. *Mascar*. Schütte has *marchar*, and no note so I figured it a typo and corrected it.

~~~~~~

6-44   We praise the wine of our hosts by showing them a gracious and happy countenance;
Nós louvamos o vinho dos ospedes com lhe mostrar gracioso e alegre rosto;

> The Japanese praise [their host's *sake*] with a face so sour,[1] they seem to be crying. *Os*
> *Japões o louvão mostrando tão roim cara que parese que chorão.*

Roim, or *Ruim* includes connotations of *perverse* and *prejudicial* as well as the connotation of broken down, crumbling, etc. which I turned into the English *sour*. What Japanese actually *do*, even today, is *grimace*. We think a good drink should be mellow. In their hearts, most Japanese would probably agree. But, strength is a desired characteristic of a drink, so a grimace showing it hit the spot is the traditional way to express gratitude for one. From the grimaces some actors make on television, even with something as weak as beer, you would think they had their first taste of 100-proof rotgut!

~~~~~~

6-45   At our tables we converse, but we do not sing or dance.
Nas nossas mezas practica-sse, mas não se canta nem balha;

> The Japanese don't converse until almost the end of the meal, warmed up, they dance and sing. *Os Japões até quasi o fim da meza não practicão, mas qentes balhão e cantão.*

This rings true. Japanese do need to be warmed up, that is drink a bit before they find their tongues. It is easier to dance or sing something they already have down. Needless to say(?), they do not dance and sing every day at their meals. This is not your average household dinner, but a party. After a half an hour of sitting without moving on *tatami* it feels good to move a little. Moreover, the songs and dance of traditional Japan, unlike most of Europe, are easily be performed by individuals with no back-up, yet still satisfy (more in the *Drama* chapter). At a memorable "Forget the Year Party" (*bonenkai*) for the Japan Translation Center in 1978, one older secretary took a tiny bivalve (*chijimi* or *asari*) from her soup and rhythmically clicked the shells together while singing something to the effect that she was a young and innocent little thing, while a country boy (a young salesman who mistakenly used honorifics with respect to his own boss while speaking to an outside third-party on the phone) took a liter-size beer bottle in hand to indicate his complementary part while dancing. I doubt anyone dared to dance quite like that for Frois and the other Jesuits!

~~~~~~

6-46   Among us, the guest goes to give thanks to the host.
Antre nós o comvidado vai dar graças ao que o comvidou;

> In Japan, the host goes to give thanks to the guest.
> *Em Japão o que comvidou vai dar graças ao convidado.*

Okada writes "this is exaggerated for the sake of contrast, but probably refers to tea ceremony etiquette." Not long after the Bungo Consultation, the Jesuits were instructed to have "in all the houses . . . a special room near the entrance door for the preparation of the *chanoyu*, the ceremonial tea," which "could not be omitted even in mission stations" and make certain to have "a tea attendant, the *chanoyusha"* who "was to be continuously on duty,"(LR maybe Valignano's 1581 *Advertimentos* in S:VMP?) and so forth, with an aim to being ready for any visitor at any time. So they had an official interest in that etiquette. Etiquette does not require explanation. But, logical reasons for the Japanese side are wanted, I think I have them. 1) It is better to give (a party) than to receive. 2) Transportation in Japan being as slow as it was (see ch.8), the guest deserves thanks for coming. 3) Many Japanese were, as I happen to be, homebodies preferring to receive visitors than go out. In this case, it is only natural that we thank them. (It is why I *never* allow guests to wash dishes.)

6-47   We esteem fried fish.
       Antre nós hé stimado ho p[eix] e frito;

> They do not like it, but love fried sea-weed.   *Elles[delle]não gostão e folgão com limos fritos do mar.*

The Iberians are still big on frying fish. Japanese roast fish or boil it, but even today rarely fry it except in *tempura,* something adopted and adapted from the Portuguese, [1] where a tiny fish or piece of squid may sometimes found. Deep-fried *konbu* (kelp, also called *kobu*) is still found today; and I would describe it as the seaweed equivalent of a thick potato-chip. But it is just one of a tremendous variety of fried or dried snacks and a far cry from the presence it was when *agekobuya* or *agekobu-uri* walked around hawking it (which is why it even made the 1604 Japanese-Portuguese dictionary). I am puzzled why Frois did not give seaweed a whole contrast, say:

> *In Europe, we eat many kinds of vegetables that grow on land and only use seaweed for fertilizer; In Japan, they not only eat a dozen types of seaweed but pay more than for land vegetables.*

Maybe *some* seaweed was eaten here and there in Europe, but usually such exceptions did not stop Frois . . . Seaweed is not only a vital source of iodine, but of many other trace elements whose value we are only beginning to appreciate [2] and, even today, many varieties are served in many ways and seaweed is still almost as popular as it was when Isabella Bird wrote:

> Seaweed is a common article of diet, and is dried and carried everywhere into the interior. I have scarcely seen a coolie make a meal of which it was not a part, either boiled, fried, pickled, raw, or in soup." (B:UTJ 1880)

1. Tempura.   I was going to explain, but Barthes is more fun:

> "It is said *tempura* is a dish of Christian (Portuguese) origin: it is a food of the lent (*tempora*); but refined by the Japanese techniques of cancellation and exemption, it is the nutriment of another time: not a rite of fasting and expiation, but of a kind of meditation…"

Here is the real difference between Portuguese and Japanese frying: "Tempura is stripped of the meaning we traditionally attach to fried food, which is heaviness" and "flour recovers its essence as scattered flower" exhibiting "a quality which seems denied to all fried food: freshness." (B:EOS)

2. Trace Elements.   James Lovelock, in *Gaia* mentions his discovery of trace elements produced by seaweed and so forth in the littoral zone that were vital for the ecology. I think we have yet to account for all of the elements important for proper nutrition and would guess the seaweed provides much more.

6-48   Fishing, among us, is a recreation for honourable people.
       O pescar antre nós o tem as pessoas honradas por desenfadamento;

> In Japan, it is thought a lowly activity and work for the base.
> *Em Japão se tem por cousa baxa e obra de jente vil.*

In Japan's oldest anthology of poetry, the *Manyôshû* (c.760), there are a few poems about noble poets going fishing where they meet goddesses in the guise of fishing girls. But nothing like the *Compleat Angler* tradition of the West would evolve. One reason why is suggested by another poem in the same anthology, in Okura's Chinese style lament for his illness where he whines [1] that there are old yet still well cormorant fishers, despite the sinful nature of *their* livelihood, while his ever-so-innocent Buddhist self is the one getting the bad karma. Later, haiku, likewise, will play the fisherman's sin against the full moon, with its Buddhist light (of the Law) capable of making even wild boars gentle! In the 20th century, however, the number of Japanese anglers multiplied as fast as good streams were ruined by the authorities,[2] with the comical result – unbelievable crowding (more fishermen than fish) – seen in photo magazines. [3]

Traditionally, almost all fishing in Japan was done from fishing boats, as work. A mid-19th century observation by an American who participated in the transport of the first Japanese embassy to the United States gives an idea of how much was done:

> The fish caught in the bay are generally more remarkable for beauty of form and color, than for delicacy of flavor; but there was no limit of the number of fishing boats constantly employed in the capture of the finny tribe, seeming almost to equal that of the unwary victims. (J:FJE)

1. *Whining Poet*   The poignant descriptions of the sweet child that died and other things make us like Okura enough to bear his whining, which reflects the influence of Chinese poetry. Japanese generally thought it improper to whine about anything but love.

2. *Dead Japanese Rivers*. Not so much the developers as the civil authorities are responsible for killing Japan's rivers in the name of safety. They are strait-jacketed in concrete to prevent any meandering.

3. *Crowded Rivers.* After finding myself constantly kayaking under fishing lines that went from one side of the river to the other, I gave up and only went out immediately after typhoons or flood-rains which scared away everyone else.

~~~~~~

6-49   The diligence with which we clean our teeth after eating;
A diligencia que nós pomos em alimpar os dentes depois de comer,

> The Japanese show in the morning cleaning them before washing their faces.
> *Dessa uzão os Japões pola menhã de os alinparem antes de lavar o rosto.*

Among the rules for dental health devised by Johannes Arculanus in the 15th century, we find

- Foods which induce vomiting should be avoided [*the acids hurt the teeth*]
- Sweet foods are forbidden.
- Clean teeth immediately after meals with a toothpick.
- After picking, rinse with wine and sage or wine, mastich, gallia, moschata, cubeb, juniper seeds, root of cyprus, and rosemary leaves.
- The teeth must be rubbed with a dentifrice before bed *or in the morning.*
  (*italics mine* http://home.uchicago.edu/~atterlep/Misc/tooth.htm.)

It is not quite as clean-cut as Frois makes it and probably never was. As it turns out, I have long done it in the "Japanese" fashion, although I did not know it was a *bona fide* custom until reading about it in Frois. Perhaps that is because, like Japanese, I do not eat a dessert and because I generally have a *nezake,* which is to say, small nightcap. Since teeth are generally scuzzy in the morning even if you clean them before sleeping, why bother?

6-50   Among us, the animals eat the plants' leaves and leave the roots.
Antre nós os animais comem as folhas das ervas e deixão as raizes;

In Japan, for some months of the year, the poor people eat the roots and leave the leaves. *Em Japão alguns mezes do ano a jente pobre come as raizes a deixa as folhas.*

This *ridiculous* contrast of grazing livestock and the dirt poor (or "water-drinkers = *mizu-nomi* to use the Japanese idiom) would seem to refer to the last crops of the year, the turnips and huge radishes called *daikon*, which, pickled, were the main (sometimes only) condiment in a poor man's miso soup in the winter. When they are being put up, there are simply too many leaves to eat – and, more important, digest! – so they are turned into mulch or used to dangle their roots from drying poles, as a person might be dangled by his or her hair. If my metaphor seems outrageous, believe me, it is nothing compared with what other Western visitors have written. First, from Kaempfer:

Turneps grow very plentifully in the Country, and exceeding large ones. Of all the produce of the fields they perhaps contribute most to the sustenance of the Natives. But the fields being manur'd with human dung, they smell so strong, that Foreigners, chiefly Europeans, cannot bear them. The natives eat them raw, boil'd, or pickel'd. (K:THJ 1690)

Provisions of this nasty composition [manure based on human waste] are kept in large tubs, or tuns, which are buried even with the ground, in their villages and fields, and being not cover'd, afford full as ungrateful and putrid a smell of radishes (which is the common food of the country people) to tender noses, as the neatness and beauty of the road is agreeable to the eyes. (Ibid)

To wit, Kaempfer blames shit for the strong flavor of *daikon* (he means *daikon* when he writes "turneps") and, elsewhere, turns around and blamed *daikon* for the strong smell of the shit! (The latter is *true*. Eat a lot of it and your offal smells woefully raw!). Even Morse, who appreciated more about Japan than anyone except, perhaps Lafcadio Hearn, had hard words for this "curious kind of radish."

It is eaten raw as a relish, and is also fermented and converted into something resembling sauerkraut, and, as a friend with me expressed it, was odiferous enough to drive a dog out of a tanyard. You recognize the odor as it is being transported through the streets, and it is hardly less offensive to encounter than the offal carriers. (M:JDD)

Personally, I love the various kinds of pickled daikon and think of them as Japan's gift to the world, so it surprised me not to find a single kind word for it from the European visitors. Even the cosmopolitan and well-seasoned Isabella Bird had nothing but invective for the *daikon*:

I have left to the last the vegetable *par excellence,* the celebrated *daikon* (Raphinus sativus), from which every traveler and resident suffers. It is a plant of renown – it deserves the honorific! It has made many a grown man flee! It is grown and used everywhere by the lower classes to give sipidity to their otherwise tasteless food. Its leaves, something like those of a turnip, are a beautiful green, and enliven the fields in early winter. Its root is pure white, tolerably even, and looks like an immensely magnified radish, as thick as an average arm, and from one to over two feet long. In this state it is comparatively innocuous. It is slightly dried and then pickled in brine, with rice bran. It is very porous, and absorbs a good deal of the pickle in the three months in which it lies in it, and then has a smell so awful that it is difficult to remain in a house in which it is being eaten. It is the worst smell that I know of except that of a skunk! (B:UTJ 1880)

Chamberlain, more fairly, describes it "as great a terror to the noses of most foreigners as European cheese is to the noses of most Japanese." *Exactly!* Cheese. What we like most as adults are those tastes we must acquire. They must run a different route through a finer part of our brain than the strawberries any child will like from the start. The sassy Edoite yellow *takuan* and the mellow rusty *nara-zuke* of the ancient capitol are, flavor-wise, as *good* in their own way as any fine *adult* cheese. I might add that they offer little by way of nutrition (calories or carbs) so they would be perfect for overweight Americans tired of eating dill pickles. But, no, they do not go with wine.

6-51   Among us, it would be insulting to eat or send someone a gift of rotten meat or fish.
Antre nós comer ou mandar prezentes de carne ou pexe podre seria afronta;

In Japan, they eat it and are not embarrassed to present it, foul smell and all.
Em Japão se come, e, asi fedendo, se manda sem pejo.

The Portuguese can also be read "they eat it, and stinking of it [or, "and so stinking"], deliver it without shame." Presumably, the bad breath that would result is the cause for eating as well as sending this crude delicacy to someone being an affront.

I assumed Frois meant *kusaya,* which is coyly defined by Kenkyûsha's Japanese-English dictionary as "a horse-mackerel dipped in salt water and dried in the sun, which has a very characteristic odor." *Characteristic?* It smells like rank carrion of the type a hound would bring home. I tried roasting some once and the odor remained in my kitchen for two weeks! But, before you think the Japanese are crazy, remember that nine out of ten Japanese today would not want to taste it, while I would bet that half of the people in Norway dare eat their *even more putrid fish* that smells so bad you look for the maggots (I had some as part of a first-time-across-the equator hazing while a work-away on a Scandinavian freighter and needed every ounce of that half bottle of vodka consumed in advance to get it down!).

Because Japanese food is, on the whole, mild, many Japanese do not like strong odors even if they are Japanese odors.   The fermented beans *natto,* which I love – which Japanese expect all non-Japanese to hate – is disliked by about half of the Japanese! (unlike most other strange flavors, *natto* is unique in that people either love or hate it from their very first taste!) But Okada does not mention *kusaya* and thinks Frois means *sushi* which, at that time, was aged – i.e. allowed to ferment – for four or five days in the Fall or Spring, or a day or two in the summer. (Like *natto* beans, one had to literally sleep on it in order to make it in the winter!)   A haiku of Issa's even describes the noises it made while fermenting!   I suspect Okada is right and I am wrong, for the name *kusaya* has "stink" (*kusai*) in it and was probably not a common gift, while sushi was.

6-52   In Europe, it would be vulgar for a respected citizen to sell wine like a cheap tavern at his house. *Em Europa seria baxeza vender hum cidadão honrado vinho atavernado em sua casa;*

In Japan, highly respected citizens sell and measure it out with their own hands.
Em Jãpao o vemdem e medem por sua mão os cidadões muito honrados.

Most *sake* was sold by dosô, who were money-lenders with earthen rooms protected against fire and well fortified against thieves. Up to 300 of these stores were in operation in Kyoto and 200 in Nara at the time (OED). The question is whether Frois's "respected citizen" means the owners of the largest of these stores *had become* major merchants who gained some social respect (not much one would think, for *warriors* and *scholars* were theoretically more admired), or, as Okada guesses, major merchants joined the game, selling *sake* alongside of these dosô (which surprised the Jesuits).

The "at his house" and "with his own hands" is puzzling. Since *most* Japanese stores were literally the front of the houses (as is still common today), I guess that would mean that the owner was selling *sake* from his home. *Were, European stores and homes, even then, generally separate?* The hands-on way of doing things is found even today in Japanese companies where the good boss wants to directly meet guests and treat them specially by doing deferential things an Occidental might prefer to leave to a lower employee. In that sense, Europe lies closer to the North African(?), Near Eastern(?) idea of men not doing manual work if he can avoid it, and big shots holding themselves aloof than Japan. But, rather than compare the respected citizen who gets his hands dirty in Japan with their less diligent counterparts in Europe, Frois makes them seem crass by introducing this difference in a contrast involving alcohol. Or, am I being unfair to Frois, here?

6-53   Europeans like to raise chickens, ducks [and rabbits?].
Em Europa folgão de criar galinhas, adens [1][coelhos e patos?] etc.;

> The Japanese don't like to do this, except for raising roosters to delight the children. *Os Japões com nada disto folgão, somente com galos pera os meninos folgarem.*

Remember that this is a chapter on food, not pets. With most hunting grounds monopolized by the wealthy in Europe, I would guess most meat the common-folk got to eat was what they raised.

Ducks, at least, were quite common around country houses in Issa's time, so I suspect they were also kept in some parts when Frois was there. *Am I wrong? Or did he miss them?* They made quite a contribution to the paddies by aerating the water and eating insects. Their wings were clipped, but perhaps they were not closely enough managed for Frois to consider them honest-to-goodness domestic animals.   Roosters were Japan's pride. Fighting was not so important as it was in South East Asia, but the beauty of the long tails for which they were bred and their diligent time-keeping was much appreciated. I had never identified them particularly with children, though the children would have liked them. Perhaps this is part of the life I confess to knowing little about, that of the nobility.   Had I been Frois, the second half of the contrast would be this:

> *Europeans keep chickens, ducks and other animals they eat.*
> *The Japanese only keep roosters and bugs for their songs and for their fighting.*

Come to think of it, the Japanese also ate a number of types of bugs (most notably *grasshoppers*, and most rarely, for medicine, *cicada*) – not those kept for the above-mentioned reasons – and it is strange Frois neglects them in this chapter which mentions "dog" twice.

1. *Adens and Ducks.* My borrowed Brazilian Academy Portuguese-English dictionary calls *aden* a "type of duck" and *pato* a just "a duck." Forgive me for not sorting it out further for this edition.

6-54   In Europe, pastry is made from flour.
Em Europa a fabrica do pastel hé da masa;

> In Japan, they throw out the meat of an orange, and with the peel and what is stuffed inside it make a pie. *Em Japão se tira o amago da laranja e com a casqua e o que lhe metem dentro fiqa pastel.*

Sweet *miso* (fermented bean-curd) stuffed inside a de-meated *yuzu,* or citron (also called a

"Chinese lemon") – not *orange* – then lightly braised is called *yuzumiso* or *yûmiso*. This "pie" was loved by some famous Buddhist priest – I cannot remember who – and is occasionally mentioned in early haiku – not to mention the 1604 Japanese-Portuguese dictionary. Today, it is sometimes made and sold in Japanese-style pastry shops (*wagashiya*),[1] and the scent of the citron skin is heavenly. It is not as common as pastry made from a skin of pounded glutinous sweet-rice surrounding sweetened bean-paste.

Frois overlooked a larger difference. As I noted with respect to brushing teeth, *Japanese did not and still do not normally eat desserts.* Desserts in Frois's time were apparently considered a mark of enjoying an affluent lifestyle by the Jesuits (Why M.A.'s *"let them eat cake!"* was particularly cruel), for right after Miguel=Valignano mentions the *"surprising variety of pastry comprising dessert"* in Europe, he says:

> That is, to sum up the food situation in a word, our Japanese food fits our narrow and skinny [infertile] land, while Europe's is understandable given its rich soil. Considering this, there is absolutely no reason to dispute [argue the superiority or inferiority of] our diets. (J/S:DM 1589)

Japanese were intrigued with European baking as they were with all "our" food. While the making of bread (still called *pan* in Japanese, after the Portuguese/Spanish), was forbidden because it "symbolized the flesh of Christ" (Etchu Tetsuya: Ibid 6-41), some types of Portuguese pastries survived and evolved.[2] Today, not only do Japanese enjoy pastry, but they enjoy what is on the whole *far better* pastry than what can be bought in the USA. However, they rarely eat it after meals. They eat them with coffee in coffee-shops or they buy them as gifts when they visit friends' houses or offices, where they are then served as they converse, much as the case with fruit. Most would be called cake. I do not know if cake (now called *bollo*) was included in *pastel* which means both "pastry" and "pie" in Portuguese.

1. Wagashiya. The *wagashiya* = japanese-pastry (&sweets)-shop differs from the French, Danish, American and other Yogashiya = Ocean[Western]-pastry-shop in Japan by rarely having space to sit and drink coffee (though some serve Japanese tea), by changing their offerings not only with the "four seasons" but with many more sub-seasons and being primarily in business to sell beautifully wrapped boxes full of dainty *wagashi* for gifts people bring when visiting someone.
2. Iberian Sweets in Japan The most common is flan called *pujin* or *pudein* and the delicate cross between a sponge cake and a pond cake called *kasutera* (from bolo de Castella, which is a favorite gift item. The weirdest is a type of brightly colored star-shaped sugar confections whose name I forget. Then again, i could be Dutch or Italian (it may be *konpeitô* of the same root as *confetti* and written "gold-rice-sugar."). A reader with a sweet-tooth is invited to gloss. I am not intrigued so much by the details as the overall mood evoked by all these sweets (often brought out in haiku). I feel *something magical in them.* Perhaps it is just because they are so pretty, but I cannot help wondering if it is the association with a people who crossed the world to be shut out of Japan and of the Japanese who first learned these things many of whom died for their belief in an imaginary world invented by "us."

6-55   In Europe, wild pig [boar] is eaten well cooked. *Em Europa se come o porco do mato cozido;*

The Japanese eat it raw, in thin slices. *Os Japões o comem cru em talhadas.*

The Japanese translations of *cozido* are "boiled," but I follow father Schütte with "well-cooked" (*gekocht*) rather than choosing between the various possible translations of *cozido* here.

Since I have never heard of this meat fermented, it is evident from what Frois writes here that *sashimi* in the modern sense of the word as *fresh and raw slices* of meat was already eaten and how remarkable land animals, not sea animals, should take the lead, especially swine, though all Japanese *porco* was wild boar, presumably clean and suitable for raw consumption because there were no domestic swine for it to mix with!   Even so, pork was almost surely only eaten on rare occasions by most people and the more commonly as part of a stew. Because the Jesuits rubbed shoulders with the nobility, we may guess these are boar taken in a fancy hunt, and perhaps some were sliced up pretty much on the spot. (誰か、猪の刺身史は？)

When we consider the incredibly diverse swine-culture of their Chinese neighbors, the Japanese forbearance from this succulent animal the English essayist Lamb later turned into gastronomic pornography, is nothing short of miraculous. At first, the Jesuits raised pigs and goats to eat; they bought cows and even slaughtered them on premises. But all this stopped after the Bungo Consultation, when it was decided that doing these things ruined their reputation for they were only done by the Chinese (probably for Chinese traders) and untouchables. "And we are taken for Chinese, dirty, low and vile" (*y nosotros quedamos tenidos por hombres chinas, sucios, bajos y viles.*) (*"Resoluciones del Padre Vistador"* in V(A):S&A). Valignano was not exaggerating Japanese culinary chauvinism. Over a hundred years later, a *Yanagitaru* senryu quips:

> *kamikaze-ni buta ya hitsuji-no hedo-o haki*

> in gods-wind
> they vomit, throwing up
> pigs and sheep

This is how Japanese black humor imagined the last minutes of the Sino-Mongolian Armada, that was done in by a timely typhoon.

..

~~~~~~

6-56   With us, missing salt for the meal is but a small inconvenience.
Antre nós carecer de sal pera comer hé pouqo incomviniente;

> Japanese without salt bloat and become sick.
> *Os Japões se carecem de sal inchão ou adoecem.*

Being salt-less was considered so excruciating an experience in Japan that there was a custom of fasting from salt (*shiodachi*) while petitioning Shinto or Buddhist gods. Okada hazards the guess that Japanese ate so much salt on a regular basis that a disruption was felt as *withdrawal*. I would add that the difference probably owes a lot to the fact that "we" automatically eat salt in "our" bread and meat (see 6-17, 6-19), so we never really lack salt even if there is no salt-shaker on the table. Also, hot steam baths meant that the nobility lost more sweat – and with it salt – in Japan.

Japanese are more salt-conscious than most of "us." One reason is simply that all school-children read about the warlord Kenshin (1530-1578), who sent salt to fellow warlord and nemesis Shingen, who was blockaded by other rivals, because real warriors fought with weapons and not food. More broadly, salt was valuable because it was scarce. According to the Tobacco and Salt Museum,

> By comparison with other heavily populated parts of the world, Japan has always been at a disadvantage, for it has no known rock-salt deposits or other terrestrial salt sources, while its relatively low median temperatures and heavy rainfall make reliance on natural evaporation impracticable.

Did the name of the Museum catch your eye? For 90 years, until 1997, Japan Tobacco Inc. had a monopoly of the salt market. Be that as it may, the placement of big scoops of salt around a building to purify it and the throwing of salt by a sumo wrestler before a match shows that in Japan there is something nobler about salt than the mere "salary" we identify with it.

~~~~~~

6-57   We ordinarily think their *shiru* [soup] salty.   *Nós ordinariamente temos o seu* xiro *por salgado;*

And they [think] ours insipid.   *E elles o nosso caldo por ensoso.*

A simple illustration of the relativity of senses that Valignano discovered.   If a reader would like to *experience* it, I recommend drinking some tap-water just after eating raw egg. You will find the water tastes absurdly sweet.[1]

1. *Raw Egg and Taste* Amazingly, raw egg also takes the edge off of salty food. To the horror of my Japanese acquaintances, I invented the practice of dropping a raw egg in my *miso shiru*. Swallowed whole with a bit of the soup (carefully, so as not to dirty the remaining soup) it improves the taste of both, *I think.*

~~~~~~

6-58   In Portugal, rice cooked without salt is used as medicine to bind the bowels.
Em Portugal se come arroz cozido sem sal por mezinha para estancar as camaras;

For the Japanese, rice cooked without salt is their regular food as bread is for us.
Pera os Japões o arroz cozido sem sal hé seu continuo mantimento como antre nós o pão.

Now, we know why the lack of salt in the rice was worth including in contrast 6-2! It is also worth mentioning parenthetically that our medical profession continued to believe in saltlessness for bowel disorders (diarrhea and mal-absorption) until the advent of the space age, when they *finally* discovered that some salt added to the sugar-water *helps* rather than hurts it get absorbed. To me, this horribly belated discovery – if I am not mistaken, it came *after* the first heart transplant! – proves how little modern medicine knows about the body's most basic operations, and shows why we still need to keep one eye open to folk-medicine (Oriental and Occidental).[1] There *had to be* traditions, where the importance of mixing salt and sugar were already known. Still, because we had salt in other things, salt-less rice might have been beneficial and Japanese also practiced the *shiodachi* (salt-fast) for certain diseases.

"Our" practice of always salting rice, however, is ridiculous. The rice of South Europe is fat and sweet like *Japonica* rather than the skinny and less tasty *Indica*.   How could Europeans not discover how to serve their own rice to bring out its flavor better? [2] If I am not mistaken, even the Indians, whose rice is less tasty, generally do not salt it (though the wealthy may add saffron and I imagine coconut and sugar is added in some places) but are content to enjoy the flavor of the rice *with* the curries and other condiments.   What made "us" incapable of combining our flavors as we chewed? And most of us are *still* like that. We insist on putting butter or salt or soy sauce *on the rice* and letting it soak in so the rice is flavored before reaching the mouth rather than putting a bit of a spicy side dish on it just before taking a mouthful or alternating mouthfuls of rice and side-dish. As someone who began in "our" mode and switched to theirs, I can testify that "we" are missing out, *for it is a richer experience to enjoy separate flavors mixing in the mouth than to have them dulled by mixing ahead of time.* To claim rice is "flavorless" and must be salted or buttered up is to confess to an improperly developed personal gastronomy.   Could there perhaps be a deeper reason, some ancestral memories that might explain the strange fear otherwise cultivated people of European descent still have for leaving their rice alone? Look what I found in William Dalrymple's depiction of "Love and Betrayal in Eighteenth Century India" –

To the Dominican fathers of the Goan Inquisition, of course, this process of acculturation was always unacceptable. Any sign that Hindu customs were being followed in a Christian house were enough to get the entire family and their servants arrested and put to torture. A list was drawn up by the Inquisition of banned Indian practices . . . . . Included in this list are such shockingly heretical practices as 'cooking rice without salt as the Hindus are accustomed to do' . . . . . (*White Mughals* (Viking/Penguin) 2002)

1. *Sugar + Salt Discovery.*   I wrote a letter to the inventor of Gator-aid because it became well-known about the same time as the medical teams in Africa began to use salt+sugar-water for the dehydrated starving. But I got no reply. If anyone know *what is what* here, please write me. From the vantage point of number of lives saved the invention(?)/discovery(?) was far more significant than the polio vaccine, yet . . .

2. *Southern European Rice*. I hope Japanese chefs will experiment with risotto rice, which is particularly fat and sweet. I cannot even buy it unless many people buy my books, for it is very expensive.

~~~~~~

6-59   Among us, mullet is highly esteemed.
Antre nós as tainhas são estimadas;

In Japan it is thought repugnant food fit for the poor.
Em Japão lhe tem asco e são pera jente baxa.

Mullet has a way of going either way, *baitfish* (as in Miami, where I grew up) or *delicacy* (as per the Greeks). The roe is esteemed in Japan and probably was in Frois's time, too. So many mullet were caught and the poor, doubtless got the part of the mullet in less demand. That is, at any rate, my theory about how mullet got a low reputation. This was to become worse in the Edo era, when the fish's form endeared them to *senryu*, where they tend to get stuck in maids using them for dildos – especially fitting because their mouths were claimed to look like the mouth of the womb – No wonder respectable folk steered clear! (*I am joking:* the world of senryu poetry did not influence anyone's diet.).[1]

Despite a half-dozen contrasts involving fish, Frois forgot the most interesting one of all: the *fugu* (globe/blow/swell-fish), which has already been introduced parenthetically in the context of attempted suicide (1-4). It is possible that what might be called the blow-fish *cult* evolved *after* 1585, as a sort of thrill-seeking by men who missed not risking their lives after the centuries of wars finally ended.[2] If so, it sunk in its roots very quickly, for Kaempfer, in 1692 wrote *pages* on it. "The Japanese reckon" the *mabuku,* or true blowfish, "a very delicate Fish, and they are very fond of it." They know that

> the Head, Guts, bones, and all the garbage must be thrown away, and the Flesh carefully wash'd and clean'd before it is fit to eat. And yet many People die of it, for want, as they say, of thoroughly washing and cleaning it. (K(S):HOJ)

Senryu mention the wisdom of washing it *at your friend's house* – for the poison is so powerful the tiniest trace remaining might contaminate the sink.

> A few years ago five persons living in Nagasaki having eat a dish of this Fish, fainted soon after dinner, grew convulsive and delirious, and fell into such a violent spitting of Blood, as made an end of their lives in a few days.

Perhaps someone poisoned the poison fish, for the usual effect is far more subtle. The poison is similar to that of the coral snake: slow working and not dramatic. Indeed, it is the basis for the Voodoo zombie. "And yet the Japanese won't deprive themselves of a dish so delicate in their opinion, for all they have so many Instances, of how fatal and dangerous a consequence it is to eat it." Another *senryu* put the dilemma like this, *"only a fool would eat blowfish, or not eat it!"* Bashô was apparently the former type of the fool.

it was nothing
nothing at all! yesterday's over:
swell-fish soup!

ara nan-to-mo na-ya kinou-wa sugite fukuto-shiru

The first half of the haiku was a light take-off on a popular song, but the total message of the poem is far from shallow: taking a risk leaves the author happy to wake up alive today.[3] The round fish, like the Buddha full of nothingness, has given Bashô an epiphany. I almost made the title *satori*. But let me *Faux Frois* this fish before proceeding further:

We never willingly eat food that might kill us;
They not only do so, but think it very gallant.

Kaempfer also mentions a regulation: "Soldiers only and military men, are by special command of the Emperor forbid to buy and to eat this fish. If anyone dies of it, his son forfeits the succession to his father's post, which otherwise he would have been entitled to." The Emperor did not get involved in law-making but the Shogun might have forbidden it, and it is a fact that regulations like this were on the books of various *han* (states/feifs). Samurai, unlike merchants and craftsman (officially), were deemed too valuable to be allowed to gamble with their lives.

Our laws do not deny certain foods to certain occupations.
Theirs deny the blowfish to soldiers and all meat to the bonzes.

I would add that the blowfish was considered uniquely good for warming the body. Issa, who made fear of the cold his trademark – he even explained his short neck as being permanently hunched up against the cold! – was a big fan of blowfish for that reason, and wrote dozens of haiku about half of which concern the expression on the face of the blowfish, which he fancied to see on many of his compatriots and vice versa.. I will introduce them in another book. Here, we shall simply Frois:

In Europe, we think any warm soup is warming.
In Japan, only soup made from the blowfish is believed to have special warming properties.

The cynic might add, yes, sweating from fear! The expense of the meat – both because it had to be fresh and because there was very little meat on each fish – also may have helped here. (I wonder if anyone has tried testing expensive placebos against cheap ones?) "The third sort" of blowfish, continues Kaempfer,

is call'd Kitamakura, which signifies North Cushion [pillow]. I could not learn the reason of this Appellation. The same Name is given to a Person that sleeps with his head turn'd to the North. The poison of this sort is absolutely mortal, no washing or cleaning will take it off. It is therefore never ask'd for, but by those who intend to make away with themselves.

Kaempfer was given the reason, but failed to ask *the reason for the reason*. It is that in traditional Japan, only a dead-man (*hotoke*) rested with his head to the North (Not a face "turned to" the North, but the head itself to the North). A hundred years later, Thunberg got it: "it being the custom with these people, to turn the heads of those that are dying towards the north." In English, we might name that blowfish *As-good-as-dead*. To Faux Frois:

Among us, no one would buy a fish to take the life Deus entrusted them with.
The Japanese think eating a certain blowfish is a capital way to go to hell.

1. *Fishy Fish.* I am about a third of the way through a book of lugubrious fish and shellfish senryu (mostly Edo era) which will be titled *The Mullet in the Maid (and the Fisherman in the Ray).*

2. *Swellfish-eating History.* I am about halfway finished compiling a book of haiku called *Swellfish Soup* but have yet to figure out how the Edo *fugu* culture got started. Fugu was mentioned in 1000 year-old medical books, but disappears in the literature (according to Aoki Yoshio: *Fugu no Bunka* (Blowfish Culture) until Hideyoshi's

famous "Order Forbidding the Eating of Blowfish" directed at the troops invading Korea (1592-9).   There was a practice of eating blowfish in Korea and it is known that Hideyoshi brought back Korean prisoners, so I can't help wondering about the possibility of the Korean connection.

3. *Bashô's Pun.* I believe he plays on the homophone "blowfish soup" = "[I/we]know[ing] happiness/luck" (*fukuto[ji]shiru*) in the poem but have not found anyone in Japan to second me on it.

~~~~~~

6-60   Among us, belching at the table in the presence of guests is thought uncouth.
          Antre nós dar arrotos à meza diante dos ospedes se tem por mao insino;

          In Japan, it is very common, and no one is fazed by it.
          Em Japão hé muito corrente e nenhum cazo fazem disso.

More vulgarity to be added to 6-31, 38 and 43.   Two hundred years later, Thunberg remonstrated: "the Japanese have the bad custom of very frequently breaking wind upwards, and [it] is by no means thought indecent as in Europe; in other matters, they are as nice as other polished nations." Three hundred years later, Alcock noted objectively that: "it takes a long habit before Europeans can bear the frequent and loud eructations, as evidence of a good meal, without a strong mental protest." Ball's remarks on *Noises, etc.* within his "Etiquette" heading of *Things Chinese* are worth quoting in full for they take into account historical perspective:

..

Guttural sounds, hawking, clearing the throat, spitting, using the fingers to blow the nose, and eructations, are not necessarily considered impolite by the Chinese. It must be remembered that they look upon such things in a quite different way than we do nowadays. We say nowadays, for it is not more than a few centuries ago that a book was published in England containing, among other things, directions on how to blow the nose neatly with the fingers. But we will not offer any more remarks on such a nauseating subject. (B:TC)

So this grossness, too, comes from China?   Let me try to do the impossible, i.e., put burping into a more graceful context by quoting a haiku+explanation from my book *Rise, Ye Sea Slugs!*

海鼠食べられて噯となり出づる　高沢良一
namako taberarete okubi to nari izuru – Takasawa Yoshikazu
(sea cucumber eating/ate[respectful passive] eructation-as/into becomes leaves/comes-out)

          eating *namako*
          indulgence that ends
          in a fine burp

I called the sea cucumber the Japanese name *namako* here rather than "sea slug" as in most of the poems (actually, it is about sea *cucumber*, but the word is too long and lacks the proper metaphorical feel) because I realized that no amount of explanation can make the burp as sweet as it is in the original with the creature clearly identified.   The added "indulgence" is my way to recover the politeness of the conjugation of the verb (eat).   While Japanese have traditionally allowed to burp to show their appreciation for good food, I do not believe it was ever *de rigor* as (I have been told) in the Near East. Unlike the slurp that is heard every day, for it is the only logical way to eat noodles or soup hot, the burp is rarely heard in Japan today.   So said, I had only known the vulgar sounding *geppu,* until reading this haiku, which uses a more formal word for "burp," namely *okubi,* which is written with a single Chinese character, also new to me, comprised of two parts, "mouth+love." In fact, one pronunciation of the word is *ai,* the same as "love." Takasawa wrote me that the burp arises because (he/the slug?) ate mud-like stuff. So, is the burp on behalf of both of them, the poet and his food?

..

endnote VI

Food

<hr>

To me, the most interesting difference in our customary manner of eating and that of the Japanese is *the way meals start and finish*. We have traditionally opened "our" meals with a prayer said by one person who is either the host (at home, the *pater familia*), or the person indicated by the host. The content is Christian and concrete, mentioning God and/or Jesus and giving thanks for specific things. When it ends, all usually repeat the amen. "They," the Japanese, cut out all the extraneous detail, giving us *a grace in a word* said by each person, alone or together, however it happens, to open their meal: *Itadakimasu*. "[I humbly/gratefully] accept=take=eat." (G:O&O) Faux Froising this:

> *We begin our meals with a prayer thanking god.*
> *They begin by thanking no one in particular.*
>
> *We have one person say the grace for all.*
> *They each say their own, which is only one word.*

Personally, I do not care for "our" way. Talking to God like that may be fine for many Christians, but it seems childish and, let me be honest, corny, to one who is not even a believer. On the other hand, it feels good to have *something* to open a meal with (What is the opposite of a *sense of closure?* a sense of *aperture?!*). So, call me odd, but I always say *Itadakimasu!* no matter where I am. The Japanese also have a grace in a word for *finishing* their meals: *gochisôsama-deshita,* a phrase in the past tense (but the long=polite verb ending it is seldom said nowadays) mentioning the host (in the abstract, by prefixes and suffixes alone) running about (*preparing the meal,* say the philologists). No one thinks much about what it means, but it is a splendid way to say "thanks!" and close one's meal.
..

> *We start our meals with various long graces depending on the occasion.*
> *They have standard graces of just one word both to start and end their meals.*

I do not know whether this Japanese practice was followed in Frois's day, and, if it was, how diligently. I believe it was followed, because Japanese Christians introduced the practice of saying grace at the end of meals as well as the beginning, but fear my documentation, probably from *de Missione*, got lost together with that copy about sitting in chairs). I suspect it goes far back in Japanese history, because Japanese are almost religious about beginnings and endings: they bind up them up neatly in words. Whenever people leave home (or a cluster of homes if it is a tight-knit neighborhood), one says *"Itte-kimasu* ([I am] going-[and will] comeback)!" And the person/s remaining shout *"Itte-rasshai* (go-[and]comeback[politely expressed])!" and when you come back they shout *"Okaeri* (welcome back)!"

> *We have nothing in particular to say whenever we go out and return to our homes.*
> *They have a word or two they always say without fail.*

食   食   食

In the Edo period of Seclusion the Japanese invented another splendid way to start a meal, to give a fresh sense of opening. This was not necessarily the reason for the invention – which is *the answer to the question* I asked in my annotation of the first contrast of the chapter – but the *result* was to get every cheap bowl of noodles off on a refreshing start. Froising it , we get:

> *Our restaurants use service of silver or stainless steel that is washed and reused.*
> *Theirs often use chopsticks that are only used once and thrown away.*

> *Our utensils come ready to use.*
> *They sometimes must break their chopsticks apart before they can use them.*

The disposable chopstick has received a lot of criticism from Western environmentalists. I once read a letter to an editor where a conceited young Yank promised to cram the disposable chopsticks up the nose of anyone caught eating with them who dared to talk about ecology! Coming from a culture which uses twice the energy per capita (despite having an equal income) of the Japanese, cannot even pass a decent gas tax, gives people *bonuses* for flying a lot instead of rewarding those who stay put, allows its population to keep growing (Japanese are less prolific), and eats higher up the food chain than all but the Argentineans (who have abundant grass pasture) – *"we" have no right to talk!* The crisp crack of a disposable chopstick, its woody texture and scent, bring the user back to the real world, the material world the ecologist, of all people, must love.

True, there is some waste. But, it is surely less than that caused by the plastic utensils served at all too many cafeterias in the USA – and these do not take us back to our roots as do the chopsticks – and it may well be no less harmful than the detergent and energy needed for hot water to wash our utensils. Moreover, old chopsticks may always be recycled as fuel for baths (in old Edo), garden aids (stuck into the soil of pots lacking holes, they prevent root-rot) or toys. If a mountain gorilla can tear off dozens of branches of leaves to make a bed every night, surely a human can afford to use tiny twig-sized sticks to eat with several times a day! What, one wonders, does our "correct ecologist" do for toilet paper!?

飲　　　　　食　　　　　飲

"Our" biggest food-related problem with Japan in the last quarter of the twentieth century was not, however, disposable chopsticks. It was *whales*. Until the middle of this century, the contrast might have been:

> *We only kill whales for the oil and throw away most of the rest.*
> *They use all of the whale and find it very filling food.*

Needless to say, their behavior was admirable and ours was not. During the Occupation, General MacArthur *encouraged* the Japanese to go out and get whales so that the people could get enough animal protein to stay healthy. But, thirty years later, we suddenly said, *Whoa!*

Conservation of cetacean resources? Yes. *But that wasn't all.* If it were, "we" would not have continued to raise a stink about Minke whales*, for there are plenty of them*. The Japanese, not illogically, responded, *you eat cows, why can't we eat whales?* Let's face it, "we" see the cetacean as an especially intelligent and good-natured creature *worthy of special treatment,* not accorded to cows and pigs. But, did we honestly admit that? *No.* "We" are not good at complex moral issues and admitting degrees of intelligence terrifies us, so we did not and still do not admit that is what it was about. (It's easier to pretend *a whale is a whale is a whale* is scarce, even when it is a lie. In the USA, if the national executive of the Japan-American Citizen's League did not exaggerate, anti-Japanese bias arising from our teaching about "cruel" and "barbaric" Japanese whale-killers even gave rise to prejudice against Japanese-American children (in L:IOJ) In Japan, on the other hand, comic books with multi-million reader circulations featured stories about how the anti-whaling mafia in the USA attacked Japan to take the world's attention off Vietnam. (Meanwhile, polls of Japanese students showed America as more feared than the Soviet Union.) When research showed that low bad-cholesterol and high good-cholesterol properties of marine mammal meat – which explains why a solid animal diet didn't hurt the Eskimos – some Japanese cynically wrote, watch and see how long before those self-serving whites start eating whales!

The whale-eater's anger is understandable, but the Japanese mass media stressed racism too much. It failed to pay attention to Greenpeace's actions against Spanish, Norwegian, and Soviet Union (all Caucasian) whaling vessels, and professed outrage at "whites" out to trash non-white food-cultures (J/G:K). The distrust spawned by this sorry exchange, which I did my damndest to make more civil, bodes poorly for the future, where diminishing marine resources and a growing global population ensure a continuing Tragedy of the Commons, particularly over food issues.

海   鼠   腸

Midword

CHINA *VERSUS* JAPAN

From the great Jesuit scholars of the
sixteenth century down to the best
sinologists of today, we can see that
there was never a more powerful
antidote to the temptation of Western
ethnocentrism than the study of
Chinese civilization.   – Simon Leys

i

battle of the antipodes

Mirror, Mirror on the wall, who is the most other *of them all?* Simon Leys, a sinologist, claims that
honor for *his* subject:

> From a Western point of view, China is simply the other pole of the human mind.
> All the other great cultures are either dead . . . , too exclusively absorbed by the problems
> of surviving in extreme conditions . . . , or too close to us to present a contrast as total, a
> revelation as complete, an originality as illuminating as China. (THE BURNING FOREST
> 1988)

In his opinion, only China allows us to know how much of our heritage is universal and how
much reflects "Indo-European idiosyncrasies." Japan, on the other hand, "even when . . . able to
challenge the power of the West militarily, . . . never disturbed theologians or philosophers, as it was
itself proclaiming that it was marginal, eccentric, and insular."(ibid.)[1] This generalization should be
qualified on two counts. First, just because Japanese have proclaimed themselves "unique among the
peoples and cultures of the world" (Anthropologist John Embree, "the anthropologist who wrote a
classic study of a Japanese village," also D:WWM) with the implication that they are utterly beyond
comprehension, do we need to take them at their word on it? And, second, does the fact (?) a culture
is "so peculiarly *sui generis*" (Pre-WW II Japan scholar George Sansom explaining why he was
attracted to Japan. D:WWM) really remove a culture from serious consideration? Because something
is unique does not mean it must remain so.

Another scholar "originally trained in Chinese literature" came to a conclusion as different from Leys'
as night and day: "it is difficult to conceive of Japan apart from China; and yet, China seems
strangely redundant when we think of Japan." (David Pollack: *The Fracture of Meaning* . . . 1986). And
Charles A Moore, "for many years senior professor of philosophy" at the University of Hawaii,
asserted that Japan "presents more intellectual and cultural challenges . . . ," no, "more challenges to
the "orthodox" points of view of *both* [ital. mine] East and West than . . . any other major tradition."
(M:JM 1967). Only Japan, he argues, does not "accept the Socratic dictum that "the unexamined life is
unfit to live" and might rather "counter by saying that it is the examined life that is unfit to live,
because it is not *life."* (ibid.) That is to say, *only Japan turns philosophy on its head.*

All parties, then, seem to agree that, compared to China, Japan is *far out*; the only difference is
whether that makes it trivial or important!

1. Marginal and Eccentric Japanese? Eliza Scidmore gives a stunning summary of the Japanese Simon Levy seems to refer to in her JINRICKSHAW DAYS (1891). In respect to "the enigma of this century, the most inscrutable, the most paradoxical of races," she laments, "to generalize, to epitomize is impossible; for they are so opposite and contradictory, so unlike all other Asiatic peoples, that analogy fails." But you can't fault her for not trying! Scidmore gives pages of contradictions as dense as this: "they are at once the most sensitive, artistic, and mercurial of human beings, and the most impassible, conventional and stolid." Or this: "while history declares them aggressive, cruel, and revengeful, experience proves them yielding, merciful and gentle." The only other place I have ever encountered people that contradictory is in Joseph Kammen: PEOPLE OF PARADOX, a book about . . . Americans!

Ian Littlewood, makes an interesting hypothesis about the relationship of Japan-as-paradox and Japan-as-contrary:

> To define what we are, we depend on what is alien. To call Japan a paradox is really to say that it threatens the existing boundaries and therefore our definition of ourselves. (L:IOJ)

> It is for this reason that the language of paradox has always been counterbalanced by a language that reaffirms these boundaries as emphatically as possible. Benedict's honourable attempt to make sense of Japan's paradoxes in terms of 'a system consistent within itself' leads her inexorably towards a model of Japanese society that is based on a series of contrasts with American society: whereas in America we do this, in Japan they do that." (Ibid)

ii

japan over china

Despite the greater prosperity and admirable institutions of government in China, which astounded the first European visitors,[2] most Europeans who knew both the Chinese and Japanese in the 16th century were more favorably impressed with the latter. St. Xavier found that the Japanese "despise riches in comparison with dignity" so that even poor nobles were treated with the same dignity as the rich, and gave the ultimate accolade: "I hardly know whether it is practiced anywhere among Christians." While admitting the Chinese he met in Japan were "in intellect . . . superior to the Japanese," he remained convinced of "the superiority of the Japanese nation over all the others at present discovered in these parts."[3] As Frois put it not long after arriving in the Miyako (the capitol, present day Kyoto) in 1565, "In their culture, deportment, and manners, they excell the Spaniards in so many ways that one is ashamed to tell about it." [4]

China may have given birth to the Chinese character, which fueled Europe's search for Universal Letters; but it is the more complex mixed writing system of Japan that the Visitador Alessandro Valignano S.J. praised as "the most elegant and the most copious tongue in the world; it is more abundant than Latin and expresses concepts better." (C:TCJ) Vilela, Organtino, Frois and others wrote pretty much the same thing. Valignano later qualified his praise of Japanese over Latin (I think not so much because it had been criticized in Europe as because of his experience running a press translating Western books into Japanese; for translation *always* makes obvious the shortcomings of the recipient language); but he reiterated and expanded his praise of Japanese as a language whose very grammar teaches civility.

More important, *the Japanese had guts. More guts than any people the Jesuits had met.*

This was partly because the Jesuits visited right on the tail end of the Warring Era (1338-1568), hundreds of years of civil strife that most (?) Japanese historians consider an anomaly in a millennium of peace. Even the common folk had come to prefer losing their lives to losing their honor and, in Xavier's words, "value arms more than any people I have ever seen." These guts allowed the Japanese to treat guests with hospitality – instead of fleeing – and made *dignity* something real. Amazingly, it survived the long Seclusion, despite the lack of real wars (the *how* of that is worthy of a book in itself!). In 1858, the Marquis de Moge, attaché for the mission of BARON GROS'S EMBASSY TO CHINA AND JAPAN wrote:

> The Japanese know the point of honour. To take his sword from one is an insult. He cannot restore it to the scabbard without having first steeped it in blood. The Chinamen burst into a laugh when they are reproached with running away from the enemy . . . . In all respects, then, the inhabitants of Japan are a superior race to those who people China. (M:BGE)

While many if not most Jesuits were concerned about the downside of this pride, this willingness to kill and die from being "dissed" – Frois called pride their Idol! [5] – the Warriors for Christ admired the Japanese for it as much as did Baron Gros (and *every* Western writer that I know of) and thought less of the Chinese for being meek. (So much for Christian values!)

Frois's chapter about Warring and Weapons has 52 contrasts, and that doesn't include the dozens of weapon-related observations found in other chapters (especially ch I, where *weapons*, with clothing, *make the man*). Chinese scholars, like the Chinese themselves, may not think much of military power,[6] but the Christian West has usually given more ear to the strong than the weak. Before Hideyoshi decided to invade China, some Jesuits actually tried to convince the Order to invade China with the help of Japanese mercenaries! (Valignano had the good sense to stop it) [7]

---

2. The Wonders of China vs. the Excellence of Japanese. Early Western reports of China are unanimous about the size and complexity of its economy. The merchant Pereira was impressed with the highly organized and efficient economy, and the Dominican Cruz elaborated further on the same (See my 11-21 notes on the use of night-soil for the gist of their argument, for the full reports of both: B:SCSC). While not using all of Cruz's insights, the indefatigable non-fiction first-person novelist Mendez Pinto borrows from his observations and fills in many more details on what, in hindsight, might be called *the* mark of a modern economy: *specialization*. China was so crowded that "if it wasn't for the immense organization and regulation of the empire's commercial life" the Chinese assured him "then without doubt the people would end up eating each other!" That doesn't necessarily mean literally – but it might.

> In the goose trade, for example, some men take the new-laid eggs and rear young geese for market; other men rear the geese to full-size then kill and sell them for cooking; others deal only in the feathers, skins and innards; yet others deal only in the eggs. Now a man who operates in one of these lines cannot deal in any of the others; the punishment for doing so is thirty lashes with no questions asked nor any opportunity to appeal or complain; neither is there any chance of bribery or influential connections being of any use to the culprit. (P(L):TMP)

This licensing system is not simply a way to make bureaucrats rich either:

> "No merchant or tradesman can do business legally without a license from the Council and when someone applies for a trading license it is quickly granted but carries an obligation to support one or

more of the disabled people who have been trained in that particular line of business." (Ibid)

Others describe the way the blind are put to work milling, but Pinto goes far further and describes how the legless work for rope-makers and the armless are fitted out with baskets to carry things and those lacking use of all four limbs are placed in monasteries where they can work as professional mourners and sick old prostitutes are kept in nursing homes supported by working prostitutes, etc..

But the most incredible thing of all was the enormous scale of the river markets, fifteen day-long fairs, or rather temporary cites with "perhaps two thousand very long, straight thoroughfares or streets marked out between two lines of boats." Besides the usual commodities in abundance: "My readers shouldn't for a moment imagine that I'm talking about quantities that would be called vast in Europe – I'm talking about two or three hundred boatloads of any particular item" – Pinto describes streets with hundreds of boats carrying birds and fish to be bought and freed for Buddhist brownie points, others with hundreds of boats specializing in wooden idols and body parts (that sick people offer to the temple when they are cured), with books and scholars to write petitions, with wild animal shows accompanied with singing and dancing, "with awnings of silk where you can watch all sorts of plays." Some boats were allowed to move about:

> Then, there are bands of armed men who travel around in very light barges and who proclaim in large voices to passers-by that if any man's honour has been insulted or injured by someone else he should come to his barge with his grievance and they will very soon see that his honour is satisfied.

> There are barges that carry large numbers of old women who serve as midwives, giving homemade medicines to drug the babies and hasten or delay the

birth. Other barges are full of nannies who look after not only waifs and strays but any other children too, for as long as the parents want. . . .

Other boats carry large numbers of nurses who deliver enemas, many of whom[which?] are not at all unpleasant. . . [Is this for real? Could anyone check the original for ch. 99?] (Ibid)

After pages of this, Pinto stops, saying that to give all the details of the floating cities would not allow him to proceed with his story and concludes:

I will just say this: there isn't a thing on God's earth that you could ask for or desire that you will not be able to find in one of these cities in far greater quantities than I have described. . . . from what I have told you, you can judge for yourself what the rest of the country is like. (Ibid)

The economy, which was, in Pinto's opinion, largely the result of the river-based transportation network, was not the only wonderful thing about China. Because the first Portuguese to spend enough time in China to really get to know it were imprisoned yet freed and paid restitution for their imprisonment under false charges – Pereira and several others, and Pinto, too, if you believe him – the Chinese legal system was, not surprisingly, highly lauded. Unlike Europe, trials were held in open courts which made lying by witnesses, dishonest notaries and prosecutors far more difficult. (In B:SCSC) While the common use of torture is not covered up – perhaps the West felt perfectly at home with it, anyway – one feels the writers have an agenda: if China is wealthy, then it qualifies to teach Europe an object lesson, for it must be doing something right. And so long as we are using it as an example, why not pad the facts a bit on the side of Utopia? Pinto even claimed that Francis Xavier

was so impressed that he said if God saw fit to bring him back to Portugal – which God did not – the favour he would wish for our own king would be for him to study the laws and statutes by which the Chinese live in peace and war. Francis firmly believed that their laws were superior to those of the Romans in their Golden Age or any of the other nations mentioned by ancient historians. (Ibid)

Pinto – or his editor – could not allow the laws to be better than "ours," for that would be asking for censorship. But since we did permit the study of classic civilization – this was, after all, the Renaissance! – it was not unchristian to suggest study of China in such a context.

So, how can I say that Japan mattered as much as China?

Basically, it is because the Japanese were recognized as our equal *as people*. Pinto's description of China and the above statement about Xavier's opinion come about halfway through his PEREGRINATION. The Japanese, soon to be met, would prove to have far better steel and, hence, swords than the Europeans and, shortly after discovering the gun – Pinto describes this event in detail,

but he is probably fusing his experience and that of Portuguese on another shipwreck – were on their way to outgunning Europe. Pinto was *very* impressed.

From this you can see just how enterprising the Japanese are, with a temperament inclined toward the arts of war, in which they take more delight than any other race on earth. (Ibid)

Pinto used the rapidly multiplying guns to prove Xavier's assertion, which he reproduces in this sentence (after the first comma) word for word. Pinto did not detail the cleanliness, elegance, sense of honor and other good qualities – far more difficult to enumerate than the riches of a Chinese market – that Valignano later will. But, it was apparently his experience in Japan that led him to drop out of the Jesuit order he had joined after knowing and serving the soon-to-be Saint, Xavier. *Why?* Was it, as Dr. Luis Sousa Rebelo writes in the introduction to Lowery's translation, simply the discovery of "a decorum, superior to that of born Christians" that made him doubt "whether Christians were fit to convert them"? We might say it all comes down to that "extemporaneous play of the Wooden Hands" (re. the European's eating with their fingers: see 6-1) in South Japan.

Maurice Collis sees this play as a representation of the inferiority of Christian civilization and culture by comparison with Japanese refinement; but Pinto's acute discomfiture during the performance suggests further meanings. The morality play served as a reminder of the gap between his own brute behavior as a trader (and worse) and the Christians' pretensions as missionaries, between creed and deed. The play marks the end of that Christian mission.

The play – hardly a morality play! – marked the end of *that* Christian mission because Belchior was ready to pull out for the time being. The King of Bungo felt the timing was bad and his baptism might trigger a civil war. But later missionaries, including Frois, returned and Bungo fleetingly became a Christian nation. A quarter century after the play it was the stage for the Bungo Consultation, where the Jesuits made history – or should have made history! – by introducing what we today call cultural relativity and deciding upon a policy of *accommodation* rather than the *reduction* (leading a people to live in the European way) found in other parts of the world. Pinto had already confessed Portuguese emotional immaturity in China (see 14-2). Yet, he repented his ways and joined Xavier. In my opinion, the sweetness, the absolute good hearts of the Japanese he was visiting in Bungo finally sank in, partly, perhaps, because the interpreting skills had improved and partly because the princess and her attendants were so cute, and the love of her parents so apparent. The humanity of these people as people really got through to him. Pinto piled on the protestations of Portuguese discomfort to help build up tension for the resolution of the play, when the wooden hands are unveiled as a means to help the poor foreigners. Even a play roasting the Portuguese was *sweet*. So I think his real hurt was more personal than the gap between creed and deed mentioned by Dr. Rebelo. I think Pinto was homesick, nostalgic for a life he had not known as an adult, the loving life of a family. And, having known enough of Japan to know he would never fit in, he realized it was time to go home and swallow the anchor.

To sum up, China *impressed* Pinto, but the Japanese really got through to him. He was sincerely *affected*. This *things*=China versus *people*=Japan equation is found clearly spelled out in the words of Miguel=Valignano (call it the Japanese-Jesuit consensus) published in *De Missione* in Latin in 1589.

> "Namely, the Chinese, with respect to the breadth of their land, the peace and tranquility, unified law, wealth and material riches are superior to us Japanese; on the other hand, the breadth of our hearts, our defense of decorum, and the degree of our nobility are superior to theirs. (dialogue 34)"

3. *Xavier on Japan and China.* Francis Xavier, for all his respect for the Japanese, nevertheless left Japan for China, where he unfortunately died before accomplishing much (unless you count his eventual Sainthood). While the difficulty of working in a land in the midst of a civil war was part of the reason for quitting Japan, Xavier's main reason for going was his understanding that China was the way to Japan's heart. He realized that, for all the popular disdain for Chinese, Japanese still respected China as the fount of their religion (Buddhism) and moral philosophy (Confucianism – which, Xavier probably thought of as a religion), so by converting China first, the Jesuits might get a *two-in-one effect*. Xavier's precocious awareness of the directionality in Japanese adoption of foreign ideas terribly impresses this writer. The man was not only a saint, but a genius.

4. *Hicks versus Kyoto.* Frois's quote continues, "And if those people [the Portuguese merchants] who come over from China have no such high regard for the Japanese, this is due to the fact that they mingle only with the merchants, not a very courteous group, who live on the coast and who, compared to the people of Miyako in cultivation are the lowest types to be found and are referred to here in Miyako as "wild men." (English trans. publ. in Eglauer ed. but found in L:AME). There were – and are – Japanese and there are Japanese. The charming manners of the people of Miyako (Kyoto) help explain the exceptional love Organtino had for the Japanese. If he had been ministering to merchants or, worse yet, pirates, he might have been less enthusiastic.

5. *Pride, Their Idol.* Willis, Englishing Frois via Maffei's Latin, sums it up well:

> " The people tractable, civil, witty, courteous, without deceit, in virtue and honest conversation exceeding all other nations lately discovered, but so much standing on their reputation, that their chief idol may be thought honour." (Of the Island Giapan, in England and Japan . . . extracted from the "History of Travayle" 1577 (W:HOT))

6. *Differing Attitudes toward Fighters.* Valignano put it like this:

In China, no one can carry weapons; here [Japan] they invariably go about heavily armed.

The Chinese are serious in the pursuit of letters and prize learning highly, showing little interest in arms; the Japanese, on the contrary, pay no regard to learning (first rendition of *Sumario*, 1579?)

The first of these contrasts was to change the year after the TRATADO was written, when Hideyoshi disarmed the peasantry with his thorough-going Sword Hunt (katanagari) and Valignano soon learned Japanese were not so uninterested in learning as he presumed. Yet even though the population was disarmed and remained so for the duration of the Tokugawa era (1603-1867), the basic contrast remained true until the mid-Twentieth century, *for the military class was considered the elite in Japan even during its long peace* (often punctuated by peasant riots put down by brigades of untouchable eta when samurai thought it beneath them), *while the soldier was considered the pits by the Chinese*, who "abhor quarrels" and "do not wish for revenge or carry arms in order to give wounds or to kill, a thing they hold to be horrible, so that to flee from such occasions is esteemed prudent and brave" as Willis put it, paraphrasing the Jesuits.

Since the samurai was also the main literate class in Japan, modernization began *as it had to* in order to succeed in an imperialistic world: *with the imitation of weapons and militarization.* And, when Japan beat Russia, one of the greatest military powers in Europe, Japan finally put an end to "one of the oftenest repeated lessons of history . . . the superiority of Europeans to Asiatics in the arts of war and peace." Or, to borrow the first line of the Introduction of Douglas Sladen's *More Queer Things About Japan*:

"The strangest thing of all is, that they have upset the course of history." (S:MQTJ)

7. *If Japanese Mercenaries Aided a Jesuit Invasion of China.* For information about this would-be invasion and the whole incredible swash-buckling era see C.R. Boxer: THE CHRISTIAN CENTURY IN JAPAN 1549-1650 (Univ. of California Press: 1967). Boxer called the idea of using Japanese mercenaries "playing with fire." He paints a horrendous picture of mercenary/pirate *wako*, "who were frequently joined by Chinese pirates and malcontents," claiming "the raids were often accompanied with every circumstance of atrocity, such as ripping open pregnant women in order to settle wagers on the sex of the unborn child. The tales told of them in this respect resemble eye-witness accounts of the Japanese rape of Nanking in December, 1937." And elsewhere, "in view of the behavior of the Imperial Japanese Army in China from 1937 to 1945, few writers nowadays would dream of contesting the accuracy of the Chinese chronicles in this respect." The behavior of the pirates and the Imperial Army should not be used to validate historical claims in this way, for the circumstances leading to both atrocities are very, very different; and such a method of argument suggests a deep-rooted cultural propensity toward cruelty which I, at least, do not find in the Japanese.

Boxer admits similarities between the Elizabethan raids on the Spanish Main and these Japanese raids on the Chinese one – both pirates traded when they had to. But, looking at Kwan-wai So's painstaking investigation of Chinese documentary material (JAPANESE PIRACY IN MING CHINA DURING THE 16th CENTURY Mich. State UP 1975), it is clear that the Chinese deserve much more credit(!) for the "Wo-k'ou" piracy. They took a much more active role – indeed were the instigators in most cases – than was previously realized. Crooked Chinese *used* Japanese in the usual way mercenaries are used, for their fighting, but also for scare-value (Japanese fighters were so feared in China that they were used as boogeymen – *Go to sleep, baby, or the Japanese will get you!*) and to conceal their own identities when smuggling and plundering their own land! The raids, then, often bore a resemblance to the fake indian raids occasionally carried out on a much smaller scale by renegade whites on the North American frontier.

If *wako* were not all Japanese, the Chinese were not always as meek as they were made out, either. This needs to be pointed out, because meekness is never praised by the writers of "our" belligerent culture. Even Kaempfer's young translator, J. G. Scheuchzer, whose father was "largely instrumental in procuring the abolition of capitol punishment for witchcraft" and – shades of Ben Franklin and Erasmus Darwin, but earlier – represents

> a company of fossil fishes which bitterly complain to each other that not only had they been destroyed and buried as a result of the just punishment of impious mankind, but that the iniquitous descendants of the iniquitous human beings who had perished in the Flood now dared to assert that these fossil fishes had never been living organisms, but were mere freaks of nature, perhaps engendered in the rocks by some occult influence of the stars,"

yes, even he, cannot refrain from mentioning the "effeminate slothfulness of the Chinese" in his introduction (1727). "Effeminate" was Kaempfer's favorite adjective for the Chinese. (K(S):HOJ)

Frois, in his *Historia* gives the only reasoned appraisal of the Chinese on this count that I know of by a European.

> Japanese and other peoples have a mistaken idea about the Chinese, so the battles of Augustino's (Onishi Yukinaga – one of the Japanese Christians Hideyoshi sent off to conquer Korea and China, mostly to get them out of his way) battles with the Chinese were a real eye-opener. People think the Chinese are weak by nature and even in countless numbers will flee in terror from a few enemy upon hearing a gunshot or seeing a drawn sword. This idea came from those Japanese [pirates] who went to rob China's coast where there were no soldiers but only farmers and townsmen who had never held a weapon so that a couple hundred Japanese could put to rout countless Chinese. It also agrees with the testimony of Portuguese about the Cantonese soldiers. They had no war experience, had never once met an enemy, and lacking a fighting spirit behaved very cowardly when they happened to get into a battle.
>
> But the unit of soldiers who came to fight Augustino [a Christian Japanese noble] were from the lands bordering the Tartars, where they engage them in constant warfare. So, as they proved on the battlefield, they were very brave and skilled in the martial arts. . . ." (J/F:Historia pt3 ch54 bk 5)

So, it depends *what* Chinese you're talking about. But, even if Frois did correct a stereotype about China as a whole, neither he nor Valignano ever praises the pacifistic side of China. The martial Westerners and Japanese could not do that until the arrival of pacifists who were clearly courageous as seasoned soldiers – the Thoreaus, Gandhis, and Martin Luther Kings of the world. They certainly were not meek like the coastal Chinese.

iii

the chineseness of japan

The first "China vs. *Europe*" listing that I know of – remember, Valignano's short-lived contrast was between "China and *Japan*" – was a long paragraph by the above-mentioned Marquis de Moge.

> In China, the compass is not made to point to the north, but to the south. It has five, not four cardinal points. The left, not the right side, is the place of honour. White, not black, is the suit of woe. Etiquette ordains we should not take off the hat, but put it on, in the presence of a superior, or of anyone whom we wish to honour. Books are printed and read, not from left to right, after our fashion, but from right to left. At dinner, fruit comes first, and soup last. As children learn their lessons aloud, all saying them over at the same time, it is the object of the Chinese schoolmaster not to keep a quiet school, but to make his little congregation as noisy as possible; and silence is punished as proof of idleness.

When a man is ennobled for a service done the state, honours so acquired do not descend, as with us, to his posterity, but, strange to say, ascend to his ancestors and ennoble them. They all become, by a retrospective action, dukes and barons and so forth, while the children and descendents of the new-made noble remain undistinguished in the common herd. Pages might be filled with similar contrasts between the habits of Europeans and Chinamen. [8] (M:BGE:1860)

As far as I know, those pages were *not* filled until Dyer Ball's Chamberlain-influenced THINGS CHINESE (1890), in which four pages are given to "Topsyturvydom" (He uses no hyphens.). If Ball follows Chamberlain, not to mention Valignano and Frois, the Chinese side of most of the dozens of contrasts mentioned precede them in reality, for things Japanese often derive from China.[9] Almost all of the following contrasts in a May 1932 *Ripley's "Believe It Or Not!"* column dealing with China are condensed from Ball and most are previously found in Chamberlain and/or Frois about Japanese.

He laughs when he is sad and cries when he is glad.
Wears white instead of black when in mourning.
Makes the lining of a suit first.
Shake hands with himself when he meets a friend.
Removes his shoes instead of his hat when entering a house.
Wears skirts and puts his vest on over his coat.
Drinks hot tea to keep cool and carries a fan in cold weather.
Does not receive a permanent name until he is dead.
Scratches his foot instead of his head when puzzled.
He is one year old the day of his birth.
He mounts a horse from the right side and puts him in the stall backward.
Builds the roof of his house first.
His fractions are upside down.
Whitens his shoes instead of blackening them.

..

Despite the fact that cultural relativism was already reforming academia, Ripley's horrid caption "the Heathen Chinee is peculiar!"[10] reveals how shamefully disrespectful our culture had become toward the non-Western world at the time. (*Ripley's* was found in Arthur Waldron's *The Great Wall of China* (1990 Cambridge UP). The ethnocentric framing (*Heathen Chinee!?*) and the lack of proper explanation made the contrasts, in themselves harmless, uniformly degrading to the Chinese.[11] The words of Nitobe Inazo, who worked so hard to bring out similarities in Japan and the West (see note 7-41), come to mind:

"The atmosphere of the Pacific seems to possess the obnoxious power of throwing above the horizon on either side not only an inverted but a perverted image." ("The East and the West" [12]

But the fact that much of what is Japanese is Chinese – as much of what is Western European is Latin (Funny how the Japanese "copied" the Chinese, while our ancestors "inherited" culture from the Greeks and Romans! [13]) – in no way detracts from Japan's antipodal character with respect to the West. China deserves credit for so much of Japan in particular and the world's culture in general that I would never belittle it; but tell me, sinologists, is there a list of Chinese opposites as long as this Japanese list of Luis Frois S.J.? And could "Chinks" possibly replace "Japs" in the following claim made by James Bond's colleague in Tokyo? (YOU ONLY LIVE TWICE, cited in L:IOJ)

The bloody Japs do everything the wrong way round.

8. *Moge's China Contrasts.* Most of the contrasts are either self-explanatory or explained elsewhere in this book. Exceptions are the five cardinal points which include a theoretical up-down axis that in no way confuses the directions, which are the same as ours, with the exception of the South being "up" on most maps, as it was once with us, too; the method of awarding titles retrospectively to ancestors, which makes more sense than ours does, because family tradition helps make us what we are and, scholars, in particular, are seldom made in a single generation, while any tradition can easily end in a generation. (In this respect, Valignano, for once, uses contrast to put Europe and Japan *on the same side*, for in his last LIBRO (1601), he notes the absence of hereditary nobility (*nobleza por generacion*) in China (carefully admitting the exception of some of the King's sons) as a natural consequence of titles gained by letters, as opposed to the power of arms, as was the case in Japan, where titles, i.e. hereditary status was passed down the generations from antiquity "in the same manner as do the hidalgos of Spain." (V:LIBRO)

While I wrote that Moge's was the earliest "Europe vs. China" *list* of contrasts, many Europe-*Japan* contrasts are found *scattered* here and there as 'Europe vs. *China*.' For example, one finds a passage in Thomas Hood's *"The War with China"* (c.1840) which contrasts Western gigantism with Chinese miniaturism:

"To look at a Chinese service" he said, "is enough of itself to make one a teetotaller. It inspires one – at least it does me – with the Exquisite's horror of malt liquor and such gross beverages. Indeed, to compare our drinking vessels with the Chinese, they are like horse-buckets to bird-glasses; and remembering their huge flagons, and black-jacks and wassail bowls, our Gothic and Saxon ancestors must have been a little coarse, not to say a little hoggish, in their draughts."

"They must, indeed," said my Father.

"Now here is a delicate drinking-vessel," continued my Uncle, taking up from the side-table a cup hardly large enough for a fairy to get into. "What sort of liquor ought one to expect from such a pretty little chalice?"

"At a guess," replied my Father, very gravely, "nothing coarser than mountain-dew."

"Yes," said my Uncle, with enthusiasm; "to drink out of such a diminutive calyx, all enameled with blossoms, is indeed like to the poetical fancy of sipping dew out of a flower! . . ." (vol.3 HOOD'S OWN or the works of ~ London 1870)

This Tristam Shandy-style discussion continues for pages until it can be conclusively ended as you might guess by John Bull in the china. Kipling's contrast of Western grossness and Eastern daintyness in a Japanese shop (ch.1 endnote) may well reflect this earlier work.

9. *Chinese Topsyturvydom.* Ball's style is clearly influenced by Alcock, Lowell Chamberlain and others who emphasized the topsy-turvyness of Japan, rather than Marquis de Moge's simple mention of "contrasts" (possibly "contradictions" in the French). His Chinese *Topsyturvydom* heading starts off in the pattern we are already familiar with for Japan:

"It is the unexpected that one must expect, especially in this land of topsyturvydom. The Chinese are not only remote from us with regard to position on the globe, but they are our opposites in almost every action and thought. It never does to judge how a Chinese would act under certain circumstances from what we ourselves would do if placed in similar conditions: the chances are he would do the very actions we would never think of performing; think the very thoughts that would never occur to us; and say what no foreigner [Occidental] would ever think of uttering. He laughs when he tells you his father or mother, brother or sister, is dead . . ."

A number of his contrasts, such as the language-related examples are unique to Chinese, but, as I show in the brackets, hardly so contrary as Ball makes them sound!

"He asks you if you have eaten your rice, instead of saying 'How do you do?' and locates his intellect in his stomach. [What is kinder than asking if the other party has eaten?] For 'goodbye' he says 'walk slowly.' [Versus "Godspeed?" – my association is the 1960's "Take it easy!"] Instead of telling you to take heart and be brave when any danger threatens, he tells you to lessen your heart; [a "small heart" means being attentive in Chinese, but not Japanese – i.e., a perfectly normal: "Take care!"] . . ." (B:TC)

While Ball admits the Chamberlain connection with respect to the title of the book in his foreword, he says nothing of the fact that, despite the Chineseness of so many particulars, the Japanese – or, at least those Occidentals who wrote about them – pretty much gained the patent on being contrary. In this respect, Ball behaves just like my impression of all too many Chinese scholars today: he *ignores* Japan.

10. *The Heathen Chinee is Peculiar.* This atrocious phrase was lifted without amendment from *"Plain Language from Truthful James,"* an 1870 poem about a Chinese hustler by Francis Bret Harte. After de-scribing the 24 packs found in the card-shark's long sleeves and the wax in his long nails, Truthful James reiterates his claim about the Chinese:

"Which is why I remark, / And my language is plain, / That for ways that are dark / And for tricks that are vain, / The heathen Chinee is peculiar, – / Which the same I am free to maintain."

Harte was *the* poet for the low-brow American up to World War II, after which folkish poetry (telling a story in rhyme) came to be pretty much monopolized by country music. While his "Cremation of Sam Magee" –

my father's favorite (which he had me read to him not long before he was cremated!) – deserves to join Kipling's best story poems, the poem Ripley plagiarizes is not even third-rate!

11. *Odious Contrast: "Believe it (and Understand it) or Not!"* Most of Ripley's contrasts are explained in the notes to this book. A few words in respect to some that are *not*.

The *whitewashed shoes.* I guess golfers weren't much of a presence in 1932. In the summer, such a color would be cool and healthy, almost as good as sandals.

The *"skirts."* This contrast had to be new – not owing anything to Valignano and Frois – because until the seventeenth or eighteenth century, many European men were still be-skirted, and the Jesuits were, as always, robed.

The *hot day hot tea.* I once had a Japanese room-mate who ate a lot of chili pepper in his hot noodles to cool off by sweating – it worked, but he was hospitalized with a bleeding ulcer. Actually, many people in sultry climates go for spicy food. (and the hottest Chinese food is in the South) Maybe *hot* is *hot.*

The *fan in the winter* makes sense if you imagine either fanning a fire and spreading heat around, or cooling down the air above (for air at face level is too hot when it is right for the feet).

And the *foot scratching* is logical enough for someone seated with a foot up as is often the case for Chinese – we should add that Chinese always have their feet in socks, (unlike the Japanese) and are fastidious about it. They are not scratching anything as dirty as might be imagined.

The *year count* – now, this is interesting! – is a normal "inclusive" way of counting, which is what we use referring to centuries when we call the 1800's "the *nineteenth* century." That is to say, to be *one* is to be *in* one's first year of life, which can be said for even the most post-mature baby. The inclusive count is also convenient, for month-wise, a baby is born ten months old, and Chinese are nothing if not decimal in orientation. (The Chinese and Japanese did not, however, use the inclusive count as often as our Roman ancestors, whose *"See you in three days!"* meant the day after tomorrow!) In China, but not Japan, individual birthdays were celebrated, but that didn't change the annual principle of aging for both people, that we take on a new year with the New Year —a child born on the last day of the year would be two years old the very next day! The Romans (and Japanese) thought likewise.

12. *"The East and the West".* Nitobe's prescient essay in THE JAPANESE NATION is cited at length in my ORIENTALISM & OCCIDENTALISM. One line in it is particularly relevant to this book: *"A mere description without an explanation is likely to lead to a wrong inference."*

13. "America as Japan" or, *Imitation in the West.* Not only was the West good at imitating=learning, but the West's West, namely the United States of America was especially so. Here is a Chinese writing in the twentieth century.

> "Psychologists divide human talents into three kinds: ability to invent, ability to put to practical use, and ability to imitate. Because America is a late-comer nation, inventive ability is not frequently seen, but America's practical and imitative talents are unusual and unmatched by other nations. No matter what the branch of science, once it is transmitted to the United States, Americans use their talents to imitate it, put it to practical use, and develop it. (LAND WITHOUT GHOSTS (A&L:LWG))"

The Wright brothers were the exception, not the rule. Henry Ford was to the Europeans who invented the automobile what the Japanese in the 1970's and 80's were to "us." Things only changed with the massive brain drain from Europe to the United States after the Nazi rise to power.

iv
the un-chineseness of japan

In THE VOYAGE OF VAN LINSCHOTEN TO THE EAST INDIES (English trans. 1598) a couple pages are dedicated to a just-so story explaining why "touching their traffique, manners, speach, and all their ceremonies" the Japanese "are cleane contrarie unto all other nations, speciallie from those of China, and till this day observe the same as an infallible [orig. *aangeboren,* or "hereditary":) law."

Once upon a time, the story began, "a great and mightie familie" in China tried to kill the King of China and usurp his kingdom. They failed and "divers of the principall conspirators" were put to death. Most of the kinsman were allowed to live and given a punishment which for the Chinese "was little better than death," banishment, for "them and all their posteritie for ever out of the countrie, into the Ilands of Iapen, which as then were not inhabited."

whereby there is so great [envie and] hatred betweene them and the men of China, that they hate each other to the death, and doe all the mischief one unto the other that they can [imagine or devise], even untill this time. The men of Iapen have done much mischief unto the men of China, and many times have fallen upon their coasts, and put all to fire and sword, and now [at this present] have not any conversation with them, but onely they trafficke with the Portingales, and to shew themselves whollie their deadlie enemies, in all their actions they are cleane contrary to the men of China, and to the same end have changed all their customes, ceremonies and [manners of] curtesie from the men of China . . . where the China useth the curtesie of salutation to a man with the head and hand, when they meet together: the Iapens to the contrarie put off their shoes, whereby they shewe them reverence, and as the Chinaes stand up when they minde to recyve any man, and to doe him reverence, they to the contraire set themselves down . . .[14]

After these two partially garbled examples, where Chinese act like Europeans – perhaps twisted from Valignano=Maffei's "us *versus* them" context to better fit his theory – Van Linschoten immediately drops all mention of the Chinese and simply lists strange Japanese customs with occasional reference to Europe ("we").   Montanus retold the legend in 1670, improving the punchline.

> . . . they so much abhor and loath the Chinese Customs and Fashions, that rather than they would resemble them in their behavior, they have taught themselves such preposterous actions, that they are not onely unlike them, but all the world beside. (M:EEJ)

– but wisely separates the Chinese-Japanese contrasts from the bulk of the European-Japanese contrasts by a few chapters, thus repeating contradictions where some Japanese traits in the latter contrast repeat Chinese ones in the first. *It is not easy to make black and white contrasts of* three *cultures!*

---

14. *The Just-so story and Another to Boot.* A footnote to Van Linschoten's text, by Arthur Coke Burnell says "this story is given in De La Porta's French version of Mendoca, and by Parke in his English version 1588." "It is not, however, in the 1596 edition of the Spanish, though, probably it may have been in earlier ones. The Italian version of the first edition does not give it." If it can be traced back before 1580, it will be the earliest clear exposition of the "contrary Japanese" we have – unless there is a letter of Frois, Vilela or Almeida out there with such opinions in it (I suspect there are). Linoschoten's contrasts come from Maffei, who took most of them from Valignano, who, as we have noted, probably requisitioned them from Frois.

The matter of where the Japanese come from has long interested both Japanese and Europeans – no one asks where the Chinese come from, or where Koreans come from, but an island people are always from somewhere – Kaempfer (1690), noted both the "forged and fabulous" story of "Linschoot" and another with a better pedigree which has an expedition of "300 young men and so many women headed by a physician" coming from China ostensibly to investigate elixirs of immortality for the emperor, but actually to escape, for he was a Nero-like

tyrant who "caus'd once a large Spot of Ground to be dug up for a Lake, and having order'd it to be fill'd with Chinese Beer, he sail'd over it in stately Barges."

Kaempfer himself thought a Chinese origin impossible not only for the entirely different "inclinations of the mind" – "peaceful, modest and lovers of a sedate, speculative and philosophical way of life" = Chinese *vs.* Japanese = "war-like, inclined to rebellions and a dissolute life . . . and always bent on high designs" – but because the languages were far too different, and instead proposed that the Japanese migrated to their Island *straight from Babylonia* because the language was particularly pure (no others like it). Yes,

> they are descended of the first Inhabitants of Babylon and . . . the language is one of those, which Sacred Writs mention, that the all-wise Providence hath thought fit, by way of punishment and confusion, to infuse into the minds of the vain builders of the Babylonian Tower. (K(S):HOJ)

I should add for readers unfamiliar with Kaempfer that *on the whole* his work is extremely scientific and based on fact-finding.

V
japan vs. *china*

When Valignano first wrote about the radical difference in European and Japanese civilization, he did indeed contrast China and Japan:

> In dress, in food, in almost every action they [the Japanese] differ so much from all other races, European or otherwise, that it almost seems as if they were consciously aimed at acting habitually in the opposite way to others, especially the Chinese, to whom they trace their origin. In everything they try to do just the reverse. The Chinese, for example, have one ruler for their whole empire . . . ; whereas the Japanese have thousands of masters to deal with . . . . In China, no one can carry weapons; here they invariably go about heavily armed. . . . The Chinese will have no friendly relations nor converse with outsiders, while the Japanese are very fond of strangers. The Chinese have the best government imaginable and are sticklers for ordered ways, while here no order or government prevails. In short, they behave in a way quite the reverse of the Chinese and indeed of any other nation. It is clear from all this that Japan constitutes a world apart, and that the people in it act in many original ways new to the rest of mankind. (trans. John J. Coyne in S(C):VMP)

Unlike Van Linschoten, Valignano's contrasts, of which there were over a dozen (which we have seen here and there in this book) were basically correct. Nevertheless, the contrasts did not remain in his later work, except in so far that they are incorporated into the Europe vs. *Japan* contrasts. Evidently, Valignano's experience in Japan – including a long time with Frois – taught him that the differences between Japan and Europe were so much greater than those with China that contrast with China was moot.[15]

Still, Valignano retains the gist of his argument that the Japanese are not only different but *want to be* different: that they seem *to study [try] in order to do everything contrary to others* (*que de proposito estudiaron de hacer todo lo contrario de los otros.*). This last line is echoed by the Hungarian-born English critic and travel writer George Mikes in 1970:

> the Japanese are human beings like the rest of us, but they will strongly resent this insinuation. They want to be different." (THE LAND OF THE RISING YEN).[16]

If Japanese, then, really are contrary – the antipodes incarnate – the question remaining is *why* this might be so. Here, we come back to their relationship with China. Frois wrote

> . . . albeit the Japans received out of Siam, and China, their superstitions and ceremonies, yet they nevertheless contemn all other nations in comparison with themselves, and standing in their own conceit do far prefer themselves before all other sorts of people in wisdom and policy. (Willes trans. of a Frois letter in his 1577 HISTORY OF TRAVAYLE)

Frois' "albeit" – if it is indeed Frois's – is, I think, wrong. It makes more sense to say that *because* of the cultural debt, Japan developed an inferiority complex and compensated with a superiority complex (as the Usanians did with their cock-a-doodle poetry (vs. England) in the nineteenth century). This, too, would, of course, be a gross oversimplification; but it would make some sense of something real that gave rise to that just-so story. [17] It makes me wonder – *How would the European psyche have developed had "we" barbarians not managed to over-run Rome and turn the ancients into ourselves?*

15. *Minimizing Difference with China.* Valignano also wrote that China bore many similarities with Europe (*tiene muchas semejanza con Europa*). It would seem that respect for Chinese was based on a recognition of similar good points – in particular involving government and social care – or recognition of human identity, while respect for Japanese was largely developed from a different-but-equal, or cultural relativity perspective.

16. *Wanting to be Different.* The extent to which Japanese are different from others – as all cultures differ from other cultures – and the question as to how much Japanese tend to emphasize their difference are different, but not all together different matters. One finds native Americans defining themselves as "what the white man is not" (see Keith Basso's PORTRAITS OF "THE WHITEMAN" – Cambridge: 1979), and one can easily imagine a tendency for the minority peoples in the Sino-cultural sphere to identify themselves in such a manner with respect to China. This tendency could then be expanded to protect the Japanese identity with respect to the new China, i.e. the West. I feel that in the latter half of the twentieth century, the excessive emphasis on difference on the part of Japanese hurt their ability to contribute toward a better world. (See my books written in Japanese, or ORIENTALISM & OCCIDENTALISM)

17. *Japanese Prejudice Against the Chinese.* The just-so story of Japanese with a chip on their shoulders against the Chinese is supported by many sources. Unfortunately, the prejudice survived the end of the Warring Era and remained in the Isolationist Tokugawa times when one might expect Japanese to be more sympathetic to another pacifistic people. In the early

nineteenth century Golownin wrote:

> "The Japanese even abominate the idea that the Chinese may have been their ancestors; their contempt of that nation goes so far, that when they mean to call any one a rogue or a cheat, they say he is a true Chinese." (G:MCJ)

And Moges in 1860 wrote that though "the Chinese consider Japan as a country tributary to the Middle Empire,"

> At Yedo, we were obliged to put a stop to our Chinese servants' going on shore in consequence of the practical jokes provoked by their dresses and tails. which were a great source of fun to the natives of Japan. (M:BGE)

When Japan reopened in the mid-nineteenth century, the Chinese were not only denigrated as cowards as opposed to the brave Japanese, but strongly reproached for two other things by all Westerns who saw both countries. First, to use Moge's words, "The Chinese are dreadfully dirty; the Japanese are cleanly to a miracle." And, second, the Chinese were too conceited to learn from others, namely the West. The Japanese apparently shared this view of the Chinese, so it is wrong to blame the West for teaching Japanese to despise the rest of Asia. *Japanese need to accept full responsibility for their own prejudices.* Still, Japanese prejudice against other Asians was not recognized as a problem by Westerners until Satow and Chamberlain pointed it out in the late-19th century and even then, they did not so much criticize it as *wrong* as point out that it boded ill for Japan's future as a colonial power.

vi
japan more chinese than china?

Radical contrasts of Japan and the West did not end with the Age of Exploration. I-saw-the-exotic-East books by 19th century Western visitors were particularly taken by the otherness of Japan as the most Eastern place in the world, and Japanese today tend to agree with them. If Usanians have called themselves a "melting pot," Japanese in the latter half of the twentieth century often called their culture a *cul de sac* of Eastern culture. *We are more Indian than India*, they claim, for Buddhism that died out there still thrives in Japan. *We are more Chinese than China*, for the Taoism there is hardly so healthy as Zen in Japan, nor the rock gardens so well developed, etc. Nay, this is true for all Asia:

> It is in Japan alone that the historic wealth of Asiatic culture can be consecutively studied through its treasured specimens" (O:IOE)

– boasts Okakura in 1903. Indeed, the Japanese are so closely identified with many of these things today that the Chinese and we who think highly of China and its civilization must constantly remind Japanophiles where all of it came from![18]   That is why I sometimes go out of the way to point out the Chinese roots of this or that item in this book and will now introduce a long quote from Frois's contemporary, the Florentine merchant Carletti:

> And it is possible to believe beyond any doubt that all these things [printing, making artillery and gun powder] came from them. And I agree to the statement that not only these, but every invention for good or for evil, of beauty or of ugliness, must have come from that region, or, at least it can be affirmed that they have in themselves the knowledge of everything, not having had it from us or from the Greeks or other nations who taught it to us, but from native creators in that huge and very ancient country which, as they say, predates by many millennia the creation of the world described by Moses, and this according to the belief that they hold, which is no less fabulous than false. (C(W):MVAW)

So, long before Professor Needham, China's priority in the arts and sciences was acknowledged. *Or was it?* Carletti's last line, if the translation is accurate, is dis/ingenious to say the least, and seems to be an equivocation intended to save its author from being accused of heresy.

18. *Chinese Roots.* One reason too little attention is given to the Chinese roots of many things Japanese is the tendency for Japan's culture to be denigrated as "imitative." If there were no such ridiculous onus attached to learning from others, the Japanese would feel freer to boast about their cultural debts. (It is, after all, always the wealthy who enjoy the most debt.) On the other hand, one reason the amount Japan has borrowed is all too obvious for those who care to look is because the Japanese are exceptionally faithful to the original. Countless scholars Japanese and non-Japanese have written about how Japan has a special skill for *adapting* what it adopts. But this is true for most cultures. Usania – at least until the recent rise of the *unmeltable ethnics* – has long been so successful at adapting things that we don't even know they were adopted! Our traditional mode of borrowing is complete incorporation. Most italicized things only remain in italics for *decades*, whereas, in Japanese, most remain obviously foreign in their stiff-looking *katakana* (カタカナ) syllabets – the equivalent of italic letters, but opposite in the sense that italics seem soft while *katakana* is harder than the usual *hiragana* (ひらがな) syllabets – *forever*. *Tempura* is one of a small number of seeming exceptions adopted in Frois's time when the italic for foreign things was the soft and beautifully flowing *hiragana*. (It is tempting to explain this change from soft to hard denotation to a new complex toward foreign things, developed during Tokugawa isolation; but it probably happened because *hiragana* came to replace *katakana* as the main phonetic syllabary used by men – women had always used it – so foreign terms were, naturally, given the less frequently used script.)

A good example of the permanence of difference in the Japanese style of "imitation" is the pipe/*kiseru*. Tobacco was introduced about twenty years after the TRATADO was written, and only ten years after that, in 1615, Englishman Richard Cocks wrote "men, woman and children" were "besotted in drinking that herb." By drinking, he meant smoking, for a 1619 journal entry says

the town of Ashia was sett on fire some 10 daies past by drinking of tobaco , where their were above 400 howses burned, and 8 of the richest men in the towne burned in adventuring over far to save their monies and goods.

Needless to say, there were many crackdowns; but tobacco was apparently harder to control than firearms, for in 1890, Chamberlain wrote "now there is hardly a man or woman throughout the length and breadth of the land who does not enjoy the fragrant weed;" but here is where he misses something:

> One of the countless ways in which the nation is Europeanising itself is by the adoption of cigarette-smoking. But the tiny native pipe – it looks like a doll's pipe – holds its own side by side with the new importation. (C:TJ)

> The diminutive pipes of modern Japan are but one among the innumerable instances of the tendency of Japanese taste toward small things. To judge from the old pictures that have been preserved, the first Japanese pipes must have been as large as walking-sticks, whereas those now used give a man but three whiffs. (Ibid)

After this, Chamberlain's discussion expands like a smoke ring as he comes to explain "the pipe as an evolutionary centre, a whole elegant little world of smoking furniture and tobacco etiquette has come into existence," without neglecting to mention how granny uses her pipe "as a domestic rod" for disciplining children "or possibly the daughter-in-law."

So what does he miss? The fact that the Japanese *kiseru* has remained basically the same (the stem, which showed some variation, grew *larger,* then returned to the original length of 6-10 inches) over the centuries, with the same basic design and bowls the same size they were *when the Portuguese introduced the habit* – the pipes themselves were South-east Asian, originally for opium (?) – while pipes in Europe evolved into quite different large-bowled and bent-stem devices. Today, the Japanese still call the *kiseru* (from Cambodian *khsier*, for a pipe=tube) a *kiseru*;

and, although few smoke them – all recognize them from television Easterns and they are idiom for *cheating with subway passes* for the end-pieces are expensive while the bamboo tube is cheap – and call the new Western devices *paipu*. I.e., by preserving the adopted item as is – while evolving the supporting universe of paraphernalia, we leave to Chamberlain to describe – then later, again, adopting another item, and preserving it, too, name and all, *Japanese "copying" tends to preserve diverse strands of culture, to create a vertically deep poliverse.* The kimono, not so different from the kimono in Frois's day, survives together with modern Western dress, even if it is usually only worn at weddings and festivals, whereas Westerners, who roll up the carpet when they progress, are oblivious to even their own old dress! Fashion and fad make it likely that only one strand in Japan is popular at a time, but the others remain, tenuously, perhaps, but they do remain for as close to forever as you will find in human culture. And *that* is what I like best about Japan.

If England today is not so closely identified with "copying" as Japan, this was not always the case. In Frois's day, English criticized themselves for aping continental culture and this criticism continued until they self-righteously criticized the United States of America for copying *them*. Be that as it may, I cannot help but introduce the fact that on Thursday, March 3rd, 1753, Adams Fitz-Adams published a fine rejoinder to those

who feared the Sinofication of England. *You have got to be kidding*, he replied,

> "the present innovations are by no means adequate to such an effect: for on a moderate computation, not one in a thousand of all the stiles, gates, rails, pales, chairs, temples, chimney-pieces, &c.&c.&c. which are called Chinese, has the least resemblance to anything that China ever saw; nor would an English church be a less uncommon sight to a traveling mandarin, than an English pagoda. I think it necessary to say thus much, in order to quiet the scruples of conscientious persons, who will doubtless be more at ease when they consider that our Chinese ornaments are not only of our own manufacture, like our French silks and our French wine, but, what has seldom been attributed to the English, of our own invention." (a Letter from H.S. in *THE WORLD* no.12)

I do not know enough about China to make any statements about its ability or inability to imitate others – to meaningfully compare – we all know the standard line which is identical in the West and Japan: *the Chinese were too proud to copy because they thought they were the center of the world.* But, I suspect the truth is far more complex.

vii
the "true orient"

But forget reality! It is more romantic to view Japan as the font of the East. Frois's contemporary Joao Rodrigues began "This Island of Japon" with a long account of the Proper Names for the nation used both within and without. Some of them, including the most commonly used one today, formalize Japan's extreme location:

> *Nichi-iki* is a dignified name much in use among the Chinese in their books and chronicles. The Chinese pronounce it Jih-yu, and it means Limit of the Sun or of the Orient, where the sun rises and the world begins, for they believe it begins there. . . .

> So to get rid of the ignominious name of the Kingdom of Servants or Slaves, they called the land *Nihon* or *Nippon*, or in the native Japanese *Hi-no-moto*, meaning the beginning or origin of the sun . . . .

> The name certainly fits these islands, for not only are they the most easterly known and form the limit of the Orient (which the ancient geographers placed 180° from the prime meridian passing through the Fortunate Isles [Canary Islands]) but also as far as India and Europe are concerned, Japan is the true Orient, as we have said, where the sun rises before reaching these countries. (R(C):TIJ) [19]

Dig through the earth, then, Rodrigues seems to be saying, and you will come out, not in China, but in Japan!

19. *Japan as Most Easterly.* The name Nihon=Japan records the geographical perspective of people who did not live there. Needless to say, Japanese standing on their Eastern coast knew the Sun did not pop up inside of their own land. I would like to know more about how ancient Japanese – who most commonly called their country

Yamato, written with the characters meaning "Big-Peace" – came to accept the name they now use. (「日ノ本」という発想の歴史とその受け取り方、つまり公認、又、非難を、知りたい。知識ある方に、本書再版に掲載してもいい＜欄外注＞を、よろしくお願いします！)

envoi
What About Marco Polo?

There is someone whose name is better known to most of us than any other traveler mentioned in this book, who went from the Far West to the Far East long before Portuguese ships spanned the globe and the Jesuit order was founded. How does he fit in?

Marco Polo says nothing about *contrary* customs. In fact, the only human artifacts that he clearly took as opposite to the West – although, even here, he did not so express it – was the Sino-Mongolian use of paper for money, which he rightly considered a practical sort of alchemy and "a magnificent palace roofed entirely with fine gold, as we might use lead for our houses and churches" in a place called *Zipangu* (Japan) "an island in the middle of the Ocean, 1,500 miles from the mainland . . . whose inhabitants have white skins and beautiful manners." (trans. Waugh: 1984) [20]

There is no lack of fabulous items. *Elephant-carrying birds!* Or, historical fact. *The first news to reach Europe of the defeat of the Tartar navy by the Japanese with the help of a typhoon.* And Polo did find a place with a *different* non-human nature: the Malabar Coast (South-West India).

Everything there is different from what it is with us and excels both in size and beauty. They have no fruit the same as ours, no beast, no bird. This is the consequence of the extreme heat. (found in G:PPI) [21]

The expression "everything .. is different" has a contrary ring to it, but is not quite the same thing as *opposite*. The only genuine topsy-turvy items in Polo's account are not of an Eastern *versus* Western nature. In Tandifu, a place between Peking and Amoy, he finds virginity was so highly valued a father "signs an agreement with the bridegroom" attesting to it, after which "the relations of both families and certain matrons" test her virginity with a pigeon's egg." We shall skip further bloody details! Let us just say, Richard Burton was vague compared to Polo.

In order to keep their virginity intact, the girls in these parts avoid all violent movement and walk with the tiniest possible steps. (Ibid)

On the other hand, twenty days into Tibet, Polo finds a culture where

"No man will marry a virgin on the grounds that if a woman has not had several lovers she must be undesirable to men and unloved by the gods. So when foreigners or strangers pitch their tents in the area, as many as forty young girls may be brought by their mothers from the village and offered to them. The more attractive are welcomed and the others go sadly home." (Ibid.)

Marco Polo was as delighted with this last practice as Herodotus was with the Babylonian Marriage

Market, and writes more, but my point is made. [20] While Marco Polo may have reached the ends of the Earth, he did not polarize it into East and West. Perhaps this is because his travels progressed Eastward by degree; culturally speaking, he never flipped over, as a man crossing the ocean would.[21]

20. Beautiful Manners. This is remarkable: *Can anyone give me the original word used for "manners" here?*

21. *The Malabar Mystery*. I overlooked this sentence about Malabar when I read Marco Polo and only pegged it down reading it a second time in Gaitonide (G:PPI), who also quotes a pioneering Portuguese apothecary, Tomé Pires on the same Malabar as follows:

> When they are ill, the patients do not eat meat: and have a diet of fish also. The chief remedy is to play the kettledrum and other instruments to the patients for two or three days and they say this does good [we seek quiet repose for the same reason]. If they have fever, they eat fish and keep washing themselves [we avoid the bath] . . . Our people when they have fevers eat fat chickens and drink wine and are cured." (SUMA ORIENTAL, in G:PPI)

Now this may not seem like much – I had to add the brackets to bring out the implied contrasts – but it is possible that the implications are clear enough that a reading could have triggered Valignano's first foray into topsy-turvy territory, a possibility that strengthens when we note the prominent and early appearance of similar medical related detail in his work. Not having read Pires' SUMA ORIENTAL, I can't say how much topsy-turvy is in it, but one more quote found in Gaitonide is suggestive:

> In Malabar, it is the custom for the woman to have her eyes on the bed during the act of coition and for the man to have his on the ceiling, and this is the general practice among great and small, and they consider anything else to be strange and foreign to their condition, and some Portuguese used to this country do not find this ugly."

I dare say if the young Valignano came across that paragraph, it would have stuck in his mind! Gaitonide also mentions a lost book on the riches and greatness of China sent to the Governor of India in 1524. If Malabar is any indication, the book may well have contained contrasts. And if Valignano saw it . . . *(Anyone?)*

22. *Undesirable Virgins*. What began as a short note turned into an essay I couldn't cut. Marco Polo's words bring to mind the discriminatory joke concerning our so-called "hillbillies," where a bride is returned for being a virgin, because "If she hain't good 'nuf for her kinfolk, she shore hain't good 'nuf for us;" but the start of Marco Polo's account suggests something not altogether rare, a

culture where perforation of the hymen is regarded as a sort of exorcism, releasing a dangerous spirit, so that it is considered wise to let strangers be the scapegoat. But his account continues:

> The traveler must give the girl a jewel when he leaves to prove she has had a lover. If a girl has twenty jewels, she has had as many lovers. The girls with the most jewels are then chosen as wives because, by common accord, they must be the loveliest. (Ibid.)

Here, we must entertain the possibility of a poor people – sometimes, entire tribes live on the margin – rationalizing a dowry scheme somewhat like what Carletti described in Japan (see note 2-1)! But, not necessarily. Originally, this custom may well have been a marriage-related beauty contest. There is a festival in Tsukuma Japan that goes back to ancient times where the unmarried women parade with pots balanced on their heads, as many pots as they had lovers that year which suggests that much! It was not found elsewhere in Japan, and, being a seasonal event, found its way into haiku. Over two hundred years after Frois died, Kobayashi Issa, the people's haiku poet, took the parade in a new direction altogether:

ima ichido baba mo kabureyo tsukuma nabe
(now, one time, aunties too/even wear them! tsukuma pot)

Tsukuma Festival
(if you've got it)

hey, old women!
you, too – why not?
wear your pots!

After noting that the bejeweled women made chaste wives, Marco Polo enthused, "It goes without saying that any young man between the ages of sixteen and twenty-four would be delighted to go to this place."

20. *Additional note*. Cultural diversity, poly or polar, is half the Marco Polo story. I was equally impressed by the other half, the similarities he discovered, again without comment. Most noticeable of all – and, I fear, a bit sad to contemplate – were a half-dozen accounts of how men in power got more than their fair share of beautiful   women   and   the   problems   it   caused!

中

VII

OF JAPANESE OFFENSIVE AND

DEFENSIVE WEAPONS & OF WAR

das armas ofensivas e defensivas dos Japõis – & da guerra

7-1   We use swords.[1] *Nós uzamos de espadas;*

And the Japanese cutlasses. *E os Japóes de traçados.*

Where is the contradiction here? Logically speaking there are *three*: 1) the former is double-edged and the latter single-edged; 2) the former has a sharp *point* and the latter an especially sharp-edge; and 3), the former is absolutely straight – note that the spade on a pack of cards is symmetrical – while the second is curved. Because the first two are covered elsewhere (1-21, for 1) and 7-7 for 2)), my first guess for Frois's intent is 3). This contrast is a good example of why description beats names: unprompted, how many of us could say why a cutlass was contrary to a sword?

Not only was 16th century Europe in constant war against itself and the Ottomans but, as if that did not suffice, it saw the full bloom of the personal duel. After the bad taste left by a famous Judicial duel before the King of France 1547, where the underdog, coached by an Italian fencing master, beat a powerful opponent by cutting his hamstring, the public redress of slights fell out of favor. [2] But private duels took up the slack with vengeance and everyone who was anyone had their Italian, Spanish or, a bit later, French fencing teacher and/or belonged to guilds that, according to one website, "taught such lethal techniques that the amount of noblemen killed in duels in the 16th century exceeded the amount killed in warfare." In this age, "we" all knew *what* swords were *what*. Iberia was in the thick of it. Some argue that modern fencing started in Spain where, in 1569, a book called *Inventor of the Science of Arms* expounded a sort of geometry of swordplay, though it is debatable its artificial schemes did much for the practice. (The real innovators are usually said to be Italian and French.)

---

1. *Sword* and *Cutlass?* The Japanese translation of the Portuguese *espadas* and *tracadas* respectively uses "sword" (*katana*) for the Portuguese *espada* and what translates literally as a "short-sword" (*tanken*) for the Japanese *traçadas*. But the actual difference in length was, if I am not mistaken, negligible. I was tempted to translate the *espada* by the name of the type of sword then current, the *rapier*, rather than "sword." Cocks, Saris and other English writers generally did not translate the names of weapons, but used the Japanese term *katans* (*katana*) for Japanese swords – that makes it a lot easier for one not well versed in 16th century weaponry. In the seventeenth century, Kaempfer's translator rendered the long and short swords carried by a samurai as "sabres and scimitars" (ridiculous, for neither curve so radically as a scimitar.) Most translations play safe and simply use the broadest generic term, "swords." In this case, I use "cutlass" partly because the characteristic of cutting is in the name, as it is in the Portuguese. The French translation uses *épée* and *sabre,* respectively.

2. *Hamstring Cut.* The notoriety of this *judicial battle* had more to do with the stupid reason for it and the King's (sorry) role in the affair than the nature of the cut for which the winner was not criticized by most. (When you are physically weak *what else can you do?*)

7-2   Our hilt is [long] enough to fit a hand;
Ho nosso puho [hé] quanto cabe [a] mão;

Theirs exceed a palm [1] and, sometimes, three.
O seu passa de hum palmo, e às vezes de 3.

One hand for "our" sword and two for theirs. The reasons have already been discussed in 1-34. Naturally, it follows that ours has a short hilt and theirs a long one, long enough, in fact, that depending on one's technique and power, the position of the hands on the hilt may vary, up and down like in baseball, golf, or pole-vaulting. Avila Giron wrote that the length of the Japanese sword blade and hilt, like the head and body of figures in European art, maintain "a due proportion." (C:TCJ) If our ideal was 1:8 head:body, the *katana* was 1:6 hilt. (The proportion he gave. To me, they appear 1:5. Perhaps he meant the *tang* (the metal part of the hilt which is not seen on a completely dressed(?) sword).

1. *Palma* Translation: The *palma* in the original was also a unit of measurement. Palm, hand and span are all such. The *palm*, unfortunately, is the most ambiguous, for there is the *side* palm measurement across the palm (about 4") – similar to the *hand* we give horses – and the *long* palm from wrist to finger tips (about 7"). Aurélio's Dictionary puts it at .22 m (8.6 inches), similar to the English *span* (thumb-tip to pinkie tip, or about 9"). The Japanese sword would have a hilt at least that long. But, three spans would be very rare.

7-3   We carry our swords on baldrics. *Os nossos trazem a espada em talabartes;*

They, [with a] hooklet [1] in/on the sash. *Elles em hum ganchinho na sinta.*

The *talabarte,* or baldric, is a sling-style belt that goes over one shoulder. Judging from some old paintings, the low side of the baldric tended to be lower than the Japanese *obi* belt, so that our swords often hung way down on the thigh (Did the mercenaries so often pictured think it debonair?).

The samurai had sashes about 3 inches wide called *katanajime,* or short-sword fasteners/ holders once used together with the classic dangling *tachi* (long sword) noted in 1-25+. Since Frois does not mention the two strings or straps used for dangling a sword from the sash, I think he refers to the style of swords "stuck in their sashes" (Avila Giron in C:TCJ).[2] To prevent the scabbards from slipping through the *obi,* the scabbard had a *kaerizuno,* a piece of metal or horn hook bound to it, which is what, I think Frois's *ganchinho* means (though his wording makes it seem like the hook is on the sash). The sashes the larger *uchigatana* swords were stuck through (i.e. under or between the wraps) grew broader year by year until they were 4-5 inches wide in the Tokugawa era (1603-1867).

Is the contrary element intended here, perhaps, between *specialized equipment* – a belt for girding swords – vs. *adaptation* of the belt in use?

1. *Hooklet*? I could not think of a diminutive for the English term. The French seems nice: *un petit crochet.*
2. *Or Am I Wrong*? Okada believes Frois means a sword hung (by cords/straps) from a hook on the belt; I doubt it because of the convex/concave contrast (1-25) suggests he had the *uchigatana* in mind. Still, it is possible Frois is talking about the largely ceremonial *tachi* here and I am wrong.

7-4   We wear our sword on one side and our dagger on the other.
Os nossos trazem a espada de huma banda e a adaga da outra;

The Japanese always wear their sword and dagger on the left.
Os Japões trazem a espada e adaga sempre da parte esqerda.

The most common short sword was called a *wakizashi* or side-stick (as in stick in the belt), so it was doubtless carried on the side, but the handle of the *wakizashi* stuck out diagonally over the belly which may explain why Avila Giron wrote "the big sword is carried on the left hip, while the smaller weapon is worn crosswise over the stomach.(C:TCJ). I translated *adaga* as "dagger" for lack of a better word (*dirk* seems too ethnic), but it refers to a small sword with a 12-24 inch blade, with a slight curve. Perhaps a small cutlass would be more accurate.

~~~~~~

7-5 Our daggers are short;
As nossas adagas são curtas;

> Some of theirs are longer than half a *katana* [sword].
> *Algumas das suas são mayores que mea* catana.

There is linguistic confusion here that will be cleared up in 7-11. Frois seems to call the second blade a *dagger* by definition.

~~~~~~

7-6 Gloves hang from our swords. *Nas nossas espadas se perdurão as luvas;*

> From theirs, a cord that serves for nothing. *E elles hum cordão que não serve de nada.*

Armored gloves were worn when fighting in Europe. In Frois's time, they were no longer as heavily armored as the Medieval gauntlet, but they were not yet abandoned.

The Japanese item may be the *sageo,* lit. "dangle-string," according to the dictionary, a "sword knot" was used to tie the scabbard firmly to the upper outside *obi* during military campaigns, but the chord ordinarily just dangled. (But, I saw another worthless string in a picture. Anyone?)

~~~~~~

7-7 The people of Europe are used to stabbing swordplay. *A jente de Europa custuma jugar de ponta;*

> The Japanese in no case do it. *Os Japões por nehum cazo.*

Stabbers and *slashers*. Where did the difference arise? Is it psychological, stabbing extroverted whereas slashing is introverted insofar that the blade is pulled over something? Japanese even today do not do much *punching* (unless they are boxers). Would a criminal psychologist find a basic difference in those who stab/thrust and those who cut/slash? Or, did the weapons came first and the mentality second? Did "ours" boast sharper points and theirs sharper edges? Whatever it is, the difference is even reflected in our idiom: we get "stabbed in the back;" they "back-cut/sliced" (*uragiri*).

Frois's "in no case" is an exaggeration. The Japanese sword's point was more than sharp enough to stab and sometimes did. The most famous swordsman and strategist in Japanese history, Miyamoto Musashi, who was born in, none other than 1585, included a couple of stab strokes, "to stab at the face" and "to stab at the heart," in his *Water Book* of instructions for sword-fighting. In respect to the latter, he wrote: the spirit of this principle is often useful when we become tired or for some reason our long sword will not cut." Although Musashi was inventive, I seriously doubt that he had to invent stabbing. [1] Still, stabbing was never a first resort in Japan. The only clear exception might have been for assassination. In that case, the classic – or at least classic *modern* – style in Japan is to grip a short sword or knife with one hand, put the other behind the butt of the handle and holding that against one's own body, throwing oneself directly against the target. But that is not sword*play*. While European Medieval swordplay was mostly hacking, this changed in the Renaissance and, with the invention of the thin rapier that evolved into the yet lighter épée while Frois was in Japan and, soon, to the remarkable foil [2]), thrusting was *de rigor*. Frois's, "play at point" (to literally translate *jugar de ponta*) is strangely apt, for it seems to predict where we were heading:

> The next century saw the invention of the fleuret, or foil as it was later known, as a practice weapon for épée. This weapon brought new rules with it that encouraged the use of proper technique and grace. One of these was concerned with a fencers 'right of way'. The idea behind this was that fencers should take it in turns to attack each yielding his right to attack when the opponent began attacking. Bizarrely this was designed to prevent two people stabbing each other simultaneously in a duel. Even more bizarrely, this idea worked, and the amount of noblemen killed in dueling dropped. (Internet: LR)

1. *Miyamoto Musashi's Inventiveness.* Since I wrote this, a friend wrote and published a biography of Miyamoto Musashi entitled *The Lone Samurai* (Kodansha International 2004). I was disappointed to learn he was born in 1584, according to Bill's calculation, rather than 1585; but I was delighted to discover just how creative Musashi was. I recall Paracelsus writing that doctors must treat each patient differently because a 1000 men, a 1000 stomachs. Well, Musashi had the same approach for every opponent he faced. He changed weapon and style of fighting to win at least 60 bouts by the time he was 30.

At his first bout, he dropped his staff dived into his opponent, lifted him up and dropped him on his head. There may be gun-fighters in "our" Wild West who can match his cool, but I wonder if any could match his creativity?

2. *The Foil.* Who could ever come up with the idea that a square tube, i.e., right angles could cut! As it turns out, there were triangular épée blades which were indented – so maybe I should say triple-edged blades – so the idea was not completely off the wall, but it still astounds me.

7-8   Among us, lords are presented with swords of very good iron.
      Antre nós se dão aos senhores de prezente espadas de muito bom ferro.

   In Japan, they are given wooden swords with sword-belts of *nuno* [cloth].
      Em Japão lhe oferecem espadas de pao com talabartes de nuno.

From ancient times, Japanese rulers wore wooden swords called *tsukuridachi, kidachi* or *kodachi* for ceremonies. In Frois's time, the *shogun* might wear one to a (war) strategy meeting. I assume symbolic significance is served by wood as well as iron and the "cloth," not silk, follows the primitive-as-festive idea discussed in 6-30 (Anyone?).

Japanese also had *bokuto,* blunt wooden swords, often oak, that served for exercise and were sometimes used in matches between heads of schools and *shinai,* the equivalent/opposite of our square-edged (post-Frois) foil, tubular swords comprising strips of bamboo, bound around at broad intervals with strips of leather, that make extraordinarily crisp, pleasant-sounding whacks when hitting together. Morse observed *kendô* classes where two groups of 50 tried to protect their leaders, each with a disk of soft pottery tied on top of his helmet. (M:JDD) Today, one-on-one *shinai* matches are part of physical education (*kendô* classes for both sexes) in all public schools in Japan. The *shinai* (*Xinai*) were in the 1604 Japanese Portuguese Dictionary, so they almost surely predated Frois.

Japan has various ceremonial weapons. The most common is not the sword, but the *headless arrows* people – in both a private and company capacity – still bring back from the Shrines as talismans to undo a bad year and hope for better fortune in the new one, and the most aesthetically satisfying are the cast-iron ritual swords – that stand point up, and have the character 心"heart" in their hilt (the second edition will picture it) – made by and for the blacksmith to consecrate his forge.

7-9   We only put swords in our scabbards.
Nas nossas bainhas não se mete mais que a espada;

Those of Japan have a place for a knife and a *kôgai* that serves for nothing.
Nas dos Japões de huma parte a faca e da outra o congay que não serve de nada.

This *kôgai* goes almost as far back as the above-mentioned wooden sword. It was an ivory or silver bar (one English language Japanese sword site calls it a "skewer") almost as long and about twice as thick as a chopstick and rounded at one end which nobles from the times of Genji used to scratch their scalp or re-arrange their hair after putting on their armor. Call it a *one-tooth comb.* Sometimes the tip had a slight notch like that of a crochet needle, "which made them look like ear-wax removers, but they were not used for that, rather for poking a bad horse" says one old document cited in the OJD. Eventually, men came to use it less, or not at all, and women took it for a hair pin, when it came to be made of gold, silver, or tortoise-shell. It still stayed on the scabbard as of old, but was seldom if ever used. The 1604 NIPO defines it as "a metal object like a tiny knife made of black lacquer or gilt copper stuck in one side of the scabbard." Rodrigues in his *Historia* called it "a certain instrument which they insert in sword scabbards and which is decorated with a flower or animal carved by skilled craftsmen." (R(C):TIJ) He also explains that they were made of a mixture of copper, silver and gold called black copper. Within decades, a new use was found for this useless anachronism. It was split in two, becoming a *wari-kôgai,* a pair of portable chopsticks for the samurai!

7-10   Our swords, though new, if they are very good, are worth a lot.
As nossas espadas, ainda que sejão novas, se são muito boas, valem muito;

Those of Japan, although new, have no value, and the very old ones are expensive. *As de Japão, ainda que novas, não tem valia, e as muito velhas são de preço.*

Our side. Needless to say, a new sword is less likely to be nicked than an old one and worth more.

New swords in Japan were hardly worthless, but the older ones were treasured both for their history and because the greatest swords were made before 1450, while the master sword-smiths still made their own iron from scratch (later, it was mass produced in mills). In Valignano's SUMARIO, three Japanese items were mentioned as the equivalent of what jewels are to Europeans: certain tea utensils, simple black and white *sumi-e* paintings and swords. He mentions swords worth thousands of *ducados* (millions of dollars in today's prices) Taladriz-Alvarez quotes Vivero on a sword worth a hundred thousand *ducado.* There is a story found in many books about a sword by the 13th century smith Kanemitsu that came to be called *Ikkoku Kanemitsu,* or "[worth] one-country-Kanemitsu!" because its owner refused a request for it by the Shogun Tokugawa Hideyoshi, though he might lose his entire province (Tôsa, the island now famous for drumming). The Shogun's emissary liked his guts and he got to keep both. Since swords have to be proven, there are also logical reasons for favoring old sword over new swords, but logic probably does not mean much here.

7-11   We wear no more than one sword and one dagger at most;
Antre nós, quando muito, não se uza de trazer mais que huma espada e adaga;

The Japanese sometimes wear two swords and a *wakizashi* in the belt.
Os Japões às vezes duas catanas e hum vaqizaxi *na cinta.*

We had some exceptions. The man who won that last judicial duel in France had several daggers because he wanted to be able to easily reach one if his opponent, who was known to be a good wrestler, tried to grab him! And, pictures show mercenaries so loaded with arms they looked like porcupines. But there were more Japanese who wore three blades than Europeans. Some wore the traditional *tachi* (long sword) dangling and stuck both an *uchigatana* (striking sword) and a smaller *wakizashi* in their belt. Others may have worn an *uchigatana* as their largest sword, a *wakizashi* as their small sword and any variety of smaller swords for a dagger. With "two swords and a *wakizashi*" we might assume the latter is the dagger (Indeed, the French translation has "[poignard]" inserted after it.). Actually, it is hard to say, for the *wakizashi,* as mentioned, had a cutting blade from one to two feet in length while the "small swords (*kogatana, tanto*)," had blades sticking out less than a foot beyond their sword-guards. So Frois is reflecting rather than creating a confusing nomenclature.

7-12   Our knives generally have wooden studs;
As nossas facas ordinariamente tem as tachas de pao.

      Those of Japan have hilts of copper or another metal.
      As de Japão tem hum punho de cobre ou de outro metal.

The Japanese knives are the "small-swords" already mentioned. Does Frois mean it is strange we have rivets of wood rather than metal and equally strange that they should have metal handles? This contrast loses me.

7-13   We cut with a knife either inward, or from left to right.
Nós cortamos com a faca ou pera dentro ou da parte esqerda pera a dereita;

      The Japanese always cut outward.
      Os Japões cortão sempre pera diante.

Left to right for a right-handed person is not very different from cutting away from oneself. So the contrast is hardly perfect. But I know what he is getting at. Once, a Japanese, astounded to find me whittling inward – actually pulling the knife with my fingers toward my thumb – warned: "[That's] dangerous! We always cut away from ourselves." As Americans all learn – or are supposed to learn – not to point a gun at themselves or others even if they think it is unloaded, Japanese apparently have a rule about pointing away with a cutting instrument. E.J. Harrison describes the etiquette of showing a good sword to a guest:

> The sword would then be handled with the back toward the guest . . . the weapon was drawn from the scabbard and admired inch by inch, but not to the full length, unless the owner pressed his guest to do so, when, with much apology, the sword was entirely drawn and held away from the other persons present. (THE CULT OF COLD STEEL in N:MAR)

The West would appear to be freer with their blades. Still it is hard to say if this contrast is rooted in etiquette. Regardless, it is pleasant to find the directional difference here the opposite of the case with saws or weaponless fighting; but, unlike these things, it is never mentioned by *nihonjinron-ka,* for an inward *pulling* West and an outward *pushing* Japan would contradict the vectors of the accepted stereotype of our respective characters.

7-14   Our beads for prayer are always made on a lathe, and our crosses, too.
As nossas contas pera rezar se fazem sempre em torno, e as cruzes tambem;

> The Japanese often make them with a knife, as well finished as by a lathe.
> *Os Japões as fazem muitas vezes com faqa tam bem feitas como em torno.*

The Japanese had lathes. A *"million* miniature wooden pagodas" (my *italics*) each containing "four Buddhist incantations printed on a long strip of paper" – i.e., tiny *stupa* – were "mass-produced on lathes" at the request of the Empress in 764. (P:GUG). Needless to say, there were devices to turn out beads 800 years later. But making items for religious use was itself a type of devotion. People carved everything from statues of the Goddess of Mercy to prayer beads. (But how were beads *held* when carving?)

7-15   We, for the most part, cut our nails with scissors.
Nós cortamos pola mayor parte as unhas com tizouras;

> The Japanese always cut them with a knife.
> *Os Japões as cortão sempre com faca.*

It is hard to say whether this was because Japanese scissors were that poor or because Japanese blades were *that* sharp! Since we *are* in a chapter on weapons and war, perhaps Frois means the latter. I think that was the point about 7-14, too, that Japanese are a knife-loving and knife-using people!

7-16   The leaves and twigs we take from trees to decorate our presents;
As folhas e ramos que tomamos das arvores pera emramar os prezeentes;

> The Japanese make artificially with their *kogatana* [1] [knives].
> *Fazem os Japões artificiais com suas congatanas.*

Japanese did not simply whittle replicas. Their foliage, if that is what it stood for, resembles the tinder sticks we learn to make as boy and girl-scouts, but with much finer and longer cuts, so that the shavings curl like ribbon. This type of wood-carving suggests the Ainu influence on Japanese culture, for the Ainu are the world's most prolific shaving artists. [2]   Isabella Bird wrote that "wands, with shavings depending from the upper end" were the "Aino Gods" and stuck in the walls, by windows, on a shelf, that is to say both adorned and charmed their dwellings. (B:UTJ vol 2)

1. Kogatana   Here, Frois uses "small-sword" for what obviously would be called a "knife" by us, as explained in 7-11.
2. Ainu Shaving.   Come to think of it, the elaborate wood shaving art resembles the bushy beards they boast! This may well be the most hair-positive people in the world (In a bushy way, rather than tamed and coiled as is found with some Indians).

7-17   Our spear heads are long and broad. *As nossas lanças tem os ferros compridos e largos;*

> Theirs, short and thin. *E as suas curtos e estreitos.*

The Japanese had *many* types of spear blades and Frois only compares the most common variety which did indeed have a very small blade. A big blade is fearsome to behold, but if thrusting through armor (metal and/or leather), or simply stabbing a body is the main intent, a thin blade can generate far more pressure for square inch.   Our spears, as suggested by the name in Portuguese, apparently owed more to the heavy lances of the knight, designed more to knock a man off a horse than to pierce the armor.

~~~~~~

7-18　　　Ours [our spears] are smooth, of the color of the wood itself.
As nossas são lizas com a cor propria do pao;

Theirs have shafts that are *urushi* [lacquer(ed)] or gilt.
As suas ou são vruxadas *ou algumas delas douradas nas asteas.*

This is a reversal of the more usual *painted Europe* and *bare Japan*. Perhaps, "our" spears were, as the older jousting lances, thought of as expendable, unlike our swords which were heavily adorned. Okada explains that spear shafts were natural wood color in Japan too, until the Warring Era (1338-1568), when black lacquer, mother-of-pearl and vermillion – the last only as a privilege for exploits in battle – became current.

~~~~~~

7-19　　　We use halberds. *Nós uzamos de partezanas;*

They, *naginata* in the shape of a sickle. *Elles de nanguinatas que são da feisão de fouces.*

Our halberds were ferocious-looking hybrids with a long spear shaft with a sharp spear-point at the tip, under which an axe-head juts out (angled in such a way as to add some slice to the hack) on one side and a prong or hook on the back of the axe-head on the other.

The *naginata* was more like a curved sword on a long shaft. The classical ones were about 40% blade and looked like sickles. Largely because of the gun, they were going out of business as a male weapon in Frois's time. The blade shrank down to knife-length by the Edo era, where they became and remained the official weapon for noblewomen – in the TV Easterns they whirl them about like huge batons – to practice with and use in defense of their lords and castles.

~~~~~~

7-20　　　We use bombards; *Nós uzamos de partezanas;*

They have no more than arquebuses. *Elles as não tem, mas uzão de espingardas.* [1]

The *bombard* was originally a stone *thrower* but came to be applied to the earliest cannon/mortars that shot stones or large shot weighing up to 200 pounds.   I hesitate to choose mortar or cannon for I am not sure the concepts were yet separate. The OED's *bombard* (n. and v.) citations reveal how hated it was: "to discharge a bumbard, to batter or murder with bumbards." The person firing it was a *bombadier.*

At last minute, I dropped the archaic "musket" (though it should be OK for translating *espingardas*), for the obsolete "arquebus," the most common word used with respect to old Japanese guns, which were indeed "hackbuts!" (see 7-52) as they were Englished by a Tudor Royal Proclamation in the very year the first guns came to Japan, which was 1543, when three Portuguese "rovers" on a Chinese trading ship landed in Japan. Two had *arquebuses* with them "and at the moment when Lord Tokita, the feudal master of Tanegashima, saw one of them take aim and fire at a duck, the gun enters Japanese history." (Noel Perrin: GIVING UP THE GUN) Within a year, his chief swordsmith had made ten guns and "within that decade gunsmiths all over Japan were making the weapons in quantity." By the time St. Xavier came in 1549, there is a record of "an order for five hundred *tanegashima*" (P:GUG) on the part of Nobunaga, the warlord who first unified Japan. [2] Moreover, Japan did not *just* copy the *espingardas*. "They increased the caliber of the guns to increase each bullet's effectiveness, and they ordered waterproof lacquered cases to carry the matchlocks and their gunpowder in," and refined "the comparatively rude Portuguese firing mechanism – developing, for example, a helical main spring and an adjustable trigger pull" as well as a "gun accessory – unknown, as far as I am aware, in Europe – which enabled the matchlock to be fired in the rain." (P:GUG)

But strangely enough, the Japanese did not show equal progress with *large* firearms. Some good cannons were made – a few, made from melted temple bells, were bought by European scrap dealers in the late-19th century where "some of the bronze may have wound up in belfries in which case the cycle was complete" (P: GUG) – but these were all field weapons: the Japanese never made decent shore batteries or armature for ships. I don't know if this is from lack of interest in these battle theatres, or Japan's comparative strength in manufacturing iron and smithing (making guns a cinch) – both of which led the world – and weakness in casting technology (making cannons durable).

There were also fire-arms fitting neither of the above-discussed categories. Enjoy this entry from the diary of Richard Cocks about a device that would be worth mentioning for the name alone.

> October 16. – The King of Crates retorned to Firando and sent to desire to see a fyre arrow shot out of a slurbo, which was donne before hym and the King of Firando to their greate content twise. He desird to have the slurbo to take a sample by to make an other, with a receapt how to make the compound for the fyre work. (DRC:1615)

1. *Espingardas*. My translation, which does not differ from all the others, is probably right, but I feel there is a tiny possibility Frois was talking about cross-bow or catapult devices called Espringals or springals in English, apparently coming from the same root and would not mind the imput of experts.

2. *Gun Diffusion in Japan*. Pinto claims that there were 600 guns made by the Japanese in the first half year from the discovery and in 1556 he was told that one medium-sized city in Kyushu, Funai, capitol of Bungo, "there were more than thirty thousand" and there were 300,000 in Japan. Scholars unanimously say every single one of these figures is a gross exaggeration. However, it is a fact that *Pinto always exaggerates on the side of the truth*. In the Battle of Sekigahara in 1600, when Tokugawa Ieyasu defeated Nobunaga's protégé Hideyoshi, an estimated __,000 muskets took part. This was __ times more firearms than had ever gathered in one field in Europe and was not matched until Gettysburg two and a half centuries later. (This example (LR and #s) is not in Perrin, but he has pages of collected evidence to the effect that within a generation of the discovery of firearms by the Japanese, many of their principalities had far more firepower than the major European powers. "The entire English army, for example, had fewer guns than any one of half a dozen Japanese feudal lords.") And the difference in fire-power may have exceeded the difference in the number of guns, for "they developed a serial firing technique [ranks shooting volleys] to speed up the flow of bullets".

~~~~~~

7-21   We carry our powder-horns on a shoulder-belt. *Nós trazemos o polvarinho ao tiracolo;*

They carry them about the neck like a relic. *Elles ao pescoso como relicairo.*

The Japanese powder-horn was called a "mouth-drug-holder" (*kuchigusuri-ire*) or a satchel (literally: "torso-rampant," why I do not know!) were indeed dangled from the neck but they were also secured to the chest and did not bounce around.   Japanese may have had to ford more rivers than Europeans.   I assumed wrongly that they would all be bamboo, for that would be easy to make; but internet photos revealed a a beautiful array of hard-wood, lacquered, bamboo and horn "powder-horns" far finer (aesthetically developed) than our comparatively folksy horns!

7-22   Our bows are medium [in size] and made of wood. *Os nossos arcos são medianos e de pau;*

And theirs, very large [and] made of bamboo. *Os seus muito grandes feitos de cana.*

With Robin Hood as my namesake, I am very aware of the fact that, in England, we had some pretty long bows ourselves though they were not nearly as long as the 7-8 foot Japanese bow.

The bows which appear in the ancient poetry of Japan are all wood, mostly catalpa or spindle treet. The lamination technology for making good composite bamboo bows is difficult, involving a number of other plants. But, this is less interesting than two functional facts Frois does not mention:

We hold our bows in the middle when we shoot them;
Japanese bows have their grip about one third of the way from bottom of the bow.

Shooting right-handed, we rest the arrow on the left-side of the bow;
They place the arrow on the right-side of the bow so it rests upon their thumb.

There are other longbows, bamboo bows and laminated bows in the world. But as far as I know, only the Japanese shoot in this way, permitting long bows to clear a horse's back. It is puzzling why the Japanese could not have copied the stronger and far more compact Mongolian bow, as they later did European firearms. Since a bow dance is still done by the Sumo grand-champion, which takes full advantage of the uniquely *wobbly nature* of the unstrung Japanese bow, the answer may be that the Japanese just had too much affection for their strange weapon. Had their bows been more powerful – like those of the Mongols (or Caribs of Florida who sent the first Iberians packing and would have held out for centuries – at least until the Gatling gun – if it were not for the newcomers secret weapon: disease) – I wonder if the Japanese would have shown so much interest in guns.

7-23   Our arrows are wooden. *As nossas frechas são de pao;*

And theirs also [like the bows] of bamboo. *As suas tambem de cana.*

Okada points out that willow arrows were also used up to the Heian Era (Think of it: *I shot an arrow in the air / and wherever it fell / a tree grows there!*). The bamboo is not the same bamboo used to make bows, for the bow is made with strips of good, thick real bamboo, whereas the arrows are made from *yadake* ("arrow-bamboo" – I'd call it *cane*), a uniformly thin (1-2 centimeter in diameter) variety (more like bamboo-grass (*sasa*)) that grows 6-19 feet high and has joints that do not bulge.

When we consider that Frois gives the type of feathers used in helmets a contrast (7-29), he might have taken a closer look at the fletching as well as the shaft:

The feathers on our arrows are slightly out of line with the shaft to make it spin and go straighter.
Theirs are perfectly straight but spin it by being convex on one side and concave on the other.

That is too say their feathers are warped and work on the principle of some of the earliest airplane wings (they rotate toward the convex side as a wing would lift that way)! When two arrows are sold, they generally comprise a set, the clockwise-rotating *haya* and the counter-clockwise *otoya*. If, it turns out that all European arrows spin in a single direction, this would give us something rare in this chapter, a true contrary and not just a difference.

Then, Frois could have looked at the heads. It is possible that Japanese arrow heads had more variety, but I do not know (gloss anyone?) [1] But, I doubt Japanese had anything as different as Ainu arrows, which had a unique hollow place for poison in the shaft next to the tip which served as the venom gland of a snake!

1. *Arrowhead Variety.* Suffice it to say that many arrowheads were large and included both backward V and backward U and crescent-shaped double-headed heads in Japan that, to me look impressive, but for warfare would be less effective than simple sharper heads. I would guess they would be good for hitting geese and making noise.

7-24   Among us, we shoot our bows with the archer clothed.
Antre nós se despedem as frechas estando o que as tira vestido;

> In Japan, someone who shoots a bow must half remove his *kimono* to bare his arm.
> *Em Japão quem tira com arco á-de despir meo* qimão *pera ficar com hum braço nu.*

The Japanese practice of "dispatching arrows" (translating Frois exactly) is clearly the strange one of the two. Frois apparently did not get close enough to the bow to see which side the arrow was shot on, but he did notice the left arm removed from the kimono, showing the left shoulder and some of the chest of the archer. This is not so bothersome a matter as might be imagined, for Japanese can yank in their arm and shoot their fist out through the lapel of their kimono while shrugging their shoulder and it is done in a second or two! It takes loose sleeves, a broad armpit and practice. Still, to see people lined up at a *kyûdo* gallery, all with one arm/shoulder bare (except for the arm-guard strapped on)! *Why, you ask yourself don't they just wear something with tight sleeves?* I would guess that archers in battle and real hunters (that not done by nobles in beautiful kimonos!) did not wear loose-sleeved robes and had no need to strip (anyone?).

7-25   Among us, no one yells out when shooting a bow;
Antre nós se tira com arco sem fazer nenhum rujido com a boca;

> The Japanese have to give a big shout when they release an arrow.
> *Os Japões em despidindo a frecha hão-de dar hum grande grito.*

"Our" side needs no explanation.

Theirs is remarkable. And it is also true for sword-fighting (see 51, below) and the modern martial arts of judo and karate. *Why do "they" do it?* Some say "to throw off the guard of the enemy for just an instant when it interferes with their cognition." When THE JAPANESE BRAIN (Tsunoda) was a best-seller, I recall reading that the Japanese heard such a yell on the verbal (left) side of their brain, unlike other people [1] who processed it in the right hemisphere as noise, so that it had more effect on them. But such a yell would not matter as much for archery (or, did it petrify deer?) as face-to-face combat. Others think it functions like exhaling quickly when weight-lifting, i.e., provides a clear physical benefit. (by sharply breathing out several times in a row, one can bend over and pick up things without harming the lower-back, too!) But, this would not apply, for they do not yell when the bow is *drawn*, but only when it is *released*! It also may function as a sort of vocal psyching up, where each blow/shout increases one's excitement level until the adrenaline is sky-high, but that, too, would be counter-productive for the calm "Zen of archery." Be that as it may, there is even a word for that surprising sharp cry, *kiai,* literally "spirit-meet." To put *kiai* into something (*kiai-o irete* is "to do something with spirit." To lose to someone's *kiai* is to be overawed (*kiai-make*) or psyched-out by them.

The *kiai* does not seem to accompany *any* sport – most Japanese tennis players don't cry or grunt any more or less than ours – and even when the sport is of the right traditional martial arts tradition, the *kiai* only accompanies *serious effort*.   I do not believe, for example, that Japanese playboys in Edo made a *kiai* when they played with small bows in their *yôkyu-ya* "willow-bow-stalls," which were a common *aimai-ya*, or "ambiguous-shop," where the female employees were often at liberty to arrange sexual favors for a fee with the archers. This activity (shooting at arrow-retrievers!) is an outstanding example of the zany low-life that was – and is – as much Japan as Zen and I cannot help but introduce it at least in a *font-size 9* note.[2]

1. *Japanese Brain.* According to this book, Japanese are not *born* with a different brain but *create* one through learning Japanese. More information in G:O&O.

2.   *Shooting Arrow-Retrievers.* "When the arrow-retriever turned her rear in the direction of the customer as she picked up his arrows, the customer tried to shoot her behind. Horseplay. As the [blunt] tip of the arrow was metal, even though the girls wore an extra layer of clothing, they would leave black and blue marks. An arrow-retriever would crawl about on all fours in front of the targets using her toes and hip movement to dodge arrows. A skilled retriever had to do all this while still maintaining the composure to turn men on by flashing her red under-skirt. This took long research and practice, and supposedly very few of these arrows shot in horseplay found their mark." (Mitani Kazuma: EDO SHÔBAI ZUE)

7-26   We use either round, gilt escutcheons or leather bucklers.
Antre nós se uza d'esqudos, rodelas douradas e adargas de couro;

The Japanese, in place of these, use a piece of board flat like a door.
Os Japões em lugar disto uzão de hum pedaço de taboa raza como porta.

Since our swords were wielded with one hand, it made sense to hold a small shield in the other. These *rondache* or bucklers were not just round but slightly rounded (convex), the better to protect the hand. Unless one is fighting a gorgon, I do not know why one would want "gilt" shields.

The Japanese were not without their small shields, too, but the door-like shields no doubt stood out for the European. In Japanese, these were called "wall-shields," for lined up, they made a protective barrier for arrows. With the adoption of firearms, these shields were replaced by bundles of bamboo which could deflect most musket balls.(Okada) But, they must have come back after the gun was banned, for even today, Japanese riot police (Koreans and Chinese, too!) still use 5 or 6-foot long, narrow shields, often improved with plexiglas windows that offer excellent protection from stones.

7-27   Our armor is very heavy. *As nossas armas são muito pezadas.*

That of the Japanese very light. *As dos Japões muito leves.*

The plate armor of our knights was notoriously heavy. Sometimes knights had to be hoisted up into the saddle using a block and pulley. It had lightened up by Frois's time but was still heavy by Japanese standards. With their long history of warring, the Japanese were also heavily armored, but weight-wise – partly because of their smaller horses and partly because of their superior design – held the line at about 25 pounds. And they, too, had lightened up over the preceding century or two.

7-28   Our armor suits are all made of steel-plate.
As nossas armas brancas são todas de aso;

Theirs are made of scales of horn and leather laced together with silk cord.
As suas feitas de laminas de corno ou de couro tecidas com retros.

The Japanese *lamina,* to use Frois's specialized (in English) term, was bound slightly overlapping like the scales on a fish or shingles. Japan also used metal. It produced "more varieties of mail than all the rest of the world put together" (George Stone quoted in P:GUG) and "we" also had something similar to "theirs" called a coat of mail (neither chain-mail, nor plate).

7-29   The plumes on our helmets are white or beige [1] and very beautiful;
As nossas prumas dos elmos são brancas ou pardas muito fermozas;

Those of the Japanese are the longest tail feathers of roosters.
As dos Japões são de penas de galo das mais compridas do rabo.

What is the big deal? From old illustrations, I gather our *plumes* stood up and had a fluffy appearance admired by all Europeans, whereas the long cock-tails dangling behind the helmet of the Japanese was, to the European mind as ridiculous as wearing a cap backwards seems to me.

Japanese roosters have the longest tails in the world – check *Guinness!* Japanese also identified the cock with a martial spirit though, compared to the Chinese and Malay, they were not much into cock-fighting. Perhaps there was also a "the time is mine!" metaphor in it (Anyone?). Regardless, the use of feathers on the helmet, or other Japanese hats, for that matter, was not nearly so common as plumes were in Europe.

1. *Translation:* My dictionaries give "brown," "dark grey" or "[a] mulatto" for *parda.* The need for a good connotation led to the choice of "beige" though I have no idea whatsoever if it is right.

7-30   Ours [helmets] have visors;   *Os nossos levão vizeiras;*

The Japanese [ones] a demi-mask of a devil. *Os Japões mea cara de diabo no rosto.*

The visor is the eye-slit piece (The colander-like mask covering the face, a *ventail).* Our knights in armor look *artificial.* The color tends toward silver and the overall effect is *robotic.* Japanese visors provide slightly larger oblique eye holes. The Shogun's or other major Lords often have crescent moon-like horns on their forehead and, as will be explained, often sported hair. But the lower half of the helmet, done in *black* metal with nostrils and maleficent mouths (open wider at each edge than in the middle) are what terrifies and they do, indeed, look *diabolical,* as Frois wrote!

7-31   Our helmets are round;   *Os nossos capacetes são redondos;*

Theirs have ears and necks made of plates.[1] *Os seus tem orelhas e pescoços de laminas.*

These "ears" stick out like those of a bat, but since "we" also had neck-pieces called "beavers" and Gorgets, I fail to see where the difference is, unless it is that said piece was not thought of as integral to our helmet as it was to theirs. I find *shoulders* the more interesting difference, for "ours" are a bit less angular than a football player's pads, while Japanese armor sometimes boasts such large shoulder fins that we are reminded of the Cadillac of the mid-20th century.

1. *Translation:* The same *lamina* translated as "scales" in 7-28 works better here as "plates," for this portion of the armor was not scaled but, from what I could see, sheet metal plates.

7-32   We must wear thick clothing beneath to put on armor;
Antre nós, pera se hum armar á-de vestir debaxo couza de pano groso;

> The Japanese, when they wear armor, are naked as when their mother bore them.
> *Os Japões, quando vestem as armas, despem-se nus como suas mãis os parirão.*

Unlike our large sheets of steel, Japanese armor (7-28, above) was not egg-frying hot like "ours," (remember how hot a car gets?), so no insulation was needed. Moreover, the Japanese armor allowed some ventilation – Japanese had muggy weather – that might be taken advantage of in such a pristine condition, though I doubt they would be without loincloths! One more contrast which Frois probably knew nothing about:

> *Our knights often go to war with the handkerchief of their patroness.*
> *Theirs keep a dirty picture in the helmet to keep them from harm.*

Apparently, there was a superstition going back to ancient China that pictures of men and women in coitus charmed. Some believe they prevented desecration of the grave for they were found in ancient caskets. Perhaps they were only there because the deceased liked sex. But they were also placed in boxes of books to keep the silverfish away. *A good rationalization for a man to buy dirty books, huh!* Then, they were said to help one achieve military success. Take them to battle. Look at them in the morning and smile/laugh (the Japanese *warau* is ambiguous). Nothing like sex to help one achieve fruition. This, too, cynics laughed at. No, it is just because the armor was a sacred thing for the samurai, so no one other than a thief would dare open one's armor chest. What better place for a man to keep his pornography than in his armor? All of this has been argued back and forth for hundreds if not thousands of years, and I have no idea how many men actually went to war with these "charms." (There is a long exposition in the *"Shunga"* heading in Chikuma Yoshihiko: *Kôshoku-Engo-Jiten* Heisei 1)

7-33   Among us, it seems one cannot go to war, unless fully armored.
Antre nós não yr hum todo armado parese que não vay à guerra;

> In Japan, it suffices to wear an armored collar to say that one goes armored.
> *Em Japão basta pôr hum colarinho ao pescoso pera se dizer que vai armado.*

Apparently neck-plates (*shikoro*) were the *sine qua non* for doing battle. It makes sense when one considers the fact that war in Japan was largely a matter of *taking heads* – they even had arrows with tips designed to do this! [1] The word *kubi,* or "neck" in Japanese also means a cut off "head" (versus an attached head, or *atama).* We get *fired*; Japanese get *necked* (*kubi ni naru*). [2] Even, today, they metaphorically risk their heads. So it is not surprising they wore impressive neck-pieces, if nothing else. Perrin relays a story about a general who cries out to a powerful enemy warrior [Shimizu] who has him beat but is trying in vain to cut off his head: "Are you flurried , sir? My neck is protected by a NODOWA [a jointed iron throat-piece]. Remove this, and take my head off." The warrior bowed and expressed admiration for the general's courage, but as he was about to remove the impediment, two of the general's squires "rushed up and, throwing down Shimizu, enabled their master to decapitate his foe and retire safely from the field." (P:GUG)

1. *Decapitating Arrowhead* I doubt if heads ever fell off necks hit by such arrows, but the 3-4 inch wide concave side of the razor sharp sickle in front could sure come close to doing that.

2. *Our Necking.* We, too, had a tradition of cutting off heads, but it was almost always done to execute people. Despite the individual nature of most such executions, "heads will roll" is always plural.

7-34   We play fifes, drums and royal trumpets in battle;
Antre nós se tanje na guerra pifaro e atanbor ou trombetas reais;

> The Japanese have no more than some raucous whelks that sound very bad.
> *Os Japões não tem mais que huns buzios rouqenhos que soão muito mal.*

Is a "royal trumpet" something like the horn used to herald the kings in Hollywood movies? Schütte put single quote marks around his "Königstrompeten," indicating, I assume, that he was not certain the word existed. At any rate, we march into battle in a din of shrill shrieking, rhythmical thud and staccato and the soaring intonation of the trumpet, whereas they sound their relatively monotonous conchs (the word usually used by English writing about Japan though it is a large whelk. It is the same shell used by mountain priests and I would bet that these Yamabushi may well have served the armies in that capacity. Since the Japanese had no brass, this was the closest they could come to the trumpet sound which for whatever reasons became identified with the military around the world. Since Japanese had a tendency to charge while roaring at the top of their voices – if TV Easterns are correct – and, as explained already, scream as they make decisive cuts/stabs/shots, they probably had less need for an additional sound-track than we did, anyway!

Okada weakens Frois's contrast, for he writes that Japanese also used drums, military bells and gongs. Perhaps, these were not played in parades as in the West, so that Frois never heard them.

7-35   We carry rectangular battle standards by hand;
Antre nós se levão as bandeiras do campo nas mãos, quadradas;

> The Japanese each carry their very long, thin ones on bamboo poles fastened on their backs. *Os Japões levão cada hum sua, metidas nas costas em huma cana muito comprida.*

Frois's Portuguese, with the "rectangular" at the end of the sentence, is poor. All the other translations have the *"very long and thin"* (*muito comprida*) modify the bamboo poles, but I suspect a comma is missing and Frois meant to describe the standards/flags, as that would make the more perfect contrast and we do not need to be told the obvious fact that bamboo is long and thin.[1] Because "we" must hold our standards, every fighter can not carry them and we have our "standard-bearers," whereas Japanese (each samurai on horseback, but not every foot-soldier or helper) may each (*cada hum sua*) carry a standard. Judging from a genre of painting called "battle-pictures," the Japanese battlefield was awash in these standards, or rather, vertical banners. This allows modern movie producers to turn mass battles into extraordinarily colorful pageants.

1. *Quadradas.* My first thought was if *quadradas* (rectangular) was not matched by *compridas* (long and thin), it might be put against the "each" carrying his own idea and mean a military unit – as our "squad" does come from "square." In that case, the standard would be born at each corner of the unit. But, I concluded a missing comma was more likely. It is *possible* that the bamboo poles are described and not the standards.

7-36   We have sergeants, squad heads,[1] decurions, and centurians;
Antre nós há sarjentos, cabos d'esquadra, decurios e senturiões;

> The Japanese do not care for any of this.
> *Os Japõis totalmente se não qurão nada disto.*

Here, Frois does not only mean the Japanese have no perfect equivalent to this hierarchy but that they are not so well organized in ranks nor care to obey in a strict chain of command as "we" did. Japan had a far larger military class than Europe – between 5-10 percent of the population versus less than 1 percent. Moreover, each warrior had his peasant help along to serve him and there were large contingents of spear and, in Frois's time, rifle-carrying footmen. So we are talking about humongous armies an order in magnitude larger than those of Europe. How all that was organized successfully is a mystery to me! (I assume it was done by locality and followed the same structure of rank found outside the military.) One thing is certain, the warlords who unified Japan when Frois was there, executed complex maneuvers which required a chain of command of one sort or another. (anyone?)

This changed when Japan modernized in the 19th century, and adopted the Western style of rank. Still, even today, military ranks are not quite as familiar to the average Japanese as they are to us. Corporate ranks, on the other hand, are more complex and familiar to all in Japan, but largely meaningless to us. I had great trouble translating when requested to find English equivalents for these various "ranks" to use on name cards used by Japanese companies.

1. *Translation.* The "squad heads" was problematic. I wondered if I should make it simply "captain," which comes from "head" (*caput*). The German translation was Gruppenführer (What a simple word! The "fuhrer of the group." The sergeant was the Feldwebel.") and the French, "chefs d'escadron."

7-37   We fight on horseback.
Antre nós se peleja a cavalo;

> The Japanese dismount when they have to fight.
> *Os Japões se apeão quando hão-de pelejar.*

We will discuss *the riding gap* in the next chapter on horses. Suffice it to say that the Japanese were far from Mongols. Moreover, they had little interest in improving their horsemanship, for fighting by sword, on foot, one-against-one was considered *the* manly way to fight in Japan. In Europe, the men fought and sported with many weapons on horseback. In the *De Missione* report, "Miguel=Valignano" describes "dusty" tournaments held inside of private courtyards – I had thought jousting was already a medieval relic, but no! – and explains to his doubting listeners, who see it as "a sure way to die" rather than entertainment, that casualties were far fewer than one might imagine because a rope (*tela*) made lanes between the horses to prevent head-on collisions, the armor was strong enough to resist bullets, but, just to be safe, the lances had dull tips and were made of poor quality wood to break easily. (The knights would break one, get a replacement, break another, . . .). But, "nothing was so thrilling to the spectator" as the fancy horsemanship, "with the horse moving at [the rider's] will, moving every which way," demonstrated by knights fighting with sword and shield in hand. Other weapons were used in the mock equestrian battles. We all know about the lance and sword, but how about bows shooting reed arrows tipped with clay balls or oranges? Imagine the knights "sometimes chasing, sometimes being chased, bending their bodies to avoid the missiles, deflecting them or making other such movements to spectacularly entertain the onlookers." (J/S:DM dialog. 11)

7-38   Our kings and captains pay a salary to soldiers.
Os nossos reis e capitãis pagão soldo aos soldados

> In Japan, everyone must pay for his own food, drink and dress as long as the war goes on. *Em Japão cada hum á-de comer, beber e vestir hà sua custa emquanto anda na guerra.*

Not only are European soldiers paid, or at least fed, but veterans got fine stipends for their service, and the amount might even be appealed, explains "Miguel." (J/S:DM dlg14) Moreover, nobles and knights who personally contributed to a war effort were given correspondingly great rewards. Earlships and the like positions of authority were largely earned in that way. The Jesuits apparently thought the lack of proper payment was one cause of the disloyalty endemic to Japan (see 7-42). Others saw this self-responsibility as a clever way for the Japanese Lord to quickly conscript and field an extraordinarily large force in comparison to his low income and limited wealth (Valignano noted that the lords in Japan are often "so poor in wealth and rent that they don't even seem to be gentry (*senores*)" (V(A):S&A pg 8) but still "resemble kings in Europe for being very powerful in people," *i.e. military man-power*. Indeed. Thirty years after TRATADO, Tokugawa Ieyasu commanded a force of 200,000 men for his Osaka "summer campaign." This figure far exceeds those in the closest parallel in Europe, the Thirty Years' War (Boxer note, in C:MKJS).

If I am not mistaken, most soldiers in Europe were what we would now call mercenaries, whereas most soldiers in Japan were closer to what we would call national guard (the samurai) called up in time of war and draftees (those under them). Depending how you look at it either system could be considered more feudal or more modern.

~~~~~~

7-39   We fight to take places, cities, villages and their riches;
Antre nós se peleja por tomar lugares, cidades e vilas e suas riqezas;

> In Japan, the fighting is almost always to take wheat, rice and barley.
> *A peleja quasi sempre em Japão hé pera se tomar o trigo, arroz e cevada.*

Okada writes that it is an exaggeration to make the crops out to be the aim of war as Frois does. I would add that the European defensive tactic of burning fields to deny them to the enemy while retreating might also have made the more valid contrast on "our" side.

But Frois is not all wrong. With a principality's – or fief's – wealth measured in terms of rice production, the crops might have been synonymous with the real estate (in which case the difference is primarily nominal). And, sometimes crops were often viewed as an end, or prize in themselves because Japanese wars tended to drag on and it made sense to take grain for one's own soldiers while depriving the enemy of food. This tactic was called *karita,* or "reap-field." It was not uncommon for the solders to actually harvest the grain! As Okada points out, this practice was common enough to be forbidden by the Shoguns.

There are even Chinese documents telling how to discriminate between Chinese and Japanese "wou'ko" (*wako*) pirate raids which identify the Japanese as the ones who are so poor they waste time stealing grain to carry back to Japan (as opposed to gold and other real treasures). According to Souyri (who cites Japanese sources in S(R):WTUP), the first raids in Korea by Japanese pirates in the 14th century were indeed by starving sailors who mainly looted granaries and harvests, but success in this lead to bigger and better=worse things . . . Still, I cannot help wonder why this particular practice was so big in Japan that it caught Frois's eye as a domestic practice. I cannot help but wonder if there may well have been something else, a sort of "rice-raid" tradition, perhaps – I think of the pony-raid of the Amerindian – in at least the Southwest part of Japan where Frois spent some of his time! [1]

1. Rice Raid Tradition?   I have yet to find *proof* of any such thing, but FK introduced me to a famous Japanese legend of a mountain sage (Hôdôsennin), an Indian who came to Japan and used teleportation to fly his begging bowl out to receive offerings and bring them back to him. Once he had it fly out to a boat carrying an Imperial tribute of rice and the bowl after being refused even a grain, went after the rice with a vengeance returning again and again ("like a flying goose") to carry off sacks of rice until none remained. More, anyone?

7-40   With us, horses, dromedaries and camels [1] carry the soldiers' gear.
Antre nós, cavalos, dromedarios, camelos, etc., levão o fato aos soldados;

> In Japan, each soldier's *hyakushos* [peasants] carry his gear and food on their backs. *Em Japão os* fiaxos *de cada hum lhe levão seu fato e mantimento aas costas.*

Camels? Spain was once occupied by the Berbers, who rode only camels and no horses. Evidently, the camel was conscripted by the triumphant Iberians but only for the less prestigious role of a carrier. (Note also that Mohammed's army rode camels and had less than 200 horses for 10,000 men. The Arabian horses largely came from Iberia where they later returned. The history goes round and round and round!)

The Japanese "soldiers" here are *samurai*. This contrast is correct, but misleading if one thinks the Japanese practice was a specifically military one. Civilians also depended more on human than nonhuman animal power for transporting both men and goods in Japan.

1. *Translation:* The Bactrian was synonymous with the   generic in Portuguese, so the "camel" means 2-hump.

7-41   Among us, killing oneself is considered a grave sin;
Antre nós se tem por pecado gravissimo matar-se hum a si mesmo;

> The Japanese in war, when they can do no more, cut their belly to show their guts.[1] *Os Japões na guerra, quando não podem mais, cortar a barriga hé grão valentia.*

If we define "us" to extend back to our Classical world, the contrast is less absolute. Who doesn't know of the proverbial Roman soldier falling on his sword?

> The ancient heroes stabbed themselves as calmly as they did their enemies, and women as well as men knew how to use the short sword" (B:JG&W)

– wrote Alice Mabel Bacon. But this practice was by no means limited to warfare. The "voluntary taking of one's life to avoid disgrace, and blot out entirely or partially the stain on an honorable name" (Ibid.) may have originated in battle as a way to prove one's bravery and avoid execution at the hands of the enemy. Since suicide might be interpreted as bravery or cowardice, the Japanese came to do it in such a difficult way (self-disemboweling) that it could only be interpreted as the former!   Or, it may go back further, to the widespread cultural practice of suicide-as-revenge (saddling another with one's spirit), but be the roots as they may, the Japanese came to make a special institution of it, where suicide served as a way to take responsibility for ones wrong-doing by oneself, and thereby prevent the laws of collective responsibility from exterminating one's entire line. As outlandish as this practice may seem, "we" have it, too. Montaigne, in his essay "Custom of Cea", not only details *whole Spanish towns* committing suicide rather than submitting to the Romans – this reminiscent of what sometimes happened when Japanese castles were over-run – but a very close parallel to the above-mentioned "special institution."

> In the time of Tiberius, condemned men awaiting execution lost their property and were denied the right of sepulture; those who anticipated it by killing themselves were buried and could make their will." (DF trans. CEM)

Yet, many if not most of the many suicides recorded in Cocks' diary and Kaempfer's History of Japan (especially the diary-like "Affairs at Nagasaki" chapter) are done for none of these reasons. "A servant made away with himself, ripping open his belly. Another servant cut his throat, for no other reason, but because he had been affronted by another servant, for which he could obtain no satisfaction from the Mayor of the town . . . by reason of its being done in the Governor's own house." (K(S):HOJ) "The night before the first of June, three people made away with themselves: two whereof hang'd themselves, one was an inhabitant of Nagasaki, for smuggling, the other, who was a monk, for reasons not known. The third, out of despair and poverty, ript open his belly." (Ibid.) Less than half of those suicides fits the official bill. Perhaps, the most incredible suicide of all was recorded – or, rather, reported – by Caron:

> . . . it hapned that a young Gentlewoman, being on her knees art the end of a Table, waiting on her Master, in the apartment of the Women, and over-reaching herself to take a flaggon that stood a little too far from her, she chanced to let a wind backwards, which she was so asham'd of, that putting her garment over her head, she would by no means shew her face after, but with an enrag'd violence taking her nibbles into her mouth, she bit it off with such fury, that she died in the place. (From a Boxer note supplying an anecdote found in the Dutch edition but cut by Manley's English translation of Caron's TD (C(B):TD) – I am puzzled: Did Boxer put it into the same olde English or find it that way? Also I suspect it is an early seventeenth century Japanese urban legend!)

It is hard to say why Japanese could kill themselves so easily. Theoretically, any people who believe in a pleasant afterlife or rebirth and have no specific strictures forbidding suicide, should do so at the drop of a hat, and Japanese pride made certain the hat had many opportunities to drop. But responsibility or sense of honor were not necessarily involved. In a 1565 *Carta*, after describing a funeral in great detail, Frois writes: "There is another manner of burying themselves, alive." (Or, as Englished by Willis via Maffei's Latin: "They have another kind of burial, especially near the sea side, for them that are not yet dead." Devotees of Amida weighed down with alms and lashed to stones go out to sea and jump overboard, the better to reach heaven. Six men and two women did this shortly before Frois visited "the isle of Hiu" and, rather than being condemned as cultists "to all such as die so, the people erecteth a Chapel, and . . . both day and night many come very superstitiously in pilgrimage." Frois records that he and Almeida – who happened to go down at the seashore to baptize a girl – were badmouthed by four or five old women (*viejas*) for not paying their proper respects to the saintly deceased when they passed the chapel! (Did Frois happen upon the blossoming of a rare cult, or was this a common aberration in Japan?.)

Still, war was the place where suicide was *most* acceptable. Suicide could show the enemy that though one may have lost the battle, one was not defeated. It was a psychological victory, whereas simply getting killed was ambiguous and surrender was a betrayal to one's side and ideals. We say lightly that the Japanese found suicide the more *honorable* way out. But, by using the word *honorable* we trivialize what was a moral issue. If the cause is bigger than the individual, is it wrong to give ones life for it? How can we (Usanians) admire "our" Nathan Hale without admiring an entire nation capable of making the same sacrifice? Captain Pessoa's heroic death in 1610, where he put a firebrand to the powder magazine blowing up himself and his ship rather than surrendering it (B:CCJ) earned him a respected place in Japanese history, while the Chinese who gave up rather than dying or killing themselves in the Sino-Japanese War of the late nineteenth century became the object of Japanese disgust (see "The Japanese and the Landscapes of War" chapter in K:AJC), as were Allied prisoners who chose life in World War II.

Because the Japanese were quick to kill themselves, before more experience with the West taught them otherwise, they assumed others (particularly if they were clearly brave men) would do likewise. If those foreigners were considered hostages rather than prisoners of war, the Japanese guards, who themselves might be forced to commit suicide if their charges did, were in a tight spot. Captain Golownin and the other Russians captured with him found some humor in this:

> When the Japanese occasionally unbound our hands, they took care to hold our pipes for us whilst we smoked, fearing that we might by some means or another convert the pipe into an instrument of suicide; but of this they soon became weary, and, after a consultation, they resolved to permit

us to hold our own pipes, on condition of our fastening to the mouthpieces a wooden ball the size of a hen's egg. We laughed at this. and explained to them that it would be much easier to choke ourselves with this ball than with the mere pipe . . . (G:MCJ)

Today, one still reads of Japanese committing suicide to take responsibility for scandals, but, on the whole, there is little to differentiate Japanese suicide from that in the West, particularly when the "West" includes Eastern European countries with double the suicide rate of Japan, as well as Catholic nations with suspiciously low rates. The biggest difference would seem to be in the way suicides are treated as a concept, how they are depicted on television. Plays and movies about the 47 Ronin (masterless samurai) who end up committing *seppuku* (formal *harakiri*) en masse are shown every year as a sort of *morality play.* These samurai pretend to lead dissolute lives, putting their own families through hell and enduring themselves every insult in the books to eventually assemble and take revenge upon a man whose insult resulted in their beloved master's forced suicide, a venture in which they succeed and, having broken the new laws of an era that no longer allowed such vendettas (this was a century after Frois), themselves, had to commit suicide.[2] I applaud such a play for we need to be reminded that there are things more important than living. But, considering the sacrifices made by the heroes' families and the parallels with people working themselves to death for the sake of heartless companies, I can understand why not a few Japanese *detest* the play and the "feudal" (a word with very bad implications to most Japanese today) values it represents. TV also shows women killing themselves to save their honor (and punish bad men) and, best of all(?), the lovers' suicide, where two people die together to be joined in paradise. The latter is common enough that even children know the term (*shinjuu:* literally "heart-inside") and sometimes enact it in play, but no one actually does it in real life, if for no other reason than the fact that very few Japanese today have a firm belief in an Afterlife.

Paradoxically, doctor-assisted suicide has, if anything, met stronger resistance in Japan than in most of the West. The main reason for the lack of organs to transplant which sends many Japanese abroad for surgery is the reluctance of Japanese doctors to allow even brain-dead patients to die. Since WW II, Japanese have done a back-flip on the sanctity of human life (aside from abortion, where there is a question as to whether the life is yet human). They *claim* that, unlike the West, where men became accustomed to controlling the deaths of animals and, by extension men, their tradition of Buddhism does not allow this, and the idea of *brain-death* itself is a Western invention depending on the separation of soul and body, which is alien to their animistic souls. I think the main issues are actually that, *first*, the tradition of forced suicide makes Japanese rightfully aware of the dangers inherent to euthanasia, and *second*, Japanese doctors are, as everyone else in Japan, simply afraid of taking responsibility, for responsibility in Japan is something absolute and doctors, understandably, fear it.[3]

1. Guts.   I could not resist my *gutsy* pun, not in the original, which spoke of showing one's *valentia,* or "valor".

2. Enduring Insults for a Vendetta.   I read a number of articles about the men who flew the planes into the World Trade Center which pointed out that, fundamentalist Muslims or not, they sure seemed to be enjoying themselves in America, they had been seen at strip clubs, etc. . . . Had the reporters read Japanese history, they might have, rather, wondered if that was part of their ruse, to throw the FBI off track.

3. Responsibility.   To my mind, responsibility in the West means doing what one reasonably can and not worrying too much about the consequences, whereas, in Japan, you must worry about the consequences because you will be held accountable no matter what. (See the endnote for chapter XIV).)

7-42   With us, treason is rare and very reprehensible.[1]
Antre nós a treisão hé couza rara e mui estranhada;

In Japan, it is so common it is almost never criticized.
Em Japão hé tão comum que já quasi nada se estranha.

While lack of proper compensation (7-38) may explain some treason in Japan, it does not fit the overall personality pattern. The main reason is not so much a lack of pecuniary incentives to remain loyal – after all, as Xavier noted immediately after coming to Japan, honor meant more to the Japanese than wealth – but the unsettled nature of that era that revealed the arbitrary nature of authority and encouraged the capricious recourse to capital punishment that made even persons *suspecting themselves to be under suspicion* liable to break and run for a new master to save the hides of their families and themselves. Ironically, the quick recourse to capital punishment itself was largely due to fear that the retainer, *suspecting he might be suspected,* might betray his master, or a servant kill his master and commit suicide. Miguel=Valignano discusses all of these factors at length in *De Mission's* Dialogue 12 and concluded that as a result,

> In our country [Japan], no-one, not the lord nor anyone under his jurisdiction can live with tranquility of mind. The one constantly dreads treachery, while the other dreads unjust punishment at the hands of his mercilessly angry lord, or owing to a plot against him. So it is not at all rare that the sound of song and dance at the height of a banquette instantly becomes a bloodbath resounding the torments of hell.

In Europe, where, we are told, people of all social levels could rest assured of fair trials, where even a peasant could sue a King for his rights, where, everyone knew and accepted their proper place as if they were members of a big family, because retainers had fixed roles for which they were well trained from infancy, unlike in Japan, where servants were both vertically and horizontally mobile and, thus, could hardly be content with their proper places (Dialogue 10); in Europe, where the King was beloved of all, where lords who were "loved and respected like parents" and "treated their subjects with mercy as if they were their very own children," where rulers and ruled alike rested easily knowing, as "Mancio" points out, that "their authority could be expected to pass safely down the generations as it had reached them from ages immemorial," unlike in Japan, "where all was extremely inconstant, where clans' fortunes rose and fell, where no position, no person, and no family was not exposed to extreme danger," in this secure place called Europe, no one feared treachery. (Dialogue 12)

Of course, the prescription for a cure was a good dose of Christianity (Dialogue 4) – Confucianism would have made equal sense, but not to the Jesuits – for Japan. (With even the succession of the Shoguns a chain of treachery, it is easy to believe that the political situation in Japan was as bad as everyone described it. It is equally hard to believe that, just fifty years after the death of Machiavelli, Europe was as tranquil a place as "Miguel" and "Mancio" made it out to be!)

The constant change, the mutability, the impermanence, the uncertainty of life in Japan was *the* most constantly reiterated theme in Jesuit letters to Rome. This was partly to explain the enormous pressure they were under and why they needed continued financial backing despite their many successes, and partly to excuse the inevitable setbacks – human disasters – that occurred with frequent loss of patrons. The Jesuits blamed Buddhism for creating this anarchic situation, but it is more likely that the situation, by seeming to prove the reality of Japanese Buddhist claims that this world was not to be relied upon – a claim that Christians also made – was one reason for the proliferation of cults such as the seaside suicides mentioned above. As some Christians, even today seem to take a perverse joy in man-made and natural disaster as proof of the truth of the approach of "Judgment Day," some Japanese Buddhists must have found this unsettled state of affairs convenient for their catechism.

Retrospectively, there is irony here. Japanese like to think of themselves as a loyal people. Most Japanese today think of the play about the faithful retainers as Alice Mabel Bacon did:

> As I watched the progress of the play, I began to understand more fully than I had before that *passion of loyalty* that made revenge the one object in life of those fourty-seven men, and which made it altogether right that they should sell their wives into the worst of slaveries, severe all domestic relations, kill their nearest relatives, and give themselves up to any or every crime or vice, if by so doing they could further the object that was foremost in their thoughts and first among their duties. (my italics: B:AJI)

In the case of this particular play, I feel that it is not so much *loyalty* as *honor* that carries the day – but, it may be that all the attention given to loyalty masks the opposite tendency – as we find in the constant reference to "individuals" conceals a boringly similar "America" – and, at least one of Japan's best-selling novelists, Sakaya Taiichi, used his considerable knowledge of the 16th century to argue in a series of books and articles written in the 1980's that loyalty never was in excess in Japan. (While Sakaya was a favorite of the business community, he could not stomach the self-serving corporate pr, which subdued workers by appealing to their traditional loyalty as Japanese in an age where more outgoing creativity was called for.) Frois's contrast also is tonic. It tells us that the beautiful aesthetic of transience was partly born of this terrifying, unnatural instability – not that Kenkô didn't make that clear – and that Japanese were hardly blessed with *wa* (harmony) from the start.

1. Estranhada. The Portuguese *"estranhada"* means literally something that is *shocking* and, depending on the context either admirable or reprehensible. The Japanese use the word *hinan,* i.e., "censured/criticized") and the French translation "trés blâmable." in it. I felt tempted to leave it at "shocking" but . . .

7-43 With us, it is the supreme infamy to be an executioner;[1]
Antre nós hé sumo vituperio ser algoz;

> In Japan, any nobleman can kill someone for justice, and they take pride in it.
> *Em Japão, matar a hum por justiça qualquer fidalgo o faz e se preza disso.*

"Our" image of an executioner is indeed a grim one. I cannot recall seeing an old picture of a European executioner without a hood over his head. On the other hand, as Frois's contemporary Avila de Giron (C:TCJ) wrote in a rarely caustic vein:

> Name a Japanese and you name an executioner – and they say it is cruel to punish children!

This was true in several senses. *First*, there was what might be called perfunctory execution, when a lord or samurai cut-down a maleficent on the spot. Obviously, it would keep people on their toes and be a good way to prove one still had the knack. Needless to say, lords who exercised this prerogative too much were not liked. *Second*, there was formal execution where a lord might choose to do so to show off his arm and test his sword – get in the first sword-test, if it were – or, for the satisfaction, because damage had been done to him (but this would be rare for low class criminals were generally executed by untouchables, the same people in charge of killing and cutting up domestic animals). *Third*, there was *seppuku,* where someone ordered to disembowel himself, might ask (or order) someone else to do him the honor of seconding him, i.e. cutting off his head. Since, the kindest cuts – made for someone who was not really interesting in showing his guts, but just getting his family off the hook by properly taking responsibility – came as soon as the short sword touched the belly, this assistance might as well be called *euthanasia* rather than execution. Since no one would want a weak arm to assist (Poor Mishima! His assist apparently wasn't able to cut through his heavily muscled neck at a stroke) to be asked to do so would indeed be an honor. It also was a good deed because samurai wished to die at the hand of someone they respected (There is a name for a second: a *kaishaku*.).

Morse, who must have sensed an anomaly between the gentle men he knew and rumors of these seemingly sadistic behavior, made more sense of the *second* type of execution by linking it to the *third*, and kindest, type. He milked "Mr. Machida, the sword merchant" for information, and learned that although the professional executioners were of the [despised] Eta class, a gentleman had a good reason for wanting "to try the temper of his blade by executing a criminal." Namely, "beheading a criminal gives a man practice" in case "any of his friends had to commit hara-kiri" and he were to be called to give the coup de grace.

Mr. Machida told me that it did not require such a very hard blow to separate the head from the body. He said the first time he performed the act he struck so hard that he broke his sword by striking a rock on the ground . . . (M: JDD)

1. Translation. *Algoz*, from the *Al-gozz*, an Arab tribe supplying executioners is a more interesting word than our Latinate term "executioner." In English, *hangman* is a good word but obviously won't do here! The Japanese, *shikei-shikkônin*, (death-penalty-enforce-person) is also a boring modern term (The only example given in the OJD is from a novel by Arishima Takero: "Do you know the name of the executioner who chopped off Roland's head?)" Is there no old generic term in Japanese? I first translated "kill someone for justice" (*matar a hum por justiça*) as simply "execute" but, not knowing if Portuguese in Frois's time had that word, chickened out.

~~~~~~

7-44   The *cambala* [1] [*yak* hair] that in India serves gentiles and moors as fans,
As cambalas que na India servem a jentios e mouros de abanos,

The Japanese use for the wigs around their helmets.
Os Japões uzão dellas pera cabeleiras ao redor dos capacetes.

When you think about it, a swishing tail is not just a fly-shoo but a fan. As described in 2-5, the Japanese imported the yak hair from China.   With the helmets, I would guess that the main purpose was adornment, but there may well be a talismanic element involved for the tail hair from yaks is seen on everything from spear-heads to smaller implements carried by religious leaders called *hossu* (the characters meaning: shooer (as in shooing away).   My dictionary calls it "a priest's horsehair flapper" ("flapper" is an old English word for shoo-fly devices – we have no new word for them!).   It is often seen in the hand of Zen patriarchs and means there is only one thing we really need, *something to guard against the various types of desires that swarm the mind like flies.*   Did the helmet wearer feel said hair was an appropriate symbol for ridding the land of pesky rivals?

1. Cambala. Okada writes that Cambala comes from "camara," meaning "white yak" in Sanskrit. Frois probably thinks it just means yak hair. Some of the hair on the helmets that I have seen is white and some black.

~~~~~~

7-45   Our razors are thick and flat. *As nossas navalhas são grosas e razas;*

Theirs are slim and curve on one edge. *As suas delgadas e curvas de huma banda.*

Okada mentions an old tale called "The (Buddhist) priest and the acolyte (和尚と小僧) where the razor serves as a simile for *ayu,* or "sweet-fish," a small river fish with a lithe and slightly curved silhouette.

~~~~~~

7-46   We grind ours with oil on hard stone.
As nossas se amolão com azeite em pedra dura;

The Japanese grind theirs on soft stone, with water.
Os Japões amolão as suas em pedra mole e com agoa.

Worldwide, water was, naturally, the more common and even the Greeks who rubbed oil on their bodies used waterstones.   Natural stones tend to clog without a lubricant and in Frois's day the European and Japanese stones were natural.   With "ours" it is best to use a mineral oil (perhaps diluted with petroleum, also called "rock-oil" in Chinese), for vegetable oils can build up and reduce the contact of the blade and the whetstone. With "theirs," the recommendation is to soak the stone in water for ten minutes or so before using. If you want to keep it wet and ready, i.e., in water, it must be cool enough not to slime the stone but not cold enough to crack it. With waterstones, much of the abrasion comes from floating particles, so a soft stone which releases many will sharpen fastest, but it will also hollow out fastest and need to be planed back in shape. Modern artificial sharpening stones are the most contrary of all, in that they generally work best dry. As is the case with corks, today, there are in-between types of reconstituted stone as well, but who knows what to put on them!

That is the overall description but if we restricted ourselves to swords, we could point out that the professional sharpener in Japan used more than one hardness of stone and that the one used first is noticeably convex rather than flat, that electric grinders are not good because they can generate a high enough temperature to adversely effect the mixed temper of the Japanese sword . . .

7-47   Among us, only barbers shave. *Antre nós os barbeiros somente rapão.*

In Japan, almost everyone knows how to do it. *Em Japão quasi todos o sabem fazer.*

As suggested in 7-14, 15 and 16, above, Japanese blades were sharper than "ours." They could apparently even shave with their short swords! No doubt their cutting culture was equally advanced, with more professional sharpeners (*togishi*) offering door-to-door service, and a greater appreciation for maintenance on the part of all than was the case in Europe. On top of that, practice with the writing brush meant that Japanese had to have had far better control of fine, unsupported hand movements, than Europeans, something vital in the days before safety razors. I would only wonder if the lower classes are included with "almost everyone" and, if so, if they could afford razors (欄外注？)

7-48   We cannot shave our beards without going to the barber;
Antre nós se hum não for ao barbeiro não pode rapar a barba;

[In Japan] Many *bonzes* and laymen shave their beards and heads by themselves.
Muitos bonzos e sequlares rapão a barba e cabeça por si mesmos.

7-49   Among us, soldiers carry the match in their left hand.
Antre [nós] os soldados trazem o murrão no braço esqerdo.

The Japanese with their right.
Os Japões no direito.

The Japanese for *murra(n)o* is *hinawa,* or "fire-string," a clearer indication of what we are talking about than the English match. It was a fuse-like smoldering string, kept ready for the firing a musket. The dictionary Englishes it as both "fuse" and "match." Since we identify a burning string with a *fuse,* that was my first choice for translation; but, considering the fact these "matches" were not necessarily the matches we imagine ("match" once even meant "lamp!") and that the rifles were and are still called "matchlocks" (as opposed to the later *flintlock*), I went with the second word though I almost went back on myself after reading the following translation of the end to a shameful raid in South China honestly recorded by Pinto:

So everyone ran down to the beach and got back to the junk without any opposition whatsoever. We were all very rich and very happy. We had also captured a lot of beautiful girls for our use later on and it was pitiful to see them coming along in groups of four and five, *hands tied up with musket fuses,* the girls all weeping and our men all singing and laughing. (my *italics,* L:PFMP)

7-50   Our matches are made of twine; *Os nossos murrões são de fiado;*

Theirs, of paper and bamboo husks. *Os seus de papel ou cascas de cana.*

This is a difference, but hardly a contradiction. (For a real difference, we need to wait for the flintlock, a 17th century European invention that may have been inspired by the flint and steel mechanical lighters Japanese nicotine addicts devised the better to light up at night.)

7-51   We can fence without yelling.
Antre nós esgrimi-sse sem falar;

The Japanese must give a shout with every blow and parry.
Os Japões a cada talho ou reves hão-de dar hum grito

We have discussed this fully in 7-25. Let me just add that it is quite an experience hearing a *kendo* class – preferably high-school girls – practicing with their bamboo swords. Someone should include it in a symphony. *Scream! Whack! Scream! Scream! Whack!*

7-52   Our Swiss soldiers discharge their arquebuses from the shoulder.
Os nossos soldados na Suisea desparão as espingardas no onbro;

The Japanese place [the butt of the rifle] in their faces, like someone aiming at enemies. *Os Japões a poem no rosto como quem aponta a inimigos*

The "our" here has two possible meanings. First, for over a hundred years squads of Swiss mercenary arquebusiers were engaged all over Europe by anyone with the money to hire them. From the way they turn up everywhere, I would not be surprised to learn that at their peak they commanded the majority of small-arms in Europe (anyone?). Second, a unit of mercenaries was engaged by Pope Julius II in 1505 and have served as the Papal Swiss Guard ever since.

Why did Japanese not use their shoulders? The butts of their guns were short.. *Why?* Did they want the gun in front of the face to keep the exploding powder further from the ears? Or was it easier to aim? Did the Swiss, then, *not* aim? Or is Frois's expression "like aiming at enemies" the idiom for a sniper? If so, did we have snipers that shot differently than the Swiss? I have read of the arquebusiers marching along, their faces all black from the powder. If so, how could the Japanese bear to be yet closer to the chamber? And considering the fact that a kick in the shoulder hurts, how did Japanese survive getting kicked in the face? *I do not know any of this.* I only know the guns remained that way for a long time, for over 200 years later, Golownin observed:

The butt ends are very small, and they do not put them to their shoulder to fire, but lay them to their right cheek and so take aim." (G:MCJ)

endnote VII

W*ar*

For all the little contrasts, there was so much missed here. For a start, how about this:

> *We raise various dogs to be mean and train them to hunt, attack and tear up our enemies.*
> *They think it an unnatural thing, worse than cannibalism to teach dogs to eat humans.*

The Iberians did not only use dogs in battle but to murder the defenseless. In the Americas, they played a special role in the extermination of the *Berdache,* or third sex, an accepted gender found among most native people. No doubt "we" would have sicced them on the abomination-loving bonzes in China and Japan if given half a chance! That does not speak well for "our" side. Neither does this:

> *We do not ask for the names of people before we fight them in a war.*
> *Their nobles and even many gentry insist upon knowing who they fight before drawing their sword.*

In the traditional battles of Japanese clans, there was a complex etiquette of doing battle, where every samurai acted in a manner found only among a far smaller number of knights in Europe. Announcing (*na-nori*) was an important part of this. It was probably true in parts of Europe, too, a couple hundred years earlier (before the cream of French chivalry was shot to pieces).

> *We fight wars outside of our countries.*
> *Japanese are happy to fight at home.*

Frois could have written this, for Hideyoshi's attempt to conquer the world (beginning with Korea) happened just *after* TRATADO (from 1592). And it was a decade-long fluke.

戦　　　　　　戦　　　　　　戦

If the *De Missione* report on the situation in Europe is taken at face value, the biggest contrast of all in the 1580s was the fact that "We enjoy domestic peace; while the Japanese are constantly at war." This was true for Japan and *Iberia* (for the Spanish took their wars elsewhere in Europe!). But, what irony! The Portuguese brought the seeds of peace to Japan. If it were not for those guns, it is unlikely that the wily Nobunaga would have succeeded in destroying his more powerful traditional rivals and the warring might have continued for hundreds of years. As it was, a mere 100 years later Kaempfer and others could describe a situation exactly opposite of that claimed by the author of *De Missione*: *They were at peace and we at war.* Forward another 250 years and topsy-turvy again. After World War II, "we" simplistically turned the losers into an *inherently warlike people,* one so dangerous the Occupying Authority had to have a special Constitution denying their right to self-defense:

..

> *The Japanese people forever renounce war as a sovereign right of the nation.* (Article 9)

Helen Mears deserves plaudits for her long (and, unfortunately boring) MIRROR FOR AMERICANS (1948), which, almost alone, took America and the West to task for this self-serving stereotyping that continued for decades. I see no need to elaborate upon her general argument that the kettle was calling the pot black: *Americans were and are every bit as militaristic as Japanese.* If we wish to think about war, I believe the biggest question is not whether we fight wars or not, but *how* and *why* we conduct them as we do. It is bad we have wars, but not all wars are bad. There are wars in which one side not only fights for a good cause but does so in a manner that is good so as not to contradict the end through the means. Japan was universally praised in the West for its fine behavior in winning its War with Russia, a leading Western military power. It was a *good* war for Japan, a good war objectively speaking, and one Japan should remember with pride.

> the Japanese have proved themselves superior to the Russians in every point – in courage, discipline, strategy, and the civilization of their methods of warfare. . . . Their demands were marvelously moderate. (S:MQTJ)

Unlike the case with WW II, Japan treated prisoners better than International standards required. It is easy for us to say that they were only trying to put on a good face, but this was no little war. It was perhaps the largest war in history up to that time. In a war like that, no nation can put on an act on all fronts. The Japanese were *that* good, period. No question about it, their martial traditions did make possible the unparalleled "disciplined courage" that allowed the war to be so well waged (Or, has anyone managed to debunk this?).   Can we speak of this type of power, responsibly exercised as "militaristic" – a word with disparaging connotations?

戦   戦   戦

In one sense, *Article 9* is very Japanese. The Japanese have, after all, disarmed *themselves* in the past. *More than once.* First, after obtaining the greatest small arms fire-power in the entire world (see note to 20, above), the Japanese "gave up the gun." Frois, in his *Historia*, gives us the first inklings of the renunciation when, in 1586, Hideyoshi "to protect his own self from any stray bullets, forbid the ownership of guns under pain of the penalty of death in the several countries neighboring his palace." Two years later, Hideyoshi initiated his more famous sword-hunt, taking all real weapons away from the hitherto armed peasantry, so that only the samurai portion of the population was armed. And, as battles slowly petered out in the first fifty years of the Tokugawa era (1600-1868), guns disappeared. They were not absolutely outlawed, but the government licensed so few to be made that they stopped multiplying and evolving. It is not quite correct to say that the samurai all returned to their swords, because many never left them – riflemen were often peasants or bonzes. The guns did not, however, become invisible, a taboo presence like Christianity. The parades observed by the Dutch invariably included many rows of colorful old-fashioned arquebus bearers. And, eventually, even the samurai's swords would have their turn.   After giving the historical and romantic context of "this magical weapon," Chamberlain explains what happened to the samurai's custom of always wearing two swords, dating back to the Warring Era, that is to say at least 500 years:

> It was abolished by an edict issued on the 28th March, 1876, and taking effect from the 1st January, 1877. The edict was obeyed by this strangely docile people without a blow being struck, and the curio-shops displayed heaps of swords which, a few months before, the owners would have less willingly have parted with than with life itself. Shortly afterwards, a second edict appeared, rescinding the first and leaving *any one* at liberty to wear what swords he pleased. But as the privilege of a class distinction was thus obliterated, none cared to take advantage of the permission, and the two-sworded Japanese gentleman is now extinct. (TJ)

..

Strangely docile?   No. *I would call it brains.* Wearing Western clothing and making a money in the world became the mark of an honorable man and the Edict made it official. In that brave new world, sword-waving became a prerogative of the military machine. A generation later, The Occupation expressed the same surprise at the docility of Japanese. *Again, I would call it brains.* The ability to recognize changed circumstances and act on it.

戦   戦   戦

In the first decade after the Black Boats pushed open their nation, samurai assassins 1), revenging real (Westerners not observing proper quarantine rules because of the unequal treaty brought in cholera that killed hundreds of thousands) or imagined slights (accidents of etiquette), or 2), hoping to create a confrontation to topple the government and create a tougher anti-foreign one, or 3), ideological xenophobes terrified the new foreign community and earned a measure of respect for Japanese as a people not to be messed with.

They did topple and change their government, after which cooler heads prevailed and Japan concentrated on development. The traveler-writers arrived. Japan was very popular as a queer place, *but no longer respected.* Prefacing his "Peace Edition" of MORE QUEER THINGS ABOUT JAPAN, written shortly after the Ruso-Japanese War ended, Douglas Sladen admitted he previously thought of the Japanese navy in their "little white men-of-war built by Armstrong" and their British Navy look-alike uniforms as "a mere parade" and "attached even less importance to the Japanese Tommies, five feet high, who were marched and countermarched in Italian uniforms by German instructors." *Sladen saw toy-soldiers; and he was not alone.* "The British merchants of Yokohama were never tired of telling you how the Japanese had been dispersed at Shimonoseki by a taste of cold steel."

Yes and *no.* It was those 47 Samurai (pretending to be resigned to being losers but really just biding their time) all over again. After Sladen learned of the bravery of the Japanese soldiers, who did not hesitate to die for their country as a martyr dies for his faith without drugs like the Dervish or "promises of Paradise like the Mahommedan [sic] who is fighting against infidels," he confessed:

> I laugh now when I think of what a lot of venerable myths we hoarded up; but I do not laugh, I almost shed tears of respect and sympathy, when I remember that ever since I have known the Japanese up to the beginning of the present war they have possessed their souls in patient, content to be branded as a toy nation – almost as a nation of cowards – until, as Minerva sprang fully armed out of the head of Jupiter, they leapt upon the astonished Russians, a nation armed cap-`a-pie, a type of martial wisdom. (S:MQTJ)

That is to say, the coming of the Black Ships placed the Japanese under a *moratorium.* A writer (or any other artist) – unless he or she is fortunate enough to be filthy rich – is someone who works late into the night while others live and love, in the hope of creating a worthwhile future where the work he or she does will finally be acknowledged. (Like Johnny Cash's *San Quentin,* we (for I write of my circumstance) suffer and, if it goes on for decades, cannot help but feel bitter to see others who "keep on moving" on the outside.) Douglas Sladen knew first-hand the collective hell the Japanese went through. Hence, the wet eyes. Still, one has to question why he and others were so blind to Japan's potential clout. I do not know how many 19th century references I have read of Golownin's evaluation of the Japanese as *unfit for modern warfare.* Between 1811 and 1813, he discovered what Perry and the first English and American Ambassadors would rediscover: *flimsy fake forts* and described a people so long at peace that they would rely on a charade for protection and, by character, timid, rather than aggressive like many Westerners. He wrote that "it requires at least a century to introduce an innovation into their military system" where "strict observance of ancient order and rules is their unalterable tactics [sic]." But, he made it clear he was talking about Japan in "a state of peace." Elsewhere, in his book, this fair-minded and insightful Russian captain made it clear that the Japanese were, nonetheless highly disciplined, determined *and could take on the world at any time if they decided to do so*; but this prescient part of his message was, for some reason (cognitive dissonance?), overlooked by the West.

Even after the Japanese showed their stuff, Golownin was still quoted in the same way as before, but this time as an example of how wrong he was! *I have yet to see a single reference to the fact that Golownin was the first to predict Japan could easily become a global power!* As far as I know, no one – least of all Golownin's countrymen – even considered that possibility until the Japanese actually defeated the Russians at sea but 50 years after the Opening. *Look, everybody, at what he wrote:*

> If the Japanese government desired to have a navy, it would be easy to build one upon the European system, and to bring it to the greatest perfection. They need only to invite into their country two or three good naval architects and some naval officers. They have good ports, all the necessary materials, a number of able carpenters, and very active and enterprising sailors. The people in general are quick of comprehension, and ready at learning. It requires no little boldness to put out to sea in such vessels as they now have. . . . We were frequently witnesses of the activity of the Japanese sailors; it is wonderful with what dexterity they manage their great boats in the violent surf . . . (G:MCIJ)

Golownin liked and admired the Japanese on many counts, but he feared an increase in the number of world powers and wrote that Japan's neighbors "must thank providence for having inspired the Japanese lawgivers" to promote isolation "and should give them no inducement to change their policy for that of Europe." He predicted that if the Japanese had a sovereign like Peter the Great, her "numerous, ingenious, and industrious people, who are capable of every thing and much inclined to imitate all that is foreign" would "become in a few years, the sovereign of the eastern ocean." In that case, he wrote, even the West coast of America would be under Japanese influence. And if the Japanese were to "adopt our policy as a model, we should then see the Chinese obliged to do the same." He was a bit off on China – unless we include 20th century developments. He feared we would "compel them" to do this.

> Attacks, for example, like that of Chowostoff [his misbehavior in the North was the reason Golownin was held by the Japanese], often repeated, would probably induce them to think of a means to repel a handful of vagabonds who disturbed a nation. This might lead them to build ships of war on the model of those of Europe; these ships might increase to fleets, and then it is probable the good success of this measure would lead them also to adopt the other scientific methods, which are so applicable to the destruction of the human race. In this manner all the inventions of Europe might gradually take root in Japan, even without the creative spirit of a Peter . . . The Japanese certainly would not be in want of teachers if they would only invite them; *I therefore believe that this just and upright people must, by no means, be provoked* . . . I do not mean to affirm that the Japanese and the Chinese might form themselves on the European model, and become dangerous to us now; but we must take care to avoid giving cause to our posterity to despise our memory. (G:MCIJ *my italics*)

Golownin's editor writes that the "extreme readiness" of the Japanese "in acquiring European knowledge is certified" by none other than our "father Luigi Froes, in 'Lettere del Giappone'" where he attests to the talent for learning on the part of the Japanese exceeded that of Europeans. Be that as it may, Golownin's warning was to little avail. *Japan was provoked.* And, wouldn't you know it, his nation was the loser! (If, 80 years later, Russia had heeded Golownin's advice and not provoked Japan into war, and lost so ignobly, I doubt that the chain of events leading to the Bolsheviks – and to Hitler's Germany – would have happened.)

戰   戰   戰

How, then, do we explain the Rape of Nanking, the medical experiments, the forced name-changing (in Korea, everyone had to adopt Japanese names!), the Bantam March? I believe that lack of fair pay-off from playing the game right with Russia, comparatively restrictive "international" restrictions on the size of their navy, racist policies hampering emigration to the West and brutal discrimination against Japanese in California nurtured hate for the hypocritical white race, and as if this was not enough, the increasingly brutal military training – the type of hazing the modern military around the world boasts of, where desensitizing takes the place of principle – of recruits already two generations removed from *bushido*-style chivalry and, in the case of what we now call the Third World, Japan's own traditional racist bent was nourished by this bitter mood. Even Chamberlain, who, like Sladen, considered Japan "more chivalrous and humane in war" than Europe, and even enthusiastically added "If there be any "Yellow Peril" it must surely consist in Europe's own good qualities being surpassed by a higher grade of those same qualities in her new rivals," was troubled by Japanese racism.

> Another particular calling for improvement is the behavior of the Japanese emigrants towards the less civilized races. Every one who has seen them in Formosa, and especially in Korea, tells of supercilious and often brutal conduct. They have imitated the white man in everything, even in his ill-treatment of what he contemptuously terms "natives." (C:TJ)

Actually, this tragic flaw was not necessarily learned from the white man. It was already noticed by the Jesuits who observed that as great fighters, valuing martial prowess and courage, the 16th century Japanese despised the neighbors from whom they had learned so much in the past. That is why Hideyoshi could send his soldiers off to Korea so easily. The Japanese did not need to imitate the white man. They were, in many ways, *one of the boys* from the start. In the end, they influenced each other badly.

戦   戦   戦

To be fair to both the Europeans and the Japanese, we should point out that they were not by any means the only war addicts in East Asia, either. In the 16th century, wars involving *hundreds of thousands* of people and casualties likewise in the *hundreds of thousands* – in at least one case, if Pinto is to be believed, costing the lives of thousands of elephants (not in battle, but eaten during a siege!) – was endemic in South-east Asia. Pinto, who lost no opportunity to point out the cruelty of his own countrymen, tells nonfiction tales of siege and rapine, revenge and sadism that curdle the blood. The Burmese (Kipling would praise their bravery) in particular and a couple people whose names I can't recall (probably Thai and Cambodians) were *every bit* as ferocious as our Far East and Far West exemplars. Here is but one of the cruelties visited upon Prome after the city's fall. Let us note that Pinto writes nothing this horrid about Japan:

> When this was over, he [the Burmese tyrant] went to stand at a window overlooking a courtyard where they brought the bodies of more than two thousand children that had been lying in the streets, and right there in front of him he had them cut into very small pieces, rolled in rice chaff and grass, and fed to the elephants. (P(C):TMP ch155)

And to crown it all, on the following day, which was Saint Bartholomew's Day, he had all the noblemen who had been taken alive – and there must have been more than three hundred of them – impaled on *caloetes* [an Indian term used by Pinto], and in that manner, impaled like suckling pigs, they too [we have skipped other atrocities] were thrown into the river. So that the means used by this tyrant to punish these unfortunate people were so unheard of, that "we Portuguese all went about gasping in horror." *Believe me, that is saying a lot!*

VIII

of HORSES

Do que toca aos cavalos

~~~~~~

8-1   Our horses are very beautiful;   *Os nossos cavalos são muito fermozos;*

The horses of Japan are much inferior to them.   *Os de Japão lhe são muito inferiores.*

We tend to connect Greece and Italy with the classic world, but when it comes to *horses* Spain has the pedigree. As a war horse, the Spanish horse was mentioned by the Greeks as being without equal, described by the famous equestrian Xenophon as "gifted Iberian horses and even mentioned in the Iliad (1100BC). They were *the* horse (for war and portrait) for most of the kings of Europe. And, right at the time Frois was in Japan, Phillip (Felipe) II, King of much of Europe from 1556-98, was busy creating the modern Andalusian or, as he thought of it, *the perfect horse* as described in classical texts dating back to the above-mentioned Xenophon (430BC). We are talking not only about graceful performance and good character but *features*, for the horse had to *look* noble and beautiful. To the ends of perceived authenticity and ethnocentrism, the *"convexo"* profile was restored – i.e., the snout of the Arab horse which had bred with the Andalusian (Southern Spanish) when the Berbers occupied *Hispania* was a bit concave (with respect to the forehead and the nostrils) and this upset the classicist who thought all noses human or equine should be Roman! Be that as it may, "the Andalusian forms approximately 80% of the bloodlines of all modern breeds including the Quarter Horse, Cleveland Bay, Appaloosa, Lipizzaner, Welsh Cob, Irish Draught, Connemara, Mustang, Kladruber, Friesian, Neopolitan, Dutch Gelderland, Hanoverian, Holstein, Fredericksborg and others."[1] And, the thoroughbred owes its start to "the infusion of twelve Spanish mares" (c 1600) by James I according to one website (most websites only mention Middle Eastern stallions, but they, too are largely Andalusian).   Today, the result of Felipe II's project is called an Andalusia in the USA and a *Pura Raza Española* (PRE) horse by the Spanish government!

With respect to Japanese horses, Frois's was a typical European opinion. His contemporary, Bernardino de Avila Giron writes cruelly: "According to our standards, their horses are not at all good and the very best one in all Japan is only fit to carry firewood." (C:TCJ). Bartolli, in his *History of the Society of Jesus* snickers that next to the magnificent Arab, "even the best horses in the Imperial [Hideyoshi's] stable were but hacks." (cited in Okada) He was restating what Frois wrote in *his* Historia. Most Europeans, Iberian or not, in whatever century one chooses concur. In 1878, the Englishwoman Isabella Bird was scathing:

> Horses are used as beasts of burden and for riding, but the Japanese horse is a mean, sorry brute, a grudging, ungenerous animal, trying to human patience and temper, with three *movements* (not by any means to be confounded with paces) – a drag, a roll, and a scramble. (B:UTJ)
>
> The traveling is the nearest approach to "a ride on a rail" as I have ever made. I have ridden or

rather sat upon seventy-six horses, all horrible. They all stumble. The loins of some are higher than their shoulders, so that one slips forwards, and the back bones of all are ridgy. Their hind feet grow into points which turn up, and their hind legs all turn outwards, like those of a cat, from carrying heavy burdens at an early age. (B:UTJ)

To be fair to Japanese *horses*, here is her appraisal of Japanese *dogs*: "cowardly yellow dogs, much given to nocturnal howling, miserable misrepresentations of the Scotch collie." Brinkley, author of an incredible encyclopedia [2] on Japan published in 1901, makes an issue of size:

The Japanese never had a war-horse worthy to be so called. The misshapen ponies which carried them to battle showed qualities of hardiness and endurance, but were so deficient in stature and massiveness that when mounted by a man in voluminous armour they looked painfully puny. (in C:TCJ)

The English trader and Captain John Saris, writing only decades after Frois, provides one of only two favorable opinions I have seen in hundreds of years of Western observations! He may not have taken any rides – and falls – for he was full of appreciation for their indomitable spirit:

Their horses are not tall, but of the size of our middling Nags, short and well trust, small headed and very full of mettle, in my opinion, farre excelling the Spanish Jennet in pride and stomacke. (again, from C:TCJ)

Even today, equestrians in the West today are so infatuated with *appearance*, with their opinion of what makes a good horse, that not only have they little interest in Japanese horses, but few appreciate the world's oldest genuine horse-centered culture, the Mongols. Go East, cowboy, if you would see the real thing! Get out into the country where little children ride before they walk! (The Mongolians are wonderful people and offer some very reasonable horse-tours.)

1. *Andalusian Information*   I must confess to relying on websites which are very enthusiastic about the horse and usually connected with breeding them.   This = http://www.preandalusians.com/EvolutionandHistory.htm l 1. (citing this ="The Origins of the Spanish and Portuguese Horse" by Holly B. Kilburn, Conquistador Magazine PP 22-28) was perhaps the most thorough, but see also http://www.equistrideinternational.com/ andalusian_history.htm.; and www.skyhorsekingdom. com/ pure_spanish_horses/ pure_spanish_horse_breed_ faq.htm.Here is the clincher on the http://www.anda-lusianfoundation.com/history/ site:

Perhaps the best quality of the Pure Spanish Horse is the willingness to work with his less than perfect human companion – the nobility and grace with which he participates joyfully in anything requested by his rider. From the drawings in the caves where early man was shown leading the prototype Spanish horse to today, the Pure Spanish Horse has been known and respected for its submission to the aids and the assistance he offers his weekend rider.(© 2001-2004 The Foundation For The Pure Spanish Horse.)

There is less information about the horse from Frois's homeland, the Portuguese Lusitano, "said to be the oldest saddle horse in the world."   (www.worldofhorses. co.uk/Breeds/Lusitano_Breed.htm)

2. *Brinkley's Encyclopedia.*   I saw it in a library just before closing in a city I was leaving. Otherwise, it might have helped me out. I cannot afford the one's sold on the web. As I would like to illustrate a future edition . . .

8-2   Ours, running, [still] stop on the spot; *Os nossos correndo parão hà risca;*

Theirs are horribly uncontrollable; *Os seos são muito dezenfreados.*

Frois does not exaggerate on either account. The Iberian horse "was designed with a short back, strong loins, able to move off quickly from a standstill (as they needed to do so in the bullring), stop quickly and change direction. The Spanish Andalusian has a capacity for lightning acceleration and yet stopping dead in his tracks." (EVOLUTION AND HISTORY OF THE SPANISH (PRE) ANDALUSIAN – http://www. preandalusians.com/EvolutionandHistory.html)

Even the long and tame centuries of Seclusion did nothing to improve Japanese horses. The unmanageability of Japanese horses of all types was a common complaint of 19th century European visitors to newly opened Japan. Isabella Bird has *dozens of pages* of invective scattered in her thousands of pages of writing on Japan – and as far as horses go, identical – Korea. Early in her Japanese travels, she confessed to having believed that Japanese pack-horses were muzzled "to prevent them from pasturing on the haunches of their companions and making vicious snatches at men." But, "now I find that the muzzle is only used to prevent them from eating as they travel." She was traveling through a region of Japan where "mares are used exclusively," and they were led by women. In other parts of Japan, there were only stallions led by men. Her first meeting with "the terrible Japanese pack-horse" – which was also generally the only horse a visitor rode – was dramatic. Excited by the crowd that always gathered when she passed through, the "horribly fierce looking creatures" went berserk and broke their "head rope." Her mount

> proceeded down the street mainly on his hind feet, squealing, and striking savagely with his fore feet . . . jumped over all ditches, attacked all foot-passengers with his teeth, and behaved so like a wild animal that not all my previous acquaintance with the idiosyncrasies of horses enabled me to cope with him. (B:UTJ)

When she and her interpreter, who had been thrown, pulled into a post for a change of horse, the stallions were so provoked by the other horses they threw the interpreter again and even the horsewoman herself, by cleverly rearing up right when she was in the process of dismounting.

> I fell on the ground, when he made several dashes at me with his teeth and fore feet, which were happily frustrated by the dexterity of some *mago* (teamster/groom). These beasts forcibly remind me of the words, "Whose mouth must be held with bit and bridle, lest they turn and fall upon thee."

One feels like one is in a rodeo and the *mago* play the clown! Two letters and a hundred miles later, she is on the back of a more "wicked horse" yet!

> His head was doubly chained to the saddle girth, but he never met a man, woman or child, without laying back his ears and running at them to bite them . . . as soon as I put my hand on the saddle [to remount] he swung his hind legs around to kick me, and it required some agility to avoid being hurt . . . The evil beast made dashes with his tethered head at flies, threatening to twist or demolish my foot with each, flung his hind legs upwards, attempted to dislodge flies on his nose with his hind hoof, executed capers which involved a total disappearance of everything in front of the saddle . . . I used to think that horses were made vicious either by being teased or by violence in breaking; but this does not account for the malignity of the Japanese horses, for the people are so much afraid of them that they treat them with great respect; they are not beaten or kicked, are spoken to in soothing tones, and on the whole live better than their masters. Perhaps this is the secret of their villainy – "Jeshurun waxed fat and kicked."

Yet for all the ill-treatment *she* received, Bird stood up for Japanese horses. In Ezo (Hokkaido), she discovered Japanese (such as her interpreter) who "never dared even to carry a switch on the main island" were "barbarous to these gentle, little-prized animals." They beat them "unmercifully over the eyes and ears with heavy sticks"(!) It was like their Buddhism didn't apply in the land of the Ainu. She found the breaking in process involved "atrocious cruelty" and didn't blame them for their tricks, such as "lying down in fords, throwing themselves down head foremost and rolling over pack and rider," etc..

The reason commonly given for the badly behaved horses is the general lack of familiarity with domestic animals and their training on the part of the Japanese. Dogs, too, were, and still tend to be undisciplined. From what I have seen (on television) of monkey training in Japan, I suspect that not only the Hokkaido horses, but *all* the horses were broken in an overly harsh way, even if people do not discipline them later.   But the need to dismount before passing or being passed by a superior in Japan probably contributed to the lack of concern for improving equine transportation, for it made the horse *all but useless for rapid transportation* and, more importantly, with almost all horses in Japan not so much *ridden* as led about by one or two footmen – because not as many people could ride and because many who could feared the responsibility in the case of accident – there was little demand for horses trained to respond in the way we expect horse's to respond, anyway.   There was some demand but it was limited. Kaempfer writes:

> The Japanese look upon our European way of sitting on horseback, and holding the bridle oneself as warlike, and properly becoming a soldier . . . they seldom or never use it in their journies. It is more frequent among people of quality in cities, where they go a visiting one another. But even then the rider (who makes but a sorry appearance when sitting after our manner,) holds the bridle meerly for form, the horse being nevertheless led by one, and sometimes two footmen, who walk on each side of the head, holding it by the bit." (K(S):HOJ)

Where it *did* matter, horses were trained well enough.   In the Shinto rite of shooting arrows (*yabusame*) at a small target at a dead run (gallop) without a hand on the rein and spectators standing dangerously close, or, competitively shooting running dogs (with padded arrows) in a crowded field of competitors, etc. would be impossible with the frightful mounts we have been reading about.   And we know there were exceptional cases, such as the Shogun Nobunaga, who Frois noted, fancied himself the greatest horseman of his age, "forcing courbettes and marching in zig-zag" in Kyoto's biggest parade (from *Historia,* found in V(A):S&A).   I do not know what breed he rode, but Valignano, who witnessed this, wished to send him top European (Napoli) horses. [1] That did not happen. But the young Ambassadors came back to Japan a decade or so later with an Arab horse that was presented to the following Shogun, Hideyoshi. [2] That was good enough.

1. *Napoli Horses*   The very large Neapolitan war-horses bred in central Italy around Naples are, to my mind, not at all beautiful like an Arabian, but would have been the most impressive to the Japanese leader, for Japan had no such huge horses.

2. *Getting One Good Horse To Japan.*   That one horse brought by Valignano and the young ambassadors may have given the Christian community in Japan several decades of tenuous grace, for it helped Hideyoshi, who was extraordinarily pleased with it, convince himself that Valignano was back, not as an envoy of the Church but as the Ambassador of the Viceroy of India bearing tribute. The expenses involved in getting this horse – one of two of four brought to Goa from the West specially for the young Ambassadors, who had requested them in Europe that Valignano chose to bring from Goa to the Shogun (one of the two died en-route) – to Japan gave Cabral, the Superior in Japan who had opposed accommodation, an excuse to backbite Valignano:

> Judging from the way that [Valignano] operates, he prefers to do everything by himself and does not want to leave any of God's work undone. Therefore, God probably is being modest and may let him do everything. This was already evident at the time that Valignano traveled with the Japanese envoys and from the tribute gifts that they brought back with them. I estimate that the tribute gifts presented to the kampaku [Hideyoshi] exceeded more than 10,000 pardao. The two horses taken from here, together with their accessories, alone cost more than 2,000 gold pardao. This is only a small portion of the money spent during the journey to Japan. That is to say, a veterinarian, horseshoer, and riding master had to be brought along as well. Also, there was much criticism concerning the transportation of the horses by ship, which resulted in scuffles among the passengers." (a 1593 letter to Father General Aquaviva found in a splendid description of the whole horse-story,   A PRESENT OF ARABIAN HORSES by Yuki Ryogo, trans. by Fumiko F. Earns, netted at www. uwosh.edu/home_pages/ faculty_ staff/ earns/yuki.html)

Shortly after coming to Japan the first time, Valignano, not realizing the social expenses of operating in Japan, had been a bit too hard on Organtino for overspending, and, now a decade later, Cabral, who (in my opinion) never realized what was what, jumped on him for doing what he felt he had to do for the survival of the mission.

8-3   Ours allow one to ride on their rumps; *Os nossos consentem cavalgar nas ancas;*

Those of Japan are not so trained. *Os de Japão não o tem por custume.*

Apparently, Europeans were not adverse to putting two people on a horse – and the body of the Iberian horse being relatively short encouraged use of the rump – while pony-sized Japanese horses were not built for more than one rider, riding anywhere.

8-4   Ours proceed abreast of one another; *[Dos] nossos vai hum apar doutro paseando;*

Those of Japan always go one after another. *Os de Japão sempre hum detraz doutro.*

I wish I could *ask* Frois to explain this one. What specific Spanish practice or practices is he thinking of?[1] Are Japanese horses of the type we have already read about, so competitive they cannot go abreast without fighting one another? Are the roads too narrow because, carts are scarce so most roads are made for foot traffic in Japan? For one versed in classical Japanese literature, all this is a comical reversal, for "horses" – or rather ponies – in Japanese poetry *always* race across the fields side-by-side (*koma narabete*)! If Frois is right, Japan changed since ancient times.

1. *Going Abreast.* At Andalusian sites we come across things like "The Cobra," where a team of three or more mares, linked either from halter to halter, or from collar to collar are paraded by a footman from one side and a four-horse hitch used in competitive driving? I do not know if either were done in Frois's time, or if he might be speaking of more than one horse being led. Or (this I would doubt) could the Iberians, like some ancient Roman nobles with their *desultorios equos* keep horses running side-by-side so they could switch back and forth in mid-battle!

8-5   With ours, the tail is extended for beauty's sake. *[Aos] nossos se entende o rabo pera fermozura;*

With theirs, it is bound in a knot. *Aos seus lhe atão com nós o rabo.*

Japanese tails were usually fixed in this manner on formal occasions when a Chinese-style saddle was used and was called "China-tail" (*kara-o*). The knotted tail was actually stuffed into a sack which was then bound to the tail. Gosh, if I had a knot tied in my tail, I might be unruly, too!

8-6   The manes of our horses, if long, are the best ornament.
As comas dos nossos cavalos, quanto mais compridas, hé mayor ornamento;

With horses in Japan, the mane is cut and rice straw attached here and there to what remains in order to enhance the horse's *isei* [presence]. *Aos de Japão lhe cortão as comas, e no que fica lhe vão atando de lugar a lugar humas palhas de trigo pera mais yxei do cavalo.*

With respect to hair, we evidently had the same standard for equine and feminine beauty, whereas the Japanese did not settle on one standard. The inclusion of two contrasts involving hair is not surprising for the Iberian horses, to give a couple internetted phrases, "had an abundant mane and tail," which "are luxuriant and naturally thick and silky." We may assume they were bred that way.

Okada cites literature suggesting Japanese had two major ways of presenting horse manes, *nogami,* meaning "field" or "wild-hair," which bore some resemblance to the European style for being long, and the *karihôshi,* or "shaved-priest" style (also called *yarihôshi*) suggested by Frois. There were many sub-styles. Sometimes it was slightly cropped and left so that the bristles stuck out like a clipped hedge, or given a *keppatsu* (bound-hair=hairdo), clipped to about 6 inches in length and bound into 33 little nubs, or made into "nine-heads," etc..

The *palhas de trigo* (straw of grain) here means rice-straw, which does not have the entirely humble connotation it does in English but was auspicious for its association with plenty) and beloved.

8-7   Our horses are all shod with iron horse-shoes and nails.
        Os nossos cavalos todos se ferrão com cravos e ferraduras.

Those of Japan are not; instead they wear straw shoes that last but half a league.
        Os de Japão a nenhum, antes lhe calsão sapatos de palha que lhe durão mea legoa.

According to the Japanese emissary to Europe, Miguel=Valignano, who assures the Japanese who stayed at home that shoeing did not draw blood or hurt a horse as they might imagine (*One wonders about the man who drove the first nail into a horse's hoof!*), Europeans "worked iron into shoes" so that "the horse's trail could be more easily followed," [1] – a new one to me! – and, *also,* in order that the shoe would "last for many rides." Apparently, the unwillingness of Japanese to immediately try horseshoes *troubled* the Jesuits because Miguel's statement ends as follows:

> Europeans really wanting to know other peoples' customs, gladly learn technology and inventions from one another, and find this intercourse not the least bit shameful. But, with the Japanese, the bad habit of finding this [learning from others] shameful is very strong. Japanese, no matter what it is, unless it is something they themselves thought up, whether they have it or not, tend to be ashamed and fear adopting it from foreigners. ([*De Missione,* dial.10.(J/S:DM) Note: the Japanese translation (supposedly from wretched Latin) is not without problem! I hope I did alright here!])

This is deliciously ironic considering the stereotyped antithesis of the humble Japanese copier and the conceited do-it-himself Occidental we are used to.   Eventually, the superiority of iron shoes on rocky surfaces and ice convinced some samurai to try to copy the Portuguese, but a century after Frois and the Embassy, Kaempfer, writing of travel preparation, makes it clear that "our European Iron horse-shoes" were still unknown!

> Shoes, or slippers, for horses and footmen. These are twisted of straw, with ropes, likewise of straw, hanging down from them, whereby they are tied about the horses' feet . . . They are soon worn out in stony slippery roads, and must often be chang'd for new ones. For this purpose, the men that look after the horses always carry a competent stock along with them, . . . tho' they are met with in every village, and even offerd them to sale by poor young children begging along the road. Hence it may be said, that this country hath more farriers, than perhaps any other, tho' in fact it hath none at all. (K:HOJ)

In 1858, Oliphant found something more poetic to say about the straw shoes his horse's feet were "swaddled in."

> . . . whenever one shoe was worn out or kicked off, another was immediately tied on; hence arises the custom in Japan of measuring distances by horses' shoes. Here you ask in how many horse shoes will I reach the residence of the Spiritual Emperor? which, after all, does not differ very much from the old problem of how many cows' tails will reach the moon. (O:EEM)

At that time, horseshoes were still virtually unknown and caused quite a sensation. (See Harris's and Heusken's journals). But Japan had changed from the time when Miguel=Valignano wrote and the generally advanced nature of Western technology was admitted, so the improvement was quickly adopted and, today, Japanese horses all wear horseshoes.

1. *Shoes for Trails?* The first reason given by Miguel= Valignano sounds absolutely bogus. But, I have read literature on *aviation history* that reveals the biggest fear many in Europe had of flying men – before they really could – was of their swooping down and absconding with young women! I kid you not! In a society where guarding female chastity was so important as in Southern Europe, I would not doubt that all fathers would want horses to leave as clear a trail as possible, or, at the very least, that it is at least possible such an explanation would have been given to the visiting Japanese by someone.

~~~~~~

8-8   With us, a lackey takes the halter in front;
Antre nós leva o moço d'esporas o cabresto diante;

In Japan, depending on the road, they carry straw shoes for the horses.
Em Japão, segundo os caminhos são, vão carregados de sapatos de palha pera o cavalo.

There is no exact equivalent of the Portuguese "boy of spurs." Had Frois written *"moço d'estrebaria,"* "stable-boy" or "groom" might have been better. Since Europeans usually did their own riding, Frois might be talking of someone who accompanies a sumpter-horse (carrying supplies for military officers) who were called "bât-boys." Or, if at an inn (your parking valet for a horse), they were "ostlers." For a general term, "footman" seemed best, but considering that the Japanese shoe carriers generally ran, a "lackey" [1] defined by OED as "a running footman, a valet" seemed best. The French translation, uses a more precise term "valets d'ordonnances."

The straw shoes of the pack-horses were usually "ty'd to the portmantles" (both sides of the rear of the saddles), but mounted gentleman no doubt preferred to have their lackeys carry them. In Japanese, too, there is an abundance of terms, some of which are specific to the person taking the halter and some specific to the shoes.

1. *Lackey* Just some of the spellings in the OED: *Lacquey, Laquay, Lacquy; Lackeis, Allakey, Allakays, Alaques*, etc.. The origin of this strange old word is unclear. It is interesting that the clearly French-sounding *valet* sounds classy, while a lackey has become a pretty sorry word.

~~~~~~

8-9   With us, the bits have their gag and rings for inside the mouth;
Antre nós o freo tem sua lingueta e argolinhas pera dentro da boca;

In Japan, they have no more than an iron [bar] passing through the mouth.
Em Japão não tem mais que hum ferro atravesado na boca.

Riding and driving bits in the West were not only complex but very diverse. I think this might be a case where horse people can guess what Frois sketches whereas we who are not horse people will not get it even if it were to be described in detail. *"Moseman's Illustrated Guide for Purchasers of Horse Furnishing Goods"* (New York – originally sold in the 1870's) shows a collection of hundreds that even puts our best little contraption, the I.U.D. to shame.

Again, as explained in 8-2, above, the demand for such control just wasn't there in Japan.

〜〜

8-10   We mount with the left foot; *Nós cavalgamos com o pee esqerdo;*

The Japanese with the right. *Os Japões com o dereito.*

It would be clearer to speak of mounting the left or right *side* of the horse, for it is unclear from the above whether the foot in question goes into the stirrup or over the horse. (Perhaps that is why in one version of Valignano's PRINCIPIO or SUMARIO, this is reversed.) Luckily, many others make it clear. Montanus:

> Having the spirit of Contradictions so much, that as we Mounting on the left side, they get up on the right side of a Horse. (M:EEJ)

Okada writes this is a result of the samurai's holding his bow in his left "bow-hand" and the rein in his right "rein-hand." Today, bowless Japanese mount from the left. I think it – *i.e.,* "our" way – which makes sense because the right arm can grasp the saddle while the left leg is usually used as the push-off leg and the right one the kicking leg. This, then, is a contrast where the simplest "natural" way is probably ours, while circumstances naturally favored theirs. The editor for the English translation of Golownin (G:MCJ) gave this contrast as an one of example of "the points in which they [the Japanese] differ from, and also those in which they agree with other nations, with whom they have had no possible intercourse." He gives us another reason to boot:

> They mount a horse on the offside, like the Arabians; the reason assigned for which is that in an action so noble and manly, it is wrong to rest upon the left foot.

It is also the only one of Frois's contrasts found in *five* contrasts concerning horses noted by Chamberlain in his "Topsy-turvy" essay:

> The whole method of treating horses is the opposite of ours. A Japanese (of the old school) mounts his horse on the right side, all parts of the harness are fastened on the right side, the mane is made to hang on the left side; when the horse is brought home, its head is placed where its tail ought to be, and the animal is fed from a tub at the stable door. (C:TJ)

It is surprising Frois did not note the location of the head and tail, for this was the *first* thing every 19th century visitor noted. Here is Alcock, the first British Ambassador, and Ms. Bacon, first foreign teacher for the daughters of the Imperial Line, respectively, on this most charming contrast:
..

> . . . the horse's head was where his tail would be in an English stable, that is facing the entrance. It certainly seems a much more rational thing to be able to go up to your horse's head, when [where?] he has an opportunity of recognizing you, rather than to his heels, with a preliminary chance of a kick and a broken leg. (A:COT)

> Horses here are put into their stalls wrong end foremost, so that I never go into the stable without thinking of the nursery rhyme, ---
>
> > "See! See! What shall I see?
> > A horse's head where its tail should be." (B:JI)

Perhaps, I thought, the Iberians did not always stable their horses like the English did, in which case Frois's lacuna is forgivable. But, in 1609, Rodrigo de Vivera y Velasco wrote:

Each horse is tethered with two chains, their croups toward the wall and their heads facing the entrance to the stables so that there might be no danger of their kicking anybody. (in C:TCJ)

The observation together with reason suggests an opposite practice. Perhaps Frois just hadn't frequented stables. I doubt if most of us today can guess which way the head and tail went in our respective cultures! But, now, that my attention has been caught, now that I know, the French object-poet Ponge's fixation on the horse's magnificent high-heeled "courtesan buttocks" begins to make more sense. Our culture apparently preferred to see a horse's ass to its head! Either Mr. Ed, who always faced the camera, was acting Japanese or sometime in the middle of the 20th century, Usanians came to place the "head where the tail ought to be!" Actually, there are reasons supporting our way, too. My equestrian sister says facing *in* rather than *out* prevented horses from swiping each other's food and from being cheeky to incoming horses. But the modern West would appear to no longer have a single way. Nowadays, most stalls are big enough a horse can face any damn way he or she pleases, and some people feed them from an inside window and others hang a bucket from the front of the stall in what was – unknown to them – the Japanese style.

The world of horses, like that of humans, is becoming grey.

8-11   Our reins are of leather and very well made;
As nossas redeas são de couro muyto bem feitas;

> Theirs are of strips of *nuno* [cloth], colored and twisted.
> *As suas hé huma tira de* nono *pintada e emrolada.*

..

According to a citation in Okada, ancient reins were white, dark blue and pale blue twisted hemp made into a triple braid. A tight braid would keep a twisted cloth rope from untwisting. The contrast seems to hint that the Japanese reins are not well made, which is unlikely, for I cannot recall ever finding a poorly made product in Japan of old.

8-12   We have a full saddle and full-length stirrups.
Nós temos sela e estribos são hà bastarda;

> In Japan, one always rides with short stirrups.
> *Em Japão não se cavalga senão só a jineta.*

When small horses run, extended stirrups can get in the way of their legs. But the Japanese seem to have their stirrups even shorter than necessary. Obviously, short is good for standing up to see over a field while hunting, shooting a bow over a horse's head, or combat. The *jineta* style (*genette* in French) was identified with crack cavalry in Europe (and jockeys today). The dictionary always includes "bent knees" in the definition, but the short stirrups imply that, so I did not add it to the translation. However, we can turn this around and say that most Europeans, because they are weak-kneed for lack of squatting, must keep their stirrups lower than would be optimal for riders with more powerful legs and have more support from a full saddle as well.

8-13   Our stirrups are iron, open in front;
Os nossos estribos são de ferro, abertos por diante;

> Theirs are wooden, closed in front, and long and thin like Moorish shoes;
> *Os seus de pao, fechados por diante, muito compridos, como sapatos de mouro.*

While the 15th century Portuguese King Don Duarte in his pioneering book on horse gear and horsemanship (*Livro da Ensynanca de Bem Cavalgar toda Sela*) included an idea of his own for stirrups with a closed front (J/F(M&J):T), our stirrups were almost without exception open.

The Japanese once used open (loop) stirrups adopted from the Chinese [1] that were not so different from "ours." These were often combined with a toe-bag. Some designs had a hard "tongue" – what we would call a "sole" – which extended in a foot-wise direction for added support.   Some "tongues" were no longer than the bag and only supported the toes, some supported the front half and, eventually, many came to support the entire sole, which made sense for Japanese footwear worn riding had soft bottoms (I think they just had *tabi* on. Anyone?). The bag and the loop were then dispensed with entirely. This was possible because the sole support does not so much *close* in front as loop up and over, (this, too, like the tip of a Moorish shoe or a Russian sled). The end of the tip loops back a bit further than the ball of the foot, which is where the stirrup strap attaches (⊂----). The open sides – or side, for the inner side was often covered – has the advantage of allowing "the rider to get his foot lose with ease in case of a fall," as Kaempfer noted.

With the exception of horses ridden for traditional rites, Japanese today use Occidental style stirrups when they ride. However, note this: when Japanese children ride stilts, which are called "bamboo-horses," today, *they still do so with their whole feet resting on the supports* – as was the case with the old stirrups – toes facing *directly into the stilt-legs* rather than sideways to the stilts in the Western manner. Someone with nothing better to do might check the correspondence between stirrups and stilts in various cultures.

1. *Chinese Stirrups.*   A twelfth century painting in the British Museum called "Young Horseman" by Ch'ien Hsüan (1235-90) shows loop stirrups. If the Chinese of old had loops and still did in the thirteenth century, does this mean the closed stirrup was a Japanese invention? Or, is it found elsewhere?

8-14   We use spurs. *Nós usamos de esporas;*

> They don't use them. They only use the *wara* [straw →brush?] on a very short segmented cane. *Elles não, somente de* vara, *que hé da cana de nós muito curtos*

I believe we are talking about *sasa, i.e.* bamboo grass and that Frois means the clump of leaves left on it when he writes his favorite word, *vara* or, "straw."

8-15   The bow of our saddles is completely closed in front.
Ho arsão das nossas selas hé todo fechado por diamte.

> Those in Japan have a hole to cling to.
> *Ho de Japão tem hum buraco pera se apegarem nelle.*

We are talking about a handhold (*tegakari*) under the front edge of a Japanese saddle – not a raised saddle horn, or pommel, but a space, or as Frois puts it "hole." If the standard European saddle (a fiction: see Kaempfer's remarks in 8-32) has an inverted "lazy U" shape, the Japanese saddle is more like an inverted "V," or, to use Bird's perfect expression, "fashioned like a saw-horse" I am not certain when the handhold was used. I imagine it would help a passenger (who is not controlling the horse but just sitting) on hilly terrain . . .

~~~~~~

8-16   We use cruppers, caparison and golden studs on the trappings;
Antre nós se uza de retrancas e caparazões e nominas;

> The horse of Japan do not have them, and only use a tiger skin with the hair-side out
> as a caparison.   *Os de Japão o não tem, somente uzão de caparazão de pelle de tigre pera fora.*

Even if we were to explain automobile parts to a pre-motoring reader, it would probably not hold his or her attention. I fear explanation of equestrian gear is the same. How many readers care to know that *cruppers* are bands that circle the rump to make certain the saddle and whatnot don't work forward? [1] Or, that the *caparison* is a richly decorated cloth that could extend from ear-tip to hoof [2] and was sometimes leather and used for defensive armor (Only Schütte's German, *Schutzdecken,* makes this clear)? The "golden studs on the trappings" are interesting for the fact that in the original Portuguese, they are simply described as *nominas.* This is *the same word* we saw in a religious context and can mean a written charm, a pouch for relics, straps wrapped around the arms for praying (i.e., *phylactery*). This suggests that the studs were not just decoration but a sort of charm.

Horses were generally less sumptuously dressed in Japan. It goes without saying that tiger skins (there being no tigers in Japan) were rare and only found on the horses of the Shogun and some of the nobility! Japanese horses appearing in festivals are another story altogether. Their decorations are varied and interesting. For example, here is a description of the horses ridden by a group of 24 Japanese nobles in a 1626 procession ("the reception of the sovereign vicegerent" [sic?] from a report of the Dutch East India Company's envoy to the "ziogoon" (Shogun), Conraedt Cramer, Englished by Ogilby) who provides, after Saris, the only other kind words I've read for Japanese horses. The men were

> . . . bravely mounted on gallant horses, proud of their little heads, short ears, and gaunt yet well trussed bodies, insomuch that the meanest their seemed to excel the most generous and bravest steed that ever Europe boasted or bred. Their saddles were all waxed or gilded; the seat embroidered with silver or gold or else spread over with tiger skins; their manes, like ours were curiously plaited with silk, silver and gold ribands. Their caparisans, that covered their breasts and haunches were a kind of network of crimson silk, full of tufts, and dangling with the motion of the wind; on their foreheads a golden horn, resembling our painted unicorns . . . (in B:MCJ)

It is possible this was a post-Frois development influenced by the Portuguese. If the parading Japanese horses had some accessories curious to Europeans, so did ordinary horses (at least in 1692, when Kaempfer visited). To wit: "a net-work of small but strong strings to defend" the head and "particularly the eyes, from flies, which are very troublesome to them." I wonder if Frois is not a bit more likely to spot things *we have* that *they do not have* more often than the *vice versa.*

1. Cruppers and Stuff Since the French translation is happy with *croupières* and the French are big on horsemanship, I thought that enough, but a picture of a "harness" in the dictionary shows no less than three different but interconnected parts to the rump part of the harness! The thickest horizontal strap (which I imagined was the crupper) which wraps right around the buttocks

under the tail is called *"Breeching,"* the two more or less vertical straps that hold it to what seems like one or two straps (looking from the side I can't tell down the middle of the back are called *"Hip-straps"* and the one or two straps are the *Crupper.* I have seen breeching on a Japanese packhorse carrying a woman depicted by Mitani Kazuma in his *Edo-shôbai-zue.* It has no hip-straps and the angle is too low to see if there is a crupper, but it makes me wonder if this was copied from the Europeans or Frois's difference holds for horses in all sectors.

2. *Caparison Above or Below?* According to the OED, a caparison is "a cloth or covering spread *over* the saddle or harness of a horse" But it is also defined as a kind of "defensive armor" (leather, usually), and that would not be over the saddle, right? Indeed, the richly decorated cloth depicted in my Shogakukan Random House is *under* the saddle. This over or under problem is driving me crazy. I hope the reader is not equally upset.

8-17   Ours [our saddles?] are made of leather and wool. *As nossas [**ressas?**] tem couro e lã;*

Theirs wood and *urushi* [lacquer]. *As suas pao e* vruxi.

Schütte writes "*ressas*" in brackets and calls it a correction (on the manuscript). "Ressas" does not, however, mean "saddles." The notes to the modern Portuguese version (1993) write it is a mistake probably meaning *redeas*, or "reins," but that would not jive with the description of reins in 8-11 above; and who can imagine wooden or lacquered reins! All the other translations simply go with "saddle," for the materials described seem correct and, at least on the Japanese side, it is perfect. I do, however, suggest another possibility: *saddle-bags* or *trunks* (Is there a Portuguese word that could be misread?), for Japanese horses carried wooden lacquered boxes. Whatever it is, one finds Japanese used less leather than we did, because they ate less of the meat the hide originally housed. The exception is, of course, the *shamisen* made from cat-skin, whereas our stringed instruments were made of wood, until the banjo was borrowed from Africa.

8-18   Our stables are always put behind or below the house.
As nossas estrebarias se poem sempre detras ou debaxo das cazas;

Those in Japan are built in front of the house.
As de Japão se fazem na dianteira das cazas.

Okada cites a contemporary document describing two stables at the residence of a magistrate, with one between the living room and reception room and another by the East gate, facing West. (貞丈雑記). Since a good house would face East or South and a reception room would clearly be in the front . . . I think Okada is right that this reflects the high value the samurai placed on their horses, yet, 11-19 (the respective locations of the human water closets) suggests another possible explanation.
..

8-19   In the houses of gentry in Europe, guests are first greeted upon coming inside;
Nas cazas dos senhores em Europa se agazalhão primeiro os ospedes nas salas;

In Japan, the first reception is in the stable.
Em Japão o primeiro recebimento hé nas estrebarias.

For guests and horses alike the Japanese method seems more efficient and friendlier. Since horse-lovers will always take you back to their stables to show off, one might as well *get it over with* while having your own horse "parked" and groomed down. Okada cites a 1586 report of a noble, who visiting Hideyoshi, enjoyed entertainment (dancing girls and other such expected at a party!) in the stable before anything else. Speaking of Hideyoshi (who, as we have seen elsewhere (?), was thought to resemble a monkey), in the New Year holiday season, the horses had a visitor of their own: *a monkey.*

The performing monkey was auspicious as a charm for all because its name *saru* means "leave" (all the bad spirits and bad luck should then hit the road) and for other reasons to be elaborated in 14-24, its most serious *job* was blessing horses, warding off disease and injury and ensuring their good behavior. Can you imagine a performing monkey visiting a stable *behind* a residence?

8-20   Our horses are cleaned with curry-combs;   *Os nossos se alimpão com almofaças;*

Those of Japan by hand or with some cords.   *Os seus com a mão ou com humas cordas.*

Okada writes there was a wooden comb used in Japan called an *akatori,* or "crud-remover," but apparently hands and cords were more common. I imagine a rough cord used by two grooms would work well, but have yet to find a picture of this.

8-21   Our horses have mangers.   *Os nossos tem manjedouras;*

Those of Japan eat in buckets.   *Os de Japão comem em selhas.*

The Portuguese word for what the Japanese horses eat from, *selha,* is problematic. It is defined in *Aurelio* as a "round wooden *vaso* (container?) with low sides," and Okada writes they generally had handles and were used to carry fish to market. Okada also wonders if the contrast was not between individual "hay-buckets" for European horses and collective hay troughs for Japanese horses. (Some Japanese trays were definitely trough-size, for I have seen old citations where people sleep in them or turn them upside down for a stage!) But, Alcock later contrasts our stable with its "*fixed* mangers" with the Japanese stable where they "*hang* their food from the roof in a bucket." (A:COT) So it may well be that *built-in* versus *portable* was Frois's intended contrast, rather than Okada's *single* versus *collective* schema.

The "manger" (*manjedouras* or "feeders" in Portuguese) is a pleasant puzzler in English – most English native speakers only know it today from the Nativity scene and have a blurry and ambiguous picture of a trough with straw acting as a cradle *and/or* the whole stable or barn where Jesus and his parents slept! – but the biggest dictionary can only tell Japanese it is a "straw-bucket." In English, a manger is a manger *whatever it is*, but what happens in translation is another story! Take this sweet episode recorded by A DIPLOMATIST'S WIFE IN JAPAN:

> I did not realize the intense difficulty of translating our thoughts into Japanese till the day after our Christmas tree, when O'Matsu came to me looking very puzzled, and said she would like to ask a question: why did Imai San (the gentleman who made the little address about the meaning of Christmas) say such a dreadful thing about "Jesu Sama"? He had said that Jesu Sama was put into a bucket, such a thing as ponies have their food in! That seemed very horrible and undignified to her. I tried to explain that in Palestine the animals did not eat in buckets; but I saw that I made very little impression. Imai San was a man, and a Japanese, and evidently my Bible history carried no weight in comparison with his. A day or two after this, I sent all the maids and children down to the convent in Tsukiji, where my friends the nuns had made a beautiful *creche* for their children. Here, in lifelike figures, were the Mother and the Babe, Joseph and the Shepherds, and the crib with its straw, all the scene splendidly decorated with pine branches and imitation snow and gold paper stars. O'Matsu came back beaming. "I understand it all now," she told me; "eyes speak better than words. Buckets, indeed!" and she laughed triumphantly . . . (F:DWJ:1899)

8-22   Ours often lie down in their master's stable.
Os nossos nas estrebarias dos senhores deitão-se muytas vezes;

> Those of Japan almost always, day and night, tied about the belly [tethered] high up. *Os de Japão estão quasi sempre de noite e de dia atados pola barriga em alto.*

The verb *atado* (tied/fastened) in the original is insufficient to explain what is what. I have found two references bearing upon this. First, Alcock:

> When not eating, however, their head is often tied up rather above the level of the neck, without any freedom or power of moving from right to left, merely to keep them quiet, which is great cruelty, and all to save a lazy groom the trouble of cleaning them if they lie down.

The belly is missing, but not allowing the horse to lie down is the same general idea. For reasons obvious from the next contrast (8-23), a Japanese stable might not make a good bed, anyway. Luckily, Bird, evidently observed the very thing *in Korea*.

> At the inn stables they [the ponies] are not only chained down to the troughs by chains short enough to prevent them from raising their heads, but are partially slung at night to the heavy beams of the roof. Even under these restricted circumstances, their cordial hatred [of one another] finds vent in hyena-like yells, abortive snaps, and attempts to swing their hind legs round. They are never allowed to lie down, and very rarely to drink water and even then only when freely salted. Their nostrils are all slit in an attempt to improve upon Nature and give them better wind. [in 1999, a device similar to an anti-snore clamp was marketed in America to do the same thing!] They are fed three times a day on brown slush as hot as they can drink it, composed of beans, chopped millet stalks . . . . I know not whether *the partial slinging of them to the crossbeams* is to relieve their legs or to make fighting more difficult. (B:K&HN)

If Bird couldn't figure out what it was all about back then, I don't know if we ever will! I seriously doubt Alcock's idea that keeping horses on their feet was to save the groom work. But I do know one thing. Horses like to lie down and, if given a chance, even dig out craters to make comfortable beds to lie in. Had Frois written in English, might it not be *hoisted up by the belly*?

8-23   Our stables are made on the ground. *As nossas estrebarias se fazem no chão;*

> Theirs have to be covered with planks. *As suas hão-de ter sobrado de taboas.*

A stable at the entrance of a Kyoto mansion Frois visited in 1565 was made of *sugi*, the fragrant smelling Japanese cedar, whose wood is used for shrines (Shinto), temples (Buddhist) and other valuable architecture. Frois noted the only part of the floors that were *not* wooden – where there were rush mats – was for the human attendants! (in Okada J/F(O):T) I have no idea *why* wood was favored and can only guess that fear of fleas and ticks may have played a role.

8-24   The horses of Europe urinate on the ground of the stable.
Os cavalos d'Europa ourinão no chão nas estrebarias.

> The horses of Japan have their urine taken by long *hishaku* [ladles].
> *Aos cavalos em Japão tomão-lhe a ourina em fixaqus compridos.*

The 1604 Japanese-Portuguese Dictionary described two kinds of long-handled ladles in stables, the *umabishaku* for scooping up water to wash the horse and the *baribishaku* for receiving the horse's stale (NIPO in J/F(O)). While horses drop their dung on the run, they must set-up (by moving their legs apart) to stale, so an attentive groom would be able to pick up the ladle in time. The handles were a little over 5-feet long, the mouth of the scoop 9 inches across and 10 deep (Okada).   One would think the carefully collected urine would be put to good use, but contrast 11-22 will claim differently!

8-25   We have mules and jennies, zebras, asses and beasts-of-burden.
Antre nós há mulos e mulas, zebras, asnos e azemalas.

In Japan, they have none of these.
Em Japão não há nenhuma de couza destas.

Precise translation was impossible. *Azêmola,* says a Portuguese-English dictionary, is a "pack-mule," a creature I cannot find in my English language dictionaries, or a "beast of burden," which puzzled me until I saw in *Aurelio* that it may mean old and decrepit horses that are put to work (as opposed to animals always used that way?). But, then again, it could be a draft-horse. *Asno* can be a donkey or an ass (both are the same *Equus asinus*) or an onager, if wild and from Asia which is possible here, considering the fact the zebra is included! Should I have made my *mulos* and *mulas* a more symmetrical *he-mule* and *she-mule*? Enough. Only a lover of the whole horsy tribe who is versed in old Portuguese and English can sort this out.

8-26   With us only jenny-mules have long saddle-cloths;
Antre nós as mulas somente trazem gualdrapas de pano compridas;

The horses of nobles in Japan have round-edged hides, and those of others are of straw. *Os cavalos dos fidalgos em Japão as trazem couro redondas e outras de palha.*

Remember the *mula* in 2-50 and the pillows that turned out to be saddle pads? If I am not mistaken, the saddle cloths above are the same thing. And it might be that "our" cloths were long for she-mules either because they side-kicked or because legs of any creature were thought to be unseemly when a woman (or a priest?) was mounted.

Doubtless, the straw was woven mat, and I would assume that it was relatively cool in the summer. The French *couvertures de toile* suggests the point of the contrast might be that such items are for working beasts and not for high-class horses.

8-27   For us it would be ridiculous for a nobleman to ride with a halter on his horse and its cord in hand; *Antre nós seria couza rediqulosa yr hum fidalgo com o cabresto no cavalo e corda na mão;*

The King of Bungo [1] and his sons often go about in this manner. *No regno de Bungo os filhos d'el-Rey andão muitas vezes desta maneira.*

Ridiculous if one's idea of riding is active, but not if you don't mind sitting back and enjoying the ride. Evidently, a good horse (there must have been some in Japan) could be trusted to do right without using the reins. To my mind, this style of riding reflects a laid-back attitude on the part of the Bungo nobility. The cord, which the French translate more precisely than the original as a *longe* (which I would have dome in English, too, if I thought anyone could read it) may well be what American Ambassador Harris described as "a third rein" put on so the groom can lead the horse. (H:JTH) His use of the word "rein" suggests it was attached to the halter in a manner that made it more servable as a rein than would be the case for our halters and *longes*, but who knows?

1. *The King of Bungo*. Bungo, a Christian stronghold thanks to the conversion of the King, was the choice part of Kyushu, the Southern Island which fronts on Korea. Here, Frois uses the term "king" (*regno* and *rei*). In his HISTORIA, he no longer does, but speaks only of rulers. [*koku-nushi* = "country-master" in Japanese – I cannot attest to the Portuguese term yet since I read the HISTORIA in Japanese (in such a situation involving terms, more of the original should be supplied, but, sob! seldom is)]. Frois explains why "king" is no longer appropriate in the prologue to the missing first volume, where it serves as the ninth of ten examples of how terms can confuse us in translation. In Japan, it is commonly written there are 66 reigns, but their rulers' power is limited. Thus, there is only one King of Japan in the meaning Europeans give the word. However, he admitted there were some exceptionally powerful rulers who might have merited the name "king," and, we may assume, the King of Bungo (who began his rule before Nobunaga conquered most of Japan) was one of them.).

8-28   When we run or mount a horse, we use one hand for the reins.
Antre nós, quando se corre ou cavalga, se leva a redea em huma só mão;

> In Japan, they have to hold both reins.
> *Em Japão se á-de levar em ambas de duas.*

In his *Journal*, the first American Ambassador to Japan, Townsend Harris was undiplomatically blunt:

> The Japanese are no horsemen; both hands are employed in holding the reins; they have no martingale, the horse therefore carries his head very high with his nose stuck out straight. They therefore have no command over him. (H:CJTH or, I mistook it for Heusken, his sec. H(V&W): JJ)

Readers who know what a Martingale is can no doubt make sense of this. And readers who don't know, like me, probably don't care. After saying that the beauty of European horses and their sensitive response to rein and spur beggar description, Miguel=Valignano describe horsemanship in a manner reflecting Frois's contrast

> Not only that, it is amazing to see how European horses, well-trained and taught good habits, smoothly respond to commands to do this or that movement or run in circles, *with the rider* holding the reins with only one hand. Now you might think I am terribly exaggerating, but this is not at all an exaggeration. (DE MISSIONE: J/S:DM 1589)

Miguel=Valignano goes on to say that "our" horses can rear up on command, jump and spin around on the spot. And, of course, "we" cannot help but boast about how *costly* the trappings are (remember those gold studs?). King Sebastian's custom-made trappings cost 500,000 gold crusados!

8-29   Our horses are only bled. *Os cavalos emtre nós se sangrão somente;*

> In Japan, they are often bled and, also, clumps of fire are put under their chins.
> *Em Japão se sangrão muitas vezes e lhe poem grandes botões de fogo debaxo dos qeixos.*

"Ours" were bled, both for certain disorders (thick blood [1]) and simply to clarify the blood and prevent illness. I do not know about Spain and Portugal in Frois's time, but an Englishman, William Dade, "recommended making an incision on the necks of horses and drawing blood on the first day of April to make them stay healthy 'the whole year'" (*English Almanacs and Animal Health Care in the Seventeenth Century* by Louise Hill Curth of the University of London www.psyeta.org/sa/sa8.1/CURTH.shtml); and farriers (smiths who shoed *and* doctored horses) had a bloodletting tool called a fleam "with several shafts that fold into a case much like a pocketknife" each with "a different size cutting blade, constructed at right angles to the shaft." (www.pbs.org/wnet/redgold/basics/ bloodlettinghistory2.html).

The Japanese only practiced phlebotomy for the relief of local symptoms. Okada writes that when Frois writes horses are "bled" here, he probably means treatment by needles (*shinjutsu*). This was a less subtle form of needling than the acupuncture we are now familiar with, for it tended to be applied directly to the trouble spot. It could draw a little blood, but was hardly comparable to our blood-letting. However, Frois mentions a lancet being used to bleed horses in Japan in 9-3, and I cannot imagine Frois could not tell the difference between a scalpel-like cutting device and a needle. Moreover, what may be the first written report of veterinary acupuncture, or VAP (from the West Zhou dynasty of 1111 BC-771 BC), refers to "jugular phlebotomy to treat some febrile diseases of horses." ("Sustainable Medicine for Veterinarians in the New Millennium" Jen-Hsou Lin, Leang-Shin Wu, Philip AM Rogers: users.med.auth.gr/~karanik/english/articles/sustaina.html).

The "fire," or *moxibustion* treatment ("point cautery") is described in 3-22 and in the next chapter. Here, let me just note that the treatment was primarily preventative – perhaps it stimulates the immune system – and done on a calendrical, *i.e.* ritual basis. Ambassador Harris had an interesting theory about the effect of all this medicine (some details seem a bit odd, but the idea can stand):

> The Governors were very fearful for my safety; they assured me that the Japanese horses were so vicious, that my life would be in danger if I attempted to ride in any different manner from their mode. They said their horses all would bite and kick. No wonder, when one knows the manner in which they use the poor brutes. *Every month* the horse is burned in his belly in a quincunx, – i.e., as the spots are placed to mark five on dice; then he is burned in the roof of his mouth in the same manner. Can we wonder that this monthly application of red hot iron should spoil the temper of a horse? (H:CJTH)

I do not know of this use of a hot iron instead of moxa, but it makes sense, for unless a horse will lie down and stay down, burning something on them, especially on the chin, as mentioned by Frois, would be difficult. Perhaps it was held in place. Japanese burned moxa on practically everything. Perhaps it has something to do with their national topography. Shiki (1867-1902):

on the second day
(national health care)

smoke rising
from mount fuji and asama:
moxibustion

fuji asama futsuka-kyû no kemuri kana
([Mt] Fuji, [Mt] Asama, second-day [of new-year] moxa's smoke 'tis)

Asama in South Japan smokes much of the year, while Fuji only does so occasionally. Shiki is turning this volcanic activity into treatment for the nation! He may also pun on another aspect of the NY's second day, a *futskayoi,* or "hangover" when people feel *nemuri,* or sleepy (The pun also fits the *gazing-upon-a-large-mountain-with-some-haze-and/or-smoke* feeling considered proper for early Spring.)

---

1. Thick Blood. I am not sure what it is, but horses, like humans could suffer from *hemachromatosis*, i.e., excessive iron and benefit from regular bloodletting as will be explained in the next chapter.

8-30   In Europe, the reins are loosened for running and tightened to stop.
Em Europa afloxão as redeas ao cavalo pera correr e as apertão pera parar;

In Japan, they are loosened to stop and tightened to run.
Em Japão as afloxão pera parar e as apertão pera correr.

The Japanese side of the contrast seems incredible. After all, common sense tells us to give a horse his head to let him go and pull back to stop him. But once we get to running, we *do* tend to pull in the reins so the horse does not over do it: so, there is an association between tightness and speed which a horse might be trained on.   Coincidently, at the very time Frois was in Japan, the revival of classic dressage, the *Haute Ecole* or "high School" of riding was being taught at academies throughout Europe.[1] Indeed, the existence of tight-reined riding in Europe was pointed out by Miguel=Valignano in DE MISSIONE:

> One reason there are many varieties of riding gear is because there are many ways of riding. Europeans generally follow one of two equestrian modes. The first is called *stapedium,* in this the reins are tightly held and the steps are quick . . . (J/S:DM dialogue 10)

This school taught riding with the taut reins still used for dressage today. From what my equestrian sister says, I gather it is like driving a car with hard steering rather than soft. You and the horse can feel each other better.

In respect to stopping, when we sit still we *do* let the reins go slack. The association is there, too.   As strange as it may seem, the Japanese way is ideal in one respect: if a horse stops when reins go slack, it would not wander when its rider fell or driver fainted. *It is like a safety device.* And, again, my equestrian sister says "a good dressage horse will usually stop if the reins are released, for the lack of information. But," she adds, "you don't need to do anything with the reins to stop a good horse. All you have to do is shift your weight slightly back and they read you."

---

1. *Riding Academies.*   While the first serious look at horsemanship was by the Portuguese King Don Duarte in 1435, the main influence in Frois's time was Federico Glisone's 1550 book (some say 1534) *Gli ordini di cavalcare,* which was reprinted dozens of times in that century. While Xenophon's *Art of Horsemanship* (360 B.C) espoused gentle training (quoting Simon, to the effect that *anything forced would not be truly beautiful*), Glisone believed horses to be fundamentally vicious, and in his famous academy in Naples broke the spirits of horses by creative methods of punishment, including "tying a cat to a long pole and placing it under the belly and hind legs" and "putting a live hedgehog under the horse's tail." (Deanna Ramsay *Early Dressage Literature to 1800* of http://www.ramsaybooks.com at IOBA standard newsletter of the online booksellers association.)   I do not know enough to generalize on the training methods and styles of riding, but thought the above of interest!

8-31   We only use oxen to till the earth. *Entre nós se lavrão as terras somente com bois;*

In Japan they use oxen or horses. *Em Japão com bois ou cavalos.*

Even without mentioning North/West Europe where, according to the histories we all read in high school, new types of harnesses had been invented in the Middle Ages that, in combination with the three-field rotational system, made *horses* so productive tillers that we achieved the superfluities of life necessary to spark the Renaissance and move Europe ahead of the rest of the world, etc. etc., even without all this, looking only at Iberia, Frois was wrong.   The oxen *had* indeed been the traditional draft animal of the Classical world as shown by the word (*boustrophedon*) for writing lines back and forth (right-to-left-right-left . . .) and of Roman Spain, where agronomists recommended it and, according to Ambrosio de Morales (1577: fol. 96) where "the ox was so closely identified with Roman agriculture that a coin was minted in Roman Spain depicting a yoke of oxen plowing on one side." And it was still "the normal work animal" in 1500 (THE LIBRARY OF IBERIAN RESOURCES ONLINE *Land and Society in Golden Age Castile* by David E. Vassberg (Ch 6 = Changes in Production and Ownership) THE SHIFTING AGROPASTORAL BALANCE). But, over the course of Frois's century, the rising population pressure and taxes forced towns to open new fields for plowing – or, rather wrest away pastures from the sheep herders, as many saw it – and use mules which moved twice as fast as oxen, which was important for plowing and commuting from town to field and field to field and, additionally, were more suitable for use in "vineyards and orchards, where a yoke of horned animals was not only difficult to maneuver, but also a potential danger to tender vines and branches" (Ibid). The first anti-mule tract, impassioned denunciation of the mule." [1] was printed in 1568, so we must assume the use was widespread before 1585. Finally, "by 1600, the mule had become the most widely used agricultural work animal, except in certain isolated or backward areas, mainly in the mountains." (Ibid)

The question is how Frois missed this? Is it just that it had not yet occurred near Lisbon and he never saw or heard of it? Or, could some cognitive dissonance been involved? Did he fail to hear of the change because he held on to an ideal classical Iberia too dearly to imagine anything in a field but an ox?

In Japan, both horses and oxen were used, but almost always only one animal to a plow. I have not heard of teams such as were used in North Europe. Water buffalo are still used in the Okinawan islands.

---

1. ***Anti-mule*** There were reasons to dislike the mule. The relatively shallow plowing led to faster degradation of slopes with shallow soil, and by helping turn pasture into plots it took away what had been more or less free food for oxen. With too little rainfall and too many rocks for three crops a year, the benefits of faster plowing were primarily only that of increasing the acreage. There was also a *bona fide* military concern. As early as the 1300's, the Castilian monarchs attempted to limit the number of mules and in 1520, "prohibited the breeding of mules in Castile" because of fear that "if the best mares were used to produce mules, . . . the quality of horses inevitably would deteriorate, and this could prove disastrous for the country's military, in an age when horses played such a vital role in warfare." * [a] (Ibid) But the argument was also carried to a higher – or, is it *lower* – plane. "In 1600, Diego Gutiérrez de Salinas published *Discursos del pan, y del vino del niño Jesús*. . . , which contained . . . a virulently anti-mule section . . . Gutiérrez called mules 'adulterous and sterile bastards', and 'corrupt monsters', who should be banished by law from Spain." (Ibid)

* **a) Horses and War.** The horse was not just the automobile but the *tank* as well. In his essay *On War Horses*, Frois's contemporary Montaigne wrote that the Romans bridled the rebellion of newly conquered people by taking away their arms and their horses, and that "The Grand Turk to this day permits no Christian or Jew, of those who are under his rule, to have his own horse." (M(F):CEM). The horse, then, was treated like the weapon it was and both developed and controlled carefully. And, if the Portuguese horse was less heralded than the Spanish one, the *Portuguese horse-trader* was another matter altogether. When the Japanese Ambassadors got back to Goa, their Arabian horses were already waiting for them,

doubtless, thanks to a Portuguese horse trader. These men popped up everywhere and, like arms-dealers today, affected military and hence political power.

The first base of operations for Europe in the East was southern India, "governed by kinglets ruling over small areas . . , but in the interior of southern India there was Vijayanagara, a powerful Dravidian Hindhu kingdom with an "absolutely impressive" capital city, which shared "our" common political enemies, the Muslim sultans. *The Portuguese wanted a monopoly on providing horses for the wars of the kings of Vijayanagara against the Sultans. In exchange they offered support against the sultans."* (Italics mine. Mia Rodriguez-Salgado and Joan-Pau Rubies: *Kingship in the Early Modern World* (London School of Economics and Political Science) www.fathom.com/course/21701738/session5.html) I do not know exactly how the horse-traders figured in this, but one Portuguese horse-trader, Domingo Paes wrote extensively about the culture in a largely sympathetic vein:

> You should know that among these gentiles there are days when they celebrate their feasts as we do, and they have their days of fasting, when all day they eat nothing, and eat only at midnight. (Ibid)

But to return to the subject, we associate the Lipizza (a Neopolitan, Arab and Karst breed begun in 1580) with fancy tricks, today. But after "they were housed in Vienna at Spanish Riding School . . . Only military officers and nobility were allowed to train there. They learned a complicated series of maneuvers originally designed as cavalry techniques used to strike fear in the heart of enemy soldiers . . . "We" were damn serious about our horses!

~~~~~~

8-32   The packsaddles of Europe are made of cloth and straw. *As albardas d'Europa são de pano e palha;*

Those of Japan are made of wood. *As de Japão são de pao.*

This is the last mention of saddles. Frois neglects to mention the most interesting contrast involving packsaddles: how they were *ridden*. A hundred years later, Kaempfer observed that on both sides of the Japanese packsaddle loom side-trunks (portmantles) carrying light and voluminous luggage and behind, helping to fasten those trunks together is a stronger back-trunk *(atozuki)* for valuables made of "thick strong grey paper." Here is the good part:

> the middle cavity between the two trunks, fill'd up with some soft stuff, is the travelers seat, where he sits, as it were upon a flat table, otherwise commodiously enough, and either crossleg'd or with his legs extended hanging down by the Horse's neck . . . (K(S):HOJ:1692)

The "soft stuff" makes it clear that Frois is not describing the entire saddles but the frames. Bird, in the 19th century, seconds and even mentions *straw*: "The pack-saddle is composed of two packs of straw eight inches thick, faced with red, and connected before and behind by strong oak arches gaily painted or decorated." (B:UTJ) As to how they were ridden, Kaempfer wrote that the traveler must be careful to remain in the center, lest he "make the Horse fall, or else the side trunks and rider." Bird, too: "The saddle is merely balanced, not girded on, and the animals are so sleepy, slow-footed, and stumbling, with a lurching, swinging gate like a camel's, that riding one is really a feat." (B:UTJ) The Western visitor had to learn t*o rest his or her feet on the horse's neck* (a haiku I found and lost on the theme of winter travel mentions the welcome heat from the horse absorbed through the traveler's soles.) But the obvious contrast here for Europeans and Japanese is as follows:

> *We always ride on a horse with our legs hanging down.*
> *They travel with their legs crossed sitting high on the horse like an Arab on a camel.*

Normally, this was, as might be expected, at a slow camel-like pace. But Morse, up in Hokkaido, observed an interesting exception:

> All along the road the Ainus we met were in the service of the Japanese, taking care of their horses in particular. When the Ainus ride they sit cross-legged and perched up high on the saddle, and whenever I saw them they were going at full gallop. (M:JDD)

..

That is the strangest riding I have ever heard of, and far from Japanese! As Alcock pointed out "It is *vulgar* and *low* to ride fast in Japan." Only drunks, officials on urgent business or people up to mischief ever risked galloping on purpose. Or, we might even say that generally speaking,

> *With us, when we are on a horse we usually actively ride it;*
> *They usually travel sitting like luggage on a packsaddle while led by teamsters.*

Kaempfer noted another contrast incidental to the different gear. Because of the side trunks, in Japan, *"the traveler mounts the horse . . . not on on side as we Europeans do, but by the horse's breast, which is very troublesome for stiff legs."* (K(S):HOJ) I should add that Kaempfer was not searching for contrasts, for he also described the "plain wooden saddle" of Japan as "not unlike the packsaddles of Swedish Posthorses." (Ibid). For that matter, he wrote that from a global perspective,

> the saddling of their horses differs but little from ours. Their saddles come nearer our German saddles, than those of any Asiatic Nation." (Ibid.)

Matsuda and Jorissen also note such a wooden saddle (covered with goat or cow-hide), called an *aubardá,* has long been used in Majorca.

8-33   We don't carry a load without a crupper. *Antre não se leva carrega sem atafal.*

        In Echizen they don't use one. *Em Yechijen não se uza delle.*

The French translation calls the *atafal* a crupper, but from the description in a Portuguese-Portuguese dictionary, I get the idea it might be the "breeches" mentioned in 8-16. At any rate, in Echizen there is nothing behind to keep the saddle from sliding forward during a quick stop or going downhill etc.. This is a bit weird because, first we already know Japanese horses have nothing back there (or was 8-16 only meant to be about horses on parade?) and second, is it really fair to contrast *one province* of Japan against "Europe?" I also do not know how salient this Echizen difference was *in Japan*. All I know is that in the Tokugawa era, soon to begin, the yearly procession of the Lord of Echizen to the capitol was to call attention to *another* unique characteristic of this Northern province: its spear-head covers made of bear-skin. [1]

1. *Echizen – Adults Only Note!* The fur caught people's eyes, while the expression "skin-covered" (*kawakamuri*) caught the salacious attention of the pundits of low culture.   Soon men with problems getting their *glans penis* fully out of the foreskin were being roasted as "*echizens*" in *senryu.* (incredibly, men with foreskin problems are *still* roasted in cartoons – and once I even heard such a comment on a crass TV show – today!) This is strange because folk wisdom had it that an Echizen man and a Kaga woman made the best lovers!

8-34   Our pack-horses wear bells and rattles;
    Antre nós os cavalos de carrega levão chocalhos ou cascaveis;

        In Japan, they wear jingles [1] like those on tambourines.
        Em Japão levão soalhas como de pandeiros.

Okada surmises the Japanese side may refer to *gyôyô,* leaf-like trinkets (literally "apricot-leaf" for the shape) that hung behind Chinese-style saddles (and, judging from similar trinkets I have heard on a Mongolian dancer, make a tinkling sound) or *kanrei,* hollow donut-like bronze bells strung up 3-4 to a ring that hit together like chimes worn by ancient *haniwa* (buried clay funereal) horses. "Maybe at this time, they or something like them, were still being used." (Okada) Kaempfer wrote a hundred years later about "small bells" hung from "the neck, breast and other parts" of Japanese horses. I think he liked details enough to have described the bells had they been significantly different and would guess that the German original might have turned into "bells" in English for lack of a better word.. *Aurelio* defines "soalha" as each one of the plates (*placas*) on a tambourine." So Frois did not really even have to mention the instrument.

One might expect to have something louder on the Japanese horse, for up to the late 19th century, an accidental death from a traffic accident in Japan could easily result in an execution – but, I may be reading the protected world of the Tokugawa into Frois's wilder Japan – where you would think horses would make a lot of noise to warn people. But, as we have seen, Japanese did not go very fast. Pack-horses would probably be even slower.   The nobility and officials who did go (relatively) fast had footmen or grooms to run ahead of them for that purpose! Alcock quipped "I had more than one who would run three or four leagues at a stretch by the side of the horse, and without distress – or used to do so before they got too fat and lazy in the foreigner's service." (A:TYJ) That is especially incredible when you know they were shouting out as they ran! Alice Mabel Bacon and Mrs. Hugh Frazer make it clear that, Alcock aside, such a human horn was needed:

> I have had my first ride this afternoon, and enjoyed it very much. It makes one feel very grand indeed to have a man run ahead all the way to clear the people out of the road. It seems absolutely necessary in Tokyo to have such a forerunner, for there are no sidewalks, and the streets are full of people, and especially of very young children, who are quite frequently burdened with smaller ones tied to their backs, so that they cannot get away with very great speed, and if the man did not run ahead to announce my coming, I could never go faster than a walk. (B:AJI)

> We arranged to try some very pretty and only half-broken ponies, and for a while it seemed doubtful whether we or they should really be broken first; then I found constant excitement in watching our groom racing along in front of the horses, lifting fat babies out of the middle of the road where they sat confidingly, leading deaf old women politely to one side, and apparently saving a life once in every ten yards. (F:DWJ)

> *We think nothing of galloping down a street with no one announcing our coming..*
> *They wouldn't think of going any speed without a footman running ahead or shouting to clear the way.*

Perhaps the bug-net I mentioned in 8-16 can also be considered a safety-feature to reduce the chance of a horse bolting and putting the life of others, and hence the driver, into peril. Yet, even without the threat of execution and the crowded conditions, *kamikaze* taxi drivers aside, Japanese are careful drivers and believe in taking responsibility for accidents (long before the USA, they had strict punishment for drunk-driving) and keep up the traditional *noise-making-for-safety* tradition. When I first visited Japan in 1971, I was surprised to find the city full of loud beeping noises. It turned out to be mandatory – and automatic – warnings for trucks and buses backing up. Since then, we have adopted the same practice.

1. *Jingles and Jingle-bells.* OED includes "jingle" as a noun without the "bell" added, but it is not the most common usage and I only used it because if I wrote "jingle-bell", I would have been tempted to preface the bell on our pack-horses with "cow-" and that would not be right. English, obviously, lacks sufficient generic terms for *bells*. I used "rattle" for *cascaveis* for the closest word I could find was *cascavel,* meaning "rattlesnake" but I could be wrong. *Help!*

~~~~~~

8-35   With us, bulls are savage and huge. *Antre nós os touros são bravos e grandes;*

In Japan, they are small and gentle. *Em Japão peqenos e mansos.*

This sudden bovinity in an equine chapter recalls a *grook* by Piet Hein: "A cow is not a horse / and a horse is not a cow / That's one similarity / anyhow!" (By memory, could be off!). Frois's bull is *bravo* and *grande.* Our word "brave" comes from the Latin for "barbarous." The Spanish *Rio Bravo,* or Wild River, like Frois's Portuguese usage is closer to the roots of the term. With the bull-fight to consider, it will not do for "our" – that is, the Iberian bull – to be gentle. In Mexico, I was *horrified* to see a gentle bull who did not want to fight *licking the television camera* before he was poked over and over by the picadors until he saw red and briefly behaved as he was expected to. Now, living in Florida, on a farm with cattle, I note the huge bull is *very gentle*, while the cows can be downright rough and even *mean* to the calves of others.[1] I doubt that all European breeds of bulls were *bravo.*

Okada writes that Japanese ox are from Korea and a different breed from that of Europe. I know that the water-buffalo I met can hurt you if they catch you with a horn while shrugging their heads (I had a close call when I found out that not all like to be touched on the horns). I do not know if these water buffalo are the same as what Frois talks about and failed to get anywhere on the internet. More information is wanted! 日本の牡牛の歴史に細かい人、よろしくお願いします！

1. *The Bull And I.* That was several years ago and now I finish the book (tentatively = until the second edition = anyway) on Key Biscayne, but I still remember the sweet temper of the bull, which came as a great surprise. It was huge but had horns that curled like a ram's. One horn was not properly embedded in his head and moved when he flicked his right ear.   The bridge of his nose was springy to the touch, like rubber, and stained the skin with black grease.   When lying down chewing his cud, he would sometimes sigh audibly, from the sound of it, wistfully, and he did not mind the dalmations licking his anus.   He loved watermelon so much that a fine one would elicit a Flehman (a lip-back nose-up long sexy sniff) and could crack it open by pressing his nose on it.

8-36   In Europe the carriers [1] load the beast and go empty-handed themselves.
Em Europa os almocreves carregão as bestas e elles vão vazios;

> Those of Japan pity the beasts and, at times, carry a third of the cargo on their shoulders.   *Os de Japão, por se doerem das bestas, levão às vezes hum terço da carrega às cos[tas].*

Okada opines: "This indicates Japanese affection for cows and horses. The Buddhist faith seems one reason for this."   Isabella Bird's observation several hundred years after TRATADO concurs:

> I have not seen any overloading or ill-treatment; they are neither kicked, nor beaten, nor threatened in rough tones, and when they die they are decently buried, and have stones placed over their graves. It might be well if the end of a worn-out horse were somewhat accelerated, but this is mainly a Buddhist region, and the aversion to taking animal life is very strong. (B:UTJ)

I think there is *also* another reason here. The Japanese, like most people in the world, were just more used to carrying things than Europeans who, if I am not mistaken, are exceptionally poor at it. Perhaps because of the broader use of the cart, by Frois's time Western people had already forgotten how to use the top of their heads or poles to carry things for long distances with little energy expenditure.   The Japanese teamsters (?) had staffs they could turn into efficient carrying poles.   I would also guess that the calcium-deficient grass of Japan would have made the horses more liable to suffering leg injuries when tired (Japanese race horses broke bones at a *tremendous* rate in the 1980's for this reason).

1. *"Carrier" Translation.* In Japanese, both those who care for horses and the men who provide cargo and transportation services with their horses – usually the same person – are called simply *mago*, "horse-child" in Chinese characters, where "child" has the nuance of our "boy," meaning a person doing blue-collar work, especially, but not always service-related. Kaempfer in English translation makes then "grooms" and "footmen," one term too narrow and one too broad for this context. "Teamster" is closer, but requires one to drive a team of horses, which is not always the case.   "Muleteer," the term that came from my Portuguese-English dictionary, seems best at first glance but we did not only use mules and the Japanese generally used horses, so I went with the bland "carrier."   Any other suggestions?

8-37   In Europe, beasts are loaded by eye;
Em Europa o fato que se carrega nas bestas hé a olho;

> In many kingdoms of Japan, they do not want to carry anything without weighing it.
> *Em muitos reinos de Japão não o qerem levar senão a pezo.*

Who can say whether this is due to a Japanese tendency to be exacting [and I would expect the same in certain European states] – or the same compassion mentioned in 8-36? I think the off-the-cuff estimates of professional carriers would be good enough but, even today, no matter the matter, it is incredibly hard to get a *guestimate* or a rough answer out of a Japanese; they usually *insist* on making you wait until they find the precise figure so, if you are like me, you sometimes wished you never asked.   I couldn't resist the direct translation "by eye," and trust the reader can guess its meaning "by feel" or "rough estimate." (The difference in the Englishing of 36 and 37 here and in the foreword reflects the fact 1) I had not seen the Portuguese at the time I began the Foreword and 2), There is more than one way to English anything.)

8-38   Among us, an unsaddled horse is led about by one man by the halter.
Antre nós hum cavalo sem sela leva-o hum homem polo cabresto.

> In Japan, a Lord's horse, though it be very gentle, has to be led about by one man with a cord in front and another with another [cord] behind, like a stayed bull.
> *Em Japão os cavalos dos* Tonos, *ainda que sejão muito mansos, á-os de levar hum homem com huma corda por diante e outro com outra por detras, como touro em cordas.*

"The master's horse was treated especially carefully" write Okada. Even a gentle horse can react when bitten by a horse-fly, so it doesn't hurt to be careful in a country of frail dwellings and crowded streets where dereliction of duty could cost a man his head.

..

8-39   Our girths fasten on the flank below the saddle.
As silhas dos nossos cavalos se apertão a huma ilharga debaxo da sela;

> Those of Japan fasten above the front saddle-bow.
> *As de Japão se atão em sima no arção dianteiro.*

Part of this may be because of the larger stature of our horses. But it also may have to do with the different manner of cinching up the girth. Japanese have long excelled in all forms of binding and fastening. Kaempfer was impressed with the way the horses could be loaded up or "unsaddled and unladen in an instant." After taking off the bed-cloths, "they need but untie a latchet or two . . . and the whole baggage falls down at once." He wrote the "latchets, thongs, and girths . . . are broad and strong, made of cotton . . . with oblong, cylindrical pieces of wood at both ends, which are of great use to strain the latchets, and to tie things hard." (K(S):HOJ) With the greater leverage possible due to those pieces of wood, the girth would not need to be worked the way we must work it to cinch up and could then fasten in a position other than the flank. However, as we have already noted, the saddles were not paradigms of stability. Perhaps a cross between Japanese fastening convenience and European overall design would have been ideal.

endnotes **VIII**

Horses

馬　　　　　　馬　　　　　馬

On a quick reading, this seemed like a lot on horses. But, while translating, explaining and, especially when quoting Kaempfer, it became clear that Frois put too much weight on describing gear minutia for one type of riding and missed travel-related items. If one read only Frois and not Kaempfer, one would imagine Basho (born 60 years after TRATADO) sitting astride a horse, alone, when it suddenly ate that Rose of Sharon by the roadside, as recorded in his famous haiku. Now, I hope you will see him being *led by a "horse-boy," sitting up high, perhaps cross-legged* on his mount, with his pen and a sketch-book in hand. Not only did Frois overlook these contrasts I added to note 8-32, but he completely neglected the whole area of wheeled cart and human-borne sedan-related transportation!

> *Among us, gentlemen most commonly get around by horse or donkey.*
> *In Japan, they are usually carried about in boxes borne by men.*

These boxes came in two basic types. As Kaempfer details, the cheap litters (*kago:* basket) – but still more expensive than traveling by horseback – dangled from a single plain pole, while the expensive ones (*norimono:* riding-thing) had "poles" made of four boards, "the bigness and length of these poles hath been determin'd by the political laws of the Empire, proportionable to every one's quality." All are covered over, with windows – often curtained (cloth or a sliding paper window) – on both sides. For a man of Volkswagen rank to be carried about in a Cadillac could get a man "a severe reprimand if not a considerable fine in the bargain," (Ibid) but women were allowed to show off as they pleased regardless of their husband's rank! Since human-carried *sedans/litters/chairs/palanquins* came to only a few parts of Europe, while Frois was in Japan, the following is doubly *faux* –

> *Our sedans have their carrying poles on the bottom side and are lifted by hand..*
> *Theirs always have the carrying poles on the top and are supported by the shoulder.*

> *Our sedans have two carrying poles to lift up like a liter.*
> *Theirs have only one so the compartment must hang.*

> *Our chairs are always wooden and solidly attached to the poles.*
> *Their cheapest sedans are baskets which sway below the poles.*

With centuries of history behind them in Japan, the sedans (almost always one-pole) were taken for granted. In Europe where they were new and never expanded beyond a number of crowded metropolitan areas, the sedan was a luxury:
..
> Then this 'killing creature' [a Georgian era fop] having first smeared his upper lip with snuff, *hailed a chair and was borne along to the door of the playhouse*, where instead of attending to the performance . . . he wandered from pillar to post, now laughing and chatting with his friends, and then pulling out by turns his watch and pocket handkerchief . . . (my *italics,* Leslie Stephen, cited in Soseki: *Bungaku-hyôron*)

Since, it would be tiring to carry something heavy by hand for long, the European sedan was only practical for very short trips, while the Japanese devices were all-purpose transportation. Even Caucasians with their thicker forearms and stronger hands than Mongolians could not overcome that difference, and of course, there was the more abundant horse (Note: A hundred or more years before Frois, most Japanese sedans were hand-carried, and it took 4 rather than 2 men). Today, with more female paramedics, in the Occident, it might make sense to redesign the litter to be carried by shoulder-pole. An added benefit is a free hand to help with support on rough terrain.

> *In Europe, carriages are a popular form of rapid transportation and always drawn by horses.*
> *In Japan, there are no carriages but slow ones drawn by oxen.*

If "we" failed to develop human-powered transport, "they" neglected animal transport. "Our" coach was invented in Kocs, Hungary in the 15th century.   While coaches and carriages and 2-wheel carts with springs – items for transporting people rather than goods – did not serve everyman until the 17th century, reading DE MISSIONE (dialogue 10), we can see they were common enough in the late 16th century to have merited a mention by Frois, especially considering that he was not adverse to contrasts involving the nobility alone. Here is Miguel=Valignano explaining the concept of a coach to Leo, who remained in Japan.

> Usually, the privileged classes use a coach [literally: "horse-car/t" in Japanese]. This coach resembles a small wooden hut with a rounded roof. Closed up inside, the noblewomen are carried [to their destination] lying down or seated on a comforter [cushioned seat?]. They are usually two-horse, but some are four, which is to say sometimes two horses are connected to the cart and sometimes four, and I think you can pretty much imagine how it looks from the picture I show you. Actually, not only women, but distinguished people, bishops or even priests with important positions ride these . . . (J/S:DM – *Translation.* The two Chinese characters "horse+car/t" are standard for "coach" but can also mean a mere cart. I wish I knew what the Latin was. Chariot, perhaps?)

Miguel=Valignano must not have been mechanically minded, for the all-important thing, the method of harnessing that permits a horse to pull hard without being winded, is left to the imagination, unless the picture – was it in the Latin version, or is it only in the dialogue? – was far more detailed than I imagine. Leo was enthralled and said he could just imagine "how good it felt to ride," and how good it might be to lounge about with six or eight friends while going down the road! But he wondered how as many as four horses might be controlled at one time.

> Oh, that is *nothing!* European horses are by nature very placid and have been road-trained . . . And, not only that, you cannot forget the knowledge and skill of the driver who sits up on a seat over the thill [look that up in your dictionary!], and holding the reins with one hand and a whip in the other, splendidly drives. (J/S:DM)

..

Then, we must read the mandatory description of the gorgeousness of it all – arranging teams of horses for the color-effect and the palatial decoration of the coaches. Europe was just *so* posh a place! Leo asks "How many of these splendid coaches are in Europe anyway?

> Lots and lots of them, you would be surprised! But, then in Europe, there are an infinite number of horses and moreover they are so beautiful, especially in Spain, the horses of Napoli and Mantua . . . . with these to pull them, you can well imagine how many coaches there are! In Rome alone, I heard there are about three thousand. In Europe, it is the ordinary way that distinguished people move about. (J/S:DM)

In Japan, the closest equivalent were the ox-wagons, or "lumbering bullock-carts" to use Chamberlain's phrase, which were not for zipping about so much as for taking noblewomen out cherry-blossom viewing or for processions, where they seem more like floats in a parade. Here, again, is Cramer describing that parade in 1626. Following those unicorn horses (see 8-16), there were

> three rich coaches, each drawn by two black bulls, covered with red silken nets and led by four footmen in white liveries; these coaches were each four fathoms high, two long and one broad, being adorned with waxen figures, and enameled with gold; on each side there were three windows . . . which were hung with rich curtains; the entry behind opened like the gate of a prince's palace, steps , ascending with turrets on each side, the windows beneath shaded with black wax, the rounds of the wheels gilded, the spokes neatly turned and inlaid with gold and mother-of-pearl, which, moving, cast beams like a looking-glass reflecting the sun, a novel and most glorious sight.

> These coaches or rather towers . . . carried in state the dayro's [same as *daimyo*] principal wives. The train of pages, all clothed in white, which attended these ladies was numerous, each of them carrying a gilded footstool and a pair of wax slippers. (in B:MCJ)

The coaches of "the emperor (*ziogoon*) [shogun, not really the Emperor] himself," equally large "but exceeding the former in riches" – followed. Then, princes and nobles on horseback and "six new fair coaches" smaller (drawn by only one ox) but "proportionally beautiful" for the *dayro's* inferior concubines. The *dayro* himself sat

> in a great square ediface surrounded by drawing-doors or windows on each corner; on the top stood a gilded ball and a cock of massive gold thereon with wings displayed. This moving house being nine foot high, was very beautifully adorned on all sides with carved imagery, each angle plated with pure gold; and the roof of it imitating the heavens, with sun, moon and stars. Fifty of the emperor's nobles carried this ambulatory palace supported on long poles. Forty gentlemen, accoutred like the ancient Greeks and Romans, armed with European headpieces, and pikes gilded at the ends, carrying in one hand a shield stuck full of arrows, had each of them an umbrella carried over them, and went before, being the *dayro's* bodyguard. (B:MCJ)

..

Not knowing how "our" kings were carried, I hesitate to make a contrast. But Frois *might* have. As the editors – Mrs Busk? the Harper Brothers? – note, this is the only report of a procession that mentions the *mikado*. While the Shôgun (*ziogoon*) was indeed in charge of the Empire, I doubt that the Japanese would equate him with the Emperor and assume Ogilby confused something. But my interest is not in sorting out *that* kind of detail. It is simply to show what kind of vehicles were around in Japan and how they were used. There were, probably, many more potential contrasts.

人   力   車

Frois cannot, however, be faulted for not mentioning the *jinrickshaw* (*jin-riki-sha*: literally, "person-power-car/t"). According to my OJD, this single or double seat between two broad-diameter light wheels with two pulling shafts and a cross-bar was invented by three Japanese (names given) *et al* in 1869. In *Things Chinese*, credit is shared by an American missionary by one account and a British chaplain (both named) by another (B:TC)! At any rate, it quickly became popular in parts of South Asia with too crowded for horses. Alice Mabel Bacon, whose fine insight on *Japanese Girls and Women* has been borrowed many times in this book already and whose *Japanese Interior* will help us in chapter 12, had a great deal to say about *jinrickshaws*, or rather, *her* jinrickshaw *man*. If it is the nature of women to fall in love with horses, it would seem that a man serving in the same capacity likewise was liable to be adored. She first seemed to notice his legs:

The garden was crowded with visitors, from the jinrikisha man in blue blouse and with symmetrical brown legs, to the fine lady in paint and powder, silk and crape, pattering along on her high, lacquered clogs. All were gazing at the flowers lost in admiration. (B:JGW)

This was an age when the adoration of well-turned male legs was still strong enough that there were people who loathed trousers for hiding them. Toward the end of her book, Bacon was still enthralled by them. She gave him and his body two entire pages of which this is the best part:

When you have ridden for miles and miles, by night and by day, through rain and sleet and hottest sunshine, behind a man who has used every power of body and mind in your service, you cannot but have a strong feeling of affection toward him, and of pride in him as well. It is something the feeling that one has for a good saddle-horse, but more developed. You rejoice in his strength and speed, put forth so willingly in your service; in his picturesque, dark blue costume with your monogram embroidered on the back; in his handsomely turned ankles; in his black, wavy hair; in his delicate hands and trim waist, -- though these are often a source of pride to you, --- but his skill in divining your wants; his use of his tongue in your service; his helping out your faltering Japanese with explanations which, if not elegant, have the merit of being easily understood; his combats with extortionate shopkeepers on your behalf . . . remain as a pleasant memory, upon your return to a land where no man would so far forget his manhood as to give himself so completely and without reserve to the service of any master save Mammon. (B:JGW)

Yasuku, the *kurumaya* [someone who pulls a *jinrikisha*], a very Hercules, who could keep close to a pair of coach horses through miles of city streets, and who never suffered mortal *jinrikisha* man to pass him. My champion in all times of danger and alarm, but a very autocrat in all minor matters, – his cheery face, his broad shoulders with their blue draperies, his jolly, boyish voice, and his dainty, delicate hands come before me as I write, and I wonder to what fortunate person he is now giving the intelligent service that he once gave so whole-heartedly to me. (B:JGW)

I think Ms Bacon's eyes were wet when she wrote this and I hope the reader has not minded the diversion from horses proper to human horses.

馬子

IX

OF DISEASES, *DOCTORS AND MEDICINES*

das doenças, medicos e mezinhas

~~~~~~

9-1 Among us, scrofula, stones, gout and the pest occur frequently.
Antre nós alporcas, dor de pedra, podagra e peste hé couza frequente;

All of these diseases are rare in Japan.
Todas estas doenças em Japão são raras.

Scrofula: Swollen lymph glands, often, but not always, associated with gonorrhea, also called "the King's [Queen's] Evil," doubtless for interesting reasons. In 1569, the year Frois convinced the warlord Nobunaga to give him *carte blanc* to preach in the capital, Charles the IX of France touched and presumably cured 2,092 scrofula sufferers. And this kept going on for centuries! [1]

Stones: Including not just *renal calculosis* (kidney stones) but other types of calculae. I cannot help wondering if prostate cancer was included in this, because there is a tenfold difference in the rate between Europeans and Japanese.

Gout: The Portuguese term used by Frois, *podagra* is still used by doctors and apparently means gout especially hard on the legs. As Okada points out, these last two diseases suggest too much meat and, I would add, not enough diuretics, like tea. Perhaps dalmations, the only dog to suffer from these diseases, would also do better eating rice in Japan.

Pest: Bubonic fever. Serves the Europeans right for killing too many cats and snakes (the latter being by far the better mouse-trap for it gobbles up baby mice in their dens). Call it a product of the Inquisition! This is not *my* idea. I saw a program about the vilification and persecution of snakes, sacred in the Ancient West, by Christianity on NHK (Japan's public broadcasting network) where this Pest hypothesis was made.[2] Religion wasn't the all of it. In England, Keith Thomas notes, physicians ordered dogs and cats killed, little imagining that might cause the fleas and ticks to transfer to human hosts! As Okada notes, the Pest also ran its course in India and China, but did not attack Japan until the late-19th century, at which time Western doctors recommended the importation of cats!

This contrast is naively egoistic. We tend to be far more aware of our own diseases than those of others! I cannot help but wonder what diseases a Japanese might find rare in Europe. One might be *senki*, a complex disease often mentioned in haiku and senryu and usually translated as "lumbago", where the legs may be put out of commission like gout, but which also causes severe pain in the groin and often enlarges the testicles. It was usually particularly bad in the winter. (In the 20th century, about half of all Japanese claimed to have stiff neck and shoulders, but I am not certain this should be mentioned next to the serious diseases Frois gives.) Then again, Japanese may have suffered from less serious disease than their European counterparts because they had a better balanced diet and were less addicted to gluttony, as Valignano and others have pointed out.

1. *The Royal Touch.* The practice of kings touching people to make them well goes back at least to the 11th century in Europe. If kings had a divine right, then they had divine powers and that includes healing. Ironically, considering the anti-Catholic=miracle frenzy in England, the kings kept at it and the Royal Touch reached its height in the seventeenth century under Charles II.
2. *Snake Phobia and Christianity Book*. Let me add one thing first. It is hard for intellectuals (like you, if you have read this far, and me) to appreciate the mindset of the

Christian fundamentalist. I saw a rat snake outside early last fall and mentioned it to the Baptist who lived downstairs. I quipped something like "Too bad they don't go for cockroaches rather than mice, but it sure is nice to see we still have them on the Key!" And he made a yucky face and said something like, "A snake! Don't you know they are bad? The *Bible* says . . ." I was thinking of asking whether or not before they were made to crawl on the ground to reflect their depravity they all went about on the tips of their tails like black mambo in pursuit or cobras defending their brood, but instead agreed that, in retrospect, hating snakes did Christianity a load of good because the drop of population resulting from the plague born by the fleas from the rodents that increased because the snakes were killed encouraged the use of labor-saving devices by which Europe conquered the world and filled it with snake-hating missionaries. After writing the above, I obtained an entire book on this subject published by NHK. It is one of those touchingly honest, matter-of-factly written but full-of-research, rankly amateur books (it makes this one look professional) and is titled *Hebi to Jujika*,(the snake and the cross). I do not have space to introduce it other than to say that Yasuda Yoshinori believes that "Christian stewardship, etc. is insufficient acknowledgment of the damage monotheism has done to the world and an *Animism Renaissance* is called for.

~~~~~~

9-2   We use bleeding. *Nós uzamos de sangrias;*

The Japanese use burning pellets[1] of herbs. *Os Japões de botões de fogo com ervas.*

In so far that cutting is considered drastic and invasive, bleeding is stereotypical Western medicine: i.e. surgery. But the *principle* of balancing humors, could by that same token, be called Eastern. The claimed effects, however, are neither Oriental nor Occidental; they are part of what we might call the perennial medicine of hope:

> Phlebotomy clears the mind, strengthens the memory, cleanses the stomach, dries up the brain, warms the marrow, sharpens hearing, stops tears, encourages discrimination, develops the senses, promotes digestion, produces a musical voice, ... (G:PPI)

> The balance of humors was governed by astrology (bleeding different parts on different days depending on ones birthday and the moon) and further justified by the wisdom of metaphor: "the more one draws upon the stagnant water from the well, the more fresh water it produces; the more the wet nurse suckles her child . . ." (*Varietes chirurgicales* (Renaissance France) in G:PPI).

There is always an equal but opposite metaphor. Nieuhoff supplies it from from the mouth of the Chinese, who, like their protégés, the Japanese, did not countenance,

> Breathing a Vein, looking upon it as a great mistake, but rather reduce the fermented Blood by cooling Medicines, to a good Temper; for (as they say) if Broth boyls in a Pot, we must not pour it out, but command to take away the Fire under it. (N(O):EC)

Burning moxa (Artemisia/mugwort) is not so drastic as bleeding. As Kaempfer writes in his thorough chapter on it, moxa burns slowly so "the pain is not very considerable, and falls short of that which is occasion'd by other Causticks." (L' Abbe writes "they lay them on the skin *for two days* and being consumed to Ashes, they fall off of themselves;" (*italics,* his: A:HCJ) I doubt if it is that slow!) To the extent it was used *as a cure*, for instant local relief, it could be called Western. "It seems to be considered a universal specific" wrote Alcock, "even the accoucheur calls in its aid, and is directed to burn 'three cones on the little toe of the right foot to facilitate delivery.'" (A:COT) Unfortunately, the Japanese and the Chinese Physicians did not always agree about *where* to burn for various complaints, so that "if their different opinions were to be brought together," Kaempfer writes, "I believe, that in some distempers there would be scarce any one part of the human body left, but that some of them would single out as the most proper to be burnt with success." Still,

> no part of the human body suffers so much from this Caustic, as the backside, all along the Spina Dorsi, on both sides down to the loins. I found the backs of the Japanese . . . of both sexes so full of scars and marks of former exulcerations, that one would imagine they had undergone a most severe whipping." (K(S):HOJ)

Later visitors attested this was still the case. Isabella Bird: "It is really the exception where the back is not scarred by its use." (B:UTJ)   Like blood-letting, moxibustion was performed as preventive medicine as well as cures.

> Here, these little mugwort cones are to be found in most houses, and people are burned in the Spring, just as in England blood-letting was formerly customary at the same season." (B:UTJ)

Kaempfer, incidentally, suggests just how important this preventative usage was believed to be by the Japanese when he discusses Christians condemned to life in jail in Nagasaki:

> All the hours of recreation these poor wretches are allow'd, are, to be taken out of the dungeons they are confin'd to twice a year, in order to be burnt with Moxa, according to the custom of the country, to wash themselves six times a year in the Tange of the Prison, and to take a walk likewise in a large and specious house built for this purpose within the Prison-walls." (K(S):HOJ)

In Europe, where "the physician to Charles IX and Henry III of France prescribed preventive bleedings monthly in young people and six times a year in the old" (G:PPI) chances are prisoners did not receive such tender loving care!

I read about *moxa* before going to Japan in 1972. So, when my father *insisted* I hurry down from his second floor hotel room to check the source of the pleasant smelling smoke coming up through eyes of the *tatami*, I guessed what it would be though I had just arrived. But, I had wrongly assumed people burned "any part wherein they feele payne," (in C:TCJ) as Richard Cocks put it. So I was surprised to discover the old lady and her even older mother burning moxa on parts of their body that bore no obvious relation to their maladies (on the arm for dental pains, etc.). But, today, few young Japanese use moxa. As a preventative, the pain probably does help keep the immune system on its toes. Perhaps such an approach could be followed in a painless way! Then again, if one believes that pain is proof that it is doing something, that would remove the *placebo* effect.

In the West, blood-letting in the traditional sense died in the last century. But, it is still used for treating hemochromatosis,[2] the most common inherited metabolic disorder of people (and sometimes a problem for other animals as well). Depending on the level of iron overload, people living with HHC may donate blood more than once a week. If, however, they also suffer from anemia (low hemoglobin), they need to undergo chelation (removing iron chemically) instead. Because studies have shown a great longevity reward for giving blood accruing even to men who do not suffer from HHC, I would guess that many people will donate blood as the safest way to reduce their iron, and whatever other harmful substances have built up.

Reading of disfiguring scars caused by moxa and premature deaths caused by overzealous bloodletting, we laugh at the idiocy of our ancestors, but our past may well have the last laugh here.

---

1. *Frois Explains the* Botões   In the prologue to his missing Summary (first book of his *Historia*), Frois cites the expression he uses here for burning pellets or cones, *botoes de fogo*, as an example of terms that are misleading without proper explanation.   Apparently, *botoes* conjured up images of larger and more painful caustic remedies used in Europe, so that where "it is written that three or four thousand *botoes* of fire are placed on the body to cure someone suffering from eye problems or rheumatism, one should know it is commonplace in Japan and take it the same way as the other things [items misunderstood because of incommensurable vocabulary and insufficient knowledge]." The so-called *botoes* are really "little balls" (*bolinhas*, mistranscribed as *lourinhas*) about "the size of large pomegranate seeds," and that "once fifteen or twenty" of

these has been piled up and burnt "in the same place, almost no pain is felt, because that place has been well mortified" (Kaempher mentions that moxa hurts the first few times, because the skin must be broken in, and that this was called *kawakiri*, or skin-cutting, a term subsequently used for a high initial tax).   And, finally, Frois's clincher: "I myself, have tried this Japanese [cure] for various aches and pains and eye disease, and had over three thousand [pellets] put on my back and knees" (J/F:Historia)

2. *Hemochromatosis?* After decades of clinically silent iron accumulation, HHC patients develop overt disease in their fourth or fifth decades: cirrhosis, skin pigmentation, cardiac failure, arthritis, endocrine failure including diabetes mellitus, and hepatic carcinoma, among other things!

9-3   Our men ordinarily bleed their arms.
Os homens antre nós se custumão ordinariamente sangrar nos braços;

> The Japanese [use] leeches or cut their foreheads with a knife and the horses with a lancet.   *Os Japões com sanbixugas ou c[om] faca na testa, e aos cavalos com lanceta.*

For the standard phlebotomy (venesection), "our" idea was to open one or more of the larger external veins.[1]   The arms were accessible and, compared to the lower limbs or the neck, better for regulating the speed of the blood-flow, which was considered important (some diseases responded better if it was rapid enough to visibly effect the system, perhaps even induce fainting).   Like the Japanese, the Jesuits should not have been big on this practice "for the Church had eschewed blood ever since the famous Council of Tours in the year 1163: *'Ecclesia abhorret a sanguine'* writes Wolfgang Michel, who curiously adds that "Luis Frois regretted that Japanese would not accept . . . phlebotomy" in this book.   I find no such opinion here, but maybe Frois did for, Michel continues,

> No one knows how to venesect, complained father Coelho in 1589, and three of the members of the order who fell ill from the strain of persecution have already died.   When in 1591 João Rodriguez was taken ill in Kyôto, he had to travel 700 kilometres to Nagasaki for treatment. (Wolfgang Michel On the Reception of Western Medicine in Seventeenth Century Japan http://www.rc.kyushu-u.ac.jp/~michel/publ/books/14/14index.html.)

Leeches were actually more popular in parts of Europe.   In England, "a leecher" was synonymous with a physician, the art of healing was called "leechcraft" and the medical/physic finger (next to baby-finger) the "leechfinger."   And it didn't stop in Frois's century.   The biggest leeching boom was in 19th century France.   "In the year 1833 alone 41,500,000 leeches were imported into France and only nine or ten million exported." (G:HOM) The leeches were eventually driven to extinction in some countries.   Now, medical leeches are most commonly used for sucking blood through reattached digits.   My chance experience with leeches in the wild taught me that they are *absolutely* painless (unlike our needless which sting, ache or both)!   I would prefer we use them to draw all blood![2]

The forehead bleeding refers to a Chinese practice carried out with a "three-corner-needle" or a *fleam,* upon the crown and occipital part of the head (since the crowns are shaven, Frois made it the forehead?) for removing bad blood, but it was not so common a practice as venesecting arms in the West and probably was only used for certain maladies.   Otherwise, Valignano (and others) would not have written: "they never bleed a person." (in C:TCJ 1582? 83?)

1. Standard Venesection.   The location of *venesection* was never so complex as was the case for *acupuncture* or *moxibustion,* but in the sixteenth century it was subject to controversy with respect to whether it should be applied to the same side of the body and near to the lesion (called *derivative* bleeding) as per Hippocrates or as per the Arabist teaching at a distance from the lesion (called *revulsive* bleeding). (G:HOM)

2. Leeching Anyone?   From a nineteenth century book: "Generally speaking, however, as in regard to the other modes of local or topical bleeding, the blood drawn by leeches is discharged too slowly to have much effect on the general system [which was desired] . . . . Infants, however, are sometimes quickly and powerfully affected, even to fainting, by the application of two or three leeches, which, so far, in them, may answer the purpose of general blood-letting, producing all the effect of venesection in the adult. There is one objection, however, to the use of leeches in children, which deserves attention; namely, the terror they sometimes occasion, with a continuance of angry feelings for an hour or two, while the operation lasts. This is a cause of aggravation in many brain affections of children, where the sensibility and irritability of the system are already greatly in excess." (Found at the Biomedical Library (biomed-ref@library.ucla.edu) Copyright© 1996 Regents of the University of California http://www2. library.ucla.edu/ libraries/biomed/ his/blood/blood.htm)

9-4   We use clysters and syringes;   *Nós uzamos de cristeis ou siringas;*

They, in no case, use this remedy.   *Elles por nenhum cazo uzão deste remedio.*

Is it not ironic that Japan, with its comparatively stronger tradition of homosexual, i.e. anal, sex should deny, and Europe welcome the enema? A "clyster" was a suppository "to cleanse the bowels or afford nutrition." (OED) Reading this makes us reflect that the "syringe" *entered* holes long before it *made* them (shots came in the 19th century) made them. Judging from what was written inside of one of my favorite books (*Tristam Shandy*), it was also used for the baptism of babies *in utero!*

The Japanese did occasionally clean themselves out, but it was from the top down. Valignano writes, in a rare contrast not found in the TRATADO, that "their purges are sweet-smelling and gentle – in this they certainly have an advantage over us for our purges are evil-smelling and harsh." (1583? in C:TCJ) Ribadeniera, a Franciscan, seconds. Aside from the various "simple medicines and potions made by boiling roots" based on "books written in China" (i.e. *kanpôyaku*) used to restore people to health, he noted "they also administer purges in candied pills so that they may be taken more easily." (in C:TCJ) So, did Japanese did not need enemas because their purges were better? I must, however, warn that not all Japanese medicine tastes good. While Japanese say that if it tastes good to you it is proof it is what you need, they *also* say good medicine should be bitter.

Today, the plethora of advertisements for "figs" (*ichijiku*) on TV in Japan, suggests they now use enemas as much as "we" do. Could this be because of Western-style toilets and diet?

9-5   With us, the doctors write prescriptions for pharmacists;
Antre nós receitão os medicos pera as boticas.

The doctors of Japan prescribe medicine from their own houses.
[Os]medicos de Japão mandão as mezinhas de sua caza.

For better or worse, "our" medicine was already specialized. Doctors in Japan were still called *kuzushi,* or "medicine-masters" and, true to their name, fulfilled their own prescriptions. This does not necessarily mean they grew, gathered and made all of it. Much was bought from merchants, but they did keep a stock. When Almeida, the Jesuit who had been a surgeon and probably a wealthy merchant [1] took over a clinic at the Our Lady of Mercy hospital in Bungo (Kyushu) in 1559, he quickly set up a pharmacy and because it depended on fluent reading of Chinese books (and ordering Chinese medicines from abroad), he put a Japanese Jesuit who was a former Buddhist monk in charge.

In 1577, Frois, himself, was pressured into playing doctor and giving out medicine – his own! – while on an eight-day lay-over in a harbor town shortly after he finished 12 years of work in the Kyoto region. "Hearing a priest was there, the pagans, as was their wont, thought because he was a European he might be a great doctor." The man next door to Frois's inn was gravely ill and the inn owner begged him to help. Frois demurred, *"If it's for the soul, I have some very good medicine . . ."* But, "in the end, they were so persistent, the padre [In his *Historia,* Frois talked about himself in the third-person] sent him a little powdered *pedra de basar* (*bezoar*: Persian for "antidote" made from many types of animal innards, but most notably from stones found in the stomachs of Persian sheep), which, as luck would have it, made him feel great, making Frois "a famous doctor" and filled the Inn with everything from sick infants to cripples on crutches over night. Our poor hero prayed for the gift of healing such as St. Pedro received, but he does not say if he got it, only that he proceeded on to Hyogo where he served as superior for the next five years. (J/F:Historia bk10ch33)

1. *Almeida*. Jesuits were not allowed to become surgeons but since Brother Luis de Almeida was a surgeon prior to joining the Society, he was allowed to practice in Japan for a few years before Rome began to limit the Society's liberties. During that time he performed "operations on chancres, ulcers, abscesses, and gunshot wounds, and trained several Japanese" who later became practitioners. According to Jacques Proust (P:ETPJ), he was of New-Christian (Jewish) blood and that helps explain why he was so open to Chinese medicine and opened the hospital to the poor who were not Christian, etc.. Judging from the written documents examined by Wolfgang Michel (*On the Reception of Western Medicine in Seventeenth Century Japan*), Almeida's pupils did not have much influence on the development of Southern Barbarian school medicine in Japan. But I wonder . . .

9-6   Our doctors take the pulse of men and women first from the right arm, then from the left.
Os nossos medicos tomão o pulso a homens e molheres primeiro no braço dereito, despois no esquerdo.

The Japanese [take] the men from the left first and the women from the right first.
Os Japões aos homens primeiro no esquerdo e aas molheres primeiro no dereito.

This fe/male difference, writes Okada, comes from Oriental yin-yang philosophy. When the print on the third digit of the index finger was read to diagnose an infant's disease, it would be on the left hand of a male and right hand of the female. And this pattern of the sinister male and dexterous female was not restricted to medicine. Male-left, female-right also applied for the use of one or another fingertip to sign documents or make oaths with a bloody fingerprint. As far as I know, both genders meditated with the left leg crossed over the right, but considering the superiority of the male in so many areas of the society, and the generally favorable connotation of right, this is puzzling. (Is there any *physiological* explanation for the different sides, or is it pure philosophy? If so, what?)

Philosophy aside, during the time Frois participated in Almeida's clinic, where they cooperated with doctors of Chinese-style medicine, Frois "wrote that he knew how to take someone's pulse in the Japanese way." (in M:MSB) That is not so easy at it sounds, for more than just "left" and "right" was involved and speaks well of Frois's sensitivity, for he was far, far too humble to claim expertise he did not have.

9-7   Our doctors look at urine to learn more about an illness.
Os nossos medicos vêm as ourinas pera terem mais noticia da infirmidade.

The Japanese, in no case, look at it.
Os Japões por nenhum cazo as vêm.

It is hard to over-estimate the importance of urine as a diagnostic tool for early modern Western medicine. Physicians in Renaissance art are commonly portrayed holding a vial of urine. One wonders all medical doctors did not end up being called *urologists*, or as a 1637 critique had it "pisse-prophets"! (S:SCP)

Urine which is milky on the surface, dark at the bottom and clear in the middle is a sign of dropsy. But ruddy urine in a dropsical patient is a sign of death (normally it betokens health). [this, an example of *prognosis* as well as *diagnosis*.]

Where the urine is frothing high up, it shows there is more pain on the left, for the left side is colder than the right. (G:PPI, my brackets)

Gaitonide quotes two entire pages of this from Talbot's *Medicine In Medieval England.* Urology (I almost wrote *uromancy!*) survived the Renaissance intact. A paragraph in *Aubrey's Brief Lives* tells about a Dr. William Butler, who was three years younger than Frois:

A Serving man brought his Master's water to Doctor Butler, being then in his Studie (with turn'd Barres) but would not bee spoken with. After much fruitlesse importunity the man tolde the doctor he was resolved he should see his Master's water; he would not be turned away, threw it on the Dr's head. This humour pleased the Dr., and he went to the Gent, and cured him.

Dr. Butler was usually on the other end of the surprise. He cured a man of Ague by pushing him over a balcony into the Thames (having arranged for a boat to be nearby, ahead of time) and another of a "red, ugly, pumpled face" by hanging him "from a Beame in the roome, and when he was e'en almost dead, . . . cutt the veines that fed these pumples and lett out the black ugley Bloud!"

Now, *there* was a man with the gift of Saint Pedro Frois wished he had! As a remarkable example of East meets West (at least in the person of Dr. Butler) *and* proof that Japanese medicine was hardly the most exotic variety, I cannot resist introducing the Formosan cure noted by Nieuhaus a century later:

> The ordering of their Sick is no less unnatural and preposterous [than parching bodies to bury them in their own house after three years]; for they use them worse than if the Devil were their Doctor; for in stead of Potion or Pill, and the like, they have but one Medicine for all Diseases, and that's a dry Halter, especially in the Village *Teopan;* far as soon as any Person falls sick, and begins to complain, lying down, and not able to walk about, and follow his Business, they presently prepare a tough Cord, in stead of Cordial; so putting the Noose about his Neck, they hoise him up to the top of the House with a Pulley kept for that purpose, then let him suddenly fall with a Jolt, which commonly proves an immediate Cure, by killing them; yet some mend upon this choking Medicine, either by the strength of Nature, or their Spirits irritated by the fright. (N(O):EC)

Southern Barbarian Medicine, as Portuguese medicine was called, brought the custom of looking at urine to Japan. Okada points out that Luis Almeida, the surgeon Jesuit already mentioned, checked the urine of the fief-lord of the Goto islands according to his October 20, 1566 letter. Presumably, this is the first recorded use of this diagnostic tool, that was common by the time Japan was opened in the 19th century, in the Orient. Today – speaking from experience – Japanese hospitals take urine for almost anything under the sun because, it makes the patient wait longer to see the doctor, there is insurance money for it, and the test is a relatively innocuous one.

~~~~~~

9-8   The body of a European, being delicate, is very slow to heal.
A carnadura dos de Europa, por ser dilicada, vai sarando muito devagar;

> That of the Japanese, being robust, heals much better and faster from grave wounds, burns, abscesses and accidents. *A dos Japôis, por ser robusta, de graves feridas, qebraduras,postemas e dezastres, sarão muito milhor e mais depresa.*

A contemporary of Fois's, Mexia, likewise wrote: "When they fall sick, they recover in a very short time without taking hardly any medicine." (in C:TCJ) Are these, together with statements by many European visitors about the light diet of the Japanese, the first indication of the concept of the *underliving* oriental, who is constitutionally tougher and can survive on less than the Occidental? Is this just a-grass-is-greener-on-the-other-side-of-the-fence type of thing? Or was it a fact perhaps the result of the Japanese having a better diet or more body-friendly clothing and postures (I really do think squatting does one as much good as walking)? Today, Japanese lead the world in length of hospital stays, so it might suggest Frois's robust race has undergone a change. Or, it might just be they can afford to stay in hospitals because of their health insurance. (Unlike the USA, where I cannot even afford to visit a Doctor!)

How does this fit with 1-1? It would seem "a good build" (*boa estatura*) is not necessarily a robust one (Muscles being more expensive to maintain?). Are "we" Europeans, then, the original thoroughbred, fast but delicate? What about the classical idea that beauty was by nature useful?

~~~~~~

9-9   We sew up wounds.
Antre nós se cozem as feridas;

> The Japanese put a little sticky paper on them.
> *Os Japões lhe poem hum pouqo de papel grudado.*

In Japan, despite the practice of acupuncture, wounds were not yet sewn up. If we wonder at their slowness to do so, considering all those sword wounds one might expect, we may wonder equally about why it took us so long in the 20th century to stop doing unnecessary stitching where good adhesive band-aids do perfectly well. Okada suggests the "glue" (*grudado* was not a noun so I used one of its adjective forms, "sticky") was really *medical ointment*. Chances are it was *both*..

9-10   All the treatment we do with cloth,   *Toda a qura [que] fazemos com panos,*

The Japanese do with paper.   *Fazem os Japões com papeis.*

Japanese paper could be almost as soft as gauze yet not break into little bits that could enter wounds and cause infection as is the case with our soft paper – including, most tissue paper sold today! Japanese could use paper and not cloth for treating wounds for the same reason they could use it to wipe up after or during sex.   I would not be surprised to learn that the paper also had the advantage of breaking down in time so it was not necessary to peal it off (i.e. the equivalent of the modern vanishing-stitches).

9-11   We burn abscesses with fire.
Antre nós qeimão-se as postemas com fogo;

The Japanese would rather die than use our harsh surgical methods.
Os Japões antes morrerão que uzar dos nossos remedios asperos da surugia.

If Hindi purified dead bodies by burning them, "we" burned ourselves alive to purify parts of them, not realizing that the trauma incurred was as often or not as deadly as the infection (and that burning itself could damage tissue in ways that could lead toward infection other than the one that was burned).   Our burning was not confined to cautery (applying hot irons) either. Scalding oil was poured into gun-shot wounds in order to remove their poison. When the oil ran out in a battle in 1537, Ambroise Pare, "the father of modern surgery" – who once bled the same patient 27 times in 4 days – found that those who had to settle for "a digestive of eggs, oil of roses, and turpentine" healed faster. Still, it took a century for the practice to die out.[2]

Frois does not write rhetorically for there surely were Japanese patients at the Bungo hospital who refused Almeida's advice on this and died. Kaempfer, a century later, was so sympathetic to the Japanese position as to seem to share it. In a chapter on "The Cure of the Colic," just before introducing the cure, acupuncture, he wrote:

> It must be owed in justice to the Japanese, that they are far from admitting of all that cruel, and one may say barbarous apparatus of our European surgery. Red hot irons, and that variety of cutting knives and other instruments requisite for our operations, a sight so terrible to behold to the patient, and so shocking even to the assistants, if they be not altogether destitute of all sense of humanity and mercy, are things, which the Japanese are entirely ignorant of." (K(S):HOJ)

Indeed, Kaempfer goes on, their moxa is "nothing else but a softly glowing tent of the Plant, which bears the name of that celebrated Queen Artemisia" and the metals used for their surgery, namely acupuncture, not hard iron but "the produce of the sun and moon" namely, "gold and silver." (Lafcadio Hearn could not have put it any more poetically!) He then gives a fine description of the instruments and operation of acupuncture that is as delicate as the thing itself. I think there was a bit of Kaempfer in many Europeans who welcomed news of different medicine in the Indies and questioned the suitability of the "harsh treatment" mentioned by Frois. Here is a question and part of an answer from THE RESOLUER, *or Curiousities of Nature, written in French by Scipio Du Pleis, Counseller and Historiographer to the French King* published in English translation in 1635:

Q – Wherefore is it to those extreame sicke, they often apply extreame remedies?

A – Because it must bee, that the remedy bee proportioned and answerable to the sicknesse, being for a certaine, that a sharpe and violent malady cannot be healed by benigne and gentle remedies in as much that they cannot vanquish neither more nor lesse, then as a Fort well ammunitioned and defended by couragious men, cannot bee wonne without great and strong forces.

1. Burn or Cauterize   I deliberately left *queimam-se* (burn) as is, rather than softening the effect with a medical term "cauterize." The hot oil works better with "burn," too.

2. The Slowness of Medicine. Why did it take so long to realize that the burning was not helpful? When, I wonder, was the first time that someone discovered what is now common knowledge, namely that maggots did a far better job of disinfecting wounds (digesting necrotic tissue) than hot cautering irons, hot oil, nitric acid or alcohol? Was this known in Japan, too? A googled tidbit: "Patients in Britain suffering from infected wounds will be able to take home a pot of maggots as part of a scheme launched today that allows doctors to prescribe them for treatment. But from today, nurses will for the first time go to patients' homes and apply them to the wound, sealing them into the infection with a dressing and leaving the maggots to feed on the dead tissue. After three days, the maggots, who leave healthy tissue alone, are removed from the wound and reapplied if necessary." (Agence France-Presse article at news.com.au *via* poe news(?) – If there is no Princess of Wales Hospital, then it is April 1.)

9-12   When our sick have no appetite, we work hard to make them eat.

Aos nossos doentes, se tem fastio,[1] trabalha-se com elles pera que comão por força;

The Japanese think this cruel, and the sick who with no appetite are allowed to die.

Os Japõis o tem por crueza, e se o doente tem fastio deixão-no asi morrer.

Analogically speaking, "we" forced food for the body on people the same way we forced food for the soul, i.e. religion, on them. One wonders if anthropologists can find a correlation here! Eating, especially eating rich food, was thought to reduce the efficacy of Chinese medicine (Okada). So, there may also have been a practical side to allowing people to follow their natural inclination. Moreover, food eaten without an appetite, or even in the face of nausea, may only exhaust the malfunctioning gastro-enteric system by increasing putrefaction and flatulence, thus hastening a person's death, where fasting may allow his organs to recoup (my personal experience) enough to make eating beneficial. But some situations (eg., where the reason for lack of appetite is trauma), support Frois's premise that fasting would kill the patient. It also leads us to a more general *Faux Frois:*

We think death something horrible that should be delayed as far as possible;
They claim to be embarassed by living too long and do not fear death.

Frois might not agree with the "we," for Westerners of deep faith did not necessarily think of death as horrible, unless they had reason to fear for their future. But, would it be right to say that forcing the sick to eat suggests that we, as a culture, had mixed feelings about death, and on the whole, placed our bets on this life? To me, the fact that Japanese faced death with equanimity even when they were not members of faiths as fanatical as 16th century Christianity (with a Heaven that was almost tangible) is as laudable as it is incredible. We talk of when death was natural in the West, and give examples of content people dying in bed surrounded by family. But comparing the attitude of the Japanese expressed in their fine death poems (by all means, read H:JDP!), with what I have read of the West, I would have to question whether most people were *ever* really at home with death in our civilization (excluding time of plague, when we are talking more of the fatalism of people in a state of shock). [2]

1. Tem Fastio.   There were two problems in translation. One was that *doente* means both "sick Person" and a "patient." I hated having to choose one. The second was the lack of an equivalent word for *fastio*. English can "have an appetite," but it cannot have the opposite, for there is no antonym for appetite in English! My first choice was to write "would fast," but the Portuguese does not make it a matter of the willing.

2. At Home With Death.   From Madrid To Purgatory presents the Spanish "culture of death," and tells how Felipe II, "spent his final days much as had his father Charles, contemplating death with his own coffin at his bedside." (E:MP) The faith of these men is impressive. At the same time, I find the details of their belief and the trappings of the final act terribly immature compared to the more subtle Japanese. Indeed, "our" religion's fixation on death and its paraphernalia remind me of a fetish. Maudlin Felipe clutching the relics of saints as he dies reminds me of the antics of the turn of the century actress Sarah Bernhardt, who made a practice of sleeping in her coffin.   Such drama does not suggest true equanimity. It seems to me that "we" have never out-

grown our childish fear of death (Remember going through a period when you feared death so much it gave you nightmares?) and I find that both endearing and disgusting, refreshingly naïve and pathetic to witness.

9-13   Our sick lie on cots or beds with bedspreads, quilts and pillows;
Os nossos doentes estão em catres ou leitos com lensões, colchões e traveseiros;

> The Japanese on a mat on the floor with a *makura* [pillow] of wood and their *kimono* over them. *Os Japões sobre huma esteira no chão com huma maqura de pao e o seu quimão em riba.*

This is simply an ordinary sleeping arrangement described elsewhere in separate contrasts regarding the bed, bed-spreads and pillows. Perhaps, Frois felt repetition was worthwhile for the *soft* vs. *hard*, *luxury* vs. *spartan* contrasts might be better felt in the context of the sickbed. The *kimono* suggests a winter sickbed, for, as explained elsewhere, there were kimono-futons.   If it were outside (a field hospital), the mat would lie on the "ground" rather than "floor." *Chão* can mean either one.

A later statement of Japanese sleeping in their clothing by L' Abbe de T. that is too general to be true for all, but true enough and well put:

> We Undress ourselves before we go to Bed; they, on the contrary, lie constantly upon Mats in their Cloaths. (A:HCJ)

9-14   In Europe, hens and squabs are used for medicine for the sick;
Em Europa se têm as galinhas e frangãos por mezinha pera os doentes;

> The Japanese think these are poison and give them fish and salted radish.
> *Os Japões tem isto por pesonha e mandão-lhe dar pexe e rabão salgado.*

Valignano wrote "everything which we would give a sick person, they forbid, and what we would forbid, they give them. And so they regard hens, chickens,[1] sweet things and practically all the foods we would give patients as being unwholesome for them; on their part, they prescribe fresh and salted fish, sea-snails and other bitter, salty things, and they find from experience they do patients good." (1582?3? in C:TCJ)   The "unwholesome" is no less than *cosa pestilencial!* (V(A):S&A) The reason would be that domestic birds were, as Alvarez-Taladriz notes, a taboo food to begin with in Japan. For a sick person to eat this meat would be to tempt fate. But he also noted that the taboo did not stop soldiers from killing domestic fowl and eating them. Alvarez also suggests that Valignano's "fresh" fish meant *raw* fish, *sashimi*. I think that is likely. Though I am not one to put down chicken soup, raw red fish is even better for people with intestinal problems because it has less fat, more folic acid and can be digested by the stomach alone. Likewise, a small portion of slightly fermented pickles – for that is what the "salted radish" is – like red wine and unpasteurized cheese, can fight bad bacteria and work to prevent run-away putrefaction in the digestive tract.

L' Abbe, after repeating Valignano's contrasts (the same as 9-2, 12 and this 14), concludes with a shiver that,

> by those methods which in our Opinion wou'd kill all our Sick in *Europe*; they recover, and live usually longer than we." (A:HCJ)

Montanus, exaggerating as usual, writes:

> . . . and as we have our Physick well prepar'd, the ascerbity or other ill tastes taken off with Correctives, they take them simple in their own likeness, able to kill our Horses . . . (M:EEJ)

I recall some awfully bitter medicine, but the reason for my knowing it was not that Japanese medicine is particularly bitter but that medicine that would be enclosed in pills in Usania are still (or, were, a decade or two ago) given in powder form – one folds a small square of paper, pours it onto the tongue and drink it quickly before coughing! Do Japanese have smaller *throats* as well as nostrils?

1. *Hens and Chickens?* This seems strange. I checked and sure enough Valignano had *gallinas* and *pollos*. Is it possible that hens that were set aside for laying eggs were called *gallinas,* whereas other hens raised for eating were categorized with roosters as *pollos*, or just plain chickens?

9-15   We pull our teeth with forceps, tongs and parrot-beak pliers [1]
Nos tiramos os dentes com botiqão, alsaprema, biqo de papgayo, etc.;

> The Japanese use a chisel and a mallet, a bow and arrow attached to a tooth and iron nail-pullers. *Os Japões com escopro e macete ou com arqo e frecha atada no dente ou com troqes [torques?] de ferreiro.*

It is fun to imagine a tooth tied by a 10-foot string to an arrow which is shot from a bow, but as Okada suggests, the bow and arrow is probably only a bow-drill.   .

1. *Translation.* I have no idea if I got it right for each word in translation has the possibility of being pincer or pliers or forceps, etc. One interesting discovery was that the *botiqão* is defined as "forceps *of a dentist*" (de *dentista*) and the the *alsaprema* as "pincer of a dentist" (and, also as "a large lever (*alavanca*) for lifting heavy weights, which is why I chose to render it "tongs"). The fact that these words were used specifically for dental tools suggests very high interest in dentistry in Iberia. A "parrot beak" tool was not in *Aurelio*. There was, however, a parrot-like nose, a plant and a particular bone by that name! Googling for help, this – yes, the very contrast! – was the best I could find: "*while the Jesuits pulled away their teeth with nippers, tooth tweezers and pliers, Japanese used chisel, mallet and arrow and elbow (this was lashed at the tooth).*" I probably could use a gloss by a truly bilingual, tool-conscious dentist! (I am hopeless. I shiver just to *think* about dentistry!)

9-16   Our seasonings and medicines are pounded in mortars.
Os nossas speciarias e mezinhas se pizão em gral ou almofaris;

In Japan, it is ground in a copper *navicula* with an iron wheel between both hands.
Em Japão se moem em huma naveta de cobre com huma roda de ferro antre ambas as [mãos].

"Our" mortars in the original have two different names, but I was unable to find two types of mortars in English, so I followed suit with the French and German translators who evidently had the same problem. The Japanese translators gamely try to match the original by creating two vessels, the first of which is described as a milk-pail (!).[1]

English has a number of terms for boats that are not boats, but none that apply here. But I could not turn the *naveta de cobre* into "a little copper boat." *Navicula*, which means small boat is, properly speaking, a sun dial where the prick (?) mimics a mast for what we might call a ship-of-time clock. I hope the reader will pardon my acting like Humpty-Dumpty and enlisting it to mean what I want it to mean! The Japanese *yagen* it refers to is is a single-grooved, slightly curved (convex) oblong mortar upon which a single wheel that serves as a pestle is held with a hand grasping the axle on each side. I cannot recall whether the wheel rotates around the axle which the hands grasp firmly or the axle, solidly attached to the wheel, rotates in the palms as the hands are moved back and forth while pressing down. Because the wheel is operated by two hands at the end of straight arms and does not require the wrist work of a mortar (We *say* "pounding" but there is a bit of *twisting* and *grinding*, too.) I believe it can do considerably more work than our mortar and pestle device. Considering the small use made of wheels for transportation in Japan, what fun to find the wheel used here! (It came with Chinese medicine from China) Since the wheel was identified with Buddhist law in Japan, I dare say it would also put some spirit into the medicine!

1. *Mortar Types.* My dictionaries are no help, but I would guess that the *gral* would be a glass or ceramic mortar for fine titration and the *almofaris* a more heavy-duty device. (*Help!*)

~~~~~~

9-17   Among us pearls and pearlets,[1] are used for personal ornament.
         Antre nós se uza das perulas e aljofre pera ornamento das pesoas.

        In Japan they only serve for being crushed to make medicine.
         Em Japão, não serve mais que de se moer pera fazer mezinhas.

Considering the uses Europe had for various stones found in other animals, this use of pearls by the Japanese is hardly surprising. In Chinese-style medicine, it served to relax the spirit, settle the soul, brighten the eyes, and cure deafness (Okada). That is to say, it was considered good for the nerves. Considering the fact it contains zinc and selenium and other trace elements, I do not doubt it. If I am not mistaken, pulverized cicada shares some of its properties. But, the strangeness in Frois's contrast is in the fact that pearls were not much valued for adornment and, thus, were destroyed to be drunken. If we are looking for an interesting medical contrast, it would be this:

> *In Europe, we pay a high price for mummia pitch or powder made from ancient bodies;*
> *In Japan, eating such a substance even for medicine would be thought ghoulish or insane.*

Mummy was a medicine in great demand since the days of the crusades. It is easy to understand why, for tar/bitumen/pitch has marvelous medical properties (especially dermatological problems where the healing is obvious). At first, tar itself (called *mummia* from Persian or *mûmîya* from Arabic) was used, but when natural asphalt ran short, that found in the hollows of corpses and finally the corpses themselves were used. Exporting corpses to Europe was big business in the 16th century and, not unnaturally, fraud was rife. When French physician Guy de la Fonteine investigated the mummy trade in Alexandria in 1564, he found fresh corpses were being dug up to satisfy the demand this patent medicine. (See Brian Fagan: *"Mummies or the Restless Dead"* in *Horizon* (Summer 1975))

1. *Pearlets.* In Frois's time, English had the word "pearlet", possibly from the Italian *perletta,* for what can be described as "a seed pearl." Portuguese maintains use of both words, *perulas* (*pérolas*) and *aljofre*. The French and German translators more practically wrote what Englishes as "pearls, large and small."

~~~~~~

9-18   Among us, if a doctor does not pass an exam, he is penalized and cannot practice;
         Antre nós, se um medico não for examinado, tem pena e não pode qurar;

            In Japan, whoever would make a living can become a doctor.
             Em Japão, pera ganharem a vida, quem quer uza de ser medico.

Certification has always been a mixed blessing for all but the wealthy. In 1589 London, there were just 38 licensed physicians for 120,000 people and about twice as many druggists, who functioned as general practitioners would today (T:RDM). The doctor-to-patient ratio proves that the exam system was more for the purpose of protecting the livelihood of doctors than the lives of the population. The heavy use of obfuscating Latin terms by the druggists was, likewise, purposefully done to prevent competition from folk practitioners and keep the prices of drugs artificially high. (Nicholas Culpepper, a truly conscientious herb-medicine specialist who fought to break that monopoly and return medicine to the folk in the mid 17c is one of my heroes). Perhaps the best thing that can be said about the monopoly of physicians, is that it saved many people from being killed by their medical care![1]

In Japan, too, the risk was known. There is an old saying that "a hundred men must die to make a good doctor." That brings a whole other nuance to the term "medical *practice.*" (Nowadays, we just aren't so honest about it. In every country I have lived in, people without connections often get tired and inexperienced interns that do little better than Frois's "anyone.") Japanese wits got a lot of mileage out of quacks, whom they called *yabu-isha,* or "bush-doctors." 200 years after Frois, *senryû* describe popular quacks as *the busiest people in Edo*, always rushing about looking ever-so-important in their sedans. It is interesting that even without exams (though various schools of doctors would doubtless accredit their own), the populace had a clear concept of *a quack* as opposed to the real thing.

1. Dangerous Medicine. Richard Wiseman's standard *"Several Chirurgicall Treatises* (1676) was popularly known as *"Wiseman's Book of Martyrs"* (!) (T:RDM) Unfortunately, physicians always found time enough for gynecology. Experienced midwives were pushed out of the way by literally dirty physicians, who ended up killing babies and their mothers for centuries. A 100 years after TRATADO, the pregnancies of Portuguese women in Goa invariably terminated fatally for both mother and child, presumably because Western male physicians did their thing (going from woman to woman without washing their hands). (G:PPI)

~~~~~~

9-19   Among us, for a man to suffer from the pox is always a dirty and shameful thing.
Antre nós adoecer hum homem de huma mula sempre hé cousa suja e vergonhoza;

> The Japanese men and women think it nothing out of the ordinary and are not ashamed of it. *Os Japões homens e molheres o tem por couza corrente e nada se pejão disso.*

Whether it came from the Americas or Africa, one thing is certain, Christians spread syphilis around the world. How convenient to have "proof" sex is sinful and a way to catch sinners and mark them for life all in one! This contrast is of a type we have become familiar with: it shows Japanese as not ashamed of things we are. In *not* bringing out the opposite instances, Frois reveals unspoken bias to the effect that only Christians are moral enough to feel shame. For example, he might have added "they would be ashamed to use their hands" in 6-1, when eating with hands was contrasted to using chopsticks, or, he might have contrasted European women who walk with their feet straight or even with their toes pointing *out*, while Japanese women would find that wanton and be ashamed not to walk pigeon-toed. But, perhaps I am being unfair. It is always easier to recognize lack of shame in others with regard to things one feels strongly about, than to discover things others find shameful that one would not even give second thought to: the *balance of shame* always falls in ones own favor. Be that as it may, the 9-19 contrast is correct as far as it goes, but it would be more interesting to add this:

> *We treat lepers in our hospitals and do not feel that their disease makes them any less human.*
> *They will have nothing to do with lepers and keep them away from all society as if they were beasts.*

Japanese may not have been ashamed of sexually transmitted diseases, but they have long been terrified of *all* incurable and visually distressing disease. That is to say, they were more sensitive to the mark *as* sin than the mark *of* sin (With the former, I stretch the meaning of "sin" to include an indefinable pollution that cannot be shaken and might better be put as a sign of being cursed, for bad people in plays, especially if they are women, suddenly find themselves severely blemished and this is thought to be partly the doings of the ghost or (if still alive) jealous soul of the wronged party). They remained, until very recently unrelenting in their attitude about leprosy, preserving a far more stringent segregation than found in the West.[2] Be that as it may, the Japanese in Frois's time may not have been particularly ashamed about *catching* a sexual disease, but the affect on their appearance would have troubled them and caused them to seek treatment before the disease played out its full course.[3]

Both of these diseases must have weighed heavily upon Frois's mind because the Jesuit hospitals in Japan had been forced to reverse their policies with respect to them. When the surgeon Jesuit Almeida ran the clinic in Funai (in the realm of Bungo), the hospital had three wings, one of which was for incurable diseases and included many lepers and some incurable syphilitics. It was so popular, patients, few of whom were Christian, came from all over Japan. Rome was not at all happy with this, for, if I understand Jacquees Proust (P:ETPJ) correctly, the policies set by the ecumenical councils allowed for assistance of the poor but not "medical activity" *per se,* much less going all out like this! For a couple decades, the hospital operations hushed up. Proust writes that "from 1562 onward there was no mention of any *medical* activity in Jesuits' letters from Japan." In Valignano's *Sumario* of 1583, he pretends nothing ever happened and suggests each region create a "house of charity" and a "hospital to take in poor and sick Christians, and also children whom the mothers customarily kill." He also recommended that the incurable, especially lepers be excluded because the Japanese found them repugnant.   This was definitely a wise move from the point of view of winning support in Japan.   But it is also the only instance I know of where the admirable policy of Accommodation decided by the Bungo Consultation of 1580 clearly backfired (at least to our moral sense). The free treatment of the poor, including gentiles, that Almeida had championed was also no longer permitted and admission restricted to "Christians from honorable and noble families." (P:ETPJ)

When AIDS exploded in our midst, Japanese had already become Western and modern and even conservative in the sense that the bourgeoisie usually is and most people had come to think of homosexuality as part of a corrupt, individualistic, sexually promiscuous Occident.[4] Perhaps because AIDS was associated with what was considered immoral behavior and was (and still is) incurable, Japan's reaction against it was greater than was the case in the USA, even with "our" gloating "We-told-you-so!" fundamentalists. Turning 9-19 on its head, AIDS became a far *more* shameful thing in Japan than in the West.   People were terrified to reveal they had it or even to get tested (The many infections through contaminated blood was the responsibility of the companies, but fear of talking out on the part of victims and their doctors delayed the response.) and, were Japanese not the world's greatest condom user, AIDS might have spread like wildfire.

---

1. *Translation:* The Portuguese for the disease is *mula,* meaning *bubo* (the chancre) as we called it after the facial marks (pock-marks), *pox.* The Japanese translated it as *yokone,* "side-root" a general term meaning "chancre" or "bubo," rather than using the proper term, *baidoku,* literally "plum-poison (the plum also meaning the bubo). Believe it or not, the name Syphilis comes from the name of a shepherd who suffers from the disease in a play written by an Italian a half century before Frois wrote the TRATADO, but the popular name seemed more fitting a translation for English, too.

2. *Segregating the Ugly.* The social stigmatization of appearance-related disease, especially if there is the possibility of genetic transmission, is one reason the effect of the atomic bomb was so much greater in Japan than most of "us" can imagine. The graphically described horrors of Hershey's *Hiroshima* can not begin to describe the living hell that many survivors and their descendents have still not completely emerged from. I think the fact the severely handicapped are not seen in public in Japan as much as in the USA, may reflect the strong desire not to look at ugly things as much as the less wasteful infrastructure (With tiny rooms, tinier bathrooms, tinier buses and trains so crowded it is hard for the healthy person standing on two legs, it is genuinely hard to make room for the weak and those in wheel-chairs.)

3. *Japanese and STD's*   Since syphilis was generally incurable, and gonorrhea, also common in Japan and called *rinbyô* (loneliness-disease!) was also as bad, I think that had Japanese been as free with sex as European visitors believed, they should have destroyed themselves within a few generations rather than keep growing. Evidently, there was considerable compartmentalization of the society, enough chastity (though one reads of sex with menstruating women in order to be cured of the latter disease, I would guess there was more self-control by the infected than found elsewhere) and/or true monogamy to prevent its spread. (Gloss, anyone?)

4. *Sexual Promiscuity.* What about the (heterosexual) bath-house sex in Japan, infamous prostitution tours abroad and strangely available child-pornography that Westerners note? Most Japanese paid little attention to these. They were, however, impressed with foreign magazines showing *full nudity* (Japan only allowed pubic hair to be shown from about 1990!) and sex (no hard porn was legal in Japan and probably still is not, though it may be found) and the news reports of hippie girls and communes and the in-your-face gay community (In Japan there are bars where one can be served by transvestites but nothing like the men that might be seen in hot-pants walking the streets of San Francisco.) *Every country thinks the other is the more promiscuous one.*

endnote IX

Medicine

~~~~~~

Compared to the other areas such as the equestrian arts, architecture or ship-building, our medicine does not come off as significantly more diverse or advanced than that of Japan, or for that matter, other Eastern nations. This was because it wasn't. *Not yet.* In Goa, we find that the viceroys, archbishops and Portuguese aristocracy preferred to be treated by the Hindi Vaidyas rather than their own physicians (G:PPI). Even the 1589 Report of the Embassy to Europe, with its constant boasting about superior European development has nothing to say about the medical science. *De Missione* does, however, have something to say about the *accessibility* of health *care*. In the context of introducing something called *societas* – what Americans now call non-profit corporations – such as the *Mons pietatis,* known as the "Mountain of Piety" (*Monte di pieta*) for the purpose of lending money to the indigent, *xenodochium,* or public inns for foreign travelers, *brephortrophium,* for the care of orphans, and *gynaeceum,* a sort of half-way house for raising the level of living and thereby reforming wayward women, Valignano=Miguel describes the *nosocomium,* or hospital,

> among which there are some with every kind of medicine and every type of equipment that give cheerful and free, complete medical care to people suffering from any complaint. Because there are many types of disease, there are many types of hospitals, or they are divided into wards, within are themselves well ordered, clean and take every consideration for the care of the patient . . . (J/S:DM)

If Sir Thomas More's *Utopia* had not already been written, one might think it all Miguel's invention. Christianity got all the credit, of course, – nothing is mentioned about Islam setting the example for the public hospital. Valignano=Leo responds:
..

> Such places would certainly be extremely beneficial. Because of them, many sins common in our country can probably be avoided in Europe. Sins such as ravishing virgins here and raising whorehouses there, using medicine, or rather poison for abortion, after which the mother murders her own dear child, and, furthermore, leaving sick men and other unfortunates to suffer and die on the road, these things anyone with a heart cannot bear . . . (J/S:DM)

While Japan did not have as many such societies as Europe – and even today is often compared unfavorably with the USA, often held up to be the exemplar nation of voluntary societies – this claim probably goes too far. Not all of Christendom was taking care of everyone half so well as the wealthiest cities, whose riches may well be the cause of poverty elsewhere, and the Tokugawa government, without the help of Christianity, thank you, would soon establish a thorough system to assist sick or injured travelers – each neighborhood had a place and a budget for so many days of care and send-off money when necessary.

病   気   病

Europeans believe miasma (pestilential airs) from swamps and dumps bring influenza;
The Japanese imagine there is a demon, who sneaks over the roofs, that brings it.

In Europe, someone in mortal danger usually sends for a priest, first;
In Japan, they always call for a doctor before the clergy.

Frois might have accomplished much more with this chapter. I think of the cultural side of disease such as the above *Faux Froises* which need no explanation. But, more than anything else, I would have liked Frois, with his Christianity as "medicine for the soul," to have taken as much notice of *how the best Japanese died* as he did of funeral customs. Here is something that took place when Frois was in Japan. Call it secular hagiography if you wish, but it really pulls at my heartstrings.

A warrior called Akaboshi was a vassal to Ryuzoji Takanobu (1529-84). The latter suspected Akaboshi of wishing to rebel against him and so took two of his children, a girl of eight years and a boy whose age is not given, as hostages. Takanobu eventually crucified them. The soldier in charge of the execution turned the children westward (toward paradise), his eyes brimming with tears. Before dying, the boy Shinroku, asked, "Where is my homeland?" "Toward the east," answered the soldier, whereupon the child replied with this poem:

Please don't face me	*Waga omote*
toward the west	*nishi ni na mukeso*
lest I should turn	*Akaboshi no*
my back upon my father	*oya ni ushiro o*
Akaboshi	*miseji to omoeba*

(Yoell Hoffmann: *Japanese Death Poems*, Tuttle, 1986)

The original poem is more poetic for, in Japanese syntax, the father comes earlier and the poem ends on the main idea: *"lest I should turn my back."* At the risk of sounding sacrilegious: Didn't this boy show a higher level of moral development than Jesus, who cowardly cried out *"My Father, why do you forsake me?"*

気　　　　　の　　　　　薬

Although I am not a Christian and am delighted that Japan, in the end, escaped being converted, I feel sorry for what happened to any useful medical knowledge Almeida brought to Japan, just as I feel sorry for the whole Jesuit mission and many if not most of the believers there. All that genuine good will and knowledge and even that explicit program of cultural accommodation of the likes Christianity had never seen and never would again until the Second Vatican took it even further to include religion in the mid-20th century (I see Ricci's work as an extension of the same). *Poof!* On the basis of an extensive search of Japanese sources which found "not a single reference to any Western work on medicine, surgery, anatomy, pharmacy is known in any manuscript dating from the long period between the advent of the Iberians in 1549 and their final expulsion in 1638," Wolfgang Michel came to the sad conclusion that the Southern Barbarian (*namban*) hospital wrote its history entirely on water.

Given the destruction of the mission hospital in Funai, the mounting persecution of Christians and also resistance within the Society of Jesus, there was no stable basis anymore for an effective interchange. So, to take issue with the standard literature on the subject to date, I do not believe the Japanese ever came to practice "southern-barbarian-style surgery" in the sense of a paradigm that could be passed on or handed down to succeeding generations. (M:MSB)

What a shame that Rome did not encourage rather than discourage the Jesuits' interest in medicine! Other physicians who came to Japan with the Dutch traders had to do it all over again. In Michel's words, "the Western art of healing was rekindled in Edo and Nagasaki in the mid-seventeenth century when a German surgeon, Caspar Schamberger, who is credited with the birth of 'Caspar-style surgery' (*kasuparu-ryû geka*), the first Japanese school of 'redhead-style surgery,' sparked a lasting interest in Western medicine, herbal lore and pharmaceutics.

妙   薬   妙

Meanwhile, the Jesuits in South America discovered *quinine*. Judging from their interest and readiness to learn about Chinese drugs, I would guess they were taught by a native of Peru. As the first specific drug for a specific illness, it gave a strong incentive for scientists to search for other cures. Brought to Europe in 1632 and in 1644 it became *the first medicine subjected to empirical testing* at the instruction of the Pope (so Rome was not entirely anti-medicine). Neuberger writes "it did for medicine what gunpowder had done for war" (G:HOM) and by quickly curing a protracted fever which the standard humor-correcting medicines/blood-letting had not affected "was the end of Galenism in medical practice." (Reader, do you realize how *significant* that is in the history of medicine?) It also played a role in one of the most shameful episodes in English history.   Known as *Jesuit's Bark* or *Jesuit's powder*, it was rumored to be an insidious poison the Jesuits brought to Europe "for the purpose of exterminating all those who had thrown off their allegiance to Rome." Here is one description of the London hysteria of the 1678 that ended up getting 35 people, including 8 Jesuits executed.

> The general outcry was indescribable . . . The Jesuits wanted to assassinate the king! The Jesuits were planning the slaughter of all the Protestants in England! The Jesuits wanted to poison the whole world . . . by means of an outlandish, so-called medicine, commonly known as the Jesuits' powder! . . . The Peruvian bark, or the facsimile of it, was paraded through the streets of London with great signs telling the gruesome story of how the Jesuits were using it to exterminate the non-Jesuit population. (From "The English Connection 'Jesuit's Powder' The author, Fr. Gene Nevins, SJ, partly citing *The English Jesuits* (1967), Bernard Basset, SJ and partly "others," all at www.company magazine.org/v144/powder.html)

> Even after the ingredient of the good drug was revealed by Louis XIV in 1681,

> the Jesuits continued to be portrayed as in league with the devil. The word *jesuitical* even made its way into the dictionary. Only when this prejudicial fever subsided did cinchona bark become an acceptable, worldwide remedy for malaria. That it was the Jesuits who had introduced it to Europe was by then forgotten. (Ibid)

If involvement in medicine sometimes got the Jesuits in trouble, it was a plus for their missions in Asia and absolutely vital in the Americas where measles and small pox and other deadly deceases from the old world killed most of the natives. This horrible tragedy that coincided with and, especially, *preceded,* the coming of the Jesuits, destroyed the credibility of the shamans and gave "our" *Black-robes* their opportunity.   While they were thinking of saving souls, the natives were thinking of saving themselves. Even baptism was thought of as charm against these horrible diseases and the relative immunity of the Jesuits to these diseases (together, I suspect, with their lack of fear of death) that permitted them to nurse the sick, doubtless enhanced their and their God's reputation. In the penultimate chapter of his tour de force, *Disease, Depopulation and Culture Change in Northwestern New Spain 1518-1764,* Daniel T. Reff points out:

Most of the medicines, herbs, rosaries and potions used by the Jesuits probably had little or no intrinsic value. However, the very fact they were used and combined with basic clinical care [getting decent food and water, kept in clean bedding, helped with body functions, protected from animals (and from committing suicide) given encouragement] meant that at least some survived that otherwise would have died. Modern medical practitioners and researchers have known for some time that clinical care can have an enormous impact on mortality rates. [After this, Reff gives examples.] (*the bracketed comments are mine* – R:DPC)

So even clinical (as opposed to medical) care can help! That helps explain a lot. Reff also notes that while the Jesuits had *a good explanation* (God's punishment for believing in the wrong gods, etc.) and *attractive public rites* to help people cope with these lethal diseases, in some cases where disease hit the natives hard *after* they were baptized, the Jesuits and their religion was blamed and baptism came to be thought of as a death sentence.   So, the total picture was complex though on the whole favorable to the missionaries.

In Japan, the importance of disease and, hence, the medical care offered by the Jesuits, was far less than in the New World, but I think it safe to say that medicine and the mission were inexorably married (though the relationship was sometimes strained) wherever the Jesuits went.

病　　　　　　の　　　　　　踊

We discuss elsewhere the difference between our vulnerability toward small pox and measles. But, this difference is not nearly so interesting as a *similarity* I just found in Souyri. I had long known that *we* danced, for I had read of "our" Dancing Mania, St. Vitus's Dance, *Danse de St. Guy,* St. Anthony's Fire, etc., attributed to mass hysteria, outbreaks of religiosity and, more convincingly, to ergotism (mold (fungus) on old grain that has toxic and, apparently psychedelic properties, that tends to accompany famine (when people will eat what they can find) and diphtheria and influenza and other diseases (caused by famine which lowers immunity and causing a worse famine by taking people out of the fields)),[1] but I had not heard of *theirs*.

> In 1134, following strong rains that caused flooding, Kyoto suffered a famine, and its residents fell victim to an epidemic . . . In 1153-4, . . . it was another disease, perhaps smallpox that mowed down the inhabitants. In the spring of 1154, crowds of people overwhelmed by adversity went to Murasakino Shrine . . . to rid themselves of the demons that had apparently caused the disease. The ancient Japanese thought that illness was caused by evil spirits possessing the body and that these spirits could be exorcised by dancing. Men and women, commoners, nobles, and outcasts all gathered . . . and danced, accompanied by flutes, bells and tambourines . . . Young servants of the shrine, dressed in ceremonial robes, performed acrobatics while the crowd danced and stamped their feet on the ground to expel the demons. he dances lasted day and night. The people seemed to have gone mad, perhaps hoping their madness would cure both fear and illness. (S(R):WTUD)

If anyone has seriously compared the dancing sick, or the dancing against illness, in Japan and the West, I'll gladly give you space for a long gloss in the next edition!

お　　元　　気　　で　　ね

THE WRITING OF THE JAPANESE AND THEIR BOOKS,

do escrever dos Japõis e de seus livros, papel e tinta e cartas

PAPER, INK AND EPISTLES

~~~~~~

10-1   We write with twenty two letters;
Nós escrevemos com vinte e duas letras;

They write with 48 *kana* abc and with infinite characters of diverse letters.
Elles com 48 no abc de cana *e com infinitos caracteres em diversas letras.*

The alphabet used by Romance languages in 1585 was four letters short of 26 because it lacked *j,* which was written with an *i, u,* written with a *v, k* with a *q,* and *w.* The letters in the Japanese *abc,* to use Frois's term for what is properly called a "syllabary," called *kana* (as opposed to *kanji,* or Chinese characters) are uniformly short, like the Greek *mora.* As *mora* is a hard word to remember, we might better speak of Japanese *syllabets* (my coinage).[1] Consonants invariably come with a vowel sound pegged on, e.g. "*ka, ki, ku, ke, ko,*" where each syllabet is written with a single letter, か、き、く、け、こ, respectively. In other words, one cannot write "k" or "s" or "t" and so forth, as there are no consonant letters, in our sense of the word. The vowels, on the other hand, can be written by themselves (a=あ, i=い, e=え, o=お, u=う in the Japanese order)) and are remarkably similar to those of Latinate tongues, both in number (five [2]) and pronunciation (as in *Buenos Aires.*) Had Frois been a modern student of ancient tongues, he might have written,

> *Our ancestors first invented stand-alone consonants and only later made letters for vowels;*
> *Their ancestors first invented stand-alone vowels and they still have no consonant letters.*

The equivalent of "our" meaningless *Alphabet Song* is a 47-syllabet poem by Abbot Kobo (Kôbô Daishi, died AD 776: the same of male-color fame) on the vanity of life, called the *Iroha,* for the first three syllabets of the poem). The missing syllabet is the controversial "n," the only consonant sound without a vowel sound pegged on – though Japanese may nasalize the palatalization in a way to give it a bit more duration/body than a pure consonant would have (and they *claim* it is as long as any other syllabet) – and thus, the only consonant that can *end* a written word in Japanese.[3]   To the ear, the syllabets "su" = す and, more rarely, "se" = せ, at the end of some verbs, sometimes tend to get only as far as the "s" part of their *sound,* but the Japanese can not express this in writing. The syllabary most commonly used today (but also used in Frois's time) is not, however, arranged as a poem, but by consonant, according to the five vowel sounds: eg. "*ka, ki, ku, ke, ko,*" followed by "*sa, shi, su, se, so,*" "*ta, ti[chi], tu[tsu], te, to,*" etc.. Its analytical arrangement, unlike our cruder alphabet, is reflected by its decimalistic name: *goju-on,* or "fifty-sounds."

English has too many phonemes to justify a syllabet – instead of 50, we would need 100's – but if your language is lucky enough to be sound-poor, a syllabet is far easier to master than an alphabet.   Children can be reading and writing with few spelling mistakes in weeks if not *days!* In the early-19^(th) century, Golownin wrote

> Every Japanese, however low his rank, knows how to write in this last character [the letters or *syllabets* of the syllabary, as opposed to Chinese characters]. They were exceedingly astonished to find that of four Russian sailors not one should be able to write. (G:MCJ)

The difference between the simple Japanese syllabets and our letters would have been at a minimum for Latin languages which were relatively easy to spell.   In these languages, the vowels are pronounced the same as the name of the vowel.   But, unlike Japanese, the pronunciation of the name of a given consonant is not necessarily the same as the bit of phoneme heard when pronouncing a word.   With Japanese, each Japanese syllabet – vowel or consonant-vowel combination – in a word is pronounced exactly like its name.   I. e., *spelling out a word only means saying it more slowly than usual.* Reader, who does not speak Japanese, can you guess what that *means?* Froising this, we get:

> *With us, parents sometimes spell out words to make them harder for children to understand;*
> *In Japan, parents sometimes spell out words to make them easier for the child to hear.*

I once heard a Japanese expert on America and its popular music explain on Japan's national public radio (NHK) that Tammy Wynette spells out D.I.V.O.R.C.E. and "C.U.S.T.O.D.Y. to "make these difficult words" *easier* for her little child to catch! I suspect he also misheard "all the *hurting* words" as "all the *hard* words," but the main reason for the mistake was the different concept of spelling out. But, there is one aspect of the Japanese syllabary that seems more complex than hours.

> *We only have one way to write our alphabet.*
> *They have two very different ways to write their syllabets, generally, and a third way for proper nouns.*
>   ..

By this, I do not only mean printed style versus cursive style (which Japanese also has, of course), but what appear to be completely different syllabaries.   The letter syllabets of one are soft and rounded, whereas the other is so hard-edged one might think it was designed for writing with a stylus or preparing print-blocks. To give an example, here is a haiku by Keigu in the alphabeticized, *hiragana,* and *katakana* versions and original mixed system (as actually written), respectively:

anonamakokayakutsundeorukamoshirenu	*keigu* [4]	(called *romaji*, or "roman-letters" by Japanese)
あのなまこかやくつんでおるかもしれぬ	けいぐ	(soft: most common letters in most writing)
アノナマコカヤクツンデオルカモシレヌ	ケイグ	(stiff, used for foreign and scientific words)
あのナマコ火薬詰んでおるかも知れぬ！	敬愚	(mix of letters, easy to read)

My haiku pen name, Keigu is a pun on the closing of a letter, "respectful-tool" = 敬具, where the last character, "tool" = 具 is changed to "fool(ish)" = 愚.   More commonly, a single name pronunciation-wise, may be written in *dozens* of ways by the various characters. For example, using the Microsoft Word standard cache alone, there are well over a hundred ways to write the name pronounced "Kenji": 賢治、健二、健治、健次、健司、賢二、憲治、謙二、賢司、謙二, and so forth. While many characters now have more than one possibility of pronunciation, they once (a thousand years ago) tended to have but one, and were used as a syllabary before syllabets were actually invented in Japan. The most studious could still read such *Manyôgana (kana* of the Manyôshû [poetry anthology] style) in Frois's time, but characters generally were not used that way any longer. Frois can be forgiven for ignoring such complexity, but he surely should have caught and included this:

> *We separate our words by spaces to read them more easily;*
> *The Japanese do not separate their words at all.*

This is one reason why it helps to use a mixture of Chinese characters and syllabets, for it creates easily readable clusters in the otherwise unbroken space. When Japanese is Romanized, we must make separate words clear. For example, the above haiku (meaning: *that sea slug / it just might be tamped / with dynamite*) reads more easily like this:

ano namako kayaku tsundeoru ka mo shirenu.

Since Frois does not mention what makes *kana* (syllabets) different from "our" alphabet, and the slight difference in number (22 *vs* 48) is far from contrary, the real contrast would seem to be between *a finite number of letters* and thos *"infinite characters,"* [5] which I'll treat in the next contrast.

1. My "Syllabet."   I invite readers who like the word to use it. The "syllabet" is particularly useful for describing *what haiku is* and *is not*. Counting *syllables* is not the same as counting *syllabets*, for the former can be much longer. In English, haiku should be based on a count of accented beats (7 or 8 total) rather than syllables.
2. Five Vowels. Technically speaking, Japanese has a couple more vowels (what makes the 48 into 50, but ゐ (*yi*) and ゑ (*ye*) are more or less dead and were already archaic in Frois's time.
3. The Only Consonant Letter. This anomaly disturbed Japanese nationalists – presumably for sharing something with Korean or Chinese – who denied the existence of "n" (ん) by insisting upon writing it as "mu" (む)!).

4. Haiku by Keigu. About 100 of the 900 haiku in the first edition of *Rise, Ye Sea Slugs!* including the above haiku #886 are by Keigu. It is really about *sea cucumber*, but "cucumber" is too long for most haiku and lacks the metaphorically proper sluggish feeling.

5. Infinite Number. Mexia, in a 1598 letter translated by Cooper (C:TCJ) also writes of "an infinite number of letters." Cooper adds "I am not sure what Mexia means when he says the Japanese have "others of their own [picture-letters]" as all the ideographs, with very few exceptions, are Chinese in origin." My guess is that Mexia *liked fish*, for there are dozens if not scores of made-in-Japan ideographs for fish.

〜〜

10-2   We study many arts and sciences through our books;
Nós estudamos diversas artes e scientias por nossos livros.

They spend their entire lives mastering their characters.
Elles toda a vida gastão em conhecer o corasão dos caracteres.

Okada notes that Rodrigues's *Arte de Lingoa de Iapam* (1604-8) claims that a total of 209,770 Chinese characters can be found! One of those "0"s probably does not belong, for estimates of "the total number of Chinese characters ever used from antiquity to present (including variant and dialect characters . . .) range up to 80,000 (Samuel Martin 1972:83)" (Hannas: 97). Rodrigues himself wrote elsewhere that "there are as many as 70,000 or 80,000 of these letters and characters" but added that "it is generally enough to know about 10,000 characters or a little less, because if these are known, many others can be understood by their composition." [1] Rodrigues means *for a learned man*, like himself. Half that many probably sufficed for most people (and, today, but half again of that). In a sense, characters are more like words than letters. *The more difficult ones, like our more difficult words, are simply not missed by most people.* But, it is true that more time is required to master them. In Dialogue 15 of DE MISSIONE, Miguel=Valignano elaborates. Yes, "our country" (Japan) does have its syllabic letters called *Cana,* but educated people do not write with it alone. In Europe, they learn only twenty-three letters − I don't know which letter was added − and "after that, they can read and write naturally and very easily."   Leno=Valignano then adds the fact that Japanese children in church schools are learning to "read and write" European tongues *in one or two months* (!). This is followed by what may be the first long complaint about the effort wasted on Chinese characters compared to the alphabet. Even the difficulty of writing homophonic Japanese vocabulary with the syllabet alone is considered – but not very deeply, because Miguel=Valignano assume that the diligent fathers can devise a system of accents and other signs to supplement the syllabet. (This would work for a few homographs that are accented differently, but most homophones are exact, so it would not help).

Still, there are studies confirming the Jesuits' impression of Japanese writing as wasteful. In 1929, Nitobe Inazo, the author of *Bushido* [2] conducted a survey which found "Japanese children spend 44% of their school days learning their mother tongue as against 31% by Europeans." He also found the reading level lagged by years and this was corroborated by the fact that "the blind acquire, in the same length of time, more solid knowledge than ordinary children – be it of history, geography or literature." (in James Unger's *The Fifth Generation Fallacy*, 1987, or a subsequent work) And it is not only the number of characters, but something the Chinese do not have to worry about, namely, learning the many ways they may be pronounced and combined with the letters.[3] Polemical linguist R. A. Miller writes: "to say that Japanese today employs a difficult, complex writing system is to risk the most sweeping understatement possible." (*Japan's Modern Myth:* 1972?)

Forty years before Nitobe, Chamberlain had already countered "the oft-repeated assertion that the ideographs waste years of school life is simply not true: – the Japanese lad of fifteen is abreast of his English contemporary in every way . . . the fact seems to be that at a certain age, the mind will absorb any system of written symbols equally well." (C:TJ) But, the other side has another more sophisticated argument that was, as far as I know, first hypothesized by Alice Mabel Bacon , namely, that the years of study needed to master the written language

> leave comparatively little time for the conducting of any continuous thought of one's own account, and so we find in Japanese scholars – whether boys or girls – quickness of apprehension, retentive memories, industry and method in their study of their lessons, but not much originality of thought. (B:JG&W)

I think that this idea,[4] which Hannas made into a book (*Asia's Orthographic Dilemma*) is dubious, for our time is not so limited and, for my part, I'd guess that time spent studying characters is not necessarily time badly spent. In fact, the best way to memorize is by inventing stories, which is to say exercising originality of thought). Moreover, I find the large initial investment *worth it*, for characters are fine for promoting a large vocabulary – I can guess the meaning of far more specialized terms in Japanese than in English – and, therefore more efficient in the long run. (For more complex argument see G:O&O) Be that as it may, nothing has been *proven* either way. That is why I am irked by the confident putdowns of Chinese characters in Japanese by alphabet-lovers. Best selling author Jared Diamond, who is wise indeed when it comes to *birdsong*, makes a fool of himself when he claims:

> Millions of people today buy designer jeans for double the price of equally durable generic jeans – the social cachet of the designer label counts for more than the extra cost. Similarly, Japan continues to use its horrendously cumbersome *kanji* writing system in preference to efficient alphabets or Japan's own efficient kana syllabary – the prestige attached to kanji is so great. (*Guns, Germs and Steel*)

> . . . the prestige of Chinese culture is still so great in Japan and Korea that Japan has no thought of discarding its Chinese-derived writing system despite its drawbacks for representing Japanese speech, while Korea is only now replacing its clumsy Chinese-derived writing with its wonderful indigenous *han'gul* alphabet. (Ibid)

Prestige value!? Japanese stopped worshipping the Chinese *centuries* ago! Sure, they appreciate the better part of what China has given the world. *We all should.* But that has nothing to do with the issue. There are *many* compelling reasons Japan continues to use Chinese characters. Because of their phonemic poverty and enormous number of homophones, Japanese have more reason than the Chinese themselves to stick with the characters. Much Japanese is unreadable by phonetic character alone. A large portion of one of the world's most wonderful literature – would be rendered unreadable. Diamond seems to have affection for a diverse ecology and so-called primitive languages, yet he shows absolutely no sensitivity for Japan's wonderful system of writing! (Korean *han'gul*, which he put in a good word for, may well be the world's most scientifically designed script, but *it is ugly*. It doesn't flow half so well as the Japanese syllabets do. Does beauty count for nothing in this world, professor?)

> *With us, even a word written by a calligrapher would not, by itself, be thought of as art.*
> *With them, a single character written in a second can be hung up like a painting and enjoyed.*

Finally, going back to Frois's time, I think the efficiency of the European side is exaggerated. Remember that written Chinese served as a sort of lingua Franca in the Far East. "We," too, needed a bridge between scholars with different national tongues and to communicate with the ancients. Some, including a certain great astronomer, thought it was a bit too much.

> Lecturing at the university of Copenhagen in 1574, the astronomer Tycho Brahe referred enviously to the precocious mathematical knowledge of his classical forebears, 'while we, unfortunately, have to spend the best years of our youth on the study of [their] language and grammar, which they acquired in infancy without trouble.' (H:CER)

1. 209,770? Large Grammar (Historia II, in Cooper; A fascinating note about the "most modern and scientific" dictionary in question, "Extract from VOCABULARIO DA LINGOA DE JAPAM, Nagasaki, 1603" mentions "about 30,000 words"). That's right. Someone misprinted.

2. *Bushido* This book on the way of the samurai was a heroic effort to find a common spirit in the martial mentality of Japan and Europe and it is wrong to think Nitobe naïve for overlooking difference. His intent was not academic. It was to sell the West on Japanese and that he did *very well*.

3. *Many Ways to Pronounce* Japanese does have many ways to pronounce the same character. The underlined part is the character's pronunciation in the given word. Eg. 男 = *otoko* (man)   男児 = *danji* (boy-child)   男色 =

nanshoku (male-color=homosexual love);   女 = *onna* (woman)   女子 = *joshi* (woman and children, dependents)   女房 = *nyôbô* ((one's) wife). Two or three ways is average, four or five is not uncommon and some enjoy even more possibilities!

4. *Too Much Study Makes Jack a Dull Boy?* Bacon's hypothesis was repeated as soon as Japan's victory over Russia was forgotten and looking down on the Japanese resumed. Dower, analyzing the ridiculous under-estimation of Japanese ability just before World War II, quotes an English Naval attaché in Tokyo who claimed Japanese had "peculiarly slow brains . . . due to the strain put on the child's brain in learning some 6,000 Chinese characters before any real education can start." (D:WWM) Could we say "our" prejudice against hard study came to the aid of our prejudice against "them?"

~~~~~~

10-3   We write across, from the left-hand to the right;
Nós escrevemos ao través, da mão esqerda pera a dereita;

> They do so vertically and always from the right-hand to the left.
> *Elles ao comprido, e sempre da mão dereita pera a esqerda.*

On January 14, 1549, Xavier wrote John III, King of Portugal about this very matter.

I send you the Japanese characters. The Japanese write in a very different manner from other nations, beginning at the top of the page and writing downwards to the bottom. I asked Paul the Japanese why they did not write as we do? "Why, rather" said he, "do not you write as we do? The head of a man is at the top and his feet at the bottom, and so it is proper that when men write it should be straight down from top to bottom. I also send you an account of Japan . . . (C:LLFX – For a modern translation, see "Head to Foot," in C:TCJ. It begins: "I am sending you a copy of the Japanese alphabet . . .")

Paul, who is mentioned in the letter, was one of three Japanese youth who came with Xavier from Malacca to spent time with him in the College at Goa, where he became "quite well instructed in the Christian doctrine." (Reading his "Account of Japan," we find Xavier gained a tremendous amount of information on the nation before going there.)   There is a Japanese saying that "the writing is the man" (*bun-wa hito nari*, "the style is the man" is the loose – and in a broad sense correct – translation) which makes Pablo Japan's head-to-foot metaphor work better in Japanese.

Acosta, in his *Historie of the Indies*, has a remarkably collected paragraph-length chapter on *the direction of writing*, which ends on this fine relative note: "To conclude, we finde foure different kindes of writings, some writte from the right to the left, others from the left to the right, some from the toppe to the bottome and others from the foote to the toppe, wherein wee may discover the diversity of mans iudgement." (A:NMH) It includes a *reason* for vertical writing:

> The *Chinois* write neither like the Greeks [left to right] nor like the Hebrews [right to left], but from the toppe to the bottome, for as they be no letters but whole wordes, and that every character signifieth a thing, they have no neede to assemble the parts one with an other, and therefore they may well write from the toppe to the bottome. Those of *Mexico,* for the same cause did not write in line, from one side to another, but contrarie to the *Chinois,* beginning below, they mounted vpward. (Ibid 1604)

I do not get Acosta's reasoning. Why should parts that assemble do so horizontally but not vertically? Japanese "assemble" their combination of syllabet and character in a manner far more liquid than our most flowing script and they do so vertically. For that matter, Japanese also write horizontally, left to right, as we do, and horizontally right to left on some Buddhist plaques (names of temples) and, most visibly, on the right-side of a moving vehicle so the writing flows from the front to the back on the right side of the vehicle as well as the left! I find the variety of directions stimulating and, after returning to the Occident after twenty years in Japan sometimes feel how a person used to a color TV might feel having to go back to black and white. To me, horizontal alone is a terrible *bore.*

If we narrow our focus, looking at the components of the words, we may note that both Chinese characters and the Japanese syllabets are individually written from the upper-left to the lower-right. For this reason, ideally, vertical lines should flow from *left to right* rather than *right to left* as is, indeed, the most common practice. Unfortunately a technical reason – try writing vertically on top of a scroll of writing paper held in the left hand while pulling it open toward the right – made this happen. I find it a shame because it means that books of mixed horizontal English footnotes and vertical Japanese text do not work well. There is one interesting reversal corollary to contrast 10-3. Speed-readers, alone, read like their antipode! To wit:

> *With us, a fast reader skims pages of horizontal text vertically,*
> *With them, vertical text is skimmed horizontally.*

~~~~~~

10-4   Where the last pages of our books are,   *Onde as derradeiras folhas dos nossos libros*

Theirs begin. *Ali começão os seus.*

If it were not for the unfortunate reversal mentioned above, this difference, at least, would not have been and what Acosta wrote about Hebrew:

> The Hebrewes contrariwise beganne at the right to the left, and therefore their bookes beganne where ours did end.

– would be equally true for Japanese, for the direction of a book follows that of the lines. When Japanese write books in horizontal lines (often done for books including many quotations from Western languages, mathematical equations and anything else horizontal), the front and the back of the book are the same as ours. But such books were not found in Frois's time. There is, moreover, one more difference associated with the direction we read. *Faux Frois:*

> *Europeans tend to turn pages from the top;*
> *Japanese from the bottom.*

While I had once drawn my hands moving to turn the pages of a book for what might be called a *meta*-flipbook, I failed to notice that reading direction changed the way we flip the pages of our books, until I read a book [1] by a Japanese friend, editions Papyrus editor Tsurugaya Shinichi, where he writes that he first noticed the difference from a painting of a French girl reading by the Japanese painter Kuroda Seiki, then confirmed it watching an unwitting Occidental working with him, . . . *me!* I tended to turn pages from the upper right hand corner, or "heaven/sky" in the language of Japanese printers (In my case, actually, it depends on the size of the book and my reading position; but my right index finger-tip does generally touch the upper part of the page), and further investigation made it a certainty. Tsurugaya notes it comes naturally from the direction we turn. (I would add, *coupled with our handedness* – left-handed readers in our respective cultures should tend to turn pages like right-handed readers in our antipodes.) And he surmises the different movement and position of our fingers helps explain the tendency for the chapter or book-title to be written on the head of the pages in Western books and the foot of the pages in Japanese books.

1. *Reading Book Sheep Lose* Adding the extra information English demands to the title of Tsurugaya's book we get "Reading a book, I Lost My Sheep" or "Reading a Book You lose Your Sheep" or "Reading Books, We Lose Our Sheep." His allusion is toward the classical Chinese story attributed to Laotse and summed up in four characters: 読書失羊, which he explains in the postscript both illustrates how deeply we can be absorbed in our reading and that we can lose sight of other things by doing so (i.e., friends, if I have neglected you while writing this book, pardon). Before reading the postscript, I thought of Socrates, who, on being asked why he did not compose books, gave this reply: "I do not transfer knowledge from the living hearts of men to the dead hides of sheep." Yes, now a book like this one requires the sacrifice of trees and sleep, but no sheep.

10-5 We hold printing in high regard;
Nós temos ha impresão por cousa singular[1];

> They almost always use manual script because their printing is worthless. *Elles*
> *quasi em tudo uzão da escritura da mão, porque a sua impresão não presta.*

Block-printing in Japan went back about 800 years, and I would bet Japan had far more books per capita than any country in Europe (anyone?). Moveable type, which Gutenberg had reinvented in Europe, had also come over from Korea, but it was rarely used and Frois doubtless has in mind the wood-blocks that were carved individually by hand. The *escritura* is a problem for it is hard to say if he means the hand-written style of the wood-block printed pages or manual copying. Because of the volume of printed books available in Japan, I assume he means the first. But it was not an either-or thing. The French translation improves Frois on the second half of the distiche by turning it into a matter of degree: "because print is not worth as much as script" (*car leur imprimerie ne se prête pas à leur écriture*). Rodrigues described Japan wood-block printing in detail:

First of all, they take a sheet of paper the same size as the proposed book and carefully write on it in the desired style, with the required number of lines, spaces and everything else. Then they glue this sheet face down on the block and with great skill cut away the blank paper, leaving only the blank letters . . . They then carve these letters on the block with iron instruments . . . They are so dexterous in this art that they can cut a block in about the same time that we can compose a page. (in C:TCJ)

Considering the fact that pulling out type from among thousands of choices would take more time than choosing from 22 (or 44 if we include our capital letters), speed might have been a major reason Japanese did *not* prefer moveable type! As Rodrigues suggests, it might have been as fast to carve blocks as set type. But I feel aesthetics was probably most important. If Japanese found crisp, clear print-style lettering beneath them, they would not have been as respectful of printing, which was accompanied by a print-style of letter the aesthetics of which was largely expended on the first letter of the chapter. Did Japanese insist upon aesthetically pleasing script [2] which literally *flowed* from letter to letter in ways not easily broken up into type? (depending which letter came next and the space available a different link would be needed). Or, is it more a matter of illustrations? Much if not most Japanese writing flowed organically about the contours (not rectangular, but of the figures) of the pictures and that, too, might have prevented the early adoption of the type.

1. *Cousa Singular* I wonder if a more literal reading of this "high regard" as a "singular thing," combined with the contrast with Japanese usage of script might mean that Europeans found the printed type attractive and worthy.

2. *Aesthetically Pleasing Script.* While I do appreciate that some types read and look better than others and respect our great type designs, I feel it is a much more limited art than what Japanese allows. And, to be honest, I do not care at all for our calligraphy. Of course I enjoy illuminated manuscript, where single letters may be turned into folk-art paintings. But calligraphy proper is all curlicues and other cute stuff. It lacks the body and soul of the Chinese, Korean and Japanese writing which is not mere *calli*, or "beauty" (that is shallow, like the face of a model) but worthy of the name *Way of Writing* that produces true art and beauty as deep and satisfying as a great painting or sculpture. (After writing this, I found

the following in Chamberlain's *Things Japanese*:

> Japanese calligraphy is artistic. Above all, it is bold, because it comes from the shoulder instead of merely from the wrist. A little experience will convince anyone that, in comparison with it, the freest, boldest English hand is little better than the cramped scribble of some rheumatic crone."

I do not agree with all his details, but the spirit is right. Chamberlain adds that considering the high esteem in which writing is held in Japan, it "seems odd" that "the signature should not occupy the same important place in this country [he lived and wrote in Japan] as it does in the West." Is it not possible that with the artistic instinct satisfied in *all the writing* the Japanese had no *need* to confine it to the one item which allows us to be creative, the signature?

～～～～～～～～～～～～～～～～～～～～～～～～～～～～～～～～～～～～～～

10-6   We write with pens of geese and birds [crows?];
Nós escrevemos com penas de pato ou de aves [de corvos?];

> They use brushes like those of an artist made of the hair of horse and rabbit on a bamboo handle. *Elles com pinceis de pintores feitos de cabelos de lebre e o cabo de cana.*

In Frois's time, a pen (penne/pennis/etc.) in English was a feather ("the rauen wyll not gyue his blacke pennes for the pecockes paynted fethers"), a flight-feather (pinion), a short, rudimentary feather, the quill or barrel of a feather, a quill-like pipe, a quill shaped like a spoon for taking snuff, the internal feather-like shell of squid, the midrib of a leaf . . . It is described by the OED as "a quill feather or part of one, with the quill or barrel pointed and split into two nibs at its lower end, so as to form an instrument for writing." A 1748 usage example from a letter of Lady Luxburough to Shenstone includes "A curse against crow-pens!" This suggests that Father Schütte's guess of *corvos* for an illegible word is correct. Doubtless, other birds were also used. The Japanese animals named are, likewise, only a small sampling of the menagerie called upon to give their hair for what was a far more versatile instrument:

As for the brush (. . .), it has its gestures, as if it were the finger,; but whereas our old pens [1] knew only clogging or loosening and could only, moreover, scratch the paper always in the same direction, the brush can slide, twist, lift off, the stroke being made, so to speak, in the volume of the air; it has the carnal, lubrified flexibility of the hand. (B:EOS)

Barthes aside, most of us feel the brush is a crude, inefficient way to write; but the physical and aesthetic satisfaction of the brush far exceeds that of the pen, an instrument that originated for the purpose of cutting rather than covering a surface (our quills resembling the *stylus* used to cut into clay tablets).   The lifelong mastery of characters (10-2, above), for the large part, was not memorization of characters – which really doesn't take *that* long – but *learning to write characters in many different styles,* styles far more different from each other than our printing and cursive, for some are closer to short-hand.   Practicing this as an art was tremendously satisfying in itself.

1. *Our* Old *Pens?* Why "old" pens? Barthes meant our pens prior to a certain new variety that had been introduced only shortly before he wrote the *Empire of Signs* and which was all the rage among "our" literate. I can still recall how excited my mother (a writer) was when she got her first one.   Reader, can you guess?

Barthes: "The ____-_____ pen, of Japanese origin, has taken up where the brush leaves off: this style is not an improvement of the point, itself the product of the pen (of steel or of cartilage), its immediate ancestry is that of the ideogram." (B:EOS)   The answer: "felt-tipped pen." *Do not ask me what the last part of Barthes' sentence means!*

~~~~~~

10-7   Our ink is liquid;
            A nossa tinta hé liqida;

            Theirs a bar which they grind when they [would] write.
            A sua hé em pãis e moe-se quando se escreve.

This *liquid* vs. *solid* difference goes back several millennia.   Both the ancient Egyptians and the ancient Chinese burnt vegetable oils for bases of their ink,[1] but the former kept the result suspended in *liquid* while the later kept it in a *solidified* form (*Why the difference? Can a chemist explain?*).

Japanese ink, or *sumi,* is usually made by the writer, who grinds the bar on the tool Frois roughly describes in his *next* contrast, thus maintaining control over the dilution of the ink. Sometimes servants, wives or children did the grinding. (I once observed a top landscape painter in Korea fast at work – a brush between each finger! – as his daughter ground his paints just fast enough to keep ahead of him). The pigment is amazingly concentrated.   Although I have never measured it, nor have I seen it sold with the promise to make so many liters of ink, my impression is that one ink-stick the size of a small candy-bar makes gallons of ink and one is more likely to lose the stick than to ever use it up.   Rodrigues writes that "the best kind is made from the smoke of sesame oil . . . which adheres to a vessel, and from this they make paste." These, then, are stamped with information, fine names and "decorated with various flowers, serpents and figures from legends . . . they add some musk while making the best sort so that it will smell sweetly when they write with it."   Some were "small, others long and others round in standard shapes" (R(C):TIJ).   Sometimes gold powder was mixed in the ink-stick.   And, more rarely, the entire stick was molded into something. (A *sumi-e* painter to whom I mailed a real cicada sprayed gold sent me in return an ink bar resembling a cicada, covered with a light gilt!)

Morse, described the process of making the ink down to the water vessel "with two minute openings, one of which you cover with your finger, thus checking the flow of water from the other opening." Valignano and Frois, both of whom were well aware of Occidentals having trouble with controlling their emotions might have enjoyed his comment:

If one is in a rage and is inclined to dash off an angry letter, he has sufficient time to cool off in getting ready to write it. (M:JDD)

Japanese did not have other ready writing instruments such as pencils, crayons or chalk either. Poets, carpenters, doctors, artists – whoever had to be ready to jot down a few simple characters or a sketch on the spur of the moment – had to have ink ready.   For this they had portable equipment called *yatate*. A tube decorated with an "infinite" variety of designs held a small writing brush, "and attached to the top at right angles, is a receptacle for a wad of cotton saturated with fluid ink." (ibid) But, there was not enough ink for an honest-to-goodness letter.

Today, people who like traditional writing instruments but are too lazy to grind ink may buy it ready-made in bottles. And, if that is still too inconvenient – for an inkstone ramp (see below) is still needed to wipe the brush – there are brushes with squeezable rubber handles full of ink (some replaceable, some throw-away) , i.e., fountain-*brushes* rather than fountain-pens!

1. The English "Ink."   Etymologically speaking, *Ink* comes from én-kaustós, or "burn-in" (Greek), but it was first used to refer to a particular ink that was purple!   Considering the subject matter, it would have been perfect for Martial's prose.

10-8   Our inkwells are made of horn and round; *Os nossos tinteiros são de corno, redondos.*

Theirs of slabs of stone. *Os seus de pedra comprida.*

In English, an inkwell used to be called an "inkhorn." Containers meant not only to be dipped into but to keep ink are, naturally, deep.

The adjective *comprida* ("long and thin") that modifies "stone" in the original I turned to "slabs," which are, in Rodrigues's words, of "suitable smooth marmoreal stone" (R(C):TIJ) and are usually rectangular, oval, or in-between and are, perhaps, ten times longer than deep.

They have a raised rim around the edge and a reservoir in the middle where the ink is ground. At one end, of this there is a small well, gracefully carved, wherein they pour the water with which the ink is mixed . . . This is rather like the stone or palette in which artists prepare and mix the colours that they use in painting. (Ibid.)

The most magnificent inkstand I know turns that small well into a grotto-like reservoir with the elixir of immortality from the Other World below the cosmic Mt. Feng-lai depicted with its three peaks, themselves part of a stylized wave-like pattern on the broad lip of the stone. Today, most inkstands have no separate well *per se,* but a graduated slope, resembling a boat-launching ramp.

10-9   Our inkwells come with lids and quill wipers; *Os nossos tinteiros tem cubertura e poidouros;*

Those of Japan do not. *Os de Japão nada disto.*

This is because, as mentioned already, our inkwells were also for keeping ink, whereas theirs were enlisted anew each time and the last of the ink dumped (or sucked up by the ink sprite captured in detail by the crystal-clear mind's eye of blind Borges).

But Japanese were not lacking in accessories as such a contrast might suggest. As Rodrigues

notes, they "place all their writing instruments in a beautiful lacquered box made for that purpose."
(Read Cooper's translation of Rodrigues: *This Island of Japan* – I dare not quote more here!)

10-10   Our papers are of only four or five varieties;   *Os nosso papel hé de 4 ou sinco layas somente;*

>   Those of Japan surpass fifty.   *O de Japão pasa de sincoenta.*

The Europeans were paper-poor, the Japanese, as part of the Chinese cultural sphere, were paper-rich. (In China, Marco Polo was amazed to find *even money was paper*, "made from bark collected from mulberry trees on whose leaves the silk worms feed," and that "throughout the empire this paper money is used in every transaction." The way the Great Khan's mint functioned, "might lead one to suppose that the Khan had mastered the art of alchemy."(*Oops*, I see Polo is not in my bibliography! Well, I promise I did not invent this!)

In Japan, paper was made from dozens of plants. There were probably more varieties of tissue paper alone than Europe had varieties of all paper. Alcock about 1860 mentioned "an infinite variety of paper" and sent sixty-seven different kinds to the [London? Paris?] Exhibition. (A:COT) I doubt that "we" will *ever* catch up!

10-11   We use only the mark of a notary public for official documents;
Nós em as escrituras publicas somente uzamos do sinal de tabalião publico;

>   The Japanese, besides their signatures, each make their own marks on their letters.
>   *Os Japões, alem do nome, cada hum faz seu partiqular sinal em suas cartas.*

Reading about 15th or 16th century notary publics, I think of the old adage about the pen being mightier than the sword. If I am not mistaken, the notary public not only attested to the fact that someone swore something was the truth, but supplied the documents that themselves served in the capacity of those that today come from law offices and courts. In other words, the notary was also a sort of lawyer if not judge and in that capacity generally grew very wealthy (for this reason, a Royal appointment was very expensive) – the person who bought himself the most posthumous masses (11,038 in 1595) in La Mancha, Vicar M Juan de Viana, was an inquisition notary reporter. As "reporter," this "all-purpose scribe and contract lawyer" (LR) was sent all over by the Crown to take testimony and make official what would otherwise be hearsay. It was as important for a town to have a notary as a priest, for until the notary wrote it down *nothing happened*, officially speaking.[1] One might say that the notary had as much power to establish the truth for *this* world as the priest had with respect to the *next*. How all this ever got started, I have no idea, but ours was a society of truth-swearing and litigation, two things that seem to go together.

The existence or non-existence of the notary public himself might have made a contrast, for while Japanese had civil magistrates in charge of various affairs, there was no exact equivalent in Japan and still is not today. (When something was sent to me in Japan from the States that needed a Notary Public, I ended up having to go to the US Embassy for one of "ours.")

The Japanese *sinal* (sign/mark/signature) in this case would mean a personal seal, something like what we have all seen stamped on prints and paintings, but generally larger and more script-like and was called a kaô or "flower-stamp/chop." Documents could be signed and stamped (just below the signature), or just stamped, but they were seldom just signed. Rodrigues wrote that the *Chinese* stamps sometimes even gave the rank of its owner in the royal household and that the seal was *everything* to a magistrate, for it was his "stamp of office," and nothing they did had validity without it. To lose it was to lose one's office, and "they are accustomed to having this seal carried in front of them in a chest slung from a pole borne by two men, and they cover it with a sunshade of yellow silk out of reverence for the king whom it represents." (R(C):TIJ) In Japan, it never went *that* far, but Rodrigues couldn't help mentioning it anyway, and neither can I!

1. *Notarizing Reality*. Notaries as well as priests accompanied the conquistadors to the New World, where their role, to hear it told in retrospect, is risible. James M. O'Toole tells it far too well for me to put it in my words:

> Picture this scene. A conquering army is proceeding inland from its fleet off shore, "in the face of the enemy." Encamped with his men before the first fortified town he hopes to reduce, the commander makes the appropriate military plans, sending a detachment around to attack from the rear while he leads the assault from the front. Before the battle begins, however, he conducts a strange ritual. An interpreter who can speak the language of the badly outnumbered townspeople stands in front of the troops and, in a loud voice and "lofty tone," he shouts out a proclamation to the opposing camp, telling them "that if blood were spilt, the sin would lie on their heads, and that resistance would be useless." The attempt to shift blame from the attackers to the defenders is common enough, and it meets the expected response of "shouts of defiance and a shower of arrows" from the opposing forces, who have probably understood little of what the orator has said in his broken dialect. But then, an even stranger thing happens. The commander causes the proclamation to be written down – duly recorded" – and a notary, who is traveling with the army precisely for this purpose, attests to the fact that the proclamation has been delivered and recorded in the proper form. Only now can the battle begin, and the town is quickly over-run.* (*Cortes's Notary: The Cultural Meanings of Record Making* Research Libraries Group 1999 Annual Membership Meeting *O'Toole cites Prescott: 1843)

After the victory, the declaration of possession was likewise notarized so Cortez could lay "fair claim" on the town of Tabasco. O'Toole notes that it is dubious Cortez thought the testimony would ever be needed – for who would contest the legitimacy? – but that "rather, the act of record-making here was important in and of itself, serving to legitimize in the eyes of the participants what had happened." Also, it bears noting that "the testimony of another soldier or even a priest was insufficient to establish that the legal requirements had been fulfilled." (He cites Richard Lee Marks: 1993 on this). *So the pen is not only stronger than the sword but stronger than the cross.*

10-12 With us, the mark of the notary public never changes;
Antre nós o sinal do tabalião publico nunca se muda;

In Japan, they change marks whenever they want to.
Em Japão se mudão estes sinais cada vez que hum quer.

Again, since there were no notary publics in Japan, and it is hard to know exactly what and how many Japanese are "they." Anyone big enough to have a chop with clout, I guess. With us, I assume the same thing could be said for our signature. In general, it is assumed to remain the same for life. That was definitely not the case with Japanese chops, which were changed when they were promoted, as might be expected because they often changed their names at the same time, and because they generally had more than one seal at a time, they could use different combinations for different letters. Okada guessed that great men had an average of about twenty "official" chops (fancy kaô,, literally *flower-stamp*) over the course of their lives.

10-13 With us, all paper is made from rags; *Antre nós todo papel se faz de pedaços de pano velhos.*

In Japan, all is made from tree bark. *Em Japão todo se faz de cascas de arvores.*

Since there are far more types of trees than clothing, this might help explain why Japanese enjoyed so many more types of paper than "we" did. Frois's "trees" here, must include some shrubs, for hemp paper was well known. Alcock adds more detail:

> Nearly all the paper in Japan is made from the bark of trees, and in some qualities it is superior to any in Europe, more especially as regards toughness. Even the fine kinds can only be torn with difficulty, and the stronger qualities defy every effort. Indeed it supplies the place of linen and cambric . . . They are not unacquainted with the process of manufacturing paper from cotton rags – indeed, I believe they would make paper out of old shoes – but the former are little used, because *the bark is preferred.* (my *italics* A:COT)

Alcock goes on to mention enterprising foreigners taking advantage of this by buying Japanese rags, which, before long, rose in price.

~~~~~~

10-14   With our letters, we cannot fully express our ideas but through long explanations;
As nossas cartas não podem manifestar os conceytos senão por grande leitura;

Those of Japan are extremely short yet very comprehensive.
As de Japão são brevissimas e muito compendiozas.

After citing this item, Cooper could not resist quipping: "Frois is certainly speaking from experience as regards the first part of this observation, for some of his letters in *Cartas* are enormously long." (C:TCJ) But Cooper knows well that the contrast had more general validity, for he also included a selection from Francois Caron (1600-73), a French born employee of the Dutch East-India Company. Caron writes that the style of writing described in the second part of Frois's observation is common to Chineses, Japanners, Correes and Torquains[?].

> A man that can contract much matter into a few lines, and intelligible, which is that which they all practice, is greatly esteemed amongst them; for such they employ to write their Letters, Petitions and the like to great persons; and truely it is admirable to see how full of substance, and with how few words these sort of writing is penned. (C:TCJ)

We would seem to be talking, then, about the telegraphic Chinese style of writing used by men. Women in Japan often used a style that was every bit as prolix as "ours."

~~~~~~

10-15   With us, writing between the lines would be uncouth[1];
Antre nós escrever antre as regras seria mao insino;

In Japan, they always *waza-to* [on purpose][2] write between the lines.
Nas cartas de Japão vaza to se escreve sempre antre as regras.

While an unglossed manuscript was considered green in the Medieval West – supposedly, some scribbled glosses on their own new manuscripts to make them seem respectable – these kept to the margins of the paper. Not so in Japan. Okada mentions a number of types of recognized *gyôkan-gaki,* or "line-between-writing" in Japan. There is the *otte-gaki,* or "chasing-writing" something like our postscript.; the *kaeshi-gaki* or "return writing," where one person's letter is returned with the reply between the lines – this one *exactly what many of us now do with our e-mail!* – the *nao-nao-*

gaki, or "this-too-this-too-writing," which simply adds more detail, . . .   And, I would add, last minute additions, for I have occasionally seen such squeezed between the lines of books printed in the nineteenth century!

If I had not read Okada's notes, I probably would have mistaken this writing between the lines for the use of phonetic syllabary written small, next to Chinese characters (*i.e.,* between the lines) to supply their pronunciation in the case of hard-to-read names, unique usage, or for the sake of poor readers, in which case they may be placed by all *kanji.* These wonderful little trainer-wheels, called *furigana,* which permit one to play with Chinese characters (a godsend for punsters) have reaped scornful comment from the West: "One hesitates for an epithet to describe a system of writing which is so complex that it needs the aid of another system to explain it." writes the historian Sansom in 1928 (in Unger:*5th Generation Fallacy*) *and,* from the East.   The novelist turned pedagogue Yamamoto Yuzo wrote:

> I doubt there is any other language that cannot be understood unless you use two lines at once to write it out . . . I envision a procession of black bugs. Why do we have to allow those disgusting bugs to crawl around the sides of our sentences." (found in Inoue Hisashi's *Shiban Bunpô,* maybe)

1. *Translation.* I think I owe the "uncouth" to DR. Thanks. It is better than "bad training" or whatever I had.
2. *Translation*. Yet another *vaza to!* Maybe someone could count up the *vaza to* and *vaza vaza* in this book! Note how it is always applied to the Japanese to emphasize that their contrariness is no accident.

10-16 Our letters are folded;   *As nossas cartas vão dobradas;*

        Japanese ones, rolled up. *As dos Japões emroladas.*

While Japanese are big on *origami,* or "fold-paper" art, letters were generally not folded. It is hard to say why rolls were preferred. Could the availability of strong yet cheap tubes in the form of bamboo have been a factor? Was there a feeling that it was not good to put lines in letters, breaking up the smooth flow of thought? Or was there a problem with the very idea of folding because of homophonic bad-luck associations? [1]   When Japan began to modernize and send mail by the packet, the old style letter boxes big enough to fit a number of rolls were abandoned as too bulky and letters which were written on paper attached to a roll, "were torn off, [loosely] wound up again, flattened by smoothing with the hand, and slid into a long, narrow envelope" (Morse:JDD) and tossed in a bag, I guess.

1. *Bad-luck Folds.* A letter simply doubled doesn't look good, one folded in three had inauspicious associations of folding and cutting the human body (*mi*=three&=body, fold=cut) and one folded four (*shi*=four=death) times suggested capital punishment, etc. so was rolling up the letter less hassle? I ask this half in humor. Chances are that people who were used to writing on rolls of paper just thought it natural to un/scroll letters.

[10-16a] We give the year in which we write a letter;
    Antre nós se põe a era em que se escreve;

        The Japanese only the day of the month when it is sent.
        Os Japões o dia somente da lua em que se manda.

Frois forgot to number this one that was evidently squeezed in.[1] The "year" is my figurative translation of *era,* in the original. For the Jesuits, spread out around the world, where letters took years – sometimes decades – to reach their destinations, the year was an essential element of dating. In Japan, letters arrived within hours or at most days from the time they were mailed. For them, the day would be sufficient. But, most European letters also presumably did not need a month, much less the year. Did Christians desiring to be perpetually reminded of their "Savior," *particularly enjoy writing the year,* and having written it, added the month, so that full dating became habitual? Formal Japanese letters were, of course, dated.

1. *Numbering Problem.* The French translators simply turn 16a into 17 and 17 into 18 and so forth, so the chapter ends up with 30 rather than 29 items. This shows an interesting problem which Frois would have faced had revised Tratado. 10-16a should have become 10-17 and 10-17, 10-17a, for contrasting eras is a spin-off of the dating of letters which is more properly the subject of the chapter. Frois put many of his spin-offs into the miscellany of chapter 14, but he must have felt tempted to put them in the other chapters next to the spawning contrast. Be that as it may, I have no idea whether Schütte included the 10-16a in his count of 611 and do not care enough to do any addition. *If anyone would care to count up all the contrasts* (mine and others) *in the book . . .*

~~~~~~

10-17   The christian era never changes from the birth of Christ until the end of the world;
A era dos christãos nunca se altera do nacimento de Christo até o fim do mundo;

Eras in Japan change six or 7 times in the lifetime of a king.
A era de Japão se muda seis e 7 vezes na vida de hum rey

In Japan, the years went back to *Start,* Year One, whenever an Emperor died and a new reign began, secular rule changed, major policy changes were made, a major disaster occurred (i.e. for the sake of better luck!), etc.. The official right to change the era rested with the Emperor, but the power often rested with someone else. If people could change *their* names at appropriate junctures in their life, why couldn't *Time,* the years, months and days Bashô was soon to call "our fellow travelers," do likewise? Still, the changes were occasionally too frequent. In the six decades before the TRATADO was written we find new eras beginning in 1521, 28, 32, 55, 58, 70 and 73. And just before the Meiji Reformation (1868), we find eras beginning in 1844, 48, 54, 60, 61, 64 and 65. This *is* ridiculous. In 1869, the *gengo* system was modified so that the era would only change with the inauguration of a new Emperor (which was used as a separate parallel system (the *dai*), anyway). Journalist Patrick Smith writes,

> Today it lingers uselessly on, too small a matter to be more than occasionally irksome, for one simple reason: Those who govern Japan prefer to keep it. It is one more reminder to the Japanese that they must regard themselves as different from others, a nation apart and all the same under their shared timekeeper, the emperor. (*JAPAN – A Reinterpretation*: 1997)

I beg to disagree. Many, I think most, Japanese *prefer* to keep it. *I* prefer they keep it, if for nothing else to remind the world that Christianity is *not* "different from the others", and there is more than one way of marking time. With the short-run calendar, for example, "our" year 2004 is Heisei 16. The Japanese newspapers generally put both year dates on the top of each page. I guess the double dating is wasteful, *but so what?* The biggest difficulty, true inconvenience, concerns the long run – even most Japanese have to use Christian dating to keep track of when was when back then, for some sort of perpetual calendar is needed. Even, here, however, there are advantages to the Japanese system, for there are all sorts of eras within eras and varieties of eras and whatnot that make a sort of verbal Venn diagram of Japanese history which, I think, is useful for the more studious part of the population. Unfortunately, it is not ideal for world-history . . .

Despite these constant return-to-start eras, I do not think Japanese were cyclic in their long-term concept of time. This is obvious from a classic poem that hopes a lord's realm will last for ages while *pebbles grow into mossy boulders* (the growing pebbles may have originated from reference to coral).[1]   I do not know exactly who settled on the zero year for Japan and how it was done [2]   but calculating back to the ascension of the first Emperor using the ancient Chronicles and bears a resemblance to "our" calculating the age of the earth by taking the begats back to Adam and, then, going further.   All I know is that on New Years Day of Meiji 26 (1894?) young Shiki (proud of his samurai past and one of the last to cut his hair) wrote: "origin two-thousand five-hundred fifty three year's spring," which is supposed to be a haiku and maybe is because he was the father of modern haiku.   With a bit of poetic license we have:

nippon banzai!

upspring the year!
two-thousand five-hundred fifty
three years here!

kigen ni-sen go-hyaku go-ju-san nen-no-haru

So long as most of the world uses Christian dating, the Japanese do well to use it, too.   But this is no reason to give up their *gengo* system. In culture-ecology, too, diversity has value of its own. At the very least, we from cultures that have long used the Christian era, should not take for granted the accident called history that has made ours the *de facto* World Calendar. We should feel a touch of *regret* for the cultural sacrifice we force others to make and apologize for it sometimes. Others are conscious of our unintended cultural aggression. When, in 1634, the Dutch (who had disclaimed religious affiliation the better to press their trade) were ordered out of Hirado to join the Portuguese on Dejima, a tiny fan-shaped island (supposedly fan-shaped because the ruler had a fan in his hand when asked about the shape) just off Nagasaki, built artificially only seven years earlier, it was the Christian era that provided the pretext for the crackdown:

> His Imperial Majesty is certainly informed that you Hollanders are all Christians like the Portuguese. You keep Sunday; you write the date of Christ's birth over the doors and on the tops of your houses, in the sight of everyone in our land. . . .   We have known long since that you were Christians, but we though that yours was another Christ.   For these reasons his Majesty orders you, through me, to demolish forthwith all your dwellings which bear the above-mentioned date (without exceptions), beginning with the latest built, on the north side and so on till the end. (in intro to C:MKJS)

At any rate, I do not begrudge the Japanese their double dating, and only wish they *also* kept their lunar calendar, where every day told us something about the moon and vice versa! [3]   I feel more comfortable reading letters or diary entries written hundreds of years ago when I know whether they were written under a new moon or a full one than more recent ones where such information is lacking.

---

1. *Pebbles That Grow*.   The poem in question, from the *Kokinshû*, became the basis for the *Kimi ga Yo*, the national anthem of Japan.   It was one of many poems introduced in the first survey of Japanese poetry ever made by João Rodrigues.   It was in his huge *Arte da Lingoa de Iapam* (1604?) and translated into English by Michael Cooper ("The Muse Described: Joao Rodrigues' Account of Japanese Poetry" *Monumenta Nipponica*, Vol.26, No.1/2 (1971), 55-75).   Cooper notes that "nothing comparable was produced until Western scholars, such as Chamberlain and W.G. Aston, began writing on the subject in the Meiji Period."

2. *Zero Year Calculations*.   In *Rise, Ye Sea Slugs!* I have already sampled the rather comical debate on dating ancient "history" in Japan.   But I did not pin down the official one.   Anyone?

3. *Lunar Calendar*.   Here, we should be more aware of the Islamic Calendar.   I recall seeing the crescent moon at high-noon on the day the World Trade Center was destroyed.   And what was the date on *their* calendar? *Do you know?*   The Islamic calendar is a pure lunar calendar, for it does not keep a New Year in any season.   To my mind, a pure lunar calendar is a bad idea for it fails to keep account of the reality of the solar, or seasonal year (one might say, it reflects a culture that fails to appreciate the ecology of the natural world), whereas a purely solar year is bad because it ignores the moon entirely (one might say it reflects a culture that fails to appreciate culture, which includes history, and aesthetics).   In my opinion, *we need to revive the mixed calendar.*

10-18   Our letters are sent sealed with wax or lacquer;
As nossas cartas vão mutradas com sera ou com lachre;

Those of Japan have a little ink put on the flap.
Nas de Japão se põe huma pequena de tinta sobre a cha[ncela?]

Another way to have translated *sera* and *lachre* would have been "bee's wax and sealing wax." The latter, by Frois's time, may have been "a mixture of shellac, rosin and turpentine, prepared for the purpose of receiving the impression of seals." (OED)

Japanese actually had more ways of sealing letters than Europeans did. Okada mentions "glue-sealing, twist-sealing, knot-sealing, cut-sealing, fold-sealing and so forth". But they did not drop and stamp warm sealing wax. A symbolic closure was achieved by making an ink mark: either an initial, a diagonal line or a diagonal line with a small line crossing it to make a sign resembling the syllabet *me* (✗), which stood for "*shime*" or "closed=tight=done," in such a manner that half is on the flap and half on the envelope. Today, it is common to stamp or initial documents in the same way, with the mark crossing the divide to make what is, to use printing terms, a registration mark. Here is a large version of the *shime:*

Let me add a contemporary difference in what computer software allows in English and Japanese.

We type words into our computers and learn if they are spelled right or wrong.
They type words into their computer and are offered many choices none of which are right or wrong.

The *enormous choice* necessary because of the Chinese characters also allows for other symbols. For example, in Japanese it is as easy as pie to type in "pai" and chose to make it Π. Or to type in "manji," the character for a Buddhist temple, and chose: 卍 (the direction is opposite that of the Nazi swastika),[1] or ⎯> and chose → or ⇒ or, better yet, "ue" meaning "above" lets us choose ↑ and "shita" or "below" yields ↓ both of which are very useful for computer discussion boards (bbs's), and "mugen" for unlimited yields us ∞. (If only we were conscious of such possibilities, we could easily do this in English by expanding the *spell-check* function to include choices for certain words. One can also get to a larger cache of symbols by typing in the Japanese for symbols, rather than relying on the "Insert" tab alone. I would give more examples but have no idea if they will all pdf into "real type" so you can see the result! My favorite is the Russian "da" (д): it makes a fine nose for little beasties.)

1. *Swastika Direction.*   A Summer 1974 *Horizon* magazine article on "Alfonso The Learned of Castille" has a period illustration of "Household Finance" that shows a Jewish moneylender. A certain symbol is hung on a little flag on the wall and here is the comment: "Swastikas, pagan symbols of the union of Earth-Mother with God-Father, did not then contrast jarringly with the Stars of David [printed on tapestry]." It was not pointed out that the swastika was the reverse of the Nazi one. It would be nice if we could learn the difference in direction and *keep the good swastika*, as the Japanese have, but I fear we may lack the calm? mental acuity? required to make the distinction. *Well?*

~~~~~~

10-19   Our letters are sent done up in packets;
As nossas se mandão feitas em maços;

Theirs are sent in oblong lacquered boxes made for that purpose.
As suas metidas em humas caxinhas compridas vruxadas feitas pera aquilo.

This is not a description of individual letter coverings but of the way *batches* of letters were transported by the couriers.   Letters in Japan were put into special waterproof containers called *fubako* or *fuminohako* (letter-boxes) rather than simply bundled together.

~~~~~~

10-20   In Europe, paper is beaten flat with an iron mallet upon a smooth stone;
Em Europa batem o papel em plaino com maço de ferro sobre pedra liza;

In Japan, they roll it up on a pole and beat it with two more.
Em Japão o emrolão em um pão redondo e ali o batem com outros dous paus

Ours seems more like making a pizza! Does the *pau redondo* or "round/cylindrical stick" on the Japanese side mean a pole of broad diameter? This contrast evidently concerns one of the last stages of paper-making. Both processes start the same way with the paper-making material soaking in water. I am afraid I never got around to researching this (a gloss on both, anyone?).

~~~~~~

10-21   We wipe ink off our pens upon black clothing;
Nós alimpamos as penas da tinta nos vestidos pretos;

Japanese suck them clean with their mouths.
Os Japões as alimpão chupando-as com a boca.

Here, I first followed Okada, having "us" use a black cloth to wipe off the pens, but after seeing Father Schütte's translation had a rare parenthetical exclamation – the only one I have found, so far – added to his translation thought "Oops!" and, re-reading carefully, saw what was happening! The "black-robes" as Jesuits were sometimes called had found a good use for their vestment. Someone who wrote as much as Frois probably never had to re-dye his robes! [1]

The Japanese side seems just as funny.   Japanese (and Chinese) did and still do put their pens in their mouths. The most common pen-in-the-mouth poems treat the hardship of being a scholar, which is to say, having to chew your icy frozen pen (which says a lot about the temperature of your humble hut) before starting work. Less common in poetry, but more common in reality is this gentle practice as described by poet Tachibana Akemi (1812-68) in his *Poems of Solitary Delights*:

> What a delight it is
> When I find a good brush,
> Steep it hard in water,
> Lick it on my tongue
> And give it its first try.

(trans. Geoffrey Bownas & Anthony Thwaite: *The Penguin Book of Japanese Verse* (1964))

I have my doubts about that penultimate line, but you get the idea. The tip of a new brush is rock-hard, for the hair is given a permanent to hold and show its shape (how the bristles come to a perfect point) and must be soaked into softness. Speaking of *steeping,* the process of breaking in a brush, like the English one of making tea, is delicate and full of details that only matter if you do it. Any post-use sucking that is done is done *after* the ink has pretty well been cleaned off by brushing it dry, and is more to smooth out the hairs and leave the brush with a sharp point again. Little, if any ink is imbibed and it has more to do with perfection of form than cleaning *per se.*

1. *Jesuits Writing.* One could probably fill a book with anecdotes about *writing Jesuits,* for they *wrote* and *wrote* and *wrote.* While their interest in the classic world brought a great awareness of drama and the spoken word, they knew the Renaissance of that world depended entirely on written language, which is to say the efforts of those who wrote. And, they knew that only writing permitted the existence of their world-wide web. So saying, an anecdote about St. Robert Bellarmine, who was saved from starvation during the Seige of Paris of 1590 in which 30,000 died of starvation because the Spanish Ambassador gave him favorite horse :

"Bellarmine wrote with a quill; he used to cheat with that quill, in a way I would not really recommend to any of us. St. Ignatius of Loyola made a wise rule that Jesuits should not work more than two hours straight without taking a little break—get up and stretch, get a cup of coffee, whatever. Bellarmine kept that rule, but in his own way. Every two hours he would flip the pen up and catch it, then keep on writing." (John Patrick Donnelly, S.J. *St. Robert Bellarmine Who Was He? What Can He Teach Us?* www1.bellarmine.edu/strobert/about/lecture.asp)

10-22   We write our letters on desks or tables;
Nós escrevemos nossas cartas sobre mezas ou taboas;

The Japanese write them on the fingers of the left hand.
Os Japões as escrevem sobre os dedos da mão esquerda.

Japanese have very good little desks (see 10-28) and used them to write on sheets of paper or notebooks, but letter writers, as depicted in many prints, generally held a slightly unscrolled roll of paper in their left hand, a brush in their right hand, writing on the convex side of the paper one line at a time with the roll providing the backing. Yet, even with the roll between, the left hand is involved in the writing process. I feel that writing on paper held by hand releases a different, connected sensibility physically, and perhaps mentally, which is not there when we write upon a desk, or the floor, where formal Japanese calligraphy is also done. There, too, we find an important contrast Frois missed:

We rest the butt of our hand upon the paper while we write.
They suspend their hand in the air, writing without support.

The brush is lightly gripped and dangles straight down so we feel it resembles a pendulum with extraordinary liberty. Alice Mabel Bacon notes what this *means* for the Japanese (and, of course, the Chinese):

To write, with a brush dipped in India ink, upon soft paper, the hand entirely without support, is an art that seldom can be acquired by a grown person, but when learned in childhood it gives great deftness in whatever other art may be subsequently studied. This is perhaps the reason why japanese value a good handwriting more highly than any other accomplishment, for it denotes the manual dexterity that is the secret to success in all the arts, and one who writes the Chinese characters well and rapidly can quickly learn to do anything else with the fingers.

I believe she has hit on something extremely important here. Writing might have far more to do with Far Eastern finger-tip finesse than the chop-stick manipulation previously mentioned. I would guess that this skill is like a second language or fiddle-playing, where the top levels of skill require that we start by seven or eight, ten at the latest.[1]

1. ***Memo: If I ever have a child,*** I will try to introduce him or her to writing unsupported as described, as well as: 1) foreign language sounds (mimicking songs from many languages), 2) fiddle playing (Chinese-style, on the hip, and not under the chin, which is wretched), and 3) chopsticks from age 5 or 6. I will also have them beat out nursery rhymes on a pair of small drums so that a variety of poetic rhythms we learn and lose take solid root.

10-23   `We seal [a mistake for "open" ?] our letters with scissors;
Nós fechamos [abrimos?] *nossas cartas com tezouras;*

They [un]seal theirs with knives.
Elles as fechão [abrem?]*com facas*

The original has a mistake. Instead of "open," Frois writes "seal." The knife is a small one with a very sharp tip generally called a *sasuga* (literally "stab-sword"), and they served as what we now call a letter-opener – kept in the writing-box with the inkstone ink-stick, water vessel, etc..

This is similar to 2-68, where the same contrast is made for cutting *thread*. If Japanese now use a scissors for cutting thread, we tend to use a knife (letter-opener) for our letters. As far as the third scissors and knife contrast, 7-15, goes, the contrast is moot for both of us now prefer nail-clippers to scissors *or* knives. Three similar differences and three different outcomes. But, why so many scissors/knife contrasts? Was it perhaps because the scissors were considered to be a mark of new technology and something Japan lacked?

10-24   We scatter sand on our paper; *Nós deitamos area em nosso papel;*

Their ink is instantly absorbed [by the paper]. *No seu logo se a tinta sume.*

Here, the Japanese way sounds familiar, while it is what "we" did that is foreign to most of us!

10-25   Our letters are very small; *A nossa letra hé muito peqenina;*

Theirs are larger than our capital letters. *A sua hé mayor que a nossa de cabidula.*

This was not so much due to our respective letters, as to the different writing devices. Now that brushes are only used for signing art gallery registers and writing old-style New Years greetings, Japanese script is written by ball-point or printed the same size as ours, despite – in the case of characters – holding ten times the visual information! Either their optometrists do much better than ours or they have better eyes.

After writing my first draft of the last paragraph, I saw something that made this contrast far more meaningful to me: one of only two extant copies of Valignano's 1601 *Libro* (V:LIBRO) in the British Library. I knew quill pens wrote well enough for, like everyone else, I had seen pictures of old documents with calligraphy that put my messy writing to shame; but I had never seen anything to prepare me for what I saw that day. *The writing was so small I could barely read it!* The capital letters were smaller than *my* handwritten small letters! Imagine, if you will, a *manuscript* with lettering as small as the print on one of those tiny pocket-books one no longer sees. *The lines were often thinner than that of the finest ballpoint!*

I can understand how Japanese do *their* bold brushwork. But I can not begin to see how *we* did *this!* The human cost must have been tremendous. Presumably, paper, transportation and ink were more important than the eyes and hands of Valignano's scribes. No wonder Frois, who spent most of his life serving as a scribe for his superiors as well as writing a multi-volume history and perhaps the most ample letters ever written, had painful arthritis by the time he was fifty! His hands must have been horribly deformed by the time he died and God knows what condition his eyes were in.

10-26   A stanza of our poems comprises four, six or eight lines;
A sentensa das nossas trovas se inclue em 4, 6 ou 8 regras;

All the songs of Japan comprise two lines, unrhymed.
Todas as cantigas do Japão se incluem em dous versos somente sem consonantia.

The name for Japanese classical verse, *waka,* literally breaks down into "peace=japanese + song" and poets were said to "sing" poetry, rather than to "make" or "write" it (The Chinese character for the verb was different than that used for singing a truly melodic song, however). Frois's use of *cantigas* for Japanese poems apparently reflects knowledge of this. While Japanese poetry, unlike Chinese poetry, did not use *obvious* end-rhyme, it is going too far to say, as Frois does, that there was no *consonancia* ("unrhymed" being a loose translation). There is ample alliteration and not a little internal rhyme which is largely "vowel-rhyme," and can be brought out through parsing. For example, my favorite *Shin-Kokinshu* (c.1205) blast against the Wind, admittedly one of the most clearly rhyming waka I know, *hana chirasu kaze no yadori wa dare ga shiru / ware ni oshieyo yukite uramimu,* may be parsed as follows:

> *hana chirasu kaze no*
>   *yadori wa dare ga shiru*
> *ware ni oshieyo*
>   *yukite uramimu*

We now have an ABAB rhyme-scheme, with some internal rhymes and assonance to boot. For the reader's amusement, my Learical translation[1] :

> pray, tell me
> where to find
> the dwelling place
> of master wind!
> i'll give him
> a piece of my mind
> i will
> that spoiler of flowers
> the wind!

Many old Japanese songs were longer than two lines,[2] but the 5-7-5 / 7-7 (or 17 / 14, because the rhythm of each line varied) syllabet arrangement was typical. Visually speaking, two *vertical* lines, or only one line, as was most common for the 5-7-5 *haiku*, suffice as artwork, whereas an equal number of horizontal lines seem more horizon than object and just do not work. If English were written vertically, I dare say we would have more short poems!

1. *Latin Title, Anyone?* I would love to put a witty Latin   title on the poem. Anyone?

2. *Longer Japanese Poems.* Rodrigues in his fine survey of Japanese poetry done 20 years aftrer Tratado, includes more variety. He mentions the tiny *kouta (small-song)* lines of chanties, Chinese style poetry, which did rhyme, that some wrote using Chinese characters alone, and even the hundred or thousand-line linked verse of *renga* and *haikai,* respectively, where different people write alternative lines, "just like capping verses." (R(C):MD) Obviously, things were a bit more complex than Frois let out, but I think Frois's contrast still holds true as a generalization.

~~~~~~

10-27   We read very rapidly; *Ho nosso ler hé muito depresa;*

They do so pausing, and in jumps. *O seu pauzado e em saltinhos.*

Despite the fact that the pronunciation of many characters depends upon context that is sometimes not grasped until the word is passed, most Japanese can read as quickly as we do, *when they read silently*. Because there are more cases in Japanese than English where thought must be given to pronunciation, reading aloud does take a bit more work. So, I would prefer *this* contrast:

> *We find it is easier to read aloud and often move our lips when reading in silence;*
> *They are completely at home reading silently but struggle to read aloud.*[1]

In English, and perhaps all European tongues, we find the poor reader has great difficulty keeping his or her mouth closed. In Japan, I have not noted this. However, there are so many possible pronunciations for some words that reading correctly aloud requires knowledge and thought.

Still, the difference is not so large as Frois suggests unless he is thinking about how Japanese read the pseudo-Chinese writing called *kanbun*. This is indeed one of the strangest and cleverest (or, *most idiotic*, depending upon your mood!) ways to read that has ever been invented, for the Japanese mark the edges of the lines, written entirely in Chinese characters, with a number of signs which indicate how to *change the previous word-order, i.e.,* grammaticise the original *as one reads*. They are, then, translating, or rather *doing simultaneous interpretation* of a sort called *kaeri-yomi,* or "return-read," and this does indeed require silent periods of figuring out *what was what* interspersed with jumps, especially when vocalizing (which it generally was not). Not only was the word order changed but the reader had to supply the part of Japanese that the telegraphic Chinese does not make explicit!

This *kanbun* writing is of intellectual interest because it shows how well (or how poorly) Chinese characters [2] by themselves allow communication between exotic languages.

1. *Silent Reading.* The legend of St. Augustine discovering silent reading for the world seems *ludicrous* to me. Can you imagine Romans reading Martial's filth (catamites with anuses split to their navels, and whatnot) aloud!? Considering the fact that much if not most of ancient Japanese writing was love poetry, where the main purpose of writing was to be able to communicate *in private,* who would want to read aloud! Or, (a half millennium later) take a look at courtesans reading love letters – a common enough theme in ukiyoe prints – how many do you find have their mouths open? (Answer: None))

2. *Chinese Characters.* As James Unger points out in several good books, *any* large vocabulary common to more than one language can serve the purpose of a common tongue, so *there is nothing magically effective about characters*. He has a point, but I wonder. Take 犬. Anyone in China, Japan or Korea knows it means "dog." Sure, we could all learn Latin and communicate the idea with the Latin term for dog (canis?). But, to do so, we would need to learn a new word = pronunciation different from our "dog," "pero," and "inu" – it would be like learning Esperanto. With Chinese characters, we need not do that. One can pronounce the word "dog" just how our language has always done. (True, Japanese *also* learned the Chinese pronunciation, but it was not necessary.). The question then arises as to the best visual device to represent thousands of ideas. I think Chinese characters do a better job of this than anything else we have.

10-28   We write sitting in chairs at high tables;
Nos escrevemos em mezas altas, asentados em cadeiras;

They, do it on low stands, seated on the floor [1] or on *tatami* [mats].
Elles em banqinhos baxos asentados no chão ou sobre os tatamis.

English lacks a word for a small table (*tablet* and *tablette* cannot be used for they mean something different altogether).   For the Portuguese *banqinho,* I considered "small table" and "tray-like table," "stool" and "foot-stool" (the latter two from the dictionary).   I fear nothing is right.   The item in mind is the traditional Japanese desk, a tiny table with folding legs and, sometimes, an adjustable angle writing surface, one of the few examples of furniture in Japan.[2]   Today, such desks are rarely seen, for Japanese use Western-style desks.   Indeed, I would bet that since the latter half of the twentieth century, Japan could boast more desks per capita than any nation in the world.   Even where their children do not have their own bedroom, the Japanese make certain they have their own desk. [3]

1. *Floor?* The original chão, which we have seen before, means both *floor* and *ground.*   I would guess more Japanese sat on the porching, or veranda that skirts their houses than on the ground, but who knows?

2. *Adjustable Desks.* My grandfather Rah brought one back to the USA about 1950, and I wonder how long back the adjustable angle type (very good for reading) goes.   Anyone?

3. *Statistics on Desks.* I have seen statistics *proving* this. Though Japanese had far less rooms and space per capita than Usanians, and their income was far less, they already had desks for almost every child.   Anyone?

10-29   In Europe, books are bound by sewing together the paper at the edge;
Em Europa emquadernão os livros cozendo o papel polas bordas;

In Japan, they are sewn at some points and the folds left as they are.
Em Japão cozen-nos polas pontas e as dobras ficão soltas.

In the West, the spine is tightly bound and even glued, as we all know.   I doubt that any reader who has not seen a Japanese book could guess how they are bound by Frois's description!   Imagine a long, long strip of paper folded back and forth on itself like an accordion.   Then imagine it sewn on one side only.   Not right at the edge but, loosely, a half an inch or so from the edge where the spine would be if there were a spine, which there never was.   The other side is just left as is. Since the leaves are not cut with these books, one can remove the thread and pull the entire book out into one long piece of paper written on one side only!   Here, it is hard to say whether Frois refers to the folds of the leaves on the side of the book opposite to where the spine would be or those on the sewn side, for both are "left as is."

endnote **X**

W *riting*

〜〜

This chapter is very unsatisfying for the word-lover because Frois really restricts himself to *the writing system* and fails to introduce any of the topsy-turvy grammar which Percival Lowell suggests in *The Soul of The East* in 1888.

> He [the Occidental] discovers that this people talk, so to speak, backwards; that before he can hope to comprehend them, or make himself understood in return, he must learn to present his thoughts arranged in inverse order from the one in which they naturally suggest themselves to his mind. His sentences must all be turned inside out. He finds himself lost in a labyrinth of language. The same seems to be true of the thoughts it embodies. (L:SOE)

The Romance languages, especially Spanish and Portuguese are more flexible about the order of the major parts of speech than English, so the word-order reversal (the Japanese object *before* the verb) is less clear-cut and Frois can be forgiven for skipping it, but he might at least have noted the opposite order of our *smaller parts* of speech:

> *Our "the," "a," "on," "with," "by," "to" etc. all come before the words they indicate;*
> *Theirs never do because they all come after them.*

After all, the use of *pre*positions rather than *post*positions holds equally for Germanic and Romance languages. As for the oft-remarked, seldom-used personal pronouns in Japanese, it so happens the Latin tongues, unlike English, can do without them (partly because it is apparent from the conjugation, and partly because these languages, like Japanese, tend to have polysyllabic words and thus are long where human breath is of the same length everywhere). So Frois did not find a difference there while an Englishman surely would have. But Frois might *at least* have mentioned this:

> *We have but one word to indicate ourselves with and two to indicate the other person.*
> *They have a dozen ways to say "I" and almost as many to say "you."*

Frois did catch some important language-related differences and put them into the miscellany in the last chapter. There is one on the different manner of using *honorifics* (14-20), one about a different attitude toward *clarity* and *obscurity* (14-36), a the respective *body-language* between unequals (14-45) and the *posture for delivering messages* (14-44). Excuse me for jumping the gun, but had Frois put the second item mentioned into *writing* terms, it might have come out like this:

> *We admire neatly written letters and our calligraphy with its ornament is very precise;*
> *They admire writing that is so messy that not one in a hundred who can read can read it!*

Japanese calligraphy, even more so than Chinese, can be so impressionistic as to verge on the abstract. At the same time, they generally follow various abbreviated script patterns which can be made out by very studious people. But when it comes to writing meant to be hung up as art (as *kakemono*), very few people have any idea what it says. This is a constant cause of embarrassment for interpreters who are asked *"What does that say?"* by foreigners visiting Japan. Speaking of question marks, Frois forgot this, too:

We have interrogatory marks and exclamation marks;
They have none of these.

The Japanese generally ask questions by affixing the interrogatory *particle* "ka" (か) to the end of the sentence. So, there is usually no need to use a question mark and a *yo* (よ)or *zo* (ぞ)or *ze* (ぜ), etc. expresses phonetically our "!" Still, questions and exclamations can be made without such particles and so today, our marks are *also* used, and more freely than we use them, for Japanese do not hesitate to line up multiple exclamation marks for greater emphasis!! And, the same thing can be said for quotations, but explaining it is too complex for this book, so I won't. Then there is this, an easy Faux Frois that I am surprised Frois himself did not include:

We have capital letters which we always use at the beginning of sentences and for proper names;
They have no capital letters, but sometimes bracket names.

While I can see how our capital letters help indicate the start of a new sentence, I do like the idea of the equality of letters, as found in Japanese, because it doesn't allow one to capitalize ones own *God* while not so honoring the *gods* of others. With no capital letters, Japanese has no small ones, too. Still, Japanese do write letters small sometimes in order to create some of their limited number of (slightly) complex phonemes such as "myo = みょ" or "kyo = きょ" where a tiny "yo =よ" syllabet is put next to larger *mi* = み or "*ki* = き" syllabets.

In Europe, old books are not written in the common tongue but in Latin, Greek or Arabic.
In Japan, people can read books written hundreds of years before, without a translation.

I do not have a very good grasp of the written culture at the time Frois was in Japan. It was evidently wide-spread but, following centuries of warring, it is hard to imagine it could have been prospering. Yet, I know that heavily illustrated stories (*kana-zôshi*) thrived and, if nothing else, the demand for news – keeping up with all that change – may have placed a premium on literacy. Anyway, with peace, letters of all types flourished and a couple hundred years later, Edo boasted *walking libraries (kashihonya)* going door-to-door with as many books as a man can carry (specially selected with an eye for that day's customers) and door-to-door joke-sellers (*kangaemono*) who left written jokes (mostly riddles) in the entrance and returned later to accept payment *if you liked them.* That tells us something. Golownin says the guards kept them awake until they got used to their reading aloud in sing-song voices all night (I am curious why these guards read aloud so much. Anyone?) and he describes something still true, the way everyone – including his guards – spent *days* writing letters for the New Years greetings. He did not say that being a diligent writer was the secret of being a popular prostitute at the Yoshiwara, that not a few prostitutes were poets . . . (But, then, it is amazing how much Golownin, in captivity, managed to find out! I have no right to complain about what he *didn't* write!) The long and the short of it is that when Japan was "opened" in the mid-19th century, it was probably the most literate country in the world. Tested literacy was not the basis for achieving posts in the government as in China but, largely owing to the efforts of the Buddhist clergy, the level of *popular* literacy was higher. It seems to me that something we might call *the joy of letters* permeated the society. *Before the modern T-shirt, where but Japan was there clothing with poems written on it?* (kimono with poems or part of poems on them were popular in the Edo era). The much maligned Japanese system of writing has, I believe, been a source of more *satisfaction* than any other writing system I know of.

In Europe, we can read aloud whatever is written down;
In Japan, much that is written down can not be read aloud.

To me, this is the most important difference between "our" writing system and "theirs." *Ours is, at heart, an adjunct of the spoken language.* It may tend to use fancier words – don't you *hate* to read essays by university students stuffed with so much polysyllabic Latin the sentences require a plunger to flush! – but, at heart, it is one and the same thing. In Japan, we who write are asked to give talks (on anything under the sun), but we are seldom asked to "give a reading" of our books because far more is lost than would be gained (by intonation).   I think Chamberlain had it right:

> The influence of writing on speech – never entirely absent in any country possessing letters – is particularly strong under the Chinese system. We mean that the writing here does not merely serve to transcribe words: – it actually originates new ones, the slave in fact becoming the master.

Chamberlain was there just in time to see the Japanese translators taking full advantage of the Chinese characters to coin words by the hundred to "designate objects, ideas, appliances, and institutions recently borrowed from Europe." He noted that

> Some of these new compounds pass from books into common speech; but many remain exclusively attached to the written language, or are at least intelligible only by reference to the latter, while at the same time they endow it with a clearness and above all a terseness to which the colloquial can never attain.

To my mind, the best part of all has nothing to do with *practicality*. It has to do with *pleasure*. By having simultaneous use of Chinese characters and a phonetic letters, one can pun to one's heart's content.. It is not just having both, but an attitude, for even when the Chinese characters served in the capacity of phonetic letters, Japanese scribes played around.   The first poem in Japan's oldest anthology of poetry, the *Manyôshû,* which is about an Emperor approaching a young woman, starts with lines about her *having a pretty scoop and basket*, which I think means "you have the female=basket and scoop=male pair, but how about yourself, my girl?" ("Scoop" has the etymological feeling of being a *digging-skewer,* so it is more male in Japanese than in English.). Here is how the words with a pronunciation meaning "pretty scoop carrying" are written and their literal meaning:

mi	*bu*	*ku*	*shi*	*mochi*
美	夫	君	志	持
beautiful	*husband*	*you?/lord?*	*desire/seek*	*have*

In old Japanese (or Chinese) "beautiful" could modify either sex, so I did not change it to "handsome," but I think you can get the idea: the amanuensis (or *transcriber* – I do not know) has scooped *the intent of the poem* while phonetically rendering it. Other Chinese characters could have been used to record the sound, but someone *chose* to have fun.   This is an exceptional example, but the principle is true for much Japanese writing: you get far more using your eyes than you can with your ears alone. As the Japanese linguist Suzuki Takao puts it – *Occidental language is radio, Japanese is television.*

XI

OF HOUSES, *BUILDINGS, GARDENS AND FRUITS*

das cazas, fabricas, jardins e frutas

~~~~~~

11-1   Our houses are tall and of many stories;
As nossas cazas são altas e de muitos sobrados;

> Those of Japan, for the most part, low and single-story.
> *As de Japão polla mayor parte baxas e terreas.*

Explanations for this difference tend to run to two extremes: the physical, namely *earthquakes*, or the psychological, namely *cosmology*. The former theory neglects the fact that South Europe is also on faulty ground. The latter assumes Japanese are earth-bound souls and see no need to reach for the sky as we, with our Heaven-dwelling God, do, i.e., *We are vertically oriented, They horizontal.*[1] I believe a something less dramatic, *climate*, is largely responsible. Sultry summers want an open house. Thus, there were "no *continuous* [corner to corner] *walls*" and in Chamberlain's words,

> The side of the house, composed at night of wooden sliding doors called *amado*, is stowed away in boxes during the day-time. In the summer, everything is thus open to the outside air. ("Architecture" in C:TJ)

If there is only a bit of external wall – enough to house the *amado*, there is no internal wall to speak of, either. Even when a room had one, in Kaempfer's words, "the least kick would break it to pieces." (K(S):HOJ) This meant there would be little support available for a second floor.[2]

Moreover, tall buildings would block the little sunlight available during the monsoon for drying the tatami and *futon*. Even with the floor-frames raised a foot or so over the ground for the sake of ventilation, mildew and fleas (11, below) were an ever present threat. In order to block the rain yet leave ventilation, the eaves must be large, so little sunlight can get in from overhead. The potted plants, that most Japanese kept and still keep *outside* rather than inside like our *house*plants, and the inner-gardens of the wealthy would all suffer from multi-story dwellings. For these reasons, Japan, despite being one of the world's most notorious construction states, nevertheless has "Sunshine laws" to ensure new development does not take away that vital drying power called sunlight.[3]

---

1. *Reaching for the Sky.* In Europe, the church took the lead in building high. In Japan, the Buddhist temples and Shinto temples did not. I am not at all convinced that belief caused the difference. The heights are, after all, magical or sacred places in the Far East, too. I wonder if the fact religion in Japan literally went to the mountain removed the incentive to build high (Why would someone a 1000 feet up a mountain want more than one story?). And the wealthy commanded the high-ground of the cities, so they, too, would have no incentive to go higher.

2. *Two Story Counter-argument.* Of course, if one *planned* to have two floors from the start, the second-floor could be the open one and cool living would still be *possible*. But this would require changing the architecture based on an open ground-floor, so it would have been hard to get started and an open second-floor would be dangerous for children and inconvenient for people used to freely stepping in and out of their gardens.

3. *Sunshine Stealing Christians*. The Jesuit's church in the capital of Japan (its official presence), made before the Bungo Consultation decided things would hitherto be done the Japanese way in Japan, was an unprecedented three-stories high and ran afoul of the Sunshine Law four centuries before it was written. (Just a guess: gloss anyone?)

~~~~~~

11-2 Our [houses are made] of stone and lime; *As nossas de pedra e cal;*

<div style="text-align:center">Theirs of wood, bamboo, straw and mud. *As suas de paos, canas, palha e terra.*</div>

Not long ago, "lime" (*cal*) meant plaster – a mixture of lime and sand – in English as well as Portuguese, so I retained the old usage in translation. This contrast is, obviously, far from absolute. Wood was not uncommon in Northern Europe. The stav churches not only are wooden but, with the raised corners on the roofs look very oriental! Moreover, lime, albeit in a different manner, was occasionally used in Japan. Almeida, writing in 1565 of the short-lived castle of Tamon in Nara:

> All these [houses of noblemen and their retainers], as likewise the circuit of the tower and its towers are built with whiter and smoother walls than ever I saw in Christendom. For they mix no sand with the lime, but only knead it with a special kind of white paper which they make for this purpose. . . .[1] To enter in this town (for so I may call it) and to walk about its streets seems to be like entering Paradise. It is so clean and white that it looks as if all the buildings had been finished that very day. (in B:CCJ)

Be that as it may, wood was, as per Frois, *the* main material for Japanese building. From the 16th to the 20th century, Japanese architecture *as a whole* was often put down for lacking grandeur (no tall buildings) and being imitative (Chinese). But the fine quality was obvious from the start. "Indeed," writes Rodrigues, "in the view of responsible people, who have seen various parts of Europe, Japanese construction in wood does not appear to be surpassed or even equaled elsewhere."(R(C):TIJ) Almeida, in the same letter quoted above:

> I went inside to see its palatial buildings, and to describe them I would need reams of paper, since it does not appear to be the work of human hands. For not only are they constructed of cedarwood, whose delicious odor delights the senses of all that enter, but all the verandahs are built of single beams about seven feet long. . . . The ceiling of these buildings looks like a single piece of wood, since no join is visible even if you look very closely. I cannot write of the other decorations for words fail me. (B:CCJ)

Frois, likewise, found Nobunaga's Azuchi Castle, which "looks as if it were built of strong stone and mortar" but was actually "constructed entirely of wood" to be "in a word . . . beautiful, excellent and brilliant," and (partly because of being on a hill) "looks as if it reaches to the clouds." (C:TCJ) To come back down to earth – or, rather, the *bamboo, straw* and *mud* part of the contrast – Rodrigues, again. "It [the wood] provided the pillars and beams, while grates of bamboo provided the ribs for clay-like mud strengthened with straw to stick on and make what walls there were." Citing the Bible, he surmises the ancient Jews also used this method because walls built by false prophets who did *not* mix straw into their building clay fall down and guesses either earthquakes or the greater difficulty of working with stone or brick discourages building with stone or brick. (R(C):TIJ) Actually, Japanese *did* have some very good stone walls independent of houses, both the natural type made by farmers and some monumental works dating back to ancient times,[2] but bricks were virtually unknown and should have been in the contrast. They did not make it to Japan until modern times, for a 19th century Japanese visitor to England described buildings with "exteriors . . . made up of cornered blocks like pillows piled on top of each other." (LR)

..

> *In Europe, we think of a house as something permanent, rooted in place like a tree;*
> *In Japan, they think nothing of moving them around and some have moved more than once.*

That *Faux Frois* is based on Rodrigues, who noted that *mobility* was a benefit conferred by wood because it was light. He and Douglas Sladen, centuries later, wrote, respectively:

A wooden building constructed in this way can be transferred elsewhere. They do this every day, moving not only houses but even cities and populous towns, as we ourselves saw many times." (R(C):TIJ)

The poor Japanese, like the snail, can move his house on his back; and the thing which surprised me most was that he did not build it a little smaller, and carry it to work with him like an umbrella. (S:MQTJ)

1. *Shiny Walls.* This paper in lime walls are now more common inside of houses. It also may contain glitter, usually silver!

2. *Monumental Work.* Emperor Nintoku's burial mound, Mozunomimiharanonakanomisasagi (百舌鳥耳原中陵), if I recall correctly, may not be so high as a pyramid used far more stones and includes a large body of water. Some castles made when Frois was there, or soon after, were actually stronger than he knew, for they had steel grates that were finished to look like wood and stone hidden beneath plaster.

~~~~~~

11-3   Ours have foundations buried under the ground;
As nossas tem alicesses fundos debaxo da terra;

> Those of Japan have a stone under each *hashira* [pillar], and they [the stones] are above the ground. *As de Japão huma só pedra debaxo de cada* faxira *e estas em riba da terra.*

To us, a pillar is round, not square. Perhaps that is why Frois chose to use the Japanese word. The *hashira* are large square beams standing at each corner and both ends of the center of the roof. All but the smallest houses also had a central *hashira* which usually retained at least part of its natural features – some were (and still are) completely natural – reassuringly powerful piece of unpainted, polished natural wood that can be seen and felt inside the house. The butt of each *hashira* resting on its stone – the bottom half of which is slightly under-ground – is visible from the outside. Usually cedar, it neither rots nor attracts termites; and, there is something metaphysically cheering about knowing *exactly what you stand upon.* Moreover, the building is more stable for *not* being attached to the ground. Describing a "*daimio's* house," Douglas Sladen justifies the seeming paradox:

> It had no foundations, but stood on a stone platform, with a sort of ball-bearings, like a bicycle. Even lofty pagodas will stand earthquakes if they are treated like this. You can see how the principle acts if you watch a woman with a cup of boiling tea in an express train. She lets the cup follow the swaying of the carriage, and the Japanese style of building lets the house follow the swaying of the earthquake. It must be very unpleasant to be in one during a good earthquake. (S:MQT)

This is a bit confusing. The reader is free to find other metaphors. I think of stone boats floating on an earthen sea. The *hashira* that rest on these stones – or, in the case of large structures, a large stone platform – are the very soul of the house (Could that be why Frois did not go with a Western term, but used the Japanese?) After they are set up, a ceremony is held:

> First they brought in all the pr'sentes sent and sett them in ranke before the middell post of the howse, & out of eache one took somthing of the best & offred it at the foote of the post, & powred wyne vpon eache severall p'rcell, . . . (Cocks 12-28-1615, longer quote in C:TCJ)

The pillars may rest freely on their non-foundations, but they are also strongly linked together on top by transverse beams. That is another reason the houses can be moved without being dismantled, as Rodrigues points out (R(C):TIJ). Then, after the pillars are linked, in no time flat, up goes the roof, *before* the walls, a most obvious contrast Frois strangely enough misses! Ball, in *Things Chinese*, catches it:

We have read of an exhibition in Western lands where a house was built upside down, and the attic built on the ground and the cellar up in the air. The Chinaman, however, does not do this, but he puts his ridge pole up first, suspended in the air and then he builds his house up to it. (B:TC)

If I am not mistaken, the Chinese, too, built not just the ridge-pole but the whole roof first. Needless to say, in a rainy place like Japan, carpenters would have it rough if this order were not preserved. Let me try to *Faux Frois* all of this:

> *We build our houses from the ground up, finishing with the roof;*
> *The Japanese build houses from the top down, starting with the roof.*

~~~~~~

11-4   Our doors, for the most part, move upon stiles;
        As nossas portas pola mayor parte andão sobre couceiras;

> Those of Japan, almost always run upon *shikii* [sill/s].
> *As de Japão quasi todas são corrediças sobre* xiqis.

Frois could have explained "our" doors better by writing that they "rotate" or "swing" (rather than simply *andam* = move/go) *around* the stile or door-post – or more simply, "with hinges" – as opposed to the way Japanese doors "run" or, better yet, "slide" upon sills." Be that as it may, there is no question that the sliding door saves space and contributes toward temperature control because it does not push in or pull out air. That is why it and not the rotating door – I don't mean the rotating door that goes around and around but all using hinges – is favored for modern buildings. (Could someone tell me if the idea for sliding doors and/or the development of electric sliding doors comes from Japan?) But, the cruder technological requirements of the Western-style door – in Japan there are carpenters who specialize in grooving and re-grooving wooden sills for the sliding doors! – make it more popular for cheap housing, even in Japan.

> *Our doors and windows usually move in different ways from one another.*
> *Japanese doors and windows almost always slide on their sills in the same way*

Japanese windows, whether door-size or, more rarely, small, slide upon horizontal sills, just like their doors. I do not know how many of ours were hinged and how many slid in Frois's time, but either way they were not like doors. The exception, as Morse noted in the 19th century, is the privy, which often has a hinged (butterfly-joint) door. This difference is not shared by the Chinese who have all hinge-door and windows with "swinging frames" (M:JH&S), or Koreans whose windows are square, with "frames hung from above and opening outside," and have a folding panel for their outer doors. Apparently Koreans evolved in an opposite direction (toward China?) from Japan on this count for inside the latter – this is Morse quoting Lowell – "for consecutive not simultaneous use" are

> a couple of pairs of sliding panels, – the survivors in Korea of the once common sliding screens, such as are used to-day in Japan. One of the pairs is covered with dark green paper and is for night use; the other of the natural yellowish color of oil-paper, and is used by day. When not wanted, they slide back into grooves inside the wall . . . All screens of this sort, whether in houses or palanquins, are provided, unlike the Japanese, with these conveniences for tying the two halves of each pair together, and thus enabling easier adjustment. (JH&S)

So the slide-door is not an exclusively Japanese item. Apparently, the Korean dwelling was once more similar, but the Koreans Sinofied themselves more, while the Japanese developed the difference.

11-5   Our partitions are stone, lime or brick.   *Os nossos repartimentos são de pedra e cal ou tijolo;*

Those of Japan are paper doors.   *Os de Japão de portas de papel.*

Japanese houses generally have no internal walls. The house is divided into rooms by lightly framed, sliding doors of paper. In English and Portuguese, the items described in 11-4 and 11-5 are both "doors." Japanese actually use different terms. The outside front-door is called a *to,* the translucent paper inner-door and veranda doors are called *shôji* and the generally opaque and lightly ornamented room-partitions *fusuma.* The *fusuma* are grooved above as well as below in such a manner that they can easily be lifted up from the tracks and turn two, three or four rooms into one without a single partition. 1891, Eliza Scidmore described the "elaborate ettiquette" of the *shôji*:

> In opening or closing them, well-bred persons and trained servants kneel and use each thumb and finger with ordered precision, while it is possible to convey slight, contempt, and mortal insult in the manner of handling these sliding doors. (S:JDJ)

There is something that troubles us about this depiction of the hypersensitive Japanese. But the matter is moot, for today, most Japanese would no more recognize the "mortal insult" than we would. Because most of these "doors" lack handles, one must still, however, take care to close them completely. Failing to do so – and all children often fail at this – brings out insulting sayings such as those we use for men caught with open flies. (Those Korean ties might be useful, here!) But etiquette is far less important than effect. Here is Alice Mabel Bacon, also in 1891:

> No thick walls and long passageways separate the nursery from the grown people's apartments, but the thin paper partitions make it possible for the mother to know always what her children are doing, whether they are good and gentle with their nurses, or irritable and passionate. (B:JGW)

Since these partitions are often kept open, on a summer day one can see right through a traditional Japanese house – indeed a syphilitic nose was called a *natsu-yashiki,* or "summer mansion," for that reason! Kaempfer, in the 17th century recognized smart design when he saw it:

> I must not forget to mention that it is very healthful to live in these houses, and that in this particular they are far beyond ours in Europe, because of their being built all of cedar wood, or firs, whereof there is a great plenty in the country, and because of the windows being generally contrived so, that upon opening of them, and upon removing the skreens, which separate the rooms, a free passage is left for the air to strike through the whole house. (K:HOJ)

All of this seems very nice, and it is (though Chamberlain, with his "draughts insidiously pouring in through innumerable chinks and crannies" might beg to differ!). A small house opened up in this way is not only healthy. It gives one the spacey feeling of a temple, or the woods cleared of yucky underbrush (a forest bed where Diana could run freely) – it is roomier than a far larger house partitioned into individual rooms. (I reverse Sladen, who emphasizes smallness by writing "a small Japanese house is no larger than a single room, and by day it is often only a single room.") This is especially true when the traditional straw roof is so thick no ceiling is needed. Such old farm houses compare favorably to the rich man's A-frame in the USA. We make a big mistake when we count and compare square-feet alone as a measure of a home's living space. Of course, there is a downside to this design. Morse writes that others

> speak of the want of privacy in Japanese dwellings, forgetting that privacy is only necessary in the midst of vulgar and impertinent people, – a class of which Japan has the minimum, and the so-called civilized races – the English and American particularly – have the maximum. (M:JH&S)

But, even in Japan, people snore. Babies, occasionally cry. Young children at play, play loudly. Some of us do want *quiet* now and then. I wonder what Morse would think of the modern Japanese office, where this open tradition means dozens of people per room, desk to desk, not even a partial cubicle between them, bombarded with loud telephone beeps, conversations and even shouts. This is all fine for superiors and inferiors to keep close tabs on each other; but it is not ideal for intellectual work. Imagine, an office full of people writing copy and editing as noisy as the New York Stock Exchange! And I am not talking about journalistic operations where such might be expected, but ordinary publishers of books! (I wish I knew if this were only in Japan, or true for many cultures.)

Assuming we could get used to the loss of privacy, would Japanese houses work in the West? While Morse found much in the Japanese home he could recommend, he had to admit it was "obviously absurd to suggest" such a structure "as a model for our own houses." *Why?* Aside from the different climate and lifestyle:

> its fragile and delicate fittings if adopted by us, would be reduced to a mass of kindlings in a week, by the rude knocks it would receive; and as for exposing on our public thoroughfares the delicate labyrinth of carvings often seen on panel and post in Japan, the widespread vandalism of our country would render futile all such attempts to civilize and refine. (Ibid)

Over a hundred years later, nothing has changed. What is it that makes "us" (in the USA at any rate) so rough we must treat ourselves like children? Or, them, so sensitive they can be trusted with delicate architecture?

~~~~~~

11-6   Our roofs are tile.
Os nossos telhados são de telha.

> Those of Japan for the most part of wood, straw and bamboo.
> *Os de Japão pola mayor parte de taboas, palha ou canas.*

The straw roofs on the farm houses in Japan look very similar to those of England. They seem an extension of the landscape, sometimes a veritable garden. Morse:

> The ridge-poles of many of the roofs in the north of Japan are covered with red lilies, and a pretty sight it is as one rides through a village to see the crests of the houses flaming with red. Around Tokyo the blue iris seems to be the favorite flower for this decoration. (M:JDD2)

But, lest we get the wrong idea, some qualifications are needed. First, this was no primitive thatching. There were many types of grasses and reeds used. Sometimes light and dark colored straws were alternatively laid so that the cleanly cut eaves (up to 3 feet thick!) were decorative. They offered *superb* insulation and came in a great variety – especially the central ridge design – of regional styles. Morse described them as far more interesting than the "stiff, straight" and monotonous "ridge-pole and eaves" where if you have seen one you have seen them all in the United States. Compare Morse, with his open eyes, to Loti, who was too Occi-centric to see the individuality in Japan and claimed that "one gets bored with the endless monotony of the little Japanese streets, with the thousands of identical little grey houses, all of them wide open as though to show off their identical interiors, the same little white mats, the same little smoke-boxes, the same little ancestral shrines." (in L:IOJ) There is some truth to this, especially in cities which are often burned down; but such hardly typified Japan.

The location of the greatest architectural originality (the ridge-pole) is not surprising, because a virtually wall-less house depends on the roof. And, even if it didn't, housing-related Chinese characters show a Far Eastern tendency to identify shelter with the roof: i.e., the *house* radical 宀 is a roof (Put a woman radical under it 安 and you have a *woman at home,* or "contentment". House itself has a "pig" under it: 家) As Mr. Sladen confirms,

The essential feature is, . . . the roof; and if it were possible to live in a roof which had no understandings the Japanese would do it, because no earthquake could make it fall down, and no typhoon could blow it away. But this has not been found practicable, so . . . (S:MQT)

Second, straw or not (temples, castles and the houses of the nobles in Japan generally had tile roofs – Frois conveniently forgot that to heighten his contrast.), Japanese roofs were *very* heavy. They were the only part removed when houses were moved.   And why were they *always* heavy? Sladen continues:

If the roof were light the commonest typhoon would play kites with it. But it can be made heavy enough to stand any ordinary typhoon. But I asked of Man Sunday, what happens in an earthquake? What's the good of having your walls so light [that it does not signify if they . . . fall on the occupants], with a roof that would squash the whole family as flat as a dried salmon? He answered, with the wisdom of the wise, that in earthquakes the roof does not kill the people in the house, but the people in the street. Judged from this standpoint, the Tokyo house is a good one.

Man Sunday's folk wisdom may be just what the humorist wants, but it is not quite right. So, why were heavy roof beams and a heavier, "more substantial" second floor *de rigor* for big houses in Japan? Kaempfer came closer to the truth in 1692.

This they do by reason of the frequent Earthquakes . . . because they observe, that in the case of violent shock, the pressure of the upper part of the house upon the lower, which is built much lighter, keeps the whole from being overthrown. (K(S): HOJ)

Kaempfer has the *reason* right, but not the *principle*. Only Morse got that down pat – at least it sounds right to me.[1] Here, he describes "two-story, fireproof buildings" in Tokyo:

On these a heavy tiled roof is used. This is believed to be of great security in earthquakes, for the inertia of the roof is such that it does not move, while the building itself may be swaying. In balancing a cane on the finger some difficulty is experienced. If a heavy book could be fastened to the top of the cane, it would be much easier to balance it, and the hand could be moved rapidly back and forth a few inches without the book moving at all. (M:JDD)

Combined with the unstable foundations mentioned in 11-3, above, we now have the whole earthquake strategy. Basically, Japanese houses tend to be top-heavy, while ours are bottom-heavy, just the opposite from what might *seem* the case from Frois's contrast of tiles and straw! (At the end of the 19th century, most of the houses in Tokyo were tile-roofed – and the tiles "so heavy that it would only take four of them to weigh as much as their master" (Sladen). Apparently, tiles spread *after* Frois.

1. *Sounds Right to Me.* I know nothing about this. Glosses from structural engineers are welcome.

11-7   Our rooms are of wood, well finished and polished.
           As nossas camaras de madeira mui lavrada e polida;

Theirs for *chanoyu* [the tea ceremony[1]] of wood just like it came from the woods, in order to imitate nature. *As suas de* chanoyu, *com a maeira asi como vem do mato, pera ymitar a natureza.*

Rodrigues wrote many inspired pages about the *sukiya* –tea hut. Since "meeting to drink *cha*" was for "the quiet and restful contemplation of the things of nature in the wilderness and desert"

all the material of this place is entirely adapted for this purpose and for eremitical solitude in the form of rude huts made naturally with rough wood and bark from the forest, as if they had been formed by nature or in the usual style of those people who dwell in woods or the wilderness. (R(C):TIJ)

The tea ceremony began as an aristocratic pastime. Such taste is understandable among literatae (and that includes many samurai) who respected sage-poets who lived pure lives in the mountains. What to me is more impressive is that the taste spread beyond the tea huts. Kaempfer wrote:

> The cieling is sometimes neither planed nor smoothed, by reason of the scarcity [rare] and curious running of the veins and grain of the wood, in which case it is only cover'd with a thin slight couch of a transparent varnish, to preserver it from decaying. ((K(S):HOJ) The "ceiling," as "ceiling" still reflected the *ciel* or "sky" origin in English spelling!)

He continues to say "sometimes they paste it over with the same sort of variously colour'd and flower'd paper, which their skreens [*fusuma*] are made of." Today, one finds that Koreans lay on floral wallpaper to a nauseating degree, but Japanese rarely do. Even the average man shows a strong tendency toward preferring natural wood grain – often, as it turns out, fake veneer; but it is the principle that counts (and Leonardo would have enjoyed either one). The tea ceremony sensibility apparently succeeded in becoming the Japanese sensibility, the national aesthetic.

In Korea, where I have spent some time, one sees a great love for natural wooden objects – from driftwood and root collections to modern art, raw wood sculpture of all kinds stands out – but one's overall impression is still one of bright basic colors (in music, what would be called *major* chords?) florid sensibility. So I had always assumed the stress on natural wood grain – something that delighted almost all Jesuits who saw it (not *one* thought it would be improved by painting, but all delighted in its luster and some in its grain) – as the main interior decoration was a uniquely Japanese, rather than Far Eastern invention. But Cruz, in the first book on China published in the West (1550), writes something very similar about the houses of common folk in China, which he found had "little luster" on the outside but were delightful inside: "as light as milk" (*alvas como leite*). The "very smooth, very even and very well worked and finished" woodwork, to use a modern expression, blew his mind. He realized "it would be an injury to paint them." (*lhe fariam injuria pintarem-na*) and confessed, "I have never seen wood as beautiful as that." (C:TCC). Yet, for reasons I do not yet understand, the Chinese did not succeed in making this their mark as the Japanese have.

Morse, whose taste I share, wrote that, generally speaking, Japanese interiors showed something American (and, I would add Korean, and probably Chinese) ones do not: *good taste.* Morse also realized how hopeless it is to teach it. Here is the concluding paragraph to his *Japanese Homes and Their Surroundings:*

> I do not expect to do much good in thus pointing out what I believe are better methods, resting on more refined standards. There are some, I am sure, who will approve; but the throng – are won by tawdry glint and tinsel; who make possible by admiration and purchase, the horrors of much that is made for house-furnishing and adornment – will, with characteristic obtuseness, call all else but themselves and their own ways heathen and barbarous.

1. *The Tea Ceremony.* The word *chanoyu* transliterates as "tea's hot-water" and means the ceremony. In Japanese, different words are used for hot-water (*yu*), water (*mizu*) and cold-water (*ohiya*).

11-8   Our rooms generally have windows of great clarity;
As nossas camaras tem jeralmente jenelas com muita claridade;

> The *zashiki* [parlor] of *chanoyu* [the tea ceremony] are windowless and dark.
> *Os zaxiqis de* chanoyu *sem jenelas e esquros.*

This contrast is misleading because, *generally speaking,* it is the Japanese house whose walls are all window, while European houses, by comparison, have little port-holes to peek out at the outside world. The only really dark dwellings in old Japan were the snowed-under houses of the snow-country and the huts of the Ainu (They were so dark, that to our loss, Morse could not make out the details within!) So the real contrast here is not about ordinary rooms, but *taste* with respect to the design of rooms used for important socializing. Perhaps Frois should have specified "drawing room" or something like that for our side.

Frois wrote in an era when the tea ceremony was at peak popularity. In 1587, Hideyoshi summoned all the tea-lovers of the nation to an unprecedented ten-day tea party(!) Judging from his character, I think it may not have been a party for many but a duty: *Come with all your priceless curios or else!* Much about this event with gaudy(?) tea ceremonies in baths and whatnot betrayed the very idea of *chanoyu* as most understood it. Meanwhile, the patron saint of the tea ceremony as we know it today, Sen no Rikyu, took up the simplicity "commanded by the poverty of the country, exhausted by ages of warfare . . . and raised it into a canon of taste" (C:TJ) before the same Hideyoshi had him put to death for reasons partly justified (*lése majesty*) and deserving a longer treatment than I can possibly give here, so I won't, other than to say that it is pleasant to think of Rikyu as *the world's first martyr for aesthetics.*

If the traditional Japanese house was open to all but the sky above, the tea hut was a closed space, which screened out the world at large. Sensory overload versus voluntary deprivation. Or, rather, a choice of a very few objects to focus on. I suspect the visual aspect was only part of it. Small windows let in less noise. [1] The quiet tea-house allowed for very quiet person-to-person communion. And, it was a democratic place, where the usual rank-related formalities were suspended. All in all, the Jesuit brotherhood highly appreciated these retreats, these tiny shrines to quiet and calmness, and many high-ranking Japanese Christians were *Way of the Tea* aficionados.

1. *Noise in Japan.* Japan is a *very* noisy place. The incessant loudspeaker – the municipality uses loudspeakers to reach everyone today, as do the local temples! and inadvertently (by accident of being loud) the schools – may be a new evil, but visitors from the West have always been impressed by the loud venders and workers. Chamberlain did not exaggerate when he complained of "the deafening clatter twice daily of the opening and shutting of the outer wooden slides." He means "the side of the house, composed at night of wooden sliding doors called *amado,* [that] is stowed away in boxes during the day-time." The "boxes" are built into short segments of wall at the edge of the room and it is not hard to quietly slide open or close the *amado.* But, no, even today, they are slid into each other or into their boxes with tremendous *gusto,* wham-bam! Moreover social intercourse that is not boringly stiff is *absolutely riotous.*

About the formality of hierarchical meetings, nothing needs to be said. It is famous. The riotous is less known abroad. It is what *any* informal public gathering tends to become in Japan. Cherry-viewing is usually a million-person cocktail party with everyone slushed. Take refuge in a bar and it is even louder. Why do you think *karaoke* was able to become a fixture? The decibels were already there! The mother of all noise-places is the *pachinko* (pinball) parlor where the working class go to relax (!), for if the balls and beeps of the machines aren't loud enough, the nonstop marching music (!) makes a rock concert seem a good place to take a nap. Even Japanese temple grounds resound with noise – *zazen* is done early in the morning before the tourist rush (and, remember, Japanese travelers swarmed Japan even in Frois's time). Of course, if you have mastered your mind, you are not supposed to register the noise anyway . . .

11-9   We treasure gems, pieces of gold and silver;
Nós fazemos tezouro de pedraria e peças d'ouro e prata;

The Japanese [treasure] old caldrons, old, broken[1] porcelain, clay vases, etc.
Os Japões de caldeirões velhos, porselanas velhas e qebradas, vazos de barro etc.

All of the Japanese items are related to the tea ceremony (see 14-21). Rodrigues describes the *dogu* (implements) aptly: "The vessels and dishes used in this gathering are not of gold, silver, or any other precious metal, nor are they richly and finely wrought; instead they are made of clay or iron without any polish, embellishment or anything which might incite the appetite to desire them for their beauty and lustre." The fact that these earthenware utensils can be "worth ten, twenty or thirty thousand cruzados or even more . . . will appear as madness and barbarity to other nations that come to hear of it." (R(C):TIJ) Decades earlier, Valignano was shown a tea caddy bought for fourteen thousand ducats, "for which, in all truth, I would not have given more than one or two maravedis." Indeed, he thought "it would only serve us as a water jar for a bird." (SUMARIO 1583) Valignano developed the relativity of gems and *dogu* at considerable length, pointing out that

> what is more surprising [than the high price] is that although a thousand caddies and a thousand *trebedecitas* [tiny tripods? or tripod kettles?] just like them were made, they would have no more value to the Japanese than they would to us, because the ones they value have to be made by ancient masters [*maestros*], and they have such [fine] eyes that they can recognize the one in a thousand [*tales ojos que entre mil los conocen propriamente,*] as our silversmiths, who can recognize and distinguish false and real jewels; and it doesn't seem this understanding can ever be achieved by a European, for no matter how long we look, we cannot even begin to understand what comprises the value or the difference. ((V(A):S&A)?)

Two things might be added. First, the Portuguese and Spaniards, no doubt with inside Japanese help, *did* manage to make "vast sums" (B:JCC) at this time by importing old pottery from the Philippines (especially caddies reputed to be especially good at keeping tea fresh in the humid season). Taladriz-Alvarez even states the pottery earned more than any other Philippine export and the amazed Spaniards at first thought some superstition must be the cause of the high demand. (V(A):S&A). And, second, many specific cups and caddies mentioned by the Jesuits are still famous today. Unlike the contemporaneous Tulip craze, if time tells, the *dogu* were for real. Today, we are far more appreciative of the value of *dogu* because of developments in the world of art since Valignano's time. Rare gems and *curios* were collected then, but art work *per se* generally was not. Churches commissioned religious scenes, the rich commissioned portraits of themselves and their possessions, and the publishers were just beginning to commission illustrations. The bourgeoisie bought paintings, hangings and sculptures *as decorations*, but most people did not think man-made things highly valuable in the way we do today – at least the Spanish did not, because if they did, they would not have kept melting down American artwork for the gold and silver alone. Now that we have an established concept of artwork, *dogu* would no longer be compared with gems. However, *dogu* do complicate matters by comprising two very different categories of art. On the one hand, there is the *dogu* made by a famous Japanese or Chinese artesian. On the other, there is the *dogu* made by the skilled (by repetition) hands of an un-named workman, possibly a child, *valued by the fiat of a connoisseur*. It would be interesting to know what percentage of the *dogu* held in Western collections comes from which type and how much we paid for them.[2]

1. *Broken* or *Cracked?* Both Japanese translations turn the "broken" into "with cracks in them." That is probably what Frois meant. Perhaps some valuable *dogu* actually have been "broken" (*quebradas*) and glued together and still retain their value as eyes-only items, but generally speaking, they were used. So it is almost certain that Frois really means small chips, whose absence makes the past more present, and the natural cracks (or cracked glaze), which add accidental beauty man alone can not create. Frois may have thought of these as sorry looking, but who knows!

2. *Dogu in the West.* I know that the West has joined the market for curio such as *netsuke*, but I wonder what the situation is with *dogu* today. In the notes to 1-28, we saw Miguel=Valignano contrast the *global* value of gems to the *local* worth of these *dogu*. Does that enormous difference *still* exist? One would not expect it to. Assuming the global economy is one, we would expect foreigners to invest in valuable *dogu,* whether or not they truly appreciate them. Are they? Since "we" fail to even pay attention to the world's greatest board game (*go*), I doubt the world is one, even today.

11-10 Our [houses?] are decorated with tissue, Gaudameci and Flemish tapestry.
As nossas [cazas?] se ornão com tapeçaria e godomecis e panos de Frandes;

Those of Japan with *byôbu* [folding-screen/s] of paper, golden or of black ink.
As de Japão com beobus de papel dourados ou de tinta preta.

Let me be blunt. "Our" decorations are just too rich and, subject-wise, too anthropomorphic(?) for my taste. Our ridiculously ornate palaces make me close my eyes and shudder to think of the personality of the people who *wanted* such interiors. So I am not the right person to describe us. Lisa Jardine has a good summary of what this stuff meant. After introducing the lavish material ("Granadan silk threads in sixty three different shades of colour," "seven types of gold thread and three types of silver thread," etc.) and the financing ("the Fugger bank had advanced all the money . . . and had then acted as brokers for its sale") that went into royal tapestry, she writes:

> Tapestries have not endured as recognized 'works of art' into our own period. In the fifteenth and sixteenth centuries they were a particularly ostentatious art-form, perfectly suited to the requirements of wealthy clients of the time: they combined exquisite design and workmanship with extremely labor-intensive (and therefore valuable) craft skills; they rendered any room in which they were hung instantaneously sumptuous; they kept large ill-insulated rooms warm and draught-free; . . . . . Furthermore, they had the advantage over frescos and paintings that they were highly portable and could readily travel with their owner . . . . . They carried his renown along with the luggage . . . (*Worldly Goods – A New History of the Renaissance*. Nan A. Talese = Doubleday: 1996)

All of Frois's items might be loosely translated as *tapestry*.[1]   Dictionaries suggest the *tapeçaria* might be cloth woven with gold or silver threads which the English of Frois's time called "tissue." Flemish art called "cloth" (*panos*) by Frois is what we identify with painting-like tapestry today, and Guadameci, an ancient tapestry from Gadamés, Tripoli, described by *Aurelio* (dict.) as "gilded, painted leather." Perhaps the intended contrast is between cloth that *hangs* and screens that *stand*. Or, it might be an extension of the last two contrasts, in the sense that paper is less substantial, or to use Jardine's adjective, *sumptuous,* than tapestry.

The byôbu screens almost always had six panels. Frois's writing is so sketchy one might assume the paper is solid gold or black, but actually both gold dust and black ink were commonly used to paint scenes or poetry, and Nobunaga had given such a screen – a very valuable black and white landscape of the capitol (Kyoto) – to Valignano in addition to talking tea with him. But these folding screens are more than mere decoration. They share the wall-making function of the *shôji* and *fusuma* described in the notes to 11-5, above.   Portable, they provide temporary private spaces or back-drops for audiences. Korean *nihonjinron* writer extraordinaire Lee O-Young contrasts the "screen-cultures" of the Far East he identifies with the free and fluid privacy of these screens with the solid-wall culture of the West, where a fixed concept of privacy begins in the cradle and ends in the basement fixations of the underground man of Dostoevsky (Yes, Russian is "West" to the Far Eastern intellectual. Wouldn't that get the Slavophile's goat!). One must quote Lee to do justice to his "post-modern" essay-style. Here are two excerpts from a book of his that probably won't be translated into English:

> The function and characteristic of a *byoubu* lies in its separation of the wall from the building. That is, the concept of the wall as unmovable has been made moveable, and given birth to its own independent culture. While Westerners made more and thicker walls for the sake of individual privacy, the people of the Eastern Trio [China, Japan and Korea], made the wall lighter and thinner in order to liberate it. Then, walls, instead of restricting people, fell under our free control. This became a reality because of none other than the *byôbu.*

> Our levels of privacy are different. In the *byôbu* cultural sphere, the individual and the group, the self and the other are not an antagonistic black and white choice. There is fusion and . . . expansion and closure depending on the circumstance of each situation. For this reason, the first-person singular of the Eastern Trio, unlike the absolutely unmoving West's, changes: *"watakushi," "ore," "boku."* [three "I's" in common use in Japan] This is not to deny the individual. It is only to say that while each panel of the *byôbu* is independent [physically of one piece and as artwork sufficient onto itself], they stand up so well *because* they link together six, ten or twelve panels at a time. (J/I:FPM:1989)

Cross-cultural metaphysics aside, *byôbu* are still used in Japanese-style homes and restaurants – where they separate parties but not the noise – but are not used as much as they deserve to be, because the very folds which allow them to stand take up too much room for Japanese offices, which are usually built on land so expensive that every inch counts, so the plain, ugly Western partition, or *sukurinu* (screen) is now more common. The sad reality be as it may, let me Frois Lee's contrast:

> *The houses in Europe have thick and unmoving walls;*
> *Those of Japan have paper walls that move about.*
>
> *Our partitions are straight and require stands or legs;*
> *Theirs zig-zag and stand up straight without those things.*

The wall most commonly mentioned by boastful Japanese *nihonjin-ron* of the 1970's and early 1980's was not the endoskeleton of a dwelling. It was the exoskeleton of the city. The standard line was that the West had castles and walled castle towns because meat-eating nomads that they were, war was the norm and people had to be constantly on guard, while Japan, being a peaceful country of farmers, didn't need walls. And this was, then, extrapolated to the Japanese house open to the outside, because the occupants were not in a state of war with nature, in contrast to the small-windowed Western house-as-my-castle (which is to say *fortress*.) This view of walls (not to mention our respective people) is a bit too pat and, as with many contrasts, it helps to have a third view to complicate the picture. Japanese might be amused to read what pioneer of fired adobe dwellings, Nader Khalili, wrote about walls *and the West*. "If we look at the West and its literature, we can see that it has always tried to tear down the walls." Occidentals don't like to be fenced in. Whereas "in the East, walls have an entirely different meaning. In Persian, "neighbors are called *hamsayeh*, people who share the shade of the same wall."

> . . . a neighborhood starts with a wall, united in shade. Each side can take advantage of the shade. One in the morning and the other in the afternoon.. In the East, a wall is built to break the wind, to create privacy, and to have the shade. (CERAMIC HOUSES AND EARTH ARCHITECTURE 1986/1999 Cal-Earth Press)

The climate is, of course, the main reason for this "Eastern" wall loving. For ". . the walls grow much faster than trees here [in Persia], and give better shade for less water. . ." (Ibid) How, then, would Khalili compare/contrast his culture *with Japan?*

~~~~~~

11-11   Ours are decorated with carpets and rugs.   *As nossas se ornão com alcatifas e tapetas;*

   Theirs with straw mats.   *As suas com colchõis de palha.*

With carpets or rugs, we think *decoration*. Or we did, at least, before wall-to-wall became taken for granted in some nations. Rodrigues wrote that the *tatami* mats were "so close to each other that there were no gaps at all between them, just as if they were floorboards." (R:TCJ) I do not know if floorboards were considered decoration or just part of the basics.   I do know that the floors in Japan are not *decorated* with *tatami*. They *are* tatami. Frois *should have* written:

..

> *We cover our hard floors with soft rugs;*
> *They never cover their floors, because the floors themselves are soft straw mats.*

These mats are not mats in the sense we imagine, for they are a good three to five inches thick, like a mattress. Rodrigues writes "three fingers thick." Eliza Scidmore mentions everything but the thickness of the mats:

The area of every room is some multiple of three feet, because the soft *tatami*, or floor-mats, measure six feet in length by three in width. These are woven of common straw and rushes, faced with a closely wrought mat of rice-straw. (S:JDJ)

Rodrigues also noted that "all the houses are built according to certain measurements on account of the mats or *tatami* with which they are laid . . ." Again, Frois missed a golden opportunity:

We fit our floor rugs to the dimensions of the room.
They fit their rooms to the dimensions of their straw mats. [1]

With us, no two houses have exactly the same floor space;
Japanese houses come in standard sizes, in multiples of their mats called ma.

Even today, the floor space of an dwelling for rent is given in terms of these standardized mats. My last abode was *roku-ma,* or *6-mat,* with a door-side kitchen and unit-bathroom. Amazing as this may seem, this standardization that began with the mats extends to other areas. The length of the mat, 180 centimeters, is also the height of "paper doors" of all types, the length of all closets and many beds. It is impressive to see a country so literally united, but at 6'2," I find the units not only inconvenient but, "as tall Saxons and Celts have found to their cost many times," downright dangerous. "H.M.'s Consul at Kanagawa fairly tried the strength of his skull against the sharp edge of the traversing beam," continues Alcock, "and measured his length backward on the ground under a blow that might have killed a weaker man." (A:COT) I am reminded of Piet Hein's *grook:* "Small people often overrate / the charm of being tall / which is that you appreciate / the charm [and safety!] of being small." But, to be fair to said beams, I should add that Alcock, in a footnote, credited one of them with saving the life of another tall Englishman by parrying the sword-blow of a would-be assassin. If the 180 centimeter high beams are not all bad, the tatami that created them is not all good either. Tatami is beautiful, soft, light and easier to keep clean than carpet, but has a problem, or two, according to Sladen:

In a common lodging house they are an Alsatia for fleas. To a flea, a Japanese mat is a fortress with thousands of doors. He burrows in it like a rabbit. The mats have the further disadvantage that the house is theirs and not yours. As your heels would be bad for it, you have to leave your boots on the doorstep of your own house. (S:MQT)

If you are wealthy enough to get new mats every few years, have a well ventilated under-floor (all Japanese house's are supposed to be built up from the ground, but not all actually are, especially when one half is sunken into a hill) and do not allow your cats to rove, *tatami* will do you no wrong. Otherwise, you will get fleas. The fleas' advantage can not be exaggerated. Even fumigation does not completely penetrate their *tatami* fortress. Living in poor circumstances in Japan – all writers without a best-seller or independent wealth live below the poverty level – I learned many fascinating things about fleas: how they don't squeeze through taut mosquito net because they insist upon jumping toward your face only to bounce off the net, how a thunderstorm's approach (drop in the barometer?) brings out their blood lust, how you can decoy for your cats by going in first and letting the fleas jump onto your smelly socks which you drop into the wash-water (the only problem with this is that you are breeding patient fleas, so each generation gets harder to catch), etc.. But I never learned to appreciate them as much as Issa whose hundred-odd flea haiku include this:

beauty is as beauty does?

the fleas in my hut
are cute as can be:
because, because
they sleep with me!

iori-no-nomi kawai ya ware-to inuru-nari
shack's flea/s cute! me-with sleep-become

Sladen's "boots on the doorstep" is wrong, for Japanese homes have no doorsteps, they have *porticos*, ante-chambers of various sizes, and that is where you leave your shoes, where deliverymen bring and wait for things. It is a liminal zone, neither truly inside nor out – but certainly out of the elements. If *tatami* cause any in-and-out problems, it is the opposite of what Sladen imagined. After all, it is *more* comfortable to have one's shoes *off* than to have them on. The problem is rather that the need to keep dirt out of the house *is hard on children.* Morse touched upon it indirectly in a paragraph on Japanese cleanliness:

> Children of the poorest classes play in front of the house, but instead of enjoying their fun on the ground a straw matting is spread for them. (M:JDD)

That would be a drag. But all in all *tatami* is child friendly. The *tatami's* softness is perhaps its biggest benefit, for children cannot get concussions by simply falling down, as they can on a hard floor. Montanus exaggerated a little when he claimed *tatami* was "stuft like a quilt, which indeed are rather their Couches or Beds, where lay themselves down," and was wrong to say this was so "that they may tread the softer;" (M:EEJ) but it is true that their thickness makes them safer than a soft rug laid over a hard floor.

1. *Universal Tatami?* After adding Faux Frois on *tatami,* I read the following in Souyri's *The World Turned Upside Down*: "In the fifteenth century, the aristocracy began to use *tatami* (straw mats) throughout their rooms and not just for seating." Here, I had assumed they went back forever. ". . . first used as a seat or bed, they became a general floor covering. . . It was not until the late sixteenth century, however, that the new interior style [not just *tatami,* but use of white paper doors, etc.] reached the wealthier classes in the provinces." (S(R):WTUD) So, with tatami as with many things, Frois wrote in a time of transition and it is amazing he pegged so much of what has become clear only in retrospect. In other words, this contrast holds true for all the upper class in Kyoto but it might not hold true everywhere in Japan.（だがなにより も知りたいことは、畳の厚さの系譜（？）です。何時から 分厚くなりました？　百年前に比べて今は？等、等。畳博 士諸君、よろしく！）

11-12 Ours [are decorated] with leather chests, Flemish coffers and cedar cabinets.
As nossas com arcas emcouradas e cofres de Frandes, ou arcas de cedro;

        Those of Japan with black baskets made of cow hide.
        As de Japão com cestos pretos feitos de pelles de vacas.

On the Japanese side, it is surprising to find even this black basket – which, according to Okada, was probably woven with a wisteria warp and hide-strip weave, then lightly lacquered – for Japanese rooms generally have a large closet (*oshi-ire:* literally "stuff-in"), which includes a shelved area and boxes for storage (valuables, however, could go under the floor or, in the case of the wealthy, into special fire-proof store-rooms), so quality space may be saved for people rather than furniture, which was regarded as so much clutter. Partly because of my difficulty with the translation above – Should it be a leather *trunk,* Flemish *chest,* etc.? – the italicized phrase in the following words of wisdom (the Japanese philosophy according to a Dutch friend of Alcock's) delight me to no end:

> You build houses ten times as large as is necessary for your accommodation, and more than your income can keep up . . . merely that you may have room to stow away *an endless succession of ugly square and oblong pieces of timber*, tortured into various shapes and uses. We build houses to live in, not for ostentation, and still less as warehouses for useless things. (A:COT)

Alcock was extremely drawn to the Japanese way for its social benefits: without the enormous first expense of marriage, an enormous "upholsterer's bill," not to mention the cost of upkeep, young men could get married on an income of ￡400 per year. "If," he remorsefully muses, "European joints could only be made supple enough to enable their owners" to live in the Japanese way, more poor people could get married. Not only could they get married, but the poor woman could be freed to go out and work, for lacking the etiquette that, in Bacon's words, "gives a Japanese woman something to do" in her empty home that "has about as much in it as a paper lantern," (B:JGW) a Western woman in a Japanese house would have time on her hands instead of wax.

Furniture "conspicuous by its absence," as Chamberlain put it ("Architecture" C:TJ), would seem to be a uniquely Japanese thing in the Far East. In Korea, almost every room has long been dominated by heavy wooden chests and cabinets profusely inlaid with mother of pearl – this furniture is to them what cattle are to many primitive folk, a representation of wealth (and an important part of marriage gifts). And in China, they even had, heaven forbid, chairs.

Today? Most Japanese have more things to fit in fewer and smaller *oshi-ire* closets (especially in the cheaply designed apartments called "mansions" that almost half of the Japanese live in) with the result being clutter far in excess of that in the West, even with the female half of the population trying to be neat. Japan today, excepting the completely traditional building in traditional use – *viz.* expensive inns – is *literally in a mess.* More interesting yet, this mess was already noticed in 1891! Eliza Scidmore:

> The very use of foreign furnishings or utensils seems to abate the national rage for cleanliness, and in any tea-house that aspires to be conducted in the foreign fashion, one discovers a dust, disorder, shabbiness, and want of care that is wholly un-Japanese. (S:JDJ)

It is strange to see the way that Westernization turns-off the good-sense switch in the Japanese mind even today. Whereas everything ugly remains hidden in a Japanese style house, one may find a *bunka-apaato* (cultured apartment – a cheap apartment house in the Western style) where the water heater, gas bombs and electric meter sit right out by the front door in plain view. Is it any wonder such dwellings are ugly inside, too? Only dust, thanks to the vacuum cleaner which no gadget-loving Japanese is without, has been largely vanquished.

~~~~~~

11-13   The people of Europe sleep up high on beds or cots.
A jente d'Europa dormem em alto em leitos ou catres.

Those of Japan sleep low down upon the *tatami* with which the house is matted.
A de Japão em baxo sobre os tatamis *com que a caza estaa esteirada.*

Many, if not most, Japanese still do.[1] And, sleeping at foot-level is very good for the little folk, who not only need not fear falling *out* of bed, but are at liberty to crawl *in* and take a nap any time they want to.   I patted myself on the back for that observation, then found Alice Mabel Bacon had beat me to it by over a hundred years. She also did so following the same progression, or association of ideas as Frois, combining the subject of 11-12 and 11-13! After explaining that the only furniture in an ordinary Japanese house (one lived in by a gate-keeper and his family) was the god-shelf, a little china cupboard, *hibachi*, tea-kettle and a "pretty bamboo vase of autumn flowers that decorated the wall" (i.e. stands in the *tokonoma* niche: see chapter *endnotes*), she enthuses:

> Certainly, the independence of furniture displayed by the Japanese is most enviable, and frees their lives of many cares. *Babies never fall out of bed, because there are no beds; they never tip themselves over in chairs for a similiar reason.* There is nothing in the house to dust, nothing to move when you sweep . . . the chief worries of a housekeeper's life are non-existent. (my *italics.* B:AJI)

People with children might consider lowering their beds rather than putting bars on them!

1. *Japanese Sleeping Habits.* My "most" might be wrong. The only survey that could be found – thanks,   FK! – on the net (it had no site affiliation and chopping off the right side of the address did not get me anywhere) broke down 60% bed and 40% futon.   Almost all of the former were satisfied with their beds whereas most of the *futon* crowd was not. My guess is that is because most people who use *futons* are poor and even if they like sleeping on the floor, not satisfied with the particular *futons* they have (I am giving my experience). I would also guess that the survey figures are skewed toward beds because it was done by internet, which favors the wealthier part of the population. So my "most" might still be right.

11-14   Our beds are always extended;
As nossas camas estão sempre estendidas nos leitos;

Those of Japan are always rolled up and hidden out of sight during the day.
As de Japão sempre de dia emroladas e escondidas onde se não vejão.

Perhaps futon have grown thicker since 1585, for today, *futon* are usually not " rolled up," but *folded* in three and put away into the *oshi-ire* closet. I find making and un-making my whole bed every day tiresome (so there is *some* housework in a Japanese house) and wanted to turn my *oshi-ire* closet into a sleeping compartment so I could leave it made; but the *oshi-ire* is always 180 centimeters (one *tatami* span) across, and that is 6 centimeters too short for me. With the beds stashed away, there is more room, and one needs only remove the door=walls and the bedroom becomes part of the living-room (If you have two rooms. As a poor man, I had but one.) So, I can understand why most young Japanese prefer Western style beds.

In good weather, the *futon* are "hung over balconies to air, coming back damper than ever, if the servants forget to bring them in before sunset." (S:JDJ) They – the *futon,* not the servants – are also thoroughly beaten. This is still true. Every modern apartment must have a place for *futon* to be aired and beaten. The only problem is when the floor above you beats down all their mites upon your wet laundry (apartment dwellers in Japan rarely have that energy-guzzling obscenity called a dryer).

11-15   Our pillows are made of feathers, linen or cotton, soft, long and thin;
As nossas almofadas são de prumagem, canh[g?]a ou algodão, moles e compridas;

Those of Japan are made of wood, and just one [type?], a palm in length.
As de Japão de pao, e huma somente, de comprimento de hum palmo.

Hard, narrow, and high as a double-pillow, Westerners found Japanese pillows a literal pain in the neck. Why do Japanese use such pillows? Morse:

> The pillow was evolved to meet the peculiar method of arranging the hair. The elaborate coiffure of the women and the rigid queue of the men waxed and arranged to last for a number of days, required a head-rest where these conditions would not be disturbed. In hot weather the air circulates about the neck, and this is very agreeable." (M:JDD)

In other words, having ones hair done was expensive and time-consuming (Since "a hairdresser's husband" is idiomatic for *a man on easy street,* we know hairdos were not free), so people didn't want their heads touching anything more than was absolutely neccessary. Mr. Sladen put it very bluntly. In Japan, "hair, like Macbeth, has murdered sleep."

> The women of Japan and Mashonaland have hit upon an almost identical contrivance to enable them to go without doing their hair for a week. It is made of wood, and looks like a door-scraper with a top taken from a cripple's crutch. When the woman sleeps she lays not her head but her neck on this headsman's block of a pillow. [(pages later) which used to remind me of Mary Queen of Scots being executed wrong side upwards, and taking her execution lying down, to use a phrase made classical by Mr. Chamberlain.] (S:MQT)

I think that not only the women of Mashonaland, but men and women in much of black Africa would have been at home with the Japanese pillow! But to continue with Japan. The pillows of the common folk were generally *all* wood; but, according to a note in Golownin (G:MCJ), "the higher or richer classes make use of a very neat box, about eleven inches high, to the lid of which an oval [I would call it *tubular*] cushion is affixed, from six to eight inches in length, and from two to three in breadth. This box contains articles which they make use of at the toilette, such as razors, scissars, pomatum, tooth-brushes, powder, &c." A pillow as a medicine cabinet!

As Okada notes, Frois mentions only wooden pillows to maximize his contrast. There were *also* hollow lacquered bamboo (woven) pillows which may still be found in some old inns. Although more giving than solid wood, they are still far too hard for most Westerners and young Japanese. All one can say is that either we are very soft-headed, or the Japanese of yesteryear must have been a very hard-headed people indeed! All of the "forms of pillow in common use" sketched by Morse – who also mentions pillows with wooden ends and basket-work middle, portable folding pillows, as well as rarer porcelain (!) pillows – show short tubular cushions "stuffed with buckwheat hulls" tied by a single string to the top of the wooden blocks. (M:JHS&S) So, it would seem that a quarter century after the Black Ships of Perry, most Japanese were already sleeping in the mode of the upper classes.

> *Our pillows are put into one or two pillow cases.*
> *Their pillows have no cases but only a piece of paper tied into place.*

The same string that ties the small conical cushion on top of the wooden stand secures the paper. With the death of the traditional hairstyle, the top part of the traditional pillow, the tubular cushion alone survived.[1] Enlarged and conical, rather than flat, like ours, they are hard enough to still give "us" trouble. Here is Ponting reporting from *The Lotus Land Japan* in 1922.

> Though I have spent many months at Japanese inns, I have never mastered the knack of keeping it [the pillow] from rolling off the futon and letting my head down with a bump. Invariably, I had to put my large camera-case at the head of the bed to keep it in place – much to the amusement of the neisan [sister = young lady] who saw it.

Today, the covering on traditional tubular pillows is cloth, often with lace near the outer edges, and extends most of the way around the pillow, leaving the ends of the pillow completely open to the air. About half of the pillows are now the shape of ours, but they tend to be cooler with barley hulls, macaroni-like bits of plastic and other airy stuffing. If we only had the brains to learn from "them," our air conditioners could be given a vacation.

1. Tubular Alone? Actually, there is another type of traditional pillow that is very hard to describe The cross-section is the same as that of a fat hamburger bun, so the pillow should be easier to prevent from rolling than a tubular one, but the pillows overall dimensions are larger so it still tends to scoot away.

~~~~~~

11-16 In Europe, pavilions, canopies and curtains of damask and silk are used.
Em Europa se uza de pavolhões, esparaveis e cortinas de damasqo e seda;

> In Japan, in the summer [they use] *kaya* [mosquito[1] net tent] of very thin *nuno* [cloth] or of paper. *Em Japão pollo verão de* cayas *muito ralas de* nuno *ou de papel.*

This is very funny if you get it, for Frois compares "our" elaborate and decorative bed fittings with their tool. But, the humble *kaya* is *by far* the more valuable device, worth more than its weight in gold, for it permits one to sleep. A summer vesper in Japan is, if I may borrow from a haiku by Issa, an announcement that one has crossed the border and entered *Mosquito Country!"* (*kane naru ya ka-no kuni-ni koyo-koyo-to*).   Alcock, who minced no words concerning his hatred for "these Poisoners of the human race, and Destroyers of all peace" on the eve of his dispatch to Japan, later found said net a happy example of the "perfect genius" Japanese have "for attaining the most useful ends with the smallest expenditure of material, and by the simplest means."   At the various inns where he spent the night when traveling (partly to test the freedom of travel granted by treaty), he attests

> We should have been devoured by the mosquitoes had the landlords not come to our rescue by the simplest of all contrivances, a mosquito [2] curtain, open at the bottom, made up in the shape of a parallelogram, is let down over the mat (6 feet by 3) selected by the sleeper, a cord is run from each of the four upper corners (into which a sort of eyelet hole has been worked), and four nails driven in to enable a servant to suspend it. Under this, the persecuted martyr creeps, tucking in the sides and ends under his cotton quilt or mat . . . (A:COT)

My main image of the mosquito net comes from haiku, in particular, one about the fun of putting fireflies inside of the "parallelogram," as Alcock describes the draped tent. Until researching for this book, I had no idea just how valuable they once were.   Originally, Japanese relied completely on smudge. The *Chronicles of Japan* (*Nihon Shoki* c.720) reports mosquito-net sewers (*kaya-no-kinu-nui*) coming over from Kure 呉 which is to say, part of ancient Korea.   Needless to say, only the nobility used them (as only "our" nobility had mosquito canopies) and even they used smudge as well for there wasn't enough netting for the retainers.   Nets only began to spread about the time Frois arrived and only became common a hundred or two hundred years later. Meanwhile, a superstition took root that they were good to stave off thunder [lightning?] (Because houses that don't need them tend to be on peaks where mosquitoes are few?).   This was not accomplished imports.

> Once, making a mosquito net was a woman's once-in-a-lifetime work, like a man's making a house, and until she had made the mosquito net for her oldest son.
>
> It was believed that a mosquito net that was not made in a single day could bring about a disaster to the family, so all of the women [in town] would gather together to sew it up, after which just those women would gather within the net and celebrate drinking *sake* and eating *mochi* (sweet-rice-cake). . . At this time, in Kumamoto prefecture's Tamano county, they hold a mosquito-net-roof-raising) and bring in a mortar and a cat, who is hit on the head because it must meow to complete the ceremony. (*my trans.* from web: LR, but it was Japanese)

Compared to the thousands of man and woman-hours that went into some of those European tapestries, I suppose a mosquito tent is not much, but the 1-day net (even with dozens of women) seems a bit too fast to me.   Did the women bring pieces with them and only need to assemble them? [2]

There are still mosquitoes, today, but most Japanese have adopted the Occidental solution of fitting mosquito nets to the windows, which is to say *screens*.   These screens are all-too-often an ugly swimming-pool blue because that is supposed to look literally cool.   For people who, like me, think screens destroy the view, there are sound-making devices which people are not supposed to hear (but I do), a traditional green-coiled smudge (You've seen it? Yes it came from Japan and I suspect was sometimes used to tell time.) that is a pleasant enough smell until it builds up and you choke on it, and a foul-smelling modern chemical that evaporates from an electronically heated tab which I suspect to be carcinogenic.   So, I prefer to feed the mosquitoes that are honest enough to show their faces in the daylight and hide within a mosquito net by night.   Most Japanese have no trouble with the above-mentioned items but, older Japanese still string them up mosquito nets for old time's sake and, I am told, enough couples feel that they are *romantic* to keep sales up.   It is also possible that an ecological conscience may spark a *kaya* revival.[3]

1. Mosquito, /Musquito etc.   To tell the truth, I have mixed feelings about the word "mosquito." The Japanese is as short as the bug is small, *ka*. It fits beautifully inside of haiku, while the English word gobbles up a fifth of the poem. But I like it for sneaking the long diminutive (for *mosca* = fly) into English and for being difficult. Re: *Lewis & Clark:* "Nor did he [Lewis] ever learn to spell his enemies' name. His usual spelling, repeated at least twenty-five times, was "musquetoe." Clark was more inventive: he had at least twenty variations, ranging from "mesquetors" through "misqutr" to "musquetors." (Stephen Ambrose: *Undaunted Courage* . . . Simon & Schuster, 1996)

2. *Mosquito Net Knowledge* What little I know so far. The nets from China were silk or cotton and Japanese about Frois's time had started making them from hemp. The eyes of these hempen nets did not need to be quite so fine as modern ones because the natural bristles on the thread prevented mosquitoes from squeezing through. Because of the loose weave (compared to most fabric that is solid) the eyes had to be fixed by applying just enough glue after weaving to prevent the threads from sliding. As a result, they could not be washed. Supposedly, hemp nets offer an additional benefit to those who sleep within their canopy. *They suck the moisture not only out of the air but from the futon.* That is they function as dehumidifiers. While strong after woven, hemp in the process of being woven is weak when dry, so the top mosquito net weavers had their factories on the side of Lake Biwako. (Info. from Anmin, a maker of hemp nets

with threads that grab each other and can be washed.) Nets remained expensive for a long time. Issa's haiku, expressing jealousy over the fine mosquito nets enjoyed by a lord's horses and describing phenomenally thick smudge in the poor parts of town, suggest that in his day (18-19 c) there were still not enough nets to go around.

3. *Mosquito Net Revival* In August of 2002, the Sugiura Hisako research club of the dept. of life-environment science at Shôwa Woman's College did what we might call an *installation* called "Mosquito-net Homes," where 18 old-fashioned pure hemp mosquito-net "homes" were placed on a tree-lined street and filled with children to demonstrate the joy of a public yet still protected (against mosquitoes, anyway) space. Professor Sugiura, who has a degree to practice architecture in France, spoke about how it showed that public space was public and that there were ways to use space other than making new buildings and the abbot of a Buddhist temple came to laud this way to protect oneself without killing bugs.   (http://www. iwatanet.com/kikuya/melmaga213.htm)

11-17 Among us, it would be below a nobleman to sweep his room.
Antre nós seria baxeza varrer hum fidalgo sua camara;

Japanese gentry do so and think it very dandy.
Os senhores Japões ho uzão e o tem antre si por primor.[1]

With the advent of the witch, the broom became so thoroughly identified with women in Europe we cannot blame men for fearing to touch them, right?

The Chinese character for a wife (妻) has a woman (女) with a broom over her head but, be that as it may, Japanese men are indeed big sweepers. If you include *raking* within the general idea, we can envision the wave patterns they make in the gravel at Zen temples, the leaves they leisurely gather to burn, . . . But, to tell the truth, I do not know about this contrast. At first I thought the broom might be confined to the tea hut which Frois has taken so much advantage of. But, look what Golownin (admittedly 200 years later) has this to say about Inns:

It is a whimsical rule that the guests must leave the apartments as clean as when they entered them; so that no person ever quits an inn, until he has seen his apartment put into proper order. well swept, and washed if necessary. In short, it would be considered an act, not only of impoliteness, but even of ingratitude, if the smallest speck of dirt was to be left behind. So precise are the Japanese in this respect, that even the Dutch, when permitted to traffic there were deemed deficient in neatness. (G:MCJ) [Note: the Dutch housewife was the terror of Europe, for she would brain a man who dared spit on her floor, and the idea of cleanliness was so celebrated in Holland that Dutch warships went about with brooms atop their masts to show they swept the sea of their enemies! (H:JJ)]

Then, again, Frois may be referring to the annual Beat-out-the-dust Day (*susubarai*), which *everyone* participated in *with gusto*. In this case, they would be literally *sweeping up*, for the rafters are only cleaned on this one day, when dust clouds were reputed to hang over the entire city, as they do after festivals in Chinese cities because of all the firecrackers. Even today, every year, everyone must pitch in and clean at the office, and television news shows us battalions of dust-masked priests and volunteers from the congregation doing what looks like a search-and-destroy mission against enormous temples using brooms and dusters with handles as long as pool-cleaning poles. These annual offensives are generally commanded by men.

1. *Primor*, again. There is that word Frois so loves that I always want to translate "cool," but fearing the word too slangy go for "dandy," while worried lest it be too light, consider "and are proud of it" for the emphasis, or "gallant" to bring out the martial spirit of the men, or "stylish" to reflect the times that were, as always, a'changing.

~~~~~~

11-18   We wipe our faces with fine towels.
Nós alimpamos o rosto com toalhas delgadas;

They *waza-to* [chose to] wipe them with rags[1] or hemp hards.
Elles vaza to com liteiros ou tomentos muito grosos.

This contrast is given in the prologue to Frois's missing summary at the end of the discussion on handkerchiefs and tissue paper. However, Frois has already contrasted handkerchiefs in 1-50. I would have preferred a unique contrast, say the *loofa* for good skin care on the part of the Japanese versus fine washcloths on the part of Europeans. But the *tomentos,* a word which suggests *down of thick short hairs* or the "tow, hurds, scutch (all meaning the roughest part, or remainder) of flax hemp, jute, etc." does not quite suggest the dishcloth gourd and Frois would probably have used a verb specifically meaning "wash." Regardless, this seems a poor contrast for this section on facilities!

It is interesting, however, to note "they" *prefer* to wipe their faces with *rough* material, while we preferred fine. Does this perhaps reflect a different attitude toward skin-care? Polishing vs scourging, perhaps? Is "our" skin too delicate (full of freckles, easily sun-burned and otherwise damaged) to permit the latter approach? The modern washcloth suggests, however, that we have come to follow the Japanese way.

1. *Liteiros*. The dictionary specifies "cotton" for this cloth, and it was indeed cotton in Japan, but since cotton was not yet known in Europe, I think "rags" alone was sufficient.

~~~~~~

11-19   Our lavatories must be behind the house, hidden.   *As nossas latrinas ão-de estar detras das cazas escondidas.*

Theirs are in front, patent to all.   *As suas na dianteira, patentes a todos.*

Here, Okada writes, Frois, desperate for contrast, is back to the homes of the commoners, for they were the ones that often had the outhouse in front (Not right by the door, mind you, but off to the side a bit, by the household garden.) The better houses, like those in Europe, had theirs out of sight in the North-side (nether regions!) of the house. Be that as it may, this practice had its merits. *First,* the toilet would be closer when one returns home. *Second*, it might bring in "fertilizer" (see 21, below). And, *third,* who says the front must be the best part of a house, anyway? The nobility's outhouses were inside an interior garden, a little paradise – there was an "upper" one and "lower" one, the former for only the lord and very favored guests, and the latter for the women of the house (Don't ask me where the other people went!). Toilets or not, the rear of the house was attractive (it had the decorative 'natural' garden) and the front, aside from the gate, nothing much. This was hard for "us" to understand, for we put our best everything out front. According to the first American Consul, Townsend Harris, the fact that "the most honorable rooms are in the rear" in Japan led to cultural misunderstanding when visiting Westerners thought they were placed in these rooms "merely to prevent their seeing anything of the people, etc." (H:CJTH).

I think the reason Frois chooses to start his discussion of toilets and excrement with this observation is because of his long stay in Miyako (Kyoto), a city which was famously upfront about collecting and recycling human waste. Kyoto even boasted public toilets *in front of shops on the Main Avenue* and at many of the cross-roads. (or, at least did in the Edo era, and *may have* in Frois's time). Polymath Aramata Hiroshi in his long essay into the origin of the *kawara, benjo* and *toire*, that is, respectively, ancient, traditional and Western style toilets in Japan, took the odor into consideration, and called these "toilet-urge-enticing devices." (J/A:NGK) – I am reminded of the sign by the public toilet photographed in the Peoples Republic of China: *"Don't be selfish* [i.e. keep it for home], *use this!"* (This would not necessarily mean waiting until one gets home either. In *Everyday Things In Modern Japan*, Susan Henley mentions 19th century travelers carrying containers for their urine, which they would try to exchange for food or money.) The Kyoto area was, and still is, known for its many fine leafy vegetables – they even have a type of cabbage (*Kyôna*) with a head large enough to feed a small village! This meant urine, with its phosphate, was in particularly high demand and was even directly bartered with greens.

As Aramata notes, people from Edo were as astounded as any foreigner to see urinals out in front of the outhouses proper, in full view of passersby in Kyoto. This *was* indeed "patent" in the original meaning of the word: *to stand wide open.* And what shocked them even more was the fact that women also used them, *standing,* hiked up kimonos, with their buttocks bent out slightly over the troughs. And these were not only servants, supposedly even the wives of wealthy merchants joined in! About a hundred years after Frois, the *senryu* poets – largely from Edo, for its largely male population found consolation for their loneliness in black humor – could not resist taking a dig at the urine capitol of Japan and its women, who were otherwise considered paragons of womanhood.

wc's galore	*perfection lost*
there are no signs saying "Urination Forbidden!" in old Kyoto	Kyoto women have a wee flaw – they stand to make water
shôben-muyô-fuda wa nai kyô-no-machi	*kyô-onna tatte tareru ga sukoshi kizu*

~~~~~~

11-20   We seated; *Nós asentados;*

And they squatting. *E elles em cocoras.*

This refers to the style of doing the "big," as Japanese call what Usanians sometimes call "number two."   Just as Frois missed the chance to comment on the direction of horses in their stalls he missed a big one here:

We face out to defecate;
They face in.

I cannot recall if this aligns us with out horses or puts us at odds with them. It does put the Japanese in a more defenseless position, but also makes embarrassment less likely, for reasons I will not try to explain. Here is another.

We urinate and defecate together;
They use separate toilets.

It goes without saying that this is ideal for collecting fertilizers. Japanese bathrooms were suitably designed for this.   In the late-18th century, Thunberg described a Japanese bathroom as follows:

> Every house has its *privy;* in the floor of which there is an oblong aperture, and it is over this aperture that the Japanese sit. At the side of the wall is a kind of box, inclining obliquely outwards, into which they discharge their urine. Near it there is always a Chinese vessel with water in it, with which, on these occasions, they never fail to wash their hands. (T:TEAA)

Said hole is flush with the floor and one does not make any contact with its edges. (Since sitting implies contact of buttocks with seat, the "sit" may be a poor translation from Thunberg's German.) These logistics – i.e., the distance from standing to the floor in the case of men – meant that even where fertilizers are no longer collected, most Japanese homes with traditional hole-toilets also have urinals, which, judging from this description, either did not exist or were not common in Europe until relatively recently.   The modern ceramic Japanese-style toilet generally has a small hood on the wall-side end rising about half a foot over floor level that serves as a spray-guard and prevents anyone peeking in the ventilation window – always floor-level and just behind the toilet (*ano iyarashii ko-mado = Edith Hansen*) – from seeing what they should not.

When somebody not used to squatting squats, he or she finds it both tiring and unstable. After the husband of the *gaijin* couple in *The Japan Times* cartoonist Roger Dahl's "Zero Gravity" boasts that he has fulfilled their agreed upon daily quota of "aerobic calisthenics," she asks: "Since when does using a Japanese-style public toilet facility qualify as a full aerobic workout?" He replies "Since prolonged breath-holding was combined with the deep-kneebend." (date lost) *This is no exaggeration.* It is hard for neophytes to squat for more than a minute or two and, because their heels fail to settle on the floor, they must occasionally grab the walls or pipes in order not to fall-over. (When I first went to Japan in 1972, I found my father, a consultant for Yamaha Boat, using a special potty-seat, rigged up over the usual floor-level basin. My father, having only one arm really needed this "training device," as he called it!) Old generation Japanese can read a book while squatting at their business as well as we can sitting on the pot and, for their part are amazed to hear *we* can do the same, for, as they note, correctly, potty seats can cut off blood-circulation.   "We," as a culture, do not understand squatting. Alcock tries:

> A Japanese quite at his ease, and *sans gene,* as naturally drops on his heels and squats, with no more a support to his person than his legs or heel can afford, as an Englishman drops into a chair when he is tired. [np] As soon as the babe leaves its mother's breast, the first thing it learns is not to walk or to run, but to squat on its heels in this baboon fashion. (A:COT)

Alcock (or his artist) did not really look close enough, for the illustration entitled "How Japanese Rest" mistakenly shows a raised heel squat. If you are *balancing* on the balls of your feet, you know not squat about squat, for the whole point of *true* squatting is to gain, not lose, stability. The feet of the accomplished squatter, heels and all, rest square on the ground. Unless you are blessed with a particularly large ass, you do not sit on your heels. The back of your upper-leg rests upon your calves. The trick to gaining the ability to squat like this depends upon getting the upper part of your foot to come closer to your shin and your knee-joints open. Baboons aside, sitting is no more modern than squatting. The difference would seem to be geographic and go way back in history. I read in a book of Loo-lore that the flushing toilets in King Minos' castle in Crete "had wooden seats." I do not know where the line between the sitting cultures and the squatting cultures may be drawn. Could it be Turkey, as was the case for the push *vs* pull-saw? Health-wise, the more natural squat surely provides more benefits. A recent rise in constipation in Japan is blamed on the Western toilet and very few Japanese have bad knees. (Or, did Westerners adopt seats *because* they had bad knees?) [1]

---

1. Bad Knees. I know from experience that even if you   smash your knee and have bits of calcium or ligament or whatever in there (With no insurance or money, I can not afford an MRI, so I do not know what is in mine, but the extreme heat suggests calcium and perhaps need of an operation), if you force your knee to open wide by sitting on your shins/heels, the frightening noise disappears for a while and movement does not overheat the knee. It seems to me that Doctors in the USA, are so obsessed about tightening knees by developing muscle that they overlook the importance of sharply bending them in order to reduce friction within the kneecap and the result is lots of operations and many bad knees. Any statistics on the knees of old people in the USA and Japan?

Extra: Frois was not very toilet-minded or he might have had more, such as:

We use water;
They use sand.

I assume we used water in Frois's day, did we?

We do not take particular measures to reduce noise;
They spread leaves in the urinal.

The use of feathers was also tried but they had the disconcerting habit of floating up to greet you.

We leave the toilet door open after use;
Theirs is always closed.

I am not sure where I got the above one from and suspect it may only apply to post flush-toilet Usania.

~~~~~~

11-21   We pay for someone to carry our night-soil away.
Nós damos dinheiro a quem nos leve o esterco f[or]ja;

In Japan, they buy it and give rice and money for it.
Em Japão o comprão e dão arroz e dinheiro por elle.

A straight exchange was common for buckets of urine, while ordure was usually bought and the food-stuff was more in the way of a bonus. In Osaka and Kyoto, according to Aramata, these waste products comprised a not-to-be-laughed-about portion of the family income. Even store clerks were reimbursed for their contribution. For a store owner with ten employees, it could amount to 20-30% of each employee's income! In Edo, on the other hand, the landlord sold the night-soil – with the urine mostly drained off (wasted) – and retained the proceeds for themselves. In parts of Japan, if enough men (over 4, perhaps) lived in a small room, *they could pay their entire rent with their waste,* which is to say, they could stay for free! (J/A:NGK) Kaempfer describes the 17th century countryside:

Care is taken, that the filth of travelers be not lost, and there are in several places, near country people's houses, houses of office for them to do their needs. Old shoes of horses and men, which are thrown away as useless, are gathered in the same houses and burnt to ashes, along with the filth, for common dung, which they manure all their fields withal. Provisions of this nasty composition are kept in large tubs, or tuns, which are buried even with the ground, in their villages and fields, and not being cover'd, afford full as ungrateful and putrid a smell of radishes (which is the common food of country people) to tender noses, as the neatness and beauty of the road is agreeable to the eyes. (K(S):HOJ)

The stench was something else again. Alcock, summarized the 18th century observations of Thunberg like this: "Japan would be a very good country to be fed in, but those who live in it ought not to have noses as well as mouths, or be in any way endowed with olfactory nerves." And again, "He somewhere else alludes to the numerous receptacles made for preserving the odious compounds until wanted 'on the highway at frequent intervals,' which, he admits, made the roads themselves impassable to people inflicted with a sense of smell, . . ."(A:COT) Thunberg, himself, put it like this:

We were, . . . whenever we passed through any village, subject to an inconvenience which embittered all our pleasures, and obliged us to keep the windows of our norimons [*norimono* = sedan] shut. A privy, which is necessary for every house, is always built in the Japanese villages towards the street, and at the side of the mansion-house; it is open downwards, so that passengers may discharge their water from the outside into a large jar, which is sunk on the inside into the earth. The stench arising . . . was frequently, in hot weather, so strong and insupportable, that no plug introduced into the nose could dispute the passage with it, and no perfumes were sufficient entirely to disperse it. (T:TEAA)

Japanese villages generally had "only one street" of a length that "frequently surpasses all belief: most of them are three quarters of a mile in length, and some of them so long it requires several hours to walk through them." Moreover, "some also stand so close together that they are discriminated from each other only by a bridge or rivulet, and their name." That is to say, we are not talking about a passing inconvenience but a constant one! Thunberg also found the liquid fertilizer hard on something Alcock forgot to mention, the eyes!

Useful and beneficial as, in other respects, I every where found this branch of the over-strained œconomy of the Japanese, it was equally hurtful to the eyes. For by the exhalations of this intolerable vapor, to which the people had gradually accustomed themselves, the eyes became so much affected, that a great many, and particularly old people, were afflicted with very red, sore and running eyes. (Ibid)

Elsewhere he mentions such eye problems also afflicted children and blamed it on "the smoke from charcoal within the houses, and the stench proceeding from the jars of urine." Obviously, *stench* does not effect eyes, but a high concentration of ammonia might! Luckily, most Japanese were inured to the stench. Even toward the end of the 20th century, they put up with the incredibly pungent smell of raw human waste coming from their *kumitori* toilet (I lived with one of these "scoop-take" toilets for eight years and either put a clothespin on my nose or held my breath every time I went!). As it turns out, this foul toilet is a modern invention: Japan, writes Aramata, took the model of the *Kentucky Toilet*, minus the best part, the septic tank. (A:NGK) Instead, the waste just collects in a big concrete cistern *directly below the toilet* from which it is collected once a year or so! I once read about how, in South Africa, a ram's head was dropped into the hole first to attract certain bugs which would completely neutralize the odor. "Scoop-take" toilets still comprise a not inconsiderable percentage of the toilets in Japan. Rather than the wasteful and un-ecological American style sewers touted for their replacement – more as a works program to improve Japan's amenity ranking in the international statistics than because of Japanese demand – someone should consider those African beetles or their chemical equivalent! Stench control aside, the Japanese arrangement makes, or rather made, far more sense than ours. Morse, alone, in 1877, recognized it as more rather than less hygienic than our practices:

Somewhat astonished at learning that the death-rate of Tokyo was lower than that of Boston, I made some inquiries about health matters. I learned that dysentery and cholera infantum are never known here . . . But those diseases which at home are attributed to bad drainage, imperfect closets [toilet systems], and the like seem to be unknown or rare, and this freedom from such complaints is probably due to the fact that all excrementitious matter is carried out of the city by men who utilize it for their farms and rice-fields. With us, this sewage is allowed to flow into our coves and harbors, polluting the water and killing all aquatic life; and the stenches arising from the decomposition and filth are swept over the community to the misery of all. . . . It seems incredible that in a vast city like Tokyo this service should be performed by hundreds of men who have their regular routes. The buckets are suspended on carrying-sticks and the weight of these full buckets would tax a giant. (M:JDD)

In his later *Japanese Homes*, Morse would qualify his remarks a little by admitting that the run-off from the fertilizer might sometime cause cholera in the South part of Japan. But, he maintained the gist of his argument: *We are fouling our own nest.* In Florida reading Morse in1999, I recall reading an article that the keys south of Key Largo were off-limits to swimming because of fecal contamination and fuming aloud: *We sure learn fast don't we!* But Morse may have exaggerated the difference between Japan and the USA, for only three years after Morse made the above observation, 103 of 222 cities surveyed in the United States put night-soil to agricultural use! And, even as late as the 1970's, about 30% of our farm villages still did (according to "New Age" magazine, Feb. 1982).[1] In one sense, however, there surely was a difference. I doubt if *any* of our systems were *ever* as thorough and efficient as those of Japan. If they were, we too would have been *paid* for waste, rather than paying for it to be removed, right? The long and short of it was that "we" thought of soil as something to be used up or at best maintained, whereas the Japanese thought of it as something to be enriched with offal and junk fish, which was also used in abundance for manure. There is good reason for it, too.

> Without manure they do not cultivate; the soil is not rich in productive materials, as it is mostly of volcanic origin. A Japanese saying is, "A new field gives but a small crop." (M:JDD)

I cannot help but recall a book on Japanese as farmers by that rare species, a right-wing intellectual, Watanabe Shoichi. (Though sometimes called the George F. Will of Japan, he has a bit more class. He translates Chesterton where Will calculates baseball statistics). He also waxes ecstatically for page after page on the subject of those *old* fields, on how big farming in America – trying to open the market – could never understand the psychological significance of intensive farming, the Japanese farmer's attachment to his land, *land created from the very bowels of his ancestors . . .* Deep shit, indeed! [2] Another sample of the real Japan:

> According to carpenter Tsukuda, who built my house, night soil was still the most important fertilizer ingredient even as late as thirty years ago when he was a student in agricultural college . . . I remember listening in amazement as he told me:

> "Part of our practical education was to wander the countryside, dipping fingers into such pits, and licking them to determine the age and quality of the contents – a bit like wine tasting?"

> (Jeremy Angel column: "Flush toilets and the Dearth of Night Soil" *The Daily Yomiuri* 1995/2/9)

While China was not all volcanic like Japan, much of it was worn out or dried out by millenniums of farming (only a portion has that bottomless soil that is far more miraculous than, say, Niagara Falls, if you think about it.). So, the Chinese had to learn how to recycle their waste, and it is their technique that the Japanese borrowed (or brought with them). Japanese tend to think they have the patent on shit, but everything written above could be repeated for China. Long before Morse, indeed about thirty-five years before Frois's TRATADO, Pereira, a merchant who endured a long captivity in China, wrote:

> The country is so well inhabited, that no one foot of ground is left untilled . . . These countrymen by art do that in tillage, which we are constrained to do by force. Here be sold the voidings of close-stools, although there wanteth not the dung of beasts: and the excrements of man are good merchandise throughout all China. The dung-farmers seek in every street by exchange to buy this dirty ware for herbs and wood. The custom is very good for keeping the city clean. (B:SCSC)

> Pereira was doubtless thinking of contemporary Lisbon, where in common with many other European cities, visitors complained "of the stench of the ordure that is continually thrown out; for not only the dust of the houses is thrown out into the streets, but the chamber-pots and close-stools, for in all the city there are no houses of office." (Note by Boxer for the above, citing a 1706 book published in London. My note: *Houses of Office!* So that's why we call it doing our business!)

Coincidentally, the *via* for the oldest surviving draft of Pereria's account "hurriedly copied by the children of the seminary attached to the College of Sao Paolo at Goa at the end of 1561" is endorsed by none other than our Frois! More detail is found in the Dominican friar Cruz's extensive tract, which Boxer appraises as "the first book devoted to China which was printed in Europe" (*Polo, you ask?* China was only part of Polo and Polo only reported part of China). Cruz used and skillfully elaborated upon Pereira's work, using his own first-hand observation or study (Eg. He explains why Chinese can plow with less force.) The excremental quote below follows a substantial essay on the incredible economy of China, where everyone must work to eat (*a quem o nao trabalhar nao no comera*) and, since everyone has great appetites (*grandes gastos),* must work like hell! – and, conversely, because they literally consume what they earn, even "tyranny may take nothing from them," so they have good reason to work – with the result that only the highest weather-beaten mountains are left alone and "nothing is ever lost in this country be it ever so vile; for the bones as well of dogs as of other beasts, they do use, making toys, and carving them instead of ivory, they inlay them in tables, beds and other fair things . . ."   *Indeed.*   Hear the premonition of an *Old Cow* in I. T. Headland's classic collection+translation *Chinese Mother Goose.*

> To head a drum they will take my skin,
> And they'll file my bones for a big hair-pin,
> The scraps of bone they will make into dice,
> And sell them off at a very low price . . .

The economy of the Chinese is legend, even to the Japanese. My Japanese friend who translated the nursery rhymes Headland collected into Japanese found this total-use "terrifying." I laughed and reminded him that the Japanese boast of their total use of whales, and use it as proof of the depth of their cultural involvement and ecological correctness.   But, I suppose, it *is* a little scary.

> Even the dung of men yields profit and is bought for money or in change of vegetables, and they carry it from the houses, in sort that they give money of money's worth, to suffere them to cleanse their houses of office, though it smelleth evil through the city. When they carry it on their backs through the city, in order to avoid the evil smell, they carry it in tubs very clean without, and although they go uncovered, notwithstanding it showeth the cleanliness of the country and cities. . . . This dung serves them for to manure their kitchen-gardens and they say with it the vegetables can be seen to grow; they mix it with earth and bake it in the sun. (B:SCSC. *Translation:* I leave the Purchas+Boxer translation as is. I only regret that the interesting idiom *al olho,* i.e. "grow right *before your eyes*" was given up for the bland "vegetables can be seen to grow." *Really, Mr. Boxer!*)

I spy one difference here. I have not heard of dung-men cleaning the privy in Japan. The original (*por lhe[s] deixarem limpar as privadas*) suggest that not only did they clean out – as in extract the dung – but actually cleaned up in China. Pinto later added some interesting detail:
..

> And the dealers who buy this stuff go through the streets making noise with a wooden clapper of sorts, like our Lazarists begging for alms, by way of letting people know what they want to buy, for they are well aware of how dirty the word in itself is and that it would be in bad taste to go crying it out in the streets. And the demand for this merchandise is so great that at times it is possible to see as many as two, three hundred sails coming into port on the tide to pick up this cargo, the way the barges in our country come in to load salt, and even so, they very often have to resort to a system of allocations at fixed prices, depending on the available supply of the commodity. And because this fertilizer is so effective, they harvest three crops a year in China. (P(C):TMP)

Pinto began his paragraph (the above is the last half) on excrement as an example of "how greed can lead men to seize upon the vilest, filthiest things to make profit" but ends up crediting it for increasing the possible number of crops by a third! As always, Pinto's exaggeration has the ring of truth: Japanese (or was it Korean? [3]) junk-collectors still used a weird type of scissors-like metal clappers to advertise their presence – rather than the usual cry giving the name of one's goods and perhaps a bit of humor – up to the 1970's. As Pinto only visited parts of South Japan, he has nothing about the Japanese *likewise* utilizing human waste, despite being less profit-oriented than the Chinese.

Bonus: Roadside fertilizer gathering rest-stops reminding us of China and Japan were also found in the Mexico. Bernal Diaz:

> On all the roads they have shelters made of reeds or straw or grass so that they can retire when they wish to do so, and purge their bowels unseen by passers-by, and also in order that their excrement shall not be lost. (in T:COA)

1. *New Age* **on Manure.** I am back-translating from one of my own Japanese books. If anyone has time to check, please check the figures, too.   Also, I wonder how the USA compares to Europe on the use of human waste.

2. Farm Protection East and West   Merle Haggard's *Amber Waves of Grass*, which asks the *gubmint* to spend some of that *fern aid* over here so we don't see "spuds stamped *'Made in Japan'*" is a fine sounding song – and, musically speaking,   part of one of the best medleys (combined with and *Farmer's Daughter*, (where the farmer talks of himself in the humble third-person, just like a Japanese!), *Mama Tried* (or how I got from the farm to the pen) then heading for good ole *Muskogee*, found in country music – but there is a big difference. In Japan, the rice is spread all over the suburbs, bringing the sound of frogs and the cooling water (remember Japan is as hot and muggy as the South East of the USA yet few people have an AC. *That* is something worth fighting for. (The problem in Japan is that the burden of the high price of this rice is mostly paid for by the poor and that reduces the value of an otherwise more just tax system than that found in anti-Robin-Hood Usania.) On the other hand, much farmland in the USA would be better given back to nature, for the rain is not there, the water tables too low and the operations in those air-conditioned cabs might as well be done on the moon. (Go, ahead, farmer, if you are reading, rebut me!)

3. *Japanese or Korean.* I bought a pair of huge scissors with dull blades convex on the outside and concave on the inside from a junk man in the early 1970's but cannot recall whether it was in Korea or Japan. It was said to be a noise-making device, though if you ask me, the noise was little for the trouble of making it. It was metal not wood, but still reminds me of Pinto's "clappers."

~~~~~~

11-22 In Europe, horse dung is thrown into vegetable gardens, and that of man into garbage dumps.
Em Europa o estero dos cavalos se deita nas ortas e o da jente nos monturos.

> In Japan, horse dung is thrown in garbage dumps and man's into vegetable gardens.
> *Em Japão o dos cavalos nos monturas e nas ortas ho da jente.*

An enormous 18th century English book called *A Compleat Body Of Husbandry* (1770 – no author, for the title page was missing) details the use of half a dozen types of ordure used as manure in Europe including that of horses, cows, sheep, hogs, pigeons, poultry and . . . man. It was used in "some parts of England, and in many Places Abroad," such as the "Vineyards of Languedoc" and "in Flanders," where it was "regularly sold" for fertilizer for "Corn" (i.e. grain) crops. Frois can be forgiven for overlooking its use for, unlike the case in Japan, it was used "oftener than is thought," which is to say it was "a Practice every where carry'd on clandestinely for nobody would care to buy that Farmer's Corn, who should be known to use it." The first sentence of the opening paragraph to the section on night-soil gives valuable insight into how "we" thought:

> There is something disgustful in the Thought of using the Excrements of our own Species for the Dressing of Lands, as it is putting them again down our Mouths: but this particular type of Dung, is not without its Efficacy . . .

It is not likely the Europeans copied this from the Japanese or Chinese, because the method of preparation was completely different. In the Orient, as we have seen, it was wet. In Europe, it was spread "for a time upon a Bed of Mould [mulch?], and let to be exposed to the Sun" to dry it out, lessen its smell and its overly "hot" quality (The "heat" or "very rich" nature of our ordure was judged the result of our eating high up the food-chain – a meat diet with alcohol being especially likely to ferment). But even treated, it was considered a filthy ore, and . . . the least manageable of all others, the most offensive to the servants employ'd in spreading it, as well as to the thoughts of those who are to feed upon the Corn that rises from its Richness.

If human excrement was not totally ignored by European husbandry, horse dung was *not* really thrown away in Japan, either. It may not have been sold in the city but thrown on a heap, but that heap was surely *used by someone* for something. It is mentioned in OJD as a fertilizer and I have read of warriors using it to cook food in their helmets, which would suggest that it served the poor in the same capacity. Moreover, it is debatable to what extent the Japanese actually had *monturas* ([garbage]mounds) in the sense we understand them. Haiku mention sweep-piles (*hakidome*) and specific piles of shell-fish shells, disposable chopsticks, or flower petals.[2] But all of these are *small and temporary*, honest-to-goodness dumps are hard to find. Morse in the late-19th century noted that

> In country village and city alike the houses of the rich and poor are never rendered unsightly by garbage, ash piles, and rubbish; one never sees those large communal piles of ashes clam shells and the like that are often encountered in the outskirts of our quiet country villages. In refined Cambridge . . . This land was so disfigured by a certain type of rubbish that for years it was facetiously called the "tin canyon"! The Japanese in some mysterious way manage to bury, burn, or utilize their waste and rubbish so that it is never in existence. (M:JDD)

A century after TRATADO, Kaempfer wrote: "The Inspectors for repairing the highway are at no great trouble to get people to clean them; for whatever makes the roads dirty and nasty, is of some use to the neighboring country people, so that they rather strive, who should first carry it away." In this respect, he specifically mentions horse dung, saying it does not "lie long upon the ground but it is soon taken up by poor country children and serves to manure the fields." Evidently, horse (and cow) dung was not as prestigious (?) as human offal, but only cow piss was clearly not used, for an old Japanese proverb equates *"the lectures of parents and cow piss: long and good for nothing!"* Thunberg, further, adds that this cleaning, or rather gleaning work was mainly done by old men and children, and "very readily, .. without stooping, with a shell (*Haliotis tuberculata*) which resembled a spoon, and was fastened to a stick. The gatherings were put into a basket and carried on the left arm." (T:TEAA)

Perhaps because Thunberg wrote "neither could I see without admiration, the industry of the farmers in manuring the lands," Alcock describes him as "an out-and-out utilitarian, in the sense of those who regard the meat and drink of the body as the great or sole end for which the many labor on this earth" and claims he described the process of making manure in great detail. Those details show that "the manure of man and beast" were mixed until "it becomes a perfect hodge-podge." Actually, Alcock gives about as much information as Thunberg, only neglecting to mention the addition of kitchen offal. But where Thunberg writes objectively that the fluid fertilizer was ladled out to six inch high plants – "so that the liquor penetrates immediately to the root," Alcock could not refrain from quipping that this "may be very advantageous to the growth of said six-inch plants, but hardly accords with delicacy of taste. Some people might object to asparagus or lettuce thus brought to perfection, and find their pleasure of eating it sadly interfered with by a certain association of ideas, foolish enough no doubt, but very difficult to be rid of." (A:COT) Still, Alcock grants Japanese are "not quite as bad [hopelessly utilitarian, leaving nary a "green meadow" or "pleasant copse" alone] as they are painted [by Thunberg, who admired such husbandry but suffered from a lack of botanical specimen], for weeds flourish at Nagasaki as elsewhere, and wild flowers, too!" Much later in his book, Alcock sneaks back to manure and supplies some information of his own about how it is spread. Despite the cheapness and abundance of the labor, Japanese economize it:

> And when they wish to manure a field, they make a tree do the duty of one man, and very much assist and economize the labor of the other by passing a rope through the handle of the pail close

to the depot of the manure, one end of which is secured to the tree, and the other held by the laborer to enable him to swing the contents over a wide area. In other cases, he is supplied with a large ladle, at the end of a ten-foot handle, which gives an equally wide sweep with little labor. (Ibid (if I ever offset this book , this is one picture to see!))

While Japanese may have had some particularly efficient methods of spreading manure, China was still the Mecca of Manure. Not only was it used for fields but for *aquaculture*. Pereira and Cruz:

> Their fish is greatly nourished with the dung of buffaloes and oxen, that greatly fatten it. (B:SCSC)

> . . . yak [[*bufula*?]] and ox dung to raise fish in tanks for a very short period of time, with which they grow before your eyes. In all the artificial ponds [*cavas*?] of the cities, they raise many fish in the same manner . . . In this way, it can be understood how fresh seafood is brought to market everyday, although it is leagues from the sea. (C:TCC – my trans. I missed this part in Boxer. I also did it without a decent dictionary.)

We still have not caught up to China's ancient agronomy. Manure was not all of it. The Chinese had great vessels in their rivers with floating bamboo cages holding thousands of ducks which they rented out by day to the rice-paddy owners to clean up the weeds and bugs. Cruz devotes a whole page to the details of this operation which is only found today in small-scale operations.[2]

*   *   *

In view of the overwhelming evidence that the wasteless economy of old Japan came from China, there is one Sino-Japanese difference I constantly came across in 19th century writings by Europeans (and soon thereafter by Japanese) that doesn't make sense. Namely, the Chinese are depicted as a dirty people living in pigsty conditions, while the Japanese are credited with being the cleanest people in the world, not just for their renowned daily bath but for the fact that even the poor lived in a neat manner. Efficiency & *neatness* seem like a reasonable pair. But efficiency & *slovenliness* seem an odd combination. One wonders how the Chinese have managed to be both. Or, were they once as neat as the Japanese?

1. *According to Haiku.* I imagine that by now, all my scholarly readers must think I am nuts to keep citing "haiku" for my documentation(?). That is just the way it is. Over the past decade I have only read a score or two of history books, but hundreds of thousands of old haiku. So, most of my knowledge came in 17 syllabet doses.

2. *Duck Power.* While too many ducks can damage the rice plants, their little duck feet also serve to aerate and increase the health of the plant. Some Japanese tried to revive this as a type of organic farming in the 1990's and I (a duck-lover) wonder how it went. Does anyone know?

~~~~~~

11-23   We lock our chests with iron locks;
Nós fechamos as arcas com fechaduras de ferro;

> They their baskets with cords, paper seals and Chinese padlocks.
> *Elles seus sestos com cordas e mutras de papel ou cadeados da China.*

The contrast seems one of solid protection with something far less. Doubtless, our locks were substantial. "We" even had lock specialists who made large, ridiculously complex "masterpiece locks" that were never used, simply to gain accreditation as master locksmiths. This was even reflected in out respective literary trope. Locks barely figured in Japanese metaphor, while it was a very common metaphor in "ours" and, if Japan had its keeper of the barriers or the gate, we had our "keeper of the keys." The Pope was "the keeper of the keys to heaven." According to the Schlage.com website,

Several centuries ago, in Spain, there was a great distrust of locks. To be safe, the householders of a block hired a watchman to patrol the neighborhood and carry the keys to their dwellings. To enter or leave a house, the resident clapped his hands vigorously to summon the watchman with his key, so, all comings and goings became a matter of public record and there was little chance for "hanky panky" in old Madrid.

By "distrust" here, the author seems to mean that copies of keys could be made by the residents which could be passed on to lovers . . . This goes back to the seclusion of women discussed in chapter 2. Reading Casanova, I can only think that the effect was counter-productive, and they might have done as well to have done away with them entirely and joined the Japanese with their cords and paper seals! (The Chinese padlock Frois mentions is a "shrimp-lock" – a bent piece of metal shaped like a shrimp stuck into a main piece – would qualify as a light-weight padlock, but would offer little practical protection to the light-weight basket most things were kept in). *Serious locking up was just not a key part of the Japanese culture.* If women in many parts of Europe were given bundles of keys upon marriage (for inside the house at any rate!), a Japanese woman received a cooking ladle. Even when Japanese doors *were* locked, it was generally by bolt, *from the inside only.* When the family went out, say, cherry-blossom-viewing, someone always remained as the *rusuban,* an "absence guard." But, even this was less to guard against robbery than to have someone there in case of fire or earthquake. When Europeans came again in the 19th century, they found Japan was still virtually lockless (We will come back to Morse on this in 14-7). Frois might better have written,

> We have many locks and lock many things;
> Japanese have few locks and rarely lock anything, even their houses.

Even *toilets* generally had no locks, so people coughed before opening the door. Today in Japan both houses and toilets are generally locked.

～～

11-24   We use secret compartments in our chests; *Nós uzamos de escaninos nas arcas;*

And they, *kakego* [drawers] in their baskets. *E elles de caquegos nos cestos.*

Judging from 23, Frois is still talking security or lack thereof. Japanese tended to trust to the conscience of others and rarely locked up things (14-7). *Kakego* today generally refers to a nest of boxes, one within another, like those Russian eggs, but the Japanese-Portuguese dictionary of 1603/4 calls them *hikidashi,* or "drawers." At any rate, they are relatively accessible and far from "our" hidden safe. While I *chose* "chest," the translation for our side could as well have been "trunks" or "boxes," so long as they are imagined hard and rectangular, for the Portuguese *arca* is one with "the ark," and the etymology, missing in English but clear in Japanese (!) – or Chinese – for Noah's salvation is 箱舟, or "box-boat." This suggests a more general contrast Frois missed, which Lee O-Young based his *Furoshiki Bunka no Posuto-Modan* book on:

> We put things into solid containers, or fill up soft ones of a predetermined size;
> They wrap up things in furoshiki.*[a pretty square piece of cloth] to fit the size of the thing.*

That is to say, that the Eastern Trio (China, Korea and Japan) usually use a square piece of cloth rather than a box, trunk, basket or sack of fixed size to carry things about – things are first set on it, then opposing corners are tied together diagonally, two at a time. Lee claims this "primary opposition" of cultural codes, i.e., "putting in" (the box principle) versus "wrapping up" (the clothing principle) goes back to primeval times, and boasts that the greater versatility of the *furoshiki* – which bring to mind morphing robot toys (largely a Japanese invention) – make the Far East more fit for the Post-Modern poliverse. The Ark, suggests Lee, is too square to save us in modern times!

~~~~~~

11-25   Our carpenters work standing up; *Os nossos carpinteiros trabalhão em pé;*

Theirs, for the most part, remain seated. *Os seus pola mayor parte sempre asentados.*

Part of this may be due to the different materials. You *go to* the stone and bricks, but wood is light enough to be carried into the workshop. But that is not all. For "us," sitting impedes all physical work but key-stroking and paper-pushing. We cannot reach out as far or move about so quickly if we are on our seat. But for most cultures – not just Japan's – sitting allows *more* work to be done. Not only does it save energy wasted on standing, but it frees up the *feet* to join in the work. We are surprised to see people doing handiwork with their feet. As Percival Lowell put it "from the tips of his fingers to the tips of his toes, *in whose use he is surprisingly proficient*, he (the Far Oriental) is the artist all over." (my italics: L:SOE) Ah, but they are only normal. People *all over the globe* used to use their feet in that way. *We* are surprisingly inept. The only feet we allow to develop their potential are those belonging to people missing arms.[1] Today, most carpenters in Japan feed their table saws, standing. But people working on sheet metal and other things not using large tables, may still be seen seated on their *tatami* with their feet out, fast at work.

1. ***Feet in the West.***   To understand the dormant possibilities in feet in the West, we need to visit the circus. Read Ricky Jay's *Learned Pigs and Fireproof Women* (to name one book whose title I recall because I corrected its translation into Japanese) for inspiring stories about the armless that suggest we shortchange our potential.

~~~~~~

11-26   Our gimlets open up holes by arm power;
As nossas virrumas vão abrindo os buracos à força de braços;

Those of Japan are always given a [a twist? a blow?] with a mallet.
As de Japões vão-lhe sempre dando com hum macete em [schütte =volta? rdg = golpe?].

A gimlet by whatever name would have been commonplace in Frois's time, but today, I would guess that most readers have only a vague idea, if any about what it is. In a word, it is a capital "T" shaped twist-drill. We assume a drill has a spiral, i.e. screw bit, like a cork-opener (also once called a gimlet) but not so screwy. These were made so that one could start screwing – just like we can do with screws – from the outset applying a bit of downward pressure and torque, using nothing but arm-power.

The Japanese gimlet had no spiral bit. Indeed, the first screws had just arrived in Japan (within the arquebuses!) and would not find other uses for quite a while, if I am not mistaken (after all, ours only served for pumps and presses for their first 500 years). Their gimlets used a different method to bore, *sharp edges*. The *mitsume-giri* had 3 edges and the *yotsume-giri,* 4. That is to say, the bit of one is triangular and one square in cross-section (they resemble the fencing blades, or *foils,* of the Occident!) I have used one of the latter and was surprised at how quickly it worked not only to make but to enlarge (far better than my rat-tail files!) holes.   The only hard part was getting started, the first half inch, where a hammer helped to drive it in far enough to gain purchase. I did not find the twisting that difficult (except when I drove it in too far by carelessness) and thus guess the missing word is not *volta,* or a "turn" but *golpe* or some other word meaning a "blow."

11-27   In Europe, we don't feed carpenters or their helpers;
Em Europa não se dá de comer aos carpinteiros nem a [seus] criados;

> In Japan, they eat where they work, and their boys, who do nothing [are also fed].
> *Em Japão comem aonde trabalhão, e [tambem]aos seus moços, que no fazem nada[, se da de comer].*

This is still true in Japan. Carpenters may bring some snacks of their own or go out for a soft drink; but the lady of the house usually brings out trays of food and tea. Today, one might think, it saves their valuable time, as they are employed by the day. But, carpenters were not paid much in Frois's time. Alice Mabel Bacon provides a more plausible reason for the practice:

> So rigid are the requirements of Japanese hospitality that no guest is ever allowed to leave a house without having been pressed to partake of food, if it be only tea and cake. Even tradesmen or messengers who come to the house must be offered tea, and if carpenters, gardeners or workmen of any kind are employed about the house, tea must be served in the middle of the afternoon with a light lunch, and tea sent out to them often during their day's work. (B:JGW)

Another factor may be considered together with this hospitality. Bacon herself gave much of her chapter on "domestic service" to it: to wit, Japanese were fundamentally more democratic than Occidentals, including Usanians, when it came to their attitude toward servants and other people doing menial work.

> In explaining to my scholars, who were reading "Little Lord Fauntleroy" in English, a passage where a footman is spoken of as having nearly disgraced himself by laughing at some quaint saying of the young lord, my peeresses were amazed beyond measure to learn that in Europe and America a servant is expected never to show any interest in, or knowledge of, the conversation of his betters, never to speak unless addressed, and never to smile under any circumstances. Doubtless, in their shrewd little brains, they formed their opinion of a civilization imposing such barbarous restraints upon one class of persons. (B:JGW)

In Japan, servants were allowed and expected to have their own minds. How ironic that our standard image of an Oriental servant as a disgustingly subservient spineless creep (not my view, but what I have seen in movies) is exactly what *we,* ourselves, demanded. *"Even in the treaty ports, where contact with foreigners has given to the Japanese attendants the silent and repressed air that we regard as the standard manner for a servant, they have not resigned their right of private judgement, but, if faithful and honest, seek the best of their employer, even if his best good involves disobedience of his orders,"* writes Bacon. "Moreover, this characteristic of the Japanese servant is aggravated when he is in the employment of foreigners, for the simple reason that he is apt to regard the foreigner as a species of imbecile who must be cared for tenderly because he is incompetent to care for himself." Or in Sladen's apt summary:

> No Japanese servant will ever condescend to be turned into as human machine. Even in the most perfectly appointed house he retains his individuality, although her may fall upon his hands and knees when he enters your presence. But he evidently believes in the Horatian maxim of his country, "Give genius a chance," for he persists in using his own brains instead of those of his master or mistress. (S:MQT)

As Sladen points out, if you are not a worrier who insists on doing things the way you expect them to be done, such a thinking servant is a treasure. But, what is disconcerting about all this is "our" attitude. Whether excused by the contract mentality of Usania or aristocratic conceit of Europe, such a denial of human dignity is hard to stomach. (See 14-20 for my paradoxical theory as to why this difference may have come to be) Granted, a worker is not the same as a servant, and I may have wandered a bit too much in my explanation. To return to the contrast, a question: Isn't it only natural to serve something to someone working on your house? I really do feel more estranged from "us" than "them" and wonder why. If I am not mistaken, this practice is fairly common in some Southern states and may also be in *parts* of the Occident.

~~~~~~

11-28   Our adze [1] is large and broad and does a lot of work;
          A nosa emxó hé grande e larga e faz muita obra;

            The adzes of the Japanese seem like toys.
            As emxós dos Japões parecem couza de brinqo.

"Our" adze (or *adz*) is basically a short-handled sharp-edged narrow-blade hoe – or, when two-sided, an anchor-like device – for working wood. "Their" adze has a handle so long and thin it looks like a cane held upside-down. Made from a single bent piece of iron, it is far more svelte than its stocky-looking Western counterpart. But, toy? *Hardly*. Aesthetics aside, I cannot speak for their relative merits and demerits except to venture that the Jesuits could not do much with them because the small diameter and round cross-section of the handle [2] would not permit one to force himself upon the instrument in the manner "we" are used to. This would not trouble the Japanese carpenter for his lumber would already be straight and he would naturally pull the blade in such a way as to require little torque or prying. That is to say, he would not need to do *muita obra* (much work) to work.

> *In Europe, an adze is just a tool for the carpenter and the cooper.*
> *In Japan, an adze is the very symbol of carpentry and they even have rituals for them.*

The OJD defines the Japanese *teono* as a tool to make roughly cut lumber even. Such a use seems a bit more limited, but close enough to what "ours" are intended for not to merit a contrast, but, I think, the most significant difference is on a different level altogether. Another OJD item *teono-hajime* (literally: "adze-start") furnished the above contrast:

> 1) The ceremony held by a carpenter on an auspicious date, when starting to construct a home or a boat. Also *Ono-hajime. Chôna-hajime.*
> 2) The [official] start of a carpenter's work in the New Year.

With this, Frois contrasts his last tool in the book. I am puzzled that he never discovered the difference in saws or planes (*push* vs *pull*-cut, as per my *Foreword*) and markers (we measured, they snapped an inked or powdered string at an angle), both of which impressed me.

1. *Adz, Adze in OED*   After writing my description, I looked it up in the OED and found it "like an axe with the blade set at right angles to the handle and curving inwards towards it, used for cutting or slicing away the surface of wood." The "like an axe" is interesting, for that is what Japanese call it, a "*te-ono*" or "hand-axe." The only problem is that a "hatchet" is also called a "*te-ono*." Verbally, context prevents confusion and in writing, a different Chinese character is used for the adze = 釿 and hatchet = 手斧(used to translate "tomahawk"). Japanese in Frois's time would not have needed to use the Chinese for they had no hatchets in the sense of small axes. For hatchet-work, they used, as they still generally do, a tool called a *nata* 鉈 which is something like the *sax* of a slater, which is to say a heavy long rectangular cleaver. You might also define it as half a machete or a hatchet that is all blade with only enough handle for a grip. It is thick on the back of the blade, razor sharp in front (watch your fingers and toes!) and what serious Japanese woodsman of the old school wear.

2. *Round Handles.*   I have long been impressed with the round cross-sections of the handle of the *mochi* (sweet-rice)-pounding hammer, which, with its long head is very unstable. It seems Japanese are deliberately making it hard on themselves! Or . . . ask me, sometime.

11-29   In Europe, the house is built as the lumber is worked.
Em Europa, asi como se lavra a madeira, asi se vai logo pondo na fabrica;

> In Japan, they first work [the lumber for] the entire house, then erect it very quickly.
> *Em Japão se lavra primeiro a caza toda e depois brevissimamente a alevantão.*

Lumber? Wood? Planks? How would you translate it? There is no contrast in it, so it does not matter. The *brevissimamente* here translated as "very quickly" is salient. Elsewhere, it is specified by Frois (or Mejia?) as "three or four days" (in note in V(A):V&S). Carletti wrote that "a house can be erected in two days." (C(W):MVAW). This is still true today. A carpenter spends most of his days *at home* planning, marking, cutting and otherwise preparing parts for assembly. If you are friends of the carpenter and visit him, you know how busy he is. Otherwise, you get a very different impression of construction in Japan. Since the ground of the site is usually broken – and the foundations laid (today, there is always some foundation, for Japanese *wallow* in concrete) – long before the parts are ready, you feel *those incompetents are taking forever!* Just then, you come home from the office one day to find the house finished! I suspect this type of construction would be ideal in the face of earthquakes and typhoons that do not take kindly to half-built buildings and the monsoon rainfall.

Still, Kaempfer writes something that indicates one part of Europe – if one thinks of it as Europe – brought prefabricated housing even further than the worked lumber of Japan.. After noting that parts of the infamously haphazard Edo were regularly laid out "entirely owing to the accidents of fire" which allowed "builders" to make the new streets according to a plan, we find this eye-opener:

> Many of these places, which have been thus destroy'd by fire, lie still waste, the houses being not built here with that dispatch, as they are at Moscow, where they sell them ready made, so that there needs nothing but to remove and set them up, where they are wanted, without lime, clay, or nails, any time after the fire. (K(S):HJ)

Chamberlain writes something that suggests what might have slowed down the Japanese carpenters enough to prevent them from impressing Kaempfer, although my prefabricating carpenter friend does not do it today:

> When building a house, the Japanese construct the roof first; then, having numbered the pieces, they break it up again, and keep it until the substructure is finished. (C:TJ)

11-30   With us, when the figures painted are many, the delight for the eyes is more.
Antre nós, quando as figuras pintadas são muitas, deleitão mais à vista;

> In Japan, the less the figures, the more they are appreciated.
> *Em Japão quanto menos figuras tanto lhe são mais aceitas.*

As Okada writes, "at this time, *fûzoku-e* (genre pictures) full of people on screens (*byôbu*) were fashionable. Apparently, to enhance his contrast with Western paintings, Frois is thinking only of *sumi-e* (black ink paintings)." There were indeed depictions of folk-life, although not quite so heavily peopled as those by the Flemish painters, battle-scenes crowded with warriors and horses, although most men tended to be shown in the mass, rather than treated as individual "figures," horrific yet entertaining panoramas of the pandemonium of Buddhist hell, and, of course, celebrities: sumo wrestlers, courtesans, and soon (within fifty years) *kabuki* stars, too. But, all of these were, I think, considered decoration and not treasured as art, as the black and white *sumi-e* was. While color had been abundantly used in classical Japanese painting, the several hundred year-old warrior culture, with its ideal of strength and discipline respected bold strokes of black and white ink. The Zen tradition became *haute culture*.

In Valignano's SUMARIO, *sumi-e* comes right after the *dogu* (tea utensils) as an example of something simple and (to the Portuguese eye) virtually worthless, that commands a high price. Valignano mentions "a paper painted with a birdy and a little tree [too bad English has no diminutive for *arbolito*!] of black ink, which done by the hand of a known ancient master brings four and ten-thousand ducados [410,000?]." Frois writes about the very picture, by a Chinese master, describing the tree more accurately as "dry" (i.e. leafless for winter, or *dead*) in his *Historia*, for Hideyoshi's desire for it and a tea utensil were held responsible for the execution of a Japanese Christian "Lucas," apparently a saintly man much beloved by his community, when a killing by a half-brother of his gave the authorities the pretext to do so (If *imitation* is the best compliment, *murder* is worst). Six years later, as Alvarez-Taladriz (V(A):V&S) points out, the painting hung by the entrance to Hideyoshi's Tea-Fest of 1592. A few years later, Rodrigues emphasized the importance of minimalism in Japan even beyond Frois:

> Although they copy nature in their paintings, they do not like a multitude and crowd of things in their pictures, but prefer to portray, even in a sumptuous and lovely palace, just a few solitary things with due proportion between them, and indeed they distinguish themselves in this respect. (in C:TCJ)

Frois's word *figuras* is problematic. They may mean *people*. The tendency of the West to literally anthropomorphize its God – that ridiculous enormous *hand* sticking out of a cloud! Is it Michelangelo's "right hand of God" the same one my catechism said Jesus rose up from the dead to "sit on?" – and idolize humans by covering walls with absurdly muscular images does indeed contrast with the nature-painting tradition of the Sino-sphere (While the Islamic world managed to contradict *both* with pure geometry! How ironic that "figure," or "figures" (*figuras)* came to mean both *bodies* and *numbers*!) As noted in 4-25, there *are* muscle-bound figures, sculpted and painted in the Sino-culture; [1] but they almost always depict guardian *demons* – more *host* than *angel* – and are not ubiquitous like our musclemen. When *human* figures are found in Japan, muscles are nowhere to be seen. What the Marquis de Mode has to say about China is equally true for Japan:

..

> The beau ideal, the beautiful of the ancient sculptors, has no existence for the Chinese mind. Among us, an expansive forehead is generally looked upon as an indication of intellectual power; but in China this is not the case. The Chinese are of the opinion that the stomach is the seat of the mind, and the consequence is that the extent of a man's mental capacity is measured by the amplitude of his abdomen. Now, I would ask, what chances the fine arts have among a people entertaining such an opinion? They will never, of course, produce anything akin to the Apollo Belvidere, but will manufacture no end of Poussahs [God of wealth/happiness and Buddhas, and other monstrosities of like kind. (M:BGE)

The chauvinistic English writer Crosland, possibly borrowing from de Mode (switching from *ideals* to *appearance* to fit his more guttural polemic), attacked the vogue for Japanese art as part of his putdown of "the dears," as he held everyone else thought of the Japanese, who were popular in his country at the outset of the 20th century.

> It is impossible that a Japanese artist should make beautiful representation of the human form, for the very good reason that the Japanese human form is not *beau*. The woman have faces like mustard plasters, the men are even worse provided . . . Japanese women have no figure. Japanese men have no stature and they are too long of body like the Scotch. What does art want of them? It is her business to reproduce beautiful things, not ugly ones. (C:TAJ)

While I contrasted the ideal of the Western muscleman and the Sumo wrestler in 1-1, the latter is not really equivalent to the former, for it is not an ideal of *beauty*. Neither male-color enthusiasts nor women in Japan longed for the sumo wrestler. Likewise, for the *Poussah* and *Buddha*: they are not ideals of personal beauty which the West confuses with "those higher faculties in human nature, which it is the true object of art to gratify and foster" but art of a more subtle, symbolic nature, reflecting a culture where the sphere was identified with perfection and *roundness* was sacred,[2] although not in the all-or-nothing manner of Near West (Judeo-Christian-Muslim) religion. It is hard for us today to imagine the way the body beautiful was worshipped by the West a century or so ago. Here is note 5 for chapter 5 of Vivien Noakes' *Edward Lear*:

> Lear said that Madame de Bunsen 'would never allow her grandchildren to look at my books, inasmuch as their distorted figures would injure the children's sense of the beautiful.'

But Frois may be talking about rich versus paltry content, rather than *human* figures, alone. Occidental (here I include Islam) artists could not bear empty space. Like the literary hack who is paid by the word, you would think they were paid by the number of items crammed into their work, with a bonus paid for the color. The high value of single black and white dead tree (with or without its "birdy") shocked the Jesuits. Rembrandt and others made studies that bear some resemblance to Japanese art, but (correct me if I am wrong) even the artists who did these sketches apparently did not think of them as pictures worthy of framing, hanging and gazing at. We didn't really *get it* until the 19th century.[3] When Lowell writes in *The Soul of the Far East*, "Far Eastern pictures are epigrams rather than descriptions," he acknowledges that the sketch is equally a work of art. The artist's "brush strokes" he wrote, "are very few in number, but each one tells. . . . The force of it grows on you as you gaze. Each stroke expresses surprisingly much, and suggests more." The reason for this are 1) The random yet not chaotic artlessness born naturally from speed; 2) The greater information or "grain" – voluptuousness, sensuality – found in each brush stroke; and, 3) The mastery inherent in the practiced stroke, which Lowell thought "requires heredity to explain." To *Faux Frois* them, respectively:

> *Among us, artists take days if not months to paint a picture;*
> *In Japan, they can complete a picture in seconds.*
>
> *We admire the way things are reproduced in our pictures;*
> *They delight in the texture of the brush mark itself.*
>
> *We write and paint with different instruments upon different materials;*
> *They paint using the very same things they do their writing with.*

That is to say, I believe that the dexterity learned with Chinese characters and the mastery of *stroke* marking Far Eastern painting are one and the same. One could say, *they paint writing and they write painting.* I wonder if the resultant minimalism gave birth to Zen in China, rather than the vice versa, as is commonly held.

1. *Musclebound Figures in the Sinosphere.* I do not know much about Chinese demons, but some of the sculptures in Japan seem to me, a layman, every bit as anatomically correct as those of our Renaissance. I wonder if any serious students of anatomy have compared these and "ours," from the viewpoint of anatomy.

2. *Round Figures in Japan*. I have oversimplified in so far that there is an older tradition of slim and elegant Buddhist sculpture, too. But I am not sure how much of this tradition would have remained by Frois's time.

3. *Nineteenth Century Discovery.* I would guess that photography, by offering perfect reproduction, sated our desire for it and allowed us to appreciate more impressionistic work for the first time, but I cannot help but wonder if there are any individuals in the West who expressed the viewpoint that a sketch could be a completed work of art prior to this. Did no one like, say, Turner's sketches better than his paintings?

11-31   We take care to plant in our gardens trees that bear fruit;
Nós de preposito plantamos em noss[os] ja[r]dins arvores que dem fructo;

The Japanese prize most in their *niwa* (garden/s) those that bear only flowers.
Os Japões estimão em mais em suas nivas as que dão somente flores.

The Iberians in general and the Jesuits in particular seem to have been *very* fruit-conscious. They continually use the metaphor of "bearing fruit" [1] when writing of their Christian mission. Cruz enthused on Chinese fruit – including three major types of oranges – and a fruit related to the lichee which one could never eat enough of. In *De Missione*, Miguel=Valignano boasted that in a single orchard in Lisbon there were no less than 76 varieties of pears! (J/S:DM) dial.17) No wonder Columbus described the shape of the earth – it was supposed to rise up high at the equator, or rather around the garden of Eden – as a pear! But Japan? Japanese was practically fruitless.

> *futokoro no ko ga kuitagaru sakura kana* – issa (1759-1823)
> (bossom [of a kimono]-child eat-wants cherry[blossom] 'tis/!/?)

> the nursing babe
> would eat them if he could
> cherry blossoms

The Japanese garden is more rational for all but the poor: we can look at far more flowers than we can eat fruit, which may always be bought and carried home, anyway. While the presence of "broken boughs of flowers" (*ori-bana, ori-eda, ta-ori,* etc.) in the haiku almanac, and thousands of haiku – not a few critical of the practice – testify to the possibility of bringing token flowers home, it simply is not the same as *the beauty of an entire plant*, which can be followed from the very first bloom to the climax and fall.

> *In Europe, we walk about looking at and gathering the flowers of spring.*
> *In Japan, they find one flower, or rather a blossoming tree and sit under it for hours.*

What really surprised the Jesuits was not so much the absence of fruit and abundance of flowers in Japanese gardens as the fact that the very tree types they cultivated for and identified with fruit were, in Japan, feted for their bloom. If "we" (in our Latin tongues or Germanic ones) don't specify we are talking about a *tree,* the word "cherry," or "plum," alone is presumes the *fruit*. In Japan, on the other hand, these trees are synonymous with their bloom – so much so in the case of the cherry that people use the generic term *hana,* (flowers/bloom) alone, to refer to the tree!

> *hiza no ko no yubisashi hajime ume no hana* – issa
> (lap-child's finger-point-start plum-blossom) [2]

sitting on her lap	sitting on my lap
his first time to point	her first time to point
plum blossoms	the plum blossoms

The premier garden tree was and is the plum – some say it is actually a variety of apricot, but we have more interesting things to discuss than the fine points of botanical nomenclature – because it blooms right on the broken back of winter, at what was in Frois's time the New Year in Japan (early Spring) and attracted the bush warbler (rightly "mistranslated" as a *nightingale* to preserve its identity with desirable singing) whose first call was awaited as eagerly as certain towns in Usania await their groundhog. Moreover, a big deal is made of the plum's scent (which I do not care for: it smells like the inside of a flower shop), said to slip inside the house, permeate all the cold corners of the room and even rise up and give the Spring moon its customary haze.   As the first blooming flower and because the plum tree's Chinese rendering combines a *tree* radical with a *mother*, the very name has a sweet domestic character, further enhanced by a homophonic affinity with birth. But, by Frois's time, the Chinese favorite, the plum, had given way to the Japanese favorite, the cherry:

dai ichi ni ki no kusuri nari hana no yama   issa
(first-of-all, spirit's medicine becomes/is: flower/blossom-mountain) [3]

and first of all
it is medicine for the soul
cherry mountain

A home cherry was also convenient for viewing. The farmers around Issa thought he was a fool for bringing one home to plant, for the flowers bloom right when they are busy working the fields, but a tree close at hand was indispensable for a haiku poet and could be just as helpful as that pair of kittens Aldous Huxley prescribed for "our" beginning writers. But, more important, cherries provided an opportunity for a Marti Gras every year. They allowed Japanese of all classes to go out flower and people-watching, as they drank their fill and, if they were the least literate, wrote themselves silly! The excesses of the cherry bash was indeed vital for the health of a largely subdued lifestyle and aesthetics. A description of luxuriance requires a 19th century writer:

To see the *sakura* in blossom for the first time is to experience a new sensation. . . . Such is the profusion of flowers that the tree seems to have turned into a living mass of rosy light. No leaves break the brilliance. The snowy-pink petals cover the branches so completely that one is conscious of the bridal veil donned for the tree's nuptials with spring. (L:SOFE:1888)

Percival Lowell's main contrast between an individualistic West and an impersonal, dehumanized (?) Far East, a Japan that took a primitive level of civilization to its full development but missed *growing up,* like "we" in the West did, is a debatable – in some aspects, reprehensible – piece of Orientalism; but the Angel is in his details.   His idealization of the Japanese love for flowering trees is absolutely brilliant:
..

If the anniversaries of people are slightingly treated in this land of the sunrise, the same cannot be said for plants. The yearly birthdays of the vegetable world are observed with more than botanic enthusiasm. The regard in which they are held is truly emotional, and if not actually individual in its object, at least personal to the species. Each kind of tree as its season brings it into flower is made the occasion of a festival. (L:SOFE)

Alice Mabel Bacon's description of a plum-blossom viewing five years later suggests that these "birthdays" were also interspecies Valentine Days:

All were gazing at the flowers, and seemed lost in admiration. In the centre of the garden grew the finest of the trees, and upon their branches were hung bits of paper on which their admirers had inscribed poems. One tree had ten poems hanging from it, although it was not the one I should have chosen as my favorite, while the tree I admired the most had not a single poetical offering upon its branches. (B:JI:1893)

We send poems to people; They give them to trees. Well, I hope Alice Mabel wrote a rhyme in English for *her* favorite; but, if she did, she kept mum about it. Today, plums are still feted and the newspapers still publish the *sakura-zensen,* or "cherry[bloom]-front in the weather section. One of my dreams is to become a cherry-bloom correspondent. and follow that front one end of Japan to the other. (If the reader wants more on blossom-viewing, check my website, for I have a book coming [4]).

1. *Bearing Fruit.* *Disfrutarse*, literally "to disfruit oneself," may well be the most popular verb on AM radio in Miami. Advertisers love it. What does it mean? "Enjoy yourself!"

2. *Pointing at Plum Blossoms* Bearing in mind the fact the Chinese character for mother 母 that is part of the larger 梅 has two nipples and that the nipple is compared to the plum-blossom, one can *also* suspect an allusion to the mother's breasts. The three の (no) suggest the name that children gave to all sublime(?) things, gods, the sun the moon (most of all the moon), *nono*. The plum and the breasts are a *nono*.

3. *The Spirit/Soul, here.* 気, *ki* in Japanese, usually spelled *qi* to make it look suitably exotic I guess, or *chi* in the Chinese way, is an ordinary word and part of a word: *genki* = well, *byôki* = sick, *honki* = serious, *kyôki* = crazy, *kimochi* = feeling, *kimagure* = a whim . . . I translated it

as "soul" here because "spirit" would have been too long for the poem. There are more allusions in the poem.

4. *Cherry Blossom Book.* It has thousands of old haiku ranging from the eros of the newly opening blossom, to terrified thoughts about death, to earthy details about drunken behavior and the accumulation of shit at the blossom-viewing sites. Unlike the case with Sea Cucumber haiku, it links up with older Japanese poetry. Had I only a wee bit more money a few years ago, you would have the book already, but I could not afford to buy the right computer, so the Japanese original (which I insist on including in all my books on/of haiku) is not yet in the Word.doc. I am still dirt-poor (cannot afford to hire help to speed things up and allow me to slow down and edit) and can only hope to get it out by Spring 2005. The title is undecided. [Note: Sorry for the ugly design! When Japanese is mixed in double columns, Microsoft Word makes lining up the sides practically impossible. -- XP needs much more work, you guys!]

～～～～～～～～～～～～～～～～～～～～～～～～～～～～～～～～～～～～

11-32   We use fireplaces.[1]
Nós uzamos de chiminés;

   The Japanese, at covered *kotatsu* [tables] in the middle of the house.
   E os Japões de cotacçus cubertos no meo da caza.

When one speaks of a *kotatsu*, "covered" goes without saying. Heat from live coals is kept (?) within the skirts of the cloth or quilting that goes over the table and extends down to the floor and beyond. The *kotatsu*, is, then, the perfect antithesis of "our" central heating. If central heating is a rug, the *kotatsu* is a pair of slippers, which does the same thing more efficiently and better, if you, like me, prefer a cool head. Speaking of slippers, you must, however, have clean socks or the stench is horrible! Otherwise, the *kotatsu* is delightful. The great traveler Bird – who had been around the British isles and the American Rockies (among other places) before visiting Japan – put the *kotatsu* into international perspective. With "the whole" of a Japanese house "being merely a porous screen from the inclemency of the weather,"

   . . . the invitation to creep under the *kotatsu* is as welcome as the "sit-in" of the Scotch Highlands
   or the "put your feet in the stove" of Colorado. (B:UTJ)

I had always thought the device a purely Japanese invention, but Okada writes it is *Chinese*. Regardless, it is the Japanese who have developed it into the most splendid heater in existence, the *hori-kotatsu*, where a pit is made in the floor – a tatami mat is removed and replaced when the *kotatsu* is put away – so one may dangle one's legs under the table while seated warm at floor level, and the modern version, the *denki-kotatsu*, where a small electrical heater is attached to the bottom of the table.

1. *Fireplaces*: The *chimines* in the Portuguese suggests the same word in English, which indeed would have been fine at the time when Frois wrote because English too conflated "chimney" and "fireplace." Pardon my modernized translation. I assume we always envision a fireplace connected to a chimney.

11-33   In Europe, the sawyers are hired, and not the saw.
 Em Europa se alugão os serradores e não a serra;

In Japan, each saw costs as much per day as each one of the sawyers.
 Em Japão tanto jornal leva a serra por dia como cada hum dos serradores.

"Our" side is the opposite of 12-21, where we hire a boat but *not the men* who come with it. The Japan side of both contrasts, however, is similar, for the men and the tool/vessel are separately hired. It would seem the Japanese liked itemized bills.

11-34 ˙ The lawn of our patios is appreciated for people to sit on.
 A relva em nossos pateos hé estimada pera se asentar a jente;

In Japan, all the grass on the grounds is *vaza to* [deliberately] denuded.
 Em Japão vazato se há toda a erva de arrancar dos terreiros.

All grass – except for bamboo, mungo grass (called *ryunohige:*dragon-whisker) and such "grasses" not made for walking on – is *weed* to the Japanese. The very word is the same. What English calls "weed-pulling" is *kusa-tori,* or "*grass*-taking." This lack of sympathy toward all things not growing in pots, gardens or crops doubtless derives from a farmer's control mentality. It is certainly true that in the USA, too, farmers have been known to raze the trees around their houses simply to gain more field and more view of it. Moreover, Japanese crops, unlike those of Europe, were in perpetual danger of being re-taken. This, writes Watsuji Tetsuro, means everything:

> Japan's most difficult season, the one which determined its architecture, the scorching heat of the dog-days, is just when vegetation proliferates and this means a fight to the death with weeds. To neglect this battle is as good as giving up farming all together. And, it is just this battle with weeds that is unnecessary in Europe. Once the ground is cultivated, the land remains submissive to humans. It doesn't try to revert to wilderness at every turn. So farm work lacks the element of battle with nature. You sow your wheat or hay and wait for it to grow up. . . . even if some weeds are found between the grain, the weeds are weaker. Eventually, harvest comes. You might say there is no need for defense, just the offensive plowing, sowing and harvesting. (*Fudoron:* 1935)

The result? The people of the Mediterranean – the font of Western culture – are naturally lazy. I threw caution to the wind and took this idea further in my 1984 book, *Han-Nihonjinron* (J/G:HNR), where I suggested that the Western idea of casting oneself into the hands of fate was to *do nothing* – like that Lilly in God's hands – while, to the Japanese, it was *work-as-usual,* for in that weed-paradise, work was taken for granted. I justified this stereotyping of our respective views of following fate as a tool for deconstructing the hoary stereotypes of an *active West* and *passive East.*

Weeding beyond all reason has also been attributed to a continental farming-culture's primeval fear of wild growth. Most Japanese – like many African nomad and farming peoples who migrated South from the arid lands into the jungle habitat of the pygmy many centuries ago – have traditionally found the woods a dark and frightening place and, even today, the woods in their neighborhoods seem remarkably free of tree-houses and trails to the likes of a little savage like me.[1] I have no idea whether this is because Japanese who came later from the continent were attacked when they encroached upon Ainu and Sanka (a short nomadic and/or hunter-gathering people whose existence has long been controversial) land, or they feared volcanic explosions and mudslides or more mysterious religious taboos (*tatari* = being cursed by going where one should not), or simply an excessive fear of the "outside" world occasioned by a neat, safe inside. They seem afraid of this chaos around them. When pressed to explain, however, most Japanese will they say their compulsive weed-killing is to prevent mosquitoes and other harmful bugs (*gaichu*) from "boiling up" (*wakideru*) during the humid season and allow more air to circulate, preventing houses from rotting.

Some Japanese, go even further and confess "we Japanese *like* mud, it makes us nostalgic for our paddy fields." And, thanks to their shoe-removing tradition, that mud does not get tramped into the house, anyway. So, not just early Spring when it can't be helped, but every monsoon, Japan turns mushy. In the 1980's, I tried calling the spindly clumps of grass coming up in front of my apartment "mud-stoppers" (*dorodomegusa*) to stop my Japanese room-mate from pulling them up, only to return home at the onset of the monsoon to find the landlord had dumped so much weed-killer on them that it looked like snow. It was a hopeless fight.   But not to worry, it does not rain all the time. You also get dust. Ah, but necessity *is* the mother of invention. The Japanese have learned to splash water around their homes to keep the dust down using large bamboo dippers, and Professor Morse further depicts buckets with holes in the bottom which were carried down the street (We sure could use this on Key Biscayne, the dustiest place I have ever lived, thanks to the never-ending construction and lack of care because everyone but me lives behind closed windows with their damn AC's on).

The Japanese approach, for all its problems, is still far more ecological than the modern Usanian one which wastes more irreplaceable fossil fuel on mowing lawns and leaf-blowers – not to mention water for watering them – than people in most of the world use to live on, while lowering the quality of "our" own life by destroying the neighborhood quiet.   I *welcome* electrical storms on weekends because there are few people who dare mow between the lightning bolts.

keeping the sabbath

lawn-mow sunday
only thunder brings us
peace and quiet!

How, one wonders, did the Portuguese of Frois's time keep *their* lawns mowed? Or did they manage to find grasses that didn't need clipping? (We see many pictures of people using scythes cutting crops, but why nothing on lawns? Were sheep brought in? Or were armies of servants on their knees clipping away?)

1. *Little Savage Like Me.* I grew up with the beach 200 yards away and a swamp 30 yards away. I spent most of my childhood up trees or under trees, hiding out and making believe, a machete in my hand a dog in the lead and a raccoon on my shoulder even when I swang from tree to tree on ropes like Tarzan. Yes, we had rattlesnakes, water moccasins, scorpions, mosquitoes and other such delightful things.

11-35   In Europe streets are low in the middle for the water to run there.
Em Europa são as ruas baxas no meo pera por ali correr a agoa;

In Japan, the middle is high, and it is low by the houses for it to run alongside.
Em Japão no meo altas, e baxas junto das cazas pera correr ao[no?]longo dell[as].

Thunberg wrote "the roads in this country are broad and furnished with two ditches, to carry off the water, and in good order all year round." The very fact he mentioned *two* ditches implies that in the late-18th century "we" still had only *one*. Here is a clear case where "we" are the party to have changed our ways, for most roads in the West with visible ditches today have the ditches on the side rather than the middle. In Texas, (another country altogether), I have found country roads that go *under* rather than over small streams – you clean off your tires coming into the LBJ ranch! – but I have never seen a road with a gulley going *down it* as Frois describes (Anywhere in Europe, maybe?). Okada cites a Japanese source indicating that Kyoto streets were especially high in the middle, "with even the [path going through the] middle of gate raised up like a *kamaboko* (fish-powder cake)." If that is true, there must have been a way for the water flowing down the street to pass under the entrances (See the next contrast!).

Thunberg also wrote something that suggests the Japanese may have had two-way traffic rules before we did!

> Their care for good order, and the convenience of travellers, has even gone so far, that those who travel up the country always keep to the left, and those that come from the capital to the right; a regulation which would be of the greatest utility in Europe, enlightened as it is, where they frequently travel upon the roads with less discretion and decorum. (T:TEAA)

The *second* time I read this, I realized that Thunberg has given us the recipe for a head-on collision! Actually, he is heading to the capital on the left-hand side of the road and those coming toward him from the capital are on *his* right. Since Thunberg was a careful on his physical observations, I suspect a mistranslation into English. Thunberg also mentions features that may not have existed in Frois's day, hedges (mostly "the tea shrub") making the roads "still more agreeable," mile-posts "set up everywhere, which not only indicate the distance, but also, by means of an inscription, point out the road" and "similar posts . . . found on the cross-roads, so that the traveler in this country cannot, easily, lose his way." He was impressed:

> Attending to all these circumstances, I saw, with astonishment, a people, which we consider, if not in a state of barbarism, at least as unpolished, exhibit, in every instance, vestiges of perfect order and rational circumspect reflection; while we, in our more enlightened quarter of the globe, are every where deficient in efficacious, and, in some places, in almost every regulation tending to the convenience and ease of travellers. Here I found every thing tend to a good end, without boast and unnecessary parade; and no where did I observe on the mile-posts the name of the governor who had erected them, a circumstance which, in fact, so little concerns the traveller. (T:TEAA)

There is an additional observation which received no comment: "all the miles are measured from one point only of the kingdom, viz. from Niponbas [Nihonbashi], or the bridge in the capital of the country, Jedo." (The bridge became the center of the central-district (Chuo-ku) of Edo and hence Japan, in 1603.) In JAPAN-THINK AMERICA-THINK (1992), Robert Collins writes:

..

> AMERICA-THINK measures distances between cities and towns from "city limits" to "city limits."

> JAPAN-THINK measures distances between cities and towns from arbitrarily selected "city centers" to "city centers." (One can go thirty miles *in* Tokyo until getting *to* Tokyo – a historic area "downtown" called Nihonbashi.) (C:JA)

11-36   In Europe, one enters a house from level ground;
Em Europa se emtra nas cazas por terra chã;

> In Japan, they make bridges with some wood or stones to pass [over into the house]. *Em Japão lhe fazem pontes com alguns paos ou pedras pera pasarem.*

Frois is explaining the previous contrast. These "bridges" let the drainage flow down the street unobstructed, while keeping the entrance high and dry. Needless to say, they also provided an aesthetic opportunity.

11-37 In Europe, doors open directly upon the street.
Em Europa saem as portas da caza patentes pera a rua;

In Japan, [they open] into their yard or *niwa* [garden], to avoid facing the street.
Em Japão pera seu qintal ou niva, *proqurando não estar fronteira hà rua.*

By opening "directly" upon the street, I mean "our" doors open and presumably show what lies inside the house to anyone who might be looking from the street. That is what the hard-to-translate *patentes* of the original implies.

The gate and the door are still generally separate in Japan, even for small houses with miniscule yards. One can think of the space between as insulation needed because the doors themselves are not very strong, the house itself has few walls, and many front doors, like the rest of the house, are left wide open all day in the summer. Also, it is a matter of custom. For someone used to it, stepping right out into the street, and vice versa, would be just too fast a transition to and fro the outside world. I, for one, appreciate that speed-bump.

But Frois's contrast only concerns *the houses of the gentry*. Many if not most of the homes of the townsmen and almost all boarding houses in Japan had no front garden. A note by Golownin's editor describes the Japan of the rest, that is the poor majority, of us (when I lived in Japan, I was poor and so I include *myself*, here.):

> In their houses, the street door always stands open; but there is a jealousy or blind put up at the entrance, formed of small net work, which prevents the inmates from being seen, without impeding their sight. (MCJ3)

In this situation, the biggest difference with Europe is that the door remains open (for the breeze is needed in the summer). Besides the blind, which is usually completely open for the bottom three feet or so, the Japanese take measures to prevent dust and heat from blowing in from the street: as described above, they regularly dash or sprinkle water in front of their homes.

11-38 In Europe, pools are made with clean rectangular, walls.
Em Europa se fazem tanqes de parede quadrados e limpos;

In Japan, they make ponds or cisterns[1] with crevices, small inlets and with rocks and little islands in the middle; and this is dug in the ground. *Em Japão fazem humas lagoaszinhas ou balsas com recantos e emseadas peqenas, com penedos e ilhaszinhas no meo, e isto cavado no chão.*

There is a world of difference in aesthetic taste expressed here. Obvious (the walls raise above ground) geometrical perfection versus natural (dug-in) scenic beauty. It is the Japanese and not the Europeans who long for the Garden of Eden, the land the farmer betrayed. Today, the Far Eastern pond – for the credit hardly belongs to Japan alone – may well be more common throughout the world than the rectangular ones which most people identify with industrial use or something equally ugly, namely swimming aimlessly back-and-forth. Still, many if not most artificial ponds in the West are boring even when they are not rectangular – does anyone think the kidney bean pool beautiful? – and I only wish that what Scidmore predicted in *Jinrickshaw Days In Japan* came true. Namely,

> a Japanese gardener will doubtless come to be considered as necessary a part of a great American establishment as a French maid or an English coachman. (S:JDJ)

Evidently, the Japanese emissaries who toured the West while Frois wrote the TRATADO were less impressed with the rectangular, clean walls (they do not mention them) than with another aspect of Western waterworks Frois happens to neglect. Miguel – here, I do not feel Valignano took the lead! – goes on and on for pages about the gardens with the innumerable devices for squirting people with "spears of water," so, "in the final event, there is not a single place in the gardens where you are safe from a water-attack!" (J/S(V):DM dialog 21) The emissaries were, after-all young, and like today, where the Japanese flock to Disneyland ... – Seriously, we all know about Versailles, but here we are talking about the grounds of the Count of Tuscany half a century earlier. These water-tricks and the countless fountains were explained, as everything else, as proof of Europe's great wealth. Still, one can't help wondering if the wise Valignano felt the childishness of his Western Civilization as he expanded upon Miguel's report.

Annotating this contrast was hard because almost everything I can find on garden history begins with the geometric excesses of the 17th century and follows with the Chinese-English idea of natural irregularity. We are not told (in most of the books I have) that both the triumphant un-natural geometric paradise *and* the refreshing wilderness (equally contrived, but, like those in the Far East, not obvious) were found in 16th century Europe. Duerr and Brueghel's evident love for natural scenes was already reflected in at least some of "our" gardens. Of course, many of "us" did not care for wilderness – "Van Mander sourly remarked that the artist [Brueghel] 'in passing the Alps' in his journey to Italy, 'swallowed the mountains and crags to vomit them up on his return on his canvases and panels.'" (H:CER). Moreover, we usually did not put sages into the wilderness, as the Chinese and Japanese did. We identified the woods with the "wildman." Still, the wild-man of Giambologna's gigantic sculpture Allegory of the Apennines (1579) looks intelligent and I have found *one* appreciation of the natural (besides Rodrigues on the Zen garden, as quoted elsewhere):

an author [2] in 1575 explains that the paths in a country house garden are 'as pleasant to walk on as a seashore when the tide is out.' (H:CER)

It goes without saying that the taste of the majority of Frois's compatriots favored the rectangularity he noted. I am not, however, satisfied with vague explanations based on "taming nature" or even the geometricism (?) of the Renaissance, and wonder if "our" rectangular farm plots as opposed to paddies that tended to adapt the shape of the land might not also have played a role in warping our taste. Another *Faux Frois* based on what Francis Bacon wrote about *his* ponds which (like many English things) belatedly reflected the continental style of Frois's time.

Our pools have pretty tiles that may be seen at the bottom because the water is clear.
They have no tiles and the only sight is fish near the surface for the water is too dark to see below.

1. *Cistern.* The original *balsas* is a problem. The Japanese translate it as a storage-pond or cistern, whereas the German and French translation mentions a "small sea." Since some connotations of *balsa* touch upon preservation, ... I just do not know.

2. *'An Author'* Only? Unfortunately, the quote in H:CER came from another book I have not yet had the opportunity to read (Strong, Roy, *Art and Power: Renaissance Festivals 1450-1650*) so I cannot be specific on the author. What a fine metaphor and sensibility!

11-39 We work hard that our trees grow straight upward.
Antre nós se trabalha muito que as arvores vão direitas pera cima;

In Japan, they *waza to* [deliberately] hang stones from the branches to make them become bent. *Em Japão vazato lhe pindurão pedras nos ramos pera as fazer yr tortas*

Since most trees want to grow straight up to begin with, the European side of the contrast brings to mind the little boy who informed Art Linkletter that *he taught the rooster a trick.* "And what might that be?" asks our host. The little boy gulps: "I taught the rooster to chase the hens." But, to Japanese, "our" trees must look strange, like they've been tampered with. "The generally weak wind in Europe," writes Watsuji in 1935,

> is apparent in the shape of the trees. They are straight and orderly as botanical specimen. The umbrella[cone]-shaped pine and pencil-shaped cypress are especially noteworthy. Perfectly composed, bun-like pines are not only found in parks but growing in fields and on mountains. Pines subject to no artifice other than having their lowest limbs lopped off, spread out their limbs equally in all directions, twigs filled out evenly, and this correct conical form is held up by a vertical trunk. For us – we to whom the very word *pine* invariably calls to mind kinked trunks and lopsided limbs – this symmetrical shape seems extremely artificial. . . . Considering further, this shape seems artificial because we are used to seeing the irregular tree forms of our native land. In our country, it is regular forms that can only be artificially produced. But, that, for the tree *is* a natural shape, and an irregular shape unnatural. So, in our country, the *artificial* and the *rational* are conflated, while in Europe the *natural* and the *rational* are. (J/W:F)

This faith in the rationality/logicality/reasonability (all these meanings are inherent in *gôri-teki*, which I translated as "rational") of nature deriving from mild wind, then, led the West to search for rules inside of nature and *voila!* Science here we come! While strong winds may have created the irregularity of Japanese pines out in the mountains, Watsuji might have given his countrymen a bit more credit for their work to make domestic trees look natural. Alcock was impressed:

> "It is perfectly astonishing to see the amount of industry and perseverance which the Japanese must have devoted to the production of these plants. There were some little fir trees, not more than a foot in height, and yet I counted upward of fifty ties, by means of which the shoots were bent backward and forward in a zigzag way." (A:COT)

Some people feel the result is stunted, ugly. *The Barbarian in Asia*, if I may describe Michaeux by his very apt title, wrote:

..

> The trees are sickly, puny, meager, rising feebly, growing with difficulty, fighting against adversity, and tortured as soon as possible by man to appear still more dwarfish and miserable.

I would rather say that Japanese trees show *more character* than "ours."   Just look at the character found in the wild Japanese pine and, I have recently discovered, the Scot pine. These have strongly individual limb-forms and even put to shame the larger cedar trees in, say, Geneva, (what does Michaeux's France have?) where one looks pretty much just like another. In *The Lotus and the Robot*, Arthur Koestler finds the stick-supported trees "looks like a procession of invalids walking on crutches" and, seeing how chrysanthemums were "made to display their petals to better advantage by the insertion of a small wire rack into the living flower" flinched: "If I lived in Japan, I would start an I.S.P.C.F.T. (Imperial Society for the Prevention of Cruelty to Flowers and Trees)." (in L:IOJ). In the 14th century, Kenkô, the bonze whose *Essays in Idleness* are considered "a central work in the development of Japanese taste," (Keene) had written the same about *bonsai*. He describes a lord who happened to observe a crowd of cripples.

> All were deformed: some had twisted arms or legs, others were bent backwards. Suketomo, noticing their strange appearance, thought, "Each is a unique oddity. They really are were preserving." He gazed on them for a while, but before long the pleasure of the sight wore off, and he found them ugly and repulsive. He thought, "The best things are the most ordinary and least conspicuous." When he returned home he realized that his recent fondness for potted plants and

the pleasure he had taken especially in finding curiously twisted specimens was of the same order of his interest in the cripples. His pleasure gone, he dug up all the potted plants and threw them away. (Trans. Donald Keene: Tuttle)

Kenkô writes "This was quite understandable;" but I am not so sure. In this contrast, Frois used the word *tortas*. The root of this word for "bent" or "crooked" is one with *tortured*. Koestler and Lord Suketomo would smile and nod. But pine growing on the side of a mountain in the face of a brisk wind *do* grow like that. And, their slow and tortured growth – especially the paucity of limbs – contributes to their incredible longevity. Granted, this is not naturally found except in the mountains or on a seashore, but if your idea of paradise is a sage one (a Chinese-style mountain-peak landscape) how could such limbs seem deformed or cruel? It also bears noting that shape – bending for the sake of appearance – is but half of the idea. The hanging stones (or other ties) are also meant to prevent the limbs from growing away from us. There is a magic to tall trees "reaching the sky," but there is something equally precious about low branches on large trees, where a life far larger than ours remains within our pitifully low human reach, literally touchable. When such a cherries bloom, we can walk around with our head in the clouds. *We can experience trees as a bird would.* But, high or low, big or small, the main effect and justification for the domestic tree is aesthetic. Some may see the the Sino-Japanese tree as Golownin's editor did; i.e. "old, distorted and deformed;" I, for one, find a very pleasing *cubism*, a cubism that satisfies more than Picasso, the much older cubism found in mountain trees and the art of Sesshu. And, related to this free-and-tall contrast another Frois skipped:

> *In Europe, the only tiny trees are seedlings which are encouraged to grow into large trees.*
> *In Japan, there are trees as small as a palm in height that are older than any living human.*

In 1826, the President of the Dutch trading company described a box 1" in diameter by 3" high according to his reckoning (or 4" long, 1 1/2" wide by 6" high according to Fischer) "in which were actually growing and thriving a bamboo, a fir, and a plum tree, the latter in full blossom." (H:MACJ) – Frois forgot to mention *bonsai*. Why? Why? Why? I cannot imagine anyone overlooking something so different, so incredible, so adorable and so old!

*   *   *

Frois's contrast of tall and straight versus short and crooked trees wants one important qualification. If the crooked tree – or I should we say one with a clear-cut character? – represents the aesthetics of Sino-Japanese culture, the straight cedar stands tall for Shinto, the traditional Way of the Gods. Today, Japanese usually write it 杉. But, once, it was more common to write 真木(*maki*) meaning "true-tree." When I read theories about Gothic cathedrals being imitations of similar trees, [1] I wonder, for Japanese, who loved their trees – they even put huge holy ropes, or festoons, around large individuals (completely untouched, ramrod straight cedar) – nevertheless, did not try to imitate them in *their* architecture. At any rate, it bears pointing out that Japan has always had a straight side, too.

1. *Why so High?* Van Loon in his exceedingly idiosyncratic 1938 book, *The Arts of Mankind,* writes, no, the idea of copying primeval forests was not it. Gothic was a result of the limited real estate in our towns, crowded within moats for defense. If that is true, we could explain 11-1 the same way, we build high because we lived in a dangerous part of the world and had enough water to build good moats and stones to build strong walls.

11-40 We wash our hands and face are washed in silver or ceramic basins;
Antre nós se lavão as mãos e o rosto em bacios d'agoasmãos de prata ou porselana;

In Japan, they are washed in a wooden *tarai* [tub], at best *urishi'd* [lacquered].
Em Japão se lava em hum taray de pao quando muito vruxado

European face-washing basins were beautifully decorated, one almost says Baroque, affairs, whereas a *tarai* is a plain item, made like a barrel, of slats reinforced with soft metal bands. Small ones are not only used to wash ones face and hands, but to scoop out water from the bath to wash oneself. Speaking of which, Frois caught a small contrast with respect to washing but missed a large one.

> *We use soap to wash inside of the bath;*
> *They wash outside of the bath and rinse off before getting into it.*

How could Frois have neglected to mention this? Perhaps he decided it was inappropriate here for he was after a difference in equipment rather than behavior and thought to kick it into the miscellany but forgot. Or, was this a difference that did not yet exist in the 16th century? But if Frois misses some contrasts that (rightly or wrongly) seem obvious, *he never misses an opportunity to point out that lacquer*. It is almost as if lacquer by itself – or, rather, *by not being a valuable metal* – was enough to make *anything* contrary! All told, lacquer appears in a dozen or so contrasts. While such a use of it implies its relative lack of value next to the gold or silver, Frois elsewhere [1] expresses his fondness for lacquer-ware. And the Mission churches used a decorated form of it called *makie* (designs which included some gold glitter) to make things for their church such as picture frames for the images of Jesus and Mary and bible stands (googled: akio haino dept of dec. arts 1997 LR).

But the greatest supporter of *urushi* was Chamberlain, who gave it five pages in his THINGS JAPANESE! The article includes the "mysterious but undoubtedly authentic" fact "that lacquer dries most quickly in a damp atmosphere." And if the room is dark "so much the more quickly will the lacquer harden." That makes it somewhat like cement, which reputedly cures best under water. But Chamberlain's best line is this: "Appreciation of lacquer is a taste which has to be acquired, grows upon one, and places the best lacquer in the category of almost sacred things." Marco Polo's Zipangu as Eldorado turned out to be, rather, the Land of Lacquer, *Uruxi*, or, as lacquer was called in English, "Japan!"

Frois's contrast is a bit disingenuous because, Okada points out, the Japanese had fancy toilet ware of their own. These lacquered vessels with *makie* paintings were not, however, for washing the *face*. They were for washing the *hands* and included a very clever device, "horns" to catch and hold back the ends of the sleeves so they would not get wet!

..
1. *Frois on Lacquer.* I have misplaced a quote somewhere! Help!

~~~~~~

11-41   We pour water on our hands from the spout of a jug in a thin stream bit by bit.
Nos deitamos a agoa às mãos polos biqos dos gumis, que saya delgada e pouqa;

> They pour it out in a torrent from a wooden pail.
> *Elles por qubos de pao que deitão hum torno muito groso.*

And, not only for washing our hands: water came out of our fountains and wine from our wine-skins in pee-like streams. Should anything be read into this?

For once, *De Missione's* central concept has been overturned. Here, Japan would seem to be the one with resources to spare. Water, at any rate was abundant.

Today, we and Japanese generally use the same type of basin or sink. There are only two places where we wash our hands in different ways. First, when entering a shrine in Japan, we find something rarely used for anything but stew in the Occident, *ladles* to scoop out water to wash our hands. Second, most Japanese flush-toilets let you stick your fingers into the water refilling the tank, which is designed to flow in a little stream through the air above the tank. Not only does it save water, but does not require one to touch any handles, so it is hygienic. Of course, you may still have to grasp a door-handle to leave the rest-room! (I fear that sanitary engineering East and West is an utter farce!)

11-42   In Europe, our roofs are ordinarily clean;
Em Europa [est[ão] ordinariamente nossos telhados limpos;

> Those of Japan are loaded with stones, wood and bamboo for wind [protection].
> *Em Japão carreg[ados de] pedras e paos e canas pera o vento.*

Much of Japan is Chicago. The same gusts of wind that make crooked trees can blow off the straw from a poor man's roof. But for all the huffing and puffing, honest-to-god tornados and even hurricane force winds – which would make such stones dangerous – are *very* rare. Big stones are still found on some remaining straw roofs and more recent corrugated tin atrocities. Not all are there for wind protection alone. According to Okada, stones and lumber were often *stored* on the roof! The main roof of finely laid straw was usually too sharply sloped for stones to rest and heavy enough by itself. So the roofs referred to here are those of tiny shacks, and a sort of awning-like extension that may be found on many larger roofs (Morse has a good picture!).

11-43   Our pines, for the most part, bear fruit;
Os nossos pinheiros pola mayor parte dão fructo;

> In Japan, while there are countless pines with nut-sized cones, they are worthless.
> *Em Japão, com aver infinitos, dão pinhas como nozes, que não prestão.*

Almost worthless. Kaempfer says "pine-nuts" were "gather'd for fewel." (K:HOJ) and I have come across many haiku and senryu about their being used to roast clams (somewhat suspicious because the pine cone was a conceit for the male gonads (*fuguri*) and the clams . . . – need I say?).

The East coast of the USA with a climate similar to Japan's, likewise does not boast pines with edible pinions. That type of pine may be found in the West with its European style climate of dry summers and wet winters. (I *love* pine nuts and would eat them every day if I were not so damn poor.)

11-44   Our cherry trees bear very delicious and beautiful cherries.
As nossas sireijeiras dão mui gostozas e fermozas sirejas;

> Those of Japan bear many small, bitter cherries and many beautiful flowers, which the Japanese appreciate. *As de Japão dão muito peqenas e amargozas sireijas e muito fermozas flores que os Japões estimão.*

How interesting that Frois would describe "our" cherries, meaning the fruit, as beautiful as well as tasty. I never thought of fruit on the tree as food for the eyes.

If there is fruit on the Japanese cherry tree, I've never seen it. Those "small bitter berries" grow after the blossoms fall, and who looks up then? What one notices instead is the pretty dappled cherry-tree shade. Until something the Japanese call the "cherry-peach" (*sakura-momo*) was imported in the 19th century, there were no real fruit-bearing cherries in Japan. Today, Japanese import and eat what they call "American Cherries," but living 20 years in Japan, I never came across a cherry pie!

On the other hand, clusters of Japanese flowering cherries now bring delight to people by the Reflecting Pool in Washington DC and a few other places in the West. We, too, it would seem, don't mind tree-flowers. But there is no question that we are less aware of them then Japanese and I wonder if it is not a problem of linguistic categories which might be Froised as follows:

> *To Europeans, a flower is something growing on the ground or close to it.*
> *To the Japanese, a flower is a flower is a flower though it be a huge tree.*

I have written a book as long as this one on cherry-blossom viewing through haiku eyes which may be published in 2005. It is that long because the practice of blossom viewing is *that* interesting. For now, just two more *Faux Frois* (For some reason, the second sounds more authentic):

> *Europeans like to walk through fields alone, breathing the fresh air and picking the flowers;*
> *Japanese go into the forest, find a blooming cherry, drink like fish and lie together under it.*

> *We think that a flower is better for blooming a long time because we can enjoy it more;*
> *They claim that the faster a flower falls the more attractive it is, and the more admirable.*

11-45   With us, when one picks a rose or fragrant carnation, we first smell it and then look.
Antre nós, quando se toma huma roza ou cravo cheirozo, primeiro o cheiramos e depois a vemos;

The Japanese, paying no attention to the smell, only delight in the sight.
Os Japões, sem terem conta com o cheiro, se deleitão somente na vista.

Unless the Jesuits imported roses and tested them on their converts, this seems a trick contrast, for the closest native Japanese equivalents (a briar rose and a pink) of what I translated as "rose" and "carnation" are practically without scent. The cherry is also scentless, but the Japanese pay almost as much attention to the scent of the official bloom of the New Year, the plum flower, as we pay to that of the rose. The difference is that the rose was literally brought to the nose or vice-versa, while the scent of plum bloom filled the air, all the way to the hazy moon, if the poets are to be believed.

11-46   We have many roses, [flowers?], carnations and herbs fragrant and very aromatic.
Antre nós há muitas rozas, fl[ores], cravos e ervas cheirozas e mui odorifeiras.

In Japan, very few of these have a fragrance.
Em Japão mui pouqas destas couzas tem cheiro.

Logic-wise, the "flowers" makes no sense. Schütte leaves it as is, so do the Japanese, but the French translators kindly kill it. Maybe Frois himself had a line through it which was eaten by the silverfish with the rest of the missing part of the word.

Besides the plum blossom already mentioned, the jasmine, mandarin orange blossom, orchard, chrysanthemum and violet all delight the nose. We do not have Japanese bending over to smell them, but they did note their scent. Issa had the violet growing wherever the micturition[1] of the goddess of Spring overflowed – a perfect metaphor considering the fact that the scent of the flower in question was considered by some (Ben Franklin, at least) to be the smell of ideal urine (as opposed to what asparagus does to you and creatable by a liberal intake of pine-nuts!). A Japanese friend, YM, after discussing the various references to scent in Japanese literature came to the conclusion that Frois had a faulty nose and that *the reason the cult of the rose did not develop in Japan was because they enjoyed a much greater variety of scent.* An interesting reversal, but considering 11-45, I have my doubts.

I must admit to being curious about a bigger contrast Frois missed. Unless I am mistaken:

We have flower gardens where many flowers boast their color and scent;
They have only chrysanthemum, which are more like pets or peony or water lilies by themselves.

We have flower-beds near our houses;
They keep most of what few flowers they have in pots or ponds.

In THINGS CHINESE, Ball notes that "the Chinese have no flowers-beds on land, but their flower-beds are in the water." All of the above-mentioned Japanese flower culture comes from China.

1. *Micturate and Micturition.* It would seem that Bill Gates would prefer we write "pee" for these words, which, like all too many, are not included in the limited vocabulary the MS Word dictionary admits. Considering the huge bite-size of Word docs (Compare it to Nisus Writer!) and the even larger capacity of our computers, the limited vocabulary offered by our software is perplexing and I can only guess that the founder of Microsoft was once shot down by an English major. OK, you've had your revenge. *Now improve your Word, sir!*

11-47   To the people of Europe, fragrant waters, like of rose, of angelica, etc. are very pleasant.
Hà jente de Europa são mui aceitas agoas cheirozas, como rozada, de flor de angeres etc.;

The Japanese are not pleased with any of these scents.
Aos Japões não lhe agrada nada nenhum cheiro destes.

I think most readers will be familiar with rose-water. Rabelais (in Engl. translation) mentions "spirit of roses, orange-flower-water and Angelica." (OED) Father Schütte and the French translators both guess that the *flor de angeres* means orange blossoms. But I doubt Japanese would have disliked *that* scent (While the blossoms and the skin are not the same, Japanese do, after all, put the peels of certain oranges into bath-water). Since Frois elsewhere has no trouble spelling *orange*, and there was an "Angelica water" also called Angel-water (OED), I follow the Japanese translations, both of which go for "flower of angel/s," or Angelica, defined in English as

med. L. = *herba angelica* the 'angelic herb,' or 'root of the Holy Ghost,' so named . . . on account of its repute against poison and pestilence, prob. from the fragrant smell and aromatic taste of its root. . . . (OED)

The Japanese were not used to scents sweeter than the incenses they were familiar with. In a word, scents that bear resemblance to what we call perfume or cologne today. A whiff of rose water (see 14-53), to a Japanese aesthete, would be the equivalent of a sip of Rosé table wine to a lover of dry Bordeaux! Even today, Japanese feel Westerners use far too powerful perfume and attribute it to "our" having such strong body odors, bathing less, or being overbearing individuals who don't mind stinking up other people's noses.

I feel there is a broad range of delicate smells which Japanese enjoy and most of "us" know nothing about. These are mostly eatable plants such as *udo, seri, mitsuba* and *myôga.* Chances are you do not know them unless you have lived in Japan.

11-48   Among us, the scent of benzoin, daisy,[1] etc. is highly esteemed;
Antre nós se estima muito o cheiro de beijoim, de boninas etc.;

The Japanese think them too strong and cannot suffer them, much less like them.
Os Japões o tem por forte e não o podem sofrer nem lhe ag[rad]a.

My English dictionary calls this benzoin "frankincense of Java," and the Chinese characters used to write it are "easy-breath-scent." (安息香 *ansokuko* in Japanese) The characters meaning "easy" or "relaxed" and "breath" without the "scent" mean *a rest*, and placed before the character for "day," rather than "scent," mean the "sabbath" (安息日 *ansokubi*). I thought it might be named for its effect on those who smell it or for its use in church, but my OJD gives the Persian *arsak* for the etymology. But this does not mean the Chinese characters were *only* chosen to match the sound. Most likely the Chinese person who named it, unlike the Japanese mentioned by Frois, found it relaxing.

In his final LIBRO (1601), Valignano qualified "Maffei's" (i.e. his own (!) earlier) remarks to the effect that Japanese senses were contrary to ours, so that what we thought smelled *good* they thought smelled *bad* and vice versa, by adding that they were not "not discontented with all of our scents, but only the strong ones like Benzoin." That this correction – not needed, of course, by Frois, who sticking to particulars did not err – went unpublished/unnoticed in Europe is shown by the topsy-turvy hyperbole of Montanus:

Whatever is most sweet, fragrant and odiferous to us of *Europe*, seems to them as abominable as the stench of Carrion, or whatever else is odious. (M:EEJ: 1670)

It seems to me that Frois has favored scent with far more contrasts than a modern writer would. *Why?* One guess would be that the Jesuits, forbidden to engage in carnal pursuits sublimated their libido into their probiscus. Another would be to deny that Frois has favored scent and point out that *we* have pretty much given up our noses because our eyes and ears are so over-stimulated in the electronic world. A third would be to hypothesize a particular Luso-Iberian interest in scent learned from their neighbors who designed gardens that would smell good in the moonlight, for the importance of scents

"was a concept of central importance in Islamic thought, Muslims who to whom it was a central concept in Islamic thought, an idea which derived from the Hadith, attributed to the Prophet: 'Scent is the food for the soul, and the soul is the vehicle of the faculties of man.' (William Dalrymple *White Mughals.* Viking 2002)

1. *Japanese Daisy.* I do not have a very sensitive nose, but I can recall thinking that a clump of flowers that *looked like daisies* in my neighborhood near Tokyo smelled like horse-shit. But it bothered me more than the Japanese . . . (This chapter has been frustrating because I have gotten three excellent books on scent translated (from English and French) into Japanese, but had none with me to refer to while writing this. . .)

endnote XI

Home & garden

~~~~~~

I will not try to find all the house and garden items Frois (and I) may have missed in the course of this chapter, but just give my three personal home favorites – one to heat the body, one to cool it and one for the delight of the soul: the *hibachi, dakikago* and *tokonoma* – and one garden favorite, the *kare sansui.*

ひ　　　　　　　ば　　　　　　　ち

A ***hibachi,*** literally "fire-kettle" or "fire-pot" is, according to the dictionary, a "charcoal brazier." Here is Ms. Bacon:

> Our *hibachi* is made of a section of a tree trunk, smoothed into a regular oval and hollowed out in the middle. . . . Into the hollowed center is set a copper pan. This is filled with light straw ashes, a little earthenware inverted tripod is pressed down into the ashes so only the three points stick up, and then in the centre, between the three points, a charcoal fire is made. This smolders away quietly under the tea kettle placed on the tripod, and gives out neither smoke nor gas. The arrangement is far superior to an alcohol lamp, as well as much cheaper, and why we do not use it in America I cannot imagine, except we are not bright enough to think of such a simple thing . . ." (B:AJI 1893)

These fires could be carefully *buried in the ashes* (which seem like a fine silt) and be waiting for you in the morning. I suspect the biggest problem for "us" would have been obtaining the right type of charcoal. That is not so simple. You can not just stick in the type of stuff you would roast a weenie with, for you would fill your room with smoke. There are charcoals of all different colors, scents, burn-speed, sound (!) and shape. (A good traditional charcoal maker in Japan is a National Living Cultural Treasure.) While tea or sake may be steeped or heated, and the faint light would have been useful for the long winter night, the main purpose of the *hibachi* was, I think heating hands. Bacon's was a section of hollowed-out tree trunk, but ceramic or metal *hibachi* were more common, so that the *Faux Frois* image I get is this:

> *We put kettles and pots on our fires.*
> *They put fires in their kettles and pots.*

I borrowed the phrase following "they" from the turn of the century humorist Douglas Sladen, who further describes them as "exactly the Italian *scaldino,* a hoop-handles saucepan for holding charcoal embers." (*"Japan, the Italy of the East"* chapter in S:MQT) He describes the fire as "a shovelful of charcoal ash, with a smouldering ember in the middle like a cuckoo's egg," and declares that "Finger-stoves would be a proper name for them." (*"Topsy-Turvy Tokyo"* chapter in Ibid.)
..
> *We have our guests take a seat by the fireplace of which there is generally one..*
> *They bring in a cushion and a fireplace for each guest.*

But when Sladen writes that "in winter, out of the sun, no Italian or Japanese is ever warm beyond the tips of his fingers," (. . . the Italy," again), he forgets about the *hibachi's* rival the *kotatsu* (11-32), a superb leg-warmer. (I am puzzled because Sladen was not the only one to forget the *kotatsu.* Even Morse does not mention it in his otherwise thorough JAPANESE HOMES AND THEIR

SURROUNDINGS (I do not have a copy here with me or I would recheck! Anyone?).   *Why?* Is it because the *kotatsu* may be a comfortable place for lazy cats and poets to sit and watch the snow, but the visual delight of the half-buried embers in the *hibachi* (called *umoribi*) made it the greater attraction? Or, do parts of Japan *lack kotatsu*?) Some people, mostly elderly, still enjoy *hibachi* today. And, I can't say that I blame them, for old people do get cold fingers and poking at coals that brighten up and even sputter back at you is so much more satisfying than switching a heater on and off! You might say they keep you company.

抱　　　き　　　籠

The **dakikago** literally translates as a "hug-basket" or "embracing-basket." It is long, hollow tubular basket of woven bamboo. It came from China originally, but is known in the West as a "dutch-wife." In the sultry summers, hug-baskets were helpful for keeping ones limbs apart and off the bed so there could be greater ventilation and transpiration. Today, they would still be important and sold in every department store if we took the environment seriously and restricted AC use, but pardon my preaching. *Faux Frois* is more fun:

> *We carry produce in baskets but do not take them to bed with us.*
> *The Japanese not only take them to bed but embrace them while they sleep.*

Its other names were "bamboo-wife," "bamboo-slave," and *she* gave birth to countless haiku in the days when haiku were part of the mirth-filled body of *haikai*. Here are a few gathered by Shiki:

an old relationship	*together for the dog-days*	*who's complaining!*
making up	my bamboo wife	so quiet
after a year apart, me and	without you, how could i make it	she's a bit too cool
my hug-basket	through the night!	my bamboo wife

a pinch in the night	*a cool hug*	*too bad she can't fan!*
is my bamboo wife	summer's when	is this sweat-rot?
jealous of beauties who come	we get the hots for	we need some cooling wind
in my dreams?	bamboo wives	my bamboo wife!

from vanity to vanity	*no sweat last night!*	*cool and empty*
a hug basket	a hug-basket	ah, hug-basket
and a mistress – yesterday	now, even my dreams	your heart so very close
versus today	are all cool	to fall

(the Japanese originals with the authors' names – and no titles, of course – are in Shiki's BUNRUI-HAIKU ZENSHU *vol.5*)

If air-conditioning should ever be outlawed, we may all rediscover our *bamboo wives*, or, now that we are in a more egalitarian society, gender-wise at any rate, *bamboo husbands*, too.

床　　　の　　　間

The **tokonoma.** With winter cold and summer heat vanquished by clever traditional engineering, it is time to consider the third item, the one that is good year round and benefits the soul:

We put sculptures on stands and hang as many pictures as we please on any wall.
They only display artwork one item at a time in an alcove built into one wall of the house.

The alcove is called a *tokonoma.* It is a small space, longer up and down than across, located directly behind the seat of honor in the living room. If Japanese culture had invented nothing else, this shrine for art built into every traditional house would be a great contribution to world civilization. It used to extend from the ceiling down almost to the floor, but now sometimes begins at about desk level. We put all sorts of things on the top of a hearth, but this display space is for *bona fide* art alone. If we eat meals in serial and they do so promiscuously (6-6), the opposite can be said about artwork. We crowd pictures together on walls; the Japanese traditionally did not hang up their entire collection (or even a part of it) at once, but regularly changed the single item on display in the *tokonoma.* This isolation of the object assures it gets attention. And the change of display guarantees we don't take it for granted. Or, in Morse's measured words:

> The principle of constant exposure is certainly wrong: a good picture is all the more enjoyable if it is not forever staring one in the face. (M:JH&S)

If Morse spoke for the Japanese way, A JAPANESE PAINTER IN LONDON, Yoshio Markino, wrote a few words in defense of "ours." When another Japanese commiserated, "I say Markino, don't you feel it is more like a shop than a drawing-room when you go to the English house? They put all their properties on their drawing rooms," Markino, as a true Anglophile, defended *us*:

> I love both way, Japanese as well as English. It is only different taste, that is all. Certainly it is very artistic taste to have only one genuine Kakemono [hung scroll-picture] on the Tokonoma, and it concentrates all our eyes there. It gives me a very pleasant feeling. But on the other hand, I don't object the English idea at all. When they are arranged beautifully it is awfully nice. Besides, we must think how long could we live in this world. Suppose one had more than five hundred pictures, and he was keeping them in Japanese way, how many times could he see the same picture in his life. How pity to hide some pictures or curios which he so dearly loves. When I think this point, I like the English way quite well. (M:JAL 1910: Chatto and Windus decided not to correct his "quaint English.")

Ideally, one would be wealthy enough to have a gallery room for dozens of pictures *and* a drawing room done in the more subdued Japanese way.

..
> *We keep the same tapestries hanging up year round;*
> *They change their hanging painting every season or, in some places every week.*

As the Japanese knew, seasonally adjusted decoration satisfies something in us, perhaps the soul we had when we lived outdoors. Theoretically, a wall full of paintings could be re-hung with every change of season, but it is impractical. A *tokonoma* encourages it. This does not mean no paintings of snow in the summer. There is no need to be simplistic. One might prefer a snow-capped mountain in the summer *for the cooling effect.* A clear link with the season is ensured anyway, by a simple flower arrangement in a vase some other device that usually stands on the base of the alcove (or, if it is small, the ledge of the niche) as a complement or offering for the painting – usually black and white calligraphy – hanging above and behind it. The two objects do not compete for attention. The effect is that of a single multi-media work and is not like our practice of hanging different pictures on facing walls or side by side on a wall. Morse also noted that filling up all wall space with pictures meant that most would not enjoy proper light. He did not think we should have to *endure* this.

> Why not modify our rooms, and have a bay or recess, – an alcove in the best possible light, – in which one or two good pictures may be properly hung, with fitting accompaniments in the way of a few flowers, or a bit of pottery or bronze? We have

never modified the interior arrangement of our house in the slightest degree from the time when it was shaped in the most economical way as a shelter in which to eat, sleep, and die, – a rectangular kennel, with necessary holes for light, and necessary holes to get in and out by. At the same time, its inmates were saturated with a religion so austere and sombre that the possession of a picture was for a long time looked upon as savoring of worldliness and vanity, unless, indeed, the subject suggested the other world by a vision of hexapodous angels, or of the transient resting-place to that world in the guise of a tombstone and willows, or an immediate departure thereto in the shape of a death-bed scene. (M: JH&S)

In other words, Morse argues that "we" thought of art like most of the Justices of the US Supreme Court thought of pornography when arguing FANNY HILL: it had to have a socially redeeming value, and failing that, was judged sinful and therefore intolerable. And like the new rich, now that we can indulge ourselves, we overdo it. We have *too much desire; too little taste.* The *tokonoma* would be a good way to train ourselves, but for the contradiction already noted by Morse, the worse one's taste, the least likely we are to realize it. Moreover, most Americans no longer even concede there is such a thing as Taste with a capital T. Today, there is only *Your* taste and *Mine.* Even a Ruskin would not make a dent on our democratic denseness. In the end, it is hard to say whether the *tokonoma* is the cause or the result of the good taste it epitomizes and the same thing could be said for the entire interior. Most Western visitors to Japan in the 19th century never failed to admit that, *taken in mass, the Japanese have better taste than we do.* Morse put it in terms of "some" versus "the throng." In the West, the throng are literally vulgar masses. This was not necessarily the case with Japanese:

> *With us, the wealthy have a monopoly on good taste.*
> *In Japan, the poor people are often as discriminating as the rich.*

The Jesuits wrote that the really dissolute poor found in the West were not seen in China and Japan. They were delighted to find *all* the people in Japan were remarkably clean, and wrote about it many times. But they did not, with the exception of Rodrigues on the tea ceremony or Zen gardens, as far as I know, comment on their equally remarkable aesthetic taste. I think it may be because *almost all Europeans at that time had no artistic taste* to speak of; they simply equated the brilliant, the sumptuous, and the richly adorned with beauty and the realistically depicted with art. Our idea of art – if we grant it that title – was, and still is, *high end.* It costs bundles. Alice Mabel Bacon put it bluntly:

> It seems as easy for the Japanese to make things pretty and in good taste, even when they are cheap and only used by the poorer people, as it is for American mills and workers to turn out endless varieties of attempts at decoration, – all so hideous that a poor person must be content, either to be surrounded by the worst possible taste, or to purchase only such furnishings as are entirely without decoration of any kind. "Cheap" and "nasty" have come to be almost synonymous words with us, for the reason that taste in decoration is so rare that it commands a monopoly price, and can only be procured by the wealthy. In Japan this is not the case . . . (B:JGW 1890)

..

What I find unique and valuable in Bacon's appraisal is that she does not think that "our" poor *necessarily* have bad taste. Not *all* of them are "won by tawdry tint" (as Morse puts it) so much as *forced* into it. Yet she does admit that our poor were not as aesthetically advanced as theirs. A few years later, in a fine chapter called "the instinct of beauty" in her lesser known book, A JAPANESE INTERIOR, Bacon notes that "the Japanese artisan" cannot help but make beautiful things "whether he makes anything pecuniarily by it or not," and opines –

> I cannot get at the bottom of the whole thing, or find out how much this instinct of beauty is the cause, and how much the effect, of the gentleness and attractiveness of the common

people here, but certain it is, that in this country there is no need of the various missions (flower missions and the like) which have been started in England and America to cultivate the aesthetic sense of the poor in the great cities; for here every poor man's table service is dainty and delicate in the highest degree . . . and as he sits at his work he usually has somewhere about the room a vase of beautifully arranged flowers. One of our workmen would starve on what supports him and his family, and yet the Japanese laborer has his aesthetic nature fully developed, and its gratification within his reach at all times. With him "the life is more than meat," it is beauty as well, and this love of beauty has upon him such a civilizing effect that some people are led to think that the lower classes in Japan do not need Christianity . . . (B:JI)

Note. The flowers were not *bought* beautifully arranged. The poor man or woman *did it.* As Menpes the painter wrote, at about the same time as Bacon,

It would be no exaggeration to say that if a common coolie were given an addressed envelope to stamp, he would take great pains to place that little coloured patch in relation to the name and address in order to form a decorative pattern. . . . The whole of Japan is one perfect bit of placing." (M:JRC)

In her earlier book, Bacon explained matter-of-factly that artwork could be bought in Japan with "the money that in this country must be spent in beds, tables and chairs;" but, here, she admits she can not really comprehend the phenomenon. Menpes, I think, *does.* Still, the last words to Bacon's paragraph are precious. As a Christian, perhaps thinking of easy divorce, abortion and such, she found the Japanese lower classes *less* moral than our lower classes, yet she also *knew* they stole and killed less and were:

. . . more gentle, more contented, more civilized I should say, except the word "civilization" is so difficult to define and to understand, that I do not know what it means now as well as I did when I left home.

Those are *humble words* that Frois, Organtino, Valignano, not to mention Mendez Pinto, would have appreciated from the heart. I think the aesthetic superiority of people, obvious to anyone with an eye, plays no little role in this change of consciousness on the part of Western visitors to Japan.

或　　　　　　矛　　　　　　盾

Yet, one thing puzzles me about my last two pages. If Japanese had such good taste, *why* did Ernest Fenollosa – who was invited to Japan in 1878 "through the influence of Professor Morse" to teach Political Economy and Philosophy at the University of Tokyo – have to save Japanese traditional art from neglect and even destruction ("it is even said that among the extreme foreignists some of these collections [of "Lords reduced to poverty"] were burned as rubbish") by the Japanese, badly bitten by the modernizing=Westernization bug? Why did he have to push to reintroduce Japanese art into the schools? (preface to Ernest F. Fenollosa's *Epochs of Chinese and Japanese Art*) Why were there people who thought of good pots as junk and kept tin cans? (LR: Read somewhere years ago!) While Bird was busy marveling at the aesthetic sense of the poor and Fenollosa was busy saving the future of Japanese art, Chamberlain, under the rubrick of "Taste" wrote:

The bluster which mistakes bigness for greatness, the vulgarity which smothers beauty under ostentation and extravagance, have no place in the Japanese way of thinking. The alcove of a Tôkyô or Kyôtô drawing room holds one picture and one flower vase . . . . The possessions of the master of the house are not sown broadcast, as much as to say, "Look, what a jolly lot of expensive articles I've got, and just think how jolly rich I must be!" . . . . The rich not being blatant, the poor are not abject. . . . . A genuine spirit of equality pervades society.

When will Europe learn afresh from Japan that lesson of proportion, of fitness, of sobriety, which Greece once knew so well? When will America learn it, – the land our grandfathers used to credit with republican simplicity, but which we of the present age have come to connect with the idea of bombastic luxury, comparable only to the extravagances of Rome . . . . But it seems likely that instead of Japan's converting us, we shall pervert Japan. *Contact has already tainted the dress, the houses, the pictures, the life generally, of the upper class. It is to the common people that one must now go for the old tradition of sober beauty and proportion.* You want flowers arranged? Ask your house-coolie. There is something wrong with the way the garden is laid out? . . . . Call in the cook or the washerman as counsellor. (C:TJ *my italics*)

I think Chamberlain exaggerates the corruption of the rich and the faithfulness to tradition of the poor. Doubtless, there were upper class Japanese as horrified by the development as Chamberlain and Fenollosa, who lacked the position of authority needed to convince others to do something about it. Unlike Fenollosa, they did not have students coming from the top families of Japan and they lacked the ability to say "You are wrong, our Occidental art is not to be confused with our technology and is in no way superior to yours." Still, to me, what happened is proof that most people, perhaps almost all people everywhere have no real taste but only mimic whatever is the prevailing idea of it. That goes equally for the businessman who claims to have no interest in art and the artist who claims to make it. In that case, Japanese of all classes did not really have better taste but were simply better at learning what was.

枯　　　山　　　水

The above characters pronounced *karesansui* or *kosansui* literally translate as "dry-mountain-water." The meaning of the "mountain-water" 山水 itself (separate from the *dry*), as given in my OJD were –

1) "Mountains and water; also, from natural geological mountain streams, the natural world in general as opposed to human secular society;
2) "Natural sights with mountains and water, with weight given to the visual scene; a natural landscape;
3) A *sansui-ga* [(Chinese style landscape painting];
4) Water found in the mountains;
5) A *sansui-teien* [Mountain-water-garden]

An example from an anonymous source for 5): *"To make mountain-water, in a place proper to a pine, stand up some boulders and dig a pond."* So, what would you guess dry mountain water means? Actually it is not a dry gulch, but something much more extraordinary, which may be introduced to best effect by Faux Frois:

Our garden's ponds and rivers may be artificially round or rectangular but they always have water; Their seas, ponds and rivers sometimes have no water at all for they are made of pebbles from the start.

The water surface on our ponds or lakes make waves when the wind blows; The waves on the surface of their pebble water are made by special rakes.

By now, I think you have guessed that the *dry-mountain-water* means a "rock garden." In an April 27, 1565 letter Frois describes "a garden with nothing more than a kind of artificially constructed mountains of stones, which are especially sought for this purpose and brought from afar" (C:TCJ) – this sounds like one of the cluttered "gardens" I have seen in Korea that, to my mind, is the Chinese style of rock garden – and a place where "the ground is covered with course white sand [what the ripples are raked into], and in other places with black stones, while some large rocks a cubit and a half in height, stand out here and there." But, he continues, "at the foot of these rocks there are a thousand sorts of roses [!?] and flowers . . ." Cooper also mentions Vilela finding Japanese gardens "inspire the spectator to contemplation," (Ibid) but I do not know if Vilela or Frois saw the exemplar, the rock-garden at Ryôanji, called "a sermon in stone" by Loraine Kuck in *The World of the Japanese Garden,* who thinks of such rocks and sand as the materials or medium by which "some abstract concept of Zen philosophy" was expressed and laments good-naturedly:

> The gardens which resulted probably should not be called "gardens," for certainly they come within no definition of that word by Occidental usage. If there were a better word we should use it, but lacking a more exact term, we must continue to speak of them as gardens. (Ibid. Weatherhill: 1968)

When she writes of these as "gardens in which landscape as the pattern was discarded," however, I must beg to disagree, for Ryôanji's garden does resemble the way islands in the sea look when viewed from a mountainside. The fact that waves are raked in should make that clear. But there is plenty of food for thought in her ten-page analysis.

> *We keep flowers growing in pots and would think someone crazy to keep a pot inside without plants. They may put nothing but sand and some little rocks in theirs and this they find very pleasing.*

Kuck writes that these *kazan* or *kazansui* (temporary/borrowed-landscapes) introduced from China "were very popular during the Muromachi period," which was when TRATADO was written. She also speculates about whether the great painter Sesshû might have had a hand in the placement, and to what degree the *kawara-mono* or riverbank people (i.e., the *hinnin,* lit. not-people who butchered, tanned skin, handled cadavers, lived near to lepers and so forth) might have shaped this particular garden. On Sesshû, she opines, *maybe yes*; on the riverbank people, she grants they may have constructed it but concludes that it was a priest or artist who *designed* it, for the *kawara* "could learn techniques by doing, but they could not create subtle parables of philosophy." Earlier in her book, she explained how the *kawara-mono* gave birth to "a class of professional garden makers which undertook to plan and carry-out an entire garden," and introduced the master garden creator Zen'ami who died in 1483, a few years before the Ryôanji garden was made, and was thought to be "the greatest in the world in stone placement." In *The World Turned Upside Down,* Pierre François Souyri, wrote in the bolder idea-centric manner of the French:

> Admired by the shôgun for his expertise, Zen'ami was from the world of the riverbanks, where his father had been a renderer. It was said he escaped that miserable environment by creating the dream landscapes that were the gardens of the time and, with them a school of landscaping. . . .
>
> The world of sand and river pebbles was projected – symbolically or unconsciously – into temples and aristocratic residences in the form of gardens made of sand and stones. Just as nothing grew on riverbanks except stunted bushes, the dry gardens, or *kare-sansui,* contained no plants. The gardens were thought to have been influenced by Zen symbolism and Chinese-style monochrome painting. Although this may be true, they may also have been simply following the aesthetic of those from the strange *kawara* world [Souyri devotes a page to describing the liminal or intermediate surrealism of riverbank life] who actually designed them. (S(R):WTUD)

I can think of nothing to add to that other than that, even if it is probably wrong, it is certainly right, in a way, and I hope Mr Souyri gives us more such speculation of which we (in the English-speaking world) have far too little!

家   家   家

XII

OF BOATS, *THEIR CUSTOMS AND DÔGU [1] [TOOLS]*

das embarqasões e seus custumes e dogus

~~~~~~

12-1 We have *naos,* galleons, caravels, galleys, pinnace, *catures,* brigatines, etc.;
Antre nós há naos, galiões, caravelas, galés, fustas, catures, bargantins, etc.;

In Japan, there are none of these.
Em Japão penitus não há nada disto.

Plenty versus poverty in ships.   Frois's homeland boasted over a hundred years of excellence at sea and these boats were both the symbol and the result of this pioneering. It didn't come easy, either. As Matsuda and Jorissen point out, when Infante Dom Henrique (Prince Henry) the Navigator died in 1460, he left his friends and acquaintances with a debt of 355000 Krones (the equivalent of gold crowns).[2] Eventually, it paid off. By leading the way in the Age of Exploration, Portugal (and, by the time Frois wrote, Spain) not only gained the prestige which the USA got for making it to the moon, but enormous material benefits that made them the envy of Europe. And those boats played a larger role in generating that wealth than we generally imagine, for most of the precious metal robbed from the "New World" did not cross the Atlantic but the Pacific, where it was traded for spices which, while not necessarily worth their weight in gold, would sell in Europe for much, much more than the gold (or copper or silver) used to buy them (Later, by substituting trinkets for precious metal when trading with innocents outside of the Sinosphere these margins climbed even higher!). Today, the names of these ships mean no more to most of us than the name of our cars or jets[3] might mean to a 16th century European, so I will keep the explanations short and reduce them to quotation-sized font.

The *nao* was the stretch-jet, supertanker of European shipping. This three-mast, three or four-deck ship with a beautiful name (from the Greek word for temple, *naos,* as Frois would have known) was a plumped up version of the caravel (below) and could carry hundreds of people and goods. As Portugal's mainstay for shipping in the East Indies, it ferried people and goods back and forth from Macao to Japan and was *the* representative "southern barbarian boat. (*nambansen*)." (F(M&J)) The *nao* was lightly armed compared to its look-alike the galleon, but still out-gunned anything in the East (see 12-9).

A *galleon's* guns were legend. In Dialog 14 of *De Missione,* Valignano=Miguel mention "the most popular type of galleon" made in the days of "the world-famous Portuguese King Sebastian" (the warrior king who deserves credit for saving Europe from the Turks), which "has one large cannon for every day of the year." Valignano=Mancio cuts in later and adds that in the Republic of Venice – sometimes "Europe" was more than Luso-Iberia – they had one (a flagship? or, a type of boat?) with 500 big guns! Even a Hollywood movie producer could not reproduce such fire-power! OED defines them as "shorter and higher than a galley," and notes we know them for doing most of the trade with the Americas (With all those English pirates out there, what but a battleship would do?)

The *caravels* are what got the West a ride on the world-wide merry-go-round. Lateen sails were found on small boats in the Mediterranean for centuries (maybe millennia). Triangular, they allow a boat to tack into the wind but, for some reason Europeans had a thing for square sails on their large ships [4] and only the concerted efforts of Prince Henrique, who knew well that our Muslim rivals got around far better than us with lateen sails got us to try them. [5] I say "us" but it took another half-century for them to catch on throughout Europe. The two or three-mast caravel was light, strongly built, and streamlined by the standards of the time, for the cabins were put fore and aft and the central deck was low and clear.   It was against the law to sell them to foreigners. Considering the expense of development, and the fact that they were strategic weapons, that was understandable. If I understand correctly, even with Spain and Portugal united under one king in the late 16th century, Spain had beg Portugal to sell them caravels (F(M&J:T).

Galleys were pretty much the thing anyone who saw Benhur might imagine. Some had several rows – or banks of oars of varying length (all these holes for oars later served for guns: I wonder if S. J. Gould noticed it). The longest were made possible by what I think is a European invention, the *apostis* "a framework standing out on each side of the hull and running parallel to it; a strong external timber, in which the thowls, against which the oars were rowed, were set." (http://70.1911encyclopedia.org/S/SH/SHIP.htm). This added leverage also allowed the use of oars of 30-50 feet (about a third inboard) pulled by 3-7 men who sat on steps (*alla scaloccio*). 208 of such hyper-long oared, single-bank galleys took on the Muslims in Lepanto. Though mostly confined to the Mediterranean, combined with sails, they also served for North Africa trade.

As for the rest, the *cature*, was a small war-boat used in the Indian sea, the *fusta* (pinnace: French) a triangular-sailed ship, and the brigantine (bargantine/burgantino) a square-sailed two-masted ship; (F(O):T) and Frois's Japanese side, being only "none of these," requires no explanation.

Today, Portugal's contribution to naval history is memorialized forever in the sailing jelly-fish we call a Portuguese Man o' War! (Although, strangely, Portuguese call it a *fragata*, or "frigate," and not a *caravela* or a *nao*.)

1. *Dôgu* here, too!? If you recall, Frois used *dogu* more than once to describe the expensive equipment used for the tea ceremony. It was surprising to find it used here, too. Did "we" lack a word meaning *tool, equipment, implement, apparatus* etc.?

2. *Henrique's Debts.*   The above was a great oversimplification. By circumventing Muslim land trade routes across the Sahara, Portugal obtained enough gold (and slaves) to start minting gold cruzados ("crusades") in 1452, eight years before the Navigator Prince died. So the first returns did not take that long to be seen. I get the impression that most of his debts came from exploration mixed up with court politics. The repercussions from an expedition to Tangier in 1437 when his younger brother was captured (Fernão died still captive eleven years later) continued for decades.

3. *Plane, Car and Ship.* It is interesting to consider what we know and do not know about the products that serve us. No one in the Occident, and most of the Orient, today can not name a few cars and planes. Yet, what about ships? Shipping handles __% of world trade by weight and __% by value, yet can you name a single ship-type in the way you can the Boeing 747? And where are they made? Do you know? (I think one problem with ships is that they are so completely monopolized by huge corporations that we on the outside have nothing to do with them. Since they are much more efficient transport than air transport, we should use them for our personal transport and trade, but an unholy alliance of big money, government and myopic unions – and now, terrorists! – force us to use un-ecological airmail. A few years ago – pre-9/11 – I got a wonderful price from a Edinburgh firm to send a pallet of books to Miami but ended up paying more than double (and losing a whole day!!!) to get them through the maze of private forwarders and hide-and-go-seek public agencies, etc. in the USA. Hopefully, fuel costs will rise astronomically to reflect its real value (long-term social/environmental costs) and sanity will return to shipping.

4. *What Made Us So Square?* I await a gloss from an expert.   I can only imagine that "we" enjoyed our muscularity – i.e., using prisoners and oar-power – too much to realize what a big handicap the lack of ability to chose ones direction to sail was; or, that we simply had a thing for square design!   Even when we should have known better, caravel such as sailed by Columbus and other ships tried to get by with only one lateen sail (the mizzen), leaving our beloved squares elsewhere. We only caught up to the Muslims and the Chinese in the nineteenth century. Come to think of it, our square sails put us on the same side as Japan with its square sail and rectangular ships.

5. *Islam in The Far East (or Oceanic, anyway).* I had vaguely known about Islamic travelers going everywhere, Marco Polo encountering Islam and the Moghul Empire in India, but despite having used Indonesia as an example of an Occidental desert religion making it in the jungle environment Japanese climate-reductionism (*fûdôron*) associated with Buddhism, I failed to comprehend the extent of the Islamic grip on the world until I read Pinto's *Peregrinations*.   They had lateen sails on decent size boats from the 8th century or so and it took "us" seven hundred years to catch on, catch up. I think there is no

question that Muslim incursions into Europe alerted "us" to the inferiority of our square rigs, but I wonder if I give too much credit to Henrique and not enough to the Venetians (whose galleys also have lateen sails) for acting on this knowledge. Has anyone carefully dated this?

12-2   Our boats have ribs and decks; *As nosssas embarqasões tem cavernas e cuberta;*

Those of Japan do not. *As dos Japões não.*

This is getting to sound like old Chinese definitions of the *sea cucumber*. It has *no* head *no* tail, *no* eyes, *no* bones, *no* scales . . . [1] Then, one wonders, what *do* Japanese boats have? Okada gives the details of the construction (from Ishii Kenji: *Nihon-no Fune*, or "the Japanese boat"), but I dare not translate so many technical terms back into English! [2] Let me just say that *the Japanese boat was more like an insect, all shell, while the more sea-worthy European vessel had a solid endoskeleton.* For this reason, the size of the Japanese ship was severely limited. But size wasn't all of it. H. Warrington Smyth, in his wonderful work of love, the *Mast & Sail in Europe and Asia* (1906):

> In their use of mast and sail the Japanese present one of their customary surprises. From an island race of such valour, industry, and capacity, boasting a civilization two thousand years old, whose history is filled with the records of fearless and strenuous enterprise, and which is so advantageously situated as is the Japanese, one would have expected remarkable developments in nautical architecture, and in maritime activity generally.

> Yet in actual fact the national high-pooped junk of Japan, the largest sea-going vessel developed in the islands, was always of clumsy construction, and had neither the quality of speed nor that of ability to work to windward.

> Although the Japanese have had considerable intercourse with China, Korea, and Formosa at various periods, it would appear that much of this was conducted in Chinese junks, and for the rest they were content to make slow voyages in their own archaic vessels, the form and rig of which have never altered in historic times.

Lest "we" get *uppity* – the perfect adjective for the Occident for the last few centuries, right? – it should be pointed out, however, that the Chinese sea-going junks of the early 15th century, of which the largest type (over 400 feet in length and a 165 feet wide) dwarfed the Western ships of the Age of Exploration, were of even more advanced structure, for, like the bamboo, or more appropriately, the whale, they had water-tight bulwark compartments – something the West "invented" in the late-18th century, dating back to at least two centuries – holes in the prow to dampen rocking movement in heavy seas, a balanced rudder, i.e. with equal parts before and after the stern post, a large after-hang, centerboards and leeboards, flat sails and other modern aspects. They got around, too (see Louise Levathes: *When China Ruled the Seas – the treasure fleet of the dragon throne* 1405-1433; and Gavin Menzies: 1421, *The Year China Discovered the World* [3]). In the words of H. Warrington Smyth:

> When our forefathers paddled along shore in open boats, the Chinaman sailed to East Africa in five-masters. (Ibid) [4]

So what prevented these Chinese from discovering the West? *Politics*. Just like politics made Japanese give up their 50 year-old love affair with the gun. In *Guns, Germs and Steel*, Jared Diamond theorizes that progress in Europe was unstoppable because of European diversity, whereas China and Japan's linguistic and political unification (the latter occurring right at the time Frois was writing in

Japan) allowed otherwise unstoppable Progress to be nipped in the bud. It is an ironic observation because the DE MISSIONE report of 1589 opined that political *disorder* in Japan, as opposed to Europe where Christian fellowship held all together amicably, was the only thing holding Japan back. There would seem to be a fine tight-rope to walk between order and disorder. Umesao Tadao, a Japanese anthropologist not cited by Diamond wrote such an *Eco-History of Civilization* (*Bunmei no Setai-shi*: 1974), which explains the success of the Far East and Far West in terms of their being close enough to major ancient civilizations arising on the Euro-Asian Continent, but far enough removed from the center to avoid being constantly over-run by migrations from droughts in the dry center of the continental mass, so that stability needed for long-term development was possible.

1. *Sea Cucumber as a Have-not.* Many of the thousands of haiku about sea cucumber (*namako*) in my book (*Rise, Ye Sea Slugs!*) play upon what the creature does *not* have, as originally defined by Chinese encyclopedias of natural philosophy.

2. *Japanese Boat Construction*. A short gloss would be welcome! Let me just say that even H. Warrington Smyth, who thought very little of the *design* of Japanese ships, lauded *the builders:*

> Probably no vessel ever built was more durable in construction or more ingeniously or better finished as regards every detail.... The chief characteristic of hull, gear, and rigging was excessive strength and cumbersomeness. (MAST & SAIL IN EUROPE AND ASIA: JOHN MURRAY 1906)

3. *Chinese Colonies in New Zealand.* I have not read Gavin Menzies's book, but Cedric Bell, a marine and works engineer surveying Roman canals and navigation in the United Kingdom (he even finds they had a "biological oxygen control system in their canals" (which I guess means that they left large rocks or shaped the canals to create aeration and allow for rush to grow, something stinky modern canals neglect to do.), writes:

> My visit and surveys in New Zealand confirmed Gavin Menzies's comments regarding the formation of colonies. The foundations of twenty-one settlements were visually located, large and small, mainly on the east coast of the South Island. By using a method involving magnetic anomalies, the foundations of permanent dwellings for approximately 19,000 people have been located. Most of these settlements had purpose built stone harbours, indicating trading. In some cases, there was evidence of iron smelting, and within sight of Mount Cook, I located a complete industrial process operation, probably handling gold. Altogether, the outlines of 31 junks have been located including 7 of the enormous 150m x 50m and 100m x 50m junks. The timbers of one smaller 47m x 11m junk were actually found protruding through a sand dune."

He continues, "The indications are that it all suddenly ended. Each colony was wiped out by a superior invading force, whilst their junks were destroyed in their harbours. Akaroa harbour was the only empty harbour found, bearing witness to a hurried flight. Akaroa also had the strongest, best-sited fort." Levathes mentions the Eunuch politics, but I cannot help wondering whether this disaster may have something to do with China's pull-out from exploration!

Bell's passage was found at a weird hyper-nationalistic Chinese site (Chinese Nationalist Alliance). After ex-plaining that retired British naval officer Gavin Menzies believes the Chinese armada (62 ships with 27,000 men) beat Columbus in discovering America, landed at the Cape of Good Hope before Vasco da Gama, and crossed the Pacific Ocean before Magellan, we are reminded:

> An interesting facet to note is that during the expeditions of the Chinese armada led by Zheng He, Hong Bao, Yang Qing, Zhou Man and Zhou Wen, the Chinese purchased and brought home plant seeds and exotic animals from areas where they landed for scientific and economic purposes but never were local inhabitants brought to China as slaves. Apart from that, they left behind plant seeds, animals as well as technology from China in places where they landed. Colonization was not the ultimate motive behind these naval expeditions. This differs from the European fleets that landed in America, Africa and the Pacific which led to colonization and suffering for the local inhabitants, the effects of which many of them still suffer until this very day.

4. *Chinese Ships* The feats of exploration and huge ships Louise Levathes describes excite, but something far more basic also deserves equal attention. H. Warrington Smyth:

> In no region of Art and Crafts have the Chinese shown greater independence of thought than in ship and boat building. The striking originality which pervades their architecture, their painting, and their life on shore, is even more characteristically displayed by them afloat. At the hands of Western travelers, the Chinese junk has received little but mockery and thinly veiled contempt; the writer treats it with his smartest ridicule, the artist in glaring caricature. Yet, examined fairly, the only excuse for such treatment seems to lie in the wide gulf which separates the thoughts and ideas of the white and the yellow races, and makes it apparently almost impossible for the one to come to any true understanding of the other.   As an engine for carrying man and his commerce upon the high and stormy seas, it is doubtful if any class of vessel is more suited or better adapted to its purpose; and it is certain that for flatness of sail and for handiness the Chinese rig is unsurpassed. Until the America visited this country, when modern flat-sail setting first asserted its superiority, the Chinese were undeniably far ahead of all other nations in their comprehension of the principles of scientific fore-and-aft sailing." (Ibid)

Smyth goes on to describe in detail a great variety of Chinese boats.

~~~~~~

12-3 Many of our boats operate by sail alone. *Das nossas embarqasões muitas se servem somente de vela;*

Those of Japan are all rowed/sculled. *As de Japõo todas se remão.*[1]

Matsuda and Jorissen write that Frois, because he is proud of his nation's *sailing* tradition, exaggerates by claiming that most Portuguese ships relied *only* on sails. But "many" (*muitos*) is hardly all. Frois's contrast stands. Generally speaking, Japanese did not rely on sails as much as Europeans. Their boats, as we shall see, had sails, but they were relatively small and poor at going into the wind. Moreover, they often operated near convoluted rocky coasts and islands with fickle wind and water currents, so man-power was indeed the common resort.

Portuguese sailing technology not only made them the first Europeans to round Africa, to get to America (Columbus may not have been Portuguese, but we should be more aware that financial support was not all he got from Luso-Iberia.) and make it around the world but helped instigate a renaissance of science. By proving the Ancients did not know everything, that there were people living in the Torrid Zone which was supposed to be too hot for life, that people really did live in the Antipodes, etc., R. Hooykaas opines, the explorers not only opened up new geography but opened up minds to a new world of empirical science. Indeed, even the lines from early-16th century Iberian poets quoted in his *Humanism and the Voyages of Discovery in 16th Century Portuguese Science and Literature* sparkle with intellectual energy. Too bad, that even as they wrote, intellectual freedom was eroded by religious censors (the first index of proscribed books was in 1546) and most men chose to make a living by fighting with arms or the word of God, rather than by thinking and creating. King Sebastian outlawed all interest – now, *that* is fundamentalism! – from 1557 until 1578 when he died. Without capitol – who would lend for no interest! – business dried up. In 1556, seven million Andalusian sheep made wool; in 1598, two million. By 1570, a quarter of the adults in Spain were clerical – close to a million people, over half the adult population of England! (M(B):HIC) I wish I had the figures for soldiers! "An edict of 1558 forbade the import of foreign books, and in 1559 Spanish students were forbidden to study abroad, except at specially exempted institutions." (Nick Boalch, School of Modern European Languages, University of Durham August 2003 http://nick.frejol.org/writings/siglo-de-oro.live) In a sense, Spain secluded itself before Japan did (and, I think, pulled Portugal down with it).

1. Row/Scull. Unlike English, Portuguese, and Japanese, for that matter, have a generic verb (*remar* and *kogu*, respectively) for row/scull/paddle. But, things are not perfect with the English verbs, for "to scull" can mean working two light oars (as per current Olympic "sculling") as well as using a single oar more or less vertically in the true sculling movement, which is what Japanese did (See 12-10)

~~~~~~

12-4 Ours are treated on the outside with pitch or *galagala* so they don't take in water.
As nossas se consertão por fora com breu ou galagala pera não fazerem agoa.

Those of Japan [do it] with only the good fit of the planks, without any other bitumin. *As de Japão com somente a boa juntura das tab[o]as sem outro bitume.*

Bitumin, ("originally, a kind of mineral pitch found in Palestine and Babylon" = OED) *impregnates*, *varnishes* and *cements*. I first translated it as "adhesive" but thinking the better of it left it as is. Frois would seem to use it in a generic sense, including the pitch, *galagala* (a Malaysian word for a mixture of tar and resin) and other such. While Japanese did not treat the whole surface, Okada writes that they did use some caulking. I might add that the precision of Japanese workmanship was assisted by the radically straight lines of Japanese naval architecture. *Curved* versus *Straight*. Frois overlooked *that* contrast. Kaempfer, a hundred years later, pegged it:

> The body of the ship is not built roundish, as our European ones, but that part which stands below the surface of the water, runs almost in a straight line towards the keel. (K:HOJ)

I must not have seen Japanese boats before going there. Or, if I did (in a Van Gogh, perhaps?), it did not sink in, for I can still recall how shocked I was by the stiff lines on their fishing boats – completely at odds with the rounded and low-in-the-water Caribbean style I love – both above and below the water line, when I first came to Japan in 1971. Japanese, on their part, were so used to hard edges that this traditional design was even copied with little change in fiberglass (!), something very wasteful considering the different properties of the material. When Japan's top boat-maker made the prototypes for my father's more rounded designs, the workmen, used to wood, beefed up *the curves* (where there *would have been* seams) with several extra layers of cloth and resin, effectively canceling out the weight-advantage gained by using a material that is stronger, rather than weaker when curved!

To the Japanese, I think, those straight lines were seen as clean and beautiful rather than brittle or hard. [1] Moreover, the lines are generally not absolutely straight but have a subtle bend that becomes increasingly gratifying to the eye with time. Still, the corners are sharp and Japanese boats (at least to me) seem masculine rather than feminine, as in the West. The same tendency towards rectangularity, is found in Japanese cars – until very recently, at the opposite pole from the softly curving Italian models. (Perhaps, something in the Japanese is finally softening.)

1. *Beauty and the Boat.*   From *Mast and Sail in Europe and Asia* (1906).

> No more favourable conditions for the production of small craft exist than in the beautiful archipelago, which is second to none in the charm and variety of its scenery and the multitude of its natural havens. The old junk, with its clumsy bulk and ineffectual rigging, seemed strangely out of place in the midst of the ordered neatness of Japanese scenery, and aroused in one's mind a constant sense of disappointment and inappropriateness. The clean schooner, modest and efficient, graceful and capable, lying peacefully in some quiet nook among the islets, or thrashing round a tree-crowned point, her modernness toned by the Eastern spell which hangs about her, seems to be totally in harmony with the whole atmosphere of her surroundings, and to form a notable instance of that power of the sailing-boat to adapt herself to man's ways and to take his character upon herself, in which she excels all inanimate things and approaches so nearly to the living.

The schooners were not foreign, but Japanese ones modeled after Pacific schooners (that is another story). *I think the ancient Japanese ship looked great with Japanese scenery,* but it is easy to understand how a true boat-lover like H. Warrington Smyth could, pace Socrates, conflate usefulness and beauty.

12-5   Our small boats are high in the stern and low in the bow;
   As nossas peqenas são altas de popa e baxas da proa;

   Those of Japan are high in the bow and low in the stern.
   As dos Japões altas da proa e baxas da popa.

In comparison to modern boats, the height of the poop (the word Frois used for stern – *popa* in Portuguese [1]) on the European boats of all sizes in this age *is amazing*. Frois has a reason for confining his contrast to small-craft, i.e., skiff and gondola-like boats. Large Japanese vessels also had amazingly high sterns, but their poop-deck was more of *an extension out over the stern* (in the traditional Chinese manner) than the top of a multi-deck aft-cabin, as was the case with ours.

A high bow seems more natural for slicing through waves without taking in excessive water. And, lacking true decks and bilges, the Japanese would want to keep water *completely out,* rather than taking it on and having it run out the scuppers as is common in the West. On the other hand, a high stern seems ideal for navigation, for a steersman can not see over a high bow, and all on the poop would be left very high and dry.

1. *The Popa Nose?* If *popa* means "low" could that explain the so-called "pope's nose" on a chicken?

~~~~~~

12-6   Ours have sails of cloth;   *A nossas tem velas de pano;*

        All their sails are straw.   *As suas todas velas de palha.*

According to Okada, Frois's "all" may be considered an exaggeration. While most Japanese small-craft may have still used woven straw-mat for sails, cotton cloth was already common and soon to largely replace the mat. I suspect, however, that Frois was still thinking small boats and the smallest of the small would have been the last to make the switch . . . somewhere in my head, I can picture one of those *funa-bikuni* (boating nuns), taking a customer aboard and lowering her straw-mat-sail for their bed! Come to think of it, fishermen probably made a practice of sleeping on their sails.

On the whole, mat was fine because a stiff sail actually worked better, so long as it was not square (as the Japanese ones were). Almost all the fast and sea-worthy Chinese ships – including the celebrated Hong Kong cargo boat – used mat sails, as did *most* boats *around the world.* Why make threads to weave with when you can go straight from the straw/fiber? Most Japanese boats only switched to cotton cloth after a sail-maker called Matsu Migieimon discovered, in 1785, a way to prepare cotton thread and weave it to allow strong, taut and light one-piece sails. This *sudare-ori* "canvas belt" (?) style-sail survives to this day. (http://www.koti.jp/marco/)

~~~~~~

12-7   Our rope is hemp, sago palm or *cairo;*   *A nossa cordoalha hé de linho, gamute ou cairo;*

          Theirs are straw.   *A sua de palha.*

Straw again! What do Japanese *not* make of it? It seems strange Chamberlain failed to give it a section in *Things Japanese.* Here, Frois mentions only the most common rope. According to the *Wakansansaizue* encyclopedia (J/F(O):T), Japanese also used *ichibii* (Indian mallow: one of the Chinese characters is "hemp"), *hinoki* (a type of cypress) bark, bracken, and, for large anchors, something comprised of the Chinese characters for potato and hemp that I cannot identify by name (anyone?).

"Our" hemp, it goes without saying, is tough (I do not know if they got it in Manila yet, but the Jesuits were there, so . . .), the sago palm, or *gamute,* is from the Malay *gomûti* and is a particularly elastic fiber and *cairo* comes from coconut husk fiber and has nothing to do with Egypt. According to the French translators, kaïr comes from the Malay-Tamil word *kayuru,* meaning "cord/rope" and was especially common in the Maldives. In his novel *Waga Tomo Furoisu* (My Friend Frois), Inoue Hisashi's Frois gives a whole paragraph of a letter over to describing the wonders of the palm-tree which stands high despite roots that don't spread out and are useful in every part, from fronds used for hats, sap used for wine, nets and rope from the bark, oil for cooking and medicine from the nuts, ladles from nut-shells, fuel from husks . . . He calls it the money-bearing tree and claims the Jesuits own plots of them, which they leave to the natives to run and that he is set to buy and set up a new one, the earnings of which will go toward supporting the Nippon (Japan) mission . . .

~~~~~~

12-8   Our anchors are of iron;   *As nossas ancoras de ferro;*

Theirs of wood.   *As suas de pao..*

The wooden anchors sank because they had stones tied to them and a cross-bar helped keep the single barb pointing down. Ours, I thought, had a minimum of two barbs, or flukes, so it surprises me Frois does not make that contrast, too. There were probably some four-fluke (Chinese-style) iron anchors already in use in Japan. A hundred years later, Kaempfer wrote that "the anchors are of Iron, and the cables twisted of straw, and stronger than one would imagine." So wood soon turned to metal but straw remained king!

~~~~~~

12-9   Our *navios* [fighting vessels] have prows with rams or beaks.
            *Os nossos navios tem na proa ou **esporão ou goroupes;***

The *fune* [ship/s] of Japan have open bows not much suited for battle.
As funes *de Japão são polas proas abertas e muito pouqo guerreiras.*

I do not know if I got just the right words for this translation. I just put in what I believe "our" boats had. Like mountain rams, ours were made for butting heads or stabbing below the belt, if the chance offered itself (the "beak" was at the waterline or slightly lower).

On the other hand, the unsuitability of the Japanese boat for war is legend. Japan had one famous ancient naval battle that sent the whole Heikei clan to the bottom of the sea where their warriors left their faces on the shell of the crab called *heikei-gani*. My impression of it is less that of boats fighting than boats as a water-stage for men (who jumped back and forth from boat to boat) to fight as they fought on land. In other words, *little ramming, little fire-power.* Otherwise, the Japan sea was generally for fishing and trade, not fighting. Of course, there was illicit trade and piracy-related clean-up attempts. And only five or so years before TRATADO, Nobunaga used iron-clad ships to cut off supply to Buddhist monks he was besieging in Osaka (L:EJ). Things were changing. But Japanese had not been in a state of constant attack-or-be-attacked naval warfare as the states of Europe were with each other and their neighbors. Some Japanese *countries* (they did not really become fiefdoms until about the time the TRATADO was written) could *field* a large number of boats in a worst comes to worst situation, but it would be more a Dunkirk-like affair depending on the many fishing and trading ships. There were, in 1585, as far as I know, no navies to speak of in the archipelago.
..

In Europe, warring and shipping was synonymous. Most of Matsuda and Jorissen's information on Portuguese ships (which helped a bit with the definitions of boat types) comes from Padre Fernando Oliveira's *Arte da Guerra do Mar* (1555). *The Art of War at Sea.* The title of Dialogue 14 of *De Missione,* cited in 12-1, above, was not "On the Ships of Europe" but *About the Ordinary Way Naval Battles Are Carried Out In Europe.*   "Battle-ship" would have been redundant. *Ship = Battle.* We are told about how the Christian coalition of Spain and Venice destroyed the Saracens (Ottoman Turks) at Lepanto [2] in 1571, by a well orchestrated attack using mainly three-oar-deck galleys. (Not that this stopped the Turks for good – the world famous King Sebastian mentioned in 1, above, was defeated in a crusade against the Moors in 1587 (the Battle of Alcacer Kebir), and the Ottoman Turks invaded Europe over and over for the next 100 years until they reached Vienna in 1683.) And if real battles were not enough, Europeans also enjoyed putting on enormously costly mock battles (An excuse, perhaps, for fireworks?).

The Japanese were well aware of their relative disadvantage at sea. Frois, in his *Historia,* records a long conversation with Hideyoshi, Shogun of the newly united Japan, where he talks openly of his intention to conquer Korea and China, humbly admits his many short-comings he hoped not to pass on to his successor when he retired, such as too much wenching and hunting (the *very next day*, Frois writes, Hideyoshi came into town with large-sized game birds dangling from 2,500 gilt bamboo poles!), agrees to keep protecting the Jesuits from the plots of their Buddhist enemies – which he did, until he wiped out the last of the militant Buddhists and decided it was the Christian's turn – and makes one request: *two large warships, with experienced Portuguese crew.* Hideyoshi was dead serious. He had already ordered enough wood for 2000 boats to be cut down. He even offered to buy the boats and pay more than the going wages for the crew. Had the Portuguese gone along with him, the history of the world might be different for Hideyoshi's invasion of Korea (1592-7), as it turns out, was largely lost at sea. Koreans, quickly conquered on land, managed to cut the Japanese supply lines and prevent re-enforcements from arriving. But it is dubious whether even the two *nao* would have helped, for Admiral Yi Sun, in what may be the greatest feat of naval history – performed on two major naval fronts, no less,– sank the Japanese fleet with a squadron of his newly invented, heavily-armored turtle-boats – a whole fleet of Monitors and Merrimacs almost 300 years ahead of their supposed time – with fire and under-water rams!

Today, reading contemporary Luso-Iberian boasts about their warships, we who are more English than Latin cannot help chuckling. In *De Missione*, which was published in 1589, there is no mention about what happened in 1588 (Experts, a question: *Were many of the Spanish ships on the expedition not up to Portuguese standards?*). Perhaps, that was partly due to the time required for the news to get to the Far East, but for the Jesuits in Japan, the manner in which the Invincible Armada met its doom (powerful gales) must have been particularly galling, for they all had doubtless heard of how the *kamikaze,* God's Wind, did in the huge Sino-Mongol armada coming to conquer Japan![1] In his *Historia,* Frois doesn't mention the turtle-boats, but attributes the naval disaster that prevented Hideyoshi from conquering China (and there are documents showing China had been all parceled up for Hideyoshi's allies – talk about counting your chickens!) to the Shogun's betrayal of the Christians and his other sins, i.e., a sinner getting his Just Punishment from God. One wonders how the Jesuits and other Catholics explained the loss of *their* Armada! [2]

1. *God's Wind.* Though it happened three centuries earlier, the memory of the Chinese (i.e. Mongol) attempt at invasion remained fresh. So fresh, indeed, that, according to Golownin's editor, Melchior Nunez, the Jesuit, who wrote to the general of the Society in 1555, declared that the Japanese were so expert in naval tactics, and possessed such a powerful naval force as completely to defeat, and nearly destroy in the space of a month, a Chinese armada of two hundred and eighty sail, manned by ten thousand troops and seamen. (G:MCJ) Unless this is about some incident that escaped me, I think Nunez is confusing ancient history for the present and forgetting the God-wind, which is usually given the most credit, but the Japanese strategists and fighters deserve some too, for there were two separate invasions (1274 and 1281) in which the Japanese proved themselves and saved their independence.

2. *Explaining the Armada.* This question is not *only* rhetorical. I would like to know. *Anyone?*

12-10   Our seamen, when rowing, are seated and quiet.
      Os nossos marinheiros emquanto remão vão asentados e calados;

  Those of Japan stand and almost always sing as they go.
      Os de Japão im pee e quasi sempre vão cantando.

Sitting *vs.* standing. So, *which is the better position to row?* Captain Sarris, in 1613, observed something that only a captain would observe, namely, that by performing "their worke standing as ours doe sitting . . . they take the lesse roome." (in S:MQTJ) I believe that a standing position should also be less tiring than the sitting one used by Europeans, for continual exercise with a bent body tires the internal organs;   the effect bears resemblance to that of absorbing body-blows in boxing.   In Southeast Asia, we see skinny old women sculling produce to market at a speed not far inferior to that of racing sculls (which, are rowed, of course!) without being winded.   I am delighted we borrowed the kayak from the Eskimo. Isn't it about time we internationalize the water wisdom of South-east Asia, by introducing *true* sculling into Olympic competition? (Because English uses *scull* to mean both the method of moving a boat by deft movements of a single vertical oar and the light, slim oars (and their tiny vessels) used in the river racing long engaged in by elite university students – did it start while their papas had slaves rowing in their galleys? – we cannot continue here without defining our terms. In this chapter, sculling means the former. Japanese *never rowed* in our common sense of the word.[1])

Quiet *vs.* Singing. *"Row, row, row your boat!"* Seriously, I thought we sang too. We did, after all, have our sea-chanties . But we must not have done it very much, for Kaempfer, who came from North Europe seconded Frois: "They row according to the air of a song, or the tune of some words, or other noise, which serves at the same time to direct and regulate their work and to encourage one another." And, significantly, he didn't write *like in this or that part of Europe*, here, as he often did. And, this contrast was indirectly verified by the Japanese diplomatic mission that visited the United States in 1871 when they (Iwakura?) note similarities between their own culture and that of the "Indians" who crossed the Bering Strait. Besides stone figures resembling Buddhist ones, baskets made of vine carried on backs, vertically long wall-hangings and the way women tied their hair –

The boats look like Japanese ones with snakes and heads [carvings] adorning the bowsprit, and they sing songs as they paddle[?]. (J/I:IR:6)

I am puzzled about the carvings, which I thought of as *Okinawan* rather than Japanese. But, regardless, we can see that *singing while paddling/rowing/sculling* was identified with Japaneseness. Six years later, the chants received the better part of the first page of Morse's JAPAN DAY BY DAY. After a 17 day trip from San Francisco, they drop anchor in Yokohama and a "long clumsy affair" of a boat manned by three Japanese came out to take them to the hotel.

..

How vigorously they worked sculling us two miles to the shore! And such a peculiar series of grunts they made, keeping time with each other with sounds like *hei hei cha, hei hei cha,* and then varying the chanty, if it were one, putting quite as much energy into the grunts as they did into the sculling. The noise they made sounded like the exhaust of some compound and wheezy engine. I felt real sympathy for them in seeing the intense energy they gave to each stroke . . . The boat was curiously arranged for sculling from the side. (M:JDD)

And Japanese seamen were not the only ones who vocalized, either. Elizabeth Bird wrote:

As I look out the window, I see heavy two-wheeled man-carts drawn and pushed by four men each . . . Their cry is impressive and melancholy. They draw incredible loads, but as if the toil which often makes every breath a groan or a grasp were not enough, they shout incessantly with a coarse, gutteral grunt, something like *Ha huida, Ho huida, wa ho, ha huida,* etc. (B:UTJ?)

Coming from Bird, whose views of Japanese singing are ludicrously harsh, the "impressive and melancholy" is an incredible compliment!!! (*See what Frois has to say about sea chanties in 13-19!*) Eliza Ruhamah Scidmore was less sympathetic:

Those coolies who pull and push heavily loaded carts or drays keep up a hoarse chant, which corresponds to the chorus of sailors when hauling ropes. *"Hilda! Hoida!"* they seem to be crying, as they brace their feet for a hard pull, and the very sound of it exhausts the listener. In the old days, people were nearly deafened with these street choruses, but their use is another of the hereditary customs that is fast dying out. (S:JDJ)

The *Hilda! Hoida!* seem suspiciously close to Bird's earlier *Ha huida,* but, Scidmore also wrote that "one's chair-bearers" in the mountain districts "wheeze out *'Hi rikisha! Ho rickisha!'* or *'Ito sha! Ito sha!'"* She was right about the falling noise-level. Today, no matter what the exertion, we usually hear only a boring *"Yosh!"* for a single time effort (eg. gramps standing up), *"Yosshou!"* repeated over and over for repeated efforts (eg. tug-o-war), and *"Yoissho!"* or, at most, *Yoi'ssho koi!"* (eg. lifting up something really heavy, or for self-conscious comic effect) for slightly more obvious signals of what we might call *diligent exertion.* But these are voiced solo, they are no longer part of a collective chant except when the *sansha* – Shinto floats – are trotted about town.

Physiologically speaking, it is *right* – beneficial – to let out a rush of air while making a sudden strenuous effort. (It contracts the groin muscles preventing hernia and, in some way I can feel but do not understand, protects against lower-back strain). Morse, however, mentions something that suggests another kind of benefit:

> Wherever I go there is perceptible in the hum of the city streets certain noises that are rhythmical. You find that the Japanese workmen hum or sing at their work, and if the work is pounding, stirring with a stick or spoon, or any uniform movement, it is done with an accent and in rhythm. These noises may be a series of grunts or an actual song. The gold-beaters and fish-choppers always beat and chop with a peculiar tempo. A curious preparation of raw fish has to be rubbed into a paste in a stone mortar . . . The movements of stirring are accompanied with a peculiar whistling sound in perfect time to the stirring, which is interrupted by long and short stirs. The blacksmiths have the hammers of the helpers tuned differently, so that an agreeable series of sounds is made, and when four are pounded in rhythm it sounds like a chime of bells. It is a curious trait in their character to lighten the burden of their labors by some pleasant sound or rhythm. (M:JDD)

My impression of late-20th century Japanese blue-collar work was *very* different. Blue collar workers are, on the average, sassier than white-collar workers, and I like that; but they are still too damned quiet and serious as they go about their tasks! Heavy momentary exertion still makes them vocalize, but otherwise they keep their mouths shut. I never heard a woman singing as she worked and only heard one young man do so – a house-mate who was a budding opera singer. On the years-end office-cleaning day at the publisher I worked for, I was always the only one singing as I scrubbed. While Japanese never were a culture which would refuse to work unless there were a band accompanying them (such cultures were once not rare!) they did sing while doing collective work – My man Issa once felt guilty about napping to the accompaniment of the rice-planting song. Indeed, in large fields, bands played when they planted. But now, I find Japanese work is depressing to look at or share in, for they think singing frivolous or are embarrassed to sing unless they have liquor for an excuse and a mike in their hand. Hearing me sing as I work, someone will say in a patronizingly sweet tone of voice *"Robin-tte yôki da ne"* which might be Englished "Aren't you the cheerful one!" (In that sense, I think of Japanese culture as sick.)

1. *Japanese Never Rowed.* I can see two situations where "our" seated horizontal-oared rowing proper would clearly be superior: war and whaling. If anyone knows of this type of rowing being used for warships by Japanese or Koreans (*How about those Turtle Boats?*) please send a gloss!

12-11 Our oars are all made from one piece of wood; *Os nossos remos são todos de hum pao;*

Those of Japan from two pieces. *Os de Japão de dous ped[aços].*

As mentioned in 12-3, with respect to the verb *remar,* here, too, the "oars" (*remos*) are problematic, for as 12-12 shows, depending how they are defined, not *all* of Japan's oars/sculls/paddles are two-piece. Frois is probably contrasting the largest type of oar here.[1]

Kaempfer describes such an oar as "being not at all streight, like our European oars, but somewhat bent, with a moveable joint in the middle, which yielding to the violent pression of the water, facilitates the taking of them up. The timber pieces and boards are fasten'd together in their joints and extremities, with hooks and bands of copper." I would, rather, say that the upper third of the shaft is splinted to the lower part to allow some give and the replacement of either half. Eliza Skidmore gives us a picture of them working in Yokohama: ". . . voluble boatmen keep up a steady *bzz, bzz, whizz, whizz*, to the strokes of their crooked, wobbling oars as they scull in and out." (S:JDJ) Like many things, the idea for two-piece sculling oars probably came from China. H. Warrington Smyth describes the arrangement on a Hong Kong cargo-boat ("one of the finest sailing lighters in the world").

> To this not only the large deep rudder, but a couple of vast sculling oars, one upon each quarter, contribute. This form of propulsion is the usual one for big heavy craft in China. The long oar, usually in two pieces, is pivoted on the quarter or stern, the fore end being held in place by a strong lanyard to the deck. Any number of the crew can work on each oar, giving to it the motion known to seamen as sculling. A vessel of several hundred tons can be propelled in this way at from three to four knots. Its great advantage is that it is perfectly quiet, not exhausting, and the oar being in line with the boat, it is peculiarly applicable to crowded anchorages or narrow waterways. The motion is really that of the gondolier when his blade is brought aft to clear an obstruction.

Without an illustration it is hard to figure out exactly what is happening in this fascinating description (Illustration, anyone?)

1. *Other Two Piece.* The medium-sized sculls and the small paddles also were two-piece, but only if you count the small cross-bar on the top of the handle. I do not think Frois counted that.

~~~~~~

12-12　Our oars have blades that are removable and broad;
Os nossos remos tem as pas postiças e são largas;

The blades in Japan are the same wood [as the handle] and long and narrow.
As de Japão são do mesmo pao e estreitas.

Now who has the single and who has the double oar? Frois uses the same *remos,* but probably refers to something different. Okada notes that the NIPO (this dictionary post-dating Frois by about 20 years) differentiates ro = 櫓 = *remos* with *kai* = 櫂 = *pangayos* and defines *kai* as "rowing from the back of the boat as with pangayos;" and that the *pangayo* is an Indian craft. [1] I could not find out how our oar blades were fastened and unfastened from the shaft, if that is what Frois means (anyone?).

The medium-sized *kai* is probably what Frois refers to, for the small one was meant for *paddling* and has a broad blade. It complicates matters a bit because the *kai* was used for both propelling the boat (in addition to a sail-power, as needed) and steering it. In that sense, it was a rudder and tiller in a single piece (for the small crossbar on top is not really a separate piece). If the next contrast did not continue with rowing contrasts, I would have assumed Frois meant to write "rudder" (*leme* – considering the virtually interchangeable "l" and "r" in Portuguese, very close) rather than *remos* (oars).

1. *Pangayo.* *Aurelio's* defines *pangayo* (prob. of African deriv.) as a majestic boat with a lanciform prow and a low stern, lots of mouth [*muita boca?*](?), sails, very fast and stable, with 2 masts and (triangular +square) bastard-rigged sails used in East Africa and India. I could not follow the train of definitions of definitions in the Portuguese and, hence, cannot give the details of the rigging. Strangely enough – for it is full of *bastard this-and-that* things, English evidently did not adopt the interesting term.

~~~~~~

12-13   When our sailors row they lift the oars clear of the water;
        Os nossos marinheiros quando remão alevantão os remos fora d'agoa;

               Those of Japan are continually rowing under the water.
               Os de Japão vão sempre remando por debaxo do mar.

The Japanese side of the contrast here perfectly depicts what I think should be the sole definition of sculling. It was done on the side by teams and the stern by a lone sculler. Kaempfer provides a slightly different angle on the way Japanese "watermen" use oars..

> They do not row after our European manner, extending their Oars streight forwards, and cutting just the surface of the water, but let them fall down into the water almost perpendicularly, and then lift them up again. (K(S):HOJ)

The horizontal versus vertical oar angles part is well-expressed, but the Kaempfer's English translation may have a mistake, for, as Frois wrote, they do *not* "lift them up." (There is a new translation of Kaempfer, but I have not seen it: Could the translator please send a gloss?). Okada has a line from Kaempfer about "just like *stirring up* the water," which is more *apropo*. If Captain Saris found space saved on ship-board, Herr Doctor Kaempfer notes that this method of rowing saves space *in the water* as well, for it enables boats to pass each other in narrow passages. Morse also notes something that must have stared Frois in the face so hard that he blanked out:

> The sailors are fine, muscular-looking fellows; wearing nothing but a breech-cloth, they are as brown as russet apples. In rowing the boat they push instead of pulling [sic] the oars, and consequently face the bow of the boat. (M:JDD)

Push versus *pull!* The best oar contrast yet. Just the opposite of the case for carpentry. Japanese also faced the side – and when sculling alone at the stern were had to look over their shoulder, but with the feet askance to one side, even then they could see where they were going, unlike our style of rowing which may be philosophically true to life, for it only lets us see where we have come from but not where we will go [1] – but is, *practically speaking*, dangerous.

                    *   *   *

Chamberlain devotes almost two pages to debating the *pros* and *cons* of our respective ways of rowing/sculling. The *pro* side admits that Japanese can "bring into action all the muscles from the feet up; and as there is no removal of the oar from the water, there is no loss of the power they exert" (quoting a Dr. Bell). But the longer *contra* side claimed that the constant use of the entire body and the fact the oars being always submerged gave the oarman no rest would to the contrary be much more tiring and give the advantage to the Western style of rowing. Chamberlain claims a well-manned 6-oared gig could out-row a *yuloing* (the Chinese word for scull/ing) pilot *sampan*, both in terms of top-speed and in terms of holding that speed for "an hour or more," which is no doubt correct for reasons Chamberlain does not give. Namely, because rowing with a large stroke – like low gear on a bicycle – is more efficient and easier than sculling very fast. But, for simply cruising along at, say 3-4 knots all day long, that *yuloing* would win hands down. Thunberg and Morse, respectively, agree:

> Their boats are not rowed, but always wriggled with one or two oars. The oar is large, and for that purpose obliquely writhed. This way of working with oars does not appear to be very fatiguing; but drives the vessel on with great speed. (T:TEAA)

Our man . . .began sculling at ten o'clock at night and kept it up with one or two intermissions until four o'clock the next afternoon, with no sleep and apparently no fatigue. (M:JDD)

I believe the logic of Chamberlain's *contra* side is wrong in so far that pushing=sculling is less strenuous work than pulling-rowing both because the weight of the whole body, rather than muscles are used and because the scullers, as I noted earlier, *do not need to bend,* which makes the motion far less tiring on the heart, lungs and guts. Sculling bears more similarity to poling or walking, movement people can do *all day*.

One contrast was missed by all but Cornwallis, who describes the way "they worked their long and somewhat bent sculls at the sides on projections from the gunwales" as follows:

this they did in perfect unison, each man chaunting a monotonous refrain, and every alternate man swinging his body in an opposite direction to the one next to him, which left the one pulling and the other pushing. The rowers thus vibrating, assisted the impetus, and preserved the steady position of the boat as she rapidly skimmed the water. (C:TJJ: 1859)

Smooth. The greater economy of space both on deck and below water make this possible.

1. *Future Lies Behind Us.* This idea came from *Word Play*, where Peter Farb wrote that Quechua put the future metaphorically *behind us* and the past *in front;* and that was noted by missionaries who had trouble with the translation of Biblical idioms such as one suggesting we "put Satan behind us." I had my doubts, but later found the *future-is-behind* perspective seconded by a West Brazilian native sign language, where the palm pushes back over the shoulder. This is not so foreign to our way of thinking as we might assume if we recall that something that we can see = envision = remember is, if it were, out *before* our eyes, whereas the future, which we (unless we are a seer) cannot see, is as good as behind us, out of our line of sight.

12-14 On our boats we are very cautious about fire.
Nas nossas embarqasões se tem grande tento no fogo;

On Japanese boats, though there's straw everywhere, they take no care of fire.
Nas de Japão, com ser tudo palha, sobre o fogo não há nenhuma guarda.

So that's why *snuff* and chewing tobacco was so big for sailors in the West! They were not permitted to smoke. On 16th century Spanish boats, according to Peréz-Mallaína,

The cooking fire was the only light that was permitted on board without being enclosed in a metal or glass lantern. During storms, the cooking fire was put out after sunset. At night, the only light that remained was the one that illuminated the compass box and one lantern shared among those on guard. Despite these precautions, there were many disastrous fires, but perhaps none like that in September 1561 [two years before Frois arrived in Japan], which destroyed twenty-three ships moored in the port of Seville. The origin of the fire was in the tomfoolery of a sailor, who eased his boredom by setting cats on fire [And I had thought burning cats was English!] . . . (P(P):SMS)

Obviously, regulations are no substitute for the quality or lack of quality of the man-power. You could no more imagine something like that happening on a Japanese ship then, than today! [1]

Did Japanese, who tended to stay near shore and lived in tinder-box houses, think that boats, with less paper and surrounded by water, were comparatively safe places for fire? Or, was it because most Japanese ships were not full of gun powder?

1. *Responsibility at Work.*   I have not worked on a Japanese ship, but I have worked in a large boat factory in Austin Texas about 1970 and I still recall the day the big guy from Tennessee took a forklift on a spin, not noticing the top of the lift was a bit too high for a certain beam which he hit going 10 miles per hour causing a dozen or so boats balanced like rockets against said beam to fall over. I cannot imagine that happening in Japan. (I suppose it is *possible,* for there *are* dumb Japanese, but they are few and far between).

12-15   With us, honorable people are always favored with the poop;
Antre nós por primor vai sempre a jente honrada na popa;

In Japan, the nobility rides on the bow, where they are often completely soaked.
Em Japão a jente nobre vai na proa onde [às] vezes se molha arrezoadamente.

I played a bit with "our" translation. "Favored with the poop" should be "ride on the poop because it is cool/classy/dandy" (Yes, *primor,* again!).

Metaphor can favor either first or last, as the classier location for big shots. With a ship, the bow should offer the clearest view, but it also was not only wet but the roughest ride. Was the samurai spirit of the Japanese upper class not daunted with such practical matters? One reason for the high poop in Western vessels is, as noted before, for the steersman (or watch) to better see over the bow. That would put the honorable people closer to the controls. Did the Luso-Iberians with their sail-loving kings like it that way? And, finally (until an expert sends a gloss), if most pooping was done directly into the sea, was the poop the best place to poop from (Did that have anything to *doo* with it?)

12-16   Our boats have round masts;   *As nossas embarqasões tem o masto redondo;*

Their *fune* [boat/s] square ones.   *As funes quadrados.*

If square sections were good, I would think tree-trunks would grow square. Unlike trees, which encounter the wind from all angles, boats do not sail backwards, so I can at least imagine a mast with a half circle cross-section. But square or rectangular! [1] One might as well have a square pole-vaulting pole! Since "square mast" also means a mast with square sails, my first reaction on reading Frois was to suspect a mistake, though "our" sails were not "round." Googling showed me, however, that square masts are not uncommon on modern sailboats(!) and are said to be easier to make then round or octagonal ones and "stiffer for their size and you can make them hollow if you want" as one boat designer put it! Another builder of a "ferro-cement yacht" adds that they are "easier to rig." And, finally, I found a Japanese website dedicated to the relatively small Japanese transport boat the *maruko-bune* of Biwako, Japan's largest lake. It said that the Japanese-style of mast was the same length as the boat and, indeed, *square.* Square was said to be stronger! (http://www.koti.jp/marco/)

1. *Rectangular Timber.*   The Japanese could translate the *quadrados* with a word, *kakuzai,* meaning "rectangular timber." The closest English can is *boards,* but they are thinner on one side.

12-17   We never demast our boats;
As nossas embarqasões nunqa se dezemmasteão;

The Japanese, when they are going to row immediately remove the mast.
Os Japões, como vão a remo, logo tirão o masto fora.

I don't know about that "never." In a typhoon, masts were sometimes cut down ("We cut the masts down with as much care as possible, but we still weren't able to stop the mainmast from falling on top of fourteen men, including five Portuguese, and splattering their brains and guts all over the place." (P(L)TMP) But, Frois means as a regular part of sailing. Kaempfer writes that the mast of the typical merchant vessel was "the same length with the ship" and is "wound up by pulleys and again let down upon the deck, when the ship comes to anchor." This "roof, or upper deck" was "flattish," and in rainy weather the mast was let down upon it, "and the sail extended over it for sailors, and the people employed in the ship's service to take shelter under it, and to sleep at night." (K(S):HOJ) Well, that suggests *one* reason for a square mast, it wouldn't roll over on a sleeping sailor!

~~~~~~

12-18   Our boats have topsails, mizzens and foresails; *As nossas tem gaveas, mezenas e traqetes;*

>Their *fune* [boats] none of them. *As* funes *nada disto.*

The *gavea* is actually the "main topsail," but I think a loose translation suffices.   One might even skip the names altogether and just say, Our ships have *zillions* of sails, theirs usually just *one*. The caravel usually had only 3, but the *nao* and galleons boasted 10 or more.

Like ancient Egyptian or Viking ships, the Japanese merchant ships had one square sail. The pleasure boats also had only one sail with one boom on *top* of the sail and none on the bottom-side, so the sail was shaped like a triangle standing on its head [1] – the exact opposite of the typical modern sailboat. This would be very safe from the point of view of *jibes*, but, one would think, unstable! It is interesting that Frois used the Japanese generic term for boat, *fune,* as if to suggest it is, or should be, a *type* of boat.

1. *Booms on Top*. This did not become a contrast because the booms on the Portuguese ships were on top too.

~~~~~~

12-19   Our boats travel by day and by night.
As nossas embarqasões caminhão de dia e de noyte;

>Those of Japan stop in port at night and travel by day.
>*As de Japão tomão porto de noyte e caminhão de dia.*

In the 20th century, long distance trucking in Japan was almost all done at night and Japanese fishing boats operating in concert with mother (factory) ships remained away from port longer than anyone; but it seems coastal shipping or fishing operations in Frois's time were strictly *day-work*.   As Okada points out, Japanese ships at this time still traded as far away as Korea, China, Annam in Indo-China and the Philippines. Frois chose to contrast coastal traffic. Ironically, within a half century, what slight sea-worthiness the Japanese ships had itself became criminal. "By the laws of the Empire, their ships must not be built strong enough to bear the shocks and tossing of huge raging waves," wrote Kaempfer, who explained the primary guarantee as follows:

..

>The stern is broad and flat, with a wide opening in the middle, which reaches down almost to the bottom of the ship, and lays open all the inside to the eye. This opening was originally contriv'd for the easier management of the rudder, but since the Emperor hath taken the resolution to shut up his dominions to all foreigners, orders were issued at the same time, that no ship should be built without such an opening, and this in order to prevent his subjects from attempting to venture out to the main sea, on any voyage whatever. (K(S):HOJ)

So a hole in the poop kept a whole nation plugged up! We laugh; but only ostensibly absurd preventative laws like this could hope to close a coastline that stretched out measures in the tens of thousands of miles. As improbable as it may seem, a close equivalent to Japan's open-stern device was found in the Americas by Morse. It has nothing to do with the travel of men or merchandise. The context is an aside from an aside on the supposed reasons cats don't have tails in Japan! I live in little Havana (Miami), but it was the first time I heard of the following:

> This idea is paralleled in Cuba, where the ears of a cat are cut off to prevent it from roaming in the cane fields. The sudden showers that fall in the tropics are annoying to cats, inasmuch as the rain gets into their ears, and this they particularly loathe. The result is that cats remain near the house, so that in case of a shower they can make a quick dash for protection. (M:JDD)

~~~~~~

12-20 Ours often keep moving without taking any account of the rain.
As nossas muitas vezes caminhão sem terem conta com chuva;

Those of Japan do not have to go when the sky isn't clear.
As de Japão em que o [tempo] não estaa claro não hão de caminhar.

As Kaempfer pointed out, the poop was not the only problem, "the deck is built so loose that it will let the [rain] water run through before the mast hath been taken down and the ship cover'd, partly with mats, partly with sails." Knowing all this, Kaempfer writes, we can't accuse the Japanese captains of "fear and cowardice" for the manner in which they repair to the nearest harbor – available on every inhabited island, and there were many – at the slightest pretext. These, again, were features of coastal shipping, but we can assume something was done to waterproof the decks on the dozens if not hundreds of boats that still ventured across the high sea at the time TRATADO was written.[1]

According to an information box at the Lake Biwa Maruko boat website already mentioned, the straw-mat sails got heavy and hard to operate when it rained. That, too, may explain why Japanese preferred to avoid the rain. It also suggests that the all-weather mat-sail boats from other countries either used different straw or wove it differently.

1. *Sea-going Japanese Ships.* I do not feel confident we know what was what. How much sea travel by Japanese was actually done in Chinese ships made up to look Japanese? A sixteenth century document cited by Kwan-wai So (JAPANESE PIRACY IN MING CHINA) claims most of the alleged Wako (Japanese=dwarf) pirates used ships with a "sharp bottom," introduced by Chinese, the "traitorous people of the Fukien seaboard." The same document claimed that even the sea-going vessels of Japan had flat bottoms unsuitable for big waves and sails that required favorable winds (only run with a following sea), so that it often took them a month to cross seas that the Chinese boats (which hoisted their sail on the side) crossed in days. For all of Japanese *macho*, it seems crazy they should stick to their own boats *if they were that* bad! Yet, *something doesn't make sense.* Souryi, citing the Kôraishi (History of Kôryo = Korea), a "fairly reliable" 1451 source, writes that in the mid-fourteenth century there were months when over 100 Japanese pirate ships were recorded plundering Korea. The rice-raids we discussed in the War chapter were but the start of it. They attacked ships bearing peasants' rent, kidnapped people for ransom and took slaves to the Ryukus (Okinawa) to resell. "Like the Vikings in the West, . . . the wakô sailed further and further up the rivers" and even began "transporting horses on their ships so they could raid the interior of the country." (S(R):WTUD) The ruling Korean dynasty collapsed and by the middle of the next century a good portion of the pirates were Korean and the Chinese had to step in, little knowing their turn would be next . . .

~~~~~~

12-21 With us, when a small boat is hired, the boatmen are not separate.
Antre nós, quando se freta huma embarqasão peqena, não se divide dos marinheiros;

In Japan, you pay as much for the boatman [1] as for the *fune* [boat].
Em Japão tanto se dá polo frete da fune *como por hum marinheiro.*

Again! We have seen the same in the last chapter with respect to the sawyers and their saw. Here, a charge for a seaman seems odd to us. In the other case, the charge for the *saw* seemed odd. In either case, we evidently expect to pay for the big thing, and have the smaller come with it.

1. Boatman. I also considered "sailor" but these small boats were largely sculled. If both were plural, I would have used *seamen*, but a singular "seaman" would not work. This part of translation I hate and would prefer to leave to a copy-editor if I only had one (It is hard to find anyone with a Japanese-enabled computer & I'm penniless!).

12-22 With us, a ship's carrying capacity is measured by its hull;
Antre nós se faz conta do que levará o navio polo casqo;

In Japan, by counting the sections of the sail.
Em Japão pola conta das esteiras da vella.

Frois is evidently talking about *classes* of ship rather than capacity *per se*, which was measured in tonnage in the West and "stones" of rice – thought of as a numerical quantity, rather than a weight – in Japan, where estates and fiefs were also ranked for prestige and taxes according to the same unit representing the output of the harvest. Japanese sails were not measured in their equivalent to our square feet or yards, but *in units of a given area*, so you have the *10-section sail* class and the *20-section* sail class and so on. Being made of mats, I assume the sections are the same standard sizes as mats found in houses [1] discussed elsewhere. (間違ったら、教えて下さい！)

1. Mat Sizes. Checking the size, I found that one mat in Edo is about a half-foot shorter than in the old Miyako, where they were almost 2 meters long! Had I only known that before! I might have moved to Kyoto where things would have fit me and who knows, I might be there still, and this book would never have been written. (It is a bit more complex because the size is actually that of square beam to square beam that they rest on, etc.)

12-23 We have carpenters specifically for ships.
Antre nós há carpinteiro detriminado pera o navio;

In Japan, *fune* [boat] masters are almost always carpenters.
Os Japões oficiaes da fune *quasi todos são carpinteiros.*

Okada writes tellingly, "this says there were apparently no specialists in ship-building, but the Japanese-Portuguese Dictionary (published about 20 years after TRATADO) has a heading for *funa-daiku* (ship-carpenter). Perhaps provincial differences were involved (Frois may not have encountered specialists). Considering the angularity of Japanese boats, I can well imagine that most were made by house-builders![1]

1. House-Boat. I found a refugee boat on the beach of Key Biscayne that was a perfect rectangle (flat-bottom, sides at a perfect right-angle) with a triangle stuck on in front. I thought, *this* was made by a carpenter! Were it not for the foam in it, the boat would not have made it across a swimming pool much less the Gulf Stream!

12-24 With us, someone who receives cargo aboard a boat hands over a freight bill to its owner who stays on land; *Antre nós quem recebe a fazenda no navio deixa conhecimento ao dono que fiqa em terra;*

In Japan, the man handing over the cargo also gives a freight bill [1] to the carrier.
Em Japão o que emtrega a fazenda dá tambem conhecimento della a quem a leva.

With regional powers being actively checked, partly through control of trade, by the Shoguns, did carriers have to be careful to have proof of exactly what was being carried and for whom?

1. *Conhecimento*. I do not know if "freight bill" is appropriate, though the dictionary gives it and "bill of lading" for translations of *conhecimento*. The original word implies an acknowledgment of what's what, a broader meaning than the English one I ended up using. Is there a better word?

12-25 Our ships' flags are square.
As nossas bandeiras dos navios são quadradas;

> Theirs is a thin strip of cloth put on a bamboo pole.
> *As suas são huma tira de pano comprida, toda enfiada em hum banbu.*

This is almost a perfect repeat of 7-35, with the *battle standards*. But, look at the Portuguese! For once, he uses *banbu* rather than *cana*! Did he feel it proper because the poles were larger? According to the OED, the Portuguese generally called very large cane *mambu* after the native Concan (?) word in the 16th century. This may be one of the first *bamboos* with a "b" in Portuguese (Note: Our idea of "bamboo" coming straight from Malay may be too simple).

Japanese ship "flags" came in two basic types. The one I think Frois means might better be called a banner. If our banners run horizontally, Japanese banners run vertically. Today, they work perfectly for advertising hung from the corners or standing by the entrance of buildings. These are strung on, or fastened by loops to the edge of a pole (now as often metal as bamboo), have a small stick at the top edge and sometimes at the bottom, too. They may flutter, but they do not move in the breeze, so they served identification purposes well. Some only hang loosely from the top of the pole, but Frois' *enfiada* (also meaning "strung on") suggests the first type. The other variety, perhaps not as common, was more like our pennant in shape, but tended to have longer tails. Fastened at one end they dangled in the doldrums or moved about dragon-like when the wind blew. Our square flags had aspects of both of these.

12-26 On our boats, nothing placed aboard becomes an augur [of disaster].
As nossas embarqasões não tem agouro em couza que nellas se meta;

> The Japanese have great fear of carrying temple bells.
> *Hos Japões o tem grandissimo em levar sinos das varelas.*

In the Far East, large bells were considered dangerous cargo popular with the Dragon God/s at the bottom of the sea, who would capsize boats to get them. *Why bells?* There is an old Chinese tale I have read about three times, but having a bad memory can only recall that there was a jealous female dragon and a bell. Also, since tall bell-towers in China were associated with dragons, maybe the dragons in the sea just want to get their fair share . . . If logic is allowed: *a large bell might actually be a strong draw for lightning!* Okada points out that horses and oxen and other 4-legged animals were a particular problem, for they were considered impure, and all impure items were jinxes.

"Our" side, reflecting the Christian party-line, was *probably* too optimistic for many of the Luso-Iberian explorers and crew, and *surely* wrong for the West as a whole. After all, the superstitious attitude of seamen in the North Sea remained largely intact up to the 20th century. This included the horrible belief it was better to leave men to drown than to save them, for that would anger the Sea God who was already smacking his or her lips. This was not reflected in the official policy for Spanish ships, where sailors were advised to "let out a great yell" as they fell to call attention to their going overboard and indicate which side it was, not to mention scaring off any shark that happened to be in the vicinity (Alonso de Chaves in P(P):SMS). Iberian ships also did not particularly mind carrying women whereas in North Europe, the presence of a *woman* aboard was believed to either incur the jealousy of the boat, which might just commit suicide against a reef or anger the feminine spirit of the deep into throwing up huge waves (The great Russian Ballad, *Stenka Rasin* has that great line about tossing a Princess overboard to placate a stormy Mother Volga).

If relics and miracles are considered, the Iberian culture seems the least modern, but when it comes to old superstitions, the Northern cultures were the more old-fashioned. This was not only true for seamen. Keith Thomas, writing of the generally superstitious mindset of the English, provides these gems

> In 1593, it was feared that the plague in London would get worse because a heron perched on top of St Peter's, Cornhill, and stayed there all afternoon.

> In 1604, the House of Commons rejected a bill after the speech of its Puritan sponsor had been interrupted by the flight of a jackdaw through the Chamber – an indisputably bad omen. (T:MNW)

~~~~~~

12-27   We think things like mermaids/sirens and mermen/men of the sea are tall tales.
Nós temos por patranhas toda a couza de serenas ou homens marinhos;

> The Japanese think there is a kingdom of lizards under the sea, that they are rational and can save them. *Elles tem que debaxo do mar há reino de lagartos e que são racionais e se salvão.*

Frois contrasts a simple world explained as *all but dead* by Christians, who believed a lot about a little, with a richer, enchanted world where most people believed a little less about a lot more. As mentioned in 12-26, not all the West was *that* disenchanted at this time. Frois makes an ironic choice in his examples, for one export item the allegedly superstitious people of the Far East made for export to the gullible West was none other than mermaids and mermen! [1] But there is truth in the contrast, for this was the time when, in parts of Europe, "we" had to pretend to disbelief, for any sailor who made too big of a fuss about The Old Man of the Sea might have been thrown into it (or burned) by his more fundamentalist compatriots, while Japanese fishermen continued to supplicant their age-old sea gods, which were, indeed, a Dragon King and a Dragon Princess. Speaking of which,
..

> *Our dragons are full of fire have hooked tails, embody hellishness and kidnap maidens.*
> *Their dragons are watery spirits considered benign unless angered who control the weather.*

While Japanese fishing villages really did support their temples and shrines with dragon and other maritime connections, they were by no means as openly religious – to the Christian mind, *superstitious* – as the Chinese.

> . . . and loud above all, the horrible row the Chinese seamen made aboard a junk about to set sail. They were invoking, we understood, the god of the pagoda by the song of gongs, to protect them from the evil spirits of the vasting deep. (M:BGE:1860)

The Japanese traditionally prided themselves on *not* raising a ruckus to the Heavens, as opposed to their cowardly neighbors, if I understand the intent of the long-controversial classical phrase denoting Japan as the *koto-age-wa senu kuni* (word-raise not do country). In this respect, it is interesting to note that St. Xavier made a name for himself by performing a two day-long non-stop prayer which was credited with saving the ship he was on from being sunk in a typhoon.

*   *   *

But a truly fair contrast would not have put the "lizards" against mermen and mermaids.   If the dragons, elemental spirits, or, rather, spirited elements of Taoism that found their way to Japan, perhaps replacing and/or incorporating the serpent-centered part of their ancient beliefs were "tall tales" or "superstition," then what is "our" rational God (and son and holy ghost) who can save us? To me, the dragon looks like a far more convincing denizen of space than our muscle-bound bearded fellow! Or, leaving God out of it, we may note that, Frois aside, the Iberian sailors' still had faith in something far more subtle than God, a host of guardian spirits harking back to pre-Christian times, as we know from the prayers of sailors collected by the commissioner in Vera Cruz, Mexico in 1586 at the instigation of the Inquisitor General of Mexico for burning because of their superstitious content. Peréz-Mallaína gives us a number – which were not specifically marked as such, but probably were – including:

> *Prayer to St. Elmo:* Holy Body, true friend of mariners, we want you to help us, and always to appear at night before us.

> *Prayer to Our Lady of Barameda:* Now that we have passed your sandbar, be pleased to have us return and pass over it again, with a good and safe voyage.

> *Prayer to St. Clare:* That she be pleased to give us clear skies night and day and bring us good weather and keep us from bad shoals, and bad fleets and bad company, and that she be pleased to bring us safely to good harbor, Our Father, Ave Maria. (P:PSMS)

Other prayers were to St. Nicholas, the Four Evangelists and Our Lady of Fair Seas. Some of these ostensibly Christian prayers invoked the natural phenomenon the Saint was identified with (St Elmo's fire), some the Saint's traditional forte (Nicholas, guardian of travelers) some the benefits implied by the name (Clare=clear), and some simply made a name to fit the item (*Barameda*=sandbar) or desire (~ of Fair Seas). The most interesting of the examples given was more abstract: spatial protection, "thus, the "four holy bodies" of the Evangelists were invoked so they could guard the four corners of the ship" (P:PSMS) or, I wonder, the compass? As salutes might also be fired for these guardians, a skeptic can also wonder if the Inquisition was thinking about saving gun-powder as well as such obviously pagan souls! On top of this,

> to avoid the evil eye, the crew members wore around their necks the well known "figs," that is, small amulets shaped like hands with the thumb placed between the index finger and the middle finger, which have been found in abundance in the remains of shipwrecks." (Ibid)

In other words, if the cross didn't work, "we" could always try giving bad spirits the bird!

~~~~~~

12-28   On our boats, we always carry water for the long haul.
Nos nossos navios se leva sempre agoa pera muito tempo

The *fune* [boat/s]of Japan each carry only two days of water.
Aas funes *dos Japões quasi cada dous dias fazem agoada.*

This is a variation on 12-19, above, day-sailing. But, one wonders why Japanese didn't consider the possibility of being swept out to see or marooned somewhere. I would guess the boats were *not allowed* to carry more water once the Seclusion began in earnest!

Perhaps a few words are in order about that Seclusion, which became almost total following a 1637 rebellion involving Christians and was advertised to the world by the merciless execution of a deputation of prominent citizens from Macau, who begged to resume trade in 1640. The only contact between Japan and the outside world allowed was through the trade-post at Dejima, a 600 ft long by 120 ft wide artificial island, planked in on all sides, with only two guarded and often closed gates, one seaward and one towards the town (Nagasaki) near the bridge. Ian Littlewood puts it well, when he writes that Japan was *"as remote as the moon;"* (L:IOJ) but the Europeans on Dejima were infinitely *more* isolated. Thunberg in 1775:

..

> . . . the ship sailed, and left behind fourteen of us Europeans, among some slaves and Japanese, in solitude, and, it might in some sort be said, confinement, we being shut up within the narrow circle of this little island of Dezima, and separated not only from Christendom, but, in fact, from the whole world besides. An European, that remains here, is in a manner dead and buried in an obscure corner of the globe. He hears no news of any kind . . . The soul possesses here one faculty only, which is the judgment (if, indeed, it be at all times in possession of this faculty.) The will is totally debilitated, and even dead, because to an European there is no other will than that of the Japanese, by which he must exactly square his conduct. (T:TEAA)

They didn't even have religious material, for when boats arrived, all Prayer books and Bibles "were collected and put into a chest which was nailed down" and "left under the care of the Japanese, till the time of our departure;" [1] and the Westerners – all of whom were supposed to be Dutch (some like Kaempfer, a German, passed) – were thoroughly checked both on board ship and when leaving the island for town. Thunberg writes that "their suspicion went even so far, as to induce them to break an egg or two from among those we brought with us from Batavia and break them." Thunberg writes the Dutch themselves were largely responsible for the severity of the searches, for "some years ago a parrot was found hid in the breeches of one of the petty officers of the ship, which, whilst they were searching the man, began to talk" and small articles were hidden in the drawers and "under their private parts." At first, the Japanese let the chief officer avoid the ignominy of being searched, but by the time Thunberg arrived this had changed:

> For many years past the captain was not only equipped with the wide furtout above described, but also wore large and capacious breeches, in which he carried contraband ashore. These, however, were suspected, and consequently laid aside; and the coat, the last resource, was now, to the owner's great regret, taken off. It was droll enough to see the astonishment which the sudden reduction in the size of our captain excited in the ignorant Japanese, who before had always imagined that all our captains were actually as fat and lusty as they appeared to be. (Ibid)

The final lock on the door of the country was linguistic. The Dutch might be permitted to trade in *goods*, but *words* were taboo:

> The interpreters are all natives of Japan, and speak with more or less accuracy the Dutch language. The government permits no foreigners to learn their language, in order that by means of it they may not pick up any knowledge of the country, but allow from fourty to fifty interpreters who are to serve the Dutch in their factory with respect to their commerce and on other occasions. (Ibid)

---

1. *Hiding Taboo Items.*   When I worked-away on a Swedish freighter, "our" pornographic magazines had to be hidden when we were in port in Japan in 1972. They were bundled up and put under the pig heads in the freezer where they safely escaped notice. One of the heads was later placed face up in the electrician's head.

12-29 When our sails tear, we sew them up immediately;
Antre nós se a vela vai rota logo hé cozida;

> In Japan, they go on with them torn or coming apart and pay no attention to it.
> *Em Japão vai sempre ro[ta] ou descozida sem se ter conta com isso.*

Since the Japanese straw sails are made in sections, as mentioned in 12-22 above, a stitch in time wouldn't make much difference. Moreover, it is probable some of those openings were, unknown to Frois, *deliberate*. After changing to cotton, it was common for sails to be –

> made of long, narrow strips of thin cloth laced together, leaving an interspace of three or four inches. The sails are very large and these interspaces relieve the pressure in high winds. (M:JDD)

> laced together vertically, leaving a decorative lacing six inches wide between each two widths. Instead of reefing in a strong wind, a width is unlaced, so as to reduce the canvas vertically, not horizontally. (B:UTJ)

Chances are that this practice was a carry-over from Frois's time. Further description of these cloth sails is found in the last sentence of the most beautiful two paragraphs of *A Diplomatist's Wife in Japan*. "Every fishing-boat from every village" took advantage of "a liberating breeze" to head out to sea.

..

> The peculiar warm sheen of the junk sails, square above and round below, made in long strips, seamed and held together in a thousand lovely patterns by the interlacing ropes strained against the breeze, gave the impression of a web of silver against the blue; and the calm majesty of the silky rush on the water's surface made me feel our great coal-fed, screw-driven liner was a blot on the universe, and had no title to travel with that fair company." (F:DWJ)

12-30 With our *fustas* [pinnace] and *catures,* we embark and disembark at the bow.
Nas nossas fustas e catures se embarqão e dezembarqão polla proa;

> With the boats of Japan, the stern quickly swings around to land and one embarks and disembarks from there. *As embarqasões de Japão virão logo a popa pera a terra e por ali se embarqão e dezembarqão.*

To pick a couple of many ships for a contrast seems rather silly. If it were only true for all, we could put it against 12-15 and note that the important people must either walk to the other end of the boat or get off *last*. A better contrast was out there, too. I will *Faux Frois* a Chamberlain (adding the unwritten side, ours):

> In Europe, boats are hauled up on the beach bow first.
> In Japan, *Boats are hauled* [up] *on the beach stern first.* (CTJ)

This is exactly what proper people do with shoes in the porticos of Japan: they leave them facing outwards to be ready for the next trip. If we "come and go," the Japanese "go and come" (*itte-kuru)*. They like to be ready to *go*.

endnote XII

Boats 船

Since I have little more to say on boats per se, let me add a bit more about the Seclusion that put a period to the Jesuit endeavor in Japan and the dreams of the Japanese. As explained already, the Seclusion made the poor sea-going vessels even more dangerous. Excluding a few merchant ships licensed to trade with Ryukyu (Okinawa), Korea and Ezo (the Ainu land that is now Hokkaido and includes islands occupied by the Soviet Union → Russia?), Japan got out of the off-shore boat game altogether. Kaempfer noted that this was not so bad as it seemed to the West:

> Another objection that could be made, is, that a Country must still be unhappy, whose inhabitants are kept, as it were, prisoners within the limits thereof, and denied all manner of commerce and communication with their neighbors . . . [but] these many and different islands [of Japan] are, with regard to the whole Empire, what different Countries and Provinces are with regard to the whole globe: Differing in soil and situation, they were to produce various necessaries of life. And indeed, there is scarce any thing that can be wished for, but what is produced in some Province, in some island or other . . . (K(S):HOJ)

More important, self-isolated Japan was not closed in spirit. The dreams of its people spanned the world. As a result, Japan had one boat which the West lacked. And, from the point of view of the land-lubber, *that* Japanese boat was better than all of the rest of the world's boats put together. I refer to the *takara-bune*, or "treasure ship" of the popular imagination. This boat was believed to carry magical treasures, secular ones like hats to make you invisible, mallets to make wishes come true, bottomless bags of gold to spring out wherever a hammer is struck (I am a bit confused about the relationship of bag and hammer), scales useful for weighing the thoughts of others, keys to open any door, rhinoceros-horn cups [1] to alert you to, or even purify, any poison, religious ones like the wheel of law, the umbrella of heaven (to float you into paradise, I think) etc. . . . (treasures usually come in sets of 8, a number symbolizing plenty and 8 sacred mountain peaks each connected with a religious treasure in India) and the 7 Chinese gods of prosperity. These Gods and most of the treasures just mentioned were imported but some (the *scales*, perhaps, for the homophone *omoi* for "thought" and "weight.") may have been added by the Japanese artists who made prints of this boat to put under the pillow on New Year's Night in the hope of having an auspicious dream on that night.

I do not know if the treasure ship of the Japanese imagination began with the enormous boats of the Chinese treasure fleet or, both were inspired by older Chinese legend. Could it be called an artistically sublimated or healthily domesticated cargo cult? I will try to have this worked out for the New Year volume of my *In Praise of Olde Haiku* (IPOOH) series which should be ready by 2005, for there is an entire chapter dedicated to this pleasant fiction.

1. Rhinoceros Horn Cup   Before coming to Japan, Thunberg happened to encounter the rhinoceros-horn cups in South Africa, where the magic was taken literally, for

> it was generally believed, that goblets made of these horns in a turner's lathe would discover a poisoness draught that was put into them, by making the liquid ferment till it ran quite out of the goblet. Such horns as were taken from a young rhinocerous calf that had not yet copulated were said to be best . . . of these goblets are made, which set in gold and silver, and

made presents of to kings . . ." (T:TEAA 1773)

A medical doctor, he experimented with horns taken from two-horn rhinocerae "both wrought into goblets, and unwrought, both old and young horns, with several types of poisons, weak as well as strong" but "observed not the least motion or effervescence." Only "a solution of corrosive sublimate, aqua phagaedenica" or the like gave rise to "a few bubbles, produced by the air, which had been inclosed in the pores of the horn, and which was now disengaged from it."

XIII

OF THE *PLAYS, SKITS, DANCE, SINGING AND MUSICAL*
dos autos, farças, danças, cantar e instromentos da muzica de japão
INSTRUMENTS OF JAPAN

13-1   Our plays are ordinarily performed at night.
Os nossos autos ordinariamente se fazem de noyte;

> The Japanese perform them almost all the time, day [*add.* and night].
> *Os Japões quasi os fazem sempre de dia – [e de noite.]*

Autos, the term used by Frois, were one-act plays.[1] Content-wise, they included the religious, topical, comical and fantastic. Structure-wise, they were pretty much the only serious drama he could have seen, because five-act tragedies and comedies had fallen afoul of the Catholic Church and were long forgotten in the Portugal of his youth. But classical drama was already well into the process of revival in Italy and the Jesuits with their humanist schools – already 70 schools in 1556 – probably did more than anyone to revive it in Iberia.[2]

..

> For the same reasons Pascal denounced theater – its capacity to move the emotions of its spectators with a lifelike replica of human existence – the Jesuits embraced theater as a pedagogical tool. Through a humanistic marriage of the heroic, secular virtues of antiquity and Christian morality, they created images both appealing to a larger public in their human drama and edifying in their intended effect. Dramatic reenactment could, through the power of declamation, gesture, and set machinery, put into living motion the kind of exalted religious images prized in painting and sculpture. (adapted from Larry F. Norman, "The Theatrical Baroque," in The Theatrical Baroque (Chicago: The David and Alfred Smart Museum/University of Chicago, 2001 www.fathom.com/course/10701023/session1.html)

> Jesuit theater began as simple dialogues but soon evolved into elaborate and complex spectacles involving music and dance. Both tragedies and comedies following classical models were produced. The average Jesuit college presented two principal public plays a year. Important church festivals such as Corpus Christi, Christmas, Epiphany, Passiontide and Easter, the patronal feast day of the college or town . . .   Among the purposes of Jesuit school dramas were oratorical and moral instruction – important elements in the training of young men whom the Jesuits intended for leadership roles. (LR)

> Drama, music, and dance were usually performed by traveling companies, but all three were also an integral part of religious liturgy. The mixture of theater and religion reached its zenith with the founding of the Jesuits' houses in Seville. Many Jesuits used theater and drama to teach virtue and dramatize the life of Jesus and the saints. Students who were taught in the Jesuits' schools became stars in the acting companies in sixteenth and early seventeenth-century Spain. The festivals of Corpus Christi were famous for combining theater and religion. Singers, dancers, and actors accompanied the floats in the Corpus processions and performed periodically in the streets, as well as in the Cathedral. One dance, the Seises, is still performed before the high altar of the Cathedral in Seville on the feasts of Corpus Christi and the Immaculate Conception. ((STUDIES IN SALESIAN

SPIRITUALITY   Elisabeth Stopp (of St. Francis de Sales at Clermont College?) orig. pub. in *Salesian Studies* 6/1 (1969) http://www4.desales.edu/SCFC/Studies/ES-Clermont.html)

Great emphasis, too, was placed on good, clear speaking, and this was further fostered by the famous and novel Jesuit practice of producing school plays in Greek and Latin on sacred or classical subjects. The idea came not from Italy but from Portugal . . . (Ibid)

In Iberia, the *comedias* were generally acted out in the courts of houses, and the first permanent theatre in Madrid was not erected until 1579 (M:HIC). The difference in location – the Japanese had halls for drama, comic story-telling, etc. – partly explains the different hours, but a different attitude toward the night (14-13) may be equally important.

The Japanese equivalent of the *auto* is almost certainly *Noh* which was at the peak of its popularity when Frois wrote. *Noh* was defined as an *auto* in the Japanese-Portuguese Dictionary (NIPO in J/F(O):T). It had at least two acts, but could have three times that many because one act seldom went more than an hour without a comic interlude, and could go on for a whole afternoon or evening, i.e. 5 or 6 hours. As a high art, *Noh* captured the interest of the rulers at the same time the Way of Tea did. A couple hundred years later, it was still performed, in the words of Okakura, on a stage "of hard, unpainted wood, with a single pine tree somewhat conventionally portrayed on the background" thus, suggesting "a grand monotony" to heighten the "infinite suggestiveness" of this "short epic drama" (O:IOE), which, Eliza Scidmore noted, might be "a trilogy, occupying four or five hours of three successive days." (S:JDJ) Still, Noh was so high an art it was probably above the interest of many Japanese. Luckily, there was more drama out there. There was a vernacularized *sarugaku* with short skits of mimicry and wordplay with broader appeal. I do not know if there was yet anything as powerful as the *kabuki* Alcock brings to life by conveying a Dutch resident's testimony about a young woman, who, like the proverbial soap opera addict of the late twentieth century, came to work still sobbing for the fate of a poor lover stabbed by a jealous husband:

'Why you little fool, it is all sham; he has not been killed at all, the fine gallant, and is most likely very busy eating his rice.' 'Oh, no, he *is* killed indeed, I *saw* the sword go into his body as he fell.' (A:COT)

1. *Auto.* From the Latin *actu-s,* or "act." Since OED does not define them properly as single act, it is safe to say the word was not used in English except in the sense of an *auto da fé,* meaning an Inquisition trial and, most particularly the death sentence and execution. Byron has a line about "the faith's red *auto* fed with human blood." That pretty much soured me on using the word. (Still, *that* auto did far less harm to the world than our 4-wheeled gas-guzzlers are). I must admit to being curious about just how long that single act could be. Was the 62,000 verse mystery "Acts of the Apostles", played in its entirety at Bourges, in a performance lasting forty days, an auto?

2. *How about England?* Shakespeare was 21 in 1585. Could anyone find, read and gloss the following for me? Peter Milward: »The papist and his poet« - "The Jesuit background to S.'s plays," in: *The Renaissance Bulletin,* Tokyo 20 (1993). Peter Milward of Sophia U. in Tokyo is always interesting. *Of course, within fifty or so years, the Puritans would kill drama in England, but . . .*

13-2   Among us, one actor with a mask makes a very slow appearance.
Antre nós sai hum reprezentador com mascara muito devagar;

In Japan, two or three with bare faces appear very quickly and place themselves before each other in the posture of fighting cocks. *Em Japão saem dous ou tres com o rosto descuberto muito depresa e poem-se huns defronte dos outros na postura em que estão galos pera pelejar.*

Matsuda and Jorissen write that Frois was mistaken about Europe (for a number of actors generally took the stage at once) unless he means someone who first took the stage to explain the play or to narrate a prologue. The French translation supplements (?) Frois by having "our" actors make their entrance "one by one" (*un à un*) and Okada guesses Frois refers to the Kyogen (translated as *farza* = farce by the NIPO dictionary) intermezzo, for Noh is generally masked. Frois's contrast would seem to be of how things began in drama. It just so happens that Kyogen served not only as an *intermezzo* but a sort of *antipasto*. In the 19ᵗʰ century, Ms. Skidmore describes a pre-Noh Kyogen entrance as follows:

> The actors enter at a gait that out-struts the most exaggerated stage stride ever seen, the body held rigid as a statue, and the foot, never wholly lifted, sliding slowly along the polished floor. (S:JDJ)

How a super strut can also be a slow slide is beyond me. This would seem to be the origin of MJ's "moon-walk." Old Japan abounded in stylized movement and its strange walking was by no means limited to the stage. Perhaps this is what Frois saw as game cocks sizing each other up.

~~~~~~

13-3   Our plays are in verse. *Os nossos autos são em trovas;*

Theirs are all in prose. *Os seus todos em proza.*

In Spain, lyrical poetry and drama went hand in hand. Latin countries in general found rhyming easy for having less phonemes to match and used a wide range of versification in their drama, including Byron's beloved *ottava rima*. The stupendous wealth of sound in English allows rhyme, but only with considerable effort, which meant plays in English had to use couplets – a rhyme scheme requiring minimal rhymes – or unrhymed blank verse, enlivened by the occasional rhymed sonnet. Couplets may have been "heroic" for a long poem, but they sound too *obvious* for spoken drama. So, the strictly metrical unrhymed stuff won out:

> But holla: here, I see a wondrous sight,
> I see a swarme, of Saints within my glasse.

The *Princeton Encyclopedia of Poetry and Poetics* says the development of blank verse culminates with Gascoigne's *The Steele Glas* (1576), from which they cite the above lines. Two years after TRATADO, Marlowe's *Tamburlaigne* would inaugurate the great Elizabethan drama. But Frois's *trovas* means "song" as well as "verse," and to me this means *rhyme* – in which case blank verse would not count. So, "we" English-speakers may be on the Japanese side of the contrast here, for Japanese, despite an equally happy *poverty of sound* (10-1), lacks the proper syntax for end-rhyme (10-26). It would seem that without rhyme, drama that is solid poetry, in the vulgar sense of the word, is impossible. Still, there is no way most Japanese drama can be defined as prose, if prose means normal speech. It is as far from that as our opera is from speech. The soon-to-come Kabuki dialogue (style-wise, hardly pulled from a hat) is largely 7 and 5-syllabet, as is most Japanese song and poetry, and the lines of Noh are *yôkyoku*, by definition a type of song.   *But must the* poetry *vs.* prose *battle be confined to words?* I am sure the following contrast could date back to 1585:

> *We move about on the stage in a more or less normal fashion.*
> *They move about in odd ways only found on the stage.*

That is to say, if we look at the *walk* instead of the *talk*, the contrast clearly reverses and it is *we* who are prosaic and *they* poetic. As Menpe put it, *"You would never see a man walk in the street as he would on the stage. And, then, the tone of voice, bearing, and attitude – everything about the man is changed."* (M:JRC) Menpes quotes, Danjiro, the greatest *kabuki* actor of his day to the effect that the poses of Western actors "suggested to me badly modeled statues."

13-4   Ours often vary and others are created from scratch;
Os nossos se varião muitas vezes e outros se fazem de novo;

Theirs are entirely determined from the start, with no [room for] variation.
Os seus são já ab initio detriminados em tudo sem se variar.

This is the drama version of 1-3 (changing fashions in Europe and lack of change in Japan). 16th century Portuguese poetry and drama had just entered a very creative phase, with new work coming out one after another. Together with the revival of classical genres, there was great attentiveness to contemporary themes, with the lyric poet (Luis de Camoas 1524-80) writing "the greatest Virgilian epic of the Iberian peninsula," (Princeton Ibid) in 10 *ottava rima* cantos, about Vasco de Gama's expedition to India! In Japan, on the other hand, *Noh's* Shakespeare, Zeami, died in 1443, a 100 years before the first Portuguese reached Japan, and Noh had become *the* drama of Japan by the time Frois arrived on the scene. Just as opera in the West soon came to stick to a score of classics, the Japanese stuck to theirs. Japanese critics usually blame the "closed" Tokugawa Era for creating a *revere-the-tradition* tradition, or should I say "copy the canon" mindset; but thanks to Frois, we can see that *in drama* it was true over a decade *before* that conservative era began.

Not that it is a bad thing to repeat. There are two very different ways to enjoy any narrative form, as something new or as something old. We in the West today tend to validate the first, "creative" way and consider it "ours." *We*, after all, live in history, *they* in endless cycles of meaningless time. So goes our catechism as moderns. We may profess surprise at people enjoying themselves by going to see the same old plays year after year. Sometimes, we are told (by the anthropologist trying to be helpful) it is the slight embellishments that hold the audience's attention. In the case of Japanese drama, the idea seems to have been to see *how this or that actor did this or that*. The point, so often missed, is that we do not *need* such apologetics. We are talking about *a performance*. We who listen to the same classical tune – no, even pop tune! – over and over again, or see the same opera dozens of times (I use the royal "we" – like Ulysses Grant, I personally have trouble sitting through an opera *even once*) should not find that so hard to understand! In the case of *Noh*, I would guess that the difficulty of catching (even for the Japanese) all of the lines, historical innuendo and puns make each performance a new, richer experience for the viewer.

Still, that single play by the Japanese princess and her friends that Pinto treated us to is enough to suggest that the Japanese could be *impromptu* and there may well have been some creative drama around the fringes missed by Frois.

13-5   Ours, being plays, not tragedies, are not divided in acts.
Os nossos, sendo autos e não tragedias, não se dividem em senas;

Theirs are always seen divided into [acts], the first, second, third, etc.
Os seus vem sempre repartidos em primeiro, 2°, 3° etc.

Again, Frois refers to the *auto*, making a contrast that, in Europe was soon to become moot. Frois's "etc." comes too early for the reader to grasp what he is driving at. Chamberlain writes that "Japanese plays (*kabuki*) are apt to run to extreme length, – five, seven, twelve, even as many as sixteen acts." Alcock mentions parties of Japanese spending "a whole day seeing either a succession of plays, or one interminable piece of ancient history, and wars and battles innumerable." And, Morse describes a play that "began at half-past six in the morning and continued in a series of acts until nine o'clock at night." Others, he wrote, took *several days* to finish and "I was told that some plays in China require a month or two for a complete performance." (M:JDD) These quotes may concern different types of drama and be hundreds of years out of date, but they all suggest a different attitude toward drama than "ours." There may, also be a method to this madness all the above visitors failed to catch. It may be that the plays in Japan were that long *because* they were broken up in a manner not to be found in the West until the age of television! Here are the 18th century Dutch findings (or, Siebold, perhaps?) as presented by Mrs. Busk.

> Three different pieces are frequently represented on the same day; not the entire pieces successively, but interchangeably in parts; first the first act of one, then the same of a second, and after this of a third; then the second act of the first play, and successively . . . preceding in this way till all the three are completed. Thus any of the audience who wish only to see one of these pieces . . . may withdraw while the pieces they do not care to see take their turn of representation, and come back refreshed to witness the next act of their favorite drama. (B:MCJ)

Perhaps the comic interlude found between acts in a Noh play which was itself a mini-act gave rise to the idea of presenting plays in this way. The Japanese intermezzo, then, would conversely be a thread of common difference weaving together this potpourri of plays. I, who have occasionally wished PBS would give me a break from a movie (perhaps a 5 or 10 minute silent film once an hour) can well understand the value of this way of doing things. There may also be a fashion factor here.

> The Japanese ladies, however, did not appear to object to the length of time required for these representations, but rather to consider it as affording a most favorable opportunity for displaying the stores of their wardrobes. They are attended on these occasions by their female servants with an ample supply of dresses, and repeatedly change their attire in the course of the afternoon and evening. (HB:MCJ)

Menpe mentioned geisha at the end of the 19th century changing the color of their lipstick thrice in as many hours. Today, Japanese women still show a strong proclivity to redressing. Wedding receptions average 3 dress changes and some have as many as 5 (only by the bride, though). All of this in itself, would seem to reflect an attitude that *life is a play.*   So, we can imagine the women using the acts of the plays they were *not* watching to re-costume themselves the better to fit the time of day or act of the play or whatever they addressed.

13-6   Our characters come out from inside a separate house where they can't be seen;
As nossas figuras saem de dentro de outra caza donde se não vem;

> The Japanese are near the stage, behind curtains of *fune* boat/s.[1]
> *Os Japões estão perto[?] do teatro metidos em cortinas de* fune.

..

The *playhouse* as we know it was not yet perfected in Europe. The stage was outside and the dressing room in a separate "house," or, in good weather, a patio. Japanese, with their broad, wide open architecture did have playhouses with various devices (most post-dating Frois) to keep performers hidden while waiting for their call. Frois's "curtains of boat/s" (*cortinas de fune*) have everyone stymied. Okada guesses he means an *age-maku,* an entrance curtain that raises up in a manner suggestive of the sail of a boat (that could be hoisted up to the upper boom, there being no lower boom with Japanese boats). From the illustrations of dressing rooms I have seen, *my guess* is that Frois means that the rectangular tent-like tops, with open sides, resembles the protected space for parties on the pleasure-craft that plied the rivers of Japan. Be that as it may, 17th century *kabuki* popularized another way of taking the stage in Japan, where the actors' dressing room is directly behind the stage, yet the entrance behind the gallery so the actors could walk up a "flower-road" *through the audience,* or *pit* on their way to the stage. The *reason* for this is given by the Dutch according to Mrs. Busk. Namely, that the audience be the more familiarly acquainted with the costume and appearance of each particular character. If this kind of knowledge be so much more difficult to be impressed upon a Japanese audience than upon any other, it is probably owing to the frequent breaking of association of the actor with his part, which association is elsewhere [in the world] maintained without interruption throughout the play. (B:MCJ)

Elsewhere, she wrote that "what is esteemed the acmé of histrionic skill is one actor's being able to perform several different characters in the same piece." *Yet another contrast!* This may still be found today. Or, at least, it seems so to me, for I was once paid to watch and write a review of a play based on a Russian novel, starring a famous kabuki actor who played the lead male and lead female part. [1]   Menpe gave yet another reason for the Japanese manner of taking stage, an aesthete's appreciation, which has nothing to do with the reason given above.

if the scene is set by the seashore, he [the Japanese playwright] will cause the sea, which is represented by that decorative design called a wave-pattern, to be swept round the theatre embracing both audience and stage and dragging you into the very heart of his picture. For this same reason, a Japanese theatre is always built with two broad passages, called *Hanamichi* (or flowerpaths) leading through the audience to the stage ... But we in our Western theaters need not trouble ourselves with all this, for we frame our scenes in a vulgar gilt frame; we hem them in and cut them off from the rest of the house. (M:JRC pre-1901)

I have no idea if this has any relation to the difference noted by Frois, but it gives us another contrast that might be expressed as *bounded* vs *unbounded* stages or *inclusion* vs *seclusion* of the actors.

1. Translation Schütte indicates that "*perto*"*do teatre* seems to say "near the theatre." But it would have to be "*within* the theater," or "near the *stage*" for the contrast to work right. I would guess that theater was more or less synonymous with "stage" here and, right or wrong, took the liberty of translating it that way.

2. Changing Roles. The actor was Tamasaburo, and he was a fine woman, but not attractive in my opinion, for his woman seemed like *a model* (which made the Japanese say "she" was *very pretty*.) while I prefer a softer, warmer variety. It helped me define what a *model* really is: *a woman easy for a male impersonator!*

13-7   Our plays are performed in the spoken tongue;
        Os nossos autos se reprezentão em practica;

        Theirs, almost always singing – or dancing.
        Os seus quasi sempre cantando – ou bailhando.

While the first recognized performance of the genre of drama that was to mark the Tokugawa era, *ka-bu-ki,* or "sing-dance-technique," did not take place until 1594, *song and dance* was long part of all traditions of Japanese drama. In fact, Okakura, in his IDEALS OF THE EAST, calls his chapter on Noh "The No-dance." Noh has more "telling" than dialogue (Frois's *practica* in plain English means "talk" and most talk is dialogue, though some may be soliliquy[1]). To the Japanese way of thinkng, Frois contradicts his assertion in 13-3 that Japanese plays are in prose, for what is sung in Japanese *is* song and song is poetry, in the Japanese style, with 5 and 7 syllabet clusters. Since the Japanese did not follow life as "we" did, poetry or not, our realistic "spoken" dramas impressed them as much as our perspective drawing. Miguel=Valignano pointed that out in *De Missione*:

Reciting their lines in male or female roles, people use many different voices depending on the topic, sometimes delighted, sometimes crying, sometimes pained, sometimes forsaken; that is to say, they can change their voices to reflect any mood. It was so skillful as to be beyond technique and I think must have come from a natural born talent. Indeed, they don't raise their voices tensely like they are singing as is ordinarily done in our country. (J/S:DM)

A few hundred years later, Ms Skidmore gave a representative Western reaction to the tense voice of Japanese drama alluded to by Miguel in the last line:

> "Their tones are unspeakably distressing, nasal [but very loud, for, like "our" opera singers, they are trained to use their diaphragms!], high-pitched, falsetto sounds, and many performers have ruined and lost their voices, and even burst blood-vessels, in the long-continued, unnatural strain of their recitatives. (S:JDJ)

Luckily, for these "tellers" – we are back to Okakura again – Noh is "full of semi-articulate sounds," such as "the soughing of the wind amongst the pine boughs, the dropping of water, or the tolling of distant bells, the stifling of sobs, the clash and clang of war, echoes of the weavers beating the new web against the wooden beam, the cry of crickets, and all the manifold voices of night and nature, where pause is more significant than pitch." While this sound/pause was going on, the actors or reciters could rest their voices and allow dance to tell, or rather, suggest the story. Here, I cannot help giving a contrast, corollary to the matter of the conversational vs. tense and/or singing voices:

> *Our actors use or exaggerate their natural pitch to express emotion;*
> *Their actors express all moods the same way and only change their intensity.*

While the tail-end of the verb in Japanese allows for marvelous tonal expression of emotion – so much so it taught me how to talk with cats (see HAN-CHAN'S DREAM when it is published!) – the Japanese sentence *as a whole* is as flat as Florida. Singing out the whole sentence in slow motion a word at a time, the usual clarity of the tail-end – and with it the individual emotional significance – is completely lost. In other words, the whole thing is so high-pitched and emotional, that only visual elements or the expressed meanings of the words tell you what the particular emotion is! At least, that is *my* impression of Noh and Kabuki. If the style of recitation were not enough of a drawback, the Japanese may of had a mental hang-up about acting. Mrs. Busk:

> the contempt felt by the Japanese towards this particular class originates in the idea that a man who will renounce his own character and assume one foreign to his nature for the amusement of others can have no sense of honour; and, as a natural consequence of being despised, the Japanese actors are said to be infamously immoral and licentious. (B: MCJ)

This prejudice would certainly make it hard for an actor to do his best! But I doubt if it really explains the contempt with which *kabuki* actors – not *all* actors! (*noh* actors have always been respected if not revered) – were held. That had more to do with the actors' *vita sexualis* which threatened straights (if I may use 20c Usanian slang to describe Confucianism) in two ways, first by the proclivity of the "female" role players for "male-color" and second, because of their tremendous popularity among women, who bought fans with their favorite actors and certainly did not count them by a number-noun used for counting animals (*hiki*) as some men evidently did! So said, if Japanese theater did not have "our" realism, the presence in Japanese of more clearly different speech for different sexes and ages and positions in life made simple caricature so easy that even if the natural acting alluded to by Miguel=Valignano might not have arisen in Japan, the words by themselves would very clearly express the identity of the character (to a Japanese, but not to a foreigner) and someone with a good memory for patterns of speech could evoke many characters without renouncing his or her own by sounding like them (Think of black and white TV: wasn't it sufficient when it was all we had?).

While I can see no difference in Japanese perspective drawings and Occidental ones today, I can still *hear* a difference in the (Western-style) drama. For whatever reason, the laughs in Japan rarely rise above the level of laughs heard in an elementary school play!

13-8   For us, it would be disturbing and an insult for one to make noise[1] during the performance of a play.   *Antre nós seria perturbasão e injuria estar hum bonzeando emquanto se faz o auto.*

In Japan, it praises and decorates the actor for there to be onlookers making great hisses/hoots/shouts. [2]   *Em Japão hé decoro e ornamento do que se reprezenta estarem alguns de fora dando humas grandes apupadas.*

"In *noraku* (the proper name for *noh*), the audience apparently used to praise the actors by raising their voices" writes Okada, for *kabuki* proper, which is known for audiences shouting out their encouragement and appreciation for the actors, had not yet evolved.

Since there are relatively few words and these are so slowly drawn out that a shout could cut clean through crosswise and hardly even nick a syllable, Noh certainly could use frequent audience participation without damage.   In Japanese folk (festival and farm) singing, a sporadic musical accompaniment or a shrill chorus of voices, usually female – is often used to spice up the melody. Often, especially in festivals, the sound is very sassy, for an element of taunt may be involved, but even then they are much appreciated and work wonderfully to increase the total energy level of the performance, much in the same way call-backs improve the total sound effect of a Southern black Baptist congregation in America.   There is even a word for it in Japanese, *hayashi.*   Until reading Frois, I assumed a Latin drama performance would be full of such *hayashi,* for flamenco is the best example of a performance which demands the same, and many Latins have a wonderful tremolo whistle to cut in with at musically appropriate times, but, not having gone to *kabuki* performances, I was surprised.[3]   Perhaps, Frois put this sort of spice and the *bonzeando* into different categories for "us" while fusing them for "them."   Or, was he surprised to find it in what was taken for a high art?   Or, did the Japanese voices indicating praise or simply excitement sound like what "we" would do to show our disgust?   The fact Usanians whistle with approval whereas most Latins do so where "we" would *boo,* shows how tricky such cross-cultural comparison is.   Had Frois been an Englishman of the 17th or 18th century, he might have written, instead:

> *We express ourselves in the galleries using an instrument called a cat-call which we buy.*
> *They show their enthusiasm during performances entirely through their own devices.*

The OED defines the *cat-call* as "a squeaking instrument or kind of whistle used esp. in play-houses to express impatience or disapprobation."   The oldest example in it is from Pepys who mentions buying one from such and such a store for 2 groats in 1669-70.   If they were sold commercially, they obviously went further back, probably to Frois's century.   An example of its use would be: "I heard a tailor sitting by my side play on his cat-call and cry out, 'Sad stuff!'" (Fielding 1732). On the whole, the intent was bad – supporting Frois's contrast where "we" identified noise during performances with criticism – but reading Addison's essay *The Cat-Call,*[4] one gets the feeling that the gallery had so much fun with it that the *cat-call* may well have been used in good humor at the appropriate turns of the play.   So, the English, at one time, may have ever so slightly approached the Japanese in their attitude toward theater.

1. *Make Noise.* It was tempting to follow the French translation *agité!*

2. *Hiss/hoot/shout?* I could have added "whistle" too. English has cheers, jeers, boos, hoots, hisses and cat-calls, but no generic term for the *apupadas.*

3. *Kabuki.* I have seen some on TV and it was enough. To me, kabuki is as bad as opera. I dislike both.

4. Addison: *The Cat-call.* This is so felicitous a piece of writing, I hesitate to rip-out chunks, but thinking that doing so may encourage the reader to delve into the neglected world of nonfiction English when it was still a fanciful art full of invention that did not limit its creativity to the mere arrangement of and commentary on "facts" or "one's feelings," I shall.   The lead is a Letter from one John Shallow, Esq. who went to a play in London. Part of it: "Upon the rising of the curtain I was very much surprised with the great consort of cat-calls . . . and had begun to think with myself that I had made a mistake, and gone to a music-meeting instead of the play-house. It appeared, indeed, a bit odd to me, to see so many persons of quality of both sexes assembled together at a kind of caterwauling . . ." Then, he asks Mr. Spectator [Addison's popular magazine = the editor], "to give some account of this strange instrument, which I found the company called a cat-call; and particularly to let me know if it be a piece of music lately come from Italy." So the editor does his research: "A Fellow of the Royal Society, who is my good friend . . . observes very well, that musical instruments took their first rise from the notes of birds and other melodious animals; and what, says he, was more natural than for the first ages of mankind to imitate the voice of a cat that lived under the same roof with them? He added, that the cat had contributed more to harmony than any other animal; as we are not only beholden to her for this wind-instrument, but for our string music in general. . . . . There are others who ascribe this invention to Orpheus, and look upon the cat-call to be one of those instruments the famous musician made to draw the beasts about him. It is certain, that the roasting of a cat does not call together a greater audience of that species, than this instrument, if dexterously played upon in proper time and place. . . But, notwithstanding these various and learned conjectures, I cannot forbear thinking that the cat-call is originally a piece of English music. Its resemblance to the voice of some of our British songsters, as well as the use of it, which is peculiar to our nation, confirms me in this opinion. . . . . Having said thus much concerning the original of the cat-call, we are in the next place to consider the use of it. The cat-call exerts itself to most advantage in the British theatre: it very much improves

the sound of nonsense, and often goes along with the voice of the actor who pronounces it, as the violin or harpsichord accompanies the Italian *recitativo*. . . It has often supplied the place of the ancient chorus . . . In short, a bad poet has as great an antipathy to a cat-call, as many people have to a real cat. . . Mr Collier, in his ingenious essay upon music, has the following passage: "I believe it is possible to invent an instrument that shall have a quite contrary effect to those martial ones now in use: an instrument that shall sink the spirits, and shake the nerves, and curdle the blood, and inspire despair, and cowardice, and consternation, at a surprising rate. It is probable that the roaring of a lion, the warbling of cats and screech-owls, together with a mixture of the howling of dogs, judiciously imitated and compounded, might go a great way in this invention. Whether such anti-music as this might be of service in a camp, I shall leave to the military men to consider." . . . What this learned gentleman supposes in speculation, I have known actually verified in practice. The cat-call has struck a damp into generals and frighted heroes off the stage. . . . . I must conclude this paper with an account I have lately received of an ingenious artist . . . He has his base and his treble cat-call; the former for tragedy, the latter for comedy; only in tragi-comedies they may both play together in consort. He has a peculiar squeak to denote the violation of each of the unities, and has different sounds to show whether he aims at the poet or the player. In short he teaches the smut-note, the fustian-note, the stupid-note, and has composed a kind of act-tune to an incorrigible play, and which takes in the whole compass of the cat-call." [Needless to say, some notes are needed to understand things like "the unities" or "fustian-note." Maybe next time!]

13-9   Our masks cover the chin all the way down to below the beard;
     Antre nós as mascaras cobrem o qeixo da barba todo por baxo;

> Those of Japan are so small that even when playing a woman, the beard can always be seen below. *As de Japão são tão peqenas que o que emtra por figura de molher, ficão-lhe sempre parecendo por baxo as barbas.*

Noh masks are tiny. They are not intended to actually disguise the actor, but just to give the audience enough to go on. If Japanese painters could not yet paint good perspective even if they wanted to, that could not be said about three dimensional objects. Japanese could be *very* realistic when they wished to be; there were statues showing each pore of the skin, with carefully implanted real hair. The *noh* mask is representative, then, of an *aesthetic choice* to be impressionistic or symbolic rather than realistic as in Europe, where, according to Miguel=Valignano the backdrops and other props were so *real* that even actual events might be expressed *just as they were*. To do this, to put on these gala productions, he wrote, they spend lots and lots of money. "Why, an estimate of 4,000 or 5,000 gold [cruzados?] would not be rare." (J/S:DM)

But remove the mask and *noh* is stranger yet: "these buckram figures, moving with the solemnity of condemned men, utter their lines like automata, not a muscle nor an eyelash moving, nor a flicker of expression crossing the unmasked countenance" writes Skidmore (S:JDJ), who might have been surprised to know that 50 years later a Japanese novelist would write that *Western* chorus and opera singers looked like *singing-machine* with their mouths opening wide and moving straight up and down like that. The funny thing is that Tanizaki Junichiro (*Inei Raisan*) is as right as Skidmore. Formal Western singing *is* very weird looking. The mouth movement resembles string operated puppets, and with them doing it in perfect unison, it looks even scarier. Only the folk tradition, *in both cultures,* lets us see humans singing naturally. But, speaking of puppets, Frois missed a big one:

> With us, the puppeteer or puppeteers must always remain out of sight.
> The Japanese puppeteers often remain in plain view on the stage.

Like the beard below the mask, we are not supposed to see the puppeteer. This is not so difficult as it might sound, for the puppeteers dressed completely in black. The same pure black clothing, including a black hood was adopted in kabuki by helpers called *kurogo* (blacklings?), who held light up to the protagonist's face or moved props around before the eyes of the audience.

13-10 Our comedies and tragedies are accompanied by soft-sounding musical instruments;
Nas nossas [c]omedias ou tragedias se introduzem suaves instrumentos de muzica;

In Japan, by goblet-shaped drums, a drum with two sticks and fife of bamboo.
Em Japão huns atabalinhos da feisão de calix e hum atabale com dous paos e hum pifaro de cana.

The Japanese instruments are no mere background noise, but function more like the sound-track of a modern thriller movie: they could get very intense and dominate tense moments.

The first type of drum is called a *tsutsumi* (wrap [drum]?) and looks like a long hourglass, or two champagne glasses cut through mid-stem and welded stem to stem. The membranes are laced with chords that cross from membrane to membrane so they may be squeezed – thanks to the narrow waist very tightly. In other words, it is a *talking-drum.* Japanese, not having a tonal language, cannot use it to talk with. So why do they have this rare type of instrument, that Europe never made? Because, the condensed emotion expressed at the tail of a Japanese sentence (or more persistently, at the end of a Korean sentence) makes obvious what Europeans only theorize about: the unarguable emotional significance of *rising* and *falling* tone. The *tsutsumi*, like a bongo, is played by hand.

The second type of drum is just a drum (*taiko,* but called *ôkawa* (big-skin) in Noh). Hit on the head it is capable of a thunder-clap. However, those sticks Frois mentions spend much time mincing out rhythm on the side of the drum, too. Both drums are particularly good at speeding up or slowing down time. Since the *taiko* drums have toured around the world, I assume readers are familiar with the way Japanese do that by telescoping or untelescoping a simple beat.[1]

The fife of bamboo. While the *NIPO Dictionary* simply translated the *fue* (Japanese flute) as a *flauta* (flute), Frois was right to use the word philologically related to "pipe" that Englishes as *fife,* a flute played by blowing over a hole from the side. The distinction is vital. The naturally shrill quality of the instrument, which makes it a favorite for military bands in the West, achieves a new level in the sound-world of the Japanese. A Japanese fifer doesn't blow, he *blasts.* This blasting has two characteristics not often found in Western music. First, it is not only worked up to, in the Western manner where sound crescendos, but often *begins* in its full fury. That is to say, it is explosive. It *hits* as strong gusts of wind often do. And, second, the fifer does not stop when the sound threatens to break, but enjoys blasting it up and over its limits. This critical break is played upon like a surfer rides a wave, and the thrill to the initiated – or, those with an ear for it – is pretty much the same.[2]

By "tragedies" and "comedies," Frois appears to admit forms of drama not mentioned elsewhere (5, above). But he may mean only that whether the subject matter of the *autos* is comical or serious, "our" music is not supposed to be intrusive.

1. Drum Beats Japanese drumming seems to me to be similar to that of the Amerindian taken to a higher level (but, it is possible the Amerindians had much that was lost in the disastrous encounter with the "Old World.") To me, the complex rhythms of the India Indian tradition are opposite to the limited Japanese repertoire, and the European drumming tradition is in-between. Glosses are welcome!

2. Explosive Flute/Fife Music. This power is felt at outdoor *omatsuri* (such as the bon dances) where I first realized how *macho* such music could be. The Cuban flute, as represented by Tito Fuentes, proves that the Occident (if Cuba is the Occident) can also create great things from a tiny hole. *To think that a flute could house a hurricane! (The guitar could not do it until it got juiced.)*

13-11   In our dances, they move to the sound of the tambourine, but do not sing;
Nas nossas danças fazem mudanças ao som do tamburil, mas não cantão;

With Japanese dances, they always have to sing to the sound of the drums.
Nas dos Japãos se há sempre de cantar ao som do atabaqe.

I am not sure exactly what Frois means by "our dances." In the NIPO dictionary, the Japanese dance called *mai*, generally performed by professionals who dance+sing legends, is translated as *baile*, whereas the dance called *odori* is translated as *dançar*. Here, we have the latter, so I imagine the *bon-odori*, or "bon-dance." Today, the singing for the bon dance is either recorded or the done by a few people using microphones. *I do not yet know if people sang as they danced.* All I know is that there is always a singing voice prominent in the music that is danced. One does not dance to voiceless music.

13-12   Ours carry bells and proceed straight ahead;
Os nossos trazem cascaveis e andão dereitos;

Those of Japan have fans in their hands, and always proceed like [?] people who have lost or go looking for something that is lost on the ground. *Os de Japão abanos nas mãos e andão sempre como [?] ou como pessaos que olhando pera o chão andão buscando o que perderão.*

Our "bells" would probably be *jingles* if we only had such a word. The straight ahead would seem to indicate dancing as part of a procession rather than a social dance. With a Japanese *bon odori*, the dancers circle a stationary band. Frois seems to be taking a close look at the slow forward progress which does include alternate right and left movement where the body is often bent (sometimes one is reminded of judo) slightly forward – in other words, Japanese do indeed look like Frois says they do. The fan is good to have for cooling off between dances and playing with. Doing the *tanko-bushi*, a coal-mining *bon dance* number, I enjoy turning my fan into a shovel.

..

13-13   Our dances are performed during the day; *As nossas danças se fazem de dia;*

Theirs almost always at night. *E as suas quasi sempre de noyte.*

Almost the opposite of 13-1, for "we" went to plays at night.

Matsuda and Jorissen take issue with this contrast, citing numerous instances of night dancing in Europe going back to 1451 (almost a hundred and fifty years earlier) in Lisbon and point out that dance was the rage in Portugal, with the 15th and 16th century called "the era that danced the night away," largely as a result of their profits from overseas. Frois may, however, be talking not about such social dances, but *performances* of dance commensurable to the Japanese *mai*. In that case, Frois can be faulted for completely neglecting *participatory dance* in the respective cultures. *Faux Frois*:

We go to dances in any season of the year.
The Japanese only dance in the hottest part of the summer or early fall.

The dance is part of the Festival of the Dead. The *bon* lanterns to light the way for the souls, the heat and the nature of drum-centered music – I don't know why, but drumbeats die in the day-light – make the night the only time for dancing.

Among us, we have dances for men and women to dance with each other as couples.
In Japan, there are no dances for couples and the very idea seems absurd.

Among us it is considered perfectly proper for men and women to touch when dancing.
Among the Japanese, for men and women to touch when dancing would be degrading.

When Miguel=Valignano mentions the existence of dances for boys and girls to do alone *or together* and dances for men and women *to do together* in Dialogue 11 of *De Missione*, Leo immediately remonstrated that the mixed dancing *certainly reduces Europe's prestige in his estimation*, to which Miguel replied that if the cheerful and open spirit of the dance were not enough, a mature character and properly serious demeanor on the part of the dancers made such a worry (Public sexuality? Seduction? Jealousy? Or, just men mixing with women?) completely beside the point. Moreover, he adds, you have to know how strongly women are honored and protected in Europe, to appreciate why this (apparently scandalous and demeaning activity) is safe. And, he goes on to explain how the slightest suspicion about a woman's being compromised can lead to a bloodbath – after which he hastily adds, *but, with judicial permission, of course* (lawless Japan *vs.* lawful Europe being the catechism). Surprisingly little had changed when ambassadors for the first Japanese mission West since the *Missione* attended a dance at U.S.A. Secretary (of War?) Cass's house in the 19th century:

> Upon enquiring, we were told that this was a "dance." As we watched the various movements of the dancers, I could not help smiling at the way the very large skirts, called crinolines, which the ladies wore, increased in volume until they became of enormous proportions when the dancers attained their top speed. . . . This continues until midnight. . . . our wonder at the strange performance became so great that we began to doubt whether we were not on another planet. . . . It seems very funny indeed to us, as dancing in our country is done by professional girls only and is not at all a man's pastime. (A:FJE)

Chamberlain gives us a far less diplomatic description of "our" dancing reflected in the eyes of the Japanese:

> Its want of dignity, together with certain disagreeable rumors to which the unwonted meeting of the two sexes has given rise from time to time, have caused the innovation to be looked at askance by many who are otherwise favorable to European manners and customs. A plain-spoken writer in an excellent illustrated periodical entitled *Fuzoku Gwaho* [customs report], says that, whereas his imagination had painted a civilized ball-room as a vision of fairy-land, its reality reminded him of nothing so much as lampreys wriggling up to the surface of the water, and (*passez-lui le mot*) fleas hopping out of a bed." ("Dances" in C:TJ)

Yet, today, the Japanese are a ballroom dancing powerhouse. So there is nothing intrinsically incompatible to Japanese in it. Indeed, the eventual success of "our" dancing in Japan was foretold by the young Japanese Ambassadors in *De Missione*. Mancio reports having to overcome his "inborn shyness toward women" and fear of dancing "like a rustic" in order to join in. Miguel also took the plunge early. Marchino describes one of the sweetest moments in Japanese-Western history:

> Mancio and Miguel broke the ice by giving it a great effort, so it *would have been* a bit less embarrassing for we who followed, had Julian, who was last, not chosen a woman for his partner who just happened to be looking his way; because she turned out to be an old lady, and all of the onlookers burst out laughing. (Dialogue 20 J/S:DM)

To this Julian replies

Had I done so on purpose, it couldn't have been better! My embarrassment was partially cancelled out by that poor old lady's, for it probably looked like I planned it that way to draw the laughter of the onlooker's away from me, with my lack of practice [*note:* Julian was sick for much of his time in Europe] to the old lady who didn't fit the scene. [1]

This is one of those episodes you *know* wasn't invented by Valignano. We can imagine how much he must have enjoyed receiving their letters about that dance and dialoging the content!

Morse, in 1877, theorizes about a supposed effect of social dance or, conversely, its absence:

The absence of rhythm in their walk is noteworthy, as with our people even school children keep step in walking. One realizes at once that the Japanese never dance together as we do. The waltz, the polka, and other old-fashioned dances requiring absolute rhythm in their movements, and the school drill of marching out of school to the music of a piano, all contribute to the marching habit. (M:JDD)

It is refreshing to have individualistic Japanese contrasted with collectivist Westerners. But, actually, in the Japanese *bon* dance, everyone not only dances to the same beat, but dances the exact same movement of the dance at the same time. So, even if Japanese did not dance as we did, couple by couple (that *does* take practice), in the above-mentioned *bon* dances they did dance altogether synchronously. I thought that the double beat of the two-stilt clogs and the tiny steps of the women were quite enough to account for the lack of a public step – some synchronization that occurs naturally when people walk together – but a Chinese who observed Americans in the first half of this century wrote that *"Westerners walk together like a formation of geese; Chinese are like scattered ducks."* (A&L:LWG p95) And Chinese did not wear *geta*. Maybe "we" were just more collected at the time!

1. *De Missione* Translation   I had trouble with the Japanese here and, assuming the Japanese translators had trouble with the Latin rhetoric, took liberties with "it ~ better." If someone has the original Latin or German translation and wishes to redo the paragraph for me, I would not mind . . .

13-14   European dancing has much movement of the feet.
Ho dançar d'Europa hé de muitos movimentos dos pés;

> That of Japan is more solemn and, for the most part done with the hands.
> *Ho de Japão hé mais grave e fá-los pola mayor parte com as mãos.*

Chamberlain, not knowing of Frois, stated the same with envious economy: *Europeans dance with their feet, – not to say their legs – Japanese mainly with their arms*. Okada, who quotes this, together with Chamberlain's next sentence – "The dress or rather undress of a European *corps de ballet* would take away the breath of the least prudish Oriental" – follows up with a *reason* for the difference: "[Our] clothing is probably the reason the legs are not normally moved a lot in Japanese dance." *Perhaps*. But, the naked Hawaiians did most of *their* dances with their hands, too. My guess is that the emphasis on arms is a Far Eastern and Pacific phenomena that has more to do with living on mats which would be destroyed by Occidental dance. Regardless, I would guess that Okada does not much care for "our" dance because his translation (unlike Frois's original) makes the leg movement *imperative*, i.e. "[you] must move [your] legs a lot." (*ashi-o ôku ugokasanakerebanaranai*)![1] The Japanese side of the contrast, however, was not at all forced: "[you] dance using [your] hands." (*te o mochiite odoru*). (J/F(O):T) But let us return to Frois's contemporaries.

After apologizing for making a bit too much of European dance, "for comparing different cultures and contrasting their customs, making one base and adoring the other is bound to bring on a reaction, and I have no intention of putting down Japan," Miguel=Valignano writes, "but if, by any chance, one [culture] were by the will of God, or by all of the races' common assent, or criticism . . ." Here, either de Sande's Latin or the Japanese translation peters out of meaning (at any rate, I can't make sense of it) ; but Miguel, continuing, soon makes sense enough: "taking dance for example, excluding a few things that might be somewhat unsuitable from the standpoint of Europeans, it shouldn't be too difficult for our country's dance to adopt the good parts of European dance and embody the true nature of dance." Leo pops in and asks: "What are those somewhat unsuitable things?" Miguel's reply:

> There are two main points. First, when someone from our country dances, he generally wears the mask of an unfortunate dead woman with wildly tangled hair, or similarly, a mask representing a soul that has left someone's body when he performs, so that instead of the cheerful thrill of dance [as in the West], it seems to produce pain and melancholy. And second, the dancing person now and then stops suddenly in mid-dance and howls, to which the audience replies with similar howls. For this reason, Japanese dance seems like a noisy and confused shrieking contest rather than something lively and interesting. If the Japanese could only get rid of those depressing masks and dance in beautiful costume to music in a scale used by Europeans, they would easily be able to achieve the European level of dance. But it is a fine thing for each country's unique customs to remain. (dialog. 11 J/S:DM)

The two points mentioned concern only a small fraction of Japanese dance. But that fraction happens to be the most active part of Japanese dance. Only the crazy, the demonically possessed whirl about and leap wildly like Europeans do in their dance. (Naturally, Japanese felt "going round and round" to quick music in the European style was "too savage to bear." *That* is precisely the part of Japanese dance that looks most like dance to Europeans. But what is amazing here is that Miguel=Valignano are dealing with a problem salient even today in Japan: the relationship of Japanese culture to a Western-biased "world culture." The same assertions followed by contradictory reassurance of cultural relativity, the same tendency to bend toward the West rather than to hold up something new and challenge the West . . . It is both delightful and depressing to find such thought over 400 years ago. But to return to Frois's contrast, it was indeed true that our dances were far more active than the Japanese ones. Yet, it was not all so sweet, so cheerful, so beautiful as depicted by the *De Missione* ambassadors. If they saw anything like the following, Valignano chose not to include it:

> One dance, the Seises, is still performed before the high altar of the Cathedral in Seville on the feasts of Corpus Christi and the Immaculate Conception. Another dance, the zarabanda, was a traditional part of the Corpus celebration that became notorious. It was so provocative, the Jesuit priest Mariana warned, that it inflamed "even very honest people." Like the escarramán, the zarabanda was a dance that represented the "abortions of Hell." Its frenzied rhythms and violent movements were more contagious than awe-inspiring, however, and spectators frequently joined in the dancing. (STUDIES IN SALESIAN SPIRITUALITY Elisabeth Stopp (of St. Francis de Sales at Clermont College?) orig. pub. in *Salesian Studies* 6/1 (1969)   http://www4. desales.edu/SCFC/Studies/ES-Clermont.html *I removed some references.*)

1. *Having to Move Legs.* I suspect that Frois's use of *hé* rather than *é* with the *de* made Okada think of *having to do something* and that he forgot to go back to correct what he wrote even when he saw the same *hé* on the Japanese side of the contrast. But, I cannot help but think cognitive dissonance is behind this minor mistranslation. It reminds me of a similar, but far worse mistranslation of a sentence in Peter Farb's *Word Play.* Farb quotes Nabokov: *"Lolita, light of my life, fire of my loins. My sin, my soul. Lo-lee-ta: the tip of the tongue taking a trip of three steps down the palate to tap, at three, on the teeth. Lo. Lee. Ta."* Then he comments "Nabokov's passage demon-strates how euphonious Lolita's name is. To pronounce it, the tongue must move in an arc through all the positions – from back to front – used to sound English vowels." The experienced but lazy Japanese translator removed the Nabokov quote altogether and paraphrased(?!) Farb as follows:

> To pronounce these letters one must make the tongue go around and around (*kurukuru mawashite*) especially to pronounce the "L" correctly over and over (*nan kai mo*). This is one of the hard things about English." (If you read Japanese, check out my book *Goyaku Tengoku* = mistranslation paradise = for more.)

13-15 Among us, music of diverse voices is sonorous and sweet;
Antre nós a muzica de diversas vozes hé sonora e suave;

> That of Japan, as all screech in just one voice, is the most horrendous that can be made.[1] *A de Japão, como todos se esganisão em huma só vox, hé a mais horrenda que se pode dar.*

Two issues – that should have been two separate contrasts – are conflated here: *harmony* and *smooth voices*. The former in its fully developed form, i.e. polyphony, is often credited to the West, and proudly ascribed to the growth of polyvalent modern culture or the analytical scientific mindset, etc.. Actually, it is traditional in Mongolia and much of continental Asia. The Far West was only a Johny-come-lately (How late is a matter for debate. Some say that even Bach – born exactly a hundred years after TRATADO – did not compose true polyphony but the "parallel running voices" of Gregorian music. I don't know enough to judge!)[2] Polyphony did not reach Japan, either, and the Japanese never discovered it for themselves (see 18, below). Then, again, I do not believe they *needed* it as much as the West did. The individual Japanese voice, human or instrumental, is *far* more complex than those of the West. It is as richly textured as a tree branch, where ours is smooth and featureless as a dowel. Morse:

> Later I learned from a [Japanese] student that our music was not music at all to them. He couldn't understand why we cut it off by jerks; to him it was "Jig, jig, jig, jig, jig, jigger, jig, jig"! (M:JDD)

For that reason, one can derive infinitely more pleasure from singing Japanese songs – acappella[3] and alone – than "ours." (*karaoke* could never have started in the West). For religious and philosophical (Platonian?) reasons, I imagine, we pursued sweetness and suavity of voice to the exclusion – save the remnants of complexity in the folk voice of the rural areas, where some ballads probably still had personality – of all nitty-gritty sound, until we ended up with polished perfection, which we escaped from by combining our "dowels" into more complex structures, i.e., polyphonic melodies and/or dressing them with melodic instrumental music. Morse is the only Westerner I know of who came to realize this – to a degree, at any rate – in the 19th century:

> We heard the most wonderful music of the flute by a Japanese court musician. . . . The enjoyment for us consisted in the delicious contrasts between note after note. The notes were long and of exquisite purity. It was a revelation to us. With harmony one gets these effects in our music, but in Japanese music there is no harmony, only melody. In the "Oratio of St. Paul," our leader, Carl Zerrahan, always became especially alert in anticipation of a delicious terminal note in one phrase in the choral "To God on High." (JDD)

> . . . then a Japanese song was sung accompanied by three kotos, three shos, and two biwas. This song was sung by the entire school. It was started by a young lady striking a long, flat, thin piece of wood with another piece of the same shape at right angles. The click was sharp and peculiar. [the sound is far sharper – that is to say shorter and more piercing yet refreshingly light – than anything our percussion instruments can do] She then uttered a long, high note without the slightest inflection, as a keynote, and the chorus began. The music was certainly very weird and very impressive, and with the peculiarly sweet accompaniment [no doubt, the *hayashi* responses I mentioned in 8, above] and curious rhythm, gave me an impression of the merit of Japanese music that I had never had before. Their music sounded distinguished as they sang it, compared with ours. (JDD)

Morse recognized that "here was a chance for some one to secure ideas in regard to the power of music in a new direction" and, about two-hundred pages later,

> As their pictorial art was incomprehensible to us at the onset, and yet at further acquaintance and study we discovered in it transcendent merit, so it seemed to me that a study of Japanese music might reveal merits we little suspected.

So, he studied a form of Japanese singing called *utai* ("singing") and concluded it was "not singing, but inflectional declamation, not unlike the conversation of the countrymen of Yorkshire." While I like Japanese folksong and music, I must admit, I don't care for *utai*. It is a *depressing* style of sing-songing – and I am someone who likes A-minor and Tammy Wynette – that Morse himself elsewhere compares to "an old man in our country, with no ear for music, alone in a woodshed, absent-mindedly trying to recall some slow-timed and rather dismal hymn tune." But, I have to hand it to Morse for trying!

*   *   *

Most Westerners did not even *try* to appreciate Japanese music of any type and give a uniformly negative opinion of it. Samuel Johnson once wrote that "of all the noises, I think classical music the least disagreeable." All Western visitors to Japan from Frois to Chamberlain – even Morse at first – unanimously thought that of all noises, Japanese music was the *most* disagreeable. Fiddles and opera have endured their fair share of insult, *but never in history has any music been so harshly and repeatedly put down as Japanese music has.* Why? Is Japanese music uniquely horrid? After all, there are hundreds, if not thousands of musics in the world. Perhaps, the fact that the Japanese culture so delighted the *eyes* of the West made our *ears* doubly disturbed not to get equal satisfaction – How can a people who sweep us off our feet in the plastic arts fail to do so in the acoustic ones? How, also, can something *that different* be disliked? "I do not mind what language an opera is sung in so long as it is a language I don't understand" wrote Sir Edward Appleton in *The Observer* (Aug.28, 1955, in Shapiro: Encyclo. of Quotations about Music); but, strangely enough, even the exotic and incomprehensible nature of Japanese music failed to help. Frois's insulting description is repeated by others *ad nauseum*.

> Although they make use of pitch, neither going up nor down, their natural and artificial music is so dissonant and harsh to our ears that it is quite a trial to listen to it for a quarter of an hour; but to please the Japanese we are obliged to listen to it for many hours. (Mexia S.J., writing about the same time as Frois. In C:TCJ)

> This instrumental music is so poor and lamentable that it seems easier to satisfy their Gods than any ways to please a musical ear. [This despite the next sentence, which shows he is the fairest of all Western observers] "Nor is the vocal part much preferable to the instrumental, for altho' they keep to the time reasonably well, and sing according to some notes, yet they do it in so very slow a manner that the musick seems to be rather calculated to regulate their action, and the motions of their body, in their ballets and dances, wherein I must own, that they are very ingenious and dexterous, and little inferior to our Western dancers, excepting only, that they seem to want a little more action and swiftness in their feet."(Kaempfer K(S):HOJ 1692)

> As we toiled up, leading our horses, we heard some very sweet notes of the *unguissu* (*uguisu*), not unlike the notes of a nightingale, and I think nearly the only bird in Japan that sings. It had one or two very sweet notes. They say the Japanese teach them to sing beautifully, which is the more extraordinary if true, as they certainly do *not* teach themselves; and, if I had not lived among the Chinese, I should have said they had the least conception of either harmony or melody of any race yet discovered. The discord they both make, when they set themselve to make what they call music, is something that baffles all description. Marrow bones and cleavers are melodious by comparison, and the notes they bring out of a sort of lute or guitar is something too excruciating for endurance. And yet they make it a study, and there are professional singers and teachers who as sedulously cultivate their art as any in Europe. The professors are often blind; to judge by their performance, I should have guessed them to be deaf also – certainly the audience should be. [Alcock elsewhere quips] "I say musicians, but they make a most unearthly noise, a perfect charivari of drum, fife, and stringed instrument, each performer apparently seeking with the greatest conscientiousness to drown the noise of his neighbor, and succeeding to perfection." A:COT 1863)

> Music, if that beautiful word must be allowed to fall so low as to denote the strummings and squealings of Orientals, is supposed to have existed in Japan ever since mythological times. . . . Be

the scale of Japanese music whatever it may, the effect of Japanese music is, not to soothe, but to exasperate beyond all endurance the European breast. Miss Bacon, in her charming book entitled *Japanese Girls and Women,* demurely remarks: "It seems to me quite fortunate that the musical art is not more generally practiced." That is what everyone thinks, though most Europeans of the sterner sex would use considerably stronger expressions to relieve their feelings on the matter. . . . Still, of course, pathology is as legitimate a study as physiology. Those, therefore, who wish to investigate more minutely the ways and means by which injury is inflicted on sensitive ears should consult the authorities enumerated below . . . ("Music" heading in Chamberlain: C:TJ: 1890)

Still, we must credit Chamberlain for *eventually* admitting to the other side of the equation:

Dislikes are bound to be mutual. Of all the elements of Europeanization, European music is the one for which the Japanese have been the slowest to evince any taste. (Ibid.)

Under his "Theatre" heading, Chamberlain gave the proof. He wrote about an attempt to introduce Japanese to opera (like *kabuki,* invented slightly after TRATADO) when a small Italian troupe visited Yokohama and were fit into a play representing "the adventures of a party of Japanese globe-trotters." The adventurers survive their encounter with "Red Indians" (I'd like to find the script for this!) and, finally, in Paris "attend the Grand Opera," where the troupe gets to show its stuff.

But, oh! the effect on the Japanese audience! When once they had recovered from the first shock of surprise, they were seized with a wild fit of hilarity at the high notes of the *prima donna,*[3] who really was not at all bad. The people laughed at the absurdities of European singing till their sides shook, and tears rolled down their cheeks; and they stuffed their sleeves into their mouths, as we might our pocket-handkerchiefs, in a vain endeavor to contain themselves. Needless to say, that experiment was not repeated. (Ibid.)

One can well imagine how surprising those arias where the prima donna sounds like she is being continuously goosed – or a cross between a howling spider-monkey and a laughing hyena? – must have been to the Japanese! The difficulty Japanese had in appreciating Western music was first given serious thought by Miguel=Valignano in *De Missione,* as we shall see in 17 and 18, below).

1. Translation: This contrast enjoys a polyphony of translations. The Japanese translators both make the "voices" *onkyô,* which means "scale," or "tone" level and write of "various tones of music." But Frois's *diversas vozes* simultaneously mean different individual human voices and the different scales of those voices. The "one voice" on the Japanese side makes it clear that Frois *is* thinking primarily about singing. I hope "voices" in English keeps both meanings. Then there is the verb *esganicam.*

Matsuda and Jorissen write "a monotone that resounds *kishikishi."* *Kishikishi* is mimesis for a *creaking* or *grating* sound.

Cooper, on the other hand, has them "howl." ("We consider harmonized music sweet and melodious; in Japan, everybody howls together and the effect is simply awful." C:TCJ)

H's suggestion, "screech," is better. I cowardly used a more human sound, "shriek," but reading Isabella Bird's words "Again the instruments wailed and *screeched* forth their fearful discords" (my *italics*) and remembering how even I – who like throaty sounds – still find some traditional Japanese music irritating, changed my mind.

Okada diplomatically avoids specification altogether, Japanesing Frois as "noisely resounds!" I cannot refrain from adding one observation. The root meaning of "our" *sonorous* is "noisy."

2. Polyphony and Harmony. In this book I conflate these two. Reading Barzun, I can see why: "The technical innovation of the 16C was to combine elements of the two musical styles, the polyphonic and the harmonic" (B:FDD) Yet the two were generally in opposition, even warring. The former so complex – and including the jamming, piling up and collision (just to borrow some words used) – that the meaning of the words could be lost made musicians happy, while the latter, what I would call accompaniment that helped bring out the words, made what we might call singer-songwriters happy. Paradoxically, some of the polyphonists managed to convey too much meaning by borrowing popular tunes with obscene words to play with. Such fun upset the faithful and almost got all instruments kicked out of church. And not long after the TRATADO was written, Frois's monarch Phillip II "banned all styles but Gregorian" [In church? Throughout the kingdom?]. It all gets to complex for me. (Glosses are welcome, especially if they can include something on non-European polyphony/harmony.)

3. Acappella. This, too! If I had a nickel for every good word the lazy folk at Microsoft failed to include in the miniscule MS Word dictionary, I would be as rich as Bill Gates and his stock-holders who chose money over words.

4. Prima Donna. *Ditto for this one! Really, MS!*

13-16   In all the nations of Europe, we find full-throated singing.
Antre as naçoes d'Europa em todas há garganta;

Among the Japanese no one sings like that.
Antre os Japões nenhum gargantea

There is a dilemma here for the translator. The temptation is to write *warble* or *quaver* for that is how the verb *gargantear* is translated by the Portuguese- or Spanish-English dictionaries. Moreover, a *garganteo* is "a tremulous modulation of the voice." But Japanese folk music (as opposed to that of the Imperial court) actually uses the grain of the voice *more* than Europeans do (It sounds like the way Ethiopians sing!). They *do* warble, i.e. make fine trembling modulations. Indeed, female professional singers were called *uguisu,* a type of *warbler* usually translated as "nightingale" because the song was considered the sweetest of all birds (today women manning the loudspeakers in politicians' sound-trucks are usually called the same!). A MUTAMAGAWA senryu provides a self-description by the Japanese: "when a warbler loses its teeth [the edge on her voice], the voice of a cicada." The latter would be an older women. So, if warbling was not something "we" had and Japanese did not, it occurred to me that Frois might be referring to *vibrato* (not the delicate quiver of young Dolly Parton, or the cat-in-heat rasp of Janis Joplin, but the mechanically uniform sounding steady tremolo of a singer trained in formal European style singing). That, however, seemed too restrictive – who says everyone sang that way in Europe? – so I wondered aloud to a Mexican friend, M, who swears that the Spanish equivalent of gargantear, means to use the full throat to *really* sing. Looking up *gargantear* in the Portuguese-Portuguese Aurelio, I found it closer to *warble* than what she said. (1) singing tones nimbly; 2) making *trinados* (trills) and, 3) singing in a languid, languorous or *amoroso* (sweet?) way.) But, 3) leaves some room for play. So she does have a point. After all, singing well in Portuguese and Spanish (*tener buena garganta*) is not to have a *voice* of honey, but "a good throat." Is it not possible that Frois, thinking of Japanese nasality, meant that Japanese had no throat=voice to speak of? [1]   Here are some quotations about what "we" once wanted from singers all found at an intriguing site (digilander.libero.it/gianuario/this_art.htm) titled: THIS ART DOES NOT SUFFER MEDIOCRITY. The host summed up the desired vocal characteristics in the 16th century as *resonance ("sonorous voice"), roundness, homogeneity, suaveness,* and *purity.*

..

> Her voice then [Tarquinia Molza] is a soprano which is not dark, not suppressed, not forced but very clear, open, very sweet, low, equal and very suave; that which in the end we could say, if it were possible to do so without transgression, is more than angelic, and that which musicians usually call round, which counts as much when it is below, as in the middle, as above. (FRANCESCO PATRIZI, Amorosa Filosofia, 1577)

> . . . round and sonorous voice [of a Singer], as much so when it is low as when it is high and in the middle range (GIULIO CESARE BRANCACCI, Letter to Alfonso d'Este, December 1589)

> The voice must expire breath little by little, making sure that it is not lost in the nose or the throat. (GIOVANNI CAMILLO MAFFEI, Delle lettere . . . discorso della voce e del modo di apparare di *cantar di Garganta* senza Maestro, Naples, 1562   [Italics mine. Note the *cantar di garganta.* I think that is what Frois means])

> The Student's voice . . . should come out clearly and purely without passing through the nose or drowning in the throat. These are the singer's most fatal defects; once they have contaminated one's technique, there exists no remedy. (PIER FRANCESCO TOSI, Opinioni de' Cantori antichi e moderni. Bologna, 1723.)

In my opinion (which will infuriate you if you are a music-school-type), European art-music – including opera – *appoppogio* and all, represents *the impoverishment of the voice* and country music's George Jones and blue-grass's Ralph Stanley – who retain some of the real soul in our music

– are worth a thousand Pavalottis. The *vibrato* is a wretched standardization of the more interesting irregularity of natural warbling, a move away from the truly plaintive call of the cricket to the droning cicada. The rest of the world may not be able to equal the range of octaves of a top opera singer or break a glass, but it can use the voice in a far more complex manner, so complex, indeed, that many of the nuances defeat all efforts to write it down (Score Emmett Miller if you can!). Most of us have simply lost the ears to comprehend such a rich and complex grain of voice and hear it as primitive cacophony.[2] Isabella Bird was an exception. Despite finding a Japanese vocal performance "most excruciating," – another one was called "agonizing" – and even complaining that the minor scale was "a source of pain" to her (as an ebullient Christian, she doubtless liked inanely cheerful major notes), she gamely kept her ears uncovered long enough to give us the best description of Japanese traditional singing ever written, one that includes what I suspect Frois's contrast misses:

> It seemed to me to consist of a hyena-like howl, long and high (a high voice being equivalent to a good voice), varied by frequent guttural, half-suppressed sounds, a bleat, or more respectfully, "an impure shake," which is very delicious to a musically-educated Japanese audience which is both scientific and highly critical, but eminently distressing to European ears. (B:UTJ)

In both this contrast and the previous one, and all of the people I have quoted, an unstated bias toward upper-class Music exaggerates the Japanese-European difference in taste. None of the Western commentators represent the folk-view. In *The Resolver* (trans. 1635) Scipio Du Pleis wrote much the same thing about *our* folk that most Occidentals, including Frois, did about the Japanese:

> Q – Wherefore is it, that the most part of those which are ignorant of Musicke, are more pleased with hearing an onely voyce shrill and tuneable, then to a Musicke accomplished with all his parts?
>
> A – It is with the ignorant vulgar in the Art of Painting which are taken more with fresh colours in pictures . . . then with . . . Michael Angelo, where all the proportions are curiously observed, and [rather] makes more business of a petulant and bawling advocate then of him which observes with moderation all the precepts of Rhetorick; likewise those which understand nothing of musick, love better to heare often a long squealing voyce, then a perfect and harmonious comfort [consort?]. (D:RCN)

For at least a half a millennium now, the upper class – and their imitators in the middle class – in Europe (and white America) have lacked a good ear for the off-note and the funky-beat. They have gained appreciation for one type of complex art form at the cost of losing others whose finesse and complexity they still fail to understand.

1. Translation: Second Thoughts.   Considering what Frois writes about the chanting of seamen being the most suitable music for European ears, maybe "warble," in the sense of wavering *while changing pitch* – I note that most is done while *more or less holding a note* in Japanese – is, indeed, more appropriate than my broader interpretation. I welcome opinions from experts.

2. Lost Ability.   An opera-lover who reads the following quote will, I think, nod knowingly:

> The double half-notes must be sung with vivacity and as rapidly as possible, on the condition that the detachment takes place in the chest. If it takes place in the throat, as often happens, confusion and disgust are generated for the listener rather than pleasure" (FRANCESCO SEVERI, Salmi passeggiati per tutte le voci sopra i Falsi Bordoni di tutti i Toni Ecclesiastici, Rome, 1615 from THIS ART DOES NOT SUFFER MEDIOCRITY (digilander.libero.it/gianuario/this_art.htm).

But, to me, it only goes to prove that the listener has lost touch with the delight of natural sound.   That single syllable Hank Williams stretched out so evocatively in *"The Lovesick Blues"* that the people at the Grand Old Opera (there's irony for you!) forced him to do, I recall reading somewhere, 9 encores for it, says it all. If you who adore the opera and its Italian singing machines are not thrilled by it and only feel "confusion and disgust," then, I would say you have lost more than you have gained in your musical studies. Of course, I am a heretic. When GIAMBATTISTA MANCINI writes that "a voice purged of all defects, of extended register, only through these qualities may be termed beautiful" (Riflessioni pratiche sul canto figurato, Milan, 1777 in THIS ART), my first thought is that such a definition of beauty leaves no room for art. It is the same as saying that machines will eventually out-sing us. To me, offsetting what *would have been faults* to create something which makes them in retrospect a plus, is what true art is about. Notes that only become good in retrospect give us the most satisfaction. We should leave perfection to Angels and, thanking God for our many flaws, enjoy improvisation while we are down here.

13-17   To us, the music of the clavichord, viola, flute, organ and *doçaina* are very sweet;[1]
Antre nós hé suavissima e melodia de cravo, viola, frautas, orgãos, doçainas etc.;

To the Japanese, all our instruments sound harsh and unpleasant.
Aos Japões, todos nossos instrumentos lhe são insuaves e desgostozos.

The *doçaina,* says *Aurelios* is a type of bagpipe popular between the 12th and 17th century. I cannot for the life of me imagine a *suavissima*-sounding bagpipe, so I left the original word!

Valignano, in his SUMARIO put this contrast in a clearly relative context. Immediately after touching on European-Japanese differences in visual sense (See "black and white" 1-30), he wrote, "And the contrariety of our hearing is no less, for our vocal and instrumental music commonly injure their ears, and they are extremely happy with their own music which really torments our hearing." Montanus rephrases: what music is "most Ravishing and Grateful to us" grates their ears "so much, that they will stop them with their fingers," while L' Abbe says straightforwardly that our music holds no charm for them while "theirs to us is nothing else, but an ungrateful Noise of Kettles and Frying Pans." Isabella Bird, who was as aware of the relativity of the ear as she was of her own heart, artfully expressed "our" torment:

> Of the musical performance, as is fitting, I write with great diffidence. If I was excruciated, and experienced twinges of acute neuralgia, it may have been my own fault. The performers were happy, and Mr. Satoh's calm and thoughtful face showed no sign of anguish. (B:UTJ)

Frois knew he exaggerated, for not a few Japanese found our music sweet from the beginning. The top rulers of Japan, Nobunaga and Hideyoshi apparently listened with pleasure (V(A):S&A, note 73) and Frois's colleague and friend Organtino was convinced there was so much appreciation for the organ and other European instruments in his district that if he only had "organs and other musical instruments, and enough singers" he could "convert all of Miyako [Kyoto] and Sakai in only a year." (Ibid. and in S:VMP). Coelho in a 1582 letter about Nobunaga's visit to Organtino's seminary testifies "of all the things introduced into Japan so far, the playing of organs, harpsichords and viols pleases the Japanese most" and explained that these things acted "as bait" to attract the pagans. (in C:TCJ) Mexia, however, wrote Japanese didn't care for organs. One wonders if Organtino, true to his name was so superb an organ player that even Japanese liked to hear him!

Five years *after* TRATADO, in 1590, Frois, himself, recorded the musical success of the newly returned Embassy. Back after eight years away from home on the opposite side of puberty – Frois notes that Miguel didn't recognize his half-brothers, and his own mother didn't recognize him, Julian's sisters couldn't guess who he was, nor could Mancio's mother recognize him – the youths, now men, "gave absolutely splendid explanations in reply to all the questions addressed to them" from the large audience of Japanese, and Frois testifies, quite a musical performance to boot. "Listening to the group sing and perform on the various instruments brought back from abroad, every one was delighted and surprised at the harmony and the correspondence maintained among the various instruments." (HISTORIA/v86) The youths learned to play a variety of instruments and how to perform them in four-part harmony together while staying in Europe. Reading this, we can't help wondering if Western music could have made sufficient inroads to influence the course of Japanese music had Japan not closed. Perspective and other painting techniques were learned from the Dutch (or, rather, from the work they brought with them) during *sakoku,* but no Japanese that I know of pursued Western techniques of making music.

Disappointed with limited success in one effort to teach and perform European, i.e. classical, music in late-19th century Japan and lacking sympathy equally for popular and aristocratic Japanese music, even Chamberlain, who, you might recall adored most things Japanese, was merciless on the subject of Japanese instruments and music. Our scholarly and accommodating Jesuits would not have dared to be *this* subjective:

> Still, of course, pathology is as legitimate a study as physiology. Those, therefore, who wish to investigate more minutely the ways and means whereby injury is inflected on sensitive ears should consult the authorities enumerated below . . . [where, normally, Chamberlain elaborated, himself]

> May this [classical music taking root] happen here before another century elapses, and then may all the *samisen,*[2] *kotos,* and other native instruments of music be turned into firewood to warm the poor, when – if at no previous period of their existence – they will subserve a purpose indisputably useful! (C:TJ)

Reading this, I cannot help wanting to know *one thing. What about the shakuhachi?* Did none of "us" notice this richest timbered of all wind instruments (that I have heard, at any rate) in the world?[3]

1. Sweet/Soft *Translation:* In the original, my "very sweet" was the extreme form of "soft," *suavissima."* In the West, "soft" has long been equated with sweetness and desirability. In 1838 Darwin, just back from the hard, cramped quarters of the Beagle, dreamed of "a nice soft wife on a sofa." Toward the end of the twentieth century, Usanians came to think of "soft" as an insult. Even women wanted to become *literally* hard-assed ("Buns of Steel," an exercise video for women!); and, more incredibly, many men began to think such hardness attractive. In music, this mania was represented by "hard rock" and "heavy metal." I hope the twentieth century will see the rehabilitation of "soft" in the world of English speakers. In the more natural Latin world, soft is still beautiful. *Suave de abajo, suave de arriba,* as the song on the radio puts it.

2. The Samisen or Shamisen. We will have more on this instrument whose popularity was rising while Frois was writing.

3. The Shakuhachi. I hope to get a gloss on the history of Western appreciation for the shakuhachi and a description of the notes which can include elements of what might in pictorial art be called asymmetrical balance, brush-texture (*hakke*), etc..

~~~~~~

13-18   We greatly appreciate the consonance and harmony of our organ music.
A consonansia e proporsão da nossa muzica de canto d'orgão[1] *estimamos em muito;*

> The Japanese find it *kashimashi* [noisy, clamorous] and do not enjoy it.
> *Os Japões a tem por caxi maxi e não gostão nada della.*

Speaking of the 16th century, Jacques Barzun writes "The period was one of musical expansion – larger choirs in churches, bigger and better organs, larger "families" of instruments and more numerous players in town bands." (*From Dawn to Decadence*) On the positive side, he quotes Thomas More's *Utopia* where "music takes the impression of whatever is represented, affects and kindles the passions, and works the sentiments deep into the hearts of the hearers." And, on the negative, Erasmus (1513), who regrets that "in college or monastery it is still the same music, nothing but music. Words nowadays mean nothing. . . . Money must be raised to buy organs and train boys to squeal."[2]   The *De Missione* ambassadors reflected the Jesuits' favorable view toward music in abundance. After Miguel=Valignano introduces nine European musical instruments (Names only, no explanation, for they brought back samples), including ones with names that sound like parts of the human body or diseases to me – *tibia* (a type of flute) and *fistula* (reed instrument?) – and claims that they make a great tune when played together properly, Leno, responds that hearing you play them the other night was very refreshing even for us (stay-at-home Japanese), "but we just couldn't feel that sweetness [Here is where I would like to see the Latin!] of which you speak." To this, Miguel, echoing one of Valignano's favorite themes, attributes it to custom:

> It shows how hard it is to shake custom and how powerful the effect of not being used to something is. And this same thing goes for singing. Since you are not yet used to the harmony of

European harmony, you cannot know the true joy and melodiousness of it. But, as our ears are already used to it, there is nothing so pleasant to hear. (J/S:DM)

Then, Miguel gives a description of the harmonizing, the different types of voices – high, medium, low and *falsa vocula* – and boasts of its complexity as an art in a manner that suggests either he (one of the other Japanese ambassadors or Valignano, himself) truly appreciated it:

Vocalizing all of that, fitting it with the instrumentals, while preserving the rules of music, or sometimes going up higher, beyond the rules . . . [Here, especially, someone please check for me!]

That "going beyond" suggests, to me at any rate, the joy of improvisation, for such a "perfect art" is a "lofty" one, "born of freemen distributing [?] and adjusting their respective voices" and, now, "diligently studied from childhood" it is making continued progress.[2] Meanwhile, Japanese song is "monotone, with no divisions of voice." After this, Leno, also sounding like Valignano, concludes "it must be a fact that our being accustomed to the music of our own country prevents us from appreciating the melodiousness of European tunes."

Actually, Japanese do have one type of accidental harmony created by Buddhist sutra chanting. In a large temple, with fifty or more people sing-songing the sutra in their natural tone of voice, each pausing to take his or her breath whenever they naturally run out, and perhaps partially synchronizing this subconsciously to the periodic chime, an effect similar but far more relaxing to the staggered singing of "Row, Row, Row, Your Boat" is achieved. I, at least, find it more interesting than any of our more orchestrated chants. But, Japan has never known anything approaching even the simple harmony one finds in any choir, many blue-grass songs, or a barbershop quartet. Even today, despite musical education in grade school that ensures they know far more about Western classical music than I ever will, most Japanese have so little actual experience with harmonizing that, when you try it with them, they immediately assume the common melody has been lost and either stop singing or good naturedly follow you. It takes some doing to convince them to wait a few seconds to catch and enjoy the harmonic effect. (This is not, of course, true for all Japanese – least of all my bluegrass-playing acquaintances! – I only relay an experience I have had on more than one occasion.)

1. Translation. *Canto d'orgão* is literally "song of [the] organ;" At first, I thought it might be songs made to be sung with the organ, but I could not confirm this and went along with the other translators. The German translation filled out the meaning of the consonance and proportion part: *symphony of tone* and the *harmony (accord)* of the music," but no one really defines what would seem to be the name for a genre of music. The word *kashimashi* refers specifically to noise made by the inclusion of too many elements; to use modern idiom, it is *too busy* or, *just too much,* and for that reason considered "cacophonous." *Kashimashii* is often written with a Chinese character made of three woman radicals, and is one of the characters most hated by Japanese feminists.

(姦しい)

2. Erasmus Quote. Perhaps the same: "We have brought into our churches certain operatic and theatrical music; such a confused, disorderly chattering of some words as I hardly think was ever in any of the Grecian or Roman theatres. The church rings with the noise of trumpets, pipes, and dulcimers; and human voices strive to bear their part with them. Men run to church as to a theatre, to have their ears tickled. And for this end organ makers are hired with great salaries, and a company of boys, who waste all their time learning these whining tones" (*Commentary on 1 Corinthians 14:19* found at www.piney. com/MuPraiseTeamAcap.html)

13-19   Ordinarily, with us, the music of the nobility is gentler than that of mean folk;
Ordinariamente antre nós a muzica dos fidalgos hé mais suave que a [da] jente baxa;

That of the Japanese nobility, we cannot bear to hear, and that of seamen pleases us. *A dos fidalgos Japões, nós não a podemos ouvir, e a dos marinheiros [hé]-nos aceyta.*

Since Europe decided that *smooth was classy* and thought nothing sounded better than castrated boys, that would be the case. The first *castrato* (in the guise of the Spanish "falsettist" Padre Soto) on record at the Sistine Chapel was 1562 (About 15 years after Frois left Europe for the Far East). It was a common practice in the 16th century – not just in Spain and Italy but in Germany and France, too – because the elaborate a cappela (in chapel) style pioneered in the previous century demanded more complexity than mere boys could hack, and the voice was preferred to that of falsettos and women (who were also forbidden to sing in church). *But what delicious irony* – the devilish practice of castration to create music thought to be angelic,[1] unnaturally deforming bodies because the natural falsetto was considered false and detested by the pure of heart.[2] Dating at least as far back as the 2nd century in Rome and continued in Constantinople. The practice was not invented at this time but, like so many things, part of the revival called the Renaissance. Italy was most castrato-positive and almost never used the word. They were called *musico* or *virtuoso* and treated with corresponding respect. But, throughout Europe they came to be treated like superstars and to act like superstars (weird dressing, ridiculously intense rivalries, tantrums, etc..). This popularity peaked in the 17th century. There is no need to go on about castratos. My point is only that "our" upper-class's unnatural desire for sweet and smooth (but ornamented) sound was so powerful that the boy-voice became synonymous with music.

The nobility in Frois's Japan was basically military class, with subdued Zen taste. The stark music of Noh was appreciated. The court music, something called *gagaku,* is less subdued in that more instruments come into play, yet sounds bad even to me. Before coming to Japan, Lafcadio Hearn was told that "There is no scale in the Japanese classical or popular music which may not be found in Greek music."[3] *I wonder.* And, I wonder if Hearn still thought that *after* going to Japan! Nakata Taizo, a Japanese *gagaku* aficionado describes the combination of three instruments like this: "When all sound together a Cosmos can be heard / Imagined by those now distant Elegant in the flickering candle of time."(http://www.gagaku.net/index.ENG.html) But, I fear I would agree with Edward Yong, who had to provide 10 minutes of mood music before a college play based on Rashomon:

> It's just a flute and drum, and I'm improvising in the style of Japanese Court Music. If anyone who attends the production thinks what I'm playing sounds absolutely horrid, tuneless, dissonant and out of tune, you're absolutely right. That's how Japanese court music sounds. In fact, what I'm playing is already a more tonal and tuneful version – I can perceive neither tonality nor melody in the original stuff.

> When I first read accounts of the western missionaries having to sit through endless hours of Japanese court music and complaining that they'd not heard anything so horrible in their lives, I thought they were just ignorant Westerners who couldn't appreciate the beauty of Asian things, even though they said they wished they were back in Cathay (China) where the music was tuneful and entertaining. Then I heard Gagaku, and I realized they were right. Coming from an environment with Vivaldi and Handel, being forced to endure hours of this must have been truly torture. Pity that so much skill (these musicians were trained for years) should be spent to produce such a hideous result. There is, however, one undoubted advantage in Japanese Court Music. There are people who can hear no melody in Chinese Classical Music. Such a person should attend a concert of Gagaku, with all the traditional instruments and dances , and then attend one of Chinese music the next night. If, after their horrid wailing, he can still find no melody in our Chinese dances and songs, he must give up looking for a tune in anything. . . .

> Apparently, Japanese Court Music is supposed to be a descendant of T'ang Chinese Court Music, and an immediate descent of ancient Hokkien Music from the Fukien province of China. I find it hard to believe the Chinese could have ever had such hair-raisingly awful music, and that when the Japanese in the 9th Century were aping Chinese culture, they tried to imitate the Chinese stuff and didn't quite get it right. There's no other explanation for it. (infernoxv.blogspot.com/ 2004_01_01_infernoxv_archive.html)[4]

..

There is no small irony in this. By definition, *gagaku* was refined and graceful, respectable music as opposed to the vulgar music of the folk. As anthropologist Robert Garfias notes, its very name (雅楽) suggests the Confucian concept of good wholesome music to keep the elements in balance, though it really derives from a different strand of Chinese music associated with court banquets (宴 楽).[5]   (http://aris.ss.uci.edu/rgarfias/gagaku/gagaku.html) The Kunaicho (The Imperial Household Agency) writes:

> The Japanese singing style and vocal arrangements for Gagaku are composed of advanced musical techniques, and have not only had a direct affect on the creation and development of modern-day music, but Gagaku itself also has the potential to develop in many aspects, as a global art form.

That is, in the world of modern music, Gagaku can raise its head up high. A few bibliographical comments about a book by musician Takemitsu, Toru (*Confronting Silence: Selected Writings*. Berkeley: Fallen Leaf Press, 1995) indirectly provides the context:

> In the discussion of his composition he talks about his concepts of sound and silence, and the influence of Gagaku (court music). Here he mentions how Gagaku was not linear like Western Music, that its sounds " . . . towered toward heaven like a tree."

> Takemitsu then goes into detail about John Cage, Merce Cunningham, and Jasper Johns and the personal and philosophical effects they had upon him. (found at theory.music.indiana.edu/isaacso/t556/takemitsu.html)

The most important question concerning *gagaku* is the degree to which it can be justly called a living anachronism, *a coelacanth of music*.   Garfias, an anthropologist who studied it in Japan a couple years called it "one of the strongest surviving music traditions in Asia." *One of*? Just how special is *that*? "Carl K. Otsuki's Gagaku Page" inadvertently reveals the paradox. On the one hand, this instrumental music was "imported from the Asian mainland" so that *gagaku* as a "living reference to the ancient Japanese art, is not only wonderful treasure but also an invaluable heritage of the ancient Asian arts" because "now we are no more able to find original music in original countries;" but on the other hand (He does not pose it in this contradictory way, but how can I help doing so?) "all imported music and its instrumentation was arranged and Japanized nicely to Japanese taste. Gagaku was reorganized as Japanese original music during the 9th to 11th centuries."   Adopted or adapted, the high degree of singularity makes me think that I really should try harder to appreciate *gagaku*. Some day, I hope to find time to fiddle with it (literally, with a three-string fiddle[6]), *for it has been my experience that participation can change musical taste where listening alone cannot*. Or, in other words, we don't only play what we like but learn to like what we play.

By music of the seamen, Frois probably means the working chants mentioned in 12-10. But he may also have heard them sing as they sat around drinking in bad weather. One might say that the inability of Japanese boats to take the rain may have given them an advantage over others.[7] Moreover, they may have sung honest-to-goodness folk-songs – chanties as opposed to chants – as they worked.

> The sailors in rowing their boats back and forth in the harbour have a peculiar song entirely unlike the sailors' songs further south [Yokohama, Kobe, etc. mainland ports] Japan. It is musical and catchy. . . . the curious chant as it comes over the water is very pleasant. (M:JDD)

Here, Morse writes nothing of the educational interest of the music, or of learning "things from the Japanese viewpoint" (a statement made while he studied *utai*). Morse speaks as every man Western. He was in Hakodate, the Southern tip of the Northernmost Island now known as Hokkaido. In a footnote, he added:

> In the extreme southern part of Japan I heard the identical song sung by the sailors of Kagoshima Gulf, and on my return to America a Russian troupe which visited Salem sang a piece called a Volga sailor's song strongly suggesting the Hakodate song. Such an air might easily spread through northern Russia to Kamchatka and find its way to Yezo [Hokkaido] through the Kurile Islands.

Frois spent much time in the Kagoshima area, so he would have heard some of these trans-Asian ballads. If I remember correctly, that type of song, tends to have a 3-beat rhythm that the

Japanese musicologists say comes from horseback-riding peoples and immediately sounds attractive to any Westerner. Played on a flute rather than sung, some can even be confused for old English ballads. (After seeing a movie on Japan – a government production – shown in the East-West Center in Japan in 1977 or 1978, I asked a number of people about the *shakuhachi* accompaniment and *most Japanese thought the melody Japanese, while the Americans, including yours truly, thought it Western!*) Since Frois predates any Russian influence that I know of, I do not think we need to credit the Russians. I believe the Koreans, who have many sweet [to our ears, too] lullabies, would be a better bet. But it might be that the same general tunes carried by Mongols, perhaps, across Asia were introduced by Russian castaways in the North and Koreans in the South.

What Isabella Bird had to say about the quality of Korean music applies here, too:

> To my thinking, the melancholy which seems the *motif* of most Oriental music becomes extreme plaintiveness in that of Korea, partly due probably to the unlimited quavering on one note. While what might be called concerted music is torture to the Western ear, solos on the flute ofttimes combine a singular sweetness with their mournfulness and suggest "Far-off Melodies." (B:KHN)

The melodies I *think* we are talking about are sweet, but not in a jolly, major way. "Far-off" is perfect. I find them Nostalgic and dreamy. As Joseph Needham wrote in his *River of Time,* a minor tone, a plaintive quality is common to *all* folk music. The philosophers (Plato or Confucius) may assume that sweet and happy (i.e. *proper*) music make people feel the same way, but the people themselves prefer a homeopathic approach: *sad music to cure sadness.*

*   *   *

Morse suggests a slightly different angle (that instruments bring out the worst in Japanese singing) and reveals a new side of working music:

> From a foreigner's standpoint, the nation seems devoid of what we call an ear for music. . . . They have no voice, and they only make the most curious squeaks and grunts when singing with the *samisen* or *biwa,* which remotely resemble our banjo and guitar. When the men sing at work, however, their voices seem more natural and hearty, and this kind of singing they actually practice, as we learned the other day at Hashishi. We passed a place we thought a carousal was going on, and we learned it was a lot of workmen practicing their songs and choruses, which they sing at their work in hoisting, pile-driving, or moving great loads. It is an interesting sight to see twenty or thirty men bending to their work and ready to pull together when a certain part of the song is reached. It strikes us a as a great waste of time to sing for a full minute or more before the slightest movement or effort is made. [Elsewhere, regarding an eight-man pile driving crew – they pull on individual ropes attached to pulleys in order to raise a pile that is "dropped with a thud" – "it seemed a ridiculous waste of time to sing the chantey, for such it was, without exerting the slightest effort to raise the weight. Nine-tenths of the time was devoted to singing!"] (M:JDD)

This is the only time I have ever come across workers meeting to practice their working songs. None of my Japanese acquaintances have heard of it either. On the other hand, we all know how neighborhoods meet to practice for singing and dancing the *bon-odori.* It is strange how little attention Frois and others have given to *bon* dances! To me, these vocals are what soar up to heaven – the *minyô* style *yagibushi,* for example –and not *gagaku,* or, for that matter our choirs.

---

1. *Castrati and Church.* How did the Church justify this? One was to maintain the fiction that a hernia operation, a fall from a horse, a bite from a large animal or the tusk of a boar was to blame and to excommunicate castrators. According to an article in the *Independent* (27 August 2001 - Copyright © 2001 Independent News-papers (UK) Ltd.)   "Now Amnesty International is calling on the current Pope to apologize to the castrati and their families down the centuries." *Is this for real?* We have enough current problems, don't we? When you con-sider the fact that most of the kids came from poor fami-lies that would have benefited greatly from their earnings, calling for such an apology is ludicrous. (most information from www.radix.net/~dalila/singers/ castrato-unnatural.html)

2. *Natural High Notes.* More from THIS ART DOES NOT SUFFER MEDIOCRITY – "Nobility in fine singing cannot come from false voices: it will come out of a natural voice that accommodates all the chords which can be used according to talent without needing breathing in order to demonstrate mastery of all the best effects that are required in this noble manner of singing." (GIULIO CACCINI, Preface to *Nuove Musiche*, Florence, 1601.) (digilander.libero.it/gianuario/this_art. htm). While this is more a definition of what was becoming the opera voice, note the antagonism toward the *false voice*. In my opinion, it explains how a culture which put men to death for "unnatural acts" could end up justifying the *castrato*:

> "... to briefly mention the sopranos, the greatest ornament music has, will Your Lordship compare the falsettos of that time with the natural soprano of the castratos which today we have in abundance?" (PIETRO DELLA VALLE, *Della musica dell' età nostra che non è punto inferiore, anzi è migliore di quella dell'età passata*, Rome, 1640.)

The 17th and 18th century were the heyday of the castrato – I would love a gloss on how the Puritans took them in England! – and the Vatican employed them up to the 20th century. By the way, the THIS ART site host wrote: "The presence today of singers of falsetto in the Italian or Italianized repertoire is completely anti-historic, anti-aesthetic and anti-technical."

3. *Japanese and Greek Music.* In 1885, Lafcadio Hearn reported on "Some Oriental Curiousities" (Now part of his *Occidental Gleamings*) at the New Orleans Exposition in Harper's Bazaar (Mar 28). He was specially interested in the report by Shuji Isawa, whom he found "learned to a degree that would do credit to a German master-composer," on investigations undertaken at behest of the Minister of Education re. the tuning of various instruments on the japanese scale. "It seems that the scale adopted for the Greek seven-stringed lyre corresponds exactly with one of the scales of Japanese popular music." After illustrating the fact with excellent diagrams, Hearn writes Isawa further observes: "This Hymn to Apollo, it appears, conforms precisely to what is known as the *banshikicho* in Japanese popular music." Indeed, they arranged and played it so "nobody present could detect any difference between the ancient Greek and the present Japanese music." Isawa hypothesized both Japanese and European music "had roots in Hindustan." An annotated biography note on an article by Miho, Hashimoto. ("*Izawa Shuji ni okeru Seiyokyoikugakusettu no jyuyo* [The doctrine of Western education acceptance by Shuji Izawa]." Japanese educational historical science. Educational Historic Society 31 (1988) : 19-37.) :
"I appreciate that Shuji Izawa put Western music at the center but he did not really recognize the different between East music and West music and try to find the similarities by force to blend those two musics. For example, lyrics were a problem to do it." (My Annotated Bibliography at homepages.nyu.edu/ ~ks742/MyAnnotated Bibliography.htm) Isawa (or Izawa, for pronunciation is often not settled) seems to have been trying to do for Japanese music in the West what Nitobe did for the martial tradition.

4. *Edward Yong* This is an awfully long quote to use without permission and I hope EY, a 26 year-old who calls himself "a Dilettante and Young Fogey" understands. For readers who might not appreciate it, let me add that Will Cuppy says horrible things about some birds and *their* song and that is precisely why he can praise others so magnificently. As Picasso once put it, you don't have to know what you like but you damn well better know what you don't. *Taste is discrimination.* It is possible that at some future time EY may learn to like *gagaku*. If so, I hope he will not criticize his younger self.

5. *Strands of Gagaku.* A superb outline at http://stripe.colorado.edu/~keister/gagaku.html gives the history as follows:

> "Music imported from Korea (3rd cent.), China and India (7th-8th cent.) /9th century: reform of many styles of imported Asian music / orchestra standardized, classifications created: /*Togaku* (music of the left; China and India) / *Komagaku* (music of the right; Korea and Manchuria) / Heian period (8th-12th cent.): *gagaku* popular at court, practiced by nobility / Vocal styles: *roei* (Chinese poems); *saibara* (*gagaku*-style folk songs); /*enkyoku* (banquet music); *imayo* (lyrics set to *gagaku* melodies). / Post-Heian: end of aristocratic power; court groups scattered; / music maintained by musical families on individual instruments."

The site also gives the modal theory, rhythmic theory, Form . . . To this, and what little I wrote above, let me add only that *gagaku* was and is played in large shrines and temples as well as at court.

6. *Three-String Fiddle.* The Japanese got the three string fiddle two ways, one from China to Okinawa, which is pure folk, and one that got into a school of gagaku. Gagaku has stranger instruments than this fiddle (the *hichiriki*, or oboe *sounds* funny and the *shô*, an irregularly-shaped bundle of bamboo tubes called a mouth-organ *looks* funny) but, nothing beats the way it is *played*. They kneel formally and rest the instrument just in front of their knees, and *to change strings rotate the body of the instrument* (that rests on a single peg) *rather than changing the angle of attack of the bow!* If ever there was a perfect musical topsy-turvy, this is it!

7. *Japanese Fishermen.* Even today (or, 1972, at any rate), when the water-proofing problem should be over, some Japanese fisherman spend a lot of time in port drinking and singing. When my father (who spoke no Japanese but was a hell of an engineer and designer) was sent to observe squid-fishing boats by Yamaha (OK, now I gave the name of the company mentioned in the last chapter), heavy rains got him holed up with the fishermen, who sure enough, drank like fish for day after day. If squid boats roll too much, the snag-hooks are yanked out and squids are lost, so my father's *mission* was to find a way to dampen the movement while not losing speed, or, if possible speeding up the boats yet further, so they would not lose too much time commuting to the best squid grounds. At any rate, I can still remember my father's amazement and awe of the fisherman's ability to swill rock-gut *shôchû*.

(I have just had a bit too much wine, myself, and I hope the reader will not mind this reminiscence. The *boat* chapter was hard on me, for I kept thinking that if only my father were still alive and . . .)

13-20 In Europe, children sing an octave higher than men;[1]
Em Europa os meninos cantão 8 pontos mais alto que os homens;

In Japan, they all hit the same note, shrieking[2] so our sopranos would be out of work.[3] *Em Japão todos em ygual ponto esganiçando-sse no ponto em que o tipre [tiple?] estaa descansado.*

This is partly because Japanese do not harmonize but sing a single melody in a single key as already noted. It also may have something to do with the fact that the physiology of sexual difference is less radically developed in Japanese, and other East Asia people so that male voices are generally not so low (obviously Tibetan throats are another story!!) and it is possible for everyone to sing along.

1. Men? I was tempted to write "adult," but such a word was little used until the mid 17th century in English and probably not much in Portuguese, either. (We sometimes say that the concept of a *child* and *childhood* is a modern invention, but these predate the adult and adulthood!) Also, as it is possible Frois might be thinking "male," I prefer to leave the generic men, but is it *grown-up*?

2. Shriek? The same "screechy" sound we found in 13-15 here is better as "shriek." Cooper renders it "shouts" here, where he made it "howls" in 13-15.

3. Soprano? The last half of the Japanese part of the contrast has some translators scratching their heads. Frois does confuse his "l" and "r" (or Portuguese has changed) from time to time, so most translators have chosen "tiple," a word meaning "soprano." The modern Portuguese translation, alone, renders it "timbre," so that the means "until they lose their timbre" (actually "until the timbre is resting"), using timbre, or "tone." But, "soprano" or "tone," there is still an idiom to guess about: "soprano/tone <u>would be *descansado*</u>". Cooper translates "In Japan, everybody sings in the same octave, shouting *on a note suitable for a soprano.* (My italics C:TCJ) The French translation is similar, making "*. . . the note one*

that, with us would be easy for a soprano." (*notes où un soprano est à l'aise chez nous.*) Okada, on the other hand, "There, the soprano *is on a [can take a?] vacation/ break.*" (*soko de wa tipure wa oyasumi de aru.*). I think *his* rhetoric means, "there, a soprano would be *out of a job*, for they all shriek on the same high note." He adds in a note that Frois was probably thinking of a boy-soprano. Matsuda & Jorissen follow Okada, who follows Schütte, (*die dem Sopram bequem est*). Schütte also added a wee bit in mid-sentence that includes the word "falsetto." [a falsetto that takes off from where a soprano rests??????? so overpowering a falsetto that a soprano would only be drowned out?] I chose to follow the German/Japanese interpretation over the English and French, for it has that humorous twist. But strictly looking at the grammar, I was tempted to follow the others, who may well be correct. If you wish to take that interpretation, I would suggest using an English idiom: "on a note that would be a breeze for a soprano." Finally, I wonder whether a third interpretation may not be possible in which the other (most common) meaning of *ponto[punto]*, "point," is taken, so that it reads: "shrieking *at the point where [even] sopranos leave off.*" That is to say, shrieking so shrill as to suggest an *alto*.

13-21 Our guitars have six strings, not counting the doubles, and are played with the fingers;[2]
As nossas violas [1] tem seis cordas afora as dobradas, e tanjen-se com a mão;

Those of Japan four, and they are played with a sort of comb.
As de Japão 4 e tamjen-se com huma maneira de pentes.

The German translation waffles with "stringed-instrument" (*saiteninstrumente*), while French boldly went for the "guitar," which has a longer classical pedigree than one might imagine,[3] though its earliest usage example in the OED is in 1621. Other lutes are not necessarily 6-string and lack the waist found on the viola, so *guitar* it is.

The 4-string Japanese instrument is a *biwa,* a beautiful teardrop-shaped lute – with the back round and the front flat, sound-holes modeled after heavenly bodies (crescent and/or circle) and a neck that bends back in a right angle at the top. Like the folk *shamisen,*[4] it is powerfully plucked – or, rather, *struck* – a *biwa* player is called a *biwa-uchi:* "*biwa*-striker" – with an enormous plectrum, usually ivory, the size and the shape of a thin hatchet head. (Frois wrote "comb" because combs used to be very high-backed and the over-all shape resembles the plectrum).   There are things only a handful of fingers can manage. For example, a single pick can not simultaneously pluck 4-strings. It cannot do many other things I could never get my fingers to do, either. But a large and heavy pick, which is indeed a good contrast with delicate finger tips, is useful in more ways than one might imagine. *First*, it prevents almost all acoustic leakage: the vibration that would be lost with fingers or a lighter pick adds to the volume, particularly with high notes. *Second*, the length translates a small movement of the wrist into a large one at the end of the pick: a lot of action for little work.   And *third*, it can serve as a defensive weapon – against a snowball in a haiku of Issa's, but, more commonly (at least in pulp fiction and Easterns!) to cut the throat of another or oneself (I doubt most were that sharp or too many strings would be cut, but the fiction is a pleasant one).   The large plectrum may be a Japanese invention, for the Chinese, from whom the *biwa* was adopted, pluck with their fingers (anyone?).

1. *Viol, Viola* In English, viols or violas are all bowed instruments. Etymologically speaking, the *viola* is indeed cognate with the fiddle: *fiddle >fithele* (OE) > *viele* (OF) > *viola*. Nothing in its name demands that it be bowed, for the word "fiddle" itself goes back to *vitul(l)a,* or *vitulare,* Latin meaning "to be joyful, celebrate a festival."   In Latin tongues, the viola can mean either a type of lute (guitar) *or* a type of fiddle (viola).

2. *Fingers*. The Portuguese have play by *mao,* or "hand," where English uses "fingers."   Same as 6-1, with food.

3. *Guitar*.   From the Greek *kithára,* or "cithara."   I would guess it shares deeper Indo-European roots with the *Sitar.* Both are fretted, differently to be sure.

4. Samisen or Shamisen.   Like many words in Japan, the 三味線, literally "3-flavor-string/s" has more than one pronunciation.   I think Japanese favor *shamisen* because it sounds better, even though it is the only instance I can think of where "three" is pronounced "*sha.*" Because the shamisen was *the* instrument for entertainers in the long Seclusion that followed soon after TRATADO, one might wonder why Frois does not mention it.   My guess is that, besides Frois's bias towards high culture, as will be discussed in the chapter notes, the shamisen was too recent of an arrival.   As far as I can gather/google, the Chinese 3-string that got to the Ryûkyû Islands (Okinawa) as early as 1390, from 江南 China, and was adapted by an Okinawan musical genius called 赤犬子(Red-dog-child) about a hundred years later and by 1562, when there was a lot of trade going on, found its way to a number of

places on the main island where dog and cat skin came to replace the snake-skin music-box (Okinawa has many *habu,* viper that do not have rattles but do make good vibrating membranes).   Strangely enough, the sites I found do not mention the relation between the fiddled 3-string and the plucked one! (gloss anyone?). A fascinating aside from Chamberlain:

> The popular or *samisen* scale is different [from the classical scale/s]. Like the scale of medieval Europe – we still quote Mr. Isawa – it has for its chief peculiarity a semitone above the tonic, which is one among various reasons for believing the *samisen,* together with its scale, to have found its way here from the Spaniards at Manila, and not from Luchu according to the recent Japanese opinion." (in "Music" C:TJ).

I do not know enough music to comment on the above, and I am confused at further assertion by a different investigator cited by Chamberlain of a missing 3rd and 6th note ("these generally omitted notes are to our ears the most important of all") where Japanese today write of a missing 4th and 7th note (the *jonanuki* scale)*;* but I can say for certain that Nihonjinron in search of contrast have noted the *short drone string* on the shamisen, and claimed this slightly dirty sound gives life to music that perfectly clean notes do not and represents what differentiates Japanese from Occidental music (Here, no one ever mentions "our" Africa-derived bluegrass instrument, the banjo, which also . . .).

~~~~~~

13-22   Among us, the nobility takes pride in playing the guitar;
Antre nós a jente nobre se preza de tanjer violas;

In Japan, it is the office of the blind, as with the accordionists in Europe.
Em Japão hé oficio dos cegos como em Europa os samfonineiros.

If Japanese noblemen and samurai were expected to be proficient at letters and the tea-ceremony as well as swordsmanship, Portuguese knights became infatuated with the troubadour art of singing ones own poems to the accompaniment of ones own plucking, something previously left to their poets and pages. For almost two centuries, write Matsuda and Jorissen, they had come to prefer music and other parlor games to tournaments and hunting, so that Prince (later, King) Don Duarte of Portugal, in the early 15th century chastised the knights for becoming effeminate in his book for teaching good horsemanship. One might say that the revival and improvement of the equine art was spurred partly by the desire to restore the nation's manliness. But, continue Matsuda and Jorissen, the guitar/lute craze by no means stopped with the nobility. In the 16th century it was popular everywhere people gathered as an instrument of solo accompaniment. (J/F(M&J:T)

In Japan, the lute was indeed identified with blind musicians. My dictionary (OJD) says they were called *biwa-hôji*, or priests of the *biwa*. And they put on a religious front – the costume and shaved head – although they were rarely actual Buddhist priests. Their specialty was not the love songs – or hymns, for the church in Portugal was not adverse to the *viola* – of the Portuguese nobility, but *almost entirely historical legend*, and that generally the same one, the Heikei-monogatari, or Tales of the Heikei, which tell of the tragic downfall of an old and beloved, highly aesthetic noble clan at the hands of a more warlike younger one.

The *biwa* was not, however, *only* played by the blind. John Saris, head of the East India Company's first trading fleet to visit Japan (Nagasaki, 28 years after TRATADO) describes what would appear to be that instrument used in a manner more like we associate with the *shamisen* on the occasion of a courtesy call on shipboard by the King of Hirado:

> The king's women seemed to be somewhat bashful, but he willed them to bee frolicke. They sang diuers songs, and played vpon certain instruments (where-of one did much resemble our lute) being bellyed like it, but longer in the necke, and fretted like ours, but had only foure gut strings. Their fingring with the left hand like ours, very nimbly, but the right hand striketh with an iuory bone, as we vse to playe upon a citterne with a quill. They delighted themselues much with their musicke, keeping time with their hands and playing and singing by booke, prickt on line and space, resembling much ours heere. (Included with the Letters of Will Adams in S:MQTJ)

The "delighted themselves" would seem to be tongue-in-cheek, for Cooper, who quotes the same passage (with only the *u*'s corrected to *v*'s), writes Saris also wrote he found "musique after the Countrey fashion" to be "harsh to our hearings." (C:TCJ) The best part of Saris's letter, however, is where he "daue leaue to diuers women of the better sort to come into my Cabbin, where the picture of *Venus,* with her sonne *Cupid,* did hang somewhat wantonly set out in a large frame. They, thinking it to be our ladie and her sonne, fell downe and worshipped it, with shewes of great deuotion, telling me in a whispering manner (that some of their companions which were not so, might not heare) that they were *Christianos:* whereby we percieued them to be Christians, conuerted by the *Portugall* Iesuits." This picture story is particularly funny when you learn that when Saris returned to England, he had *a stock of pornographic books and paintings* that "were discovered and publically burnt on 10 January 1615." (L:IOJ) Ian Littlewood calls Saris "a clod" for not following Will Adam's advice and thus losing out on the chance to establish a trading base in Japan. This may (or may not) be fair, but I wish Saris had stayed in Japan longer and written a book about it, for he was a damn good reporter. He did mention one more concert:

> The old King came aboord againe and brought with him diuerse women to be frolicke. These women were actors of comedies, which passe there from iland to iland to play, as our players doe here from towne to towne, hauing seuerall shifts of apparrell for the better grace of the manner acted: which for the most part are of Warre, Loue, and such like. (Ibid)

I included these long quotations because they show how someone not looking for contrast may find similarity ("*as we use to* play upon a citterne," [1] "*resembling much ours* heere," "*as our players doe* here") in the same field where another finds difference.

---

1. Citterne. A *Cithern/Cittern* according to the OED was "an instrument of the guitar kind, but strung with wire, and played with a plectrum or quill. The method of playing takes us closer to the Japanese one. In England it often had a grotesquely carved head and hung in barbershops and the Tyrolese form is called (why I know not!) a zither. I found one mention of it in a 16th century Iberian context. "Their [the parish churches in Cuenca Spain in the 1520's] sanctity was violated by criminals who, exploiting their right to asylum in a church, lodged themselves inside, gambled, brought in women, played *cittern*, and used the temple as a hideout from which they could attack their enemies with impunity." (Sara T. Nalle *God in La Mancha: Religious Reform and the People of Cuenca*, 1500-1650 THE LIBRARY OF IBERIAN RESOUCES ONLINE)

13-23 Our clavichords have four strings and are played with keys;
Os nossos cravos tem 4 cordas e tamjen-se polas teclas;

Those of Japan have a dozen strings and are played with wooden picks made for that. *Os de Japão tem 12 cordas e tanjem-nos com humas unhas de pao feitas pera isso.*

The European instrument is a proto-piano, of which there were many types before the huge modern piano came into being. The number of strings makes me want to call it a keyed-up dulcimer, because we have already been told it sounds sweet (17, above).

The Japanese *koto,* a long zither that looks like a crate for an alligator is played by both sexes, but despite the considerable strength needed to depress the strings (to vary the tension) and carry the instrument, it has traditionally been *the* instrument for proper young women to play (perhaps because, like a piano, it stays home?). In 18th century Edo, *senryu* joke about the *koto* as an instrument played and appreciated by such women. The *koto* comes with them when they get married, after which it grows cobwebs, for no husband has any interest in listening to them except when he is a captive audience, i.e. *too drunk to flee!* In that case, he may even use it for a *samisen,* that is to say:

girl thing / guy thing

i'll be damned!
a drunk in a blither dances
to a . . . zither!

baka na koto namayoi koto de odoru nari
([a] foolish thing: [a] drunk zither-to dance does/becomes)

Forgive the *color*, not in the original! I imagine the harp was similarly regarded in Europe. Yet, sweetness is not intrinsic to the instrument. As there are bluesmen who bounce bottles of beer on their macho pianos, there are *koto* players who really rock out. I have seen Korean women playing with incredibly powerful nail-picking (shellacked nails?) and click-striking (for lack of a better word) as one would send off a cockroach – jamming so ferociously they seemed to be fighting! – one smoking a cigarette all the while. But the general sweet tinkling (?) quality of the *koto* – the one that makes it the darling of the environmental=background music today – made it the instrument that least bothered Occidentals.   My favorite is the 1-string, for it is both easier and harder than playing anything else. There were various sizes and types of *koto* with various numbers of strings, but they generally settled upon 13 by the time Japan was opened again, and Ms. Bacon describes it as follows:

..

an embryo piano, a horizontal sounding-board, some six feet long, upon which are stretched strings supported by ivory bridges. (B:JGW)

I would think that the fact that *each string had its own, extremely tall bridge* (which, to me, bear some resemblance to the Eiffel Tower!) would be worth a contrast, but let me stick to Frois's contrast. The *picks* he mentions are, in Japan, almost always used. Again, a whole contrast would be possible, for if *our picks are flat,* these *koto* "nails" or "talons" are *tubular* and fit completely over the last digit of the finger – the verb used (*hamaru*) is the same for putting on a ring – with the size sometimes adjusted for the user by pouring hot rosin inside which dries to fit (how I don't know). They stay on better than guitar picks, but still would fly off if played as freely as those Koreans played.

13-24   Among us, the blind are very pacific;
Antre nós os cegos são muito pacificos;

> In Japan, [they are] very pugnacious, carrying staffs and *wakizashi* [dagger/s], and are
> real paramours. *Em Japão muito brigozosos, trazem bastões e* vaquizaxis, *e são muito namorados.*

The blind in Japan have always worked as musicians, masseurs, pimps and money-lenders. In
their latter capacity, some numbered among the wealthiest individuals in Japan. In the Edo era, some
even bought – that is to say freed – high level courtesans, something that cost the equivalent of
millions of dollars today. And, as is true for the rich anywhere in the world, they were popular with
the women. The Portuguese (*namorados*) I translated as *"real paramours,"* – it could as easily have
been "real ladies men," real womanizers, or love-makers. Two YANAGIDARU *senryu* on these blind
men:

<table>
<tr><td align="center">not blind to beauty!</td><td align="center">you gotta hand it to him</td></tr>
<tr><td align="center">for women
no one has a better eye
than the head</td><td align="center">for women
no one has a better eye
than the blind-boss</td></tr>
</table>

(onna ni isso me no aru zatônobo)

The "head" is my make-do for "seat-head," or *leader of a troupe*, which was the lowest of the
four main ranks of one of the two main orders of the organized blind (but still, a *zatô* had the right to
sit in the highest spot if performing with sighted musicians).   In his capacity as a pimp, the blindman
was regarded as an extraordinary judge of what we might call woman-flesh.

the mistress
of blind boss – skin value
over face value

(kengyô no mekake kao yori hada no koto)

The original mentions *kengyô,* a rank up from a *zatô* and, like zatô does not have the word
"blind" in it. What is a translator to do? These main ranks were further broken down into an absurdly
complex 16 ranks.   The order's history goes way back to ancient times, the Genji-Heikei wars.
Kaempfer writes at length about this. Alcock sums it up in a sentence: the "two sects of the blind . . .
[are] founded by two great celebrities of Japanese history – one the third son of a Mikado who wept
himself blind for the death of his mistress, and the other by a defeated general in the civil wars, who
tore out his eyes that he might not be provoked to take the life of a generous victor . . ."   With
organization came special privileges and monopolies. The organization is a complex pyramidal
"common-wealth" with "their General" residing in Miaco (Kyoto, the capital). The top officers have
the "power of life and death" over members, but "no person can be executed" without the approval of
"the Chief Justice of Miaco."   The two orders are quasi-religious, like the Buddhist sects, they
probably did not hesitate to skirmish in order to guard their turf in that rambunctious age when the
Jesuits arrived in Japan.

The *pugnacity* was also no lie. If the violence naturally arising from sect *vs.* sect was not
enough, the blind had a reputation for being sharply tempered and nursing a grudge. With all their
money and women to protect, those canes came in handy as cudgels, especially in the dark when they
were the only one who could "see" what was happening.

blind vengeance

in jealous rage
the head returns home
with bated cane

yaku zatô tsue o koroshite kaeru nari

The original is better, for the pun is double. In Japanese, to bate one's breath is not only to hold it to keep quiet, but idiomatically to "kill" it.

           *   *   *

On the neighboring peninsula, too, the blind were not thought of as handicapped and a burden for others. They lacked the organization and did not share the same office they had in Japan, but they were nevertheless able to make a good living. In Korea, as we have seen, shamanism was big business – fortune-telling, exorcism and benediction all in one – and one of the two principle classes of Shaman was blind. Isabella Bishop:

> The *Pan-su* are blind sorcerers, and those parents are fortunate who have a blind son, for he is certain to be able to support them in their old age. (B:KHN)

So long as we are on it, in China, Cruz wrote that blind men were generally given work involving brute force, such as turning power-wheels for mills, while the women became prostitutes – as was often the case in Japan – who also were taught to play various musical instruments to increase their attractiveness and, thereby, earnings. (C:TDCC) He did not say that they studied massage, as was the case for many blind of both sexes in Japan. In one way or another, people generally worked in the Far East, rather than begging as was common in most of the world, including the West.

For fairness sake, I should point out that not *all* blind got respect in Japan. Blind singer-prostitutes, the *goze,* are usually *beaten* in *senryu.* Superstition said it was good luck to hit the *goze* one slept with!

~~~~~~

13-25 Noblemen in Europe sleep at night and play by day;
Os fidalgos em Europa dormen de noyte e folgão de dia;

> The Japanese noblemen sleep by day and have their parties and play at night. [1]
> *Os Japões fidalgos dormem de dia e tem suas festas e folguedos à noyte.*

An essay of the marvelous Sir Thomas Browne (1605-82), comes to mind, where he wrote that we should go to bed with and rise with the sun *as God intended,* for to do otherwise was "to play the part of our Antipodes." If the Far East is antipodal to us, as far as nobles go, he was wrong! From reading *The Tale of Genji,* I long knew that in ancient times, the noblemen used to play the roving Tom at night while poets sat still and viewed the moon; but I did not know the upper class had a *generally* nocturnal lifestyle and wondered if Frois might not be exaggerating, until I read a 1563 letter, where he gives a long description of what amounted to a friendly round-the-clock siege by the nobility of South Japan, who came –

each day to hear mass at the house at three o'clock at night: because it is the custom of these gentlemen [*senores*] to sleep very little at night; and they waited until four when father Cosme d' Torres came to give it . . . . And because, after being baptized they hadn't had the opportunity (for the time had been so short) to hear the mystery's of the mass and of the sacrament of the Eucharist, one night they were with brother Juan Fernandez from three to five . . . another time they called for him at midnight and remained with him until dawn, asking many questions about matters of faith, saying that he had to know them . . . to respond to the bonzes when they questioned them. (CARTAS)

That pretty much cinches it, at least for the Southern part of Japan. The Chinese nobility, likewise, were evidently great night-people. Cruz described great birthday parties which lasted

through the entire night, because all of these peoples live in obscurity without the knowledge of God (*Deus*), and, likewise, all their parties for all parts of India [the East Indies] and China are held at night. There is a great abundance of food and wine and they spend the whole night in eating and drinking and diverse playing with diverse [musical] instruments. (C:TCC in my translation, ch-45.)

One wonders if Cruz really believed his reason for Far Eastern people partying *at night,* or if he was just exercising his Christian wit. In a sense, the night was *bad.* As Golownin wrote, the Japanese did visit their "bagnios" at night: "The lovers of such places generally visit them from sunset to sunrise." And, even more to the night's discredit, it was a prime time for the competition, Buddhists, because the moon reflected the merciful Light of the Law and, rather than the sun, was identified with the it. Here is a haiku by Teitoku (age 16 in 1585) on what happens during the time of year when staying up late was, indeed, *de rigor* for any cultured gentlemen:

harvest dreams?

sowing the seeds
of everyman's noon nap
the fall moon

minabito-no hirune-no tane ya aki-no tsuki
(all-peoples' noon-nap-seed, 'tis: fall-moon)

Had the moon and moon-viewing not had the Buddhist connection, Frois might have written the following contrast about what must be the world's most innocent night-time entertainment:

..

In Europe, only farmers astronomers and calendar-makers pay much attention to the moon.
In Japan, the gentry vaza vaza [wazawaza*: on purpose] stay up late to watch and fete it.*

Actually, the large number of writings against sleeping in found in Europe suggest that "our" noblemen, even Iberians, did have a tendency to stay up late at night. The Augustinian Fray Luis de Leon's LA PERFECTA CASADA (the perfect bride/wife), published just two years before Frois' TRATADO, wrote that if nature sends us light it must be good for us to wake up "and this is not negated by the habit of those people whom the world now calls gentlemen, whose principle preoccupation is to live in order to rest and regale their bodies, sleeping in until mid-day." Perhaps the biggest contrast with Japan would, rather, be in the vehemence of our opposition to this practice thought by some to be "part of a gentleman's status," as opposed to the tolerance of the Japanese (with respect to nobles, not peasants!). De Leon makes it clear that the problem was not only what one did at night, but the damage done to body and mind by sleeping in –

for the discord in life arises and has its origin in an even greater discord which is to be found in the soul and which itself is also the cause and origin of many base and ugly discords. For the blood and humours of the body, excessively kindled and harmed by the heat of day and sleep, not only damage one's health but they also hideously affect and infect the heart.   And it is something worthy of admiration [i.e. of great surprise] that being in everything else great followers, or better still, great slaves of pleasure, these men forget their pleasure only in this matter and through the vice of sleeping miss out on what is most pleasurable in life, which is the morning. (L(J&L):LPC)

This passage is followed by a page on the pleasure to be found when one wakes up early. *It is no mere first worm, but what may well be the best description of the magical multi-sensed beauty of dawn ever written!*

1. *Play By Night.* In retrospect, I think it fair to Japanese to mention the greater humidity in the hot months as a factor. The 90% naked laborer could keep cool with his or her sweat, but the upper-class liked to go out *dressed* and the performers, likewise, were fully costumed. That would simply not have been possible 4-6 months per year in Japan. It might also be fair to give an indication of some of the things that happened in night in Iberia in the 16th century. When the city of Cuenca petitioned Charles V to order Ramírez and the corregidor to audit the municipal charity box's account books for the last twenty years in 1527. Ramírez charged that the sanctity of the diocese's churches and shrines (*ermitas*) was commonly violated; ermitas were the apparent scene of so many sins that Ramírez prohibited the foundation of any new sanctuaries. With the excuse of attending all-night vigils on certain holy days, many people would spend the night at ermitas, where the vigils disintegrated into feasting, dancing, singing of secular songs, adultery, and fornication. Corrupt priests would encourage these all-night vigils by agreeing to hold illegal predawn masses, for which they would be paid. (See: Sara T. Nalle *God in La Mancha: Religious Reform and the People of Cuenca, 1500-1650* THE LIBRARY OF IBERIAN RESOUCES ONLINE). But, to be fair to Frois, Spain may have pretty much cleaned up its act by 1585.

13-26 In Europe, we do not eat and drink during soirees, plays and tragedies.
Em Europa em serões, autos e tragedias não se uza de comer e beber;

In Japan, these are never put on without wine and *sakana* [appetizers].
Em Japão nenhuma couza destas se faz sem vinho e sacana.

True, Matsuda and Jorissen admit, no eating and drinking took place in the chapels and monasteries often used for these events in the West, but there were light acts called *entre-mezes* (intermezzos) and *momos* (mummery/miming – "strange body movement" write M&J in Japanese) sandwiched into banquettes or balls, so drama and food were not complete strangers.

13-27 Among us, the leaps of the *fulia* [joyful dancing][1] and tambourines [thrown] into the air are customary; *Antré nós os saltos nas fulias e pandeiros pera o ar hé custume;*

They are very astounded by it, and think it mad and barbaric.
Elles o estranhão muito e o tem em nós por doudice e barbaria.

The grammar for "our" side is confusing. Basques *did* throw tambourines according to Schütte and the French translators, so I went that way, but the Japanese translators have people leaping into the air to the little belled drums (tambourines) of the *fulia*. There is a touch of unintended irony implicit in the name of the dance which is one with "folly."

As Miguel=Valignano pointed out in *De Missione*, Japanese dancers jumped and whirled about to depict a deranged soul. Contented people stay still. To expand this further, it may be that the very idea of *jumping for joy* was foreign to the Japanese.[2]   Reading this contrast, one wonders who put on the show that astounded the Japanese. Did Japanese see Portuguese sailors dancing with each other? Or, did they try to teach it to Japanese? Or did Japanese see it in the Philippines? Or, did the Jesuits – who were, as we have seen, big on drama – ever leap into the air themselves?

1. *Translation.* A dance can not be translated. We can not call the *fulia (folia)* other names, even if the *jig, flamenco,* and the *polka* are all hot-blooded up-tempo dances. So it remains in the original Portuguese.

2. *Showing Joy.* What we do and do not do can be very strange – I wonder how many decades our late-20th century invention of *fist-pumping* as a sign of triumph and joy will remain, or whether the World is now, god save us, stuck with this obnoxious mannerism forever. (Since Hollywood imposes it on times where success/winning was expressed with open hands and magnanimous (sometimes tearful) expressions, is it not possible that other types of expression will be forgotten?) To be honest, I feel the clenched fist should have been left to protestors and not co-opted by athletes and then the general population , for it literally incorporates a hard, aggressive, and tense attitude toward life. When I see baby children learning to express joy by punching the air and grunting out a "Yes!" rather than waving their hands freely about and gurgling with delight, I worry for the future of the human race.

13-28 Among us, it would be ridiculous for a very noble man to ride bareback without a barrette.
Antré nós yr hum fidalgo muito nobre a cavalo descalso e sem barrete seria doudice;

In Japan, it is an ordinary custom to go about in this manner.
Em Japão hé custume ordinario andarem desta maneira.

Sweet Jesus! Bareback and hatless! Oh, the scandal of it! This contrast, which ought to have been in the Horse chapter was apparently concocted to balance those leaps that made us look ridiculous to the Japanese. *Look,* says Frois, *you do things that look ridiculous to us, too!* (Maybe he envisions a mixed class of European and Japanese students for his *Tratado*?).

The higher the class of the man, the better his equestrian outfit. That would generally be true in Japan, too. But, Japanese had a second concept of quality experience. Is there not something to be said for the feel of a bare back between ones thighs and the air whipping over one's shaven pate? Like those bare wooden cups, I find this practice of the noblest of the nobles proof that Japanese – as a culture if not as individuals – appreciated the pricelessness of primal experience. For all their complex culture, their layered civilization, the awareness that *nothing can beat the bare basics* managed to survive.

13-29   In Europe, plowing is done by one man with a pair of oxen;
Em Europa anda lavrando hum homem com hum par de bois;

In Japan, one ox with two men do the plowing.
Em Japão pera lavrar vai hum só boy com dous houmens.

No drama or dance here, either. Evidently, after proceeding from *foolish in dance* to *foolish with horse*, Frois recalled the oxen in the Horse chapter.   In the Japanese case, one of the men might lead the ox (for the nose ring worked and they had no goad), but I doubt it was done that way all of the time.

endnote **XIII**

Plays

Not all entertainment in a society is formal, i.e. performing expected things in the proper places and times. Take the following happening (?) recorded by Edward Morse:

> An illustration of the tolerance of the people and the good manners of the children is shown in the fact that no matter how grotesque or odd some of the people appear in dress, no one shouts at them, laughs at them, or disturbs them in any way. I saw a man wearing for a hat the carapace of the gigantic Japanese crab. This is an enormous crab found in the seas of Japan, whose body measures a foot or more in length and whose claws stretch on each side four or five feet. Many looked at this man as he passed and smiled. It was certainly an odd thing to wear up[on the head when most of the people go bareheaded. (M:JDD)

After seeing the illustrations of the street vendors of Edo with chili-pepper salesmen sporting red chili-pepper dress and a four foot chili-pepper sack, bear-fat unguent salesmen looking out of the mouth of a bear mask, a Chinese-style candy seller riding a fake horse, a Japanese-style candy vender who is dressed like a fox and dances if you purchase anything, a dumpling seller wearing a boat with a boat-nun doll in it (who sold dumplings), a beggar dressed as a ghost with a fake knife through his throat, etc., after seeing all that (as Mitani Kazuma draws them, based on old prints and paintings in 江戸商売図絵), we realize that Japan was once a truly dramatic place to live. Unlike Europe – or the USA of my youth (1950's, early 60's) – eccentric behavior did not give others the excuse to throw things at you or beat you up (Paradoxical as it may seem, the USA did not grow up and learn to tolerate difference until the late 1960's, a time wrongly remembered as juvenile. *Think about it.* The flower-child was more mature than the adult who *demanded* crew-cuts, etc.).

歌　　　　舞　　　　伎

..
That was, however, post-Seclusion Edo. I do not know if such diversity, creativity, and the civilized forbearance that made it possible existed in Frois's time. But I cannot help suspecting Frois has short-changed us a bit in the low-culture department. While he was good at observing *little* things, such as which fingers are used for picking noses, or the respective sides on which we sniff melons, he missed many *low* things, perhaps because he had little interest in the low life, or even if he did, felt it best not to reveal it. He mentions the chants and chanties of the watermen, but that is about it. Popular entertainment receives short thrift. This is too bad because Frois might have helped shed light on the beginning of *kabuki* and the institution called *geisha* on the one hand, and the Japanese equivalent to our balladeers on the other. In respect to contrast 13-4, respecting the presence or lack of innovation, Cooper opines:

> As regards the traditional Japanese theatre, Frois' observation remains true to this day, for *Nô* and *Kabuki* dramas are still staged without any variation. Cocks makes several references to the latter, spelling the term indifferently *Cabicke, Caboki, Caboqui, Caboque* and *Cabuqui*; in one place he describes the *caboques* as "women plears, who danced and songe." (C:TCJ *my italics*)

And, I would add, *cabuks, cabokes* and, strangest of all *dansing beares!* (*Beares!?* OED was no help there! Why *beares*? Anyone?)   It is touching to read of Cocks' cordial relationship with the performers and his Japanese business associates:

> I gaue the *cabukis* 1 bar *coban* [an oblong coin, the perfect shape for passing from one hand to another!] & two *ichibos* [a unit] of gould. Shezero the *caboke* sent me a Japon cap, & I gaue her that brought it 5 *mas* 4 *condrin,* paid p'r Goresano.

> And we had the *cabokis* after supp'r ashre, whoe plaid and dansed till after midnight & then went away, being 8 women, & 6 or 7 men.

> I gaue the *caboque* Shezero an *ichibe* & a silk *catabra,* and sent the mr. of them a bar *coban.*

> The *cabokes* came out to sea after vs in a boate brought a banket. So I gaue them a bar of *coban* to make a banket at their retorne to Edo . . .

> The China Capt. envited both vs & the Hollanders to dyner this day, where we had greate cheare w'th dansing beares.

> I sent ij *taies* to the dansing beares, in small plate, they coming to our garden w'th a banket when we planted our trees.

> Skidayen Dono & his consortes had the feast of Baccus for their junk this day, dansing thorow the streetes w'th *caboques,* or women players, & entred into our Eng'sh howse in that order, most of their heades being hevier than their heeles, that they could not find way hom w'thout leading. (some examples chosen at random from Cocks 1616/7 and 1620/1)

The problem is the relationship, if any, between these entertainers, who seem the forerunners of popular entertainers, i.e., geisha, and Kabuki which, together with Noh, has come to represent Japanese drama. The first recognized Kabuki *performance* took place, according to the OJD, in 1603, when a certain *miko,* or shrine maiden from an Izumo (Shinto) temple danced a sutra in Kyoto. Her dancing – her imitators? – became very popular and the authorities, fearing a deleterious effect on the public morals, forbade it and the *wakashû-kabuki* ,performed by *bishonen,* or "beautiful youth" quickly replaced the women and in twenty or thirty years, that, too, was forbidden and kabuki actors were restricted to grown men. By the end of the 17th century, it rivaled Noh as major theatre. Here is a take on female kabuki by Edo expert Tanaka Yûko.

> In performances called *onna* (female) *kabuki*, 50 or 60 girls around 16 years of age would dance about the stage waving the sleeves and hems of magnificent kimono (usually made from Chinese silk) perfumed with aloes (generally imported from Vietnam). Each time they waved their sleeves the exotic scent wafted down from the stage. The *yûjo* [lit. "play-women," later the name for women of the pleasure quarters] would sit on stools plucking their shamisen, whose sound commingled with that of drums and flutes, while the dancers sang, "We are but visitors to this dream of a floating world." It was said that people in the audience were so transported that they would declare that the world is an illusion and profess their indifference to wealth, property, and life itself.

> The impact of these performers on the large crowds that congregated in populous urban centers doubtless dwarfed anything produced by earlier itinerant entertainers. Indeed, it seems that these performances turned Kyoto's Rokujô-Misujimachi and Edo's early pleasure district into crucibles crackling with the combined energy of dance, music, and sensuality, and the shogunate regarded this as a threat to the social order. In 1612, the government arrested and executed 300 *kabukimono*. (TANAKA Yûko Vol. 30, No. 6, December 2003 *Japan Echo* "Development of the Geisha Tradition.")

There is no way that Cocks was talking about kabuki drama as we now know it; and I find it impossible to believe that all those banquette-bearing and obviously delightful *kabokes* described by

Cocks derived from the one performer in fifteen years or even from those large performances – or did the crackdown mentioned in Tanaka's article do to the performers what the crack-down in New Orleans did to jazz: *spread it around the country?*   Tanaka does make one thing clear. The word connected with entertainment that "we" all think we know today, *geisha,* is a very recent invention:

> During the Edo period [1603-1867] . . . scholars of Confucianism, Shintô, poetry, and astronomy, as well as doctors (including surgeons and dentists), were all known at times as *geisha* [art/skill-person]. Masters of such martial skills as sword fighting, archery, equestrianism, gunnery, spear throwing, horse training, and blade testing were called *bugeisha, bu* meaning "military." And in the Meiji era (1868–1912), *geisha* was occasionally used in reference to teachers of foreign languages. . . . In the world of *kabuki, geisha* referred to the dancers, likewise distinguished from the *yakusha* [actors]. In time, the word *geisha* came to be used to refer to people who entertain others not on the stage but in private quarters, and it is this meaning that fits most closely with the geisha with whom we are familiar today. (Ibid – my brackets and italics)

Yet, the *kabuks* of Cocks seem remarkably like our (?) geisha! I feel we are talking about a country with plentiful *popular* entertainment with multiple roots that may be summed up in anything smaller than a large book. Pierre François Souyri mentions puppeteers (*kugutsu*), jugglers and other

> itinerant artists who went from inn to inn. The performers' wives (*kugutsume*) sang *imayô* – improvised songs, appreciated both at court and by the lower classes – and danced wearing colorful, shimmering costumes . . . The *kugutsume* were also prostitutes. Ôe no Masafusa, a great scholar of the late eleventh century, describes these characters . . . as people "who ignored the state, did not fear the provincial administrators, did not pay rents, and lived for pleasure." (S(R):WTU).

There is a gypsy, or "traveler" feeling here. The *kugutsume* are mentioned again in a description of "dancers and courtesans" a couple centuries later, together with *asobime,* who performed on water," enticing travelers entering port by boat with "songs and colorful clothes . . . comparable it was said to that of young women of the aristocracy," and courtesans called *shirabyôshi* (who are, I might add, often encountered in poetry) who "went to nobles' manors to sing and dance" or could be sent for. (Ibid) Judging from the before and after, all of these, and more, were around *in one form or another* in 1585.

傀　　　偶　　　女

The lack of attention to popular music was not due to Frois's individual bias. He shared the collective bias of the Haughty Culture (if you will pardon a pun that is true) East and West. Until very recently, one can find book after book on music which takes it for granted that *Music* is classical in much the same way that one can find many books on *Religion* that are actually about a single example, Christianity. I do not know how much of the following is Mrs. Busk and how much the Dutchman Meylan, but this passage is very revealing:

> The Japanese are passionately fond of music; and their traditions assign it a divine origin. According to this tradition, the goddess of the sun, upon a certain time, in resentment at the violence of an ill-disposed brother, retired into a cave, leaving the universe in utter confusion and darkness, and music was invented by the gods to lure her forth from her retreat. But though the presence of daylight is indubitable evidence that the device succeeded, Japanese music seems but poorly to correspond with the high purpose of its birth. It has indeed produced a variety of instruments . . . but the Japanese have no idea of harmony . . . (B:MCJ:1845)

To the Western mind, music means – or, rather *meant*, for we have seen a bit of change in the latter half of the 20th century – beautiful harmony which evokes divinity. Forgetting the problem of harmony, it needs to be pointed out that the very idea of an original "high purpose" juxtaposed *against* the reality of a low-brow music would amuse Japanese, for the common understanding is that the Goddess Amenouzumenomikoto, commonly known as Amenouzume coated her face white (the popular etymology for the word "interesting" – *omoshiroi,* or face-white – in Japanese) *and did a striptease* to that music which caused such a commotion among the delighted gods that the Sun-Goddess opened the boulder to see what was happening at which time the "Strong-arm-god" stuck his hand in and kept the cave entrance open. I leave the matter of whether such a beginning is of *high* or *low* purpose to the reader. Suffice it to say that "we" (literary Occidentals) have had a weird, restrictive idea about the nature of music that shared more with Confucian idealism than with Japanese reality.

逆   様   舞

It is important not to judge a culture on its high forms of art alone. Despite those repeated performances of the same Noh dramas (13-4), and the same tendency to canonize seen in *Kabuki,* lower art kept changing. Look what Kaempfer writes about the "processions and shews" in a Nagasaki festival slightly over a 100 years post-TRATADO, *i.e.,* in the Tokugawa era that was, until the research, or rather rethinking, of Tanaka Yuko and others in the 1970's and 80's, supposed to be lacking in originality:

> The spectacles, machines, songs and dances must be new every year, and it would be thought beneath the dignity and majesty of that great God [?], if repeating, upon occasion, the same story over again, they did not at least dress it up after a new fashion. (K(S):HOJ)

The Japanese have two sides. The traditional, unchanging side is easier to spot. It is found in the more formal arts, the arts foreigners, even Jesuits in the 16th century, usually go to see because they are what the upper-class appreciates, and because they are officially *Japanese culture*. But, the Japanese *also* have a tradition of change, of improvisation. That, *too*, is their culture. It holds true for their skits (see the Wooden Hands: 6-1n), for their dance and for their music. Mrs. Busk's 1845 book includes this summation of Meylan:

> . . . the girl must be lowborn and lowbred indeed who cannot accompany her own singing upon the *syamsie* [*shamisen*]. And this music is often *extempore*, as there is scarcely ever a party of young ladies together in which there is not some one of them capable of *improvising* a song. (B:MCJ)

Actually, the presence of a limited number of patterns which the performer knows inside and out is what *permits* such artistic freedom. It is what makes the blues work so well. So long as you come back and touch base on those blues notes, there is nothing you cannot do. With a more diverse form (such as rock, which is closer to classical music because it has many quite different melodies), such *play* is impossible. *That* is the paradox of music and, for that matter, all art. Be that as it may, look how a couple *geisha* and their *maiko* (*geisha* in training) – after putting on the usual "fan dance" and "cherry-blossom dance" and "autumn dance" have been dutifully performed – improvised in order to express their surprise at the topsy-turvy West in 1881 (Note: That is four years before Gilbert and Sullivan create their mankind that "seems to be walking on its head"). I love the story so much, that the print for the quote will be *enlarged* rather than reduced:

The closing dance – a veritable jig, with whirls and jumps, rapid hand-clapping, and chanting by the maiko [young apprentice geisha] – ended in the dancers suddenly throwing themselves forward on their hands and standing on their heads, their feet against the screens.

"That is what we call the foreign dance: it is in foreign style, you know. You like it?" asked the interpreter on behalf of our guests; and our danna san [host, in this case] had the temerity to answer that it was very well done, but that it was now going out of fashion in America." (Eliza Skidmore: (S:JDJ))

The *danna-san* [host] has diplomatically pretended not to have appreciated the Japanese trying to dance Western style. (I cannot tell if Skidmore is being tongue-in-cheek on this or didn't really get it – if you recall (13-27), such jumping did not exist in Japanese music). He knew a spoof when he saw one and provided the perfect witty response (I wish I knew who he or she was!). One which, if it were properly translated, doubtless made the performers howl with laughter (once they've had a bit to drink, Japanese howl with the rest of us) ! Good Japanese parties, especially ones attended by geisha, are more than anything else, occasions for the exchange of wit. And, unlike "our" cocktail parties, you need not be on your feet.

雅　　　　　　楽　　　　　　話

What would be the ultimate expression of instrumental topsy-turvy? Chamberlain gives it, with the possibly facetious qualification that "this is but one among many instances of the strange vagaries of the Japanese musical art." Let me enlarge, again.

The perfection of Japanese classical music may be heard at Tôkyô from the Band of Court Musicians attached to the Bureau of Rites. Having said that it may be heard, we hasten to add that it cannot be heard often by ordinary mortals. The easiest way to get a hearing of it is to attend one of the concerts given by the Musical Society of Japan . . . at which the Court Musicians occasionally perform. A more curious ceremony still is the performance by these same musicians, at certain Shintô festivals, of a *silent* concert. Both stringed and wind instruments are used in this concert; but it is held that the sanctity of the occasion would be profaned, were any sound to fall on unworthy ears. Therefore, though all the motions of playing are gone through, no strains are actually emitted!

A footnote to the 1905 edition of *Things Japanese*:

The existence of these "silent concerts" was set in doubt by a critic of the first edition of this work. Never heard, or rather seen, by ourselves, we describe them on the authority of Mr. Isawa, who, in a private communication on the subject, reminds us that such esoteric mysteries would not be willingly alluded to by their old-fashioned possessors, least of all in reply to the scientific enquiries of a foreigner, and that the very explanations given – supposing any to be given – would probably be couched in ambiguous language . . .

XIV

OF D̲IVERSE̲ *AND EXTRAORDINARY THINGS THAT WOULD*

de algumas couzas diversas e extraordinarias que se não podem bem reduzir aos capitolos praecedentes

NOT FIT WELL IN THE PREVIOUS CHAPTERS

~~~~~~

14-1 We strike the fire with our right hand and hold the flint in the left;
Nós ferimos o fogo com a mão dereita tendo a pederneira na esqerda;

They strike with the left hand and hold the flint with the right.
Elles o ferem com a esqerda temdo a pederneira na dereita.

The way Frois puts it, "our" way is natural, for it is easier for right-handed people to strike with that hand. Knowing that even samurai under 40 needed a license (*hiuchi-bukuro-gomen*) to carry fire-making paraphernalia in Frois's time and thinking that suggested fire outside of the hearth was something more formal (?) than we might imagine, I guessed there might be a logical, i.e. historical, or even metaphysical explanation[1] for this seeming left-handedness. As it turns out, Frois was, strictly speaking, *half*-wrong. Japanese did indeed usually hold the flint with their right hand. But, they also struck *with* it. The other hand held a blackboard eraser-shaped piece of wood with a runner of metal (a piece of a *sickle* = *kama* = *blade* from a region of Japan I forget the name of was thought the best) embedded in it. Since this "striker" was larger and heavier than the flint, the flint, or firestone, did the striking. *Frois pulls a fast one by defining the striking hand as the one that does not hold the flint!*[2]

The reason I wrote "usually" is because Japanese *also* held the flint in the *left* hand and struck with the right. They did this when they held a bit of inflammable cotton down with their thumb on a stone with a convex side while they struck the edge with the blade of the striking device. In this case, it makes sense to keep the stone still so the sparks would not be wasted in the air. More commonly, however, the "striking" device with the metal blade was held vertically over a nest of inflammable material (wood shavings, cotton or whatever) and *the stone held in the right hand* struck downwards to shoot the sparks along the metal blade and down into the nest. This same method of spark-throwing, called *kiribi* (cutting/separate/start-fire/s), was also used for healing, exorcism and, in Edo at least, for charming departures. In that case, however, the device with the metal blade was held up *horizontally* by the left hand and the stone struck out along the blade to throw the sparks out in front like a subtle flame-thrower. In the case of the send-offs, the sparks were supposed to shoot over the right shoulder of the departing party.[3]

1. *Metaphysical Reasons.* For example, in the RESOLUER (1635), the advisor to the French King explains that a lightning bolt is pictured held in the left hand because it is a gift from God's right hand. (D:R) Since I never found such a metaphysical reason for what Frois described, I kept searching until I found the real one. **2. *Frois Might Be Right.*** If things changed later and Frois was right. I would be delighted to be proved wrong.

3. *Sparks for Good Luck.* According to a website run by someone who sells these devices, spark-throwing had the crisp feeling Edoites went for. Also, he claims that craftsmen, story-tellers and performers who value tradition and, politicians, sumo-wrestlers and hostesses(?)whose work involves a degree of risk still appreciate such a send-off. (I was going to look it up again but forgot. Google 火打ち＋切火＋鎌& you'll find it.)

14-2   We show much emotion on losing our fortune or when our houses burn down;
Antre nós se mostra muito sentimento da perda da fazenda e qeima das cazas;

The Japanese suffer all of this appearing to take it very lightly.
Os Jappões no exterior passão por tudo isto muito levemente.

While the stoicism we call Spartan and the fatalism we call Medieval were, and still are to a lesser degree, embodied by the Japanese, *they* consider *themselves* emotional or "wet" compared to "dry" and rational Western people. By specifying *no exterior,* or, "on the outside," Frois did not confuse the calm expressions of the Japanese with whatever feeling lay within. That was wise, for psycho-philosophically speaking, an argument could be made (and I have read it made for Swedes, somewhere) that strong emotions are, by definition, repressed; they require a pressure-cooker to build up steam, so that "we" (the excitable South European) have the weaker emotions. Be that as it may, the same thing Frois observed has been observed over and over. Heuskin, translator and secretary for the first American Ambassador ("Consul-General") to Japan, shortly after their arrival to Japan in 1856:

> A frightful hurricane laid waste the coast of Japan. All the junks in the Bay were cast against the shore. Almost a third of the town of Shimoda was destroyed. When the next morning, I sighted the destruction of the night, the masts scattered on the beach, the debris of ships and houses, I was astonished by the behavior of the Japanese. Not a cry was heard. Despair? What! Not even sorrow was visible on their faces. On the contrary, they seemed quite indifferent to the typhoon and everyone was already busy repairing the damage caused by the tempest. (H:JJ:10/21)

The same thing was said more recently about Japanese in the aftermath of the Kobe earthquake. And the question that arises – if one is honest and dares to ask such questions – is *who is acting more naturally, us or them?* Is it right to marvel over how they control their emotions – or, in Montanus' opinion, are born with a more "magnanimous [meaning large enough not to worry about things] Soul?" Is it not possible that *they* are behaving in a more logical and, biologically speaking, *fit* fashion than we are and that our lack of self-control is, rather, the odd thing? *What good does it do to cry over spilt milk?* What makes our hysterionics *seem* so natural to us that we never point it out? I can think of several possibilities. *First*, we never outgrow our childhood temper tantrums (see 14-57) so it feels right.   *Second*, we are inward-looking so it is all we know (as noted already, we held out our open palms in a relaxed manner when we won anything only 50 years ago, but now, as uniformly as robots, pump tightly clenched fists and think it is as natural as breathing!). And, *third*, we place excessive value on material things. So saying,[2] I *can* understand that Japanese coolness might be mistaken for a lack of human sensibilities. It might be instructive to see where Japanese *do* get visibly emotional. Morse mentions a "story-teller" who –

> partly recites and partly sings his story, accompanied by another performer who plays the samisen, keeping up an extraordinary vocal accompaniment with curious guttural sounds, short notes, high squeaks, even sobbing sounds and astonishing ejaculations appropriate to the parts depicted in the story. . . . The samisen, too, is made to form an important auxiliary, for all kinds of sounds are evoked from it – crescendo, sobs, abrupt notes and weird notes – by running the fingers up and down the string while vibrating it.

This sounds like a blues guitar and depicts a point overlooked in the last chapter. *Our lute plays various melodies clearly and very well; Their samisen is not much on melody but excels at imitating various noises.* But my point here is to convey to the reader what Morse said about *the effect* of that recitation and noise-making:

Strange as it may seem, people are affected to tears by pathetic recitals in this style.

So Japanese *can* lament in public, provided the lamentation *is not for themselves*. Westerners find it hard to imagine a people so (apparently) hardened to personal misfortune, *yet* not at all hard! Elsewhere, Morse mentions this very paradox. After a fire burned down an entire block, he stopped to sketch and noticed –

> The quiet way in which the sufferers of these calamities take their misfortunes is interesting; not a face that is not amiable and smiling. It is curious to see women cry at theatres and yet be so stoical . . . (M:JDD)

I cannot resist a *Faux Frois:*

We are quick to lament for ourselves, our families and our friends;
They don't lament for themselves or their own, but cry readily for fictional characters.

Perhaps the most charming comments on Japanese stoicism ever made are in Alfred Fowler's THE CURIOUSITIES OF KISSING (1905). After declaring the "wonderful control of all emotions" the most distinctive emotion of the Japanese, acknowledging the fact that "deep volcanic fires glow beneath these stolid faces," and mentioning "suppression" over time (Social-Darwinism) to explain why "these genuine gentle folk, wonderful to relate, neither swear nor storm, neither curse nor kiss!" he offers a magnificent, and considering the subject of his book, magnanimous thought:

> Imagine, the saving in serenity in a society that scorns both cursing and kissing.

Another Western writer, not sharing his Victorian civilization's reverence for sweet, soft and shy repression, wrote the antipodal philosophy to everything traditional Japan stood for, without mentioning or even thinking about Japan:

> With wife or husband, you should never swallow your bile. It makes you go all wrong inside. Always let fly, tooth and nail, and never repent, no matter what sort of figure you make. (D.H. Lawrence: FANTASIA OF THE UNCONSCIOUS)

He, too, is partly right. He is right for most of "us," in most situations. But, he is wrong from a societal viewpoint, not because of social good gained by holding back, but because practice at taking things calmly over the years can actually make you calm so there is not that much bile to have to swallow. For this reason, I believe that the difference Frois mentioned was *not* only exterior.

1. Translation: A smoother translation might have been "pass through all this with little outward expression," but I wanted to try to keep the positive *muito levamente*. I almost translated it "very blithely," but chickened out.

2. Saying So. I am afraid I come down hard on "us" more often than on "them". When I write *in Japan*, I tend to defend "us" and take the air out of Japanese sails. I prefer to move readers to self-reflection than to self-celebration.

~~~~~~

14-3   With our houses, when there is a fire, people rush in with water and dismantle neighboring houses; *As nossas cazas quando se qeimão acoden-lhe com agoa e com desfazer as cazas dos vizinhos;*

> Japanese climb up on other roofs and fanning with winnows, shout to the wind to go away. *Os Japões poem-se nos outros telhados a abanar com supis e gritão ao vento que se vá.*

This is a fascinating contrast. One even wonders if the might have had a particular charmed chant. Okada, however, suggests Frois may have been misled by paintings of large fan-like devices used to *block* flying sparks. I would add that the things he mentions people doing for "our" houses were *also* done by Japanese. If anything, Japanese have long been the world-leaders at *deconstruction*.

A 100 years after Frois, Kaempfer mentioned that fighting a fire that had already consumed several houses "they know no better remedy at present, but to pull down some of the neighboring houses." (K:HOJ) Indeed, removing fuel was *the main method* of fire-fighting in Japan from time immemorial. Morse, who first found the weak Japanese water-pumps ridiculous and thought Western methods of fire-fighting better, changed his mind when he became more familiar with the realities of fire spreading between crowded tinder boxes. He wrote that one reason Japanese houses came apart so easily was to enable them to be rapidly demolished in the path of a conflagration – a new angle on the architecture – and, as you will see, suggested a better contrast for Frois respecting the use of water:

> Mats, screen-partitions, and even board ceilings can be quickly packed up and carried away. The roof is rapidly denuded of its tiles and boards, and the skeleton framework left makes but slow fuel for the flames. The efforts of the firemen in checking the progress of the conflagration consist mainly in tearing down these adjustable structures; and in this connection it may be interesting to record the curious fact that oftentimes at a fire the streams are turned, not upon the flames, but upon the men engaged in tearing down the building! (M:JH&S)

Kaempfer also mentioned something Morse, for all his interest in architecture, does not.

> Almost every house hath a place under the roof, or upon it, where they constantly keep a tub full of water, with a couple maps [blueprints to help with deconstruction or rooms of a large mansion?], which may be easily come at, even without the house, by the help of ladders. (K(S):HOJ)

But, despite these proto-fire-extinguishers and the quick disassembly, fires on dry, windy winter days were often unstoppable. The worst, in 1657, destroyed half of Edo and killed over 100,000 people. Not surprisingly, Japanese had fire on the mind. According to Chamberlain,

> so completely did this destructive agency establish itself as a national institution that a whole vocabulary grew up to express every shade of meaning in matters fiery. The Japanese language has special terms for an *incendiary fire*, an *accidental fire*, *fire starting from one's own house*, a *fire caught from next door*, a *fire which one shares with others*, a *fire which is burning to an end*, the *flame of a fire, anything* – for instance, a brazier – *from which a fire may arise*, the *side from which to attack a fire* in order to extinguish it, a *visit of condolence after a fire*, and so on. We have not given half. (*italics* mine C:TJ)

I have scared a landlord out of her wits by mentioning how much I like *fires* – a neighbor was always burning trash out in front and I too did it – *by using the wrong term*. The dictionary said *kaji* was a "fire," how was I to know it only means "a fire that burns up a house"? I should have used a different word altogether, *takibi*. Chamberlain was not exaggerating when he said "we have not given half." These two simple terms were not among the ones he mentions! [1]

---

1. Fire Terms   One of mine was part of one of Chamberlain's which he provided as follows: *tsuke-bi, soso-bi, jikwa, morai-bi, ruisho, shita-bi, hinote, hinomoto, keshi-kushi, kwajimimai. Sosobi* should be *sosôbi*, lest it be mistaken for a fire within a woman's private parts (Just kidding, for that is what *soso* would mean) and the *kwa* is written *ka* today. My favorites, not here, are *umoribi*, the buried fire of a hitachi, the *hi* of which is fire, and *hanabi*, literally "blossom-fire," which is to say *fireworks*.

~~~~~~

14-4   With us, to call someone a liar to his face would be a great libel;
    Antre nós hé suma injuria dizer a hum homem no rosto que mente;

> The Japanese laugh it off as gallantry.
>   *Os Japãos rin-se disso e o tem por galantaria.*

Japanese valued *face* as much as the Latin culture Frois knew best, but had a more sophisticated attitude toward *lying*. Tact, they knew, often requires it, and they greatly admired a good bluffer.[1] But it is possible Frois's contrast has a simpler explanation. Even today, Japanese lightly say *"uso-tsuki!"* or "liar!" (as a version of the more common *"uso!"* or "[it must be a] lie!") when someone tells them something interesting. We are talking about an idiom meaning *You don't say!* Imagine a modern day *Japanese* Frois:

> *With us, to call someone a "mother-fucker" to his face would be unthinkable;*
> *English-speakers do so and laugh it off as cool behavior.*

The above was my off-the-cuff response to Frois's contrast. But the issue is deeper than idiom. Judeo-Christians with their tendency to make oaths on their holy book or on the name of their God have an *exceptionally* black and white attitude toward lying. Over a 100 years after TRATADO, in a little town called Salem, a number of innocent people would be executed because they would not lie and admit they were witches (in which case they would have been spared!). Once, *the truth was more important to us than life* – now people will lie to avoid a traffic ticket. "Our" attitude was magnificent, but, when compared to the vast majority of human cultures, extremely rare, *i.e. abnormal.* On the other hand, Japanese lived in a society, which placed so high a premium on being secretive as to be an anomaly. Here is Valignano. After explaining how wonderfully self-controlled the Japanese were,

> On the other hand, they are the most false and treacherous people of any known in the world; for from childhood they are taught never to reveal their hearts, and they regard this as prudence and the contrary as folly, to such a degree that those who lightly reveal their mind are looked upon as nitwits, and are contemptuously termed single-hearted men. (1583? in C:TCJ)

Rodrigues was later to develop this line of thought further, writing that the Japanese had "three hearts: a false one in their mouths for all the world to see, another within their breasts only for their friends, and the third in the depths of their hearts, reserved for themselves alone and never manifested to anybody." (C:TCJ) Regardless of whether this secrecy derives from the negative influence of insecurity deriving from the long Warring Era, or the positive value given to hiding emotion as a sign of maturity, Japanese preferred to remain silent about many things. In this situation, not the liar but the person who insists upon asking the question that forces one to lie is resented. In other words, foreigners hear more lies from Japanese than Japanese do because they unwittingly force them to lie.

Shortly after the Opening of Japan in the mid-19th century, the upper classes of Japan took it upon themselves to represent their country, or hold foreigners at bay in one way or another. Wasn't it Beirce who described a diplomat as *someone who lies for his country*? Well, all of these Japanese were self-appointed diplomats, so what do you expect! Of course, this gave Japanese an even worse reputation for lying than the Jesuits gave them. The English Ambassador Alcock, who, as we have seen, was on the whole favorably impressed by Japan, raged on and on about Japanese lying, about how "it is evidently easier for them to make an incised wound into their stomach than to speak the truth;" and lamented "If anyone is in danger of forgetting how precious a bond of society this is, he has only to come to Japan where this is unknown. He took deep offense at an "official gentry" telling him: "I told you last month that such a thing had been done, and now I tell you the thing has not been done at all. I am an officer whose business it is to carry out the instructions I receive, and to say what I am told to say. What have I to do with its falsehood?" and, while admitting such lying was common at his (the far Western) side of the great Continent too, but with one difference: "it is not considered right to avow the fact, with the same cynical indifference to what may be thought either of it or the avowal." (A:COT) While I can understand Alcock's feelings, to my uninformed mind, the Japanese side comes off here as the more honest one, for honestly admitting to lies!

---

1. *A Good Bluffer.* The Japanese term *haragei* – literally "belly/guts/soul-art/performance" comes to mind. The dictionary explains it as acting on the strength of your personality. This basically means bluffing your way through a situation.   That is something that takes both gumption and skill. Put this way – *as a bluff* – I think most of us will be able to see how *lying* can have a gallant dimension!

14-5   We can not kill [someone] unless we have the authority and jurisdiction to do so;
Antre nós não mata senão quem tem alsada e juridisão pera isso;

In Japan, anyone can kill [someone] in their own house.
Em Japão cada hum pode matar em sua caza.

This was one of the first things Xavier observed about the Japanese in the same paragraph where he praised them as "white, courteous and highly civilized."

> Every man, whether a gentleman or a common fellow, has such control over his sons, servants and other members of his household, that he can kill any of them on the smallest pretext any time he likes, and seize their land or goods. They are absolute lords of their land, although the chiefest among them frequently league together for defense against their suzerains, who are thus often prevented from doing as they wish. [1] (in B:CCJ)

Frois puts it like this in a letter of 1565 Englished by Willis:

> No public prisons, no common gaols, no ordinary justices: privately each householder hath the hearing of matters at home in his own house, and the punishing of greater crimes that deserve death without delay. Thus usually the people is kept in awe and fear.

Xavier and Frois do not exaggerate. Valignano even more clearly specifies that "each man is so absolutely master of his house and those under his rule that he can cut or kill them *justly or unjustly* without having to answer to anyone."(my *italics* and trans from V(A):S). Alvarez-Taladriz, in a footnote to the SUMARIO says Valignano protested that power and that "among Christian gentry/lords (*senores*) the custom was greatly humanized. D. Augustin Konishi established three special judges in order to investigate the causes of deaths." That was marvelous. But, we should grant one thing to the Japanese. They, too, were killing with authority and jurisdiction.[2]   Carletti:

> The system of subjugation is such that each one can kill someone because of his position, without danger of being questioned why, and superiors have that authority over their vassals, masters over their servants and slaves. (C(W)MVAW)

Besides this right-to-kill, the feudal lord could banish his vassals. But, the authority was not absolute in the way Westerners might imagine. Here is Schütte, S.J., the man who rescued Frois's TRATADO from oblivion, on this vital point:

> On the other hand, in accordance with Japanese legal usage, he had no jurisdiction over the vassals of his feoffees[?]; these were subject to the orders of their immediate masters alone. (S:VMP)

In other words, there was a clear-cut chain of command which precluded the top authority from exercising his fiat over everyone. This was good if one's immediate master were the better man, but not when the higher-up was. One could appeal, but it would be likely cost your life even if the appeal won. Moreover, the appealer's family, and perhaps even his neighbors might have to die for the crime against hierarchy! (I speak of the Tokugawa era, but it probably held true to a degree at this time, too).

1. *Defense Against Their Suzerain?* At the time Xavier wrote, a large part of Japan was still controlled by the Ikkô and Hokke sects' self-government and quite aside from that, the peasants decided some things (as we will see in 14-7, below) *by themselves* whatever the Lords might say. As explained earlier, the peasants could threaten to vote with their feet and abandon their land.

This freedom was being throttled at the time Frois wrote for feudal autonomy was incompatible with the new increasingly centralized authority.

2. *Killing With Authority.* Recently, I found that a Spanish scholar (Gabriel Vázquez) responding to Valignano's question as to whether the Fathers should attempt to do something to change the ancestral custom (the lord's authority to execute subjects or to allow subjects to do revenge-killings against other subjects) in much the same way I did above. He suggests it would not be necessary to act when there was slim chance of succeeding and possible to think that "whoever kills in this manner is not doing so by individual authority but by that of the sovereign prince." (P(B):EPJ) As Jacques Proust notes, it is hard to say such a king existed. But Vázquez's larger point, that where custom gives authority, men have it, legally speaking, seems right. But all this is conceptual. It is hard to stay cool reading what Richard Cocks wrote in 1615. When he and his friends went to "a lodg the king had lent us" they

> "fownd a yong gerle of som 11 or 12 years of adge, dead on the back side under the walle, and doggs feeding on her, havinge eraten both her legges and her lower partes, with one hand, being newly kild but a littell before. It is thought som villen raqvished her

and after kild her, or else, being a slave, her master had kild her upon som displeasure and cast hert out to be eaten of dogges, an ordenary matter in these partes, the lives of all slaves being in the masters handes, to kill them when he will, without controle of any justice." (C:DORC)

But I would warn the reader to remember that Cocks is writing on conjecture and that in parts of Europe, where the upper class was not supposed to be a rule upon themselves, they may well have behaved far worse than they did in Japan. I cannot imagine anyone in Japan getting away with what the sadistic Hungarian noblewoman Elizabeth Báthory did, right at the time Frois wrote! Either the peasants en masse, or the authorities would not have allowed the abduction, torture and murder of hundreds of young women like that. Likewise, for the countless murders and torture of young boys by the Frenchman Gilles de Rais over a hundred years earlier.

14-6   We are terrified to kill a man, but think nothing of killing cows, chickens and dogs;
Antre nós hé espanto matar a hum homem, e nenhum matar vacas, galinhas ou cãis;

The Japanese are afraid to kill animals, but kill men as a matter of course.
Os Japõis se espantão de ver matar animais e matar homens hé couza corrente.

Valignano wrote the same (*sans* cows and chickens) about the Japanese in his 1583 SUMARIO:

> The fourth bad quality is that they are very cruel and easily kill, for they kill their subjects for slight things and think no more of cutting off a man's head or cutting a man in half from one end to another than they would a dog [in another rendition he writes *a pig*], so much so that many, if they can do it without danger to themselves, encountering a poor man may cut him through the middle just to see how his *katana* (sword) cuts. (my trans. from V(A):S&A)

Since Valignano did a magnificent job of explaining the *good* qualities of the Japanese, he had to do equally well with the *bad* qualities, too, if he didn't want to put the Christian world in a bad light and upset the censors in Rome. But after Maffei translated his observations into Latin and they became a hit among the intellectuals throughout Europe, Valignano either felt bad about slighting the Japanese or worried that he had created such a bad image that it would hurt support for the church in Japan, for in his LIBRO PRIMERO of 1601 (& in V(A):S&A note) he desperately tried to explain that Japanese were *not* cruel killers as might be inferred "from what Maffei wrote."

..

> even if it cannot be denied that the Japanese with the profession that makes all soldiers [meaning the samurai or *buke* that formed Japan's gentry] can kill with ease . . . they cannot be called cruel and barbaric for their killing is in battle or at the order and command of their lords, as executers of justice . . . And because they will not let themselves be killed without taking vengeance [first?] when they can, it naturally follows that many times they must use dissimilitude when killing. . . But, excepting killing done in time of war or at the command of their lord, they live very peacefully with very few killings and duels, thus, they are not naturally cruel. And, while there are cases where someone kills a poor man to test a sword, this is very rare, because there is great [i.e. capitol] punishment [*grandísima pena*] for homocide, or even for fighting with others, and [they] only test their swords on those who are dead by justice. (V:Libro in note (A):VS&A)

Now that is *much* more fair than his words in SUMARIO! While there were aberrations, such as the second Tokugawa Shogun Iyemitsu's nocturnal sword-testing expeditions (years after LIBRO), the rules against dueling strengthened as Japan unified, a process already underway in Frois and Valignano's time, so that within decades, *just drawing a sword* in town was what we now would call a felony, and might get the *bushi* executed! (Many students of history in Japan are rightly incensed by the ridiculous amount of swordplay at the drop of a hat shown on television Easterns[1]). Not that any of this mattered in Europe, where Montanus in 1670, borrowing from Valignano's earlier work, wrote of how "sometimes, having no Quarrel, in a meer Frolick, they [Japanese] will try whether the Edges of their Blades be so tender, as to be bated, or turn upon one anothers Heads."

If one didn't mess in politics and were lucky enough not to be in a war, Japan was a safe place even then, on the tail of the Warring Era. Valignano continued to qualify himself, or rather, disavow his own *hard view* of Japan. *Harakiri* was to save the lives of their family, and not out of an outlandish cruelty so fantastic as to extend even to themselves (if the word had existed, it would have been *masochism*) as he had written earlier. Similarly, infanticide was not "even crueler" but only done by the poorest people because they thought it less cruel than letting them live in misery (Ricci, in China, facing the same was later to add that the idea was that the infants might be luckier in their next reincarnation: i.e. "Pythagorean"=Buddhist belief played a role in it (S:MPMR), and this was, after all, done by *our* gentile Romans. And speaking of Romans, Valignano added, the supposedly cruel Japanese did not make mass games out of gladiatorial and marine combat where people were proud of killing each other in front of others, nor did Japanese rulers take pleasure in having men fight lions and tigers for the joy of seeing how many men they could kill. All in all, Valignano explained, the Japanese did have a barbarian government, as must be for a nation that is not Christian, but they were not *as* barbarian as "our" Romans!

..

> And, so I conclude, by the experience I have of this people, and having read many histories of mankind, that there cannot be found a people more moderate and modest in their actions and less bad and less cruel than the Japanese, nor more subject to reason and capable of receiving our Holy Law and to set forth on the road to the good and find salvation. (Libro 1601 or in V(A):S&A n)

Yet, all in all, killing was all too common in Japan at the time of TRATADO. Valignano may have exaggerated a bit when he wrote earlier that "since a man can kill anybody of his own household and wars are so frequent, it seems a majority of them perish by the sword" (PRINCIPIO? in B:CCJ), but if execution was included as "killing," then the number of men who had committed homicide was evidently high enough to interfere with Jesuit recruitment, for *perpetrasse homicidium* was a count against entry into the order. It was, then, not a matter of propaganda, but a practical problem taken up as part of the strategy for accommodation to the Japan of the Bungo Consultation. Schütte S.J.:

> Valignano suggested to the general that, in view of conditions prevailing in Japan, this impediment should be so interpreted as not to affect those who had slain someone before their conversion to Christianity, or who after conversion had done so at the command of their master, or who had put to death one of their own servants in accord with the existing law [i.e., in accordance with justice and therefore justifiable under natural law]. ((My comment in brackets) S(C):VMP)

Nihonjinron (books on Japaneseness) written by Japanese intellectuals in the 1970's and 80's usually attributed the Japanese reluctance to kill animals (which includes not putting their dogs to sleep) to their lack of experience with livestock, not being part of a Christian culture where God gave man the right to play God with other animals, Buddhist spare-all-life faith, Shinto fear of pollution, or being a particularly peaceful farming people who simply cannot stomach the sight of blood. This also was, conversely, used to explain away massacres in World War II. Namely, Japanese soldiers went berserk because killing was so far from their nature, unlike those calloused Westerners who could easily enslave and kill people in cold blood *because* of their long experience with livestock and its extension, slavery. These intellectuals ignore the relative cheapness of human life for hundreds of years preceding and following Frois's stay and preferred to point out a 300 year period earlier in Japanese history (the Heian era (794-1185)) where there was no capital punishment and running people out of town and exiling them was considered bad enough). Incredibly, they forget the reality of hundreds of years of publicly displayed bodies and heads. They even forget the graphic scenes of killing and suicide in Japanese drama which astounded 19th century European visitors and shown the Japanese were far from delicate when it comes to gore.

> . . . the wonderful endurance of the hacked victims, and the streams of red paint and red silk ravellings that ooze forth delight the audiences, who shout and shriek their "*Ya! Ya!*" and "*Yeh! Yeh!*" (S:JDIJ)

> The play itself was a little too gory to suit our present taste, as there were two suicides and three murders performed upon the stage, with every ghastly detail of blood, muscular contortion, death rattle, and final rigidity given in the most carefully worked out and realistic manner. (B:AJI)

And that same sentiment (?) was to give birth to squirting blood (including sound effects!) splattering paper doors and partitions on TV Easterns, until they were cleaned up in the 1980's.

*   *   *

Although Buddhism, as have seen, does not ultimately determine precisely what can and cannot be killed, its emphasis on preserving *all* life as opposed to the anthropocentrism of the Judeo-Christian morality, no doubt played a role in creating the difference – or illusion of difference – behind this contrast, which was first noted by Frois in a charming letter about Nara (the old capitol when Kyoto (now the old capitol) was the capitol) in many ways identical to another letter by Gaspar Vilela dated that same year: 1565 (Either the two wrote from a common outline or one copied the other's and added and subtracted to fit his own taste. I do not know if it was a test of powers of observation and writing abilities or insurance – similar letters sent by different routes so that at least one would get through).

Frois found "three things notable about Nara." First, "a pond as broad as a musket-shot filled with innumerable fish dedicated to the Pagoda [temple]." Anyone who ate one was said "to turn into a leper." The second, was "the great multitude of chickens on the grounds of the same Pagoda, which no one would kill, for it was taken to be the gravest sin, and when killing a man was not taken for a sin." And, the third was "the Pagoda deer who roamed the streets of the town like dogs in Spain." To bother them would be to incur a great fine and to kill one would be punished with death and "if one were found dead on the street unless it could be proven beyond doubt to have been sick, the entire block was razed and the stores lost." (Frois first showed his ability for listing here, for Vilela had the great Buddha statue listed with two of the above animals as the first of the three wonders, *and then* mentioned the third animal. The statue is indeed a bigger wonder than the chickens, but Frois showed better editorial sense in mentioning it separately and preserving one category, sacred animals.)

But if religion can help explain the Japanese tendency to refrain from killing most animals, our religion cannot even begin to explain why "we" were *so cruel* to them (the incredibly gory games played with live cats in much of Europe in Frois's time are sickening, worse than the behavior we often find in the boyhood of a serial murderer today). Yet, in the last half of the 20th century, "we" were more eager to protect animals than the Japanese, who killed off even their little bears (hardly grizzles) and cemented up their rivers (the last Japanese otter went extinct decades ago) in the interest of total public safety, and almost always kept their big dogs on a small chain around the clock. Only in respect to euthanasia do Japanese reflect their old selves. Many, if not most, are against putting down pets. On the other hand, "we" (at least Usanians), are so extremely callous about *human* life that we have allowed our murder rates to climb sky-high and have created a society that takes it for granted that a large part of our population (such as yours truly at this writing) cannot afford to see a doctor.

1. *Fighting and Easy Killing.* Exception to the Rule. The reader must be getting fed up with me contradicting myself from chapter to chapter page to page and even paragraph to paragraph. Let me, however, add that while the amount of killing, the locations and the parties involved in TV Easterns tends to grossly exaggerate the amount of gratuitous bloodshed, there were duels fought, generally in locations where a duel would not get anyone in trouble, and they could be to the death. In his recently published biography of Miyamoto Musashi, *The Lone Samurai*, William Scott Wilson depicts a world that for all of its spiritualization (my word for some of the description of the mastery of the way of the sword) bears no small resemblance to the world of the gun-fighter. We even have characters roaming Japan wearing ridiculous outfits bearing boasts about being "Greatest Martial Artist in the Land." To some of these guys, life, including their own, was indeed cheap. But, the aim of these fighter was generally to gain enough of a name to establish a school to train people who would uphold law and order for one or another lord, so . . . Come to think of it, some of "our" gun-fighters turned into marshals, too . . .

14-7   With us, one is not killed for stealing, unless it be above a certain sum;
Antre nós se não mata por furto senão até huma certa cantidade;

In Japan, one is killed no matter how trifling the sum.
Em Japão por qualquer couza ainda que seja muito peqena.

All accounts of Japan from Xavier, before Frois, to those of the newly-opened Japan of the 19th century mention the draconian laws against stealing in Japan. Frois, in a 1565 letter Englished by Willis: "They detest all kind of theft, whosoever is taken in that fault may be slain freely of anybody" (W:HOT). Carletti: "And in my time many suffered crucifixion on the slightest pretext, such as theft of a radish or some similar trifle . . . But they pay no more heed to the death of those who suffer in this way than we should to the killing of a fly" (C:TCJ). Cocks: "This day a Japon was roasted to death, runing rownd about a post, fyre being made about hym. The occation was for staling a small bark [boat] of littell or no vallue."(C:TCJ) The logic of this severity was two-fold. *First*, theft is theft. A Japanese proverb says something like "he who would steal a penny would steal a pound." And, *second*, the law had to be fair to all. That ruled out fines, for as Kaempfer wrote "if punishments could be bought off with money, it would be in the power of the rich to commit what crimes they please, a thing in their opinion, and in its very nature, absurd and inconsistent with reason and justice." Finally, Japanese disliked corporal punishment and jails . . .

Few, Westerners, however, mention the children hung for bread-crumbs that stain our own history. As Cooper wrote in his notes "It would be well to recall, however, that 'in England, until early in the 19th century, punishments for crime were ferocious' (E.B.,VI.p173) and we can agree with Gladstone's observation, written in the second half of the 18th century: "It is a melancholy truth, that among the variety of actions which men are daily liable to commit, no less than one hundred and sixty have been declared by Act of Parliament to be felonius without benefit of clergy; or, in other words, to be worthy of instant death. So dreadful a list, instead of diminishing, increases the number of offenders.' (*Commentaries* [Oxford 1769]" (in C:TCJ))

What is fascinating here is that *in Japan*, at least, the draconian laws [1] (and large rewards posted for murderers) evidently worked! Captain Will Adams, who spent the last half of his life involuntarily in Japan, put it like this: "And their citties you may go all ower in ye night with out any trobell or perrill." This was written about 20 years after the TRATADO. It was even more true in the orderly nation Kaempfer observed a 100 years later, and over 200 years later when Golownin admitted to his Japanese guards that a little peaceful city (Japan) was better than one (Europe) where the "inhabitants were rich, and had abundance of necessaries and luxuries, but they unhappily lived in constant quarrels, and there were so many rogues among them, that people durst not venture in the streets of a night for fear of being murdered." (G:MCJ) And Golownin's Japanese guards were not wrongly informed. Here is an 18th century description of London:

London is really dangerous at this time: the pickpockets, formerly content with filching, make no scruples to knock people down with bludgeons in Fleet Street and the Strand, and that at no later than eight o'clock at night. But in the Piazzas, Covent Garden, they come in large bodies armed with *couteaus,* and attack whole parties . . . (from a 1744 letter from a poet named Shenston [?] quoted in Natsume Soseki's BUNGAKU-HYÔRON)

After the spate of assassinations died down, all of the 19th century visitors highly praised Japan's safety, the conditions that allowed Isabella Bird to travel freely everywhere with no more than an 18 year-old translator for her companion. Morse, who was amazed at the lack of rowdiness in Japan, gives some interesting statistics. If you think the great disparity in our murder rates is a late-20th century phenomenon, think again! An acquaintance of Morse's in Michigan, hardly a dangerous part of the USA sent him a report on health conditions/mortality-rates, etc.

Among vital statistics I found that eighty-seven murders had been committed in that year. As the population of the State of Michigan at that time was only slightly lower than the population of Tokyo, I asked Mr. Sugi how many murders had been committed in Tokyo for the year. He said none, indeed, only twelve murders and two cases of political assassination had been committed in Tokyo in the last ten years. (M:JDD)

Statistics for theft mean little, for, unlike homicide, the difference between the "dark figure of crime," (the actual amount of crime as ascertained by study and survey) and the official ones is generally too large to allow for meaningful comparison. But it is possible to compare after one has lived in a country for a while.

It is delightful to be in a country where the people are honest. I never think of keeping my hand on my wallet or watch. On my table, with door unlocked [there were no locks], I leave my small change, and the Japanese boy or man coming in fifty times a day leaves untouched everything he should not touch. (M:JDD)

Realizing the honesty of the people in the fact I had never seen a lock, key or bolt on any sliding screen in Japan, I resolved to risk the experiment, so left eighty dollars in an open tray in a room which was probably occupied a dozen times during my absence and to which access could be had by every domestic and guest in the house. We were off for a week's trip, yet on my return every bit of change to the last cent, and the watch, of course, were in the open tray as I had left them. When one recalls the warnings and admonitions in printed notices on the doors of American and English inns in comparison to this experience, one is compelled to admit the innate honesty of these people, and this is only one of the many examples I could cite. It must amuse a Japanese when he visits our country to see dippers chained to the fountain, thermometers screwed to the wall, doormats fastened to the steps, and inside every hotel various devices to prevent the stealing of soap and towels. (Ibid)

I should add that Morse did not purposely tempt the Japanese. He had asked if he could leave his valuables while he went out on a junk and had been astounded to find they did not put them in a safe-box. One example he gives elsewhere, of a produce stand left untended with a box of change, I have seen and used in Tokyo on many occasions. In this case, even if someone was secretly watching – which wasn't likely – no one could possibly notice if one pretended to pay or actually stole some of the change. So one cannot simply say that fear of the law ingrained by centuries of capitol punishment, or exceedingly strong shame at being found out, i.e. external sanctions are responsible for the good behavior. A person who can put himself into another's shoes, that is to say an honest-to-god *conscience*, i.e. the moral gyroscope that is the mark of an inner-directed person must be responsible. So, honesty with respect to things and lying words would seem to have comfortably coexisted. Harris, the first American Ambassador to Japan, had experienced the same diplomatic prevarications that Alcock had, but still wrote (echoing the conclusion of Kaempfer and Golownin):

I sometimes doubt whether the opening of Japan to foreign influences will promote the *general happiness* of this people. It is more like the golden age of simplicity and honesty than I have ever seen in another country. (H:CJTH)

During the Tokugawa period, the law itself, if anything, grew crueler with time, until German law codes were adopted in the late-19th century. So we have the apparent contradiction of an incredibly good people with law and order that makes even the Old Testament's eye-for-an-eye a model of clemency. One the one hand, this may be coincidence, on the other, as ridiculous as it sounds, one can not help but wonder whether a millennium of killing people for petty thievery increased the fitness of the most timid, thus affecting the very genes of these people! This idea is by no means mine. Take this excerpt from a speech Morse gave on Founder's day at Vassar college, 1894.

> If we admit, as we must, that our manners at times are of necessity insincere, we find with the Japanese so many acts of the most unselfish nature blended with their good manners that one might be inclined to believe that the courtesy of the Japanese is a part of their nature and that such conditions had come about by a process of selection. With the sharp definition of classes in feudal times coupled with the dominance of the proud Samurai class over those below, it is possible that those who would not manifest good manners and a kindliness of demeanor have been exterminated and thus by a process of selection the well behaved have survived. Frankness compels me to confess that when confronted by the overbearing impertinence of public officials, the flippant serving girl and many similar kinds of people, and the pernicious influence this behavior exerts upon our children, I have sometimes wished for the power of some selective action to weed out the rude and impertinent from our midst and do it at once. (M:IGM)

Morse, who had been the first to lecture on Darwinism in Japan, then assured his audience that "the selective action however is surely going on though like the mills of God, it grinds slow. In hundreds of occupations the man who cultivates good manners not only keeps his place and is advanced, but makes a host of friends and well-wishers to help him in times of stress, while the rough boor is forced into occupations where the death rate is high." In those days, when poor men had to suffer late marriage or remaining single for life, Morse had a point. Nowadays, the least responsible, the least likely to defer satisfaction for learning, those most likely to have bad manners and lack self-control – not to mention fight, steal and kill – men or women alike, breed so young, so often and so successfully (few abortions and ample aid for childcare) that selection in America now *favors* the folk you see on Jerry Springer and Ricki's shows. It is not necessarily a matter of genetics. It is the dominance of this or that lifestyle in a culture that is *definitely* affected by what people have more or less children. In the 20th century, "we" *claimed* that learning was the way to the future, but, by our policies, have favored the growth of the offspring of those who took little stock in the same.

1. *Killing the Thief.* One week before putting this book to bed I came to see I missed something *big* in my explanation. I knew from the journals of the haiku poet Issa of the extraordinarily cruel torture and execution of gamblers that had taken advantage of his rural community by the same, but I felt it had something to do with the nature of Issa's tough Shinano countrymen or the Tokugawa era with laws of collective responsibility and so forth (encouraged from above) and did not fully comprehend the depth of the *tradition* of strict punishment *by the peasants* until I read Souyri's *The World Turned Upside Down.*

> Kujô Masamoto, a great dignitary of the imperial court who was visiting his estate in Hine, expressed his indignation over the barbarism of village justice in notes that he took during his stay. . . . . He had invited peasants from one of the villages on his estate to his residence . . . During the banquet, one of the villagers was robbed of a valuable dagger. To catch the thief, Masamoto had the village chiefs meet in the sacred space of the local shrine and "appeal to divine nature" through the test of boiling water. Frightened, the guilty party stepped forward. Masamoto quickly exercised his Lord's right to justice, depriving the peasant of his rights in the village and ordering that management of his household . . go to his son. But the other peasants . . . decided a few days later to exercise their own brand of justice. A group went to the thief's house, killed him, his wife, and his three sons, and burned down his house. Masamoto was appalled . . . he had no way to stop them. (S(K):WTU trans. Käthe Roth)

The other incident that Masamoto related was a theft committed during a period of famine – aggravating circumstances – in the winter of 1504.

> . . . the villagers of Iriyama were reduced to digging in the dirt to uncover the roots of ferns, which they ground to a powder from which a thin gruel could be made. The powder was distributed to each family according to how many mouths it had to feed. One night, the powder was stolen, but the young villigars standing guard surprised the thief as he fled and killed him on the spot. A judgment then took place: the villagers killed the thief's parents and children. Kujô Masamoto was revolted by such cruelty. But he always had food on his plate when he was hungry . . . (Ibid)

I do not know whether or not the villagers had to be that strict to survive or not, but this suggests that "our" (my?) concept of harsh justice as an invention of the *haves* holding down the *have-nots,* or as a corollary of the samurai's sharp sword, is not sufficient for understanding Japan.

14-8   With us, if we kill another with just cause or for our own defense, we are spared;
Antre nós, se hum mata a outro e teve justiça, ou foi por sua defensão, salva-se;

In Japan, if someone is killed, someone must die, and if he fails to appear, another is killed instead. *Em Japão, se hum mata, á-de morrer aquelle, e se não aparese, matão outro por elle.*

The apparent discrepancy between getting away with murder as noted in 14-5, above, and automatic death for killing here is explained thus: The former concerns the rights of someone who kills someone under his or her authority, while this concerns those who kill a superior, an equal (excluding war) or an inferior who is the charge of another without the other's permission. Here, the contrast is about the absence on our part and presence in Japan of a type of *collective responsibility*. Here is Cocks about a theft in which he had been the victim:

Soe they made a comvne serche throwe the towne for the theefe Man, &, not finding hym, comitted his father, mother, & brother to pr'son, w'th an other, his m.r w'ch sould hym [indentured him as a servant], whoe the ten of the streete are bound to answer for his forth coming, &, in fallt of fynding out the theefe, must answer w'th their lives or geue vs content for what is stolne. (1620 currant [1621] 03. (22.))

This is not necessarily a bad idea. But, as we have seen with the footnote to 14-7, collective responsibility could be worse. Even if the criminal *were* found and killed, his relatives, neighbors or employer might be executed. Hideyoshi, a peasant who come to rule Japan when Frois wrote the TRATADO was a big one for this concept and used it to speed the unification of the nation (If someone was found not to have turned in his weapon as required, the whole neighborhood would suffer for it) and, reprehensibly, for vendetta and personal gain. In the 1589 *De Missione* (dial. 12), Miguel=Valignano came down hard on collective responsibility, in particular, the execution of a wife for her husband's crimes that she knew nothing about was simply "not right;" and "law should not help give a lord the opportunity to exercise his cruelty and avarice." Because there were no clear edges on where responsibility stopped at that time – or if there were it didn't stop selfish leaders – as Leno pointed out in the dialogue, "it made the violation of an individual's rights something matter-of-fact." Needless to say, it was used against Christians when Christianity was outlawed, because a house that harbored a Christian could get a whole town destroyed.

The type of collective responsibility Frois mentions created a dilemma for the Jesuits in their capacity as advisors to Christian rulers in Japan. The twentieth of forty-five "thorny problems of conscience" Valignano submitted to Rome, which was first sent to the scholar Father Gil Vázquez is about this. Valignano explains that the reason someone else from the same country as the murderer is demanded if the murderer is not caught is "because if no one is caught, the inhabitants of the dead person's country would be permitted to kill on their own authority any inhabitant whatsoever of the murderer's country [and this might lead to further complications]." (in P(B):EPJ) It was not always "any inhabitant" for the more common form of substitute punishment was one which allowed a vassal to be executed in one's place, or "the parent or child of the vassal executed in *his* place." (Okada) This could be a merciful measure because it would allow the member of the family more important to the welfare of the other members to be spared; but it could favor the powerful and that was against the egalitarian spirit of Japanese law (12-7), so it was eventually stopped.[1] But to return to Valignano – his question:

When a pagan governor asks a Christian governor to hand over this sort of hostage, what shall he do, given that if the murderer is not discovered, by not delivering the innocent who is demanded, he risks his own life, not to mention the numerous other problems that would ensue? (Ibid)

To this Vázquez replies:

If the harm would come only to the [Christian] governor if he did not hand over the innocent [being demanded], he is not permitted to surrender the person; however, if a threat to the country itself would be incurred, then it would be permissible. . . (Ibid)

The advice seems reasonable, but I can see how someone could plot to remove a Christian governor by creating a situation that forces him to put himself in harm's way (risk almost certain assassination).

*   *   *

To return to the macro view, collective responsibility units could be countries, towns, blocks (as seen with the sacred deer) groups of families, families and relatives, or families. The five-family responsibility unit became standard in 1721 and was only replaced by a modern criminal law modeled on the German in 1871. If we harp upon the negative aspect of collective responsibility – and forget about the bottom-up tradition of collective justice – we might say that the government treated commoners like enemy in occupied territory! But, as horrific as it seems, such a system of responsibility may have played a major role in, eventually, making Japan such a safe place. Consider the implications of this paragraph by Kaempfer, who gave by far the most detailed explanations of what some have called Japan's "police-state" of any visitor.

If quarrels, or disputes, arise in the street, whether it be between the inhabitants or strangers, the next neighbours are oblig'd forthwith to part the fray, for if one should happen to be kill'd, tho' it be the aggressor, the other must inevitably suffer death, not withstanding his *moderamen inculpatae tutelae*, pleadings of *se defendendo*, or the like. All he can do, to prevent the shame of public execution, is to make away with himself, ripping open his belly. Nor is the death of such an unhappy person thought satisfactory, in their laws, to attone for the deceased's blood. Three of those families, who live next to the place wherre the accident happen'd, are lock'd up in their houses for three, four or more months, and rough wooden boards nail'd a-cross their doors and windows, after they have duly prepar'd themselves for this imprisonment, by getting the necessary provisions. The rest of the inhabitants of the same street, have also their share in the punishment, being sentenc'd to some days, or months, hard labour at publick works . . . The like penalty, and in a higher degree, is inflicted on the *Kumi Gasijra* [*gashira*], or heads of the Corporations of that street . . . It highly aggravates their guilt, and the punishment is increas'd in proportion, if they knew beforehand, that the delinquints had been in a quarreling humour . . . The landlords also and masters of the delinquents partake in the punishment for the misdemeanors of their lodgers, or servants. This rigorous proceeding . . . seems to be grounded upon the same principle with the *Canon Facientis dist.86. Facientis culpam* . . . He is doubtless guilty of the same Crime with the delinquint, who neglected to prevent it, when he could have done it. (K(S)HOJ:1692)

With such a system of collective responsibility, the rowdy behavior tolerated as inevitable in the Occident would be nipped in the bud by people worried about their own interests. Blaming the bullied as well as the bully would not be right, but, there would be few bullies if such a system were applied to parents in the West because they would not allow juvenile behavior to grow into a habit. If a bully picks on another student, have the bully's parents' flogged. If a kid extorts money from another kid have the parents repay it a hundred times, etc. Crime would have nowhere to start.

As with so much else, the Japan's system was modeled after China's, where houses were "numbered and divided into groups of 'ten and ten' households" (L:AME), but it seems to me that the Japanese emphasized the responsibility of the group to work out their troubles by themselves so they would not escalate into a criminal act, while the Chinese emphasized the responsibility to report on one's neighbors.   Still, the Shogunate eventually developed an internal spy system which horrified "Commodore Perry's historian," whom Alcock quoted: "Everybody is watched. No man knows who are the secret spies around him . . . This wretched system is even extended to the humblest of the citizens." (A:COT) This may be exaggerated a bit. Alcock also quoted another American to the effect that "the system of espionage, an abomination to foreigners, loses much of its repulsion when viewed from a Japan stand-point. . . . It exercises a wholesome restraint upon delegated powers, sitting light upon intelligent and upright officers, who regard these spies with no more disfavor than our treasurers their auditors. . . . Japan, it must be confessed, furnishes the best apology for despotism that the world affords." (A:COT) The historian should, however, have noted this did not harm family relations because relations were not expected to report each other. (The 1871 revision even made informing on relatives a felony with a 2 1/2 year sentence if true and life-sentence if false!)

The idea that *if someone is killed, someone must die* gave rise not only to collective responsibility but to a sort of objective sentencing. The latter doubtless encouraged people to be very careful not to exercise their negligence; but is nevertheless, terribly sad to think about. The merciless impersonality of the Japanese Law – what we now call "mandatory sentencing" – was to anger and sadden Western residents in the newly opened country.   In YOUNG JAPAN, John Black tells of a Japanese commoner who hits back at a rowdy drunk Western sailor, who manages to hit his head on the pavement and die. To the horror of the Western community, who thought the sailor only got what was coming to him, the man was tried and executed for manslaughter by the Japanese authorities. Feeling partly responsible by the fact the sailor was one of their "foreign community," and sorry for the widow, they raised her a large annuity. (This is very nice, but on a wider scale, the Western governments were forcing Japan to accept cholera without quarantine and otherwise pushing them around and doing their damndest to plant the seeds that would bear the fruit that would fall on Pearl Harbor!)

1. *Strict Laws.* Lost the date for the end of this practice of substitute punishment. (*Anyone?*) These various types of laws where people other than the criminal could be punished once were found in most of the world including old Europe, but, for better or worse, Japan kept them longer than the West.

14-9   With us, there is no crucifixion;   *Antre nós se não crucifica;*

In Japan, it is something very common. *Em Japão hé couza muito uzada.*

In THE JESUITS (orig. *The Power and the Secret of the Jesuits*) René Fulop-Miller brings up crucifixion in the context of the martyrdom of the Jesuits in Japan:

> With calm resignation, they allowed themselves to be imprisoned, tortured and crucified, for the Japanese had learnt of this form of execution, which was hitherto unknown in Japan, from the sermons of the Jesuits on the crucifixion of Christ, and now it afforded them derisive satisfaction to nail to the cross the priests of the crucified Savior. ((F&T):TJ)

A good story, but, in Japan, being *crossed* (as Will Adams put it: prob in S:MQT) was a common form of capital punishment that went back hundreds of years before the Jesuits arrived. It served as "hanging is in our land"(in Okada). The crosses are not identical. The Japanese cross is more of a "丁" than a "＋", and the word used for the punishment, *haritsuke*, lit. "stretch-fix," is unrelated to the one used to describe the "＋" shape. Originally, it was about stretching out the person to be executed and could even be on the ground. By Frois's time, the person was generally tied (not nailed) to a standing piece or pieces of wood. But imperfect or not, the equivalence was apparently unsettling to Europeans. In *De Missione*, when Miguel=Valignano describes justice in Europe, explaining that the crime and not the soul of the criminal is being punished, so they can have a last confession and beg the mercy of God and go to death with a quiet heart, he claims rather ingeniously, that they are executed in a number of relatively kind ways, and are never "burned [boiled?] to death in a kettle or crucified." Miguel does not elaborate on why *crossing* was considered more cruel and unusual punishment than other European methods of punishment, but moves directly into metaphysics.

> After all, the cross is the symbol of our salvation by Christ and is, therefore something revered and exalted by all." (Dial.12)

One can understand where they are coming from. The association of *crossing* with the execution of common criminals (as it was in Rome, originally, right?) in Japan was sometimes turned against the Christians. Frois mentions Buddhist polemicists gleefully saying things like:

> the fathers say outright that the one they claim to be the creator of heaven and earth and the savior of mankind was a man who was crucified with two thieves! In Japan, only bad people are crucified, so you can imagine what sort of man this so-called savior was! And even stranger, they worship this crucified man as a god and praise him, and they and others who are converted put the cross on the end of their rosaries, or wear it as a remembrance or draw it on paper for their evangelizing and kneel before it with their hands pressed together in prayer. (F:HISTORIA 7)

Compared to some of the other accusations they made (digging up bodies in graveyards to eat and being tools of the devil) against the priests, it is mild criticism. Even in China, where crucifixion was *not* common, the image of the cross with the bloody body of Jesus on it was a problem. Ricci's cross almost got him a beating when the Eunuch who looked after the Emperor's interests thought it "a wicked thing you have made, to kill our king." That is to say, they saw it as we might see a figure pounded full of nails, as a device used for black magic. "As one Chinese friend said to Ricci, it was really "not good one to have someone looking like that"[mistake in my quote?]; another suggested that the Jesuits "crush into powder any other crucifixes they had with them, so there would be no memory of them." So the Jesuits in China pretty much had to stick with the prettier image of Virgin Mary. The result of this was that many Chinese believed that the Christian God was a woman with child! (S:MPMR) While I have not heard that the Japanese were *that* upset by the crucifixion scene – perhaps for the reason inherent in the title of Ivan Morris's fine book THE NOBILITY OF FAILURE, as well as their having stronger stomachs – they, too, probably had their doubts, for images of Virgin Mary were far more popular than Jesus there, too. The Japanese Embassy to the West in the early 1870's, gave an excellent summary of the significance of religion in the West. Iwakura found the Occidentals enthralled by their tall-tale-like (荒唐) religion with "voices coming from the sky and executed prisoners reviving."(J/I:IR) The Japanese visitors found it hard to understand what gave rise to the tears shed by the religious kneeling down wailing at the feet of the executed Jesus.

> In every municipality in Europe and America, we find pictures of the dead prisoner, blood-stains all over him, being lowered off the cross. These are hung on hall-walls and house-niches and gives people the sensation of passing a graveyard or lodging at an execution ground. If this isn't *kikai* [eerie, monstruous, outrageous, spookie, weird] what in the world *is*! And the Occidentals find it *kikai* that the East does *not* have them . . . (J/I:IR)

As Carletti described it 300 years earlier, the Japanese, unlike the Romans, provided some support between the legs and under the feet, and tied people to crosses "with iron straps hammered into the wood" or, "bound the entire body" to the cross with ropes *before* lifting up the cross and sliding the base into a prepared hole. (Sometimes the hole was not deep enough for Frois tells of the crucifixion of a good Christian man ostensibly for the crimes of a half-brother, but actually because his tea *dogu* were coveted by the Shôgun Hideyoshi, where the cross actually tipped-over!) Then, at a judge's order – this is where the last-minute reprieve comes in the TV Easterns – lances were simultaneously stabbed up and through the bodies from the right and left, with the intention of piercing vital organs and hastening death. It was not always so merciful. Carletti saw people left alive on crosses and "they similarly crucify women with babies still nursing at their breasts, so that both the one and the other die of privation." He describes hellish scenes:

> along all the streets and roads . . . . one sees nothing . . . . but crosses full of men, of women, or of children . . . ." (C(W):MVAW).

The last was a description of the martyrdom of 26 Christians at Nagasaki. They were left up until they fell apart, a warning to all. God knows, we did worse things to many more witches. But even ignoring the killing fields of our religion, capitol punishment was *visible* everywhere. We, too, left *examples* hanging up for all to see. Descriptions of gibbet-filled London – if you don't know what a *gibbet* is, look it up! – every bit as horrendous as anything you can find in Japan may be found in Yi Fu Tuan's *Landscapes of Fear*. One exceptionally *pleasant* (!) episode related to such display is found in AUBREY'S BRIEF LIVES (I don't want to be rude, but the native English-speaker who has not yet read this classic has no right to read about Japan!) concerning the head of Sir Thomas More, which was set "upon London Bridge"[1] after he was beheaded:

> There goes this story in the family, viz. that one day as one of his daughters was passing under the Bridge, looking on her father's head, sayd she, That head haz layn many a time in my Lapp, would to God it would fall into my Lap as I passe under. She had her wish, and it did fall into her Lappe, and is now preserved in a vault in the Cathedral Church at Canterbury.

Okada made one comment about crucifixion in Japan that was new to me: before Frois's time, the body was often crucified head down. Now *that* is a contrast!

---

1. "*Upon London Bridge*." Readers who are not English might lack a clear picture of what this means. A sixteenth century painting of London – no special event, just a typical panorama – by C.J. Visscher shows about 20 heads each stuck on its own pike (spear-like pole), mostly inclining outward diagonally from on top of the ramparts of what I would call a guard-tower capping an arch people would have to go under to cross the bridge. I imagine there must either be a guard sitting down out of sight within the garden of heads on high or they were poisoned for not a crow was in sight. The heads must not have always worked to set an example, for we can imagine some young ruffian happy to have his moment of fame even if it would be posthumous! In at least one case, the exposure clearly backfired. After the newly ordained Catholic cardinal (a gentle old man) was cruelly executed by Cromwell and Henry the VIII, here is what happened: "His head was parboiled and displayed – as the heads of traitors commonly were – on a pole on London Bridge. But as many people crowded around to look upon Fisher's head with reverence – some even declaring that it 'grew fresher and more comely day by day' – that 'almost neither horse nor cart could pass over the Bridge,' and it soon had to be removed by the authorities." (*Tower of London* by Christopher Hibbert and the Editors of Newsweek Book Edition 1971)

14-10   With us, domestic servants are reprehended and other help punished by whipping;
Antre nós se reprendem os criados e se castigão os servos com asoutes;

In Japan they are reprehended and castigated by being beheaded.
Em Japão a reprensão e castigo hé cortar a cabeça.

There may be a paradox here. Judging from what Valignano wrote, the Japanese dared not beat their servants, for even servants had high self esteem and might revenge the insult by killing their master and committing suicide. So, this excessive punishment may have been the result of what we might call equality of honor in Japan!

Although there were notable exceptions – the famously sadistic Shogun Nobunaga, who met and liked the Jesuits, reputably decapitated a servant girl for leaving the stem of a fruit on the tatami – the Japanese were, on the whole, kind and closer to their servants than we were.

14-11   We have prisons, wardens, bailiffs and constables;[1]
Antre nós há troncos, alcaides, meirinhos e biliguins;

Japanese have none of these, nor caning, de-earing, or hanging.
Antre os Japões não há nada disto, nem asoutar, desorelhar,[2] nem em[for]car.

It is clear that as far as prisons go, the West was far more developed (?), unless we include the clever devices – little cages in the street and whatnot – soon to be used in the large Japanese Pleasure Quarters to publicly hold Johns who wouldn't pay for their play. However, Alvarez-Taladriz notes that Japan once *had* prisons, until "they lost the feeling for" them during the long period of civil wars with decentralization and military justice. He adds that Valignano, who observed Japanese had no prisons in his SUMARIO (1583), wrote in his ADICIONES (1592) that the institution was reestablished. In Dialogue 12 of DE MISSIONE, written in between the aforementioned, Miguel+ Leo=Valignano discuss the contrary attitudes and how they might be related to the differing situations:

Miguel – . . . . Also, [in Europe] no one rashly hands out death sentences; it is only done when the facts have been considered over a long period of time. Because Europeans know that their punishment is [*or,* will be] based on just laws, they do not feel great distress at being led to prison. . . . Europeans have actually seen people often leave the jail as free men without punishment according to the judges just understanding of each and every man's deeds.

Leo – Hearing that, we Japanese can only wonder at the patience of the Europeans! From what you say, Europeans don't find imprisonment that great of a pain. But if you take the people in our country, they are of such a spirit that they would spend their blood and give up their lives to avenge a single day of imprisonment [*or,* rather than spend a single day in prison].

After this, Miguel explains that Japanese fight to the death rather than go to prison because they know that prison means they are bound to be executed, probably at the whim of the lord, rather than justice. (The last explanation suggests that either the Japanese translation or the Latin rendition is a bit off, hence the bracketed suggestions).

Punishment, however, is a different matter. Not to be beaten, Okada lists 10 methods extant in Frois's time, including crucifixion rightside-up and upside-down, skewering, ox-splitting [quartering by ox-power?], cart-splitting, roasting, pot-boiling, mat-wrapping and the only one as bad as "our" flaying: the "saw-pull," where – if the TV Easterns I've seen are accurate (which, on the whole, they are *not!*) – those who passed by were actually required to take a pull at a saw slowly cutting through a man buried by the side of the road(!),[3] and the above-mentioned ear-removal. Ironically, Frois actually met the Shogun (Hideyoshi) whose army brought back so many ears and noses from Korea that large mounds were needed to inter them only a few years after TRATADO! (*Anything* can get a memorial mound in Japan, from the souls of whales to sit-down comic (*rakugo*) routines – I swear, I saw a mound in Tokyo for routines about drunkenness and adultery that were interred during wartime so soldiers on the front could fight in peace knowing the folk back home were being good!) Could a Portuguese have given Hideyoshi the idea?[4] As to why Japanese did not hang people, I can only guess that it was because hanging was pretty much thought a way for women to kill themselves, and that may have ruled out its use as a proper method of punishment.

Caning. We have already seen that Japanese do not cane/whip their children. Now Frois claims the same thing holds true for adults. While there is a stereotype dating back before TRATADO of Chinese who whip and beat people bloody *versus* Japanese who slice their heads cleanly off, it is doubtful that Japanese *never* used corporal punishment in Frois's time. They certainly used all sorts of fiendish devices to torture Christians into renouncing their faith over the fifty years or so *after*

TRATADO, and, apparently, many of these were put into service against people who got behind on their taxes. In 1592, Kaempfer attested to the innovative spirit abroad throughout the world in the field of torture:

> Criminals are now brought to a very quick confession by a new instrument of Sino Cami's own invention, being a bench full of short sharp points, over which criminals are drawn, not unlike the witches-stool at Lemgow, the extream pain and torment of which, would make the most innocent man confess, what he never was guilty of [Since it is sometimes said – an overgeneralization, in my opinion – that Japanese only executed those who admitted their guilt, this *would* be a convenient device!]. (K(S)HOJ)

In the mid-19th century, Ambassador Harris noted that "whipping is inflicted with a small bamboo or rattan over the shoulders or back." Perhaps they did *some* corporal punishment in Frois's time, too, but it was too little to be noticed next to the whip-eager West and the cane-eager Chinese. Kaempfer noted that "Japanese are only in prison until they are tried" and gave a reason for Japanese rarely using imprisonment for punishment that fits what Frois writes about walking (1-27), but is not so convincing as the explanation given by Leo=Valignano, above.

> The Japanese cannot understand our imprisonment for punishment. They say for a man to be in a good house and have enough food and clothing cannot be a punishment to a large portion of men, who only care for their animal wants and have no self-respect; and, as they never walk for pleasure, they cannot think it hard to be deprived of wandering about. (56-10-25)

1. Translation. "Our" vocabulary was very hard for me to make sense of.

Tronco as one of those *stocks* people used to be put in was much higher up the usages in the dictionaries but, combined with the word that follows, clearly meant *prison*.

I needed the OED (!)* to tell me specifically that ***Alcaide*** (*alcayde*) was "the commander of a fortress" (from Arabic) or "warden of a prison." My small Portuguese dictionary tells me it is an idiomatic "dead horse" and my large one is no more specific than "an ancient official of justice" (and a Brazilian meaning is "an old and ugly person!").

The ***meirinhos*** are bailiffs and a bailiff, if you have not been in the graces of the law, means a *summoner*.

Biliguin appeared only as "a small fly" (!) in my Portuguese dictionaries so I follow the Japanese translation which suggests a person whose job is capturing/arresting people. Checking from the Japanese back I get "a policeman, hound (myrmidon) of the law, a petty officer of the law" or "a raiding constable." In the USA, a deputy might bring in a prisoner, but "constable" has a nice ring to it so I took it. I cannot help wondering if we have this right!

* **Note**: as amazing as it may sound, the OED often gets to the root of Portuguese words even the Bible-dimensioned 1,500 page *Aurelio* Portuguese-Portuguese does not.

2. Translation. Looking for the verb *desorelhar*, or *dis-ear*, I found a much more interesting word to share:

desolhar (*dis-eye*), i.e. to free persons from the evil eye!

3. Sawing People. My OJD has both *nokogiribiki* (saw-pulling=cutting) and *nokogiribiki-sarashi* (saw-pulling-exposure) in it. While it is famous because the sadistic Nobunaga sentenced a man who had taken a potshot against him years earlier to it (on the TV drama, the guy is a rather stupid, nice guy, who had no idea what he was doing, so you feel so sorry for him), the OJD says it was meant *specifically for people who kill their master or parents* and that, at first, fine-toothed bamboo saws were placed on each side of the condemned (needless to say, a cut from the front would defeat the purpose of the torture) and passersby could take a cut if they wished to do so (The requirement to saw seen on TV was probably due to Nobunaga's sadism extending beyond the criminal). Later, cuts were made in the shoulders and the blood rubbed on the saw-blades that were placed by the criminal who was removed after a a second day of exposure, crucified and speared. I suppose I could look this up and get more details, and do likewise for other tortures mentioned, but I do not relish the idea of being the expert cited on some sadistic website, so I must demure.

4. Collecting Parts. The central document of "our" civilization, records a gross collection practice (encouraged by "our" God) of cutting off and bringing back the foreskins of the vanquished foe. The most famous was Saul asking David for a *mohar* of 100 Philistine foreskins – hoping to scare him off – for his daughter's hand in marriage. David went out and collected 200 to win Michal's hand in marriage. In most cases, these were probably tallied up, then heaped into mounds after battles (as done by the Moghul Empire) rather than used for a bride-price. At any rate, compared to that, ears, noses, or scalps are polite trophies.

14-12 With us, stolen goods are returned to the owner by the court;
Antre nós, o furto que se acha se torna por justiça a seu dono;

> In Japan, when stolen goods are found, they are confiscated by the court as if they were lost. *Em Japão o tal furto achado toma-o a justiça pera si por perdido.*

Okada cites a contemporary document showing that *by law* stolen goods were supposed to be returned to their owners in Japan and stipulating that in the meantime they were to be held by the bailiff or placed in a specified place, but adds, perhaps it was the custom for the bailiff to confiscate stolen goods. I.e., the law and practice may have differed. In *De Missione* dialogue 12, after Valignano=Leno points out that any tiny misdemeanor can be used as a pretext to confiscate property, Valignano=Mancio replies that

> Such things are not surprising. Japanese, being heathens, don't think about the legality or illegality of things like Christians do. Even though the law says that another's things should be returned to the original owner, the Japanese, not thinking of things in the context of an eternal future, don't obey; and think that governing people is not for the public interest but their own private interest.

As politically turbulent Japan rapidly unified, there was evidently a lot of confiscation going on under one pretext or another. It was also, however going on in Europe. Some inquisitors were infamous for teaming up with local lords to rob others legally through carefully manipulated witch trials. And, more important yet, Mancio's reasoning is faulty because it ignores the fact that those who were not governing, by all accounts, stole *less* than their Christian counterparts in Europe.

14-13 With us, man, woman and child are afraid of the dark;
Antre nós, homens, molheres e meninos tem medo de noyte;

> In Japan, to the contrary, neither the old nor the young have any fear.
> *Em Japão polo contrairo grandes nem peqenos nenhum medo tem.*

If Frois's contrast and my impression of old Japan are correct, most Japanese felt safe in the light of the full moon, for it was identified with the cleansing mercy of Buddha. While "our" moon spawned werewolves, the Japanese moon made even savage boars take a break from ravaging farms and fall sweetly asleep. The Milky Way is identified with the home of souls and there is a Star Festival for the *loving stars* (the Herder and the Weaver) every year. As the seventh was a half-moon night, it was relatively bright in the evening. I assume that much of Frois's "dark" refers to such nights, bright enough to find one's way around. Did many Europeans, or at least Iberians, fear the demonic night so much that they even called bright nights "dark" and shuddered at the thought of going out? Or, were "we" just too unruly and prone to violence when not placed under the giant crime-light in the sky, the Sun? In Lodovico Augustini's *The Imaginary Republic*, written between 1575-1580, the citizens are forbidden to wander the streets or gather in the piazza after nightfall "in the interest of law and order." (H:CER). As far as pitch-black nights go, I wonder. Japanese have always had a greater variety of ghosts than we do, many were denizens of the night and I cannot believe parents never used them to get children to go to sleep. During the Tokugawa era, when these ghosts evidently had their heyday, it would seem that fear got the upper edge. In the *senryu* collections dating back to less than a hundred years post-TRATADO, there are poems reminding us of one of Goya's best known *caprichos*, "After the lamp dies, horrific wisdom comes out" (*cho-ga kiete-*

kara osoroshii chie-ga deru: MUTAMAGAWA).   By the end of the ghost-ridden Seclusion, we might even speak of a reversal between *them* and *us*. To wit, Bird in 1877 and Skidmore shortly later:

> The Japanese are terribly afraid of darkness; the poorest people keep a lamp burning all night. In these regions they will not walk along the roads after dark unless in companies. I have been compelled to make an early halt several times because the *mago* [horseboy=muleteer] would not for double pay encounter the supernatural risks to be met with in returning at night. At Shingoji I was awoke by a great disturbance because a bald-pated monster with goggle eyes and a tongue hanging out of his mouth had looked over the folding screens, a trick he often plays. (B:UTJ)

> The outer veranda is closed at night and in bad weather by *amados*, solid wooden screens or shutters that rumble and bang their way back and forth in their grooves. These *amados* are without windows or air-holes, and the servants will not willingly leave a gap for ventilation. "But thieves may get in, or the *kappa!* they cry, the kappa being a mythical animal always ready to fly away with them.[1] In every room is placed an *andon* or night lamp. (S:JDJ)

The Japanese today usually close the *amado*, not to keep out the *kappa* but because of a fear of catching night-chills or something by draughts while sleeping. Since the room is pitch-black with the *amado* closed, one can understand why, as Bird wrote, "No Japanese would think of sleeping without having an *andon* [a type of dim lantern she calls "wretched 'darkness visible'"!] burning all night in his room." (Personally, I love a pitch-black room and, after twenty years in Japan, have difficulty with the light coming through curtains in the USA). Alcock also writes of streets "too dark and unsafe to be much frequented after night fairly sets in," so it would seem that Japan was not always, everywhere and at all times perfectly safe. And he added something amazing, but considering the thoroughgoing law and order of the Tokugawa era totally believable:

> Every one by law, as in China, is bound not to stir out after dark without a lantern on which their name is printed. (A:COT)

Okada believes Frois is not describing Japanese as a whole but the character of the children of the samurai who were raised to be brave. The passage he cites from the samurai classic *Hagakure* reminds parents that cowardice even in childhood may turn into a lifelong blemish and that it would be *negligence* (*fukaku*) for them to put their young children (幼少) into a funk over thunder, allow them to fear the dark or tell them scary stories. Since most Japanese deliberately spook their little children to encourage them to cling to them or make it easier to prevent wandering,[2] this advice is very apt indeed. Then, when the child gets a bit older, they were positively challenged, made to visit cemeteries alone at night and so forth until they learned to become fearless.[3]

1. Kappa. Generally *kappa* are liable to pull people into the water and drown them, so it seems strange to encounter them in this setting, unless the room is next to a nice sized pond. But no more on *kappa*, for I have or will mention them elsewhere (viz: *The Mullet in the Maid*).

2. Boogymen. I have known Japanese mothers and grandmothers, as sweet as they are, to use *me* to gently spook their one or two year old children. And, I can recall a neighbor running about shouting *Abunai! Abunai*

dakara! (Danger! It's dangerous!) in order to find a little boy who wandered. The idea (though I doubt the mother was thinking about what she was thinking) was to frighten the child into running back to mother. This type of thing, for good or bad, tends to make children timid and attentive to adults.

3. Tough Little Samurai. I may have read about those cemeteries in Fukuzawa Yukichi's autobiography, but I forget. Glosses welcome.

~~~~~~

14-14   We are generally afraid of snakes and dislike holding them;
Antre nós geralmente tem medo aas cobras e asco de lhe pôr a mão;

The Japanese pick them up easily, without fear, and some eat them.
Os Japões as tomão com a mão muito facilmente sem temor, e alguns as comem.

It may be accidental that the generic term for "snake" in Portuguese is "cobra," [1] but it seems indicative nonetheless of "our" jaundiced view of snakes, that held all *poisonous*, if not in body, *in spirit*. With the snake a major presence in the pagan religions of Eurasia, it was turned into the symbolic fall-guy, or scapegoat for all who resisted "our" brazen monopolization of the sacred and banishment of all gods but our own. As the symbol of evil, the snake was also the first victim of our war against the natural world. It may well be we share an instinctive primate fear of snakes, but Judeo-Christo-Islamity magnified this to an absurd degree. Or, is this fear, in part derived from our unconscious guilt at what we have done? This was, of course, a death warrant for the snakes of the Occident and, as mentioned elsewhere, a command to the rats whose fleas carried the plague to multiply and fill the earth.

Most Japanese were, of course, afraid of poisonous snakes. In Okinawa, there are hours when people are afraid to go out into the fields. Yet the poisonous snake population is not large for they are in high demand for making musical instruments and putting in *shôchû* (a powerful liquor made of sugar-cane, yams or other things) or whiskey. The rattlesnake-like viper called a *habu* is thought especially good for stamina (=virility). Even today, airline-size bottles of whiskey with a bit of viper extract can be found on the counter of almost every liquor store in Japan. Perhaps this was once true in parts of Europe, too, for one of the Japanese visitors, Thunberg, in Roggeveld (South Africa) in 1774, wrote matter-of-factly that "not a day passed that we did not catch several [serpents], and put them into the brandy kegs." (T:TEAA)

Though many snakes were considered edible in Japan, albino snakes were taboo, for Shinto held them to be sacrosanct messengers from the Earth (earth-dragon etc.). Still, Japanese did not get as close to snakes as Indians with their cobra cults,[2] unless one chooses to include some rather perverted *senryu* of the 18th century that mention doctors using frogs to lure snakes out of human cavities where they were supposed to have lodged. Supposedly, women powdered and rouged to look like Benten, goddess of prosperity (and a synonym for a beauty), in the seedy part of Edo trained snakes to crawl into their privies as part of a strip-show and sometimes had trouble getting them to leave. Eventually, this much seems to be fact (meaning I recall reading it in at least 3 books), the shows stopped after authorities cracked down on them as "cruelty to animals." The Russian Captain Golownin, whom I find absolutely trustworthy, described what was probably the standard snake trick (not so risqué as the one that excited *senryû* poets) if it can be called that, in the early-19th century. After finishing his account of "the industry of the Japanese" he described a snake-lady as an example of "the idle people" that "there are among them as among all nations."

> The following method, by which idle people, especially women, gain money, deserves particular mention. They catch a number of snakes, of different sizes and colours, from which they extract the sting so skillfully, that they cannot do any mischief. Then they strip themselves quite naked, cover merely the parts which decency teaches even savages to conceal, and wind snakes round their arms, legs, and their whole body. In this manner they make themselves a motley covering of the open, hissing serpent's heads; and in this dreadful and brilliant costume, they ramble about the streets, sing, dance, and play all manner of anticks, to obtain a reward, or rather charity. (G:MCIJ)

On the other hand, 60 years later, Isabella Bird was riding on a packhorse led by a woman –

> We traveled less than a *ri* (about a kilometer) an hour, as it was a mere flounder among rocks or in deep mud, the woman in her girt up dress and straw sandals trudging bravely along, till she suddenly flung away the rope cried out and ran backwards, perfectly scared by a big grey snake, with red spots, much embarrassed by a large frog which he could not let go, though, like most of his kind, he was alarmed by human approach and made desperate efforts to swallow his victim and wriggle into the bushes. (B:UBJ)

Evidently, with snakes as with many things, there are sexual and, more important, individual differences, as well as national ones!

1. *Translation.* I checked on the equivalent of "serpent" in Portuguese and found it referred to all snakes but especially poisonous ones, whereas cobra was defined as neutral in this respect, so I went with the plain "snake."

2. *Indians and Cobras.* I have seen four things (on television) about India that impressed me: 1) Women cutting fruit against still-standing knives (see *Midword*);

2) A child being washed with the body slapped around as if it were putty; 3) a man making sure to spit out every drop of water used to gargle on the plants in his garden; 4) people taking cobras home for a night and releasing them the next day. *This latter interspecies ritual is wonderful,* but beyond me. I grew up with rattlesnakes around and must admit to killing them and feeling fine about it!

~~~~~~

14-15 To sneeze is, with us, a natural thing and we think nothing of it;
O espirrar antre nós hé couza natural e de que se não faz cazo;

On the isles of Gotô, it is thought to be an omen, and anyone who sneezes that day can not speak to the *tono* [feudal lord]. *Nas ilhas do Goto se tem por agouro e não pode falar ao* tono *quem aquelle dia espirrou.*

"Gesundheit!" "God bless you!" and other such exorcism lest one sneeze out one's soul or otherwise harm oneself or others suggest that some in the West, too, have traditionally ascribed *supernatural* significance to sneezing. But, sneezes may have gotten a bit more attention in Japan than in Europe, for there is ample literature on masking sneezes with words and vice versa. According to the OJD, the literary word for "sneeze," *kusame* (as opposed to the modern word *kushami*), may have originally meant either "That I don't rot!" (neg. subj. of *kusaru*) or derived from "Eat shit!" (*kuso kurae*), both charms against bad spirits. Proof *kusame* was used as a charm is found in the 14th century Buddhist priest Kenkô's *Tsurezuregusa*. Here is essay #47, as translated by Donald Keene:

> A certain man on his way to Kiyomizu was joined on the road by an aged nun. As they trudged along, she kept murmuring, "*Kusame, kusame,*" until finally he asked her, "Sister, why do you say that?" Without even deigning to answer, she kept up an unending stream of repetitions of the word. He persisted, and when she had been asked several times she at last became angry and said, "What a nuisance of a man! Don't you know that unless you say the magic word when somebody sneezes he'll die? The young master I brought up is an acolyte now on Mount Hiei.[1] He may be sneezing at this very moment, for all I know. That's why I said "*kusame.*" This was certainly a case of unusual devotion. (*Essays in Idleness*: Columbia University Press 1967/Tuttle 1987)

But Frois, here, does not say "Japan," but *the Gotô islands*, which are about 40 kilometers closer to China than Hirado, Japan (Frois's directions). As a contrast, it is ridiculous. Imagine substituting, say, "the Isle of Mann" for "Europe"! As is often the case for out-of-the-way places, East or West, it was an incredible hotbed of superstition. Frois discusses the superstitions on the "three tiny islands" of Gotô (the name transliterates as "Five-isles," either Frois overlooked 2 or they sank) in three delightful pages of his *Historia*. If I am not mistaken in my dates, the section concerns the efforts of Cosme de Torres in 1554. First, Frois mentions how much the people of the Goto islands hated smallpox, which was almost as bad a problem in Japan as the plague was in Europe. Then he described the strict quarantines they observed when someone was stricken which he compared to Japanese funeral practices where the family of the deceased could not make contact with other people for months. He must have felt both of those practices were superstitions because he leapt from them directly to the sneezes!

> Another weird superstition found among the residents of the Goto islands is that they find a sneeze to be extremely ominous. For that reason, when someone has to go see the Lord or for some reason is invited to visit him, he may reply [by messenger or letter?] "I am dreadfully sorry, but as I sneezed this morning, I cannot come" and escape from the duty of visiting that day. Or, if he was actually on his way to see the lord and happened to sneeze on the way, he would have to return home and not speak to his lord on that day. (J/F:Historia ch13)

Apparently, the islanders also closely abided by the calendar of auspicious and inauspicious days – Frois neglects to write that the calendar was common to all Japan, it was only the degree to which they heeded it that was noteworthy – and, being poor, lived in great fear of and constantly propitiated the Devil. As Frois describes it, they were "ridden with Devilish superstitions." His main example of such "superstitious customs" is far more fascinating to us than the sneezing, for it seems to be tailor-made for what we now think of as responsible stewardship of the earth. Since Frois's long *Historia* is not likely to ever be translated into English, let me give this part in full, for it deserves to be known. In the last sentence, Frois, indirectly and incredibly, recognizes the benefit of "superstition" for what we would now call *ecology*.

> Wherever they are, whatever type of place it is, when they cut the wood to fuel their salt-pots [apparently, salt (a symbol of the boondocks and exile in Japan) was one of their export items], in order that their pot not be cursed by the gods, they leave untouched an especially verdant and pleasant place, be it an entire hill or a part of the mountain=forest that is covered with particularly tall and valuable trees, for the gods. No pagans take so much of a twig from these trees though it only be for medicinal purposes. If some one were to cut even a little from those trees, it would end up costing him a lot. This is not only because of some sort of disaster or curse of the gods, but because that person must make amends [2] in the form of ceremonies and money to fulfill his duty for the sin of cutting off tree limbs [on such a mountain] by planting a fixed number of trees. Because of that, and because when times are hard the people pledge to the gods [not to cut certain areas], the many places they dedicated to the gods are covered with green and there is beautiful scenery for the people. (Ibid)

Today, it is the *number* of sneezes that matters in Japan. *One* may mean someone is saying something bad about you, *two* that someone is saying something good about you (or vice-versa, I always forget) and *three* – well, you're getting a cold! Or maybe there are *four*.[3] Whatever it is, repeated sneezes in an office always get attention. Omen or natural thing, Japanese are still particularly attentive to and averse to sneezing. Many Japanese men and almost all Japanese women stiffle or completely kill them. If they want to pop their eardrums, it is their business, but the perpetual sniffling (they rarely *blow* their noses, for that, too, is thought disgusting!) drives this foreign honker bananas!

1. Mount Hiei. I believe Kenkô made the mountain the one he did for his story because its name may be punned with *hie*, or "a chill." Since acolytes practicing austerities on such mountains had a high death rate, fear he might catch a cold and die was not unreasonable even if the old nun's manner of coping with it was!

2. Tree Amends. The ancient Celts were far stricter than the gentle people of Gotô, for, if Frazer was right, they nailed the offender's navel to the stripped tree and wrapped his guts around it! (See the *Golden Bough*)

3. Sneezing Schemes. If anyone wants to make an international collection of sneezology, be my guest. I have found a Mexican one where one sneeze is *salud* (sneeze out that germ and be healthy?), two is *dinero* (money: what if I do it on purpose?), three *amor* (ditto, I am single) and four, an allergy.

14-16 We use gold and silver coins;
Antre nós [se u]sa de moedas d'ouro e prata;

In Japan, they circulate in pieces and [are valued] by weight.
Em Japão correm em pedaços sempre a pezo.

Okada says that sometimes standardized coins were made by territorial lords, but usually not. Apparently, Japan was not sufficiently unified to agree on regional standards, much less "national" ones. European countries, on the other hand, generally used coins stamped with the sign of the king or republic. The Japanese ambassadors brought back many pretty samples of this money according to

Miguel in dialogue 28 of *De Missione*. While this contrast makes Europe seem modern, we should not forget the use of paper money by the Mongol government of China described with astonishment by Marco Polo hundreds of years earlier!

14-17 We in Europe always use a balance; *Nós em Europa sempre uzamos de balansas;*

And, the Japanese [use] a *dachem* [(Chinese) scale]. *E os Japões de dachen.*

A balance is the type of weighing device that uses two plates or dishes called scales. A *dachem* or *dachen* was derived from the the Malaysian name (*daching*) for a Chinese scale adopted by the Portuguese. It was a small lever-scale (close to a *beam-scale*, where a small weight is moved closer or further from the fulcrum to change the leverage but not quite the same). The Chinese carried them "aboutt them to wey their monies," while larger ones were used to weigh commodities and sometimes even two "stillyards" (scales?) were used at once to weigh a heavy thing, according to Peter Mundy in 1637. His editor explained that a balance was "a beam made to move freely on a central pivot with a scale pan at each end" while a dotchin (*d'achem*) "consisted of a lever with unequal arms which moves on a fulcrum." This definition was found in Boxer's notes to Gaspar Da Cruz's *Things of China*, where he writes that "everyone hath scales of his own . . . for each laboureth by all means to deceive the other, so none do trust the scales and weights of the other." Not that one's own scales will help much when hens are filled with water and have sand [and other things] in their crops, etc. ! (B:SCSC)

[14-17/18]   Our copper coins are whole; *Antre nós a moeda de cobre hé inteira;*

In Japan, they have holes in the middle. *Em Japão furada polo meo.*

Another of Frois's unnumbered contrasts (Schütte made it 18a, the Portuguese made it nothing and the French gave it a proper number so that rest of the items in the chapter are a number higher than those Frois assigned to them). To me, what is more interesting than the hole itself is the fact that it is square rather than round as one might expect for money that might be strung up. In the Warring States period an enormous quantity of these round copper coins with square holes were imported from China and continued to circulate in Japan until Frois's time and then some. They were the most popular currency in Japan because of their crisp design and the words printed on them: 永 楽 通 宝 (*eirakutsûhô*) = *eternal-ease/pleasure-commute[pass-through]-treasure*, or 開 元 通 宝 = *open-origin-commute-treasure*, or 乾 降 通 宝 = *dry[drought]-[or] wet[downpour]-commute-treasure*. One character was on each side of the square hole. They were, in a word, *auspicious*. To Faux Frois it:

··
With us, good luck may bring us money.
With them, money may bring good luck.

14-18 In Europe, copper coins are accepted as a matter-of-course;
Em Europa se toma correntemente a moeda de cobre;

In Japan, they must be chosen, and must be old, of such and such color and markings. *Em Japão á-de ser escolhida, e á-de ser velha e de tal cor e tais cunhos.*

With hundreds of years of domestic and foreign-made coins of diverse purity – in particular many poor copies (a good fake wouldn't be a problem, right?) of the lucky Chinese *eiraku* coins just mentioned – in circulation, in Japan, every man had to behave like a coin collector! This is bad. People should not have to waste time on little things. (But not so bad as the situation in the USA today, where we are constantly forced to waste our time – which is irreplaceable – choosing which of a zillion services to use, thereby losing far more than any possible gain, which in the long run usually turns out to be bogus to boot!)

14-19   In Europe, it is uncommon to use copper coins as a gift;
Em Europa commumente se não faz prezente com moeda de cobre;

> In Japan, they are very commonly sent in boxes as a *rei* [formal thank-you gift] to lords. *Em Japão hé muito corrente ir fazer* rei *aos senhores com caxas.*

According to something quoted by Okada, in the Tokugawa era, it was common to give a single gold coin and a dozen or so silver ones and other coins of various dimensions and put a closed piece of paper with that information on an accompanying stand (*tsukedai*), but "in the old days" there was no stand and "it was normal to give small change (銭)." The *old days* were those of Frois. My guess is that because the coins were considered lucky, they were probably would be divided up and used for the monetary New Years gift (*toshidama*) the lord gives his underlings. With fortunes constantly gained and lost in the upheavals of that time, I also imagine that *luck* would have meant far more than money! (On reflection, it is more likely that with the country settled down, lords became strong enough to demand *real* rather than *token* "gifts."

These copper coins were also strung up like beads on a necklace. Today, they are sometimes given to children or as prizes in neighborhood lotteries, in their reincarnation as freshly minted 5-yen coins. They do not have the above-mentioned lucky words printed on them, but their denomination has an intrinsically auspicious value: In Japanese, *go-en* (five yen) happens to be a homophone for "good fortune!"

14-20   We express honor through our nouns/names; *Nós pomos a honra nos nomes;*

> The Japanese express it all through their verbs. *Os Japões a põe toda no uzo dos verbos.*

Frois is a bit off. With far more conjugations for etiquette (levels of politeness) than for tense, it is true that Japanese can do much more with their verbs than we can. They even have different verbs with identical meanings to use depending upon whom they speak to and whom they speak about. But Japanese do not *only* rely on the verb. For some words, they *also* have different levels of nouns. And they have honorific prefixes and suffixes to be pegged on to nouns or (even on adjectives) fore and aft. Moreover, it would have been more accurate to write "honor and humility" for one can both talk *up* another and talk *down* oneself with equal ease in Japanese (Very easily, but doing it well is very hard for me at least). Frois had to know he was vastly oversimplifying, for even Valignano, probably basing his understanding largely on what he learned from others, had written as follows about Japanese some years earlier and got the nouns, too:

..

> . . . it is more abundant than Latin and expresses concepts better. As well as possessing a great variety of synonyms, it also has a kind of natural elegance and dignity; and so *you may not use the same nouns and verbs when talking with different people* . . . (1579?82?83? in C:TCJ *italics* mine)

Only the prefixes and suffixes are not yet specified. In 1601, after obtaining a deeper understanding of Japanese – or, after being criticized? – Valignano qualified his remarks on Latin and elaborated on those honorifics:

> It is also true that the tongue of Japan is very copious and elegant. While preferring it to Latin would be odious [as Maffei, i.e. Valignano, himself, did earlier!], it could be said that it is the more courteous and dignified [*cortes y honrosa*], because it has certain particles of honor for verbs as well as nouns that greatly assists in making it courteous and . . . *it also has another manner of courtesy: that no one, though he be great and powerful, can when speaking of himself can use any of the particles or verbs of honor [i.e. honorifics], but must use verbs and words that are common and humble when speaking in the first-person* [Alvarez-Taladriz's citation suggests this was first observed by Gago in 1562] and can only use them [the honorifics] when speaking of others; and conforming to the persons and things they speak of which they speak, they must use words and particles of honor, respecting, when they speak, not only the persons with whom they speak, but of the people and things about which they speak, and, in conformance with this, must use verbs that are common or of honor. (*My italics* V: Libro in V(A): S&A n)

This is a splendid summary. Even the practice of honoring or disparaging *things* is not overlooked. I would have loved it had Frois at least picked up on the aspect of Japanese mentioned by Valignano that I italicized and written, say:

> *In Europe, the great men of our society speak as befit great men;*
> *In Japan, even the greatest men must speak humbly of themselves.*

It should be pointed out, however, that the Jesuits, even when they themselves were great men, believed in humility, whereas Frois personally knew a couple shôgun who were maniacal egoists who may not have always followed the Japanese rules of speech （いかがでしょう？この仮説は）. Perhaps that is why he neglected to mention the same. There is one aspect of learning to speak Japanese that differs from the situation with European tongues. As Mexia wrote in 1584: "there is another thing which I do not think is to be found in any other language – that a person learns rhetoric and good breeding along with his language, for nobody can learn Japanese without knowing how he must address the great and the lowly, the nobles and the commoners, and the decorum to be observed with them all, for they have particular verbs and nouns and ways of speaking for one class and the other," (C:TCJ) or, as Rodrigues put more succinctly a couple decades years later, "it is impossible to learn the language without at the same time learning to speak with dignity and courtesy." (C:TCJ) Actually, it is also true for other languages where different levels of language are clear to all. *Eg. Malay.* But, all of this is hard to follow in a Western language lacking the equivalent grammar. It is hard for us to imagine that the verb "to be" may have various forms depending on levels of formality, politeness and whatnot (the term *honorifics* does not really cover the half of it). Percival Lowell *tries* to imagine and comes up with this unsympathetic picture:

> . . . but what excuse can be made for a phrase like the following, "It respectfully does that the august seat exists," all of which means "is," and may be applied to anything, being the common word – in Japanese it is all one word now – for that apparently simple idea. It would seem a sad waste of valuable material. (L:SOFE:1888)

His ludicrous "phrase" is a single complex word, *gozaimasu,* still in common use today! But who cares about the "waste" of a few syllabets? *It sounds nice.* Remember. Japanese sentences *end* with the verb, at the end of that conjugation. If you do *not* use varying speech levels, play with those conjugations, it can get awfully monotonous. *Da* is also *is* in Japanese. But who wants to hear *da, da , da* all the time? Not me! Translated, even the simplest element of Japanese *honorifics*, the wee and subtle particles – (mostly *prefixes* such as "*o*" or "*mi*" or "*go*" which do before a word), primarily signifying simply that something is someone else's rather than one's own, but *also* containing a kernel of courtesy or respect – when Englished, turn into heavy, ie. *obvious*, artificial and fawning adjectives.

O-cha, becomes "honorable tea," *o-kao* becomes "exalted visage" and *o-kuruma* becomes "august sedan" etc.. Bird, who gave examples like this from letters, as conveyed to her by Chamberlain, writes to her reader, "they will interest you from the extreme orientalism of their expressions."

No! No! No! They are Orientalized *by default.* They do not convey the essence of the Japanese but are *"an unconscious act of revenge by the English language against forms of speech it is unfortunately incapable of matching."* (G:O&O) The translator, who has the choice of ignoring the politeness/respect or making Japanese sound inane is a traitor *no matter what he or she does* (See my book *Orientalism & Occidentalism* for a deeper discussion of why exotic tongues cannot help but create misunderstanding). To her credit, Bird surmised that "possibly they do not go very far beyond "your obedient humble servant." *That is right.* In fact, they do not sound half so fulsome. But at the same time, Japanese does have more obvious politeness in it. I should try to Frois the difference, I get:

> *We must always chose our words carefully in order to be polite and respectful.*
> *They learn polite and respectful ways of speaking that can be applied at the appropriate time..*

Rodrigues *liked* the way "respect and courtesy" for rank – before democracy, rank was not looked down on – were pegged on to the very grammar of Japanese. So did *everybody* back then. Today, when equality is idealized, even in Japan, some people have mixed feelings about this. Moreover, the complexity of such language – strictly speaking, the redundant ways of "saying the same thing" takes time to learn – is thought of as a barrier to global understanding. But, believe me, neither the Japanese nor any Orientals have ever sounded *oriental* in their own languages.

14-21   We wash our hands to touch something precious;
   Nós lavamos as mãos pera tocar alguma couza preciosa;

> The Japanese wash theirs to view *dogu* [implement/s] of *chanoyu* [the tea ceremony].
> *Os Japões as lavão pera verem os* dongus *de* chanoyu.

Contrast 11-9 says that *dogu* were as precious to the Japanese as gems are to "us." By putting *dogu* against *something precious* here, we are indirectly told that *dogu* are not precious by "our" way of thinking. Rodrigues describes the context of this washing.

..

> As they walk along the path through the wood up to the *cha* house [hut?], they quietly contemplate everything there – the wood itself, individual trees in their natural state and setting, the paving stones and the rough stone trough for washing the hands. There is crystal clear water there which they take with a vessel and pour onto their hands . . . (R(C):TIJ)

Since even someone who might not touch the most valuable utensils would wash his hands, Frois writes "view." Note that the prelude to the tea ceremony bears much resemblance to visiting a Shinto shrine – or Buddhist temple, for they often resemble shrine's in this respect – one takes a nature walk and cleans one's hands in water ladled from a trough bored into a boulder (or, better yet, a natural convexity in the boulder). The only difference is that the tea people are conscious of the masterfully arranged, generally small, if not miniature, natural elements and savor them and their choreography, whereas the shrine-goers are just enjoying their walk to the shrine and may or may not pay attention to the cedar, boulder, mountain peaks and, perhaps, sea. Although it is true that *dogu* will be handled and drunk from, we hear nothing of soap here; the intent is more like that of the shrine or temple-goer: *spiritual purification.* Perhaps we should add that in both sacred grounds and the tea hut, there was a spirit of equality not present in the extremely rank-conscious outside world (a world which paradoxically included the authorities of the religion and tea-ceremony), so washing, also, symbolized (though not obviously) *a temporary removal of the trappings of difference.*

It is possible, however, that Frois here is only thinking of a situation where someone asks to view – which means pick up and feel in the case of tea cups – a valuable *dogu* in someone's possession.

~~~~~~

14-22 Europeans kill boar mounted, with pikes, greyhounds and arquebuses;
Em Europa se matão os porcos montezes com chuças, galgos e espingardas;

The Japanese often chase them with *catanadas* [blows of *katana*=swords].[1]
Os Japões muitas vezes a coço às catanadas.

Even if the Portuguese calls them *porcos,* which sounds *piggy* and cute, we are talking about what some believe to be *the* most dangerous game on earth. [1] Facing a boar with a sword is more dangerous than facing a lion with a spear, for a sword is shorter and the former beast is less likely to flee if wounded. The tusks are also perfectly designed to cut a femoral artery and kill a man. Okada's only comment is: "this is a scene drawn from a scroll painting." I do not know if he means that Frois provides evidence for the reality of such a scene on a painting, or if it means that Frois has gotten this (wrong) idea from a picture! The only such scene I have on-hand shows mounted Japanese with spears, with only one exception, a man seated backwards on top of a huge boar that threatens to break through the lines, raising a knife as if to stab the boar in the buttock or the back of a leg. (Readers, please keep your eyes peeled!)

1. Catanada. Amazingly, this is bona fide Portuguese and I need not have included it in italics. The Japanese *katana,* sword or saber, spelled *catana* became Portuguese and in *Aurelio* has no less than six meanings! *Catanada* has a separate listing and means "a blow or stroke of a sword" or, "a severe reprimand."
2. Most Dangerous. Or, the African bush ox. Or, the grizzly bear.

~~~~~~

14-23 With us, killing flies with the hand is [considered] filthy;
Antre nós matar moscas com a mão hé sujidade;

In Japan, princes and lords do it, pulling off their wings and throwing them out.
Em Japão o fazem principes e senhores e tirando-lhe as azas as deitão fora.

Apparently, we thought flies vermin *before* we had a germ theory. I guess it wasn't hard to see what they sometimes sat on.

I cannot imagine anyone snatching flies from the air by their wings, so the Japanese side has me stymied. Surely, these men were not cruel enough to *torture* Winter flies sitting on window paper. Or, were they? Or, was this a clever way for pious Buddhists to avoid killing? You whack them just hard enough to knock them out but not kill them. Then you pull their wings off quickly while they are still unconscious. Then you toss them outside. Lacking wings they cannot get back inside. And if the ants finish them off, then the bad karma is on the ants. Is that it, perhaps? (A Japanese friend thinks this shows how spoiled and mentally deranged young nobles were. Anyone else? 誰か、欄外注を、お願いします！これは面白いぞ！) Or were the wings pulled off for a more practical reason, to reduce friction so the body could be thrown or snapped further away?

In Japan, to be "so old you can only chase a fly with your chin" was a common conceit – could this have made fly-catching a national past time, *a way to prove one was not yet over the hill?* Or did the guilt occasioned by Buddhism backfire and stimulate men to chance their fate? I have no idea, but I do know there are *thousands* of haiku on the subject, indeed the very category of "(summer) fly" is sometimes called, or at least subtitled *hae-uchi* or *hae-o utsu,* i.e., "hitting flies." Even Issa, so well known for his "Oh, *don't* swat the fly!" haiku (see 4-42) has far more about actually swatting the fly!

mercy me, it was rubbing its hands!

on my porch
even begging flies
get killed!

en-no-hae te-o suru tokoro-o utare-keri
(veranda's fly, hand rubbing [= praying for mercy] place=when, swatted [+completion])

na-mu-a-mi-da-bu-tsu!

a sutra
for every fly
i swat

hae-hitotsu uteba namuamidabutsu kana
(one fly, if=when hit, namuamidabutsu tis)

If any readers want more fly fare, please read my next book of collected, annotated and translated haiku, *Fly-ku!* Perhaps it will already be published by the time you have read this far.

~~~~~~

14-24 European monkeys, for the most part, have tails;
Os bojios d'Europa pola mayor parte tem rabos;

In Japan, there are many monkeys but no tails and seeing them [tails] is a novelty.
Em Japão com aver muitos não há nehum que o tenha e pera elles hé couza nova.

Had Frois been alive in the early Eocene, he might have found lemuriform primates in Europe, but the only non-human primates of "our" own to make it into human history are the Barbary apes of Gibraltar [1] and, *guess what!* – they are tail-less macaque, like those of Japan! But, all sorts of monkeys, mostly with tails, did make it to Europe, where they were greatly enjoyed as pets and performers. I have seen a picture of what I took to be a capuchin monkey on the shoulder of a "Southern Barbarian" visitor to Japan and Frois doubtless saw or witnessed Japanese astonishment to find the monkey had what Europeans took for granted, *a tail.* That is to say, Frois's "European monkeys" are not really European monkeys but the monkeys most commonly known to Europeans or the European *image* of a monkey, as transmitted from ancient times (the classical world imported many animals from Africa).

So long as the monkey is on my back, let me add that primatology was enlisted in *nihonjinron* in the 1970's and 80's (see Donna Harraway: *Primate Visions,* and the appropriate chapter of Peter Dale: *The Myth of Uniqueness*), and I have personally overheard young Japanese at the zoo relating the character of Japanese and Western primates to our respective characters (The Japanese *Macaca fuscata* a far tenser hierarchical animal than the easy-going "Western" chimp). Be that as it may, I have two *Faux Frois* monkeys to add:

With us dogs and cats are considered natural enemies;
The Japanese say the same about dogs and monkeys.

To us, a monkey is a symbol of ugly and uncouth behavior.
To Chinese and Japanese monkey's stand for self-control

The former does not surprise, for on the one side, monkeys/macaques do enjoy making monkeys out of dogs and, in Japan, are known for kidnapping puppies and on the other, a nosey watch-dog, unlike a cat, would constantly get in a monkey's way. The latter does surprise us. The "self-control" comes from Chinese philosophy which uses *the horse* as a symbol of the hard-to-tame *id* full of unruly desire and *the monkey* as the *super-ego* that struggles to restrain it. Unlike the dog and the monkey idiom which is known by all, this is only known to scholars and I would not know it had I not translated a book with a *sumie* painting of a small monkey tugging on a line attached to the Chinese character for "heart" (心) painted so as to suggest a horse!

*   *   *

If Frois was the only visitor interested in Japanese monkey tails or lack thereof, that was not true for *another* animal tail in Japan. The absence, scarcity, or shortness of *cat* tails in Japan was a common subject in 19th century European travelogues, for they were supposedly lost at the hands of superstition. Chamberlain finally put the tourists' worries to rest: "let it be known the peculiarity is a natural one."[2]

1. *Gibraltar Macaques.* Some think they made it across the Strait of Gibraltar from Morocco, 15 miles away. Others think British sailors brought them. Others think they were once indigenous to southern Spain. An article claims "no one is quite sure where they go when they die" either, for "no one has ever found the remains of any of the colony's deceased apes . . . they . . . know when it is their time and disappear into the wilds of the mountain to some undiscovered ape graveyard." They are treated well for Churchill once said England would rule the island so long as the apes were there. And because they are popular with tourists. Indeed, "if an ape becomes ill, it is treated at the local military hospital. Citizens of Gibraltar, military aside, are usually not allowed this privilege." Like the macaque in Japan, "they amuse themselves by breaking windshield wipers off cars and other acts of petty vandalism" and must be caught and taken "back up to their dens. . . . One local policeman noted that noisy drunken sailors from the old days were less of a problem to get into the car than a fun loving Barbary ape. The sailors usually stayed put once their celebrations were curtailed. As for the apes, the minute they're set free on top of the mountain they turn around and head back downtown again." (James Smith: *Monkeying Around on the Rocks The Barbary Apes of Gibraltar* from Gibraltar Tourist Information www.goworldtravel.com)

2. *Cat Tails in Japan.* I have more of this in *Han-chan's Dream: An essay in felinity* which will be published when I find a large publisher that believes in it enough to let me use color illustrations *and* keep the price down by doing a large printing.

14-25   We count by quill [writing numbers down] and tallies;   *Antre nós fas-se a conta por pena ou tentos;*

Japanese use *jina* [1][abacus].   *Os Japões a fazem com* jina.

François Caron wrote: "They reckon with little pellets, stuck upon little sticks upon a board . . wherewith they will add, multiply, and divide, with more facility and certainty then we with Counters." (C:TCJ) More precisely, metal or bamboo rods [2] set in two rows, or decks, on a wooden frame. Until about 1850, the upper row of rods on a Chinese abacus (*suan-pan*) held 2 beads and the lower 5 (called a 2/5 abacus), but the Japanese used a possibly Korean adaption, a 1/5 abacus until 1930, when they changed to a 1/4, which is what is in common use today. The 2/5 had 13 columns (the *ones* are on the right, then the next, *tens* if you wish, and so forth, while beads in the upper-deck generally count *five*) across, whereas the 1/4 has 21. That is too say, the Japanese one is long and slim. There are also differences in Chinese and Japanese fingering, with the former using the thumb and the first two fingers and the latter only the thumb and first finger. Whatever, the abacus beats the pen. Its users can calculate as fast if not faster than a computer, for entering a number *ipso facto* tabulates it. So, when your long-hand calculator begins to work out the answer, the *soroban,*[3] as Japanese call it, is already done! Not surprisingly, people *still* use it in the small stores and, sometimes, even in the post offices and railroad ticket offices in Japan. The only thing hard to understand is why *we* have not used it.[4]

The oldest known counting board (abacus) is the Babylonian Salamis tablet dated ≑ 300 B.C. Basically, there are groves inscribed in marble for stones to be lined up in. The first real abacus (suan-pan) is said to have evolved about 1200 A.D. in China. Meanwhile, the abacus is said to have disappeared in the Middle Ages when written calculation spread,[5] but that was before the Chinese improved it. The Europeans could have readopted it in the 16th or 17th century had they had the brains to have done so. Some, mentioning the common vertical orientation of the suan-pan and the Roman hand-abacus guess that early Christians brought the abacus to the East. But Chinese had written vertically for thousands of years, so that is not even circumstantial evidence. I also note that *all* the websites I visited, *all* the articles I read claim that it was the 17th century or, *at earliest* "circa 1600 A.D." when the Japanese adopted the Chinese (or Korean?) abacus. *Take note, you guys! It was already common in* **1585**.

Recently – I quote an undated *Newscientist.com* article by Jim Thomas entitled "Atomic Abacus" – James Gimzewski, head of a group of researchers at the IBM Zurich Research Laboratory, came across a ticket vender using a *soroban* in Japan and, eureka! his team soon had a nano-sized abacus using football-shaped buckminsterfullerene molecules, or buckyballs, as the beads with copper guide rails a millions times thinner than human hair as the rods [Can copper be that thin?!]. Meanwhile, Makoto Komiyama of the dep. of chemistry and biotechnology at Tokyo University "built a molecular abacus of his own" promising "to increase computer memory capacities to undreamed-of levels and even lead to molecular computers."

1. *Jina,* the Word.   Sometimes *gina*. It is a mystery. Perhaps it is a Southeast Asian term picked up by the Portuguese before they got to the Far East. Anyone?

2. *Bamboo Rods.* If you imagine a piece of bamboo *as is*, please think again. Bamboo is a very hard material from which rods, skewers and toothpicks may be made. The fibers are such that a rod with a bead sliding on it would last and last and last.

3. *Soroban,* the Word. I like the sound of the word used for the Japanese abacus. The etymology is ambiguous, but who cares!

4. We Haven't?   I recall reading that at least one European country does learn it in grade-school and also that the Russian early-modern 10/10 abacus was the best known in the West. *Gloss anyone?*

5. *Writing* vs *Bead Moving*. While I will admit to having met *soroban* users who had lost the ability to do simple calculation in the head, the problem is not intrinsic. A googled snippet:

> "At the Edinburgh Centre for Mathematical Education we have been investigating the use of a Japanese abacus, the soroban, as a means of developing mental calculation skills. Using a soroban encourages mental imagery and computation in conjunction with the physical movement of the beads. It therefore offers opportunities for learners to engage with the concept of number and strategies for mental calculation."

That doesn't sound too bad. The best summary of what the soroban can do well and what the brain can do well (if it is an extraordinary brain) is by the great physicist and bongo-drummer Feynman in his best-selling autobiography. The excerpt may be found at this extraordinarily elegant yet thorough abacus site http://www.ee.ryerson.ca:8080/~elf/abacus/index.html

14-26   We give many presents to show our love;
Antre nós dar de prezente diverzas couzas se tem por mais sinal de amor;

In Japan, few gifts show more class.
Em Japão quanto são menos hé mayor primor.[1]

Giving little is not just a case of Japanese moderation, good taste and philosophy (Rodrigues on the *sukisha,* tea-masters: "their ideal is to promise little but accomplish much, to praise sparingly but achieve a great deal . . . finally, to desire to err by default rather than excess"(R(C):TIJ?)). In Japan, gift-giving was – and, to a degree, still is – as formalized as that of many primitive peoples. Every little gift must be matched in a given amount of time. Giving a lot would set off a vicious cycle of exchange every bit as hard on the pocketbook as a potlatch. Indeed, like a potlatch, it could and was used with belligerent intentions.

Westerners residing in Japan today find it hard to simply give people things because it inevitably becomes a big deal and the party one hopes to help ends up impoverished from buying an equally expensive return-gift. Indeed, one of a wife's traditional (?) duties is keeping tabs on the value of every present and matching it with a return gift. Wealthy professionals who are showered with gifts by clients have special recycling arrangements worked out with a specialized business which might be called gift brokers who take back some gifts, recycle some and resell others. Japan is not the ideal place to live for someone who likes to give when he or she can and take when they need to take and doesn't like to keep tabs on this sort of thing.

But, I could be wrong on my reading of Frois. It might be just that such a strong connection was made between high-quality and small number in Japan that classy gifts and few gifts were equated. Actually my reading of *primor* favors this second interpretation.

1. *Primor*, again! Okada translated *mayor primor* as "more polite" (better etiquette = *reigi tadashii*). That suggests he thought along the lines of my first interpretation. Matsuda and Jorissen translate "the quality is heightened," (*hinkaku ga takamaru*) which supports my second. The French translation is "the homage is grand." (*plus l'hommage est grand.*) For some reason, French pulls this off best.

14-27 We have no custom of giving presents of medicine;
Antre nós não se uza dar mezinhas de prezentes;

In Japan, it is a common thing to give medicine in clam [1] shells.
Em Japão hé cousa muito corrente dar mezinhas em cascas d'amejias.

I find Japanese and Korean clams (young ones less than 4 inches in diameter) among the most beautifully marked shells in the world. They completely live up to their scientific name: *Meretrix,* or painted woman! (And, unlike the grosser American clam do not make me sick) Most of the clams used for gift containers, however, were artificially painted, i.e. standardized.[2] Today, they no longer make presents of medicine – except, occasionally, a medicinal wine something like our Campari – and no longer use shells for packaging any gifts. (The idea of shells for packaging is so unfamiliar to us that a copy-editor (?) for the French translation inadvertently turned the clam = *pruaire* into prune = *prunier*.)

This contrast is a fine observation, but, one much larger contrast was overlooked, unless "we" were still like the Japanese in the 16th century. To wit: *Japanese gave gifts where we would give payment for almost all services rendered.* With us, until very recently, a poor farmer might pay a Doctor with produce; but, in Japan, the rich, too – or, rather, *especially* the rich, gave Doctors and teachers and others they respected a gift, or rather, a token of gratitude rather than payment per se. As Ms. Bacon pointed out, contracts and exact charges for professional services were considered disgustingly crass by both sides:

In Japan, a present of money is more honorable than pay, whereas in America pay is more honorable than a present. (B:JG&W)

Today, the Japanese still use *o-rei,* or honorariums, more than we do. But note that these presents tend to be cash. This use of cash is itself worthy of a *Faux Frois:*

We give clothing and toys and other carefully chosen things to people;
They give cash for everything from children's New Year's presents to weddings and funerals.

This American was taught that giving money was vulgar. But note, the cash *must* be enclosed in a traditionally decorated, formal money-giving envelope (sold in any convenience store). Moreover, *money must always be wrapped up.* (I have been chastened for being impolite enough to leave change on someone's desk without putting it in an envelope.) But the best example of contrariness – real topsy-turvy – in present-giving *today* involves neither seashells nor money:

Among us, men give women flowers or chocolate on St. Valentines Day;
In Japan, the women always give chocolate to the men

There is also something called *giri-choko,* or "dutiful-chocolate," which female employees give to male employees working together in a firm to be certain everyone has chocolate on his desk. This can then be repaid on *huaito-dei,* White-Day, a week or two later, because, if I am not mistaken, an ad campaign by a major dairy producer convinced men to give back "dutiful white-chocolate" to the women.

1. *Translation:* Frois used a word (*ameija*) referring to clams in the broadest sense (bi-valves). Okada uses the Japanese word for cockle-shell (*torigai*), but I have read about the use of *clam* shells for medicine, so I'll go for it.

2. *Artificially Painted Clams.* Not all Japanese today know about the use of clam shells for medicine but all are familiar with another use of painted clam shells. They were painted gold, then adorned with a tiny portrait of a poet together with his or her poem and sets of these shells were then used for parlor games. *Faux Frois:*

> *We throw away the shells we eat.*
> *The Japanese paint poetry on them.*

14-28   With us, a visitor ordinarily brings nothing;
Antre nós ordinariamente se costumão as visitasões sem levar nada;

In Japan, visitors for the most part always must bring something.
Em Japão [quem] vai visitar pola mayor parte sempre á-de levar alguma couza.

This is still true today. Remember to bring a full load of trinkets if you visit Japan. Audubon birdcalls, if you can find them, are my first recommendation. Or, buy the usual pastry, fruit or alcohol on the way to someone's house. There are always stores primarily for this purpose close to the station (If you are in Japan you can use mass transit rather than wasting resources on cars with bumper stickers about saving the environment. Thus even the town that fails to create a center cannot help but enjoy one and it is the train station).

14-29   With us, things brought as presents can not be enjoyed by the same person who brings them;   *Antre nós das cousas que hum tras de prezente, não se pode ao mesmo convidar com ellas.*

In Japan, it is a sign of affection between the one who gives them and the one who receives them to try [1] them on the spot. *Em Japão em sinal de amor o que as dá e o que as recebe as hão logo de provar ali.*

As the gift is usually food, you must be sure to bring something you like, so you can enjoy giving your cake and eating it too!

1. *"Try Them"* Translation. Frois wrote "have to try them," but I had trouble squaring it with the first part of the sentence and considering that he sometimes uses the "have to" (*hão*) in the weak sense that a given behavior is customary, and as such must generally be followed, it might sound too forced in English. The Japanese translators write "taste," which reads better than "try" (*provar*) but gifts are not *always* food – they can be clever devices, and whatnot. . . Perhaps, I should have thrown away the attempt at a close translation and written "enjoy," instead.

~~~~~~

14-30   We embrace on parting and arriving from elsewhere;
Antre nós se uza de abraços ao despedir ou vir de fora;

The Japanese do not embrace at all, and laugh to see it done.
Os Japões totalmente o não uzão, antes se rim quando o vem fazer.

The Japanese are, as Frois's words suggest, one of the least touching people of the world. Any embracing they did, was done by adults in private. Neither men nor women went about with their arms over each others shoulders or holding hands.[1] Even children were not generally hugged. Passing through a crowd, they made a strong effort not to touch anyone. Rather than physically squeezing through as is common in many cultures, if someone was in the way, they always said something or, if the other person were looking, might use a slight karate-chop-like gesture that a way needed to be opened. (Yet, today, Japanese on trains tolerate being packed together far tighter than Western people can bear. It is an interesting paradox.[2]) Knowing this, my only surprise was not finding anything about *kissing* in the TRATADO. In 1585, even the stiff English still kissed like Hungarians.[3] Did the Spanish and Portuguese *not* do so? Or was it taken for granted to be part of the above-mentioned embrace and thus not mentioned? The Japanese, at any rate, soon came to expect *kissing* from Westerners, if they did not already in Frois's time, for Kaempfer wrote in his account of an audience with the Emperor [or was it the Shôgun?] in 1692 that

> Then they made us kiss one another, like man and wife, which the ladies particularly shew'd by their laughter to be well pleas'd with. (K:HOJ)

That delegation was completely male. It seems that visiting the antipodes can be a trying experience. Crossing the equator for the first time, I, *too* had to kiss a male. To be precise, it was the painted toes of the ugliest sailor (Neptune's wife, Juno) on *La Traviata* (a Russian-built Swedish bulk freighter with the OW line) I worked away on.

The Chinese, who also did not embrace or kiss in public, found our *skinship* (a fine 20th century Japanese term) as odd as the Japanese did. A picture from a Chinese magazine article c.1890 shown in *Land Without Ghosts*, a book on how Chinese viewed the West, depicts families and relations in France saying good bye before a trip. The caption includes the following:

> Prostrating oneself, kneeling, and bowing – each expresses civility through regulation of limbs. This is called civility of manners. Shaking hands, brushing cheeks, and kissing are also exchanges of civility by making bodies come together. This may be called civility of sentiments. Westerners esteem sentiment the way Chinese esteem etiquette. Civilities are different but the desire to be polite is the same. (A&L:LWG)

The nuanced relativism is fascinating. The caption continuing mentions a young daughter-in-law who was scolded by the elder brother's wife for sleeping in and missing the chance to kiss her father-in-law goodbye, as etiquette demanded. Perhaps I over-associate, but I cannot help but recall a common figure in Chinese popular poetry (nursery rhymes etc.): the lecherous father-in-law chasing around the daughter-in-law who defends herself by squirting him with milk from her breasts, etc.. And, *here,* the Chinese reader chuckles to himself, she is *supposed* to kiss him! The caption writer could not resist a few more words on kissing itself:

We have also heard the way to kiss requires making a chirping sound. In the Western language/s it is called '*quasi.*' Those who do not know how to translate say the sound is like a fish drinking water, but this is wrong. (Ibid)

Hygienic types have suggested that even a handshake is too much contact and that we should copy the Japanese here. People who feel that humans need more touching, however, may find the Japanese physical standoffishness pathological. While not overly hygienic, Thoreau would have liked the Japanese way and found it refreshing. When he was visited by some preachers from somewhere out West (California, if I recall correctly) who not only hugged him too familiarly but presumed to know him better than he knew himself, he recoiled and spat that when they dived into his belly they ought to take care not to break their necks upon the shallow bottom.[4]   Call me *cold*, but I would second Thoreau.   But this coldness can be overdone.   If we confine ourselves to the physical, than all humans are cold fish compared to our closest primate relation, the bonobo,[5] who turn every greeting into a veritable feel-fest of mutual masturbation and sex. No, we are forgetting something important: *words*. Japanese enjoy more crisp stock phrases for greeting and coming and going, entering and leaving situations than English.   To a person sensitive to language, such words can be just as satisfying as "our" physical methods of greeting and send-off (not that the Japanese do not combine their words with bowing and other physical yet not touching body-language – it is that the words might be said to provide the touch).   And, for the cultured classes, these words were not only spoken. *They often involved writing!* Reading the haiku saint Basho (1644-1694), we find almost half of his poems composed for greeting and parting situations – mostly using natural allusion or allegory to express gratitude, joy, respect, remorse, sorrow, etc.   *Faux Frois:*

> *We exchange standard pleasantries and talk about people when we meet and part;*
> *A Japanese of parts must make up an appropriate poem about nature to express his feelings.*

And, in respect to another parting about which Frois might well have written but did not:

> *Before we die, we give the priest our last confession;*
> *Japanese compose and leave the world a poem.*

1. *Holding Hands* I was disgusted to hear a Usanian warrior in Iraq interviewed on NPR presume to teach Iraqi men not to hold hands, because he wrongly associated it with homosexuality. Talk about *The Ugly American!*

2. *Touching on the Train*. There are two possible takes on this. One is that being pressed up against people on trains compensates for the lack of touch elsewhere, so that unconsciously Japanese *need it*. The other is that, this is proof of the strength of the Japanese character, the discipline to put up with discomfort not found in the spoiled Occident. Or, is it purely economic: *What else can one do?*

3. *English, Hungarians and Usanians.* From the late 15th century to the early 16th century English were famous for being the kissiest people. Visitors from the continent enjoyed the way they not only kissed you coming and going but even extended their kisses to the pets. This is hard to reconcile with the stereotypically cold Englishman, no? One of my godfathers is a Hungarian and I can still remember how, as a boy, I was not especially pleased to be kissed on two sides by a scratchy beard! It was almost as bad as the more perfumed of my grandmothers. These are things I might have been spared had I grown up in Japan. Seriously, when I returned to the USA after almost twenty years in Japan as an adult, I was astounded to discover that the embrace reserved in my youth for grandmothers and Hungarian godfathers had become commonplace! The same decades that brought us the disgustingly aggressive fisting of the air to indicate triumph had us hugging everybody! *Talk about cultural schizophrenia!* Call me a nostalgic Rip Van Winkle, but I would prefer less of both behaviors!

4. *Thoreau*. I do this from memory, for thanks to extreme poverty and sickness at a time of moving, my almost complete preparation of five large anthologies of Thoreau's work are somewhere, possibly lost, in Japan and I am afraid to investigate lest the shock of losing it hurt my work on haiku. If you like Thoreau, please keep your fingers crossed for me!

5. *The Bonobo*. The bonobo ape, which shares about the same percent of genes with us as the chimp but is more similar physically, engage in sex (hetero-, homo- or self) once every hour or two. *Males tend to greet by rubbing butts with each other*, or *having coitus with females*, whereas *females* (who are socially more dominant than chimp females) *greet other females by rubbing each other frontally* (stimulating the clitoris until orgasm if I am not mistaken), a behavior the Japanese researchers who discovered it call *hokahoka* (a psychological onomatopoeia with heating connotations) and Usanian researchers prosaically call GG-rubbing (G=genital). Considering Frois's contrast, how interesting that the discovery of this species of ape with very physical greetings should be none other than the Japanese! (The Germans knew of bonobos, which were considered pigmy chimps, from 1928 and carried out studies on a few bonobo in a Munich zoo in the 1930's but the Japanese researchers discovered what they were for the first time in the 1970's.) On the other hand, how lucky that Japanese rather than "our" pc-biased researchers found them! Our culture is so hopelessly moralistic that sex cannot be treated with the equanimity required to see what is what. The first Japanese University bonobo site I found on the net showed a photo of a female with what looked like a

very happy expression with a baby on her back, a male adult against her rump and one of her legs lifted up and reaching back so her foot could squeeze the balls of the male, something, the researcher explains matter-of-factly in the caption, *they often do when nearing orgasm.* Maybe I am wrong, but I doubt one of "our" university sites would *allow* such objective reporting. Be that as it may, who is not touched by the sensitive bonobo's apparent ability to empathize (obvious from the way the infirm or blind are treated), in contrast with the often heartless behavior of the crude chimp? If we want to better understand where we, as a species, came from, should not the defense of this habitat (in the Congo) of our endangered fellow primate be the highest priority for anthropologists, cultural anthropologists, psychologists, psychiatrists and others? *Why then are the funds involved to date so small?*

14-31   We use our hands to play ball; *Antre nós se joga a pela com a mão;*

The Japanese play with their feet. *Os Japões a jogão c[om o p]ee.*

Speaking of feet and hands, I must add that whereas the chimpanzee grabs and pulls one toward itself to bite, the bonobo is said to use its feet to kick one away, defensively.

See the next contrast about what we were doing long before we had baseball, basketball or soccer. The Japanese game *kemari,* literally, "kickball," was played "from time immemorial." Native Americans (who share blue-spots on their rear-end with the Japanese) were also mostly into kicking sports. The world might be divided into *kicking* and *throwing* sports cultures.

14-32   We do our play with the ball against a wall from above;
Antre nós se fazem os piqes da pella em parede pera riba;

In Japan it is done on the ground, striking it always with the ball from below.[1]
Em Japão se fazem no chão, dando sempre com a pela pera baxo.

Europeans had long bounced balls off castle walls and churches (Okada). This, combined with the throwing devices of the central Amerindians evolved into *jai-lai.* It is hard to say exactly how the European game was played in Frois's day. Marques writes there is no description of the ball games, that "it probably was one of throwing the ball, perhaps with intent of knocking down some obstacle or simply hitting a distant point;" but he also writes that (King) Joao I considered it very useful in training for arms "because this game makes the members of the body supple," something which suggests the game must have been far more active than his guesses indicate!

The Japanese game *kemari* is no longer played (unless someone can prove it is the root of soccer). On TV Easterns, at least, we see a prettily decorated small ball repeatedly kicked up – like we play with a soccer-ball trying to keep it in the air – by young nobles wearing silk formal clothing. Rodrigues explains the game as follows:

> The balls are inflated and are the size of a man's head. This is played a great deal by the nobles and *kuge* [peers: imperial line, as opposed to shogunate or fief-related nobility], and many of them gather in a circle wearing on the right foot a certain shoe with a blunt point; it is a fine sight to see them

kick forward the point of the foot and hit the ball upwards, and then do various tricks and clever feats with it without letting it touch the ground. Among the *kuge* there is a noble family which is head of this art for it belongs to the royal household and palace. The same applies to archery, riding and various other liberal arts. (Cooper trans. R(C):TIJ)

I continued quoting beyond the proper subject of this contrast because Rodrigues has pointed out a Japanese practice that deserves a *Faux Frois:*

> We have heads of various public institutions, religious orders and learned societies;
> The Japanese have heads for everything from poetry to tea-making to sword-identification.

Rodrigues explains all of this as an aside in his long essay "On Entertaining With Cha," because the "teacher or head of this religion or art" [the tea ceremony, including the construction of the tea hut and *dogu,* etc.] was called a *suki-no-oshô,* where *suki,* means fine-discrimination and *oshô,* is a term generally used for the head of a zen temple. He explains that some heads are "promoted and chosen by the king, . . . others are recognized as such by their superiority over everybody else in an art." For the former type, he mentions "the head of the poets in every kind of Japanese verse." And, for the latter, Japanese chess and *go.* Sometimes it was a hereditary office, and sometimes elected.

> . . . in their lifetime they select the best of their disciples and instruct them so that they may succeed them. They teach them the principle rules and secrets of their art and issue them a patent confirming their succession therein, just as the ancient philosophers used to do in the succession of their academies. The same also happens in the mechanical arts, in which somebody is always chosen as the one natural master of the art by election, approbation or hereditary succession. Sometimes, indeed, there are some nominated as such by themselves without anybody awarding it to them, and they are called *Tenka-ichi,* [literally, heaven-beneath-one] that is, the leading person of the kingdom in such an art . . . Such people are wont to place a notice or inscription above the door of their house, for example, *Fude Tenka-ichi,* that is, "the best manufacturer of writing brushes in the kingdom," etc. This also applies to fencing masters who possess sufficient self-confidence to call themselves unique in their art . . . (R:TKJ)

This is significant because Rodrigues wrote it at the very start of the Tokugawa, the closed period of Japan's history which is usually *blamed* for spawning this system where every art has its master-families (*iemoto*) who dictate over it. Some may find this suffocating. I am impressed to find a society striving for and admitting excellence though I must admit the titles still used today (by Japanese, Chinese and Koreans) for the masters of the board-games make my eyes open wide with wonder whenever I see them. We have chess-masters and the grand-master. That is nothing. They have, besides dozens of levels and ranks, and titles including words like "sacred" (聖) [2] But to return to the foot-ball, the game described by Rodrigues resembles the play which Latin Americans do for hours with soccer balls (Strangely enough, Norte Americano soccer players do not do it so much!) In Cooper's footnote to Rodrigues, we find this gem:

> In 905 a record was set up in the presence of the emperor by a group of courtiers kicking the stuffed ball 260 times without letting it touch the ground. (R:TIJ)

Nothing in the note explains why Rodrigues wrote of an *inflated* ball and the note a *stuffed* one. There is surely a China-connection here, because Dyer Ball gives an entire page to a form of foot-ball he calls shuttle-cock. The shuttle-cock comprises 8 to 20 layers of skin, the outer two being snake and inner ones "said to be shark's skin" with three duck-feathers. The kicking styles can get very elaborate, but the most common involves "the inner side of the sole of the right shoe." A version of this is done under the left calf and

> the most usual form of this stroke is as follows: the left leg is doubled round so that the foot is in front of the body and about ten or twelve inches from the ground: this is done while the shuttle-

cock is descending: and, when it is almost near enough to hit, a spring is taken off the ground with the right foot last, and the shuttle-cock is immediately hit by the inner side of the sole of the right foot from under the left calf. . . . Another stroke is made with the sole of the right foot from behind the body . . .

I will refrain from quoting him on the more complex kicks! "The object of the play is, of course, to keep the shuttle-cock up as long as possible." Just like in Japan with that *mari*.

1. *Translation*. The Portuguese for the Japanese side is ambiguous. Both Japanese translations and the French follow the German and have the ball bounding-off the ground, while one Portuguese native-speaker (H) had them "hitting the ball always downwards." The only problem is that I have not found any description of such a style of *kemari* play. So I bet upon the grammar stretching to mean that while the play was done standing on plain ground (with no wall being used) the ball was kicked "*from* below." However, reading the description of "Tennis play in Mexico" in the encyclopedic PLEASANT HISTORY OF THE CONQUEST OF THE WEST INDIES ("if the ball toucheth the wall it loseth." – There is also something about "skynne upon eache buttocke" but the microfilm was too dark to read what came before or after.), it occurred to me that there is also a slight chance the ball's touching the wall or ground respectively would constitute a point. And there is an even slighter chance Frois meant to specify the ball could be kicked by curving the leg so as to hit it with the bottom of the foot. But, I seriously doubt the ball was ever dribbled under foot as the other translations allow, because traditional games generally don't change quickly, and Rodrigues's description was less than two decades after TRATADO.

2. *Titles in Go and Shogi*. For some reason, I had trouble finding the titles on the Net! Anyone?

14-33 We have mills, water-wheels and horse-powered grinders;
Antre nós há moinhos, asenhas e atafonas;

In Japan, all flour is ground with a hand mill using arm-power.
Em Japão tudo o que se moe hé com roda de mão à força de braço.

To me, the fact that little dogs spent their entire days and lives working turnspits for "us" tells it all. In 1585, there was already a disparity in horsepower – the West was using more energy per capita than the Japanese who generally ground flour or beans with a *te-usu* (hand-mill), as opposed to the Chinese style *fumi-usu* (tread-mill). But in the Tokugawa era that would soon follow, Japanese developed many types of mechanical power and complex automata enjoyed great popularity, so they were ready to reproduce steamboats, railroads and whatnot when Perry pushed open that door.

14-34 In Europe, people socialize and recreate with others in plazas and streets;
Em Europa se comonicão e recreão os homens polas praças e ruas;

In Japan, [they do it] only in their houses, and just walk along when they are on the streets. *Em Japão somente em suas cazas, e polas ruas sempre vão de caminho.*

In Europe, squares and parks where people could socialize had a long history going back at least as far as 5th century Greece, and buildings in Europe surrounded an open public square. Searching the history of public spaces on the internet brought one nice story (*the Corpus Christi parades where dawn-to-dusk plays were performed on stages with wheels that went from one public square to another, performing one act at each!*) for a hundred horrible ones (*hanged in the public square; usually burned alive in the public square; publicly beheaded in the public square; slow-roasted upon an open fire in a public square; hung by the heels in a public square,* etc.). So, it would appear that executions were "our" favorite recreation or people who have websites have axes to grind.

On the other hand, Japan had no such public places to socialize. This changed, to a degree, in Edo (Tokyo) in the centuries to come. Still, at the end of the 18th century, Issa complained about the need to buy green – pay for tea or something to get out of the hot treeless streets of Edo where walled-off daimyo residences took up miles of street-front. In most of Japan, I would think it was only a short walk to a temple ground or a recreational establishment of one sort or another. But, these places were, perhaps, not for socializing with others in the sense Frois's word *se comunicão* suggests. This does not mean, however, that Japanese did little socializing. They just did more between people in common professions (I think of the networks of poets whose activity tended to be far more social – done in groups – than was the case in Europe) who would arrange to meet somewhere, maybe a hall at a temple, or someone's house, and less with complete strangers.

Even today, many Japanese municipalities are not eager to develop central *outdoor spaces*. I do not think it is just the cost of the real-estate. The town I lived in did not even have a bench in front of the train station (the closest thing to a center) for they feared teenagers would congregate. But, at the same time, they had an incredible number of good little restaurants, coffee-shops and bars which they use for socializing rather than bringing people home as is done in the USA. That is to say, my experience has been the reverse of Frois's! I am not alone in this, either. The Japanese aversion to bringing guests home is a common complaint coming from foreign visitors! The excuse given by Japanese and foreign language newspapers in Japan is usually the lack of room, shabby dwellings and desire not to mix family and business matters – since most socialization is with others in the same company in Japan. I thought this was a post WWII phenomenon, but Townsend Harris's journal suggests the reversal may have already occurred by the mid-19th century.

> I told them they had a queer way of showing friendship and hospitality; that I had been in the country four months and a half, and had never been invited to enter the house of a Japanese, and that they had even refused to dine with me on my country's New Year's Day . . . and closed by saying that in America such conduct would be called inhospitable. (H:CJTH)

Harris's loneliness may in part derive from his high position, which warranted isolation to the Japanese way of thinking, and the official policy of keeping foreigners at arm's length. But, I feel that it is mostly that Japanese were very private. While they may have entertained *themselves* at home, perhaps they rarely if ever invited other people there (except for the New Year's visit). Yet, 64, below, suggests they were different in Frois's time.

In one sense, Frois's contrast still holds true. When it comes to talking with strangers – not, foreigners, who are a special class, but even other Japanese – Japanese are the least social people I have known. They tend to socialize entirely within their own cliques and, aside from the mama-sans at the bars who are almost always witty, there is relatively little of the easy-going *exchange of jokes and insults between strangers* that makes going out so much fun in most countries. Then again, Japanese may simply not have gone out much (except for pilgrimages). Here are some remarks from the Iwakura Embassy, a Japanese diplomatic mission that toured the West in the 1870's, that touch upon this contrast (and indirectly demonstrates the Japanese enthusiasm for topsy-turvyism from their side)! The comments were occasioned by a visit to Woodwall Gardens (sp?).

> East/West cultural traits or dispositions categorically differ with each other, as if they come out opposite: the Occidental enjoys outside contact [*gaiko*]; the Oriental shrinks from it. It is not only a remnant of our Seclusion. It is because we pay little attention to making fortunes and feel little urgency to trade. Occidentals enjoy going out and taking trips . . . Orientals enjoy remaining idle inside . . . *Occidentals study the science of the material and Orientals the science of the immaterial.* . . . That every Occidental city has botanical and zoological gardens and we have our *uegiya* [nursery/nurseryman] and beast-shows, excepting the difference in scale, superficially seems a point of resemblance; but the facilities' purposes are radically opposed . . . ([*italic* was emphasized in the original] J/I:IR 1876)

We can see here that Orientals=Japanese are pegged as stay-at-homes and Occidentals as literally outgoing – just as Frois put it almost 300 years earlier. And, to link this going-out to the park, Iwakura's point was that when Westerners went out, they gained valuable material knowledge as they enjoyed themselves. The Japanese "zoo" was a mere freak show, while Western parks served the interest of material science, instructing children about the natural world, and this promotion of material science and progress was what lay behind the wealth and poverty gap separating West and East. Since this is book is neither about parks nor progress, I will not translate any more of the two-page-long commentary. [1]

1. *Iwakura Embassy Book* The comments are probably translated elsewhere. I found on the Web that the entire report is translated but the price for the book (or, rather, volumes) was *astronomical!*

~~~~~~

14-35   With us, a feigned smile/laugh is considered frivolous;
Antre nós ho rizo finjido se tem por liviandade;

> In Japan, refined and [a mark of] good comportment.
> *Em Japão por primor e boa condisão.*

In Portuguese, *riso,* and in Japanese, *warai* means both "smile" *and* "laugh." In English we must specify one or the other. I suspect that "smiling" is what Frois is thinking of, but considering the fact *risinho* is used for smile in 48, below, can not completely rule out "laugh" either.

> When a servant is rebuked or scolded he must smile like a Chinese cat. This etiquette in smiles is very misleading at first. I often used to think that Také, my *riksha*-boy, meant to be impertinent when he insisted on smiling while I was angry with him; but when he told me of the death of his little child with a burst of laughter, I knew that this was only one of the tidbits of etiquette in this topsy-turvy land. (S:MQTJ)

I will not bother quoting any more observations by Westerners about the "strange way" Japanese and other Far Eastern people smile or laugh when they have done something wrong, are tense, or sad because someone has died in their family, etc., because these observations are a dime a dozen. Let me just observe that *if one is going to maintain a stiff upper lip about things, it is more graceful to do so in the form of a slight smile than in a scowl or a frown, is it not?* Moreover, such a smile is actually a close relative of the grimace – as reflected, I think, by "grin and bear it" – so it has a valid physio-psychological pedigree and is not really *artificial* as "we" claim.

Essays on "the enigma of the Japanese smile" – I recall coming across a few – strangely overlook the Koreans and Chinese [1] who do the same, though not so often if they are more outspoken. The Sinosphere appreciates self-control and equanimity, which is to say, not looking troubled. Note: *Buddha shares that smile.* Christ, as we have recounted above, is depicted looking pretty damn wretched. In that sense, Christ was Occidental. Perhaps, there is greater difference between the way Japanese and other Far Eastern people express themselves in private (when their faces show what Ekman calls "universal emotion" (intro. to C. Darwin: *The Expression of the Emotions in Men and Animals*)) and in public – as compared to Usanians, at any rate – but there is nothing strange or topsy-turvy about it; and, I think it bears noting that Japanese are no more aware of their slight smile than are most Occidentals of their unnaturally strong tendency to stare into the eyes of other people. A *senryu* goes: "the prostitute / is made up, right down / to her smile" (*warai-gao made keisei-wa koshiraeru*). The allusion in the original, punning on the verb used for cosmetic application, suggests the common saying about such a woman's tears being of the crocodile variety. Is that not proof that *other* Japanese did not think of *their* smiles as made up?

It is interesting that Frois concentrates on the contrast in *facial expressions*, both in not revealing grief in calamity (14-2) and now in this matter of smiling. He never writes, "We always complain; They never do." Valignano almost does when he writes: "they [the Japanese] never come to discuss their troubles . . ." (*nunca vienen a contar sus trabajos ni agravios . . .*). (V(A):S&A). Confession was doubtless exceedingly difficult for Japanese, and a relief for them!

1. *Chinese Smiles.* I have observed far more Chinese with what seems to be genetically built-in smiles than Japanese, Koreans or Europeans. Does my observation have any validity? Has any one researched this? Do people with turned-up mouths tend to come from any particular part of China?

14-36   In Europe, clarity of language is sought and ambiguity avoided;
Em Europa proqurão clareza nas palavras e jojem da eqivocasão

> In Japan, ambiguous words are good language and held in high estimate.
> *Em Japão as equivocas hé a milhor lingoa e são as mais estimadas.*

In the timeless classic ENGLISHMEN, FRENCHMEN, SPANIARDS, the ambiguity of our native tongue is held to be the mainstay of British diplomacy and well suited for the "allogical" (not illogical) national temperament. But, in England, aside from antagonism toward the cold unbending logic of the French, some of whom do indeed claim that "what is not clear is not French" – a prescriptive claim under the guise of a fact that only goes to prove other Frenchmen *are* using ambiguous language! – one does not find the clear-cut, conscious and unabashed *defense of ambiguity* found in modern Japan.

Okada opines Frois is talking about "the honorifics that reached their most complex state of development at the time" which "took a form that avoided clear ways of saying things and favored expressions that were indirect and inconclusive." I would add that opinions were not completely spelled out not only for the sake of avoidance but because doing so insults the intelligence of a friend or an enemy. Moreover, I would not link Frois's observation to honorifics alone. Ambiguity was also couched in the double and triple negatives which might accompany but are not the same as honorifics. And, I would not be surprised if Frois regarded things like "Excuse me" (*shitsurei desuga*) meaning "And could you please tell me to whom I am talking" and "I'll think it over" (*kangaete-okimasu*), meaning "You might as well give up asking because there is almost no chance it is possible" – to use a couple expressions common today – as "ambiguous" *when actually they are not*: for the Japanese and the fluent foreigner know exactly what they *mean*. (What *I* mean is that we must be careful about overdoing this *ambiguity* stuff for Japanese do, after all, have to communicate). Be that as it may, Frois is the first person I know of to make this particular contrast, which is generally explained today as proof that Japanese are close-knit and need not explain themselves *ad-nauseam* and have the good sense to allow for some play on the part of the other party by people who like ambiguity, and as the result of years of warring and fear for losing one's head by being clear by people who do not appreciate it (All in 14-36 is expanded upon in G:O&O).

14-37   With us, a respected man would be thought deranged to hang the pelt of a fox or jackal [1] from his belt; *Antre nós trazer hum homem honrado huma pele de rapoza ou adibe pindurada detras na cinta, te-lo hião por doudo;*

> In Japan, noblemen bring them with them when they have work to do, or their lackeys bring them, for them to sit upon.   *Em Japão os fidalgos quando fazem obras as trazem, e os pajens, pera se asentarem nellas.*

Growing up on tatami, Japanese prefer sitting *down* to sitting up on chairs. *Ergo*, fur on the ground would beat a hard log for a stool. But, this custom may have a less natural, i.e. historical, explanation which harkens back to the usual place, China (where there was no tatami and people more often than not sat on stools). From the Orestes' PICTORAL CHINESE-JAPANESE CHARACTERS account of the origin of the character for *tail*:

> In ancient times in China, people of the common class used to carry, when working outside, traveling on foot or going places, a kind of fur cushion hung behind at the waist like an animal's tail to sit upon when in need of rest.

Vaccari also notes that Japanese miners still carried "a similar thing made of straw." (V&V:PCC) The *nobleman* aspect of the contrast would appear to be the uniquely Japanese part. Frois's description of Japan's first country-unifying shogun Nobunaga would seem to shed some light on the proliferation of pelt fashion in Japan:

> He decreed that while the work [building Nijo castle] was in progress none of the monasteries either inside or outside the city should toll its bells. [i.e. no telling of time!] He set up a bell in the castle to summon and dismiss the men, and as soon as it was rung all the chief nobles and their retainers would begin working with spades and hoes in their hands. He always strode around girded about with a tiger skin on which to sit and wearing rough and coarse clothing; following his example everyone wore skins and no one dared to appear before him in court dress while the building was still in progress. (in C:TCJ)

Needless to say, the castle was built in record time.

1. *Jackal?* No, they did not have jackals in Japan. The Japanese translators use the word "mountain-dog," which can mean "wild-dog," but usually means the Japanese "wolf." If Frois meant "wolf," he might have used the word available for it in Portuguese.   So, I suspect he really is talking about *tanuki,* a canine with small feet, a fat body and a fox-like head with less pointed ears and a raccoon face and bushy tail. But I went with the known word "jackal," as per the German and French translations. どうだい？狼でなく、狸の可能性はないか？

~~~~~~

14-38 In Europe, an open crown for mass is only worn by a bishop;
Em Europa coroa aberta de missa não a tras senão os sacerdotes;

> In the Gokinai [central Japan, around Kyoto] area, *komono* [petty servant/s] who carry a lord's shoes wear one. *Nas partes de Goquinay as trazem os comonos que levão os sapatos a seus senhores.*

The profile of this open crown, or hat with an almost flat front and a back, called a *miter*, resembles the top of a bishop in chess. The barnacle-shaped *eboshi* cap worn by petty servants was not as highly decorated, but too similar for Frois to resist this practically meaningless contrast! I suppose it was funny to consider underlings with tall hats which were generally symbols of high position and Frois's envisioned audience being fellow clergy . . .

~~~~~~

14-39 In Europe, we go forward when playing a board game;
Em Europa as tabolas que se jogão se vão lançando pera diante;

> In Japan, they always pull [their pieces] back toward themselves.
> *Em Japão se vai sempre tirando por ellas pera tras.*

In this contrast one might expect to find in the last chapter, Frois would seem to be comparing our chess or checkers to a parchisi-like game called *sugoroku*. He must have known, or cared little about board games or he would have made more contrasts, such as:

> *Our chess pieces are always ours;*
> *Their shôgi [Chinese-style chess] pieces are turned over when taken and join the other side.*

> *Our chess pieces are discriminated by shape;*
> *Theirs are identified by Chinese characters meaning "castle," "elephant," etc. written on them.*

In the heyday of *Nihonjinron* (1970-1990), the way *shôgi* pieces do not die, but are recycled in this way was sometimes tied into stereotypes of gentle relativistic Easterners versus cruelly absolutist Westerners. The use of writing to indicate pieces used in a popular game shows how deeply the written word permeated Sino-Japanese culture. If *shôgi* is the etymological sibling of *chess*, as closely related as, say, the chimpanzee to the bonobo, *go,* then, would be *Homo sapiens*, for it is known as *the* top intellectual board game in the East, and is clearly a cut above chess and shôgi.

> *Our chess pieces are diverse of type and movement;*
> *Their more complex board game,* go, *uses only identical black or white stones;*

> *Our chess game starts with all the pieces on the board and has no handicap;*
> *Their* go *game begins with no pieces on the board, unless one player is given a handicap.*

> *Our chess pieces move about, so that each piece might be said to have a history, or a trail.*
> *Their* go *pieces are called* ishi, *and true to their name, remain in place like stones.*

> *In chess, we try to checkmate the king;*
> *In go, they compete to capture the most territory.*

> *With chess, the winner is obvious;*
> *With go, it is sometimes necessary to tabulate the respective territories to know the winner.*

> *Our pieces always set within square spaces on the board;*
> *Theirs always set on the interstices of the lines rather than on the space between.*

> *We keep our pieces in rectangular boxes or leave them lined up on the board;*
> *They keep them in round bowls and never leave them on the board.*

Perhaps because all board games in Japan were used for gambling (*go* has a good handicap system which allows amateurs to play pros), the Jesuits, despite their love for learning, failed to appreciate the superiority of *go* to chess – *Try it and see if you still want to play chess!* – and didn't bring it back to us (Perhaps a Ricci scholar can explain why someone as bright as he obviously was failed to export it from China either!!!) Even Golownin, who I would think just the man for *go* – his captivity was the perfect opportunity to learn – only refers to it in a footnote:

> They make use of a very large draught board and four hundred men, which they move about [*sic.* They are not moved but *placed,* probably a mistake in the English translation, for Golownin is usually precise] in many different directions, and which are liable to be taken in various ways. Our sailors played at draughts according to the usual European way; the Japanese immediately imitated them, and the game was soon generally known throughout the whole city, and the Russian terms were adopted in playing it. (G:MCJ)

Neither, for that matter, did Morse or Chamberlain. Even Dyer Ball, who devoted a page to shuttle-cock and another to the chess-equivalent game in THINGS CHINESE, short-changed *go* (*wai-k'ei*) with a single short paragraph and the lame excuse that "We have not space for a full account." And today, many people in the West try a *go*-like game, Othello, but rarely try the real thing. *Why? What is wrong with us?* Even in the 1970's and 80's when Japan was *the* country to copy, why in the world didn't more people in the West try *go*? [1]

1. Let's Go *GO!* For learning, I recommend David Fotland's user-friendly *Manyfaces* software. If there is a wealthy person out there who would like to make history by bringing the world's best board game to the attention of the West, please establish a multi-million dollar prize! In the United States, for example, you might offer a million dollars to both the over-all champion and the highest placing Usanian. If you invest in *go* equipment companies and sell the rights to Japanese television, you will more than earn back your prize money, too.

14-40 In Europe, hawks and falcons almost always have hoods over their eyes;
Em Europa os asores e falcões estão quasi sempre com caparões nos olhos;

In Japan, the eyes are always uncovered.
Em Japão sempre tem os olhos descubertos.

Frois must have seen a lot more hawks staring back at him in Japan than in Europe – and a glance at old prints bears this out – but the difference may not have been absolute (Okada finds a citation of a hood on a Japanese hawk, but it is almost three decades after Frois and might have been learned from the West.) Hawks probably deserve a whole chapter, like horses, for the attention the nobility gave to them in both Europe where an Emperor (Frederick II) wrote a fine book on them, and in Japan where there are dozens of terms for their feathers alone. The most touching animal-related poem in the overwhelmingly human – love-affair – centered *Manyoshu* (Japan's oldest anthology of poetry) is an eulogy for a hunting hawk that the poet raised in his living room parts of which remind me of one of "our" most touching animal eulogies, Skelton's incredible "Phillip Sparrowe."

14-41 We wash turnips with our hands; *Antre n[ós] lavão-se os nabos com as mãos;*

Japanese women wash them with their feet. *As molheres japoas os lavão com os pees.*

Herodotus in his description of the contrary culture of Egypt wrote that "They knead dough with their feet but mud with their hands," as opposed to the unmentioned Greeks, or rest of the world who do the opposite. The difference between "us" and "them" is sometimes paralleled with gender. In Meiji 27 (1895) the poet Shiki was to write a pair of haiku about washing rape leaves:

men, they
stick in a pole to wash
winter greens

women, they
tread in a tub to wash
winter greens

bô irete fuyuna o arau otoko kana
pole inserted, winter-rape=greens wash man tis

oke funde fuyuna o arau onna kana
tub treading, winter-rape=greens wash woman tis

I do not know if this is because men's feet are considered dirty and they are more likely to have thin shanks with poor circulation which makes immersion in cold water for extended periods impossible, or because women have weak arms. I do know that if "we" were Scots and the turnips laundry, the whole contrast would flip over (n.1-49+).

14-42 Our sacks of wheat and barley are made of cloth; *Os sacos de trigo e sevada antre nós são de pano;*

The Japanese ones of straw. *Em Japão de palha.*

No one is growing hay for sacks in Japan. Rice straw, wheat straw, etc. – all are "hay" and all are kindly helping to carry themselves to market. I would guess that in Europe such hay would be eaten by the more abundant livestock. I would like to know how both bags were re-used or recycled.

14-43   When we warm our hands, the palm faces the fire;
Nós quando aqentamos as mãos pomos as palmas pera o fogo;

> When the Japanese warm them, the back of the hand faces the fire.
> *Os Japões quando se aqentão virão pera a parte do fogo as costas das mãos.*

Logically speaking, the palms and insides of the fingers are feeling organs full of nerves, while the back of the hand has the big blood vessels and the bones to heat up. Who can say what makes most sense? But, there may be psychological reasons here. As noted earlier, Japanese have a tendency to "face" danger with their backs rather than their fronts. They are also more likely to walk with their toes in than out, as we are taught to do (exposing the outside rather than the instep of the foot). We/they also differ in this respect:

We beckon others with our palm up motioning upwards and back with one or more finger tips;
They beckon others with their palm downward, moving their fingers down and back.

Perhaps they do this because we tend to make inferiors rise and they to make them get down as noted in 2-60. But I would not be surprised if a correlation between these last three mentioned mannerisms and the one in this contrast could be found. If you would like to do *pure research* in cultural anthropology, this would be the right type of question for a worldwide survey.

14-44   With us, a long message is given while standing or kneeling;
Antre nós, dando-se hum recado comprido, estaa hum im pé ou de jiolhos [1] dando seu recado;

> In Japan, it is with both knees on the ground, and almost prone, with one hand on the *tatami* [mat] and the other turning up its sleeve and gently rubbing it. *Em Japão está com ambos os jiolhos em [te]rra e quasi de bruçsos com huma mão estribida nos tatamis e com a outra mão á-de arregaçar aquelle braço e estar-se levemente coçando nelle.*

I usually associate fly-like rubbing with the Chinese rather than the Japanese. As Cruz wrote "the common courtesy is, the left hand closed, they enclose it within the right hand, and they move both hands repeatedly up and down towards the breast, showing that they have one another enclosed in their heart." (TCC in B:SCSC) In Japan, only the merchant – considered the most Chinese trade – seems to have done a lot pf rubbing. And in Japan, it is not an etiquette with an explanation such as that given to Cruz in China. Like the disconcerting practice of hissing between the teeth still found among old Japanese men, it would, rather, seem to be *a way of showing one is as tense as one should be* in a formal situation, facing one's superior. The Japanese seem to have had an unconscious agreement that *underlings should look tense at all times*. While most young Japanese no longer do these things, one still feels that Japanese feel, however unconsciously, that being tense is the most important part of being respectful.

1. On Bended Knee/s. The Portuguese plural today suggests both knees, but seeing the way Frois specified *ambos,* i.e., "both" knees for the Japanese, it makes sense to assume he means "our" standard one-knee kneel.

14-45   With us, men stand up straight with one foot in front of the other while talking;

Antre nós, quando se fala em pee, estão os homens direitos e com hum pé diante do outro;

> In Japan, when two men talk, the inferior must line up his feet side by side, cross his arms at his belt, bend his body forward and respond to what the other says by making bows like the women of Europe. *Em Japão, se [estão] dous, o que hé inferior á-de ter os pés juntos, a[s mã]os cruzados na sinta, o corpo inclinado pera diante e, segundo que o outro fala, á-de estar fazendo mizurinhas como as molheres d'Europa.*

There are actually *three* contrasts here. The *first* and least significant one is the matter of the position of the feet. Unless, that is, we can find an explanation for "ours." Did the vaunted beauty of the classic *contrapposto* stance, albeit made for statues, come to be copied by Renaissance schools while side-by-side legs were considered stiff and lacking grace? Or, were we taught to put our best (right) foot forward when we spoke? Or, were we taught to plant one foot ahead of the other in case the talk turned into a fight, so we could not be easily pushed over and could quickly move forward or backward? *Without knowing the answer to these questions,* [1] I can only move on to the *second* unstated contrast and note the comparatively greater equality of body language in Europe compared to Japan. You will note in the Japanese case, as described above, only the inferior "must" do this or that. The implication would seem to be that the superior stands (or rides) however he wants as he talks.

The *third* contrast, the bows, deserve a whole paragraph (though I fear I may already have introduced the concept in the chapter on *Writing,* it is worth *more* notice). It reflects the fact that "we" tend to speak in sequential monologues, while Japanese converse in bite-sized chunks of sentence, punctuated with the listener's "yeahs" and grunts (usually *hai!, ha!, he!, ho!,* or *un!*) each of which is accompanied by a bob of the head and a slight body-bow – more emphatic on the part of the inferior (but the superior also nods a bit) – so Japanese speaking to Japanese can be discriminated from non-Japanese from a hundred yards away – the ones who look like chickens pecking grain. If the listening party forgets to, or doesn't know enough to grunt, the Japanese speaker may even stop talking. This is not only a Japanese phenomenon. I have read about an English anthropologist who, despite considerable knowledge in speaking the native tongue, was having trouble getting more than short sentence replies out of his informants in an African village (I forget what book I read it in and the name of the people – I only remember the anthropologist was *very* British) and mistakenly thought them reticent, for exactly the same reason.

1. Proper Stance while Conversing. I was amazed to find *nothing* about "our" right-before-left conversation stance etiquette on the net (It's all *contrapposto* this and that!). If I were in a city with a major library, I would start by looking up Bulwer's 17c book on body language, gestures in ancient rhetoric, etc. . . *Anyone?*

14-46   With us, the towel that serves the face is different from the one that cleans the feet;

Antre nós hé diferente a toalha que serve do rosto e a com que se alimpão os pés;

> The Japanese, when washing their bodies use the same towel for everything.
> *Os Japões, quando lavão o corpo, huma mesma toalha serve pera tudo.*

Before reaching the last line in Chamberlain's "Topsy-turvydom" entry, I thought of adding a Faux Frois: *We use a washcloth to wash; the Japanese also use it to dry themselves.* But, he beat me:

Strangest of all, after a bath, the Japanese dry themselves with a damp towel. (C:TJ)

"Strangest of all? No, not at all! Depending upon your lifestyle, *it makes perfect sense.* Theoretically, a huge dry towel is best; but the Japanese washcloth-towel-in-one is better for a poor bachelor in a country with high humidity. You see, when you wash yourself, you also wash your towel, so you never have to launder it and need not wait for it to get completely dry before using it again. I can imagine, though, that those of "us" who would *never* think to use the same towel for a face and feet, would be totally disgusted at "their" side (which, I guess includes *me*, for I have done it).

~~~~~~

14-47 We clean our nostrils with the thumb or index finger;
Nós alimpamos as ventas do naris com o dedo polegar ou index;

   They have small nostrils and use their little finger.
   Elles, polas terem peqenas, o fazem com o dedo meiminho.

Finally, our favorite! Frois really had a thing with nostrils! He already mentioned small Japanese nostrils in 1-4! Here he adds fingers. It is hard to say for sure what he means by "clean." Are we talking about diligent ablutions with fingers going into nostrils while washing the face? Or, are we talking about the behavior that always feels fine when you do it yourself but looks gross when others do it, namely nose-picking? (This is how it is usually translated, for the best of reasons: because it is funniest). Or, does Frois mean that the fingers in question are used to cover one nostril to spray out the contents of the other.   Regardless, I would guess that nostril size may not be the main reason. Using a baby finger is *classier.*   And since we already use our pinkies for the ear, it also makes sense to use the same digit.   And, speaking of ears, Japanese have wooden wax scoops (*mimikaki* or *mimikujiri*), that look like a cross between a crochet needle and a spoon – the Chinese character 了 is differentiated from other characters pronounced *ryô* by calling it the *mimikaki-ryô,* or "ear-scoop-*ryô* – which never fail to amaze, and often frighten, the Occidental:

   We clean out our own ear wax and have nothing special to do it with; [1]
   Japanese men have their mother or wife do it with a specially designed wooden scoop.

Since mothers do it for their children, the Japanese wife is able to baby her husband that way. Usually, he rests his head on her lap. Since the scoops are wooden, thin and hard, it goes without saying that they would be dangerous in the hands of a rough person or in the ear of a child who couldn't keep still. As such, they would be, like paper partitions, impossible in "our" relatively crude world (and a manufacturer would be sued for injuries).   If that is not enough, these tiny devices generally have some downy white feathers on the other end.   According to LD, the feathers come in handy because "Asians tend to have flaky white mimi kuso [ear-crap] . . . while Caucasians have brown waxy (hence the name) earwax, " which down-feathers would not budge.[2]

1. *Occidental Ear Cleaning.* But what exactly did we *do* before Q-tips!? Gloss, anyone?
2. *Crap on Ears*. I have no Asian blood, but some months after I used wart medicine to burn off a large sebaceous dermatitis from the inside of my ear, I was plagued with flaky white crap in, or rather on, my ear, and it continued for a couple years. So, thanks to my poverty (I would prefer to use medicine with salicylic acid but without some of the evidently harmful chemicals in wart medicine but, living in the USA, cannot afford to see a doctor and the pharmacists do not know how to make simple and harmless medicines, so I must sometimes use inappropriate medicine), I have been able to experience a Far Eastern ear (right one only) at first hand.   Dr. Pangloss was correct, there is good in everything that befalls us.

14-48   We exchange courtesies with a serene and grave demeanor;
       Antre nós as cortezias se fazem com rosto sereno e grave;

      The Japanese always, infallibly, with artificial smiles.
      Os Japões sempre infalivelmente com rizinhos finjidos.

      14-35, narrowed down. But here, the Portuguese *risinho* is definitely a smile rather than a laugh. If it is as easy or easier to hold a grin than to maintain a grave demeanor (that, for some of us is always in danger of changing into a laugh), who says the smile is the more artificial demeanor? Isn't a grave face equally artificial? The only thing I can not quite reconcile to this image of the smiling Japanese is the early photographic image (singular, for all are the same) of Japanese as glum-looking as your glummest Occidentals. What did the camera *do* to the Japanese? Are they copying *us?*

      Today, I believe that we Occidentals usually smile when we exchange greetings, don't we? Usanians, at least, seem at least as smiley as the Japanese. But, I am not a very people-oriented person, and hope more sensitive readers can enlighten me on these things.

14-49   Our kegs of wine are placed on boards on the ground and well sealed;
       As nossas pipas de vinho estão estão sobre paos em riba do chão muito bem tapadas;

      The Japanese keep their wine in large open-mouthed vessels and keep them buried in the earth up to the mouth. *Os Japões tem o seu vinho em jarras com grandes bocas destapadas emterradas até boca na terra.*

      Heat from the atmosphere cannot work its way through ground as well as through air. Earth-cooling would beat a cellar in the hot summer and in the winter, because Japanese used little heating. Obviously, the dirt did not come quite up to the lips of the vessel, for they had to be high enough to prevent dirt from getting in!

14-50   Our pelts are colored with dye;
       As nossas peles tomão sua cor com tintas;

      The Japanese color theirs very well with the smoke of straw.
      Os Japões as pintão muito bem com fumo de palhas somente.

..

      English has no generic term for what might be called "straw of *anything*." Okada writes that one of the main "straws" in use was pine needles and that thick paper was glued on white pelts so that smoking created a clear print of the family crest.

      This contrast made me think: *Do we* – in the Occident or Japan – *today have any idea how our clothing is colored?* Now, *that,* is a contrast with our mutually foreign country, *The Past.*

14-51   Our bamboo in Europe serves for little but spindles;
As nossas canas, tirando rocas pera fiar, servem em Europa de mui pouqas couzas;

> That [bamboo] of Japan is eaten as a morsel in *shiru* [soup] and serves for bows, arrow shafts, flooring, roof-tiles, ladders, vials for oil, wine flasks, blinds, tea whisks and many other things. *As de Japão servem de iguaria pera se comer no xiro, servem de arcos, frechas, solhado da caza e telhas do telhado, escadas, almotalias d'azeite, [va]zilha pera o vinho, esteiras, escovas pera o chá, e de outras muitas couzas.*

I *worship* bamboo and wonder if there is anything it can *not* serve for! Rather than list more conventional uses, let me mention just a few of my own:, for, among other things, I have pole-vaulted with it, made a fiddle bow, a fiddle (as do the Chinese) and kayak paddles, floored an anteroom floor that only required cleaning a few times a year (split the bamboo in half and put the convex side up and the dirt and lint gathers below while the top remains clean), fit a length to each arm so I could walk like an ape (good for the lower-back), invented and made a pick-stick (using the arrow-making variety) which could pick real staccato because the teeth passed perpendicular through a slit extended to the upper edge of the bamboo so they had room to bend, and made beautiful ball-point pens from the tip – imagine using a pen that was blown back and forth against the sky (though, it cannot match a quill that has flown across the ocean) because only the tip of the main stem is narrow enough yet hollow (the stems are not).

14-52   Our presents are sent in little boxes without any decoration/ribbons;
Os prezentes que antre nós se mandão em bocetas vão sem nenhum atilho;

> In Japan, they are tied with string or covered with paper, and in *Ximo* [*Shimo*] they are sent in bottles wrapped in women's belts. *Em Japão se atão com fio ou grudão com papel, e no Ximo vão as vazilhas atadas com sinjidouros das molheres.*

As far as I can tell, "we" were very slow to learn how to wrap presents. Lacking cheap and attractive paper, we were more likely to put gifts into a trunk or a cloth bag to carry them and leave them bare.   In the 1830's, a wrapping paper was made from straw in Tuscany, by the mid-19th century, the idea of wrapping things in paper had become commonplace – when Claude Monet visited Zaandam, he purchased from a Dutch grocer a stack of Japanese color prints he was using to wrap-up butter and cheese which he took to Paris, where they became the rage – and, by the end of the century, colored Christmas tissue and printed gift wrapping paper was sold commercially, or else, I am wrong and Hallmark invented it in 1917 . . . [1]

The Nagasaki (Shimo) area custom of wrapping up gifts with women's belts (beautiful *obi*?) was a singular practice. I doubt not that a strange manner of wrapping gifts can be uncovered somewhere in Europe as well.   But, one thing is certain, the Japanese of *origami* fame, are indeed the most avid wrappers on earth. Every culture has one or two areas where creativity runs wild. In Italy, I am told it is the variety of flush devices on toilets. In Mexico, *I know* it is the dashboard of buses. (Other entries are welcome!) To shop in Japan is to be *amazed* at the variety and beauty of the packaging. From Frois, we know that this has a long history and that it began with gifts.

1. *Wrapping Gifts.* I would have thought the idea of presenting gifts beautifully would have found its way from Japan to the West far earlier than what I can gather from the net. Can anyone provide new perspective on this?

14-53   We refresh our faces with rose-water; *Nós resfriamos a testa com agoa rozada;*

The Japanese do it with a handful of wine. *As Japões com o vinho que tomão na mão.*

Throughout the book, Frois uses the same word "*vinho*" for what we usually call "wine" and for *sake*. The Japanese must translate from Portuguese using different terms, because wine in Japanese (*budô-shu*) has "grape"(*budô*) clearly in it, and *sake* is made from rice. More, precisely, they use the Chinese character 酒 for *sake* and in tiny lettering next to it give the pronunciation for *vinho*. Sake on the face must not have been as common a practice in Japan as rose-water in Europe for Okada, after explaining that rose-water had some alcohol in it, opined that the *sake* was probably refreshing/bracing for the skin, as it, too, had alcohol.

14-54   We require a spoonful of sweetmeat or a succade to drink a dipper of water; *Antre nós pera huma pessoa beber hum pucaro d'agoa se lhe dá huma qulher de confeitos, ou huma talhada de conserva;*

In Japan, it is enough to have one sweetmeat, or something of its size per [1] *sakazuki* [*sake* cup]. *Em Japão pera tomar o* sacanzuqi *basta dar-lhe hum só confeito ou couza do seu tamanho.*

Water was usually not drunken alone in Europe (6-33). Usually, *sake* is accompanied by salty tidbits, not sweet ones, which is why, I think, Frois writes "or something of its size" (not, *même importance,* as in one translation). Okada, noting the Europeans *also* had appetizers with their drinks wonders about the worth of this contrast. If I am not mistaken, the reference to "size" suggests what Frois' intended contrast might be, namely, a *sake* cup is much tinier than a *púcaro,* or ladle/dipper/mug/glass ("a small vase with a handle"). We drink a lot per morsel while they have only a sip with each. If this is the case, the "enough" (*basta)* is something rare in Frois, facetious irony.

Confeito did not make it into the OED, unless it is *confection*, of which one type is what we want and gives "dainty, comfit and sweetmeat." *Confeito* did, however, get into the OJD, where, as *konpeitô,* it has almost a whole column (there are four columns per page). It is written in Chinese characters 金平糖 or, "gold-level/peaceful-sugar." It also came to be the name of a type of snail or conch and a bumpy colorful fish, for Portuguese *confeito* was like that, though the Japanese sweetmeat which Frois calls *confeito* was probably square or the natural shape of whatever it was.

1. *Per Cup?*   The Portuguese translates "take the *sakazuki*," which is Japanuguese, if I may coin a phrase.   Where English might say "take a drink," Japanese say "take a sake cup."

14-55   We in Europe offer a bouquet of roses to show our affection to our friends; *Nós por a[miz]ade oferecemos em Europa a hum amigo hum molho de rozas;*

The Japanese only a single rose or pink.[1]
Os Japões huma roza ou hum cravo somente.

Ah, give me a culture whose people give One Rose and believe in ten-thousand gods before one whose people give ten-thousand roses and believe in One God! It is hard to say if this difference arises from different aesthetics, the flower version of paucity vs. abundance of figures in a picture (11-

30) and the tokonoma-style of introducing a single work at a time (ch.11 note), from the fashion of giving *less* gifts (14-26), or simply from the lack of a tradition of cut flowers – other than those used for truly artistic creations, i.e. ikebana – and no concept of a *bouquet* [1] – in Japan.

> The vases which hang so gracefully on the polished posts contain each a single peony, a single iris, a single azalea, stalk, leaves and corolla, all displayed in their full beauty. Can anything be more grotesque than our "florist's bouquets," a series of concentric rings of flowers of divers colours, bordered by maidenhair and a piece of stiff lace paper in which stems, leaves, and even petals are brutally crushed, and *the grace and individuality of each flower* systematically destroyed. (*my italics* B:UTJ)

Reading Isabella Bird's strong statement, I find a possible symbolic explanation for the gift of a single flower. As one, it suggests the person receiving it is likewise the only one in the giver's mind. In modern times, the Japanese came to adopt the Occidental bouquet. Were Frois with us, he would surely write this instead:

> *We carry bouquets with the flowers right-side up as they grow;*
> *In Japan, they are carried with their heads dangling down.*

The Japanese claim they do this not to damage the flower heads in movement, but I wonder if it was originally not a matter of modesty (hiding the sight and scent until the present is delivered). Regardless, I cannot imagine whipping out an upside-down bouquet for anyone! There was, however, no set etiquette that I know of for carrying *one* flower. It might even be carried in a basket or a sleeve-as-pocket in which (judging from haiku) it was sometimes forgotten. There was, however, one notable exception to the wee flower *vs* bouquet contrast that Frois neglects to mention. *Tree blossoms* were presented *by the branch*. In that case, not a snippet but a large branch would be the best present.

> *We present stalks of flowers representing the production or life of entire plants.*
> *They present branches of bloom broken off from trees.* [2]

1. *Pink Translation* The flower that was not a rose, in the original Portuguese was *cravo,* or "carnation." The only problem is that there were no carnations in Japan at the time. Japanese translators gave what they knew Frois was referring to, a pink (*Dianthus Chinensis*), written with the characters "rock-bamboo," while pegging on the Portuguese word's pronunciation alongside the characters! This flower is lacey about the edges like a carnation but only has a single layer of five petals, i.e. it is not at all *meaty* like the carnation, which, as it turns out, was imported from Holland shortly *after* Frois and called, in Japanese, a "Dutch-pink," or *oranda-nadeshiko..*

2. *Blooming Branches.* I will introduce much more about these branches of bloom, some from the point of view of the trees, in a book with thousands of old haiku about cherry blossom viewing to be published in 2005.

14-56   We toss a lot of gum benjamin [1] directly upon the fire;
Nos deitamo[s] muito beijoim immediatamente sobre o fogo;

> The Japanese place an extremely thin plate of silver on hot coals and put a few pieces of aloes [2] the size of kernels of wheat on it. *Os Japões poem sobre a sinza qente huma laminazinha de prata muito delgada e sobre ella huma pouca d'aguila tamanha como dous ou 3 grãos de trigo.*

I do not know if the abundance of European per-fume was due to its use to consecrate space and fumigate disease-causing bad airs or simply because of "our" tendency toward *lots of* this or that, as already mentioned in several contrasts. In Japan, on the other hand, Okada notes that benzoin was only used in combination with other aromatics and, more interestingly, that the idea was to *hear* the tiny kernel of scent, which was sometimes even smaller than a grain of rice, indeed one variety was said to be "as thin as [a hair from a] horse-tail[hair]" or "mosquito-leg," and the tray, a Chinese invention, was called a "silver-leaf" but could also be glass, crystal or gold. Needless to say, such miniscule kernels would not fill a room with smoke. Indeed, with the exception of the place where people pray for things at temples and funerals, where all who attend light-up a stick of joss for the departed, the Japanese only encounter such fumes as mosquito smudge. 20th century Occidentals, who tend to think of incense as Oriental, have found Japanese reticence or even displeasure (*"Uh! It's like somebody died!"*) with respect to burning incense sticks in their rooms hard to understand. (I am thinking of *my* experience in Japan in the early 1970's.) But some sort of more subtle disconnect, a different attitude that was not just quantitative, goes back centuries. Menpes gives a surprisingly Zen explanation, which one might confuse for Suzuki, Blyth, Herrigel or Watts had it not been written in the 19th century.

> No Japanese ever smells incense; he is merely conscious of it. Incense is full of divine and beautiful suggestion; but the moment you begin to vulgarize it by talking, or even thinking, of its smell, all beauty and significance are destroyed. (M:JRC)

I think that using it to make a room smell like, say, *coconut* or *pine*, or something considered good for you,[3] as we – some of us – do, would be included in this idea of vulgarity. But, even as I write, I recall the notable exception to this apparent disinterest, a certain phenomenon that "has been a favorite ever since AD 1500" among the wealthy aesthetes of Japan? (C:TJ) Okada's mention of "hearing" the incense hinted at it, because the Incense Party was called a *kikikô* or *bunkô,* or "hear-scent." Let Chamberlain, who never missed an odd thing Japanese, explain:

> The gist of it is this: – The host produces from among a score of different kinds of incense, five kinds, to each of which he affixes at pleasure a new name founded on some literary allusion, and each name receives a number. The various kinds are then burnt in irregular order, sometimes in combinations of two or three kinds, and the guests have to write down the corresponding numbers on slips of paper by means of certain signs symbolical of the chapters in a celebrated classical romance called *Genji Mono-gatari.*[4] He who guesses best wins a prize. When the nose gets jaded by much smelling, it is restored to normal discrimination by means of vinegar.

> . . . serious treatises have been written on the subject . . . coming next to tea ceremonies in the estimation of men of taste, ['incense-sniffing'] was a pastime at once erudite and aristocratic, and which no Japanese would have thought of joking about. Nor need a European joke about it. Have we not rather cause for wonder, perplexity, almost awe, in the spectacle of a nation's intellect going off on such devious tracks . . . Such strict rules, such grave faces, such endless terminologies, so much ado about nothing! (C:TJ)

1. *Benjamin?* The Chinese characters for benzoin read "ease-breath-scent" and its nicknames in English are "gum benjamin" and "friar's balsam." OED describes "a dry and brittle resinous substance, with a fragrant odour and slightly aromatic taste, obtained from the *Styrax Benzoin,* a tree of Sumatra, Java, etc." called "frankincense of Jawa" by Ibn Batuta c 1350. "Benjamin" is a corruption: *Benzoin→ Benjoin→ Benjamin.*

2. *Aloes?* There are two aloes, the bitter medicinal one is more recent. Here the reference is to the fragrant resin of the Agalloch derived from the East Indian Aloexylon and

Aquilaria. This aloe was usually written *aloes.*

3. *Aroma Therapy.* I have only known two Japanese to burn incense. One had spent considerable time in India and the other was a construction worker who liked to party with a young hippie crowd. Doubtless, aroma therapy has arrived in Japan but, like vegetarianism, think that it is probably not so popular as in the USA.

4. *Genji and Scent.* Evoking the Classic Heian Era of Genji, gives the party a Renaissance air. I have mentioned Genji and scent somewhere. *Perhaps LD could add a full gloss for the next edition?*

14-57 We are passionate with anger running free and impatience hardly tamed at all;
Nós temos a paxão da yra muy solta e a impacientia mui pouqo domada;

They, in some strange manner, control themselves and thus are moderate and prudent. *Elles em estranha maneira a tem moderada e são nisso muito moderados e advertidos.*

Too bad Frois didn't speculate about *what* exactly that special method of self-control was! Or, conversely, why he thought "we" boil over so quickly. While there are parts of Japan where people fly off the handle quickly, and splendidly uptight parts of the West; but the contrast, on the whole, still holds. And it is the main reason why General MacArthur's "nation of twelve year olds" has always felt, with far more justification, that we are far younger than that! In THE CHRISTIAN CENTURY IN JAPAN, Boxer writes –

> he [Valignano] notes that "the Japanese are slow and deliberate in their dealings, and . . . never display outward resentment or impatience, even when they are inwardly upset. They do not lightly murmur or complain, nor do they speak evil of one another. They are very secretive in their hearts. They are greatly addicted to formal manners and empty compliments, but know how to bid their time in silence very patiently. Whereas we on the contrary are usually quite the reverse. For we are hasty, choleric, free and easy in our speech, and straightway disclose our thoughts and minds, . . ." It is amusing to find a Jesuit – traditionally the embodiment of reticence and guile[1] – writing thus, but the celebrated French Jesuit, Jean de Fontaney, wrote the same strain about the Chinese and Europeans more than a century later. (B:CCJ)

Missionaries, wrote the French Jesuit (as Valignano had written earlier) had to be patient and sweet tempered if they were to be respected. If even these Jesuit missionaries were children compared to the Japanese and Chinese who judged maturity on the basis of one's self-control, most other Westerners came across as *raging maniacs*. Mendez Pinto describes how nine Portuguese in the middle of China comported themselves in the mid-16th century:

> This dispute was born of a certain vanity that exists among the Portuguese, something that I can't explain other than by our having low boiling points in matters of honour. This was the point of honour at stake: two of our number happened to start arguing about which family enjoyed higher standing in the King of Portugal's household, the Madureiras or the Fonsecas. One word led to another . . . They were both in such a rage that finally one of them clouted the other man about the head and in reply had his cheek slashed open with a knife. Then the first man grabbed a halberd and sliced off the other's arm and in the meantime the other seven of us had started fighting among ourselves to settle this miserable argument. (P(L?):TMP)

They all got whipped and thrown in jail – had they been in Japan, they would have been executed. Pinto puts a great speech in the prosecutor's mouth:

> That men of the same race from the same country, who speak the same language and are subject to the same king and the same religion, that such men fight and kill each other mercilessly without any good reason whatsoever is something that can only be understood if they are the slaves of the Voracious Serpent from the House of Hell . . . the court should isolate these men from any contact with our people as if they had a contagious disease, and banish them to the mountains of Chabaki . . . (Ibid)

In another prison they spent there time "cursing the Madureiras and the Fonsecas and, above all the devil himself who had ensnared us in this mess." That is to say, the punishment did nothing for them. Their character changed not an iota. When they finally made it to the South of China and the sea, they began quarreling again and came "close to killing each other " because "a characteristic of the Portuguese is that we are very fond of our own opinions." The "noodlelum" in charge of them "was so shocked by our savagery" that he refused to take their letters and gifts back to the king and "the captains of the two junks wanted nothing to do with us either and they set sail without us." Pinto was generous to find the fault in his own countrymen – don't you just love that! – but Frois's contrast is more accurate, for the Portuguese were hardly the only louts in Europe. They drank less and were probably on the whole better mannered than the English and Dutch. A few tidbits from Cocks' dairy about Englishmen in Japan about a half-century after Pinto.

January 16. – Mr.Nealson in his fustion fumes did beate Co Jno., our *jurebasso* [interpretor], about the head with his shews in the streete, because he came not to hym at his first calle, and yet had a *jurebasso* of his owne as good a linguist as he. This man seeketh quarrellls against all men, which is no small trowble and greefe unto me, I having much adoe to please all and yet cannot.

Aprill 16. – There were rymes cast abrode and song up and downe towne against Matinga [Cock's concubine] and other English mens women. Wherupon matters being brong in question to put them all away, noe proofes could be fownd against them, but a mater donne of spyte by their evell willers, . . .

January 10. – I understand that in my abcense at Emperours cort that the Hollanders misused me in speeches, . . . And after, Mr Sayer and Jno. Portus going along the streete, yhe Hollanders cast a cup of wyne in the faces of them. Where upon they grew into wordes, and fell together per the eares; in which broyle Jno. Portus broke a Hollanders pate with his dagger.

There were also drunken murders and major plots such as the Portuguese trying to blow up their gun-powder, etc., but it is in these smaller items that we see "our" character best: We have met the *yahoos* and, by God, they were us! To be fair, the Japanese were not always angels either. It would seem that a border city was a border city even in Japan, for toward the end of Cocks' letter [forgot to copy the date] to the Governor of the East India Company, he wrote:

And as som of our men goe along the streetyes, the Japons kindly call them in and geve them wine and whores till they be drunk, and then stripp them of all they have (some of them stark naked) and soe turne them out of dores. And some they keepe presoners, forging debtes upon them, which som of our men sweare they owe not; yet it is noe beleeving of all, for som of our men are bad enough; yet out of dowbt the abuse is greate and never seene till the last yeare and this.

But, even here, the Japanese are not rowdies. They are not out of control. They are in control, but happen to be criminals. This fundamental difference Pinto stressed and Frois contrasted was put into modern racial terms by the Iwakura Embassy to the West in the 1870's:

The peoples of Europe are generally categorized as "the white race" or Caucasian race, Asian peoples "the yellow race" or "Mongolian race." Roughly considering the temperaments of these two races, whites, being afire with desires, are wild for religion and have little power to control themselves, or, to put it in a word, are a *yokubukaki* [avaricious/rapacious] race; yellows have weak desires and are strong [good] at controlling their temperament, in a word, they have little avarice [rapaciousness]. Accordingly, the purport of government also must be opposite: in the West, there is a politics of protection [(?) *hogo*], and in the East one of morality. (I:TZT)

In the early-20th century it was further confirmed by a most unlikely source. The Report of the Missions Investigating Committee "appointed to tour the world and supply an unvarnished report of the true condition of affairs in Oriental lands amongst the peoples usually termed "heathens" by the INTERNATIONAL BIBLE STUDENTS ASSOCIATION at its convention held September 1-10, 1911, with respect to the Japanese, was that

We found the people industrious, peace-loving, polite and kind to each other, and towards foreigners. Although our visit was in the holiday season, when, according to their custom, over indulgence in liquor would be pardonable, nevertheless our entire party, scattered for the purpose of wide observation, noted only twelve intoxicated persons, and three of these were Europeans. Parental love and care were in evidence everywhere. We heard not a harsh expression from parent to child, nor to any one, and witnessed only one altercation, and it trivial. Everybody seemed industrious, minding his own business, and happy. Our united comment was, Would to God as favorable conditions prevailed in Europe and America! We noted nothing resembling profanity, and upon inquiry were told that they use no profanity, and that their strongest expression is "beka" [*baka*] – fool.

We did not, however, conclude that the fretfulness, unhappiness, quarrelsomeness and rudeness and boisterousness frequently in evidence in Europe and America are attributable to Christianity.

On the contrary, we surmised that Divine Providence had sent the message of the Gospel in the direction of the more rude or combative race, which received the letter and form of Christianity in a measure, without generally entering into its spirit of meekness, gentleness, patience, long-suffering, brotherly kindness and love. (www.agsconsulting.com/htdbnon/r5007.htm)

What splendid rationalization. I wonder if this is how Pinto saw it almost 400 years earlier!

14-58   In Europe, if for some reason a married or single woman happens to find shelter in a lord's house, she is helped and kept safe; *Em Europa se huma molher cazada ou solteira por algum cazo fortuito se acolhe a caza de algum senhor, ali hé favorecida e ajudada e posta a salvo;*

> In Japan, if a woman goes to the house of any *tono* [lord], she loses her liberty and becomes his captive. *Em Japão como se acolhem a casa de qualquer* tono *perdem a liberdade e ficão suas cativas.*

I do not get it. Was Europe, despite woman's relative lack of liberty we have seen in chapter II, this much kinder to women? I could understand if Frois had written "some *tono*," but *qualquer* = any = all!? It so happens that what Frois describes is common on TV Easterns in Japan, today: a woman begs the *tono* to right things for her wronged husband, or for a loan to pay for a sick child's medicine, only to be sexually assaulted (after which – or, during which – she commits suicide and is revenged by the hero, a martial artist do-gooder who usually is not the husband but feels guilty for not doing something to help the lady more earlier, etc). The coincidence makes one wonder, but surely all the *tonos* of Japan were not *that* monstrous. I believe Frois must have been upset about more than one shameful incidents that occurred in the recent past and took out his helpless anger with this contrast. (これは、酷い話でしょう！日本人の史家の御意見・欄外注を、よろしくお願いします。)

14-59   With us, people who have made up beg apologies from one another and embrace; *Antre nós os que se fazem amigos se pedem perdão ou abraçam;*

> In Japan, the one to blame rubs his hands before the other and drinks from his *sakazuki* [*sake* cup]. *Em Japão o culpado esfrega as mãos diante do outro e bebe o seu* sacanzuqi.

Hand rubbing, as mentioned in 14-44, is a sign of being contrite, and the other offers him *sake* to say, "I forgive you." and reaffirm vows of friendship. I would bet there were parts of Europe and classes of people who *also* drank rather than embraced to make up.
..

14-60   With us, the iron [blade] of a hoe is broad and shallow; *Antre nós as emxadas são largas e curtas no ferro;*

> Those of Japan are very thin, long and curve. *O ferro das emxadas de Japão he muito estreito, comprido e concavo.*

I prefer the Japanese hoe blade. The slight curve – I say "curve" rather than *concave* because it is only concave on the up-down axis [1] – improves the bite and driving in much deeper, it can pull out long-rooted weeds more easily. The slight curve in the hoe blade makes as much sense as the slight curve in the Usanian ax, which made it superior to the old world axes. Unfortunately, the handles on *all* hoes in Japan *and* in the West are too damn short. It is as if someone had the idea that the men of the soil should always be short men who should bend low, and I (a tall man who finds hoeing a great satisfaction, so long as I can stand straight) resent it!

1. *Concave Thought.* Had the blade been curved from the sides, like a scoop, I would have followed the Portuguese and written concave! How strange! Are there any definitions of concave which specify such a thing?

14-61   European flutes are made of wood and have a hole to play/blow into;
> *As frautas d'Europa são de pao e tem buxa por onde se tanjem;*

> Those of Japan are of bamboo, open on both ends.
> *As de Japão são de cana e são abertas todas por baxo e por cima.*

The Japanese flute works like the South American *cana,* one blows across the end of it, rather than through a hole that guarantees your breathe strikes it at the perfect angle. Because the bamboo is thicker on the large Japanese flute (the *shakuhachi* mentioned in chapter 13) it is hard for most people to even get a noise out of it! Once mastered, however, the greater freedom of attack that causes so much initial suffering permits nuances the Western flute performer cannot even dream of. (Another advantage of open ends is no place for spit to build up.)

14-62   With us, the hair of domestic servants is kept short and the manes of horses allowed to grow;   *Antre nós trosqião-se os moços de serviço e deixão-se crecer os topetes dos cavalos;*

> In Japan, the horse's is cropped and the *komono's* [=underling's] is allowed to grow. *Em Japão, trosqião-se os topetes dos cavalos e deixão-nos crecer aos* comonos.

One thing seems certain from this and other contrasts we have seen; the imposition of short hair on persons of inferior position in Europe was so broad-spread a practice that the presence of hirsute help in Japan must have shocked Frois. To think that almost 400 years after Frois, growing up in the New World, the establishment still tried to keep our hair short! Women in the Occident have pretty much broken free in terms of clothing (bifurcated or not) and hair (long or short), but most men still live in what amounts to servitude if not slavery.
..

14-63   Portuguese grapes and figs are for us pleasing and very delicious;
> *As uvas e figos de Portugal são pera nós fructas aceytas e muito gostozas;*

> Japanese abhor figs, and do not particularly enjoy grapes.
> *Os Japões avorrecem os figos, e não gostão muito das uvas.*

According to Okada, "*figos*" (written with the characters meaning "no-flower-fruit" in Chinese) were also used by the Portuguese to indicate Japanese persimmon (*kaki*), but since Japanese liked them and because Japanese figs are tiny and not very good by any measure, Frois is probably talking about *dried or sugared figs* brought in by the traders.

14-64 With us, there is no custom of a domestic servants inviting their master and mistress to their house; *Antre nós não hé costume convidarem os criados em suas cazas a seus senhores e senhoras;*

In Japan it is often done, sometimes from obligation and sometimes otherwise.
Em Japão o fazem muitas vezes, humas por obrigasão e outras sem ella.

It is one thing to feed the carpenter working at your house (11-27) and quite another to visit the house of your help.   Perhaps this was on the servant's holiday or the day when servants were changed or their service extended (generally, they had one-year contracts). But I do not know, for this is the only mention of boss's visiting their servants' houses that I have ever come across!

In the late twentieth century, visiting people to one's home was itself rare in Japan. I worked with a dozen or so people for almost twenty years and another dozen or so more for ten years and only saw one of their apartments, and that when a company party (at a restaurant) kept a number of us from making the last train. That, makes this practice doubly notable. The only question, and it is a big one, is whether it was egalitarian, which is to say a social visit pleasant to both parties or authoritarian, i.e. an inspection of the quarters by the employer/master.   （ここも、識者よ、頼みます！）

14-65 In Europe, household servants do not accompany their master wearing his clothing;
Em Europa os criados não vão com os vestidos de seus senhores acompanhando-os;

The *tono* [sire/s] of Japan lend their servants their clothing and gilt *katana* [sword/s] for the sake of their own *isei* [pomp/prestige/splendor]. *Os* tonos *em Japão emprestão seus vestidos e catanas douradas aos criados pera seu yxei.*

..

Contradicting Frois's claim that European servants don't wear their master's clothing, Matsuda and Jorissen cite Nola's *Libro de Guisados* (1529): "forgetting the humility of old Portugal, maid-servants have adopted the new style of wearing the same good clothing as their Mistresses" and de Melo's *Carta de Guia de Casados*(1650) which "criticized this, saying that it would make it hard to tell apart a mistress from her servants, make the latter haughty and that it is sufficient for a good master to see that his or her help is dressed in clean clothing." (J/F(M&J):T). I am not sure we are talking about the same thing here. When Frois writes "the clothing of their masters'" (*os vestidos de seus senhores*), he does not necessarily mean that the clothing is identical and the servants are acting uppity trying to ape their superiors. His point is that in Japan, the master or employer makes a real effort to outfit the servants as he or she feels that their looking good reflects the fortunes of the house, and that some even go so far as to give men gilt-handled swords (since Japanese do not ordinarily wear such swords, I would guess he means for ceremonies or parade-like moves from one place to another). The De Melo quote suggests that, in the splendorific Baroque era, some Europeans began to think more like Japanese and cooperated in making their servants look good, but Frois could hardly be expected to predict that!

endnote XIV

Diverse

~~~~~~

On the whole, I think the Japanese – at least, as I explain them in this book – come across better than *us*. I am happy with that, partly because it is true, and partly because "our" national (I speak as a Usanian, but the same could be said not only for most Europeans but a surprisingly large number of Latin Americans who tend to call all Far Eastern people *"Chino."*) conceit can always use some deflating. In my books, published in Japan/ese, on the other hand, I made more of an effort to defend *us*, because in the heady 1970's and 1980's, Japanese intellectuals avoided hard thought about their *own* future by Occidentalizing (engaging in what might be called intellectual bashing of the West) and this, I felt, was bad for the world they would be playing a larger and larger role in. In other words, writing in Japanese, I tend to be hard on the Japanese, and writing in English I tend to be hard on English-speakers (and people of cognate Indo-European culture). Which is why, I guess, I am not your most popular author.

But, as I wrote the notes to the three items in this chapter touching upon and *praising the greater self-control the Japanese have over their emotions than Westerners do*, I felt there was one bad thing about Japan – something I didn't care for, at any rate – that needed to be expressed if this book would be fair. *What is it?* First, let me say what it is *not*. It is *not* the usual putdown of Japanese conformity. Since Japanese have more self-control and are on the whole more literate than "we" do, their world-view and opinions tend to be more individual than "ours" (This especially goes for my fellow Usanians most of whom *seriously believe* they are giving you an *original* opinion when they are only spouting off one of a number of old saws. They have no idea how *difficult* it is to come up with anything original.) Where it counts most, *inside*, "we" are generally the more conformist than Japanese. Our greater freedom is illusory. Nor, is it Japanese lack of creativity. Who *says* we have more? (I will debate this another time, if/when I publish my *One-String Experiment*. This book has reached its 740 page maximum limit for POD!)

No, the problem with Japanese is that their stoicism toward their own lot can give rise to what seems like, or *is,* callousness toward the lot of others. Here is something Kaempfer saw in 1691.
..

> In the middle of a field we found a Monk dying. The poor man lay on his face, thoroughly soak'd with water, it having rain'd pretty hard, but gave as yet some signs of life, and doubtless might have been reliev'd. Such a miserable object, one would think, should have mov'd the hardest stones to pity, but it had no effect on the merciless Japanese. (K(S):HOJ)

Remember, Kaempfer saw and liked Japan and even argued that the people seemed so happy that it might be a good idea for the country to remain closed even if some of the benefits of international discourse are lost (Perhaps the fact this was found and translated back into Japanese, helps explain why the arguments the Japanese give Golownin on the matter sound so familiar!). Yet, he cannot help marveling at "the merciless Japanese." *And this was not peculiar to the Tokugawa era.* I have saved one, possibly two lives, myself, when no one had the decency or guts to act (In one case, a yakuza was repeatedly kicking an unconscious man in the head on a train platform and in the other a drunk fell clunk onto the track when a train was coming). Less spectacularly, I have watched lost children wailing and wailing with no one helping them. The I-don't-want-to-be-troubled side of the Japanese has attracted the attention of many foreign visitors. I once read an article by one particularly gutsy, or rude, Occidental who pretended more than once to have a heart-attack on a train platform, just to see if anyone would help!

So *why are they like that?* I can think of any number of reasons. *First*, they themselves expect no help (Here the Golden Rule works the wrong way!). *Second*, Japanese are terribly timid. If they are too timid to hurt a stranger, they are also too timid to help one. To put it another way, it takes courage to be bad, or to be good.   *Third*, many if not most Japanese are like rich people in the West. As a number of psychological surveys (where someone has been sent out begging door to door) have shown, the wealthy tend to be smug and less likely to assist people than the poor. Perhaps, the same self-control that allows them to defer gratification and control their rowdy side, also reins in their natural sympathy, or conscience, before it can act. And, *fourth*, they have an all-or-nothing sense of responsibility, whereas we have a greyer form of incremental responsibility.

This last item requires an example to explain. One day, I had just left work – at an avant-garde publisher – on the way to give a short talk and participate in a panel discussion before hundreds of veterinarians (all because I mentioned life with a cat in one of my books and wrote a few articles!) when I found a large, apparently well-fed and badly injured dog on the sidewalk by the six-lane street. I rushed across the street to the vet training school that just happened to be there and explained the situation. After leading a veterinarian and his students to the dog, I ran to the train station and arrived just in time to talk and luckily, my first soy-bean shot from the lectern to the small fry-pan I hung on one side of the auditorium hit its target (It was one of my tools for teaching cats to behave).   *The next day, my superior at work lectured me on my bad behavior.* The gist of it was that I had acted *irresponsibly* because the vet-school called the publisher – being right across the street, they knew my face – and asked: "Who is going to take responsibility for this dog, which your *gaijin* (foreigner) picked up?" *What was I to do!?* I had an appointment I couldn't be late for, the dog lay bleeding with glazed eyes on the sidewalk and the vet-school was right across the street. I compromised and did the best I could under the circumstances, and I think most Americans would agree that *I acted as responsibly as I could.* But my superior (someone interested in moral philosophy, Leibniz, no less!) strongly criticized me for *not thinking of the responsibility incurred and bringing about a troublesome situation.* "If you get involved in something, you have to take full responsibility for it, do you understand?" I *do* understand, but I beg to disagree with her.

After experiencing this type of thing a few times, most Japanese in my shoes would have walked right by that dog, pretending one thing or another to themselves to assuage their consciences. It left a sour taste in my mouth, which has still not completely gone away.

The question is whether people can be less all-or-nothing about responsibility than the Japanese, yet still exercise splendid self-control. Or, whether these good and bad things inevitably come together.

雑   雑   雑

Given the title of this chapter, I had first thought to use this Note to add diverse Faux Frois's missed by Frois. But, I hope you will forgive me for, finally, *pooping out.* What readers send will be pegged on below, in subsequent editions.

"We" _____.
"They" _____.

POSTWORD

"the jappyknee oppositioner"

While we wos a waitin' I spyd wun ov Mr. Harper's artists a skethcin' away like phun, makin' a pictur ov the yard, and ov the peeple, and ov the white-washed plank-walk for the Jappyknees to cum ashoar on, and the sogers, and the stemeboat we wos on, Jappyknees and awl, includin' me. But awl at wunst he seed sumthin' on the bote, and stop'd drawin', and begun to larf like phun. I looked tew see what on airth he was a larfin' at, and thair was a Jappyknee oppositioner a sketchin' away like phun teew. I deon't wundur Mr. Harper's artist was kinder knocked aback tew see this feller, and I would like tew see the tew picturs, side by side, jist tew see which feller was best. (Benjamin Downing, 3rd. *Harper's Weekly, May 26,1860*)

The writer observed the coming of the first Japanese Embassy to the United States. What he said about the painters was true for the whole affair, with the only difference being that the Americans were concerned with the bad behavior of their *own* citizens as well as the manners and deportment of the Japanese. *Harper's Weekly* writers mention "the gentleman who smashed his hat over their eyes in Baltimore; the lady who filled up the window in Philadelphia, the shouting, staring, insulting crowd which has dogged them everywhere" and laments that, unlike the always dignified visitors, we exhibited such "barbarian and savage behavior" that the "princes" might regret their allowing the country to be opened. But, he need not have worried, the Japanese were far more impressed by the tremendous amount of flowers the women showered on them – "How lucky we are!" – after they learned it was "the highest expression of kindness on the part of the fair sex." The Japanese understood perfectly well why they were mobbed.

..

> None of the Ambassadors from Europe excite any curiosity here, as they are almost the same in manners and customs as the Americans. Moreover, the latter themselves were once Europeans, whereas we belong to an entirely different civilization, the Government, manners and customs of which widely differ from those of America. We can quite understand how great the interest and curiosity aroused by our party must be.
>
> The day appointed for our presentation to the President of the United States of America has at last come. . . . What immense crowds there were! The streets were like seas of human beings; the windows and balconies were thronged with people eager to get a glimpse of the procession. I could not help smiling at the wonder in their eyes, which reached a culminating point when they caught sight of our party wearing costumes that they had never seen before or even dreamt of. I might say that the whole procession seemed to the people of Washington to be a scene out of fairyland, as, indeed, their city appeared to us. It was however, not without a feeling of pride and satisfaction that we drove, in such grand style, through the streets of the American metropolis as the first Ambassadors that Japan had ever sent abroad . . . (A:FJE)

How *refreshing* to read of a culture, a nation of people equal to the West for as long as they've known us! From that first Embassy, we know that what was true when Frois lived in Japan was still true when Perry jammed his foot in the door. Perhaps the West enjoyed a momentary superiority in military hardware, but, as Golownin had predicted a century earlier, that was nothing a bright and well educated people couldn't fix in a generation or two. Indeed, less than fifty years later, Japan whipped Russia and turned world history on its head. The defeat of Japan in World War II put world history back on its Occidental feet; but, this time, it took Japan only one generation to knock it back on its butt where it has stayed for the full count. (If Japan's economy is not flying especially high as I write, China's is gaining ground rapidly. The point is that people with a tradition of study and the deferment of satisfaction, which is to say self-discipline, are bound to come out ahead, eventually.) OK. *I exaggerate a bit.* I find myself bored and disgusted by "our" criminally wasteful (Usanian) culture and *wish* more creative and responsible people would offer more attractive alternatives.

Equal or not, the world has become depressingly uniform. The same East Asian leaders who call human values "Asian values" all too often do so while wearing a Western suit. The only exceptions are Islamic leaders, whose ability to stand up to the West (a *good* thing) comes from a common tradition of absolute religion (a *bad* thing: it is still fast at work destroying cultural diversity in Africa and Asia today), and the occasional sartorial maverick – I think of the Japanese finance minister, who gained notoriety (?) by wearing his nation's traditional dress to America in the 1980's or 90's (He also brought along his daughter on what was an official government business). In other words, Far Eastern culturalists talk the talk, but rarely walk the walk. And their suits are the least of it. The young Asian, who could be forging his or her own tradition, literally *redressing the world*, has a knack for picking up the ugliest fashions from the West. The striped deformation called a jogging shoe, usually worn two sizes too big, shirts colored in every which way but right, and even trousers with the waist worn far below the belt, . . .

My complaint is nothing new. Most Westerners who wrote about Japan in the late 19th century said the same thing about the quickly changing dress and, for that matter architecture and art. They thought giving up a beautiful culture for an ugly secondhand version of another one was a big mistake. (Only music, as we have seen, being the exception. Almost *all* Westerners wanted Japanese music to *die*.)

My complaint is only different because, in the 19th century, one had grounds to argue that the Japanese had to mimic Occidentals if they hoped to join the ruling class of the world. *Today, this is no longer true.* The idea of cultural relativity has sunk in deep enough in the West, and the East has enough economic clout that there is no longer a need to *pass*. Aside from some difference remaining in the culinary arts and religion, this tolerance, or rather, freedom, is largely wasted.   What hides in the closet remains there, growing cobwebs. My guess is that until Japanese men tie their hair up on top of their head (as, I might add, our Picts used to do) and wear robe-like clothing – that is to say, until they are bold enough to come out in person – nothing much will happen. If the philosophers of *mu* (nothingness) and animism in the cultural capitol of Japan can convince other Kyotoites to *wear* rather than spout their metaphysics, the world will have another pole.

..

Difference is a dangerous game to play, whether you emphasize your own or that of others. You must love your uniqueness enough to keep it alive yet not become so self-infatuated that you force it on the world. You must notice the difference of others but take care lest your awareness becomes another's prejudice. Valignano did everything a man could do to convince his superiors that Japanese were as different as different can be from us, and our cultural match. He did it in order to show why the Japanese mission needed more money and time than the people back in Rome might otherwise imagine. He did it to justify a policy of Accommodation, of doing things *their* way, and training *them* to run the Japanese church. Yet, after being published in Maffei's Latin translation, his different-but-equal cultural antipodes quickly mutated into the all-too-familiar exotic wonderland, the worst of which – probably Montanus, for the fulsome illustrations of idols and *harakiri* – bring to mind the *freak show.*

But we need not be too shy. We need not avoid mention of difference for fear of creating prejudice. Even though Valignano's qualifications in 1601 of his earlier generalizations about Japan's bad traits did not find their way into the public forum, his clearly expressed *respect* for the Japanese and their culture (all but *religion* and *sex*) was never completely lost. One finds scattered words of praise for the Japanese character and polity in almost every book written in English over the following four centuries. *The depiction of the Japanese and their culture as a paragon of contrariety did not make them our inferiors. If anything, by removing the Japanese from our scale of culture, it saved them from being treated as unfairly as culturally closer traditions have been.* (The same way a bird or a horse can be attractive but not an ape, for apes look too much like us to be measured by a separate ideal of beauty.) *If Orientalism implies a single cultural yard-stick, than it might be argued that only Japan, and to a lesser degree, China, were not fully Orientalized.*

That is my take on it. Now I must admit to being very curious to learn how the cautious world of academia responds to this TRATADO, which, it is safe to say, contains far more "we this" and "they that's" than have ever been gathered into a single book. Indeed, if my *Faux Frois's* are included, I wouldn't be surprised if there were over 1000 contrary distiches!

While I tried to keep things balanced as I went, sometimes by qualifying the extent of the difference and sometimes by offsetting with examples from "our" side, which might be overlooked by most readers, I really have no idea what impression of the Japanese this book will leave on my readers. Because of my poverty, I could not afford to print out a single copy of this book for myself, much less more to send around for opinions. So all I have are a few comments on individual chapters sent to acquaintances as attachments. Let me be honest. *This is spooky.* I *think* I am educating as I entertain. But, for all I know, I could be creating *more* prejudice instead of less. Since most of my previous books attempt to deconstruct stereotypes of difference and involved no risk whatsoever of being taken the wrong way, this has been a new and trying experience for me. My pride (?) as a recognized destroyer-of-stereotype extraordinaire (I was pretty well-known for this in Japan in the 1980's) told me to destroy all the contrarieties (especially what I call "antithetical stereotypes") I could, while my instinct as a translator was to defend Frois's claims with all my heart.

It is funny, but despite the unforgivable way Frois treated Buddhist "idols" (he destroyed them), *I really came to like the guy.* An acquaintance, the famous novelist and playwright Inoue Hisashi, wrote a 100 page novelette called *Waga Tomo Furoisu,* or, "My Friend Frois" (If anyone would like to translate it, I will append the whole damn thing – with Inoue's permission – in lieu of the biographical information I should have prepared but did not because I hate writing biography, whenever I find a large publisher to work with or gain the funds to do offset myself.). I can appreciate that. I ended up pretty much on Frois's side, for all but the chapters on religion. Moreover, as hinted at in the Foreword, once differences become a collectable item, *it really is hard not to join the game!* You might say I joined Frois and had my fun! I had intended to make amends for this difference-mongering by pegging on a 5-page appendix describing 16 *Ways to Make a Difference* – to make it seem like "we" and "they" are far more different, far more contrary than we really are – on to the tail of this book. As the sexy female voice on the most recent Coca Cola commercial on the Miami Cuban radio puts it *Es mejor pedir perdón, que pedir permiso.* (Have your fun, *then* apologize.) As it turns out, however, it is not here. I published *Orientalism & Occidentalism* first, and pegged it on *it* (See *Appendix 2*), instead. Read it, if you wish to know the tricks of the trade and bring critical judgment to bear upon the differences found in this book.

If I quoted more old books than properly called for, it is because my heart was not in my century. I lived half of the 20th century longing for the fairy-land that used to exist in both the East *and* West. When I look into the mirror, I want to see that "Jappyknee oppositioner," in a *kimono* or some other *wafuku* staring back at me. The only problem is that, if he is looking for difference, he might not like what *he* sees, for I might be wearing the same! (Like Alan Watts, I feel strong opposition to a culture that insists on confining the male-sex in bifurcated clothing and am often found wearing a robe or wrap-around skirt.) ✎

..

p.s.

Excluding those old *Harper's* quotes and that catch-phrase from the Coca Cola commercial, I am not very happy with my *PostWord*. Something seems lacking. Or even disingenuous. There is a big difference, after all, between me and Lafcadio Hearn (he could *write!*) and Alan Watts (he had *charisma!*). Both had a deep knowledge of their own ancient cultures and respected "theirs" as well. I have little more respect for traditional culture *** than I do for whatever we have now. And I know damn little about either. I never learned Greek and Latin and my understanding of things Japanese is awfully biased toward the one thing I really like, *old haiku* and a fox with a raccoon face called *tanuki* because I became friends with three generations of one tanuki clan. And, I am afraid that, whatever nice things some people have written about me, even my knowledge of *that* (the haiku, not the *tanuki*) is full of holes. Trying to *explicate* 611 contrasts – which, including "our" side means 1222 items – was just too much for my limited resources, inside and outside of my brain. Each chapter brought with it a different kind of frustration and the desire to turn it over to an expert *to do the job right*. Of course, this still may be done. I envision each expertly expanded chapter as a book in itself, with plenty of illustrations (an average of one for every item). *What do you think?*

Confession: I may talk up traditional culture and appreciate aspects of it, *but I do not love it*. Let me give an example. I saw a traditional play at a local hill-top temple in Ikuta (near Tokyo) about 10 years ago. It was of Shinto origin, called *kagura*, literally "god/s-music/fun" (神楽). I noticed people getting up – coming and going – as these officially celebrated "Human Cultural Treasures" performed. I listened carefully. Not having heard Japanese until I was an adult, I am not bilingual. Amazingly, I could pick up every word. The problem was that the dialogue was *boring*. It was pleasant enough but not at all witty. *No wonder no one was paying attention!* I could think of puns they could add to most of those sentences which would not harm the plot at all and keep everyone in stitches. Instead of thinking, *how wonderful this ancient form has been preserved for us*, my thoughts were: *this is crap!* Drama should be fun. I'll bet it was full of puns *a thousand years ago*, but lost them over the intervening years when no one had the guts to complain. I was *angry*, just as angry as when I noticed that the drains on the freighter I worked on lacked a sufficient crater around them to keep the water flowing out when that side of the boat was up. I do not have the necessary skills to be an engineer, but I could imagine *that* far.

Can you follow me? I do not have what it takes (patience? modesty?) to do good traditional work, be it scholarship, drama or science, but I have the uncanny ability to immediately spot everything that is wrong in anything and the frustrating ability to see how things could be better *if only this or that*. As a result, I cannot be satisfied to *curate* culture. I am pleased we have noble and diligent souls to do that, but I cannot. I must *create* culture, but lacking money and the time to try to convince others to follow along, the end result is that I can do nothing. Nothing, that is but think. *Hell is to be dirt-poor with a never-ending stream of ideas knocking on your door pleading for assistance you can not afford to provide them*. There is not a day I do not fall asleep wishing I were 100 or 1000 people so I could do justice to my dreams (or that I had enough money to hire others to do so) and do my part to make the world a better place.

Take the computer, for example. If I only had a hand in developing it, we would be joyfully contesting each other, drawing *life-from-birth-to-death* or *strange-flowers-from-seed-to-fall* in 100-frame flipbooks (actually, I have many more ideas for various lengths of flipbooks from 2-100 frames, the software requirements for fast and easy creation, and the methods to popularize the activity, but this is not the place to elaborate), but the mentality of the MS and Apple people (*no difference* from my perspective) was one of "constructing" rather than drawing, so we have gotten *nowhere* interesting. *Ditto*, for the music. CAD (computer-aided-design) and music synthesizing – as opposed to hands-on programs, where the computer lets us *improvise* – are one and the same concept and one and the same mistake. When I think about the creative potential that computers *could have released* but have *not* over the past couple decades, again, *I blow my top*. I realize that not 1 in 100 readers will have the least idea of what I am driving at. Q: is there no one out there with money *and* an imagination!? (I get so tired of hearing of the super rich doing the same old things and pretending to be innovative when all they are being as irresponsible – if not *criminal* – as a sauna in an airplane! Obviously, the monomaniacal mindset needed to *make a man rich* and that which could make those riches *bloom* into *something creative and good* are not of the same type.) If anyone reading has money and wants to try an experiment, please let me know. Lend me what one CEO makes in a year and I'll show you a new world (I know this sounds vague, but I have many projects ranging from new string instruments+playing-devices that could free us of the guitarization of music and allow people with good ears to *play by feel*, to a new method of suspending a hat over the head in a cooler manner, sleep comfortably 5-10 degrees warmer or read the newspaper in bed in zero degree weather, comfortably, etc..)! I am serious, *try me!*

What has *happened*, here?

I think *Frois* is to blame. He covers so many subjects, that I am constantly reminded of my frustration with being shut out of this and that world – all require money/time to play – has finally spilled over! I will just have to put a heavier top on my boiling mind, and clamp down hard for a while, because more books await finishing and I cannot afford any more distraction.

This just keeps getting worse and worse. I doubt this weird complaint will be found in the 2nd edition!

Ah, I remember. A final question. All of Valignano's European-Japanese contrast-mongering has been summed up as *an apology for the Jesuit policy of adaptation.*. Not that difference requires an apology, but, in that case, could we not, say, call Frois's TRATADO *an apology of an apology and my work an apology for that?*

Be that as it may, *obrigado*, Brother Frois, *obrigado!*

***

No respect for tradition? The past? The exception is people. People long dead, who thought well and did well. I revere them. My eyes can grow moist for them.

Biblio*graphy*

Dr. Thunberg, who might be remembered by the reader for his comments on night-soil if nothing else, visited a professor in "Amsterdam, 1770," and made use of his library. "Here," he wrote, "I perceived the unspeakable advantage of a professor having a library so near at hand, which affords him an opportunity of arranging it in scientific order, and of comparing the different subjects in his collection with the figures and descriptions of different authors, of which it is frequently necessary to consult not only one or two but a hundred." After discussing the limited hours and "inconvenience of frequent applications" rather than having one's needed books close at hand, he concluded,

> These important considerations render it advisable for professors to furnish themselves, as far as they are able, with libraries of their own; and also show, that notwithstanding all that has been said of the utility of large public libraries, much is wanting to render them as extensively useful as is pretended. (T:TEAA)

Today, public libraries have, theoretically speaking, become far more useable to the researcher who can quickly copy pages of material in the library or from checked-out books but, in the United States at least, the public library system still offers surprisingly little to the scholar of anything the least bit arcane. Fortunately, access to Worldcat (a large interlibrary loan system including most university libraries) is gradually becoming easier for those of us not fortunate enough to have university access so it will soon be possible to reduce the "unspeakable advantage" considerably, but the poor outsider still works under a considerable handicap. (Eg. Just recently, I found *Alessandro Valignano: man, missionary, and writer* by M. Antoni J. Üçerler, SJ, in a Blackwell magazine, but lacked the money to "purchase immediate access to this article for 30 days through our secure web site for US$25.00 using a credit card.") I was able to avail myself of the Library of Iberian Resources Online, for it is truly open and free (*hurrah! hurrah!*); but I could not use *Monumenta Nipponica,* which *would have been* a tremendous help, for they require some sort of number/affiliation I could not figure out how to get. And, as a poor man, I could not and still cannot even afford to reunite myself with my own limited library, for lack of space and the cost of shipping! And, I could not afford to take the time to keep trying to obtain books and magazines, or visit libraries, simply because I live on borrowed money to write and every day fall deeper into debt (a tiny debt, to be sure, for I have no house, no car, no stocks, no nothing to borrow against, which is what makes it hard to continue). So I just read what I *could* and, as you will see, *wrote what I had time to.*

Doubtless, the reader will already have noticed that I am not one to cite page numbers. Simply put, I do not believe it a good idea, in most cases. *Here is why.* At Georgetown, I observed students who read *very* little write term papers with *beautiful bibliographies* that pleased their professors (while I, who really read, barely got through). That happens because they can borrow the citations, *page number and all*, from one or two meticulously footnoted books. With this *Topsy-turvy 1585*, that will not be possible. The lazy student will either have to cite me *ad nauseam,* or actually *read more books* (or visit internet sites, as the case may be) to try to find the page number of the part I cite! It is also the case, that for someone like me, who can only find time for three showers and one shave a week – I am working around the clock and often do not leave my room once in the whole day – recording page numbers – or, worse, re-finding them could be the straw that . . . I've just got to scrimp *somewhere.*

However, *I do like to give credit where credit is due.* And I am delighted to give what time/space I can to acknowledge my debts and guide others to good books. I hope that the scholars among my readers will find enough in the *Annotations* to forgive me for not following convention on my citations. And, sorry for the *10+8-size font.* I had it *10.5+9,* but the book went over the 740 page POD printing limit!

Books in Western Languages

A:HCJ = Abbe (trans. N.N.): THE HISTORY OF THE CHURCH OF JAPAN written originally in French by L' Abbe de T. London 1705 (vol 1) and 1707 (vol 2). *The "Description of Japan" comprising the first 42 pages of the main body of the book has a couple pages of contrasts, the largest such listing between Valignano/Frois and Chamberlain, which is mostly borrowed from Valignano's SUMARIO, but seems to supplement it with material from Xavier, Frois and others.* The extremely Japanophilic *Description (See the Foreword part v. note 3) is followed by a church history and a heart-wrenching second volume which might better be titled the History of Martyrdom in Japan!* (I never could find Charlevoix in English and wonder if this might be him. If not, can any one find out who this is?)

A:NMH = Acosta, Ioseph (trans. by E.G.): THE NATURAL AND MORAL HISTORIE OF THE EAST AND WEST INDIES. London 1604 (vol 12?) (from a UMI microfilm) *Cooper (C:TCJ) mentioned his writing on the Chinese writing systems. His comparison of various writing systems was indeed good, but disappointingly short!*

A(S):AI = Al-Bîrûnî (Edward C. Sachau trans.) ALBERUNI'S INDIA (orig. London 1888; New Delhi 1964). I suppose that bibliographic propriety should make *Sachau* author of a book with such a title but this is not a book *about* what Al-bîrûnî wrote (a type of book we have all too many of) but the thing itself. *But Sachau does deserve our gratitude for translating what this extraordinary polymath wrote about the religion, science (including some math far beyond me), literature and all-round mindscape of Hindu civilization in the early 11th century, based upon a stay of 13 years in India undertaken expressly to learn about the same. This is not only the best contemporary introduction to medieval India ever written but a pioneering work of ethnic studies, or cultural anthropology. While mostly descriptive, the occasional thoughts are delightful. For example, after mentioning that the Hindus have a thousand words for the sun and the Arabs nearly as many for the lion, he goes on for a page questioning whether copiousness of vocabulary is really a good thing or not, coming up with several good reasons why less words would be preferable. The only thing in his* India *that might trouble the modern reader are the occasional disclaimers to the effect that as good/interesting as such and such may seem, these are deluded heathen and things are not relative. We saw the same with the Jesuits reporting on Japan and China, and I sometimes wonder the same thing: Are these genuine misgivings or words intended to protect the writer his superiors or other less tolerant zealots?*

A:COT = Alcock, Sir Rutherford: THE CAPITAL OF THE TYCOON: a narrative of three years residence in Japan (Dates of residence, anyone?). (2v) The Bradley co (NY) (Original is 1863). *A remarkable work by England's first Ambassador to Japan. My plentiful citations by no means exhaust its riches. Someone should edit it down to half-length and reprint it today. As elaborated in my Foreword vi, parts of the book were read in England years before its publication.*

Alvarez   I only read selections from Jorge Alvarez's 1647 report found in C:LLFX, below. I have not had the opportunity to read all. (Glosses are welcome from anyone who has.)

Alvarez-Taladriz → See V(A):S&A

A:FJE = the America-Japan Society: THE FIRST JAPANESE EMBASSY TO THE UNITED STATES OF AMERICA 1920 / 1977. *The first Japanese embassy was sent to Washington in 1860 by the Shogunate that fell by the time the ambassadors returned.* THE MURAGAKI DAIRY *(transl. Miyoshi Shigehiko) and the many news reports from the American press included in this book, show both the sincerity of the US government and the rowdiness of its population.* (I believe I read recently about a full translation of this embassy's report)

A(M):LLT = Anonymous (W.S. Merwin trans.: THE LIFE OF LAZARILLO DE TORMES (c.1554) Anchor 1962. *The introduction by Leonardo C. De Morelos gives this novel published simultaneously in 3 cities established the literary genre of the picaresque or roguery novel. There is some brilliant irony and superb realistic detail. De Moreles mentions Quixote and other picaresque* fiction, *but I think it equally important to note that it may have helped inspire Pinto to honestly record his and his countrymen's knavery on the high-seas.*

A&L:LWG = Arkush, R. David and Lee, Leo O. trans./ed.: LAND WITHOUT GHOSTS: CHINESE IMPRESSIONS OF AMERICA FROM THE MID-NINETEENTH CENTURY TO THE PRESENT. Univ. of California Press, 1989. *A good selection of writing, presented chronologically, with some biographical material on each author.*

A:HOG = Armstrong, Karen. A HISTORY OF GOD – The 4,000 Year Quest of Judaism, Christianity and Islam. *Patient scholarship, impeccable judgment and kindness are palpable on every page of this 'brilliantly lucid'* (The Sunday Times has it right) *introduction to and apology for "our" God with a capital G.*

A(D):AL = Aubrey, John (Oliver Lawson Dick, ed): AUBREY'S BRIEF LIVES (late 17th century). Martin,

Secker and Walburg, Ltd. 1949. (Penguin Classics 1987). *If you are even part English and haven't read Aubrey, you probably have no right reading* me. *Even if you hate history, you will enjoy many of these short biographies. Sir Walter Raleigh's tryst with the maid – "Swisser Swatter Swisser Swatter!" she cries – alone is worth the price of the book.*

Aurélio = Novo Dictionário AURÉLIO, or, NOVO DICIONÁRIO DA LÍNGUA PORTUGUESA by Aurélio Buarque de Holanda Ferreira and a team which includes people with even longer names. Editora Nova Frontera 1st ed 15th Imp. 1985? Rio de Janeiro. *This large dictionary gives more spellings of a word and more connotations than the other Portuguese dictionaries I have seen and has some Japanese-derived words only common in Brazilian Portuguese, of which one came in handy for Frois. I like it, and found it easy to use in combination with a smaller Portuguese English dictionary.*

A: TJ = Aveling, J.C.H.: THE JESUITS. Dorset Press (Stein & Day) 1981/7. Aveling *claims that the long-standing Jesuit view of Valignano's support for accommodation to the great cultures of the East and his role in the training, placement and support of Ricci, Acquaviva and other great Jesuit missionary-extraordinaires was over-rated by historians and that newly accessable material in the Gesu [?] archives show his "great limitations of outlook, his hidebound European prejudices, his lack of sympathy for , and interest in native cultures, his extreme harshness of judgment and his changes of front." Aveling's discussion of clothing and accommodation suggest he – Aveling, not Valignano – did not understand that it may be* more *accommodating to wear ones foreign clothing than to try to pass as native (see my note in Foreword part iv). I think Aveling detests and misjudges Valignano because of his support for Hideyoshi's invasion of "Chinese Korea" that endangered Ricci's fledging mission in China. He evidently has no idea of the pressure exerted by Hideyoshi, i.e., the serious risk faced by Japanese Christians had Valignano not complied as far as he did (which was not so far as to supply the boats that might have made the invasion a long-term success). Did he expect Valignano to risk the lives of tens if not hundreds of thousands of Japanese Christians for the sake of Ricci's dream!*

B:AJI = Bacon, Alice Mabel: A JAPANESE INTERIOR. Houghton, Mifflin and co. 1893. *Between information given in her earlier JGW and Morse's later book on Japanese homes, a good portion is redundant, unless you choose to read this first, in which case it is fine..*

B:JGW = Bacon, Alice Mabel: JAPANESE GIRLS AND WOMEN (1890?). Gordon Press (NY) reprint of Houghton Mifflin 1925 ed. *Informal and charming, in the it's-only-a-letter style so often adopted by women in the nineteenth century, this is one of the finest pieces of cultural anthropology ever written and deserves to be as famous as Benedict's* THE CHRYSANTHAMUM AND SWORD. *A transparently sweet soul, Bacon taught young women with Imperial blood and was doubtless beloved by them. (The 2nd and 3rd ed are 1891, so I guess on the 1st as 1890 – More important, there are many reprints.)*

B:TC = Ball, J. Dyer: THINGS CHINESE (orig.1890). Kelly &Walsh, ltd (Shanghai, HK and Singapore: 1925.) *On the whole, Ball is not up to Chamberlain and his* Things Japanese – *as writing on China in general tends to be less inspired than that written on Japan – but he does* very *well with some items.*

B:D = Barr, Andrew: DRINK – *a social history of America.* Carroll & Graf Publ. inc. (NY) 1999. *Once upon a time Americans drank from whiskey bottles rather than water fountains because the latter had not been invented and they were terrified of cold water. History is stranger than fiction!* (I suppose this book is a bit too marginal to deserve space here, but it is full of quotations from period sources which prove the past is a foreign country and I like *that.* Speaking of which, I would surely have found something to quote from David Lowenthal's *The Past is a Foreign Country* if only my library were with me!)

B(H):EOS = Barthes, Roland (Richard Howard trans.). EMPIRE OF SIGNS (1970) Hill and Wang 1982. *Barthes would write about a fictive "Japan" and not about Japan, but his readers, I fear, may forget about the italics for his "unheard of symbolic system" is not " altogether detached from our own," but clearly opposite and, as such, real by virtue of of reference to* us. *So said, there is nothing more entertaining than an essay that boldly turns appearances into ideas and does not stop with a single witty metaphorical phrase (in the style of the usual travel writer) but turns it into a paragraph or an entire chapter.*

B:FDD = Barzun, Jacques: FROM DAWN TO DECADENCE – *500 Years of Western Cultural Life 1500 to the Present* (2000) HarperCollins. *An idea-centered and opinionated (a good thing to my mind, for opinion makes writers try harder to convince) history that essays a dozen or so particularly crucial times+places including* The View From Madrid Around 1540. *There are chunky quotations in boxes on almost every page and* best of all, *plentiful recommendations of books scattered throughout. Got this one at a garage sale!*

B:UTJ = Bird, Isabella L.: UNBEATEN TRACKS IN JAPAN (2v), John Murray (London) 2ed 1880 (1st same year). *Bird is great and this is her classic. Observant, opinionated, witty and brave – what more does one need in a good travel writer? She saw more of the boondocks of Japan than any other Western visitor I know of.*

B:KAHN = Bishop, Isabella Bird: KOREA AND HER NEIGHBORS (1897). Fleming H. Revell co (NY) mdcccxcviii??? (something is a bit off) *Her long description of Korean ponies and Korean superstitions would be worth the price of the book if it were reprinted which probably won't happen, and her story of the inner workings of the Japan-influenced coup, which includes first-hand acquaintance with the Korean royalty is uniquely informative. Recently* Bishopped, *she includes her native* Bird.

B:YVAB =   Bishop, Mrs. J.F. (Isabella Bird): THE YANGTZE VALLEY AND BEYOND. Same publisher, 1899. (reprinted by Ch'eng-wen Publishing Co., Taipei, 1972) *Married or not, still indefatigable.*

B:MM = Blyth Reginald. MUMONKAN. *I will not bother writing more here.. Anything by Blyth is erudite and enjoyable. If you don't know about him, check him out.*

B:CCJ =   Boxer, C. R..: THE CHRISTIAN CENTURY IN JAPAN 1549-1650. U. of California Press, 1967. *Incredible tour de force! Boxer is as interested in warfare and piracy as he is in the interesting Jesuits, so much of the book is as exciting a read as Pinto. I can only complain about his twice mentioning the Nanking massacre in notes on his* historical evidence of cruel behavior by Japanese. *The circumstances are too different, and the Japanese behavior in the Russian Japanese War too good to warrant such simple long-term claims* (but I am glad UCP did not edit that out).

B:SCSC = Boxer, C.R. ed. SOUTH CHINA IN THE SIXTEENTH CENTURY: Being the narratives of GALEOTE PEREIRA, FR. GASPAR DA CRUZ, O.P., FR. MARTÍN DE RADA, O.E.S.A. (1550-1575), printed for the Hakluyt Society (London) 1953. *Boxer uses old English translations as far as possible in order to retain the delightful language lost in a modern translation, but he also makes unobtrusive changes as necessary for accuracy's sake and supplies his usual masterful notes as needed. These guys really observed China and, I think influenced Valignano's understanding of Japan.* (The reason some Gaspar Da Cruz quotes are in my trans. is because I found the original before obtaining this book.)

Bulletin of Portuguese-Japanese Studies.   *Well-edited and right up my alley. Hope to see more of them!*

B:A = Bulwer: ANTHROPOMETAMORPHOSIS. (1652) (first is 1650). *This classic with an original name running a full page, comes under many abbreviated names. The one I have quoted from here is missing the first part of the title and is available in microfilm* (at the BL) as "A view of the people of the whole world" (1654). *It lacks the wonderful preliminary poem I read decades ago in the LC. Another version with the title beginning "The Artificial Changeling." lacks the illustrations. If a well-funded patron can be found, I hope to publish a modern version with all of the parts in one! The book gathers together all the newest information about what people did to their bodies all around the world, but, unlike early modern anthropology, looks at European practice as well. I knew that "we" used to value the male leg. I did not know that one could write pages on the differing ideals of the male calf in Europe, nor that we actually stroked our calves to make them handsome!*

B:MCJ = Busk, Mrs. W. (or M.M.) ed.: MANNERS AND CUSTOMS OF THE JAPANESE (in the 19th century from the accounts of recent dutch residents in Japan, and from the German work . . .). Harper & Bros, 1841. *How do you write the bibliography for what would seem to be a stolen book? If I had not checked a second time with a very specific search on Worldcat, I would have thought that this book was translated and edited by the Harper brothers themselves rather than an Englishwoman, for they give her no credit whatsoever for what is an* excellent *job of translation, selection and annotation, and have the gall to boast – as only New Yorkers can? – that "the English copy has been carefully revised and corrected, and the work will be found, from the novelty of its matter and on other accounts, exceedingly entertaining." That is true. The book (original from John Murray (London) the same year) is a fine read no thanks to them. The only problem is that the seamless editing of the English edition (which I latter saw in the BL) and American, alike, often makes it hard to tell* who wrote what. *The information is not limited to the 19th century, but goes back to Kaempfer in the late 17th century. I think this book gave me some Siebold, who, despite his fame, was hard to find in English –* (I note that the author for this book was left blank in the fine bibliography at the end of Knapp:1897, and at least one recent English book.)

CP = Commonplace. Things so commonly known no Japanese would use a citation. *I should use this more.*

C(W):MVAW = Carletti, Francisco (trans. Herbert Weinstock): MY VOYAGE AROUND THE WORLD (early 17th century). Pantheon, 1964. *This Florentine merchant's work is a delightful compliment to the Jesuits' more high-brow observations. It is marvelous how matter-of-factly he elaborates upon South Asian sexual practices (especially things implanted in the penis) and admirable how he strongly criticizes both the inhuman traffic in slavery and the branding (!)which he had to do "under orders from a superior" in Cape Verde. The RAGIONAMENTI (chronicles) connection to Frois/Valignano is broached in the introduction to this book (note in Foreword v.).*

C:MKJS = Caron, Francois and Schouton (ed. C.R.Boxer): A TRUE DESCRIPTION OF THE MIGHTY KINGDOMS OF JAPAN AND SIAM (1663 English edition. Schouton describes Siam.) The Argonaut Press (London), 1935. *A plain-written description of some facets of Japan a generation after Frois by a man who worked up from Cabin boy to 2nd in charge of the Dutch East India Company. Caron's description of the gruesome tortures undergone by Catholic Japanese is as long as his book is short.*

CARTAS = (Au = I guess The Society of Jesus?)   **CARTAS** QUE LOS PADRES Y HERMANOS DE LA COMPANIA DE IESUS, QUE ANDAN EN LOS REYNOS DE IAPON . . . (1547-1571) casa de Iuan Iniguez (Castilla and Aragon) 1575. *What a wealth of writing! I wish I had found more time to read! The microfilm was old and the folio pages too large for the copier so I lost many page numbers* (this was one reason I gave up on page numbers). *If you find any mistakes in my credits for these letters to the Company from Jesuits in the Far East mistaken, please let me know!*

C(T):HML = Casanova, Giacomo (trans. Willard R. Trask). HISTORY OF MY LIFE. The John Hopkins UP. 1971. *This man who will do virtually anything to seduce all the beautiful women he meets all the while trying to convince himself and his readers that he is trying to help her is reprehensible. But, there is so much about life in the 18th century, wit and, yes, wisdom in his memoirs that even women might find it a worthwhile read.*

C:TJ = Chamberlain, Basil Hall: THINGS JAPANESE (first ed. 1890). *I have actually used a Tuttle reprint, with the pages in pieces, lacking a title page, index, etc called JAPANESE THINGS after the 1905=5th, revised edition, perhaps? A fine witty and tasteful book which generously cites many other fine books as it covers most Things Japanese (the latter editions are good for he increased these references, or rather reviews). I hope the horrid reversal of the name of the book has reversed back again by now! I got confused on how I should cite the name, but decided to acronym it as it should be! As exampled in my Foreword, Chamberlain is indeed the most prolific Topsy-turvyman since Frois, but he was not at all unique in this, as I show.*

C:CBD Chambers, Robert: CHAMBER'S BOOK OF DAYS (1869) *This wonderful book (which I would put next to* Aubrey's Lives *as the best window on our past) includes Matters connected with the Church Calendar, Phenomena connected with the Seasonal Changes; Folk-Lore of the United Kingdom connected with Times and Seasons; Notable Events, Biographies, and Anecdotes connected with the Days of the Year; Articles of Popular Archeology of an entertaining character, tending to illustrate the progress of Civilization, Manners, Literature, and Ideas in these kingdoms; Curious, Fugitive, and Inedited Pieces.* Mike Hillman is to be commended for putting it on-line, so we who cannot afford to buy the book can take enjoy and use it, and with the ability to *Search!* (I wrote him and was surprised to find mine the first fan letter! (Really! When you find good things, let people know, for others may not!) With a bit of help from some college students, he hopes to have the whole book up by the end of 2004.

C:JIL = Cockburn, S.: JAPANESE IDEAS OF LONDON. London 1873. *This book written in far-from-heroic couplets is supposed to be a letter from "a Japanese scout" to his wife in Yokohama, but other than the word Yokohama, I find nothing to suggest the English author read a single article about Japan. His wife's name is Chinesey ("Fow Chow") and things he thinks typically English, such as a coldness on the part of men to those without proper introductions and a population packed "like herrings in barrels all pickled and hacked" are, if Cockburn had only known, even truer with respect to Japan!*

C:DORC1 = Cocks, Richard: THE DIARY OF RICHARD COCKS (1615-1622) Haklyut Society reprint. *I used the* E.Thompson ed. *version (Burt Franklin, NY_), but found out later that the version published in Japan was far better, for it did not remove the sexier parts. (If the Haklyut Society is still out there, I hope they will give us the real thing). Cocks, who was manager of the English factory/trading post in Japan, provides the side of life the Jesuits did not know and is worth reading for his incredibly wild (even by unsettled English standards) spelling alone! I have misplaced my bibliographical note but think the unexpurgated version published in Japan that I read standing in a bookstore scribbling notes was*:

C:DORC2 = Diary of Richard Cocks, 1615-1622 : diary kept by the head of the English factory in Japan / [edited by The Historiographical Institute, The University of Tokyo]. Tokyo : The Institute, 1978-1980.

C:LLFX = Coleridge, Henry J. THE LIFE AND LETTERS OF ST. FRANCIS XAVIER. London. new ed 1881   *This good book includes the Japanese convert Paul's description of Japan and an abbreviation of Alvarez's account sent to Xavier. I wish I could have found all of Alvarez's account.*

C:JA = Collins, Robert J. JAPAN-THINK AMERICA-THINK. Penguin 1992. *This "Irreverent Guide to Understanding the Cultural Differences Between Us" contains hundreds of opposites, some well-treated; but the humor is, on the whole, not dry(?) enough or cultured(?) enough for the discriminating reader. Aside from the narrow scope, it is the only example of one of "us" doing the type of thing that Japanese do without bothering to use the adjective "irreverent."* (I dare say Penguin would do better with a short version (say, 200 pages?) of this TOPSY-TURVY 1585. Anyone with Penguin connections out there?)

C:RTI = Cooper, Michael, S.J. RODRIGUES THE INTERPRETER – an Early Jesuit in Japan and China. Weatherhill 1974. *A biography of a barely educated Portuguese boy who arrived in Japan at age 15 or 16 and eventually came to play a central role in Jesuit affairs in Japan, worked closely with Shogun Ieyasu, the first ruler of the Tokugawa dynasty, and wrote important works of Japanese grammar, culture and history. Cooper is always thorough and entertaining to read. He does not neglect Rodrigues's* *shortcomings, even as he wonders how this important figure of history was so long neglected in the West.*

C:TCJ = Cooper, Michael (compiled and annotated): THEY CAME TO JAPAN – An Anthology of European Reports on Japan, 1543-1640. Univ. of California Press (1965/81). *One of the best anthologies ever written. One reason I use so much post-1640 material is that Cooper has managed to find so large a percent of the best of the older material – the most interesting passages, too – that it is hard to avoid replicating his work! He tends to translate loosely which is generally for the good (overly literal translations often show the translator did not have enough confidence in his or her understanding to make hard choices); the quote I corrected in the introduction is a rare exception. Cooper must have been very young when he wrote this, for he is still active. What fine judgment and erudition for a young scholar!* (I only wish he dated citations of Valignano instead of simply giving the modern source: Wicki!).

Cooper trans. This Island of Japon by Rodrigues→R(C):TIJ). Unfortunately, I have NOT yet seen: M. Cooper 2002, *Joao Rodrigues's account of sixteenth-century Japan* (London: The Hackluyt Society) and wonder if it has more, including anything useful for this book.

C:TJJ = Cornwallis, Kinahan: TWO JOURNEYS TO JAPAN.   1859. *I found this book in Alcock, who mentioned someone having sent it to him for an opinion, which was that he doubted the author had ever been to Japan, for* "if so, I felt I ought to lay down the pen in despair, for I had not even a hope of having anything half so wonderful to narrate, were my residence in Japan to be prolonged a hundred years – which Heaven forbid!" (A:COT *– Alcock found the deprivation of beef and mutton hard on his "English constitution" and was ready to return.*) *It is true that Cornwallis' book begins with a series of happenings that remind one of Pinto. In a few dozen pages a bronze casting of a Japanese sea-god is found in a sea-cave and later stolen by the Yankee Yahoos who don't know "the laws of Meum and Tuum," a samurai commits* hara-kiri *on the spot when a gruff Yankee skipper "performed with his heavy expedition boot a violent ceremony" on his backside (the man was only doing his duty of following them), and the author himself shoots a rare Japanese wolf (not knowing it was rare when he did so) now found, he claims, in the Smithsonian* (Can anyone check this out for me?). *Yet, most of this two-volume book – which does not continue in so Pinto-esque a vein –* seems *as trustworthy as . . . Alcock. Many of the little details* ("My host introduced me as *America," being invited to a home after someone noticed him sketching, and so forth) are* perfect. *Cornwallis also deserves to be remembered (Alcock doesn't even give us his name and subsequent authors don't mention his book) for his bold humanist stance:* "Why send your money to convert the heathen, when you have a community at home more vicious and depraved, and destitute, both morally and physically . . ." *than in Japan, which* "affords a heaven of contentment as compared to our own." *His specific criticism of the wretchedness of many in London – still true today, in the year 2000!* (I had to pass through beggars to make it to the BL) *– is identical to that made by the first Japanese visitors to the West. The book ends with anti-missionary, pro-Japanese poems.* "Japan! let not invaders desecrate thy land; / Why should the idols which thy people serve./ As thy forefathers served be now cast down? . . ." *There is also a description of a Pacific island, which ends:* "Nookoora will soon be laid desolate and its people wither away . . . all the wretchedness and calamity of our enlightened system of society will hiss upon the yet unpolluted air of that far-off Eden." *I write at length partly because I think it a good bet that young Lafcadio Hearn read and was influenced by this forgotten book. Still, Cornwallis has one serious shortcoming: he never cites the work of others* (Touché for Alcocks). *After a long bath episode at his Japanese friend's house, he concludes* "The act of taking a warm bath in the presence of witnesses, was another new feature in the order of things. But it was the custom of the country. What black is to us, white is to the Japanese in more matters than mourning garments." *This is the earliest post-Opening topsy-turvy statement published in book form that I know of, but both the* "customs of the country" *and the bath connection suggest the author read Alcock's report with the material cited in the foreword of this book.*

C:TAJ = Crosland, T.W.H.. THE TRUTH ABOUT JAPAN. London 1904. *This author had already written* THE UNSPEAKABLE SCOT *and* LOVELY WOMAN, *both savage attacks of wit upon types he considered grossly over-rated. With a tremendous volume of work painting Japan and the Japanese culture in glowing colors, Crosland's poison pen aimed to even the score. Unlike the other two books, however, this book had some serious political implications. He argued that Japan's victory over Russia had dire implications for Great Britain's Far East interests, quoting a Professor K. Ukita to the effect that it was Japan's mission to set up a confederation of Asian nations.* "Asia for the Asiatics" *he warns,* "might become a *fait accompli* in far less time than the European thinks for [sic]. Furthermore, we might hear something about "Europe for Asiatics," and the yoke might change necks." *Crosland was right to be concerned about* new brooms sweeping clean, *for Japan did prove to be an authoritarian colonial power. But his argument is hopelessly stained with racism:* "Russia, after all, is a white nation. It is not seemly that a yellow race, however "plucky" and however "sturdy" should be permitted to bait her." "The ha'penny papers have vied with one another in the invention of endearing epithets for him – "little Jappy Atkins", "little Jap Tar," "the Englishman of the Orient," . . . "A stunted, lymphatic, yellow-faced heathen, with a mouthful of teeth three sizes too big for him, bulging slits where his eyes ought to be, blacking brush hair, a foolish giggle, a cruel heart, and the conceit of the devil – this, O bemused reader, is the authentic dearly-beloved "Little Jap." *I quote this at length because its attitude was very rare and represents a reaction against what we might call friendly Orientalism. I wonder if Crosland's devil's advocate exercise had a major influence on the political betrayal of the Japanese by the British which was soon to follow and which, more than anything else, put Japan on the route to Pearl Harbor.*

C:TCC = Cruz, Frei Gaspar da (Rui Manuel Loureiro ed.): TRATADO DAS COISAS DA CHINA (Evora 1569-70). Cotavia (Lisboa), 1997. *After struggling through this in Portuguese, I was half-disappointed to find it in Boxer:SCSC! The first book on China published in Europe. As obvious from my quotes in this book, Cruz was overwhelmed by the scale of the commerce and the depth of the industry of the people.*

---

*DR = Daniel Reff, correspondence. Please see Acknowledgments. For his books, see R.

D:A-J = Dalby, Liza et al: ALL-JAPAN: THE CATALOGUE OF EVERYTHING JAPANESE. William Morrow and co., 1984. *A more selective introduction of things Japanese than that of Chamberlain, and with many illustrations. Where I learned that the folding fan was a Japanese invention. It would be nice if the book were expanded many times over though I doubt that, even then, it could live up to the claims of its title, which, knowing LD's fine discrimination, probably was not her idea!*

D:EBJ = Dalton, William. AN ENGLISH BOY IN JAPAN. London, 1858. *Dalton obviously read Busk's collection of Dutch writings, Kaempfer, Willis's Frois letter (the unique spelling of the romanized Japanese for the mountain priests gives it away) and, probably, Golownin.*

D(B):DLS = Defourneaux, Marcelin (Newton Branch tr). DAILY LIFE IN SPAIN IN THE GOLDEN AGE. George Allen and Unwin, 1970. *A bold and creative* wet *style of history, the book begins with an invented letter about Spain by a very opinionated Frenchman and includes many entertaining quotes throughout.*

De Missione → see Japanese book J/S:DM.

D:GGS = Diamond, Jared. GUNS, GERMS, AND STEEL . W. W. Norton & co, 1997. *A good attempt to explain developmental differences by geo-ecological conditions, i.e.,historical determinism, but asides on Chinese characters contain regrettably crude ABCentricism.*

Dicionário Escolar Inglês-Português, Português-Inglês = Oswaldo Serpa (Ministerio da Educaçao e cultura FENAME Rio de Janeiro 7th ed 1973? *I used this mostly to read* AURELIO. *It is limited but well edited for what it does have and when I cite a Portug. dict., it was often this workhorse.* (Saw a few more, too)

D:WWM = Dower, John W. WAR WITHOUT MERCY. Pantheon, 1986. *Perhaps the best book published about bad stereotypes, period. The prejudice leading up to and used during WWII by Americans and Japanese which Dower elaborates includes a strong topsy-turvy element. I hope a future edition can include a bit more on the Japanese boasts about their own unique military spirit and threats that were published in English (and their impact), for that would complete an otherwise perfect book.*

D:RCN = Du Pleis, Scipio. THE RESOLUER, OR CURIOUSITIES OF NATURE written in French by ~. (orig. date anyone?) London, 1635. (You must spell "resolve" with a "u" to find it in the catalog). *An invaluable glimpse into the mindset of Europe, this book is as much fun as Plutarch's MORALS* (which, if you are not familiar with it, teaches us such things as the reason why a stallions tail makes a better bow-string (or was it a fiddle bow?)). *It will teach you all sorts of things, such as* "from whence comes it, that the tears of a Boare are hot, and those of a Deere are cold," *why elephants and camels prefer muddy water:* "because that seeing their Images in the cleare water, they are afraid . . ." *and* "wherefore is it that hot water is sooner cold in the Sunne, then in the shadow." *etc.. I cannot recall how it got into this book.*

E:MP = Eire, Carlos M. N.. FROM MADRID TO PURGATORY: the art and craft of dying in sixteenth-century Spain. Cambridge University Press, 1995. *There was a saying* "De Madrid al cielo," (from Madrid to heaven) *or, after seeing Madrid, only Heaven remains (see Venice and die) but, in reality, only the souls of a tiny spiritual elite went straight up,* "for most people" *Eirie explains,* "death was not a journey from Madrid to heaven so to speak, but from Madrid to purgatory."

E:DD = Elison, George. DEUS DESTROYED: THE IMAGE OF CHRISTIANITY IN EARLY MODERN JAPAN. Harvard UP, 1973. *Some history on the attitude of the Jesuits in Japan and more on the way the Japanese viewed the Jesuits and Christianity, with ample translation and analysis of arguments written against Christianity by two Japanese and Portuguese apostates. Elison's treatment of Valignano is excellent – and it is so rare to find a book like this giving the other side of the argument at length that I hate to quibble – but I feel his short summary of Frois' TRATADO is more flippant than fair* (though, so well-done, that, ingrate that I am, I borrowed it for my book explanation.).

F: DWJ = Frazer , Mrs. Hugh: A DIPLOMATIST'S WIFE IN JAPAN. (v1) Hutchinson & Co; London, 1899. *The wonderfully poetic first letter I quoted from is, unfortunately, the beginning of a far less inspired book.* (The Japanese call this "dragon-head-snake-tail"). *So please do not bother to burden inter-library loan for it!*

F(S):T(K) = **Frois, Luis (Josef Franz Schütte S.J. trans/ed.) TRATADO**. The actual name of this book, the first to put Frois's original in print is KULTURGEGENSÄTZE EUROPA-JAPAN (1585). Jochi (Sophia) University Press (Tokyo), 1955. *Schütte S.J. deserves all our gratitude for discovering and saving the TRATADO of Luis Frois from oblivion! Printed in Japan, it has no Japanese. It has the Portuguese original [Frois's misspelling left as is and indications given for places in the manuscript where the whitefish won or Frois apparently nodded], a German translation, ample background on Frois, Valignano and their work, and a fair number of notes about problematic vocabulary.* (If any fluent readers of German feel that there is anything in that Frontal matter that should be cited anywhere in this book, please send me the gloss!)

F(C):T(EJ) Frói s, Luís = (TRATADO) = **EUROPA-JAPAO UM DIÁLOGO CIVILIZACIONAL NO SÉCULO XVI.** (Comissão Nacional para as Comemorações dos Descobrimentos Portugueses / Lisboa: 1993). [The Commission would seem to get the credit on all the listings I have found, but Worldcat provides the following additional information: apresentação de José Manuel Garcia ; fixação de texto e notas por Raffaella D'Intino.] *A tastefully designed book – tall, slim, on artsy paper, as I would like to publish were it not for budget problems – with a short, proper introduction, a pithy historical essay and definitions of the Japanese vocabulary used by Frois, but no other notes to speak of. My all-caps hide the clever* EuropaJapao *of the original. Modern Portuguese speakers who find the original given in my book hard to follow had best buy a copy of this.* However, *something bothers me. This book is only found at 5 libraries on Worldcat. Compare that to 51 for Schütte's German trans., 26 for the French one, 15 for Matsuda+Jorissen, and 6 for Okada . . . There really should be a Portuguese edition that gets around. If the lack of notes makes it too dry for the non-academic reader, I would be delighted if a new version using modern Portuguese were to use the annotations in this book to spice it up, for it does not seem right that Portuguese speakers do not have easy access to Frois* (I first had the modern Portuguese in this book, but switched to the old because I did not want to compete with any modern Portuguese edition;). *Let me add that the modern Portuguese in this 1993 book was very helpful, for Frois's old and sometimes misspelled words were not easy to look up* (eventually I learned which letters to substitute, etc., but at first I had no idea!).

F(CSG):T(T) = Frois, Luis. (Xavier de Castro & Robert Schrimpf trans., presented by (?) José Manuel Garcia: **(TRATADO) TRAITÉ DE LUIS FRÓIS, S.J. (1585)** sur les contradictions de moeurs entre Européens & Japonais (Editions Chandeigne, Paris: 1993). *It is interesting to see the word* contradiction, *which does not work in English, preserved in the title! Though I do not rightly read French, I can tell that it is a very smoothly reading, indeed lively translation* (So I occasionally quote it) *and gets a few things right that others missed. Whoever was responsible for searching out the Far Eastern Portuguese (Malay, etc.) words deserves particular commendation. Unfortunately, there are far too few notes in this beautiful book. Instead, it offers 10 pages of Álvarez, and something I have never read by Nicolas Lanzillotto* (Gloss,anyone?).

Frois's TRATADO in Japanese → J/F:T entries in Japanese book section, below. My heaviest debts are to these annotated translations.

F(F&T): TJ = Fulop-Miller (F.S. Flint and D.F. Tait trans) THE JESUITS (The Power and the Secret of the Jesuits 1930), Capricorn Books (NY), 1963. *Although mistaken with respect to the roots of crucifixion in Japan and some other things, the book is a good read. It makes far more sense to call Ricci's Mandarin persona* Doctor Li, *and later* Holy Doctor Li, *than the graduate Li, as Aveling does. (Of course, it is hard to know whether to credit the author or the translators for such matters.)*

G:PPI = Gaitonide, P.D.: PORTUGUESE PIONEERS IN INDIA: spotlight on medicine. Sangam Books (Manchester) 1983. *I am not certain if this book proves what it sets out to prove, namely the large contribution made by Indian medicine to the West, but it does not matter, for the history of the Portuguese in India and essays of the respective systems of medicine are gems.*

G:HOM = Garrison, Fielding H. An Introduction to the HISTORY OF MEDICINE W.B. Saunders Company 1913/1966 – *After describing various historical medicines, the progress of Western medicine is traced with evident delight one doctor/pioneer at a time. A personable tour d'force.*

G:ET = Gill, Robin: EXOTIC TONGUES – Loving English through Japanese and vice-versa. I have no idea when I will finish and publish this, but it is one reason, I did not go overboard to supplement Frois's rather lacking treatment of linguistic opposites. Better to leave something for next time.

G:OAO = **Gill, Robin D. ORIENTALISM & OCCIDENTALISM** – is the mistranslation of culture inevitable? Paraverse Press 2004.   *The very identity of Japanese is built upon contraries, that is to say identifying themselves as the opposite of "us." That is a tendency found in much of the non-West* (see Basso's *Portraits of "The Whiteman"*). *This book shows how (mutually) exotic tongues exacerbate this. I borrowed some phrases and ideas from this manuscript (eg. itadakimasu as "a grace in a word.") The list in the appendix of sixteen ways in which differences are exaggerated and antithetical stereotypes created complements my TRATADO notes where I have given into the temptation to introduce a bit more difference, a bit more strangeness than I should have!* (I have written this elsewhere, but it is worth repeating.)

G:RCM   Glassman, Hank "THE RELIGIOUS CONSTRUCTION OF MOTHERHOOD IN MEDIEVAL JAPAN. 2001 Princeton U library has the dissertation (There is also a Religious Studies program Stanford University connection.) *Found on the internet. The original Good research, splendid reading. I'm surprised it hasn't become a bona fide book already!*

G:MCIJ = Golownin, Captain (Vasilii Mikhailovich), R. N. (3v): MEMOIRS OF A CAPTIVITY IN JAPAN 1811-1813 (Henry Colburn & co. London 1824). Oxford University Press, 1967. *Russia once had the best human resources on the planet. To read the words of Captain Golownin and Captain P. Rickford of the Imperial Russian Navy (whose account of the affair is included in v.3) is to love them. This is the only first-hand information on Japan in its isolated era that doesn't come from the Dutch trade mission! Someone* must *make a movie of this drama which, against all odds, has a happy ending!*

G:WDW: Goreau, A.   THE WHOLE DUTY OF WOMEN. *Find this book and enjoy one of the most incredible war of words the world has ever known. Horrible but witty put-downs of women and equally if not more witty and powerful comebacks on the part of women, and most of this in verse. Mostly 17th century.*

G:EOJ = Gulick, Sydney L.   THE EVOLUTION OF THE JAPANESE. New York, 1903. *This seems a remarkably deep work, but I only saw it for ten minutes and it was closing time at the library in a city I was leaving.* (If I were only wealthy, I would have bought a copy and it probably would have been quoted within.)

Historia → For Frois's Historia, see J/F:HISTORIA in the Japanese section.

H:CER = Hale, John.   THE CIVILIZATION OF EUROPE IN THE RENAISSANCE. Antheneum 1994. Like Barzun (B:FDD), impressive for being more interested in ideas than dates.   With everyone writing about the discovery of the New World, I was especially delighted to read the history of the "Discovery of Europe" and the chapter on "civility" has instructed me more than could be included in Topsy-turvy. Better had I tread it earlier! While not using boxes to highlight quotes like Barzun, this too is a cornucopia of primary material.

H:CJTH = Harris, Townsend (ed. Mario Emilio Cosenza), THE COMPLETE JOURNAL OF TOWNSEND HARRIS – first American consul general and minister to Japan. Doubleday & Co. (published for Japan Society, New York), MCMXXX. *I am sure this fine literate consul would have written a lot more – as much as Alcock – if he had not suffered from mal-absorption and the diminished productivity it entails (If only he had the constitution of his Hollywood persona, John Wayne! (Hollywood is often criticized for thinking romance requires physical beauty. Why not criticize it for linking accomplishment with physical strength?). He had not only read Kaempfer – as every one going to Japan did – but evidently knew something of Valignano, for when the Japanese tried to prevent his meeting with the head of the nation on the basis of there being no precedent for it, he replied:* "What about Valignani?" *who indeed had visited Nobunaga and later Hideyoshi and Tokugawa as the representative for Rome, and India, respectively! (did I get that right?)*

H:JAI = Hearn, Lafcadio: JAPAN – AN ATTEMPT AT INTERPRETATION (190_). Charles E. Tuttle Company, 1955/69. *Besides the attention given to the topsy-turvy, Hearn considers Japan's future in a world of aggressive Western powers and, among other things, predicts Nazism:* "Western civilization will have to pay, sooner or later, the full penalty of its deeds of oppression. Nations that, while refusing to endure religious intolerance at home, steadily maintain religious intolerance abroad, must eventually lose those rights of intellectual freedom which cost so many centuries of atrocious struggle to win. . . . With the return of all Europe to militant conditions, there has set in a vast ecclesiastical revival of which the menace to human liberty is unmistakable; the spirit of the Middle Ages threatens to prevail again; and anti-semitism has actually become a factor in the politics of three Continental powers . . . " *The church, evidently, was not only guilty of closing its eyes to Nazi monstrosity; but, if Hearn is correct, one of its parents. Hearn had only one working eye, but thanks to his Japanese experience, a truly binocular world-view.*

H:S = Hearn, Lafcadio = SHADOWINGS. Little, Brown and co..1900. *The cicada and Japanese female names are two of the more interesting topics in this book, which like all of Hearne's books is interesting. If I had more Hearn on my current book-shelf, I would have cited him more!*

H:ETP = Hanley, Susan B. EVERYDAY THINGS IN PREMODERN JAPAN. Univ. of California Press, 1997. *This book, which I read too late to take much advantage of, shows that in some ways pre-modern was modern indeed. The chapter on "urban sanitation and physical well-being" includes much information on the recycling of human waste.* (I wrote the above 4 years ago and could kick myself for not borrowing the book again!)

H(G):HH= Herodotus (trans. David Grene): HERODOTUS'S HISTORY Univ. of Chicago Press (date, next time). *Herodotus is worth reading. Topsy-turvy is not all of it by any means. To me the story of how one king (or was it a General) took a year off a campaign to engage his troops in chopping up and killing a large river because it "killed" his favorite horse (drowned in crossing it) alone was worth the price of the book (somewhere in my library in Japan).*

H(V&W): JJ = Heusken, Henry (Jeannette C. van der Corput & Robert A. Wilson trans/ed.) JAPAN JOURNAL 1855-1861. Rutgers U. P. 1964. *The poetic and open expression of the first half of the journal by the translator/secretary for the first US consul in Japan is* astounding *for a man in his twenties. If he were not assassinated by a Japanese nationalist, there is no telling what Heusken may have eventually accomplished. The original diary of this Dutch-American was written in French. Heusken is the one who tells us that the American consul Harris told the Japanese they were wrong to claim no ambassador had ever been allowed to meet the Shogun personally:* "It would not be the first time that the head of State receives an ambassador of a foreign nation. Among others, Father Valignani, bearer of a letter from the Viceroy of Goa, has been received by him." (from August 27, 1857 entry)

H:HJD = Hooykaas, R.: HUMANISM AND THE VOYAGES OF DISCOVERY IN 16TH CENTURY PORTUGUESE SCIENCE AND LETTERS. North-Holland Publ. co 1965/79. *Many good quotations show how the discovery of what ancients did not know was interpreted, i.e. how it influenced "our" inventiveness.*

H:CCTT = Huc, M. L'Abbé: CHRISTIANITY IN CHINA, TARTARY AND THIBET (v2) D&J Sadlier &co (Montreal), 1884

K(S):HOJ =   Kaempfer, Engelbert, MD (J.G. Scheuchzer trans.): THE HISTORY OF JAPAN (Together with a Description of the Kingdom of Siam)(1690-2). James MacLehose and Sons (Glasgow), Macmillan co (NY) MCMVI. *With neither the (still missing) first volume of Frois's HISTORIA, nor Rodrigues's history of the church* (first volume: *TIOJ) yet published, Kaempfer's work provided the most complete picture of Japan available outside of the Jesuit's archives until the mid 19th century! Kaempfer did a phenomenal job considering he was only in Japan for a couple years, and that mostly on Dejima, the artificial island built for foreigners. Unlike Montanus (M:EEJ), he observed and recorded things not found in the earlier Jesuit writing. Perhaps because of Montanus' dwelling on Japanese contrariness, Kaempfer writes no topsy-turvy generalizations, but sticks to the facts, which, however include hearsay from Japanese). His translator provides an incredibly knowledgeable introduction, showing he was conversant with everything hitherto written on Japan. There is also a long biographical note on the translator and his family which include the fact that one letter from his father (a professor of Physics, a father of modern natural history and "largely instrumental in procuring the abolition of capital punishment for witchcraft") to the Royal Society (Feb. 8,1722/3) discussed the height of a mountain, cataracts of the eye, icy dendrites, a membrous kidney, curious Swiss crystals, the anatomy of a male badger, a lunar eclipse, a worm found in the skin of a weasel, flies and ants at Baden and little beetles from Mexico. Like Charles's grandfather Erasmus Darwin, he was a student of fossils and had an acerbic wit. One treatise has a school of fossil-fish remonstrate about the dastardly humans who got them destroyed and buried by provoking the Flood with their sinning, and* then *dared to assert the fossils were mere freaks of nature. This Zurich Professor's son, who surely would have accomplished many great things, died before him, shortly after completing this translation.* (There is a good very recent translation, but I have not seen it.)

K:AJC = Keene, Donald. APPRECIATIONS OF JAPANESE CULTURE. Kodansha International (1971) 81.. *Keene writes not only responsible and readable, but entertaining literary criticism that always has something new, even for the specialist.*

K:JDE = Keene, Donald: THE JAPANESE DISCOVERY OF EUROPE 1720-1850. Stanford U, 1969. (I fear I never managed to get this one! If you have it and find anything to use as a gloss in this book . . .)

K(K):EI = Kenko (Donald Keene trans.): ESSAYS IN IDLENESS – THE TSUREZUREGUSA OF KENKO (orig1330-32) Tuttle, 1987(1967 Columbia UP). *If you have not read this, do. Together with Sei Shônagon's Pillow Book, this is the most entertaining Japanese classic book you will find.*

K:KJ = Kipling, Rudyard (Hugh Cortazzi and George Webb ed.): KIPLING'S JAPAN. Athlone, 1988. *One editor, an expert on Japan and one on Kipling. Fine notes. I only wish our publishers would see fit to* USE *good footnotes, rather than placing them where one must jump back and forth!*

K:FMJ = Knapp, Arthur May: FEUDAL AND MODERN JAPAN (v2). L.C. Page and co (Boston) 1897 (1896). *A delightful book, content and design-wise. The small number of typeset Chinese characters found in the text on the chapter on "the written language" look better than anything else I have seen. The electrotyping by Geo. C. Scott & Sons for Colonial Press was superb.*

K:HWJ   Kurihara, Toshie: HISTORY OF WOMAN IN JAPANESE BUDDHISM / NICHIREN'S PERSPECTIVES ON THE ENLIGHTENMENT OF WOMAN published (on line) by the Institute of Oriental Philosophy. *Splendid summary, scholarly yet not academic.*

L:AME = Lach, Donald F.. ASIA IN THE MAKING OF EUROPE. vol 1. The University of Chicago Press. *Together with B:TCC, the best overall picture of the meeting of the continents. Incredible detail on so many subjects, the books (there are more volumes) are an education in themselves – some day I hope to read them all. Lach stands alone (and is absolutely correct) in his assessment of Frois' writing as* not *being given to verbosity.   One may write at great length, but provided the writing is full of "concrete data and detail" (1-pg.683), it cannot rightly be criticized as verbose.*

L:JIA = Lanham, Charles: THE JAPANESE IN AMERICA. NW University Publishing Co (1872). *Lanham, Secretary for the Japanese Legation in Washington, did a fine job editing what is largely pr for Japan. The book comprises 1) testimony (about the high intelligence, courage, sense of honor and universally polite nature of the Japanese, and the technological advances already made cleverly left to actual speeches by Americans and citations from American newspaper articles), 2) essays by Japanese students that were sent in to Mori Arinori, and 3) Mori Arinori's American Summary, which includes mention of our collective activities such as house-raising, apple-paring, sugar-making (frolics), corn-huskings, clam-bakes, shooting sheep-shearing and plowing matches, . . . A speech by Marquis Ito includes a fascinating paragraph of what might be called allegorical revisionism:* "The red disc in the centre of our national flag shall no longer appear like a wafer over a sealed empire, but henceforth be in fact what it is designed to be, the visible symbol of the rising sun, moving onward and upward amid the enlightened nations of the world." *This is the earliest instance I know of Japan* as *the rising sun, rather than the* birthplace of *the sun! Meanwhile, a student, Yashida Hisomaro noted that* "the terms oriental and occidental have not been used with strictly scientific accuracy; for the United States of America are east of Japan, and yet Japan is called an oriental nation, though in fact it is occidental in relation to them."

LR = (Lost Reference, or Forgotten Source.) *Read sometime in the past; the title either forgotten or the book not found in time to confirm whether it was indeed the source of the information.* (Sorry!)

L:TSC = Las Casas, Bartholomew de (trans M.M.S.): THE SPANISH COLONIE OR BRIEFE CHRONICLE OF THE ACTS AND GESTES OF THE SPANIARDES . . . (1641?49?) William Brome (London) 1583. *I had read about Las Casa's for years and finally came upon this fine translation by accident in a microfilm while searching for something else. Wow! The polemic is far bolder, more powerful than I had imagined. Never has cruelty been described in so many metaphors! The date of the English translation is the same year that Valignano's Summario of Japan was sent to Rome..*

L:AJN = LaViolette, Forest E.: AMERICANS OF JAPANESE ANCESTRY (1945/ Canada Institute of International Affairs). Arno Press (NY) 1978. *A good "study of assimilation in the American community."*

Lazarillo→ Anonymous

L:IOJ = Lehmann, Jean-Pierre: THE IMAGE OF JAPAN – from feudal isolation to world power, 1850-1905. George Allen & Unwin (London), 1978. *An exceptionally well-balanced book using ample period text to analyze the ambivalent Western feelings about Japan's modernization.*

L(J&L):LPC = León, Fray Luis de (tr. ed. John A. Jones and Javier San José Lera): LA PERFECTA CASADA – A Bilingual Edition of ~ (the role of married women in 16th century Spain) (1583). The Edwin Mellen Press. 1999. *This Augustinian and "leading humanist of Spain's Golden Age" also did the first Spanish translation of Solomon's* Song of Songs, *for which he got in a bit of trouble with the Inquisition! As Jones's and Lera's long and fine introduction explains, the original* perfect married woman *was published together with the longer work* De Los Nombres de Cristo, *but proved such a hit that it ended up separate and reprinted over and over. Unlike the horrific polemic over the role and nature of women that one finds in England shortly later, this Dominican father treats us to cool classical rhetoric* ("if there is anything under the moon that deserves to be prized and esteemed, it is a good wife; in comparison to her, the sun itself pales and the stars darken.") *combined with extremely creative metaphor* ("as climbing up a sand-hill is for the feet of the elderly, such is a garrulous wife for a quiet husband") *– and the longest (over a hundred pages!) sustained argument against cosmetics and essay of personal beauty I know of.*

L:WCRS = Levathes, Louise E.: WHEN CHINA RULED THE SEAS: the treasure fleet of the dragon throne 1405-1433. Oxford UP, 1994. *Ships the length of two football fields with many modern features! A book suitable for general readers about the spectacular rise and fall of Chinese sea-power.*

L:VJHVL = Linschoten, John Huyghen Van: THE VOYAGE OF JOHN HUYGHEN VAN LINSCHOTEN ((1596) from the old english translation of 1598, first vol. by Arthur Coke Burnell, Haklyut Society reprint 1885?) reprint Lenox Hill (Burt Franklin) 1970. *It is hard for me to tell who to credit for what with this book, but it is a fine olde read!*

L:IOJ = Littlewood, Ian: THE IDEA OF JAPAN. Secker & Warburg, London, 1996. *Much fine 19th & 20th century writing is cited and with no little wit; but, in my opinion, the unfavorable or patronizing element of the Western images and myths of Japan is somewhat over-emphasized – despite the well-balanced introduction – perhaps to ensure the book belongs to the popular discipline (?) of [anti]Orientalism.*

L:SOFE = Lowell, Percival: THE SOUL OF THE FAR EAST. Houghton, Mifflin and co. 1888. *This is an outrageous attempt to use Japanese as proof that the essence of the West is individual-enhancing and the East individual-effacing. Lowell's wild and often poetic metaphysics is amusing, but Morse, who was in Japan at the same time, observed Japanese much more closely! Lowell mysteriously dedicates his book "to the rose" – a very Occidental flower – in Japanese only* (Bara-no hana ni)!

M:JAL = Markino Yoshio: A JAPANESE ARTIST IN LONDON. George W. Jacobs (Philadelphia) 1910. (and Chatto & Windus) *The only book I have read full of awkward English, left unpolished to deliberately show it was the genuine work of one who is not a native speaker.*

M:DLP = Marques, A. H. de Oliveira (tr.S.S. Wyatt): DAILY LIFE IN PORTUGAL IN THE LATE MIDDLE AGES. (U of Wisconsin Press: 1971) *Despite the fact that in Frois's time Portugal had almost the population of England and Spain had over twice as much, the British Library has not a single book about the reign of Phillip II (who ruled not only Iberia but much of Europe while Elizabeth I reigned in little England). There are such books, but they made the mistake of getting themselves published in the USA (the U of Wisconsin has a London branch, so its books generally are found here). This book was the closest I could come! The author shows particular care with clothing, ample illustrations depict what print alone cannot show.*

M(B):HIC = Martins, J.P. Oliveira (tr. Aubrey F.G. Bell): A HISTORY OF IBERIAN CIVILIZATION (1879). Oxford UP 1930. *As the translator writes, this is "history seen through a temperament." It reminds one at times of a later classic, Cash's THE MIND OF THE SOUTH, a gothic portrayal of the people of the Southern part of the United States.*

M:AWE = Massarella, Derek: A WORLD ELSEWHERE – Europe's encounter with Japan in the Sixteenth and Seventeenth Centuries. Yale U P, 1990. *Massarella's attempt to balance Boxer's CHRISTIAN CENTURY . . . by giving more space to English contacts (as opposed to Iberian) and ten full pages of their intimate relations with the Japanese is fine, but Boxer is still the book to read. Massarella gives little more space (one paragraph) to the Bungo Concensus than do writers on China, who at least have the excuse of saying they are, after all, dealing with China.*

Matsuda & Jorissen (their trans. of TRATADO and analysis) → J/F(M&J):T

M:RPJ = Matsuda, Kiichi: THE RELATIONS BETWEEN PORTUGAL AND JAPAN (Lisbon) 1965. *Half of this book by the translator/annotator of one of the Japanese translations of TRATADO is a pithy but masterful summary of the history of the earliest Portuguese and Japanese relations, and what happened to Christianity there. (It is why I don't try to include much history in this book: others do it so much better than me!). The second half, on the influence of Portugal on Japanese culture could be expanded.*

M:MFAJ = Mears, Helen: MIRROR FOR AMERICANS – JAPAN. Houghton Mifflin co., 1948. *This long polemic takes Americans to task for demonizing the Japanese, pointing out that they are no more militaristic than we are, and argues for a kind Occupation.*

M:JRC = Menpes, Mortimer (and Dorothy): JAPAN, A RECORD IN COLOUR. London 1901. *Dorothy Menpes claims to simply present her father's impressions of Japan, but I wonder if it is simply a transcription. This book is* the *most Japan-praising book of all – more so even than Morse, for Menpes is a lover not a critic. This book is one long aesthetic adulation of a nation where people care about where they* place *things, whether they be actors, postal stamps or trees; and an extended criticism of the bad taste of the West.. While I agree with most of the argument, I can sympathize with Crosland's reaction to it, as well!*

M:MSB = Michel, Wolfgang: THE MEDICINE OF THE SOUTHERN BARBARIANS IN JAPAN (http://www.rc.kyushu-u.ac.jp/~michel/publ/books/)   *This is a thorough and very readable survey of the history of Western Medicine in Japan. (It was first published in Japanese as part of Michel, Wolfgang: Kômôryû geka no tanjô ni tsuite [On the Birth of Kômô-style Surgery]. In: Yamada, Keiji / Kuriyama, Shigehisa (ed.): Rekishi no naka no yamai to igaku [Disease and Medicine in History]. Shibunkaku Shuppan, Kyôto, March 1997.)*

M:LRY = Mikes, George: LAND OF THE RISING YEN. Andre Deutsch 1970 (Penguin 1973) *Lines like "The Japanese are human beings like the rest of us, but they will strongly resent the insinuation" and "I am for untidiness and a modicum of dirt" make Mikes' irreverent, but never mean, criticism a delight to read.*

M:BGE = Moges, Marquis de. BARON GROS'S EMBASSY TO CHINA AND JAPAN IN 1857-58. London (Richard Griffin & Co) 1860. Baron Gros and Lord Elgin's Embassy and War-party *might more accurately describe the Chinese part of the book! The author is the attaché to Gros's mission. He not only notes background, business and results, but all the fascinating hearsay (eg. a half page on the preference of tigers for Chinese flesh, likewise for the drunk-friendly facilities of Ascension Island) – not to mention translated anti-Western polemic – he can find. Unlike most attachés, he has opinions about everything. Because the party enjoyed the privilege of open access to the homes of the governors, generals and even temples – "everything was bared to our eyes" – in the wake of the European military victory, the China part of the book is enriched with a plunder of observations, if I may coin a new term of venery! The translator of the "authorized translation" is not given.*

M(F):CEM = Montaigne, Michel de (Donald M. Frame trans) :THE COMPLETE ESSAYS OF MONTAIGNE (c1570~88).. Stanford U P, 1943 /85 *I can not imagine writing a book without a quote from the* Essais. *If you have not read Montaigne's Essays, do. Find out how far we have* not *come in 500 years!*

M:EEJ = Montanus, Arnoldus: AN EMBASSY TO THE EMPEROR OF JAPAN [also, *Atlas Japannensis*]. (Engl. transl: 1670). *This book allegedly about the Dutch Embassy, but actually a hodge-podge of Japan-lure, the best part of which repeats Valignano's contrasts, adding commentary that makes them seem even stranger, and serves up the whole with scores of magnificent illustrations by an artist who obviously never went to Japan. A large number of these all-to-plainly show the European fixation on, and misunderstanding of, " idol worship" (see forward-note _), and all give the Japanese the only body European artists were capable of imagining: thick and muscle-bound with Popeye-like forearms (this last especially strange because very, very few Japanese have the massive forearms found in not a few Caucasians). Our* Frois *appears under one of his strangest names:* "Father *Lodowick Frojus* relates in his letter from *Canga,* an Island in *Japan, . . .*" that the "Empress" had a "Chappel in her own Palace" where she "worships *Amida.*" I cannot recall any Empresses in Frois, but, then again, I have a poor memory . . .[The edition I saw at the BL is dedicated to Prince Charles by John Ogilby ("Master of His Majesties Revels in the Kingdom of Ireland") who writes: "These strange and novel relations concerning both the ancient and present estate of the so Populous and Wealthy Empire of Japan being a Book of Wonders, dedicated with all humility lies prostrate at the Sacred Feet of your most serene MAJESTY, . . ."]

M:JM = Moore, Charles E, ed. THE JAPANESE MIND. University of Hawaii Press: 1967 *Very readable papers by academics (including a world-class physicist) about what Japanese logic (if there is such a thing) has to offer (something different?) in the greater (Western?) world of philosophy. I would recommend reading T:SJT before reading this and my G:O&O after reading it.*

M:JJ = Moran, J.F.: THE JAPANESE AND THE JESUITS – Alessandro Valignano in sixteenth century Japan. Routledge, 1993. *Valignano is given due credit for the great work he did for his Church in the Far East. Moran also sympathetically describes poor Frois writing, writing, writing for Valignano, while the latter was sending his own treatises to Rome, but holding on to those of his overworked amanuensis. If a reader wishes to understand Frois' circumstances better, see Moran's book – for, sorry to be repetitive – I hate to write biography. The historical importance of the Bungo Consultation, i.e.* Accommodation *made official, is not, in my opinion, forcefully enough expressed; for that reason, I feel that Schütte's* VALIGNANO'S MISSION PRINCIPLES *is still* the *book on Valignano and what he did that most deserves to be general knowledge.*

M:IGM = Morse, Edward S. ON THE IMPORTANCE OF GOOD MANNERS. 1894. *This speech to the graduates of Vassar might be the first attempt at* Learn-from-Japanism *in the USA. Harvard charged me an arm-and-a-leg to see the micro-film or fish or whatever. Take care if you Worldcat it!*

M:JDD = Morse, Edward S.: JAPAN DAY BY DAY 1877, 1878-9, 1882-3 (2v). Houghton Mifflin Company, 1917. *Even if the book, which was taken from thirty-five hundred pages of journal by the author himself, were not blessed by 777 illustrations, Morse's ample and absolutely unaffected observations would be fine reading. He writes as a scientist, sympathetic but neither romantic nor paternalistic toward the Japanese, whom he felt had as much to offer the West – if not more – than the vice-versa. Because of this, the book is ageless. There is a 1990 reproduction by Cherokee Publishing Company. A major publisher should give it to us in paperback at a decent price.*

M:JHTS = Morse, Edward S.: JAPANESE HOMES AND THEIR SURROUNDINGS. Harper & Brothers, 1904. *A fine book, well illustrated by the author and worth reprinting.*

M:CL = Mungello, D.E.: CURIOUS LAND: JESUIT ACCOMODATION AND THE ORIGINS OF SINOLOGY. U of Hawaii Press, 1989. *Unfortunately, the role of Valignano and the Japanese experience in the development of a policy of Accommodation is completely overlooked. As the original title (*Studia Leibnitiana, Supplementa 25 (1985) by Fritz Steiner Verlag Weisbaden) *suggests – Leibniz wrote of Chinese ideographs – the book does better with Ricci and Chinese philosophy and language and their effect on European thought.*

N:GIL Nalle, Sara T. GOD IN LA MANCHA: Religious Reform and the People of Cuenca, 1500-1650 THE LIBRARY OF IBERIAN RESOURCES ONLINE *Full of both statistics and local color, entertaining quotes from the mouths of the people as recorded by the notaries. You feel like they are standing right before you.*

NIPO = Nihon-Portuguese, i.e. Japanese-Portuguese dictionary of 1604. *I wish I had a copy but I don't.*

N:MAR = Nelson, Randy F. ed. THE OVERLOOK MARTIAL ARTS READER. The Overlook Press (NY) 1989. *A fine "anthology of historical and philosophical writings." Lafcadio Hearn on judo was a new discovery for me.*

N(O):EC = Nieuhoff, John (John Ogilby): AN EMBASSY FOR THE EAST-INDIA CO. TO . . . . THE GRAND TARTAR CHAM EMPEROR OF CHINA. 1673. *I cannot understand how one man Olgilby could have managed to translate and print this enormous three volume set and the almost as large two volume set of Montanus while also serving as the cosmographer, geographer and master of revels in the Kingdom of Ireland for His Majesty. This book has some of the same horrendous pictures of idols found in Montanus, but also includes some reproductions of actual Chinese pictures of Taoist legend and Buddhist* deities! Nieuhaus, *"the steward to the Ambassadors"* not only recorded his trip and findings but, like Montanus, collected others writing and even gives us a nice chunk of Kircher (all properly credited) who had not visited China [?]. The folklore explanations of the magical natural world of the Orient (obviously gathered from local sources with relish) equals the best – i.e .most fabulous – passages of Pliny. Indeed, Pliny is often quoted. The Gods of the Formosan's and the Chinese are listed and described in great detail without any moralizing.. In fact, the details in the description of Formosan festival – especially a page-long one description of how a shamanness drank, pissed ("if the Priestess chances to Urine thorow the Roof of the Church, then the Spectators promise to themselves a fruitful year") *and "tabored" on her private parts* ("which Taboring the Spectators observe with as much Zeal, as in our Countrey the Auditors give ear to the Preaching of a Sermon") – *are* very *impressive and should stand up to anything modern anthropology can offer. The author also repeatedly decries the harsh way the new Mongol rulers treated the people in South China.*

OED = **The OXFORD ENGLISH DICTIONARY.** *Why mention it? Because I only realized just how much help it was for* TRANSLATING *a few months before finishing this first edition* (for that reason, it helps the last half of the book more than the first). *What I discovered is that it had not a few, but* many *old Portuguese words not even found in* AURELIO! *Before I had searched for some words I thought* also *might have been English. I was too timid. If any of you happen to be translating from old Portuguese or Spanish or French or German, try the OED, if you have not already, and you will thank me for the advice. Needless to say, you must use your imagination with the spelling, but that is half the fun of it.*

OJD → J/OJD, in the Japanese section.

Okada = his annotated trans. of TRATADO → **J/F(O):T**

O:IOE = Okakura, Kakasu: THE IDEALS OF THE EAST WITH SPECIAL REFERENCE TO THE ART OF JAPAN. John Murray, 1903. A prefatory note tells us that *"Mr. Murray wishes to point out that this book is written in english by a native of Japan."* Regardless, it is not so interesting as his writing on *The Way of the Tea!*

O:EEM= Oliphant, Laurence: Earl of Elgin's Mission to China and Japan, v2 1860, New York, Harper & Brothers, (first US edition). [I misplaced my note and cannot recall which edition I saw]. *The first volume on China is one military and political action after another. Unlike his French counterpart Moge, Oliphant has almost nothing to say about the Chinese. Yet the second, on Japan, is 90% culture and history. Oliphant cites nearly every major writer on Japan that precedes him. One can see there is by now a cultural Japanology, largely favorable to Japan, whereas Sinology is dead. Oliphant only found one theme for the Chinese: dirty or not, they are a hard-working people. Oliphant argues that it is ridiculous to* complain *about this; instead, we should find a way to take advantage of what one would think ought to be regarded as a* blessing.

P:AOE = Palliser, D.M.: THE AGE OF ELIZABETH under the late Tudors 1547-1603. Longman (London) 1983/92. *A thorough but a bit too dry history.*

P(P):SMS = Peréz-Mallaína, Pablo E. (Carla Rahn Phillips trans.). SPAIN'S MEN OF THE SEA: DAILY LIFE ON THE INDIES FLEETS IN THE SIXTEENTH CENTURY. John Hopkins, 1998. *A well-researched book written with fine tongue-in-cheek humor, beautifully translated. An illustration of sailors hauling on a cable shows them using devices to grasp the rope such as Morse was later to credit the Japanese for!*

P:GUG = Perrin, Noel: GIVING UP THE GUN: JAPAN'S REVERSION TO THE SWORD 1543-1879. G.K. Hall & co (Boston) 1979. *An excellent essay proving that good sense counts more than language skills, because the author slowly gathered material with the help of translators and . . . read it and see for yourself!*

P:EAE : Picaza, Jorge, MD.: "The European-Amerindian Encounter: An immunodeficiency lesson" in *Mercy medicine,* vol.2 #4 1984. *The citation is from* Oviedo FG. HISTORIA GENERAL Y NATURAL DE LOS INDIOS. Mexico City: Fondo de cultura economica, 1950. *Picaza describes diseases to which the Europeans were the more vulnerable as well as the usual destruction caused by "our" diseases to "them."* (a fine article found while organizing papers of Dr. Harvey Blank, MD.)

P(C):TMP = Pinto, Fernao Mendez (Rebecca D. Catz trans./ed.) THE TRAVELS OF MENDES PINTO. (written1560-80, publ. 1614) U. Chicago, 1989. *The full edition, with ample notes, especially on the vocabulary that are very helpful. Everyone should read Pinto at least once.*

P(L):TMP = Pinto, again. (Michael Lowery trans/abridge and Dr. Luís Sousa Rebelo intro) THE PEREGRINATION OF FERNAO MENDES PINTO . . . Carcanet Press (Manchester) 1992. *The abbreviated parts are summed up and the book is long enough for most readers. I am surprised this Pinto is not out in paperback, for Pinto's honest-to-goodness (and badness) history reads like Don Quixote crossed with Candide and The Arabian Nights.*

P:LJ = Ponting, Herbert J. THE LOTUS-LAND JAPAN. London & NY, 1922. *Not bad, but nothing much.*

PRINCIPIO = See V(W):HPP.

P(B):ETPJ = Proust Jacques. (Elizabeth Bell trans.) EUROPE THROUGH THE PRISM OF JAPAN – Sixteenth to Eighteenth Centuries. U of Notre Dame Press, 2001. *The good judgment used in the selection of themes and the grace of the essays remind me of Rodney. Needham's* Exemplars. *Like Perrin's* Giving Up the Gun, *it proves that (not having)reading knowledge of Japanese is less important than brains and taste. Among other themes, the relationship between the Jesuit Almeida being a New-Christian (Jewish roots) and his practice of medicine in Japan, the reaction of "one of the most famous casuists of the time" to Valignano's list of predicaments faced by the Jesuits in Japan (situations arising from the difference in the cultures).*

R:DPC = Reff, Daniel T. DISEASE, DEPOPULATION, AND CULTURE CHANGE IN NORTHWESTERN NEW SPAIN 1518-1764. *This classic book documenting the demographic and cultural consequences of the spread of Old World disease is, on the whole, for anthropologists and historians and students, but the penultimate chapter "Cultural Change and the Dynamics of Missionization," is a fine (= readable and recommended to all who wonder what happened to native peoples when they met "us.") survey/analysis of various theories about what precipitated and sustained native acceptance of the Jesuit missions. The most important point Reff makes is that disease in almost all cases preceded the missions and so decimated the cultural institutions(including towns which were abandoned) as to provide the chroniclers (all Jesuits, for it was the policy to keep records) with a misleading image of primitive societies that fed the "civilization vs. savagery" myth (bad positive feedback), that eventually worked its way down to "our" patronizing attitudes toward underdevelopment and inner-city culture, for that matter.*

R(R&A&D):HOT = de Ribas, Andrés Pérez (Trans. of 1645 Spanish orig. by Daniel T. Reff, Maureen Ahern and Richard Danford): HISTORY OF THE TRIUMPHS OF OUR HOLY FAITH Amongst the Most Barbarous And Fierce Peoples of the New World. 1999. U. of Arizona Press. *In Book 7 ch.1 of this huge work, the author wrote "My motivation for writing this Treatise was augmented by the fact that I learned that a modern-day heretic had published a treatise against the Company, saying that its missionary sons seek out and choose ministries only among the richest, noblest and most powerful peoples and republics such as China, Japan, and other similar nations." (According to Reff's footnote, said treatise is probably John Barclay's* Euphormionis lusinini satyricon, *or* Satyricon, *second only to* Don Quixote *as an important work of fiction in the seventeenth century according to one scholar cited.) In his* HISTORY, *De Ribas more than proves that the Jesuits in North Mexico endured great privation and died by the droves while carrying out their missions among the "barbarous, wretched and miserable people" of North Mexico, who, he hastened to add, were not despised for this. De Ribas's* HISTORY *not only has anthropological sketches of dozens of cultures, which include not a little delightful detail, but tales of incredible courage in a land that in some ways remind me of the highlands of New Guinea described by its first explorers. This is for New Spain what Frois's* Historia *is for the history of Christianity in Japan: the primary document to see.*

R(C):TIJ = RODRIGUEZ, JOAO (Michael Cooper trans./ed): THIS ISLAND OF JAPON (book 1 of *Historia da Igregja do Japao:*1620-33). Kodansha Int'l ltd (Tokyo and New York). *The first part of Rodrigues's History of the Church in Japan, this may be the best single introduction to Japan ever written. I think it may well have utilized Frois's missing summary to his HISTORIA.*

R:MD = Rodrigues João (Michael Cooper trans. intro) "THE MUSE DESCRIBED: Joao Rodrigues' Account of Japanese Poetry" Monumenta Nipponica, Vol.26, No.1/2 (1971), 55-75). (A selection from Rodrigues' huge *Arte da lingoa de Iapam* (dated 1604, prob. not printed until 1608)) *If you are interested in the history of the translation of Japanese poetry, this is where it started. Most of the examples of poetry in the book come from the first poem in Japanese collections of poetry, which generally were quite witty or in some way representative. Rodrigues introduces the concept of poetry about seasonal themes to the West for the first time and chooses a fine poem to example the difference between the literal and metaphorical meanings.*

R(L):TOES = Rodriguez, João (Jeroen Pieter Lamers trans+intro): TREATISE ON EPISTOLARY STYLE – João Rodriguez on the Noble Art of Writing Japanese Letters. (selection from *Arte da lingoa de Iapam* (1604-8)) Center for Japanese Studies, U. of Mich. 2002 *Good translation, good introduction and good notes, but for $50. one should get* all *of Rodrigues/z's GRAMMAR, not just a part. Luckily, U. of Georgia Worldcat'ed it down to me in Miami, or I would have missed it as I missed the rest of the 40-odd monographs on Japan published by said press.* (Imagine how long my annotations would be had I money to buy such books!)

Ross, A.C. = A VISION BETRAYED 1994 Edinburgh. ***Unfortunately, I missed this!*** *At last minute, I read a book review suggesting Ross made overly large claims for the depth of Valignano's challenge to Eurocentric understanding of culture. But, my guess is that I would prefer this to Moran's.*

R:TKM = Rudofsky Bernard. THE KIMONO MIND. Van Nostrand Reinhold Company 1965. *The subtitle calls it an* informal *guide to "Japan and the Japanese," but* "irreverent" *would be a better adjective. Rudofsky likes ideas, so intelligent readers can enjoy him, but the abundance of tasteful illustra-tions fail to offset the all-too-often unfair and occasionally tasteless swipes at the Japanese character.*

---

de Sande → See the Japanese books J/S:DM

S:HOJ = Sansom, George: A HISTORY OF JAPAN, 1334-1615. Stanford UP:1961. *A standard.*

S:JDJ = Scidmore, Eliza Ruhamah: JINRICKSHA DAYS IN JAPAN. Harper & Bros, 1891. *If Skidmore is not an adventurer of Bird's class, she is an even better writer. She is the one who called the Japanese "a nation of poseurs – all their world a stage, and all their men and women merely players" long* before modern cultural anthropologists came up with the concept of a theatre-state. [[]]

S(C):VMP = Schütte, Josef Franz S.J. (John J. Coyne, S.J. trans): VALIGNANO'S MISSION PRINCIPLES FOR JAPAN (v.1). The Institute of Jesuit Sources (St. Louis), 1980. *Schütte not only found and presented Frois's TRATADO to the world, but, with this book, gives Valignano the full treatment he deserves. Any scholar pretending to understand the Jesuit's policy of Accommodation in Japan and China, and the Bungo Consultation [that became the Consensus?] that hammered out the modus operandi and vivendi to make East-West cultural equality a reality for the first time since the Renaissance (my claims, not Schütte's), must start from this in-depth but easy-reading study. (I was shocked to find the British Library, which boasts that it is the top academic library in the world did not have a copy. Then again, they lack many good books written in English, merely because they dared to be published outside of the U.K.. I put a note explaining that without this book they cannot call themselves a research library and, a recent check on Worldcat shows they have it!) This book may sound very specialized, but it is a far better read than most books published by academic presses and I would hope that a place like, say, the University of California, should consider a reprint. (Dan Reff introduced it to me in 1998, but I was unable to find it* again (almost reread it in a Society of Jesus library in London, but before I could get around to the letter they wanted (they have accommodated themselves to this awful English practice) I was in Edinburgh). To bad, for a second reading would have improved this book.

S(M)PBSS = Sei Shonagon (Ivan Morris trans/ed): THE PILLOW BOOK OF SEI SHONAGON (c 1000 AD) Columbia U P 1967/Penguin 71. *As they say about seeing Venice, read Shônagon then die. I think Sei Shônagon would appreciate my putting it that way!*

S:QTJ = Sladen, Douglas. QUEER THINGS ABOUT JAPAN. Anthony Treherne & Co., Ltd., 1903.

S:MQT = Sladen, Douglas (and Norma Lorimer): MORE QUEER THINGS ABOUT JAPAN, Anthony Treherne & co. (London), 1905. *I read and enjoyed Sladen's first book twenty years ago, but was unable to obtain it by library loan. But, that is well, for he is so amusing I end up quoting him too much! In this book, which he shares with Ms Lorimer (whose contribution is mostly a rehash of Alice Bacon), Sladen provides the reader with a bonus, "the famous letters of Will Adams,"not to mention a retranslation of a Japanese Life of Napolean"!*

S:JPMC = So Kwan-wai: JAPANESE PIRACY IN MING CHINA DURING THE 16TH CENTURY. Michigan State U, 1975. *Chinese documents show that much if not most of the Japanese piracy was actually done with Chinese cooperation and leadership.*

S(R):WTU Souyri, Pierre François (trans. Käthe Roth) THE WORLD TURNED UPSIDE DOWN – Medieval Japanese Society. (Columbia University Press 2001. Orig is 1998). *I knew that villages in Japan got in rock fights with other villages, but put it in a Homo ludens context (a relatively benign form of ritualistic primitive warfare at worst); here, I found it was nothing so pretty and had more to do with societal breakdown (I found myself thinking LA youth gang or somewhere in the Near East). That sort of occasional detail, and the survey of the religious communes, degree of autonomy won (and later lost) by many peasants was fascinating and more than made up for what began as an overly complex history – one warlord after another (to a generalist like me). Valignano stressed how turbulent Japan was and this book makes it clear why that is an understatement! And, thanks to Souyri, we can know more what it was all about (esp/ the taxes/underpinning). Besides impeccable citations, there is a thorough glossary of Japanese used for names and terms. While the author could not resist quoting Valignano on* contrary *Japan, the title refers to inversion of the social hierarchy, with the warriors that served in the Heian Era turning into the rulers.*

S:MPMR = Spence, Jonathan D.: THE MEMORY PALACE OF MATTEO RICCI. Viking, 1984. *Having read Francis Yates, I had long known that the art of memory used obscenity to impress the mind with associations, but until reading Spence, I did not know the first major book published by the Jesuits in Rome was the* Epigrams *of Martial – expurgated or not, we are talking about stuff that makes Lenny Bruce seem like an angel! This artistically styled biography and appraisal of Ricci's achievement in China has something new for every good reader. Valignano is treated at length, but, as explained in the notes to the China Midword, his significance and his feelings regarding the Japanese, understandably but not*

completely justifiably, bend to fit Spence's affection for Ricci and China.
S:MOA = Steadman, John. THE MYTH OF ASIA (A Refutation of Western Stereotypes of Asian Religion, Philosophy, Art and Politics) Simon and Schuster. 1969. *I cannot for the life of me understand why this book should be so unknown. The first book to grasp the complexity of Orientalism – it described the diverse stereotypes (some good and some bad) and analyzed the ways by which differences become generalized and exaggerate – Steadman deserves more attention than a certain man about whom enough has been* said.
(To me, this weird discrepancy proves that academia, for all its pretensions to objectivity, is basically a matter of *fads*.)
S:SCP = Sutton, Richard L.: SIXTEENTH CENTURY PHYSICIAN AND HIS METHODS – a Mercuralis on diseases of the skin (1986) The Lowell Press, Kansas City, Missouri. *A translation of a book by Hieronymus Mercuralis' about what is now called dermatology written in 1572. The anti-Pisse-prophet book cited comes from Sutton's introduction (he takes it from a "delightful discussion" in an article by J. H. Keifer (trans. Amer. Assoc. Genitourin. Surg. 50:161-172 1958). The "Identifications" – what most might call a glossary of terms – at the end of the book contains much of general interest about early Western medicine.* (If I have not had my general library with me, I have had access to my late step-father's library. Yes, Harvey Blank was a dermatologist. A famous one at that.)
S:GT = Swift, Jonathon. (ed Greenberg) GULLIVER'S TRAVELS. (1726) W.W. Norton & co. 1970. *Japan is clearly the model for one scene and provided ideas for others. Since I do not think Kaempfer was very Topsy-turvy, I believe it is not right to assume Swift read Kaempfer early on (before the English translation appeared). I bet he read Montanus.* (Note: Norton critical edition anthologies should be given the best place in every bookstore, because of the additional matter that beats that off their more favored rival. (Judging from the Norton website, it does not realize how good its critical editions line is.)
SUMARIO ➔ **See V(A):S&A.** But note that there is also Frois's lost **Summary** mentioned in J/F:Historia.

T:SIH = Taylor, Gordon Rattray SEX IN HISTORY (1954) . *Find this extremely readable classic(?) on the Internet. It would be a great way to get students to start reading history!*
T:RAD = Thomas, Keith RELIGION AND THE DECLINE OF MAGIC (1971). *While I had a few quotes, my book is in Japan. If it were here, I could not have resisted the plentiful and interesting primary material (extremely choice quotes) and the chapters on religion would have been so full of England that nothing from Iberia would have fit or the book would have to be 10 pages longer. And, if you read it, also peek at Valerie Flint's RISE OF MAGIC in Europe, which argues that the church was more attentive to and incorporated more pagan 'magic' than Thomas suggests.* (That book, too, is in my stranded library).
T:MNW = Thomas, Keith. MAN AND THE NATURAL WORLD Changing Attitudes in England, 1500-1800 (1983). *Likewise for this book. I have read a horrid review by a well-know Usanian scholar to the effect that Thomas failed to rise to summary, but I recall reading one of that scholar's books which was boringly monotone for having everything in his own words (as Usanians are taught to do). Give me Keith Thomas who gives us the words of the past in the words of the past, any day! A word to academics from an amateur (me): We readers are perfectly capable of thought. You need not summarize to death. You do not even need to analyze, though analysis is welcome. But you* must *give us primary material, for that is what we rarely get to see. It is not fair that you hog those riches. So, thank you Sir Thomas, (he was knighted some years back) for letting us share with you!*
T:TEAA = Thunberg, Charles Peter, M.D.: TRAVELS IN EUROPE, AFRICA AND ASIA (made between the years 1770 and 1779). Engl. trans. printed for F. and C. Rivington and sold by W. Richardson, London 1795/96. 3 or 4 vol. (I only found three) of which vol.3 is all Japan. *Thunberg whom Alcock championed as the world's greatest Japanophile, clearly thought highly of Kaempfer's more substantial work and was able to add but little to his general observations on Japan. Like most writers on Japan, he is quite amusing when most opinionated. Thunberg also contributed a lot to Botony, but I have not examined that work.*
T:COA = Todorov Tzvetan (Richard Howard trans.): THE CONQUEST OF AMERICA HarperPerennial: 1984. (1981 Editions du Seuil). *This book stressing mis/communication is the best modern book on what happened when the Iberians met the "Indians." The book is dedicated to the memory of a Mayan woman devoured by dogs (after she kills herself rather than submit to sex with captain Alonso Lopez de Avila.)*
T:SJT = Tsunoda, de Bary, Keene compiled: SOURCES OF JAPANESE TRADITION v2. Columbia University Press, 1964. *This book of readings is part of Theodore de Bary's "Introduction to Oriental Civilizations" series, and gives the reader a far better feel for the intellectual traditions in non-Western civilization than any analytical one-topic book could.*

V&V:PCC = Vaccari, Oreste and Enko: PICTORAL CHINESE-JAPANESE CHARACTERS. Vaccari's Language Institute (Tokyo), 1950/70.
Valignano = for *De Missione* ➔ J/S:DM in the Japanese books.
Valignano=Miguel/Leon, etc., as above, ➔ J/S:DM
Valignano (1601) , or (1602) or 1603 ➔ V:LIBRO, below (but also sometimes cited in V(A):S&A).

Valignano (1579)(1582?)(1583) → V(W)HPP or some quotes from C:TCJ or from V(A)S&A.
Valignano (1583) (1592)(1602) → V(A)S&A
V:LIBRO = Valignano, Padre Alexandro, LIBRO PRIMERO DEL PRINCIPIO y progresso de la religion christiana en jappon . . . Compuesto por el Padre Alexandro Valignano, 1601. (Ms. British Museum Add. Mss.9857) *Comments in this work which soften and explain earlier criticism of the bad qualities of the Japanese, show that despite all the hardship encountered by the Church in Japan, Valignano had not hardened but rather came to understand and appreciate Japan over the years. This is contrary to the impression left by Spence (S:MPMR.) In order not to confuse this manuscript with the HISTORIA DEL PRINCIPIO below, I used the first word in its title LIBRO, rather than calling it "Principio" as does Alvarez-Taladriz. In order not to confuse anyone I will* try *to change my references to* **Valignano 1601.** *I use the date I saw o/for the Ms at the BL. But it is sometimes given as (1602) and (1601-3). When I use 1601, I generally mean the copy I read. Regardless, all trans. are mine from Spanish.*
V(A):S&A = Valignano, Alejandro S.I. (ed. José Luis Alvarez-Taladriz): SUMARIO DE LAS COSAS DE JAPÓN (1583), ADICIONES DEL SUMARIO DE JAPON (1592). Sophia U. (Tokyo), 1954. *Much of it is a summary of the good and bad character and customs of the Japanese, with some of this given in what might be called prosaic distiche, i.e. simple contrast. The editor supplies ample information – "learned and remarkable notes" (Schütte) – mostly about claims similar to those that have been made by Valignano found in previously written Jesuit letters, but also about anything where Valignano may later have changed his emphasis. A fine work of scholarship. If you read Spanish, this book is* the *book on Valignano's contrary Japan. If I ever pay off my debts, I will buy a copy of this one.*
V(W):HPP = Valignano, Alessandro (ed. Joseph Wicki S.I.): HISTORIA DEL PRINCIPIO Y PROGRESSO DE LA COMPANIA DE JESUS EN LAS INDIAS ORIENTALES 1542-64 Institutum Historicum S.I. (Rome) 1944. (1579~1603?). *I had very little time with this book and the copies of pages dealing with Japan were a bit too small to catch the page captions, etc. If I recall correctly, it has the earliest summary written by Valignano in 1579, which was largely about India and may have included the topsy-turvy China vs Japan, the next rendition which gave Japan more space and compared it to Europe, instead, and the next, which refined that in 1583. From this point (in 1998)I called the earlier work* PRINCIPIO *and the 1583 SUMARIO. Since Sumario is the same in Alvarez-Taladriz, it was not confusing when I cited him, but Cooper (C:TCJ) usually writes "Historia del Principio" and, looking at the biblio, I find it hard to say if he means via Wicki or Alvarez-Taladriz, but I think he means the 1583 version, I call SUMARIO. PRINCIPIO for the earlier renditions became a problem for Alvarez-Taladriz uses it when he mentions what I called LIBRO(see, above). Sometimes, after the passage of years, I cannot recall which is being referred to and, not having the ability to gather all the books together, just hope I got most of it right! Angel readers with time on their hands and a love for details are invited to correct me!*
V:RCJ = Vivero, G. San Antonio y R. de: RELACIONES DE LA CAMBOYA Y EL JAPON. (Cronicas de la America, Historia 16?). *Vivero would seem to have fallen in with very bad company, for he is the only early observer to find Japanese vicious in drink.! At the time I read him, I fear my Spanish was not yet warmed up enough to get everything in his book.*

W:HOT = Willes, Richard.(also Willis) HISTORY OF TRAVAYLE (1577) in ENGLAND AND JAPAN (pref. M. Paske-Smith). J.L. Thompson & Co. (Kobe), 1928. *The History can also be found on microfilm and its full name is The (Pleasant) History of Travayle in the East and West Indies. Japan is but a tiny part of a huge world history. Wiles writes only a few words on Japan prefacing his translation of "my old acquainted friend" Maffei's Latined version of a 1565 Frois letter. According to P-S' preface, since Marco Polo was not Englished until 1579 (There is a wee mention of a fabled land called Zipangu), this book was "the first notice in English of Japan." So, our "Father Froes" was the father of Japanology in English. The above-cited book includes a wonderful letter from "Edward VI of England to the Kings and Princes of the East requesting friendship and commerce," sent East with Sir Hugh Willoughby in 1553, but never arriving in Japan, where, of course, no one could have read it, anyway. There are some long passages on what economists would later call* comparative advantage *– "they permit us to take of theyr thyngs, such whereof thaey have abundance in theyr regions, and we agayne graunt them such thynges of ours whereof they are destitute" – sweetened by the thought that this was true because "God of heaven and earth, greatly provydying for mankynd, would not that al thinges should be founde in one region, to the ende that one should have neede of an other, that by this meanes frendshyp myght be establyshed among all men and every one seeke to gratifie all." Amen!* (I wonder if any economists have noted and commented on this.)

XAVIER → C:LLFX, above.

..

Books in *Japanese*

..

J/A:NGK = Aramata Hiroshi. NIHON GYÔTEN KIGEN (Japan-shocking-origins) Shûeisha: 1994
J?De Sande → See J/S
J/E:NBJ = Ebisawa Arimichi transl. *Nambanjikyôkaiki* (c.1700); *Jakyô Daii* (1648); *Myôtei mondo*
(1605); *Ha-deusu* (1620) *Tôyô Bunko* = Heibonsha 1964/1989. *I was just looking for a copy of Ha-deusu*
(Destruction/Destroying Deus), the famous attack on Christianity and the Jesuits by the apostate Fukan
Fabian, but his Myotei-Mondo *a lively attack on Buddhism, Taoism/Confucianism and Shinto was actually*
much more fun to read and revealing, for anyone could have predicted that a mind that hyperlogical would
end up at odds with Christianity unless it were given extraordinary attention. Unfortunately for the Jesuits,
that was not the case. The Nambanjikyokaiki *whose author I did not make out* (academic books in Japan can take so
long to explain things that I run out of patience finding out the basics) *is a lively folk-history of the "Barbarian Temple's*
Prosperity and Destruction" by someone who was anti-Christian with excellent notes by Ebisawa.   The
1648 writing is a remarkably cogent summary of the basics of Christianity. (If you read Japanese, read this rather
than Elison, for the bunko is cheap and, wow! 3 in 1.)
J/F:HISTORIA = Frois, Luis. (trans. by Matsuda Kiichi and Kawasaki Momota)   kanyaku
FUROISU-NO NIHON-SHI (complete translation Frois's Japan-History) 12v. Chuokoronsha, 1977-
80. This is a full translation of Frois's *Historia de Japam, which is actually a history of the Church in*
Japan, but probably includes more first-hand information on the Japanese rulers (who the Jesuits knew
personally) than any other single source, which, of course is why a major Japanese publisher has put it out
in pocket book. I only thoroughly read the first part, the introduction for the Summary *volume that was*
supposed to begin the history (I feel Rodrigues might have read that Summary*).   Even though the*
introduction is a few scant pages, it is extremely significant for reading between the lines of TRATADO, for
it proves Frois was not naïve about the implications – i.e., misunderstanding – arising from terms that do
not translate or, worse, seem to translate but really differ.   I believe that the lost Summary *would have*
explained *many of the things I, in my wilder way,* explicated *in the course of this book.   That part (for that*
matter, the entire history except for any excerpts that might have been included in Cooper and others)is not
available in English, so I translated (from the Japanese) a nice chunk of it for a note to part iii of my
Foreword. I believe it is also translated into some non-English European tongues. As most of the
remainder of the history is about the propagation of Christianity in Japan, something about which my
interest is marginal at most, and I had too little time to read thoroughly anyway, I may have missed quite a
number of interesting tidbits of information scattered throughout. The Japanese translators provide a
plethora of excellent notes, but I am not always certain of the date of my citations because the volume #
does not appear on the page and even though the chapters do, and I copied the table linking chapters to
dates, I realized too late – after the loaned books traveled 3,000 miles back to their library – that there
was more than one chapter count in the 12 volume history!   Recently, I got the pocket-books, and
rechecked a few citations, but the chapter scheme is still too confusing. Good luck finding anything! One
thing: The important *Prologue* to the lost *Summary* is placed in the back of the first volume.
J/F(O):T = Frois, Luis (Okada Akio trans./ed.: TRATADO:1585) YOROPPA-BUNKA TO NIHON-
BUNKA (European Culture and Japanese Culture). Iwanami Shoten (Tokyo), 1996 (1965). *My copy is the*
*thirteenth printing of the pocketbook. The original was first published together with another work (*Nihon
ôkoku-ki*), as part of a series on the* Age of Exploration *(Dai-kôkai-jidai-gyôshô vol. XI) in 1965 under the*
title: Japan-Europe Cultural Comparison *(nichi-ô-bunka-hikaku). About half of the 611 items are annotated,*
with annotations averaging several lines. They tend provide a bit more information on Japan than Europe,
perhaps because many Japanese today know little about their own history, or because Okada had more of
an opinion about his side.   I find many useful and cite or quote them in my notes.   I even considered
translating Okada's book, but, since the Western reader needs different information than the Japanese
reader and Okada failed to address many items I felt had to be solved, thought it better to write my own.   I
vaguely recall thinking some of his notes too long when I first read his 200 page book decades ago, but
seeing how long my notes got . . . I no longer have grounds to complain.

**J/F(M&E):T = Frois, Luis (Matsuda Kiichi and Engelbert Jorissen trans./ed: TRATADO:1585):
FROISU-NO NIHON-OBOEGAKI** – nihon to yoroppa no fûshû no chigai (frois' notes on japan – the difference in the customs of Japan and Europe). Chuô-shinshô, 1983. (The *ss*'s in Jorissen are actually a big *B*-like letter and the J pronounced *Y*.) *Actually, this book, unlike the case with Okada, has Matsuda and Jorissen down as co-authors rather than translator-annotators. While most of their translation is virtually identical with Okada's (even the mistaken 2-29 and trickier 2-59), and there are 102 pages of critical essay versus only 77 pages for the TRATADO (squeezed into one chapter!) there is ample supplementary information on things European. Unfortunately for the reader (if you, like me want notes on the same page as what they treat) they are stuck in another chapter and only cover some chapters. The route by which the manuscript arrived at the Museum, its relationship to Francesco Carletti's* Voyage Around the World *(which borrowed much from it) and its authenticity are carefully analyzed for the first 60 pages of the book – this is particularly well done and if I were a better scholar might have been more carefully noted in this book – and the veracity of Frois's observations (this is how the supplementary info. on Europe is* used) *for 30 pages at the end. Like Okada's book, this was published as a pocket book.*

J/F = Fukan Fabian. → F/E:NBJ and E:DD.

J/G:EKN = Gill, Robin: EIGO-WA KONNA-NI NIPPONGO (english is that japanese!). Chikuma-bunko, 1989 (Kirihara-shoten, diff. title: 1984). *Finds similarity underlying language-related antithetical stereotypes and challenges stereotypes held by Japanese on both languages.*
J/G:GT = Gill, Robin: GOYAKU-TENGOKU (mistranslation paradise). Hakusuisha, 1989. *An indictment of the mistranslation of books and culture in Japan, and a reading of Peter Farb's WORDPLAY, which was horribly mistranslated, this book also developed themes from EKN, above..*
J/G:K = Gill, Robin KORA!MU! Hakusuisha. *A collection of my essays, mostly previously published elsewhere. It includes an article I wrote defending the anti-whaling movement from horrid charges made in the leading magazine (Chuokoron) in which it was published.*
J/G:HNR = Gill, Robin: HAN-NIHONJIN-RON (anti-japanesesness-arguement). E.O. Reischauer preface. Kousakusha, 1984. *Deconstructs environmental reductionism more widespread in Japan than in the West and attempts to get beyond antithetical stereotypes of East and West to consider lifestyles ideal for humans and their planet..*
J/G:NRT = Gill, Robin: NIHONJIN-RON TANKEN. TBS Britannica, 1985. *An attempt to cure what I called "The Uniqueness Syndrome," the Japanese fixation on themselves and the West as antithetical.* Also good medicine against the difference-mongering I enjoyed here, so I mention them with genuflective intent. *Mea culpa, mea maxima . . .*

J/I:FPM = I, Oryon (= Lee O-young)= FUROSHIKI-NO-POSUTO-MODAN. Chuokoronsha, 1989. *My riposte to this Japanese-Korean-Occidental book of contrasts was published in the same publisher's monthly magazine Chuokoron. People sometimes get the wrong idea of my criticism. I usually do not bother with someone unless I like their work. I doubt if Lee has ever written a single boring sentence. The English language world could use some such essayists!*
J/I:WTF = Inoue Hisashi: WAGA TOMO FUROISU (my friend frois). Nesco (Bungeishunju) 1999. *A delightful novellete of Frois' life almost entirely comprising letters, based upon fact but crafted with artistic license. A letter from Frois to Vilela written over 10 years before Valignano's SUMARIO and 15 years before TRATADO has almost a dozen topsy-turvy contradictions. [Does anyone have this on hand? I would like a copy to see what those first differences were! Inoue cites the Japanese translations of books full of correspondence between Jesuits I have not read. But, it is a novel, so . . .]. So Inoue apparently judges the idea came from Frois rather than Valignano Among the deceased Frois' scanty personal effects, Inoue writes, there was one sheet of Japanese Sugiwara paper with the words* par in parem imperium non habet: *"equal has no right to rule equal."*
J/I:IR= Iwakura Tomoi: *tokumei zenken taishi bei-ó kairan jiki* ("special rights plenipotentiary ambassador america-europe tour report," or, commonly: THE IWAKURA REPORT) 1872. *The reporting is, on the whole, heavy-going, for the mission was to learn about the West's industry & economy. But the summaries of different social topics are occasionally interesting and the ample engravings which seldom forget to include natural scenery are splendid. I cannot recall if it was this report or the Muragaki report (* A:FJE)*, above, that had a recent full translation priced, if I recall correctly, at about $1,000.!!!.*

J/Lee O-young → See J/I

J/N&T:SCK : Nakano Miyoko and Takeda Masaya: SEKIMATSU CHUGOKU-NO KAWARABAN.

Fukutake shoten 1989. *A translation of selected feature stories from a late 19ᵗʰ century Chinese tabloid by the top Japanese scholars of what I would call interesting and often significant Chinese subjects.*

J/OJD: NIHON-KOKUGO-DAI-JITEN. Shogakukan. *This 20-set (or 10-set small print)dictionary is more interesting than even Johnson's dictionary, because the literary examples in Japanese are entire, thanks to the brevity of Japanese poems! Believe it or not, many are senryû and very risqué. Because this is the only Japanese dictionary useful 90% of the times I look up an obsolete or archaic word, I call it THE ONLY JAPANESE DICTIONARY, OJD for short. Because of the resemblance to the OED, it is easy to remember, too. Okada relied heavily on it, too (I often found the same example, where I wanted another!)*

J/O:KGB = Ôhara Rieko: KUROGAMI NO BUNKA-SHI (cultural history of black-hair) 1988. *Hundreds of illustrations of Japanese hairdos (90% women), all of which have names and a short description.*

J/R:ALJ = Rodrigues, Joao (Doi Tadao trans.): NIHON DAI-BUNTEN (ARTE DA LINGOA DE JAPAM). Sanseido, 1955 (Nangasaqui-no Collegio de Japao da Compania de JESV, 1604). *Or, to give the English title provided:* A GREAT JAPANESE GRAMMAR. *I seriously doubt that anyone wrote so substantial a book on English grammar! And, not only is there grammar, but more information on poetry than I have ever seen in a modern grammar book! It is astounding that a translation (based on the Bodleian Library copy) of this huge book could be published before Japan's economy had recovered from the long War.* (I once saw this, but must have not been getting enough sleep, for I cannot recall it! Library reading is very hard on me, for the quiver in fluorescent lamps makes me drowsy. I always ate very spicy curry before going to the BL, but sometimes it was not enough.)

J/S:DM (DE MISSIONE) = de Sande, Duarte [Eduardo] de trans., (au=Valignano) DE MISSIONE LEGATORUM IAPONEN (Macao 1589 (i mistakenly may write **1590** sometimes) More precisely, the Japanese trans. of the same from Latin by Izui Hisanosuke: Tensho nenkan ken'o shisetsu kenbun taiwaroku; Sande, Duarte de, Tokyo : Toyo Bunko, 1942. Also with Nagazawa Nobuhisa, Mitani Shouji and Sunami Ichiro trans./notes published by Yushodo Shoten (Tokyo), 1969. *This is an introduction to Europe in dialogue form, created by Valignano with the help of abundant reports he received from his brainchild, the Japanese Embassy to Europe (1582-1588) We cannot know exactly what information and opinions came from the four young Japanese envoys Mancio Ito, Miguel Chijiwa, Martin Hara and Julian Nakaura (Michael=Miguel, Martinus=Martino, Iulianus=Julian and Mancius=Mancio) and what from the apparent editor/author Valignano and other sources. So I credit "Miguel=Valignano," "Mancio =Valignano"etc.. I quote heavily because DE MISSIONE is not available in English and is the only Japanese opinion on the subject of many of Frois's contrasts found so far, even if it is biased by passing through Valignano in Spanish, put into dialogue form and further changed into poor Latin by De Sande* (whose humble apologies = his head was immersed in Chinese = are touching), *rather than coming directly from the pens of the Japanese youths. The Japanese team did a prodigious amount of research for their notes* [as extensive as Alvarez-Taladriz for Valignano's *Sumario*, but with many more Japanese sources], *which I appreciate much more than the stilted translation-style Japanese. A team comprising a native English speaker who is a Latin+Renaissance expert and a Japanese capable of helping with the notes for the Japanese side should English this book!* (Some have argued that De Sande was the author, not only because his name was on it but because of the "lusitanismo" (Portuguese style) of the dialog. I agree with J.E. Moran's article "The Real Author of *de Missione*" (Bulletin of Portuguese Studies, June 2001 (vol 2). that it must be Valignano because reading it, I never felt otherwise and because of proof such as the letter to Aquaviva from Valig. explaining why he did what he did – made the dialog completely Japanese talking to Japanese – quoted by Moran, who also shows how Valig., who wrote in Spanish, tried to satisfy the sensibilities of the Portuguese Jesuits.)

J/U:BNS = Umesao Tadao: BUNMEI NO SEITAISHI-KAN (a historo-ecological view of civilization). 1974. *Some of what Diamond did in D:GGS was already done by Umesao.*

J/U:KNS = Umesao Tadao: KYOTO-NO SEISHIN (Kyoto's Espirit). Kadokawa-sensho: 1987. *Umesao thinks Kyoto is no mere tourist city, but a center, if not the center for Eastern civilization. Europeans talk about Americanization as a* culture *problem, but Umesao argues Kyoto has bigger fish to fry: it would defend a* civilization. *Anthropology generally stops with* culture, *but Umesao only begins there.*

J/W:F = Watsuji Tetsuro: FÛDO (1935/44). Iwanami Bunko, 1983. *A classic book about the effect of climate on culture with a focus on explaining Japanese and Western differences, but also treating Japanese vs. mainland Asian and North European vs. South European differences. FUDO has enough cultural anthropology to make it exceptionally interesting for a book of history/philosophy.*

..

APPEAL (FOR SECOND TIME!)

Anyone who has read right down the bibliographies is a good man or woman. So, I once again beg for your assistance,

1) Finding and correcting errors – I will have an on-line Errata Page (I would like this to be done on a live page, but have not yet succeeded in making one on my website.) – and you will be free to point things out in signed correspondence or anon., as you prefer.

2) More interesting, adding glosses, likewise anon. or by name as you prefer. If the latter, you will also be free to put in a line or two about your own book or research or whatever else you wish to advertise! *Scholarship as Mutual Aid* – why not!

I regret that there are many books I failed to find and read. *Anything not in my explications that you feel would enhance this book is welcome.* For example, I would bet there is something in the work of von Siebold, the German physician and scientist who taught and learned a lot from Japanese (except for the little found in B:MCJ), and Giovanni Antonio Menavino (quoted in Cochrane: *Historians and Historiography of the Italian Renaissance*) who wrote about the Turks being superior to Europeans in 1551. Both of these could well have made some topsy-turvy remarks. There must be others whose existence is still unknown to me. Not working at a University and living far below the poverty line, my situation is not ideal for accessing books and most scholarly magazines are out of reach. There must be dozens of article in *Monumenta Niponnica, alone!* I ought to know and a few in the marvelous young *bulletin of Portugues/Japanese Studies* (eg. one on Jesuit church architecture in Japan and China). Because I have invested years of research preparing for a multi-volume work of haiku and would prefer to concentrate on that and *not* search out more material for Frois myself, I welcome leads, but *would prefer receiving relevant passages which I can plop right into the page* either as a note or in the main text or in the margin, if/when I find a major publisher willing to work with me (With MS-WORD, I find it too tricky to use side-tracks in addition to multi-column notes. Also, I took this up to the 740 page limit for POD-style printing.) *Authors* of these articles or books – all those expensive books from Curzon and Michigan I missed – who could use the publicity are urged not to wait, but write *quickly* so as to put in a word of pr for themselves (not possible if a *third-party* cites them in a gloss). I will list glosses received on the 1585 Gloss page at my website. *Please check that page before looking up something or writing me to be sure someone else hasn't already done the same.*

3) If you find this, or any Paraverse Press books, worth introducing to others, *by all means do so,* for otherwise they may never learn of it! I do not generally send out books for reviews unless they are requested, because such books are almost never read and I hate finding them in second-hand book stores. Bug your friend with radio, magazine, or newspaper connections, for we do not yet have them. Despite a generous 5-page review (in the most prestigious haiku magazine in English, *Modern Haiku*) by the top editor-writer in the world of English language haiku (William J. Higginson) which recommended *Rise, Ye Sea Slugs!* over Blyth, Henderson, Yasuda, etc. (all the greats of the past 50 years!), I have yet to get *a single personal letter through to the editors of any major magazine or newspaper, much less a review.* (Yes, I put choice tidbits from reviews and blurbs *proving* it deserves attention in a short letter, but I never get a personal reply.) The FBI is not the only institution poor at sifting out information to get the best to the top. The mass media that criticizes the FBI has itself been swept away by the flood of information, with the result that reviews generally cover the same handful of publisher-conglomerates and authors. It gets so *boring* that I have stopped reading them. *Book review editors, please take note!* Thanks to *POD printing*, publishing, like music, is finally free of the biggies. *If only you would open to new authors and publishers* (we are out here!), *this could be a golden age of letters . . . and review!*

ACKNOWLEDGMENTS

I generally find this the easiest part of a book to write, for it is always so nice to have a place to thank people. This time it is a bit harder for I feel I must start by an acknowledgment that is partly an apology *cum* explanation. When I mentioned Frois's *Tratado* to Professor of Comparative Studies Daniel Reff in 1998, he suggested we do a book. At that time the *Tratado* was only one of several Japanese books (for I had Okada's translation of *Tratado*) I was thinking about translating. But, thanks to Dan's interest, I switched into high gear for Frois. He was working on Jesuit activities in the New World (see R(R,A&D):HOT, above), introduced me to Schütte: *Valignano's Mission Principles,* which was a real eye-opener, and taught me the word *distich,* which I must confess to not knowing. We planned to do *Tratado* together, but I ended up going overboard (researching the Japanese side *and* the European, and finally invading Dan's Jesuit territory), as you can imagine from reading this book, while he was slowed down by other obligations and found my idea for three versions (hyper-short pocket book, medium length academic, and long-frois, as I called what became *this* book) hard to take. At any rate, being in debt and with an income far less than my rent, by the end of 2003 I realized I simply could not afford to do more research without publishing *soon* and having, in the meantime, become a publisher (which costs practically nothing), a long book became practical. I had no choice but to do it *my way* – long-version first – something that sounds fine in a song but can be hard on other people. Since I failed so miserably on pinning down page numbers for citations, the academic (critical edition) would have been difficult, even had it been the only one and we agreed on whether or not to have a Portuguese expert as a third author . . . Be that as it may, I apologize for anything that needs apology. Thank you, Dan, for getting me started, the letter that enabled me to read Valignano's 1601 work at the BL, the incisive and probing questions about some of the chapters, of which I only wish there could have been more (and likewise for your brilliant student KT – I wish she could have read and commented on the whole thing rather than only a chapter!) and your work (together with H) on the translation which helped get me back into thinking critically in English (in 1998, my vocabulary was not quite *there* after 20 years of writing in Japanese!). And thank you, Prudence (my sister in Columbus), for introducing me to Dan (*viz* DR).

My debts to other researchers is acknowledged already, directly and indirectly. If the reader would understand them better, the Bibliography is annotated. Without Father Schütte's discovery and transcription into readable print of the *Tratado* (F(S):T), this book would not exist, but my largest debt *in terms of understanding the content* is to Okada's heavily annotated translation of *Tratado* (J/F(O):T), followed by Cooper's *They Came to Japan* (C:TCJ), and quite a bit further down the line, Matsuda and Jorissen's translation of *Tratado* (J/F(M&J):T), the *De Missione* translation (J/S:DM), Matsuda + Kawasaki's translation of Frois's *Historia* (J/F:HISTORIA), and *Valignano's* writing (especially: V(A):S&A).

Indeed, no one (not even Dan) has read even half of this book that just kept growing! It is *too bad* – all books should have many readers *before* the final draft (so I think of this first edition as a sort of *reading copy* and the next one, the second edition, improved by *your* comments and glosses, as the real *final draft*). So, when I say that the wild hypotheses and unscholarly if not irresponsible opinions I express on many subjects are *no one's responsibility but my own,* that is not only a standard disclaimer, lest others unlucky enough to be acquainted with me should be unfairly criticized for whatever irresponsible things *I* write, but a statement of fact. A sad and lonely fact: *I have no editor.*

Reference-wise, Mary McCarthy at the Santa-Fe + St Leo library made my stay with my other sister in Gainesville (actually, Newberry, Watermelon Capital of the World) *extremely productive.* Thank you, Susan, for putting me up so long and allowing me a big chunk of bookcase. Worldcat (inter-library loan) is not automatic. One must be good at choosing the universities to beg the book from and Mary had a high batting average. I probably got as many if not more good books through Mary as I did during my several months camping out at the British Library and I am very grateful to her and the kind, mostly Southern and none-to-wealthy universities who were especially cooperative. (Unlike rich Harvard which charged an arm and a leg for a tiny micro-fiche). The public library in Miami, where I live now, has improved with Worldcat and got me some good books recently, for which I thank them, and I am eagerly awaiting their changeover to an on-line system of requesting, so I will have more to thank them for in a future book, if I remain here. I almost forgot the cheerfulness of some non-British workers (Pakistani, perhaps?) at the British Library, and Mark and Carmel for the cheap flat that let me afford to stay within striking distance. More recently, Kristina Troost at Duke's Perkins Library helped me obtain the *Monumenta Nipponica* (Rodrigues's introduction of Japanese poetry) and Catarina Marot Mendez of the Biblioteca National de Portugal was kind enough to respond to a few language-related questions, which gave me confidence, though informing me that she was the only reference librarian, in the USA sense of the word, in the Library for the rest were para-professionals who had to be paid for their assistance! Some kind fellow members of the PMJS were kind enough to provide a few leads in response to questions, as was one librarian at the LC, but I fear (being poor and lacking access to a university library) I was unable to take advantage of their suggestions!

On the local side, thanks to Jacque (sp?) of France on Key Biscayne for buying me the French translation of *Tratado* and answering my questions re. the French (and his son Alexis, for his help, too!); Alexandra for answering questions about Schütte's German and lending me her dictionary, though I must say, I find German dictionaries a *horror* (they are so "root" oriented that most words must be looked up part by part!); Camila and her daughter Gabriela for living without *Aurelio* and their other Portuguese-English dictionary for 4 months as of this writing; my mother for likewise doing without her OED (mine is in Japan); Pablo for cover help with my last book (it was after pdf'ing so I could not thank him), and, I almost forgot, ER, whose uncanny ability to find the word on the tip of my tongue when I phone him for it is much appreciated!

On the Japan side, I thank Hiroko-san, the owner of a small used-book store, for helping me round up a number of books over the past year or so; "Tenki-san," host of the charming haiku website Ukimido, for setting up a Frois Questions and Answer's Site (フロイス問答場) and all those who visited it to answer questions (or answered them elsewhere). The overall champion is Furiko-san. I hope that after this is published, it gets enough attention to draw some professional historians and specialists in some of the fields Frois covers to the website, for there are still all-too-many unsolved questions! I also thank Midorikawa Machiko for letting me try the PMJS bbs, though (涙), I got no response.

I am most grateful of all to those web-sites *that offer information easily accessible to all*, such as Iberian Resources On-line and the University of Washington's Nagasaki-magazine (old copies, any way – but it is better than nothing). For anyone who is too poor (in time=money) to travel, or has ecological qualms about it, the ability to find information on the net – rather than simply find out *about* the existence of information – cannot be overstated. As anyone who has read this book knows, my debts are far larger than the annotated bibliography lets out. Perhaps, I can do better in the next edition. LD, who read the first chapter, wrote that she had one stylistic bone to pick with me and that was my constant use of the verb "google, because it will eventually date me." I appreciate her faith in the longevity of this book, but will continue using it because it feels natural. Rather than snorkeling around, you goggle+oogle, or *google*. And, besides, I have derived great benefit from their intelligently designed search-engine, so using the verb is a deliberate show of gratitude.

At the end of the introduction to his *Epochs of Chinese and Japanese Art*, one of many books read but not cited here, Fenollosa acknowledges the help of eight of his Japanese colleagues and pegs the following onto the tail: *"Other scholars to whom I owe tribute might be enumerated by the dozens. Marco Polo is surely worth something."* (Some way or another, *my* Marco Polo slipped the bibliography: *Oops!*)

r.d.g. – On Key Biscayne without AC on the longest day of 2004.

Reviews of Previous Work by the Author

re: *Rise, Ye Sea Slugs!* 1000 holothurian haiku (2003)

"Gill **appeals to readers who revel in ideas and expansive footnotes.** . . . Some of the most engaging commentary on haiku (and senryu and the occasional tanka or kyôka) ever to see print. . . . one of the most original minds to take up the related subjects of haiku and cross-cultural communication. . . . may be our best English-language window yet into the labyrinth of Japanese haikai culture. . . As a translator, I find Gill's approach stimulating and challenging. **He has raised the bar very high in terms of a translator's responsibility** (. . .) to the text. . . . **If you have read Yasuda, Blyth, Henderson, Ueda, and Shirane, then read Gill**. **He will expand your mind. If you have not read those guys yet, then read Gill first. He's more fun.** – William J. Higginson, dean of haiku editors in the USA and author of the international classic *Haiku World,* in *Modern Haiku* (a 5-page review in vol. 35.1 winter-spring 2004)

"You may think you need a system of bookmarks to keep on the subject, but it is easiest to just give your mind over to Gill and follow his incredible journey on printed pages. . . . If you ever thought haiku were not erotic, this book alone could change your mind forever. **If you read it, I can guarantee you will not be the same when you finish it!** . . . Incredible work." – Jane Reichhold (host of the marvelous Aha! poetry web-ring) in her *Lynx* (February, 2004)

"Gill's tone is relaxed and informal and he doesn't take himself too seriously or struggle for academic respectability, but he is still **precise in his own way, and insanely erudite**. . . . All told, it's **an original undertaking carried out with style**. . . . [An example haiku in the review]: *a few drinks / and i am a sea slug / out of water* Gijô (1741) – Danny Yee in Dannyreviews.com (solid reviews of eclectic books Down-under)

"This book gets my vote for **the most original literary theme of the decade**." – Jim Nollman, author of *Dolphin Dreamtime*, in Interspecies (his fine ecological newsletter Spring 2004).

"**Already a classic** . . . like the work of Blyth." "The *ante y después* of critical studies of haiku" (The Sino-japanese phrase *kuzenzetsugo* would work, but what can English do with *antes y despues*?) – Vincente Haya, author of *Corazon de Haiku* from 2 postings at El Rincon de Haiku (an online haiku forum in Spanish).

re: anti-stereotype books published in Japanese only.

"**I bow my head to the author's linguistic prowess.**" – Inoue Hisashi (on a reader's card) – a top Japanese novelist and playwright. [re. *Omoshiro hikaku bunkakô*, later republished as *Eigo wa konna ni nippongo* = English is This Japanese! (Chikuma bunko)]

"What felt good about reading it [Han=nihonjinron = anti-Japanology, (Kousakusha: 1984) was that the book **doesn't get bogged down in Japan, but develops into a theory of culture** [bunkaron] . . . it is **remarkable for not being prejudiced either for or against the past**." – Itasaka Gen (review in *"Honyaku no Sekai"*), a Japanese literature scholar who formerly taught at Harvard and later became the president of Tenri University.

"**The author's Thoreauvian naturalism is splendid** . . . and the book [*Han=nihonjinron*] leaves you feeling better than reading ten of those popular Japan-as-Number-One type books." – Matsuoka Seigow (review in an NTT book) – one of Japan's top editors and well-known avant-garde thinker.

"**A splendid deconstruction** [on Ibid] **of longstanding stereotypes of Japanese national/cultural character** (nihonjinron) that, wearing the academic guise of cultural anthropology and topographic/climatic reductionism, (fudoron), have titillated our pride." – Kyodo News Service (review carried nationally).

"Whether due to the flexibility and uniqueness of the perspective or the continual dissimulation of the author's Japanese writing, this book [*Nihonjinron Tanken* TBS-Britannica (1984)] is simply thrilling. Introducing example after example of things from other cultures that have been held to be unique to Japan, **the author's point is that we must not allow our obsession with "Japaneseness" to stop us from facing up to the human agenda in this Age where we are capable of spoiling the earth.**" – TSUMURA Takashi (also Kyodo), a well known practitioner and advocate of Eastern medicine and meditation.

(The reason I did not try to get these or my other books translated is because I tailor my books to the understanding of my imagined audience. Books that would make sense to everyone tend to be trite – or, stylistically speaking, overly plain – for they must be both redundant and general.)

More reviews and links at http://www.paraverse.org